Handbook of
AGING
AND THE
SOCIAL
SCIENCES

THE HANDBOOKS OF AGING
Consisting of Three Volumes:
Critical comprehensive reviews of
research knowledge, theories,
concepts, and issues

Editor-in-Chief: **James E. Birren**

Handbook of the Biology of Aging
Edited by Caleb E. Finch and Leonard Hayflick
Handbook of the Psychology of Aging
Edited by James E. Birren and K. Warner Schaie
Handbook of Aging and the Social Sciences
Edited by Robert H. Binstock and Ethel Shanas

Editorial Committee

Vern L. Bengtson • Robert H. Binstock • James E. Birren • Jack Botwinick • Harold
Brody • Sheila Chown • Carl Eisdorfer • Caleb E. Finch • Leonard Hayflick • George L.
Maddox • Isadore Rossman • K. Warner Schaie • Ethel Shanas • F. Marott Sinex •
Dorothy Wedderburn

Handbook of
AGING AND THE SOCIAL SCIENCES

Editors

Robert H. Binstock
Ethel Shanas

With the assistance of Associate Editors

Vern L. Bengtson

George L. Maddox

Dorothy Wedderburn

VNR **VAN NOSTRAND REINHOLD·COMPANY**
NEW YORK   CINCINNATI   ATLANTA   DALLAS   SAN FRANCISCO
LONDON   TORONTO   MELBOURNE

Van Nostrand Reinhold Company Regional Offices:
New York Cincinnati Atlanta Dallas San Francisco

Van Nostrand Reinhold Company International Offices:
London Toronto Melbourne

Library of Congress Catalog Card Number: 76-25584
ISBN: 0-442-20798-0

Manufactured in the United States of America

Published by Van Nostrand Reinhold Company
450 West 33rd Street, New York, N.Y. 10001

Published simultaneously in Canada by Van Nostrand Reinhold Ltd.

15 14 13 12 11 10 9 8 7 6 5 4 3

Library of Congress Cataloging in Publication Data

Main entry under title:

Handbook of aging and the social sciences.

    (The Handbooks of aging)
    Includes index.
    1. Gerontology—Addresses, essays, lectures.
I. Binstock, Robert H. II. Shanas, Ethel. III. Se-
ries.
HQ1061.H336   301.43′5   76-25584
ISBN 0-442-20798-0

CONTRIBUTORS

Kurt W. Back, Ph.D.
James B. Duke Professor, Department of Sociology, Duke University, Durham, North Carolina

Walter M. Beattie, Jr.
Director, All-University Gerontology Center; Professor, School of Social Work, Syracuse University, Syracuse, New York

Vern L. Bengtson, Ph.D.
Laboratory Chief, Laboratory for Social Organization and Behavior, Andrus Gerontology Center; Associate Professor of Sociology, University of Southern California, Los Angeles, California

Robert H. Binstock, Ph.D.
Stulberg Professor of Law and Politics, Department of Politics and The Florence Heller Graduate School; Director, Program in the Economics and Politics of Aging, Brandeis University, Waltham, Massachusetts

Leonard D.Cain, Ph.D.
Professor of Sociology and Urban Studies; Associate Director, Institute on Aging, Portland State University, Portland, Oregon

Frances M. Carp, Ph.D.
Project Director, The Wright Institute, Berkeley, California

Neal E. Cutler, Ph.D.
Laboratory Chief, Social Policy Laboratory, Andrus Gerontology Center; Associate Professor of Political Science, University of Southern California, Los Angeles, California

C. L. Estes, Ph.D.
Associate Professor, Sociology Program, Department of Social and Behavioral Sciences, School of Nursing, University of California, San Francisco, California

Howard E. Freeman, Ph.D.
Director, Institute of Social Science Research; Professor of Sociology, University of California, Los Angeles, California

Charles M. Gaitz, M.D.
Head, Special Clinical Services Division, Texas Research Institute of Mental Sciences, Houston, Texas

Jack Goody, Ph.D.
William Wyse Professor of Social Anthropology, St. John's College, University of Cambridge, Cambridge, England

Chad Gordon, Ph.D.
Associate Professor of Sociology, Department of Sociology, Rice University, Houston, Texas

Gunhild O. Hagestad, Ph.D.
Assistant Professor, Department of Behavioral Sciences; The Committee on Human Development, The University of Chicago, Chicago, Illinois

Philip M. Hauser, Ph.D.
Lucy Flower Professor of Urban Sociology; Director, Population Research Center, The University of Chicago, Chicago, Illinois

Robert B. Hudson, Ph.D.
Assistant Professor of Politics and Social Welfare, The Florence Heller Graduate School for Advanced Studies in Social Welfare, Brandeis University, Waltham, Massachusetts

Richard A. Kalish, Ph.D.
Professor of Behavioral Sciences, Graduate Theological Union, Berkeley, California

Juanita M. Kreps, Ph.D.
Vice President and James B. Duke Professor of Economics, Duke University, Durham, North Carolina

Sanford A. Lakoff, Ph.D.
Chairman, Department of Political Science, University of California at San Diego, La Jolla, California

Peter Laslett, Ph.D.
Cambridge Group for the History of Population and Social Structure, Trinity College, University of Cambridge, Cambridge, England

Martin A. Levin, Ph. D.
Associate Professor of Politics, Department of Politics, Brandeis University, Waltham, Massachusetts

Marjorie Fiske Lowenthal
Professor and Director, Human Development Program, Department of Psychiatry, University of California, San Francisco, California

George L. Maddox, Ph.D.
Director, Center for the Study of Aging and Human Development; Professor and Head, Division of Medical Sociology; Professor of Sociology, Duke University, Durham, North Carolina

Bernice L. Neugarten, Ph.D.
Professor of Human Development, Department of Behavioral Sciences; The Committee on Human Development, The University of Chicago, Chicago, Illinois

Matilda White Riley
Fayerweather Professor of Sociology; Chairman, Department of Sociology and Anthropology, Bowdoin College, Brunswick, Maine; Sociologist, The Russell Sage Foundation, New York, New York

Betsy Robinson, M.A.
Human Development Program, Department of Psychiatry, University of California, San Francisco, California

Irving Rosow, Ph.D.
Professor of Medical Sociology, Langley Porter Institute, University of California, San Francisco, California

James H. Schulz, Ph.D.
Professor of Welfare Economics, Program in the Economics and Politics of Aging, The Florence Heller Graduate School for Advanced Studies in Social Welfare, Brandeis University, Waltham, Massachusetts

Ethel Shanas, Ph.D.
Professor of Sociology, Department of Sociology, University of Illinois at Chicago Circle; Professor of Health Care Services, School of Public Health, University of Illinois at the Medical Center, Chicago, Illinois

Harold L. Sheppard, Ph.D.
Director, Center on Work and Aging, American Institutes for Research, Washington, D.C.

Gordon F. Streib, Ph.D.
Graduate Research Professor, Department of Sociology, University of Florida, Gainesville, Florida

Marvin B. Sussman, Ph.D.
Professor and Chair, Department of Medical Social Science and Marital Health, The Bowman Gray School of Medicine, Winston-Salem, North Carolina

James A. Wiley, Ph.D.
Human Population Laboratory, California State Department of Health, Berkeley, California

FOREWORD

This volume is one of three handbooks of aging: the *Handbook of the Biology of Aging*; the *Handbook of the Psychology of Aging*; and the *Handbook of Aging and the Social Sciences*. Because of the increase in literature about the many facets of aging, there has been an increasing need to collate and interpret existing information and to make it readily available in systematic form, providing groundwork for the more efficient pursuit of research. The phenomena and issues of aging cut across many scientific disciplines and professions, and a review of research necessarily involves many experts. A decision was made, therefore, to develop a multidisciplinary project, the purpose of which was to organize, evaluate, and interpret research data, concepts, theories, and issues on the biological, psychological, and social aspects of aging.

It is expected that investigators will use these books as the basic systematic reference works on aging, resulting in the stimulation and planning of needed research. Professional personnel, policy-makers, practitioners, and others interested in research, education, and services to the aged will undoubtedly find the volumes useful. The new handbooks will also provide a compendium of information for students entering and pursuing the field of gerontology and will, we hope, also stimulate the organization of new courses of instruction on aging.

The Editorial Committees generated the final outline of each volume, suggested contributors, and discussed sources of information and other matters pertinent to the development of the work. Committee recommendations were reviewed by the Advisory Board and the Editor-in-Chief.

Project Advisory Board

Vern L. Bengtson
Robert H. Binstock
James E. Birren
Sheila M. Chown
Caleb E. Finch
Leonard Hayflick
K. Warner Schaie
Ethel Shanas
Nathan W. Shock
F. Marott Sinex

James E. Birren, *Editor-in-Chief*

Editorial Committees

Handbook of the Biology of Aging

Harold Brody
Caleb E. Finch (Co-Editor)
Leonard Hayflick (Co-Editor)
Isadore Rossman
F. Marott Sinex

Handbook of the Psychology of Aging

James E. Birren (Co-Editor)
Jack Botwinick
Sheila M. Chown
Carl Eisdorfer
K. Warner Schaie (Co-Editor)

Handbook of Aging and the Social Sciences

Vern L. Bengtson
Robert H. Binstock (Co-Editor)

George L. Maddox
Ethel Shanas (Co-Editor)
Dorothy Wedderburn

There are many individuals who contributed to the successful completion of this publication project: Phoebe S. Liebig, Project Coordinator; Julie L. Moore, Research Bibliographer; Project Assistants Barbara H. Johnson, Aelred R. Rosser, Rochelle Smalewitz, and Robert D. Nall; Editorial Assistant V. Jayne Renner; Copy Editors Robert D. Nall and Judy Aklonis (social sciences), James Gollub (psychology), and Peggy Wilson and Carolyn Croissant (biology); Julie L. Moore, Indexing; and Library Assistance, Emily H. Miller and Jean E. Mueller. It is impossible to give the details of their many and varied contributions to the total effort, but they reflect the best traditions of respect for scholarship.

The preparation of the handbooks has been a nonprofit venture; no royalties are paid to any individual or institution. The intent was to give the books a wide circulation on an international level and to reduce publication costs.

The project was supported by a grant from the Administration on Aging under the title "Integration of Information on Aging: Handbook Project," Grant Number 93-P-75181/9, to the University of Southern California, with James E. Birren as the principal investigator. The Editor and his associates wish to thank Dr. Marvin Taves, who encouraged the development of the project as a staff member of the Adminstration on Aging, and also the agency itself, which perceived the value of such work and provided the grant for its support.

JAMES E. BIRREN

PREFACE

The purposes of the *Handbook of Aging and the Social Sciences* are to provide comprehensive information and major reference sources, and to suggest contemporary research issues on the phenomena of aging. To achieve these purposes the social aspects of aging are viewed through the perspectives of the social sciences, broadly conceived.

This *Handbook* is intended for use by researchers, professional practitioners, and students in the field of aging. It is also expected that the book can serve as a basic reference tool for scholars and professionals who are not presently engaged in research and practice directly focused on aging and the aged. Accordingly, the volume has been designed as a compendium of what is now known about the social aspects of aging and of suggested central issues for further research.

The present *Handbook* represents a somewhat different approach to the organization of knowledge about aging than that used by Clark Tibbitts in his pioneering effort in editing the *Handbook of Social Gerontology* published in 1960. The Editors of this volume believe that knowledge about the social aspects of aging can be best understood and developed within the framework of the social science disciplines. Each discipline approaches the study of aging and the aged in terms of its own constructs and subject matter, contributing its unique strengths to an understanding of the topic. This multidisciplinary focus, we believe, substantially enriches the intellectual resources available for understanding the social dimensions of aging.

The *Handbook* is organized into five sections.

The first section, *The Social Aspects of Aging*, considers the origins and scope of interest in aging as a social phenomenon, some of the presuppositions that underlie the study of age-related changes, and the life span context in which aging takes place. A second section, *Aging and Social Structure*, deals with changes in the age structure of populations, with the role and status of the aged in various societies, and with contemporary intergenerational relations. In the third section, *Aging and Social Systems*, the contributors discuss differences among age strata in a variety of social systems, and how aging persons affect and are in turn affected by family life, housing and institutional arrangements, the economy, patterns of work, retirement and leisure, the law, and political systems. Under a fourth general heading, *Aging and Interpersonal Behavior*, the authors consider social networks, role changes through the life span, and death and dying. Finally, a section on *Aging and Social Intervention* treats the political and strategic issues involved in contemporary and future societal efforts to provide and deploy income, health and social services, and other social resources to the aging.

The topics treated in the 25 chapters of this volume have been sifted through the analytical screening of the best available experts in the various disciplines. These contributors successfully met a number of difficult challenges. Whenever possible, the authors brought to bear knowledge and points of view available from outside the United States. They provided historical perspectives on their topics, and they constructed their presentations so as to ensure that the usefulness of the volume would not be limited by specific time referents. Most impressively, they were able to present their knowledge and viewpoints succinctly and to relate their treatments to those of their fellow authors.

In developing the subject matter for this volume and in the selection of contributors, the Editors were assisted by James E. Birren, Editor for the *Handbook* project, and by an Editorial Committee of three Associate Editors: Vern L. Bengtson, George L. Maddox, and Dorothy Wedderburn. The Associate Editors also helped substantially in the process of editorial review. The first draft of each chapter was read and critically reviewed by at least one Associate Editor and one Editor. Comments and suggestions from these readings were organized and forwarded to the authors for their consideration in undertaking revised drafts.

If this volume has any special merit it is due to the seriousness with which the chapter authors accepted their assignments and to the good will with which they responded to editorial criticism and suggestions. To these colleagues, the Editors and Associate Editors would like to acknowledge their special appreciation.

ROBERT H. BINSTOCK
ETHEL SHANAS

CONTENTS

PART THREE

Aging and Social Systems

PART FOUR   401

Aging and Interpersonal Behavior

PART 1 THE SOCIAL ASPECTS OF AGING

1
SCOPE, CONCEPTS AND METHODS IN THE STUDY OF AGING

George L. Maddox
Duke University
and
James Wiley
University of Illinois, Chicago Circle

Explicit interest in human aging and in the aged has increased markedly among social scientists during the past three decades. This chapter will trace the development of this interest and will selectively highlight major themes and issues which will be discussed in detail in subsequent chapters. The recent history of social scientific study of aging illustrates two issues particularly well: (1) the fusion between basic and applied research and (2) the application of multidisciplinary and interdisciplinary approaches to complex scientific and social phenomena. We will begin with a brief discussion of the emergence of research on aging and the aged first as a social problem and then as a social scientific problem. Social scientists initially focused their attention on the aged and viewed with concern, and occasionally alarm, demographic trends and societal arrangements which seemed to militate against, if not preclude, the social integration of older persons. Adaptation in late life was viewed as quite problematic. However, the early discussion of aging as a social problem identified most of the contemporary issues in the social scientific study of human aging: the

social and cultural as distinct from the biological meaning of age; age as a basis for the allocation of social roles and resources over the life span; the bases of social integration and adaptation in the later years of life; and the special methodological problems of studying time-dependant processes over the life cycle and of interpreting observed stability and change.

Our overview of the emergence of these themes and issues will be followed by brief and selective illustrations of notable research on aging in each social scientific discipline. We will conclude with a discussion of methodological issues which deliberately focuses on several issues currently of distinct relevance for the study of aging—age as an explanatory variable, cohort analysis, and the measurement of environments. We take for granted that the elements of sound research design and multivariate statistical techniques of data analysis are basic and important in studies of human aging, but not distinctively so. Our limited space will be devoted to issues we consider especially important in contemporary social scientific research on aging.

AGING AND THE AGED: SOCIAL PROBLEM AND SCIENTIFIC ISSUE

Thomas S. Kuhn (1970) has argued persuasively that science as it is normally pursued is a strenuous and devoted attempt to force nature into the conceptual boxes supplied by professional education. The propositions presented in the paradigms of normal science identify significant facts, match fact and theory, and organize the perspectives which purport to describe and explain various aspects of reality. Scientific research does not ordinarily aim to produce conceptual or phenomenal novelty and, when successful, produces neither. Rather, scientists are essentially puzzle-solvers whose paradigms suggest which puzzles are interesting and solvable and which are not. Hence, prevailing paradigms of a scientific community often tend, Kuhn argues, to isolate scientists from problems which are not reducible to puzzle form and which do not have a definitive solution. Unlike engineers or physicians, scientists need not choose problems because they need solution or choose their problems without regard to the availability of the concepts and techniques necessary to solve them. Social scientists are more likely than others, Kuhn suggests, to defend the choice of problems in terms of their social significance, but this is not common even among them.

Kuhn's observations are relevant to understanding the study of aging. Recognition of aging as a social problem is recent; recognition of aging as a social scientific problem is more recent still. The social scientific study of aging needs but currently lacks widely shared paradigms which would provide common conceptualization of issues, standard measurements, and clearly defined agendas for the systematic testing of hypotheses derived from theory. Applied, problem-oriented studies of the societal consequences of aging predominate; but increasingly sophisticated theory and research techniques are now available to social scientists for use in describing, monitoring, and forecasting social issues posed by an aging population. No single theoretical perspective organizes substantive research on the social aspects of aging. In fact, methodological issues have dominated the attention of social scientists in recent years. Major theoretical advances in our understanding of aging appear to depend on the development and application of analytic techniques for sorting out the relative importance of cohort, environmental, and aging effects on behavior in late life.

The Aged as a Social Problem

Public curiosity about aspects of the human life cycle is quite old, but the systematic study of aging is quite new. Students of intellectual history have noted that every period of history highlights a particular division of human life and designates a privileged age. Ariès (1962) argues that youth was the privileged age of the seventeenth century, childhood of the nineteenth, and adolescence of the twentieth. Although old age is yet to be a time of privilege in modern societies, the aged and aging were discovered as social problems in late nineteenth century Europe and as social scientific problems in the second quarter of the twentieth century in the United States.

As early as the 1930's, the personal troubles commonly associated with late life were being described frequently as a social problem and the aged as a problem group in the United States (Tibbitts, 1960a; Maddox, 1970). A core idea of the social problem perspective is the perception of unnecessary human suffering which threatens prevailing social values and is remediable by collective action (Weinberger and Rubington, 1973). The changing demographic structure of populations in western industrial societies (see, e.g., Browning, 1968; Siegel and O'Leary, 1973; United Nations, 1973) was the common point of departure for those who initially viewed with alarm the social implications in increasing life expectancy and an increasing number of older persons whose health and welfare needs would obviously strain existing social arrangements. A Social Science Research Council research planning report (Pollak, 1948), the work for which was begun in 1941, noted that contemporary demographic trends were "fraught with social complications" especially in societies which historically value competition; extol individuality; stress productivity; are deeply suspicious of public welfare programs; experience changes in the structure and function of families; and insist on universalistic standards of performance regardless of age. Human suffering among aged persons in the form of incapacity, isolation, and poverty were considered to be prevalent enough to warrant social concern and social action (see also Burgess, ed., 1960).

The way a society defines its social problems and discusses their solutions, reflects, at least implicitly, a perspective; the perceived nature of a problem affects both the solutions one can imagine to be relevant and the solutions one is likely to pursue. Weinberger and Rubington (1973) have suggested five common perspectives on social problems which can be usefully applied to both early and contemporary references to aging or to the aged as a social problem. The two major perspectives they propose are designated *social pathology* and *social disorganization*. Three additional perspectives concentrate on various aspects of social power and its uses—these they designate *value conflict*, *deviance*, and *labeling*. While the literature on aging as a social problem is largely descriptive and átheoretical, each of these perspectives has appeared at one time or another.

The *social pathology* perspective has its roots in biology and its rhetoric features the concept of disease. From this perspective, social problems are basically explained by faulty individuals, and their solution requires that individuals be changed. Unhealthy social conditions do exacerbate the behavior of individuals whose behavior is problematic; but in the final analysis, flawed individuals must be treated in the interest of achieving a healthy society. An illustration of a social pathology perspective on problems of aging is found in discussions of the extension of the human life span (e.g., Conference on Extension of Human Life Span, 1970). Such discussions typically emphasize the eradication of disease and modification of cellular aging as the most important task in reducing social problems associated with aging. In contrast, the SSRC report on research planning (Pollak, 1948) notes the deterioration of physical and mental capacity with age but focuses instead on restrictions of social opportunities as a more basic issue, an emphasis which reflects a *social disorganization* perspective on the social problem of aging. Social

change and cultural conflict lead to breakdown of social rules and restriction of opportunities. The actions required to reduce problems of aging involve the restoration of social consensus about the equitable distribution of social resources. Society must accommodate the aging individual, not the other way around.

The remaining three perspectives on social problems discussed by Weinberger and Rubington agree that social problems cannot be adequately reduced to faults which lie ultimately in either the individual or in society. These perspectives all call attention to the complexity of social transactions, to the diversity of individuals which blurs distinctions between normalcy and deviancy, and to deviancy and conflict as the natural and inevitable products of social interaction. Thus, unusual behavior should be understood and appreciated rather than simply condemned and punished.

From the *value conflict* perspective, social problems associated with aging and the aged cannot be adequately understood in terms of either individual pathology or social disorganization. Arnold Rose (1968) argued, for example, that the fate of older persons in the United States is largely independent of their personal characteristics; rather, the problems of older persons stem less from social disorganization than from the use of dominant middle-class, middle-aged life-styles and values to judge the behavior of the old (see also Rosow, 1967). Although the empirical support for Rose's contention has been challenged, his perspective on the problem of old age is clear. He locates the problems substantially in the structure and values of society rather than in the older individual.

This contention is also relevant for understanding the fourth perspective on social problems, *deviancy*. For a very long time, the analysis of social problems traced the explanation of the nonconforming individual to personal characteristics. If, for example, one begins with the view that the behavior of the middle-class, middle-aged individual constitutes normalcy, then behavior in late life not in conformity with these expectations might reflect changing ability to meet expectations, changing motivation to do so, or both. The expected response to observed deviance from social expectations is that such behavior should be disapproved, corrected if possible, and, if not correctable, isolated. In recent years, the growth of a socio-logical view of deviancy has involved, according to Matza (1969), the replacement of an empha-sis on correction by an appreciation of the pre-sumed deviant subject, the purging of a concep-tion of pathology by stress on human diversity, and the erosion of the simplistic distinction be-tween deviant and conventional behavior. The perception of aging in late life as deviant, some-thing to correct if possible, makes empathy and understanding, much less appreciation, difficult, if not impossible.

It is interesting to read Cumming and Henry's *Growing Old* (1961) as a critique of the ten-dency to insist that older persons remain socially active and as an appreciation of the in-evitability of withdrawal and death. If late life, as they argue, is inevitably characterized by the progressive mutual and inevitable withdrawal of individual and society in anticipation of death, then this withdrawal is or can be functional. The imposition of the behavioral norms of middle life on older persons is therefore inap-propriately intended to correct perceived devi-ance. One of the principal contributions of functionalism in social scientific studies of be-havior, Matza has argued, is that notions of pathology should be purged in favor of compre-hending and appreciating human diversity. The argument of *Growing Old*, quite independant of the adequacy of the data it marshals in sup-port of the disengagement thesis, about which we will have more to say later, does illustrate an appreciation of types of behavior in late life usually considered to be deviant.

The last perspective discussed by Weinberger and Rubington is *labeling*. This perspective stresses the construction, and hence the possi-bility of reconstruction, of social reality by in-dividuals with the power to do so. Untenable diversity is what the powerful definer says it is. The determination of deviance lies therefore in the power of groups to enforce their definitions at least as much as it lies in the behavior of the individuals in question. Bernice Neugarten (1972) has documented the particular social construction of the age-related social norms which constrain the behavior of individuals over the life span. Society provides guidelines which

permit an individual of a given age and sex to know whether he is "on track, on time" in edu-cational and career development, for instance. Age-related normative expectations can and do inform members of a society that children are supposed to be in educational institutions, but adults not usually, and older adults certainly not; that retirement from work at age 65 is normal; or that sex after 60 is not something one should expect or even talk about. The per-ceived capacity, the motivation to respond, and the behavioral response to age norms affect social evaluation of the older individual and hence self-evaluation. Rosow (1967) has argued that prevailing expectations about behavior in late life tend to be negative and restricting, so much so, in fact, that older persons tend to avoid applying the label *old* to themselves whenever possible, but tend to be so labeled anyway by others. Rosow interprets avoidance of the label *old* as an indication that older in-dividuals correctly perceive the normative pre-scriptions associated with late life; to label one-self as old or to accept that label concedes that the prevailing negative stereotypes of older people are applicable.

In sum, we have reviewed aging and the aged in terms of various social problem perspectives in order to indicate that: (1) references to aging and the aged as social problems are frequent in the early social scientific literature; (2) the analysis of aging and the aged from a social problem perspective is primarily implicit; (3) illustrations of all five social problem perspec-tives as summarized by Weinberger and Rubing-ton are found in the literature on aging; and (4) among social scientists, the social pathology perspective has been less attractive than per-spectives which emphasize the construction of social reality and the power of social groups to define social reality in ways which are disadvan-tageous to older persons.

Aging as a Social Scientific Problem

Interest in aging among social scientists has not, however, been confined to an emphasis on social problems, although this emphasis is con-tinually observed to the present time. In fact, social scientific interest in human aging is evi-dent in the early 1940's; and 1945 constitutes an intellectual watershed of interest in the scientific as distinct from the social problem aspects of aging. The work of Linton and Cottrell anticipated this shift in emphasis. Ralph Linton's (1942) seminal article on age and sex categories noted that, while "old man" and "old woman" were designated in all societies, we actually know very little about the factors which affect the problematic or successful transition into late life. In the same year, L. S. Cottrell, Jr. (1942) anticipated the issue which was to preoccupy social scientific studies of aging for the next three decades. This issue was adjustment or adaptation to age roles, its determinants and consequences.

We can assert here, intending to elaborate subsequently, that the earliest social scientific discussions of adjustment or adaptation in late life never concentrated on chronological age as a simple predictor and consistently stressed the necessity of a multivariate approach to understanding behavior in late life. Early investigators clearly appreciated the complex problem of person/environment fit, and, to some extent, understood the complications of cohort analysis (see, e.g., Folsom and Morgan, 1937; Pollak, 1943; Folsom, 1946; Frank, 1946).

Tibbitts (1960a) documents, however, that while a number of studies of aging were undertaken prior to 1950, these studies tended to be inventories, surveys, and observations intended primarily to alert and aid in the solution of practical problems of welfare and health among the aged. Among social and behavioral scientists, only in psychology did an identifiable professional group specifically interested in aging as a process emerge; this was the Division of Later Maturity and Old Age created by the American Psychological Association in 1946. The Social Science Research Council appointed a multidisciplinary committee on social adjustment in late life, in 1941; this committee eventually produced a significant report without, however, having much direct impact on established social scientific disciplines. Collections of social scientific investigators emerging at the University of Chicago and the University of Michigan in the 1940's and at the University of California (Berkeley and San Francisco) and Duke University in the 1950's laid the foundation for subsequent social scientific research.

And, although conceptualization of aging as a social scientific issue in the 1940's ran far ahead of empirical research, issues outlined in the literature of the 1940's and 1950's eventually proved to be basically sound.

John E. Anderson as late as 1960 called attention to the continuing difficulty of enlisting social scientists to study aging but correctly described the evolution of the social sciences toward empiricism and toward interest in explanation. Insofar as social scientists were interested in age at all, they were interested increasingly in social and behavioral aspects of aging, as well as in the characteristics of the aged. L. K. Frank (1946) in his perceptive lead article in the first issue of the *Journal of Gerontology* argued that the groundwork for a synoptic, holistic conception of aging which would necessarily draw on the specialized investigation of many different disciplines had already been laid. Frank knew the limitations of chronological age as an independant variable, noting "the extraordinary variations among individuals of the same chronological age." He also argued that an adequate foundation of the process of aging would involve what he labeled field theory, i.e., a system of separately distinguishable parts and activities which together constitute a whole and which, in turn, structure the behavior of organisms as they act, react, and interact in changing environments. Frank thus anticipated the contemporary rediscovery of the relevance of ecology for understanding the process of aging and the behavior of the aged.

The publication in 1948 of the Social Science Research Council's research planning report *Social Adjustment in Old Age* edited by Otto Pollak marked another important transition from concern about the aged to the study of aging as a process. The report reflected almost a decade of work by an interdisciplinary committee, which began in 1941. By 1943, the committee had focused its attention on social adjustment in old age as the most significant issue for social scientific research. This decision set a course which was to be pursued by many social scientists for the next two decades. The SSRC report intended to provide a common frame of reference to research investigators. It concentrated initially, for example, on alternative definitions of age. Should we focus on chronological or functional age? The response was clear; while chronological age may provide a convenient marker for locating problems and associated social phenomena, the meaning of age is in important ways a dependent variable. The meaning of *old* varies by social and cultural context. Chronological age is at best an indicator which marks substantial variation in both capabilities and behavior.

The scientific issue of interest in the SSRC report is, in fact, not the aged or even aging but the multiple ways in which individuals adapt in late life. No *a priori* assumptions about whether most older persons do or do not achieve adequate adjustment were made. Into the equation which will most adequately predict adjustment the authors of the report put needs, capacities, predispositions (preferred life-style), and social opportunities. Attention was also given to possible ethnic and subcultural differences in modes of adjustment. An important observation was also made about the origin of problems in late life; for example, the report stated that "actually many old age problems originate not in changes in physical and mental capacities but in changes in social opportunity" and, "both the individual and social factors are usually involved in the solution of the resulting problems." The emphasis of the report thus stressed transactions between person and environment, an emphasis which has reappeared in current studies of aging.

Another seminal document in the early social scientific literature on aging which anticipated current interest in multidisciplinary research on aging is the proceedings of a conference held at the University of California, Berkeley, in 1950. The proceedings, edited by Harold E. Jones (1950), included summaries of current and projected research at three universities (Chicago, Syracuse, and California, Berkeley), in two private organizations (Moosehaven and Teachers Insurance and Annuity Association) and in one European country (England). While some attention was given to biological aspects of aging, the emphasis was on social factors, including comments by Gregory Bateson on cultural aspects of aging, by Clark Kerr on the implications of an aging population, by Mason Haire on psychology, by Lloyd Fisher on politics, by Peter Steiner on econom-

ics, and by Seymour Lipset on sociology. The proceedings underscore the decidedly multidisciplinary strategy that characterized early social scientific proposals for research on aging. Moreover, specific methodological issues of particular current relevance for research on aging were discussed, including the importance of longitudinal studies and of special problems of sampling, research design, testing, and subject motivation. The potential relevance of research for policy formation on issues of public health, income, maintenance, welfare, and social adjustment was also considered. Interest in empirical research on aging was clearly stressed throughout the Berkeley report.

The sophisticated level of conceptualization presented in this early report is impressive. Age was understood to be a dependent as well as an independent variable; and chronological age, it was argued, masks substantial individual variation. A host of individual and environmental factors affect reactions in late life. Methodologically, the participants in the Berkeley conference distinguished between age differences and age changes, knew why longitudinal studies are useful and necessary, and anticipated the need for cohort analysis.

At the end of the 1950's a multi-university consortium had projected three volumes which would document the scope, methods, and conceptualization of studies on aging. The first of these volumes to appear was the *Handbook of Aging and the Individual: Psychological and Biological Aspects* edited by James E. Birren (1959a). Two additional volumes appeared shortly afterwards, the *Handbook of Social Gerontology: Societal Aspects of Aging* edited by Clark Tibbitts (1960) and *Aging in Western Societies* edited by E. W. Burgess (1960). These volumes constitute excellent bibliographic coverage of studies on aging in the two decades prior to their publication and document the principal characteristics of studies of aging noted above: a multidisciplinary emphasis, an appropriate tension between emphasis on problems of the aged and the scientific study of aging, a distinction between age change and age difference, and a keen awareness that chronological age is a variable with limited utility in social scientific research.

While these three volumes should be consulted for information about the scope, methods, and concepts of the studies at the beginning of the 1960's, James E. Birren's (1959b) opening chapter in the handbook edited by him is especially noteworthy because of the clarity with which scientific issues are identified and discussed. Birren's discussion of age as a variable in research is germane for research investigators generally and summarizes succinctly the dominant view at the end of the 1950's. An aging mechanism, he argued cautiously, "may be defined as an invariant relationship in which, with present knowledge, time cannot be excluded as a parameter for all transformations of that relationship." He concluded that it is difficult to contemplate, much less demonstrate, such invariant relationships for the complex range of biological, sociological, and psychological phenomena of interest to gerontologists. This is so because both distant as well as proximate factors must be considered in explaining observed behavior. There are many indications that age status and age norms are social facts which define the allocation of roles, resources, and honor as well as the expectations about behavior which constrain observed behavior; as a consequence, *age* becomes a dependent as well as an independant variable. Chronological age has been demonstrably useful in the construction of life tables and is an administratively useful general index of the residual life expectancy of healthy individuals at any specific age. Otherwise, chronological age has limited utility in the understanding or prediction of the behavior of adults. In fact, aging connotes three distinct phenomena: the biological capacity for survival, the psychological capacity for adaptation, and the sociological capacity for the fulfillment of social roles. Insofar as the various indices of these various aspects of aging are relatively autonomous, the linking word *age* loses its usefulness. Or said another way, as research permits increasing specification of biological, psychological, and sociological variables which describe, explain, and predict behavior, chronological age will persist primarily as a crude but convenient reference for purposes of general discussion and administrative classification.

Birren, as well as others, knew in the late 1950's that patterns of aging and age changes are masked when cross-sectional research data are used; Birren specifically anticipated the need for research designed to assess cohort differences and the cultural-boundedness of research confined to a single society or subgroup within a society. He further anticipated the imbalance in increasingly fine-tuned conceptualizations and measurements of individual differences and the crudity of conceptualization and measurement of environments. It is possible, he concluded, that human behavior is organized more intermittently and is more determined by situation than we have been prepared to believe or to demonstrate. Vital or maintenance biology, as he called it, may well be a necessary but not determining condition of behavior. And our understanding of human adaptation must include the possibility of discontinuities in behavior over the life span.

A decade and a half later, research on aging continues to explore, with only partial success, the implications and applications of the sophisticated conceptualization of human aging in print at the beginning of the 1960's.

A BRIEF REVIEW BY DISCIPLINE

Tibbitts' *Handbook of Social Gerontology* (1960b) and Burgess' *Aging in Western Societies* (1960) are landmarks in social scientific research on aging. The bibliographies and summaries in these volumes provide a convenient, reasonably comprehensive and useful introduction to the relevant work of anthropologists, economists, political scientists, and sociologists in the United States, and to a limited extent, in Western European countries. The notable review of gerontological research which marked the beginning of the 1960's was matched at the end of that decade by three volumes edited by Matilda W. Riley and supported by the Russell Sage Foundation. *Aging and Society: An Inventory of Research Findings* (Riley and Foner, 1968) selected, condensed, and organized an enormous body of empirical research on social scientific aspects of human aging. The strategy of presentation is interesting and useful. Illustrative tables of findings from published research are reported and annotated, and each chapter concludes with summaries and suggestions for future research. A second volume, *Aging and the Professions* (Riley, Riley, and Johnson, 1969), interprets the findings of the inventory for a variety of fields concerned with the well-being of the aging and the aged and with the prevention and management of problems associated with late life. The third volume, *A Sociology of Age Stratification* (Riley, Johnson, and Foner, 1972), constitutes an integrated effort to explain the use and significance of age for the allocation of social resources and opportunities over the lifespan. These major volumes are broadly interdisciplinary and comprehensively reference a large number of monographs, research reports, and articles in periodical literature.

While the subsequent chapters of the present volume will provide detailed documentation of research and research findings in a wide variety of disciplines, it is useful to provide here an overview of the themes and issues that have appeared in particular social scientific disciplines. Since the other chapters will develop specific issues in detail, no attempt is made to provide exhaustive references. Our purpose is to illustrate representative issues, themes, and concepts. In these brief accounts, continuing interest in social problems associated with aging will be apparent in spite of increasing emphasis on aging as a social scientific problem. Concern with issues of social policy affecting the welfare of the aged is particularly apparent in economics and political science. Age as a basis for the allocation of social roles and resources is stressed in sociology and anthropology; both these disciplines have been particularly interested in the possibility and probability of the social integration of older individuals in their adaptation to personal and social change. The dominant methodological issues of all the social sciences focus on the distinction between age differences and age changes and on the importance of distinguishing the effects of age, cohort, and immediate environment in explaining behavior over the life cycle.

Anthropology and Comparative Sociology

Comparative research is basic to the scientific enterprise and its search for invariant relationships among phenomena of interest. For the social scientist, an anthropological and comparative sociological perspective suggests a fundamental and necessary challenge to all propositions about human behavior that are claimed to be culture-free and hence universally applicable.

The premier comparative study of aging in various societies is Leo W. Simmons' (1945) *The Role of the Aged in Primitive Societies*. The general argument of this early review and interpretation of published anthropological materials is that the status of the aged varies among societies; the allocation of resources and honor to older persons in a given society is negatively related to the development of technology and occupational specialization, or more generally, modernization. This general argument has reappeared in various guises for almost three decades and has a recent expression in the Cowgill and Holmes' (1972) *Aging and Modernization*.

The empirical evidence for testing propositions about the social determinants of age status remains, however, quite limited. Palmore and Manton (1974) have presented evidence from 31 countries which challenges the prevailing conclusion; they suggest that as societies move beyond a transitional stage of rapid modernization, discrepancies between the status of the aged and the nonaged decrease, and the relative status of the aged appears to rise. Hence, it is important to distinguish between the short- and long-run outcomes of social change and to take account of this possibility in designing research.

International contacts among investigators, stimulated by the International Congresses of Gerontology, have encouraged comparative cross-national research. A good example is the comparison of social and behavioral aspects of life among older persons in Denmark, Great Britain, and the United States (Shanas, Townsend, Wedderburn, Friis, Milhøj, and Stehouwer, 1968; see also Tibbitts and Donahue, 1962). Probability samples in each of three industrialized societies have provided data which document convincingly an unexpectedly high degree of social integration and life satisfaction among older persons. Although some differences in the perceptions, attitudes, behavior, and social circumstances of older persons are reported in the three societies, the similarities dominate. Another illustration of comparative cross-national research is the six-city (Vienna, Milan, Bonn, Nijmegen, Warsaw, Chicago) study of adjustment to retirement (Havighurst, Munnichs, Neugarten, and Thomas, 1969). The principal objective of this study was to assess the effect of occupation, socio-cultural environment, and involvement in various social roles on life satisfaction. Social expectations about behavior and options for involvement in late life did vary by city, and these factors affected social participation. But the positive relationship between role involvement and life satisfaction suggested by most research in the United States was confirmed in each city for both occupational categories.

Cross-national studies of economic issues associated with aging and the age composition of populations have begun to appear (Shanas et al., 1968; Schulz, Carrin, Krupp, Peschke, Sclar, and Van Steenberge, 1974). These studies have described provisions for income maintenance and the social and economic situation of older persons in the United States, Great Britain, and Denmark and also in the United States as compared with Sweden, West Germany, Belgium, and Canada.

There is a considerable amount of research that is implicitly comparative; that is, a number of European investigators have tested and confirmed, in their own countries, generalizations about various aspects of behavior in late life in the United States. This is the case in Rosenmayr's work on family relationships in Austria (1968) and in other publications of the Institute of Sociology, University of Vienna. It is also the case in a large number of social and social psychological investigations in Europe summarized by Ursula Lehr (1972). In general, these studies provide additional confirmation that the descriptions of the aged and the factors which affect the aging process in at least the western industrial world are very similar.

Cultural values — for example, a preference for youth, for nuclear rather than extended families, for productivity, for individualization, for independence, for activity — can and do help explain observed variations in the behavior of older persons. And some cultural configurations

should be more stressful to some individuals than to others in late life; this was in fact the observation of the Social Science Research Council Report (Pollak, 1948) almost three decades ago. This is also the argument of Clark and Anderson (1967) in their contemporary study of older persons in San Francisco.

The Clark and Anderson study, part of a series edited by Alexander Simon at the Langley Porter Neuropsychiatric Institute, University of California Medical Center, San Francisco, is in the tradition of urban anthropology, a mixture of ethnography and survey research. Although the dominant proposition of their research is that the cultural values of the United States make growing old a difficult challenge, the fact is that most of the older persons studied appeared to be adapting reasonably well; that is, they show a "rich and wide variety of adaptations." Social integration of older persons they found, is not only possible but also probable. Social isolation, negative self-conceptions, low morale, and mental illness are the exceptions, not the rule. The Clark and Anderson research provides additional evidence in support of the positive relationship between social functioning and personal satisfaction; hence these investigators are appropriately critical of disengagement theory. They are probably correct in concluding that the disengagement argument tends to misread autonomous behavior of the healthy, middle-class elderly as withdrawal and tends to underestimate the negative effects of illness and subsequent age segregation on behavior.

Economics

The economic depression of the 1930's focused public attention dramatically on issues of employment, income maintenance, and social welfare. The special relevance of these issues for older persons was anticipated by Abraham Epstein's (1928) The Challenge of the Aged, was discussed in detail at the First National Conference on Aging in 1950, and has been reviewed periodically since that time (Corson and McConnell, 1956; Steiner and Dorfman, 1957; Orbach and Tibbitts, 1962; U.S. Senate Special Committee on Aging, 1969).

It is a matter of fact that older persons are at high risk for not being in the labor force and experience a substantial drop in income at the time of retirement. If their retirement income remains constant, they are particularly vulnerable both to inflation and to the rapid growth of the economy. Older individuals are thus disproportionately represented among persons considered to have inadequately low incomes. The economic problem of late life has been more obvious than the solutions (Gordon, 1960). Issues of social equity are involved in questions of income distribution; determining how much income redistribution is enough and how to finance adequate incomes for retired persons in a society which is characterized by a decreasing work life and an increasing number of years in retirement are complex political as well as economic issues (McKinney and DeVyver, 1966).

There have been repeated attempts to document patterns of income, consumption, and saving over the life span since 1941 (Steiner and Dorfman, 1957; Goldstein, 1960; Kreps, 1969). These attempts make it clear how difficult it is to disentangle the issues of level of living (goods and services which can be purchased with a given income) and standard of living (goods and services which should be available to maintain a valued life style). It has been demonstrated that older persons are not a homogeneous category economically; categorical solutions to problems of income maintenance based on age alone are thus debatable and controversial. In fact, economists appear to be in general agreement that *ad hoc* solutions to problems of income maintenance in late life cannot be satisfactory in the long run and are not indicated. The fundamental economic problems of late life stem from social and public policy, explicit or implicit, regarding the distribution of work, income, and leisure over the life span (Steiner and Dorfman, 1957; Kreps, 1963; Kreps, 1971). These are fundamental political issues, not simply economic ones; they remain unresolved but may be amenable to solutions (Schulz *et al.*, 1974).

In a comparative economic study of the United Kingdom, Denmark, and the United States, Dorothy Wedderburn (Shanas *et al.*,

1968) found that the basic determinants of income in late life were the same in the three countries. Income was related to continued employment and the availability, level, and form of government benefits. Personal resources, while a useful supplement, were not a substitute for governmental provisions. Diversity of economic circumstances among the elderly was noted in the three countries; but variance in income among individuals was greater in the U.S. than in Britain and much greater than in Denmark. In spite of differences in public policy regarding income maintenance in the United Kingdom, United States, and Denmark, total societal allocations in each country as a proportion of gross national product were similar; the proportion in 1962 was 2.3 percent in the United States, 2.9 percent in Denmark, and 3.3 percent in the United Kingdom.

Political Science

The social visibility of the elderly increased rapidly in this century as their numbers increased and the magnitude of their health and welfare needs became evident. Particularly in the depression years of the 1930's, the income, welfare, and health problems of older persons challenged the adequacy of existing institutional arrangements. Considerable public discussion of income maintenance and related issues of social security began in these years and have continued for over three decades.

Older persons as a social category are of political interest because there is the possibility that shared concerns about their interests and well-being might be converted into political movements. The Townsend Movement of the 1930's suggested the possibility of a politics of age and a potent bloc of older voters; but political science research has documented the improbability of such developments either then or now (Holtzman, 1963; Pinner, Jacobs, and Selznick, 1959; Holtzman, 1954). The political behavior of older persons has been a particular interest in the United States as indicated by a great deal of research on age, aging, and political behavior (Riley and Foner, 1968, pp. 463-479, provides a review of relevant research; Foner, 1972, discusses theoretical issues). In balance, the political attitudes and interest of an older citizen in the United States, for instance, do not particularly differentiate him from adults generally; he is more likely to be affiliated with a party than most adults, and is as likely to vote as adults generally and more likely to vote than young adults. A focused debate on aging and political conservatism has illustrated with particular clarity a basic methodological issue of general relevance for social scientific research on aging; this is the necessity of distinguishing the effects of age, cohort, and time of measurement. Political science research on aging and political behavior provides some of the best illustrations currently available of empirical research in which these various effects may be parcelled out. The most frequent conclusion about aging and politics is that, in balance, age and aging have not proved to be particularly useful predictors of either political behavior or attitudes (Campbell, 1971; Douglass, Cleveland, and Maddox, 1974). There is simply no evidence that a politics of age is in prospect in the United States (Binstock, 1972; Marmor, 1973; Binstock, 1974).

Sociology

While some sociologists as early as the 1940's commented on the aged as a social category and on the social significance of age status and age norms, sociological interest in the life cycle in general and in the middle and later years of life has never been substantial. Interest in the development of children and adolescents has been common and is well established (see, e.g., Eisenstadt, 1956). Interest in adult development is uncommon and recent (see, e.g., Brim and Wheeler, 1966; Riley, Riley, and Johnson, 1969; Shanas, 1971; Cain, 1959; Streib and Orbach, 1967). The early work of Chen (1939), Folsom (1946), Linton (1942), Cottrell (1942), Landis (1942), and Pollak (1944) discussed aging and the aged as topics warranting sociological interest and research, but over a decade passed before systematic sociological studies on aging appeared. Sociological research was frequently done in multidisciplinary settings and was published in monographs rather than in sociological journals. For example, publications on aging from Duke University included the work of sociologists as well as biomedical and psychological investigators; at the same university, economists and other social scientists cooperated in a program of socioeconomic studies of aging (Kreps, 1963; McKinney and DeVyver, 1966; Simpson and McKinney, 1966). Multidisciplinary longitudinal studies of biomedical, psychological, and social adaptation in middle and late life among samples of subjects living in the community, begun in 1955, continue to the present at Duke (see Palmore, 1970, 1974).

In the middle and late 1950's, interdisciplinary research programs which included sociologists or social psychologists were launched at the Langley Porter Neuropsychiatric Institute, University of California Medical School, and at the University of Chicago. The Langley Porter studies focused on the determinants and consequences of mental health and illness in late life (Lowenthal, 1964; Lowenthal, Berkman et al., 1967; Clark and Anderson, 1967; and Simon, Lowenthal, and Epstein, 1970). The University of Chicago's Committee on Human Development began a series of studies, the best known of which are reported in three volumes describing the Kansas City Studies of Adult Life (Cumming and Henry, 1960; Neugarten and Associates, 1964; and Williams and Wirths, 1965).

Sociologists in the Duke, Langley Porter, and Chicago studies all concentrated to a substantial degree on adaptation in late life, conceptualized variously as morale, mental health, or life satisfaction. The dominant perspective which emerged in these studies was that social integration in late life is not only possible but also probable and that social integration predicts morale (or mental health or life satisfaction). The exception to the dominant perspective was, of course, Cumming and Henry's (1961) concept of disengagement. They argued that intrinsic and hence inevitable changes in personality in late life predicted increasing anormativeness and decreasing activity; this personal withdrawal coincided with functional societal needs for a succession of cohorts in important social roles. Optimal aging was said to require disengagement, expressed both in terms of reduced activity and reduction of affective attachment to social objects.

Critiques of disengagement as an explanation of optimal aging preoccupied investigators in the 1960's and was the premier issue. The general consensus reached was that, on both theoretical and empirical grounds, disengagement was one of several alternative life-styles equally capable of producing satisfaction (or morale) in late life. While disengagement was the dominant issue of the 1960's, it was not the only issue. Important studies were also conducted to specify relationships between work and retirement, the forms and consequences of kinship and generational interrelationships, and the forms and consequences of community participation in late life (Simpson and McKinney, 1966; Shanas and Streib, 1965).

In closing these brief comments on research on aging in sociology, we note two monographs which, when compared with the social psychological emphasis of the Duke, Langley Porter, and Chicago studies, are radically sociological. The first is Irving Rosow's *Social Integration of the Aged* (1967). Rosow argues that the probability of the social integration of older persons is significantly affected by the availability of age-peers of similar social status. Prevalent negative stereotyping of old age has led, he concluded, to a situation in which age segregation is not only a likely outcome but also a social condition in which alienation can be minimized, at least among socially disadvantaged elderly persons.

A second distinctly sociological volume warranting special comment is the third volume of the Russell Sage series on *Aging and Society* (Riley, Johnson, and Foner, 1972). *A Sociology of Age Stratification* recommends a theory of age stratification which parallels sociological work in socioeconomic stratification. Age is viewed by these authors as a fundamental social mechanism by which resources are allocated over the life course. Age cohorts tend to have fundamentally different experiences in their interaction with their past and present environments. This is one of the reasons why the assessment of cohort effects

must be considered along with both age effects and environmental effects in the explanation of observed behavior. The Rosow and the Riley, Johnson, and Foner volumes call attention to a badly and oddly neglected aspect of sociological studies of aging—the measurement of environments. This is a point which will receive attention later in this chapter.

THEMES AND ISSUES IN THE STUDY OF AGING

In the previous sections of this chapter we have provided a brief historical sketch of the emergence of social scientific interest in aging, noted the persistent interest in the aged as a social problem, and briefly illustrated various interests in the aged and in aging as they appear in different social scientific disciplines in recent decades. Selected themes and issues which have been explicit or implicit in our discussion will be highlighted and interpreted briefly in this section. Specifically, we will focus on: (a) aging and social integration; (b) successful adaptation; (c) age as a social characteristic; (d) society as a succession of age cohorts; (e) environment as a variable in understanding behavior; and (f) the continuing search for a unified theoretical perspective for the social scientific study of the life cycle. We see these as major issues which, among others, will be addressed in varying detail and with documentation in the chapters which follow.

In the final section of this chapter, we will concentrate on two methodological issues of particular relevance in the social scientific study of aging: the disentangling of age, period, and cohort effects in data analysis and the methodological implications of selecting the life span as a unit of analysis.

Aging and Social Integration

Four decades ago the projected rapid increase in the proportion of older persons in industrialized urban societies was viewed with concern, if not alarm. In such societies social differentiation and specialization characterized both individuals and social institutions; productivity tended to be valued and to provide an important basis for assessing individual merit. Older people were therefore perceived to be very vulnerable in modern society. The social integration of older persons appeared to be problematic on both theoretical and evidential grounds to many of the social scientists who gave the matter any consideration at all. And the answer continues to seem problematic to social scientists as contemporary as Irving Rosow. The values of modern industrial urban societies do appear to favor youthfulness; social roles in late life do appear to be ambiguously defined, inviting the inference that late life is roleless; and access to important social goods and services does appear to be restricted for many older persons.

But evidence of the social integration of older persons in all urban industrial societies has now been well documented; and, in balance, evidence of integration outweighs evidence of isolation. While no one would argue that older persons are exempt from discrimination, few would argue that older persons are singular targets of social inequity. Basic legal rights of older persons have been maintained; political participation of the older citizens is not strikingly different from other adults; most older persons live in private households; kinship relationships between generations demonstrably exist at a level which is higher than prevailing theory would have suggested; and social and economic security in the later years, while problematic for a substantial minority, is achieved to a tolerable degree for the majority. We do not argue that late life is an unproblematic or socially attractive period of the life cycle. Rather, we argue that current evidence indicates that older persons are more likely to be socially integrated than not. Age *per se* is not an adequate predictor of social integration. The agenda for future research in aging, we believe, should concentrate on identifying factors in addition to chronological age which facilitate or impede social integration. Even if age, or age-related characteristics such as illness and poverty, were demonstrably an impediment to social integration in a given society, one would still need to explore the transience and modifiability of such a finding. We see no necessary connection between age and social integration on either theoretical or evidential grounds.

Successful Adaptation

The relationship between aging and successful adaptation (variously morale or life satisfaction or mental health) is perhaps the oldest, most persistently investigated issue in the social scientific study of aging. The consensus which has emerged is impressively consistent: successful adaptation in late life is demonstrably the rule, not the exception, in a wide range of societies. Consensus does not exist about why this is the case. In the 1960's it was popular to pit activity theory against disengagement theory as alternative and contradictory explanations; the one purportedly emphasized social integration and involvement as the explanation of life satisfaction and the other, withdrawal of affective attachment and withdrawal from conventional involvement in social roles. Both perspectives, however, predicted successful adaptation as the expected outcome. And both perspectives were partially correct. What we have learned from longitudinal studies of successful adaptation in late life is that there are multiple pathways to this common outcome. While, in balance, research documents that the relatively more socially involved members of a cohort of older persons are more likely to report satisfaction, a disengaged life-style can also be found, but not commonly. Moreover, a disengaged life-style, when observed, appears to be continued from adulthood into late life and is not a product of late life. The capacity to maintain life satisfaction in the face of decreasing social involvement is an interesting phenomenon warranting study.

Age as a Social Characteristic

All societies mark and measure distance from birth in some fashion and in a variety of ways allocate social roles and resources on the basis of the resulting age grades. Societies do tend to be stratified by age, and age statuses do tend to be associated with age norms which define preferred or expected behavior. These observations provide a useful perspective for predicting and understanding regularities in human behavior at various points over the life cycle. However useful this perspective may be in orienting an observer, many important questions remain to be answered. The most basic question is the relationship between chronological age and the social meaning which is attached to distance from birth. Cultural and social preferences have rather clearly affected age status and related age norms variously over time in the same society and from one society to another. Chronological age may be useful in categorizing individuals for administrative purposes, but it is not a very precise predictor of adult behavior. The demonstrated tenuousness in the relationship between chronological age and adult behavior underlies the now common distinction between age differences and age changes and more recently the significance attached to age cohorts. Age norms observed in a society are intended to constrain behavior and presumably do so; one consequence of this is that behavior displayed at a particular chronological age cannot be assumed to be a totally reliable indicator of the range of possible behavioral responses. Observed differences in behavior among persons of various ages, therefore, cannot confidently be attributed to changes which inevitably occur over time. Discussions of society as a succession of age cohorts also suggest why the demonstration of changes in behavior unambiguously attributable to chronological aging is quite difficult.

Society as a Succession of Age Cohorts

While the methodological implications of age cohort analysis in studies of aging will be addressed specifically in the last section of this paper, a brief substantive comment is appropriate here. Individuals born at approximately the same time constitute a cohort who, at least figuratively, move through the life cycle together. We call attention to the phrase *born at approximately the same time*. The decision of investigators to define a cohort in terms of a single year or some longer period appears to be based primarily on practical rather than theoretical considerations. Cohorts differentiated by year of birth are conventional in the construction of life tables. Cohorts differentiated by five-year age spans are conventional in social scientific research in which census data are used.

At any point in time, a given society can be described as a collection of cohorts succeeding one another as they move through the life cycle. If, for instance, we define a cohort simply in terms of a particular chronological age, such as 65, we would observe that a new cohort achieves this age each year. Over a period of time we might observe that successive cohorts achieving age 65 are numerically larger or smaller, have completed more or fewer years of education, are in better or worse health, or are more or less homogeneous in a variety of ways. If we observed this succession for, say 20 years, the collection of survivors in the various cohorts would constitute a collection we might call "the elderly between the ages of 65 and 85." However, our continuous observations would have made us quite aware of inter- and intracohort differences at age 65. Unless we were willing to treat the observed differences at age 65 for the various cohorts as irrelevant or as likely to be negated by the passage of time after age 65, we would be very reluctant to explain any differences in behavior observed between a 65-year-old and an 85-year-old adult simply in terms of changes related to age. There is yet another reason for caution in using age to explain adult behavior.

Environment

If successive cohorts arriving at the same chronological age are different in ways that affect their behavior and subsequent life course, then we must entertain the hypothesis that the environments in which members of a cohort matured were different in some consequential ways. It is plausible to believe that the effects of distal environments in the experience of members of a cohort affect their experience of, and response to, immediate environments. Interestingly, while there is consensus among social scientists regarding the importance of environmental effects on behavior, no consensus is apparent regarding the conceptualization and measurement of environments (see, e.g., Willems, 1973; Lawton and Nahemow, 1973; Schooler, 1970). Efforts to conceptualize and measure environments have been complicated further by continuing uncertainty about how to assess the relative importance of perceived vis à vis objective aspects of environment. Psychologists have, in recent years, been increasingly willing to concede the limitations of explaining behavior in terms of personality traits and to stress the importance of interaction between personal preferences, predispositions or traits, and environmental stimuli. Social scientists, while flattered by this concession to the relevance of their perspective, have not developed the conceptualization and measurement of environments to the extent that psychologists have developed the conceptualization and measurement of personality. This inability to conceptualize and measure environment is a serious impediment to further research on behavior in late life.

Toward a Theoretical Perspective

Systematic development and application of theory are activities which, for the most part, have been and continue to be strikingly absent in the social scientific study of aging. Until recently, social scientific research has tended to be indifferent to theory (Cain, 1959, 1964; Streib and Orbach, 1967; Shanas, 1971), concentrating instead on the description of behavior in late life or on the social contexts within which the aged live and the aging run their life course. The prime exception to this characterization is, of course, Cumming and Henry's statement of disengagement theory. But, as noted above, the initial statement of disengagement theory was seriously if not fatally flawed by what appeared to most social scientists to be an unwarranted biological reductionism and serious inadequacies in the evidence advanced in support of propositions derived from the theory. Consequently, Cumming and Henry's argument became the foil against which social scientists reacted rather than an intellectual tool to be reshaped through use. Leopold Rosenmayr in a recent unpublished work (1974) is probably correct in observing that disengagement theory, which stressed the intrinsic and hence inevitable progressive deficits in the potential for performance in late life, was presented at an inopportune time. That is, the theory was presented just at the time when scientific investigation was documenting the unexpected capacity and potential for performance of many older persons and demonstrating the effect of environmental opportunities and constraints on performance over the life span generally and in late life specifically. A dynamic multidimensional view of the interaction of individuals and environment emerged in the 1960's in the social sciences. This view led logically to a consideration of both individual and cohort differences in behavior which could not be satisfactorily explained by reference to either chronological age or social structure alone. Social scientists in the 1960's were apparently convinced that the phenomena they wanted to explain involved complex transactions between individuals and the sociocultural as well as physical environments within which and with which they interacted. Social scientists studying aging were not an exception; they found static, descriptive accounts of aging and the aged increasingly unproductive and uncongenial.

A perspective which is particularly consonant with contemporary emphasis on dynamic, situational, transactional aspects of behavior is found in social exchange theory. Described as one of the most significant theoretical orientations in the social sciences in recent decades (Buckley, 1967; Singelmann, 1972), exchange theory illustrates the converging interests of several disciplines in the processes by which societies allocate roles and resources and in the interaction among individuals. A substantial literature now exists which describes the origins of social exchange theory in economics and anthropology (Nord, 1973; Ekeh, 1967-70; Buckley, 1967); its applications to decision and game theory (Meeker, 1971); its impact on sociology and social psychology, principally through the work of Homans, Blau, and Newcomb (Buckley, 1967); and its intersection with social psychological theories of symbolic interaction and structural balance (Singelmann, 1972; Abbott, Brown, and Crosbie, 1973; Zajonc, 1968). The potential and possible applications of this theoretical orientation to the study of aging remain to be explored. But the multidisciplinary origins of social exchange theory, its focus on issues of role and resource allocation, and its emphasis on the dynamics of social processes recommend its consideration by research investigators in aging.

As an economic concept, *exchange* evokes association primarily with utilitarian interaction and relationships between costs/rewards and supply/demand. The usefulness of conceptualizing behavior in terms of costs and rewards, however, derives from the fact that individuals so frequently behave as though they intend to maximize outcomes they value. Therefore, three propositions derived from classical economics seem applicable to the study of behavior generally: (1) the more often a person rewards another for an activity, the more often the other will emit this activity; (2) the more valuable the reward, the more often the activity will be emitted; but (3) at some point the frequency of reward leads to satiation and discontinuation of even rewarded behavior. These propositions have an obvious similarity to reinforcement theory in psychological behaviorism, the reductionistic, mechanistic assumptions of which have been appropriately criticized. However, social exchange theory uses the elemental exchange paradigm as a point of departure, not as an end in itself. What an individual values, how he calculates costs in relation to rewards, the decision rules he employs, and the standards of fair exchange against which he evaluates the outcome of interaction all have a decidedly social component. These social components may be embodied in the normative expectations of social groups and transmitted both formally and informally to group members. Once the social origins and normative component of social exchange relationships are understood, social research based on classical economic exchange theory, game theory, and decision theory provides useful insights into the observed complexity of social interaction (Buckley, 1967).

Exchange relationships may be predominantly calculative, individualistic, competitive encounters. But this need not be necessarily so. Anthropologists who have studied the exchange of gifts have repeatedly noted that such exchanges are intended to enhance social integration and emphasize the interests of collectivities rather than individuals. Norms of reciprocity and reciprocal behavior are widely observed. An individual may learn to value noneconomic as well as economic outcomes of exchange. He may seek psychic as well as material rewards. He may be guided by altruistic as well as by egoistic sentiments. He may use a variety of reference groups in assessing the equity, the fairness, of the outcome of social exchanges. Social exchange theory thus highlights both the situational structuring of options and resources which constrain interaction and the tendency of participants to maximize their values in such a way that a fair outcome results. Exchange relationships are inevitably affected by and affect power relationships in groups; however, differential rewards in interaction are not necessarily unfair and may in fact be required by prevailing expectations about fair exchange among persons of unequal social status. Social contracts can and do exist between age cohorts, for example, which may be as specific as income transfers between those in the work force and those outside and as general as understandings about the bases of affection and respect between generations.

No theory can be expected to accommodate all interesting and important social phenomena equally well. Social exchange theory does, however, appear to have particular relevance for a number of important issues in the social scientific study of aging, and a social exchange perspective is already at least implicit in some instances. Consider, for example, studies of intergenerational relationships, kinship networks, and intercohort relationships within societies. The existence of modified extended kinship networks has been demonstrated by documenting the extent of economic exchange that in fact takes place and also by documenting that, among kinsmen, shared sentiments are not totally dependent on spatial proximity. Intimacy at a distance is possible, and observed emotional detachment between generations is revokable under specific conditions. Or consider the anomalous finding that in spite of the many indications that late life is a time of personal and social loss and that old age evokes many negative stereotypes, chronological age simply does not predict life satisfaction very accurately. This is the case regardless of how life satisfaction is measured. Such a persistent finding invites the inference that many, if not most, individuals in late life experience a fit among needs, personal values, and social options which produces outcomes evaluated as tolerably fair. What any particular older person would consider as a tolerably fair social exchange is, of course, not necessarily equivalent to what a social philosopher would consider to be equitable. Social exchange theory concentrates on observed expectations about fair exchange in order to account for behavior which persists in spite of the appearance to an outside observer that the behavior is unrewarding. Similarly, one must account for why younger cohorts in a society persist in allocating resources to older cohorts whose most obvious claim to those resources is past productivity. Notions of equity are involved in such considerations. But more than that, one must suspect that there are psychic rewards for the members of younger cohorts whose self-esteem is enhanced by insisting on a fair allocation of resources to members of older cohorts. Correspondingly, members of older cohorts may well derive psychic rewards by agreeing, as they appear to do, that when resources are scarce, allocations should favor younger cohorts.

Social exchange theory would also lead us to expect that individuals seek those situations in which rewarding outcomes are most likely to be experienced. The observed fit among personal needs, values, and environmental opportunities for satisfying those needs and for achieving valued outcomes predicts satisfaction. This is why we expect that, whenever possible, individuals seek out situations in which they expect a maximum fit.

The ultimate test of good theory is its usefulness in organizing our thinking about and understanding of phenomena of interest. At this time, social exchange theory provides a relatively rare linkage among social scientific investigators studying social aspects of aging.

METHODOLOGICAL ISSUES

Our review of themes, issues, and concepts in the study of aging raises several questions whose methodological implications will be considered more fully in this section. We will first present a brief analysis of relationships among *age*, *period*, and *cohort* in studies of aging. This analysis will provide a framework for discussing three specific topics which were prominent in the preceding sections of this chapter: the limitations of chronological age as an explanatory variable; interpretations of age, birth cohort membership, and period of measurement as sources of variation in behavior; and the measurement of environments. In the final part of this section, we will discuss some of the methodological implications of defining life span as a context for the study of aging.

Age, Period, and Cohort

Birren (1959b) has noted, in his essay "Principles of Research on Aging," that there is an "aura of inelegance" surrounding research on aging. This aura hangs about social science studies of aging in particular, because relationships between age and variables of interest to the social scientist rarely exhibit the invariant properties that characterize age curves in certain other disciplines. The apparent effects of age are almost always confounded with the effects of other variables correlated with age. One kind of confounding arises from the interaction between aging individuals and changing environments. The existence of ". . . mechanisms which accumulate the consequences of secular trends in individuals or in institutions or both" (Birren, 1959b, p. 9) provides sufficient theoretical ground for the hypothesis that age differences are the result of differences in the environmental histories of age groups. This line of argument rivals *aging* as an explanation of observed differences between age groups. The same idea is made explicit in Ryder's concept of *cohort* (Ryder, 1964a, 1964b, 1965, 1968). The key to the cohort approach is the proposition that *position in the stream of historical environments, indexed by date of birth, differentiates one cohort from another with respect to broad classes of behavior*.

Inconsistencies between the findings of

studies of age differences and studies of age changes (Schaie, 1965; Ryder, 1964b) motivated the first studies of the relations between age and cohort. Schaie's attempt to resolve these inconsistencies in his (1965) "General Model for the Study of Developmental Problems" led him to specify three formal sources of variation in measurements on individuals: *age*, the number of elapsed standard time units between date of birth and date of observation; *period*, the date of observation expressed in standard time units from a fixed origin; *cohort*, the date of birth in standard time units from the same fixed origin. Because individuals are nested within cohorts, the concept of "cohort effect" is a between-individual concept. "Age effects" and "period effects" can be defined as within-individual effects, even though they are completely confounded within individuals.

Schaie's Table 1, reproduced here as our Table 1, shows how observations can be classified with respect to the three factors. This table is organized so that the rows identify cohorts and the columns represent periods of observation. The age factor is represented in the diagonals of the table.

This table illustrates two kinds of restrictions on combinations of age, period, and cohort. Let

$$C = \text{date of birth},$$
$$P = \text{date of observation},$$
and $\quad A = \text{age}.$

Each observation can be indexed by the triplet (C, P, A). Since there are no observations prior to the date of birth, the condition $P \geqslant C$ must

hold for every triplet. Given a maximum age, say $A_{\max}$, it follows that P must be less than or equal to $C + A_{\max}$. Therefore, there exist no observations whose indices violate the condition

$$C \leqslant P \leqslant C + A_{\max}.$$

This restriction accounts for the empty cells in Table 1: they represent logically impossible combinations of date of birth and date of observation. The second, and more fundamental restriction, is the identity

$$A = P - C,$$

which holds for the indices of every observation. Thus, "age" in Table 1 is uniquely determined by "date of birth" and "date of measurement."

Linear dependence among age, period, and cohort has two primary consequences. (1) To the extent that each factor is a distinct bundle of casual influences on the dependent variable, most simple contrasts of the data values represent *mixtures* of effects. For example, comparisons across age groups at a fixed period represent mixtures of age and cohort effects. Similarly, contrasts over age groups within a cohort mix age and period effects. (2) One of the three factors is formally redundant. This means that a two-factor model can replace a model which incorporates the three sources of variation, since the redundant factor can be eliminated by substitution.

Schaie (1965), and later Baltes (1968), recommend factorial arrangements of developmental data with respect to two of the three factors. There are three possibilities. Data may be organized in a cohort by age table (Schaie's

TABLE 1. AGES OF SELECTED COHORTS AVAILABLE TO AN INVESTIGATOR IN 1960, AT 20-YEAR INTERVALS.

Date of birth	DATE OF MEASUREMENT										
	1860	1880	1900	1920	1940	1960	1980	2000	2020	2040	2060
1860	0	20	40	60	80	100	–	–	–	–	–
1880	–	0	20	40	60	80	100	–	–	–	–
1900	–	–	0	20	40	60	80	100	–	–	–
1920	–	–	–	0	20	40	60	80	100	–	–
1940	–	–	–	–	0	20	40	60	80	100	–
1960	–	–	–	–	–	0	20	40	60	80	100

SOURCE: Adapted from Schaie (1965), p. 93.

cohort-sequential model and Baltes' bifactorial developmental model), in a cohort by period table (Schaie's cross-sequential model), or in an age by period table (Schaie's time-sequential model). In each of these forms, the data can be analyzed by analysis of variance techniques. If, as Schaie maintains, age, period, and cohort are separate causes of variation in the dependent variable, then estimates of parameters derived from two-factor designs can be regarded as biased or confounded, because they contain effects attributable to the "missing" third factor. In his criticism of Schaie, Baltes argues that emphasis on three factors is misplaced, because age, period, and cohort are not defined independently (i.e., $A = P - C$). He suggests a reduction of the three-factor developmental model to a two-factor model incorporating age and cohort.

Another strategy is to specify a model which is additive in the age, period, and cohort effects. Mason, Winsborough, Mason, and Poole (1973) suggest this procedure for analyzing data organized in an age by period table. The model is described by the equation

$$Y_{ij} = K + A_i + P_j + C_{(j-i)+I} + E_{ij}$$
$$i = 1, \ldots, I \text{ age groups,}$$
$$j = 1, \ldots, J \text{ periods}$$

where Y_{ij} is the mean response for the ith age group and the jth period, A_i is the effect of the ith age group, P_j is the effect of the jth period, and $C_{(j-i)+I}$ is the effect of the $(j-i)+I^{\text{th}}$ cohort; K is a constant, and E_{ij} is a random error term. Note that the index for the cohort effect is a linear function of the indices of the age and period effects. A 'convenient set of restrictions on these parameters is

$$A_1 + \cdots + A_I = 0,$$
$$B_1 + \cdots + B_J = 0,$$
$$C_1 + \cdots + C_{I+J-1} = 0.$$

Mason *et al.* show that although the parameters of the general model are not estimable, there exist more restricted versions of the model whose parameters can be estimated. In particular, it is possible to obtain least squares estimates of the parameters under the assumption that any pair of age, period, or cohort effects are equal. This model has been used very effectively in Knoke and Hout's (1974) analysis of American political party affiliation.

We can summarize the "age-period-cohort problem" and the typical way it is conceptualized as follows: (1) the assessment of age, period, and cohort *effects* begins with operational definitions of age as chronological age, cohort as date of birth, and period as date of observation; (2) there is a formal dependence among these operational definitions; effect estimates based on them are formally confounded; (3) the problems that arise from this confounding can be confronted in two ways— by eliminating one of the three factors or by constructing a three-factor model with special restrictions that circumvent the usual consequences of dependence among the three components.

The principal cause of the age-period-cohort *problem* is the habit of basing the assessment of age, period, and cohort effects on formally dependent operational definitions. The three concepts are given different labels and regarded as alternative explanations of variation in behavior because it is believed that they represent distinct patterns of causal influence. Period effects and cohort effects, in particular, presuppose causal hypotheses connecting environmental variations with behavioral responses. This suggests that definitions of age, period, and cohort effects might be usefully stated in terms of explicit causal processes.

Period. Defined as date of measurement, period is really a surrogate for those unmeasured but potentially measurable elements of the environment that are thought to be causally related to some concomitantly observed dependent variable. Laying aside for the moment the question of redefining age and cohort effects, we note that the replacement of "period" with appropriately timed measurements of environmental variables is sufficient to remove the confounding between age, period, and cohort. There is no reason to suppose that age, cohort, and "environment" are linearly dependent.

Cohort. Most discussions of the cohort concept that go beyond the minimal "date of birth" imply that cohort differences arise from some kind of interaction between age and changes in the environment. Consider for example, Ryder's justification of cohort effects:

> The minimum basis for expecting interdependency between intercohort differentiation and social change is that *change has variant import for persons of unlike age, and that the consequences of change persist in the subsequent behavior of these individuals and thus of their cohorts* (1965, p. 844) (italics ours).

Ryder's statement suggests three conditions for the development of cohort differences: (1) the existence of age variations in response to environmental changes; (2) a tendency for behavior established in response to the environment to persist over time; (3) environmental instability. One example of these conditions is the following: (1) and (2) a behavior is established in early childhood as a response to environmental conditions, and subsequent environmental changes and changes in chronological age do not modify that behavior; (3) there is a wide variation in environmental conditions over time. Since successive cohorts bear the permanent stamp of their childhood environments, variation in those environments produces cohort differences. Human characteristics which stabilize in early life, but which are nevertheless subject to environmental influence during the period of most rapid growth, fall within the class of processes that could generate strong cohort effects (see Bloom, 1964).

Age. Those who object to the use of chronological age as an explanatory variable in models of behavior may do so on many different grounds. The most common objection is that the age-behavior relation conceals interesting causal processes. The formal confounding of age and cohort in cross-sectional designs, of age and period in longitudinal designs, and of age, period, and cohort in the usual three-factor classification of data (in each of these cases confounding can be removed through redefining period and cohort effects as causal hypotheses linking environment and response) are merely extreme cases of inability to distinguish between rival explanations of variation in behavior. It is the causal assertions

implicit in references to *period* and *cohort* that make us suspicious of the role of age in explanations of behavior: Would we observe age effects in an appropriate multivariate model of behavior—a model that specifies past and present environmental influences on the dependent variable? If we find age effects in such a model, we can respond in two ways: (1) the list of environmental factors is incomplete; the age effect will vanish with a more complete description of the environment; or (2) there is a tendency, *ceteris paribus*, for the response to change in standard ways as individuals age—in Wohlwill's words "... we are dealing with behavioral variables for which the general course of development (considered in terms of direction, form, sequence, etc.) remains invariant over a broad range of particular environmental conditions. ..." (1970, p. 52).

It appears that the role of age, period, and cohort in explanations of behavior can be illuminated by introducing variables that characterize changes in the environment. We have used the term *environment* in a nonspecific way, referring to any forces external to individuals which tend to shape or influence their responses. The *form* of explanation implied by our definitions of age, period, and cohort effects can be well-illustrated without identifying the forces or influences that constitute the environment of a particular behavior. We assume that the characteristics of the environment that affect a given response are known and measurable and that the relations between the response and the environmental variables are linear. The latter assumption is made to simplify the mathematical exposition of our argument. It is our intention to use these assumptions and the foregoing definitions of age, period, and cohort effects to formulate a model for response variables that change over age and time.

Figure 1 introduces the components of a multivariate model in which past and present environments and age combine to produce variations in a response. The dependent variable in this model is R_{ta}, the response measured at time t of an individual at age a. The component labeled S_t is the environment

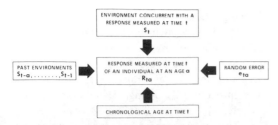

Figure 1. A multivariate model for response with components that produce age, period, and cohort effects.

concurrent with that response. A causal relation between S_t and R_{ta} generates a "period effect." The possibility that variations in past environments are causally related to variations in the current response is recognized by including the sequence $S_{t-a}, S_{t-a+1}, \ldots, S_{t-1}$ among the list of independent variables. This component of the model builds environmental history into the response and thereby supplies a mechanism for generating cohort effects. Chronological age is included as an independent source of variation to cover the case of responses which show standard developmental changes over a wide range of environments. Finally, there is a random component, e_{ta}, representing variation in the response which is not related to age or the environmental variables.

Figure 1 fails to make explicit two important possibilities. First, the contribution of environmental variations may change—perhaps diminish—in importance as the time-lag between distal environment and response increases. Second, increases in chronological age may make persons more or less vulnerable to proximal environmental influences. In short, the weights attached to past and present environments may shift in complex ways as individuals age and as time passes.

Let us formulate a model for the *average* response of a population of individuals who are age a at time t, which includes the components specified in Figure 1 and allows the influence of environmental variables to change with age and time-lag between the environment and the response. We will suppose that a single variable S_t is sufficient to characterize the environment at each time t. We use the following notation:

$\bar{R}_{ta}$ = the mean response (the mean is taken over individuals) of a population at age a at time t,

$\bar{S}_t$ = the mean value of S_t (it is assumed that $\bar{S}_t$ is the same for each age group),

$\bar{e}_{ta}$ = the mean value of e_{ta} for a population at age a at time t,

b_a = the hypothetical mean value of the responses for populations at age a when there are no environmental effects,

b_{ai} = age-lag-specific weights for past and present environmental variables.

The equation for $\bar{R}_{ta}$ is

$$\bar{R}_{ta} = b_a + \sum_{i=0}^{a} b_{ai} \bar{S}_{t-i} + \bar{e}_{ta}. \quad (1)$$

The summation

$$\sum_{i=0}^{a} b_{ai} \bar{S}_{t-i} = b_{a0}\bar{S}_t + b_{a1}\bar{S}_{t-1} + \cdots + b_{aa}\bar{S}_{t-a},$$

carries the influence of past and present environments. The number of $\bar{S}$'s in this sum increases with age, and the weight attached to a given $\bar{S}$ can change with age. The magnitude of environmental effects may vary according to age of occurrence and time interval between environment and response. The parameters b_a vary with age but not with period. They represent environmentally-independent age effects. (The Appendix gives a more complete exposition of the formal structure of the model.)

A simple age-period-cohort model can be generated by placing restrictions on the coefficients of equation (1). Period effects are induced by changes in the environment which affect the response without time-lag. They can be represented by the expression $P\bar{S}_t$, where P is a constant. A cohort effect is created by the persistence over age and time of an earlier period effect. The process can be represented as a lagged effect, $C\bar{S}_{t-a+v}$, where C is a constant and v is the fixed age of onset of the cohort effect. Note that the index value $t-a+v$ is constant within a cohort. Age effects are represented in this model by the parameters b_a. These are, by definition, independent of environmental sources of variation in a response.

For $a > v$, we write

$$\overline{R}_{ta} = b_a + P\overline{S}_t + C\overline{S}_{t-a+v} + \overline{e}_{ta}.$$

This three-factor model is only one of many different models which can be derived from equation (1). The Appendix to this chapter includes a sample of models obtained by making alternative assumptions about the coefficients b_a and b_{ai}.

A number of methodological issues can be conveniently discussed within the framework of the model represented by equation (1).

1. *The role of age in explanations of behavior.* There are two kinds of age effects embedded in the model. First, there are environmentally-neutral age effects, denoted by the b_a. Chronological age plays the role of an independent variable through these parameters, but in a context where it must compete with environmental factors to explain the variation in a response. This type of age effect dominates in situations where the same age pattern of responses is observed more or less independently of the environment. An hypothesis of inexorable decay in physical and psychological factors with advancing age can, for example, be represented by imposing a suitable trend on the values of the b_a. The second kind of age effect, represented by the b_{ai}, determines the short-term and long-term impact of environmental change on the response. Here age interacts with environment to produce a response, in the sense that age controls the effect of environmental change. Carlsson and Karlsson's (1970) concept of age variations in "proneness to change" is an example of the second type of age effect, as is Berger's (1960) notion that the extension of adolescence increases the age range over which individuals are subject to the influence of certain kinds of events.

2. *The interpretation of cohort differences.* Cohort effects are produced by the conjunction of age differences in susceptibility to permanent change and variation in the environment. Their existence presupposes a mechanism that carries forward the effects of causal processes which were initiated prior to the date a response is observed. In equation (1), cohort effects are generated by permitting long time lags between environment and response and by allowing the weights (b_{ai}) to change so that the effects of past environments can decline, remain stable, or even increase in magnitude. Intercohort differences have a very complex structure in the general model and cannot be summarized by a single parameter for each cohort.

3. *The measurement of the environment.* The introduction of exogenous environmental variables into models for responses which change with age and time accomplishes three things: it eliminates formal confounding between age, period, and cohort effects; it forces a clear statement of the causal hypotheses that underlie period and cohort effects; it clears the way for a rational assessment of the importance of chronological age as a predictor of behavior. There are, of course, many candidates for the position of environmental variables in such a model. Among the most prominent "environments" in social science are family structure and parental behavior, "... the structure of expectations and relationships through which [an individual] sequentially passes" (Clausen, 1972, p. 459), and macrohistorical events or eras.

The Life Span as a Unit of Analysis

The appearance of a series of volumes bearing the title *Life-Span Developmental Psychology* (Goulet and Baltes, 1970; Nesselroade and Reese, 1973; Baltes and Schaie, 1973) marks the acceleration of a movement toward the designation of the human life span as a fundamental unit of analysis for social and psychological enquiry. This concept, like that of cohort, has important methodological implications. The implicit proposition that justifies this emerging field of study is this: *there exist basic social and psychological processes that are serially dependent and continuous throughout the life span.* In accord with this hypothesis, we should be inclined to avoid isolating phenomena associated with later parts of the life span from events that occur in earlier periods. Furthermore, methodological efforts should be bent toward devising ways to identify, measure, and model processes that are defined over a broader range of ages than is typical for research on old age.

We will discuss in this section three methodological aspects of life span research: (1) some possible justifications of the use of life span as a unit of analysis; (2) the relation between characteristics of the life span and models of change; and (3) an example of model building that takes into account the life span.

The most elementary rationale for life span research derives from the methodological principle that restriction of a variable's range biases estimates of its relation to other variables. Studies which attempt to estimate the relation between age and other human characteristics should, according to this principle, extend the range of the age variable as far as possible. Only in cases where the characteristic is not defined over certain ages, or where the age curve is linear, can we be confident that a limited sample of ages is sufficient.

At a more theoretical level, it is possible to justify life span research by proposing hypotheses that connect events throughout the life span via causal chains. Long chains of causation can be specified by defining variables (states of the system) at convenient points in the life span and linking them together with causal hypotheses consistent with the order of the variables in time. Different degrees of lagged causation can be associated with the idea of a causal chain. Processes which store up and then spread out the effects of past states may require specification of causal links that connect events at widely distant points in the life cycle. Causal chains also vary with respect to determinacy. We can conceive of *tight* chains which carry the causal import of past events with little attenuation and predictable long-term effects and *loose* chains in which the effect of past events is quickly obscured by the intervention of random shocks. The tightness of a chain and the extent to which it incorporates historical influences are not independent. The discovery of a determinant sequence of causal influence may obviate the need to incorporate much of the past in the explanation of present states.

The dominant sociological view of the life span as a series of partially age-graded roles (Cain, 1964; Ryder, 1965; Clausen, 1972;

Riley, Johnson, and Foner, 1972) also provides a basis for life span research. In this model of the life span, serial dependence is produced by making the entry into roles conditional on performance in temporally prior roles. Failure, deviance, mediocre or exceptional achievement—each affects the probabilities of entry into subsequent roles, especially if these events are formally recorded. Every society has some way of "remembering" socially relevant aspects of an individual's biography, and that information is used to structure his current opportunities. In modern societies, individual role histories are efficiently assembled by records-keeping departments of impersonal bureaucracies.

Whatever theoretical suppositions inspire the life span concept, its ultimate justification rests on empirical demonstrations of connectedness between events at different points in the lifetimes of individuals and cohorts. The scholastic formula *post hoc, ergo propter hoc* does not provide a proper basis for integrating studies of aging with investigations of other stages in the life span. Partition of the life span into discrete units for separate study may be reasonable if it can be shown that the processes under study are confined to a particular age interval and are independent of events located elsewhere in the life span.

The social sciences now possess a considerable array of formal structures for the analysis of change. These include probability models which describe the over-time behavior of qualitative systems (Coleman, 1964a, 1964b) and dynamic structural equation models for analyzing multiple time series (see, for example, Theil, 1971; Kmenta, 1971; Goldberger and Duncan, 1973). These models were not specifically formulated to account for change in systems that age, accumulate experience, and finally die. A reasonable model of *change over the life span* must incorporate some of the characteristics which distinguish the life span from the ageless, ahistoric systems described by most social science models of change. We consider some of these characteristics below.

One of the most prominent characteristics of the life cycle is its length. There is a plausible basis for expecting a relation between life expectancy (considered exogenously determined) and the structure of the life span. An increase in life expectancy extends the time horizon for decision-making about key events in the life cycle (e.g., when to marry, when to have children (Browning, 1968)). Rational individuals would be expected to change their behavior when faced with a different schedule of mortality rates (Ben-Porath, 1970). The principal assumption here is that the optimum spacing of events over the life cycle varies with the length of life. Alternatively, we may drop the notion of an exogenously determined life span and regard the length of life as a function of its content. Both hypotheses suggest that length of life should be an important parameter in models of the life course.

A longitudinal record of the life span motivates speculations about cause and effect that do not normally arise in the analysis of cross-sectional data. Two kinds of questions occur frequently: (1) questions about the nature of the dependence between past and present events, and (2) questions about the temporal stability of relations between variables. We can conveniently discuss these issues in connection with a simple baseline model of change: a stationary, first-order Markov chain.

Markov chains were first used in social science as models of intergenerational mobility and movement of the labor force among industries. They have also been proposed as models for the occupational mobility of individuals throughout their work lives. It is instructive to derive a Markov model for cohort occupational mobility, beginning with a scheme which merely records the occupations of individuals at various points in the life span. The following derivation is due to Pullum (1970).

We first assume that each occupation at each point in time can be assigned to one and only one of K persistent categories. We know the occupation (and thus the occupational category) of men at time t who are age 20–24 at last birthday. If we follow the cohort through the next five years and record the occupations of the surviving members at time $t + 5$, we can compute the proportion $p_{ij}(t, t + 5)$ of persons in category i at time t who are in category j at time $t + 5$. The number $n_i(t)$ of individuals in category i at time t and the number $n_j(t + 5)$ of individuals in category j at time $t + 5$ are related through a simple matrix equation:

$$[n_1(t + 5), \cdots, n_K(t + 5), d(t, t + 5)] =$$

$$[n_1(t), \cdots, n_K(t), 0] \begin{bmatrix} p_{11}(t, t + 5), \cdots, p_{1K}(t, t + 5), m_1(t, t + 5) \\ \vdots \qquad\qquad \vdots \\ p_{K1}(t, t + 5), \cdots, p_{KK}(t, t + 5), m_K(t, t + 5) \\ 0 \qquad \cdots \qquad 0 \qquad\qquad 1 \end{bmatrix}$$

$$(\text{or } N(t + 5) = N(t)P(t, t + 5)).$$

The matrix P and the row vectors N have been extended to account for mortality between t and $t + 5$. The expression above is an identity which must hold by virtue of the definition of N and P. By chaining these expressions, we can describe the vector N at five-year intervals from t until the extinction of the cohort: $N(t + s5) = N(t)P(t, t + 5)P(t + 5, t + 10) \ldots P(t + (s - 1)5, t + s5)$. A Markov chain model can be derived from this sequence of identities by making two assumptions: (1) the probability of transition from category i at time t to category j at time $t + 5$ is independent of category membership prior to time t (the first-order Markov property): (2) the matrices P are all equal (the stationary property).

In order for condition (2) to hold, mortality rates must remain constant over the life span of the cohort—a demonstrably false assumption. However, this problem can be avoided by defining P and N in terms of the surviving population. A more serious challenge to the stationarity assumption is the possible decline in rates of occupational change with age. If the probability of entering a given category depends on the history of past occupations, the Markov condition is also invalidated. Evidence from studies of intragenerational mobility and migration casts doubt on both assumptions: the rates of transition between occupations tend to vary with age and occupational history (see Pullum's 1970 review). Fortunately, the basic Markov model can be extended in various ways to incorporate nonstationary and higher order lagged effects (Bartholomew, 1967; Singer and Spilerman, 1974).

The kinds of extensions required in applying the Markov chain to life span processes are likely to arise again in more complex cases. Nonstationarity is a familiar problem in developmental psychology in the guise of changes over age and time in the coefficients relating unobserved latent variables to their observed indicators. A solution to the problem of factor variance seems to be a necessary prerequisite to the construction of developmental curves for latent variables (Baltes and Nesselroade, 1970). Recent research suggests that such a solution will require new specifications of the traditional factor model (Kenny, 1973).

Life span processes appear to be intrinsically nonstationary. However, we frequently suspect that the change we "observe" may be an artifact of inadequate models and measurements. Most measurements of individual differences have been constructed to measure the status of the individual at a given point in time and are not well suited for the measurement of change (Harris, 1963). Measurements whose error characteristics change over time in complicated ways can generate spurious estimates of change. In some cases, instability can be eliminated by redefining the variables. A judicious reorganization of occupational categories, for instance, might reduce nonstationarity in occupational mobility (McFarland, 1970).

Aging is often considered to be a cause of nonstationarity because so many relationships between variables seem to be affected by age variations. The model constructed in the preceding section of this paper postulates, for example, that the structure of the relation between environment and response varies with age. We will not know whether nonstationarity due to age variations is significant until the processes which constitute aging are specified and fitted into models of change. Omitted variables are always potential reasons for tem-

poral instability in the structure of models of change.

Complex patterns of dependence between present and past states, including long-lagged relations, can be justified in many ways. One rationale is a possible increase in predictability. The construction of higher-order Markov chains in which the transition to present occupation depends on a sequence of prior occupations would surely improve the prediction of occupational category. This kind of model is intellectually unsatisfying even when it results in better prediction, however, because it fails to specify how lagged effects arise. According to Coleman, the introduction of lagged relations ". . . is more like blind curve fitting, in which an increase in predictability of an extrapolation is sought through an increase in the number of points used" (1964b, p. 10).

Dissatisfaction with lagged effects is generally associated with a sense of mystery about their origin. One mechanism that can explicate lagged relations is suggested by Rozelle and Campbell (1969): processes of accumulation and storage of food, energy, information, or money to be used at a later point in time. Thus, consumption at time $t + k$ could be more strongly related to income at time t than to income at time $t + k$. In many cases of this type, a careful redefinition of the variables can eliminate the lag. But the interpretation of long lags over the life span requires more than the concept of storage processes. A strong relation between two variables distant in time sometimes implies the existence of a causal chain consisting of short-lagged relations. The more determinant the chain, the stronger the relation between the long-lagged variables. A clear implication of this construction is that we can eliminate long lags by careful specification of the intervening variables.

The long lags encountered in our formulation of cohort effects offer a third type of interpretation. The purest type of cohort effect depends on a causal process in which the proximate environment determines the response without lag at a specific age; thereafter the response simply persists without modification from change in the environment. This process implies a strong lag correlation between the only causally effective environment and all subsequent response measurements, without positing a causal chain in the strict sense.

A good example of model building of relations between variables at different points in the life span is Duncan's work on the relation between socioeconomic background and achievement (Duncan, Featherman, and Duncan, 1972). Duncan's strategy is to specify the variables in his model so that they fit into unambiguously ordered stages of the life cycle. Thus, he defines *family background variables* (parental education and occupation, number of siblings) that affect *intervening variables* (ability, motivation, peers, school characteristics, and educational attainment) which in turn determine *socioeconomic outcome variables* (occupational status, income). A number of *career contingencies* (age of entry into the labor force, migration, marital status, fertility) arise, but their temporal location relative to the other variables is too vague for them to be allocated to a distinct stage in the life cycle. A relabeled version of Duncan's basic model is diagramed in Figure 2.

Background variables play a key role in this model since they are the only fully exogenous variables in the system. The school and peer group variables are interposed between the background variables and the job variables. The double arrows linking career contingencies to the other stages indicate that the causal order among these sets of variables is often ambiguous. We have added another set of variables, the post-job variables, at the end of Duncan's chain to extend the range of the model over a greater portion of the life span.

Age and time are only indirectly implicated in this model. Age indexes cohort but is otherwise excluded from the model; its part in the determination of socioeconomic status is absorbed by the concept of "stage in the life cycle." Time also plays a passive role; it is merely a backcloth on which the stages are ordered.

The designation of stages of the socioeconomic life cycle is a key strategy in this model. It is a highly useful assumption in the study of processes that are clearly concentrated in particular intervals of the life span. However, structuring the model so that it takes advantage of what appears to be a natural clustering of variables in time forgoes the considerable benefits of defining variables so that they may vary continuously in time. Certainly, time and age would be treated differently in a continuous model, and background variables would recede in importance as current exogenous variables were introduced.

CONCLUDING REMARKS

Our review of the scope, concepts, and methods in the study of aging documents significant advances in recent decades. A new interest in aging as a social scientific problem has supplemented an initial interest in the aged as a social problem. All social scientific disciplines now have a substantial literature addressing a wide range of issues related to the later years of life and to aging as a social process.

A consensus now exists that *age* is a very imprecise concept which has distinct biological, psychological, and social components. These components simply do not correlate in a precise way, and this fact must be taken into account in research on aging. Societies surely take into account changes in the biological capacity

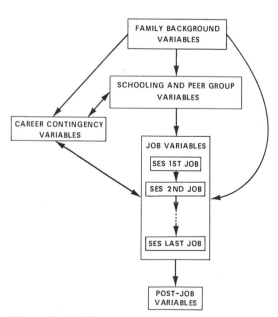

Figure 2. A diagram of Duncan's basic model of the socioeconomic life cycle.

of individuals to survive and their psychological capacity to adapt in late life. But social competence to perform social roles in late life is not a simple function of biological and psychological capacities; and the social integration of older persons and their personal satisfaction are demonstrably the rule, not the exception. Environmental factors, both distant and immediate ones, affect behavior in late life, but our capacity to demonstrate precisely the extent of these effects is currently quite limited.

We are now certain that scientific investigators must distinguish between age differences and age changes. Rather elegant methodological strategies are now available to permit us to conceptualize how we can disentangle the effects of age, cohort, and environment in understand-

The summation in (1A) represents the effects of past and present environment on current response. Each $b_{ai}(j)$ represents an appropriately dimensioned row vector of weights to be applied to the elements of a specific $S(j)$. As the number of past environments increases with age, the number of vectors of weights and the number of terms in the sum must correspondingly increase.

A concrete example shows how the model generates responses over age and time. Let us trace the response of the jth individual over ages $0, \cdots, k$ and over periods $p, \cdots, p+k$, given measurements $S_p, \cdots, S_{p+k}$ on the environment. At age 0 the response is

$$R_{p0}(j) = b_0(j) + b_{00}(j)S_p(j) + e_{p0}(j).$$

For ages 1 through k, we have

$$R_{p+1,1}(j) = b_1(j) + b_{10}(j)S_{p+1}(j) + b_{11}(j)S_p(j) + e_{p+1,1}(j)$$

.
.
.

$$R_{p+k,k}(j) = b_k(j) + b_{k0}(j)S_{p+k}(j) + b_{k1}(j)S_{p+k-1}(j) + \cdots + b_{kk}(j)S_p(j) + e_{p+k,k}(j).$$

ing processes of aging and the behavior of aged persons. While the methodological strategies are available, the data required by these strategies are not. The matching of our methods of research and analysis with appropriate data is our primary task in the years ahead.

APPENDIX

Formulation of The Response Model

First we will formulate the model for individual responses and then derive an aggregate version by averaging within age group and period. We require the following components: $R_{ta}(j)$, the response of the jth individual at time t and age a; $S_t(j)$, a column vector whose elements represent a quantitative description of the jth person's environment at time t; a linear function which transforms the jth individual's *past and present* environments into his current response; $e_{ta}(j)$, a random disturbance in the response of the jth individual at time t and age a. The equation for the jth individual's response is

$$R_{ta}(j) = b_a(j) + \sum_{i=0}^{a} b_{ai}(j)S_{t-i}(j) + e_{ta}(j).$$

(1A)

The first term on the right side of each equation depends on age alone. If the other coefficients were set equal to zero, these coefficients would determine the age curve of the responses, apart from random disturbances. The weighted sums of S's represent the effects of the jth individual's current and past environment. Note that the weights vary with age *and* lag time between past environment and current response. This characteristic is important because it allows flexibility in the specification of the age pattern of weights and because it permits many kinds of persistence and decay in the effects of past environments. Consider, for example, the sequence of coefficients $b_{00}(j)$, $b_{11}(j), \cdots$, $b_{kk}(j)$ that carry the effect of S_p, the environment at age 0. In the event that the effect of early environment attenuates with the passage of time, we expect decay in the size of these coefficients over time. If the change induced at age 0 (time p) is irreversible, these coefficients should be constant.

The model represented by equation (1A) can be formulated at several different levels of aggregation. Defined at the individual level, there are many more parameters than observations. A common assumption is that the coefficients have the same value for every individual. In this case the model can be rewritten omitting

TABLE 2. RESTRICTIONS ON THE MODEL.

$$\bar{R}_{ta} = b_a + \sum_{i=0}^{a} b_{ai}\bar{S}_{t-i} + \bar{e}_{ta}$$

Type of Model	Restrictions	Restricted Model
A. One-Factor models		
1. Age Effects:	$b_{ai} = 0$ all a, i	$\bar{R}_{ta} = b_a + \bar{e}_{ta}$
2. Period Effects:	$b_a = b$ all a	
	$b_{ai} = \begin{cases} p & i = 0 \\ 0 & i > 0 \end{cases}$	$\bar{R}_{ta} = b + p\bar{S}_t + \bar{e}_{ta}$
3. Cohort Effects:	$b_a = b$ all a	
	$b_{ai} = \begin{cases} c & a = i \\ 0 & a > i \end{cases}$	$\bar{R}_{ta} = b + c\bar{S}_{t-a} + \bar{e}_{ta}$
B. Two-Factor Models		
1. Age and Period Effects:	$b_{ai} = \begin{cases} p & i = 0 \\ 0 & i > 0 \end{cases}$	$\bar{R}_{ta} = b_a + p\bar{S}_t + \bar{e}_{ta}$
2. Cohort and Period Effects:	$b_a = b$ all a	
	$b_{ai} = \begin{cases} c & i = a \\ p & i = 0, a > 0 \\ 0 & \text{otherwise} \end{cases}$	$\bar{R}_{ta} = \begin{cases} b + c\bar{S}_t + \bar{e}_{t0}, & a = 0 \\ b + p\bar{S}_t + c\bar{S}_{t-a} + \bar{e}_{ta}, & a > 0 \end{cases}$
3. Cohort and Age Effects:	$b_{ai} = \begin{cases} c & a = i \\ 0 & a > i \end{cases}$	$\bar{R}_{ta} = b_a + c\bar{S}_{t-a} + \bar{e}_{ta}$
C. A Three-Factor Model: Age, Period, and Cohort Effects:	$b_{ai} = \begin{cases} c & i = a \\ p & i = 0, a > 0 \\ 0 & \text{otherwise} \end{cases}$	$\bar{R}_{ta} = \begin{cases} b_0 + c\bar{S}_t + \bar{e}_{t0}, & a = 0 \\ b_a + p\bar{S}_t + c\bar{S}_{t-a} + \bar{e}_{ta}, & a > 0 \end{cases}$
D. Age-Specific Zero-Lag Model:	$b_{ai} = \begin{cases} p_a & i = 0 \\ 0 & i > 0 \end{cases}$	$\bar{R}_{ta} = b_a + p_a\bar{S}_t + \bar{e}_{ta}$
E. Complex Models with Lagged Effects		
1. Distributed Lags:	$b_{ai} = l_i$ all a	$\bar{R}_{ta} = b_a + \sum_{i=0}^{a} l_i\bar{S}_{t-i} + \bar{e}_{ta}$
2. Cumulative Growth:	$b_{ai} = g_{a-i}$	$\bar{R}_{ta} = b_a + \sum_{i=0}^{a} g_{a-i}\bar{S}_{t-i} + \bar{e}_{ta}$
3. Cumulative Growth with Distributed Lag:	$b_{ai} - l_i g_{a-i}$	$\bar{R}_{ta} = b_a + \sum_{i=0}^{a} l_i g_{a-i}\bar{S}_{t-i} + \bar{e}_{ta}$
4. Lag with Uniform Geometric Decay:	$b_{ai} = d^i g_{a-i} \quad 0 < d \leqslant 1$	$\bar{R}_{ta} = b_a + \sum_{i=0}^{a} d^i g_{a-i}\bar{S}_{t-i} + \bar{e}_{ta}$
5. Lag with Age-Specific Geometric Decay:	$b_{ai} = d_{a-i}^i g_{a-i} \quad 0 < d_a \leqslant 1$	$\bar{R}_{ta} = b_a + \sum_{i=0}^{a} d_{a-i}^i g_{a-i}\bar{S}_{t-i} + \bar{e}_{ta}$

the index j from the coefficients b_a and b_{ai}. The response and associated environmental measures continue to be defined at the individual level.

With the assumption of constant coefficients, equation (1A) can be consistently aggregated to describe the *average* response of a population of individuals at age a and time t (Theil, 1971, p. 556 ff.):

$$\bar{R}_{ta} = b_a + \sum_{i=0}^{a} b_{ai} \bar{S}_{t-i, a-i} + \bar{e}_{ta}. \quad (2A)$$

The sequences $\bar{R}_{ta}$ and $\bar{S}_{ta}$, for $t - a = $ constant, are the average response history and environmental history of a particular cohort.

This is a square matrix with zeros above the main diagonal. The first column consists of age-specific weights which transform current environment into current response. Coefficients which carry the influence of past environments 1 to K units distant from the present are arranged in succeeding columns. Each diagonal (i.e., set of coefficients with $a - i = $ constant) carries the influence of one past environment into the present response.

It is possible, under some conditions, to estimate the coefficients b_a and b_{ai} from observed values of $\bar{R}$ and $\bar{S}$. Suppose we have a sequence of responses for the same age group at times $t = 1, \cdots, K$: $\bar{R}_{1a}, \bar{R}_{2a}, \cdots, \bar{R}_{Ka}$. Writing each response as a function of environment, we have

$$\bar{R}_{1a} = b_a + b_{a0}\bar{S}_1 + b_{a1}\bar{S}_0 + \cdots + b_{aa}\bar{S}_{1-a} + \bar{e}_{1a}$$

$$\bar{R}_{2a} = b_a + b_{a0}\bar{S}_2 + b_{a1}\bar{S}_1 + \cdots + b_{aa}\bar{S}_{2-a} + \bar{e}_{2a}$$

$$\vdots$$

$$\bar{R}_{Ka} = b_a + b_{a0}\bar{S}_K + b_{a1}\bar{S}_{K-1} + \cdots + b_{aa}\bar{S}_{K-a} + \bar{e}_{Ka}.$$

We can carry aggregation one step further by defining the average environment at time t to be the same for each cohort (i.e., $\bar{S}_{ta} = \bar{S}_t$).

For the purposes of exposition, we confine our discussion to average responses, and we assume that the average environmental variables are homogeneous over age at each period. The resulting class of models is given by

$$\bar{R}_{ta} = b_a + \sum_{i=0}^{a} b_{ai} \bar{S}_{t-i} + \bar{e}_{ta}. \quad (3A)$$

The b_a vary with age only. These may be interpreted as environmentally-independent age effects. The b_{ai} are age-lag-specific coefficients that transform present and past environments into the metric of the response. The set of all coefficients b_{ai} can be arranged in an age by lag matrix:

$$
\begin{array}{c}
\\
\\
\\
\text{Age} \\
\\
\\
\\
\\
\end{array}
\begin{array}{c}
\text{Lag} \\
\begin{array}{ccccc}
0 & 1 & 2 & \dots K \\
\end{array} \\
\begin{array}{c}
0 \\ 1 \\ 2 \\ . \\ . \\ . \\ K
\end{array}
\left[
\begin{array}{ccccc}
b_{00} & 0 & 0 & \dots 0 \\
b_{10} & b_{11} & 0 & \dots 0 \\
b_{20} & b_{21} & b_{22} & \dots 0 \\
. & . & . & . \\
. & . & . & . \\
. & . & . & . \\
b_{K0} & b_{K1} & b_{K2} & \dots b_{KK}
\end{array}
\right]
\end{array}
$$

The coefficients relating the past and present environments to the response are the same in every equation. So long as the number of data points (K) exceeds the number of coefficients ($a + 2$ for *one* environmental variable), estimates of the coefficients can be obtained through least squares regression analysis. The use of ordinary least squares assumes that the random error terms are independent and that there is no long-term linear trend in the environmental measures.

Table 2 presents several models which can be derived by placing restrictions on the coefficients in equation (3A). Models of type A, B, and C show how the concepts of age, period, and cohort effects can be operationalized within the framework of equation (3A). Models of type E and D represent more complex kinds of relationships between environment and response.

REFERENCES

Abbott, C., Brown, C., and Crosbie, P. 1973. Exchange as symbolic interaction: For what? *Am. Soc. Rev.*, 38, 504–506.

Anderson, John E. 1960. Research on aging. *In*, E. W. Burgess (ed.), *Aging in Western Societies*, pp. 354–375. Chicago: University of Chicago Press.

Ariès, Philippe. 1962. *Centuries of Childhood*. Translated by Robert Baldick. New York: Alfred A. Knopf.

Baltes, P. B. 1968. Longitudinal and cross-sectional sequences in the study of age and generation effects. *Hum. Develop.*, 11, 145–171.

Baltes, P. B., and Nesselroade, J. R. 1970. Multivariate longitudinal and cross-sectional sequences for analyzing generational change: A methodological note. *Developmental Psychology*, 2, 163–168.

Baltes, P., and Schaie, W. (eds.) 1973. *Life-Span Developmental Psychology: Personality and Socialization.* New York: Academic Press.

Bartholemew, D. J. 1967. *Stochastic Models for Social Processes.* New York: John Wiley.

Ben-Porath, Y. 1970. The production of human capital over time. *In*, W. L. Hansen (ed.), *Education, Income, and Human Capital*, pp. 129–147. New York: National Bureau of Economic Research.

Berger, Bennett M. 1960. How long is a generation? *British Journal of Sociology*, 11, 557–568.

Binstock, R. H. 1972. Interest group liberalism and the politics of aging. *Gerontologist*, 12, 265–280.

Binstock, R. H. 1974. Aging and the Future of American Politics. *Annals of the Am. Acad. of Pol. and Soc. Sc.*, 199–212.

Birren, J. E. (ed.) 1959a. *Handbook of Aging and the Individual: Psychological and Biological Aspects.* Chicago: University of Chicago Press.

Birren, J. E. 1959b. Principles of research in aging. *In*, James E. Birren (ed.), *Handbook of Aging and the Individual: Psychological and Biological Aspects*, pp. 3–42. Chicago: University of Chicago Press.

Bloom, B. S. 1964. *Stability and Change in Human Characteristics.* New York: John Wiley.

Brim, O. G., Jr., and Wheeler, S. 1966. *Socialization After Childhood: Two Essays.* New York: John Wiley.

Browning, H. L. 1968. Life expectancy and the life cycle—some interrelations. *In*, R. N. Farmer, J. D. Long, and G. J. Stolnitz (eds.), *World Population— The View Ahead*, pp. 227–251. Bloomington, Indiana: The Bureau of Business Research, Graduate School of Business, Indiana University.

Buckley, W. 1967. *Sociology and Modern Systems Theory.* Englewood Cliffs, New Jersey: Prentice-Hall.

Burgess, E. W. (ed.) 1960. *Aging in Western Societies.* Chicago: University of Chicago Press.

Cain, Jr., L. D. 1959. The sociology of aging: A trend report and bibliography. *Current Sociol.*, 8(2), 57–133.

Cain, Jr., L. D. 1964. Life course and social structure. *In*, R. E. L. Faris (ed.), *Handbook of Modern Sociology*, pp. 272–309. Chicago: Rand McNally.

Campbell, A. 1971. Politics through the life cycle. *Gerontologist*, 11(2), 112–117.

Carlsson, G., and Karlsson, K. 1970. Age, cohorts, and the generation of generations. *Am. Soc. Rev.*, 35, 710–718.

Chen, Arthur. 1939. Social significance of old age. *Sociol. & Soc. Res.*, 23, 519–527.

Clark, M., and Anderson, B. G. 1967. *Culture and Aging: An Anthropological Study of Older Americans.* Springfield, Illinois: Charles C. Thomas.

Clausen, J. A. 1972. The life course of individuals. *In*, M. W. Riley, M. Johnson, and A. Foner (eds.), *Aging and Society: Vol. 3, A Sociology of Age Stratification*, pp. 457–514. New York: Russell Sage Foundation.

Coleman, J. S. 1964a. *Introduction to Mathematical Sociology.* New York: The Free Press.

Coleman, J. S. 1964b. *Models of Change and Response Uncertainty.* Englewood Cliffs, New Jersey: Prentice-Hall.

Conference on Extension of Human Life Span. 1970. *Geriatric Focus*, 9(6), 1, 7–10.

Corson, J. J., and McConnell, J. W. 1956. *Economic Needs of Older People.* New York: The Twentieth Century Fund.

Cottrell, L. S., Jr. 1942. The adjustment of the individual to his age and sex roles. *Am. Soc. Rev.*, 7, 617–620.

Cowgill, D., and Holmes, L. (eds.) 1972. *Aging and Modernization.* New York: Appleton-Century-Crofts.

Cumming, E., and Henry, W. 1961. *Growing Old: The Process of Disengagement.* New York: Basic Books.

Douglass, E., Cleveland, W., and Maddox, G. 1974. Political attitudes, age, and aging: A cohort analysis of archival data. *J. Geront.*, 29(6), 666–675.

Duncan, O. D., Featherman, D. L., and Duncan, B. 1972. *Socioeconomic Background and Achievement.* New York: Seminar Press.

Eisenstadt, S. N. 1956. *From Generation to Generation.* New York: The Free Press. 2nd ed., 1971.

Ekeh, P. P. 1967–1970. Issues in exchange theory. *Berkeley J. Sociol.*, 12–15, pp. 42–58.

Epstein, A. 1928. *The Challenge of the Aged.* New York: Macy-Masius, Vanguard Press.

Folsom, J. K. 1946. Old age as a sociological problem. *Am. J. Orthopsychiat.*, 10, 30–42.

Folsom, J. K., and Morgan, M. 1937. The social adjustment of 381 recipients of old age allowances. *Am. Soc. Rev.*, 2, 223–229.

Foner, A. 1972. The Polity. *In*, M. Riley, M. Johnson, and A. Foner (eds.), *Aging and Society: Vol. 3, A Sociology of Age Stratification*, pp. 115–159. New York: Russell Sage Foundation.

Frank, L. K. 1946. Gerontology. *J. Geront.*, 1(1), 1–12.

Goldberger, A. S., and Duncan, O. D. (eds.) 1973. *Structural Equation Models in the Social Sciences.* New York: Seminar Press.

Goldstein, S., 1960. *Consumption Patterns of the Aged.* Philadelphia: University of Pennsylvania Press.

Gordon, M. S. 1960. Aging and income security. *In*, C. Tibbitts (ed.), *Handbook of Social Gerontology*, pp. 208–260. Chicago: University of Chicago Press.

Goulet, L. R., and Baltes, P. B. (eds.) 1970. *Life-Span Developmental Psychology: Research and Theory.* New York: Academic Press.

Harris, C. W. (ed.) 1963. *Problems in Measuring Change.* Madison, Wisconsin: University of Wisconsin Press.

Havighurst, R. J., Munnichs, J. M. A., Neugarten, B., and Thomas, H. (eds.) 1969. *Adjustment to Retirement: A Cross National Study*. Assen, Netherlands: Van Gorcum.

Holtzman, A. 1954. Analysis of old age politics in the U.S. *J. Geront.*, 9, 56–66.

Holtzman, A. 1963. *The Townsend Movement*. New York: Bookman Associates.

Jones, H. E. (ed.) 1950. Research on aging: Proceedings of a conference held on August 7–10, 1950, at the University of California, Berkeley, for the Social Science Research Council.

Kenny, D. A. 1973. Cross-lagged and synchronous common factors in panel data. *In*, A. S. Goldberger and O. D. Duncan (eds.), *Structural Equation Models in Social Science*, pp. 153–165. New York: Seminar Press.

Kmenta, J. 1971. *Elements of Econometrics*. New York: Macmillan.

Knoke, D., and Hout, M. 1974. Social and demographic factors in American political party affiliation. 1952–1972. *Am. Soc. Rev.*, 39, 700–713.

Kreps, J. (ed.) 1963. *Employment, Income and Retirement Problems of the Aged*. Durham, North Carolina: Duke University Press.

Kreps, J. 1969. Aging and financial management. *In*, M. W. Riley, J. Riley, and M. Johnson (eds.), *Aging and Society: Vol. II, Aging and the Professions*, pp. 201–228. New York: Russell Sage Foundation.

Kreps, J. 1971. *Lifetime Allocation of Work and Leisure: Essays in the Economics of Aging*. Durham, North Carolina: Duke University Press.

Kuhn, T. S. 1970. *The Structure of Scientific Revolutions*. 2nd ed. Chicago: University of Chicago Press.

Landis, J. 1942. Social psychological factors of aging. *Soc. Forces*, 20, 468–470.

Lawton, M. P., and Nahemow, L. 1973. Ecology and the aging process. *In*, C. Eisdorfer and M. P. Lawton (eds.), *Psychology of Adult Development and Aging*, pp. 619–674. Washington: American Psychological Association.

Lehr, U. 1972. *Psychologie des Alterns*. Heidelberg: Quelle & Meyer.

Linton, R. 1942. Age and sex categories. *Am. Soc. Rev.*, 7, 589–603.

Lowenthal, M. F. 1964. *Lives in Distress. The Paths of the Elderly to the Psychiatric Ward*. New York: Basic Books.

Lowenthal, M. F., and Berkman, P. L. *et al.* 1967. *Aging and Mental Health in San Francisco: A Social Psychiatric Study*. San Francisco: Jossey-Bass.

McFarland, D. D. 1970. Intragenerational social mobility as a Markov process: including a time-stationary Markovian model that explains observed declines in mobility rate over time. *Am. Soc. Rev.*, 35, 462–476.

McKinney, J. C., and DeVyver, F. T. (eds.) 1966. *Aging and Social Policy*. New York: Appleton-Century-Crofts.

Maddox, G. L. 1970. Themes and issues in sociological theories of human aging. *Hum. Develop.*, 13, 17–27.

Marmor, T. R. 1973. *The Politics of Medicare*. Chicago: Aldine-Atherton.

Mason, K. O., Winsborough, H. H., Mason, W. M., and Poole, W. K. 1973. Some methodological issues in cohort analysis of archival data. *Am. Soc. Rev.*, 38, 242–258.

Matza, David. 1969. *Becoming Deviant*. Englewood Cliffs, New Jersey: Prentice-Hall.

Meeker, B. F. 1971. Decisions and exchange. *Am. Soc. Rev.*, 38, 485–495.

Nesselroade, J. R., and Reese, H. W. (eds.) 1973. *Life-Span Developmental Psychology: Methodological Issues*. New York: Academic Press.

Neugarten, B. L. 1972. Personality and the aging process. *Gerontologist*, 12(1), 9–15.

Neugarten, B. L., and Associates (eds.) 1964. *Personality in Middle and Late Life*. New York: Atherton Press.

Nord, W. 1973. Adam Smith and contemporary social exchange theory. *J. Econ. and Sociol.*, 32, 421–536.

Orbach, H., and Tibbitts, C. 1962. *Aging and the Economy*. Ann Arbor: University of Michigan Press.

Palmore, E. B. (ed.) 1970. *Normal Aging: Reports from the Duke Longitudinal Studies, 1955–1969*. Durham, North Carolina: Duke University Press.

Palmore, E. B. (ed.) 1974. *Normal Aging II: Reports from the Duke Longitudinal Studies, 1970–1973*. Durham, North Carolina: Duke University Press.

Palmore, E. B., and Manton, K. 1974. Modernization and status of the aged: International correlations. *J. Geront.*, 29(2), 205–210.

Pinner, F. A., Jacobs, P., and Selznick, P. 1959. *Old Age and Political Behavior*. Berkeley: University of California Press.

Pollak, O. 1943. Conservatism in late maturity and old age. *Am. Soc. Rev.*, 8, 175–179.

Pollak, O. 1944. Discrimination against older workers in industry. *Am. J. Sociol.*, 50, 99–106.

Pollak, O. 1948. *Social Adjustment in Old Age: A Research Planning Report*. Bulletin 59. New York: Social Science Research Council.

Pullum, T. W. 1970. What can mathematical models tell us about occupational mobility? *Sociological Inquiry*, 40, 258–280.

Riley, M. W., and Foner, A. (eds.) 1968. *Aging and Society: An Inventory of Research Findings*. New York: Russell Sage Foundation.

Riley, M. W., and Foner, A. (eds.) 1970. *A Sociology of Age Stratification*. New York: Russell Sage Foundation.

Riley, M. W., Johnson, M., and Foner, A. 1972. *Aging and Society: Vol. 3, A Sociology of Age Stratification*. New York: Russell Sage Foundation.

Riley, M. W., Riley, J., and Johnson, M. (eds.) 1969. *Aging and the Professions*. New York: Russell Sage Foundation.

Rose, A. M. 1968. The subculture of the aging: A topic for sociological research. *In*, B. C. Neugarten (ed.), *Middle Age and Aging: A Reader in Social Psychology*, pp. 29–34. Chicago: University of Chicago Press.

Rosenmayr, L. 1968. Family relations of the elderly. *J. Marriage & Fam.*, **30**, 672–680.

Rosenmayr, L. 1974. Elements of an assimilation-yield theory: an exchange model for gerosociology. A paper read at the 8th World Congress of Sociology, Toronto, Canada.

Rosow, I. 1967. *Social Integration of the Aged.* New York: The Free Press.

Rozelle, R. M., and Campbell, D. T. 1969. More plausible rival hypotheses in the cross-lagged panel correlation technique. *Psych. Bull.*, **71**, 74–80.

Ryder, N. B. 1964a. Notes on the concept of a population. *Am. J. Sociol.*, **69**, 447–463.

Ryder, N. B. 1964b. The process of demographic translation. *Demography*, **1**, 74–82.

Ryder, N. B. 1965. The cohort as a concept in the study of social change. *Am. Soc. Rev.*, **30**, 843–861.

Ryder, N. B. 1968. Cohort analysis. *In*, D. Sills (ed.), *International Encyclopedia of the Social Sciences, Vol. 2*, pp. 546–550. New York: Macmillan Company and The Free Press.

Schaie, K. W. 1965. A general model for the study of developmental problems. *Psych. Bull.*, **64**, 92–107.

Schooler, K. K. 1970. Effect of environment on morale. *Gerontologist*, **10**(3), 194–197.

Schulz, J. H., Carrin, G., Krupp, H., Peschke, M., Sclar, E., and Van Steenberge, J. 1974. *Providing Adequate Income in Retirement.* Hanover, New Hampshire: Brandeis University Press.

Shanas, E. 1971. The sociology of aging and the aged. *Sociol. Quart.*, **12**, 159–176.

Shanas, E., and Streib, G. (eds.) 1965. *Social Structure and the Family–Generational Relations.* Englewood Cliffs, New Jersey: Prentice-Hall.

Shanas, E., Townsend, P., Wedderburn, D., Friis, H., Milhøj, P., and Stehouwer, J. 1968. *Old People in Three Industrial Societies.* New York: Atherton Press.

Siegel, J. S., and O'Leary, W. E. 1973. Some demographic aspects of aging in the United States. *Current Population Reports Special Studies*, Series P-23, No. 43.

Simmons, L. W. 1945. *The Role of the Aged in Primitive Societies.* New Haven: Yale University Press.

Simon, A., Lowenthal, M. F., and Epstein, L. 1970. *Crisis and Intervention: The Fate of the Elderly Mental Patient.* San Francisco: Jossey-Bass.

Simpson, I. H., and McKinney, J. C. (eds.) 1966. *Social Aspects of Aging.* Durham, North Carolina: Duke University Press.

Singelmann, P. 1972. Exchange as symbolic interaction: Convergences between two theoretical perspectives. *Am. Soc. Rev.*, 37, 414–424.

Singer, B., and Spilerman, S. 1974. Social mobility models for heterogeneous populations. *In*, H. Costner, (ed.), *Sociological Methodology 1973–1974*, pp. 356–401. San Francisco: Jossey-Bass.

Steiner, P. O., and Dorfman, R. 1957. *The Economic Status of the Aged.* Berkeley: University of California Press.

Streib, G., and Orbach, H. 1967. Aging. *In*, P. Lazarsfeld, W. Sewell, and H. Wilensky (eds.), *The Uses of Sociology.* New York: Basic Books.

Theil, H. 1971. *Principles of Econometrics.* New York: John Wiley.

Tibbitts, C. 1960a. Origin, scope and fields of social gerontology. *In*, C. Tibbitts (ed.), *Handbook of Social Gerontology: Societal Aspects of Aging*, pp. 3–26. Chicago: University of Chicago Press.

Tibbitts, C. (ed.) 1960b. *Handbook of Social Gerontology: Societal Aspects of Aging.* Chicago: University of Chicago Press.

Tibbitts, C., and Donahue, W. (eds.) 1962. *Social and Psychological Aspects of Aging.* New York: Columbia University Press.

United Nations General Assembly. 1973. *Questions of the Elderly and the Aged: Conditions, Needs, and Services, and Suggested Guidelines for National Policies and International Action.* A/9126.

U.S. Senate Special Committee on Aging. 1969. *Economics of Aging: Toward a Full Share of Abundance.* Washington, D.C.: Government Printing Office.

Weinberger, M. S., and Rubington, E. 1973. *The Solution of Social Problems.* New York: Oxford University Press.

Willems, E. P. 1973. Behavioral ecology and experimental analysis: Courtship is not enough. *In*, J. R. Nesselroade and H. W. Reese (eds.), *Life-Span Developmental Psychology: Methodological Issues*, pp. 197–217. New York: Academic Press.

Williams, R. II., and Wirths, C. G. 1965. *Lives Through the Years.* New York: Atherton Press.

Wohlwill, J. 1970. The age variable in psychological research. *Psych. Rev.*, 77, 49–64.

Zajonc, R. B. 1968. Cognitive theories in social psychology. *In*, A. Lindzey and E. Aronson (eds.) *The Handbook of Social Psychology*, Vol. 1. 2nd ed. Reading, Massachusetts: Addison-Wesley.

2

AGE AND THE LIFE COURSE

Bernice L. Neugarten

and

Gunhild O. Hagestad

The University of Chicago

INTRODUCTION

To the anthropologist and the sociologist, age is a major dimension of social organization. To the social psychologist, it is a major dimension by which the individual organizes his life course and interprets his life experience. Both the sociology of age and the social psychology of aging are commanding increased attention, with the first exemplified by the recent volume on age stratification (Riley, Johnson, and Foner, 1972) and the second exemplified by the book on middle age and aging whose subtitle was "A Reader in Social Psychology" (Neugarten, 1968b).

The present chapter draws from both these fields as well as from anthropology. We shall be concerned with the age organization of society as a sociocultural reality and as a significant context for studying the life course of individuals. The emphasis will be not upon the formal elements of the age structure such as demographic distributions, age strata, and cohorts, nor upon the age organization that characterizes various social institutions such as the work force, the polity, or the educational system, because these topics are treated elsewhere in this *Handbook* (see especially Chapters 3, 7, 8, 11). Instead, the focus will be upon the age organization of society as a dynamic,

socially meaningful, and psychologically meaningful system. From this point of view, it may be said that in all societies, lifetime, or biological time, is divided into socially relevant units. Lifetime becomes translated into social time, and chronological age into social age. Age classes, age grades, and age-status systems emerge as social constructions. The interactions between age groups is socially regulated; the allocation of persons of different ages to given social roles comes to reflect the underlying age-status system; and age norms form a pervasive network of social control.

In considering the life course, the emphasis will be upon social timetables, and how social age regulates the individual's behavior and self-perceptions. Individuals develop a mental map of the life cycle; they anticipate that certain events will occur at certain times; and they internalize a social clock that tells them whether they are on time or off time. They also internalize other cultural norms that tell them if their behavior in various areas of life is age-appropriate.

Within this framework, we have selected only a few key topics for discussion here. Because research is scanty in most of the areas mentioned, we shall be addressing questions more often than answers. And although age status and the social psychology of age are also important in childhood and adolescence, our attention will be focused upon adulthood.

The Index of Chronological Age

Before moving to the issues of age and the life course, a few introductory comments should also be made regarding the definitions of age.

The life course is usually viewed as a progression of orderly changes from infancy through old age, with both biological and sociocultural timetables governing the sequences of change. It is often pointed out that a multidimensional approach is needed in studying time-related patterns; that social, biological, and psychological age should be separately measured; and that chronological age is a poor index of any of the three.

In the first instance, chronological age is at best only a rough indicator of the individual's position on any one of numerous physical or psychological dimensions because of individual differences in development.

In the second instance, and from the subjective point of view, age is meaningful only in relational terms, as in signifying that one is younger or older than someone else, closer or farther from birth or death, or in marking progress compared to other persons in one's reference group. In the same way, the subjective experience of a given segment of metered time varies according to the events encompassed. The discrepancy between calendar time and subjective time was pointed out nearly a century ago by Janet (1877) who argued further that the apparent duration of a period of time is relative to the total duration of one's life, and that, accordingly, 1 year out of 20 seems longer than 1 out of 80.

In the third instance, from a sociocultural perspective, chronological age is meaningless unless there is knowledge of the particular culture and of the social meaning attached to given chronological ages. It is an obvious example that in modern America the girl who has lived 16 calendar years is a schoolgirl, while in a simple village society she may be a wife and mother of two children.

Despite these shortcomings, chronological age is an indispensable index in our society, and from a historical perspective, perhaps an increasingly important one. As institutions beome more bureaucratized, and as administrative procedures become more complex, the needs for record keeping and for simple ways of categorizing people make age an increasingly convenient marker.

It is of some importance, furthermore, that legal definitions couched in terms of chronological age have become more important in determining the boundaries of successive life periods. Changes in legal definitions reflect, but also help to create, changes in the economic, political, and social status of age groups. For instance, when a young person becomes legally responsible for his crimes, he comes also to be regarded as an adult in other ways; and when a person becomes legally eligible for Social Security benefits, he comes to be regarded as old. Cain (1974) has called attention to the paradox that at the same time in history that researchers are pointing to the inadequacy of chronological age as an index of social functioning, it is nevertheless becoming the determinant for assignment to one or another social age group.

Whatever its limitations—and in the context of the present paper, whatever our wish for an easily understood measure of social age—we have no choice but to use chronological age in much of the discussion to follow.[1]

AGE-GRADING IN MODERN SOCIETIES

Although simple societies have been described in which only two age classes exist (the uninitiated and the initiated, or in our own terms, children and adults), most societies have defined at least three age grades or age strata (children, adults, and the aged), and some have delineated six or more (Prins, 1953). We shall not attempt to summarize the extensive anthropological

---

[1] Rose (1972) has attempted to measure social age as one among several measures of the individual's functional age. Because the components of his scale are those which correlate highest with chronological age, and the individual's position on the scale is used to compare him with others of the same chronological age, Rose's conceptualization is quite different from the one to be developed here. Our use of the term *social age* refers to the individual's position in an age-grade or age-status system.

literature on age-grading; we will draw from it only a few generalizations that are of particular relevance here. (See Cain, 1964 for a useful summary of that literature.)

In societies where the division of labor is simple and the rate of social change is slow, a single age-grade system becomes formalized, cross-cutting all the major institutions of that society; and as the individual moves from one age grade to the next, he simultaneously takes on a new set of family, work, religious, and political roles. In such societies, there is, as it were, a match between the social age grades and the periods of the life course.

In more complex societies, plural systems of age-grading arise that are differentiated in relation to particular social institutions. These institutions vary in the extent to which age grades are explicit and formal; and the individual's movement in one subsystem is not necessarily synchronous with his movement in another. Thus, in modern America a man is an adult in the political system when he reaches 18 and is given the right to vote, but he is not an adult in the family system until he marries and becomes a parent (events which occur several years later), nor is he an adult in the economic system until he becomes a full-time worker (an event that for many men is postponed even several years more).

At the same time, there is a more generalized, more informal, age system; and whether or not a man makes these role transitions in family or work, he is recognized first as an adolescent and then as a young adult, and there are accompanying changes in his behavior and in the behavior of others toward him.

THE CONCEPT OF AGE STATUS

Anthropological and sociological research has demonstrated that rights and responsibilities in most societies are distributed to a large extent by various kinds of ascribed status, particularly by age and sex. As already pointed out, members of a society are categorized into age grades, and the social age structure becomes a basis for regulating the relationships between members. Age grading facilitates the social use of individuals' physiological and psychological capacities; it forms a basis for the division of labor; and in this sense, it gives social meaning to biological development. At the same time, age-status distinctions that accompany age-grading aid in the distribution of valued resources, such as material goods, knowledge, power, and prestige. Thus, age serves also as a basis for a second type of social differentiation, a form of social stratification.

Ever since Linton (1936) defined status as a person's position in a particular interaction pattern, the term *status* has tended to have a dual meaning in sociology. It has, on the one hand, been defined as the basis for assigning valued resources, i.e., social ranking, and on the other, as a basis for differentiating social behavior, i.e., role differentiation.

Age Status as Rank

There is a lack of empirical research on how, in modern societies, transitions in the age system involve altered status in the hierarchical sense. We know very little about the way in which age criteria actually operate alongside other criteria in determining social rank. (See Chapter 7 in this *Handbook* for a different treatment of this topic.) Shanas, Townsend, Wedderburn, Friis, Milhøj, and Stehouwer (1968) concluded from their cross-national study that the elderly comprise "a kind of potential or embryonic 'class' accommodated uneasily in the present class structure," which is one way of saying that it is not clear where the old are to be ranked in relation to other age categories.

One approach to the question has been that of historians, sociologists, and anthropologists who have described in broad terms the relations between age groups in different societies and at different points in history. For example, Simmons (1945) has dealt with the status of the aged in simple societies, and Beauvoir (1972) and Laslett and Goody (Chapters 4 and 5 in this volume), with the position of the aged at various times in European history. Much of this literature has been written in terms of the relations between generations, as discussed in Chapter 6 in this *Handbook*. From a long-range perspective, some observers believe that inequities and conflicts between age groups are now increasing; that new divisiveness and new antagonisms are appearing that can be called *ageism* (Butler, 1969). Some have said that the Western world is entering a period of social change in which the struggle is for age rights, as compared to earlier struggles for political and economic rights, and that the struggle is being joined by young and old alike. Some believe also that ageism will become greater in the future, as the world contends with overpopulation, decreased energy resources, and the myriad problems that will flow therefrom, such as the rising economic costs of social and health services that will be needed by the increasing numbers of older persons (Rosow, 1975). Others take a different view of history, seeing more equitable social systems arising, and in particular, an improvement in the status of the aged as modernization is achieved. From the latter perspective, in whatever ways societies solve their broader man-environment problems, older people will share equitably with younger people in whatever goods are produced. Still others are calling attention to the ethical problems that may arise in the future in allocating goods and services to various age groups (Neugarten and Havighurst, 1976).

Whatever the future may bring, presently available studies of older persons in other societies raise doubts about the stereotyped view that the aged have lost status as a consequence of urbanization and industrialization (Maddox, 1970). Whether the aged in America are given less deference or less respect today than, say, 100 years ago remains a matter for speculation, for there is little empirical evidence by which to judge the matter. The relations between younger and older persons were perhaps more formal in the nineteenth century than in the twentieth, but the extent to which systems of etiquette reflect patterns of economic or political power is a moot point.

It is apparent that this is an area in which conceptual clarification is badly needed before empirical work can progress. In his seminal work on class, Max Weber (1946) argued forcefully that hierarchical status is a multidimensional phenomenon. He suggested three basic dimensions: access to valued material resources or what he called "life chances"; respect and prestige; and finally, the ability to control the behavior of others, i.e., authority and power. If status is treated as multidimensional, the possibility arises of what Lenski (1954) refers to as status inconsistency, the situation in which an individual or a group hold different rank on the various dimensions. This is a highly relevant consideration in discussing such themes as the status of youth or the status of the aged, where often there has been too little attention given to the definition of terms and where, as a consequence, conceptual vagueness increases. Examples include a paper on cross-cultural views of the aged by Slater (1964) and papers on aging and modernization edited by Cowgill and Holmes (1972) where the discussions include deference, respect, power, and material comfort, without distinctions made between them.

It is commonly argued that in our society the aged are devalued and treated as second-class citizens, while in other societies they are given considerable deference and respect. Yet there are ethnographic accounts which demonstrate that in a culture which pays them deference, the old may nevertheless have limited access to food or other material comforts (Guemple, 1969; Harlan, 1964). In the same vein, it is repeatedly said that ours is a youth-oriented society; yet it is in the same society that we speak of youth as powerless and in which the old have been the only age category singled out for such benefits as free medical care and subsidized housing.

One of the few studies in which age status has been operationally defined is one by Palmore and Whittington (1971). Using U.S. census data they showed that with regard to income, employment, and education, the gaps between younger (14 to 64) and older (65+) individuals had widened from 1950 to 1970, with the old becoming more disadvantaged. In a follow-up study (Palmore and Manton, 1973), the same indices were used to demonstrate how age needs to be viewed in conjunction with other dimensions such as sex and race; for while age inequality was greatest on the index of education, sex inequality was greatest on the indices of income and occupation. Continuing studies based on criteria such as these are needed, especially because successive cohorts of older persons will have dramatically higher levels of education than the present aged, and because the economic status of older persons has improved dramatically in the United States in the few years since 1970 (Foner, 1975; Schulz, Carrin, Krupp, Peschke, Scalar, and Van Steenberge, 1974).

Age status Reflected in Attitudes. In contrast to these analyses based on income and education, most empirical studies of age status are studies of attitudes, particularly attitudes toward the aged. A study by Cameron (1969) showed that both young and old respondents regard the middle-aged as superior in wealth and power, but a recent review of attitude research, while mentioning many studies of attitudes of young toward old, cited only two studies of attitudes of the old toward the young (Cryns and Monk, 1973). While many investigators conclude that attitudes toward the old are negative, and therefore that the old enjoy lower status than other age groups, it has been suggested by a few others (Seltzer and Atchley, 1971) that negative attitudes and stereotypes about the old may not in truth be so clear and that gerontologists themselves may be oversensitive to stereotypes of old age, anticipating them where they may not in fact exist.

Relating to this point, a recent national survey (Louis Harris and Associates, 1975) showed not only little evidence of ageism in the attitudes expressed by the public at large, but also that older persons described their actual situations (economic levels, social interactions, self-concepts) much more favorably than the public presumed them to be. The latter finding is reinforced by similar surveys carried out in England and in West Germany (Ageing International, 1974). Eisele (1974) has suggested that ageism, now that it has been recognized and labeled, has already led to various attempts to counteract it. He and others (e.g., Cain, 1974) point to the fact that the aged in America in the 1970's are coming to enjoy a set of economic privileges that, while intended to combat the undeniable poverty and other types of economic discrimination that prevailed among them in the 1950's and 1960's, may

now be operating to provide them with a favored status as compared to other age groups.

Along the same lines, others have pointed to the great range of differences among older people (for example, that their income shows a much greater dispersion than that of younger groups) and to the fact that at least in some segments of American society, older people are becoming a visible and contented leisure class, helped along by the greater permissiveness toward the new life styles of the retired and by a change in national values from instrumentality to expressivity and from a work ethic to a leisure ethic. On the other hand, a leisure class of the aged, to whatever extent it presently exists, may disappear again in the future, if a no-growth economy continues, if the proportion of older persons continues to increase, and if the participation of older persons in the labor force is once again required—conditions which are being forecast for the United States for the decades after 2020.

This discussion of age status as hierarchical rank makes clear that even along this vertical dimension alone, age status is a multifaceted phenomenon.

Age Status as Role Differentiation

Age serves not only to rank persons hierarchically, but it serves also as the basis of prescribing, proscribing, or permitting various social roles. Because age-related roles are discussed elsewhere in this volume (see Chapters 8 and 18), we shall comment on the topic only briefly.

Riley, Johnson, and Foner (1972) have dealt at length with the role structure of society in relation to age strata, focusing on roles as specific structural elements, upon processes of role allocation, and upon changes over time in both the role system and role incumbents. As each new cohort moves from childhood to old age, its members are assigned to specific roles according to age, and they learn, through complex processes of socialization, the behaviors that are expected of them in each role.

Authors concerned with the social psychology of the life cycle have emphasized the need to focus on changing patterns of role involvement across the life span (Gordon, 1971). Some investigators have focused upon role patterns in one or another life period. For example, Havighurst (1957) demonstrated the relative stability of role performance in middle age, and Havighurst, Munnichs, Neugarten, and Thomae (1969) described different role patterns after retirement among men in different Western societies. But there are few empirical studies in which persons have been followed through adulthood with regard to the restructuring of roles. In a statement reflecting the Van Gennep (1908) tradition of looking at role transitions as "ceasings" and "becomings," Rapoport and Rapoport (1965) point to the utility of concentrating on critical points of major role transitions when both personality and social systems are in a somewhat fluid state and when new structures are in the process of being established.

However, mapping such transitions in modern society presents complex problems. First, a heterogeneous society has a multiplicity of timetables with regard to role entry and role exit. (We shall return to a discussion of timetables in a later section.) Second, many adult roles are achieved rather than ascribed, and as a consequence, many role transitions are self-initiated (Hagestad, 1975). In other words, while the individual in a simple society has a life course which is to a great extent laid out for him, the individual in our society, within socially set limits, creates his own life course. Thus, both the nature and the timing of major life roles involves a complex interaction between individual choices and the range of social options available, a point that has been emphasized in much of the recent discussion of women's lives in today's society.

It is important to note, furthermore, that some roles are entered by achievement but exited by ascription, such as the spouse role that is ended by widowhood or the work role ended by mandatory retirement. Those role changes that are self-initiated probably occur most frequently in the period from early adulthood through middle age, while role changes that lie beyond the individual's control are most frequent in the earliest and latest decades of life. For these and related reasons, adult role transitions in modern society are complex processes, and much of the research done to date fails to reflect this complexity. (See Chapter 18 in this *Handbook* for an elaboration of this point, as well as the points to follow.)

Because of such role losses as retirement and widowhood, some authors have tended to take the "victim approach" in their discussions of the role portfolio of the older person, as reflected in the recurrent theme of rolelessness in old age (Bengtson, 1973; Blau, 1973; Burgess, 1950; Rosow, 1974). Accompanying the theme of rolelessness is often the theme of normlessness. Rosow (1973) argues, for instance, that the lives of the elderly are socially unstructured; and Cumming and Henry (1961), that the normal process of disengagement means a reduction in the normative control of behavior.

While the loss of formal roles is undeniable in the lives of most older persons, and a shrinkage of life space occurs for the very old, it is nevertheless true that many informal roles remain, and that the typical older person is not without a role set nor without a set of "others." In most cases he participates in a number of family, leisure, and neighborhood roles, as has been shown in the study just cited by Havighurst *et al.* (1969). Another factor is that the quality of roles, whether formal or informal, changes over time. Many roles in our society allow for considerable "role making" (Turner, 1962). This holds true particularly for roles anchored in primary groups. It is appropriate, therefore, to focus on what Goslin (1969) has called role negotiation; that is, change in the quality of a role relationship initiated by the partners themselves.

Thus, when status is defined as role differentiation, the subtle changes that occur in age status as the individual moves through the periods of adulthood are not to be understood by mere enumerations of his formal roles.

With regard to normlessness, it does not follow that the loss of certain roles must lead to loss of normative control. For example, an older person who is both retired and widowed participates in many encounters such as that between customer and salesclerk. The encounter may involve intensive exchanges that range from political issues to dress styles to the welfare of one's children. The participants determine not only the content of the exchange, but also the extent of social influence transmitted.

AGE AND SOCIAL INTERACTION

The foregoing discussion of age status as role differentiation has suggested the limitations of that approach in understanding age and social interaction. There are additional ways in which the latter topic can be pursued.

Societies with clearly defined age grades set parameters for inclusions and exclusions across a wide range of life activities, thus creating in-groups and out-groups based on age. A classical example is the Nyakusa described by Wilson (1951). When groups of boys reach age 10 to 11 in this East African society, they create their own village, and for the remainder of their lives they share activities with their age peers. Erny (1973) describes the African Bambara who have a special term, the same as that used for twins, to distinguish persons who were initiated into adulthood at the same time.

The same general phenomenon is present in modern societies, although it takes varied forms in different institutional settings. Many authors have shown that in American society there are numerous structural barriers to interaction among persons of widely different ages, and they voice concern over what they see as a trend toward age segregation, seeing it as a problem that pertains particularly to the old and to the young. The report of the Panel on Youth of the President's Science Advisory Committee (1973) argues that two institutions, the family and the school, have become increasingly age homogeneous. Because children have been born earlier in the marriage and have been spaced more closely together, they have been growing up with siblings who are close to themselves in age and with parents who are relatively young. Educational institutions are said to create youth ghettos, with interaction increasingly limited to age peers.

Some writers have pointed out that because of such structural and spatial barriers, members of our society are being deprived of valuable socialization experiences. Lofland (1968) stresses that lack of face-to-face interaction between members of different groups is conducive to the formation and maintenence of age stereotypes; and Shanas *et al.* (1968) are among those who see the issue of segregation as a central problem facing the aged. Although it is difficult to argue against the claim that we have been producing youth ghettos, it may be more difficult to demonstrate extensive ghettoization of the old, for it is a very small proportion of older people who live either in age-segregated housing or in retirement communities.

It is a commonplace observation that some communities are relatively age homogeneous—not only retirement communities, but also suburbs composed of young families, and in special instances, in communities of students that grow up around universities—but it is noteworthy that such communities have seldom been studied with regard either to the formal social and political patterns that differentiate them, or to the informal patterns of interaction between individuals. Starr (1972), for example, discusses the community as an age structure, but her essay demonstrates the lack of empirical studies on these topics.

One noteworthy exception is the work of Barker and Barker (1961) who charted the interaction of persons of various ages residing in a little town in the United States and in one in Britain. They showed not only the differences between age groups (adolescents, adults, and the aged) in the range of social settings utilized and in the kinds and durations of interaction patterns (e.g., as stranger, onlooker, guest, member, or leader), but also striking differences between the two communities. The aged in the American town exhibited much greater range, depth, and duration of social interactions than did their English counterparts.

Other exceptions include the ethnographic study of a retirement community (Jacobs, 1974) that described the interaction patterns of the residents, and two well-known studies of age-segregated housing (Hochschild, 1973; Rosow, 1967) which show that these residential settings facilitate friendships and a sense of community among older people.

Age and Friendship

The fact that older people living in age-segregated housing have more friends than those living in nonsegregated settings illustrates a more general finding that people of all ages tend to demonstrate age-homophyly in the choice of friends (Hess, 1972). Bonds of friendship are said to develop, as a rule, between persons whose interests and experiences are similar, and who consider themselves peers. To the extent that age similars have had common experiences, and to the extent that age is a factor in peership, age becomes one of the bases for friendship.

In this connection, Hess (1972) suggests that age is a more important basis for friendship selection at those life stages where the individual's role cluster is least differentiated, or in other words, where other bases for a sense of peership are fewer. If older people have a narrower role set than middle-aged people, it might be anticipated that they are more likely to choose same-age friends.

The fact is that there has been very little research on friendship patterns in adults of different ages (Brown, 1975), and in particular, research that clarifies some of the ambiguity of the term *friendship*. A friend may mean a neighbor, a colleague, a casual acquaintance, or a confidante. The ambiguity suggests that generalizations regarding age-homophyly should be regarded with caution. Ours is a society in which friends are often presumed in advance to be age-peers. As a consequence, close relationships may exist between age dissimilars, but they may not be labeled friendships, either by the individuals involved or by the researcher. For instance, a close relationship between a younger and an older man may be characterized, not as "he's my friend," but as "he's my father figure."

Social psychologists usually treat the topic of sociability, if not as a form of friendship, then as a closely related form of social interaction, and it is often remarked that age-graded sociability patterns are characteristic of adults, just as they are of children and adolescents. Such adult patterns may stem directly from peer group formations begun in youth. In a rural Hungarian village, for instance, the age peer group set the framework for sociability during adolescence, then the pattern faded in importance during the adult years, then in old age it became important again as a source of social contact and emotional support (Fél and Hofer, 1969). While sequences like these are probably infrequent in urbanized societies where mobility rates are high, empirical evidence is lacking.

The proximity and availability of possible friends may, of course, be as important a factor as sense of peership. Because our society is age-graded in the ways described here, patterns of availability may themselves be the outcome of age-grading practices that occur in such settings as the school, the work place, and the community.

AGE NORMS AND REGULARITIES IN BEHAVIOR

We have been describing a conceptual framework, the age-status system, as one of the ways to look at social organization, and we have been illustrating some of the ways in which age creates predictable patterns of social interaction. Regularities are produced because norms regarding age-appropriate behavior become established, and persons become socialized so that they behave according to the norms.

Norms vary in their degree of institutionalization and the strength of sanctions attached to them, from those stipulated by law to those reflected by informal consensus regarding the "proper way" of doing things. For example, at the door of a discotheque a young person who cannot show that he has reached the requisite age is violating an institutionalized age norm, and he is refused admission. Inside, a middle-aged man who begins to dance in what others regard as an abandoned manner is subjected to frowns and mocking remarks.

Much research remains to be done on age norms, formal and informal. Laws, the most formal of norms, set age floors and ceilings in various institutional spheres: for compulsory school attendance, for marriage without parental consent, for entry into the labor force, for eligibility for Social Security benefits. Investigators have only recently begun to look at the ways in which, all across the life span, laws link rights and responsibilities to chronological age. An impressive amount of work has been done, for instance, on the legal rights of juveniles; and in the last few years, on the legal rights of the old (see Chapter 14 in this *Handbook*).

In exploring *informal* noninstitutionalized norms, one method is to look for regularities in life patterns and to see how life events are scheduled in relation to age. Because events in the family cycle are more easily defined and more comparable across large groups of persons than are events in the work cycle of in other areas of life, data available for studying age-related patterns in adulthood have usually been those that relate to family events. Norton (1974), for example, has aggregated information with regard to women's ages at successive points in the family cycle (marriage, birth of first child, birth of last child, marriage of last child, widowhood) as presented in Table 1.

Although Table 1 shows differences in successive cohorts of women, the median ages have stayed remarkably the same. Data such as these do not reflect the wide variations that occur among individuals, but they are useful in suggesting that normative patterns exist and stay relatively stable over time, even in modern societies.

In this connection, the more telling question is whether there has been increasing or decreasing variance around these modal patterns in successive cohorts. Unfortunately the requisite data are not often available. Carter and Glick (1970) have shown that for age at first marriage the variance around average ages for both men and women decreased in successive cohorts over a 25-year period ending in 1966. Thus, for at least this one event, there had been increasing age regularity with historical time. Uhlenberg (1974), on the other hand, in analyzing family patterns of successive cohorts of white women, indicates that the modal pattern (stable marriage,

motherhood, and survival to age 50) became more prevalent in successive cohorts of women born from 1890 to 1930, but now, with increasing numbers who do not marry or who are childless, and with increasing rates of divorce, this trend has probably come to an end. Other such studies would help in pursuing the questions of whether age norms, in the sense being discussed here, are becoming more or less salient, and whether age is becoming a more or less meaningful dimension in studying the life course.

Age normative patterns operate also in the world of work, although variations are so great between occupations that it is difficult to generalize. In occupations that are vertically structured, there is usually a timetable for advancement that is roughly correlated with age, and in occupations that are horizontal (whether blue-collar or white-collar, craft or profession), the periods of being an apprentice or a novice, then a fully skilled worker, then a retiree, all follow general age patterns. Although each occupation may have its own timetable, most men and women within a given occupation are found to be at about the same place at about the same age.

Because occupational status is closely tied to social class status, it is relevant in the present context that a study of social mobility in men, carried out in the mid-1950's, showed that those men who had moved up the social ladder compared to the position of their fathers had

TABLE 1. MEDIAN AGE OF WHITE EVER-MARRIED MOTHERS AT SELECTED STAGES OF THE FAMILY LIFE CYCLE[a]

| | YEAR OF BIRTH OF MOTHERS | | | |
| | 1900 to 1909 | 1910 to 1919 | 1920 to 1929 | 1930 to 1939 |
Subject				
First marriage	21.1	21.5	20.7	19.9
Birth of first child	23.0	23.7	22.9	21.5
Birth of last child	31.0	31.9	31.2	29.2–30.2[b]
First marriage of last child	52.3	53.2	52.5	50.5–51.5
Marriage ended by death (usually of husband)	63.7	64.4	64.7	64.8
Average no. of children born	2.98	2.94	3.21	3.22[b]

SOURCE: Norton, 1974.
[a]The corresponding ages for husbands are about 3 years older.
[b]Projected completed fertility.

consolidated their new social class positions by the age of 40 (Coleman and Neugarten, 1971, Ch. 11).

Some age norms relate to the nature and timing of major life roles; others do not. As in the example of the discotheque, there are norms that govern leisure behavior, language, dress, sexual behavior, and other aspects of general life-style that are not tied to specific roles. There are both large and small ways in which the individual, whatever his age, is expected to act his age.

The Awareness of Age Norms

That informal norms with regard to timing are recognized as social realities has been demonstrated in a series of empirical studies begun in the late 1950's by Neugarten and her associates. One such study showed that middle-aged people, residing in a midwestern city, perceived adulthood as composed of four life periods, each with its characteristic pattern of behavior: young adulthood, maturity, middle age and old age (Neugarten and Peterson, 1957). Respondents described the progression from one period to the next along five underlying dimensions: health and physical vigor, the career line, the family cycle, psychological attributes ("middle age is when you become mellow"), and social responsibilities ("old age is when you take things easy and let others do the worrying"). Thus, age expectations are present in various areas of life and provide a frame of reference in which experiences are perceived as orderly and rhythmical. There were individual differences among respondents, and perceptions varied somewhat by age, sex, and social class (working class men and women saw middle age and old age beginning earlier than did middle class respondents), but there was an unexpected degree of overall consensus.

Interviewees responded easily to questions such as, "what is the best age for a man to marry?" or "the best age for a woman to become a grandmother?" or "when does a man have the most responsibilities?" or "when is the prime of life for a woman?" There was greatest agreement in responses to items that related to the timing of major role transitions.

For instance, most middle class men and women agreed that the best age for a man to marry was from 20 to 25; most men should be settled in a career by 24 to 26; they should hold their top jobs by 40; be ready to retire by 60 to 65; and so on.

There appears, then, to be a prescriptive timetable for the ordering of life events. Age expectations seemed more clearly focused on the period of young adulthood, as if the normative system bears more heavily upon individuals as they move into adulthood than when they move into middle or old age. (Similar findings are reported by Kedar and Shanan, 1975.) There was greater consensus with regard to age-appropriate behavior for women than for men; and the higher the social class of the respondent, the later the ages associated with all major life events.

These studies were repeated with other groups of respondents living in different cities: with a group of young men and women in their 20's; with a group aged 70 to 80; with a sample of middle class blacks aged 30 to 50. Although variations appeared, the same general patterns emerged each time.

Individuals themselves are aware of age norms in relation to their own patterns of timing. It is not only that they make role transitions when they think they have reached the "best" age or when they think they "ought," but respondents can report easily whether they were early, late, or on time with regard to one life event after another ("I married early," or "I had a late start because of the Depression"). Similar findings are reported by other investigators. Sofer (1970), for example, found that business executives held a clear notion of where they should be in their career development at a given age, and they defined success partly in terms of being early or on time. Thus, individuals internalize a social clock, and age norms act as prods and brakes upon behavior, or, to use Lyman and Scott's term (1970), the norms operate to keep people on the time-track.

In still another study it was found that middle-aged and old people see greater age constraints operating in the society than do young people (Neugarten, Moore, and Lowe, 1965). They regard age-appropriateness as a reasonable criterion by which to evaluate behavior; and believe that to be off-time with regard to major life events brings with it negative consequences. In the young there is often a certain denial that age is a valid dimension by which to judge behavior.

It remains to be seen to what extent such perceptions are changing, but it seems a safe generalization that even in a heterogeneous society, informal age norms form a pervasive network of social controls.

From a societal perspective, then, the age norm system does not only provide mechanisms for allocating new recruits to major social roles; it also creates an ordered and predictable life course, it creates timetables, and it sets boundaries for acceptable behavior at successive life stages. The fact that differences exist between groups and between individuals, a point to which we shall presently return, does not negate the sociocultural realities and regularities we have been illustrating here.

HISTORICAL CHANGE IN THE AGE SYSTEM

As implied at earlier points in this discussion, age-status systems and age norms change with the flow of history. A comprehensive analysis of social change as it affects age patterns lies outside the scope of this paper, but alterations in the age organization should be viewed as the accompaniment of demographic, technological, political, and economic developments (Neugarten and Moore, 1968).

As the American society has changed from the agrarian to the industrialized, from small town to metropolis, there has been growth and redistribution of the population, with changing proportions of young and old, and with a striking increase in longevity. There have been far-reaching alterations in the economic system, the family system, and the political system, all of them leading to changes in the age-organization of social institutions and to a new rhythm of the life course.

The dynamic character of the age system is due in part to differences in the initial characteristics of successive cohorts, such as their relative size and sex ratios. It has been pointed out, for instance, that political youth movements have appeared when unusually large cohorts of young people are present in a society. Another example is that wars produce changes in the sex ratio, with the result that many women are excluded from marriage and parenthood at the same time that their participation in the labor force becomes more important to the economy (Rosset, 1964). Economic fluctuations affect birth rates as well as opportunity structures, thus affecting the timing of both family and work sequences. Women have been more likely to incorporate work in their life course in periods of general economic expansion. Giele (1973), for instance, has shown that downswings in the economy lead to increased sex role differentiation, as shown in decreased proportions of women who pursue professional careers.

The effect of economic conditions upon the timing of events in the life course can be illustrated by comparing individuals currently in their 40's with those in their 20's. The former belong to the small cohorts born in the Great Depression years, persons who finished their education and entered adulthood in an era of economic expansion. Because they were relatively few in number, and because they faced a society in which career opportunities were plentiful, their work careers were accelerated, and many are now occupying positions of considerable influence at relatively young ages (Elder, 1974, 1975). They have been followed by enormous numbers of youth who belong to the postwar baby boom, whose education has been prolonged, and who seek to enter the labor force in a time of a depressed economy. Many of these young persons are experiencing delays in their work careers, and their timetables in both the work and family areas will be different from those of their fathers.

The point has often been made that cohort differences must be given prominence also with regard to persons reaching old age. As Cain (1967) has pointed out, much of existing gerontological research is based on cohorts born in the 1880's and 1890's, of whom one-fifth were immigrants, who tended to come from rural backgrounds, who had an average of eight years of education, and who grew up in a climate in which social Darwinism and a Victorian set of values prevailed. These were, by and large, people who went to work at an early age, who married only after their economic roles had stabilized, whose child-rearing responsibilities stretched across many years of their lives, who retired late, and who died relatively soon after retirement. As new cohorts of the aged appear, their characteristics are markedly different; and the timing of life events is different.

In the sections to follow, we shall focus more closely upon changing rhythms of the life course, but at this point it need only be reiterated that social change affects timing and timetables just as it affects the life course in all its other aspects.

The Increasing Number of Life Periods

One of the ways the timing of the life course has been altered is that the number of recognizable life periods has been increasing, at least as described by historians and other observers. For instance, it has been argued (Ariès, 1962) that in Western societies it was not until the seventeenth and eighteenth centuries, with the growth of industrialization, the appearance of a middle class, and the emergence of formal educational institutions, that childhood became a discernible period of life with its special needs and characteristics. The concept of adolescence, while it can be traced to Rousseau's *Emile* first published in 1762, did not take on its present meaning until the last part of the nineteenth century nor did it become a widespread concept until the twentieth (Bakan, 1971; Demos and Demos, 1969; Gillis, 1974). A new stage called youth has emerged in the last few decades (Keniston, 1970; Panel on Youth, 1973), as the transition from childhood to adulthood has been increasingly prolonged and as a free-choice period now occurs for a growing number of young persons between high school and first job or marriage.

It is also within the last few decades that new differentiations have begun to be made within the second half of life. Middle age has now been clearly delineated, due not only to increasing longevity and improved health, but also to the historically changing rhythm of events in the family cycle. With children being born earlier in the life of the parent, then growing up and leaving home earlier, there is a period for parents before retirement, one that begins around age 40, when they are regarded as middle-aged. The perception is widely shared that persons no longer move abruptly from adulthood to old age, but instead go through a relatively long interval when physical vigor remains high, when family responsibilities are diminished, and when commitment to work continues but specific work roles may change, as when women reenter the labor market in their 40's and 50's and when men's work patterns become modified.

Still another division seems to be appearing, that between the young-old and the old-old (Neugarten, 1974). The young-old have emerged, again because of increasing longevity, but more particularly because of the drop in age of retirement. The young-old, drawn mainly from those aged 55 to 75, is a group who are relatively healthy and vigorous, relatively comfortable in economic terms, and relatively free from the traditional responsibilities of both work and parenthood. Better educated than earlier cohorts of the same age, politically active, and with large amounts of free time available, this age group seeks primarily for meaningful ways of self-fulfillment and community service.

The extent to which persons see their own lives in terms of these newly delineated stages has not been directly investigated, although there is at least one study in which persons aged 40 to 55 not only identified themselves as being middle-aged, but described in some detail the unique characteristics of this period as compared to preceding periods in their lives (Neugarten, 1968a). A scale for measuring age-grade consciousness in college students has been developed by Johnstone (1970), but so far as we know, such scales have not been developed for use with older adults. It seems reasonable, nevertheless, to presume that as the names for newly-appearing age groups are used in the mass media, persons may come to identify with them, and to perceive the rhythm of their lives in somewhat different terms than before.

Cohort Differences in the Timing of Role Transitions

If one looks, not at life periods, but more specifically at major role transitions in areas of life such as education, family, and work, it is apparent that underlying social, economic, and demographic changes have produced differences in the timing of role transitions in successive cohorts of men and women. We have already alluded to this fact, but it warrants further elaboration.

It is a commonplace observation that an increasing proportion of youth remain in school through their teens, with the consequence that entry into the labor market is delayed, In 1910, 9 percent had stayed in school and graduated from high school by age 18; but in 1971, it was 79 percent. Similarly, in 1910, 2 percent of the age group had stayed on through college and graduated with BA degrees; but in 1971, it was 21 percent (U.S. Office of Education, 1971, 1972).

Changes with regard to education appear also in the second part of the life course, for more middle-aged and older persons are becoming involved in formal educational activities. While from some points of view the percentages are still distressingly small, it is nevertheless noteworthy that in a national survey in 1974, some 5 percent of persons aged 55 to 64 and 2 percent of persons aged 65+ reported that they were enrolled in an educational institution or taking courses through a library or a museum or by television (Louis Harris and Associates, 1975). Because those most likely to be enrolled are those who have already achieved high levels of education, and because successive cohorts of older people will have had more education in their youth, the proportions of older students are likely to accelerate in the next few decades. Thus, new points of exit and entry into the student role are marking the differences between cohorts (Parelius, 1975).

Other shifts relate to the family cycle. Referring again to Table 1 of this paper, we commented on the similarities in timing of family events when seen in the broad context of the life course, and how the data reflect normative patterns that exist in the society. The data also show differences between cohorts, with a drop in age at marriage, at birth of first child, and despite an increase in numbers of children, a drop in age at birth of last child. (The cohort of women born in 1910–19 were marrying during the Depression years of the 1930's and showed a temporary reversal in these trends.) For newer cohorts of women, other changes are likely to be recorded by the time they near the end of their family cycle: an upturn in age at first marriage has appeared in the past few years; a decline in numbers of children per family together with reported lower levels of births expected; and, in particular, a rising rate of divorce.

For present cohorts, changes in the family cycle are occurring also in the second half of life. Women have an increasing number of years remaining after their day-to-day involvement in the mother role is over; and great-grandparenthood is now a role that can be anticipated by the majority of adults in the United States. An effect less often discussed is the increasing frequency with which both children and parents grow old together, sometimes producing members of two generations in the same family who simultaneously suffer major illness or disability (Brody, 1966; Falk, 1972).

There have also been marked changes in the work cycle. The twentieth century has seen a steady decline in the proportion of men's lives spent in the labor force, with entry into work roles delayed because of prolonged education, and with exit accelerated because of a drop in age of retirement. Furthermore, the increased size and bureaucratization that characterizes the business world has been accompanied by a lengthening of the early phases of white-collar career lines. For example, the average age of the business elite rose steadily from 1870 to 1950 (Harris, 1969), a trend that is perhaps reversing in the 1970's as increasing numbers of executives retire early.

For women there are often two periods in the labor force, one before and one after the early child-rearing years. While in a given calendar year, work force participation by age forms the shape of an inverted U-curve for men, it forms the shape of an M for women. Women's participation in the labor market has gone through two major changes since 1900. First was the increased numbers of middle-aged women in the work force—the proportion of married women workers aged 45 to 64 doubled in just the 20-year period from 1950 to 1970. The second is the increased numbers of young mothers who remain in the work force.

The new life course pattern that has emerged for women, in which family and work roles are coordinated throughout adult life, is a pattern which, if continued, will produce an approximation of the inverted U-shaped curve for labor force participation. A cross-sectional view of the labor force may, however, be misleading with regard to the number of years being spent in the work force by successive cohorts. This is the familiar problem of cross-sectional versus longitudinal approaches, a problem that yields only to the method of cohort analysis.

Data such as these, while limited here to the areas of education, family, and work, make clear the marked differences to be found between cohorts with reference to the timing of role transitions.

MULTIPLE TIMETABLES

The historical trends described above do not tell us directly about the succession of events as they actually occur in the lives of individuals; how, for instance, an event in the work cycle has followed or preceded an event in the family cycle, and how the progression has followed an altered rhythm in persons of successive cohorts or in persons who belong to different groups within a single cohort. For this purpose, life history data are needed whereby interweaving of events across various areas of life can be studied with regard to timing.

We are defining the life course as the progression through successive roles and statuses, a view shared by others who have treated the life course from a sociological perspective (Cain, 1964; Clausen, 1972; Elder, 1975; Riley, Johnson, and Foner, 1971; Ryder, 1965), but we shall continue to keep the focus narrowed to issues of timetables and timing. From this perspective, perhaps the most relevant fact is that in a modern society, different institutions have their own timetables, and there is only

partial overlap. The consequence for the life course is that age-related changes in roles are not synchronized, a point made earlier. Roth (1963) described the life course as "an interacting bundle of career timetables," and Elder (1975) uses the phrase, "a concept of interdependent life paths which vary in synchronization."

The greatest synchronization is likely to be found in our society, as in others, around the period of early adulthood, where a pile-up of role transitions occurs and thus a pile-up of status passages (Glaser and Strauss, 1971). In the span of approximately ten years, the individual is expected to finish his education, start a family, establish himself in an occupational role, and become active in political and civic roles. Some authors have suggested that the recent trend has been for these major role changes to be compressed into a narrowing span of years, with increasing congruence among institutional spheres (Hill, Foote, Aldous, Carlson, and Macdonald, 1970; Modell, Furstenberg, and Hershberg, 1975).

Overall, however, we have few studies of how different institutional timetables are related during adulthood. The interaction between the economic and family spheres was clearly seen in rural Europe, when ownership of the farm passed from father to son, and when the son did not come of age and marry until the father died or voluntarily relinquished ownership. Although sociologists have studied interactions between family and work roles in urbanized societies, they have not often dealt specifically with these relationships in terms of timing. Myrdal and Klein (1968) and Held and Levy (1974) have discussed timing problems when women seek to integrate work careers with family careers, and Chinoy (1955), Wilensky (1961), and others have suggested that working class men begin to shift attention from work to family earlier in their lives than do middle class men. But once again, these discussions are not anchored in life history data *per se*.

Group Differences in Timing

Despite the lack of appropriate data, we can be sure that with the multiplicity of timetables and with the considerable degree of individual choice available in our society, there will be a great deal of variability around whatever modal patterns are discernible. We have already spoken of differences between cohorts, but within a given cohort, a number of patterns will be produced by the interaction of age and such variables as sex, race, ethnicity, and social class.

One set of data is illustrative. In a study of the life histories of a representative sample aged 50–70 residing in a midwestern city in the mid-1950's, a close relationship was demonstrated between social class and age at successive life events (Olsen, 1969). For both men and women, the higher the social class, the higher the median age for each of the following events: completion of formal education, leaving the parental home, first full-time job for men, marriage, birth of first child, birth of last child, first child

leaving the parental home, first child married, and first grandchild born. Figure 1 shows the regularity of these social class differences in the sample of women. For men the patterns showed similar social class distinctions.

This study was based on a relatively limited sample, and it focused primarily upon the family cycle, but it illustrates the kinds of studies that would be important in pursuing the question of timing in the life course. With regard to the question of variance, the Olsen data, as might be anticipated from our earlier comments, indicated greater variance around the later events than around the earlier.

Social class differences in timing are reflected also in other studies (Huyck, 1973) and in national data that show, for instance, that women and to a lesser extent, men of higher-

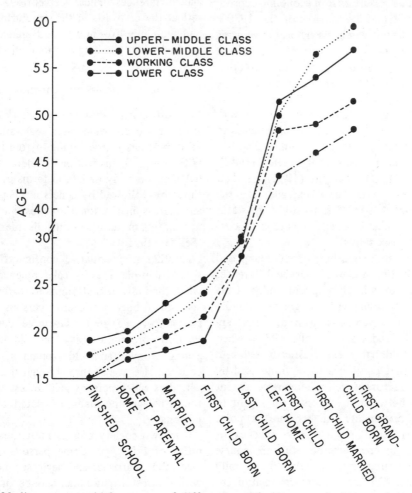

Figure 1. Median ages at which women of different social classes reached successive events in the family cycle. (From Olsen, 1969.)

than-average educational levels tend to be the late marriers and therefore the late parents, as well as the late entrants into the labor force. Such differences would presumably be reflected also in regard to the timing of events in the second half of the life course.

In addition to those related to social class, there are other group differences in timing. Kitagawa and Hauser (1973) have demonstrated that even with social class held constant, blacks in United States have a shorter life expectancy than whites; and Uhlenberg (1974) and Norton (1974) have elucidated the systematic differences in the family patterns of black and white women. Youmans (1973) has described patterns of aging that vary in urban and rural areas, and Elder (1974) has demonstrated the effects on the subsequent life course of children who did and who did not suffer from economic deprivation in the Great Depression of the 1930's. More such studies would be helpful in showing how role and age-status transitions are mediated by a whole range of social, economic, and other variables that affect patterns of timing.

Sex Differences. We have commented at various points in this paper on the differences in the life course of men and women. The differences are so pervasive that Cottrell (1942), Linton (1942), and Parsons (1942), in their classic papers on age and sex, all make the argument that it is fruitless to study age status in isolation since it operates always in conjunction with sex status.

For reasons that stem both from biology and from socialization, there are marked differences between the sexes in phasing and timing of the life course, beginning with the greater total life expectancy for women—a gain that first appeared in United States in the 1930's when deaths in childbirth were drastically reduced, but a gain that continues to be influenced by many other factors as well. There are consistent differences between the sexes with regard to age-related constraints on behavior, a point made earlier, and in the relative saliency of institutional spheres, whereby the life course for women is timed more in relation to family events, while for men, more in relation to occupational events. However, a recent paper by Van Dussen and Sheldon (1976) suggests that the traditional life cycle for women is now disappearing.

In a study already referred to (Neugarten and Peterson, 1957), men and women perceived different punctuation points across the life span. Men reported a succession of minor dividing points, but women reported one that outweighed others in significance, and they tended to describe adulthood in terms of two somewhat disconnected lives, one before and one after age 40. In various studies of middle age (Neugarten, 1968a; Soddy and Kidson, 1967), the sexes report different perceptions of timing with regard, say, to time-left-to-live in relation to time-since-birth; and in a study by Back (1971) of the metaphors for time and death, sex differences were much more striking than age differences. These perceptions obviously reflect the contrasts in the structuring of men's and women's lives and the differences in phasing that occur all along the life course.

Individual Timetables and Off-time Events

In addition to cohort and other group differences, there are wide individual variations and idiosyncracies in the timing of role transitions. Within a given institutional sphere, an individual may be early or late in terms of the social timetable followed by others in his peer group; and across institutional spheres, an individual may have a more or less time-disordered pattern (Seltzer, 1975).

Another nonnormative configuration is one that Guemple (1969) calls renewal activity, when the individual attempts to regress in social age and to become a peer of persons who are in a younger age grade. Guemple describes an Eskimo community in which old men marry young women and old women adopt young children. He argues that through these renewal activities older persons gain access to some of the privileges normally restricted to younger persons.

Our own society creates numerous opportunities of this type. Some persons enter May-December marriages and begin second families, with the result that a man may become a father again at the same time that he becomes a grandfather. There are second careers in which a retiree becomes an apprentice; and in institutions of higher learning, there are middle-aged and old college freshmen. Very little research has been done on the interpersonal world of men or women who engage in such renewal activities. Are they faced with essentially the same constraints and opportunities as their chronologically younger peers?

Off-time Events. We have suggested that social timetables serve to create a normal, predictable life course. Role transitions, while they call for new adaptations, are not ordinarily traumatic if they occur on time because they have been anticipated and rehearsed. Major stresses are caused by events that upset the expected sequences and rhythms of life, as when the death of a parent comes in adolescence rather than in middle age, when marriage is delayed beyond the appropriate age, when occupational achievement is delayed, or when widowhood occurs early.

To be off-time usually creates problems of adjustment for the individual, either because it affects his sense of self-worth, or because it causes disruption of social relationships. In either case, the consequences of a role change that accompanies a major life event depends on whether or not the same change is prevalent among one's associates. Thus, Blau (1961) found that women who were widowed relatively early, and men who retired earlier than their colleagues, had greater disruptions in their social relationships than did those men and women for whom the events occurred on time.

Like other realities which are so much taken-for-granted that their significance becomes apparent only in the breach, the fact that social timetables are significant in the lives of individuals can better be seen by studying persons who have been off-time rather than those who have been on-time. A number of studies bear this out. It is well known that marriages contracted in adolescence more frequently end in divorce than those contracted in young adulthood. Studies of U.S. Army officers by Huyck (1970) and by Lowe (1964) revealed systematic differences between those who were on time and those who were not. (Because the U.S. Army is a formally graded hierarchy, the investigator can create an objective measure of time in grade, and can determine who is on-time and who is off-time.) In the second of these studies, the two groups differed not only with regard to evaluations of their careers, but also with regard to self-esteem, mobility aspirations, anticipated adjustment to retirement, perception of status in the civilian community, and degree of social integration in the community.

Rose (1955) reported that middle class women who had married at too young or too old an age, in their own eyes, were more likely to be dissatisfied with their lives when their children were grown than were women who had married between the ages of 20 and 30. And in addition to the study by Blau (1961) previously mentioned, other investigations indicate that women widowed at relatively young ages have higher rates of psychiatric complaints and greater problems of social adjustment than women widowed at later ages (Baler and Golde, 1964; Lopata, 1972; Parkes, 1964). Similarly, a powerful predictor of post-retirement adjustment is whether the withdrawal from the work role was expected or unexpected (Barfield and Morgan, 1969; Streib and Schneider, 1971).

On the other hand, being off-time may have its benefits. Nydegger (1973) showed that men who were early fathers suffered strains which affected their role performance, but late fathers were more effective and more comfortable in the role than either the on-time or the early. The indication was that men were more effective as fathers if parenthood did not coincide with the demands of early career building. Thus, by delaying some role transitions, the individual may avoid an overload of role demands. Riley, Johnson, and Foner (1972) discuss the erratic performance of young workers from this same perspective, suggesting that such performance may reflect role overload because of other simultaneous transitions into adulthood.

Similarly, some of the reported fear of success in young women (Horner, 1972) may reflect the strain that comes from preparing for a work career at the same time the young woman is preparing for a family career. The advantage of taking one thing at a time was expressed, for instance, by women who had returned to school in their middle years and who saw themselves advantaged over younger students because they had fewer role changes to negotiate (Likert, 1967).

Still another factor is what Hollander (1964) has called idiosyncracy credit: that is, when off-timers escape negative sanction because they have recognizable handicaps that come, say, from poor socioeconomic or educational backgrounds. Some persons are given idiosyncracy credit when they have performed according to societal demands in one sphere and are therefore delayed in another. For example, colleges were quite ready to accept off-timers who were veterans returning from service in World War II, just as they are now ready to accept middle-aged women whose early adulthood was preoccupied with family responsibilities.

Here again we have few systematic studies of the timing of role changes in relation to the positive and negative sanctions that accompany them.

IS AGE BECOMING MORE OR LESS SIGNIFICANT?

We have been saying that age is a term with many meanings, whether viewed from the societal perspective or from the individual perspective. On the one hand there are multiple age-status systems, multiple and asynchronous age-linked roles, multidimensional sets of age norms; and on the other hand, multiple definitions of age, multiple timetables, and multiple ways in which individuals adjust to, deviate from, or set about changing the rules regarding age-appropriate behavior.

Some observers have asked if age is becoming a more or a less significant dimension of social organization, and if it is becoming a more or a less significant dimension of the life course. The questions have no simple answers, for in some ways our society is becoming more age-conscious, in some ways, less.

We have suggested that age segregation is growing, bureaucracy is bringing with it the increasing use of chronological age in sorting and sifting people, age criteria are being codified into law, special government programs are being aimed at the young and at the old, and

age is becoming accentuated in the formation of interest groups and subcultures.

Juxtaposed to this picture is an opposite one, for although there are few studies in which the extent of change has actually been measured, ours seems to be a society that has become accustomed to 70-year-old students, 30-year-old college presidents, 22-year-old mayors, 35-year-old grandmothers, 50-year-old retirees, 65-year-old fathers of preschoolers, 60-year-olds and 30-year-olds wearing the same clothing styles, and 85-year-old parents caring for 65-year-old offspring. To the extent that the strength of age norms is reflected in the variability around modal patterns, we seem to be moving in the direction of what might be called an age-irrelevant society; and it can be argued that age, like race or sex, is diminishing in importance as a regulator of behavior.

It is the mark of a complex society that both pictures are true. It is also a reasonable prediction that in the decades that lie ahead, the pictures are likely to become neither more stable nor more coherent. It is for these reasons that the area of inquiry we have called age status and the life course will continue to attract the attention of the social scientist.

REFERENCES

Ageing International. 1974. Images and conditions of aging, **I**, No. 4, 6.

Ariès, Phillipe. 1962. *Centuries of Childhood.* New York: Alfred A. Knopf.

Back, Kurt, W. 1971. Metaphors as test of personal philosophy of aging. *Sociol. Focus,* **5**(1), 1–8.

Bakan, David. 1971. Adolescence in America: From idea to social fact. *In, Daedalus,* Fall, 1971. Twelve to sixteen: Early adolescence.

Baler, Lenin A., and Golde, P. J. 1964. Conjugal bereavement: strategic area of research in preventive psychiatry. *Working Papers in Community Mental Health,* Vol. 2, No. 1. Boston: Harvard School of Public Health.

Barfield, Richard E., and Morgan, James N. 1969. *Early Retirement: The Decision and the Experience.* Ann Arbor: University of Michigan Press.

Barker, Robert G., and Barker, Louise S. 1961. The psychological ecology of old people in Midwest, Kansas and Yoredale, Yorkshire. *J. Geront.,* **16**(2), 144–149.

Beauvoir, Simone de. 1972. *The Coming of Age.* New York: Putnam.

Bengtson, Vern L. 1973. *The Social Psychology of Aging.* New York: Bobbs-Merrill.

Blau, Zena S. 1961. Structural constraints on friendships in old age. *Am. Soc. Rev.*, **26**, 429–439.

Blau, Zena S. 1973. *Old Age in a Changing Society*. New York: New Viewpoints.

Brody, Elaine M. 1966. The aging family. *Gerontologist*, **6**, 201–206.

Brown, Benson B. 1975. The relation of age to friendship. Unpublished paper on file, Committee on Human Development, University of Chicago.

Burgess, Ernest. 1950. Personal and social adjustment in old age. *In*, Milton Derber (ed.), *The Aged and Society*, pp. 138–156. Champaign, Illinois: Industrial Relations Research Association.

Butler, Robert N. 1969. Ageism: Another form of bigotry. *Gerontologist*, **9**, 243–246.

Cain, Leonard D., Jr. 1964. Life course and social structure. *In* R. E. L. Faris (ed.), *Handbook of Modern Sociology*, Ch. 8. Chicago: Rand McNally.

Cain, Leonard D., Jr. 1967. Age status and generational phenomena: the new old people in contemporary America. *Gerontologist*, **7**, 83–92.

Cain, Leonard D., Jr. 1974. The growing importance of legal age in determining the status of the elderly. *Gerontologist*, **14**(2), 167–174.

Cameron, Paul. 1969. Age parameters of young adult, middle-aged, old, and aged. *J. Geront.*, **24**, 201–202.

Carter, Hugh, and Glick, Paul C. 1970. *Marriage and Divorce: A Social and Economic Study*. Cambridge, Massachusetts: Harvard University Press.

Chinoy, Ely. 1955. *Automobile Workers and the American Dream*. New York: Doubleday.

Clausen, John A. 1972. The life course of individuals. *In*, Matilda White Riley, Marilyn Johnson, and Anne Foner (eds.), *Aging and Society*: Vol. 3, *A Sociology of Age Stratification*, pp. 457–514. New York: Russell Sage Foundation.

Coleman, Richard P., and Neugarten, Bernice L. 1971. *Social Status in the City*. San Francisco: Jossey-Bass.

Cottrell, Leonard S., Jr. 1942. The adjustment of the individual to his age and sex roles. *Am. Soc. Rev.*, **7**, 617–620.

Cowgill, Donald O., and Holmes, Lowell D. 1972. *Aging and Modernization* New York: Appleton-Century-Crofts.

Cryns, Arthur G., and Monk, Abraham. 1973. Attitudes toward youth as a function of adult age: A multivariate study in intergenerational dynamics. *Int. J. Aging Hum. Devel.*, **4**, 23–33.

Cumming, Elaine, and Henry, William E. 1961. *Growing Old*. New York: Basic Books.

Demos, John, and Demos, Virginia. 1969. Adolescence in historical perspective. *J. Marriage & Fam.*, **31**, 623–639.

Eisele, Frederick R. 1974. Age discrimination: Definitions, victims, techniques. Paper presented at the Annual Meeting of the American Sociological Association, Montreal.

Elder, Glen H., Jr. 1974. *Children of the Great Depression*. Chicago: University of Chicago Press.

Elder, Glen H., Jr. 1975. Age differentiation and the life course. *In*, Alex Inkeles, James Coleman, and

Neil Smelser (eds.), *Annual Review of Sociology*, Vol. 1. Palo Alto, California: *Annual Reviews*.

Erny, Pierre. 1973. *Childhood and Cosmos: The Social Psychology of the Black African Child*. New York: New Perspectives.

Falk, Jacqueline M. 1972. Some unanticipated results of family planning in previous generations. *In*, A. R. Doberen (ed.), *The Family Unit: Proceedings of the 3rd Annual Population Symposium*. Green Bay: University of Wisconsin.

Fél, Edit, and Hofer, Tamas. 1969. *Proper Peasants: Traditional Life in a Hungarian Village*. Chicago: Aldine.

Foner, Anne. 1975. Age in society: Structure and change. *American Behavioral Scientist*, **19**, 144–165.

Giele, Janet Z. 1973. Age cohorts and change in women's roles. Presented at the Annual Meeting of American Sociological Association, New York.

Gillis, John R. 1974. *Youth and History.* New York: Academic Press.

Glaser, Barney G., and Strauss, Anselm L. 1971. *Theory of Status Passage*. Chicago: Aldine.

Gordon, Chad. 1971. Role and value development across the life cycle. *In*, J. A. Jackson (ed), *Role: Sociological Studies, IV*, pp. 65–105. London: Cambridge University Press.

Goslin, David A. (ed.) 1969. *Handbook of Socialization Theory and Research*. Chicago: Rand McNally.

Guemple, D. L. 1969. Human resource management: The dilemma of the aging Eskimo. *Sociological Symposium*, **2**, 59–74.

Hagestad, Gunhild O. 1975. Role change and the life course: Toward a conceptual framework. Unpublished paper on file, Committee on Human Development, University of Chicago.

Harlan, William H. 1964. Social status of the aged in three Indian villages. *Vita Humana*, **7**, 239–252.

Harris, Louis, and Associates. 1975. *The Myth and Reality of Aging in America*. Washington, D.C.: National Council on the Aging.

Harris, P. M. G. 1969. The social origins of American leaders: The demographic foundations. *Perspectives in American History*, **3**, 159–346.

Havighurst, Robert J. 1957. The social competence of middle-aged people. *Genet. Psychol. Mongr.*, **56**, 297–375.

Havighurst, Robert J., Munnichs, J. M. A., Neugarten, Bernice L., and Thomae, Hans. 1969. *Adjustment to Retirement: A Cross-National Study*. Assen, Netherlands: Van Gorcum.

Held, Therese, and Levy, René. 1974. *Die Stellung der Frau in Familie und Gesellschaft*. Frauenfeld: Huber.

Hess, Beth. 1972. Friendship. *In*, Matilda White Riley, Marilyn Johnson, and Anne Foner (eds.), *Aging and Society*: Vol. 3, *A Sociology of Age Stratification*, pp. 357–393. New York: Russell Sage Foundation.

Hill, Reuben, Foote, Nelson, Aldous, Joan, Carlson, Robert, and Macdonald, Robert. 1970. *Family Development in Three Generations*. Cambridge, Massachusetts: Schenkman.

Hochschild, Arlie R. 1973. *The Unexpected Community*. Englewood Cliffs, New Jersey: Prentice-Hall.

Hollander, E. P. 1964. *Leaders, Groups, and Influence*. New York: Oxford University Press.

Horner, Matina. 1972. Toward an understanding of achievement related conflicts in women. *J. Soc. Issues*, 28(2), 157-175.

Huyck, Margaret, H. 1970. Age norms and career lines in the careers of military officers. Ph.D. dissertation, University of Chicago.

Huyck, Margaret H. 1973. Social class and age cohort patterns in timing of education, family, and career. Paper presented at the Annual Meeting of the Gerontological Society, Miami Beach.

Jacobs, Jerry. 1974. *Fun City: An Ethnographic Study of a Retirement Community*. New York: Holt, Rinehart & Winston.

Janet, P. 1877. Une illusion d'optique interne. *Rev. Phil.*, 1, 497-502.

Johnstone, John. 1970. Age-grade consciousness. *Sociol. of Educ.*, 43, 56-68.

Kedar, Hannah S., and Shanan, Joel. 1975. The phenomenological structure of the life span from adolescence to senescence as spontaneously reported by different age-sex groups. Paper presented at the 10th International Congress of Gerontology, Jerusalem.

Keniston, Kenneth. 1970. Youth as a stage of life. *Am. Scholar.*, 39, 631-654.

Kitagawa, Evelyn M., and Hauser, Philip M. 1973. *Differential Mortality in the United States: A Study in Socioeconomic Epidemiology*. Cambridge, Massachusetts: Harvard University Press.

Lenski, Gerhard E. 1954. Status crystallization: A non-vertical dimension of social status. *Am. Soc. Rev.* 19, 405-413.

Likert, Jane G. (ed.) 1967. *Conversations with Returning Women Students*. Ann Arbor Center for Continuing Education of Women, University of Michigan.

Linton, Ralph A. 1936. *The Study of Man*. New York: Appleton-Century-Crofts.

Linton, Ralph A. 1942. Age and sex categories. *Am. Soc. Rev.*, 7, 589-603.

Lofland, John. 1968. The youth ghetto. *J. Higher Educ.* 39, 121-143.

Lopata, Helena. 1972. *Widowhood in an American City*. Cambridge, Massachusetts: Schenkman.

Lowe, John. 1964. A study of the psychological and social impact of age-expectations on an age-graded career—the army officer. Unpublished paper on file, Committee on Human Development, University of Chicago.

Lyman, Stanford M., and Scott, Marvin B. 1970. *A Sociology of the Absurd*. New York: Appleton-Century-Crofts.

Maddox, George L. 1970. Themes and issues in sociological theories of human aging. *Hum. Develop.*, 13, 17-27.

Modell, John, Furstenberg, Frank F., and Hershberg, Theodore. 1975. Social change and life course development in historical perspective. Paper presented at the annual meetings of the American Sociological Association, San Francisco.

Myrdal, Alva, and Klein, Viola. 1968. *Women's Two Roles: Home and Work*. 2nd ed. London: Routledge and Kegan Paul.

Neugarten, Bernice L. 1968a. The awareness of middle age. *In*, Bernice L. Neugarten (ed.), *Middle Age and Aging*, pp. 93-98. Chicago: University of Chicago Press.

Neugarten, Bernice L. (ed.). 1968b. *Middle Age and Aging: A Reader in Social Psychology*. Chicago: University of Chicago Press.

Neugarten, Bernice L. 1974. Age groups in American society and the rise of the young-old. *Ann. Amer. Acad.*, pp. 187-198 (September).

Neugarten, Bernice L., and Havighurst, Robert J. (eds.). 1976. *Social Policy and Social Ethics in an Aging Society*, in preparation.

Neugarten, Bernice L., and Moore, Joan W. 1968. The changing age status system. *In*, Bernice L. Neugarten (ed.), *Middle Age and Aging*, pp. 5-21. Chicago: University of Chicago Press.

Neugarten, Bernice L., Moore, Joan W., and Lowe, John C. 1965. Age norms, age constraints, and adult socialization. *Am. J. Sociol.*, 70, 710-717.

Neugarten, Bernice L., and Peterson, Warren A. 1957. A study of the American age-grade system. *Proceedings of the Fourth Congress of the International Association of Gerontology*, Vol. 3, pp. 497-502.

Norton, Arthur, J. 1974. The family life cycle updated: Components and uses. *In*, Robert F. Winch and Graham B. Spanier (eds.), *Selected Studies in Marriage and the Family*, pp. 162-170. New York: Holt, Rinehart & Winston.

Nydegger, Corinne N. 1973. Late and early fathers. Paper presented at the Annual Meeting of the Gerontological Society, Miami Beach.

Olsen, Kenneth M. 1969. Social class and age-group differences in the timing of family status changes: A study of age-norms in American society. Ph.D. dissertation, University of Chicago.

Palmore, Erdman B., and Manton, Kenneth. 1973. Ageism compared to racism and sexism. *J. Geront.*, 38(3), 353-369.

Palmore, Erdman B., and Whittington, Frank. 1971. Trends in the relative status of the aged. *Soc. Forces*, 50, 84-91 (September).

Panel on Youth, President's Science Advisory Committee. 1973. *Youth: Transition to Adulthood*. Washington, D.C.: Government Printing Office.

Parelius, Ann P. 1975. Lifelong education and age stratification: Some unexplored relationships. *American Behavioral Scientist*, 19, 206-223.

Parkes, C. M. 1964. Effects of bereavement on physical and mental health: A study of the medical records of widows. *Brit. Med. J.*, 2, 274-279.

Parsons, Talcott. 1942. Age and sex in the social structure of the United States. *Am. Soc. Rev.*, 7, 604-620.

Prins, A. H. J. 1953. *East African Age-Class Systems*. Groningen, Djakarta: J. B. Wolters.

Rapoport, Robert N., and Rapoport, Rhona V. 1965. Work and family in contemporary society. *Am. Soc. Rev.*, 30, 381-394.

Riley, Matilda White, Johnson, Marilyn E., and Foner, Anne (eds.) 1972. *Aging and Society:* Vol. 3. *A Sociology of Age Stratification.* New York: Russell Sage Foundation.

Rose, Arnold M. 1955. Factors associated with the life satisfaction of middle-class, middle-aged persons. *Marr. Fam. Living*, 17(1), 15–19.

Rose, Charles L. 1972. The measurement of social age. *Int. J. Aging Hum. Devel.*, 3(2), 153–168.

Rosset, Edward. 1964. *Aging Process of Population.* Oxford: Pergamon Press.

Rosow, Irving, 1967. *Social Integration of the Aged.* New York: The Free Press.

Rosow, Irving. 1973. The social context of the aging self. *Gerontologist*, 13, 82–87.

Rosow, Irving. 1974. *Socialization to Old Age.* Berkeley: University of California Press.

Rosow, Irving. 1975. The aged in a post-affluent society. *Gerontology*, 1(4), 9–22.

Roth, Julius A. 1963. *Timetables.* Indianapolis: Bobbs-Merrill.

Rousseau, Jean J. 1966. *Emile.* New York: E. P. Dutton (originally published 1762).

Ryder, Norman B. 1965. The cohort as a concept in the study of social change. *Am. Soc. Rev.*, 30, 843–861.

Schulz, James, Carrin, Guy, Krupp, Hans, Peschke, Manfred, Sclar, Elliott, and VanSteenberge, J. 1974. *Providing Adequate Retirement Income.* Hanover, New Hampshire: University Press of New England.

Seltzer, Mildred M. 1975. Suggestions for the examination of time disordered relationships. *In*, J. F. Gubrium (ed.), *Time, Role, and Self in Old Age.* New York: Behavioral Publications, forthcoming.

Seltzer, Mildred M., and Atchley, Robert C. 1971. The concept of old: Changing attitudes and stereotypes. *Gerontologist*, 11(3:1), 226–230.

Shanas, Ethel, Townsend. Peter, Wedderburn, Dorothy, Friis, Henning, Milhøj, Poul, and Stehouwer, Jan. 1968. *Old People in Three Industrial Societies.* New York: Atherton Press.

Simmons, Leo W. 1945. *The Role of the Aged in Primitive Society.* New Haven: Yale University Press.

Slater, Philip E. 1964. Cross-cultural views of the aged. *In* Robert Kastenbaum (ed.), *New Thoughts on Old Age*, pp. 229–236. New York: Springer.

Soddy, Kenneth, and Kidson, Mary C. 1967. *Men in Middle Life.* London: Tavistock.

Sofer, Cyril. 1970. *Men in Mid-Career.* New York: Cambridge University Press.

Starr, Bernice C. 1972. The community. *In*, Matilda White Riley, Marilyn E. Johnson, and Anne Foner (eds.), *Aging and Society:* Vol. 3, *A Sociology of Age Stratification*, pp. 198–235. New York: Russell Sage Foundation.

Streib, Gordon F., and Schneider, Clement J. 1971. *Retirement in American Society: Impact and Process.* Ithaca, New York: Cornell University Press.

Turner, Ralph H. 1962. Role-taking: Process versus conformity. *In*, Arnold M. Rose (ed.), *Human Behavior and Social Processes.* Boston: Houghton Mifflin.

Uhlenberg, Peter R. 1974. Cohort variations in family life cycle experiences of United States females. *J. Marriage & Fam.* 36, 284–292.

U.S. Office of Education. 1971, 1972. *Digest of Educational Statistics.* Washington D.C.: Government Printing Office.

Van Dussen, Roxann A., and Sheldon, Eleanor Bernert. 1976. The changing status of American women. A life cycle perspective. *American Psychologist*, 31 (2), 106–116 (February).

Van Gennep, Arnold. 1908. *The Rites of Passage.* Reprint. 1960. University of Chicago Press.

Weber, Max. 1946. Class, status and party. *In*, Hans H. Gerth and C. Wright Mills (eds.), *From Max Weber: Essays in Sociology.* New York: Oxford University Press.

Wilensky, Harold L. 1961. Orderly careers and social participation in the middle mass. *Am. Soc. Rev.*, 24, 836–845.

Wilson, Monica. 1951. *Good Company: A Study of Nyakusa Age Villagers.* London: Oxford University Press.

Youmans, E. Grant. 1973. Age stratifications and value orientations. *Int. J. Aging Hum. Devel.*, 4, 53–65.

PART 2 AGING AND SOCIAL STRUCTURE

3

AGING AND WORLD-WIDE POPULATION CHANGE*

Philip M. Hauser
The University of Chicago

INTRODUCTION

Man or a close relative has occupied this planet for some four million years. As the only complex culture-building animal on the globe he has, among other things, generated four developments which have profoundly affected his attitudes, values, behaviorisms, and institutions. These developments may be termed the population explosion, the population implosion, the population displosion, and the technoplosion. They may be regarded as the four elements of the social morphological revolution—the transition from a folk, collectional, and agrarian society, the "little community," to the urban, metropolitanized, industrial "mass society." Among other impacts, the social morphological revolution has greatly increased the number and proportion of older people in society, profoundly transformed the milieu—physical, economic, social, and political—in which they live, and significantly altered the roles they play in society.

The population explosion, widely understood at the present time, refers to the remarkable acceleration in the rate of world population growth and, as will be shown, comprises two explosions, one in the present economically advanced areas and the other in the developing

*Prepared with the assistance of Patricia Anderson, candidate for the Ph.D. in Sociology.

regions. The population implosion refers to the increasing concentration of population on relatively small portions of the earth's surface— the phenomenon better known as urbanization. The population displosion refers to the increasing heterogeneity of population which shares not only the same geographic locale but also, increasingly, the same life space—social, economic, and political activities with insistence on equality of opportunity. The technoplosion refers to the accelerated pace of technological change.

These four elements of the social morphological revolution are interrelated. The explosion has fed the implosion. Both have affected the displosion. The technoplosion has been both antecedent and consequent of the other developments and has generally preceded and induced significant social and cultural change.

These developments have had and are still exerting major impact on older persons. In the process of transition from the little community to the mass society, a process still under way, both the older person and the society of which he is a member manifest many problems which may be better understood and dealt with if they are regarded as products of the social morphological revolution.

WORLD POPULATION DEVELOPMENTS

First to be considered are the general population trends for the world as a whole and for the more developed and less developed nations, respectively. The data presented provide the framework within which aging and the extension of life can be seen in comprehensive context.

The Population Explosion

The world has experienced great acceleration in the rate of population growth. During the more than three centuries of the modern era, explosive growth was experienced mainly by the one-fourth of the world's population now in the economically advanced nations—in Europe and, in general, in areas of European settlement. In this first population explosion, rarely did growth rates reach or exceed 1.5 percent per annum through natural increase, that is, the excess of births over deaths. The remaining three-fourths of mankind in the developing nations in Asia, Latin America, and Africa did not experience the population explosion until after World War II, thus only during the past generation. This second population explosion is of much greater magnitude than the first. The developing nations as a whole are increasing at the rate of 2.5 percent per annum, and the most rapidly growing developing nations are increasing at rates up to about 3.5 percent per annum.

The implications for absolute population increase of the highest growth rates of developing nations, more than twice the level of the highest experienced by the economically advanced nations, may be better grasped by contrasting the periods required for population doubling. At growth rates of 1 to 1.5 percent, the economically advanced nations required from about 47 to 70 years to double their populations; at growth rates of 3 to 3.5 percent, the developing nations will double populations in about 20 to 23 years.

By reason of the population explosion, the rate of total world population growth rose from about zero in 1650 to an average of 0.4 percent per annum for the half century 1700 to 1750, to an average of 0.5 percent per annum for the half century ending in 1850, to an annual average of 0.8 percent in the first half of this century, to 2.0 percent per year at the present time. As a result, total world population has increased tremendously. It required most of man's time on the planet to generate a population of one billion persons—a number that was not reached until around 1800. But it required only 130 years to add a second billion, by 1930; 30 years to add a third billion, by 1960; and only 15 years to add a fourth billion.

The population of the economically advanced nations increased from about 201 million in 1750 to 347 million in 1850, to 858 million in 1950, and to about 1.1 billion in 1970. The developing nations (see Table 1) increased from 590 million in 1750 to 915 million in 1850, to 1.6 billion in 1950, and to 2.5 billion by 1970.

Looking ahead, if fertility remained constant, total world population, according to the United Nations projections, would reach 7.8 billion by the end of this century. Of this number, about 1.5 billion persons would reside in the presently more developed countries and about 6.4 billion in the less developed countries. The tremendous implications of present growth rates by level of development may be grasped by indicating that their continuation would produce a world population of about 1.8 trillion by the year 2150, of which only 1.9 billion would reside in the more developed nations.

The United Nations, in addition to the above assumption of constant fertility rates, has calculated three additional variant population projections based on differing assumptions on the reduction of fertility. Under the low fertility assumptions, world population would reach 6 billion persons by 2000, of which the more developed countries would have about 1.4 billion and the less developed countries about 4.5 billion. The medium fertility assumptions would produce a world population of 6.5 billion, 1.4 billion in the more developed countries and 5.1 billion in the less developed countries. The high fertility assumptions would result in a world population of 7.1 billion, of which 1.5 billion would be in the more developed and 5.7 billion in the less developed nations.

Although the United Nations prefers, and there is a general preference, to accept the medium variant as the best estimate for future population, there is also good reason to regard the high variant as plausible. That is, based on the relatively small amount of fertility reduction

TABLE 1. ESTIMATES OF PAST, PRESENT, AND FUTURE WORLD POPULATION FOR MORE AND LESS DEVELOPED REGIONS, 1750 TO 2000.

| Year | POPULATION (MILLIONS) | | | PERCENTAGE | |
	World	More developed countries	Less developed countries	More developed countries	Less developed countries
1750	791	201	590	25.4	74.6
1800	978	248	730	25.4	74.6
1850	1,262	347	915	27.5	72.5
1900	1,650	573	1,077	34.7	65.3
1950	2,486	858	1,628	34.5	65.5
1970	3,632	1,090	2,542	24.9	75.1
2000					
Constant variant	7,843	1,454	6,390	18.5	81.5
High variant	7,125	1,454	5,672	20.4	79.6
Medium variant	6,515	1,454	5,061	22.3	77.7
Low variant	5,998	1,454	4,545	24.2	75.8

SOURCE: For 1750 to 1900, J. D. Durand, "The Modern Expansion of World Population," *Proceedings of the American Philosophical Society*, Vol. III, No. 3, June 22, 1967; For 1950, United Nations, *The World Population Situation in 1970*, United Nations, New York, 1971; For 1970 to 2000, United Nations, *World and Regional Population Prospects: Addendum, World Population Prospects Beyond the Year 2000*, ECOSOC, World Population Conference, 1974 (E/Conf. 60/BP/3/Add.1), 16 May, 1973, (Mimeo.), pp. 3–16.

achieved to date by the less developed countries despite national family planning programs, the constant variant cannot be ruled out as impossible during the remainder of this century. If this proposition is accepted, then the United Nations high variant may be regarded as a "medium" projection, with the United Nations medium variant as a "low" projection. However, no matter which of these projections is taken as the best estimate, it is clear that, short of the catastrophic, the world is faced with great population increase to at least the end of the century, an increase that has tremendous implications—social, economic, and political—and one that will significantly affect the number, proportion, and way of life of older persons.

Whichever of the United Nations projections is utilized for anticipation of the future it is clear that the present less developed countries will increase their proportion of the world's population during the remainder of this century. In the year 2000, under the assumption of constant fertility, the less developed countries would have 81.5 percent of the world's peoples compared with 75.1 percent in 1970; under

the high variant, 79.6 percent; under the medium variant, 77.7 percent; and under the low variant, 75.8 percent.

The reason for the explosive increase in population growth may be quickly summarized. It is explained by the "theory of the demographic transition" which, although it has been subjected to much criticism in recent years, still stands firm in its major thesis. This thesis holds that the great acceleration in population growth rate is attributable primarily to great reductions in mortality while fertility remained high and declined only with considerable lag. In the first population explosion restricted to the more developed countries, mortality began its decline with the beginning of the modern era, 1650, but accelerated greatly after mid-nineteenth century. In the second population explosion which did not reach the 75 percent of the world's population in the less developed countries until after World War II, mortality declined much more precipitously as a result of which much greater growth rates were generated. The more rapid decline of mortality in the less developed countries is explained by the diffusion from the more developed countries to the less developed countries—in the post-World War II era—of the forces lowering mortality.

The Population Implosion

Man did not achieve fixed settlement until as recently as the Neolithic Period, some 10,000 years ago. Population agglomerations large enough to be called towns or cities began to develop between 5000 and 3500 B.C. Prerequisite to large population concentrations were, among other things, technological and social organizational developments. Mankind did not achieve enough in the way of technological and social organizational development to make a city of 100,000 possible until Greco-Roman civilization, and a city of 1,000,000 was not possible until the beginning of the nineteenth century.

It is not possible to trace world urbanization until about 1800. At that time, only some 2.4 percent of the world's peoples lived in cities of 20,000 or more. By 1900, some 9.2 percent of the world's peoples lived in such places; by 1950, about 21 percent. In 1970, using local definitions of "urban," which vary by nation, 37.2 percent of the world's peoples lived in urban places; about two-thirds of the population in the more developed countries (65.7 percent) and one-fourth (25.0 percent) in the less developed countries. United Nations projections indicate that, with present trends, more than half of the world's people will live in urban places by 2000 (51.1 percent); about four-fifths of the people in the more developed countries (80.7 percent); and over two-fifths of the people in the less developed countries (42.6). In little more than one human generation, between now and the end of the century, more than half of the world's peoples may become subject to "urbanism as a way of life." This augurs profound changes in values, attitudes, behaviorisms, and institutions with, as will be shown, great import for older persons.

Both the forces making for urbanization and its consequences differ in the more developed countries and the less developed countries. In the more advanced nations, urbanization was both antecedent and consequent of advances in productivity and levels of living. As Adam Smith noted, the larger the population agglomeration, the greater was possible the division of labor. This led to increased specialization, easier application of technology, and the use of non-human energy, economies of scale, external economies, and minimization of the frictions of space and communication. All this may be summarized by saying that urban centers in the more developed countries represented the most efficient production and consumption units yet developed. Moreover, in the more developed countries urbanization led to "urbanism as a way of life."

In the less developed countries, urbanization has been the product of quite different forces with, in the main, different consequences. To begin with, most less developed countries are characterized by "primate cities"—one major city generally without the accompanying system of smaller cities which make up the urban hierarchy in the more developed countries. The primate city, in contrast with the city in the more developed countries, was the product not so much of indigenous economic development as of colonial-imperial development in which it served as an entrepôt between the mother country and the colony. Only the core of the primate city bore a close resemblance to the city in the more developed countries. Its periphery remained more a congeries of indigenous population groupings often differentiated by race, ethnicity, religion, or language in pluralistic societies. With the collapse of colonialism after World War II, the growth of cities in the less developed countries was more the result of "push" factors from the rural countryside than the "pull" factors of economic advantage which stimulated rural to urban migration in the more developed countries. Among these push factors were: the troubled and insecure rural area occasioned by invasion and liberation during World War II; the search for security when independence generated, at the outset, communal conflict and social and political instability; the explosive population growth brought about by exogenous rather than indigenous decreases in mortality which produced population increases the land was unable to absorb. To be sure, there were also some pull factors in play—the social lures of the city and, to some extent, possible improvement, little as it was, in economic conditions. By comparison with urban growth in the more developed countries, the less developed countries became "overurbanized" in the sense that population agglomerations were not accompanied by corresponding increases in industrialization, productivity, and levels of living.

The consequences of urbanization visible in the more developed countries have not followed the same pattern in the less developed countries. Increased size, density, and heterogeneity were not necessarily accompanied by "urbanism as a way of life." The explanation of this difference in consequences is to be found in Durkheim's concept of "moral density," by which he meant interaction and communication. To the extent that cities in the less developed countries comprised an agglutination of disparate population groupings with relatively little social interaction, "urbanism as a way of life" was not a resultant of urban growth.

The above discussion constitutes a framework for tracing the changes in the life-style and role of the older person who is disproportionately buffeted by the frictions generated in the transition from the little community to the mass society. It helps to explain why the role of the older person in the less developed countries, even in the urban setting, differs from that of the older person in the more developed countries.

The Population Displosion

The world population displosion is more difficult to quantify, but it is nonetheless a significant element in the social morphological revolution. The displosion refers not only to increasing population heterogeneity but, also, to increasing sharing of social, economic, and political activities. Diverse populations have, of course, shared the same geographic locale as far back as antiquity, as in ancient Rome; but they have not shared social, economic, and political activities on an egalitarian basis. Differences in race, ethnicity, culture, language, and religion have in the past been accompanied by rigid forms of social stratification—slavery,

caste, or some system of subordination and superordination. Under such conditions each group "knew its place," and intergroup hostility and open conflict were minimal. In the contemporary world, however, since the end of World War II and the advent of "the revolution of rising expectations," the accompaniment of diversity with differential social, economic, and political opportunity has generated social unrest, political instability, and overt conflict throughout the world.

In the preurban, preindustrial world, populations lived, in the main, in small communities relatively homogeneous and autonomous with minimal social contact and interaction with diverse groups. In consequence of the population explosion and implosion and the emergence of the mass society, however, diverse populations came into increasingly greater contact and interaction. Moreover, technological developments, especially in communication and transport, brought diverse peoples into contact and interaction even across large spatial distances. It is probably no exaggeration to state that transport and communication advances have produced more social contact and interaction among widely differing populations during the past century than occurred in previous millennia of human history. Alienation, hostility, and conflict have become among the visible manifestations of the population displosion. This is evident in the conflicts, to mention a few, between Catholic and Protestant in Northern Ireland, tribes in Africa, Malays and Chinese in Malaysia, English and French descendants in Canada, Hindus and Muslims in the Asian subcontinent, and blacks and whites in the Union of South Africa, Rhodesia, Great Britain, and the United States. In the contemporary world, a correlation between population diversity and socioeconomic opportunity and status vitally affects the role and lot of older people.

The Technoplosion

Accelerated technological development has generally both preceded and required social change. As has been noted, improvements in transport and communication technology have exerted great influence on intergroup relationships. Other technological innovations have altered the way in which man makes a living and the containers in which he spends much of his time—residences, offices, factories, recreational facilities, and educational and cultural institutions. Technological developments have affected the behavior of all persons including old people—some with positive and others with negative consequences. For example, the changed nature of work has decreased the need for muscular power in many types of work, which may increase the usefulness of older persons with diminishing physical strength. On the other hand, rapid industrial developments have outmoded many occupations and have disproportionately forced older workers out of established career lines or entirely out of the work force. Furthermore, as technological advances have increased the need for workers with higher educational levels, older persons, by reason of the inverse correlation between age and education, have been adversely affected.

In general, rapid technological change has altered the physical and social setting in which persons spend their lives and has required often painful adjustments on the part of all persons, and especially of the aged. Needless to say, the adjustments required of old persons up to the present have been much greater in the more developed countries than in the less developed countries.

The world population developments described provide the setting within which world-wide aging and the extension of life have occurred. These processes are next reviewed.

AGING AND THE EXTENSION OF LIFE

Aging

The aging of a population is indicated by increased average (or median) age and by a larger proportion of old persons. For the world as a whole, the factors which influence the age structure of a population are fertility and mortality and their interaction. For any subdivision of the world, net migration is also involved in the aging of the population.

It has been shown that, although lower birth and death rates both contribute to aging, that is to the development of an older population, declines in mortality contribute relatively little as compared with decreases in fertility. Moreover, changes in mortality and changes in fertility have differing effects on the base of any population (lower ages) and its apex (older ages). Furthermore, such fertility and mortality changes may be independent or interrelated depending on specific developments.

A decline in the birth rate decreases the number of young people and, therefore, increases the proportion of old. If the birth rate remains low, the age structure tends to become fixed but with a greater proportion of older persons than contained in the original population. If fertility continues a downward course, the proportion of old persons continues to increase.

A decrease in the death rate can have differential impacts, depending upon the ages at which such mortality decreases occur. If the decline is the same at all ages, the age structure will remain the same, although expectation of life, the average number of years lived, will increase. Such an increase eventually will result in a larger proportion of older people. If the death rates decline mainly at the younger ages, which has occurred historically, the proportion of young will immediately increase. However, as expectation of life is increased, survivorship to older ages also occurs, and the proportion of older persons increases in the longer run. If, however, the decline in death rates occurs at the older ages, there will be an immediate increase in the proportion of older persons. The population will remain aged and grow even older if the death rates at older ages continue to go down.

The combined effect of decreases in both birth rates and death rates is to increase the proportion of older persons in a population. This is what has actually occurred in the economically advanced nations as their fertility and mortality both decreased.

The age structure of a population is also affected by migration. Unfortunately, migration is difficult to measure. Migration statistics, therefore, are often incomplete or are unavailable for many nations. In general, however, the evidence indicates that under most conditions, migration is relatively unimportant in comparison with decreases in fertility and mortality in the changing of population age structure.

In a country which is experiencing emigration, if all the emigrants were drawn proportionately from all ages, there would be no effect on age structure. This is generally not the case, however, because migration is usually selective by a number of characteristics, including age. If the emigrants are younger than the population from which they depart, the population of origin immediately grows older, especially if birth rates and death rates remain the same, and emigration is great. During the process of emigration, the population may grow younger at the outset, and then older as survivors of nonmigrants reach old age. Such fluctuations generally cannot be detected unless the rate of emigration is quite high.

The impact of immigration on the age structure of a country receiving migrants is just the reverse of that outlined above. The receiving population could grow younger or older depending on whether immigrants were younger or older than the resident population.

Extension of Life

It is useful to recognize the distinction between "aging" of a population and "the extension of life." "Aging" refers to an attribute of a population, "extension of life," to a characteristic of a person. From the moment of birth the individual has no alternative but to grow older. An aggregation of individuals, a population, however, may grow younger as well as older, depending upon the interaction of fertility, mortality, and migration. A decrease in the birth rate results, as indicated above, in a smaller number and proportion of young, relatively rapidly increasing the average (or median) age of a population and the proportion of older persons. A decrease in the death rate, apart from its effect on age structure, increases the average number of years lived by the person.

Also important to recognize is the distinction between "life span" and "expectation of life." The former is the theoretical length of time the human mechanism can survive under the best of conditions. The latter is the average number of years of life remaining for the person at any specified age from zero years of age at birth or from any greater age. Determination of the span of life is essentially a biological problem with available evidence indicating that it has changed but little, if any, during the past two millennia. The expectation of life is measured by analysis of observed death rates at each age, either at an instant in time (normally over one or more years) or over the actual life of a group of persons born at the same time (the same year or interval of years).

Analysis of death rates at each age makes possible the construction of a "life table" which includes a calculation of "life expectancy" or average number of years of life remaining at each age. If the life table is constructed on the basis of death rates as of an instant in time, it is known as a "synthetic life table" and gives the average number of years of life remaining if the population continues to die at the observed death rates at each age at that time. If the life table is constructed from observed death rates at each age of a population born in the same time period and observed over the entire lifetime of the group, it is known as a "longitudinal" or "generation" life table. Because of greater availability of data, most figures on life expectancy, including those used in this chapter, are based on synthetic rather than on generation life tables.

With decreases in mortality, expectation of life, not the span of life, has increased. As death rates have declined over time, there has been a great increase in the proportion of the life span which persons born actually live. Thus, extension of life is possible even if a population grows younger as measured by decline in average (or median) age. For example, with the post–World War II baby boom, the average age of the population of the United States declined, but the expectation of life continued to rise.

MODEL POPULATIONS

The effect of changing birth and death rates on the aging of a population, on extension of life, and on assessment of dependency can be illustrated by the consideration of model populations with different levels of fertility and mortality (Table 2). First summarized is the

TABLE 2. MODEL DEMOGRAPHIC PROFILES UNDER VARYING FERTILITY AND MORTALITY LEVELS.

Population characteristic	Primitive-stationary[a]	Pre-modern[b]	Transitional[c]	Modern[d]	Modern-stationary[e]
Birth rate	50.0	43.7	45.7	20.4	12.9
Death rate	50.0	33.7	15.7	10.4	12.9
Annual growth rate—percent	0.0	1.0	3.0	1.0	0.0
Age structure					
Percent under 15	36.2	37.8	45.4	27.2	19.2
Percent 15–64	60.9	58.8	52.0	62.4	62.3
Percent 65 and over	2.9	3.4	2.6	10.3	18.5
Average age	25.5	25.1	21.8	32.8	40.0
Dependency ratio	64	70	92	60	61
Youth dependency ratio	59	64	87	44	31
Aged dependency ratio	5	6	5	16	30
Percent surviving to age 15	41.0	55.9	78.8	95.6	98.9
Expectation of life at birth	20.0	30.0	50.0	70.0	77.5
Children ever-born to women age 50	6.2	5.5	6.1	2.9	2.1
Average number children surviving to age 20	2.3	2.9	4.7	2.7	2.0

[a] Mortality level 1.
[b] Mortality level 5.
[c] Mortality level 13.
[d] Mortality level 21.
[e] Mortality level 24.
SOURCE: Ansley J. Coale and Paul Demeny, *Regional Model Life Tables and Stable Populations*, Princeton, New Jersey: Princeton University Press, 1966. (Based on stable populations for "West" female.)

process of aging in each of the five model populations examined. Next the same is undertaken for the extension of life. Finally, in this section, changing dependency ratios are observed under the varying demographic dynamics for each of the model populations.

For analytical purposes, five model demographic profiles may be distinguished which may be termed the "primitive-stationary," the "pre-modern," the "transitional," the "modern," and the "modern-stationary." These models have been arbitrarily selected and designated by the writer from regional model life tables calculated by Ansley J. Coale and Paul Demeny (1966). The "primitive-stationary" model is selected to illustrate a population in which, under primitive conditions, fertility and mortality is determined by nature. Arbitrarily selected is a high birth and death rate of 50 (50 births and deaths, respectively, per 1,000 persons per year), vital rates which would result in zero population growth. This is a condition that must have obtained during much of man's occupation of this planet.

The "pre-modern" model shows what the demographic profile would be if it had a birth rate of 43.7, a death rate of 33.7, and a growth rate of 1 percent per annum. This represents a population in which the culture building of man has begun to reduce death rates and in which some minimal forms of fertility control have occurred. Factors which operated to reduce mortality undoubtedly included the emergence of national governments which tended to reduce internecine warfare, expand markets and, with improved technology and productivity, decrease the impact of famine and pestilence. Such a small reduction in fertility as is indicated would be mainly the result of abortion and primitive methods of contraception control.

The "transitional" model represents a society in which considerable reductions in mortality had been effected while the fertility level remained high; and by reason of the extension of female life through the child-bearing years and improved morbidity accompanying decreased mortality, the fertility rates would rise above the pre-modern level. In such a population, famine and pandemic and epidemic diseases would have virtually been eliminated, public sanitation and personal hygiene would have been considerably developed, and modern medicine would have begun to make its impact. The growth rate of such a population would soar to 3 percent per annum.

The "modern" model depicts a society not only in which mortality has been greatly reduced by the advances of modern medicine but, also, in which man has intervened to control the birth rate, mainly by means of contraception. It is a population in which man rather than nature controls both fertility and mortality. It has a birth rate of about 20, a death rate of about 10, and a growth rate of 1 percent per annum.

Finally, the "modern-stationary" model provides a glimpse into the future. Given the mathematical axiom that infinite growth is impossible in a finite space, zero population growth is inevitable (over time). The future, which will be reached by the more developed countries ahead of the less developed countries, will witness a birth and death rate each at a level of 12.9 (assuming a life expectation at birth of 77.5 years) which will result in zero growth. The zero growth of the modern-stationary population will be much more efficient, in the sense of being achieved with much lower fertility and mortality, than was the case in the primitive-stationary population.

The age structure and extension of life accompanying each of these models is next examined.

Aging in the Model Populations

The interaction of changes in birth and death rates results in declining average age from 25.5 years in the primitive-stationary population, to 25.1 years in the pre-modern, to 21.8 years in the transitional population. Thus, as man increasingly wins control over nature in respect of mortality first and then fertility, the average person grows younger. With the emergence of modern society, however, and great fertility reduction, average age increases by over 50 percent to 32.8 years. With the modern-stationary population profile, yet to be

achieved, average age would continue to rise to a level of 40.0 years.

The aging of the population, as indicated by the rising average age, is also demonstrated by the changing age structure. The proportion of persons 65 and over, only 2.9 percent of the total population in the primitive-stationary model, rises to 3.4 percent in the pre-modern model. However, in the transitional model with the sharp reduction in mortality, mainly in infant mortality and in mortality among the young, the proportion of older persons drops to 2.6 percent. In the modern model with the large decrease in the birth rate, the proportion of older persons soars to 10.3 percent. With continued fertility decline to reach zero growth, the proportion of persons 65 and over would rise to 18.5 percent.

The proportion of young persons under 15 also changes dramatically with the changes in fertility and mortality displayed in the models. The proportion of youth under 15, 36.2 percent in the primitive-stationary population, rises to 45.4 percent in the transitional population as the birth rate remains high and the death rate plummets. After that, with declining fertility, the proportion of young diminishes to 27.2 percent in the modern population model and would further decrease to 19.2 percent under the vital rates of the modern-stationary model.

With the offsets occasioned by increasing proportions of old persons and diminishing proportions of youth, the proportion of persons of intermediate age, 15 to 64, remains relatively stable, at about 62 percent, beginning with the modern model. In the three earlier models, however, the proportion of persons 15 to 64 decreases from 60.9 percent in the primitive model to a low of 52.0 in the transitional model. The age structure of the transitional model with a large proportion of young and a relatively small proportion of persons of intermediate (working) age has significant economic implications as will be indicated.

Extension of Life in Model Populations

Whereas the decline in fertility is the main factor in the aging of a population, it is the decline in mortality which has extended life. With a death rate of 50 in the primitive-stationary model, expectation of life at birth is only 20 years. With the lower death rate of 33.7 in the pre-modern model, life expectation at birth rises by 50 percent to 30 years. As the death rate further drops to 15.7 in the transitional model, expectation of life increases to 50 years. In the modern population model, the death rate of 10.4 is accompanied by an expectation of life of 70 years. Finally, under the assumptions of the modern-stationary model, a life expectancy at birth of 77.5 years would accompany a death rate and birth rate of 12.9. Such an expectation of life presses quite closely on what appears to be the span of life and could not be expected to increase much thereafter without extraordinary advances in biological knowledge and medical practice.

Most of the decrease in mortality shown in the models occurs in the death rates of the young, including infants. The documentation for this observation is given by the percent surviving to age 15 in the respective models. In the primitive-stationary population, only 41.0 percent of persons born live to age 15. Survival to age 15 increases in the successive models to 55.9 percent, 78.8 percent, and 95.6 percent in the modern population model. Under the assumption of life expectation of 77.5 years in the modern-stationary model, 98.9 percent of all persons born would survive to age 15.

A major impact of the extension of life may be seen in the relation between children ever-born and their survival to age 20—to the age at which they are still likely to live with their parents. In the primitive-stationary model, the average number of children ever-born to women by age 50 is 6.2, but with high mortality only 2.3 children survive to age 20. In the successive models, of 5.5 children born, 2.9 survive to age 20; of 6.1 children born, 4.7 survive; of 2.9 children born, 2.7 survive; and of 2.1 children born, 2.0 survive to age 20. The proportion of children ever-born surviving to age 20 increases from 37 percent in the primitive model to 93 percent in the modern model and would further increase to 95 percent in the modern-stationary model.

Dependency in the Model Populations

Age structure information makes possible an assessment of dependency. Ideally, dependency would be best measured by relating the number of dependents or persons not in the work force to persons in the work force. Such data are generally not available, especially for developing countries. Consequently, the practice usually followed by demographers is to substitute for the nonexistent data the ratio of persons above and below working age, often taken as below 15 years and 65 and above, to persons of working age, those 15 to 64 years old. Conventionally, this relationship is expressed as the number of dependents per 100 persons of working age. It is also possible to show the number of young and old dependents, respectively, per 100 persons of working age.

In the primitive-stationary model, the dependency ratio is 64, comprising 59 young and 5 old dependents. The total dependency ratio rises in the successive models to a peak of 92 in the transitional model, of which 87 are young and 5 are old. In the modern population model, total dependency declines to 60. This decline is the result of a 50 percent decline of young dependents, between the transitional and modern models, to 44, and a more than tripling of old dependents, to 16. Under the conditions of the modern-stationary model, total dependency would remain almost the same as in the modern model, rising by only one dependent to 61. But the number of older dependents would almost double to reach a level of 30 and almost match the youth dependency ratio, which would fall sharply to 31.

It is clear that problems of aging, extension of life, and dependency vary considerably among the five model populations studied. These variations provide insight into the actual patterns which can be observed for the world as a whole and for the more and less developed countries, respectively.

ACTUAL POPULATIONS

The demographic models presented above illustrate how changes in fertility and mortality which have generated the population explosion affect aging, the extension of life, and dependency. Next to be considered is the actual situation in the contemporary world as a whole and in the more developed and the less developed areas. The data are those published by the United Nations for the period around 1970.

The World

The demographic profile of the world as a whole is that of the combination, of course, of the profiles of the more developed countries and the less developed countries. Since about 70 percent of the total population resides in the less developed areas, the world picture is dominated by them (Table 3).

The growth rate of the total population on the globe is about 2.0 percent per annum, a rate which would double the population in about 35 years. The growth rate comprises a birth rate of 33.8 and a death rate of 14.0.

The average age of the world population is 26 years. The world population is a relatively young population with 37.0 percent under 15 years and only 5.2 percent 65 and older. Persons of intermediate age (working age) constitute 57.8 percent of the total. Expectation of life at birth in the world as a whole is 53.1 years. Of all persons born, 85.9 percent survive to age 15. Of the 4.7 average number of children ever-born to women by age 50, 4.0, or 85 percent, survive to age 20. In the world as a whole the dependency ratio is 74, made up of a youth dependency ratio of 65 and an aged dependency ratio of 9.

Of great interest, of course, are the differences between the more developed countries and less developed countries. These differences become more meaningful when related to the model population profiles considered above. At the outset it may be observed that the profile of the more developed countries closely approximates that of the "modern" model whereas that of the less developed countries bears close resemblance to the "transitional" profile.

TABLE 3. DEMOGRAPHIC PROFILE OF THE WORLD CLASSIFIED BY ECONOMIC DEVELOPMENT *CIRCA* 1965–70.

	World	More developed countries	Less developed countries
Birth rate	33.8	18.6	40.6
Death rate	14.0	9.1	16.1
Growth rate	2.0	1.0	2.4
Age structure			
Percent	100.0	100.0	100.0
Under 15	37.0	26.8	41.4
15–64	57.8	63.5	55.3
65 and over	5.2	9.6	3.3
Average age (median)	26	33	23
Dependency ratio, total	74	59	81
Youth (under 15)	65	44	75
Aged (65 and over)	9	15	6
Percent surviving to age 15	85.9	95.0	82.0
Expectation of life at birth	53.1	70.4	49.6
Children ever-born	4.7	2.7	5.6
Average number surviving to age 20	4.0	2.6	4.6

SOURCE: Adapted from United Nations, *The World Population Situation in 1970*, New York: United Nations, 1971 (Department of Economic and Social Affairs), Population Studies, No. 49.

The More Developed Countries

The more developed nations are increasing at 1.0 percent per year with a birth rate of 18.6 and a death rate of 9.1. Comparable data in the modern model are 1.0 percent for growth, 20.4 for the birth rate, and 10.4 for the death rate.

Average age in the more developed countries is 33.0 years, almost identical with the 32.8 years of the modern model. Persons under 15 make up 26.8 percent, and those 65 and over, 9.6 percent of the peoples in the more developed countries. In the modern population model the comparable data are 27.2 percent for the young and 10.3 percent for the old. Persons of intermediate age constitute 63.5 percent of the more developed countries' population as compared with 62.4 percent in the modern model. In the developed nations, expectation of life at birth is 70.4 years as compared with 70.0 years in the modern model. Survivorship to age 15 is 95.0 percent, that of the modern model, 95.6 percent. Of the 2.7 average number of children ever-born, 2.6 survive to age 20 in the more developed countries. In the modern model, of the 2.9 average number of children ever-born, 2.7 survive to age 20. Finally, the dependency ratio in the more developed countries is 59, made up of a youth dependency ratio of 44 and an aged dependency ratio of 15. Comparable data for the modern model are 60, 44, and 16.

The Less Developed Countries

The less developed countries are increasing at the rate of 2.4 percent per annum, a rate below the 3.0 percent in the transitional model. The birth and death rates are of about the same general order of magnitude in the developing world and the transitional model, the birth rates being 40.6 in the former compared with 45.7 in the latter and the death rates being 16.1 and 15.7, respectively.

Average age in the developing nations is 23, compared with 21.8 in the transitional model, and the age structure is quite similar. Youth under 15 make up 41.4 percent of the developing world's population compared with 45.4 percent in the model; older persons are 3.3 and 2.6 percent; those of intermediate age are 55.3 and 52.0 percent.

Expectation of life at birth in the actual population of the less developed countries at 49.6 years is almost identical with that in the model, 50.0 years. Survivorship to age 15 is 82.0 percent in the former and 78.8 in the latter. Of the average of 5.6 children ever-born to women by age 50 in the developing world, 4.6 survive to age 20. In the transitional model, of the average of 6.1 children ever-born, 4.7 survive to age 20.

In general, the correspondence between the demographic profile of the less developed countries and that of the transitional model is quite close, with the differences largely the result of the rapid progress being made towards the modern model by some among the developing nations (e.g., South Korea, Taiwan, Malaysia, Singapore, and Hong Kong).

The More Developed Countries vs. the Less Developed Countries

The less developed nations with a growth rate of 2.4 percent per year stand to experience a population doubling in less than 30 years. In contrast, the more developed nations with a growth rate of 1.0 percent would require about 70 years for a doubling of their population. The much lower birth rate of the more developed countries, 18.6 compared with 40.6, augurs a much more rapid aging of population; and their lower death rate, 9.1 compared with 16.1, points to a greater extension of life.

By reason of the lower birth rate experienced by the more developed countries, the average person in those countries is considerably older than the average person in the less developed countries, 33 compared with 23 years; and the proportion of persons 65 and over is almost three times that in the less developed countries, 9.6 compared with 3.3 percent. In contrast, the less developed countries have a much larger proportion of young, 41.4 compared with 26.8 percent. They have a smaller proportion of persons of intermediate age, 55.3 compared with 63.5 percent.

These differences in age structure result in

significantly different dependency ratios. The less developed countries have 81 dependents for each 100 persons of working age, in contrast with 59 for the more developed countries. Of the 81 dependents in the less developed countries, 75 are young and only 6 are aged. In the more developed countries, of the 59 dependents, only 44 are young and 15 are old. In the more developed countries, then, the aged dependency ratio is 2.5 times that in the less developed countries.

The lower death rate in the more developed countries than in the less developed countries has resulted in a much greater extension of life for the former countries. Expectation of life at birth in the more developed countries, 70.4 years, is almost 21 years greater than that in the less developed countries, 49.6 years. Whereas only 82.0 percent of persons born in the less developed countries survive to age 15, 95.0 percent do so in the more developed countries. Of the average of 2.7 children ever-born per woman by age 50 in the more developed countries, 2.6 or 96 percent survive to age 20. In the less developed countries, of the average of 5.6 children ever-born, 4.6 or 82 percent survive to age 20.

It is clear, then, that actual patterns of aging, extension of life, and dependency for the more developed countries closely resemble those observed in the modern population model, whereas those for the less developed countries closely resemble those in the transitional model. Next, let us turn to the consideration of projections of the demographic profiles of the world as a whole and of the less and more developed countries, respectively.

PROJECTIONS OF DEMOGRAPHIC PROFILES

Using the various United Nations projections it is possible to present for the year 2000 demographic profiles paralleling the models and actual population situation presented above (Table 4).

The World

According to the medium variant projection, the growth rate of the world in 2000 would be 1.7 percent per annum, a decrease of 15 percent from the present rate of 2.0 percent. The world birth rate of 25.1 would be down from 33.8

TABLE 4. DEMOGRAPHIC PROFILE OF THE WORLD CLASSIFIED BY ECONOMIC DEVELOPMENT IN THE YEAR 2000 (MEDIUM VARIANT).

	World	More developed countries	Less developed countries
Birth rate	25.1	17.5	27.4
Death rate	8.1	9.6	7.6
Growth rate	1.7	0.8	2.0
Age structure			
Percent	100.0	100.0	100.0
Under 15	32.9	24.9	35.2
15–64	61.0	63.7	60.3
65 and over	6.1	11.4	4.6
Average age (median)	29	35	27
Dependency ratio, total	64	57	66
Youth (under 15)	54	39	58
Aged (65 and over)	10	18	8
Expectation of life at birth	66.5	73.2	65.3
Children ever-born	3.3	2.5	3.5
Average number surviving to age 20	3.1	2.4	3.3

SOURCE: Adapted from United Nations, *World and Regional Population Prospects: Addendum, World Population Prospects Beyond the Year 2000.*

in 1970, a decline of 26 percent. The world death rate of 8.1 would be down from 14.0 in 1970, a decline of 42 percent. Average age in the world as a whole would be 29 years, up from 1970 by 3 years, or by 12 percent. The aged 65 and over would make up 6.1 percent of the population, up from 5.2 percent in 1970. The young, under 15, would drop from 37.0 percent in 1970 to 32.9 percent in 2000. Persons of intermediate age would rise from 57.8 percent in 1970 to 61.0 percent in 2000. Thus, the aged between now and the end of the century would increase by 17 percent, the young would decline by 11 percent, and persons of intermediate (working) age would increase by 6 percent.

The world total dependency ratio would decrease to 64 by 2000, from 74 in 1970. Aged dependency would rise from 9 to 10; youth dependency would decline from 65 to 54. While total dependency decreased by 14 percent and youth dependency by 17 percent, aged dependency would rise by 11 percent.

Life expectancy in the world as a whole in 2000 would be 66.5 years, an increase of 13.4 years of life, or a rise of 25 percent. The total number of children ever-born to women by age 50 would in 2000 be 3.3, as compared with 4.7 in 1970, a decrease of 30 percent. The number of children surviving to age 20 would be 3.1. Thus, the survivorship of children ever-born to age 20 would increase from 85 percent in 1970 to 94 percent by the year 2000.

More Developed Countries and Less Developed Countries

The world profile is, of course, the weighted average of the profiles in the more developed countries and less developed countries. The growth rate of the more developed countries is projected to be 0.8 percent in 2000, as compared with 1.0 percent in 1970, a decline of 20 percent. In the less developed countries, the growth rate in 2000 would be 2.0 percent per annum, down from 2.4 percent, or a decline of 17 percent.

The birth rate of the more developed countries in 2000 would be 17.5, down from 18.6 in 1970; in the less developed countries, 27.4,

down from 40.6. The death rate in the more developed countries would be 9.6 in 2000, up from 9.1; in the less developed countries, 7.6, down from 16.1. The birth rate of the less developed countries, then, is projected to decline by 33 percent during the remainder of this century, that of the more developed countries by 6 percent. Whereas the death rate of the less developed countries is projected to decrease by 53 percent, that of the more developed countries would increase by 5 percent. This does not mean, however, that mortality would be greater in the more developed countries than in the less developed countries. The projected increase in the death rate of the more developed countries would occur even as mortality at each age went down because of the aging of the population and the fact that older persons have higher death rates than younger persons. Similarly, the lower death rate of the less developed countries, as compared with that of the more developed countries, in 2000, would simply reflect the younger age structure of the former.

These last observations are confirmed by consideration of the respective age structures. By the end of the century, the average age in the more developed countries would be 35 years, an increase of 2 years, or 6 percent over average age in 1970. The average age in the less developed countries would, by 2000, be 27 years, up 4 years over that in 1970, or a rise of 17 percent. Nevertheless, the average person in the more developed countries in 2000 would still be 8 years older than the average person in the less developed countries.

Old persons in the more developed countries would make up 11.4 percent of the population in 2000, as compared with 9.6 percent in 1970. In the less developed countries, the comparable figures would be 4.6 and 3.3 percent. Youth in the more developed countries in 2000 would constitute 24.9 percent of the total as compared with 26.8 percent in 1970. In the less developed countries, the comparable figures would be 35.2 and 41.4 percent. Persons of intermediate age would, in the more developed countries, constitute 63.7 percent of the total in 2000 compared with 63.5 percent in 1970. In the less developed countries, the comparable figures would be 60.3 and 55.3 percent. Thus, the proportion of older persons during the remainder of this century would, in the more developed countries, rise by 19 percent as compared with an increase of 39 percent in the less developed countries—if fertility drops in accordance with the projections. In contrast, youth would decrease by 7 percent in the more developed countries and by 15 percent in the less developed countries. Persons of working age would increase by only 0.3 percent in the more developed countries and by 9 percent in the less developed countries.

In the more developed countries, by 2000, the total dependency ratio would be 57, down from 59 in 1970; in the less developed countries, it would be 66, down from 81. The aged dependency ratio in the more developed countries would rise to 18 from 15, and to 8 from 6 in the less developed countries. Contrariwise, the youth dependency ratio in the more developed countries would decline to 39 from 44, and in the less developed countries, to 58 from 75. Accordingly, while total dependency in the more developed countries decreased by about 3 percent and youth dependency by 11 percent, aged dependency would increase by 20 percent. In the less developed countries, while total dependency would drop by 19 percent and youth dependency by 23 percent, aged dependency would rise by 33 percent. Despite the greater rate of increase in aged dependency in the less developed countries than in the more developed countries during the remainder of this century, the aged dependency ratio in the latter would, in 2000, still be more than twice as great as that in the former.

Expectation of life at birth in the more developed countries would by 2000 be 73.2 years, 2.8 years above that in 1970, a rise of 4 percent. In the less developed countries, life expectancy would rise by 15.7 years to 65.3 years, an increase in average years of life of 32 percent. In the more developed countries, the number of children ever-born to women by age 50 would be 2.5 in 2000, down from 2.7 in 1970. Comparable data for the less developed countries would be 3.5 and 5.6. In the more developed countries, of the children ever-born, 96 percent would survive to age 20, 2.4 of the 2.5 born. In the less developed countries, as

evidence of rapidly declining mortality, 94 percent would survive to age 20, 3.3 of the 3.5 children born.

According to the United Nations projections, then, the less developed countries would, by the end of the century, be down the road in the demographic transition but still with a long distance to travel. In addition, it must be emphasized that the projected progress toward a modern demographic profile is based on an assumption of declining fertility, and the empirical evidence necessary for justification of the assumption is not yet at hand.

Within the context of the population projections considered, which differ greatly for the more and less developed areas, let us next turn to the projections of older persons.

Projections of Older Persons

Projections of the total population of the world and of the more developed countries and the less developed countries have been presented above. Drawing on the United Nations medium variant projections, the outlook for persons 65 and older is now examined.

In 1970, of the total of 3.6 billion persons on the globe, approximately 190 million were 65 and older. Of these old persons, about 105 million were in the more developed countries, and about 85 million in the less developed countries. Despite the fact that the more developed countries made up only 30 percent of the world's population, by reason of the more rapid aging of their peoples they had 45 percent of the world's older people.

According to the United Nations calculations, annual rates of growth of persons 65 and over would, for the world as a whole, decrease from 2.7 percent per annum in the quinquennium 1970-75 to 1.8 percent per year between 1980-85 and then rise to a level of about 2.5 percent per year, with some fluctuation, during the remainder of the century. The world rates are, of course, the resultant of the differing rates in the more developed countries and the less developed countries, respectively. In the more developed countries, the growth rate is estimated at 2.4 percent per year between 1970 and 1975, a rate estimated to decline to 0.4

percent during the quinquennium 1980–85 and then rise to 2.0 percent in the following two quinquennia before declining to 1.1 percent in the last quinquennium of the century. In the less developed countries, the rate of increase in older persons per annum, 3.2 percent between 1970 and 1975, will rise to 3.5 percent for the last two quinquennia of the century.

The fluctuations in the annual growth rate of older persons in the more developed countries is mainly a reflection of previous fluctuations in fertility. The higher and rising rates in the less developed countries follow from their prior higher fertility as well as rapidly declining mortality.

By the year 2000, the projected growth rates would produce a population 65 and over of 396 million, more than a doubling of older persons in the world. In the more developed countries, old persons would total 166 million, in the less developed countries, 230 million. While older persons in the more developed countries increase by 58 percent between 1970 and 2000, those in the less developed countries will almost triple. In consequence, whereas the less developed countries had only 45 percent of the world's aged in 1970, they would have 58 percent by the century's end.

REGIONAL VARIATIONS

The data presented above, while depicting the world situation and that of the more developed countries and less developed countries, respectively, obscure regional variations in the present demographic situation and in the outlook. These will be next considered in summary form.

The United Nations, in its most recent projections (1973), has subdivided the world into eight broad regions as follows: East Asia, South Asia, Europe, USSR, Africa, Northern America, Latin America, and Oceania. These regions may, in the main, but not exactly, be divided into the "more developed countries" and "less developed countries" classifications. East Asia, for example, includes Japan and Hong Kong, and South Asia includes Singapore. The population of each of these areas, their proportions of the world's total, and their numbers of persons 65 and over are given in Table 5 for 1970 and projected to 2000.

Between 1970 and 2000 world population will, according to the medium United Nations projections, increase by 79 percent, but population in the less developed countries will increase by 98 percent, about double, while population in the more developed countries

TABLE 5. POPULATION AND OLDER PERSONS OF WORLD BY EIGHT UNITED NATIONS REGIONS, 1970 AND PROJECTED TO 2000 (MEDIUM VARIANT).

| | TOTAL POPULATION | | | | PERSONS 65 AND OVER | | | |
| | Number (000,000's) | | % distribution | | Number (000,000's) | | % distribution | |
World and region	1970	2000	1970	2000	1970	2000	1970	2000
World	3,632	6,515	100.0	100.0	190	396	100.0	100.0
East Asia	930	1,424	25.6	21.9	40	99	21.0	24.9
South Asia	1,126	2,354	31.0	36.1	36	99	18.8	24.9
Europe	462	568	12.7	8.7	52	71	27.1	17.8
U.S.S.R.	243	330	6.7	5.1	19	39	9.9	9.8
Africa	344	818	9.5	12.6	10	27	5.5	6.8
Northern America	228	333	6.3	5.1	22	31	11.6	7.8
Latin America	283	652	7.8	10.0	10	29	5.5	7.3
Oceania	19	35	0.5	0.5	1	3	0.6	0.8

SOURCE: Total Population, from United Nations, *World and Regional Population Prospects: Addendum*, *World Population Prospects Beyond the Year 2000*, p. 13; Persons 65 and over, from same for year 2000; for year 1970, estimated from United Nations, *The World Population Situation in 1970*, pp. 46–50.

will increase by only one-third (33 percent). Among the eight broad geographic regions, three will more than double: Africa, with a projected increase of 138 percent; Latin America, with 130 percent; and South Asia, with 109 percent. The five remaining regions will grow relatively slowly: Europe by 30 percent; the Soviet Union by 36 percent; East Asia by 53 percent; Oceania by 84 percent; and Northern America by 68 percent.

These differential growth rates will, of course, result in changes in the distribution of the world's population. The three most rapidly growing regions will increase their share of the world's peoples: South Asia from 31.0 to 36.1 percent; Africa from 9.5 to 12.6 percent; Latin America from 7.8 to 10.0 percent. The four remaining large regions will shrink as a proportion of the world's total: East Asia from 25.6 to 21.9 percent; Europe from 12.7 to 8.7 percent; the USSR from 6.7 to 5.1 percent; Northern America from 6.3 to 5.1 percent. Oceania, with only 0.5 percent of the world's population in 1970, will have the same proportion in 2000.

Older Persons

The three most rapidly growing regions will also experience the greatest increase in persons 65 and older. Older people in South Asia, increasing at 3.4 percent per year in the period 1970 to 1975, will accelerate in growth rate to 3.7 percent per year in the last quinquennium of the century; Africa from 3.0 percent per year to 3.6 percent; Latin America, with an annual rate of increase of 3.6 percent between 1970 and 1975, will decline to a 3.0 percent per annum increase by 1995–2000, a level still above that of four of the five more slowly growing regions at the end of the century (except for East Asia, 3.1 percent). In contrast, the five more slowly growing regions will, with the exception of East Asia, experience sharp drops in their annual increases in older persons: Europe, with some fluctuations, will register a decline from 2.2 percent in the first five-year period beginning with 1970 to 0.7 percent per year by the last five-year period of the century; the USSR will show a decrease from 3.3 to 1.7 percent;

Northern America from 1.6 to 0.2 percent; and Oceania from 2.3 to 1.0 percent. East Asia will experience about the same annual rate of growth of her aged, about 3.0 percent, with some fluctuation, through the period.

The proportions of older people will increase in almost all the regions of the world. The proportion of older persons in Europe will increase from 11.4 percent in 1970 to 12.5 percent in 2000; in the Soviet Union from 8.2 to 11.7 percent; in Oceania from 7.3 to 8.6 percent. In East Asia the proportion of older persons will rise from 4.3 in 1970 to 7.0 percent in 2000. In Northern America the proportion of old persons will be at the same level in 2000 as in 1970, 9.4 percent. The proportion of old persons in South Asia will rise from 3.0 to 4.2 percent; in Africa from 2.8 to 3.2 percent; in Latin America from 3.8 to 4.4 percent.

The differential rates of increase in the proportion of older persons among the regions of the world is the result of past fertility, projected fertility, and mortality. In North America, for example, the fact that the proportion of older people is the same in 2000 as in 1970 reflects the sharp decline in fertility during the depression of the 1930's which produced relatively small numbers of survivors to age 65 by the year 2000. It is clear that the regions most characterized by economic advance and which have already experienced relatively large decreases in fertility will have the greater proportion of older persons by the end of the century. It is also clear that the regions mainly characterized by low levels of economic development will experience increases in their proportions of older persons, if their fertility indeed does decline as assumed in the United Nations projections.

By 2000, of the total of 396 million persons 65 years of age and older, 99 million, or 25 percent, will be in South Asia and East Asia, respectively; 71 million, or 18 percent, will be in Europe; 39 million, or 10 percent, will be in the USSR; 31 million, or 8 percent, will be in Northern America; 29 million, or 7 percent, will be in Latin America; 27 million, or almost 7 percent, will be in Africa; and 3 million, or less than 1.0 percent, will be in Oceania.

The regions which will experience the greatest

increase in their proportion of older people will be East Asia with a 63 percent increase in prospect; the USSR with 43 percent; and South Asia with 40 percent. These areas will be faced with the greatest adjustments to the problems accompanying aging. Africa and Latin America with relatively small decreases in fertility in prospect will have moderate increases in their proportion of old persons of 14 and 16 percent, respectively. Europe and North America, with already relatively low fertility and a relatively large proportion of aged persons, will experience either relatively little change (Europe, 10 percent increase) or no change (North America).

When zero population growth is achieved, the proportion of older persons will significantly increase, depending then mainly on what advances may have been made in lowering mortality and increasing life expectancy. As has already been indicated, if an expectation of life of 77.5 years is achieved, the proportion of persons 65 and over would reach 18.5 percent. With a life expectancy of 70, the proportion of old persons would reach 15.2 percent at zero growth.

Regional variations in proportions and numbers of older persons represent, of course, the weighted average of country data within each region. Next reviewed, therefore, are the data for individual countries to the extent that they are available.

INDIVIDUAL COUNTRIES

Since policy and program in respect of the aged is a matter for individual nations, data are presented in Table 6 for the 81 countries for which information is available on total population, age structure in broad groups, crude birth and death rates, and life expectancy by sex as of about 1970. The countries are arranged in order of highest proportion of persons 65 years old and over. Of the 81 countries, the German Democratic Republic has the largest proportion of older people, 15.6 percent, and Mali has the lowest proportion, 1.6 percent. The median country, Lebanon, has 5.0 percent of her population 65 and older.

The United Nations has defined populations as "aged," "mature," and "young" on the basis of their proportions of old people. The "aged" nations are those with over 7 percent of the population 65 and over, the "mature" between 4 and 7 percent, and the "young" under 4 percent. On this basis, of the 81 countries, 34 are aged, 13 are mature, and 34 are young.

TABLE 6 TOTAL POPULATION, BROAD AGE STRUCTURE, CRUDE BIRTH RATE, CRUDE DEATH RATE, AND LIFE-EXPECTATION AT BIRTH FOR EIGHTY-ONE COUNTRIES IN OR AROUND 1970.

| Country | Year of census or estimate | Population (000's) | BROAD AGE STRUCTURE (PERCENT OF POPULATION) | | | 1970 crude birth rate | 1970 crude death rate | LIFE-EXPECTATION AT BIRTH, 1970 | |
			Under 15	15–64	65 and over			Male	Female
German Democratic Republic	1971	17,068.3	23.3	61.1	15.6	13.9	14.1	69.2	74.4
Austria	1970	7,390.9	24.5	61.3	14.2	15.1	13.2	66.5	73.3
Sweden	1970	8,076.9	20.8	65.4	13.7	13.6	9.9	71.7	76.5
Federal Republic of Germany	1970	60,650.6	23.0	63.6	13.4	13.3	11.6	67.6	73.6
France	1970	50,768.4	24.0	62.7	13.4	16.7	10.6	68.6	76.1
Belgium	1970	9,650.9	23.7	63.0	13.3	14.7	12.4	67.7	73.5[a]
England and Wales	1971	48,815.0	23.9	63.0	13.1	16.0	11.7	68.7	74.9
Norway	1970	3,888.3	24.4	62.6	12.9	16.2	9.8	71.0	76.0[a]
Scotland	1971	5,217.4	26.1	61.6	12.3	16.8	12.3	67.1	73.2
Denmark	1970	4,928.8	23.3	64.4	12.3	14.4	9.8	70.8	75.7
Switzerland	1970	6,269.8	23.7	64.7	11.6	15.9	9.0	69.2	75.0
Czechoslovakia	1970	14,361.6	23.0	65.6	11.5	15.8	11.4	66.2	73.2
Hungary	1970	10,315.6	21.0	67.6	11.4	14.7	11.6	66.3	72.0
Greece	1971	8,768.6	24.9	64.0	11.2	16.5	8.4	67.5	70.7[a]
Ireland	1971	2,978.0	31.0	58.1	10.9	22.8	10.6	68.1	71.9[a]
Northern Ireland	1971	1,534.0	30.0	59.2	10.8	21.1	10.9	68.3	73.7
Italy	1971	53,770.3	24.4	65.0	10.7	16.8	9.7	67.9	73.4
Netherlands	1971	13,194.5	27.0	62.7	10.3	18.4	8.4	71.0	76.4
United States	1970	203,211.9	28.5	61.6	9.9	18.2	9.4	66.6	74.0
Bulgaria	1971	8,536.4	22.6	67.5	9.9	16.0	9.0	68.8	72.7

TABLE 6—Continued

Country	Year of census or estimate	Population (000's)	BROAD AGE STRUCTURE (PERCENT OF POPULATION)			1970 crude birth rate	1970 crude death rate	LIFE-EXPECTATION AT BIRTH, 1970	
			Under 15	15-64	65 and over			Male	Female
Spain	1970	34,037.8	27.8	62.5	9.7	19.6	8.5	67.3	71.9[a]
Finland	1970	4,622.3	24.2	66.4	9.4	13.7	9.5	65.4	72.6[a]
Portugal	1970	8,668.3	28.3	62.5	9.2	18.0	9.7	65.3	71.0
Iceland	1970	204.9	32.3	58.8	8.9	19.7	7.1	70.8	76.2
Poland	1970	32,642.3	26.2	65.3	8.6	16.7	8.1	66.9	72.8
Romania	1970	20,252.5	25.9	65.5	8.6	21.1	9.5	65.5	69.8
New Zealand	1971	2,862.6	31.8	59.7	8.5	22.1	8.8	68.4	73.8[a]
Australia	1971	12,755.6	28.8	62.9	8.3	20.5	9.0	67.9	74.2[a]
Canada	1971	21,568.3	29.6	62.3	8.1	17.0	7.3	68.8	75.2
Yugoslavia	1971	20,523.0	26.9	65.2	7.9	17.6	8.9	64.8	69.2
Soviet Union	1970	241,720.1	30.9	61.4	7.7	17.5	8.2	65.0	74.0
Argentina	1970	23,362.2	29.9	62.6	7.5	21.9	9.5	64.1	70.2
Barbados	1969	253.3	36.3	56.3	7.4	21.9	8.6	62.7	67.4
Japan	1970	103,720.1	23.9	69.0	7.1	18.9	6.9	69.0	74.3
Israel	1971	3,045.6	33.0	60.2	6.8	26.8	7.0	69.6	73.0
Puerto Rico	1970	2,712.0	36.5	56.9	6.5	24.8	6.6	69.0	75.1
Chile	1970	8,853.1	39.0	54.9	6.0	29.6	9.4	60.5	66.0
Cuba	1970	8,495.4	37.0	57.1	5.9	26.6	7.5	66.8	
Lesotho	1969	889.6	42.6	51.5	5.9	38.8	21.0	43.5	
Botswana	1971	598.1	45.8	48.8	5.4	44.2	22.6	41.0	
Lebanon	1970	2,126.3	42.7	52.4	5.0	26.5	4.5	b	
Morocco	1971	15,153.8	46.2	49.2	4.7	49.5	16.5	50.5	
Yemen, Democratic	1970	1,435.9	39.8	55.6	4.6	50.0	22.7	42.3	
Jamaica	1970	1,865.4	46.0	49.6	4.4	34.4	7.6	62.6[a]	66.6
Algeria	1966	12,096.3	47.2	48.4	4.4	49.1	16.9	50.7	
Turkey	1970	35,666.5	42.5	53.4	4.1	39.6	14.6	53.7	
Union of South Africa	1970	21,443.2	40.8	55.2	4.1	40.3	16.6	49.0	
West Malaysia	1970	8,801.4	42.8	53.3	3.9	33.8	7.3	63.8[a]	66.3
Hong Kong	1970	3,959.0	37.1	59.0	3.9	19.0	5.0	66.7	73.3
Trinidad and Tobago	1970	1,026.7	41.2	55.0	3.8	24.3	6.8	62.2[a]	66.3
Uganda	1969	9,548.8	46.2	50.0	3.8	43.2	17.6	47.5	
Panama	1970	1,428.1	43.4	52.8	3.7	41.1	8.8	57.6[a]	60.9
Mexico	1970	48,225.2	46.2	50.1	3.7	43.2	8.9	61.0	63.7
Ghana	1970	8,559.3	46.9	49.4	3.6	46.6	17.8	46.0	
Kenya	1969	10,942.7	48.4	48.1	3.6	47.8	17.5	47.5	
Sri Lanka	1971	12,711.1	41.8	54.6	3.6	29.4	7.5	61.9[a]	61.4
India	1971	547,949.8	41.8	54.7	3.5	42.8	16.7	41.9[a]	40.6
Brazil	1970	93,204.4	41.8	54.7	3.5	37.8	9.5	b	
Jordan	1971	2,383.0	47.5	49.1	3.4	49.1	16.0	52.6[a]	52.0
Liberia	1971	1,571.5	41.6	54.9	3.4	51.0	16.0	50.8	57.4
El Salvador	1971	3,549.3	46.2	50.4	3.4	40.0	9.9	56.6	60.4
Singapore	1971	2,110.4	37.7	58.9	3.4	22.8	5.4	68.2	
Philippines	1970	36,684.5	43.2	53.4	3.4	44.7	12.0	48.8[a]	53.4
Republic of Korea	1970	31,469.1	40.3	56.3	3.4	35.6	11.0	59.7	64.1
Pakistan	1968	104,599.6	45.9	50.9	3.2	50.9	18.4	53.7[a]	48.8
Paraguay	1970	2,386.0	46.4	50.4	3.2	44.6	10.8	59.4	
Syrian Arab Republic	1970	6,144.1	46.0	50.9	3.2	47.5	15.3	52.8	
Guyana	1970	763.4	44.2	52.6	3.2	38.1	6.8	59.0[a]	63.0
Peru	1970	13,586.3	45.0	51.9	3.1	41.8	11.1	52.6[a]	55.5
Iran	1971	30,159.0	47.2	49.7	3.1	45.4	16.6	50.0	
Dominican Republic	1970	4,006.4	47.5	49.4	3.1	48.5	14.7	57.2[a]	58.6
Haiti	1971	4,243.9	43.2	53.7	3.1	43.9	19.7	44.5	
Nicaragua	1971	1,911.5	48.3	48.8	2.9	46.0	16.5	49.9	
Niger	1969	3,909.0	44.5	52.6	2.9	52.2	23.3	41.0	
Ecuador	1972	6,508.0	47.2	50.0	2.8	44.9	11.4	51.0[a]	53.7
Venezuela	1970	10,398.9	47.1	50.5	2.4	40.9	7.8	63.8	
Honduras	1970	2,582.0	46.8	50.8	2.4	49.0	17.1	49.0	
Greenland	1965	39.6	46.2	51.5	2.3	24.3	5.6	57.0[a]	64.2
Zambia	1969	4,057.0	46.3	51.5	2.2	49.8	20.7	43.5	
Kuwait	1970	738.7	43.2	55.0	1.7	43.3	7.4	64.4	
Mali	1970	5,047.3	49.1	49.3	1.6	49.8	26.6	37.2	

SOURCE: United Nations, *Demographic Yearbook*.
[a]In or around 1960.
[b]Data not available.

Because the countries for which no data are available are predominantly less developed countries, the number of young countries is understated.

Among the 34 nations in the aged category, 10 have 12 percent or more of their populations comprising older persons, 8 have 10 to 12 percent old persons, 11 have 8 to 10 percent old, and 5 have 7 to 8 percent old. The median proportion of older persons among the aged nations is between 10.7 and 10.3 percent. The United States, it may be observed, is among the aged nations but is still relatively young with 9.9 percent 65 and over. It is noteworthy that almost all of the aged nations are among the more developed countries and in either Europe, Northern America, or Oceania. The only aged nations not in the above 3 areas are Argentina, Barbados, and Japan. Among these exceptions, only Japan is economically advanced. In all likelihood Argentina falls among the aged nations by reason of heavy past immigration and Barbados by reason of heavy current emigration. Both barely fall into the aged category.

Of the 13 mature countries with respect to age, Israel heads the list with 6.8 percent of her population 65 and over; and the Union of South Africa is at the lowest end of the list, with 4.1 percent old. Five of the 13 nations are in Africa, 4 are in Asia (Southwest), and 4 are in Latin America, including the Caribbean.

Of the 34 young nations, West Malaysia and Hong Kong, among the more developed of the less developed countries, are the oldest, with 3.9 percent of aged. The 2 youngest countries are Mali, with only 1.6 percent, and Kuwait, with only 1.7 percent, 65 and older.

Twenty-five of the young countries have from 3 to 4 percent aged; 7, from 2 to 3 percent; and 2, below 2 percent. All of these nations are among the less developed countries, with West Malaysia, Hong Kong, and Singapore, however, beginning to reach the more developed level. Of the 34 countries, 10 are in Latin America, including the Caribbean, 4 are in Central America, 7 are in Africa, 12 in Asia, and the remaining country is Greenland.

Among the "aged" nations, the crude birth rate in 1970 ranged from 13.3 in the Federal Republic of Germany to 22.8 in Ireland, with a median birth rate of 16.8; and the death rate ranged from 6.9 in Japan to 14.1 in the German Democratic Republic, with a median death rate of 9.5. Life expectancy among the aged nations ranged for females from a high of 76.5 years in Sweden to a low of 67.4 in Barbados, with a median life expectancy of 73.6 years, and for males from a high of 71.7 years in Sweden to a low of 62.7 in Barbados, with a median of 67.8 years.

Among the "mature" nations, the crude birth rate ranged from a low of 24.8 in Puerto Rico to a high of 50 in Yemen, with a median birth rate of 38.8. The death rate ranged from a low of 4.5 in Lebanon to a high of 22.7 in Yemen, with a median death rate of 14.6. Life expectancy for females for countries for which the data were available varied from levels of around 41 in Botswana to 75.1 in Puerto Rico; and for males from a similar low to a high of 69.6 in Israel.

Among the "young" nations, the crude birth rate varied from a low of 19.0 in Hong Kong to a high of 52.2 in Niger, with a median birth rate of 43.6. The death rate ranged from a low of 5.0 in Hong Kong to a high of 26.6 in Mali, with a median death rate of 11.7. Finally, expectation of life at birth varied from a low of about 37.2 years in Mali to a high of about 68.2 for both sexes combined in Singapore (66.7 for males and 73.3 for females in Hong Kong), with a median life expectancy of 52.7 years for males.

Clearly, in light of the great differences in the proportions of old persons, policy and programs in respect of older people must be adapted to actual conditions in individual countries at the present time and in relation to the outlook for the future. Problems of aging in relation to policy and programs will next be considered.

IMPLICATIONS OF AGING AND EXTENSION OF LIFE

The social morphological revolution, still underway, is transforming the world in which man lives from a "little community" to a "mass society." In the process of transformation, both the social order and the person are being subjected to accelerating rates of change generating unprecedented strains and problems. Both the aging of populations and the extension of life are among the products of this revolution and as such are relatively new phenomena which man is still striving to understand and manage. Since the four elements of the social morphological revolution have had differential impact over varying periods of time, there are great variations on the globe in their effects on the nature of societies and on the values, attitudes, and behaviorisms of man. Among the variations manifest are those relating to the number and proportion of older persons, the roles they play, the status they possess, and the problems they confront.

The differences between the more developed and less developed nations and world regions presented above by no means represent the full spectrum of variations in demographic profiles. But, in general, the less developed countries tend to have the characteristics of "little community" societies and the more developed countries, those of "mass societies." As a matter of convenience, if not necessity in terms of available data and space, the implications of aging and the extension of life will be considered separately for the elements in this dichotomization of the world. However, before proceeding to consideration of the role, status, and problems of older persons in these respective types of societies, the general impact of the population explosion, implosion, displosion, and the technoplosion will be briefly summarized.

The effects of increasing size, density, and heterogeneity of populations have been widely discussed in the literature by such sociological pioneers as Durkheim, Tonnies, and Weber and, more recently, by Park, Burgess, McKenzie, Wirth, Redfield, Mannheim, and many others, including contemporary scholars. Most of these authors have been aware of the interplay of these population factors and technological change.

The impact of increasing population size and density on the social order and the person is relatively easy to trace. As numbers and concentrations of population increase, the potential for social contact and interaction increases at an exponential rate. In a circumscribed geographic area of a circle, say, with a radius of 10 miles, with a density of one person per square mile (not too different from that which obtained in what is now the United States before European settlement), the total number of inhabitants would be 314. In contrast, in the same land area, a population density of 10,000 persons per square mile (close to that of central cities in the United States) would have 3,140,000 inhabitants. This tremendous increase in population in a confined land area, by greatly multiplying the potential human interaction, can have effects in the realm of the social comparable to that of mutation in the realm of the genetic. Actual impact is, of course, a function of the extent to which the potential for social contact and interaction is actually achieved. The consequences of increased size and density of population accompanied by greater social contact and interaction can be briefly summarized as manifest in the person, the family, and the social order.

On the personal level, contacts in the mass society become secondary, segmental, and utilitarian, rather than primary, integral, and sentimental as in the little community. Personality tends to change from a relatively rigid structure molded by the traditional social heritage to more fluid flexible patterns, arising from the necessity to exercise choice and from rationalism in behavior, as the hold of tradition loosens and new problems emerge.

The family, the basic social institution, changes in structure, size, and function in the mass society. The extended family of three or more generations tends to shrink to the nuclear family and is accompanied by alteration in living arrangements of horizontally related kinfolk. The size of the household and family diminishes not only by reason of the transition to the nuclear family and neo-local residence but, also, because of declining fertility and, despite decreased infant and child mortality, smaller numbers of children to be reared. Interpersonal relationships among family members are modified as the roles of spouses, parents, and children are transformed in the more complex social order with various groupings competing for their time and attention. Of special significance is the modified role of the wife as her role changes from female to human being—that is, as she becomes eligible for participation in the spectrum of activities previously open only to men. The new role of women, as will be noted below, has adverse effects on labor force participation and income flow of older men. Many of the functions of the traditional family are attenuated or disappear. In the mass society the family is no longer a production unit and tends even to lose some of its role as a consumption unit. Much of the function of the family in the socialization of the child is diminished as formal educational institutions from pre-nursery school through higher education proliferate and as the multiplication of peer group organizations command the interest of the child.

The family in the mass society also plays a less prominent role than in the little community in religious, recreational, affectional, and security functions. Religiosity is, in general, diminished in the more sophisticated urban world; recreation increasingly tends to become commercialized, although television has tended more recently to bring the family back into the home, if not necessarily to the same programs. Even the affectional function of the family is modified as evidenced by increasing divorce rates and turnover in spouses. Of special significance for older persons is the loss of the security previously provided by the family, especially economic security, as the nuclear family no longer has physical or social space for older persons.

On the social level, cohesion in the mass society becomes a function of interdependence engendered by increased specialization and division of labor; it is no longer the mechanical product of the social heritage of a relatively homogeneous and closed little community. Social institutions in the urban setting become "enacted" rather than "crescive"—that is, the product of collective experience over time. As older institutions become attenuated or disappear, new institutions are created to cope with unprecedented situations and problems. The traditional social institutions are subjected to forces which modify their structure, their role, and their hold on the behavior of the person.

In the mass society, government is characterized by increasing interventionism as organizational complexity, interdependence, and frictions increase. In the more developed countries, the transition from the little community to the mass society has been characterized by the emergence of complex formal organization—bureaucracy—not only in government, but also in business, labor, voluntary associations, and in virtually all organized aspects of the mass society.

Rapid technological change has not only transformed the physical world in which man lives, as evidenced in the urban and metropolitan environment but, also, it has greatly altered the way in which man makes his living. It has changed the nature of work, it has placed unprecedented premiums on training and education, greatly prolonging preparation for adulthood, and it has accelerated the obsolescence of skills and career lines, increasing the risks of technological displacement in employment.

In this macrocosmic consideration of the impact of the mass society, it must be emphasized that the transition to it from the little community does not proceed in an orderly and synchronized manner. The social morphological revolution and its elements proceed with different tempos in different sectors of the society, among the world regions, and within nations. In fact, one of the basic characteristics of the transition is to be found in the coexistence, at any one time and in any one society, of different degrees of change. The more rapid the rate of change, the greater becomes the probability that diverse sectors of the social order will be characterized by anachronistic relationships and dissonance which may be reflected in the attitudes, values, and behavior of the person.

In the transitional process, the reorganization of the person, the family, and the social order is preceded by disorganization. It is manifest in increased delinquency, crime, alcoholism, and drug addiction; in the "sexual revolution," in family disorganization and disruption in separation and divorce; in intergroup hostility and conflict; in unemployment, underemployment, poverty, consumer exploitation, and inflation; in political cleavage over "big government," in problems of intergovernmental relations, and in political corruption. It is manifest also in physical problems such as those of environmental degradation, the slum, congestion in the circulation of goods and persons, and in problems of urban design. These types of problems were either frictional by-products of the social morphological revolution or were greatly exacerbated thereby.

These considerations, then, set forth the general perspective within the framework of which the problems arising from aging and the extension of life will be considered. This will be done separately for the more developed and the less developed countries.

Impact in the More Developed Countries

In the more developed countries and especially in their larger and older urban and metropolitan centers, the consequences of the social morphological revolution on older persons can be readily observed.

First of all, as the data show, the number and proportion of older persons have dramatically increased and so, also, has life expectancy. The presence of large numbers of older persons and the attainment of greater age are, then, relatively recent phenomena in the experience of mankind. Moreover, in the transition from the little community to the mass society, the definition of "old age" has been a cultural variable. In a society with a life expectancy of 40 years, the "older person" is likely to be much younger than in a society with an expectation of life of 70 years.

The number and proportion of old people are, in themselves, among the determinants of their role and prestige. In the little community, the scarcity value of older persons undoubtedly contributed to the age deference patterns which characterize it. In contrast, in the mass society in which one in seven persons is 65 or older, and the prospect is that it will be one in five in the not too distant future, the scarcity value of older people is lost, and their prestige is accordingly diminished.

The prestige of older persons is, however, more seriously adversely affected by the transformed nature of the social order. In the little community, the old person is the source of wisdom based on the rich experience longevity has made possible. The older person in such a society, generally characterized by mass illiteracy and with minimal, if any, accumulated literature, is the repository of knowledge transmitted by word of mouth from generation to generation. In the mass society, in contrast, in which are found printing presses, schools including universities, and various forms of specialized institutions—libraries, research centers, museums, and the like—the older person's role as a source of knowledge and wisdom is greatly attenuated. Furthermore, by reason of the inverse correlation between age and formal education, the knowledge of the older person is likely to be "out-of-date" and, in general, greatly discounted. The combination of increased numbers and proportion and the emergence of new and more powerful sources of knowledge diminishes the prestige of the older person and greatly changes his relationship with younger persons.

In the mass society in which relationships become increasingly segmental, based on utility rather than sentiment, the role of the old person is also adversely affected. Especially is this the case when the older person, with the emergence of the nuclear family, no longer has access to the warmth and security afforded by the extended family. With separate living arrangements, older persons are more "on their own" in economic as well as social terms; and in the mass society they are caught in the vortex of impersonal and diminished extra-familial social contacts as their friends and colleagues fail to survive the passage of time.

The increased premium placed on training and education in the complex mass society, rapid technological change, and the increased labor force participation of women undermine the economic security of older men as life is extended. Because the need for training and education has increased and greatly prolonged the period required for preparation for adulthood, the older person in contemporary mass society is generally less well trained and educated than younger persons. In addition, such training and education as he may have received may be outmoded by reason of rapid technological change. This is why the increasing number and proportion of women in the labor force, the result of the changed nature of work and the transformed social role of women, has been accompanied by a great decrease in the labor force participation of older men. The young well-trained and educated female is often more in demand for employment than the less skilled, obsolescently skilled, or less well-educated older male.

Loss of employment and underemployment of the older male worker are not the only threats to his economic security. Inflation, over time, which has characterized modern societies, and especially high rates of inflation, erode the value of savings and pensions to alarmingly low levels.

The adverse effects on the aged of the emergence of the mass society have to some extent been offset by other accompaniments of modernization. Technological advances have eased the burden of hard physical labor and through increased productivity have raised levels of living for much of the population including older people. Moreover, such advances have created new work opportunities for women. The emergence of unions and their growing power have led to "seniority" rules which have afforded some protection to older workers.

The development of old age pension plans in the private sector has also helped to provide income flow for older persons, although, as in the United States, such plans may have many loopholes which require remediation. The increased intervention of government on behalf of the disadvantaged, including older persons, in the form of such programs as unemployment insurance, public old age pensions, and Medicare have to some extent provided formal substitutions for the economic security formerly given by the extended family. Despite these offsets, however, the fact is that the economic hazards of old age have increased and have by no means been eliminated. In the United States, for example, the 1970 Census returns show that over twice the population of persons 65 and older were officially classified as poor compared with the proportion of poor among the total population, 17.9 percent as against 8.0 percent. Among families headed by older people, twice as many were poor as compared with the proportion of poor families in the total population, 16.4 compared with 7.4 percent.

The extension of life in the more developed countries, accompanied as it has been by accelerating rates of social as well as technological change, has subjected mankind to unprecedented need for adjustment to new conditions over the life space. Today's octogenarian was, in the main, born into a preurban, preindustrial order and has witnessed and been forced to adapt as best he could to the emergent mass society. The extension of life has also been accompanied by increased chronic illness and often disabling physical impairments, which were largely precluded when death occurred at earlier ages. These personal, social, and physical problems account for the emergence in the more developed countries of the rapidly growing fields of gerontology and geriatrics and for the growing functions of government in respect of older persons. The more developed nations are still responding to the problems of the aged and are still formulating policies and programs designed to mitigate, if not fully to resolve, the more pressing difficulties which confront them. Needless to say, there is considerable variation among the more developed countries in the extent to which they have thus far dealt with these problems. The United States, although the most affluent of all nations, is among the more retarded in government acceptance of responsibility for making the life of persons reaching old age the "golden years."

Professor Ernest W. Burgess (1960), one of the pioneers in gerontology, directed attention to two aspects of adjustment to old age, "personal" and "social." The "personal" refers to the adjustment the individual must make, the "social" to the adjustment society must make.

The personal adjustments required on the part of the elders are those arising from the changes in living arrangements; the greater life expectancy of women than of men; the handicap of relatively little training and schooling; the changed nature of work; the loss of relatives and friends who fail to survive to old age; the greater incidence of chronic disease and physical impairment; decreased active participation in voluntary organizations, recreational activities, and the like. Dr. Burgess also pointed to the need for adjustments in attitudes, feelings of happiness and usefulness, and zest and interest in life itself.

Research has demonstrated that the major factors which facilitate good adjustment in old age include maintained income flow, retention of earlier social status, good health, continued family and friendship relationships, effective use of leisure time, and continued concern with and planning for the future. For some, but under the impact of the mass society a declining proportion, belief in an afterlife and church attendance also contribute to good personal adjustment.

The specific types of social adjustment needed are based, of course, on the problems which confront old people. In general, the societal adjustments needed, both in the private and public sectors, are those designed to facilitate personal adjustment. The more important programs required include income maintenance, health care, housing, facilities for leisure time activity, and adult educational programs. A number of societies have gone far in making such social adjustments—especially those in which a "welfare state" is not regarded as a form of undesirable "socialism" or "communism." It is noteworthy that the United States, perhaps the most individualistic as well as the most affluent of the more developed countries, is increasing its degree of social adjustment on behalf of the aged even while proclaiming the need for "rugged individualism" and decrying the "welfare state."

The need for social adjustment in the more developed countries is especially acute in respect of minority groups. In all societies in which population diversity is accompanied by differential social and economic opportunity, the lot of older, as well as of younger, persons is worse for the minority populations. In consequence, minority group aged are much worse off than the aged in the dominant majority population. In the United States, for example, in 1970, 50.2 percent of black elderly were poor as contrasted with 17.9 percent of all elderly. Likewise, of all black households with heads 65 and over, 41.6 percent lived in poverty, compared with 16.4 percent of all households with aged heads. For minority populations, the solution of the economic problems of the elderly, as of the entire group, requires a basic social adjustment, namely, equality of opportunity. The population displosion, by reason of which minorities are insisting on egalitarianism, may hasten this form of social adjustment or, if it does not come about, lead to dangerous levels of social unrest and open conflict, not excluding guerrilla warfare.

Other forms of social adjustment called for are those designed to prevent many of the problems of aging as well as to deal with them. Such programs would entail increased public investment in human beings from birth on. They would include improved general education, especially for minorities, so that basic skills, salable skills, and civic skills would enable persons to assume the obligations as well as the rights of citizenship. Furthermore, they should include provision for continuing adult education to update training and education and to minimize the obsolescence of skills and job displacement. Such programs would also provide for the maintenance of adequate income flow, health care, housing, and slum elimination to prevent the crippling effects of social and economic disadvantage throughout the life space.

In the private sphere, there is need to re-examine existent practices in respect of retirement so that older workers can, if they wish and are capable, ease into retirement through various stages of part-time activity. There is need for integration of private pension plans into national systems which assure the retention of pension rights no matter when or where earned. There is need also to eliminate existent practices prejudicial to the employment of older workers and to prevent their disproportionate unemployment and underemployment.

Impact in the Less Developed Countries

The less developed countries, still characterized by "little community" societies although they have large absolute numbers, are not yet confronted by large proportions of elderly. Moreover, even in their urban areas, despite population size and density, there is relatively little evidence, as has been noted above, of "urbanism as a way of life." In consequence, although mortality is rapidly decreasing and life expectancy is increasing, the less developed countries do not at the present time number among their more serious problems the problems of an aging population. The less developed countries are rather confronted with desperate levels of poverty that plague most of their populations including their relatively small proportions of older persons.

The less developed countries are, in the main, still societies characterized by "age deference"—societies in which old people possess great prestige and respect. This status of the aged stems no doubt in part from their scarcity value as well as from their traditional respected roles as family heads and repositories of knowledge and widsom.

In the period which remains in this century, the relatively high birth rates which are likely to continue in the less developed countries will not greatly increase the proportion of old, but, as has been indicated above, there will be a great increase, a tripling, in the number of elderly. Between now and the century's end, however, there is not likely to be much attenuation, at least among the peasant masses, of the extended family system. There is, therefore, not likely to be much change in such security as older persons enjoy in the extended family, but there is likely to be an appreciable increase in chronic illness and physical impairments of older persons by reason of increase in their life expectancy. Consequently, the less developed countries may have greater need for increasing the provision of geriatric services than for gerontological services for several decades ahead.

The increased urbanization anticipated in the less developed countries during the remainder of this century points to the eventual prospect of urbanism as a way of life. If fertility should decline more rapidly than is anticipated and if the trend towards urbanization continues, then the relatively rapid aging of the population which would occur would in the urban setting generate new and difficult social and economic problems. Against this eventuality, it would be good policy for the less developed countries to utilize the experience of the more developed countries so as to lubricate the frictions of rapid population aging in urban areas. It is in the urban areas that problems of aging and extension of life will be more evidenced and exacerbated by the transition, even though slow, from little community to mass society patterns of life. Moreover, it is in the urban areas that the more acute transitional problems will be discernible in the problems of in-migrants from rural to urban areas as they are forced to adjust to urban living.

Furthermore, the in-migrant often finds his area of first settlement is a shanty town, in which the decadence of the less developed urban environment is manifest in its most extreme form. Consequently, superimposed on problems of adjustment, there may be severe problems of health and nutrition, and of extreme poverty and squalor in living conditions. In such a setting, the in-migrant frequently displays personal disorganization as the subjective aspect of social disorganization. It is in the in-migrant family that the greatest incidences of personal and social pathology are found—delinquency, crime, prostitution, mental illness, alcoholism, drug addiction, etc. Moreover, rural in-migrant workers often lack rudimentary skills for industrial work, possess high rates of illiteracy, and are otherwise ill-prepared for city living. Throughout the developing countries, the need to increase literacy and to provide minimum vocational training for urban employment for in-migrants and especially for aging in-migrants is acute. In fact, the provision of adequate educational and vocational training, both to the in-migrant and to the more permanent inhabitant of urban places, as preparation for problems of old age, as well as to meet immediate needs, is among the most critical social problems which confront the developing areas.

Rapid urbanization is accompanied by increasing tempos of cultural, social, and personal change. A number of scholars have maintained that less developed areas with non-Western cultures possess ideologies and value systems that tend to resist change in general and, therefore, changes of the type induced by urbanization. A rapid rate of urbanization, as contrasted with a slow one, conceivably increases the frictions of transition from non-Western to urban (and presumably Western) value systems. It is, of course, disputable whether Western values identified with urbanism as a way of life are an antecedent or a consequence of industrialization and urbanization, and whether they are the only values consonant with urban living. Conceivably, the difference between non-Western outlooks produces different kinds of "urban mentality" and interpersonal and social relations in the urban setting. Whatever the answer to the question may be, it is undoubtedly true that rapid urbanization increases the tensions and frictions of adjustment in value systems from preurban ways of life. It will be readily agreed that the personal adjustment required by in-migrants to urban areas will, in general, be more difficult for older than for younger persons.

In the less developed countries which contain diverse populations, the population displosion will, no doubt, worsen the problems of aging and extension of life. Differential social and economic opportunity associated with cultural, linguistic, religious, racial, or ethnic difference will, if prolonged, intensify communal conflict and will disproportionately adversely affect the elderly who, in general, are more vulnerable than younger persons to social and economic hardship.

In the less developed countries, in general, the personal adjustment of older persons will for some time be easier than in the more developed countries by reason of the shelter afforded by the extended family and the relative gradualism in prospect in the transition from the little community to the mass society. Social adjustment, however, may be expected to be much more difficult than in the more developed countries because of tremendously limited resources and the constraints of the traditional order.

Under the continued pressures of the social morphological revolution, however, the less developed countries will be forced to make social adjustments on many fronts, including that of the aged. In this process they may be able to avail themselves of the experience of the more developed countries and so make minimal the costs of the transition. For the remainder of this century, at least, however, limited national resources, acute poverty, and rigid traditional orders will obstruct efforts to resolve the many social and economic problems with which the less developed countries are confronted, including the problems generated by aging and extension of life.

SUMMARY

World-wide aging and the extension of life have been considered within the framework of total population trends. It has been noted that the social morphological revolution generating the transition from the "little community" to the "mass society" has not only affected the number and proportion of older persons but, also, has greatly transformed their roles and the social and economic milieus in which they live. Unprecedented problems—personal, social, and economic—have accompanied the aging of populations and the extension of life in the more developed nations and are beginning to emerge in the less developed countries.

Aging and the extension of life, as relatively new phenomena in the human experience, are requiring new forms of policies and programs, both in the public and private sectors.

The relatively new fields of geriatrics and gerontology are focusing on the problems and needs of older persons and are providing impetus to the creation of policies and programs designed to cope with the personal, social, health, housing, and economic problems of aging and life extension.

The more developed countries have to date experienced larger numbers and proportions of older persons and have had increasingly to develop policies and programs to cope with their emergent problems. The less developed countries, now beginning to experience the impact of population developments, may also be faced with the prospect of rapidly increasing numbers and proportions of the aged. Although it is to be hoped that the less developed nations can profit from the experience of the economically advanced nations, their present widespread poverty and their dismal economic prospect, at least to the end of this century, do not hold forth great promise for progress in their adequate coping with the problems of aging and extension of life.

REFERENCES

Burgess, Ernest W. (ed.) 1960. *Aging in Western Societies*. Chicago: University of Chicago Press.

Busse, Ewald, and Pfeiffer, Eric (eds.) 1969. *Behavior and Adaptation in Late Life*. Boston: Little, Brown.

Coale, Ansley J. 1956. The effects of changes in mortality and fertility on age composition. *Milbank Memorial Fund Quarterly*, **34**, 79–114.

Coale, Ansley J., and Demeny, Paul. 1966. *Regional Model Life Tables and Stable Populations*. Princeton: Princeton University Press.

Dublin, Louis, Lotka, A. J., and Spiegelman, Mortimer. 1949. *Length of Life*. rev. ed. New York: The Ronald Press.

Hauser, Philip M. 1953. Facing the implications of an aging population. *Social Service Review*, **XXVII**, No. 2, 162–176.

Hauser, Philip M. (ed.) 1969. *The Population Dilemma*. 2nd ed. Englewood Cliffs, New Jersey: Prentice-Hall.

Hauser, Philip M. Mobilizing for a just society. *In*, National Conference on Social Welfare, *Social Welfare Forum*. New York: Columbia University Press, forthcoming.

Hauser, Philip M., and Shanas, E. 1952. Trends in the aging population. *In*, A. I. Lansing (ed.), *Cowdry's Problems of Aging*. St. Louis: Williams & Wilkins.

Kitagawa, Evelyn M., and Hauser, Philip M. 1973. *Differential Mortality in the United States: A Study in Socioeconomic Epidemiology*. Cambridge, Massachusetts: Harvard University Press.

Lorimer, Frank. 1951. Dynamics of age structure in a population with initially high fertility and mortality. *Population Bulletin*, *No. 1*. New York: United Nations.

Palmore, Erdman (ed.) 1970. *Normal Aging: Reports from the Duke Longitudinal Study*. Durham, North Carolina: Duke University Press.

Sauvy, Albert. 1954. Le vieillissement des populations et l'allongement de la vie. *Population* **9**, 675–682.

Shanas, E., and Hauser, Philip M. 1975. Zero population growth and the family life of old people. *J. Soc. Issues*, **30**, No. 4.

Sheldon, H. D. 1958. *The Older Population of the United States*. New York: John Wiley.

Tibbitts, Clark (ed.) 1959. *Aging and Social Health in the United States and Europe*. Ann Arbor: Division of Gerontology, University of Michigan.

United Nations. 1956. *The Aging of Populations and Its Economic and Social Implications*. Population Studies, No. 26.

United Nations. 1973a. *Demographic Yearbook 1972*. New York: United Nations.

United Nations. 1973b. *The Determinants and Consequences of Population Trends*, Vol. I. Population Studies, No. 50.

U. S. Bureau of the Census. 1973. Some demographic aspects of aging in the United States. *Current Population Reports*, Series P-23, No. 43 (February). Washington, D.C.: Government Printing Office.

4

SOCIETAL DEVELOPMENT AND AGING

Peter Laslett

Cambridge Group for the History of Population
and Social Structure

INTRODUCTORY, HISTORICAL SOCIOLOGY IN RELATION TO AGING

Historical sociology is the study appropriate to the examination of societal development and aging, that is, the question of how the process of aging and the position of the aged have changed over time. But historical sociology is the newest and least developed of the social sciences, first emerging as a distinct study in the middle of the 1960's. Little can yet be expected, therefore, in the way of considered conclusions: the area of knowledge is still very small, and theoretical principles are scanty and mostly untried. What is advanced in this essay must be very tentative and subject to rapid obsolescence.

There are three sources of historical information on aging:

1. Running records of births, marriages, and deaths.
2. Census documents of the statistical era and census-type documents from earlier times.
3. Literary and plastic materials.

Literary and Plastic Data on Aging in the Past

The third of these sources has easily the greatest chronological span and goes as far back as the earliest representation of human individuals whose state of maturity can be recognized—in the cave paintings of southern Europe, perhaps, or in the iconography of the Egyptian treatment of the dead. But little can be made of such evidence until the epoch is reached when written materials survive in sufficient quantity to give meaning to pictures, statues, and monuments and to provide a representation of aging and the aged which can be both interesting and revealing, though usually fragmentary. The span of centuries open to examination, therefore, is confined for practical purposes in the case of Europe to the 2, 500 years which have elapsed since surviving Greek and Hebrew writings were first set down, and for Asia presumably since the Chou dynasty in China, going back some 500 years further. This is an exceedingly shallow tract of time from which to make assertions about human development.

Until the recent growth of historical demography, literary and plastic materials were virtually the only sources which were consulted when questions of aging were considered, and the class of evidence for the past most favored by the sociologist, the psychologist, or the gerontologist was probably what might be called high literature. Appeal was made, therefore, to Cicero's *de Senectute*, or to Vasari's life of Titian, or to Shakespeare's *King Lear*, or even to Jane Austen's Mr. Woodhouse, when a contrast was to be drawn between what happens now and what used to happen, or when some particular recommendation was thought to need historical legitimation. When this subject was pursued outside the European arena, similar use was made of similar materials, such as, for example, the early Japanese novel. These tales were apparently just as realistic in their portrayal of the old, their attitudes, and attitudes towards them, as any of the classics of our own cultural tradition, perhaps even more so.

But high literature is only a small part, and in some ways a rather deceptive part, if taken on its own, of materials of this kind. If, however, diaries, letters, poems, sermons, plays, novels, and so on are supplemented by medical observations, legal regulations, and court cases, by recordings made for economic and political purposes, and by funerary practices and funerary iconography as well as by works of art it is notable how much relevant evidence can be assembled. There are attractive instances of this in the writings of the French historian Philippe Ariès (see, for example, his work on childhood and family life, 1962; and especially his study of Western attitudes towards death since the Middle Ages, 1974). These sources are, of course, the only ones capable of yielding any information on the attitudes of persons towards the aged and aging and on the outlook of aging individuals, for any period in the past.

Our experience as historical sociologists, however brief it may be, has taught us to be wary of all inferences from literary and plastic evidence, unless it can be checked from evidence outside itself, especially numerical evidence: this brings us to sources 1 and 2.

Numerical Data on the History of Aging

From running records of births, marriages, and deaths (source 1), we can now recover, under rather special circumstances, fairly reliable estimates of rates of mortality at various ages: hence the expectation of life and (by the use of demographic theory) proportions of various age groups in the population can be roughly estimated. These running records are ordinarily those attached to baptism, marriage celebration, and burial rather than to the vital events themselves. Nevertheless, birth rates and marriage rates, together with rates of remarriage and ages at marriage and remarriage, can be recovered with considerable reliability. To be able to reckon these vital statistics for as long ago as the middle decades of the sixteenth century, as has been done for English villages, or from the late seventeenth century for French villages, is an open invitation to examine the effect of societal development on aging since those earlier generations, from the demographic point of view. Now that exactly similar results are appearing for Japan in the 'late feudal' era of her social development (that is, Tokugawa times, from our early seventeenth to our late nineteenth centuries), we can at last make a beginning in the direction of two dimensional comparison, across time and between cultures, in the matter of vital statistics.

In order to study the personal and familial situation of older persons in former times as distinct from their expectation of life and so on, it is necessary to go to our second numerical source, census and census-type documents. These also exist for dates as early as the mid-sixteenth century for England and for other countries too. Some examples, all unfortunately imperfect, are already known from the Middle Ages and from earlier times, including one from the second century A.D. in Roman Egypt (Hammel and Laslett, 1974). Where repetitive listings of high quality are available, the life cycle and domestic group cycle can, in principle, be accurately determined, otherwise, this has to be inferred from cross-sectional data, that is, individual listings giving ages (examples of this exercise are Berkner, 1972; Hammel, 1972). If repetitive detailed listings can be found along with vital registration, and other materials of a 'literary' and a plastic kind joined to them, then the historical sociologist has his best opportunity for analyzing aging in the past, and indeed for examining the whole nexus of familial and kin relationships. The examination of social development actually altering the position of the aged can of course only be undertaken if bodies of revealing data of this kind are gathered from before and after the significant change. The one change so far envisaged as likely to have an effect of this order has been industrialization.

Limitations on Historical Sociology as to Aging

The most telling opportunities for carrying out such definitive exercises in historical sociology are likely to occur within the statistical era, that is, since about the year 1800 in European countries, where the State has been recording births, marriages, and deaths, as well as carrying out regular censuses. Unfortunately, however, while our interest is in the transition between preindustrial and industrial, the process of industrialization itself usually includes the initiation of these centralized official and reliable statistics.

The drastic restriction as to the capacities of historical sociology to tackle such a subject as aging should now be clear, both those which arise from its youth as a study and those which are inherent in all historical enterprises. They can never create their own data, but merely discover what has been left behind by our human predecessors.

The reader must be left in no doubt on one capital point. The sustained and detailed work just described as being possible has not yet been done. We report here on much more preliminary outcomes.

SOCIETAL DEVELOPMENT AND AGING, THE CURRENT THEORETICAL SITUATION

Absence of Formal Theory

There appears to be a lack of formal theory specifically devoted to societal development and aging, which stands in sharp contrast to the wealth of theoretical speculation on some subjects in the social sciences. This is no doubt to be expected because of the primitive state of historical sociology and because of the quite recent development of gerontology itself. There nevertheless seems to exist a series of quasi-theoretical assumptions, which may affect the outlook of those responsible for welfare policies as well as that of gerontologists. These assumptions correspond to popular attitudes to a large extent, and if they are not those of experts on aging, they seem often to be believed by the aging and the aged themselves. What follows is an attempt to write out this existent body of informal theorization in a dogmatic form.

Informal Existent Dogmatic Theory

Four sets of propositions are taken here to constitute this body of existent informal theory of a dogmatic kind on societal development and aging: historical propositions, normative propositions, functional propositions, and domestic propositions. The major historical dogma, the most important because the subject itself is historical, is that there has been a *before* and an *after* in the matter of aging, and that the transition between the two has been from one uniform situation to another. This transition is associated with industrialization, modernization, and/or (following Marxist historical theory) the rise of the bourgeoisie and of capitalist social forms. It may be noted that in Marxist historical analysis, capitalist productive arrangements and ideology existed well before industrialization, which raises issues as to where in past social development the division between *before* and *after* is to be placed. A more formidable complication is the tendency to equate the *historical* distinction between a given society at a time when industrialization was absent and at a time when it was present with the *geographical* distinction between nonindustrial societies in our contemporary world and industrial ones. However conceived, though, the assertion is that aging was different in the *before* than it became in the *after*.

The second set of dogmatic propositions, the normative ones, lays down that in the *before*, aging was an accepted part of the system of belief, and the aged themselves were both entitled to respect and were universally accorded it. In the *after*, aging has been rejected as unworthy of any note: the aged are allotted no prestige, and society tends to proceed as if the aged did not exist, or as if it would be better if they did not exist. These informal, normative dogmatic claims follow closely as might be expected, upon a number of dogmas under our third head, the function of the aged.

In these functional propositions it is maintained that in the *before*, the aged had specified and valued economic and emotional roles, which particularly attached to grandparents, and the multigenerational household was an approved institution which had important, even indispensable, functions. In the *after*, however, according to this presumed series of dogmatic assertions, neither aged persons, nor surviving ancestors, grandparents, or otherwise, have any obvious function as representatives of the approved and traditional; and in fact they have become obstacles to the adoption of "modern" ways of life. Compulsory retirement, universal in high industrial society, typifies the relegation of older people to a position of inactive insignificance. The aged decidedly lack any economic utility, and the multigenerational household has no advantage of any kind; it has no welfare functions, for these are now undertaken by political agencies.

The fourth set of dogmatic generalizations, the domestic, begins by asserting that in the *before*, the constitution of the domestic group was specified by universally accepted social assumptions, and the group was expected to allot membership to all senior persons within the kin network of its head, including parents and siblings of his spouse. These beliefs about the *before* are of considerable importance to gerontology as a whole and seem to be capable of some elaboration, even providing an order of priority to the duties which the household had to perform toward surviving members of generations preceding that of its head, or toward members of the head's generation, if they happened to be old.

The first priority was to ensure that the head's own parents, or his wife's, should be accorded membership in the domestic group, if this became necessary for any reason, such as widowhood, debility, or economic decline. The elderly parent accordingly always had a right to live in the household of one of his or her sons or daughters, though it seems to be conceded that it might be a matter of negotiation as to which of the children would undertake the responsibility. This prime obligation operated on sons and daughters when they were grown-up. It might well require that instead of forming his own household at marriage, or on succession to the active direction of the family farm or "business," one son should stay at home with his wife and with their children as they arrived so as to maintain the household of his parents, whether or not that parent remained the household head. This domestic regulation would completely dictate the decisions of an only son.

The same duty might require a daughter to bring her husband into the parental household. In both cases it seems to be contemplated that if an independent household had been set up elsewhere, the child might be expected to return to the domestic group of his or her aging parents if necessary, bringing spouse and children. Further implications are that marriage might have to be postponed in reference to these duties, especially for daughters, who indeed might be compelled to put off or even abandon their prospects of having their own families in order to stay at home and look after aging and/or infirm parents, and who might even have to return home for this purpose from a position of independence elsewhere, whether or not they were married.

The principle that every surviving member of an earlier generation in the *before* had to be provided with a place in the family of one or other surviving offspring could be defeated if no surviving offspring existed. This brought the second order of obligation on the domestic group into play, which (in this set of dogmatic assertions) required that the household should fit in aging members of the kin other than the parents of the head or of his spouse, beginning perhaps with aunts and uncles, but not stopping at great aunts and great uncles and including second cousins and so on. For the dogmatic principle at issue is that in the *before*, no aging relatives, least of all an aging parent, should have to live alone, or with inadequate company, or perhaps worst of all, in an institution.

Though the provisions included in this fourth, domestic, set of dogmatic quasi-theoretical assertions can become quite complicated as they apply to the *before*, they are quite straightforward in the *after*. Nowadays, in capitalist, bourgeois, postindustrial or high industrial society, no doubt also in post–Revolutionary socialist societies, the domestic group has been drastically redefined, and its earlier principles abandoned. In the *after*, a family (the notion of household becomes less and less appropriate) consists exclusively of a man, his wife, and their children, if present, living alone and independently. No one else has any right of any kind to belong to it. The right to marry at will and to leave home for that purpose is also absolute. Members of former generations and older persons generally, therefore, have no expectation that offspring will ever bring a spouse to live in their families rather than leaving to establish another family; they cannot hope to become a member of any offspring family under any circumstances, least of all to be received within the family of more distant connections. Aged persons and grandparents live with each other, if they can, or they live alone, or they go into institutions. The duties of caring for them, insofar as they are recognized at all, are fulfilled by economic assistance or by visiting and being visited, never by permanently changing the strictly specified shape of the domestic group.

Comment on Existent, Informal Dogmatic Theory

The unifying concept of this body of dogma, insofar as it can be said to have one, is that of a transition between a *before*, which existed at some time in the past (or "our past," the past presumably of the national society to which the speaker belongs, since the possibility that traditional societies may have differed in respect of aging does not seem to be contemplated), and an *after*, which exists today. This transition is deeply interfused with a sense of loss: society has been impoverished by ceasing to take account of aging, and the aged themselves have been brutally deprived.

The historical sociologist has come to recognize these sentiments as belonging to what has been identified as *the world we have lost* syndrome, in which the deficiencies of the present are referred to the destruction of an idealized society at some point in the past. (See Laslett, 1965, a work in which the phrase *the world we have lost* is taken in several senses, though never intentionally in a recommendatory or

sentimental one.) The parallel and connected belief, or misbelief, in the universality of the large household in the past may be taken as another instance of this tendency. This is a dogma which historical sociologists are not finding easy to expose to reasoned reassessment (see Laslett, 1972). The location of this will to construct a compensatory ideal projected backwards in time in the minds of people not given to critical analysis, and its presence in fairy tales, in journalism, in television scripts, and in fantasy material of other kinds are presumably reasons for its persistent vitality.

A discovery which helped to show up the belief in the universal presence of the complex household as misplaced in respect of the past, at least of the past of the English-speaking peoples, was that well under 10% of all households in preindustrial England seem to have contained more than two generations. Moreover, kin of all types, quite apart from grandparents and grandchildren, were infrequently found in the household (Laslett and Wall, 1972, see especially pp. 149–155). These facts themselves cast doubt on any supposition that there was ordinarily an easy, familiar and familial relationship between the aged and the young, especially as it can be shown that if our English ancestors had wanted to live in multigenerational households, they could easily have established many more than seem to have existed amongst them. It also implies that the multigenerational household can hardly have been an institution universally valued for its functions. Nevertheless, the issue of the situation of the aged before and after modernization is not the same as the issue of the size and structure of the domestic group, and the relationship between the two is somewhat complicated.

It could be argued that there are ways in which the aged have indeed lost as a result of this societal development. This might be so even if their loss has not been as serious as is implied by the dogmas just recited, which attribute to the older members of English society in the past a position which might well be termed mythical.

Elementary demography asserts that in the societies of the past, as in all other "underdeveloped" or "preindustrial" societies, old people must have been rarer and the experience of aging less common than in industrial societies today. High fertility and high mortality brought this about; the first ensuring that the numbers of the old should have been small in relation to the population as a whole, and the second that expectation of life should have been lower. (See Pressat, 1972, Chapter 9, especially pp. 277–282, for a demonstration that the aging of a population is almost entirely due to a decline in fertility, and not, to any extent, due to a rise in the expectation of life.) Aging, therefore, is unlikely ever to have been a problem, except perhaps locally, in the societies of the past, and the aged cannot often have represented a burden, in spite of the very much lower levels of production and social resources which then prevailed. The consequence may well have been that the comparative rarity of old men and old women, and the exceptional character of their experiences, gave a value to them in earlier times which they no longer possess and entitled them to a respect which has disappeared.

It is a commonplace of literary surveys of the literary and plastic evidence, especially when such material is drawn indiscriminately from the past of cultivated societies and from "primitive" societies in the contemporary world, that this value and respect was supposed to have been attached to aged persons for a whole range of familial, social, and even religious reasons. There are conspicuous and interesting exceptions, though, where quite the reverse is indicated by the sources (see e.g. Simone de Beauvoir, 1970). In these contexts, aged people are neglected, despised, and sometimes even disposed of.

The ambiguity and contrariness of sources of this kind, however, become exasperating to the interpreter, especially since there is so little point in applying numerical arguments to them. We are unlikely to get much nearer the truth by counting and comparing contexts in which aging seems to be respected and those in which it seems to be condemned. But we can begin to appreciate the actual experience of old people in the past if we try to establish numerically, as far as we can, how much less common they were than they are now, and so how much less

likely to be felt as a burden and how much more likely to be valued for their rarity. Figures of this kind, as has been stated, are now reasonably accessible, though still few in number.

We can go rather further in our examination if we direct our attention to circumstances which may have been of greater consequence to the security and welfare of the aged, that is, the extent to which they continued to live in a familial situation. This involves discovering how often they retained their spouses and children, and how likely it was that they would otherwise be accepted as members of the families of their children, their kinsfolk, and their juniors in general. Rough statistics of this kind can now be recovered from a selection of our exiguous sources, unfortunately only from a very few even in the case of England, which is so far the only country where evidence has been systematically collected.

Nevertheless, with even the limited numerical evidence in hand, we are in a better position to make a choice between the favorable and unfavorable elements in the literary materials and to pronounce on the informal dogmatic theory of the aged in relation to societal development which has been sketched out above. I shall be so bold as to preface our survey of such numerical data as have so far been won from the recalcitrant raw materials with an alternative general theory of societal development and aging.

AN ALTERNATIVE GENERAL THEORY OF SOCIETAL DEVELOPMENT AND AGING

Revision and Rejection of Stereotyped Assumptions

A revised hypothetical general theory of aging and societal development in recent centuries begins with the historical dogma about a *before* and *after*. The notion of a single transition is wholly too simple, especially when it is identified with that overall, predominantly economic development through which traditional societies become modern, advanced societies. It is true that some traditional societies have in fact undergone a process during which modernization was accompanied by a crucial change in the proportion of the aged in the social structure. Several of the many ethnic and economic regions which constitute the present U.S.S.R. are possible examples, as well as others in central and eastern Europe. Japan is another. In none of these countries, it may be noted, was the coincidence at all precise, and in the case of Western societies, as in that of Britain, particularly, the two developments have been almost entirely separate in time.

In France, the U.S.A., and especially in Britain the really extensive changes in the proportions of the aged in the population took place a century or more after the onset of industrialization and the onset of the dissolution of traditional society. This was because the demographic transition, during which the regime of high fertility and high mortality characteristic of traditional society gives way to the regime of low fertility and low mortality characteristic of a modern industrial society, was not contemporaneous in these societies with the start of industrialization, but instead came sometime afterwards. In any case, the sustained continuance of low fertility, which is responsible for the very high proportions of the aged in all "advanced" societies, could not in principle have had its effect until 50 years or so after fertility began its definitive fall. In England and Wales, as we shall see, the decline in fertility commencing in the 1870's was not reflected in a substantial rise in the proportion of the aged until the years after 1911 and did not bring about an outstanding alteration until the 1930's, '40's, 50's, and especially the 1960's.

In England and Wales, therefore, if it is legitimate to make assumptions about a *before* and an *after* at all, it is on the understanding that something like a century and a half or more of intricate change took place before the one gave way to the other. If we are to talk of transformation, moreover, it is very recent times which we must have in mind, not the notorious years of early industrialization associated with young Queen Victoria, and least of all the time when capitalism or bourgeois attitudes and practices first became established.

We shall also observe, to make matters more complicated, that England cannot be taken as necessarily typical of Western experience, except during the final stages; it certainly is not indicative in detail of what happened in France. Indeed, we shall consider indications that the actual behavior of old people in respect of residence may have differed from area to area in traditional European society, and that England may have been somewhat exceptional in its uniformity. In what follows it must be borne in mind that English conditions are being discussed.

Although it might be worth retaining in a highly modified form the notion of a *before* and an *after* in respect of the history of societal development in relation to aging, in England and amongst English speakers, very little of the remainder of the informal dogmatic theory we have set out can enter into a revised hypothetical general theory. It is true that the fragmentary though suggestive evidence which we shall cite indicates that the aged in preindustrial England were more frequently to be found surrounded by their immediate family than is the case in the England of today. It is possible that they were given access to the families of their married offspring more readily than is now the case. This may be thought surprising in view of the infrequent occurrence of multigenerational and of complicated households of all kinds. But we shall find that these circumstances can be persuasively accounted for without having to suppose that in traditional England deliberate provision was made for the physical, emotional, or economic needs of aged persons, aged relations, or aged parents in a way which was in any sense superior to the provisions being made by the children, the relatives, and the friends of aged persons in our own day, not to speak of the elaborate machinery of an anxiously protective welfare state.

As for the rest of the informal dogmatic theory, it is for the most part illusory as far as England and the English past are concerned, and in its pure form perhaps for the whole of the West. There is little need to remind readers of this volume that the majority of aged persons in these areas today are not found in fact to be in the position described above as characteristic of the *after*, whatever the stereotypes. Retirement may be widespread and peremptory in high industrial society, but its effect varies with the interest of the job which has to be abandoned, the skill and effectiveness of the individual concerned, his health, and his economic position. It is certainly not always felt as a deprivation, or even as a diminution of consequence. Nor are the old so drastically bereft of prestige and respect; they do have recognized functions, especially in respect of their families and their children; they are supported, emotionally, and otherwise, by their offspring, sometimes by their siblings, and even by more distant kin.

Elderly and aged persons may live apart from their close relatives in our society, but they very often manage to live near enough to them to be in intimate contact. This is an arrangement which they are known to appreciate because it combines interchange with independence (see the relevant chapters of this handbook; Tunstall, 1966; and Shanas, Townsend, Wedderburn, Milhøj, Friis, and Stehouwer, 1968). We must not be led to suppose that the sufferings of some of the aged and the miseries of the minority of the anomic amongst them who come into contact with the welfare services are a proper indication of the conditions of old people generally in contemporary high industrial society. So much for the *after*.

The *domestic* generalizations of the informal dogmatic theory as to the *before*, while not all inaccurate, cannot be confirmed as a whole from the available English historical evidence and certainly do not bear the interpretation which has been put upon them. Some of the assumptions can be rejected out of hand. It can be shown, for example, that the second order obligations of the family supposed above to have existed in traditional English society, which would require it to give succor and even family membership to aged relatives other than the parents of the head, were entirely absent as a recognized social duty. The famous Elizabethan Poor Law of 1601 specifically confined responsibility for the relief of the elderly to their children alone. In spite of the supposedly bilateral character of English kinship, moreover, the case law developed by the judges on this basis succeeded in confining all such duties to "natural" connections, and thus excluded all relatives by law, even stepfathers and stepmothers.

The behavior of children in the matter of marriage affecting the welfare of their own parents can also be shown to have been very different from the dogmatic assumptions. Family reconstitution demonstrates that English children had no traceable disposition to wait until the parents died before they took spouses: in fact, the marriage of orphaned children appears to have been later than that of those whose parents were alive. No doubt most daughters and some sons did conduct themselves so as to assure the comfort and security of their aging parents as far as they could, but we have found it difficult to confirm that they would return home for that purpose from their jobs or their holdings in other localities. Movement of failing fathers and mothers into the households of their married offspring certainly did go on, but it was not a very widespread occurrence in the evidence we have so far surveyed, and it was certainly not a universal pattern.

Two General Principles in an Alternative Theory

The first general principle in an alternative theory is a negative one and has implications which go far beyond the issue of aging. It presumes that in the traditional English social order, at least at its final stages, the membership of the coresident domestic group as we now call it was never specified in such a way that any person other than the head or spouse of the head had a right to belong to it.

It is not even clear that the offspring of the head lived by right in his domestic group, although up to the age of seven they were regarded as "nurse children" and could not be separated from their parents. The inference can be made, and there is evidence for it in the surviving data, that, after seven years, children might be removed from the domestic group, with no right to be restored to the parental family. If this were so, how could it be supposed that elderly parents rightfully belonged to the households of their mature children, married or unmarried, or that such children could be required by social custom and neighborly opinion to live with those parents if necessary?

The authority of the father in traditional England was real enough, especially amongst the elite. But if he could command his children whether, or when to marry, or where to live, and even do so successfully, this was evidently not effected on the ground that the approved shape of the coresident domestic group itself demanded it. In practice, as we have said and shall try to demonstrate numerically here, English parents showed little disposition to keep children at home after marriage or to require them to return after marriage or after being launched in the world elsewhere. They could certainly not appeal to norms of household composition in order to effect such things: all the evidence goes to show that these conventions favored quite opposite actions and attitudes. The ordinary story of the family-household after the child-rearing stage was of offspring leaving successively, though not necessarily in order of age, until the parents finally found themselves alone if they survived. There is a telling contrast here with the traditional familial system of an area like South China, for example, where no child left the parental household except under clearly specified conditions because the recognized rules of familial behavior required coresidence wherever possible, and where no father or mother of grown offspring would ever live alone. Some part at least of what has been called the "world we have lost syndrome" must be attributed to English and English-speaking peoples being led to believe that their familial past has been the same as that of people like the Chinese.

If the stem family arrangements so widely assumed, at least until recently, to have been common or even universal in traditional Europe had in fact been so in England, then the patriarch in charge, or even his widow, might have had the sanctions at hand to require a grown and often married child to live at home, and to provide a supporting circle of family members when retirement arrived (see Berkner, 1974). But this form of the domestic group seems to have been of singularly little importance amongst the English in the generations just before traditional society began the process of transformation.

Where membership of the domestic group was conferred upon solitary, necessitous, or infirm parents or kinfolk in England in earlier times, therefore, it may be supposed to have been done because of the advantages of the presence of elderly relatives, or because of the dutiful-ness, the affection, or the charitable disposition of the heads of the households concerned, rather than for any socially sanctioned expectation that such an action should take place. As for the advantages, they must have existed even before the rise of the factory took the working mother some distance away from the home during the whole of the day and created the need for perpetual child minders. The remarkable alacrity with which fathers with young children are known to have remarried in an older English society, to have sometimes sent their orphaned youngsters to live with a grandmother, and even to have occasionally packed up and taken the whole family back there until a new wife could be installed all confirm what common sense suggests, that the older generation were of use in child rearing. There are signs that widowed mothers were imported into the households of young and growing families; perhaps some widowed fathers too.

But so little was it the accepted thing for the parents of married persons to be living with them that we sometimes find such coresidents described as "lodgers" rather than as family members, and even as a "lodger, receiving parish relief" (Laslett, 1972, p. 35, footnote p. 50: the lodger concerned was the aged father of the head of the household). In the one or two sets of data where we can follow such vicissitudes in peasant England, we find examples of sons succeeding to the family occupation (perhaps even to the family cottage) and actually leaving their widowed mothers and their sisters to live in the poor law institutions. The extreme poverty of such persons as these must be borne in mind before judging such cases, but it must not be overlooked that the legal duty of a child to assist his parents never seems to have been construed as an obligation to receive or maintain him or her in the household.

Nevertheless, this general theoretical proposition about aging and societal development should not be taken to imply that children usually did little or nothing to assist or to entertain their aging parents out of love and respect when and how they could, in traditional English society. There are good grounds for supposing that in fact they aided them in this way, although we are certainly not yet in a position to estimate how much money was transferred to their parents, how often they visited them, and how frequently and strenuously they exerted themselves to live near them or to find accomodations which would enable the parents themselves to come within easy reach. The wisps of evidence we have suggest that in some families elderly persons and children did live in close proximity, in others not. But we cannot hope to decide from the present state of our knowledge how successful our ancestors were in making such provisions, taking account of the very different situation of younger, independent people in that era of exiguous resources, poor communications, and widespread illiteracy, which made keeping in touch with home and relations generally so much more difficult. The most likely conjecture from what we do know is that they behaved very much as we behave now in this respect, no better and no worse.

The second general principle in an alternative hypothetical theory about aging, in relation to social development in England and in the Western world generally, is that the position of the elderly in the late twentieth century social structure is historically novel. If the aged present a "problem to be solved", it is a problem which has never been solved in the past, because it did not exist in what has been called the *before*. The value of historical sociology to the creation of policy in the present is in denoting how far we differ from past people and how much we are the same. With respect to aging, the theory is that we are in an unprecedented situation: we shall have to invent appropriate social forms, for they cannot be recovered from our history. It follows that elderly people and the gerontologists who help to create policy for them are at a serious disadvantage while they continue to accept a world we have lost which it would make sense to try to restore. It could be said with greater conviction, if our knowledge had been greater, that the familial history of peoples other than the English, or of areas other than the western European, does provide examples of the treatment of the aged and aging which might give us guidance and provide precedents. But in all of these areas and at all of the times we know about, the numbers of the aged were very much less than those present in high industrial society today. Our situation remains irreducibly novel: it calls for invention rather than imitation.

The rest of this essay will be given over to the presentation of some of the evidence on which this tentative alternative general theory of aging and societal development has been based, and a remark or two will be made of a comparative kind, hinting at the rather different general view which might have emerged if our evidence had been equally derived from non-Western as well as from English sources. The preliminary and uncertain character even of the English data themselves will be apparent to the reader, and the status of our general hypothesis must be judged accordingly.

HISTORICAL DATA FOR A TENTATIVE THEORY OF AGING AND SOCIETAL DEVELOPMENT

The painfully recovered facts which underlie the statements made in the previous three sections about the *before* in contrast to the *after* will be presented in the form of eight tables, one figure, and a commentary. In view of what has been asserted about the differing dates of modernization and of demographic transition, it will be appreciated why there has been difficulty about dates before which the societies in question could be justly said to be "traditional" or preindustrial," and after which they could be said to be "modern," or in full progress towards modernization. This has led to some discrepancies between the various sets of figures, but it is to be hoped that the message of these rather crude statistics has not been obscured.

Life Expectation and Proportion of the Elderly in Traditional Societies in the Past

A selection of the few available estimates of the expectation of life in some traditional societies in the past is presented in Table 1. The variations in these estimates from period to period are sometimes surprising to those to whom the demography of earlier societies is unfamiliar. It is now a commonplace in historical sociology, however, that in the same village, county, or even country, fertility, nuptiality, and mortality can be expected to change quite drastically between generation and generation, up and down. For this reason, the exceptionally high figure reported for the Plymouth Colony is not particularly surprising, although the early American settlers may well have lived longer

TABLE 1. EXPECTATION OF LIFE IN SOME TRADITIONAL SOCIETIES OF THE PAST.

Country	Date	Expectation of life at birth (years)	Expectation of life at (years)
England			
Colyton, Devon	1538–1599	45	
	1600–1649	42.5	
	1650–1699	34	
	1700–1749	c.40	
	1750–1800	c.45	
Colonial America			
Plymouth Colony	17th Century	"as high as 50 years in some places" (Wrigley, 1969)	
Massachusetts and New Hampshire	18th Century (Wigglesworth)	28.15	
			(10) 49.23
			(20) 34.21
			(30) 30.24
			(50) 21.16
			(60) 15.43
			(70) 10.06
			(80) 5.85
France			
Crulai, Normandy	1675–1775	30 ± 2	
Whole Country	Late 18th Century	28.8	
	1821	c.41 (women only)	
Switzerland	Late 18th Century	20–30	
Spain	Before 1797	26.8	
Germany			
Breslau	1690's	27.5	(10) 40.2
Japan			
One Village	1671–1725		(10) 50.0 (males)
			38.3 (females)
	1726–1775		(10) 49.9 (males
			48.1 (females)
Another Village	1717–1830		(1) 46.9 (males)
			50.7 (females)
Italy			
Verona	1761–1766	28	
Milan	1804–1805	30	
Bologna	1811–1812	26	
India	1891–1901	23.8	
	1901–1911	22.9	
	1911–1921	20.15	

than their European contemporaries. We do not have nearly enough evidence to estimate the limits of such variation, but it is clear that no single figure for life expectation in preindustrial times generally would make sense.

On the whole, figures for the duration of life are higher rather than lower than might be thought probable, and this is particularly the case with estimates for later ages, as is illustrated by Wiggleworth's famous figures for New England in the later eighteenth century. It may well turn out in fact, when the evidence is all in, that the life expectation of western Euro-

pean peasants in the middle and later years of life could be quite high under favorable economic, nutritional, and climatic conditions, not all that much inferior to what it is generally today.

This is important to the question of aging in relation to social change not only because it may mean that the experience of being old came to more people—that is, to persons no longer children—than might be supposed, but also because it implies that the family group lasted rather better. The duration of marriage in preindustrial England was of the order of 20

TABLE 2a. PROPORTIONS OF AGED PERSONS (BY SEX) IN SOME TRADITIONAL SOCIETIES IN THE PAST.

Location	Date	Population	AGED 60 AND ABOVE				AGED 65 AND ABOVE				AGED 70 AND ABOVE				AGED 75 AND ABOVE				AGED 80 AND ABOVE			
			M	F	Both	Sex ratio	M	F	Both	Sex ratio	M	F	Both	Sex ratio	M	F	Both	Sex ratio	M	F	Both	Sex ratio
S.E. Europe																						
11th Century (Excavated Graveyard)					9.9				2.5													
Italy																						
Arezzo	1427		15.9	15.9	15.9	104	10.0	10.2	10.1	105	8.1	8.6	8.4	109								
Venice	1601–10				10.7																	
	1691–1700				11.6																	
France																						
Mostejols	1690	439	9.6	8.9	9.3	123	5.7	6.9	6.1	93	4.3	3.9	4.1	126	1.8	1.8	1.8	100	1.3	1.5	1.4	100
Longuenesse	1778	332	8.5	9.7	9.1	76	5.9	8.0	7.0	104	2.0	5.1	3.7	25								
	1790	387	10.2	5.5	7.7	191	6.4	4.5	5.4	133	3.2	3.0	3.1	100								
Belgium																						
Lisswege	1739	796	4.5	5.1	4.8	100																
	1748	702	3.6	3.4	3.9	117																
Denmark																						
Bjorre Is.	1650	1,032			7.7																	
Zealand Prov.	1650	129,000			7.0																	
(Natl Census)	1787		8.0	9.3	8.7	85					2.6	3.4	3.0	74					0.4	0.7	0.6	56
	1801		8.8	9.8	9.4	87					2.9	3.6	3.2	79					0.5	0.8	0.7	69
Iceland																						
(Natl Census)	1703		5.8	9.2	7.7	52	3.6	6.1	4.6	48	2.2	4.1	3.3	44	1.2	2.5	1.9	40	0.8	1.6	1.2	45
	1729		12.4	16.7	14.7	82	9.0	12.7	11.0	60	5.8	8.6	7.3	57	3.2	4.9	4.2	55	1.4	2.2	1.9	54
	1787		6.5	8.7	7.8	58					1.6	2.5	2.1	48								
Germany																						
Löffingen Gemeinde	1777	2,500			8.7																	
Switzerland																						
Meltmenstetten	1634				5.1																	
Zürich, S. Peter	1637				7.2																	
Albisrieden Zumiken	1634				3.4																	
Wiesendangen	1721				6.3																	
(Ober-u Unter)	1764				9.9																	
Bern	1764				10.3																	

Place	Date	N															
Austria																	
Abtenau	1632	4,000+	5.4				2.8	3.3	3.1	82	2.2	2.1	2.2	100	1.3	0.9	1.1
Estonia																	
(Village Census)	1782		6.8	5.7	6.3	118											
	1795		4.3	4.7	4.8	89											
Hungary																	
Kölked	1816	638	5.7	4.6	5.0	113											
Serbia																	
Belgrade	1733	1,357	5.2	3.4	4.7	133	2.6	1.5	2.1	77	1.8	1.3	1.5	137			
Japan																	
15 places	1671–90		6.7	6.8	6.7	100											
15 places	1711–40		8.9	8.4	8.7	115											
	1761–90		11.5	11.8	11.7	107											
	1811–40		8.6	9.7	9.1	93											
Nishinomiya	1713	653	9.2	9.9	9.7	106	6.3	6.9	6.6	104	4.3	3.6	4.0	136			
Colonial U.S.A.																	
Bedford and New Rochelle	1698	385	5.7				1.8				0.8							

years for most couples, but it could last for 35 years or more for a fifth or a quarter of them (see Laslett, 1975, in criticism of the view of Ariès that married life was too brief to ensure familial stability). This in turn improved the chances of old people made solitary or helpless having the home of one or other of their children to go to and stay in.

At the time of writing (June 1975), the Cambridge group for the History of Population and Social Structure is not in a position to provide any very useful figures for elderly persons, of 60 years and over, or aged persons, of 65 and over, who had at least one married son or a married daughter alive to go and live with, given marriage ages, number of children and so on, prevailing in preindustrial times. Clearly, there must have been considerable variability from family to family, place to place, time to time, and even greater variability when England is contrasted with other cultural areas. Neither can we say how many relatives of any kind such people would have; how often, for example, an elderly or aged spinster would have a similar sister or brother she could live with: the numbers of old people with no living relatives, or even with no living child, married or unmarried, must have been small at all times. Without larger more precise knowledge of this kind, our evidence is less useful than it might be, especially when we compare the situation then with the situation now. The intention, however, is to make such estimates for varying demographic rates and so on with the use of microsimulation by computer.

Even with this information at hand, however, we shall still have to try to determine, or to guess, how many of the surviving children of an elderly person would be in contact with him or her, in a position to give house room, with the resources to do so, and with a motive as well, of a child-minding character or of any other. These circumstances underline, once more, how preliminary our present knowledge is, and how much there is yet to do to get any *precise* notion of the situation of the aged today in comparison with the situation in earlier times.

Tables 2a and 2b contain a collection of figures which have been recovered from lists of inhabitants for individual cities, towns, or villages,

TABLE 2b. PROPORTIONS OF AGED PERSONS (BY SEX) IN CERTAIN PLACES IN ENGLAND BEFORE 1800.

			AGED 60 AND ABOVE				AGED 65 AND ABOVE				AGED 70 AND ABOVE				AGED 75 AND ABOVE				AGED 80 AND ABOVE			
		Population	M	F	Both	Sex ratio	M	F	Both	Sex ratio	M	F	Both	Sex ratio	M	F	Both	Sex ratio	M	F	Both	Sex ratio
Ealing	1599	427	7.0	4.5	5.9	133	1.7	1.0	1.4	130	0.4	1.0	0.7	175								
Chilvers Coton	1684	780	6.6	6.7	6.7	104	3.6	2.4	3.0	61	1.9	1.0	1.4	71								
Lichfield	1695	2,861	6.4	9.4	8.1	160	3.4	4.6	4.1	86	2.1	2.5	2.3	66								
Stoke-on-Trent	1701	1,627	8.2	9.1	8.6	87	5.0	5.3	5.2	100	2.6	3.6	3.1	98								
Corfe Castle	1790	1,239	9.8	9.5	9.7	100	6.6	6.3	6.4	133	3.4	3.5	3.3	127								
Ardleigh	1796	1,126	7.2	4.4	5.9	215	3.4	1.8	3.1		2.4	2.0	2.2									
Grasmere	1683	310	8.4	10.3	9.4	81	3.9	7.1	5.5	81	3.2	5.2	4.2									
Buckfastleigh	1698	1,111	6.4	5.7	6.0	116	2.6	2.4	2.5		1.6	1.7	1.6									
Ringmore	1698	188	19.3	19.4	19.1	80	10.8	11.6	11.2	75	6.0	7.8	6.9									
Trent	1748	375	6.6	10.3	8.0	60					1.7	3.6	2.7	43								
Shrewsbury	1770	1,046											5.6				2.7		1.3	0	1.6	
	1780	1,113											3.6				2.0		0.6	1.3	0.8	
Ackworth	1757	603	10.3	8.5	9.1	150					2.5	2.8	2.6	100					0.6	1.4	0.6	
	1767	728	8.5	11.0	9.9	67					2.6	3.8	3.3	60							1.0	
	1772	678	8.5	12.7	10.6	21					2.6	4.4	3.5								1.0	
Ashton-Under-Lyne	1773	7,956			5.9								1.7								0.3	
Chester	1774	14,713	14.2	12.2	13.1	100							4.3						1.4	0.6	1.0	
Sandwich	1776	609									6.0	4.6	5.5	113								
Carlisle	1780	7,677			9.1																	
	1788	8,677			9.1																	
Manchester	1773	13,786			3.4								1.9									
Maidstone	1782	5,755									4.2	5.9	5.1								0.6	
Taunton	1791	5,472											4.7								1.5	
Wigton	1791	1,650			16.3						3.0	4.8	4.0	50								
Bocking	1793	2,943									3.3	2.1	2.6									

together with those from several national or provincial censuses, and one outcome from palaeodemography—the estimation of the ages of the skeletons excavated from an eleventh century graveyard. A noteworthy feature of the results of calculating the proportions in the higher age groups of the populations concerned is that they are also nearly all relatively high in relation to what one might expect in traditional societies. Only 7 of the 56 figures for the percentage of persons aged 60 and above are as low as the percentage reported in Tunisia in 1966 or in Brazil in 1970, two contemporary industrializing societies (compare Table 5: only 2 are as low as the figure for Indonesia in 1964-65). The variation from place to place, though noticeable, is certainly rather less than might be expected. These variations do not seem to be entirely the result of the smallness of the population studied, since that of Venice was in the tens of thousands. England, with the interesting exception of Manchester in 1773 in the very dawn of the factory era, seems to have had a consistently high proportion of the elderly.

These statistics, then, might be held to confirm the impression given by the estimates of the expectation of life, that is, that a fair number of people reached the higher ages in historic times, and that fertility may have been consistently lower than the levels now reached in underdeveloped societies in our day. The probable reason for this is not without significance to the overall contrast in marital habits which has been proposed as distinguishing western European areas from other areas of the world: later age of first marriage for women (see Hajnal, 1965; Laslett, 1973). They tend to modify the contrast between the *before* and the *after* in a somewhat surprising way, as well as even the assertion that the aged were not likely to have been a burden in preindustrial society, an assertion not easily maintained in the case, of, say, Arezzo in 1427.

It should be insisted, however, that the absolute reliability of all these figures is questionable, since they come from societies where the reckoning of ages must have been much less accurate than it is today in advanced societies, or even in countries like Indonesia or Tunisia. Older people are known to have exaggerated

their ages when they talked to the listtakers of the past, and to have declared themselves at the decadal years to a great extent. This undoubtedly had the effect of inflating the numbers over 60 and probably even more at the advanced ages.

Social Development in the Past and Sex Ratio, Marital Status, and Proportion of the Elderly and Aged

In Tables 3a and 3b are set out a small selection of figures for the proportion of married, widowed, and single amongst the older age groups, by males and females. The reason why the number of communities is so few, even fewer than in Tables 2a and 2b, is that for England and Wales a concerted search over a decade and more has so far (1975) failed to uncover further documents giving the relevant information. In the case of other countries (for example, Germany), it is known that a great deal more evidence exists, but it has not yet been analyzed. Comments on these data therefore must be even more tentative than on the other sets of figures presented here. Nevertheless, it may be worthwhile to draw attention to some of the features of these data.

Variability is clearly considerable in these statistics, as must be expected for such minute numbers. But the indications are, for what they are worth, that elderly and aged women were no less liable to be widowed then than they are in Western countries in our own day. In 1960, 50 percent of all women were widowed above the age of 65 in Britain, 53 percent in the United States, and 43 percent in Denmark (Shanas et al., 1968, p. 12). The same effect is observable for men, if a little less pronounced: the contemporary figures for widowers above 65 are 22 percent in Britain, 19 percent for the United States, and 23 percent for Denmark. There is evidently little ground here for believing that widowhood was less common in the English past.

It is interesting, however, that the really sharp contrasts come in Table 3b and for two places outside the European west, Belgrade and Nishinomiya, where over 80 percent of women of 65 and above are given as widowed. A mere 13 per-

TABLE 3a. MARITAL STATUS OF ELDERLY AND AGED PERSONS BY SEX AND AGE CATEGORY IN CERTAIN PLACES IN ENGLAND BEFORE 1800, IN PERCENTAGES.

		AGED 60 AND ABOVE		AGED 65 AND ABOVE		AGED 70 AND ABOVE	
		Male	Female	Male	Female	Male	Female
Ealing, Middlesex	Married	62	70	33	33	0	50
1599, pop. 427 (16 males,	Widowed	19	20	67	67	100	50
12 females aged 60 and above)	Single	19	10	0	0	0	0
Chilvers Coton, Warws.	Married	74	58	75	40	71	50
1683, pop. 780 (24 males, 23	Widowed	19	42	25	60	29	50
females aged 60 and above)	Single	5	0	0	0	0	0
Grasmere, Wstmrld.	Married	75	41	80	50	75	60
1683, pop. 310 (11 males,	Widowed	16	58	20	40	25	40
12 females aged 60 and above)	Single	8	0	0	0	0	0
Lichfield, Staffs.	Married	80	41	81	23	76	19
1695, pop. 2,861 (79 males,	Widowed	12	58	19	77	24	81
131 females aged 60 and above)	Single	8	1	0	0	0	0
Stoke-on-Trent, Staffs.	Married	62	37	58	25	45	20
1701, pop. 1,627 (65 males,	Widowed	27	55	31	70	40	73
75 females aged 60 and above)	Single	11	8	11	5	15	7
Corfe Castle, Dorset	Married	58	40	60	37	57	32
1790, pop. 1,239 (60 males,	Widowed	34	48	38	55	38	68
77 females aged 60 and above)	Single	8	12	2	8	5	0
Ardleigh, Essex	Married	67	50	75	64	70	57
1796, pop. 1,126 (43 males,	Widowed	33	45	25	36	30	43
20 females aged 60 and above)	Single	0	5	0	0	0	0

NOTE: Not all individuals in these places have marital status recorded. Those of uncertain status have been classified as single.

TABLE 3b. MARITAL STATUS OF ELDERLY AND AGED PERSONS BY SEX AND AGE CATEGORY IN CERTAIN PLACES OUTSIDE ENGLAND BEFORE 1800, IN PERCENTAGES.

		AGED 60 AND ABOVE		AGED 65 AND ABOVE		AGED 70 AND ABOVE	
		Male	Female	Male	Female	Male	Female
Longuenesse, N. France	Married	64	44	67	31	33	12
1778, pop. 333 (11 males,	Widowed	27	56	22	69	33	88
16 females aged 60 and above)	Single	9	0	11	0	33	0
1790, pop. 387 (18 males,	Married	61	54	67	56	67	50
11 females aged	Widowed	22	46	25	44	33	50
60 and above)	Single	6	0	8	0	0	0
Belgrade, Serbia	Married	69	7	80	7	70	14
1733-4, pop. 1,357 (28 males,	Widowed	12	90	13	86	20	72
50 females aged 60 and above)	Single	19	3	7	7	10	14
Nishinomiya, Japan	Married	67	17	50	16	46	0
1713, pop. 653 (32 males,	Widowed	33	83	50	84	54	100
30 females aged 60 and above)	Single	0	0	0	0	0	0

NOTE: Not all individuals in these places have marital status recorded. Those of uncertain status have been classified as single.

cent of the men lack spouses in Belgrade, and this is a result of earlier marriage for women, together with the greater age gap between spouses (see Laslett, 1972, pp. 52–53; Laslett, 1973). In Japan, the remarriage of widows was perhaps less common. Almost nothing can be learned from the tables about the probability of being a bachelor or a spinster in later life at these places. This is because the evidence so often leaves unclear the distinction between the unmarried and the widowed.

Table 4, with its accompanying figure, provides an account of the actual course of change in the proportion of the elderly in the population for England and Wales on the one hand, and France on the other. This covers the whole period of industrialization, from the eighteenth century until 1971, together with a conspectus of comparative figures from other Western, industrialized countries. The pattern which is presented by these data is conspicuous and interesting.

The singular constancy of the proportions of the elderly in England and Wales up until the year 1901 should first be noted, together with the indication that these proportions were lower

TABLE 4. PROPORTIONS OF ELDERLY PERSONS IN ENGLAND AND WALES AND IN FRANCE (BOTH SEXES) SINCE THE LATE 18TH CENTURY (WITH SOME FIGURES FROM OTHER COUNTRIES FOR AGED PERSONS).

		ENGLAND AND WALES			FRANCE		
Date	% 60 and above	Men	Women	Both	Men	Women	Both
1776					7.2	7.3	7.3
1786					7.8	8.1	7.9
1796					8.6	8.7	8.6
1801					8.7	8.8	8.7
1811					9.0	9.0	9.0
1821		7.3	7.6		9.6	9.8	9.7
1831					9.5	10.4	10.0
1841		6.8	7.4	7.2	9.2	10.4	9.9
1851		6.9	7.8	7.4	9.2	11.1	10.1
1861		7.0	7.8	7.3	9.9	11.4	10.7
1871		6.6	7.8	7.4	11.0	11.9	11.7
1881		6.9	7.8	7.3	11.7	12.5	12.1
1891		6.8	7.9	7.2	12.0	13.2	12.6
1901		6.8	8.0	7.3	12.3	13.5	13.0
1911		7.3	8.6	7.9	11.6	13.5	12.6
1921		8.7	10.0	9.3	11.5	14.5	13.7
1931		10.7	12.3	11.5	12.7	15.1	14.0
1936					13.4	16.0	14.7
1946					13.8	17.9	15.9
1951		14.6	17.7	15.9	13.5	18.8	16.2
1961		15.3	17.9	16.2			
1968					15.7	21.6	18.8
1971		15.9	21.9	18.7			

AGED PERSONS (% 65 AND ABOVE, BOTH SEXES)

Date	England and Wales	France	Germany	Italy	The Netherlands	Sweden	U.S.A.	Canada
1850	4.6	6.5			4.7	4.8		
1900	4.7	8.2	4.9	6.2	6.0	8.4	4.1	5.1
1930	7.4	9.3	7.4		6.2	9.2	5.4	5.6
1950	10.8	11.8	9.7		7.7	10.3	8.1	7.8
1969/70	13.0	13.0	14.0	11.0	10.0	14.0	10.0	8.0

during those three generations than they had been in traditional times. So far from bringing about a surplus of the elderly, it would seem that industrialization in England can have had very little effect in that direction for a full century. But change, when it did begin, soon became extraordinarily marked, and it could justly be said that the proportions of the aged have been completely transformed in the 60 years since 1911. Change was greatest in the 1940's, '50's and, '60's.

There is a close resemblance in this development over time with the course of mean household size in England, which was noticeably constant over the period of industrialization, in fact from the seventeenth century until 1901 (see Laslett, 1972, pp. 139-144, Figures 4.3, 4.4). Between the 1920's and the 1970's, then, the elderly in England became markedly more numerous, and the disproportion in the numbers of old women as compared with old men,

consistently small in the nineteenth century, suddenly grew. Meanwhile, household size was becoming smaller, so that the percentage of those living in households of one or two persons more than tripled; many of these solitaries and pairs being older people. It might be said that action in the story of societal development and aging in England and Wales was long in coming but when it did arrive, in the lifetime of the aged people still with us today, it was swift and fundamental.

This may be thought to be a surprisingly dramatic story for such a subject as this, and since it is apparently the first time that such a story has been told, it might be natural to suppose that what happened in English society would be typical. The parallel series of figures from France and the scattered numerical details from other countries in Europe and North America show that this cannot be so.

In France, the proportion of the elderly in

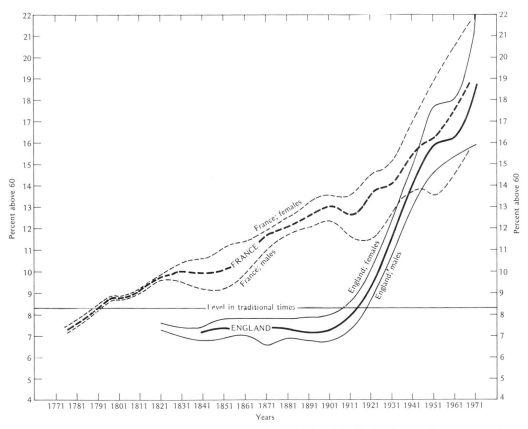

Figure 1. Proportions of elderly persons (aged 60 and above) in England and Wales and in France since the 18th century.

the population was not as consistent during the nineteenth century, over the years when industrialization was beginning, as it was in England and Wales, and it was noticeably higher. The difference in the ratio of the proportion of the elderly by sex varied too. There was a curious rise in this statistic during the years 1821-51, when it could be claimed that France first began to industrialize on any scale, since in that country the process came later than in England. And so the different story continued until the 1950's, when development coincided completely in England and in France for the first time. Meanwhile, it is evident that neither country could be taken as representative of western Europe, though England and Wales may have been at one extreme, where, as in Germany, the proportion of older people remained low until the end of the nineteenth century, and France at the other extreme, where, as in Sweden, the proportion was already high by 1900. The body of evidence from very recent decades as to proportions of the elderly and aged, sex ratios, and so on, shows a tendency toward convergence in what we have called high industrial societies, especially and perhaps paradoxically between England and France.

The passing of traditional society in England is supposed to have begun by the 1770's, the earliest decade in our figures, though there is reason to question how far the process can have gone for the first 70 or 80 years in changing the lives of the majority of English persons. It is clear, nevertheless, that for at least half a century, elderly people in England remained as scarce as they had ever been, or even scarcer, yet social transformation was going on apace. This further demonstrates the point which has been made already, that industrialization and the demographic transition were quite distinct in time in England. Yet in France the relationship was not quite the same, and it would seem that in the United States and elsewhere it was different again, both as to the proportion of the elderly, its size and fluctuations, and as to the inception and progress of industrialization. If we considered countries or areas outside the West, Russia, perhaps or Japan or China, we should probably get quite other relationships.

Historically, then, there is no set pattern between the *before* and the *after* insofar as it concerns the number of elderly persons, whatever may be the case in respect of countries undergoing industrialization in the late twentieth century.

Table 5 has been inserted to show how different the situation can be now, in countries at various stages of the demographic transition and of industrialization as well.

Household Position of the Widowed, the Elderly, and the Aged in Traditional English Society

The three final tables attempt to portray the domestic situation of elderly and aged persons in one country, the first to undergo both modernization and industrialization and the first to be studied from the point of view of the present paper. The great difficulty here is to get enough data to illustrate the principles already laid down about this, the most important part of our subject. Accordingly, we have begun with a table drawn from lists of inhabitants which do not specify ages. While we possess these in tens, we have less than a dozen English documents in all with data which provide useful age statistics. Table 6 sets out the household position of widowed persons (age not given) in 61 English settlements. Although it is not advisable to use widowhood as a reliable indicator of age—indeed up to half the women aged 45-49 could be widowed in an Elizabethan village—these figures indicate an interesting and important principle. This is that once a man or woman had become a householder or a householder's wife in England in traditional times, he or she tended to stay at the head of the family, in spite of the vicissitudes of life in that insecure world.

Even these figures are dubious of course because of the problem of identification by sex and situation; all men and women living with their children and without a spouse in the household, for example, have to be counted as widowed, so that some numbers of deserted spouses, especially deserted wives, must be present in the data of the table. Still we may attach some importance to the figures which

TABLE 5. PROPORTIONS OF ELDERLY AND AGED PERSONS IN CERTAIN INDUSTRIALIZED, INDUSTRIALIZING, AND NONINDUSTRIAL COUNTRIES IN THE 1960'S AND '70'S.

	AGED 60 AND ABOVE				AGED 65 AND ABOVE				AGED 70 AND ABOVE				AGED 75 AND ABOVE				AGED 80 AND ABOVE			
	M	F	Both	Sex ratio	M	F	Both	Sex ratio	M	F	Both	Sex ratio	M	F	Both	Sex ratio	M	F	Both	Sex ratio
United Kingdom 1971	15.9	21.7	18.9	69	10.3	15.7	11.1	62	5.8	10.0	8.2	55	3.2	6.1	4.6	46	1.4	3.1	2.3	41
United States 1970	12.6	15.6	14.1	81	8.5	11.2	9.7	72	5.3	7.5	6.3	68	3.0	4.5	3.7	64	1.4	2.3	1.6	60
Poland 1971	11.1	14.9	13.1	70	6.9	10.1	8.5	65	3.7	6.1	5.0	51	1.7	3.2	2.5	51				
Brazil 1970	5.0	5.1	5.1	96									1.7	1.9	1.8	87				
India 1971	6.1	6.0	5.9	110	3.3	3.4	3.3	106	2.1	2.1	2.1	104	1.0	1.1	1.0	100	0.6	0.6	0.6	96
Tunisia 1966	5.8	5.3	5.6	115	3.7	3.3	3.5	116	2.1	2.0	2.1	112	1.2	1.1	1.2	116	0.6	0.6	0.6	108
Indonesia (September 1964–February 1965)	4.8	4.2	4.5	110	2.3	2.2	2.3	103	1.5	1.4	1.4	100	0.6	0.7	0.6	93				

TABLE 6. HOUSEHOLD POSITION OF WIDOWED PERSONS BY SEX IN 61 PLACES IN ENGLAND BEFORE 1821.

	HEADING HOUSEHOLDS CONTAINING					IN HOUSEHOLDS HEADED BY						
	Unmarried offspring	Married or widowed son	Married or widowed daughter	Only those not offspring	Sub-total	Son or daughter	Son- or daughter-in-law	Other kin	Other persons	Solitary	In institutions	Total
Widowers												
Number	120	9	5	24	158	12	2	9	18	12	0	211
Percent	57%	4%	2%	11%	74%	6%	1%	4%	9%	6%	0	100%
Widows												
Number	243	7	5	50	305	48	17	19	41	65	6	501
Percent	49%	1%	1%	10%	61%	10%	3%	4%	8%	13%	1%	100%
Both												
Number	363	16	10	74	463	60	19	28	59	77	6	712
Percent	51%	2%	1%	10%	65%	8%	3%	4%	8%	11%	1%	100%

indicate how few "widowed" persons were living alone, or in institutions; to those which show that having a married son or daughter living in the family was rare; and to those which imply that living in a household headed by such married offspring was considerably commoner, but still only affected about a tenth of all "widowed" people. The "other" persons in whose households the widowed are found were a miscellaneous lot, and included a good proportion of unrelated people with whom they were simply lodging. But some amongst them may have been married daughters unrecognized by us.

These uncertainties, it seems to me, cannot disguise the message of the table. Widows and widowers in preindustrial England lived for the most part where they were before they became widowed. The loss of a spouse did not always or even usually lead to the break up of the household and certainly not to its being absorbed into another household. We know that those who administered the Elizabethan Poor Law would assist a widow in keeping her family together, though we do not know how often this venture failed. There may, for instance, have been widowed persons present in these 61 English communities concealed from us because they lived as servants.

Table 6 is of value also because it gives a comparative context and some very welcome confirmation of the numerous facts about the household position of the aged persons in preindustrial England which have been marshaled in Tables 7a, 7b, and 7c. If, for instance, 6 percent of all widowers and 13 percent of all the widows can be supposed from the figures in Table 6 to have been living alone, it is reasonable that we should find that 5 percent of the widowers over 60 years old in Table 7c, and 16 percent of the widows of that age, should also be found to be solitary.

The difference between men and women was no doubt due to the greater facility with which widowers remarried, and this is one of a number of interesting contrasts between the sexes amongst the elderly in historical communities. Though we find three-quarters or so of persons above 60 to be living as heads of households, and so establish the principle that the old as

well as the widowed were left to continue in their families as before, it transpires that over four-fifths of old men were in that position and only some two-thirds of old women. This was because more widows than widowers were solitary, in earlier times, as indeed they are now, and because more widows lived with their married children although they did not quite so frequently form a household with their unmarried offspring as widowers did.

Old men, on the other hand, showed a slightly greater tendency to live as lodgers and in institutions if they lacked spouses. Here we must recognize that some of the individuals were certainly bachelors. Indeed, one 80-year-old inhabitant of the hospital at Lichfield was called "maidenly Harry" in the listing document.

The interest of the array of figures in Table 7 lies in the contrast between the domestic situation of the elderly in preindustrial society and their domestic situation in the England and Wales of our own day. We have found it difficult to establish comparison in just the terms which would be most revealing, and the best we can do for the time being is to be found in Table 8. Here the ages are higher, 65 and above, and only 5 settlements can be included from traditional England. The resemblances and differences are so interesting that it is hoped that these places are in fact reasonably representative. We shall rather rashly refer to the aged persons in this little group of places as "traditional English society," and the carefully selected sample (from Shanas *et al.*, 1968, see Tables VI.16, VI.17) studied in the 1960's as "England today."

While two-thirds of married couples over the age of 65 live on their own with each other in England today, in traditional England this was not the case. Half of the married women were in that position, but rather fewer of the married men. More aged married men in fact lived with spouse and unmarried children than lived with their wives alone in the old social order, though this slight difference is not statistically significant. In England today only a quarter of aged married persons of either sex have their "families" of children still at home.

Here we reach the same important point again, that, in the traditional world, full family life,

TABLE 7a. HOUSEHOLD POSITION BY SEX AND MARITAL STATUS OF PERSONS AGED 60 AND ABOVE IN SIX PLACES IN ENGLAND BEFORE 1800: NUMBERS AND PROPORTIONS OF ELDERLY MARRIED PERSONS LIVING:—

	As head (or his spouse) with unmarried children		Not as head with unmarried children		As head (or his spouse) with married children		Not as head with married children		As head (or his spouse) with grandchildren		As head (or his spouse) with servants		As head (or his spouse) with spouse only		As head (or his spouse) with kin and/or lodgers		Not as head with kin of any kind		As lodger or in unclear status or position in the household		In institutions	
	M	F	M	F	M	F	M	F	M	F	M	F	M	F	M	F	M	F	M	F	M	F
Ealing, 1599	9	1	0	0	0	0	0	0	0	0	1	2	4	3	0	0	0	0	0	0	0	0
Chilvers Coton, 1684	5	8	0	0	2	0	0	0	1	1	0	1	5	1	2	2	0	0	0	0	0	0
Lichfield, 1695	27	20	0	0	4	5	0	1	0	0	2	2	13	15	4	4	0	0	0	0	0	1
Stoke-on-Trent, 1701	22	14	0	1	2	1	0	0	2	1	3	3	10	9	0	0	0	0	0	0	0	0
Corfe Castle, 1790	13	10	0	0	0	0	0	0	6	7	0	0	6	7	4	1	0	0	0	0	0	0
Ardleigh, 1796	11	4	0	0	0	0	0	0	3	1	1	1	6	4	2	1	0	0	1	0	0	0
Total	87	57	0	1	8	6	0	1	12	10	7	9	44	39	12	8	0	0	1	0	0	1
Proportion	51%	43%	0%	1%	5%	5%	0%	1%	7%	8%	4%	7%	26%	29%	7%	6%	0%	0%	1%	0%	0%	1%

TABLE 7b. HOUSEHOLD POSITION BY SEX AND MARITAL STATUS OF PERSONS AGED 60 AND ABOVE IN SIX PLACES IN ENGLAND BEFORE 1800: NUMBERS AND PROPORTIONS OF ELDERLY WIDOWED PERSONS (INCLUDING DESERTED SPOUSES AND NEVER MARRIED) LIVING:—

	As head with unmarried children		Not as head with unmarried children		As head with married children		Not as head with married children		As head with grandchildren		As head with servants		Solitary		As head with kin and/or lodgers		Not as head with kin of any kind		As lodger or in unclear status or position in the household		In institution	
	M	F	M	F	M	F	M	F	M	F	M	F	M	F	M	F	M	F	M	F	M	F
Ealing, 1599	0	1	0	0	0	1	0	0	0	0	1	0	0	1	0	0	0	3	1	0	0	0
Chilvers Coton, 1684	6	3	0	0	0	2	0	2	0	1	2	0	0	1	1	0	0	0	1	1	0	0
Lichfield, 1695	9	30	0	0	0	2	0	8	0	0	0	2	1	13	4	10	0	0	4	4	11	14
Stoke-on-Trent, 1701	7	13	0	0	1	2	0	7	1	0	1	2	3	6	1	4	1	1	6	13	0	0
Corfe Castle, 1790	6	1	0	0	2	2	1	3	1	2	2	1	1	7	2	8	1	1	10	4	0	0
Ardleigh, 1796	6	1	0	0	2	0	1	1	0	0	1	0	0	1	0	1	0	0	4	3	5	2
Total	34	49	0	0	5	9	2	21	2	3	7	5	5	29	8	23	2	5	26	25	16	16
Proportion	32%	26%	0%	0%	5%	5%	2%	11%	2%	2%	7%	3%	3%	15%	7%	12%	2%	5%	24%	13%	15%	9%

TABLE 7c. HOUSEHOLD POSITION BY SEX AND MARITAL STATUS OF PERSONS AGED 60 AND ABOVE IN SIX PLACES IN ENGLAND BEFORE 1800: PROPORTIONS OF THE ELDERLY HEADING HOUSEHOLDS, OR LIVING OTHERWISE.

	MARRIED		WIDOWED				
	Male	Female	Male	Female	All males	All females	All persons
Heads or spouses of heads	100%	98%	52%	48%	82%	69%	75%
In household headed by others	0 ⎫		28%	27%	10%	17%	14%
Alone	0 ⎬ 2%		5%	16%	2%	9%	6%
In institution	0 ⎭		15%	9%	6%	5%	5%
Total	100%	100%	100%	100%	100%	100%	100%

defined in this way, lasted proportionately longer for most persons than it does in the present world, for those who got married—a very high but uncertain proportion—and for those who became widowed as well. We may dwell a little, with these tables in front of us, on the probable reasons for these important circumstances, although at the present time we cannot be very precise in our discussion or entirely confident in the conclusions.

Under the demographic conditions and with the familial rules which prevailed in preindustrial England, numbers of children were quite large, if variable: completed family sizes varying, at different times and places, from four or five to six, seven, or eight. Offspring were born relatively late in the childbearing stage, both of the husband and of the wife, in contrast, that is to say, with parts of the world where the European marriage pattern did not prevail. Although they finally left home with such remorseless promptness, if not necessarily in age-order, these children went on arriving until well into the 30's or even the 40's of the life span of their mothers. Therefore, some of them would still be in the parental household when the parents entered into old age.

Many of the families would be broken by death, but the children would remain with their widowed parents; remarriage, as we shall see, was frequent, especially for fathers widowed during the childbearing stage (see Laslett, 1975 on orphans: a quarter or a third of all orphans were living with remarried parents). As old age proceeded, solitary couples and solitary widowed people grew more common,

and living as lodgers or even in institutions began to be the fate of a few of the senescent. But two further circumstances helped to ensure that these conditions were confined to a few. First there was the tendency for a proportion of the surviving grandparents, especially widowed grandmothers, to be taken into the families of their married offspring. Second was the fact that the expectation of life of the old in that society was lower than it is today, not as much lower as expectation of life at birth, but enough to curtail the final years when familial living might have been more difficult.

In the above rather dogmatic general account of the situation of the old in preindustrial England, nothing has been said of those who never married, but these, as will be seen, make no appearance in our tables because we cannot identify them adequately.

There are contrasts between the situation now and the situation then which are evident and clearly marked: according to Table 8 we have double the number of widowed persons living alone in our day than they did in preindustrial times. But some parts of the pattern described have to be extracted from our tabular information by comparison and inference. Table 7a shows, for example, that 30 percent of married males and 36 percent of married females over 60 were living with spouses only (4 and 7 percent respectively with servants as well). Table 8 reveals that by age 65, 44 percent and 49 percent of married men and women were living with spouses alone. We can therefore infer that, during the five years which

TABLE 8. HOUSEHOLD POSITION BY SEX AND MARITAL STATUS OF AGED[a] PERSONS IN ENGLAND IN FIVE PLACES BEFORE 1800 COMPARED WITH BRITAIN IN THE 1960'S.

	CHILVERS COTON 1684		LICHFIELD 1695		STOKE-ON-TRENT 1701		CORFE CASTLE 1790		ARDLEIGH 1796		TOTAL		PER-CENTAGES		BRITAIN, 1960'S PER-CENTAGES	
	Men	Women	Men	Women	Men	Women	Men	Women	Men	Women	Men	Women	Men	Women	Men	Women
Married persons																
Living with:–																
spouse and unmarried children	3	2	8	6	12	2	7	2	5	4	35	16	46%	37%	24%	24%
spouse and married children	1	0	3	0	1	1	0	1	0	0	5	2	7%	5%	5%	1%
spouse only	5	2	8	5	4	3	11	9	3	2	31	21	44%	49%	67%	68%
others	0	0	1	2	0	1	2	0	2	1	5	4	7%	9%	4%	7%
Widowed, etc. persons																
Living with:–																
unmarried children	1	0	3	14	5	8	4	1	0	1	13	24	23%	20%	18%	20%
married children	0	2	1	10	3	13	2	7	2	2	8	34	14%	28%	23%	17%
others	1	1	9	16	5	8	7	11	5	5	27	41	48%	34%	22%	18%
Living alone	0	1	1	10	4	8	3	4	0	0	8	23	14%	19%	37%	45%

[a] Aged 65 and above.

elapsed between their parents passing from 60 years to 65 years old, the numbers of last remaining children went down quite sharply, and that this left their fathers and mothers on their own. Nevertheless at 65, as Table 8 makes plain, half as many again are living alone in the England that we know today.

The contrast between the contemporary world and the traditional world is well marked in these respects in Table 8, but there are interesting resemblances as well as differences. Married persons over 65 were only very little more likely, it would seem from this evidence, to be living with their married, as distinct from the unmarried, children, than is the case today. With such wavering statistics, in fact, it may well be that there was no difference at all, especially for the males. So much, once again, for the outmoded stereotype of two or more married couples usually being present in the same domestic group in the *before* but not in the *after*.

In traditional England elderly married persons seem to have resembled their successors in another important respect. They were members of the households of persons other than their children just about as often as they are today. The heading "Others" in Table 8 is inclusive and covers lodging and being in institutions as well as being present as a member of a family household.

A few, we cannot unfortunately say how many, of the "others" were kinsfolk and represent the whole sum of the *residential* responsibility which related persons, apart from members of the immediate family, undertook for the care of old people. In the case of the "widowed" (which covers the never married and those deserted by their spouses), the proportions living with these others are quite high, much higher than today. A comparison with Table 7, which in a sense breaks down this category for the over 60's, seems to imply that it represented lodging to a much greater extent than living with kin (though, which is exasperating to the researcher, we have already seen that the two situations, lodging and living with kin, may not have been always distinguished in that society).

The deserted, and those who had never married, were perhaps the most likely to be living as lodgers, a form of residence which seems to have become more common for people of this sort as they grew older. To find that up to one-half of all spouseless old men— that is, "widowed etc." males in Table 8—were in this (presumably) entirely *unfamilial* situation, and one-third of the women too, is somewhat surprising, even after what has been claimed here about the lack of any responsibility upon the household in that social order to give shelter to distant relatives in need.

It could be said, on the other hand, that one was much less likely to be solitary as an aged widow or widower in earlier times. This seems to have been the case because of the lodging arrangements we have just described rather than because of any greater propensity for widowed people to live with their own children, married or unmarried. Sharing a household with married children compares in a rather complicated way between the traditional world and our own. Widows now are in this position considerably less often than they were then, but widowers today are actually much more frequently found with their married children than they were in the *before*. The comparison with Table 7 shows that this practice also seems to have grown as age advanced.

Little then seems to be left in favor of any prejudice against the contemporary English family for expelling the really old, or for failing to take them in, at least when the comparison is made with the English familial past. Even the advantage, in general, reckoned for widows and widowers in traditional England in Table 6, and for these over 60 in Table 7, that is, the advantage of being left to live with unmarried children, seems from Table 8 to have been eroded by age 65. Not many more of the spouseless had such offspring still resident than they do in our own contemporary world. When we are able to allow for the difference between the preindustrial situation and our own in respect of the numbers of children surviving to the old age of their parents, we will be able to make a more realistic comparison between the two epochs in respect of the aged, even with the present unsatisfactory data. It is possible that in this way a case might finally be made for believing that the aged would then have been less alienated from the family group than they are observed to be today, given that the same residential conventions had survived from traditional times. But I doubt if any such attempt at demonstration would be convincing.

We have described the old in preindustrial England as having in general been left as they were, and where they were, watching their children grow up and leave home never to return, and not receiving into their households their own elderly relatives for company nor joining those relatives for the same reason. The crude, cross-sectional data on which our tables are based, cannot tell us about the previous experience of the individuals described, and we do not know how many of the few found living with their married children had allowed, or encouraged, those children to bring their spouses into the house, or how many had joined those children in their households, abandoning their own family homes. We can, however, form a provisional if not a numerical impression of what usually happened in the study of change over periods of years in village society. This is an exercise which is occasionally possible in historical or traditional English communities (see, for example, Laslett and Harrison, 1963, analyzing the seventeenth century villages of Clayworth and Cogenhoe, an essay which is in the course of revision and republication).

These materials seem to bear out what has been claimed. None of the parents as they grew older between 1676 and 1688 in Clayworth, for example, were rejoined by a son or a daughter, married or unmarried, coming home to help them as their health and their strength failed. Quite a number of these aging heads of households were being denuded of their children during this period of time, and one or two were actually reduced to living on parish relief, or even in the Poor Law institution, while their children set up home for themselves in the village. The handful of instances in which married children did live with their parents seem to have come about because a son brought his wife, or a daughter brought her husband, into the house for a year or two or a month or two after marriage. Except for the unfortunates

who had to go into institutions, the rule of continued independent residence by the old seems by and large to have been maintained.

But there are significant signs of exception to this rule, and the evidence also hints at the existence of a further practice which likewise implied change of residence for some persons, and which could have been connected with the fear of loneliness in age. The exception applies to the widowed amongst the old, and especially to the women: it seems clear that they were sometimes brought into the households of their married children, of both sexes, and clear too that this practice was connected with the rearing of the grandchildren. (Grandchildren, it may be noticed, are quite often found, in the English evidence, living with their grandparents rather than with their own fathers and mothers, though many of these children may have been illegitimate.) These are the circumstances which seem to account for the figures of widowed parents living with married children set out in Tables 6 to 8. The expedient against loneliness was remarriage: in Clayworth in 1688 there were 67 extant marriages, and of these, 28 were remarriages (3 third marriages, 4 fourth marriages, and 1 fifth marriage). If you were in danger of solitary old age, you married again, if you could. This happened in England in spite of the possibility that there may have been some feeling against remarriage, and in other countries and cultures, it happened even more.

Historial Data and Aging: Commentary and Conclusion

It has been insisted that the notion of a *before* covering both contemporary and historical preindustrial society is entirely misleading. So also is any assumption about uniformity in respect of the position of old people in the societies which represent our own past, the past, that is, of English-speaking peoples and especially of late 20th century North Americans. Whereas the English, of English descent, can look back on what seems to have been a uniform past in respect of aging, the Europeans can do so to a lesser extent, and North Americans least of all. Before we conclude this essay in the preliminary analysis of aging and societal change, we may glance at a little of the newly available evidence from one or two other past societies, so as to get some idea of how variable they have been in their treatment of the widowed and the old.

Beginning with France in the seventeenth century, there is, for example, the village of Montplaisant in 1644, with some 350 inhabitants situated in the Dordogne (South Central). There were only 12 widowed persons there, and 11 of these were heading their own households: the 12th was a solitary widow. All 4 of the widowers and 4 of the 8 widows were, in fact, the first named in households which contained their married sons, households which seem to have been complex, some indeed very complex. All this is in sharp contrast to the English pattern we have examined, though when we reach 1836 we find in Montplaisant fewer multiple households than in 1644. In that later year, however, a singular circumstance appeared: the widowers, 4 out of 5 of them, were living with their married sons, but the widows, 5 out of 9, with their married daughters; no widower is found with his daughter, no widow with her son. Perhaps a chance effect of small numbers this, but indicating nevertheless how these practices might differ from small community to small community. In northern France at the same time, the aged were in the English situation, which (as far as we can yet tell) was by no means confined to England.

If we go on to take a German village, in the Baltic area in 1795, (Grossenmeer with 880 people), we find no solitary widowed persons at all, and a conspicuous difference between the sexes: 10 widowers to 44 widows. Two-thirds of these persons were living with their married children, equally divided between married sons and married daughters, but only 2 of them as heads. These arrangements differ markedly from the English and differ from Montplaisant too. In all these cases remarriage must have been frequent, even more frequent in Grossenmeer amongst the men, and in Montplaisant for both sexes, than it was in Clayworth. Remarriage seems to have been at its most intense to our knowledge in Lisswege, a Belgian village near Bruges in the early eighteenth century, where a widowed person seems to have been a rarity.

Going outside the boundaries of western Europe, we can find villages with even fewer widowed persons, and with even lower levels of residence with unmarried children. At Vändra in Estonia in 1683 (population 967), the only widower recorded was at the head of a household of a married son, and all the eight widows were living as members, not as heads, in the households of married sons as well. Households, if household is quite the word, were huge in that settlement and often very complicated. The situation was the same in villages in Latvia in the eighteenth century.

For the settlement of Kölked, in Transdanubian Hungary, in 1816, we have age evidence. There were 13 males and 17 females over 60 amongst the population of 636, less than 5 percent, of whom 6 of the men and 13 of the women were widowed. All the elderly males, married and widowed, were at the heads of the households of married sons, as well as one of the widows: 5 of the other widows were living in the families of married sons, and the rest of the elderly women were variously disposed. Only 5 of the women were in the "English" position, that is, in charge of a household containing their unmarried children. Once more, households were often complex in Kölked, but in settlements not far away they were as simple as they have been found to have been almost everywhere in England, with the aged in much the same position as we have described for the English.

The one cultural area outside Europe from which information on the old is beginning to be available for the past is Japan. Here we find examples of a situation which occurs very seldom in our own European data, the situation in which old people, and especially widows, have yielded the headship of the household to their *unmarried* children. Widowhood was commoner in Japan than might have been expected, and remarriage seems to have stopped altogether at the later ages: most old people evidently lived with their married sons. Some of these sons were adopted rather than offspring in the European sense: adoption was a rarity in the West, about which virtually nothing is known.

We do not yet know enough to say whether local variation was common in Japan. Indeed, it must be clear that the sum of our present information goes only to the stage of providing a little of a comparative framework in which to place the English and the western European pattern of aging. Our own ancestors lived in their own distinctive way in this respect, but it will be a long time before we can say quite how much they differed from the rest of the world. We cannot yet pass any judgement at all on the *common situation* of the aged in nonindustrial society generally, amongst humanity as a whole, as has often been done by those who have previously pronounced on aging in relation to social development.

It has been conventional in discussions of aging and the household in the European past, as far as these things have been systematically discussed at all, to insist on two features so far scarcely mentioned here, the stem family form of the household, and the tradition of retirement. It has recently been shown, for example, that in certain eighteenth century areas of Austria and Germany, a stem family arrangement prevailed amongst a sizable minority of households, allotting to the old a familial situation which gave to retirement an institutional form (see Berkner, 1972, 1974). These arrangements meant demotion from the headship and even, in a sense, expulsion from the family group. This might be said to be a less "familial" way of treating the aged, or even a more inhumane one, than the practices described for traditional England. But this pattern, which has also been found in twentieth century Ireland, did succeed in allotting a position in space to the outdated farmer or laborer, a space given the name "the west room" on Irish farms.

This is not the opportunity to pursue the controversy about the extent to which social scientists have exaggerated the prevalence and importance of these arrangements. The "west room" of the Irish is now treated with some scepticism by the social scientists, for example. Nor have we the space to survey the evidence now being assembled about the position and role of the aged during the long generations which elapsed between the *before* and the *after* in English historical development. The aged, it has been commonly assumed, acquired a new role in the early factory era, a role as child-minder. It is becoming known, however,

(Anderson, 1972) that it was not always the parents and parents-in-law of the mill-girl wives who kept the home going during the long shifts at the loom, but friends and neighbors as well, not all of them old. So conspicuously different, moreover, were the factories from what went before, that the numerical importance of these arrangements has also been very easy to exaggerate. We simply do not know what happened to the old people living in a society undergoing industrialization but not themselves directly caught up in the process. This is a matter of capital importance because our immediate past, in high industrial society, is not that of traditional times at all, but that of the industrializing nineteenth century.

One further question only can be broached. How far was it an advantage to the widowed and the old in the traditional world to be kept in the familial situation? Did they in fact have the same appreciation of independence as their successors in our day?

We have one stray result to present in this connection from our English evidence. Amongst the privileged, widowed persons were less, not more, likely to be living with their married children than amongst those below them in the social scale (Back, 1974). Those who could afford to do just what they wanted about their aged parents did not have them at home. They seem to have set them up with their own servants in their own households. Or was it rather that the old gentlemen and old ladies themselves amongst the rich and powerful saw to it that they did not have to live with their married sons and daughters, but maintained their own establishments with their own staffs? This detail is the more significant in that the English gentry, like all privileged classes, were more and not less likely to have their relatives of other kinds living with them in extended or in multiple households. But the practice was not entirely confined to the gentry. We can see much more modest people providing servants for their aging parents in the evidence from those English villages which can be studied over time.

The conclusion might be that then, as now, a place of your own, with help in the house, with access to your children, within reach of support, was what the elderly and the aged most wanted for themselves in the preindustrial world. This was difficult to secure in traditional England for any but fairly substantial people. It must have been almost impossible in many other cultural areas of the world.

REFERENCES

Anderson, M. 1972. *Family Structure in 19th Century Lancashire.* Cambridge: Cambridge University Press.

Ariès, P. 1962. *Centuries of Childhood.* Translated by Robert Baldick, London: Cape. 2nd ed., 1973.

Ariès, P. 1974. *Western Attitudes Towards Death.* Baltimore: Johns Hopkins University Press.

Back, Kurt. 1974. Unpublished typescript on class differentials in the household position of widowed persons in traditional English society.

Beauvoir, Simone de. 1970. *La Vieillesse.* Paris.

Berkner, L. 1972. The stem family and the development cycle of the peasant household. *Am. His. Rev.,* 77.

Berkner, L. 1974. Inheritance, land tenure and family structure at the end of the 17th century. Paper read at the International Conference of Economic History, Copenhagen.

Hajnal, J. 1965. European marriage patterns in perspective. *In,* D. Glass and D. Eversley (eds.), *Population in History,* London: Arnold.

Hammel, E. A. 1972. The zadruga as process. *In,* P. Laslett and R. Wall, *Household and Family in Past Time,* pp. 333–373. Cambridge: Cambridge University Press.

Hammel, E. A., and Laslett, P. 1974. Comparing household structure over time and between cultures. *Comparative Studies in Society and History,* 16 (1), 73–109.

Laslett, Peter. 1965. *The World we have lost.* London: Methuen. New York: Schriber. 2nd ed., 1971.

Laslett, P. 1972. Introduction. *In,* P. Laslett and R. Wall, *Household and Family in Past Time,* pp. 1–89. Cambridge: Cambridge University Press.

Laslett, P. 1972. Mean household size in England since the 16th century. *In,* P. Laslett and R. Wall, *Household and Family in Past Time,* pp. 125–158. Cambridge: Cambridge University Press.

Laslett, P. 1973. Typescript in course of publication on the European family pattern and socialization process.

Laslett, P. 1975. Typescript in course of publication on the adequacy of the household in pre-industrial Europe for socialization purposes.

Laslett, P., and Harrison, J. 1963. Clayworth and Cogenhoe. *In,* Bell and Ollard (eds.), *Historical Essays presented to David Ogg.* London: Black.

Laslett, P., and Wall, R. 1972. *Household and Family in Past Time.* Cambridge: Cambridge University Press.

Pressat, R. 1972. *Demographic Analysis.* Chicago: Aldine-Atherton. London: Arnold.

Shanas, E., Townsend, P. Wedderburn, D. Milhøj, P., Friis, H., and Stehouwer, J. 1968. *Old People in Three Industrial societies.* London: Routledge.

Tunstall, Jeremy. 1966. *Old and Alone.* London: Routledge.

Wrigley, E. A. 1966. Family limitation in pre-industrial England. *Economic History Review,* XIX (1), 82–109.

Wrigley, E. A. 1969. *Population and History.* London: World University Library.

Wrigley. E. A. 1972. Mortality in pre-industrial England. *In,* D. Glass and R. Revelle (eds.), *Population and Social Change.* London: Arnold.

5
AGING IN NONINDUSTRIAL SOCIETIES

Jack Goody

St. John's College, Cambridge

The process of aging obviously affects every type of social group, and indeed every type of social relationship, in all societies, whether industrial or not. This chapter attempts to sketch some of the general features that mark the process of aging and, more specifically, the position of the aged, in nonindustrial societies, that is, those in which the economy is based upon hunting and gathering, pastoralism, or agriculture, including the nonindustrial sectors of industrial societies.

THE STRUCTURE OF DOMESTIC GROUPS

Nonindustrial societies are marked by economic systems where production is carried out by domestic groups. This does not imply the absence of cooperation between such groups, nor of exchange in objects (e.g., trade) and people (e.g., marriage). But unlike industrial societies where the domestic group is largely a consuming group, the 'family unit' (to use a vaguer alternative) carries out the basic productive tasks; this is so in most agricultural societies, even where the domestic group does not own the land it farms. Besides their role in production and consumption, we also need to examine the reproductive and residential aspects of domestic groups and their relevance for the study of aging.

Such productive groups are always small. The largest farming groups I have encountered were those of the LoWiili of West Africa, where average size was 11.1 (Goody, 1972a). Here, the division of farming groups was delayed because brothers continued to farm together even after the father was dead; 83 percent of adult males farmed with another adult kinsman.

Such a situation is far from usual. A more common figure is one around 4.7, which Laslett (1969; Laslett and Wall, 1972) found as a fairly consistent mean for household size (i.e., the consumption rather than the productive unit) in England from the sixteenth century until as late as 1911. The size of the farm family is clearly related to its composition and this in turn is related to "the points of family fission", i.e., to the timing of the departure of sons or daughters (or both) from their natal household; in principle, one could calculate the average of the length of residence with the senior generation. If all children moved out before marriage (as generally occurs in urban Western society), then clearly the senior generation are left on their own for a considerable part of their lives, which maximizes independence but exacerbates the question of "care." If, however, some or all of the children stay in the household, then the problem is greatly mitigated, at least from the parental standpoint. For the latter will simply

117

continue to live on where they lived before, together with their junior kinsmen. At this level of composition, the mode of production is closely linked to the situation of the aged.

THE TRANSMISSION OF RESOURCES

This relationship is radically different in the nonindustrial and industrial worlds because, in the former, an individual is directly dependent upon his own senior generation for the acquisition of rights in the basic means of production. In hunting societies, where economic resources are largely open, these rights and opportunities are somewhat diffuse; livelihood depends upon acquiring skills and having generalized rights to exploit a territory. But in agricultural societies, control over resources becomes more individualized; a man acquires a right to exploit farm land which had previously been farmed by a senior kinsman, usually a member of the same unit of production. The degree of individualization depends upon the scarcity of resources. In economies based upon hoe agriculture, technology places limits on the area a man can farm so that there may be no great pressure upon the land; where an open frontier exists, parental control is likely to be less. But the harnessing of animal energy through the plough enables a man to cultivate a much larger area, and the investment required by irrigation means increasing the value of that land; both processes lead to shortages for others; greater differentiation leads to greater dependence upon the position and the holding of one's forefathers. The same is true of many pastoral societies, though here the fragility of the basic productive resources (the possibility of the destruction of the herd through war or pestilence) tends to lay more stress on the economic interdependence of kin and neighbors.

The relative scarcity of resources affects the nature of the control exercised by the senior generation over the junior, whether these resources are used for productive or reproductive purposes. Where a man needs a substantial bridewealth to marry, he could get this only from senior relatives; equally with the provision of a dowry for a woman. The ability to earn money and hence to provide for one's own marriage is often seen as weakening the authority of the senior generation over the junior.

Clearly the question of the timing of the transfer is of critical importance in the maintenance of authority, in influencing the points of family fission, and in ensuring support for the aged. The transmission of property between kin (as distinct from purchase on the open market) encourages continuity on the land, involving some degree of coresidence, or at least of contiguity, of adjacent generations. Its transmission at death (i.e., inheritance) provides both a carrot for the young and a surety for the old.

It is not only the timing but the kind of inheritance that influences the provisions made for the aged. The 'direction' of inheritance (i.e., fraternal, conjugal, or intergenerational; close or distant; patrilineal, matrilineal, or bilateral) helps to determine who will work (and hence live) with whom, and this fact affects the size and composition of domestic groups as well as the question of care. The point is illustrated by comparing the LoWiili of Northern Ghana, a patrilineal people who, as has been noted, had average farming units of 11.1, with an adjacent group, the LoDagaba, who inherited moveable property between matrilineal relatives, i.e., in the absence of a full brother, it was a sister's son that would come and claim a man's wealth, his livestock, and the contents of his granary. Among these latter, sons were naturally reluctant to continue farming with their fathers after adolescence, since any surplus of grain they accumulated would be used to purchase livestock that might be claimed by others. So young men broke away (at least in an economic sense) to farm on their own, and family fission tended to take place at an earlier point in time, the average number of persons in a farming unit being 7.0.

Even in the latter society, however, it was the job of one son (or group of sons, since children of the same mother usually farmed together) to stay with the father after the others had left. This obligation was balanced by compensating advantages in the division of property; since the younger son stayed with the father, he benefited from the system of "preferential ultimogeniture" (Goody 1958, 1962). In parts of England and France, a similar preference was given to the child that sat by the hearth (the astrier, or hearth-heir); if there were no sons, an unmarried daughter might stay and inherit the whole tenement, the other daughters having been married off with their portion or dowry (Pollock and Maitland, 1898, p. 281). In other parts of Europe, the eldest son was preferred; in each case, transmission of the means of production (and other property) was linked with obligations towards the old; rights involved duties, and the transactions were "reciprocal." Indeed, they often continued after death; in societies that practiced ancestor-worship and conceived the dead as continuing to influence the lives of their descendants, it was often the specific duty of the heir to maintain communication with the departed, by prayer, by blood-sacrifice, or by offering the first fruits of the harvest. This close relationship between inheritance and dependence becomes even clearer in looking at the institution of retirement.

RETIREMENT

The decreasing powers of the aged, at least in the economic sphere, lead inevitably to a reduction of their role in the fields, the pastures, or the woods. On the other hand, the formal transfer of these resources weakens their control over the junior generation, with the possible result of neglect or nonsupport. The situation is most clearly stated in Shakespeare's *King Lear* where the ruler divides his realm among his daughters but is unable to accept their exercise of this newly acquired power. No longer able to command their obedience, he is dependent upon their love; yet their gratitude is of far less value than he anticipated.

Why should he have placed himself in this weak position by handing over his kingdom in this manner? Firstly, to rid himself of the worries of office and to hand authority to "younger strengths":

> 'tis our fast intent
> To shake all cares and business from our age;
> Conferring them on younger strengths, while we
> Unburden'd crawl toward death.

Secondly, to prevent "future strife" by publishing now "our daughters' several powers", on which the marriage of at least one of them depended. In making this arrangement, the king handed over effective authority to his sons-in-law but retained his now empty title.

> Only we still retain
> The name, and all the additions to a king;
> The sway, revenue, execution of the rest,
> Beloved sons, be yours:

At the same time, Lear puts forward a detailed claim for support of a kind that resembles the 'circuit' of rural Scandinavia.

> Ourself by monthly course,
> With reservation of an hundred knights,
> By you to be sustain'd, shall our abode
> Make with you by due turns.

But while the early transfer of property or office between the living (*inter vivos*) relieves the tension that exists between the generations and manifests itself in the Prince Hal situation (that is, in the desires and actions of the heir directed against the property of the holder), it also weakens the position of the retired, by depriving them of a sanction of great strength.

The problem of retirement has two separate aspects, one relating to withdrawal from productive activities, the other to the transfer of control over resources.

The withdrawal of the old from productive activities, which in centralized societies often marks a man's appointment to a chiefship, is largely a matter of age. However, the possibility of withdrawal is also linked to the presence of descendants (viewed as dependents and subsequently as supporters). Given support from the younger generation, a man can withdraw from farming and devote himself to other pursuits. But in the conditions of high mortality which mark most nonindustrial societies, only some 60 percent of men will leave behind them a male heir (Goody, 1972a), even when a strategy of maximum reproduction is pursued. In other words, some 40 percent of men will not have this particular opportunity to retire, 20 percent because they have no surviving progeny, another 20 because they have only girls.

In the simpler societies, retirement in the sense of the transfer of control is rare. Aging invariably lessens one's ability to perform the productive tasks, leading to a measure of withdrawal, even though other important jobs still remain in the hands of the elderly. In the non-economic domains, especially those dominated by ideas of kinship or religion (where selection is delegated to or sanctioned by one's forebears or one's gods), individuals generally continue to perform their offices and roles until the end.

However, a specific concept of retirement is found in some societies where agriculture is relatively developed, where social differences are advanced, and where resources are consequently restricted. In such societies, the early retirement of the senior generation may be demanded by the workings of the social system. For where it is necessary to make a "match" for a son or daughter, in order to see that one's progeny are well taken care of, and that one's name and honor are not abased by an alliance with a family of lower status, a man may have to promise each of his children a proportion of the estate when they marry or reach "maturity." For daughters, this transaction is known as dowry, and it is often linked with a dower, an allocation of property to the wife by the husband, so that she is provided for in her widowhood. This allocation may take the form of money ("with all my worldly wealth I thee endow"), of a house (the dower house), and occasionally of land.

The allocation of property at the marriage of son or daughter may take a variety of forms. In early eighteenth century Provence, marriage contracts defined the property that both husband and wife brought into the marriage. Where they joined the household of either spouse, then the contract specified details about lodging, food, and maintenance, as well as the conditions of separation (*insupport*). The donor retained control of the property allocated in the contract, but he promised the couple the whole or part of his heritable wealth, at the same time as agreeing to support them and their children (Collomp, 1972).

In Europe we usually find that marriage demands the actual transfer of control to the new family, in the manner described for rural Ireland (County Clare) in the 1930's. "The dowry or marriage portion," wrote Arensberg and Kimball, "is . . . a phenomenon universal in European peasant life . . . After the 'walking of the land' and the making of the bargain, the two

parties to marry go to a solicitor . . . The 'writings' is a legal instrument conveying the ownership of the holding to the son. It is usually both marriage settlement and will" (1961, p. 115).

But at the same time as handing over legal control, the father makes some provision for his own maintenance, in case he too should suffer from "nonsupport," for this type of arrangement is the complement of that found in Provence. The provisions include the right to the "grass of a cow," to food and the use of the hearth, and perhaps to the use of a room in the house, known in some parts as the "west room." To take care of possible disputes, "certain very hardheaded stipulations are often included, allowing for the conversion of these rights into cash support."

This type of retirement system was widespread in peasant Europe; in parts of England, the end room was set aside; in Scandinavia, Germany, and Czechoslovakia, the old people sometimes moved into a separate house adjacent to the main buildings. The arrangements for support varied in their content and in the degree to which they were detailed; this elaboration in legal documents was clearly a function of literacy; in communities without writing, the continued support of parents who had handed over authority, property or both, depended upon more diffuse sanctions, often of a religious nature, the pietas of individuals, the judgement of the community, and beliefs in the supernatural: "Honor thy father and thy mother: that thy days may be long upon the land which the Lord thy God giveth thee" (Exodus 20:12).

This system was by no means confined to Europe. In parts of rural Tibet, a man retired "from the headship of the family when his eldest son has reached full age and taken a wife . . . Usually a retired father lives as a dependent householder in a separate house. On each holding there is a plot of land with a kind of dower house to which the father . . . retires" (Carrasco, 1959, p. 31, referring to Spiti, around 1870). While retirement appears to take this form only in agricultural economies of a relatively advanced type (i.e., peasant societies), it is also a marked feature of pastoral societies. As men acquire dependents, so they can build up their herds; size is closely related to the amount of available labor. As the sons grow up, fathers may indicate their own cattle, their future inheritance, which they often take over at marriage or when they in turn have sons to help. Thus, the senior generation gradually divests itself of livestock as the children marry, keeping only such animals as they alone can look after.

This process is particularly clear among the Fulani. While the sons are engaged in establishing themselves on their own, "the father's personal power and skill as a herdsman and as a begetter have been waning . . . he is steadily losing dependants as they get married. Allocations of cattle have depleted his herd." At the same time, the mother hands over her decorated calabashes, symbolic of her milking rights, to her daughters, "until finally, on the marriage of her last daughter, her stock of decorated calabashes and her responsibilities as a mother, housewife and dairywoman came to an end." They even abandon their own homestead and reside as dependents, the woman being of some use in caring for the infants, but "an old man is regarded as of little use. He may help in making rope, but he has no voice in planning the movements of the cattle of the household. Old people in this situation spend their last days on the periphery of the homestead, on the male and female sides respectively. This is where men and women are buried. They sleep, as it were, over their own graves, for they are already socially dead" (Stenning, 1958, pp. 98-99).

PATTERNS OF CONSUMPTION

In dealing with the transfer of productive resources in the context of declining physical strength, we have inevitably touched upon the elderly as consumers; it is this position that has to be maintained by means of joint households, contracts of transfer, or even the kind of circulating arrangement by which the old made a circuit among their married children. In Scandinavia this was known as *Flaetfoering*. When a man divided his property, the law permitted him to make a circuit, spending the number of days with each in exact proportion to the quantity of goods he had received, a formula that sounds like a typical piece of written formalism based upon local custom. That it was accepted

as a model can be seen from *King Lear* (it is more likely to happen with daughters than sons) as well as from the visitations made by English monarchs to the estates of their nobility.

We have noted how the fate of an individual in old age oftens depends upon his wealth in offspring. It is the indigent old for whom special arrangements, such as the right of gleaning, have to be made. In ancient Israel these rights were more extensive than in the simpler societies (e.g., Africa), doubtless because the greater differentiation that more advanced agriculture permits often aggravates the problem of the aged, for example, by introducing a category of landless "laborers" or servants, who may have a reasonable standard when they are employed, but whose old age is marked by severe poverty. In Israel, the right to glean was supported by firm, religiously sanctioned, taboos.

> When thou cuttest down thine harvest in thy field, and has forgot a sheaf in the field, thou shalt not go again to fetch it: it shall be for the stranger, for the fatherless, and for the widow: that the Lord thy God may bless thee in all the work of thine hands.

Equally, the olive orchard and the vineyard had their gleanings for the poor (Deuteronomy 24: 19-22).

The other way that the elderly maintain their patterns of consumption, despite their lowered ability to produce, is through communal distributions. These may take the form of meals cooked for festive occasions, as in West Africa for the birthday of Mohammed; on a domestic level, feasts such as Christmas or Pesach sanctify the offering of food to strangers, particularly to the poor. These offerings may take the form of individual gifts of food, money, or other wealth, associated with the achievement of religious merit, of God's grace, or simply of secular prestige: the *sadaq* of Islam, alms given for religious purposes, charitable gifts of all kinds. In a more general sense, hospitality (as its cognates indicate) was often an aspect of the obligation of the better off toward those in worse circumstances. In the simpler societies, the elderly are provided for in their role as priests of cults, sacrificers to the dead, or senior members of restricted associations (e.g., "secret societies"). For the officiants at shrines not only receive offerings on behalf of the god, they also acquire a share of the sacrifice together with any special portions which are seen as too dangerous for the young. Taboos that affect the hunter or the husband may well be irrelevant for those to whom these aspects of their life exist only in the past. With regard to associations, a common feature is the way in which the contributions of food and money required from members becomes an investment in future benefices; a man enjoys the payments of all future members, and the longer one lives, the more one receives.

An explicit aspect of the Bagre society of the LoWiili is to act as a friendly society; an old man may be given clothes which have been specially bought with the money collected by the neophytes at the time of their initiation. In addition, costly materials are used to cover the funeral stand when a member dies, emphasizing that he was neither poor, nor alone, but representative of an association that took good care of his material as well as his spiritual needs (Goody, 1972b, pp. 41–42). Of course, the same kind of service can be performed by kin groups for their members; such associations however provide an added source of support, especially for those without descendants; the Bagre, say the LoWiili, *is* your father and your mother, and, appropriately, kinship terms are applied to those who organize these occasions.

Similarly, in centralized societies, kinship terms are often applied to chiefs, who may also be required to assist the old. The more centralized the state, the more extensive these provisions. Among the Inca and the Aztec, food and clothing were supplied from the public storehouse (Simmons, 1970, p. 25). Poverty and destitution were avoided because of the regular order of tilling the soil; first the land assigned to the Sun was cultivated (for religious purposes); second, those of widows, orphans, sick or aged, or persons otherwise unable to work, as also the land of absent soldiers. After the land of the poor and distressed had been attended to—and only then—the people worked their own lots, neighbors assisting each other (Markham, 1871, pp. 5–6).

In China, some residential provision was made for old women. In Nanching, one adult woman

in six was living in an "old maid house." Even if a widow returned to her natal home, she sought to die in such an establishment since they provided supernatural comfort; after death her spirit could return to these houses, which had their own tablets, altars, and sacrifices for the dead woman (Yang, 1947, p. 85).

PATTERNS OF REPRODUCTION

Much of the discussion about the position of the aged in simpler societies has turned upon the question of the control of women by older men. The control takes the form of allocation and use. Allocation is a matter of arranging and approving marriages; use is a question of plural marriage, more especially of polygyny.

The arranging of marriages may be done by prescribing partners, though such rules apply to categories rather than individuals, so that there is room for further manipulation in the selection of a specific spouse. The extent to which the senior generation plays a part in such arrangements varies greatly. In more differentiated (dowry) societies, the emphasis is often placed upon securing a partner of the right "standing" in terms of property and origin. Where marriages are arranged through a relatively standardized bridewealth, then the control has less to do with the actual spouse than the age of marriage. Bridewealth and polygyny, which are closely correlated, both imply a delayed marriage age for younger men and the accumulation of spouses among the older ones. This general feature of polygyny (as practiced in virtually all African societies) varies in its intensity. Among the Konkomba, young men have no choice but to get betrothed to infant girls since all other potential spouses are preempted. Consequently, they do not marry till the mid-30's but soon build up a polygynous household by virtue of the enforced abstinence of the younger generation.

But the accumulation of powers (in the most general sense) by the older generation (the "elders") is always modified by the process of senescence. Even where there is no relinquishing of rights by the very old, the exercise of those rights is qualified by physiological facts. The accumulation of rights in women is a particularly obvious case. The higher the rate of polygyny, the greater the difference in marriage age between men and women. Moreover, in polygynous unions, men will tend to choose younger and younger women, especially if they are able to enforce their choice through political power. Such women will have less and less chance of leading lives that satisfy them sexually (not to mention companionship) and hence will be more open to the advances of others. The problems of running the larger polygynous households are notorious, even with the help of high walls and eunuchs; in some parts elders with large holdings of women allowed others some limited access in order to keep the situation under control, for a wife in the hand, even if unfaithful, was better than one in the bush.

Thus, the process of accumulation is never without problems. In a study of marriages in a Ghanaian village (LoWiili) over a 15-year period, I found that while the older men had more wives than the younger, their holdings were diminishing, through death, divorce, or return to kin, which losses were not being replaced (Goody, 1969). Indeed, in the nearby state of Gonja, as among the matrilineal Ashanti to the south, most wives returned to their natal kin after the menopause, abandoning the conjugal state to look after (and be looked after by) their brothers (Goody, 1973). In this case a man's holding of wives decreased rapidly after middle age.

Clearly, the question of accumulation is a variable both within and between societies. But even in the case of the nomadic Samburu of East Africa, which Spencer describes as a gerontocracy, the same tendency can be discerned. Spencer defines gerontocracy in terms of control over women. "Literally, the term gerontocracy means government by old men; but by defining power as the possession of wives, all those societies in which the older men are polygamists and the younger men are bachelors become gerontocracies" (1965, p. 300). His figures show an increase in the number of wives per "stock owner" (i.e., "household head") until the penultimate age-group (57–70 years), and thereafter a decline. As Spencer points out, in justifying his assertion of a linear relationship, the homestead of an elder may also contain the wives of his sons; when these are included as "effective wives," they clearly "increase in number with the age of the stock owner" (1965, p. 14). But this shift from an individual to a household count cannot serve as an index of *gerontocratic* accumulation and therefore cannot be used to support a linear theory of "the older, the more" type. Indeed, Spencer himself recognizes that "where a married man is living in his father's homestead, it is often he who directs its affairs, either because the father is staying elsewhere in another of his homesteads, or because he is a very old man and has allowed this son to take over these responsibilities" (1965, p. 14).

Many age-group systems accentuate the dominance of junior by older grades. One aspect of this dominance can be seen in the procedures by which adolescents are formally initiated into adulthood, a process which is similar to that found more widely as a means of entry into various associations, colleges, and army units, in a variety of societies. These procedures often involve not only education but also tests that subject the novice to the same hardships the senior generation themselves have had to undergo at an earlier stage.

One aspect of this "hazing" is the control of juniors by elders, a control which is more or less explicit depending upon the society and the individual. It can also help to organize the gerontocratic accumulation of wives. At least as important as the economic "exploitation" of young by old is the unequal access to sexual or anyhow to conjugal partners. In any society that allows polygyny (the marriage of a man to more than one wife simultaneously), older men tend to have more spouses than the younger; number of wives is associated with duration of marital career. Given that the sex ratio of potential partners is roughly in balance, polygyny depends upon men having a shorter marital career than women; and to have more at one stage is to have less at another. Usually this imbalance is achieved by a late marriage age for men; that is to say, it is the young who have less. Indeed, in some age-group systems, such as that of the pastoral Samburu of Kenya (who in many ways resemble the better-known Masai), the members of junior grades are unambiguously defined as bachelors; similarly, members of the warrior grades of the southern Bantu (e.g., the Zulu regiments) had to remain unmarried. The opposition between sex and war (or hunting) promoted the interests of the senior generation. Among the Samburu, for example, the age-group system focused largely on the *moran*, the most junior group of young men who are forbidden to marry until they can be replaced by a new age group, by which time many of them are well over 30 years of age. It is through this prolonged bachelorhood that a high degree of polygyny is maintained (Spencer, 1965, p. 313). Meanwhile, the young girls, who are their age mates, are the subject of competition among the bachelors as lovers. "Notions of honour and clanship are developed to a brittle extreme which brings them against one another in what might be described as gang warfare between the clans. A wide range of activities from dancing to fighting and stock theft becomes intelligible in the context of their relationship with these girls and their prolonged bachelorhood" (Spencer, 1965, p. 314). The system of age classes which gives an obligatory character to the late age of marriage is seen as keeping under control the conflict between generations arising from delayed marriage, strains that are diverted to the age-class system. But the system also ensures the supply of young girls to older men, which only aggravates the intergenerational tension.

From the age specific rates of polygyny, Spencer derives what he calls a "gerontocratic index" for ranking groups according to the extent to which polygyny is a privilege of old age. The index is arrived at by dividing the polygyny rate for men over 40 by that for younger men; a high value suggests that older men have a large number of wives compared with younger ones.

This process of accumulation which, with the modifications we have noted, is characteristic of polygynous societies, means that older men marry younger wives, a phenomenon that one finds in the "serial polygyny" of many monogamous societies. While the element of sexual attraction is important, so too is the fact that by this means old men provide themselves with care in their old age and at the same time increase the proportions of widowed (and in the case of monogamous societies, divorced) women in the total society. The association of care for the elderly with the role of women is linked to the provision of domestic services, as well as to the aggressive part males play in social life; women are *domestiquée* in contrast to the *sauvage* male.

The situation may be reversed where women control property that is attractive to, or utilizable by, men, in other words, in societies where women inherit property from males as well as from females, a system which I speak of as "diverging devolution," best exemplified by the dowry. Heiresses, including widows, become attractive as partners to junior men, because of the property they have inherited from their parents or their husbands.

Marriages of this kind may well create tension not only generally between the generations but more specifically between father and son. Among the Fulani "adult sons are very critical of their father if he marries a young wife. They have less objection to his marrying an older woman, whom they regard merely as a helpmate for their aging mother and not as a woman with whom he will have regular sexual relations with the likelihood of her bearing children. Indeed, it is felt that if an old man marries a young wife she, being sexually frustrated, will engage in prostitution . . . Such a marriage may be referred to as . . . 'marriage of lust'" (Hopen, 1958, pp. 125–126) which may be viewed as an attempt to retain control over the family herd. On the other hand, the marriage of an elderly man to a young woman arouses minimal public disapproval when he is wealthy or has no living sons. Once again we see how the position of the aged is directly affected by the "family lottery," the number and sex of an individual's offspring.

RESIDENCE

In looking at the question of the role of the aged in the producing, consuming, and reproductive activities of the domestic group, we have inevitably touched upon the question of residence. Briefly summarizing a more complex situation, we can say that in the simpler societies, the members of one sex, usually the male, continue to live throughout their lives in the groups in which they were born. There is no problem of residential fission, no problem of the old being separated from the young. For the other sex (usually the female), the organizational alternatives for old age are remaining with one's husband or rejoining one's natal kin group, alternatives which are often closely linked with the system of inheritance and descent. Despite the dominance of virilocal residence (the wife joining the husband) in patrilineal societies, it should be insisted that the alternative is not isolation but a return to kin.

In agricultural societies age differentiation may lead to a separation of the young, for example, in the age villages of the Nyakyusa. In more complex societies, as we have seen, the question becomes more critical; in peasant communities the splitting of dwelling groups is often connected with the control and ownership of the farm, and especially with the early retirement of the head, either to separate rooms or to "an old people's house." In some of the more developed states, arrangements exist for the support or shelter of the indigent aged in special institutions distinct from the family, provisions which look toward the much more extensive extrafamilial arrangements of industrialized societies.

THE CALCULATION OF AGE

In non literate societies there is no conceptualization of absolute age calculated by time elapsed from a fixed position such as date of birth, since the reckoning of a birthday and its annual commemoration of time past, age attained, is dependent upon the existence of a calendrical system based upon an era, i.e., a point at which time begins, at least for the purpose of time-reckoning. In order to maintain such a mode of recording the passage of time, a graphic system is a virtual necessity. In theory, individual lives can be reckoned by stones in a bag or by notches on a tree; the counting of lengths of reign by dropping gold nuggets in a brass vessel has been reported (and queried) for at least one preliterate dynasty, the Brong of Ghana (Meyerowitz, 1952, p. 29). More usually, individuals place themselves comparatively (he was born before me), in relation to some irregular natural event (before the

flood), or in some loose way by reference to the passage of the seasons (he has seen 80 summers). Most frequently the reckoning of age is done by means of age categories or, in certain parts, of age classes and age groups.

AGE ORGANIZATION

The most usual form of differentiation is the age category, the various stages of life that are seen as characterized by rather diffuse activities and obligations. These labels Eisenstadt (1956) sees as generalized role dispositions into which specific roles may be built; they are the actor categories of child, adolescent, adult, and elder, current in a particular society. *Age grades* are more specific; here age-defined roles are linked into a graded system, which stresses movement from one to another, defining the relations between the grades and sometimes providing a specific occasion for the transfer by means of a *rite de passage*. Where a particular age grade is given importance, as with the grade of elderly men in some Australian peoples, then we may speak of the members as forming an *age class*; recruitment is made on an individual basis, depending upon a person's physiological state, such as puberty, or his social status, such as marriage or parenthood. In rural Ireland, during the long period between adolescence and becoming the head of a farm, men were known as "boys" and "married boys", a divided grade that could last until a person was 40 years of age. On many social occasions, such as a wake or a party, men cluster according to their subgrades, separated off from the gathering of family heads, seeking the companionship of their coevals in extrafamilial situations.

Such classes may take a more definite form when entry occurs not individually, but jointly, as with many ceremonies of initiation, where the participants are seen as having a special relation of friendship, egality, even quasi-kinship, one with another. Such is the case among the Nuer of the Southern Sudan and the nomadic Turkana of Kenya, where men acknowledge a common status based upon membership of a class, even though these units may not be corporate groups in the full meaning of the word: the class never gathers together or acts as a unit, nor does it pass through a series of grades. This further stage of formalization is known as *age groups*, consisting of a "permanent collection of people who recognize a degree of unity, . . . engage in particular activities, accept mutual obligations, and function as a group in relations with outsiders. Age-groups are usually named, may possess property . . . and are internally organized for decision making and leadership" (Gulliver, 1968, p. 159). In nonindustrial societies, organized groups of this kind were mainly to be found in sub-Saharan Africa, among some Plain Indians of North America, and among certain peoples in Brazil and India. Gulliver distinguishes two kinds of age-group system, the transitory and the comprehensive. The first comes into being to organize the activities of younger men and sometimes women, often operating for educational purposes, teaching the young about ritual or sexual behavior and the like. Among the centralized states of the southern Bantu, age groups were organized as regiments and labor battalions for the state.

Comprehensive age-group systems, where adolescents form a new group in which they remain throughout life, passing from age grade to age grade, are relatively rare. The classic case is that of the Masai where a man moves, along with his group, from junior to senior warrior, and thence to executive elder, to senior elder, and finally to "retired old man." In this particular case, and perhaps only here, the whole of Masai public life is administered through the age groups; the social system is built around the process of aging in a highly integrated manner. Other such comprehensive age-group systems work mainly in a ritual context and also tend to be found among societies without centralized political institutions.

Age differentiation does not of itself involve the physical separation of age categories, classes, or groups, though such separation may be incidental to the organization of age regiments with their barrack rooms or the allocation of special sleeping huts to young men. The separation of the young tends to lead to the separation of the old, at least temporarily. In some situations, such separation becomes more permanent. Among the Gonja of northern Ghana, a young man will often deliberately decide to build his house on the outskirts of the village, away from the compound of his father, so that the old residence, hallowed by years of family living and communal sacrifice, tends to fall into disrepair, while that of the physically vigorous sons presents a more prosperous picture.

THE ELDERS AS A CLASS

French anthropologists working in the Marxist tradition have recently paid much attention to the relationship between *ainés* (elders) and *cadets* (here, juniors), examining the ways in which the latter are "exploited" by the former, especially in relation to control over women. Part of the discussion, in the writings of Meillassoux (1964), Terray (1969, 1975), Rey (1971), and Dupré and Rey (1969), has centered upon the question of whether this relationship should be treated as one of "class." Clearly a very inclusive concept of class is in question. Moreover, the concept of the exploitation of the young by the old tends to be treated as a constant rather than a variable, thus neglecting not only the great differences between societies (Sahlins, 1972; Douglas, 1962; Lee, 1968, p. 36; and Richards, 1961, p. 402) but also the great differences in a relationship over time; there is often an explicit element of reciprocity arising from the fact that the contribution of the young toward the well-being of the old is balanced by the earlier contribution of parents to the care of the young. "Reciprocal altruism," it has been suggested, is a positively selected trait among humans as among other species, but it only operates over a given span of time (Trivers, 1971, 1974).

AGE AND THE SOCIAL SYSTEM

In the following sections I want to deal with the role of the aged in the kinship, political, and religious spheres; their economic roles have already been sufficiently discussed.

Kinship

From the numerical standpoint, the aged will have no ascendants (except the ancestors), few coevals, and many descendants; they sit on a lonely pyramid, playing the roles of grandparent rather than sibling or parent. The relationship of grandparent to grandchild is generally a benevolent one. Whatever conflicts persist into old age between adjacent generations, the ties between alternate generations are usually relaxed. As far as women are concerned, the ease of the relationship is often associated with the care a grandmother provides. In rural societies everywhere, the "work" contribution of women is often directly linked to the presence of an elderly parent who can care for the children; in the absence of servants, such services are of great value. Grandfathers make a less immediate contribution to the domestic economy. Nevertheless, these relations contrast even more strongly with parental ones being characterized by what has been called "joking."

From the standpoint of terminology, two interesting facts emerge. Firstly, terms for the second parental generation are frequently not "basic," i.e., they are derived from the parental ones (e.g., grand*father*). Secondly, they are usually "merged"; one term is often used for both a man's grandparents of the same sex, even in systems that stress unilineal kinship (i.e., through the father *or* the mother). The first feature emphasizes the developmental aspects of kinship roles; the second indicates the overriding stress on age (or rather generation) at the end points of the developmental cycle; lineage differentiation ceases to be the dominant criterion.

The position of the old in domestic groups is somewhat different from that in wider kingroups. In these more inclusive groups, the authority structure is often closely linked to age (or generation) so that elders (and often women) may find themselves in key positions, especially in the political and religious spheres.

Politics

Politics is an area, even in industrial societies, where old age is rarely an impediment to office. In the Western world, political leaders are often active long after others have retired, and the same is true in nonindustrial societies. Indeed, where "blood" (or filiation) is part of the requirement of office and legitimizes the choice of incumbent, a man may well be separated from his position only by death. Even senility may not lead to his retirement. In the kingdom of Gonja, in northern Ghana, there was a special office to which a decrepit paramount was entitled, the Bure chiefship; in fact, it was rarely, if ever, filled, and I have seen a divisional chief, scarcely able to speak, being carried into his courtroom to take part in the decision-making process. His judgement, delivered to the assembled audience by the spokesman, appeared to be that official's interpretation of "the sense of the meeting." Nonetheless, it was seen as coming from the lips of the chief rather than of his advisers. These instances of recumbent rulers and incompetent incumbents are clearly related to the divinity of kings, discussed in another context by Sir James Frazer and Marc Bloch. If authority is legitimized by association with the cosmological system, it is less easy for subjects to reject; equally, it is more difficult to strip the aged of the insignia of office, though real power may lie elsewhere. In any case, the maintenance of the old in political office delays the problem of succession and puts off the disorder that so often marks these periods of transition. An interest in peace postpones the transfer of title.

Religion

The position of religious roles is similar to that of political ones; indeed, the two are sometimes united in one person. Perhaps the continuing role of the aged is even more important here; while elderly kings are moving out of the political system, elderly priests are moving into the religious sphere. Since the power of the elders does not rest upon the strength of their arms, they no longer command obedience through their achievements in man's central activities, in fighting, in production, nor yet in sex. The dominance of the elders must be maintained by "tradition," inertia, familial continuity, by the pietas of those below. A factor of great importance is the ritual strength which continues to reside in the old.

This factor operates on three levels. Firstly, there is the accumulation of knowledge, not confined to religious matters. Secondly, the elder is the "natural" intermediary with the ancestors. In any system where the ancestors are the objects of worship (and even of cult), the elders are not only the nearest to the ancestors in genealogical terms (and in this respect are living ancestors with "one foot in the grave"), they are also progenitors of the maximum number of descendants, the apical ancestors of the living. On both these grounds they are the most appropriate persons to conduct sacrifices and other forms of communication with the other world. So the aged are not only the present givers (since they usually perform the sacrifices or the prayers), they are at the same time the future receivers (when they join the heavenly throng). This statement holds true of most societies (and they are virtually all) that have some notion of the persistence of the human persona after death, at least of the soul or spiritual part. Elders are close to ancestors; filial piety is blessed by the gods as well as by the philosophers; and supernatural sanctions are often intrinsic to a society's attitude toward, and treatment of, its aged members.

Thirdly, the very weakness of the senior generation makes their curses and their blessings more powerful. The ability to change the world by words alone is often seen as characteristic of those who cannot change it by other means; hence, the curse of the beggar, the gypsy, the outsider, and the weak has much greater force than that of the soldier, the chief, or the politician; it is equally so with the young and the old. In other words, the obligations of the young toward the old, which in one sense balance the obligations of parents towards children (earlier in the life cycle but simultaneous from a societal standpoint), is reinforced by a belief in the ritual powers of the latter, through their knowledge, their closeness to the ancestors, and their power to curse and bless.

AGE, KNOWLEDGE, AND LEARNING

There is one aspect of old age in societies without writing to which little attention has been paid. Whatever innovations and changes a new generation succeeds in introducing into a par-

ticular society, they are directly dependent on their immediate predecessors for acquiring their language and their culture. While this is true of all societies, in nonliterate ones the vast majority of communications have to be face-to-face; whereas with writing, indirect communication through books and other graphic techniques becomes of increasing importance. Given books, the old appear no longer necessary, indeed even redundant, as repositories of wisdom. Learning is not confined to the familial context. In oral societies, the aged are always an important resource for information about the past and hence about tradition and the right way of doing things; they remain "useful" not simply as repositories of family lore but as repositories of social life itself. This is particularly so of communicative acts that become relevant only at long intervals. For example, the performance of the 60-year ceremony of the Sigi of the Dogon must depend very greatly upon the childhood memories of old men, without whom the ceremony might disappear, or anyhow suffer a sea change. Other central rites of society, such as the funeral ceremonies of chiefs, depend for their continuity upon the supply of old men and women, who thus provide a cultural fund of a very significant kind. Their memories are other people's culture.

Even when industrial societies return to visual and oral modes of communication by the use of radio and television, transmission is taken out of the familial or communal context. It is not the senior generation in one's own family or kin group that remain the significant others, the important reference points in one's personal system of orientation.

This chapter has attempted to present some general aspects, analytic and substantive, on aging in nonindustrial societies. I have given little emphasis to the fact of "geronticide" reported for various hunting and nomadic peoples because too much stress has already been placed on this side of things. Comparative age is clearly of great significance in the simpler societies, though increasing social differentiation automatically reduces its importance: a young royal is more important than an old commoner. The position of the old is always influenced by the decrease of effective powers, but this loss may be compensated by the gain in other spheres, particularly the religious one. A specific concept of retirement exists in most peasant societies, since it is often intrinsic to the system of marriage and "class." But while the aged are sometimes grouped into age classes, it seems inadequate to consider them to be a "class" in the socioeconomic sense, especially as this suggests that they are the exploiters rather than the exploited.

ACKNOWLEDGMENTS

I am particularly indebted to L. W. Simmons' survey of the aged in primitive societies as well as to P. H. Gulliver's article on age differentiation in the *Encyclopedia of the Social Sciences*.

REFERENCES

Arensberg, C. M., and Kimball, S. T. 1961. *Family and Community in Ireland*. Gloucester, Massachusetts: Peter Smith.

Carrasco, P. 1959. *Land and Polity in Tibet*. Seattle: University of Washington Press.

Collomp, A. 1972. Famille nucléaire et famille élargie en Provence au XVIIIe siècle. *Annales E.S.C.*, **4–5**, 969–977.

Douglas, M. 1962. Lele economy as compared with the Bushong. *In*, G. Dalton and P. Bohannan (eds.), *Markets in Africa*, pp. 211–233. Evanston, Illinois: Northwestern University Press.

Dupré, G., and Rey, P. P. 1969. Réflections sur la pertinence d'une théorie des échanges. *Cah. Int. de Sociologie*, **46**, 133–162.

Eisenstadt, S. N. 1956. *From Generation to Generation: Age Groups and Social Structure*. Glencoe, Illinois: The Free Press. London: Routledge.

Goody, E. N. 1973. *Contexts of Kinship*. Cambridge: Cambridge University Press.

Goody, J. 1958. The fission of domestic groups among the LoDagaba. *In*, J. Goody (ed.), *The Developmental Cycle in Domestic Groups*, pp. 53–91. Cambridge: Cambridge University Press.

Goody, J. 1962. *Death, Property and the Ancestors*. Stanford, California: Stanford University Press.

Goody, J. 1969. "Normative," "recollected" and "actual" marriage payments among the LoWiili, 1951–1966. *Africa*, **39**, 54–61.

Goody, J. 1972a. *Domestic Groups*. Addison-Wesley Module in Anthropology, 28. Reading, Massachusetts: Addison-Wesley.

Goody, J. 1972b. *The Myth of the Bagre*. Oxford: Clarendon Press.

Gulliver, P. H. 1968. Age differentiation. *In, International Encyclopedia of the Social Sciences*. Vol. I. New York: Collier-Macmillan.

Hopen, C. E. 1958. *The Pastoral Fulbe Family in Gwandu*. London: Oxford University Press.

Laslett, P. 1969. Size and structure of the household in England over three centuries. *Population Studies*, **23**, 199–223.

Laslett, P., and Wall, R. (eds.) 1972. *Household and Family in Past Time*. Cambridge: Cambridge University Press.

Lee, R. 1968. What hunters do for a living, or, How to make out on scarce resources. *In*, R. Lee and I. DeVore (eds.), *Man the Hunter*. Chicago: Aldine.

Markham, C. R. (ed.) 1871. *First Part of the Royal Commentaries of the Yncas*. Vol. ii. London: The Hakluyt Society.

Meillassoux, C. 1964. *Anthropologie économique des Gouro de Côte d'Ivoire*. Paris: Mouton.

Meyerowitz, E. L. R. 1952. *Akan Traditions of Origin*. London: Faber and Faber.

Pollock, F., and Maitland, F. W. 1898. *History of English Law*. Vol. II. Cambridge: Cambridge University Press.

Rey, P. P. 1971. *Colonialisme, Néo-colonialisme, et Transition au Capitalisme; exemple de la 'Comilog' au Congo-Brazzaville*. Paris: Maspero.

Richards, A. 1961. *Land, Labour and Diet in Northern Rhodesia*. 2nd ed. London: Oxford University Press.

Sahlins, M. D. 1972. *Stone Age Economics*. New York: Aldine-Atherton.

Simmons, L. W. 1970. *The Role of the Aged in Primitive Society*. Hamden, Connecticut: Archon Books.

Spencer, P. 1965. *The Samburu. A Study of Gerontocracy in a Nomadic Tribe*. London: Routledge & Kegan Paul.

Stenning, D. J. 1958. Household viability among the pastoral Fulani. *In*, J. Goody (ed.), *The Developmental Cycle in Domestic Groups*, pp. 92–119. Cambridge: Cambridge University Press.

Terray, E. 1969. *Marxism and Primitive Societies*. Paris: Maspero. Reprint. 1972. London/New York: Monthly Review Press.

Terray, E. 1975. Classes and class consciousness in the Abron Kingdom of Gyaman. *In*, M. Bloch (ed.), *Marxist Analyses and Social Anthropology*, pp. 85–135. London: Malaby Press.

Trivers, R. L. 1971. The evolution of reciprocal altruism. *Quart. Rev. Biol.*, **46**, 35–57.

Trivers, R. L. 1974. Parent-offspring conflict. *Amer. Zool.*, **14**, 249–264.

Yang, M. C., 1947. *A Chinese Village: Taitou, Shantung Province*. London: Routledge & Kegan Paul.

6
GENERATIONS AND INTERGENERATIONAL RELATIONS:
Perspectives on Age Groups and Social Change

Vern L. Bengtson
and
Neal E. Cutler*
University of Southern California

The role of generational succession in social organization and change has been a recurrent theme in the history of social theory. In mankind's first writings, biological descent from a particular progenitor was a principal indicator of the individual's place in the social order, just as genealogies represented the primary means of demarcating periods of history (as reflected, for example, in the *Genesis* record of a group emerging from nomadic tribes into a more complex nation state).

But ranked descent within lineages—the first and simplest definition of generation—proved to be an inadequate frame of reference as later social historians attempted to explain relations among time, aging, and patterns of continuity in social structure. Nineteenth century scholars

came to define generations as age-peers who shared common historical and other social characteristics, often exhibiting a "collective mentality" and distinctive life patterns which set them apart from other contemporaneous groups (Mannheim, 1952 [1928]). The idea of social and historical generations, arising among individuals who shared common location in both historical time and in life-cycle development, suggested an important means of understanding patterns of differentiation within society and the causes of social change (Esler, 1972).

Recently there has been a resurgence of interest in the concept of generations. Contrasts between age groups became the topic of popular concern as evidenced in discussions of the "generation gap" frequently seen in the mass media. In the past decade many social scientists have begun to examine anew the interface between social and chronological generations. Analyzing contrasts in behavior among individuals of different ages, or as evidenced in the same person tested at three or more points in time, gerontologists in particular began to stress the importance of differentiating between three factors:

*Original data reported in this chapter are from studies supported by several sources: The National Science Foundation's RANN program (#ERP-72-03496), the Administration on Aging (#93-P-57621/9), the National Institutes of Mental Health (#MH 18158), and United Parcel Service's 1907 Foundation. The authors wish to thank Glen Elder and Kent Jennings for their suggestions on an earlier draft of this paper.

changes over time attributable to maturation or aging; those that are created by historical or period effects; and contrasts reflected in characteristics persisting throughout the life span of a specific age group (often termed "cohort" or "generational" effects.)

The distinction between *chronological* (or biological) and *social* generations is crucial. Despite increasingly frequent use of "generational" explanations in current social and behavioral science, often this distinction is not clearly drawn. The result has been some confusion in attempts to understand the role of generations in patterns of social change and stability through time. The purpose of this chapter is to explore four major issues in current generational analysis. First, what *is* a generation: or, to be more precise, what are the major perspectives or definitions of this construct found in current examinations of trends or contrasts related to aging or the passage of time? Second, at the macrosocial level of analysis, in what ways do contrasting groups identified by the various criteria of generational membership differ with respect to specified attitudes or behaviors? How does a generational perspective assist social scientists in explaining such observed contrasts? Third, what are the microlevel patterns of interaction and influence observable between generations, especially with regard to older family members? Finally, what are the prospects for the emergence of a social or historical "generation" of the elderly, analogous to other "generations" identified among youth during the past decade or in earlier historical periods?

There are three major ways in which the generational concept has been employed in theory and in research. First is the *cohort* perspective, a focus which emphasizes demographic attributes of age groups. Born during a given period of history, a particular age cohort experiences in similar ways the consequences of historical events. This view emphasizes the role of age groups in macrosocial differentiation. A second approach, generation as *lineage*, offers the most appropriate perspective for examining micropatterns of continuity and discontinuity through the socialization process, especially as evident within the family context. A third orientation to generations, focusing on subunits of age cohorts as *historically conscious agents of social action*, offers insight into the social construction of age categories and their role in historical movements. It highlights potential elements of conflict among contemporaneous age groups and, among the alternative generation concepts, attempts to deal most directly with the episodic nature of social change and the connections between social change and age groups.

In this chapter we will examine conceptual issues involved in the construct "generation." One theme is that all three conceptualizations (age cohort, lineage, and generation unit) make contributions in their own right. To use the vernacular, the "generation gap" should be conceptually decomposed into three constituent elements: cohort gap, lineage gap, and generation unit gap. Each perspective offers different insight into the problem of time, aging, and change in social structure. But it is important not to confuse the essential elements of the three, and to be aware of where they overlap and where they are distinctive.

A second theme of the chapter is that the three basic manifestations of the generation concept are of considerable relevance to gerontologists as major alternative perspectives to the maturational explanation of age trends and apparent age changes. Observed age differences cannot necessarily be attributed simply to developmental age change; each of the three orientations to generational analysis sensitizes the observer to alternative explanatory systems. The tendency to proffer single-hypothesis explanations for age-group differences or trends over time, as frequently reflected in past gerontological and social change analyses, is inadequate. Awareness of multiple factors and multiple perspectives is necessary in order to untangle the complex relations among time, human aging, and alterations in social organization and behavior.

THE PROBLEM OF GENERATIONS: CONCEPTUALIZING TIME, AGE GROUPS, AND SOCIAL STRUCTURE

The problem of generations, as addressed by philosophers and poets throughout history, centers on understanding the effects on social structure of aging and the succession of age groups. What is the relationship between the continuous succession of one generation by another and the frequent but irregular emergence of distinctive social movements and behavioral styles across historical periods? The varied answers to this classic human dilemma reflected different approaches to concepts of time, age groups and aging, and social structure as applied by scholars across the centuries (see Feuer, 1969; Marías, 1968; Spitzer, 1973).

Pre-Socratic social theorists, seeking rational explanation for changes they observed in the political and social order, turned to the age-related facts of birth, succession, decline, and death as exhibited by successive generations of individuals. To these and early modern European scholars, the cycle of generational emergence seemed a sensible way to account for the growth and decline of dynasties, ideologies, religions, even artistic styles; these alterations in social structure and culture often appeared to follow some periodic rhythm. However, most such explanations which simplistically linked cultural progression to the biological succession of generations proved to be inadequate even for prescientific scholars. Social historians in the nineteenth and early twentieth centuries turned to more elaborate models of within-generation elites as active agents of socio-political change (Dilthey, 1924; Mannheim, 1952 [1928] ; Ortega y Gasset, 1933 [1923]).

For various reasons, the efforts of these philosophers and social historians did not come to be incorporated into the mainstream of theory regarding social change, at least not in American sociology. Within the past decade, however, many social scientists have returned to the theme of temporal placement—in terms of historical time and life-course or developmental time—as a means of better understanding trends and changes in behavior and social organization. In particular, such issues have been addressed by gerontologists employing a comparative life-cycle perspective to issues of behavioral change over time.

While the broader historical and life-span comparative framework represents considerable advantages, it also brings with it new problems. In particular, there is the problem of *interpretation*: when patterns of age differences in social attitudes and behavior are discovered, they may be attributed not only to the effects of matura-

tion or individual aging but to other factors as well. Parallel developments in psychology (Baltes, 1968; Schaie, 1965); sociology (Elder, 1974, 1975; Mason, Mason, Winsborough, and Poole, 1973; Riley, Johnson, and Foner, 1972); economics (Lansing and Sonquist, 1969); and political science (Cutler, 1969; Jennings and Niemi, 1974, 1975) have indicated that comparisons among age groups which might at first inspection appear to document *life-cycle or developmental differences* may in fact be more appropriately explained in terms of *demographic* or *birth-cohort* factors, or be manifestations of even more general *historical* or *period-specific* trends. Or, when viewed from the perspective of social movements, these effects may be intertwined with other aspects of differentiation in a manner producing *historically-conscious generation units*—subgroups within birth cohorts with particular ideologies leading to collective action or distinctive life-styles. In short, age differences observed at a single point in time do not always signal age changes in a developmental or aging sense; nor are they necessarily indicators of social change at the broader level of cultural history. It is here that the concept of "generation" is often employed.

Levels of Analysis: Temporal and Structural Considerations.

The principal goal in generational analysis is to apply a comparative framework to the problem of age groups, succession, and change in social structure. The apparently distinctive attitudes or actions of youth or the elderly can be better understood when looking across dimensions of social time and space, comparing one age group with others in contemporary society, or contrasting a given age cohort with those of the same age in previous decades (Bengtson and Starr, 1975; Elder, 1975; Esler, 1966).

But in order to examine such issues it is necessary to specify explicitly the levels of *temporal* location and of *social-structural* location involved in the description of age groups and social configurations. It is also necessary to recognize that the construct of generations involves both *microlevel* and *macrolevel* applications, distinguishing between the individual and the broader social system.

Unfortunately, the term *generation* is currently employed in the social sciences in a variety of ways (see Troll, 1970). This has led to considerable difficulties in comparing the conclusions of scholars who use a "generational" explanation. The central problem involves varying *levels of analysis*, often unrecognized by the investigator, concerning temporal and social-structural location. This can be seen in examining the central contributions of the three major perspectives of the concept "generation." Each has different implications with respect to the analysis and interpretation of change over time, and to the relationship between aging and social stability or change.

Generations as Cohorts: Historical Location and Age Group Differentiation

Most gerontologists and demographers have tended to treat generational location as a social membership category similar to class, race, or sex, deliberately eschewing the term *generation* (Riley, Johnson, and Foner, 1972; Ryder, 1965). The substitution of "age stratum" or "age cohort" represents an explicit attempt to focus on the macrolevel of analysis and to avoid any intermingling of the lineage implications of generation. Nonetheless, although demographers often focus on the basic population composition of successive cohorts, the concept of generation has taken on a more extensive meaning as used and adapted by sociologists (e.g., Glenn and Hefner, 1972), psychologists (e.g., Nesselroade and Baltes, 1974; Schaie, 1965; Woodruff and Birren, 1972), and political scientists (e.g., Abramson, 1974). These analyses point to the behavioral and social change which results from a particular interaction of demographic facts *and* historical circumstances.

Thus, the cohort conceptualization of generation focuses explicitly on a macroperspective of social stability or change and of the role which aging and age groups play in understanding both the current and the future configurations of social systems. Within a specified historical period, society is represented by a continuous flow of successive birth cohorts. At any given time, the age structure of a society represents different cohorts, each at a different stage of its life-cycle development (Riley, Johnson, and Foner, 1972, ch. 1 and 2). Thus, to understand the genesis of behavioral orientations among "old people," one should recognize that these orientations represent the intersection of (a) a particular birth cohort which is (b) at a particular chronological or developmental age, with (c) the events and nature of a society at that point in time. Mannheim (1952 [1928]) notes that this intersection is unique, for each historical period will be confronted by a different group of individuals who represent different birth cohorts and different first-hand historical experiences. Thus, even if maturational processes were to stay the same, one is dealing not only with different historical influences but also with different people—born, reared, and maturing in an historical context which contrasts with that of today's older person (Cain, 1967).

The interconnection between the flow of successive birth cohorts and system stability or change is further indicated by what may be called the process of cohort differentiation. *Intercohort* differentiation, along such dimensions as differential fertility, contrasts in average age of marriage, and differentials in economic opportunity, influences the magnitude of the size and the compositional contrasts between adjacent cohorts. Such contrasts may precipitate social conflicts when, for example, a large birth cohort (the "baby boom") following a small birth cohort finds school and job opportunities relatively less available than they were for the preceding cohort.

Intracohort differentiation, although less frequently discussed, is also an important implication of the cohort generation perspective. Although members of a birth cohort may be exposed to a common set of sociopolitical events at a common point in their life-cycle development, racial, class, or geographic factors may affect the way in which these events are experienced (Laufer and Bengtson, 1974). The orientation of the cohort may reflect the general circumstances of the cohort's intersection with history; yet subgroups may react quite differently to what Heberle (1951) has called "decisive sociopolitical events" (see, for example, Elder, 1974; Esler, 1966).

Thus, the processes of cohort differentiation work to identify the members of a cohort with respect to social location. Identifying age groups and their relation to social change in this way focuses on the historical intersection of (a) individuals born at a particular time; and (b) the unique socialization experience of those individuals at a common time in their psychological, biological, and social development.

Generations as Lineage Differentiation: The Family and Socialization

A second major conceptualization of the construct of generation concerns *lineage position*: ranked descent within a family. Emanating primarily from anthropological studies of power and prestige in kinship-based social systems, generation in this context focuses on differentiations between, and interaction patterns among, parents, children, and grandparents within the family unit (at the microlevel) and between aggregates of parents and children (at the macrolevel). The processes of intergenerational transmission, of continuities and discontinuities evident as the product of socialization, are a particular focus of analysis. Thus, the lineage connotation of generation involves a slightly different consideration of temporal birth location ("age") than does the "age-cohort" conceptualization.

An elementary process requisite to the continued function of any social system over time concerns the transmission of orientations and attributes from one generation to the next. The lineage perspective on generations (which, as will be noted below, need not be limited to analysis of intrafamily relations) provides an explicit perspective on dealing with these basic aspects of social behavior. The focus is on age groups in a socialization-based context of interaction in which the aging process produces a succession of roles which have substantial influences on behavior orientations (see, for example, Bengtson and Starr, 1975; Reiss, 1968; and the chapters by Neugarten and Hagestad, Riley, Rosow, and Back in this volume). Patterns of adaptation to the changing roles and the potential for resultant conflict or consensus are important topics of interest.

While gerontological research has often focused on the chronological age dimensions of the individual's development and maturation, the lineage perspective directs attention to significant changes in the interpersonal network in which the individual is enmeshed. But life-cycle and lineage-related roles are not invariantly correlated with chronological age. While some individuals become parents at 20, others have children for the first time at 30; in some families grandparenthood comes at age 45, while in others it is delayed until 65. Thus, in the lineage perspective the processes of social aging are seen through the inspection of ways in which significant social roles themselves become the indicators of life-cycle change. Such a perspective is quite different from that of the strict cohort conceptualization or the unadorned chronological-biological view of aging.

The lineage approach to generations also calls attention to the crucial process of socialization. At the microlevel the focus is on preparation of the individual to take on the succession of roles, and of correlated changes of the individual's attitudes and behavior. At the macrolevel, the focus is on cultural stability or change over time as the result of such socialization.

The intricacies of intergenerational transmission are beyond the scope of this overview (see Baltes and Schaie, 1973; Clausen, 1968; and Goslin, 1969 for reviews). However, four points should be emphasized in passing. First, socialization is in many respects a bilateral process involving mutual influence. Although social location is identified in terms of hierarchical role relationships and although typically the older generation is seen as the socialization agent of the younger, the old may also learn much from the young (Goslin, 1969; Mead, 1970). And, in a continuously changing society, both learn together as changes created by technological innovations, demographic shifts, and sociopolitical events alter the social system and the individual's perceptions of it (Bengtson and Black, 1973).

Second, the actors in an intergenerational relationship are dynamic representatives of their birth cohort—dynamic in that each generation is acting out its own developmental agenda. As the actors themselves age with the passage of time, the social dimensions of the parent-child relationship are continuously renegotiated (Bengtson and Black, 1973).

Third, the levels of analysis described previously become mutually reinforcing: microlevel socialization processes evident within families are affected by the macrolevel events of historical periods. While young and old may respond to the environmental stimuli differently, each in accordance with their own developmental agenda, such events will nonetheless affect the relationship in what may be termed the psychohistorical nature of the socialization relationship which varies across generational cohorts (Bronfenbrenner, 1961; Cutler, 1975; Elder, 1974).

Fourth, the implications of transmissions across generations should not be limited to parent-child dyads. Socialization in its basic meaning refers to the transmission of information from incumbent to neophyte. Although used principally to refer to the parent-child relationship, the lineage perspective may more generally be employed whenever an age-graded exchange within a particular dyad is implied. In increasingly complex, industrialized societies, social institutions other than the family have come to have important training functions for the younger generation; consequently, the developmental agenda and generational stake concepts noted above influence age-based lineage relationships in a wide variety of societal contexts. It is necessary to note the possible tension between parents and other socialization agents. These too can be examined as macrolevel phenomena, contrasting aggregates of parents and children (see, for example, Jennings and Niemi, 1975; Bengtson, 1975).

Generations as Historical Consciousness: Mannheim and Generation Units

Both conceptualizations of the generation construct discussed so far rely primarily on objective or positivistic indicators of generational location: birth-cohort on the one-hand, lineage position in age-graded socialization relationship on the other. Both consider the historical context in which the age groups mature and accede to adult roles; both, explicitly and implicitly, thus attempt to deal with aging and social change. But neither perspective, in focusing on objective or chronological conditions creating a "generation," is totally convincing in accounting for the very issue which has made the "problem of generations" a classical human theme: the periodic emergence of distinctive political movements or social styles, crystallized by specific age groups.

The perspective on generations which most directly addresses the issue of age groups as dynamic, change-producing collectivities arising at certain points of time is the tradition of Karl Mannheim (1952 [1928]). Indeed, recent revival of interest in the concept of generations in empirical social science is greatly attributable to his seminal formulation of generational dynamics. Mannheim's work reflects the intellectual tradition of Continental social historians who used the tools of logical analysis to develop early sociology. Perhaps Mannheim's most influential contribution to modern social science is his translation of classical idealistic philosophy into sociology: reality, as man experiences it, is socially defined. Thus, the basis for human behavior is an awareness or "consciousness" of positions and expectations, and of the possibility for collective action in altering existing social institutions. This perspective has significant implications for those studying aging for it reminds us of the social construction of age positions and the collective definition of age groups (Bengtson, Kasschau, and Ragan, 1976; Elder, 1975).

For Mannheim, a generation represents a unique type of social location based on the dynamic interplay of *demographic facts* (being born during a certain period) and the particular configuration of *sociopolitical events* which occurred during the period of that cohort's coming of age. Mannheim went beyond this "objective" characterization of generations, however, to include the crucial "subjective" element which created, of some birth-cohorts, a "true generation." This element he termed *historical consciousness:* a sense of group identity and purpose coming from an awareness of participation in history.

The idea that components of emerging birth cohorts can, and occasionally do, develop a consciousness of themselves as a unique group with a distinctive ideology and political purpose was supported by Mannheim in his analysis of the episodic emergence of social movements in the late nineteenth century. Mannheim noted that each successive youth cohort has "fresh contact" with existing social institutions and ideology. The new perspectives result in an inevitable questioning of the established social order and, under certain circumstances (such as "politically traumatic" events), lead to the formation of a "generation unit" which is the active, dynamic force in the forging of social movements and, occasionally, revolutions. Mannheim thus contrasted the "actual generation" and "generation unit" from the contemporaneous youth cohort experiencing "fresh contact" of which they are a part:

Youth experiencing the same concrete historical problems may be said to be part of the same actual generation; while those groups within the same actual generation which work up the material of their common experience in different specific ways, constitute separate generation units (Mannheim, 1952 [1928], p. 304).

Mere contemporaneity does not, in itself, produce a common generational location. "Only where contemporaries are definitely in a position to participate as an integrated group in certain common experiences can we rightly speak of a community of location of a generation" (p. 119). This can be termed a "generation effect" in the strict meaning of social change: a distinctive consciousness or ideology which will persist throughout the life-cycle biography of that group.

A final point of Mannheim's conceptualization concerns the impact of period events in the formation of "collective mentality" or ideological generation units. Whether a youth cohort produces its own "distinctive unity of style" (regardless of whether it consciously emphasizes its character as a generation unit) depends upon the tempo of technological or cultural change. The more rapid the pace of technological or political change, the greater the probability that "particular generation location groups will react to changed situations by producing their own entelechy" (p. 125).

This idea has been found particularly useful by sociologists and political scientists examining the manifestations of youth protest and counter-culture styles of the 1960's, when a unique configuration of demographic events (a large birth cohort) coincided with widespread disaffection with political policies and adult institutions (the Vietnam War, educational policies, Civil Rights) to produce a "generation of dissent" (Braungart, 1974; Fendrich, 1974; Langman, Block, and Cunningham, 1973; Starr, 1974; Weider and Zimmerman, 1974).

Mannheim gave a very specific meaning to the concept of "generation unit"—as a component of a birth cohort or age group which holds a common relationship to a political, social, economic, and cultural system, and which has organized self-consciously to change that system. But Mannheim's use of the concept becomes theoretically vague concerning such questions as: where does one look for these carriers of social change? why do they arise in some periods of history and not in others? what causes an age cohort to achieve "consciousness"? whatever happened to the Youth Movements of the 1960's? The imprecision of Mannheim's use of the concept probably has contributed to its generally limited use (Buss, 1974; Goertzel, 1972). In fact, the occasional use of the concept "generation" as an action category in social change has led to considerable skepticism by more quantitatively oriented social scientists—for example, demographers and developmental psychologists (Laufer and Bengtson, 1974).

As a more general result of this vagueness, many social scientists examining aging have emptied the concept of generation of its active political meaning—as best understood in the context of the Marxian tradition of class consciousness within which Mannheim developed his sociology of knowledge—and have treated generational location simply in birth-cohort terms. The crux of Mannheim's concept of generation units, however, lies in its intermingling of birth-cohort categories, historical experience, and political consciousness. The social action consequences of the confluence of these factors represents a more elaborate analytic framework than is typically contained in the cohort approach to generational analysis.

INTERGENERATIONAL CONTRASTS IN ATTITUDES AND OPINIONS: THE COHORT PERSPECTIVE

As reviewed in the previous section, there are three major meanings of the concept of generations as used in philosophical and scientific analysis. This section explores in more detail the cohort approach to the problem of generations. In particular it focuses on problems of *interpretation* which arise in examining age-related or time-trend explanations. We will return to the lineage and Mannheim perspective on generations in subsequent sections.

The cohort approach to generational analysis focuses attention on aggregates of individuals who, having been born in the same period, are socialized in a common slice of social history. As they age they "carry" with them the impact of their early experiences and, consequently, their interpretations of and orientations toward a variety of social issues. But since people do change the question becomes: do observed attitudes and behavior represent the effect of *N* years of aging, or do they represent the long-standing beliefs of those born *N* years ago who hold attitudes reflecting the period of adolescent or early adult socialization? Similarly, the scholar must consider the possibility that historical events affect the attitudes of all age groups equally, i.e., that neither aging nor generational differences are operative in a particular configuration of attitudes. In short, the student of aging and generations must consider a *maturational* or developmental *aging* hypothesis, a generational or *cohort* hypothesis, and finally, the *historical* or *period* hypothesis.

Until recently, the prevalent approach in social scientific analysis involving age differences was to examine a given attitudinal phenomenon in the context of just one of these three competing hypotheses. And in many cases, the hypothesis fails to be disconfirmed simply because the investigator did not have evidence of the competing substantive hypotheses for comparison. For example, studies of aging and alienation, or cohort differences in political attitudes, cannot by themselves provide conclusive evidence validating a maturational or a generational hypothesis *unless* evidence for the three com-peting hypotheses are included in the analysis (Cutler, 1974a). Thus, it is important to recognize that conclusions about any of the three age-related explanations should be understood in the context of the research design and data base in which they were advanced—typically, without the empirical test of competing explanations.

The purpose of the present discussion is to illustrate the facility of generational cohort analysis in resolving conflict among the three alternative age-related hypothesis. In doing so we will confine our presentation to three case-examples which are well represented in extant research: political party identification, political alienation, and attitudes toward governmental involvement in the provision of medical care. A more general and comprehensive review of the relationship of age factors to society and politics is found in Chapter 15 of this volume; a discussion of methodological and statistical models relevant to cohort analysis is outlined in Chapter 1 (see also Baltes, 1968; Hyman, 1972; Mason *et al.*, 1973; Schaie, 1965).

Generations and Political Party Identification

Competing hypotheses. It is popularly believed that aging *brings about* a more conservative perspective in social and political orientations. An interesting controversy in recent studies of political attitudes is based upon this assumption of age-induced conservatism and focuses on age patterns of public support for the Republican and Democratic parties in the United States. Each of the three competing hypotheses of generational cohort, maturation, and period effects, taken by itself, could be supported by available data. When evidence for just one of the explanations is presented, it is possible to conclude that it is *the* appropriate explanation of age-based patterns of party identification.

Some analyses have concluded that *maturation* is the main underlying factor and have presented evidence pointing to life-cycle maturational changes favoring the Republican Party. Crittenden (1962), for example, examined data from a series of national Gallup surveys taken in the 1940's and 1950's. In each year the older age groups were seen to be more Republican than the younger age groups. The analyst concluded that the explanatory hypothesis was that of maturational aging: "Aging seems to produce a shift toward Republicanism in the period 1946 to 1958.... The pattern appears to be linear" (Crittenden, 1962, p. 654).

The *generational cohort* explanation, by contrast, is stressed in a study which looked at the contemporary party identifications of young voters who entered the political system during the Depression-New Deal era. Campbell, Converse, Miller, and Stokes (1960) found that this cohort of voters maintained a Democratic party identification of a much stronger nature than would be predicted from such variables as age change and socioeconomic factors. The analysis concluded that the events of the early 1930's had precipitated the creation of a heavily-Democratic generation of voters whose identifications were, in the aggregate, substantially maintained throughout the life cycle of members of that group (p. 155).

Historical or *period* effects have been noted in trend studies which have found various historical alternations of patterns in party identifications in the United States in the recent past (e.g., Scammon and Wattenberg, 1970; Pomper, 1975). The results of recent presidential and congressional elections clearly document changes in the popularity of the two major American parties. Political analysts and pundits have noted dozens of political, economic, social, and psychological factors which plausibly account for at least some of these changes in the structure of partisan attachments over past elections (e.g., Axelrod, 1972; Converse, Miller, Rusk, and Wolfe, 1969; Pomper, 1972).

Of particular relevance is the role which generational trends might play in this sequence of political changes. Aside from the attractiveness of particular candidates or party platforms, to what degree are changes in patterns of attitudes attributable to the entrance of new generations of citizens into the electorate (Abramson, 1975; Cutler and Schmidhauser, 1975)? Certain elements of contemporary politics might affect the orientations of these new cohorts but not so strongly affect the firmly-held opinions and party attachments of older voters (Carlsson and Karlsson, 1970). *The basic point is that any analysis of these possibilities must take all three hypotheses into account since each one, by itself, potentially offers a plausible explanation of social trends.*

Evidence of multiple effects. The issue of trends in partisan attachments has received substantial scholarly attention in recent years, and the question of the measurement and meaning of age differences has represented an interesting area of controversy. Indeed, the generational perspective on patterns of party identification has played a major role in recent reviews of generational phenomena (Cutler, 1975; Spitzer, 1973) and in recent textbooks on research methods (Hyman, 1972, Chapter 7; Kirkpatrick, 1974, Chapter 5).

The basic evidence presented above supporting the maturational explanation represents a single-hypothesis analysis of age influences on patterns of party identification. As noted, Crittenden concluded that the relatively greater portions of Republicanism among the older groups was the result of the maturational dynamics of aging. A subsequent study, however, reanalyzed these data using a formal cohort analysis approach (Cutler, 1969). By looking at the pattern of aging longitudinally across cohorts, rather than by the cross-sectional comparison of old and young within each year, a different pattern of Republicanism over the 1946–1958 period was discovered. The conclusion of the later study is that there is no evidence of a consistent trend associated with aging favoring the Republican Party during this period; if anything, the data modestly supported a generational cohort effect.

A subsequent analysis of the same issue employed a more expansive data base (1945 to 1969) and a statistically more controlled application of cohort analysis (Glenn and Hefner, 1972). In analyzing their data, a portion of which is presented in Table 1, the investigators examined each cohort across time (and aging), rather than examining different age groups at one or more cross-sectional points in time. As the data demonstrate, there is no general movement toward Republicanism associated with aging. The dominant pattern is that of differences *between* the modal responses of the suc-

TABLE 1. PARTY IDENTIFICATION OF SEVEN COHORTS AT FOUR-YEAR INTERVALS, 1945-1969. (% REPUBLICAN IDENTIFICATION)[a]

Cohort number	Birth years	1945	1949	1953	1957	1961	1965	1969
1	1876–1885	48	38	39	46	43		
	(ages)	(60–69)	(64–73)	(68–77)	(72–81)	(76–85)		
2	1886–1895	40	33	35	39	41	34	39
	(ages)	(50–59)	(54–63)	(58–67)	(62–71)	(66–75)	(70–79)	(74–83)
3	1896–1905	33	31	31	36	35	29	33
	(ages)	(40–49)	(44–53)	(48–57)	(52–61)	(56–65)	(60–69)	(64–73)
4	1906–1915	31	30	30	30	28	27	29
	(ages)	(30–39)	(34–43)	(38–47)	(42–51)	(46–55)	(50–59)	(54–63)
5	1916–1925	23	22	29	29	23	21	26
	(ages)	(20–29)	(24–33)	(28–37)	(32–41)	(36–45)	(40–49)	(44–53)
6	1926–1935				31	23	24	26
	(ages)				(22–31)	(26–35)	(30–39)	(34–43)
7	1936–1945						20	23
	(ages)						(20–29)	(24–33)

[a]Percentages for each age group were computed for the four categories of Republican, Democratic, Independent, Other. Adapted from Glenn and Hefner (1972), Table 1, pp. 36–37.

cessive cohorts rather than noticeable age changes *within* cohorts. On the basis of this evidence and other aspects of their study, Glenn and Hefner conclude:

> Therefore, the thesis that cohorts experience an absolute increase in Republicanism as a consequence of aging receives no support from our data. . . . the positive association of Republicanism with age, consistently revealed by the cross-sectional data gathered at various times during the past 30 years or so, reflects intercohort (or "generational") differences rather than the effects of aging (p. 35).

> This study should rather conclusively lay to rest the once prevalent belief that the aging process has been an important influence for Republicanism in the United States (p. 47).

Generations and Political Alienation

Competing hypotheses. Much has been written about societal alienation in general as well as political alienation in particular. In 1969 a bibliography compiled by the National Institute of Mental Health listed 250 articles on the subject; a recent discussion of the relationship between political alienation and political behavior cites over 50 studies germane to the topic (Schwartz, 1973, Chapter 1). In various studies each of the three age-related hypotheses— maturation, generation, and period effects— have been examined. When only one of the hypothesized effects is included in a study, the conclusion may be improperly reached that aging or generational differences or historical period effects is responsible for observed patterns of alienation.

Maturation or life-cycle interpretations of alienation are represented by several studies of alienated youth. Flacks (1967), for example, focused on the role which alienation played in the protest political behavior of upper-middle class students in the mid-60's. Several studies have noted that among young people actual or perceived powerlessness is strongly related to alienation (e.g., Seeman, 1959). Thus, it is not surprising that studies such as those by Freidenberg (1959), Keniston (1965), and Whittaker and Watts (1969) have found that youth is a major locus of alienation in American society.

Studies of older people have also examined the maturational genesis of alienation. Many of the real or perceived losses in status, resources, and abilities which are associated with aging have been seen to contribute to an aging-based explanation of old-age alienation (e.g., Agnello, 1973; Martin, Bengtson, and Acock, 1973). Still other analyses of alienation have found that, perhaps for different reasons, both the young and the old represent the locus of alienation in contemporary American society (Miller, Brown, and Raine, 1973).

The *generational cohort* interpretation of political alienation has been supported by discussions indicating substantial discontinuities between age cohorts. Such labels as the "beat generation" or the "lost generation" allude to groups of individuals whose alienation affected them throughout their lives, not just in youth. A study of student activists of the mid-1960's concluded that they did not merely represent alienated youth; rather, the birth cohort represented by the student activists constitutes a distinct generation (Flacks, 1967; Keniston, 1968).

A review of several "generation gap" studies of youth (Bengtson, 1970) suggests that the gap between young and old sometimes represents differences in maturational level and life-stage responsibilities. Thus, in many instances, the differences between parents and their children are temporary phenomena rooted in developmental processes. Other analyses, however, argue that the observed discontinuities between young and old are so large, and substantively so important, that the contrast will never be closed. Such "Great Gap" proponents conclude that the alienation of youth is so great and so strongly connected to an inhumane and unjust political system that it should not be expected that the alienated youth will mature into traditionally involved adults (Friedenberg, 1969; Slater, 1970).

Trends in alienation can also be attributed to the societal events which comprise social and political history—a *period* interpretation. As was the case for party identification, specific events may effect levels of alienation aside from the impact of aging or generational influences. Thus, the assassination of leaders, the conduct of an undeclared and unpopular war, and the disclosure of massive immorality at the top levels of government can each contribute to increases in political alienation throughout society. Indeed, a correlational analysis of data covering the years 1952 to 1968 disclosed that trends in political alienation in the United States reflect period effect changes in the population as a whole, changes not attributable to identifiable age, region, sex, education, or income groups (House and Mason, 1975).

Evidence of multiple effects. Many studies of alienation present data which plausibly support one or the other of the three competing age-related hypotheses. For the present discussion, however, the issue becomes that of the degree to which any of the hypotheses is valid when all three are tested together in a data base which includes the same population, the same operational measures of the phenomenon, and the same analytic procedures.

A recent study attempting to incorporate such considerations (Cutler and Bengtson, 1974) applied a formal cohort analysis to a set of three items measuring political alienation, over the period 1952 to 1968. The structure of the cohort analysis facilitated the examination of aging, generational, and period effects. Some of these data are presented here in Table 2, reporting agreement with the statement, "People like me don't have any say about what the government does."

The pattern for this item, and the results of the study as a whole demonstrated that, for the 1952 to 1968 period, fluctuations in political alienation tended to affect all age and cohort groups similarly. All groups (except Cohort C, born between 1916–1923) witnessed a decrease in political alienation between 1952 and 1960, followed by a substantial increase in alienation between 1960 and 1968; in all cases the level of alienation in 1968 is greater than it was in 1952. The same pattern is seen whether one examines young life-stages or old life-stages (the rows in Table 2), or cohorts born at different points in time (the diagonals, Cohort A *vs.* Cohort E). Thus, the authors conclude that a *period or historical effect* is the most appropriate interpretation of these data, a conclusion supported by a statistically different approach to age analysis (House and Mason, 1975).

Generations and Social Policy Attitudes: Government Involvement in Medical Care

Competing hypotheses. The degree to which attitudes toward specific areas of social policy are related to age phenomena may depend primarily upon the nature of the issue. Many issues concern financial allocations which pro-

TABLE 2. COHORT ANALYSIS OF POLITICAL ALIENATION
1952-1968. (% GIVING ALIENATED RESPONSE)[a]

Age Group	Cohort Label	1952	1960	1968
	A			
21-28		31	10	31
	B			
29-36		28	26	34
	C			
37-44		25	25	37
	D			
45-52		29	29	40
	E			
53-60		35	27	49
61-68		40	32	54
69+		41	37	53
TOTAL		31	27	41

[a]Percentage agreeing with the statement "People like me don't have any say
about what the government does."   Adapted from Cutler and Bengtson
(1974), Table 1, p. 169.

vide specific benefits (or liabilities) to identifiable age groups. In such circumstances, it
might be expected that age will prove to be a
significant variable in the analysis of changes
or trends in the attitude.

One such policy orientation concerns government involvement in medical care programs
(the issue of costs and financing) and the role
which the federal government ought to play in
this issue. Since old people tend to be both
poor and ill, it might be initially expected that
an individual's support for federal programs
aimed at lowering the cost of medical care or

providing medical care insurance will increase
as a function of age.

Yet, as before, we must consider all three of
the competing hypotheses by which age may be
related to trends in a given orientation. The
maturational explanation is quite plausible as
we might expect support for medical care
programs to increase as the individual matures
into a life-stage characterized by increasing
medical bills and decreasing financial resources.
On the basis of studies of the national electorate in 1956 and 1960, Campbell (1962) concludes that older voters, more so than younger

voters, are supportive of federal medical care programs. He further concludes that the pattern of support represents an instance of a *group benefits* orientation—an orientation toward political issues which is framed not in ideological terms but in terms of whether or not the policy or program will benefit a particular group of which the individual is a member.

A more formal analysis of this issue (Schreiber and Marsden, 1972), using a sequence of similarly-worded items from presidential election surveys spanning the years 1956-1968 concludes that support for a governmental role is associated with increasing age. The study indicates that although there are some period shifts in the electorate's overall support for the issue, from a low of 64 percent in favor (1964) to a high of 75 percent in favor (1960), the age pattern is relatively consistent within each of the survey years: there is a general age-related increase in support for government programs of medical aid. In each year the younger age groups exhibit lower support, and the oldest age group (65 and over), the highest amount of support.

The *generational* hypothesis may also provide a plausible interpretation of any age-connected patterns in this area. Evidence of this interpretation is found in a recent cohort analysis of the traditional dimension of liberal-conservative ideology in domestic American political attitudes: federal involvement in economic and welfare programs, including the federal medical care issue. This analysis found cohort differences both in the support of the ideology and in the degree of ideological constraint or homogeneity across several discrete policy issues (Kirkpatrick, 1974).

Finally, *period* effects must also be considered since the United States has seen substantial changes over the past three or four decades in many areas of social policy. Twenty-five years ago, government-sponsored medical aid was dismissed as "socialized medicine" and supported only by a minority of the nation's population. But like other social welfare issues, government involvement in the financing of medical care came to be an issue whose time had come, first in the Medicare context and more recently in various legislative and govern-

mental proposals for more expansive federal involvement in this area (Marmor, 1973). Thus, period effects in attitude change on the issue of medical care must be considered as a plausible hypothesis, to be comparatively evaluated with the maturational and the generational hypotheses.

Evidence of multiple effects. One recent investigation examines the effects of maturation upon attitudes toward the medical care issue (Cutler and Schmidhauser, 1975). The results of a cohort analysis, spanning the years 1956 through 1972, are summarized in Table 3. Unlike the analyses of party identification and political alienation (presented in Tables 1 and 2), the purpose of these data is not to trace opinion patterns across the entire life cycle, but to isolate patterns in a small segment of the aging process and to examine that segment, in a replicative fashion, across successive cohorts.

If the maturational hypothesis suggested by Campbell and by Schreiber and Marsden is valid (i.e., because of a self-interest or group-benefits orientation, old people become increasingly supportive of governmental involvement in medical aid programs), then support for the issue should increase *within* a cohort as the cohort is examined at the older end of *its own* life cycle. Convincing evidence of the maturational hypothesis would require that: (a) the *level* of support among aged cohorts should be greater than for youthful cohorts, (b) the amount of age-related *increase* in support should be greater for the cohorts observed in old age than cohorts observed in early adulthood, and (c) this pattern of old age support should be found *consistently* in differing periods or contexts.

The data in Table 3 substantially confirm the maturational hypothesis: (a) in general, each cross-sectional election survey tends to show that respondents in their 60's more strongly endorse governmental involvement in the financing and provision of medical care; (b) the cohorts observed in their 60's display greater *increase in support* (or less diminution of support in those years where the historical trend was downward) than do the cohorts in their

TABLE 3. ATTITUDES TOWARD FEDERAL GOVERNMENTAL MEDICAL AID PROGRAMS[a]. (% IN FAVOR)

Age group	1956[b]	1960	1964	1968	1972
21–24	70	77	67	67	
25–28		69	62	56	56
change:		−1	−15	−12	−11
61–64	69	84	64	72	
65–68		85	73	76	69
change:		+16	−11	+12	−4
Total Sample	70	77	65	67	61
change:		+7	−12	+2	−6

[a] Adapted from Cutler and Schmidhauser (1975), Table 18.5. Data were made available by the Inter-University Consortium for Political and Social Research, through the USC Political and Social Data Laboratory.
[b] The questions read, for 1956 and 1960: "The government ought to help people get doctors and hospital care at low cost." For 1964 and 1968: "Some people say the government in Washington ought to help people get doctors and hospital care at low cost; others say the government should not get into this. Have you been interested enough in this to favor one side or the other?" For 1972: "There is much concern about the rapid rise in medical and hospital costs. Some feel there should be a government insurance plan which would cover all medical expenses. Others feel that medical expenses should be paid by individuals through private insurance like the Blue Cross. Which side do you favor?"

20's; (c) even in the context of the 1956–1972 fluctuations, there are similar patterns of aging at the younger and older ends of the life cycle. When the entire electorate decreased its support of government medical aid programs in 1964, the older cohorts exhibited less decrease than did the younger. Perhaps more telling confirmation of the maturational hypothesis is given between the years 1964 and 1968, when the difference for the whole electorate was negligible (an increase of 2 percentage points). In this period the older cohort increased its endorsement of the issue by 12 percentage points, while the younger cohort in the same period exhibited a net decrease of 12 percentage points.

The Importance of Comparative Perspectives on Time, Aging, and Trends in Opinions

This section has presented a brief sequence of case studies of public attitudes in order to demonstrate three competing hypotheses describing age effects—the maturational or aging effect, the generational or birth cohort effect, and the period of historical effect. While cross-sectional descriptive studies can provide evidential support for any one of the hypotheses, our discussion has endeavored to demonstrate that for each of the three sets of attitudes investigated, all three hypotheses are plausible. Only for studies in which the three competing hypotheses are *simultaneously* examined can the most compelling explanation from among the three be identified.

In reviewing the three cases presented here, several summary points should be made:

1. In each case, plausible maturational, generational, and period hypotheses are available.

2. The three cases of party identification, political alienation, and medical aid attitudes each resulted in the "validation" of a different one of the three hypotheses. The party identification analysis provided some evidence that a generational effect describes recent Republican-

Democrat differences in the United States. For political alienation it was apparent that period effects were predominant, since all life-stage and cohort groups responded similarly during the period. In the case of attitudes toward government involvement in medical aid programs, it appears that aging does lead to an increase in support for such programs.

3. The various cohort analyses present a mixed pattern of confirmation and disconfirmation of the evidence of cross-sectional studies. For party identification the cross-sectional analysis supported the maturational hypothesis while the cohort analysis supported the generational hypothesis. For attitudes toward governmental medical aid programs, the cohort analysis confirmed the interpretations deduced from cross-sectional analysis.

Thus, generational analysis, in general, represents an analytic approach to the systematic evaluation of the three competing age-related hypotheses. Depending upon the attitude or behavior orientation being investigated, the analytic approach is capable of either confirming or rejecting any of the three hypotheses, as this sequence of case examples has demonstrated. The fundamental lesson is that studies which focus only on one of the three hypotheses to the exclusion of the other produce incomplete and potentially misleading results. Even if the one hypothesis is, by itself, confirmed rather than rejected, the investigator cannot evaluate the power of that hypothesis relative to the possible explanatory power of the others. Generational analysis suggests that comparative analysis of age groups, across time periods and across birth cohorts, must be undertaken to understand the dynamics of aging and age-related phenomena.

INTERGENERATIONAL INTERACTION AND INFLUENCE: THE LINEAGE PERSPECTIVE

At the level of microsocial analysis, the problem of generations can be viewed in terms of (a) socialization—exchange of information between the young and the old regarding skills, knowledge, or orientations necessary or valued in the social setting; (b) power and responsibility—control over desired resources and the delicate negotiations characterizing intergenerational interaction on expectations, roles, and autonomy; (c) welfare—caretaking of dependent members of the domestic group who are not able to sustain themselves through their own efforts. Since earliest recorded history, these themes have been the source of comment and moralizing; they represent classical issues which are made ever contemporary and personal by one's own involvement with them.

Most research concerning intergenerational relations has focused on the younger family member and his interaction with elders. Yet the issue of solidarity and conflict between aging parents and their middle-aged children is important both as a subject of scientific inquiry and as a practical social problem. More importantly, gerontologists can learn much about older persons and the social processes of aging by employing the focus of lineage generational relationships, either at the microlevel (specific family relations) or at the macrolevel (relations between generational aggregates).

Three questions stand out in considering lineage generational analysis in gerontology. What perceptions do older people have of cross-generational relationships—both within the family and within the broader society? What is the nature and extent of interaction between aged individuals and their families—patterns of help or exchange, contact, and affection? How much consensus—and how much conflict—exists between older parents and their middle-aged children or grandchildren?

Perceptions of Intergenerational Relations: Cohort and Lineage Considerations

In the protest-filled decade of the 1960's, there appeared a new cliché, the "generation gap," which described the apparent contrasts and conflicts among different age groups (Friedenberg, 1969). One analysis describing this decade (Bengtson, 1971) suggested that the problem of generations impinged on contemporary older individuals in two ways. First is evidence of differences between the behaviors and standards of the aged individual's own cohort and those of younger age groups. These contrasts can be attributed to differences in levels of maturation (aging) and to contrasts in historical experience, as was discussed in the previous section. Born during a particular period in history and sharing certain sociopolitical events, those individuals who are over 65 have orientations that are often perceived as contrasting with those of younger members of the society. To paraphrase the popular jargon, this may be termed a "cohort gap."

Second are differences between generations within the family. Here, possibly, the differences are more personally relevant, since they are related to the wishes and fulfillment that parents often seek for children and grandchildren. Within the family, the aging individual may see the currents of change and conflict in the broader society as impinging on him personally and as disturbing or questioning lifelong principles that have for many years governed his behavior. Such family differences may be termed a "lineage gap."

Relatively little attention has been given to either type of generational difference, as far as elderly persons are concerned. There is, however, a growing body of literature in family sociology relevant to gerontology (Bengtson and Black, 1973; Hill, Foote, Aldous, Carlson, and MacDonald, 1970; Shanas and Streib, 1965; Shanas, Townsend, Wedderburn, Friis, Milhøj, and Stehouwer, 1968; Streib, 1965, 1972; Sussman, 1965; Sussman, Cates, and Smith, 1970; Treas, 1975; Troll, 1971; Willmott and Young, 1960). A corresponding tradition has been established in political socialization (Cutler, 1976; Dodge and Uyeki, 1962; Jennings and Niemi, 1968, 1974, 1975; Lane, 1958; Langton, 1969; Renshon, 1974). Still, it is clear that theoretical models and conceptual foci are at a relatively early stage of development, both in terms of interlineage and intercohort relationships.

Attribution of "closeness" or "distance". One important consideration in the analysis of intergenerational relations is the perception of relationships across generations. On the one hand, attributed differences may be seen in stereotypes held by one age group of the other or in generalized desirability of traits for one age group as contrasted to another (Ahammer and Baltes, 1972). On the other hand, they may be evidenced in the evaluation of interaction between age groups—the "closeness" or "distance" one feels from a member of another generation. Little research has examined this dimension of interage interaction or studied systematically the content of such contrasts.

One survey, however, affords some data which taps perceptions across generational boundaries in both cohort and lineage terms (Bengtson, 1971). In this study three parameters of person perception were examined: (a) age of the *perceiver*; (b) age of the *referent* or *target group*; (c) the *social context* of the perceiver-referent relationship (primary group versus generalized collectivity). Respondents were asked to evaluate the closeness of the relationship between members of various referent groups (youth-middle aged, middle aged-elderly, youth-elderly) in two social contexts: the "broader society" (cohort) and "your own family" (lineage).

The results, summarized in Table 4, indicate three things. First, the "cohort gap" perceived between generations in the broader society is considerably larger than the "lineage gap" perceived within the respondent's own family (comparing grand means reported on the last line in the two tables). Second, the age of the *perceiver* makes some difference in the degree to which a "gap" is seen: the youngest age group (in this study, 16–26 years of age) perceives the least closeness, particularly at the family level (at the cohort level, the old and the young attribute similar levels of distance). Grandparents see the greatest degree of closeness within the family. Third, the age of the *referent* constitutes a considerable difference: a greater "gap" is perceived between the youth and the elderly than between the other dyads.

The principal conclusion, then, is that the nature of cross-generation perceptions varies depending on several factors, the primary of which is the context of the referent group (primary relationship versus broader collectivity). For the older family member, this contrast is particularly pronounced: "Yes, there *is* a generation gap, but not in *my* family."

TABLE 4A. MEAN PERCEPTION OF "COHORT GAP" BY GENERATION OF RESPONDENT[a].

| | REFERENT | | | | | | |
| | Between G3 – G2 | | Between G3 – G1 | | Between G2 – G1 | | Total by generation of respondent |
Respondent	$\overline{X}$	s.d.	$\overline{X}$	s.d.	$\overline{X}$	s.d.	$\overline{X}$
G1	3.62	1.37	3.90	1.63	3.00	1.31	3.51
G2	3.20	1.12	4.25	1.31	2.81	1.11	3.42
G3	3.28	1.35	4.42	1.44	2.95	1.19	3.55
Total by generation of referent	3.38	1.29	4.17	1.48	2.92	1.21	3.49

[a]"Some people say there is a 'generation gap' between age groups in American society today. How much of a 'gap' do you think there is between the following groups?" (The groups referred to are the column headings in this table.) Subjects gave responses on a six-point scale from "no gap whatsoever" (scored 1) to "very great gap" (scored 6).

TABLE 4B. MEAN PERCEPTIONS OF THE "LINEAGE GAP" BY GENERATION OF RESPONDENT[b].

| | REFERENT | | | | | | |
| | Between G3 – G2 | | Between G3 – G1 | | Between G2 – G1 | | Total by generation of respondent |
Respondent	$\overline{X}$	s.d.	$\overline{X}$	s.d.	$\overline{X}$	s.d.	$\overline{X}$
G1	2.19	1.24	2.06	1.23	1.81	1.19	2.02
G2	2.35	1.04	3.62	1.53	2.72	1.28	2.89
G3	2.96	1.34	3.75	1.62	2.70	1.23	3.14
Total by generation of referent	2.46	1.24	3.07	1.65	2.38	1.30	2.64

[b]"In your family, how great is the 'gap' between the three generations, in your opinion?"
SOURCE: Bengtson, 1971.

Factors affecting perceptions of intergenerational contrasts. A variety of explanations have been offered to explain the contrasts attributed to differing generations. Summarizing some of these factors, one set consists of *sociocultural disparities* between age cohorts. (a) Each generation is born into a different historical period, shaped by different social events, and each cohort may vary in size and composition from its predecessor. (b) Social institutions change over time, and thus the various developmental roles sequentially experienced during the life course (student, parent, provider, etc.) have different meanings for members of successive generations. (c) Status in social institutions tends to increase with the years, giving the older person both greater rewards and a greater stake in the *status quo*.

A second set of factors includes *biological and psychological* factors associated with life course development: (a) changes with advancing maturity in the relative importance of various needs; (b) changes in perception, cognition, and sensation with advancing age; (c) changes in life outlook and response to social stimuli, brought about by the personalistic ways in which each individual experiences the events of his life.

At a higher level of abstraction, these sets of life course changes taken together can be said to give each generation a different *developmental stake* in the other (Bengtson and Kuypers, 1971). Parents and children have an investment ("stake") in their relationship which varies according to how the relationship enables the attainment of personal goals. In the case of the adolescent and his middle-aged parent, the parent may be concerned with the creation of social heirs. Aware of his own mortality and fearing that his contribution or significance may be lost, the parent may wish to perpetuate valued ideals and institutions in his offspring. To this end, the older generation may tend to deny or minimize evidence of intergenerational differences. By contrast, the younger generation is concerned with developing distinctiveness—individuated identity. The goal of the youth is to create values and institutions for themselves, and their elders' attempts to perpetuate existing values and institutions may be perceived as an imposition rather than well-intentioned advice. Their developmental stake causes them to exaggerate or maximize intergenerational differences.

The developmental stake perspective, based on the observation that different generations have contrasting representations of their common relationship, represents an application of Waller's (1938) "principle of least interest" developed in studies of dating behavior: the actor with the least commitment to maintaining the relationship will be in the best position to bargain for influence, for he has the least to lose if the relationship is broken. By contrast, the actor with the greatest commitment must often make concessions to the will of the other in order to avoid an implied threat of severance. This principle has interesting implications for the position of older members of the generational relationship; the exercise of parental authority carries with it an implied threat to the stability of the relationship, and so parents may tend to minimize differences (Bengtson and Black, 1973). In the case of the older family member, it may lead to a reluctance to make any requests for assistance of adult

children, as has been shown in several studies (Streib, 1965), because such demands put the elder family members at an even greater disadvantage in terms of exchange.

Intergenerational Solidarity and Older Family Members

An important determinant of the process and product of any human group is the solidarity or cohesiveness among individual members. The family, of course, is a special type of small group, and the extent to which family members like each other, do things with, and agree with one another has significant implications for the individuals who comprise it. A useful term to describe the parent-child dyad as it develops and changes through time is *solidarity*, a concept drawing from the works of the earliest sociologists down to the present.

Intergenerational solidarity can be conceptualized as comprised of three elements: *association* ("objective" interaction or activities); *affect* ("subjective" interaction—the degree of sentiment between members); and *consensus* (agreement in values or opinions). These concepts serve as a way to organize the emerging literature concerning intergenerational relations involving older family members (see Bengtson, Olander, and Haddad, 1976).

Objective solidarity (association). The bulk of empirical analyses of older family members has focused on patterns of interaction and exchange. For example, a widely-held misconception concerning the elderly—that the elderly become isolated from their children or feel a sense of loneliness as they enter the later stages of the life cycle—has been refuted by many studies. Shanas *et al.* (1968) reported that at least 84 percent of the elderly parents in the national probability sample of three industrial societies lived within one hour of at least one child, and that 85 percent had seen at least one child "within the previous week." Similar findings were obtained by Litwak (1960), Adams (1968), and Rosow (1967). The conclusion is that a great majority of the elderly parents and middle-aged children live in relatively close proximity and interact frequently.

But what of the *nature and type of interaction* patterns between the two generations? And what of the possible *differences in perceptions* of such interaction on the part of the elderly as contrasted with the middle-aged? A number of studies (Adams, 1968; Hill *et al.*, 1970; Sussman, 1965; Troll, 1971) have reported that elderly parents and their children do exchange a variety of services (babysitting, gardening, shopping) as well as money and other resources; that aged parents will turn to middle-aged children for assistance before they will ask for help from siblings; and that the exchange is fairly symmetrical, both generations giving and receiving assistance (for a different perspective see Hill *et al.*, 1970). But almost all research in this area has relied on the report of one generation—either the elderly or the middle-aged member of the dyad. As is suggested in the preceding discussion of intergenerational perceptions, it is necessary to gather information from both members of the generational dyad in order to allow for the inevitable, if unintentional, differences in perceptions that result from the "developmental stake" which colors the assessment of each lineage member.

From one study involving 2,044 members of three-generation family lineages (sample described in Bengtson, 1975) come several suggestions concerning associational solidarity involving older family members. Reports from both the elderly and middle-aged concerning the nature and frequency of intergenerational interaction yielded two dimensions of interaction or "objective solidarity" (Black and Bengtson, 1973): *informal activities* (recreation, conversation, talking about important matters, helping and being helped) and *ceremonial or family ritual activities* (large and small family gatherings, reunions, birthdays).

Both generations reported relatively high levels of both types of activities. No significant general differences appeared between the reports of the middle-aged and the elderly in the perception of frequency of contact, although one specific difference concerned the giving and receiving of help. When estimating the amount of help given by the middle-aged child, the child himself reported a higher level than did

his parent. Moreover, the parents reported giving less help to the children than the children reported receiving.

Subjective solidarity (affect). A more difficult and less researched issue in the lineage intergenerational relationship concerns the level of sentiment or liking between dyad members. In the three-generation study described above, parents and children were asked to report their perceptions of affect toward the dyad partner and from the dyad partner. These were assessed on each of five issues (degree of understanding, trust, fairness, respect, and affection) which the individual felt characterized the relationship.

The analysis of these data produce two notable findings. First, relatively high levels of perceived solidarity are exhibited by both dyad members. The mean for the elderly parents is 50.9 and for middle-aged children, 48.1, on a scale from 10 to 60. Second, the data reveal a slightly higher perception of subjective solidarity on the part of the elderly parent.

In summarizing these two dimensions of solidarity, it appears that the elderly parents report higher levels of subjective solidarity (affect) while the middle-aged children report higher levels of both giving and receiving help (objective solidarity). This is consistent with the developmental stake concept discussed earlier, which implies that each member of the dyad has a differential investment in the dyad which colors his perception of the relationship. While the elderly report higher levels of affection, they minimize the amount of assistance or exchange of services. This is congruent with their greater "stake" in the relationship, in which the dimension of affect or sentiment is more important than the dimension of assistance or help.

Consensual solidarity (agreement). A third aspect of lineage relationships concerns the degree of consensus or conflict in beliefs or orientations external to the family. Political issues, religious practices or ideologies, global value orientations—these are often the topics of family traditions, on the one hand, or of protracted disagreements and conflict on the other. To what extent do elderly family members appear similar or different to their middle-aged children, and to their grandchildren, in matters of opinion and orientation? How do such intra-family congruences or differences compare with intercohort contrasts—given the recent spate of popular literature concerning the "generation gap"?

While many studies have focused on the real or attributed contrasts between cohorts in opinions and orientations, few analyses have addressed the issue of lineage or parent-child continuities in the face of cohort contrasts (for exceptions, see Connell, 1972; Jennings and Niemi, 1975), and fewer still have focused on differences between the elderly and their descendants (for exceptions, see Fengler and Wood, 1972; Hill et al., 1970; Kalish and Johnson, 1972; Streib, 1965). From the empirical evidence to date, however, several tentative observations can be made.

The first concerns contrasts and similarities between elderly parents and their middle-aged children. On some issues the similarities between these two generations appear marked, e.g., values regarding fatalism and optimism (Hill et al., 1970) and global orientations concerning collectivism vs. individualism (Bengtson, 1975). Indeed, on the latter value orientation, the variance attributable to predicting the middle-aged child's orientation from that of the parent was 15 percent—a relatively high degree of predictability.

For other variables, however, parent-child contrasts were marked: values regarding child-rearing (Hill et al., 1970) and on general orientations toward materialism vs. humanism (Bengtson, 1975). Whether the similarities evidenced can be attributed to transmission or socialization effects operating long into adulthood is, of course, equivocal: they may be due to common location within the social structure or to the impact of commonly-experienced historical or period effects; that is, the similarities may have developed in parallel rather than in series (Connell, 1972). Similarly, it is not possible to determine whether the contrasts are reflective of life-cycle (maturation) or cohort (generational) effects which outweigh potential similarities resultant from socialization influences or other correlates of family lineage.

A second observation concerns contrasts or continuities evidenced among nonadjacent generations: grandparents and grandchildren. Some surveys have pointed to surprising similarities between youth and their grandparents, e.g., in orientations toward materialism vs. humanism (Bengtson, 1975) and in norms regarding expressive behavior (Kalish and Johnson, 1972). Such considerations have caused several observers to consider the young and the old as "generation gap allies" (Kalish, 1969) or as representing a potential coalition against the middle generation. However, in the three-generation study of values (Bengtson, 1975), the similarities between grandparents and grandchildren could not be attributable to lineage effects (less than 1 percent of the variation was accounted for by family membership) and rather appears to be the result of common cohort situational variables.

A third implication of intergenerational solidarity may be inferred from analyses of inheritance in explicit legacy-making. Elderly individuals often invest a considerable amount of energy in arranging disposition of their estate after death. The analysis of Sussman, Cates, and Smith (1970) suggests that these intergenerational transfers often follow carefully considered norms of reciprocity and equity by the families involved. Sussman, Cates, and Smith note that there is a conscious effort to effect a smooth continuity with minimal hassles among descendants over claims and priorities (p. 291). Their study of inheritance patterns of 659 family systems suggests a great deal of care is given to the just distribution of intergenerational property inheritance.

Conclusion: Socialization and Lineage Generations

From the microlevel perspective of intergenerational relations, five points appear especially relevant when considering the older individual. First, it must be remembered that the nature of family intergenerational relations changes through time. Both in terms of interactional patterns (objective solidarity) and in terms of affection and regard (subjective solidarity), the relationship alters over time. Both members of the dyad are in continuous and bilateral negotiation concerning the issues at stake—socialization, power, welfare—and the relationship itself is continuously altered over time as the participants themselves change with aging (Bengtson and Black, 1973). Nowhere does the dynamic and processual quality of social systems become more evident than when examining a particular family unit over time (whether months, years, or decades).

Second, the level of both objective and subjective solidarity is perceived by family members as high in contemporary American families. But third, the perception of these factors varies between generations; the elder perceive slightly more affection, the younger see more exchanges of services. These differential perceptions of intergenerational interaction can be accounted for by an awareness of contrasting "developmental stakes": personal investments in the relationship which are a function of developmental concerns and which color the assessment of it.

Fourth, the patterns of similarity and contrast in attitudes and values are complex; but it seems safe to say that there is no marked indication of conflict in orientations between aged parents and their grandchildren. In short, the "generation gap"—perceived at both cohort and lineage levels—turns out, upon careful inspection, to be a dubious set of contrasts reflecting more consensus than cleavage.

Fifth, many principles and concepts in macrosocial analysis must be taken into account and are particularly useful in understanding the microlevel concerns of generational inquiry. The historical setting of intergenerational interaction, the facts of differential birth cohort composition and characteristics, the availability of roles, and the nature of institutions and values in the surrounding culture—these contextual issues influence relations between generations and place boundaries around the ongoing processes of transmission and interaction.

EMERGING GENERATION UNITS OF THE ELDERLY: PROSPECTS FOR POLITICAL AND HISTORICAL CONSCIOUSNESS

In addition to the traditional age cohort and lineage conceptualizations of "generation,"

there is a third perspective which focuses specifically on the social construction of age groups and their subsequent effect either on social change or stability. The most comprehensive treatment of this topic has been suggested by Mannheim with the phrase "generation unit." This refers to groups of individuals within an historical cohort who share a collective mentality and define themselves as a collective with common perspectives and concerns and who become the initiators of social change. To be sure, neither the cohort nor the lineage approach to generational analysis assumes that all members of an identifiable generational grouping are homogeneous with respect to social orientations. The specific living experiences and immediate contexts of members of both cohort and lineage groups will shape their perceptions and their reactions to the society and polity. Generational analysis, in other words, does not replace, but rather complements, social class, ethnic status, and other stratification factors known to shape sociopolitical orientations. These traditionally recognized differentiations and groups—and the relationships among them—may well describe the essence of the generational experience.

The utility of the generation unit concept in a gerontological context can be seen in answers to the following questions: what evidence is there that the generation unit can be linked to patterns of social stability and change? is it possible to specifically identify generation units among contemporary populations? what does generational analysis in general, and the concept of generation unit in particular, allow us to say about the future role of older persons in social and political systems?

Our task here is not to predict the future but to consider selected examples of issues and data which have a bearing on the interaction among generation units, the older population, and sociopolitical change. As Binstock (1974) has noted, observers often become polemic concerning political changes stemming from increasing numbers of older people. The sensationalism of an "old age voting bloc" must be avoided. A generational perspective is of assistance in helping to avoid such pitfalls.

Identification of Generation Units: Within-Cohort Differentiation

The first issue concerns identification of generation units within birth cohorts. As mentioned in the first section, Mannheim himself provides little direction in this area; thus, the task has been left to more contemporary analysts. For example, in his report of several analyses of student political activity in the mid-1960's, Flacks (1967) refers to the "revolt of the advantaged" in discussing the role which alienation appeared to play in the protest activities of wealthy and well-educated upper-middle class students. The point which Flacks makes is most relevant to a consideration of differentiation among age groups: although the societal and political forces which set the stage for the protests of the 1960's were "available" to all youth, it was often the socioeconomically advantaged and college-enrolled youth who, for a variety of resource and opportunity reasons, became the focal point of political activity. These college students could be described as a generation unit within the larger cohort of college-age youth in the 1960's.

Several recent reviews of youth-based social and political protests have demonstrated that no single characterization of youth in the 1960's would be completely descriptive of all members of the cohort. Rather, a range of styles can be discerned from among the many empirical studies which focused on the phenomenon. Laufer and Bengtson (1974), for example, noted the following four generation units among contemporary youth: the activists, the revivalists, the communalists, and the freaks (Bohemians). While all of these youth may be considered members of the same generational cohort, they are clearly not of the same generation unit. The different identifiable generational units have differing orientations toward society, and they have different postures toward the issue of involved social change.

Demographic Factors: The Foundation for Sociopolitical Units Among the Elderly

Demographic data indicate the phenomenal growth in the older segment of Western societies. Where in 1900 the over-65 population

represented only 4.1 percent of the population of the United States, they were 6.8 percent in 1940 and 9.9 percent in 1970. Between 1960 and 1970, while the national population increased by 12.5 percent, the over-65 population increased by 21.1 percent (Brotman, 1971). According to census estimates based on the fertility assumption of zero population growth, by the year 2020 the over-65 population will number in excess of 40 million and will represent 13.1 percent of the national population (Cutler and Harootyan, 1975).

A more significant illustration of population change which may affect future social and political activity is reflected in the "dependency ratio," the number (or proportion) of people in a "dependent" age category divided by the number in the "supporting" age category (Shanas and Hauser, 1974; Shyrock and Siegel, 1971). In standard demographic analysis, the 18–64 age group is defined as the work force population, and those under 18 and over 65 are considered to be the dependent population. The logic of the dependency ratio can be used to compute alternative index measures, depending on whether the numerator contains just the young, just the old, or both groups. In the present discussion, the old-age dependency ratio (65+/18–64) will be used.

Table 5 indicates the trend in the dependency ratio for the years 1930 through 1970 and includes the estimated dependency ratios through

TABLE 5. OLD AGE DEPENDENCY RATIOS, 1930–2050.

1930	1940	1950	1960	1970	2000	2020	2050
.097	.118	.133	.167	.177	.177	.213	.257

Dependency Ratio = 65+/18–64.
SOURCES: (1930–1940): U.S. Bureau of the Census, *U.S. Census of Population: 1940, Characteristics of the Population*, Table 8, p. 26. (1950–1970): U.S. Bureau of the Census, *Statistical Abstract of the United States 1972*, Table 37, p. 32. (2000): (based on Series E projections) Herman B. Brotman, "Projections of the Population to the Year 2000," Statistical Memo #25, Department of Health, Education, and Welfare, Administration on Aging, June 1973, p. 3. (2020, 2050): (based on Series E and Series W, respectively) prepared by Dr. David M. Heer, Population Research Laboratory, University of Southern California, February 1974.

the year 2050. As these data indicate, there is substantial increase in the proportion of the older population as compared to the supportive working population. The dynamics of the dependency ratio depend, of course, on the relative sizes of population cohorts born at different times. The Baby Boom of the 1940's becomes the Gerontology Boom of the years 2000 and 2010. During the time that a proportionally large Baby Boom cohort is in its productive working years, especially when older people during those years constitute a relatively smaller cohort, the relationship between supports and demands may not produce conflict. But when the social and political system is faced with the Gerontology Boom at a time when the work force population has relatively decreased, age-based allocation claims may very well become the focal point for increasing political-economic conflict, thereby precipitating generational units among both the elderly and the working population. Economists are increasingly recognizing this interaction of demographic, economic, and political factors in the context of aging. Among economists interested in gerontological concerns, Kreps (1965) has referred to the "economics of intergenerational relationships," and Morgan (1975) has discussed the "intergenerational social contract" implicit in extant social security pension systems in which a worker of today expects the future generation to support his pension tomorrow (see also Walther, 1975).

Political Factors: Potential for Increasing Engagement Among Older Cohorts

While the demographic data indicate that there will be more older persons in the first decades of the next century, and that they will represent a growing proportion of the national population, such information in and of itself does not predict increasing old-age involvement in social concerns. A third part of the picture, therefore, involves cohort patterns in the public's level of formal education—an individual characteristic which has been seen in a great deal of previous research to be linked to participation (Milbrath, 1965; Verba and Nie, 1972).

In Table 6, each of six national sample surveys has been divided into high and low education groups, the criterion for high education being the completion of high school. The change from 1952 through 1972 for the electorate as a whole can be seen in the "total" row. The data for the over-65 group reveal even more significant changes. The older group in the 1952 sample was educated at the beginning of the century, when mass public education was not yet generally available. As the more educated cohorts age, the average educational level of older persons is increased, as is seen by a

TABLE 6. AGE COMPOSITION IN EDUCATION.

Age group	1952 Lo	1952 Hi	1956 Lo	1956 Hi	1960 Lo	1960 Hi	1964 Lo	1964 Hi	1968 Lo	1968 Hi	1972 Lo	1972 Hi
21–24	45	55	33	67	39	61	30	70	19	81	14	86
25–34	47	53	34	66	36	64	29	71	21	79	22	78
35–44	58	42	48	52	36	64	34	66	34	66	26	74
45–54	67	33	59	42	47	53	50	50	39	61	40	60
55–64	76	24	65	35	68	32	62	38	55	45	55	45
65+	81	19	78	22	71	29	67	33	71	29	70	30
TOTAL	62	38	51	49	48	52	45	55	41	59	38	62

"Lo" Education is defined as no education through incomplete high school;
"Hi" Education is complete high school (or equivalency) and higher.
SOURCE: Each year was taken from the University of Michigan Center for Political Studies presidential election national survey. The data were made available to the authors by the Inter-University Consortium for Political and Social Research through the USC Political and Social Data Laboratory.

comparison of the 65+ groups in 1952 and 1972.

Finally, by extension, the educational level of old people at the beginning of the next century can be seen. The youngest age group in the 1972 sample will all be at least 65 years old by the year 2016. Thus, older people by the year 2020 will be a much better educated group than the aged of yesterday and today. Where the 65+ group in 1952 was divided 19 percent to 81 percent in terms of high-low educational attainment, the 65+ group by 2020 will be divided 86 percent to 14 percent—a rather substantial reversal. From the perspective of social change, then, the potential for involvement and activity will be greater for tomorrow's older people than it has been in the past.

In short, the stage has at least been set for the more active social and political participation of tomorrow's older population. To anticipate more directly the participation of the Gerontology Boom of the next century, it is instructive to briefly examine patterns of political participation among contemporary age groups (see chapter 15 for a more detailed exposition of this topic). The data indicate that *old age is not a period of political quiescence.*

In terms of participation in voting, there is little evidence—as might be predicted by disengagement theories—that participation substantially declines in old age. While a slight drop-off has been noted among those over 65 (for females more so than males), contrasts between males and females and differences between groups varying by educational attainment were substantially larger than differences between age cohorts (Foner, 1972).

Further evidence of the lack of any inherent decrease in participation on the part of old people has been documented by Verba and Nie (1972), who examined both voting behavior and more general modes of political participation. Since it is known that current cohorts of older persons have fewer economic resources than younger cohorts, corrections for socioeconomic factors were employed. "When we use the corrected scores, the decline in participation found in the older group almost disappears on the overall participation measure and it disappears completely for voting partici-

pation" (p. 143). Since these and several other studies find socioeconomic differences more pervasive than age differences, the improvement in the educational status of tomorrow's older population noted in Table 6 takes on increased importance.

Age Consciousness and Generation Units Among the Elderly

In considering the potential for the emergence of generation units among the aged in future years, four contextual factors have thus far been noted. First, the older population in America and throughout Western Europe has been rapidly and continuously expanding. Second, the proportion of old people relative to other age groups, as indexed by dependency ratios, has continued to show marked increase. Third, secular changes in educational opportunities mean that tomorrow's cohorts of older people will be much better educated than old people of previous years. Fourth, the available evidence fails to support a "disengagement" view of older persons; to the contrary, political participation appears to continue into the sixth and seventh decades of the life cycle (Cutler, 1977; Cutler and Schmidhauser, 1975).

To this sequence of factors which provide the political, demographic, and social context for the possible emergence of generation units among the elderly, we now turn to a final issue: the *subjective perceptions* of older persons which potentially serve as the basis for generation units. As mentioned previously, a number of different styles and cultures appeared in young adults in response to the social and political context of the 1960's. While we cannot predict what styles of action may emerge within the population in general and the aged in particular in the next century, we can point to certain emerging differentiations among contemporary older persons and indicate some of the social and political consequences of these subjective differentiations. In particular, we are here concerned with the notion of subjective age identification. To the degree that youth have become conscious of themselves as youth, social styles and political movements have emerged at different points in history (Feuer,

1969; Spitzer, 1973). The question is whether similar age consciousness exists within the older sector of the population and, if so, whether such consciousness has any identifiable correlates and consequences.

Of course, the general question of age consciousness is not new to social gerontologists (see Ragan and Dowd, 1974; and the chapter by Streib in this volume). Measured in a variety of ways, age consciousness or subjective age identification has been found to vary among groups of older persons and to be correlated with such personal variables as life satisfaction, adjustment to old age, health, sex, and socioeconomic status (McTavish, 1971; Peters, 1971). Until recently there have been few studies which address the issue of age consciousness among different segments of the elderly—contrasts which could serve as the basis of emergent generation units within the older population of the future.

One recent study relevant to this issue (Cutler, 1974b) was based upon a national attitude survey of the American electorate which included a measure of subjective age identification along with a large complement of questions concerning social, economic, and political issues. Subjective age, of course, is not perfectly correlated with chronological age, since not all young or old necessarily identify themselves as young or old; some identify with the opposite group, while many do not identify with age at all. Using the broad age categories of 18-35, 36-59, and 60+, the study found that 38.1 percent of the young group identified as young, while 38.4 percent of the chronologically old subjectively identified as old. The correlation (gamma) between objective and subjective age was found to be .60.

While it is true that 38 percent of old and young each subjectively identified with their age-peers, we, of course, cannot predict with any certainty that as today's young become tomorrow's old, they will maintain a psychological affinity for their age group. Nonetheless, such a possibility cannot be dismissed. Equally important to the present discussion, however, are the attitudinal consequences of subjective age identification among the contemporary old. Toward this end, a sampling of issues contained in the national sample survey described above is presented in Table 7 as related to those chronologically old who express a subjectively old age identification and those who do not.

The pattern of responses in Table 7 portrays attitude and perception differentials among the elderly. In general, it appears that among those older persons who subjectively identify themselves as old, there is somewhat greater support for federal governmental action in the area of inflation and medical care, and a corresponding desire to see a reduction of federal expenditures for military purposes. While older persons in 1972 do not see themselves as particularly liberal, the subjectively old are somewhat more liberal than those who do not so identify themselves. At the level of personal fiscal perceptions, the subjectively old are less optimistic with respect to their current and future economic position as compared to those older respondents who are not subjectively old. The seventh and eighth items in Table 7 indicate that the subjectively old are not ideologically committed to all "liberal" positions since they are less in favor of abortion and of the federal government's involvement in antipollution activities. A subsequent analysis indicated that there are not only differences in the direction of opinions between the two subgroups of the chronologically old, but that on some issues the two groups differ in how they organize the pattern of several opinions on the same issue.

The main point of these data is not the particulars of the differences, but the fact that differences within the chronologically old do exist along this subjective dimension. These opinion distributions underscore the main point of this part of our discussion in demonstrating the potential subjective basis for emergent generation units among the elderly. All of the respondents represented in Table 7 are in the same general chronological stage of the life cycle (60 or over), and all have experienced approximately the same slice of history at approximately the same time in their lives. Yet the variable of subjective age identification indicates that this group is not homogeneous with respect to a variety of social, political, and economic attitudes and perceptions. In short,

TABLE 7. SUBJECTIVE AGE IDENTIFICATION AMONG OLDER PERSONS AND SELECTED SOCIAL, POLITICAL, AND ECONOMIC ISSUES IN 1972[a].

Issue	SUBJECTIVE AGE IDENTIFICATION	
	As old	None
1. GOVERNMENT ACTION ON INFLATION		
% Should Act	97.9	89.5
2. FEDERAL MEDICAL PROGRAMS		
% In Favor	71.7	51.9
3. CUTS IN FEDERAL MILITARY SPENDING		
% In Favor	41.5	26.4
4. SELF-IDENTIFICATION AS LIBERAL OR CONSERVATIVE		
% Liberal	21.2	16.4
5. PERSONAL FINANCIAL CONDITION, NOW *vs.* YEAR AGO		
% Better Now	44.0	59.6
6. PERSONAL FINANCIAL CONDITION, NOW *vs.* NEXT YEAR		
% Better Next Year	46.2	50.0
7. ABORTION ALLOWABLE UNDER CERTAIN CIRCUMSTANCES		
% Agree	22.0	33.6
8. GOVERNMENT ACTION AGAINST INDUSTRIAL POLLUTION		
% In Favor	67.6	73.0
ALL RESPONDENTS AGED 60+	38.1%[b]	54.5%

[a]These data, analyzed by the authors, represent the responses of those respondents aged 60 and over in the University of Michigan Center for Political Studies national survey of the 1972 presidential election. The election survey was made available by the Inter-University Consortium for Political and Social Research through the USC Political and Social Data Laboratory. Total N for the 1972 survey is 2700. More complete analysis of these data may be found in Cutler (1974b).
[b]Not included here are the 7.4 percent of the 60+ group which identified as young.

subjective age identification at the older end of the life cycle does make a difference in public orientations—as was demonstrated for youth in the turbulent years of the 1960's.

We cannot be sure, of course, that the results of a cross-sectional analysis of responses in 1972 will be predictive of possible differentiations among the aged in the year 2020. Yet these data do provide a basis for the anticipation of such differences when set in the context of the following set of observations: (a) generation units among adolescents and young adults in previous years have been seen to be the basis for collective action; (b) subjective age identification at the older end of the life cycle, as seen in the data presented here, is also associated with attitudinal differences; and (c) old age organizations such as the Gray Panthers, the National Council of Senior Citizens, the National Caucus of the Black Aged, and the American Association of Retired Persons are purposely attempting to raise age consciousness among the elderly in support of political programs (Jackson, 1974; Pratt, 1974; and Chapter 15 by Hudson and Binstock in this volume). Indeed, there is evidence that membership in old-age homogeneous organizations, as compared with membership in age heterogeneous organizations, has a positive impact on the age consciousness and political orientations of older persons—even when the organization is basically nonpolitical (Trela, 1971).

These points provide some basis for suggesting that old age represents a stage in the life cycle when generation units can emerge. And while not every birth cohort partakes of a revolutionary spirit, it is nonetheless the case that the potential for social movements and political action is located in such generational units. It should not be anticipated that the various factors discussed here will yield an attitudinally cohesive voting bloc of senior citizens which will polarize all of American politics around a small number of economic and political issues. As others have also noted (e.g., Binstock, 1974; Campbell, 1971), older persons will still tend to maintain their allegiances and identifications as Democrats and Republicans, white and black, rich and poor, etc.

What is suggested by the sequence of factors reviewed here is that as a greater proportion of the population is included in the older age categories, as future generations of old people have the educational resources and political experience to actively participate in political controversies concerning issues of social and financial allocation, and as age consciousness and subjective age identification among the elderly increase—under these circumstances generational analysis predicts the emergence of generation units among the elderly. And while not all old people will evidence age consciousness, those who do become the focus of generation units potentially represent a significant force for social and political change.

For social gerontology the perspective of generational analysis should provide an increasingly important set of analytic and conceptual tools for the consideration of evolving future configurations of the elderly and for anticipating and understanding the role of older persons in the evolution of society.

REFERENCES

Abramson, P. R. 1974. Generational change in American electoral behavior. *Amer. Pol. Sci. Rev.*, **68**, 93–105.

Abramson, P. R. 1975. *Generational Change in American Politics*. Lexington, Massachusetts: D. C. Heath.

Adams, B. N. 1968. *Kinship in an Urban Setting*. Chicago: Markham.

Agnello, T. J., Jr. 1973. Aging and the sense of political powerlessness. *Public Opinion Quarterly*, **37**, 251–259.

Ahammer, J. M., and Baltes, P. B. 1972. Objective versus perceived age differences in personality: How do adolescents, adults, and older people view themselves and each other? *J. Geront.*, **27**, 46–51.

Axelrod, R. 1972. Where the votes come from: An analysis of electoral coalitions, 1952–1968. *Amer. Pol. Sci. Rev.*, **66**, 11–20.

Baltes, P. B. 1968. Longitudinal and cross-sectional sequences in the study of age and generation effects. *Hum. Develop.*, **11**, 145–171.

Baltes, P. B., and Schaie, K. W. (eds.). 1973. *Developmental Psychology: Personality and Socialization*. New York: Academic Press.

Bengtson, V. L. 1970. The generation gap: A review and typology of social-psychological perspectives. *Youth and Society*, **2**, 7–31.

Bengtson, V. L. 1971. Inter-age differences in perception and the generation gap. *Gerontologist*, Part II, 85–90.

Bengtson, V. L. 1975. Generation and family effects in value socialization. *Am. Soc. Rev.*, **40**, 358–371.

Bengtson, V. L., and Black, K. D. 1973. Intergenerational relations and continuities in socialization. *In*, P. Baltes and K. W. Schaie (eds.), *Life-Span Developmental Psychology: Personality and Socialization*, pp. 208–234. New York: Academic Press.

Bengtson, V. L., Kasschau, P. L., and Ragan, P. K. 1976. The impact of social structure on the aging individual. *In*, J. E. Birren and K. W. Schaie (eds.), *Handbook of the Psychology of Aging*. New York: Van Nostrand Reinhold.

Bengtson, V. L., and Kuypers, J. A. 1971. Generational differences and the developmental stake. *Aging and Human Development*, **2**, 249–260.

Bengtson, V. L., Olander, E., and Haddad, A. 1976. 'The generation gap' and aging family members: Toward a conceptual model. *In*, J. F. Gubrium (ed.), *Time, Self, and Roles in Old Age*. New York: Behavioral Publications.

Bengtson, V. L., and Starr, J. M. 1975. Continuity and contrast: A generational analysis of youth in the 1970's. *In*, R. J. Havighurst (ed.), *Youth: National Society for the Study of Education Yearbook*. Chicago: University of Chicago Press.

Binstock, R. H. 1974. Aging and the future of American politics. *Annals of the Am. Acad. of Pol. and Soc. Sc.*, **415**, 199–212.

Black, K. D., and Bengtson, V. L. 1973. Solidarity across generations: Elderly parents and their middle-aged children. Unpublished paper presented at the Annual Meeting of the Gerontological Society, Miami, Florida.

Braungart, R. G. 1974. The sociology of generations and student politics: A comparison of the functionalist and generational unit models. *J. Soc. Issues*, **30**, 31–54.

Bronfenbrenner, U. 1961. The changing American child. *J. Soc. Issues*, **17**, 9.

Brotman, H. B. 1971. The older population revisited: First results of the 1970 census. *In, Facts and Figures on Older Americans*, No. 2. Washington, D. C.: Administration on Aging SRS-AoA Publication #182.

Buss, A. R. 1974. Generational analysis: Description, explanation, and theory. *J. Soc. Issues*, **30**, 55-71.

Cain, L. D., Jr. 1967. Age status and generational phenomena: The new old people in contemporary America. *Gerontologist*, **7**, 83-92.

Campbell, A. 1962. Social and psychological determinants of voting behavior. *In*, W. Donahue and C. Tibbits (eds.), *Politics of Age*, pp. 87-100. Ann Arbor: University of Michigan Press.

Campbell, A. 1971. Politics through the life cycle. *Gerontologist*, **11**, 112-117.

Campbell, A., Converse, P., Miller, W., and Stokes, D. 1960. *The American Voter*. New York: John Wiley.

Carlsson, G., and Karlsson, K. 1970. Age cohorts and the generation of generations. *Am. Soc. Rev.*, **35**, 710-718.

Clausen, J. A. 1968. Perspectives on childhood socialization. *In*, J. A. Clausen (ed.), *Socialization and Society*, pp. 130-181. Boston: Little, Brown.

Connell, R. W. 1972. Political socialization in the American family: The evidence re-examined. *Public Opinion Quarterly*, **36**, 321-333.

Converse, P. E., Miller, W., Rusk, J., and Wolfe, A. 1969. Continuity and change in American politics: Parties and issues in the 1968 election. *Amer. Pol. Sci. Rev.*, **63**, 1083-1105.

Crittenden, J. A. 1962. Aging and party affiliation. *Public Opinion Quarterly*, **26**, 648-657.

Cutler, N. E. 1969. Generation, maturation, and party affiliation: A cohort analysis. *Public Opinion Quarterly*, **33**, 583-588.

Cutler, N. E. 1974a. Aging and generations in politics: The conflict of explanations and interference. *In*, A. R. Wilcox (ed.), *Public Opinion and Political Attitudes: A Reader*, pp. 440-462. New York: John Wiley.

Cutler, N. E. 1974b. The effects of subjective age identification among old and young: A nation-wide study of political, economic, and social attitudes. Unpublished paper prepared for the 27th Annual Meeting of the Gerontological Society, Portland.

Cutler, N. E. 1975. Toward a political generations conception of political socialization. *In*, D. C. Schwartz and S. K. Schwartz (eds.), *New Directions in Political Socialization*, pp. 363-409. New York: The Free Press.

Cutler, N. E. 1976. Political socialization research as generational analysis: The cohort approach versus the lineage approach. *In*, S. A. Renshon (ed.), *Handbook of Political Socialization Research*. New York: The Free Press.

Cutler, N. E. 1977. Demographic, social psychological, and political factors in the politics of age: A call for research in political gerontology. *Amer. Pol. Sci. Rev.* **71**.

Cutler, N. E., and Bengtson, V. L. 1974. Age and political alienation: Maturation, generation and period effects. *Annals of the Am. Acad. of Pol. and Soc. Sc.*, **415**, 160-175.

Cutler, N. E., and Harootyan, R. A. 1975. Demography of the aged. *In*, D. Woodruff and J. E. Birren (eds.), *Aging: Scientific Perspectives and Social Issues*, pp. 31-69. New York: D. Van Nostrand.

Cutler, N. E., and Schmidhauser, J. R. 1975. Age and political behavior. *In*, D. Woodruff and J. E. Birren (eds.), *Aging: Scientific Perspectives and Social Issues*, pp. 374-406. New York: D. Van Nostrand.

Dilthey, W. 1924. Ueber das studium der geschichte der wissenschaften vom menschen, der gesellschaft und dem staat. *In*, W. Dilthey, *Gesammelte Schriften*, Vol. 5, pp. 31-73. Leipzig and Berlin: Teubner.

Dodge, R. W., and Uyeki, E. S. 1962. Political affiliation and imagery across related generations. *Midwest Jour. of Pol. Sci.*, **6**, 266-276.

Elder, G. H. 1974. *Children of the Great Depression*. Chicago: University of Chicago Press.

Elder, G. H. 1975. Age differentiation and the life course. *In*, A. Inkeles (ed.), *Annual Review of Sociology, Vol. 1*. Stanford: Annual Reviews Press.

Esler, A. 1966. *The Aspiring Mind of the Elizabethan Younger Generation*. Durham, North Carolina: Duke University Press.

Esler, A. 1972. Youth in revolt: The French generation of 1830. *In*, R. J. Bezucha, *Modern European History*. Lexington, Massachusetts: D. C. Heath.

Fendrich, J. M. 1974. Activists ten years later: A test of generational unit continuity. *J. Soc. Issues*, **31**, 95-118.

Fengler, A. P., and Wood, V. 1972. The generation gap: An analysis of attitudes on contemporary issues. *Gerontologist*, **12**, 124-128.

Feuer, L. 1969. *The Conflict of Generations*. New York: Basic Books.

Flacks, R. 1967. The liberated generation: An exploration of the roots of student protest. *J. Soc. Issues*, **23**, 52-75.

Foner, A. 1972. The polity. *In*, M. W. Riley, M. Johnson, and A. Foner (eds.), *Aging and Society: Vol. III: A Sociology of Age Stratification*, pp. 118-132. New York: Russell Sage Foundation.

Friedenberg, E. 1959. *The Vanishing Adolescent*. Boston: Beacon Press.

Friedenberg, E. 1969. Current patterns of a generation conflict. *J. Soc. Issues*, **25**, 21-38.

Glenn, N. D., and Hefner, J. 1972. Further evidence on aging and party identification. *Public Opinion Quarterly*, **36**, 31-47.

Goertzel, J. 1972. Generational conflict and social change. *Youth and Society*, **3**, 327-352.

Goslin, D. A. 1969. Introduction. *In*, D. Goslin (ed.), *Handbook of Socialization Theory and Research*. Chicago: Rand McNally.

Heberle, R. 1951. *Social Movements*. New York: Appleton-Century-Crofts.

Hill, R., Foote, N., Aldous, J., Carlson, R., and MacDonald, R. 1970. *Family Development in Three Generations*. Cambridge, Massachusetts: Schenkman.

House, J. S., and Mason, W. M. 1975. Political alienation in America, 1952–1968. *Am. Soc. Rev.*, **40**, 123–147.

Hyman, H. H. 1972. Cohort analysis. *In*, H. H. Hyman, *Secondary Analysis of Sample Surveys: Principles, Procedures, and Potentialities*, pp. 274–290. New York: John Wiley.

Jackson, J. J. 1974. NCBA, black aged, and politics. *Annals of the Am. Acad. of Pol. and Soc. Sc.*, **415**, 138–159.

Jennings, M. K., and Niemi, R. G. 1968. The transmission of political values from parent to child. *Amer. Pol. Sci. Rev.*, **62**, 169–184.

Jennings, M. K., and Niemi, R. G. 1974. *The Political Character of Adolescence*. Princeton: Princeton University Press.

Jennings, M. K., and Niemi, R. G. 1975. Continuity and change in political orientations: A longitudinal study of two generations. *Amer. Pol. Sci. Rev.*, **69**, 1316–1335.

Kalish, R. 1969. The young and old as generation gap allies. *Gerontologist*, **9**, 83–89.

Kalish, R., and Johnson, A. 1972. Value similarities and differences in three generations of women. *J. Marriage & Fam.*, **34**, 49–54.

Keniston, K. 1965. *The Uncommitted: Alienated Youth in American Society*. New York: Harcourt, Brace & World.

Keniston, K. 1968. *Young Radicals*. New York: Harcourt, Brace & World.

Kirkpatrick, S. A. (ed.) 1974. *Quantitative Analysis of Political Data*. Columbus: Charles E. Merrill.

Kreps, J. 1965. The economics of intergenerational relationships. *In*, E. Shanas and G. Streib (eds.), *Social Structure and the Family*, pp. 267–289. Englewood Cliffs, New Jersey: Prentice-Hall.

Lane, R. E. 1958. Fathers and sons: Foundations of political belief. *Am. Soc. Rev.*, **24**, 502–511.

Langman, L., Block, R. L., and Cunningham, J. 1973. Countercultural values at a Catholic university. *Soc. Prob.*, **20**, 521–532.

Langton, K. 1969. *Political Socialization*. New York: Oxford University Press.

Lansing, J. B., and Sonquist, J. 1969. A cohort analysis of changes in the distribution of wealth. *In*, L. Soltow (ed.), *Six Papers on the Size Distribution of Wealth and Income*, pp. 31–70. New York: National Bureau of Economic Research.

Laufer, R., and Bengtson, V. L. 1974. Generations, aging, and social stratification: On the development of generational units. *J. Soc. Issues*, **30**, 181–205.

Litwak, E. 1960. Reference group theory, bureaucratic career and neighborhood primary group cohesion. *Sociometry*, **23**, 72–84.

McTavish, D. 1971. Perceptions of old people: A review of research methodologies and findings. *Gerontologist*, **11**, Part II, 90–101.

Mannheim, K. 1952. The problem of generations [1928]. *In*, D. Kecskemeti (ed.). *Essays on the Sociology of Knowledge*, pp. 276–322. London: Routledge & Kegan Paul.

Marías, J. 1968. Generations: The concept. *In, International Encyclopedia of Social Sciences*, Vol. VI, pp. 88–92. New York: The Free Press.

Marmor, T. R. 1973. *The Politics of Medicare*. Chicago: Aldine.

Martin, W., Bengtson, V., and Acock, A. 1973. Alienation and age: A context-specific approach. *Soc. Forces*, **54**, 67–84.

Mason, K., Mason, W., Winsborough, H., and Poole, W. 1973. Some methodological issues in cohort analysis of archival data. *Am. Soc. Rev.*, **38**, 242–257.

Mead, M. 1970. *Culture and Commitment: A Study of the Generation Gap*. New York: Basic Books.

Milbrath, L. W. 1965. *Political Participation*. Chicago: Rand McNally.

Miller, A. H., Brown, T. A., and Raine, A. S. 1973. Social conflict and political estrangement, 1958–1972. Unpublished paper prepared for the Convention of the Midwest Political Science Association, Chicago.

Morgan, J. N. 1975. Economic problems of the aging and their policy implications. Paper prepared for the Gerontological Society Conference on Public Policy Assessment of the Conditions and Status of the Elderly, Santa Barbara, California.

Nesselroade, J. R., and Baltes, P. B. 1974. Adolescent personality development and historical change: 1970–1972. *Monographs of the Society for Research in Child Development*, **39**, 1–80.

Ortega y Gasset, J. 1933 [1923]. *The Modern Theme*. New York: W. W. Norton.

Peters, G. R. 1971. Self-conceptions of the aged, age identification, and aging. *Gerontologist*, **11**, Part II, 69–73.

Pomper, G. M. 1972. From confusion to clarity: Issues and American voters, 1956–1968. *Amer. Pol. Sci. Rev.*, **66**, 415–428.

Pomper, G. M. 1975. *Voters' Choice: Varieties of American Electoral Behavior*. New York: Dodd, Mead.

Pratt, H. J. 1974. Old age associations in national politics. *Annals of the Am. Acad. of Pol. and Soc. Sc.*, **415**, 106–119.

Ragan, P., and Dowd, J. 1974. The emerging political consciousness of the aged: A generational interpretation. *J. Soc. Issues*, **30**, 137–158.

Reiss, I. L. 1968. How and why America's sex standards are changing. *Trans-Action*, **5**, 26–32.

Renshon, S. A. 1974. *Psychological Needs and Political Behavior*. New York: The Free Press.

Riley, M. W., Johnson, M., and Foner, A. 1972. *Aging and Society: Vol. III, A Sociology of Age Stratification*. New York: Russell Sage Foundation.

Rosow, I. 1967. *Social Integration of the Aged*. New York: The Free Press.

Ryder, N. 1965. The cohort as a concept in the study of social change. *Am. Soc. Rev.*, **30**, 843–861.

Scammon, R., and Wattenberg, B. J. 1970. *The Real*

Majority. New York: Coward, McCann, & Geoghegan.

Schaie, K. W. 1965. A general model for the study of developmental problems. *Psych. Bull.*, **64**, 72–107.

Schreiber, E. M., and Marsden, L. R. 1972. Age and opinions on a government program of medical aid. *J. Geront.*, **27**, 95–101.

Schwartz, D. C. 1973. *Political Alienation and Political Behavior*. Chicago: Aldine.

Seeman, M. 1959. On the meaning of alienation. *Am. Soc. Rev.*, **24**, 783–791.

Shanas, E., and Hauser, P. M. 1974. Zero population growth and the family life of old people. *J. Soc. Issue*, **30**, 79–92.

Shanas, E., and Streib, G. F. (eds.). 1965. *Social Structure and the Family: Generational Relations*. Englewood Cliffs, New Jersey: Prentice-Hall.

Shanas, E., Townsend, P., Wedderburn, D., Friis, H., Milhøj, P., and Stehouwer, J. 1968. *Old People in Three Industrial Societies*. New York: Atherton Press.

Shyrock, H., and Siegel, J. 1971. *The Materials and Methods of Demography*. Washington, D. C.: Government Printing Office.

Slater, P. 1970. *The Pursuit of Loneliness*. Boston: Beacon Press.

Spitzer, A. B. 1973. The historical problem of generations. *Am. His. Rev.*, **78**, 1353–1385.

Starr, J. M. 1974. The peace and love generation: Changing attitudes toward sex and violence among college youth. *J. Soc. Issues*, **31**, 73–106.

Streib, G. F. 1965. Integenerational relations: Perspectives of the two generations on the older parent. *J. Marriage & Fam.*, **27**, 469–476.

Streib, G. F. 1972. Older families and their troubles: Familial and social responses. *Family Coordinator*, **21**, 5–19.

Sussman, M. 1965. Relationships of adult children with their parents in the United States. *In*, E. Shanas and G. Streib (eds.), *Social Structure and the Family: Generational Relations*, pp. 62–92. Englewood Cliffs, New Jersey: Prentice-Hall.

Sussman, M., Cates, J., and Smith, D. 1970. *The Family and Inheritance*. New York: Russell Sage Foundation.

Treas, J. 1975. Aging and the family. *In*, D. S. Woodruff and J. E. Birren (eds.), *Aging: Scientific Perspectives and Social Issues*, pp. 70–91. New York: D. Van Nostrand.

Trela, J. E. 1971. Some political consequences of senior center and other old age group memberships. *Gerontologist*, **11**, 118–123.

Troll, L. E. 1970. Issues in the study of generations. *Aging and Human Development*, **1**, 199–218.

Troll, L. E. 1971. The family of later life: A decade review. *J. Marriage & Fam.*, **33**, 263–290.

Verba, S., and Nie, N. 1972. *Participation in America*. New York: Harper & Row.

Waller, W. 1938. *The Family: A Dynamic Interpretation*. New York: Dryden.

Walther, R. J. 1975. Economics and the older population. *In*, D. Woodruff and J. E. Birren (eds.), *Aging: Scientific Perspectives and Social Issues*, pp. 336–351. New York: D. Van Nostrand.

Weider, D. L., and Zimmerman, D. H. 1974. Generational experience and the development of freak culture. *J. Soc. Issues*, **30**, 137–162.

Whittaker, D., and Watts, W. 1969. Personality characteristics of a nonconformist youth sub-culture. *J. Soc. Issues*, **25**, 65–89.

Willmott, P., and Young, M. 1960. *Family and Class in a London Suburb*. London: Routledge & Kegan Paul.

Woodruff, D. S., and Birren, J. E. 1972. Age changes and cohort differences in personality. *Developmental Psychology*, **6**, 252–259.

7
SOCIAL STRATIFICATION AND AGING

Gordon F. Streib

University of Florida

Social stratification involves the patterned inequality which is characteristic of all societies. The stratification component refers to the fact that there are strata, layers and classes that may be demarcated and that have differentiating characteristics and privileges. Central to the definition of stratification are the core values—the beliefs and rationalizations which justify the institutional structure of the society. A search of the literature for an analysis of how aging is related to social stratification reveals that this topic has not received systematic attention. This singular neglect makes it imperative to map out some of the major dimensions of the interrelationship of these two areas. The discussion in this chapter rests on two main assumptions: (1) various age cohorts are differentially valued, both by individuals, by aggregates, and by collectivities; and (2) the heterogeneity of the aged means that there is marked within-cohort differentiation of stratification.

THE BASIC DIMENSIONS OF STRATIFICATION

Social stratification may be viewed both in terms of process and structure. The dimension of process involves ranking and evaluation: it is concerned with judgments of whether people are richer or poorer, more esteemed or less esteemed, powerful or weak. The analyst of social stratification who is concerned with the dynamics of process must also be concerned with mobility, both upward and downward, for one of the distinguishing features of stratification in the latter part of the life cycle is downward mobility. Two other forms of mobility, career mobility and generational mobility, take on special pertinence in the latter part of the life cycle.

From a structural point of view, social stratification involves the consequences of these ranking processes: the outcomes which solidify in time into class structures, elites, and castes.

Social stratification as process and as structure is probably as old as the culture of mankind. It is only within the last 100 years that systematic attention has been given to the study of the complexities of rank differentiations. The analysis of social stratification takes on added complexity when one adds aging as a variable.

The universality of stratification still leaves open the question of which criteria are to be employed in sorting out the strata and classes in a given society. All studies of social stratification acknowledge the importance of economic factors—income, wealth, and occupation—as primary considerations in any social rankings. This straightforward generalization requires qualification in order to analyze more completely and more precisely the significance of economic factors.

Most studies of stratification maintain that those who adhere to a Marxian interpretation assign greater importance and significance to economic factors than do other analysts, who see economic considerations in relation to other variables. Marx never set forth a systematic account of his ideas concerning social class, but almost everything he wrote had implications for the understanding of social inequality (Bendix and Lipset, 1953; Bottomore, 1966; Kahl, 1957). The core of Marx's theory of social stratification may be summarized in three statements: (1) social classes are derived from the positions people hold in the system of production; (2) a new social structure will result from inevitable class conflicts; (3) there will be the eventual development of a type of society which will be classless.

A tremendous amount of writing has been stimulated by Marx's ideas—some of which supported his theory and some of which was highly critical of it. Max Weber (1946), one of the most eminent of Marx's critics, was among the first to offer both a comprehensive and focused plan for understanding social stratification. Weber used a three dimensional approach to stratification—class, status, and power. The economic factor is the starting point for practically all discussions of the first dimension, class. Whether one views the class system from a Marxian or Weberian standpoint, or some other orientation, most students of stratification, regardless of their ideological perspective, assign prime importance to the economic base. Other criteria of stratification may be important—race, ethnicity, religious affiliation, and kinship—but economic position forms the basic structure and most of the other forms of stratification are derived from it.

The second major dimension of stratification proposed by Max Weber is that of status. It is closely related to one's economic or class position; however, there are other aspects which are involved so we must consider status as a distinct phenomenon analytically and empirically. When Weber made his distinction of class, status, and power groups, he emphasized that

one of the major properties of status groups is "honor" (Weber, 1946, p. 186). Status also includes such concepts as styles of life, prestige, social rank, and evaluations which, although related to economic position, involve other criteria than those based strictly on economics. Status groups, or as Weber called them, "status communities," are identified by a number of important social behaviors, such as friendship, visiting networks, marriage choices, consumption patterns, and a general style of life.

Power is the third dimension of social stratification in Weber's analytical scheme. Power, as employed here, denotes the idea of influence, particularly that manifested through governmental structures, political parties, and the political process. However, economic factors are significant determinants of power, as they are of status. In a modern democratic state, power is manifested primarily through control of the machinery of government. Because the government has the legitimate authority to pass laws, to enforce them, and to tax, those individuals and groups who exercise political and governmental power are able to influence the behavior and destiny of other people, or as Weber wrote, their "life chances."

AGE AS A DIMENSION OF RANKING

In this chapter we will take the basic position that economic factors are of prime importance, although they are modified, interpreted, and embellished by status, by power, and also by social psychological considerations: perceptions, attitudes, and personality. But in discussion of social stratification and the aged, we must give attention to age itself as a component of ranking and evaluation because of the fact that various age cohorts are differentially valued by individuals and groups both within societies and across cultures (Riley, Johnson, and Foner, 1972).

The subject of age stratification will be covered more fully in Chapter 8. There are several questions derived from studying class stratification which can illuminate the emerging field of age stratification. Riley (1971) has focused upon four important comparative subjects: (1) the individual's location in the class or age structure; (2) the social relationships within and between the class or age strata; (3) the issues and problems related to upward or downward mobility and the differences between mobility and cohort flow; and (4) the impact of the processes affecting individuals and their effects upon the macrostructure of a changing society.

It has been observed that peoples in most cultures affirm the unique and special qualities of the old. Folk wisdom and social science (Simmons, 1945; Cowgill and Holmes, 1972) indicate that age may be associated with characteristics that are positively valued by man: maturity, wisdom, compassion, spirituality, and self-acceptance. Almost all of these traits are qualitative characteristics which are nonquantifiable, although most people probably make judgments about their degree of attainment. Yet, most people would prefer to have these characteristics at a younger stage in the life cycle, for they are not the exclusive possession of the aged.

Generally, old age is not valued highly because it is associated widely with decline in physical attractiveness, vigor, health condition, sexual prowess, and perhaps some mental abilities. And most important from an actuarial basis, it is associated with the expectation of fewer years of life itself. In a fundamental sense, this is the consideration which makes the aged lose status—even though they may have many positive characteristics. The inescapable fact of human mortality forces all other aspects of ranking to fade into lesser significance when evaluated in relation to life itself. Stating it boldly and simply, almost all peoples when asked to rank the dimensions of stratification—income, possessions, education, prestige, political power, honor—would choose extension of life over these other traits. And some persons who are most hostile to the aged as a category are those who are fearful of their own eventual decline and demise. They have not come to terms with their own mortality and shun contact with anyone who might remind them of their future condition.

CLASS, STATUS, POWER, AND AGING

How does age alter or modify some of the basic dimensions of stratification? In this section we will discuss the changes associated with age according to the Weberian scheme of class, status, and power. Our overall approach to stratification considers age and sex as intervening or modifying variables which qualify correlations or conditions reported for earlier phases of the life cycle. Most writers on stratification give little if any consideration to the way in which aging might modify the class position of individual or members of groups or strata. The intellectual giants of the nineteenth century whose ideas are still pervasive and significant, Marx and Weber, did not consider the way in which aging and the aged complicate social stratification in modern societies. They were concerned in the main with the way in which stratification issues were joined at the peak periods of life from adulthood through middle age. Their neglect of this subject is understandable, for during their lifetime the concern for the aged was just developing. Indeed, the life span and the age structures of German and English societies were such that very few persons, even those as prescient as Marx and Weber, recognized the growing significance of aging and the age structures.

Class Position in Aging

Occupation. One of the major dimensions of stratification is one's occupational position. Many studies of stratification use this as the major criterion of classification (for example, Shanas, Townsend, Wedderburn, Friis, Milhøj, and Stehouwer, 1968; Porter, 1965). Therefore, retirement may cause a definite lowering of social stratification ranking in some individuals. However, the retiree still retains his job skills and body of knowledge even though he no longer exercises his occupation. His self-evaluation and the regard in which he is held by society is higher than that of the unemployed, untrained person. Moreover, there is a definite carry-over effect of the employment situation, especially in the professions. A physician retains his prestige as a medical expert even though he has ceased to practice; a judge is often called "Judge" and considered an expert on law; a person of high military rank keeps his title and prestige.

Social class as measured by occupation has a

certain stability throughout the life span. Svalastoga (1959, p. 308), for example, has made an interesting analysis of the Danes, in which he shows a gradual increase in status over the years until about age 60, and then a decline. The sharpest status rise is from 20 to 30, and the decline begins at 60 and drops sharply after age 70. Stability of class position as measured by occupation is only one component of stratification in later life.

Income. The reduction in income is one of the most consistent class changes which occurs in aging and is related, of course, to the loss of occupation. How does this affect the individual's class position? In the years immediately following retirement, there is no evidence that the class position is drastically altered. In the Cornell Study of Occupational Retirement, it is significant that although the average person had a decline in income of 56 percent, a quarter to a third of the retirees stated that their retirement standard of living was better than during most of their lifetime (Streib and Schneider, 1971, pp. 85–86). The data show that the percentage of people who say they worry about money was essentially the same before and after retirement. In answer to the question, "Do you consider your present income enough to meet your living expenses," from 60 percent to 87 percent of the different cohorts said that it was enough, despite the fact that their income was about half of its previous level.

A more recent longitudinal study of old age assistance recipients in California by Tissue (1972) adds additional information on income adequacy. Not surprisingly, Tissue reports that the aged poor see their hardships largely in terms of inadequate income. However, it was discovered that one-third of the respondents having an income of $200 or less per month still felt they had no significant money problems. Tissue found that current economic dissatisfaction was not related to previous socioeconomic status. He states, "In short, perceived economic difficulty is no more common to those who 'skidded' into old age than those who have always been relatively poor" (Tissue, 1972, p. 337).

These studies show that we must consider not only objective income, but its subjective aspects (Bultena *et al.*, 1971). Furthermore, a 50 percent decline in income does not mean the same thing to different income levels. The businessman whose income drops from $40,000 to $20,000 may feel "deprived," but he suffers no real status loss or change in class position. He is still more privileged economically than 90 percent of the rest of the population. The retired teacher whose income declines from perhaps $16,000 to $8,000 may complain of feeling pinched financially, yet in comparison to a young family of four or six persons existing on $8,000 he is fortunate indeed. His style of life and class identification remain the same as they were in his middle years. The really deprived segment of the population, whose income may drop, for example, from $5,000 to $2,500 may be in a critical situation. However, from the standpoint of class, if they have endured a lifetime of poverty, they experience simply a more critical situation but not a real *loss* in class position. Their circumstances are a continuation of what they have always known.

There is, however, a group that experiences "new poverty"—those who enjoyed the middle class position in their earlier years and find themselves with few or no resources in later years. This would include the working man who did not receive the pension he expected, or the widow whose husband's pension ceased upon his death—those who have only income from Social Security to live on after having received comfortable incomes in previous years. These people suffer a real decline in class and perhaps also in self-conception.

However, in all reports on the income of the elderly, it seems obvious that sheer dollar amounts do not represent precisely the adequacy or inadequacy of their income in comparison to other groups. Many elderly couples and single persons are able to exist on very small amounts and apparently feel no decline in class level. Why are the elderly able to get along on such small incomes? Are they simply keeping a "stiff upper lip" when they say their income is enough? This is an area that needs much more research, for we do not know enough about the resiliency and adaptability of people to cope with declining income.

However, we have several tentative explanations. First, most of the elderly have a stock of goods and equipment that they have accumulated during a lifetime. They often own a house, and they need to spend less for new furniture, appliances, and equipment.

Secondly, the elderly often benefit from a considerable amount of interhousehold transfers. Children, relatives, friends, and neighbors supply food, goods, and services. Many elderly acquire their entire clothing replacements through gifts at Christmas, birthdays, and Mother's Day, etc.

In addition, they may have absorbed and internalized some of the general attitudes of society: that retired persons *should* receive a lower income than working persons. Rainwater's (1974) study of the social meanings of income shows this clearly. When 600 people were asked what was a fair recommended minimum income, they listed the recommended level for a retired person at two-thirds that of a worker of age 42. The Bureau of Labor Statistics, in setting budget standards, reflects a similar judgment when they state that older people "need" less. They say that a working couple over 65 years of age "needs" about 85 percent of the income of a 35 to 54-year-old couple, while a retired couple "needs" 72 percent as much.

And finally, a process of disengagement could be operating. The elderly often voluntarily curtail their needs, activities, and consumption patterns in accord with their declining energy, declining interests, and declining income. The work of Tissue on perception of self- and income adequacy offers insights into the varying ways that disengagement occurs.

The most significant variable in his study related to perception of economic hardship is whether a person retained a younger or older self-image. Persons who are young or who feel young and act young state they have more economic problems than those who regard themselves as old or actually are old (with one minor exception). Finally, people who perceive money problems are also those who feel a frustration in satisfying consumer needs. In the California study, the aged who wished to travel, to buy clothing, to entertain friends, to buy furniture are more likely to report money problems than those who have less interest in such things.

Tissue (1972, p. 339) summarizes the issue, "A youthful age image with a desire for consumer items produces the highest problem rates, whereas an older age image, matched to a lack of consumer interest, is least productive of hardship." Thus, a person with an older self-image may manage comfortably on a smaller income because he has "disengaged from consumerism," so to speak.

Runciman's work on relative deprivation in Britain shows that the demands of the elderly are more modest than those of other poor groups. He (Runciman, 1966, p. 271) writes: "While there is a widespread view among younger people that the elderly have done rather badly financially, the old themselves have modest demands."

Property. Closely related to income is the amount of property a person has accumulated. Property has not only material value but also symbolic qualities which often become accentuated in old age. For the older person, the home, the furnishings, the possessions may encompass a lifetime of values, feelings, and emotions. In the calculus of old age, this may be more significant than the dollar income.

In the United States, about 70 percent of families own their own homes at retirement (Riley, Foner, Moore, Hess, and Roth, 1968, p. 91). This is important both financially and symbolically. Kent and Hirsch (1971), in studying low income black and white families in Philadelphia, reported that nearly half of the sample owned their own homes. When the researchers asked why some of these very low income people did not apply for Old Age Assistance, one of the reasons frequently given was that they were afraid they would lose their homes. The investigators (Kent and Hirsch, 1971, p. 116) state, "the present generation of old people place great value on home ownership. They received their early socialization at a time when to own one's home was one of the major goals of the American people."

Education. A fourth important determinant of class is education and training. This is significant because these are measurable attributes that cannot be taken away from a person, and which can be used as a precise indicator of rank. However, it is true that in the case of the aged, a considerable proportion have education and training that has become obsolescent in a changing society. At the same time, the person with higher educational attainments retains certain objective advantages which can never be removed. Higher educated people, in particular, retain attributes which help them to maintain and even increase their social standing in the community vis-à-vis less educated older people.

Status and Aging

The second major dimension of stratification is that of status, prestige, or esteem. What are the attributes or characteristics which contribute to high or low rank along these dimensions?

Membership Groups. Status is likely to reflect one's memberships and group affiliations because these are inextricably linked to one's family and kin ties and to the way in which family characteristics are ranked and evaluated in the local community. Obviously, these affiliations are not completely independent of the characteristics discussed above under economic or class level. Generally, there is a correlation between class and status position, but in some cases they do not completely correspond. Status also involves informal affiliations such as friendships and cliques, and the interactions which originate from these social sources. The prestige of many of these persist for the older person even if he or she withdraws from active participation. For example, a person who belonged to an exclusive country club still retains the aura of membership even though he may no longer attend and pay dues. He once attained the "stamp of approval," and this can never be taken away even though he may no longer have the income, health, strength, or interest to continue the association.

Similarly, Lipset (1968) speaks of "accorded status"—the honor and prestige which is given to individuals. There is considerable continuity and persistence of this type of status. For example, the retired actor or sports hero is still given considerable attention on the basis of his past fame. Unlike the objective or material or monetary aspects, the accorded status may continue throughout the retirement period of life.

Style of Life. Status is also a reflection, in part, of one's style of life. This is, of course, related to income but may also be related to education. One of the paradoxes in later life is that persons can suffer severe declines in income, yet still retain essentially the same style of life. This means that they may live in the same neighborhood, keep the same friends, and pursue the same hobbies and interest (on a reduced scale).

Their expenditures for essentials may remain the same, but their discretionary income is reduced. The individuals themselves may be keenly aware of various economies, but their reduced economic position is not readily obvious to the outside world, and they appear to retain the same class position. In addition, an aspect of the process of disengagement may "assist" in the tapering off phases, so that they may, for example, take fewer and shorter vacations, drive their car less, and buy a new model less frequently.

In the three nation study of the elderly in the U.S., England, and Denmark (Shanas *et al.*, 1968, p. 256), the investigators observed that there were three distinct styles of life: the white collar, the blue collar, and the agricultural workers. These three major categories had different family life-styles in middle age. "These same differences, reinforced by time, continue into old age," Shanas *et al.* report (1968, p. 256). They noted national differences, for in Denmark, middle and working class elderly people appear to merge in a common classless pattern, while the agricultural workers maintain a distinctly different style of family life.

Subjective Status. Finally, there is subjective status as a major dimension of stratification. This involves a person's own sense of where he thinks he ranks on the social hierarchy. There is a positive relationship to the two other major dimensions of stratification, objective (e.g., economics) and accorded status, although not a perfect correlation. For example, Coleman and Neugarten (1971, pp. 112-113) found a fairly high correlation between objective indicators and subjective evaluation, but there were differentials in the correlations. At the upper class level, the objective factors were rather poor predictors of subjective positions.

Power and Aging

Turning to the power dimension in relation to aging, we observe that there are two major ways that age can manifest itself: first, through a disproportionate holding of important offices by older people and second, by the power that older people may wield individually or collectively to express their concerns either through voting, or through interest and pressure groups. The first type is illustrated by the way in which seniority operates in most legislative bodies in the United States. One can think of state legislators, congressmen, and U.S. senators who by virtue of their seniority (which is highly correlated with age) are able to exercise disproportionate influence on the legislative process (Mathews, 1954). Inasmuch as elective officials are not subject to any formal retirement process, except as expressed by the will of the electorate, some aged persons are able to exercise disproportionate power.

In appointive positions, such as the judiciary, regulative commissions, and administrative agencies, there are often formal rules for retirement. However the normal retirement age, whether 65 or 70, may be waived in the case of exceptional persons, or those who have unusual power over the persons who appoint them. (One thinks, for example, of the late J. Edgar Hoover, who directed the Federal Bureau of Investigation for over half a century.)

Generally speaking, these persons do not conceive of the elderly as their special constituency and rarely use their power to enhance the specific interests of the aged. Rather, elected officials often attempt to create the impression of being middle-aged and try to place some social distance between themselves and their age-peers.

The question often arises as to whether the aged could not exercise enormous power at the polls, if they should act as a power bloc. We agree with the interpretation of Binstock (1974, p. 199): "There is no sound reason to expect the aging will gain power by voting cohesively in the future." While interest groups may galvanize from time to time on a special issue, it seems unlikely that they will form a continuous pressure group. Despite the marked growth of some membership organizations (Pratt, 1974)

and the emergence of new "militant" senior power groups, it does not seem likely that they will develop into one cohesive organization in the decade ahead.

Finally, there is another facet of the way in which older persons exercise a disproportionate influence in political and economic affairs, namely, through the leadership in the trade union movement (where there are no fixed retirement ages or where such retirement rules are not invoked) and through the ownership and control of vast private fortunes. In these two cases, however, they do not exercise influence on behalf of their age cohort. For a fuller discussion of power and aging, see Chapter 15.

A discussion of power would not be complete without a mention of power on the microlevel—in the environment of the family. Throughout history, old people have exercised power because they own and control property and have the final decision as to the disposition of their wealth. While we often think of the exercise of power as involving large fortunes, it must be pointed out that even very small amounts of wealth and property can be powerful "weapons" in the family and kinship system. Although 90 percent of legacies are under the $60,000 taxable limits (Sussman, Cates, and Smith, 1970), these smaller amounts can be a real consideration in the treatment which older persons receive. Many elderly persons have enjoyed attention and concern from their relatives, as they kept them guessing about the provisions of their last will and testament.

STRATUM CONSCIOUSNESS

The study of social stratification offers the opportunity to bring together the traditional concept of class consciousness and the newer concept of age consciousness. In this section of the chapter, we will first develop these two concepts and then show how they are interrelated to each other. We will also try to analyze the ways in which group solidarity stems from group consciousness and how solidarity is necessary for group action. The development of group consciousness based on class or age can, as Mannheim pointed out, provide persons with a "common location in the social and historical process" and may lead to a "characteristic mode of thought and experience" (Mannheim, 1952).

Class Consciousness

The first step in our analysis is to demarcate the concept of class consciousness. This tends to be an individual's feeling of where he fits in the stratification system. Moreover, class consciousness may vary at different points in the life cycle, and it may be influenced by community and historical contexts. Finally, class consciousness is important because it is found in different forms at different levels of the class system. The class consciousness of the top strata, for example, may involve a variety of feelings and motivations: snobbery, exploitation, *noblesse oblige*, compassion, etc. Conversely, among the most deprived class or strata, one may also find a variety of feelings and attitudes associated with awareness of one's class identity, such as resignation, deference, or "knowing one's place."

One of the significant issues in the study of social stratification is whether one conceives of the system as composed of social classes or of social strata. The distinction between the two rests upon the degree to which people see a class as having some boundaries and involving a degree of group solidarity. Many writers use the word *social class* when they are really talking about social strata, which are ill-defined layers or categories in a hierarchy. Both the concept of class and of strata are ill defined and hard to distinguish in the United States as compared with some other industrialized societies.

This distinction is important both from the standpoint of the analyst and from the standpoint of the person himself. Rosenberg (1970) is one of the few investigators who has given systematic attention to the images older persons hold of the class system. His study of the white working class in Philadelphia shows that lower income persons (all respondents had family incomes of $7500 or less) see the class system as closed. These older persons believed that automation prevents advancement, and getting ahead is out of one's hands. The image of a closed class system is correlated with the neighborhood economic context, for the old men in

this study living in the poorest neighborhood are more likely to have an image of a closed class system.

A number of investigators (Rosenberg, 1970; Olsen, 1974) have found that there is always a certain percentage of persons who find it difficult to formulate a conception of the class system. A simple description is that class consciousness tends to be higher among those who are least rewarded by the society. Rosenberg (1970, p. 167) says, "These underdogs place the blame for lack of advancement squarely on the class system and where their own careers are concerned have the least difficulty of any group of breadwinners of conceiving of the operation of the society in terms of class factors."

Another factor that may be involved in the degree of class consciousness present is the general economic conditions that prevail. Rosenberg's study was carried out in a postwar period of prosperity. The studies of Pope (1941) and Jones (1941) carried out during economic depression show a higher level of class consciousness. Therefore, one would expect that the underprivileged aged might have a heightened sense of class consciousness, and their inability to work or to anticipate an improved economic situation would increase their apathy and antagonism to the *status quo*. In writing about periods of economic depression, Leggett (1968, p. 25) has said, "Not only the poverty of the average person but the vivid contrasts in wealth, the relative decline in workers' standards of living and the widening gap between what the worker expected and the middle class obtained were undoubtedly relevant."

Another issue related to class awareness is the way in which class consciousness changes over time. Schreiber and Nygreen (1970) have analyzed eight different national surveys and conclude that working class identification increased irregularly in the U. S. from 1945 to 1960 and finally reached a plateau slightly higher than the original point. These data suggest that the period effect is not very great during the 15 years after World War II.

Age Consciousness

A concept analogous to class consciousness is age consciousness—the awareness and feelings of one's chronological development. Throughout human history individuals have been aware of their own growing old and of those in their communities who lived to be old. Poets, playwrights, and philosophers have written with sensitivity and insight about age consciousness, but the phenomenon has taken on a different dimension in the last half century, principally in industrialized societies. Age consciousness has new meaning because of the greatly increased number of aged in the population, the institutionalization of retirement, and the development of voluntary and interest groups concerned with the aged.

There are two major facets to age consciousness: the first is the awareness of one's own aging processes—primarily a psychological phenomenon. The second facet is more sociological—awareness of the fact that others are growing old, and that one may have something in common with them as persons who have reached a similar point in the life cycle.

The first question to ask is: precisely who are the aged? How does the analyst demarcate the aged as a category or stratum from other segments of the population? The simple objective way is to use a chronological criterion, as age 60, 65, or 70. This is the means usually employed for most administrative purposes—insurance, retirement, pensions, and social security. Among gerontologists (Kelleher and Quirk, 1973), and also among lay persons, there is an effort to use functional criteria rather than chronological age for determining a person's age status. But it is a minority position, and although there are valid grounds for considering such bases, it is doubtful if functional criteria will be widely used in the near future.

Another development which has direct bearing upon issues related to social stratification and age stratification is the division of the older population into two or three different categories (Neugarten, 1974). (1) The young-old are those who are 55 to 65 years of age. In most instances, they are still gainfully employed and at the peak of their earning power and social recognition. (2) The middle-old, aged 65 to 75, includes a large proportion of the retiree population. These people have

experienced a substantial cut in income and have given up their lifetime occupation. However, many of them are in good health and have an abundant supply of a precious resource—time. (3) The old-old are persons over 75 and often include those who are the most frail, the sickest, the most isolated, and the most impoverished segment of the population. It is this group who constitute the core of what might be labeled the "problem population" among the elderly and are considered by those who refer to the low status of the aged.

The use of functional criteria is a process followed not only by experts but by the aged themselves in self-rating evaluations. Indeed, numerous surveys have found that a very large proportion of 65-year-old persons consider themselves "middle-aged." Until quite late in the life cycle, this tendency persists for persons to identify themselves with younger groups. Some interpreters (Rosow, 1967) have stated that this represents denial of one's true age status. In view of such interpretations and findings concerning refusal to identify with one's age mates, it would seem that old age consciousness is a weak basis for group solidarity and group action.

The Aged as a Conscious Minority Group

This leads to a discussion of the question of whether the aged constitute a conscious minority group in our society. There have been some gerontologists who maintain that the aged are discriminated against and constitute a minority group. (Barron, 1953; Palmore, 1969; Palmore and Whittington, 1971). Such an approach requires careful definition and conceptualization, for the term *minority group* has the possibility of being employed as a technical term and as an image-producing term. The latter usage is akin to the definition of the aged as a social problem, or as "victims" of social forces or of deprivations and discriminations imposed or invoked by other categories of persons in the society. Some persons view compulsory retirement as analogous to job discrimination on the basis of sex, race, or ethnicity. They do not recognize that over half of the persons who retire say they are unable to work because of declining health. Thus, most people are "victims" of their own biology—not "victims" of society.

A sociological evaluation would conclude that the aged are not a genuine minority group, for they do not share a distinct and separate culture (Streib, 1965). Moreover, membership in the category of persons designated as the aged is not exclusive or permanent but awaits all members of a particular society who are fortunate to live long enough. Age is not as distinguishing a social group characteristic as sex, occupation, or social class. Many of the aged do possess distinctive physical characteristics, but these do not usually justify or result in discriminatory treatment by other persons or groups.

Furthermore, many of the aged do not identify with their age mates, and they tend to have a low feeling of group consciousness. While membership organizations of senior citizens have grown greatly in the last decade, such groups have relatively low hostility towards out groups.

Some persons have charged that the aged are segregated in "geriatric ghettos." However, retirement communities are joined voluntarily and can be left at any time. Furthermore, numerous surveys and qualitative evidence indicate that many of the elderly prefer to live with their age-peers.

Although the aged participate in the voting process more frequently than some other age groups until the age of about 75, Binstock (1974) and others (Riley et al., 1968) have pointed out that to date there is limited evidence suggesting strong solidarity on political matters.

Ragan and Dowd (1974, p. 154) believe that the aged are a *potential* political force. However, they conclude, "Age-group political consciousness—the identification by the aged of their common political interests and potential for common action—is not clearly manifest among the current cohort of older persons."

A contrasting point of view is presented by Laufer and Bengtson (1974, p. 199). They state: "We would argue that structural conditions which prodded youth to be open to change and self-conscious exploration of identity may now be reappearing among older

people." They believe that the need to reorganize identity at advanced stages of the life cycle raises the prospect of collective action.

Morris and Murphy (1966) have proposed that stratum consciousness be viewed as a series of steps or stages which have a cumulative property to them: (1) stratum awareness, or perception of separateness from other age groups; (2) stratum affiliation, or sense of belonging; (3) stratum consciousness, or identification of interests in conflict with those of other strata; and (4) stratum ideology and/or action. In the case of the aged, it would appear that the first step, stratum awareness, may be more commonly perceived, but the next three steps are less likely to occur. In spite of widespread publicity given to the Gray Panther movement, for example, this involves only a minute percentage of the elderly. While some gerontologists and other writers speculate about the marked potential for group action by the elderly, to date there is little evidence of its manifestation.

Jacobs offers a challenge to the notion that establishing a group identity of the aged and the resultant political action would be wholly beneficial for the aged. He believes that such a development would have negative consequences that would outweigh any possible benefits to be derived. He states (Jacobs, 1974, p. 75), "While group identity can be viewed as positive with respect to organizing a set of persons toward purposeful actions, an identity based upon the virtues of old and that is achieved by "putting down" youth and segregating the aged from youth in retirement settings . . . will not lead to the fulfillment of group goals through the group's greater involvement with the general culture."

SPECIAL CONTEXTS OF STRATIFICATION AND AGING

It has been stressed that the aged are very heterogeneous and that various age cohorts are differentially evaluated. Four subject areas have been chosen for further analysis to illustrate cohort differentiation: sex, great wealth, residential density, and ethnicity.

Stratification and the Aging Woman

The way in which sex differentiation is involved in the allocation of power, prestige, and other resources must be considered in studying stratification in relation to aging. Holter has said (1970, p. 227): "Gender differentiation, which is always ascriptive, is probably felt as more inconsistent with the general stratification system based on achievement compared to one based on ascription." The implications of considering age and sex simultaneously are starkly shown in the way in which pension and social insurance schemes discriminate against women in many cultures.

The way in which sex status enters into distribution of power and privilege has until very recently been neglected in the stratification literature. Lenski (1966, pp. 402-406) is one of the few writers who has given specific attention to "The Class System Based on Sex."

Haug (1973) has pointed out that a woman's class position is generally assessed on the basis of the man's position. With two wage earners in the family, the question arises as to how the female's position affects the family rank. First is the matter of the income supplementation, and second, the possibility of status inconsistency in the family if the women's occupational status or educational attainment is different from that of her husband.

After the husband retires, the economic situation of the family is much stronger if his wife continues to work than if they depend on his pension alone. If she retires and receives a pension too, their economic situation is even more advantageous.

Widowhood may be a particularly important factor in the status of women at the end of the life cycle because of relatively greater frequency at later ages. The widow is in an ambiguous position if her status has been dependent principally on her husband's rank. If he has left her a large estate, this one factor can overcome almost all other stratification considerations. But if he has left her with no support and if his pension ceases upon his death, she may be one of those in "new poverty"—forced to adapt to a new style of life consistent with her downward mobility. She may have only a reduced social security check as her means of support. Of course the widow who works can maintain a more adequate economic position. However, given the fact that many women care for their husbands in case of a final illness, it may be hard to reenter the labor force.

The status implications of widowhood have been studied by Lopata (1973). She found that widows were often reluctant to keep up community and neighborhood friendships and associations after their husbands' deaths. Many withdrew from social life, particularly from events they would have attended as a couple. One woman, reflecting the lower status she experienced as a result of this withdrawal, observed that she felt like a "second class citizen" (Lopata, 1973, p. 191).

Lopata also reported that better educated women often found widowhood very threatening to their self-identity, for their activities and world view are constructed around the life of their husband and his work associates. The lower class women, in contrast, were less involved in the world of their husbands. The couples communicated less with each other, and the husband's death was not as damaging to the self-identity of the wife.

Finally, a further loss in status is experienced by older widows who have to give up their own home and share a domicile with their children. This is a loss both in the eyes of the community and in the widow's self-perception. The fact that she is no longer mistress of her own household and no longer surrounded by the possessions which she has spent a lifetime accumulating represents a severe loss of status in her microenvironment. Some families have eased this situation by having the daughter or daughter-in-law return to work when the mother moves in so that there is not the friction of "territorial rights" in the kitchen. This problem of power at the microenvironmental level occurs in only a small percentage of cases, as most women prefer to live by themselves rather than move into the home of a child.

In order to present a full picture of stratification as it relates to age and sex, one must mention the fact that statistics show that half of all millionaires are women. Why are there so many women millionaires? There are no systematic answers but one can speculate. First, the greater longevity of women means that they inherit their husband's wealth and thus control the fortunes accumulated by another during a lifetime. Secondly, because almost all men marry women younger than themselves, many women live for years as widows. Because of these life cycle circumstances, there is a change in the sexual allocation of income and wealth from the pattern which is normative at earlier ages.

Age and the Very Rich in the U.S.

Many analyses of social stratification and the aged concentrate on the fact that the aged form a disproportionate section of the poor in most societies. However, it is a paradox that the aged are also disproportionately represented in the very rich segment of the population. The average age of millionaires in the U.S. is about 60, and there is not much difference in the age of male and female millionaires. A study by *Fortune* magazine of the very wealthiest persons in the U.S.—the 66 centimillionaires—indicates that the median age of this group was 65 years of age (Louis, 1968).

The concentration of great wealth and high income among a small number of the aged raises some important questions about how the stratification system functions: (1) how does it happen that people can accumulate large fortunes? (2) how is this wealth transmitted at death and (3) what is the relation of great wealth to class consciousness and age consciousness?

The answer to the first two questions is obviously the tax structure of a capitalistic society which enables people to enjoy a high income and accumulate great wealth during their lifetime, and then because of the inheritance taxes and trust funds, to transfer large fortunes from generation to generation.

The third question revolves around the issue of the kind and degree of age consciousness and group solidarity. As noted earlier, a continuing controversy in the gerontological literature is whether the aged are a minority or quasi-minority group. Writers who argue for a minority group perspective tend to concentrate their attention upon the poor and underprivileged

aged. On an aggregate basis, one does not dispute the fact that many of the elderly must live under conditions of extreme deprivation. However, the aged are a heterogeneous group and include many who are comfortably retired, and a few who are extremely rich and privileged. The lack of solidarity among the aged is demonstrated by the fact that the wealthy elderly people do not use their power and influence specifically to reduce the underprivileged status of their age mates. They generally do not attempt to press for the redistribution of resources or improvement in status of the victim category. They identify with their class and with their own family and kin groups—not with their age cohort. Thus, it seems that there is age solidarity and group consciousness principally if there is a shared victim status—and as soon as persons move out of the underprivileged group, their age group consciousness diminishes. As they move to the most privileged segments, it seems to vanish.

Furthermore, it would seem that the underprivileged are not too critical of the desire of the wealthy to pass on their wealth to their children and kin, for this is exactly what they would want to do if they themselves were wealthy. Even very poor people desire to "leave something" to those they love. They would rather have more generous old age benefits from federal sources but still keep intact a large part of our inheritance laws.

In a survey of homeowners in Los Angeles County, respondents were asked whether they desired to leave an inheritance to their children. Although the median income of the 65–75-year-old group was only $3,620, 72 percent said they desired to leave an inheritance. The principal reason was parental pride and tradition. "Many respondents who, apparently, could not afford it were attempting to leave something to their heirs and were thereby reducing their own comfort and enjoyment in old age," the investigator states (Chen, 1973, p. 44).

Retirement Communities and Stratification

A new and growing trend which has implications for social stratification of the aged is the development and acceptance of retirement communities. These have been regarded both positively and negatively by gerontologists and other observers. Some consider them to be "geriatric ghettos" and accuse society of casting out its older citizens, so they are "out of sight." Those persons who feel that the aged should remain in the mainstream of life and attempt to remain productive until the end regard retirement communities as an unhealthy withdrawal from life. Other critics have denounced them as being hedonistic in spirit and devoted only to pleasure, recreation, and leisure activities.

However, there is a differing point of view—namely that the retirement communities constitute a status buffer. They provide a protective environment which tends to shield the older person from the acknowledgment of downward mobility or a loss of status. Persons engaged in the world of production may consider that the retiree has declined in status—that he is out of the mainstream, a "back number," as retirees often express it. Within the retirement community, the residents interact principally with those in the same situation. They do not need to envy those who go off to work each day. They do not need to keep up with younger people who are full of ambition and vigor. They do not need to receive pity when they slow down. They can enjoy leisure without feeling abnormal, for all of the residents are in the same situation. Generally, they have a positive viewpoint of their status, when surrounded by persons who have experienced the same role losses. Their situation is reenforced by their attitudes and values. It should also be emphasized that people join such communities voluntarily and may leave if they choose. Thus, the communities are composed of people who have made a conscious choice that this style of life is their best alternative. If they elect to stay in the community, they are usually enthusiastic about their decision.

Bultena and Wood (1969, p. 216) report that persons who moved to retirement communities had significantly higher morale than those who moved to regular or age-integrated communities. And Neugarten (1966) has suggested that by making old age a more attractive period of life, retirement communities may raise the general prestige of the elderly.

One woman of Sun City observed (Malcolm, 1974), "Retired people don't belong in a busy working society because they make pests of themselves, so we came to a retirement community where everyone is at leisure. It's nice to have a place to go to have fun and maybe act a little foolish—I never learned how to ride a bike or swim until I came here—and no one will laugh at you because you're older."

This attitude of sensitivity to ridicule by younger people is undoubtedly a factor influencing some who choose retirement communities. The residents are protected from the amused condescending attitude of younger people when they attend dances, learn new skills in classes, participate in sports, etc.

There are clear socioeconomic differentials between those who migrate to a retirement community and those who remain in their home communities. First, the residents are mainly more affluent middle class or upper-middle class persons who have the funds to relocate in another part of the country. Carter and Webber (1966) reported higher educational levels and above average income for elderly migrants in their detailed Florida study. Therefore, the residential communities are a relatively homogeneous segment of the population. In terms of status and life-style, they follow an emphasis on leisure, friendship, and recreation. In fact, the residents of retirement communities could be called a "new leisure class" (Michelon, 1954).

The internal stratification system within retirement communities tends to be democratic, for people are not impressed by previous accomplishments or what people "used to do." As Jacobs stated in his study of a retirement community of 5600 people, "This general indifference to the former status of their neighbors was, I believe, outstanding" (Jacobs, 1974, p. 65).

There is no clear evidence on whether retirement communities exercise political power as a bloc in relation to the larger political structure. It has been asserted that these enclaves of older persons constitute a cohesive bloc who might adhere to a conservative low-tax voting behavior on local issues. However, there is no evidence to date of such bloc voting. There is the potential for a cohesive political force present in these communities, which might be crucial if it were mobilized and if the issues or candidates were presented in terms emphasizing the interests of the aged.

From a political standpoint, these retirement communities represent an interesting phenomenon since most of the residents are not employed and potentially have more time for political activity than persons in the labor force. However, impressionistic data indicate that the persons who are active politically are those who in their former occupations or communities had some involvement in the political process.

There is some evidence that age density may also act as a crucial variable and status buffer in the microenvironments of large cities. Rosow's (1967) study of Cleveland clearly shows that small environments which are age-segregated have positive social psychological consequences for the residents. Although younger people may complain that it is "depressing" to see a community with a large proportion of aged, such an environment offers many supports for the elderly themselves. They are more apt to help each other in case of trouble, to form visiting patterns, and to offer neighboring services than in a completely heterogeneous community. Rosow (1967, p. 78) says, "The common assumption in gerontology that residential proximity readily stimulates friendships between the generations is simply not borne out by the facts . . . the number of old people's local friends varies directly with the proportion of age peers."

Furthermore, Rosow observed class differences, for he noted that blue collar elderly are more apt to make and maintain friendships in communities with a high proportion of aged. He found that people in preferred positions and those with less role loss are more independent of local relationships, but persons with lower statuses and with more role loss are the most locally dependent.

The studies of Rosow are also supported by the research of Hochschild (1973) on a public housing project and Johnson's (1971) studies of a working class mobile home community.

Ethnic Stratification in Old Age

The Black Aged in the United States. Racial and ethnic dimensions complicate the analysis of stratification in old age. There are two main issues which must be discussed: (1) whether ethnic stratification is a distinct or different form of stratification and (2) the relationship of ethnic stratification to other hierarchical systems: occupation, income, and education. A related issue is the label or term that one employs to designate the ethnic stratification subsystem.

Lieberson (1970) states that the primary criterion for distinguishing ethnic groups is political autonomy since ethnic groups have a potential for setting up their own political entities. Efforts to establish separate nations or political unions on the basis of age or sex would be futile since neither could maintain itself as a separate society.

The separation of ethnic groups is a function of how majorities judge and relate to them and also how the ethnic minority regards itself as an entity and in relation to the larger social structure. In this discussion we will limit ourselves principally to the black ethnic minority in the United States because they comprise the largest minority group and to people of Spanish heritage, the second largest minority.

A subsidiary issue is the label that is employed to designate the ethnic subgroup. For example, the word "caste" has been used by some students of the American Negro population. This term has come into disuse because it implies a rigidity of the hierarchical system which may not apply to the U.S. Quasicaste has been proposed by Blau (1974) as a designation for a structure which is ascriptive, hierarchical, and restrictive of social intercourse. He proposes. a decomposition of the elements of caste so that it is possible to discover the extent to which a group displays caste ingredients.

Billingsley (1968) has used the term "Negro community" as an ethnic subsociety. He points out that in the United States and throughout other parts of the world (Billingsley, 1968, p. 168), the Negro people are viewed as a group or a category set apart from other peoples and sharing conditions, attributes, and behavior in common. On the other hand, great variations of conditions, attributes, and behavior are obvious in so large and diverse a group of people. Thus, when one studies a complex ethnic subsociety, one has the problem of determining the autonomous nature of the society and simultaneously the heterogeneous nature of the people. The complexity of this social reality has been pointed out by Billingsley. He states that Negro families in the United States have to be analyzed in terms of the social environments created by: (1) the social class system within the ethnic subsociety and (2) the region of the country, crudely stated North and

South and (3) the place of residence, namely urban or rural. Lieberson (1970, p. 179) described the phenomenon in these words, "If we consider a society in which there are various combinations of age, sex, economic and ethnic stratification, it becomes clear that the relative importance of each stratification system may vary considerably. This proliferation of status combinations can provide a powerful empirical clue to the nature of these stratification factors as determinants of, say, income."

A factual overview of some of the salient socioeconomic characteristics is presented from the 1970 U.S. census showing comparisons of blacks, whites, and Spanish-speaking persons in Table I. The aged blacks are the least privileged of the three groups: their median income is less, and a higher percentage of black aged

TABLE 1. INCOME AND INCOME SOURCES OF BLACK, SPANISH, AND WHITE AGED IN THE UNITED STATES

	GROUP		
	Black	Spanish	White
Median individual income			
female, 65–69 years	$1,170	$1,270	$1,608
70–74 years	1,098	1,248	1,525
75+ years	974	1,189	1,362
male, 65–69 years	1,956	2,659	3,817
70–74 years	1,711	2,101	2,892
75+ years	1,503	1,735	2,229
Percent persons with income under $2,000			
female	83.4	77.3	67.5
male	59.8	47.4	34.0
Percent persons without income			
female	14.0	21.0	13.0
male	5.9	5.8	2.9
Median family income by family type husband (65+ years old)- wife	$3,250	$4,373	$5,050
female, 65+ years old- head	2,904	3,897	5,772
Percent of all aged families living in poverty	38.8	25.4	15.6
Percent of all aged unrelated individuals in poverty	71.7	58.1	48.8

SOURCE: U.S. Bureau of the Census, *Census of Population, 1970: Detailed Characteristics*, Final Report PC(1)-D1, United States Summary (Washington, D.C.: Government Printing Office, 1973).

families live in poverty. However, more blacks in families headed by a 65 year old have earnings from employment than do whites or the Spanish speaking.

There are other social characteristics which have a bearing upon one's social position and which reflect stratification variables. For example, mortality rates for blacks are higher (Kitagawa and Hauser, 1973); more blacks than whites are widowed; and more blacks have a spouse absent.

Aggregate statistics for all groups—whites, blacks, Spanish-speaking—offer only a general picture, and there is a need as Jackson (1974) has pointed out to refine our knowledge so that we can compare homogeneous subsets within the black population and between the black and other demographic categories.

There remains the difficult and complex issue of determining how much significance should be attached to economic as compared to ethnic and racial factors in the overall stratification analysis of the aging population. There is a school of thought which does not accept a class-caste or ethnic distinction but claims that economic advantages are the fundamental factor in hierarchical relations (Reissman and Halstead, 1970; O'Kane, 1969). This approach glosses over the importance that may be created by race and ethnicity because of attitudinal, emotional, or symbolic characteristics attributed to the racial minority. There are, of course, conditions where different economic segments of an ethnic subcommunity will unite on issues involving ethnic stratification instead of pursuing their independent economic interests. This requires further empirical study. Recent examples of the attempt to unite an ethnic group regardless of economic status is evidenced by the organization of a National Caucus on the Black Aged (Jackson, 1974).

Rokeach and Parker (1970) offer evidence that cultural differences between economic groups are greater than those between races. A study involving a national probability sample of 1400 adults found that there are considerable value differences between the rich and the poor, but these differences do not distinguish Negroes from whites. When socioeconomic position is controlled, that is, when poor whites and poor Negroes are compared with one another, the difference in values becomes smaller or disappears.

There are basic similarities between Negroes and whites in the nature of the prestige hierarchies assigned to different occupations. In 16 different stratification studies, basic similarities of perception of occupational prestige were found. Siegel (1970, p. 169) states: "... Negroes appear to be evaluating occupations in the same world as everyone else evaluates them and to be employing essentially the same information and the same combination of criteria as everyone else."

The basic unit in most stratification systems is the nuclear family, for it is there that a person receives his initial position in the system. In old age, the family may be a source of economic and social support. Thus, it is appropriate to consider how familial factors are intertwined with the status of the older black. Hill (1971a, p. 93) points out that it is the role of the elderly that is primarily responsible for the strong kinship bonds in most black families.

One sharp difference between the black and white women over 65 who are heads of families is the frequency with which they take children under 18 into their families. Of black families with female heads 65 and over, 48 percent had related children under 18 in their families in comparison to 10 percent of white women (Hill, 1971b, p. 41). Billingsley (1968, p. 21) notes that the Negro family has proved to be an amazingly resilient institution. He refers to such "augmented families" as an example of how the family survives in the face of oppression and sharply reduced economic and social support. The pattern of older women taking in young related and unrelated children is not only beneficial to the child but may provide a social role and also a little income for the elderly woman.

The Aged Spanish-Americans. The social stratification patterns of the United States' second largest minority, the Spanish-Americans, have some similarities to those of the white majority and also to other ethnic minorities, but there are some special features which must be mentioned. This section will be limited to a discussion of Mexican-Americans, for space does not permit presentation of data on other groups of Spanish heritage, such as Puerto Ricans or Cubans. One issue of some sensitivity is what the Mexican or Spanish-Americans call themselves or wish to be called by others: Spanish-Americans, Mexican-Americans, *latinos*, *chicanos*, Latin Americans, etc. (see Grebler, Moore, and Guzman, 1970, pp. 583-584).

The first feature of the stratification system arises from the group's history, for the contemporary class structure is a blending of features of the American class stratification system and residues of stratification from the Spanish-Mexican period. The Mexican-American class structure has vestiges of a "quite rigid caste system based upon elitism and 'purity of blood'" (Grebler, Moore, and Guzman, 1970, pp. 320-321). While the Southwest was under Spanish rule and long after, the ranking system was as follows: "Spanish outranked native-born Mexicans of Spanish descent, who in turn outranked mestizos or mixed-bloods, who in turn outranked Indians. . . . 'Blood' continues to this day to be a status-preoccupation in Mexico despite an official ideology emphasizing 'Indianism,' and despite the fact that only a small minority of the population is classified as 'pure' Indian or 'pure' white." At present, this class system based on race and wealth is disintegrating, but this occurs in varying rates in different parts of the Southwest.

A second major feature of the stratification system is the demographic pattern: there is a smaller proportion of aged in the Spanish-American group than in the white or black population. This is due to a lessened life expectancy and a high fertility rate. Thus, the median age of the Spanish-surname group is 20 in comparison to 30 for the Anglos and nonwhites, (Grebler, Moore, and Guzman, 1970, p. 123). Another important aspect of the demographic pattern related to stratification is the dependency ratio for the three major groups in the Southwest, as shown in Table 2. The high dependency ratio for the Spanish-Americans is due to the high percentage of children under 15 years of age. It will also be noted that the dependent aged of the

TABLE 2. DEPENDENCY RATIOS[a] OF THREE POPULATION CATEGORIES, SOUTHWEST, 1960.

	Anglo[b]	Spanish surname	Nonwhite
Total dependent	85	121	98
Dependent young	68	112	87
Dependent aged	17	9	11

[a]Combined number of persons under 20 and 65 or over, related to the population 20 to 64 years of age.
[b]Statistical category—white other than Spanish surname. Adapted from Grebler, Moore, and Guzman, 1970, p. 16, Table 2-1.

Spanish-surname group is approximately one-half that of the Anglos.

A third major feature of the Spanish-speaking peoples is an extended family system which is characterized by a greater emphasis on familistic attitudes than in other groups. As Grebler, Moore, and Guzman, (1970, p. 351), state ". . . the major theme dominating the classic portrayal of the traditional Mexican family is the deep importance of the family to all its members. The needs of the family collectively supersede the needs of each individual member." This emphasis means that there are strong emotional relationships, kinship ties, financial assistance, and exchange of work and advice which is probably greater than in most white and nonwhite families.

This is particularly pertinent in regard to care of the aged, for traditionally it is shameful to seek aid outside the family, (Grebler, Moore, and Guzman, 1970, p. 352). However, sometimes the concern for the aged may limit the development of the young person or potentially mobile individual.

Leonard (1967, p. 257), writing about the older Spanish-speaking people of the Southwest, states: "Far from feeling useless and dependent in old age, older Spanish-speaking persons consider themselves needed persons performing important roles in advising sons, daughters and others. Some of the older persons consider themselves important links to the past, charged with the task of acquainting younger people with Spanish history and tradition. Having such key responsibilities, they do not feel useless or burdensome, even though they depend on charity or on what sons and daughters can provide. Few would argue that key advice in the area of morals and history is not worth the price of food and shelter."

Leonard points out that there is a deep sense of courtesy in Spanish-American culture. Older people are often given places of honor in the household with special chairs set aside for them in the homes of children. This gives them a sense of importance in the group.

When one spouse of an older couple dies, the surviving parent frequently joins the home of the son or daughter. William Madsen (1964) observes that this situation almost always leads to a conflict in roles and a division of loyalties.

It must be emphasized that Leonard studied rural Mexican-Americans, where perhaps the traditional Mexican culture patterns remained in operation. Studies by the Andrus Gerontology Center at the University of Southern California of urban Mexican-Americans, blacks, and Anglos in Los Angeles showed that older Mexican-Americans had the most negative perceptions of the three groups regarding the quality of their lives in terms of feelings of sadness and worry, that life is not worth living, and that things were getting worse with advancing age. They state that subcultural patterns of aging need to be reexamined, for the cultural norms of family cohesiveness and positive attitudes toward old age may not protect the aged Mexican-American from very unhappy feelings about aging (Ragan, Bengtson, and Nunez, 1975).

Thus, the pressures of the mainstream of American culture in urban areas may modify some of the traditional strengths of the Mexican-American culture in providing satisfactions for the aged.

One might say that at present there are two class systems: one inside the Spanish-American community and one outside—that of the larger American society. Furthermore, the stratification systems of towns and cities may vary so that the analyst needs to be cognizant of local variability in class systems. In some communities there may be more of a castelike

situation, and in other places the castelike structures have been or are being modified. In large California and other Northern cities, there is the emergence of dual system for Anglos and for Mexican-Americans in which ethnic identification is optional.

In larger communities, where the local history does not include residues of castelike structures and attitudes, and where the Mexican-Americans are a comparatively small proportion of the population, options may be available like those extended to most American ethnic groups of European origins.

In studying the class system in Los Angeles and San Antonio, two cities in the Southwest with a high percentage of Mexican-Americans, the researchers employed income as the major indicators of class position. Income is the least biased indicator within the ethnic class system. Moreover, it has the advantage when analyzing a relatively poor population that comparatively small increments show a greater effect than small increments in education or occupational prestige (Grebler, Moore, and Guzman, 1970, pp. 325–326).

The Spanish-American aged suffer from a dual handicap in being from an ethnic minority and in experiencing the poverty which is part of the general milieu of the group. Yet the older Spanish-American has many supports— both financial and emotional—because of the close familistic system of his culture. As the next generation of Spanish-Americans becomes acculturated and moves into the mainstream of American life, changes will undoubtedly occur in the family structures which may result in increasing isolation of older family members.

In conclusion, we would state that the black and Spanish-speaking peoples cannot be designated as a true caste. The dynamic and changing nature of American and other societies suggests that the rigidity of the hierarchies, the ascriptive nature of caste, and the amount of social interaction results in a quasi-caste system. The general historical trend is toward integration of ethnic minorities. There are, of course, elements of prejudice and discrimination in the operation of the social system which result in differential rewards and privileges, and the consequences of these movements tend to perpetuate a quasi-caste system. Furthermore, groups within the ethnic minorities emphasize and desire separatistic social patterns and social philosophies with ethnic identity and separatism.

PERSPECTIVES ON CROSS-NATIONAL STRATIFICATION OF THE AGED

Up to this point in the chapter, the material presented has been concerned mainly with stratification in the United States. Therefore, let us review stratification and aging in a cross-national perspective. Is there something different in other societies or in the nature of aging in other societies that would result in a different picture of stratification than that found in the U.S.?

Western Societies

A useful source of information on social stratification cross-nationally is *Old People in Three Industrial Societies* (Shanas *et al.*, 1968). This careful study of Great Britain, Denmark, and the United States offers valuable information on social class of the aged in these three industrialized countries. The comparative utility of the study is increased because of similar sampling methods, a common interview guide, the same timing, and a team of researchers who employed the same analytical framework in presenting the data. Only a sample of their rich data can be summarized here.

First, in all three countries, income derived from the government is of basic importance for the elderly. A corollary to this finding is that economic support from the family is of minor importance in all three countries.

The Danish aged are better off than both the British and United States aged, relative to the standard of living of other groups in each country. However, the aged in the U.S. are absolutely better off than in the other two countries, due to a higher general standard of living.

In all three countries, there is considerable diversity of economic circumstances among the aged, but the differences are far greater in the U.S. than in the other countries, due to the extremes of wealth and poverty in the U.S. Asset ownership is more widely held in the U.S. and Denmark than in Britain.

Race is not a differentiating factor in the two European countries, but the heterogenous picture in the United States is partly due to the differences between white and nonwhite aged.

In all three countries, the retired couples have about one-half of the income of those who are fully employed. However, in Denmark, the elderly tend to work longer, for fewer persons are retired compulsorily, and the age of usual retirement is later. Further, in Denmark pensions are regulated according to who needs help the most, for example, persons over 80 years of age receive a supplementary payment. Finally, this favorable set of policies in Denmark may be associated with the fact that a greater percentage of retirees report themselves satisfied with their incomes than in the other two countries.

Shanas and her coauthors (1968, p. 447) state: "All in all, the cross-national study suggests that at this time different patterns of employment and retirement seem to be more explicable in terms of difference in pension ages, economic and social structure, relative size of incomes and asset holdings, and disability rates than in terms of individual attitudes and national personality traits or value systems."

Social Stratification and Aging in the Soviet Union

It is essential to include the Soviet Union in our discussion of social stratification so that we have comparative information and analysis on the stratification of the aged in a socialist, industrialized society where all of the means of production, the services, and facilities are owned and controlled by the government. Furthermore, the Soviet administration has the power to enforce its programs. "Objective needs" in the U.S.S.R. are determined by the party, not the individual or group (Feldmesser, 1968). How does this affect the status of the aged?

McKain (1972, p. 151) stresses the genuine concern by the ordinary Soviet citizen for older people in the U.S.S.R. He says, "Despite the emphasis on the future and the emphasis on youth, older persons are not neglected. The love and respect that older people enjoy in a peasant society have been carried over into Soviet society and new ways have been found to guarantee a good life for the elders."

It is necessary to outline first some aspects of stratification in the Soviet Union in general terms before we describe the situation in regard to stratification of the aged. Soviet sociologists and ideologists assume (at least publicly) that their society and government is in a transitional state and eventually will reach the goal of real equality—a classless society. Concepts of lower and higher strata do not apply, it is claimed, to the Soviet socialist society. What is the objective situation concerning differentiation of groups in the Soviet Union? There is a scarcity of accurate and complete information on income differentials, but one can make a few observations. Lipset and Dobson state that income inequalities in the Soviet Union are probably less at present than in the period before World War II (Lipset and Dobson, 1973, p. 126). Yet there are still considerable differences in income between people at the top of the occupational structure and those in lower positions. In the early 1960's, a director of a steel plant might earn 400 rubles a month, a director of a scientific institute might earn 600, and an ordinary typist would be paid around 60 rubles.

Two Soviet sociologists, Gordon and Klopov, have stressed the emergence of a hereditary occupational strata in a 1972 article (Lipset and Dobson, 1973, p. 172). This is another kind of evidence suggesting that there are inequalities even in a society structured around the goal of equality.

Another way of empirically studying occupational differences is by studies of prestige which reveal that the occupational prestige structure in the Soviet Union is practically identical with those of nonsocialist countries like the United States (Inkeles and Rossi, 1956; Hodge, Treiman, and Rossi, 1966). Thus, in the U.S.S.R. we have, in effect, what

might be called an "ideal" and "real" system of stratification.

What are some clues as to the stratification system in old age? One might speculate that in a socialist society, the aged would receive fullest honor and consideration and support in acknowledgment of their years of productivity for the benefit of the nation. Under a system where the amassing of any kind of personal wealth is disapproved and largely prohibited, one would expect generous pensions upon retirement. However, pensions have been pitifully small until the 1960's (Geiger, 1968, p. 204), and it was mainly the responsibility of the children to support their parents.

There is fragmentary evidence which suggests that income differentials and better housing from earlier periods continue into later life. There is clearly a "pension elite" in the Soviet Union. Lipset and Dobson (1973, p. 129) state, "There are high retirement awards made to 'persons who have rendered exceptional service . . . in the areas of revolutionary, governmental, social and economic activity . . . and in the fields of culture, science and technology.' "

Article 120 of the Constitution of the U.S.S.R. established that "Citizens of the U.S.S.R. have the right to maintenance in old age and also in the case of sickness or disability. This right is insured by the extensive development of social insurance of industrial, office and professional workers at state expense, free medical service for working people and the provision of a wide network of health resorts for the use of the working people" (Muravyova, 1956, p. 3).

This creates "conditions for security in old age," according to Muravyova (1956, p. 3). The general pension age is 60 for men and 55 for women. In the case of persons employed in very strenuous work, underground, or in hot shops, men are pensionable on reaching age 50 and women at age 45. The amounts of old age pensions are the same for men and women, ranging from 50 percent to 100 percent of earnings, averaging at about 70 percent of all wages (Keefe et al., 1971, p. 234).

There are some aspects of the Soviet work and retirement system which tend to differ from those of other industrial countries—

namely, that because of a shortage of labor, there is an interest in having older workers stay in the labor force for as long as possible. Indeed, special attempts have been made to lure older citizens back into the labor force. Depending on their employment, they receive their full pension in addition to their weekly wage (Acharkan, 1972). This undoubtedly contributes to the economic advantage of those who have the health and energy to keep working.

However, as Ivanovna and Nikolayevna (1972, p. 244) have pointed out, "The actual placement of aging workers does not always correspond to their qualifications and professions, their physical and moral status." They add that older men and women "more often hold jobs where they can work in free tempo and rhythm under conditions of individual distribution of daily programs during the working time. All these professional and production factors put together determine to some extent the high proportion of aged women in gardening, vine-growing, melon-growing (19.3%), cattle shepherding (8.2%), communal services (11.8%), and non-specialized jobs in agriculture (12.7%). The women-pensioners are widely represented among doctors, heads of public health institutions, actresses, producers, musicians (6.7%–8.1%)." Ivanovna and Nikolayevna (1972, p. 243) also observe that older men who continue to work tend to be employed in low status occupations as janitors, watchmen, beekeepers, etc.

An increase in employee's pensions resulted in a sharp drop in pensioners who worked—from 50 percent in 1956 to 9 percent in 1962, according to the Soviet gerontologists. Thus, Russian workers would seem to prefer to retire if they have an adequate income.

Hollander (1973) observes that old age does not appear to be a major social problem in the Soviet Union at present, for the severe housing shortage continues to hold the older and younger generations together to a far greater extent than in the U.S. Thus, families are forced to live together because there is absolutely no alternative. In addition, the grandmothers frequently play an important role in running the household and raising the children, while the mothers are at work.

Social security coverage was provided for only about half of the Soviet population until 1965 when pensions were introduced for collective farmers; almost all workers are now covered (Keefe *et al.*, 1971, p. 234). However, rural pensions are about one-half those received by urban workers (Smith, 1976, p. 208). The Soviet family has adapted to the lack of adequate pensions for the aged and the shortage of homes for the aged by the use of a three-generational extended family form. Geiger (1968, p. 205) summarized the situation in these words:

> In the marketplace of mutually desired services it has been a good bargain; in exchange for a home, the aged have taken over, according to capacity, the functions left undone by the working wife and mother. In past years this arrangement has been such a standard practice that it was defined as desirable . . .. All benefit from this arrangement, including the Soviet regime itself, which saved itself the expense for many years of becoming a true welfare state.

Two Soviet gerontologists (Solovyev and Petrichenko, 1972) speaking before the International Gerontological Congress in Kiev in 1972 extol the role of the elderly in helping young couples in family planning, taking care of the children, planning the budget, and running the household. Solovyev and Petrichenko (1972, p. 271) state, "The aged play a special role in the sphere of moral relations with the view to insure the sense of duty, dignity, agreement, diligence and collectivism in the members of the family. They educate the young generation to this aim on the high moral and humane principles." It is difficult to know if the elderly really have such high status as is portrayed here. It seems to mirror aging in the "ideal world" rather than in the real world. The gerontologists add that when older people help in the household duties, "the young people get more time to participate in social life, thus raising their cultural level." (This might be considered a dubious mark of status of the elderly to some observers.)

One paradoxical aspect of the Soviet situation in regard to status of the aged must be pointed out: although the babushka (the grandmother) is often essential to the family in caring for the physical needs of the child, there is a subtle but pervading denigration of her influence in the realm of intellect or values. She is considered to represent traditional outmoded values, and there is subtle pressure for the young person to ignore her influence and form his values from the peer group, the school, and the party, according to Geiger (1968, p. 312).

Alienation is not particularly an issue in the Soviet Union. Persons in the U.S. are concerned about feelings of personal happiness and usefulness and consider alienation to be highly undesirable. As a society, Americans berate themselves for permitting citizens to be alienated. In the Soviet Union, however, according to Hollander (1973, p. 399), "Neither powerlessness nor alienation is much of an issue . . . Powerlessness is taken for granted among the population at large. Alienation is not a pressing public or private concern. There is little self consciousness about it; a certain amount of alienation is probably taken for granted—as a more or less natural condition."

The Soviet Union does have one problem that is characteristic of some developed societies—namely the increasing percentage of middle-aged and old population in rural areas. The young people are anxious to get out of the country because of the physical isolation, a 30 to 50 percent lower level of wages of farm workers in comparison to factory workers, more limited supply of consumer goods, and longer working hours (Benet, 1970; Smith, 1976). Furthermore, it is difficult for the Kolkhoz peasants to get passports for travel or for change of residence. One way these restrictions can be evaded is for young people to leave the farm before the age of 16. Hollander (1973, p. 341) observes: "There is some similarity to the vicious circle of poverty in the United States and the hopelessness of Soviet rural areas. However in the Soviet case a move to the city is probably a more decisive improvement than similar moves are for the American poor." The willingness of the babushka to move in with her grown children and take care of the grandchildren when she is needed may be a consequence of the grim living conditions in rural areas.

Thus, inequality exists even in the Soviet Union which has as one of its premises a classless society. Despite great efforts, ideological and structural, to create a society of greater equality for older citizens, the analyst concludes that there are differentials between the privileged old and the impoverished, and there are also differentials between the old and those in the work force. It seems a truism that in any society marked by shortages, it is the working segment of the population that receives the first consideration. Thus, despite the *intentions* of the Soviet system that each citizen is entitled to the basic necessities and a life of dignity, the workers are accorded the highest honor, and the aged are somewhat secondary in the prestige level.

A NEW DIRECTION FOR RESEARCH—STATUS INCONSISTENCY

The analysis of social stratification as it pertains to the latter third of the life cycle involves complex issues which this chapter has only begun to conceptualize. The knowledge base is limited, and it is hoped that this work and related chapters on age stratification, on income, on the economy, and on the family, for example, will delineate important new areas for further theoretical and empirical research. Most analysts of stratification accept the multidimensional nature of stratification. The tripartite scheme of Weber—class, status, and power—which has been used by many scholars, has been discussed previously. Other investigators have focused on a variety of observable indicators: ethnicity, sex, income, occupation, education, and property. Surprisingly, age is not included in the array of variables. Yet stratification in the latter part of the life cycle must recognize age as the strategic characteristic which is linked causally to other features and is a primary reason for downward mobility. In fact, much of the literature on retirement is actually a study of the differential loss of status and its consequences, or status inconsistency.

Status inconsistency can be defined as the dissimilar ranking on different dimensions of stratification (Lenski, 1966). It deals with the horizontal or nonvertical aspects of stratification. It may also be viewed as the way that different components may be weighed or balanced in relation to one another.

Status inconsistency is a useful concept in studying the stratification of the aged because it takes account of the fact that older persons may experience changes in their rankings on one hierarchy but not on another. For example, most older people have a marked decline in income, but not all experience downward movement in style of life. Most older people eventually retire from work, but their educational attainment remains the same. In fact, the work of Svalastoga (1972) on the measurement of responsibility shows that education is a better measure of prestige than the number of subordinates. Hence, status in retirement may not decline as much as some would expect, for education is not lost even though the person no longer has subordinates.

The concept of status inconsistency has particular pertinence for studying social stratification of the aged, although it should be pointed out that the concept has limitations in other spheres. As the studies have accumulated over the years, the research results, particularly on ethnicity, are ambiguous and even contradictory. Moreover, as Lebowitz (1974) and others (Hartman, 1974; Jackson and Curtis, 1972; Knoke, 1972; Olsen and Tulley, 1972) have pointed out, there is a need for futher substantive and methodological work to refine the concept and to differentiate the effects of status inconsistency. Whether age is to be regarded as an independent or as an intervening variable is open to debate, but at present it would seem that there is more usefulness in assigning it as a modifier or intervening variable.

There is need for research on the degree to which social deprivation and psychological strain result from differential downward mobility. Various studies have noted that when the aged become involved in status inconsistency, they appear to be more accepting of the situation and more adaptable to the consequences than do persons encountering status inconsistency at other phases of the life cycle.

Further research is needed to delineate the possible reasons for this behavior. At present it is possible to offer only speculations: for example, the aged have had a lifetime to perfect their coping mechanisms, so that they have learned to come to terms with anomalous situations. Another explanation could be that their feelings of self-identity are often more firmly established than those of persons at earlier stages of the life cycle (Lowenthal, Thurnher, Chiriboga, and associates, 1975).

The research of gerontologists at the University of Southern California may offer another clue as to why some elderly can tolerate status inconsistency—namely, the development of an integrating theme of life for some older people—that of "aging as a career." These researchers have noted that the process of survival itself can be considered a triumph. Small and ordinary routines of living that seem insignificant to younger people constitute sources of pride and accomplishment to the elderly. "Meaning is provided by the sense that each day is lived autonomously in the community, with independence, dignity, alertness and control over one's faculties and mobility" (Bengtson, 1975, p. 60).

The study of social stratification of the aged has been too long neglected. Perhaps the further refinement of the concept of status inconsistency in the latter part of the life cycle—both conceptually and substantively—will add new depth to our knowledge of hierarchies and gerontology.

REFERENCES

Acharkan, V. A. 1972. Development of the law on Social Security of Older Working Persons in the U.S.S.R. *Abstracts, Ninth International Congress of Gerontology, Kiev, U.S.S.R.*, 3, 173.

Barron, Milton L. 1953. Minority group characteristics of the aged in American society. *J. Geront.*, 8, 477–482.

Bendix, R., and Lipset, S. M. 1953. Karl Marx's theory of social class. *In*, R. Bendix and S. M. Lipset (eds.), *Class, Status and Power: A Reader in Social Stratification*, pp. 6–11. New York: The Free Press.

Benet, Sula. (ed.) 1970. *The Village of Viriatino: An Ethnographic Study of a Russian Village*. Garden City, New York: Doubleday (originally published in Moscow, 1958).

Bengtson, Vern L. 1975. *The Social and Cultural Contexts of Aging: Implications for Social Policy*. Progress Report to National Science Foundation. Los Angeles: Andrus Gerontology Center, University of Southern California.

Billingsley, Andrew. 1968. *Black Families in White America*. Englewood Cliffs, New Jersey: Prentice-Hall.

Binstock, Robert H. 1974. Aging and the future of American politics. *Ann. Amer. Acad.*, 415, 199–212.

Blau, Peter M. 1974. Parameters of social structure. *Am. Soc. Rev.*, 39, 615–635.

Bottomore, T. B. 1965. *Classes in Modern Society*. London: George Allen and Unwin.

Bultena, G. L., and Wood, V. 1969. The American retirement community: Bane or blessing? *J. Geront.*, 24, 209–217.

Bultena, Gordon et al. 1971. *Life After 70 in Iowa: A Restudy of the Participants in the 1960 Survey of the Aged*. Sociology Report 95. Ames, Iowa: Iowa State University.

Carter, Howard W., and Webber, Irving L. 1966. *The Aged and Chronic Disease*. Monograph #9. Jacksonville, Florida: Florida State Board of Health.

Chen, Y. P. 1973. A pilot survey study of the Housing-Annuity Plan. Offset. Los Angeles: University of California, Graduate School of Management.

Coleman, R. P., and Neugarten, B. L. 1971. *Social Status in the City*. San Francisco: Jossey-Bass.

Cowgill, D. O., and Holmes, L. D.. 1972. *Aging and Modernization*. New York: Appleton-Century-Crofts.

Feldmesser, R. A. 1968. Stratification and Communism. In, A. Kassof (ed.), *Prospects for Soviet Society*, pp. 359–385. New York: Praeger.

Geiger, H. K. 1968. *The Family in Soviet Russia*. Cambridge, Massachusetts: Harvard University Press.

Grebler, L., Moore, J., and Guzman, R. 1970. *The Mexican-American People*. New York: The Free Press.

Hartman, M. 1974. On the definition of status inconsistency. *Am. J. Sociol.*, 80, 706–721.

Haug, M. R. 1973. Social class measurement and women's occupational roles. *Soc. Forces*, 52, 85–98.

Hill, R. B. 1971a. A profile of black aged. In, J. Jackson (ed.), *Proceedings of Research Conference on Minority Group Aged in the South*. Durham, North Carolina: Duke University.

Hill, R. B. 1971b. *The Strengths of Black Families*. New York: Emerson Hall Publishers.

Hochschild, A. R. 1973. *The Unexpected Community*. Englewood Cliffs, New Jersey: Prentice-Hall.

Hodge, R. W., Treiman, D. J., and Rossi, P. H. 1966. A comparative study of occupational prestige. In, R. Bendix and S. M. Lipset (eds.), *Class, Status, Power*, 2nd ed., pp. 309–321. New York: The Free Press.

Hollander, P. J. 1973. *Soviet and American Society: A Comparison*. New York: Oxford University Press.

Holter, H. 1970. *Sex Roles and Social Structure*. Oslo: Universitets forlaget.

Inkeles, A., and Rossi, P. H. 1956. National comparisons of occupational prestige. *Am. J. Sociol.*, 61, 329–339.

Ivanovna, S. E., and Nikolayevna, S. N. 1972. Demographic shifts in modern society and labour activities of the elderly population. In, D. F. Chebotarev et al. (eds.), *The Main Problems of Soviet Gerontology*, pp. 240–251. Kiev, U.S.S.R.

Jackson, Elton F., and Curtis, Richard F. 1972. Effects of vertical mobility and status inconsistency: A body of negative evidence. *Am. Soc. Rev.*, 37, 701–713 (December).

Jackson, Jaquelyne, J. 1974. N.C.B.A., black aged and politics. *Annals*, 415, 138–159.

Jacobs, Jerry. 1974. *Fun City: An Ethnographic Study of a Retirement Community*. New York: Holt, Rinehart & Winston.

Johnson, S. K. 1971. *Idle Haven: Community Building Among the Working-Class Retired*. Berkeley: University of California Press.

Jones, Alfred W. 1941. *Life, Liberty, and Property*. Philadelphia: J. B. Lippincott.

Kahl, J. A. 1957. *The American Class Structure*. New York: Rinehart.

Keefe, Eugene K. et al. 1971. *Area Handbook for the Soviet Union*. Washington, D. C.: Government Printing Office.

Kelleher, Carol H., and Quirk, Daniel H. 1973. Age, functional capacity and work: An annotated bibliography. *Industrial Gerontology*, 19, 80–98.

Kent, D. P., and Hirsch, C. 1971. *Social and Economic Conditions of Negro and White Aged Residents of Urban Neighborhoods of Low Socio-Economic Status*. Vol. I. Final report submitted to the Administration on Aging. University Park, Pennsylvania: Pennsylvania State University.

Kitagawa, Evelyn M., and Hauser, Philip M. 1973. *Differential Mortality in the United States: A Study in Socioeconomic Epidemiology*. Cambridge, Massachusetts: Harvard University Press.

Knoke, David. 1972. Community and consistency: The ethnic factor in status inconsistency. *Soc. Forces*, 51, 23–33.

Laufer, Robert S., and Bengtson, Vern L. 1974. Generations, aging and social stratification: On the development of generational units. *J. Soc. Issues*, 30, 181–205.

Lebowitz, B. D. 1974. Concept formation and concept rejection: The case of status consistency. Paper presented at the Annual Meetings of the American Sociological Association, Montreal, Canada, August, 1974.

Leggett, John C. 1968. *Class, Race and Labor: Working Class Consciousness in Detroit*. New York: Oxford University Press.

Lenski, G. 1966. *Power and Privilege: A Theory of Social Stratification*. New York: McGraw-Hill.

Leonard, O. E. 1967. The older rural Spanish-speaking people of the Southwest. In, E. G. Youmans (ed.), *Older Rural Americans*, pp. 239–261. Lexington, Kentucky: University of Kentucky Press.

Lieberson, S. 1970. Stratification and ethnic groups. In, E. O. Laumann (ed.), *Social Stratification: Research and Theory for the 1970's*, pp. 172–181. Indianapolis: Bobbs-Merrill.

Lipset, Seymour M. 1968. Social Class. In, *Interna-*

tional Encyclopedia of the Social Sciences, pp. 296–316. New York: Macmillan and The Free Press.

Lipset, S. M., and Dobson, R. B. 1973. Social stratification and sociology in the Soviet Union. *Survey*, Vol. 19, No. 3 (88), 114–185.

Lopata, Helena. 1973. Self identity in marriage and widowhood. *Sociol. Quart.*, **14**, 407–418.

Louis, Arthur M. 1968. America's centimillionaires. *Fortune*, **77**, 152–157.

Lowenthal, Marjorie Fiske, Thurnher, M., Chiriboga, D., and associates. 1975. *Four Stages of Life*. San Francisco: Jossey-Bass.

McKain, Walter. 1972. The aged in the U.S.S.R. *In*, D. O. Cowgill and L. D. Holmes (eds.), *Aging and Modernization*, pp. 151–165. New York: Appleton-Century-Crofts.

Madsen, W. 1964. *The Mexican-Americans of South Texas*. New York: Holt, Rinehart & Winston.

Malcolm, A. 1974. Special to the *New York Times*, March 24.

Mannheim, Karl. 1952. The problem of generations. *In*, Paul Kecskemeti (ed.), *Essays on the Sociology of Knowledge* by Karl Mannheim. London: Routledge & Kegan Paul.

Mathews, Donald R. 1954. *The Social Background of Political Decision-Makers*. New York: Random House.

Michelon, L. C. 1954. The new leisure class. *Am. J. Sociol.*, **59**, 371–378.

Morris, R., and Murphy, R. J. 1966. A paradigm for the study of class consciousness. *Sociol. & Soc. Res.*, **50**, 297–313.

Muravyova, N. A. 1956. *Social Security in the U.S.S.R.* Moscow: Foreign Languages Publishing House.

Neugarten, B. L. 1966. The aged in American society. *In*, H. S. Becker (ed.), *Social Problems: A Modern Approach*. New York: John Wiley.

Neugarten, Bernice L. 1974. Age groups in American society and the rise of the young old. *Annals*, **415**, 187–198.

O'Kane, J. M. 1969. Ethnic mobility and the lower-income Negro: A socio-historical perspective. *Soc. Prob.*, **16**, 302–311.

Olsen, Marvin E. 1974. Social classes in contemporary Sweden. *Sociol. Quart.*, **15**, 323–340.

Olsen, Marvin E., and Tully, J. C. 1972. Socioeconomic ethnic status inconsistency and preference for political change. *Am. Soc. Rev.*, **37**, 560–574.

Palmore, E. 1969. Sociological aspects of aging. *In*, E. Busse and E. Pfeiffer (eds.), *Behavior and Adaptation in Late Life*, pp. 33–69. Boston: Little, Brown.

Palmore, Erdman, and Whittington, Frank. 1971. Trends in the relative status of the aged. *Soc. Forces*, **50**, 84–91.

Pope, Liston. 1941. *Preachers and Millhands*. New Haven: Yale University Press.

Porter, J. 1965. *The Vertical Mosaic: An Analysis of Social Class and Power in Canada*. Toronto: University of Toronto Press.

Pratt, H. J. 1974. Old age associations in national politics. *Annals*, **415**, 106–119.

Ragan, Pauline, Bengtson, Vern L., and Nunez, F. 1975. Variation in quality of life indicators among aging blacks, Mexican-Americans, and Anglos. Paper delivered at the Pacific Sociological Association Annual Meeting, Victoria, British Columbia.

Ragan, Pauline K., and Dowd, James J. 1974. The emerging political consciousness of the aged: A generational interpretation. *J. Soc. Issues*, **30**, 137–158.

Rainwater, Lee. 1974. *What Money Buys: Inequality and the Social Meanings of Income*. New York: Basic Books.

Reissman, Leonard, and Halstead, Michael N. 1970. The subject is class. *Sociol. & Soc. Res.*, **54**, 293–305.

Riley, Matilda White. 1971. Social gerontology and the age stratification of society. *Gerontologist*, **11**, 79–87.

Riley, Matilda W., Foner, A., Moore, M. E., Hess, B., and Roth, B. K. 1968. *Aging and Society: Vol. 1, An Inventory of Research Findings*. New York: Russell Sage Foundation.

Riley, Matilda W., Johnson, M., and Foner, A. 1972. *Aging and Society: Vol. 3, A Sociology of Age Stratification*. New York: Russell Sage Foundation.

Rokeach, M., and Parker, S. 1970. Values as social indicators of poverty and race relations in America. *Annals*, **388**, 97–111.

Rosenberg, George S. 1970. *The Worker Grows Old*. San Francisco: Jossey-Bass.

Rosow, I. 1967. *Social Integration of the Aged*. New York: The Free Press.

Runciman, W. G. 1966. *Relative Deprivation and Social Justice*. London: Routledge & Kegan Paul.

Schreiber, E. M., and Nygreen, G. T. 1970. Subjective social class in America, 1945–68. *Soc. Forces*, **48**, 348–356.

Shanas, Ethel, Townsend, P., Wedderburn, D., Friis, H., Milhøj, P., and Stehouwer, J. 1968. *Old People in Three Industrial Societies*. London: Routledge & Kegan Paul.

Siegel, Paul M. 1970. Occupational prestige in the Negro subculture. *In*, E. O. Laumann (ed.), *Social Stratification: Research and Theory for the 1970's*. Indianapolis: Bobbs-Merrill.

Simmons, L. W. 1945. *The Role of the Aged in Primitive Society*. New Haven: Yale University Press.

Smith, Hedrick. 1976. *The Russians*. New York: Quadrangle.

Solovyev, N. ya, and Petrichenko, A. E. 1972. Old age, family and society. *In*, *Symposia Reports*, Vol. 2, pp. 270–273, International Congress of Gerontology, Kiev, U.S.S.R.

Streib, G. F. 1965. Are the aged a minority group? *In*, A. W. Gouldner and S. M. Miller (eds.), *Applied Sociology*, pp. 311–328. Glencoe, Illinois: The Free Press.

Streib, G. F., and Schneider, C. J. 1971. *Retirement in American Society: Impact and Process*. Ithaca, New York: Cornell University Press.

Sussman, M., Cates, J., and Smith, D. 1970. *The Family and Inheritance*. New York: Russell Sage Foundation.

Svalastoga, K. 1959. *Prestige, Class and Mobility*. Copenhagen: Gyldendal.

Svalastoga, K. 1972. Measurement of responsibility. *Social Science Information*, 9, 75–85.

Tissue, Thomas. 1972. Old age and the perception of poverty. *Sociol. & Soc. Res.*, 56, 331–344.

U.S., Bureau of the Census. 1973. *1970 Census of Population P.C.(1)-D1 United States Summary. Detailed Characteristics*. Washington, D.C.: Government Printing Office.

Weber, M. 1946. Class, status and party. *In*, H. H. Gerth and C. W. Mills, (eds.), *From Max Weber: Essays in Sociology*. New York: Oxford University Press.

PART 3 AGING AND SOCIAL SYSTEMS

8
AGE STRATA IN SOCIAL SYSTEMS

Matilda White Riley*

Bowdoin College and Russell Sage Foundation

Age and aging, widely studied as characteristics of individuals, are often overlooked as fundamental aspects of social structure and social dynamics. Yet, in every society both the population and the roles are stratified by age, much as they may be stratified by class or sex. The age strata, which shift and change as society changes, are among the bases of social organization that shape sociocultural life and the historical course of mankind (Sorokin, 1968). A person's activities, his attitudes toward life, his relationships to his family or to his work, his biological capacities, and his physical fitness are all conditioned by his position in the age structure of the particular society in which he lives. And as this structure changes, people age in different ways. Growing old in the United States today is not the same as growing old in Colonial America or in ancient Greece, for the proportions of people in the oldest strata have multiplied, and the life-course sequences of roles in the family, the work force, or the community have been transformed. Thus, human beings of different ages cannot be understood apart from

the age strata of the society in which they are inextricably involved, nor can human aging be understood apart from the societal processes and changes affecting these strata.

While full understanding of the relationship between aging and society is a distant goal, the purpose of this chapter is to outline a conceptual framework for approaching the task. A framework is needed as a tool for organizing and analyzing the available information about age strata in social systems and for formulating the central questions to be answered. It is needed to stimulate further investigation of age stratification systems. It is needed to help check on our current interpretations of the place of older people within the societal macrocosm and as a guide to appropriate interventions when inequity and injustice prevail. The heuristic framework presented aims to meet such needs. It constitutes a working model of conceptual elements, assumptions, and propositions—a paradigmatic outline of abstract ideas, designed to generate specific formulations and clear understandings.

The conceptual model is drawn from the sociology of age stratification developed collaboratively with Marilyn Johnson, Anne Foner, and others (more fully set forth in Riley, Johnson, and Foner, 1972). From this perspective, age strata are seen as the link between human aging

*This chapter was prepared as part of the Russell Sage Foundation Program on Age. The author is indebted for many of the major ideas to her longtime collaborators, Marilyn Johnson and Anne Foner; and for suggestion and criticism on earlier versions to John W. Riley, Jr., Robert K. Merton, and others.

and social change. In reviewing the perspective, we note in this chapter how people and roles are stratified by age at particular periods of time, how the strata are interrelated and intersect with single groups and institutional spheres, how they change and vary across time and space, and how the full set of coexisting age strata moves concurrently across time. We also suggest how people in different age strata are shaped by, and in turn shape, both the roles and the environing age-graded system; how people behave, think, and relate to one another in different ways according to their ages; and how, as age-typical patterns develop in the routines of daily life, age-appropriate norms and roles come to be defined and institutionalized. We consider how, and with what consequences, age strata emerge from the incessant interplay between the changing society and the developing lives of its members.

In introducing such broad topics, the first section of the chapter outlines the conceptual model as it can provide insights into many aspects of old age and aging, including such specific topics as old people's relations to their families and communities, their place in the economy and the polity, and their patterns of work, retirement, and leisure. In this model, we conceive of society as a shifting age structure of roles, in which age (or life-course stage) defines the locations of individuals alive at any one time. The differences—biological, psychological, or social—that appear in every society among people of differing age are seen as the complex resultant of dual processes, both intertwined with social change, aging, and the succession of cohorts (generations). The second section of the chapter states certain formal principles as a guide to use of the conceptual model in interpreting knowledge about age stratification systems as they impinge on older people. The final section examines selected implications of the model as age affects the individual and society and notes key questions requiring investigation. Pointing to the need for further conceptual clarification and specification, we stress certain themes implicit in the model as basic to a sociological understanding of old age today and in the future. Paramount among these themes are: the inevitable and irreversible nature of the processes of aging and cohort flow that, con-

strained by social conditions and norms, produce age strata in the population; the universality of these processes; the special interrelationships of people and social structures within and between the age strata at particular periods of time; and the strains toward change arising from the arhythmic relationship of these age processes to other societal dynamics.

A CONCEPTUAL MODEL

In order to explore the power of this view of age stratification for explaining many aspects of age and aging, we outline a conceptual model in which both the people and the roles in a society are seen as analytically distinct and as divided into strata according to age. That is, there are differences in the numbers, capacities, motivations, and attitudes of the people in these age strata. And there are also differences in the roles (or positions) available to old and young and in the normative expectations, facilities, rewards, or deprivations which define these roles.

As parts or levels of a social system (a society or smaller group), these people, roles, and strata are interdependent. They are in continuing dynamic interaction with each other and with the environment to produce social stability or change (cf. Riley and Nelson, 1971). From Shakespeare through Erikson (1950, 1968) to Ariès (1962), many have variously defined several "stages" of the life course, or—from our stratification perspective—several age strata within which people at different stages of their own lives coexist and relate to one another within the same social system. Yet the numbers of strata and their age-related boundaries differ from one time and place to another. Indeed, they are often defined only vaguely (note, e.g., definitions by Neugarten and Moore, 1968; Bengtson, Furlong, and Laufer, 1974). Intuitively, one can easily distinguish between a stratum composed of infants (or even a fetal stratum in which life is just beginning) and a stratum of old people arrived at the age when, under modern conditions of mortality control, it is deemed appropriate to die. In some societies only a few (perhaps three or four) strata may be distinguished; whereas many strata (from infancy, childhood, adolescence, youth, middle age, to early old age, and late old age) may be distinguished in highly differentiated societies or within their particular groups and subsectors (cf. Neugarten, 1974; Neugarten and Datan, 1974).

Age is often merely an index of life stage, carrying with it varying probabilities of behavior and attitudes (just as dates index pertinent historical or environmental events). In itself, age is a continuous measure; when the population of a country is arranged by chronological age, from newly born infants to the oldest people alive, age is a continuum. Hence, *partitions of the population by age acquire meaning as age strata only as they index socially significant aspects of people and roles.* Indeed, one use of our model is to determine empirically the extent to which phenomena indexed by age do exhibit discrete and socially meaningful boundaries.

Formation of Age Strata: An Overview

Pertinent to any definition of particular systems of age stratification is the general question of how age strata arise. In exploring this ques-

tion, social scientists often erroneously postulate the single process of aging—or even just "growing up" or just "growing old." Actually, two basic sets of processes, which we shall describe, are continually at work to produce these strata: age processes—which involve the people in society; and societal dynamics—which involve the changing age structure of roles.

Age Dynamics and Societal Dynamics. The rudiments of strata formation are indicated schematically in Figure 1. The age processes are suggested by the horizontal bars, which represent the life span of three selected cohorts. Each cohort consists of people born at the same time. The people within the cohort age. That is, over time they pass through a socially structured sequence of roles from birth to death (such as dependent child, student, worker, spouse, retiree), learning to adapt to new roles and to relinquish old ones, accumulating knowledge and attitudes and social experiences, and undergoing biological and psychological development and change. As they age, they change. While particular individuals are aging and dying, a re-

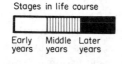

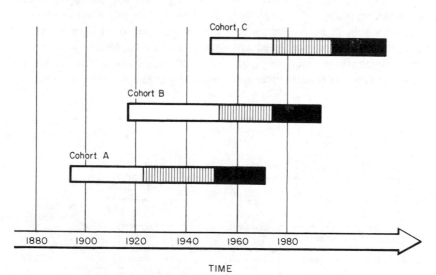

Figure 1. Processes underlying the age strata. (From Riley, Matilda White, Johnson, Marilyn, and Foner, Anne. 1972. *Aging and Society: A Sociology of Age Stratification, 3.* New York: Russell Sage Foundation, p. 10. Reprinted by permission.)

lated process is taking place: new cohorts of people are continually being born (cf. Cain, 1964). Each new cohort, because it is born at a particular time and confronts a unique sequence of roles and environmental events, has a distinctive character; hence the people in different cohorts tend to age in different ways. At given periods of time (such as 1940 or 1960 in the diagram), the successive cohorts fit together to form the age strata in the population.

In continuing interplay with the age processes in the population are societal changes in the age structure of roles. At given times (suggested by the vertical lines in Figure 1), we can think of the age structure of roles as a kind of screen through which the different cohorts of people are concurrently passing. (For example, in a school, different cohorts of children are performing in the respective roles of first-grader and of twelfth-grader.) Age is a criterion for entering and leaving certain roles, and age affects the nature of role prescriptions and role rewards or punishments. Over time, the role structure itself (such as the organization and operation of the grade system in the school), far from being fixed, is undergoing modification and change. And the differing life-course patterns of people in successive cohorts are not only influenced by—they in turn influence—the role structure in society.

Both age processes and role changes, while interdependent and mutually affecting one another, are directly subject to the exigencies of environment ("history," both social and natural, in Figure 1). Institutions, roles, and aging individuals are all affected as society undergoes

wars, famines, periods of prosperity or depression, changes in science and the arts, and so on.

The age strata can be understood, then, as a cross-section slice through these two sets of concurrent and interpenetrating processes: (1) the alteration of age-graded roles in society, as historical events occur and institutional structures change; and (2) the aging of people who inhabit these roles, and the continual dying out and replacement of one cohort by another.

Elements in the Model. The diagram in Figure 2 suggests how the two sets of age-related processes are continuously at work within the population and the role system, respectively. (In addition, the diagram shows how people are linked to roles through processes of allocation and socialization, to be discussed later.) Corresponding to these processes are two pairs of structural elements (diagrammed in the boxes) that can be viewed in cross-section at given periods of time, as both people (the population structure) and roles (the role structure) are differentiated by age (cohort membership and life stage), and both make age-differentiated contributions to the social system. We refer to these elements as "structural"—not because this aspect of our approach is static, but because the elements are interconnected within the society. (Although the design for analysis of the age structure at a single period is cross-sectional, it employs not merely a single cross section but also a sequence of cross sections to trace the age strata through history.)

By utilizing these structural elements, we can consider, at the macroscopic level, the division

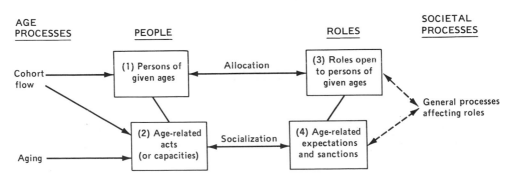

Figure 2. Elements in a conceptual model of age stratification. (From Riley, Matilda White, Johnson, Marilyn, and Foner, Anne. 1972. *Aging and Society: A Sociology of Age Stratification, 3.* New York: Russell Sage Foundation, p. 9. Reprinted by permission.)

of every society into age strata, the interrelationships among these strata, the synchronic changes and variations across time and space, and the implications for social structure and social change and particularly for the status of older people. At the microscopic level, we can also regard these strata from the viewpoint of the individual. We can show the ways in which the particular stratum to which he belongs at a given time affects the complex of roles he is expected to play, the rights and privileges accorded to him in each role, the manner in which individuals at varying ages differ in their capacity to perform these roles and in their reactions and adaptations, and the specific implications for the older person's relation to society.

Age Strata and Social Change.

Before considering these basic elements in more detail, let us first note the dramatic character of their interrelationships and their crucial implications for social changes affecting the age stratification system. All the structural and processual elements are in continual interaction with one another, changing in diverse ways. We think of the age-related processes as an intricate system of feedback loops, in which each process interacts with the others, with changes in the role structure, and with the changing environment (with the surrounding "historical" factors—social, physical, and biological—that impinge upon the social system from outside). Implicit in the notion of system is the principle that any change in one part influences each other part and is in turn influenced by each (cf. Henderson, 1937). These complex interdependencies can result in manifold disequilibria in the age strata. Although such disequilibria may in some instances persist in similar fashion through the lives of many cohorts, they are most likely to distinguish cohorts from one another either through temporary disturbances or through long-term change; and, as cohorts age in different ways, the nature of the age strata changes.

Some Examples.

A major objective of a sociology of age stratification is to plot the continuing dialectic between age dynamics and societal dynamics and to trace the connections between changes (or variations) in age strata and the related changes (or variations) in environing factors. A few examples, many of them familiar, can only hint at the broad sweep and complexity of this task.

Changes in any one of the *structural elements* shown in Figure 2 can generate pressures for change in other elements as well; thus, an increase in the numbers of school-age children (element 1), as in the United States after the second World War, can increase the number of places required for them (3) in the schools; or an increase in the numbers of senescent persons (1) can increase the number of geriatric caretakers required (3). An increase in the performance capacity of an age category (2), as through improved levels of health or through retraining of older workers, can allow more roles for an age stratum by mitigating the age restrictions on role entry (3). Slackened expectations for performance by older workers (4), as in wartime, can also serve to relax age restrictions in hiring (3). Or higher rewards (4) for an age stratum, as for schoolchildren, can increase motivation and raise performance levels (2) for that stratum.

Such structural changes in the age strata are mediated through changes in corresponding processes. E.g., changes in cohort size may affect socialization and allocation, as the nature of schooling and structure of education were influenced by the baby boom cohort; changes in practices of socialization, as in preparation for widowhood, modulate capacities for performance over the subsequent life course; changes in allocation, as in work force allocation, may influence the motivation to control reproduction (depending upon the demand for breadwinners in the family) or may influence the will to live on in retirement; or changes in the aging process are incurred by modifications in any of the related processes.

Moreover, changes in the environment, or in those biological processes that are basic to our model though outside its purview, can operate sometimes as "cause," sometimes as "effect" of particular aspects of age structure and age dynamics—typically involving an entire chain of reactions within the age structure itself. Thus, to cite a few examples, the age structure of roles may be affected by: the general tendency toward increasing role differentiation in the United States, as this alters the numbers or types of age-specific roles available; a war that, by reducing the ratio of young adult males to females, influences the norms surrounding the appropriate age of marriage; or crop yields in an agricultural society, as these might produce unusual demands for the field labor of the very young or the very old. Similarly, for example, the age structure of the population may be affected by: wars that govern the sizes of particular age strata, not only through mortality, but also by influencing nuptiality and fertility; science and technology (through their impact on medicine, air pollution, or standard of living), that can influence the aging process and the consequent age-related performances; or the general upgrading of the society that may change the gap between old and young in educational attainment.

Equally important to the model is an understanding of the broad societal changes, as well as specific changes in biological and physiological functioning, that can occur as the consequences of interaction among changes in the age strata and in the age stratification of society. For example, the increasing joint survival of husband and wife into the middle-aged strata may have the consequence of strengthening the autonomy of the nuclear family at all ages. Or a change in the relative sizes of the age strata, by changing the societal distribution of such age-related characteristics as health, can influence the overall performance capacity of the society and its dependency burden (cf. Hawley, 1959, pp. 378–380). Or further institutionalization of expectations and rewards in the leisure time roles available to older people could affect leisure facilities and roles available in the total society and could result in changing the values for all age strata. Or if more old people became engaged in active occupations, this engagement might heighten their vitality and reduce certain of the deficits of senescence, thereby freeing for other uses the societal facilities and resources now devoted to support of the aged.

A little reflection on these intricate interrelationships will emphasize the disruptions experienced at both the societal and individual levels because new participants are continuously being born, living out their lives, and dying; and because each new cohort requires continuous reassignment and retraining to perform essential tasks. Within the macrocosm of the total society, the flow of cohorts fits individuals together, however disparate their respective backgrounds, so as to stratify the society by age. And the current interplay among coexisting cohorts (the age strata) at given periods of history, while tending to preserve many aspects of the social order, also presses for the emergence of new or altered structures.

Processes Underlying the Age Strata

We shall now pause for more detailed and precise definition of the elements in the conceptual model, returning first to the social processes and then to the nature of the resultant age strata. Some repetition is unavoidable, since it is only through careful definition and specification that these fundamental concepts can be linked together into testable propositions that illuminate the nature of age stratification.

Cohort Flow. The age strata in the population at a given time (such as 1960 in Figure 1 above) can be conceived as a composite of the several cohorts, with each cohort the dynamic counterpart of a different stratum. The strata are differentiated through the process of cohort flow, which consists of the formation of successive cohorts, their modification through migration, and the gradual reduction and eventual dissolution of each cohort through the death of individual members (cf. Ryder, 1963, 1964, 1965).

A cohort has already been defined here as an aggregate of individuals who were born (or who entered a particular system, such as a hospital or the community of scientists) in the same time interval and who age together. Each cohort starts out with a given size which, save for additions from immigration, is the maximum size it can ever attain. Over the life course of the cohort, some portion of its members survive, while others move away or die until the entire cohort is destroyed. Each cohort starts out also with a given composition; it consists of members born with certain characteristics and dispositions.

Over the life course of the individual, some of these characteristics are relatively stable (a person's sex, color, genetic makeup, country of birth, or—at entry into adulthood in our society—his level of educational attainment are unlikely to change). Even in respect to such stable individual characteristics, however, the composition of the cohort changes over its life course, since certain segments tend to survive longer than others (in recent experience, for example, women longer than men, whites longer than blacks).

The flow of cohorts (barring the complete disruption of the society) is an inevitable and irreversible process. When successive cohorts are compared, they resemble each other in certain respects, but differ markedly in other respects: in initial size and composition, in age-specific patterns of survival (or longevity), and in the periods of history covered by their respective life spans.

Aging. The strata at any given period differ not only in the cohorts to which they belong but also, as can again be seen from Figure 1, in stage of the life course (or chronological age). Strata are differentiated through the process of aging (including biological, psychological, and social aging), which involves all the individual members of every cohort (irrespective of date of birth) as they proceed and change over their life course (cf. Clausen, 1971). It is noteworthy that, since aging occurs throughout all the interdependent strata in the society, in a sociological model the term cannot be confined solely to later stages of the life course. It is noteworthy too that the age strata are direct reflections, not of individual changes over the life course from birth to death, but of changes in composition over the life course of the cohort—that is, the aggregate changes in all the aging individuals who compose the cohort. Thus, a distinction must always be made, as in all social system analysis, between the (microlevel) aging of individuals and the (macrolevel) aging of cohorts (discussed further below).

Individual aging has been defined here to involve performance in a sequence of socially prescribed roles, accumulation of experience, and psychological change and development (as well

as various organically-based changes). Over the life course, individuals acquire certain capacities and motivations but lose others, and (often without regard to capacities or motivations) enter some roles but relinquish others. Aging constitutes mobility from one age stratum to the next, much like social class mobility, save for its inevitability and irreversibility. Viewed as mobility, aging is revealed as entailing many strains affecting the mobile individual, the group he leaves behind (such as his family of orientation), and the new group that must absorb him (such as his wife's family when he marries).

Aging, inevitable and irreversible like cohort flow, is far from a uniform process. The nature of aging among human beings as members of society is markedly affected by many factors—psychological and social as well as biological: by the individual's characteristics and dispositions, by the modifications of his characteristics through socialization, by the particular role sequences in which he participates, and by the particular social situations and environmental events that he encounters. It therefore follows that patterns of aging—and the consequent nature of the age strata—can differ, not only from one society to another and from one century to another, but also among successive cohorts in a single society. For any given cohort, the pattern of aging will reflect the particular historical background of the cohort, the special patterns of its compositional segments (by sex, color, or socioeconomic status, e.g.), and the special definition of age as a criterion for role assignment and role performance.

Thus, the two processes of aging and cohort flow are linked together and operate in tandem to sort people (the members of society) into age strata.

Role Changes. The age stratification system, as it derives from the continuing interplay between age dynamics (cohort flow and aging) and societal dynamics, consists of roles as well as people. The numbers and kinds of roles open or closed to people in the several strata and the age-related norms governing these roles, are affected not only by processes endogenous to our model but also by far-flung processes and changes in history and the environment. Such exogenous processes, though crucial to the model, often exceed our immediate focus on age. E.g., in the United States, the secular decline in the age at which males leave the labor force, which is central to our concern with the newly-differentiated retirement role, is also associated with broader trends (such as declines in agricultural employment or in self-employment) that transcend the place of age in the system (cf. Riley, Foner, Moore, Hess, and Roth, 1968, Chapter 3). Or the long-term extension of formal education, which has institutionalized the age-specific roles of high school or college student, is further traceable to many factors other than age (cf. Coleman *et al.*, 1974). Our age-specific model cannot deal directly with all such environing factors but will often treat as "given" broad changes in the role structure which underlie our immediate focus on shifts in the age criteria for role allocation or for role definition, on changes in age-ascriptive roles, or on the emergence of new boundaries between strata.

Difference in Timing. Of central importance to the formation of strata, however, are the differences in rhythm and timing between age dynamics and these societal dynamics that determine age-related role opportunities and rewards (or deprivations). There is a definite rhythm to the flow of people through the society, as they are born, live out their life span, and die. This flow is staggered across time (as suggested by the horizontal bars in Figure 1). By contrast, the role processes, which have no comparable rhythm or periodicity, traverse the coexisting age strata at given periods (as in the sequence of vertical lines in Figure 1). This fundamental and universal lack of synchronization in the formative processes has important consequences for the nature of age strata and, as we shall see, for the relationships among people who are differentially placed in the age stratification system.

The Nature of Age Strata

Against this background of process and change, we can now view in further detail the age strata themselves, the people and roles that constitute them, and their implications for individuals and for society.

Age Strata in the Population. As the first of the structural elements in Figure 2 above, people (conceived here in sociological terms as actors in a social system) form strata composed of persons of similar age; and the total population is made up a series of such age strata, as Figure 3 illustrates for the United States. Within a population, the several age strata can vary in size and composition, as there may be more people in the younger than in the older strata, or the ratio of females to males may increase from younger to older strata.

More specific aspects of our model of the age strata in the population include the following obvious but basic points: an aggregate of individuals (or of groups) who are of similar age at a particular time is called an age stratum (or an age category). The divisions between strata may be variously specified, either precisely or approximately, and in terms either of the chronological age of the members (as in Census age categories) or of their stage of biological, psychological, or social development. The strata within a population form an ordered series from younger to older.

Age-related Acts. Not only do the age strata differ from one another at any given period in population size and composition, but they differ also (element 2 in the model) in the contributions they can make to the activities and processes of the groups and the society in which they are found. That is, both actual performances and orientations and the capacity and motivation to perform are affected by age in complex ways. E.g., older people may be less responsive than younger people to technical reasoning because they have forgotten the strategy for learning (life course stage), because they have a generally poorer educational background to start with (cohort membership), or as a self-fulfilling prophecy because their teachers offer little encouragement to the old (role expectations).

Age Structure of Roles. Just as age divides the population into age strata, age is also built into

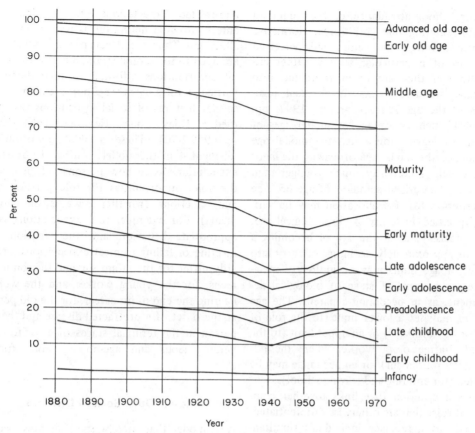

Figure 3. Distribution of U.S. population by age strata, 1870–1970. (From Bogue, 1959, pp. 96–97, compiled from 1950 Census of Population, Vol. II, Part 1, Table 98: data for 1880–1950; from 1960 Census of Population, Vol. I, Part 1, p. 148: data for 1960; from 1970 Census of Population, Vol. I, United States Summary, p. 269: data for 1970. Reprinted by permission from Riley, Matilda White, Johnson, Marilyn, and Foner, Anne. 1972. *Aging and Society: A Sociology of Age Stratification, 3.* New York: Russell Sage Foundation, p. 421.)

the social structure as a criterion for entering or relinquishing certain roles (or positions in society and its various groupings). Age can operate directly as a criterion; e.g., in the United States a person cannot vote until age 18 or become President until age 35; or he may be required to retire at age 65. Age can also operate indirectly as a role criterion through association with other factors; e.g., biological stage limits motherhood; or being old enough to have completed high school tends to limit entry into college; or the rapid reaction time required for certain occupations can exclude the aged. Thus, age criteria form a basis for allocating persons to positions in the social structure, thereby affecting the boundaries between age strata.

As regulated by age criteria, roles open to

persons in the several age strata (element 3 in the model) vary in type (according to the institutional spheres in which they are embedded), in the particular complexes or constellations of role types that are simultaneously accessible, and the numbers of each type available (e.g., in the number of jobs open to workers under age 20 or over age 60).

More specific aspects of our model of the age structure of roles—parallel in many respects to the age strata of people who pass through these roles—include further clues to the operation of age criteria. As an aspect of the social structure, most age criteria are socially normative (cf. Neugarten, Moore, and Lowe, 1965), permitting or requiring people of given ages to perform particular activities—as in the prescribed ages for school attendance or the minimum ages for entering the work force. Normative age criteria reflect the values and perceived exigencies of a particular society. Other criteria, though they are often translated into normative standards, constitute factual regularities in the age strata (Sorokin, 1947, pp. 191–194), such as average or modal ages of entering or leaving roles—e.g., the modal age of dying; or the modal age of leaving the labor force, which is currently much younger than the widely prescribed standard of age 65. Age as a criterion for role allocation may be variously specified in terms of chronological age, either precisely, as in the age of becoming a voter, or approximately, as in age of entry into college; or age limits may be indirectly specified, e.g., in terms of stage of biological development, as in becoming a parent. The age criterion may set a lower limit (to the role of voter or of "drinker") or an upper limit (to the role of draftee or of worker where there is mandatory retirement); or an age range may be specified (for entering and leaving school).

Age is a criterion that links together complexes of roles that are otherwise differentiated. E.g., old age may place individuals simultaneously in the roles of retiree, member of friendship group, and grandparent (cf. Rosow, 1967). Complexes of age-linked roles form an ordered series within the society. However, the ordering of roles by age—though it often results in inequalities—is not necessarily defined socially as a hierarchy. Instead, this ordering may be viewed by members of the society as a set of equivalent, though differentiated, role-complexes. E.g., the educational and leisure roles differentially available to the young may (or may not) be assessed as balancing the political and occupational roles available to mature strata (Riley and Johnson, 1971; Foner, 1973; cf. Back and Bourque, 1970, whose "draw their lives" graphs suggest a perceived decline in the quality of life after a plateau between age 50 and 70). Even when a hierarchy of inequality is perceived, the ordering may not follow the chronology of the age strata, as in modern societies the middle-aged stratum may be considered the apex.

Age-related Expectations and Sanctions. Age enters into role definition as well as into role allocation. Thus, age affects not only what roles are open to the several strata, but also the societal contributions afforded to incumbents of particular roles by other group members or by special features of social institutions (as specified in Riley, Foner, Hess, and Toby, 1969, pp. 959–970). These societal contributions (element 4 in the model) consist of normative expectations as to how persons will behave in the role, opportunities for role performance, and sanctions (whether rewards or punishments). For example, role expectations as to appropriate behavior, and the sanctions for meeting or failing to meet expectations, ordinarily differ for the infant son and the son in his teens, for the young worker and the worker nearing the end of his career, for the old person at the onset of a protracted disease and the old person in the terminal stages of it, or for age-heterogeneous and age-homogeneous friendships.

Age Strata and Other Societal Divisions

Any model that merely specifies how people and roles are differentiated by age is incomplete. For people and roles are also organized in groups and in institutional spheres within the society. Age is only one of several bases of social stratification. Thus, full development of the implications of age stratification also requires an understanding of how the age strata intersect with other societal divisions. If one visualizes the people and the roles in the society as divided by horizontal lines into age strata, then these age divisions cut across, or sometimes coincide with, the other divisions of the society: the divisions into lower-level structures, solidary groups, or institutional spheres, as suggested in Figure 4 (like families, work organizations, communities, the polity, or the economy); and also the broader division into subpopulations by sex, class, or race. The extent that the age strata cross-cut or converge with these other divisions affects the impact on the society, e.g., on tendencies toward age solidarity or cleavage, and on the individual,

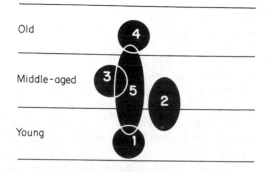

Old

Middle-aged

Young

1 – High school peer group
2 – University
3 – Work group
4 – Senior center
5 – Family

Figure 4. Relation of groups to age strata (a schematic view). (From Riley, Matilda White, Johnson, Marilyn, and Foner, Anne. 1972. *Aging and Society: A Sociology of Age Stratification, 3.* New York: Russell Sage Foundation, p. 400. Reprinted by permission.)

e.g., as he must handle an entire complex of age-linked roles, or as his relationships are marked by love or hate, dominance or submission.

Age Strata and Group Membership. Since people located in the several age strata are simultaneously organized as members of various groups, they participate in a complex of roles in different groups and institutional spheres. Each of these roles affects the behavior and attitudes typically expected of individuals, as well as the rights and privileges accorded to them.

The extreme case (reportedly approximated by a few nonliterate tribes) is the *age-graded society* in which the age boundaries of all the major roles within an age stratum coincide, so that people within an age stratum tend to belong to the same groups. In an otherwise relatively undifferentiated tribe, e.g., each male may belong to one of several "age sets," composed respectively of boys, warriors, and elders. Membership in an age set is a key indicator of a person's status, and most of the important

roles are allocated and regulated through these sets. To the extent that an age stratum involves the whole range of major age-graded roles and normative expectations, the stratum may be considered an age status.

In highly differentiated modern societies, there are no societal-wide "age grades" strictly analogous to the simple model, and groups often show wide variations in age boundaries. Figure 3, in which age strata are schematically delineated, suggests the nature of this variation. Some groups are contained within a single stratum (they are age-homogeneous). Other groups cut across lines dividing age strata (they are age-heterogeneous); in turn, an age-heterogeneous group (e.g., a church or a school) may itself be stratified internally by age.

Modern approximations of a generalized age status may be defined by the expectations of a predominant role. E.g., the emergence of "adolescence" as a distinct status describing an entire stratum is apparently tied to prolonged schooling and delay of entry into the work force; or "old age" may be roughly defined by retirement or by widowhood.

Age Strata and Subpopulations. Members of the several age strata belong not only to particular groups, but also to particular subpopulations affecting social life, such as social classes, sex categories, or races (Sorokin, 1968, p. 409; Sorokin, 1947, p. 181). Neugarten (1963; see also Cumming, 1963, pp. 385–391) regards sex as so crucial a division that special theories of aging are required for men and for women; and age patterns differ also by socioeconomic status, race, and ethnicity. There are tendencies in our own society for age lines to correspond with certain other division (Blau, 1974). Thus, educational level declines with age, the foreign-born are highly concentrated in the oldest strata, or sex ratios tend to be correlated with age. Yet few of these lines converge completely in any highly differentiated, pluralistic society, and individuals who are alike in age may be widely separated in other subpopulations of a matrix criss-crossed by myriad societal divisions (cf. Foner, 1973).

Articulating Processes

Within the complex structure of society, where roles continually change and people endlessly shift in and out of roles, how are the streams of individuals articulated with the roles in each of the age strata? Referring back to Figure 2, we are reminded that the facts of aging, death, and the infusion of new cohorts into the population involve a continuing flow of manpower into age-specific roles and the training of new recruits to meet age-specific expectations. Figure 2 also indicates that two processes, allocation and socialization, work together to bring into conjunction the four sets of structural elements in the model.

Allocation. Allocation is treated here as a set of mechanisms for the continual assignment and reassignment of individuals of given ages to the appropriate roles. Diverse allocative procedures and agencies operate to enhance the opportunities and rewards in certain roles, while closing off access to others (or rendering them undesirable). Although allocative procedures are sometimes rooted in nonsocial phenomena, such as biological or vital processes or territorial location, they are generally sociocultural in character.

Nonsocial processes may effect allocation by impinging on the individual's relationship to role partners, as an individual is allocated out of the marital role and into widowhood via the death of a spouse, or neighbors may lose one another as role partners through migration of one of the pair. Even when allocation is mediated through nonsocial processes, supplementary procedures are widely used to symbolize or validate the social aspect of conferral (or withdrawal) of a role. E.g., registration and baptism legitimate the assumption of parenthood, at the same time marking the entrance of the child into state and church; death certificates and burial rites legally or religiously validate termination of the life course. The purely social procedures of allocation range from the highly formalized legal or bureaucratic processes of military conscription; through mechanisms of competition and negotiation involving hiring and firing, promotion and demotion; to in-

formal customs and folkways as these may operate (within the biological limits of fecundity) to produce the characteristic age gap between parent and offspring, or between an individual and his siblings.

Allocative processes operate through structured sets of relationships in which the allocator (such as an employer), because of greater experience or seniority in the particular group, is often older than the candidate. These relationships tend to be asymmetrical (with certain exceptions, such as friendship), with candidates lacking allocative power over the agent of allocation. Hence, the relative ages of allocators and candidates often demarcate relations of power or competition within or between age strata, entailing special strains.

Socialization. The second articulating process, socialization, serves to teach individuals at each stage of the life course how to perform new roles, how to negotiate allocative procedures, how to adjust to changing roles, and how to relinquish old ones. The massive available literature (e.g., Goslin, 1969a; Clausen, 1968) implicitly connects socialization with the progress of individuals over the life course. In addition, like allocation, socialization involves varied structures of age relationships. While infants are always younger than their parents or other socializers, mature students or on-the-job trainees are often taught by persons younger than they. Moreover, socialization tends to be a reciprocal process, in which the teacher learns a good deal from the person being taught (an often-overlooked aspect of socialization, early recognized by Mannheim ([1928] 1952, p. 300). Particularly in periods of rapid social change, the older strata can learn much from the younger.

When allocation and socialization are viewed in terms of our conceptual model, a marked parallelism between them becomes apparent. Both must be apprehended as integral components of the life course, and both involve special structures of age relationships. Thus, cross-section views of the age strata at particular periods reveal a multiplicity of role relationships among individuals of varying age who are also in varying stages of socialization and allocation and who confront one another as candidates or allocators, or as socializees or socializing agents for particular roles.

In sum, our model of age stratification variously selects for attention those aspects of a social system in which age is importantly implicated. Structurally, we have emphasized age as a factor for dividing the population into strata with differentiated contributions, as well as for defining criteria for occupying roles and specifying the expectations, facilities, and sanctions associated with particular roles. Correspondingly, two sets of processes that underlie this age structure are those impinging upon the population to produce age strata and mobility across strata; and those societal processes affecting the age-related structure of roles; while a third pair of articulating processes effect the allocation and socialization to roles of people at various ages.

INTERPRETING RESEARCH FINDINGS ON AGE STRATA

In this paradigmatic sketch of the processes underlying age strata in a social system, we have touched upon many themes and questions with implications for individuals and for society. Before considering certain of these implications, we must note a few formal principles, highlighted by this conceptual model, that govern its use in analysis and in interpreting research findings on age stratification.

Cross-Sectional Data as the Translation of Processual Data

One key principle of wide utility in analysis derives from the assumption in our model that age strata are the joint products of societal processes and the pair of age processes, aging and cohort flow. In research, the age strata are typically examined through cross-sectional information, and we deal with aging and cohort succession, not as abstract processes, but as empirical processes occurring in particular historical and environmental contexts—i.e., the age dynamics are merged with societal dynamics. Hence a special nomenclature is needed.

We use the shorthand terms "life-course differences" (within a cohort) and "cohort differences" in life-course patterns (among successive cohorts). The expressions "life-course differences," "cohort differences," and also "strata differences" for the cross-sectional differences among strata of special concern in this chapter merely indicate what comparisons are being made, whether or not the data at hand reveal differences or lack of difference.

Principle 1 holds, then, that (at least in a closed population) the differences (or similarities) among old, middle-aged, and young at a given time can be completely described in terms of life-course differences and cohort differences. Table 1, specifying this principle, shows how selected cohort and life-course tendencies are translated into the cross-sectional age patterns (strata differences), frequently obtained from survey data (cf. MacMahon, Johnson, and Pugh, 1963).

TABLE 1. TRANSLATION OF PROCESSUAL DATA INTO CROSS-SECTIONAL DATA.

	Tendency in cross-sectional data (strata differences):
If trends have produced:	
a. Increases in successive cohorts (cohort differences are +)	Younger > older
b. Decreases in successive cohorts (cohort differences are −)	Younger < older
If life-course patterns show:	
c. Increases with aging (life-course differences are +)	Younger < older
d. Decreases with aging (life-course differences are −)	Younger > older

NOTE: The apparent anomaly that cohort differences and life-course differences seem to have opposite effects on strata differences occurs simply because, among "successive cohorts," the more recent cohorts constitute the younger (rather than the older) strata.

SOURCE: Riley, Matilda White; Johnson, Marilyn; and Foner, Anne. 1972. *Aging and Society: A Sociology of Age Stratification*, Vol. 3. New York: Russell Sage Foundation, p. 58.

Cohort Differences. First, the translation into strata differences of certain types of cohort differences is illustrated in situations (a) and (b) of this table. Consider situation (a). If there is an increasing trend over time, so that successive cohorts are marked by rising levels of a characteristic—by rising levels of educational attainment, e.g.—then a slice through the age strata at a particular time will reflect this rise in a special way. There will be a consequent heightening of the educational levels for the younger as compared with the older strata. Situation (b) is the converse. If successive cohorts experience declining levels of a characteristic—such as declining death rates from tuberculosis—then the cross-sectional slice will reflect heightened effects of the disease in the older as compared with the younger strata.

Life-course Differences. Second, consider how life-course patterns are reflected in cross-sectional data, illustrated in situations (c) and (d) of Table 1. Suppose that, as in situation (c), the size of vocabularly increases over the life course. Then this characteristic will tend to rise with increasing age among the strata observed at a particular time. Conversely, if, as in situation (d), speed of response declines over the life course, the strata will tend to show in cross-section a decrease by age.

Combined Cohort and Life-course Differences. We have been discussing each set of diachronic (processual) patterns singly, as in Table 1. But, according to Principle 1, both cohort differences and life-course differences are simultaneously at work. Their combined consequences for particular sets of cross-sectional data can either reinforce or counteract one another. Thus, a combination of situations (a) and (d) can jointly increase the tendency for younger strata to exceed older strata—for example, if cohort increases in the tendency to drink alcoholic beverages were coupled with a decline in drinking over the life course. However, if the decline (as in drinking) over the life course (d) were to be coupled with decreases over successive cohorts (b), then the cross-sectional differences between young and old yielded by

(d) would tend to be reduced by (b). Indeed (if the two sets of decrements were equal), the strata differences might disappear entirely or they might become the reverse of the life-course decline.

In converse fashion, the joint operation of situations (b) and (c) can heighten the tendency for the younger strata to be lower than the older strata in cross-sectional measurements. This would occur, e.g., in religiosity if a cohort decline were accompanied by increases with aging. If, however, an increase associated with aging (c) were to be accompanied by cohort increases (a), as in the proclivity to vote, then the cross-sectional differences in this proclivity would tend to be reduced.

The combined effects of cohort and life-stage response may, of course, be more than simply additive. In some of the more complicated situations than those listed in Table 1 (such as situations complicated by curvilinear patterns), the two types of response interact with each other. Thus, young and old may react in different ways to the same societal event, not merely because they differ in life-stage, but also because their differing cohort membership conditions the ways in which life-stages are experienced. E.g., changes in political party allegiance might show older people shifting toward one party, but younger people shifting in the other direction toward an opposing party, a finding evocative of tantalizing questions: did the older people react differently to the events of the period because they were older or because of their cohort membership? how might cohort membership and aging influence each other in mediating the impact of social change? Whatever the answer to such questions, where life-course differences and cohort differences mutually interact, the nature of the cross-sectional patterns are not predictable from separate examination of the two sources of diachronic variation.

Some Criteria for Interpretation. Such close inquiry into this general principle helps to clarify some of the complexities underlying the data obtained in a single cross-sectional study to describe the age strata (cf. Schaie, 1965; Baltes, 1968). We can now also specify as *corollaries of Principle 1* two special situations in which such data can be interpreted appropriately (Cohn, 1972). First, the strata differences can be understood as a reflection of cohort differences when it is reasonable to assume that there are no appreciable life-course variations in the measure under scrutiny (such as age-specific differences among adults in level of education). Second, and conversely, the differences among strata can properly be attributed to changes over the life course when cohorts can reasonably be assumed to be substantially alike in a certain respect (as in the ages marking decrements in visual acuity). That is, cross-sectional patterns in the age strata are interpretable whenever relevant fact or theory permits the necessary assumptions.

Some Potential Fallacies. Often, however, there is no clear basis for assuming either that there is no variation over the life course or no difference among cohorts. Here the unwary investigator is in danger of misinterpreting the cross-sectional information on age strata. He runs the risk of committing a "life-course fallacy" by overlooking the possibility of cohort differences, or a "generational fallacy" by overlooking the possibility of life-course differences. Life-course fallacies are especially prevalent in the literature since it seems "natural" to explain differences among strata in terms of the aging process alone. E.g., the cross-sectional data on intelligence were originally interpreted to mean a retrogression (beyond the late teens) due exclusively to aging, until a few longitudinal studies challenged this simplistic interpretation (Riley *et al.*, 1968, pp. 255–257). Here the fallacy may stem from the sharp differences in educational level among successive cohorts. Because educational level and performance on intelligence tests are highly correlated, these cohort differences would affect the cross-sectional findings profoundly. Indeed, much current thinking about aging as a process in strata formation may need revision, as sophisticated investigation points to the potential power of cohort differences in interpreting a wide range of age-specific patterns (e.g., in the etiology of tuberculosis, Frost, 1939; in cognitive functioning, Nesselroade,

Schaie, and Baltes, 1972; in tolerance of nonconformity, Davis, 1974).

Processes and Structural Change

For purposes of analysis, we have summarized under Principle 1 the processes underlying differences among age strata as observed at a single period of time. Now we turn to the relationship of these processes to change or stability in the age strata, observable in cross-sectional age data when two or more periods are compared.

The kinds of data widely used to analyze trends by age (in marital status, income, and all the many attributes characterizing the age strata) are suggested schematically in Table 2. Comparison down the columns shows pervasive strata differences, but comparison across the rows shows a distinct difference between the

TABLE 2. PERIOD ANALYSIS REFLECTING DIFFERENT LIFE-COURSE AND COHORT PATTERNS.

Fictitious figures show proportions of persons in each stratum having a particular characteristic. (Date of birth in parentheses)

Example 1 (Zero life-course differences)

PERIOD OF OBSERVATION

Age	1930	1940	1950	
30	30	40	50	(1920)
40	20	30	40	(1910)
50	10	20	30	(1900)
	(1880)	(1890)	(1900)	

Example 2 (Zero cohort differences)

PERIOD OF OBSERVATION

Age	1930	1940	1950	
30	20	20	20	(1920)
40	25	25	25	(1910)
50	30	30	30	(1900)
	(1880)	(1890)	(1900)	

two examples in the table. In Example 1, there are period increases in every stratum, but there is no change ("period differences" zero) in Example 2. What additional principle is suggested here?

A shift in perspective on these data is profoundly revealing. Examination of columns and rows directs attention to the strata. Reexamination of these same data along the diagonals redirects attention (as in cohort analysis) to life-course patterns (reading along each diagonal) and to cohort differences among these patterns (comparing diagonals). How does such reexamination account for the differing trends in the two examples? In Example 1, where there are period increases, there are also consistent cohort increases (e.g., at age 30, the most recent cohort—born in 1920—is higher than its predecessors). By contrast, in Example 2, where there are no period differences, there are also no cohort differences. It is to be noted here too that, in the absence of cohort differences, the consistent life-course patterns do not in themselves yield structural change.

With this example in mind, we can now state *Principle 2*: Any change in the age strata between two or more periods of observation reflects the cohort difference in the life-course patterns of those cohorts existing at the particular time periods. An important, if not immediately transparent, *corollary to Principle 2* can also be stated: If there are no differences among cohorts, then there will be no differences among periods, regardless of the life-course patterns. In sum, changes in the age strata are produced by intercohort, not by intracohort, patterns. Differences in age strata from one period to another are the consequences not of aging, but of intercohort differences—in level, slope, or shape—of life-course patterns. E.g., the well-known transformation in the age pattern of work force participation, as long-term economic development has been examined by drastic decreases in participation by older men and younger boys, has occurred because each new cohort of young men has tended to start work at a later age than its predecessor, but to stop work at a younger age. As Ryder (1964, p. 461) puts it, social change occurs to the extent that "successive cohorts do do something other than merely repeat the patterns of behavior of their predecessors."

Levels of Analysis

Such principles, relating life-course patterns and cohort patterns to the age strata, point to the differing levels of the social system to which attention may be directed. Any particular analysis may focus primarily on the age-stratified society as a whole, on the age stratum (or cohort in cross-section), or on the individual as a member of either or both; or the focus may be multilevel, examining the interdependencies between strata and society or between society or stratum and the constituent individuals (Riley, 1963, Unit 12).

Cross-sectional data, when used to cut through these system levels at given periods (corresponding to our view in Figure 1 of the staggered cohorts moving through time), are applicable to the different levels in distinctive ways (cf. Ryder, 1964; Riley and Nelson, 1971). At the macrolevels of society or strata, cross-sectional data are crucial for describing age patterns and relationships, for examining trends and changes in the strata, or for assessing the effects of new policy or practice at the time of intervention. At microlevels, where individuals are directly involved, cross-sectional data are needed to locate people of given ages with reference to coexisting other people of the same, or differing, age (e.g., in studying the relation between grandparents, their adult offspring, and their peers; or in studying how middle-aged persons regard the financial dependency of the very young and the very old). However, in tracing the underlying processes of cohort flow and aging, the data (again in correspondence with the conceptual model) refer to the macrobiographies of the cohorts that form the strata. They are not simply reducible to the microbiographies of individuals, nor can they be directly interpreted at the individual level. For the changing age strata comprise the "collective" individual biographies, the net result of the myriad shifts and changes of the aging people within each stratum. A few examples will illustrate these important, though often misunderstood, distinctions in social system levels which affect understanding of age strata.

Macrolevel Changes in Strata. Consider the Census data on marital status in the United States as analyzed by the demographers I. B.

Taeuber and C. Taeuber (1971, pp. 284–304) for the decades 1890 to 1960. These data show for each age category the proportion of the population who were currently single, married, or widowed. Taken together, these data, because of their collective reference to the age strata, disclose dramatic societal changes in family structure, with near revolutionary social and economic implications. For example, the middle age strata (30 to 34, 35 to 39) show continuing increases in the proportions currently married. Meantime, the proportion single at age 20 to 24 dropped drastically over the 70-year interval, reflecting the increasing proclivity toward marriage of new cohorts entering this stratum. And the proportions widowed were declining in the age stratum 65 and over (and even more sharply at age 55 to 64), as successive cohorts entered these later-life strata. Further information—still referring to the strata—might be used to explain the decrease in widowhood, given the tremendous increase in the married population who were "at risk" (cf. Susser, 1969). Additional information is clearly needed on rates of remarriage among the widowed and on the increases in length of life, which affect both the proportions of spouses dying and the chances of survival for the widowed (on the vexatious problem of mortality, cf. Uhlenberg, 1969).

This example, admittedly complex, suggests how changes in the strata may be interpreted by reconstructing the history of the coexisting cohorts moving through the system. As in most actual analyses of the changing age strata, the focus is on macrobiographies of cohorts and on rates (however refined), rather than on individuals as actors in the system. Although numerous difficulties must be overcome, macrolevel analysis has a unique advantage in the study of age strata: it can transcend those phenomena immediately comprehensible to most individuals involved. It concentrates instead on factors in the society, past and present (such as the economic factors associated with the income of older people, or the intricate web of attitudes and practices that legitimate retirement), which often operate below the level of awareness to constrain people's thoughts and behavior (cf. Durkheim's [1897] 1951 classic analysis of social integration as a factor in suicide).

Microlevel Changes in Strata. Although the strata are macrolevel phenomena, full apprehension of their nature and dynamics requires information about the component individuals—information difficult to extract from the typical data in the sequence-of-cross-section samples drawn from the same cohorts. Sometimes, therefore, alternative types of data are used that trace the *same* individuals within age strata from one time to the next, either through retrospective questioning (cf. K. E. Taeuber, 1965); or through longitudinal analysis of samples from several age strata, as in the lifespan studies of psychological variables by Schaie and Strother, 1964, or in the Duke panel (for an early description, see Maddox, 1966). While each type of data has special limitations (Riley, Johnson, and Foner, 1972, Appendix), information on the biographies of individuals comprising the strata (cf. Berger and Berger, 1972) can enable the investigator to take the viewpoint of the aging individual (cf. Weber's concept of *Verstehen,* [1922] 1947, p. 100), and to learn how he experiences his position and his interactions within the age stratum. Such information is often essential too for understanding the ways in which individuals change as they pass through each stratum, as they switch political party allegiance, e.g., or as individual women move in and out of the labor force. At the stratum level also, information on the shifts and rearrangements of individuals is useful: e.g., an older stratum might differ markedly from a younger one in the frequency of dropping in and out of the labor force, yet the two might appear from the cross-section data to be alike in *net* labor force preparation rates (for discussion of this principle, see Riley, 1963, Vol. II, pp. 134–135).

Some Pitfalls in Microlevel Interpretation. Where pertinent biographical data on individuals are not accessible, the researcher relying on cross-section age data (as from the rich stores currently accumulating in data banks) must note the possible pitfalls and fallacies if only to avoid them. One difficulty, that we call the "net shift fallacy" (a special case as applied to change of "aggregative" or "ecological" fallacy), occurs when collective data that refer to the stratum or cohort are interpreted inappropriately to refer to the individual. This fallacy can arise in analysis of reversible, rather than irreversible, characteristics. E.g., in the Taeubers' analysis of changing marital status using Census categories, the status of "single" (never married) is irreversible over the life course of the individual: a person, once married, cannot again become never married. For the single persons in an age stratum, then, the past marital history seems clear. Not so for married persons, who may or may not have remarried after previous divorce or widowhood, because the status of married (and also the status of widowed) *is* reversible over the life course. Becoming married (or widowed) is a repeatable event. Thus, to draw inferences from their current status about the past marital history of the married (or the widowed) in an age stratum is to risk an aggregative fallacy.

Net shift (or aggregative) fallacies can arise when shifts over the life course of individuals are concealed in the cohort data (as these shifts tend to counteract each other). A second, closely related, difficulty (or "compositional fallacy") occurs when changes in the kinds of people composing a cohort are erroneously interpreted to mean life-course changes that individuals personally bring with them into an age stratum. E.g., higher levels of job satisfaction in the older than in the younger strata (repeatedly observed in the United States— Gurin, Veroff, and Feld, 1960, p. 170; Executive Office of the President, 1973, p. 124) do not necessarily mean that people, as they age, become increasingly satisfied with their jobs or shift around until they find jobs they like; for these strata differences (which may also reflect cohort differences) may be due in part to changes in the kinds of people remaining in the labor force, as the less satisfied workers retire (cf. Streib and Thompson, 1957, p. 184).

As another major source of the compositional fallacy, consider the impact of death on a cohort. Like retirement from the labor force, death tends to operate selectively, so that certain categories of individuals (such as females, married persons, those in higher socioeconomic brackets) are more likely to survive than their counterparts (males, the not-married, the low-ranked). Selective mortality means, then, that certain characteristics which are irreversible with respect to the individual are reversible with respect to the cohort. E.g., many individ-

uals afflicted in childhood with an incurable disease will die before they grow old—and, once these afflicted individuals have died out of the cohort, the later-life death *rates* from this disease will decrease. This could scarcely lead to the inference that the afflicted person's risk of death from this incurable disease decreases as a result of aging! The appropriate interpretation refers, of course, not to the *individual's* life course, but to the declining proportions of afflicted survivors over the life course of the *cohort*. In other examples, the rising proportion of women over the life course of the cohort might create the erroneous impression that older individuals become increasingly susceptible to sex-linked characteristics, like religiosity or certain mental disorders (cf. Riley, Johnson, and Foner, 1972, pp. 602–607). Such instances suffice to emphasize the general point that the earlier experiences of individuals in an age stratum cannot always be inferred directly from the macrobiography of the cohort.

In short, as a developing conceptual model is revised and elaborated to embody accumulating knowledge about age strata, it can lead to forms of analysis and interpretation designed to achieve theoretical congruence. Guided by a model, appropriate forms of analysis can avoid much of the naïveté and uncertainty often besetting gerontological studies (the potential fallacies, the struggles with the "identification problem" as discussed, e.g., by Mason, Mason, Winsborough, and Poole, 1973; or by Stinchcombe, forthcoming) and can accomodate such aspects of the model as the several distinctive system levels, the succession of cohorts as macrobiographies composing the strata, or the interactions and relationships of individuals pursuing their daily lives within the age-stratified society.

SOME IMPLICATIONS OF THE MODEL

For a workable understanding of age stratification, we have sketched in the first sections of this chapter the broad outlines of a highly general conceptual framework and have selected formal principles guiding any application of this framework. Such concepts and interpretative principles can be useful in social research, public policy, and professional practice only as they can be specified. Our abstract provisional model needs to be refined and elaborated, as well as revised, in order to define the properties of people and their environment indexed crudely by chronological age and date and to state testable hypotheses about the casual linkages among these properties. Much material for such specification is at hand in the broad array of facts and the many interpretations of these facts in this volume and throughout the social science literature on age.

This final section of this chapter notes a few of the more concrete concepts and propositions discernible in a less abstract model through careful scrutiny of the available materials. We touch upon four selected aspects of the model: the ways in which strata emerge from the interplay between the changing society and the developing lives of its members; the special interrelationships of people and social structures within and between the age strata at particular periods of time; the strains and imbalances that arise from poor articulation of people and roles within the strata; and the pressures toward change inherent in the arhythmic relationship between age dynamics and other societal dynamics. We use examples (many of them developed in subsequent chapters) merely to suggest how the emerging model, through continual specification and revision, can be employed as a tool for new research and analysis, pointing to key questions requiring investigation; for comparing and codifying the variations in the age strata under widely differing sociotemporal contexts; and for generating a full-fledged theory of age stratification.

Individuals and the Age Strata

One aspect of the model requiring specification is the interplay between the changing age strata and the daily lives of the people involved. What is the nature of this interplay? What is life like for people in each of the age strata or at the boundaries between strata? And how do people, as they interact, press upon the roles within the strata to shape and change them?

Individuals within the Strata. People at differing ages constitute and mold the social system and are in turn affected by it. We have seen

how society as a whole, and its shifting roles, can be imagined as a web through which individuals of various ages are passing. At any historic moment, this web stretches across the entire population, regardless of age. Thus, many aspects of the role structure—differences among strata in the number and complexity of roles, the opportunities to remain in a stratum and acquire experience over varying time spans, the discontinuities between roles in contiguous strata—all help to shape the capacities, motivations, and performances of individuals who, though unlike in age, coexist within the same society. It comes as no surprise, then, that individuals differ, not alone because of differing cohort membership and life-course experience, but also *because they are located in different age strata.*

No society provides individuals of different ages with an equal array of roles, defining these roles clearly and affording adequate facilities and rewards to motivate the expected performances. Instead, while the nature of the differences varies from time to time and from place to place, the age strata are unequal both in the roles available and in the facilities and rewards for role performance. This changing age structure of roles, as Merton (1957, p. 123) puts it, "constrains individuals variously situated within it to develop cultural emphases, social behavior patterns, and psychological bents." Thus, subcultures form within the strata.

As one example of the effect of societal conditions upon age strata, let us consider how older people respond to retirement. While many welcome the new role and increase their interest in various activities, many others evidence low morale or find it difficult to keep occupied. Their time budgets take conspicuous note of just sitting, standing, looking out the window, or napping (Riley et al., 1968, Chapter 17.5.a). Are such responses peculiar to the state of being old, or can they be traced to the particular social context of older people in today's society? E.g., would a situation in which jobs are generally unavailable evoke from the young responses similar to those noted among retired older people?

Some answers to this question are available from studies that probed into just such a situation—into the general unemployment in several countries during the Great Depression (Riley *et al.*, 1969, pp. 972-974). Among these unemployed, a few found functional equivalents for their lost jobs (such as home repair or gardening), others became resigned to unemployment, and still others were defensive or deviant in their reactions. But of all the responses to the severity of this unemployment crisis, withdrawal or *disengagement* (to use the term dramatized by Cumming and Henry, 1961) was by far the most common, often giving way to complete apathy and indolence, sometimes erupting into physical or mental illness, sometimes deteriorating into complete unemployability. In short, the responses of younger workers are strikingly parallel to those of older workers when circumstances are similar—when, as in many cases of retirement at early ages today, loss of the work role is widespread, of long duration, and often imposed upon the individual quite apart from his own choice. In all age strata, social structural barriers can destroy the motivation to perform in accustomed roles.

This example, in which it is not age alone that elicits particular responses, demonstrates a central point: that many of the attitudes, satisfactions, and performances that constitute subcultures among the age strata are evoked by societal conditions and changes rather than simply by processes inherent in biological, psychological, or social aging.

We mention just two of the many questions posed by the existence of these age-related subcultures as people confront the age-stratified role structure and respond in varying ways. First, since the roles open to the several strata vary in number and complexity of their interconnectedness, how does a person who has reached a given age accomodate? Is there an optimum number of roles he can handle adequately without undue strain? The person with many roles to play—such as the middle-aged man in the contemporary United States—may be overwhelmed by multitudinous obligations, conflicting demands, and expectations of high-level performance (cf. Goode, 1960; Brim, 1966). By contrast, the older person with relatively few roles open to him may suffer from a superfluity of time from involuntary role deprivation (cf. Bredemeier and Stephenson, 1962, p. 131).

Just as individuals may be diversely affected by the number and complexity of roles within a stratum, they are also affected by the age scope of the stratum. When the role structure is viewed in cross-section, each age stratum can be imagined as a band that is more or less broad in scope (from age 60 to 80, e.g., or from age 60 to 61), and this age scope bounds the length of time a person experiences the events and the roles associated with the stratum. Increasingly, the concept of duration in a role becomes important as a postulated casual mechanism in our model, as duration becomes gradually disentangled from the coincident process of aging. Thus, increases with age in commitment to a political party, a job, a neighborhood, or a friendship may often be due, not to aging *per se,* but to accumulated experience in a role regardless of age. And duration in socially valued roles, with concomitant opportunities for extended performances and investment of self, requires a broad span in the years set by age criteria for entering and leaving the role.

Individuals at the Boundaries. Age operates as a criterion also for establishing the divisions between any two strata, divisions experienced as life-course transitions by people approaching them. The nature of particular transitions and the human toll they take depend upon how the boundaries are delineated and on how continuous or disjunctive the roles in adjacent strata may be.

The transfer from one stratum to the next can be either sharp or gradual, sometimes taking place by stages. Exit from work can occur through tapering off or it can consist of a complete break between the last full day of work and the first full day of complete retirement. Marital rites can be performed in a few moments or they can extend over long periods—perhaps decided while the spouses-to-be are still children, negotiated over a period of years, and finally consummated many years later through some official feast or marriage ceremony (Van Gennep, [1908] 1960). Similarly, boundaries at different life-stages and different sociotemporal conditions can be flexible or rigid. Flexibility in age criteria can give individuals greater freedom of choice than permitted under rigid standards and can also provide organizations with maneuverability in adapting to changing needs or supplies of manpower at particular ages.

The impact of role transitions on individuals depends further on the degree of compatibility or continuity between the role complexes in contiguous strata. Individuals making the transfer from one stratum to the next must not only prepare in advance to cross the threshold, but they must also adjust to the new sets of roles at the next higher age level. The new set may either provide direct substitutes for former roles, compatible with the values and attitudes of the previous complex; or alternatively, it may present entirely different norms that require restructuring of orientations or activate defense mechanisms leading to potentially deviant adjustments. Thus, much depends upon the degree of normative consonance between roles available in adjacent strata (Benedict, 1938; Riley *et al.*, 1969, p. 971).

The Emergence of Boundaries. If age criteria constrain the thoughts and acts of people, influencing the structure of society and the particular kinds and durations of experiences to which people are exposed, these criteria were themselves set by people. A key aspect of the conceptual model in need of further specification is the process whereby new age boundaries are established and old ones changed.

One approach to understanding this process involves the full complexity of history. Why, e.g., within the modern family, has the stratum of jointly surviving husbands and wives been widening over the past century while the scope of the child-rearing stage seems to have been narrowing? One answer lies in the association of these changes with broad historical trends toward greater longevity, independent housing, or the contraction of the child-bearing phase. Or why has the boundary between youth and adulthood been rising over the century (Ryder, 1974, p. 48), until we now witness the emergence of a new stratum of "youth" as distinct from "early adolescence"? These changes are undoubtedly related historically to the upgrading of the roles to be learned, the prolonged period of socialization (through the extension of higher education), and the productivity of an economy that has been able to operate without the labor of the young.

Another approach to understanding the emergence of age boundaries is through the everyday process of interaction in which, as millions of apparently unrelated decisions are negotiated and daily behaviors become routinized, age-related patterns gradually emerge. Consider the finding (Heshka and Nelson, 1972) that, in natural outdoor conversations, younger and older people stand closer together than middle-aged people do. Or consider the large numbers of middle-aged women recently returning to school in the United States. Such factual age patterns can, if perpetuated, evolve into normative criteria through the well-known processes of institutionalization in the social system and internalization by the people involved (cf. Parsons, 1951, pp. 204–205; Goslin, 1969b, pp. 7–10; Berger and Luckman, 1966, pp. 169–171). Normative boundaries, as they become customary, are often translated into contract or law (cf. Cain, 1974)—as negotiated retirements finally lead to a mandated age for retirement; or as the changing age distribution of mortality, having established an "appropriate" age to die, may raise questions of legalized euthanasia.

Pressures for Change. One major way in which large numbers of individuals can effect change in the age strata is through *age incongruity*, the violation of age-related expectations or of age criteria for role incumbency. There are, of course, many sporadic instances of behaviors that are popularly viewed as age-inappropriate or deviant, such as first marriage or working at an entry-level job at age 50 or 60. When such age-incongruent behaviors engage large numbers of people, however, they may come to be accepted, rather than deviant, and indeed may produce major changes in the social structure (Foner, 1973). Thus, any widespread and persistent tendency to return to school or college at ages previously adjudged "too old" would involve not only the restructuring of educational institutions, but also greater flexibility of movement between education and work, alterations in the familial division of labor, and a general loosening of the age stratification system (cf.

Coleman *et al.*, 1974; Parelius, 1975; Riley, 1974).

Such blurring of the boundaries of age strata may come about through direct attack to the extent that age (like race or sex) comes under critical scrutiny as an ascriptive basis of allocation. For example, the continuing decline in the age of leaving the work force might conceivably be halted if the mandatory retirement age were widely challenged or the laws against age discrimination in hiring widely enforced. As Marilyn Johnson (1973) puts it, "If age is to remain a principal basis for distinguishing the social activities and opportunities of individuals, achievement values demand that it be linked with some regularity and immutability to *actual* differences in capacities and motivations of people of different ages."

Unlike such pressures to weaken the age strata, the multiplicity of boundary inconsistencies (discussed below as an integrating factor at the level of the social system) may influence individuals to strengthen the strata through attempts to align their boundaries. Consider the young entrant into the status of adulthood who confronts legal age requirements that may vary by several years for criminal liability, drinking, driving, marriage, school-leaving, voting, eligibility for military service, residence outside the parental household, or eligibility for welfare. When complexes of roles heavily inhabited by persons of like age are defined at the boundaries by inconsistent age criteria, there is an undoubted push (such as the push to lower the legal age of voting) toward change in the criteria.

Integration *vs.* Segregation of Age Strata

Age affects daily life not only by sorting people into age-specific places within strata and at the boundaries in the social system, but also by integrating or segregating them from one another. Age as a basis for channeling social relationships is an aspect of the conceptual model that especially lends itself to further specification because sociological principles of social class stratification and social mobility are pertinent (cf. Sorokin, [1927] 1959; Foner, 1974; Riley, 1971). Here we simply note how, and with what consequences, age can serve to link persons of similar age as well as roles having similar age criteria, and to segregate (or differentiate) persons (as well as roles) that differ in age.

Age Integration. *Within* particular strata, age often operates as an integrative mechanism both for society and for its individual members. Members of an age stratum tend to resemble one another in life-course stage and in cohort membership. Thus, biologically and in participation in the role structure, they share a common past, present, and future. They are alike in the sheer number of years behind and the potential years ahead. They also share a common historical (environmental) past, present, and future. E.g., those aged 30 in 1940 had all experienced World War I and the Great Depression. were currently exposed to World War II, and confronted the future of the 1940's through the 1970's. As Mannheim ([1928] 1952) puts it, they share common positions in society.

Similarly, age integrates complexes of roles that are otherwise differentiated (see Figure 4 above). E.g., middle age is a life-stage in which the roles of worker, spouse, and parent of dependent offspring are often joined. And these complexes of roles, quite apart from patterns of individual variation, are also responsive to history—as history affects the role system and its age-specific elements. As Parsons once put it, age, like sex, constitutes "one of the main links of structural continuity in terms of which structures which are differentiated in other respects are articulated with each other ([1942] 1949 p. 218n.; cf. Linton, 1942).

Thus, at a given period in history, individuals of similar age find their way into, and learn to play, roughly similar sets of roles. To an extent, then, the common positions and mutuality of experience among age-peers can operate as an integrative force within each stratum, tending to foster shared orientations, interaction toward common goals, or the development of organized groups (cf. Laufer and Bengtson, 1974). Solidarity can be promoted where age-peers are in a position to communicate about their similar tasks, needs, and problems, and about the exacerbation of these problems at points of major life transition. In the United States, outside of family groups, people in all age strata tend (though by no means exclusively) to have friends who are similar to themselves in status characteristics—notably age—that signal mutuality of experiences, tastes, or values. As the sociological literature shows (Hess, 1972), such choice of age mates is only a special case of the widespread phenomenon of "homophily" (similarity among friends in status or in values— Lazarsfeld and Merton, 1954).

In many circumstances, however, age-based solidarity is problematic. For age strata can themselves be highly differentiated according to other bases of stratification (such as sex, class, or ethnic affiliation) that may command the predominant loyalties. Moreover, the consequences of within-stratum solidarity are not all positive: whereas for the individual such solidarity may mean emotional support and opportunity for interaction and communication, for the society it may, as Blau (1974) points out, foster potential cleavage between the internally cohesive strata.

Age Segregation. *Between* strata, age operates quite differently, often segregating sets of people from one another and differentiating many of the roles they play. Persons in different age strata differ both in life-course stage and in cohort membership. Only because they all share the same present situation do they confront one another across the stratification boundaries that separate them. Roles and role complexes are also differentiated by age, as the roles of student, worker, and retiree (though somewhat overlapping) are typically separated by differences in age criteria. Moreover, certain *relational* roles, such as parent and his offspring, are inherently differentiated by age. Such relational age gaps between roles tend to persist in the social structure over time (history), as the chronological difference between a man and his son necessarily remains fixed throughout their joint lifetimes.

Potentials for Conflict and Change. Consequent upon the differences among the strata, divisive tendencies, though often latent, are apparently universal. Sorokin speaks of the struggle between generations as "a continuously flowing river" that "constantly undermines and reconstructs the social institutions" (Sorokin, 1947, p. 193; see Eisenstadt, 1956, for special types of societies in which revolt of young against old seems endemic).

Among the major sources of possible strain or conflict are age inequalities of facilities and rewards that become defined as inequities. Socially-valued roles open to certain age strata may be denied to others, and tensions are produced by denying to some members of society what they think they are entitled to. To some extent, however, an age differentation of preference, that parallels the age differentiation of rewards, may reduce the sense of inequity, as persons at different life-stages and with differing cohort experiences regard different things as rewarding (Riley and Johnson, 1971).

In addition to distributive inequities, a second potential source of strain among age strata is incompatibility of values. Certain standards, ideologies, and attitudes differ among strata, reflecting differences in life-course stage and the unique slice of history experienced by each cohort. And divergences in values can lead to change through outright conflict, through the spread of deviance from institutionalized patterns, or through shifts in the balance of established but contradictory patterns.

Conflict-reducing Mechanisms. Yet strain or cleavage between strata, like solidarity within strata, is not inevitable. For there are diverse forms of interdependence and deference that can integrate people in the several strata, overriding their differences (cf. Sussman, 1955; Streib and Thompson, 1960; Shanas, 1969). Moreover, there are age-related aspects of the social structure and its underlying processes that operate to mitigate or prevent age conflict (cf. Foner, 1974).

Paramount among these mechanisms is the inevitability of the aging process itself. Though persons in the several strata differ in life-stage, each can share with the others all past stages in retrospect and all future stages in anticipation. Thus, the old, remembering their own adolescent problems, may sympathize with the difficulties of youth. Moreover, the same persons who are in one age stratum at a given time pass into another stratum at a later time, linking together the age-differentiated roles. E.g., a student revolt cannot develop permanent personnel and leadership because the members move out of student roles and into adult roles. Indeed, if age strata tend to be segregated by cohort flow (because new people are continually coming into the youngest strata to replace those who are dying out of the oldest), the strata tend to be united by the process of aging (because the same people now in one stratum have experienced younger strata and anticipate older ones).

Another conflict-reducing mechanism is the extension of solidary groupings across the boundaries of age strata (cf. Figure 4 above). Members of a pluralistic society, by belonging to many age-heterogeneous groups, are exposed to the varied viewpoints of the several age strata, as we have seen. In such situations, the firmly held views peculiar to one's own stratum are difficult to maintain, as interactions across age boundaries continually reinforce the processes of reciprocal socialization. Further, even if persons of different ages do hold divergent views, their affective ties and shared interests can suppress open expressions of hostility. At times the common goals of these other groups become more salient than the goals of an age stratum, much as social class differences tended to narrow the generation gap in the late 1960's. Thus, when other affiliations cross-cut age strata, unity within an age stratum is reduced and solidarity between age strata enhanced.

Reduction of Conflict and the Political Context.
Foner (1974, pp. 193-195) postulates that such age-related conflict-reducing mechanisms are more effective when the major issues of political controversy are material rather than ideal—when they concern the distribution of economic resources rather than freedom, justice, human rights, or other ethical principles. Since material issues give salience to social class interests that involve people of all ages, they are more likely than ideal or moral issues to bring into play those cross-cutting solidarities (like the family or the shop) that supersede age cleavages. By contrast, broad, general questions touching all major spheres of life evoke differences between young and old. When

such ideal issues predominate in political life, as during periods of affluence, the potential for age conflict rises. In line with Foner's hypothesis, the fact that ideal issues are not always paramount in the polity helps explain the sporadic nature of sharp conflicts between strata.

Imbalances between People and Roles

Such ideas and theories about one aspect of our conceptual model, social relations within and between strata, emphasize the widespread connection between age and two major sources of potential change inherent in any society: unjust distribution of facilities and rewards, and malintegration of values. Another aspect of the social system, also a source of potential innovation and change, is the balance—or the imbalance—between the roles and the role players that compose the age strata. Clearly, the match may be poor: there can be societal discrepancies in the numbers or kinds of people and roles available in particular strata; and there can be gaps between role expectations and individual motivation or capacity for performance at particular ages. While the processes of allocation and socialization operate continuously to bridge such discrepancies and gaps by articulating people and roles, many inbalances in the age structure are beyond the reach of these processes.

Supply and Demand for Personnel.
If we think of the numbers of roles and the supply of age-appropriate role-players in terms of "supply" and "demand," the two may often, at least in principle, be compatible. Some roles, as defined in a particular society, are limited in quantity only by the size of the population of the appropriate age. The supply of friendship roles, e.g., seems limited only by the capacities and willingness of individuals at particular ages to form and maintain friendship relations and by the supply of role players available in particular age strata (see, e.g., Blau, 1973, Ch. 5; Lowenthal and Haven, 1968; Rosow, 1967; Rosenberg, 1967). Or—again in principle—where age allocation is universal and compulsory, as in school attendance, the number of available roles is determined by the population in the affected

strata. In order for the balance to be maintained here, the social-structural facilities, including the complementary roles of teachers, must expand or contract in response to the demographic factors (fertility, mortality, and migration) regulating the numbers of children.

In practice, of course, this principle of age-specific numerical balance between people and roles often fails to apply, as a few contemporary examples attest. Increases in the numbers of teachers to meet the spiraling demand occasioned by the postwar baby boom later resulted in a surplus of teachers when the rate of new school entrants began to decline. Or the sex mortality ratio among old people, by limiting the numbers of available men, forecloses to many elderly widows the possibility of remarriage. Or the hierarchical structure of corporate enterprise restricts the number of top managements roles relative to the supply of ambitious older men.

Role Expectations and Performance. Manifestly, the question is not simply one of balancing the quantity of people and roles, for quality is also involved. Even when the people and roles within an age stratum are numerically commensurate, there are many failures of correspondence between role performance by the age strata and role expectations. Consider just a few of the performances, styles, or behaviors that distinguish particular age strata in the United States but seem to have no clear counterpart in the age structure of role expectations. Item: social norms dictate maintenance of independence in old age, but many old people lack the facilities of income, health, or education needed for independence. Item: the tendency for husbands and wives in the middle strata to engage in social visiting as couples only can prevent the single, widowed, and divorced from meeting expected patterns of behavior in friendship roles (Hess, 1971). Item: in many types of routine jobs, the youngest workers display the lowest levels of actual performance (in consistency of work, regularity of attendance, or even in some instances of productive output—Riley et al., 1968, pp. 426–434).

These examples hint at some of the ways in which individuals may be underqualified—or sometimes overqualified—for the roles they play. In work performance, the comparatively high levels attained by older workers, despite their frequent handicaps in physical functioning or in educational background, may perhaps represent "overachievement," while the relatively poor records of younger workers in jobs demanding neither wisdom nor long experience may represent "underachievement." Many roles are widely recognized as utilizing only a small fraction of the input of which individuals are capable. For the stratum of young adults today, the roles open in work, as in voting and other activities, often fail to offer the desired rewards, or to provide opportunities for enactment that are commensurate with the capacities and training of role incumbents. Similarly, for untold numbers in the oldest stratum, normative expectations are often set too low to evoke optimum performance: witness the remarkable extent of individual variability in the behaviors and characteristics of old people (the oldest stratum in this country contains both the richest and the poorest, both the most powerful and the utterly powerless, both the senescent and those with no noticeable organic decrements).

Sources of Imbalance. Thus, as numbers and kinds of roles in the age structure of a society continually change, these changes may fail to synchronize with contemporaneous changes in numbers and kinds of role players at the requisite ages. In some strata people may be overdemanded or underdemanded, and pronounced gaps between role expectations and performance may occur. Structured imbalances in the age strata can arise from many sources, including: improper phasing of socialization and allocation; emergence of new roles and disappearance of others; societal changes in the way roles are defined or organized; changes in fertility, migration, or mortality, or in the social controls over any one of these processes; rising levels of age-specific aspirations unmatched by rising opportunities. As imbalances develop, they often persist because of rigidities or slow rates of change in the role structure or in the population.

Some Consequences of Imbalance. When roles and role players are poorly matched in an age stratum, the resultant tensions and strains can lead to various forms either of adjustment or of change. Many processes, apart from those of allocation and socialization, operate within the population or the role structure to redress age-related imbalances.

Supplies of people are modulated through environmental conditions such as famines or earthquakes, or through such social interventions as contraception or control over pollution or disease. Complex modifications in the age structure of roles are made (by special design, through intricate negotiations between allocators and candidates, or as aspects of broader changes) through alterations (1) in the numbers and kinds of roles available; (2) in the requirements of these roles; or (3) in the age criteria for role incumbency. E.g., young mothers can occupy work roles if maternity leaves are provided; or leisure in old age can be made more enjoyable if socially approved; or, under shifting pressures from role applicants, substitute roles may be provided such as volunteer or consultant for older people, or paramedical specialist for the medically trained young veteran. As Waring (1973) has shown, processes that redress the balance between cohort size and available roles include modulating the *rate of cohort flow*, as the flow of young people into the work force may be decelerated by protracting the period of education, or the movement of adult workers through and out of the work force may be accelerated by providing pensions and lowering the retirement age. Changes in rate of cohort flow often involve changes in the social structure that affect not merely the one stratum immediately implicated, but the entire age-graded role system.

Change. Where adjustments fail to equilibrate roles and people in the afflicted strata, however, unresolved strains can produce frustration for individuals, remedial demands, or potential deviance that may pervade a stratum (cf. Glaser and Strauss, 1971, p. 73), as well as contradictions, discord, and other internal pressures for change in the society. And resultant changes can take any one of the usual forms, from evolutionary development or innovation to revolutionary alteration or chaotic disruption.

Inherent Potentials for Social Change

The final aspect of the conceptual model we select for discussion here leads us back to the basic relationship between the tempo of mankind and the tempo of society. Aging and cohort succession each has its special rhythm, as we have seen. But no such regular rhythm or periodicity has been shown to control the changing role structure through which the population flows (cf. Sorokin, 1941, Vol. 4, p. 505; Nisbet, 1969; Smelser, 1968, p. 266).

Intrinsic Tensions. Because the rhythmic flow of people is channeled through an unpredictable structure of roles, a constant tension inheres in the age strata and in the articulating processes themselves. Age dynamics are not synchronous with societal dynamics. And many of the consequent tensions and imbalances are beyond the reach of socialization and allocation. Indeed, additional pressures for change can be exerted by imperfections in these processes, as allocation and socialization may be out of phase with each other, as socialization may qualify people inadequately for the roles available, or as allocation may fail to assign the numbers and kinds of people appropriate to meet current needs.

The potential for innovation thus appears intrinsic in the lack of synchronization between age dynamics and societal dynamics. Over the life course of each new cohort, aging as a social phenomenon is made possible by the articulating processes that sort out individuals, train, and assign them to roles. And, as cohorts endlessly succeed one another, they respond to historical transformations in role sequences at the same time that they contribute to these transformations.

Repercussions on the Society. Many of the pressures for change implicit in this difference between cohort timing and societal timing leave their imprint upon the entire society, affecting all its strata. Thus, differences between cohorts in one social sphere can have far-reaching consequences for other spheres. E.g., the long-term changes in age of labor force participation among women have been affecting their roles in the home as wives and mothers. Or innovations emanating from a single stratum can sometimes ramify rather quickly through the other age strata, without awaiting the lag over a long series of new cohorts. E.g., increasing leisure in retirement might serve to modify the Protestant Ethic to fit the notion of a "good society" in which every individual has opportunity to develop and exercise his capacities (White, 1961). It is not impossible, then, that the oldest stratum may provide the models for entirely new values which, though now regarded askance as "deviant" or "dysfunctional," may come to be institutionalized as values of the future and to be implemented in a new structuring of social life.

Only through examination of the interface between the changing life-course sequences of individuals and the changing age structure of society can we glimpse such problems of synchronization, or the integral connection between age stratification and social stability and change. Karl Mannheim ([1928] 1952, p. 292) once dramatized the theme through a tantalizing mental experiment. Imagine, he said, a society in which one generation lived on forever, and none followed to replace it! In this experiment, the age strata are scarcely discernible.

In sum, this outline of a sociological perspective on the age strata points out a special challenge to the oncoming cohorts of gerontologists—not merely to pursue current lines of inquiry, but also to reorganize and reexamine existing knowledge in a new way. We suggest specifically a view of society stratified by age, which, on the one hand, defines bases for inequality and conflict and, on the other hand, defines social positions that influence men in their performance of socially-demanded operations. We suggest a review of social change and stability which, while merging Marxian emphases on conflict with Durkheimian emphases on integration, focuses on still another dynamism: on aging and the succession of cohorts that follow their own rhythm, that entail special processes and structures for allocation and socialization of personnel, and that in themselves constitute strains and pressures toward innovation. Such an approach, we submit, can illuminate central aspects of age strata within the statics and dynamics of society and the implications of the full set of age strata for older individuals and for the aging process. At the same time, such an approach can suggest potential solutions to wide-ranging practical problems of great immediate concern.

REFERENCES

Ariès, Philippe. 1962. *Centuries of Childhood: A Social History of Family Life*. Translated by Robert Baldick. New York: Alfred A. Knopf.

Back, Kurt, and Bourque, Linda B. 1970. Life graphs: Aging and cohort effects. *J. Geront.*, **25**, 249–255.

Baltes, P. B. 1968. Longitudinal and cross-sectional sequences in the study of age and generation effects. *Hum. Develop.*, **11**, 145–171.

Benedict, Ruth. 1938. Continuities and discontinuities in cultural conditioning. *Psychiatry*, **1**, 161–167.

Bengtson, Vern L., Furlong, Michael J., and Laufer, Robert S. 1974. Time, aging, and the continuity of social structure: Themes and issues in generational analysis. *J. Soc. Issues*, **30**, 1–30.

Berger, Peter L., and Berger, Brigitte. 1972. *Sociology: A Biographical Approach*. New York: Basic Books.

Berger, Peter L., and Luckmann, Thomas. 1966. *The Social Construction of Reality*. Garden City, New York: Doubleday.

Blau, Peter M. 1974. Parameters of social structure. *Am. Soc. Rev.*, **39**, 615–635.

Blau, Zena Smith. 1973. *Old Age in a Changing Society*. New York: New Viewpoints.

Bredemeier, Harry C., and Stephenson, Richard M. 1962. *The Analysis of Social Systems*. New York: Holt, Rinehart & Winston.

Brim, Orville G., Jr. 1966. Socialization through the life cycle. *In*, Orville G. Brim, Jr. and Stanton Wheeler, *Socialization After Childhood: Two Essays*, Vol. 3, pp. 156–157. New York: John Wiley.

Cain, Leonard D. 1964. Life course and social structure. *In*, Robert E. L. Faris (ed.), *Handbook of Modern Sociology*, pp. 272–309. Chicago: Rand McNally.

Cain, Leonard D. 1974. Political factors in the emerging legal age status of the elderly. *Annals*, **415**, 72–79.

Clausen, John A. (ed.) 1968. *Socialization and Society*. Boston: Little, Brown.

Clausen, John A. 1971. The life course of individuals. *In*, Matilda White Riley, Marilyn Johnson, and Anne Foner, *Aging and Society: A Sociology of Age Stratification*, Vol. 3, pp. 457–514. New York: Russell Sage Foundation.

Cohn, Richard. 1972. On interpretation of cohort and period analyses: A mathematical note. *In*, Matilda White Riley, Marilyn Johnson, and Anne Foner, *Aging and Society: A Sociology of Age Stratification*, Vol. 3, pp. 85–88. New York: Russell Sage Foundation.

Coleman, James S. *et al.* 1974. *Youth Transition to Adulthood*. Chicago: University of Chicago Press.

Cumming, Elaine. 1963. Further thoughts on the theory of disengagement. UNESCO *International Social Science Journal*, **15**, 377–393.

Cumming, Elaine, and Henry, William E. 1961. *Growing*

Old: The Process of Disengagement. New York: Basic Books.

Davis, James A. 1974. Tolerance of atheists and communists in 1954 and 1972-73. Mimeographed. National Opinion Research Center: Social Change Project.

Durkheim, Emile. (1897) 1951. *Suicide.* Translated by John A. Spaulding and George Simpson. Glencoe, Illinois: The Free Press.

Eisenstadt, S. N. 1956. *From Generation to Generation; Age Groups and Social Structure.* Glencoe, Illinois: The Free Press.

Erikson, Erik. 1950. Eight stages of man. *In*, Erik Erikson, *Childhood and Society*, pp. 219-234. New York: W. W. Norton.

Erikson, Erik. 1968. Life cycle. *In*, David L. Sills (ed.), *International Encyclopedia of the Social Sciences*, Vol. 9, pp. 286-292. New York: Macmillan and The Free Press.

Executive Office of the President: Office of Management and Budget. *Social Indicators 1973.* Washington, D.C.: Government Printing Office.

Foner, Anne. 1973. Age in society: Structure and change. Unpublished paper read at the Annual Meeting of the American Sociological Association, New York.

Foner, Anne. 1974. Age stratification and age conflict in political life. *In, Am. Soc. Rev.*, 39, 187-196.

Frost, Wade Hampton. 1939. The age selection of mortality from tuberculosis in successive decades. *Am. J. Hyg.*, sec. A, 30, 91-96.

Glaser, Barney G., and Strauss, Anselm L. 1971. *Status Passage.* Chicago: Aldine-Atherton.

Goode, William J. 1960. A theory of role strain. *Am. Soc. Rev.*, 25, 483-496.

Goslin, David A. 1969a. *Handbook of Socialization Theory and Research.* Chicago: Rand McNally.

Goslin, David A. 1969b. Introduction. *In*, David A. Goslin, *Handbook of Socialization Theory and Research*, pp. 1-21. Chicago: Rand McNally.

Gurin, Gerald; Veroff, Joseph; and Feld, Sheila. 1960. *Americans View Their Mental Health: A Nationwide Interview Study.* New York: Basic Books.

Hawley, Amos H. 1959. Population composition. *In*, Philip M. Hauser and O. Dudley Duncan (eds.), *The Study of Population*, pp. 361-382. Chicago: University of Chicago Press.

Henderson, L. J. 1937. *Pareto's General Sociology.* Cambridge, Massachusetts: Harvard University Press.

Heshka, Stanley, and Nelson, Yona. 1972. Interpersonal speaking distance as a function of age, sex, and relationship. *Sociometry*, 35, 491-498.

Hess, Beth. 1971. Amicability. Ph.D. dissertation, Rutgers University.

Hess, Beth. 1972. Friendship. *In*, Matilda White Riley, Marilyn Johnson, and Anne Foner, *Aging and Society: A Sociology of Age Stratification*, Vol. 3, pp. 357-393. New York: Russell Sage Foundation.

Johnson, Marilyn. 1973. Recent inquiries on age. Unpublished paper read at the Annual Meeting of the American Sociological Association, New York.

Laufer, Robert S., and Bengtson, Vern L. 1974. Generations, aging and social stratification: On the development of generational units. *In, J. Soc. Issues*, 30, 181-205.

Lazarsfeld, Paul F., and Merton, Robert K. 1954. Friendship as social process: A substantive and methodological analysis. *In*, M. Berger, T. Abel, and C. H. Page (eds.), *Freedom and Control in Modern Society*, pp. 18-66. Princeton, New Jersey: D. Van Nostrand.

Linton, Ralph. 1942. Age and sex categories. *Am. Soc. Rev.*, 7, 589-603.

Lowenthal, Marjorie Fiske, and Haven, Clayton. 1968. Interaction and adaptation: Intimacy as a critical variable. *Am. Soc. Rev.*, 33, 20-30.

MacMahon, Brian, Johnson, S., and Pugh, Thomas F. 1963. Relation of suicide rates to social conditions. *Public Health Reports*, 78, 285-293.

Maddox, George L. 1966. Persistence of life style among the elderly: A longitudinal study of patterns of social activity in relation to life satisfaction. *Proceedings*, 6, 309-311. Vienna: 7th International Congress of Gerontology.

Mannheim, Karl. (1928) 1952. The problem of generations. *In*, Paul Kecskemeti (ed. and translator), *Essays on the Sociology of Knowledge*, pp. 276-322. London: Routledge & Kegan Paul.

Mason, Karen Oppenheim, Mason, William M., Winsborough, H. H., and Poole, W. Kenneth. 1973. Some methodological issues in cohort analysis of archival data. *Am. Soc. Rev.*, 38, 242-258.

Merton, Robert K. 1957. *Social Theory and Social Structure.* Glencoe, Illinois: The Free Press.

Nesselroade, J. R., Schaie, K. W., and Baltes, P. B. 1972. Ontogenetic and generational components of structural and quantitative change in adult cognitive behavior. *J. Geront.*, 27, 222-228.

Neugarten, Bernice L. 1963. Personality changes during the adult years. *In*, Raymond G. Kuhlen (ed.), *Psychological Backgrounds of Adult Education*, pp. 43-76. Chicago. Center for The Study of Liberal Education for Adults.

Neugarten, Bernice L. 1974. Age groups in American society and the rise of the young-old. *Annals*, 415, 187-198.

Neugarten, Bernice L., and Datan, Nancy. 1974. The middle years. *In*, Slavano Arieti (ed.), *American Handbook of Psychiatry*, Vol. 1, pp. 592-608. New York: Basic Books.

Neugarten, Bernice L., and Moore, Joan W. 1968. The changing age-status system. *In*, Bernice L. Neugarten (ed.), *Middle Age and Aging*, pp. 5-21. Chicago: University of Chicago Press.

Neugarten, Bernice L., Moore, Joan W., and Lowe, John C. 1965. Age norms, age constraints, and adult socialization. *Am. J. Sociol.*, 90, 710-717.

Nisbet, Robert A. 1969. *Social Change and History.* New York: Oxford University Press.

Parelius, Ann P. 1975. Lifelong education and age stratification: Some unexplored relationships. *American Behavioral Scientist*, 19, 206-223.

Parsons, Talcott. (1942) 1949. Age and sex in the social structure of the United States. *In*, Talcott Parsons, *Essays in Sociological Theory, Pure and Applied*. Glencoe, Illinois: The Free Press.

Parsons, Talcott. 1951. *The Social System*. Glencoe, Illinois: The Free Press.

Riley, Matilda White. 1963. *Sociological Research*. New York: Harcourt, Brace & World.

Riley, Matilda White. 1971. Social gerontology and the age stratification of society. *Gerontologist*, **11**, 79–87.

Riley, Matilda White. 1974. The perspective of age stratification. *School Review*, **83**, 85–91.

Riley, Matilda White, Foner, Anne, Hess, Beth, and Toby, Marcia L. 1969. Socialization for the middle and later years. *In*, David A. Goslin (ed.), *Handbook of Socialization Theory and Research*, pp. 951–982. Chicago: Rand McNally.

Riley, Matilda White, Foner, Anne, Moore, Mary E., Hess, Beth, and Roth, Barbara K. 1968. *Aging and Society: An Inventory of Research Findings*, Vol. 1. New York: Russell Sage Foundation.

Riley, Matilda White, and Johnson, Marilyn. 1971. Age stratification of the society. Unpublished paper read at the Annual Meeting of the American Sociological Association, Denver.

Riley, Matilda White, Johnson, Marilyn, and Foner, Anne. 1972. *Aging and Society: A Sociology of Age Stratification*, Vol. 3. New York: Russell Sage Foundation.

Riley, Matilda White, and Nelson, Edward E. 1971. *In*, Bernard Barber and Alex Inkeles (eds.), *Stability and Social Change: A Volume in Honor of Talcott Parsons*. New York: Little Brown.

Rosenberg, George S. 1967. Poverty, aging and social isolation. Mimeographed. Washington, D. C.: Bureau of Social Science Research.

Rosow, Irving. 1967. *Social Integration of the Aged*. New York: The Free Press.

Ryder, Norman B. 1963. The translation model of demographic change. *In*, Norman B. Ryder (ed.), *Emerging Techniques in Population Research*, pp. 65–81. New York: Milbank Memorial Fund.

Ryder, Norman B. 1964. Notes on the concept of a population. *Am. J. Sociol.*, **69**, 447–463.

Ryder, Norman B. 1965. The cohort as a concept in the study of social change. *Am. Soc. Rev.*, **30**, 843–861.

Ryder, Norman B. 1974. The demography of youth. *In*, James S. Coleman *et al.*, *Youth Transition to Adulthood*. Chicago: University of Chicago Press.

Schaie, K. Warner. 1965. A general model for the study of developmental problems. *Psych. Bull.*, **64**, 92–107.

Schaie, K. Warner, and Strother, Charles R. 1964. A cross-sequential study of age changes in cognitive behavior. Unpublished paper read at the meeting of the Midwestern Psychological Association, St. Louis.

Shakespeare, William. *As You Like It*, II, vii.

Shanas, Ethel. 1969. Living arrangements and housing of old people. *In*, Ewald W. Busse and Eric Pfeiffer (eds.), *Behavior and Adaptation in Late Life*, pp. 129–150. Boston: Little, Brown.

Smelser, Neil J. 1968. *Essays in Sociological Explanation*. Englewood Cliffs, New Jersey: Prentice-Hall.

Sorokin, Pitirim A. (1927) 1959. *Social and Cultural Mobility*. New York: The Free Press.

Sorokin, Pitirim A. 1941. *Social and Cultural Dynamics: Basic Problems, Principles, and Methods*, Vol. 4. New York: American Book Co.

Sorokin, Pitirim A. 1947. *Society, Culture and Personality*. New York: Harper & Brothers.

Sorokin, Pitirim A. 1968. Social differentiation. *In*, David L. Sills (ed.), *International Encyclopedia of the Social Sciences*, Vol. 14, pp. 406–409. New York: Macmillan and The Free Press.

Stinchcombe, Arthur. *Cohort Analysis of Surveys*. Forthcoming.

Streib, Gordon F., and Thompson, W. E. 1957. Personal and social adjustment in retirement. *In*, Wilma Donahue and Clark Tibbitts (eds.), *The New Frontiers of Aging*, p. 184. Ann Arbor: University of Michigan Press.

Streib, Gordon F., and Thompson, W. E. 1960. The older person in a family context. *In*, Clark Tibbitts (ed.), *Handbook of Social Gerontology*, pp. 447–488. Chicago: University of Chicago Press.

Susser, Mervyn. 1969. Aging and the field of public health. *In*, Matilda White Riley, John W. Riley, Jr., and Marilyn E. Johnson (eds.), *Aging and Society: Aging and the Professions*, Vol. 2, pp. 114–160. New York: Russell Sage Foundation.

Sussman, Marvin B. 1955. Activity patterns of post-parental couples and their relationship to family continuity. *Marr. Fam. Living*, **17**, 560.

Taeuber, Irene B., and Taeuber, Conrad. 1971. *People of the United States in the 20th Century*. Washington, D.C.: Government Printing Office.

Taeuber, Karl E. 1965. Cohort population redistribution and the urban hierarchy. *Milbank Memorial Fund Quarterly*, **43**, 450–462.

Uhlenberg, Peter I. 1969. A study of cohort life cycles: Cohorts of native born Massachusetts women, 1830–1920. *Population Studies*, **23**, 407–420.

Van Gennep, Arnold. (1908) 1960. *The Rites of Passage*. Translated by Monika B. Visedom and Gabrielle L. Caffee. Chicago: University of Chicago Press, Phoenix Books.

Waring, Joan. 1973. Disordered cohort flow: A concept for the interpretation of social change. Unpublished paper read at the Annual Meeting of the American Sociological Association, New York.

Weber, Max. (1922) 1947. *The Theory of Social and Economic Organization*. Translated by A. M. Henderson and Talcott Parsons. Glencoe, Illinois: The Free Press.

White, Winston. 1961. *Beyond Conformity*. New York: The Free Press.

9
THE FAMILY LIFE OF OLD PEOPLE

Marvin B. Sussman

Bowman Gray School of Medicine

INTRODUCTION

This chapter has several basic themes:

In complex societies if aged persons are to survive successfully they must deal with bureaucracies, especially those which provide human services. The family of these elderly persons often serves as an unobtrusive mediating link between the older individual and societal institutions and organizations.

There are continuous difficulties in describing what is a family. The many perspectives are a consequence of the ways "family" is used by functionaries of organizations and institutions and by the members themselves. This situation exacerbates the existing problems of communication, comparative analysis, and meaningful analytic description of primary group relationships, those between an elderly person and his "family."

Related to the problems of describing a family is the variety of family forms in contemporary society—structures and attendant interactional patterns which differ from the traditional nuclear family of procreation of husband and wife with the husband in the principal role of provider and the spouse as homemaker. Some of these forms such as family kin network are not "new" while others have a twenty-first century aura. These forms provide new options and problems for the elderly.

In the past, intergenerational transfers within family systems provided one basic form of economic and symbolic bonding of the elderly with their children and grandchildren. The persistance of this linkage is examined in the light of society-wide generational transfers which rely more on programs and bureaucracies than the family and kin network to provide care, services, and economic sustenance.

Effective elderly person-family bondings in the latter decades of this century and well into the twenty-first will be a consequence of reallocation and reorganization of societal resources with an emphasis on the utilization of incentives. These economic and human service supports made available to member units of kin networks can reduce financial and psychological constraints to the formation of intergenerational households based on meaningful reciprocities and exchanges. The use of incentive packages to family units as alternatives to institutionalization of the elderly family member is proposed.

THEORETICAL BASES

The theoretical constructs most appropriate to bonding of aged persons, family units, and bureaucratic organizations are social exchange and linkage. Exchange theory (Homans, 1960, 1961; Kelley and Thibault, 1954; Bengtson and Black, 1973; Bengtson, Olander, and Haddad, 1975) provides the most viable explanation of primary group relationships. Filial responsibili-

218

ties characterized as protective, care, and financial *duties*, those ... "required by law, by custom, or by personal attitude" (Schorr, 1960) provide boundaries and conditions for interaction based on a profit/cost, reward/punishment, "developmental stake" equation (Black and Bengtson, 1973a).

The components of exchange—cost, reward, profit, reinforcement—have roots in hedonistic doctrine, utilitarian economics, and the psychological theory of reinforcement. Avoidance of pain and obtaining pleasure are the objective of interaction; profit is also the object of human activity and profit is reward minus the cost; making a profit leads to repetitive behavior, with reinforcement of the profit-making endeavor. If the quest is satiated, coupled with severely diminished drives and motivation, contributory responses emerge—costs outweigh rewards, and efforts are made to extinguish the unprofitable interaction.

Studies on the formation and structural properties of small groups (Sherif, 1966; Kelley and Thibault, 1954; Thibault and Kelley, 1959) have indicated that rewards for members in interaction may be unequal and that individuals stay in the group because the relationships provide some reward despite the uneven exchange and are perceived to be more satisfactory than other alternatives. This may be the "tension line," an invisible boundary of acceptable dyadic and group relationships (Rapoport and Rapoport, 1975; Shaw and Costanzo, 1970).

Another important proposition of exchange theory is distributive justice. Individuals should be rewarded proportional to their costs and receive profits proportional to their investment. The pervasiveness of this conceptual element is discussed in relation to family inheritance patterns, later in this chapter. The "sense" of distributive justice is a family property. It not only guides an individual's presentation of self and interaction but is a behavioral expectation. Those children who provide affection, attention, association and services, i.e., "generational solidarity" (Black and Bengtson, 1973a), to elderly members are expected to receive more than their legal share of any inheritance. It is a sibling shared value and expression of distributive justice (Sussman, Cates, and Smith, 1970).

Individuals in exchanges which result in unequal rewards are said to be in a *power* relationship. There are dependence, compliance, and subordination on the part of Actor A and independence, command, and superordination by Actor B in the social exchange (Blau, 1964; Weber, 1947). Social interaction is a continuous process of losing or gaining power credits or resources for use in subsequent transactions.

As Dowd (1974) indicates "... the problems of aging are essentially problems of decreasing power resources ... money, approval, esteem or respect, and compliance." Esteem and compliance are the most often used credits in exchange relationships among the aged. Esteem is a short-lived commodity because of the decreasing utility of expressing past achievements repeatedly in the face of group needs. Under "normal" conditions of social exchange—as in previous life-cycle stages where the individual amassed, distributed, and lost credits in social exchanges; where a "you win some and you lose some" posture was possible—compliance was often a resource. For the elderly person, however, it becomes an unidirectional process, used because there are few options and still fewer resources. The pressures on the elderly person to comply are exerted by societal norms and reflected in the superordinate postures of institutions and organizations and in the increasing dependency of the elderly person on the family.

Family, Bureaucracy and Elderly Linkages

The connectedness of most elderly members with their families and kin networks is unbroken despite industrialization and modernization (Paillat, 1976; Munnichs, 1976; Rosenmayr, 1976; and Piotrowski, 1976) and the more recent emergence of new and variant family forms and life-styles (Sussman, 1972; Libby and Whitehurst, 1973; Smith and Smith, 1974; Sussman, Cogswell, and Marciano, 1975).

Societal complexity with its differentiated occupational structure, social segregation, and accelerated geographical mobility may automatically constrain linkages of generationally and bilaterally linked kin. Concomitant "role exit" (Blau, 1973) of elderly persons exacerbates the feelings of alienation and isolation among many of them. However, for those aged persons who have had substantial involvement in kin family networks over the life span, even segmented in relation to time and nonpropinquitous because of occupational and social mobility, there is a "pull" factor to restore and reinforce such ties in the later years. Such older persons have more options in their exchanges; they may be wanted for themselves and the services they can potentially perform.

For elderly individuals with a poor record of kin network activities there may be a "push" to reconstitute close family relationships. With fewer options, the older person, in turning to other family members, especially children—a likely occurrence since institutionalization is viewed as a last resort for different reasons by elderly persons and establishment elites—becomes dependent and committed to the exchange relationship (Blau, 1964). The individual, in this circumstance, has few or no other choices. The family linkage to the elderly person is thus of critical importance and one which has extreme influence on the elderly member's relationship with nonfamily individuals and organizations. The increased dependency on family lessens the older individual's autonomy and independence in dealing with bureaucratic organizations.

Since World War II the ideology of pluralism in family structures in complex societies has been espoused and varied family forms and lifestyles, if not legitimized, are at least tolerated (Sussman et al., 1971). It would be expected or at least hoped that these new optional structures and styles would provide the elderly member with environmental alternatives to living alone or with children or in institutions. With a few exceptions, however, where elderly persons are reported to form communal households because of limited economic resources and physical handicaps, the revolution of new family formations has passed them by.

This conclusion is derived from a review of extensive studies of the past ten years on emergent new and variant family forms and lifestyles such as communal households, group marriages, and intimate networks—those which differ from traditional nuclear and kinship forms (Cogswell and Sussman, 1972; Ramey, 1972; O'Neill and O'Neill, 1972; Sussman, 1975). None of these variant forms provide

proof that they are willing to handle the crises, dependencies, disabilities, and deviances of their members, regardless of age. Their ideologies and practices presume that each participant has the ability to contribute to the group and thus to achieve highly desired parity relationships and near equitous reciprocities. Self-actualization is achieved through group interaction. The potential presence in one of these new family forms of an individual who cannot contribute fully and who is identified as a liability for any reason is counter to the new ideology. Moreover, enlisted recruits who are not sound in mind and body and competent to carry their fair share of the load in exchanges can jeopardize group survival.

These new family forms are strikingly similar to military units in relation to requisite structural properties and selection of role incumbents. Both these family forms and the military demand competence or the material with which to develop competence as a starter. If individuals become liabilities, e.g., do not "fit," as it is commonly expressed, the usual solution is to discharge or to effect a resignation. Such voluntary groups (the United States now has a voluntary military) cannot afford to take on "problem" members at the outset, since they are beset with almost insurmountable internal and external problems and issues—the molding of an effective internal structure with appropriate institutionalization of commitment, motivation, and identification of its members. In dealings with outside groups, the task is to survive in the face of outside aggression and potential cooptation.

New family forms like communal or group marriage households have a greater need to screen initially and, if in error, to segregate potential deviants because, unlike a military unit, the new family form is unsanctioned, usually unpopular, and with no institutional roots. It cannot call upon outside sources for help when in need or trouble. Moreover, many of the volunteers in such groups have opted out of traditional family forms because they wanted to escape dependent and obligatory relationships. The existentialist philosophy of these new forms requires optimal role performance to achieve self-actualization via interaction and group achievement.

It appears that "family and kin," however

defined, and as they have existed in the past, will continue in the future to be those primary groups who will respond in service and kind when members call or are in need. The traditional nuclear family form may have its greatest rationale for universality and continuity because of its function in taking care of its sick, disabled, deviant, and deficient members. The extended nuclear family is an all purpose caretaking system.

The legally constituted and franchised family found in complex societies is continuously engaging in linkage activities with bureaucratic organizations in behalf of its elderly members. There is no option to do otherwise. The state, through its massive structure of institutions and bureaucratized agencies, has created multitudinous support programs for its dependent citizens. The necessity to deal with them is obvious if aged members are to obtain even a partial share of their entitlements.

The family is still important to the aged person and will continue to be so for the next decade or two, although zero population growth in the twenty-first century may shear the older person of surviving relations and make the elderly member dependent upon a welfare bureaucracy (Shanas and Hauser, 1974). Today, the "family" of the aged individual often is found to be in an interstitial position between the elderly individual and the organization. Old people use their children and relatives both as a means of reentry into the social order and as a buffer against the pressures of bureaucracy. The extended family seems to be the mediator between the aged and formal organizations. Children and relatives act as information resources for the elderly, informing about housing, pensions, medical care, and other available options and entitlements. At the same time, it is the children and relatives who assist the aged in dealing with the bureaucratic structure of housing authorities, pension schemes, and hospitals and clinics. Many of the relationships between old people and their kin seem to be on the level of help in coping with bureaucratic structures. Such bureaucratic structures differ from society to society and even within societies at different periods of time.

It would appear that differences in bureaucratic structures affect not only the quantity but also the quality of family relationships in old age. For example, the quality of the relationship between old people and their kin in societies in which children have direct responsibility for the support of the aged may differ from that in societies in which responsibility for support is indirect, with direct responsibility taken by the state through its various programs of financial and service support. On the other hand, it may be that there is no difference. The quality of family relationships in old age may be independent of the nature of bureaucratic structures, the requisite linkages, and the family's investment in developing competencies to handle bureaucratic organizations; it may instead be solely dependent on the more intimate family interaction. Earlier patterns of reciprocal exchanges and especially affectional relationships, then, may be the prime determinants of the quality of relationships in old age.

The connectedness of aged members (65 years or older) to family are corroborated by the statistics regarding their living arrangements. In 1970 in the United States, only 4 percent were institutionalized, the majority—79 percent of the men, and 59 percent of the women—live in family situations and most in their own homes (Population Reference Bureau, 1975).

In complex societies elderly women, because of their greater longevity and fewer available potential mates for remarriage, are more likely to live alone as widows and divorcees. Thus, they are most active in linkage activities within kin family networks. The factors of age and

TABLE 1. PERCENT OF ELDERLY MEN AND WOMEN IN VARIOUS LIVING ARRANGEMENTS, 1970.

Living Arrangement	Men	Women
Family	79	59
Head of household	71	10
Wife is head of household	x	33
Other relative is head of household	8	16
Alone or with nonrelative	17	37
Head of household	14	35
Living with a nonrelative	3	2
Institution	4	4

COURTESY: Population Reference Bureau, Inc., 1975, p. 16: Taken from Administration on Aging. Facts and Figures on Older Persons, No. 5 (Washington, D.C. Department of Health, Education and Welfare Pub. [OHD] 74-20005) pp. 4–6.

number of children ever born seem to be the most important predictors of moving into a family member's household when living alone becomes untenable because of diminished health and mobility (Chevan and Korson, 1975). The older the person, the less likely it is that his health and mobility status is adequate for solo living. The more offspring the person has, the more likely it is that he or she will take up residence in a child's household, thus delaying institutionalization as long as possible.

These data indicate that the linkages of elderly persons with their families are of two types: those which occur in the majority of cases, among members living in separate households; and those which exist between members of the same household, an arrangement for a minority of elderly persons. Meaningful family linkages do not require living in the same household but do require a network involving productive exchanges of reciprocal benefits for all family members. Complete intimacy expressed through continuous face-to-face interaction may not be the most desirable arrangement. Contact and relationships at discrete times may be preferable and more preservative of the network. Rosenmayr and Köckeis (1965) have referred to this desire of elderly persons to live close to relatives but not with them as "intimacy at a distance."

Institutionalization of the aged is not required for the majority of aged persons who may have such ailments as heart disease, rheumatism, and arthritis, the most common afflictions of old age. Even if such persons cannot maintain a totally independent existence, their incapacitation does not require institutionalization. Shanas (1971), in a study of the health care needs of the elderly, found that only 2 percent of the noninstitutionalized persons over the age of 65 are bedfast. All others were at least semiambulatory and capable of participation to some degree in the world around them. The continued psychological well-being of the aged, similar to the needs of persons at all stages of life, is largely dependent upon a high level of activity, involvement with other persons, and with interests beyond their own personal lives. Meaningful participation in a family group is a major source of such activity for the elderly (Adams, 1971). To the aged, institutionalization, whether voluntary or involuntary, may be seen as a final surrender to the recognition that they can no longer care for themselves and that the hope of regaining the activity level lost due to illness or natural aging processes is forever gone. These beliefs are a major reason for postponing as long as possible the entering of homes for the aged or hospitals for the chronically ill.

One innovative recommendation is to improve hospital rehabilitation programs sufficiently so that the aged can be returned to the community as soon as possible. The primary procedure is posthospital care in the home on the premise that home care is far more beneficial than institutional care for all but the most severely disabled (Steinberg, 1971).

In the stage of aging between independence and the need for prolonged total care (if such need should arise), there is often a period during which necessary supportive care is best supplied by adult children or other relatives. Many families now fill this need. Others, however, might be able and willing to provide care for their elderly kin if various supports were available to ease the burdens that such care imposes. A modest proposal will be made subsequently on how to develop a complementary system to the institutionalization of elderly members and one which would foster involvement of elderly living alone with the other members of their family network through harnessing, utilizing, and reallocating existing service and economic resources. Since the term *family* has been used liberally, the issues of definition, description, and perception of family require some analysis.

FAMILY DEFINITIONS AND DESCRIPTIONS

Introduction

How does one describe or define the family and use it in research (Sussman, 1973)? This task is not easy. The most salient conclusion is that there is a lack of consensus on defining or describing family.

On the academic level variations can be attributed to the different ways scholars perceive and conceptualize "family." In the empirical world definitions are made on the principle of utility as determined by bureaucracies with some reference to the canons of statutory and common law. Society's organizations and institutions, especially those which are concerned with the provision of human services, have definitions that fit their mandate, ones usually rooted in legislation which expresses social policies determined by ruling elites—in American society, the people's representatives. Implementation involves establishing guidelines for determining eligible populations and procedures for dispersement of services and moneys and for data collection and evaluation. In due course definitions of family are established, usually based on some idealization of what the family is or ought to be. Once a definition is established, bureaucratic norms require rigid adherence to that definition, whether or not it is descriptive of reality and despite the fact that it may have unanticipated negative consequences for those so labeled.

Professionals in human service systems begin with a mandate for the provision of various services to eligible clients and then proceed to develop a description of "family" rehabilitation. The basic rationale is that when disability, for example, occurs to one family member, it has a "domino effect" upon all others in the household unit.

The rehabilitation unit at the Arizona Job College, as an illustration, is capable of "treating" 120 whole families simultaneously; each family has its own household at the college. Approximately ten families graduate each month after an average stay of six months.

All families in this program are below the poverty level; they are multiethnic in background: approximately 55 percent are Chicano, 19 percent white, 17 percent Indian, and 9 percent black. One of the program's aims is to reduce for other family members the potentially denigrating effects of disability that may occur when the demands for care and attention of the disabled person make it difficult for the other members to perform their normal roles. A related objective is to improve the capabilities of all members to perform roles satisfactorily in various life sectors. The program provides for 25 different services such as housing after leaving the center, vocational training and job placement, budget management, child care,

home management, medical treatment, transportation management, and legal services.

Because of a mandate to undertake "family rehabilitation," rigid criteria were established for acceptance into the program, including a narrow (traditional) definition of family. Of the five requirements, three are pertinent to this discussion.

1) The primary wage-earner must have a physical or mental disability which is a handicap to employment.   2) The total family income from all resources must fall below federally established poverty guidelines, and the family must be willing to leave the welfare rolls if accepted into the program. 3) The family must be a *whole family* composed of a legally married father and mother with dependent children. It must also include other legal dependents who are determined to be a "natural" and longstanding part of that family's structure. (Reprinted from, "Why Not Family Rehabilitation?" by Louis Y. Nau in the *Journal of Rehabilitation*, 1973, 39(3), p. 16.)

The program designers have accepted a societal imagery of what is a whole family. By definition they exclude variant forms such as single-parent families and cast some doubt on the latter's capabilities to be successfully rehabilitated. They are seemingly unaware of other structural forms such as dual-work, three-generation, extended family network, and communal families where the need for creative rehabilitation programs may be as great as in intact families (Sussman, 1971; Cogswell and Sussman, 1972; Sussman and Cogswell, 1972).

Using a definition of family that fits one's personal predilections or the requirements of an organization appears to be a natural thing to do and intrinsically may not be bad. However, it can be unsettling and can create a sense of ambiguity to members of families who may be bombarded, and in some instances feel attacked, by these multiple definitions. In communications and encounters with bureaucracies, there is pressure to comply with the organization's particular definition in order either to stay out of trouble or to receive a reward. One possible cost of such compliance is a limitation in options for role development, identification, and expression within the family. Role taking by members, then, is dictated by the demands of nonfamily structures. A cost that is a plus, using our earlier language, is that varied definitions and concomitant demands require families to become experts in adaptation and in developing the competence of its members to handle these requisites of bureaucracies.

Workable Definition of Family

These are but a few of the caveats associated with the issue of "what is a family and from whose perspective?" The problem is more complicated by the lack of clarity and the synonymous use of such terms as household, domestic functions, family, and marriage. For purposes of further discussion of older people and families and on the assumption that commitment, attachment and emotional exchange, and reinforcement are basic processes or needs for individual and group survival (Ball, 1972; Hall, 1974), a two-part definition is proposed. The first component is a "living together" group of individuals suggested by Ball to be "the actual social arrangements of the contemporary everyday-anyday world: these may be defined as any cohabiting domestic relationship which is (or has been) sexually consequential, i.e., gratification for members, or the production of offspring. These are the relationships most often associated with the emotions of love and the home" (Ball, 1972, p. 302). Ball argues for abandonment of a kinship-based definition of family that includes legal and religious sanctions and the obligations of kinship because of marriage and blood ties. The advantage of a living-together definition, the "everyday family," is the inclusion of sanctioned or unsanctioned variant family forms involved in domestic functions, emotional and sexual cohabitation that is the reality of today's existence.

Anthropologists in studies of family structure have attempted to differentiate between a conjugal and consanguine principle in kinship organization. Ralph Linton (1936) explains, "A society may capitalize the sexual attraction between adults and do all it can to give permanence to mated relationships (conjugal)*, or it may capitalize the associations formed on an asexual basis during childhood, reinforcing

*Insertion of terms (conjugal and consanguine) is done by the author for clarification.

them into adult life. Such asexual relationships are most readily established between individuals brought up in the same functional family unit, i.e., real or socially designated brothers and sisters (consanguine)."

The "everyday family" previously described approximates the consanguinal form; it is structurally most suited to accommodate nontraditional bondings such as homosexual, lesbian, and communal. This family form also possesses potentialities for experimentation in interaction styles, the development of heightened intimacy, quality emotional relationships, and shared responsibilities for maintenance within prescribed social and physical space. For both microanalytic and research purposes, this definition has appeal.

This empirical definition, however, leaves unrecognized a major perspective for viewing family that accounts for societal legitimization and religious sanction of marriage, laws defining rights and responsibilities of those entering this status, and those kinship ties that link the individual of a living-together family with other persons some distance away. Within this extended boundary there can be intimacy at a distance (Rosenmayr, 1976); emotional support especially along generational lines (Hall, 1974); and some assistance in domestic functions, especially economic aid (Sussman, 1965).

Society demands a formalization of structure and processes so that it can handle the conflicts engendered by individuals living together when these need third-party mediation or arbitration. The concern to provide reparations for the injured person and to protect the weak and helpless, however often erroneously determined or identified, nevertheless requires some system of universal definition, implementation, and control. The society, to protect the members from themselves and to insure orderly transfers of status and power from one generation to the next, has in effect become a third party to marriage and private agreement and an overseer of family activities and behavior.

The conjugal family form, referred to in the idiom as nuclear ". . . consisting of a nucleus of spouses and their offspring surrounded by a fringe of relatives" (Linton, 1936, p. 159), is best fitted for the societal component of this bipartite definition. It emphasizes that the core of the family is the husband and wife around which all life functions. This unit is easy to establish by contract, is most visible, and the obligations, instrumental and affectional bonds and ties with other kinship units, can be more readily ascertained than in the consanguinal form where ". . . we can picture the authentic family as a nucleus of blood relatives surrounded by a fringe of spouses" (Linton, 1936, p. 159).

These other kinship units with whom conjugal families relate and interact consist of various relatives or kinsmen such as grandparents, uncles, aunts, nieces, nephews, grandchildren, and cousins obtained by marriage or tied to one another by blood. These are conventional kin. Two other types of kin, discretionary and fictive, who are "just like family," are part of this extended system (Ball, 1972). Discretionary are those distant relatives with whom one develops close and intimate relationships, ones not normally expected because of their location in the kin network, e.g., a spouse's sister-in-law or cousin. Fictive are those "non-kin," usually friends (Ball, 1972, p. 300), whose relationships with the members of the conjugal unit are "as family." They are adopted members who take on obligations, instrumental and affectional ties similar to those of conventional kin.

There are no legal requirements or cultural traditions in American society to make this kin network of conventional, discretionary, or fictive members functional. It is an optional system in competition with society's organizations and institutions for the participation and loyalty of family members. Conjugal family members—supported by some concern for their familial responsibilities—enter into economic, help, and emotional exchanges with kin members largely voluntarily. The selection and intensity of these bondings are based on personal selection and on the real and perceived values attached to the exchanges by kin members. Both definitional components should be used in explanation and analysis of micro and macro family phenomena.

KIN FAMILY NETWORKS AND VARIANT FAMILY FORMS

Kin Family Networks

In the discussion thus far on definitions no mention has been made of the individual's own definition of family, namely, the answer to the question, "whom do you consider to be family?" The response to this question is far more critical in evaluating the meaning, significance, and probabilities of family relationships of older persons than those estimates made by organizational functionaries or described by social scientists. This self-definition of family is a prelude to any study of kinship structure which employs as principal measures residential propinquity; type and frequency of interaction; mutual aid; familism, affectional bonds, and value transmission (Sussman, 1960; Troll, 1971). Structural analysis of kinship systems is a complicated and time-consuming process because of a multidescent pattern in the United States where one can claim up to four lineages (Schneider, 1968). In this sense one "chooses" the generational line or lines, i.e., the relatives with whom he wishes to be identified. This comparative freedom to relate to those kin with whom one is reciprocally compatible or finds attractive—in that there are no legal statutes, common laws, or cultural prescription to obligate oneself to be connected with relatives—indicates the major relevance of self-descriptions of family and kin and the need to tap these in empirical work to obtain meanings to kinship behavior and the voluntary nature of the kin network.

The kin structure in most complex societies is composed of household units each containing a family form—e.g., intact, single-parent, dual-career—whose members are related by blood or marriage and who in some instances may be a "fictive" kin. The network is a voluntary system characterized by reciprocal exchanges. There are no legal rules or cultural ideologies as requirements for belonging. Moreover, one can opt out of the network, but, if one remains a member, then in time there develop expectations of interpersonal exchange, emotional support, and forms of aid and assistance under various conditions. Mutual expectations of reciprocity evolve to encompass the whole system. This network, similar to other voluntary organizations and to some not so voluntary, competes for the time, interest, and investment of its members. It cannot "demand" adherence to norms of filial piety. However, it has a distinct advantage over other human-built social structures in that kin loyalty and identification, buttressed by general societal expectations of appropriate behavior where "family" is involved, have powerful attractions. The immemorial adage of "blood is thicker than water" seems to hold even in this postindustrialized period. In societies undergoing rapid changes from rural to an industrial based economy, such as Egypt, Iran, and Pakistan, family bondings are the primary structures vis-à-vis mechanisms for making bureaucracies functional and tolerable.

Describing the "functionality" of the kin network in terms of specific structural properties is an initial step in establishing the meaning and significance of the kin network for aged members. The suggestion of Kerckhoff (1965) is to use proximity and help exchanges as principal components of a structural kin network taxonomy. He proposes three measures of functionality: "nuclear isolated" where member units are in close proximity but have no or very few contacts; "modified extended" where families are spatially dispersed but have high scores on contacts, interaction, and exchanges; and "extended" where units are residentially propinquitous and high in functionality.

It is obvious that mapping of the network using this simplified set of categories, fully recognizing the operational issues in determining "functionality," can ascertain the relevance as well as the quality of such involvements for the older person. The test of relevance is whether the network provides the intimate human interaction and empathetic reciprocal response on the emotional level, conditions critical to survival, the sustenance of mental and physical health, and "a more meaningful existence" (Jourard, 1971; Lowenthal and Haven, 1968; Moriwaki, 1973; Noelker, 1975). While other forms of structure can provide this social interaction that results in intimacy and empathy, and it has been suggested that friendship among peers is a possible solution (Rosow, 1967), the viability of the network as an optional system for handling the primary emotional needs of the elderly is at test. Relevance rests in whether it is actually achieved. If the outcome is intimacy and empathy, then quality has been obtained.

The functionality of the extended family system is so extensive among blacks that its existence is tantamount to survival of the individual as well as black culture and tradition (Shimkin, Louie and Frate, 1973; Shimkin, Shimkin and Frate, 1975). The pervasiveness of the extended family as a source of information, support, intimacy, and interaction in one Mississippi county required directors of a health research program to conceptualize the constraints and supports for delivery of services to an impoverished population in terms of extended family networks in lieu of individual analysis. In this situation, ascertaining goals and their pursuit of motivations and drives of stress-producing events and diagnosing adaptive mechanisms used by blacks required structural and contextual analyses of extended family systems (Shimkin and Shimkin, 1975).

A review of reported researches on family systems in black societies indicates that the extended system is the primary one among blacks and is found in urban as well as in rural environments (Shimkin, Shimkin and Frate, 1975). The Shimkins' synthesis of working papers of the Pheasant Run Conference, 1967, concerned with black extended family systems derived 12 tentative conclusions on black family structure, values, and behavior. Two are especially germaine to this presentation. "A widespread and functionally important institution of black society in the United States is a bilateral descent group, with more loosely related spouses and with extensions to various kinds of fictive relatives, which is called 'family'; and characteristically, this family is centered, perceptually and in terms of action initiatives, on its representatives of the oldest living generation, who are symbols of unity, objects of respect and moral authority, sources of fosterage and objects of care for all members" (Shimkin and Shimkin, 1975). The readiness of extended families to commit their total resources to help the elderly person, including the social and economic costs of terminal care, is both alarming and amazing to researchers and policy makers because it is nonmodal according to their value system and experience, and in the long run, may be devastating in its consequences for the economic stability of the extended family (Shimkin and Paterson, 1969).

Similar patterns of connectedness and support of black aged members on all socioeconomic levels are reported by Jackson (1971a, 1971b, 1972a, 1972b, 1973). Elderly members have legitimate claims for help and extended kin will "squeeze blood from a turnip" to provide assistance (Jackson, 1972a). The generational ties are strong and are reinforced through adult-to-adult interaction where wisdom and experience are shared and where a parity model replaces the usual superordinate-subordinate model of parent-child relationships. This generational link requires further analysis.

Intergenerational linkages have proven to be the most salient component (and most researched) of the kin network. A proposal to catalyze involvement of more bilateral and extended kin by utilization of an "incentive" package will be presented later in this chapter. Stage of the life cycle, sex of individuals, presence of generational kin, and propinquity are related to interactional patterns, intimacy, and empathy.

Parents and young married couples are closely linked in interaction, communication, and systems of mutual aid involving services and financial help, the flow being generally from parents to children, especially among the middle classes (Sussman, 1953; Aldous and Hill, 1965; Adams, 1968, 1970; Feldman, 1964). With increasing economic and psychological independence of the young married exacerbated by geographical separation and buttressed by ideologies which attempt to reconcile the contradictions of the ideal and real, independence and dependence in human relationships induce some hiatus in generational relationships until the retirement of parents which is perceived as old age, the period of decreasing vigor and health (Troll, 1971).

Support for this cyclical shift in closeness and interaction is derived from clinical evidence of role reversal of children and older parents regarding dependability and dependence and from statistical data regarding residency patterns. Maturation of married children with experience, "filial maturity" (Blenkner, 1965, 1969), is demonstrated by a competence and capability to take on supportive and, if necessary, caretaking roles with one's parents as the latter become less independent. The reciprocal of this is the older person's comfortable feeling

that children can be "counted on" when needed and lessens the pervasive pathological concern of "being a burden" to children.

There are statistical data from several studies to support high levels of intergenerational activities between married children and older parents (Cumming and Henry, 1961; Kerckhoff, 1966; Shanas, 1962, 1967, 1968; Sussman, 1960; Youmans, 1963). The majority of older persons, over 85 percent in most studies, live less than an hour's distance away from a child, and almost 30 percent are living in a child's household, with the percent rising in rural areas. Some middle-aged (40–60) children are in key "orchestrating" positions for multiple activities and functions within generationally linked kin networks (Shanas, 1962). They may be providing a home for an aged parent: looking after a divorced daughter and her child; seeing their children through college; providing guidance and sometimes a home to other relatives who migrate in for jobs, school, marriage; and running a "boarding" house for families of married children who never seem to leave home. The significance of these exacting adult socialization roles of middle generation parents for maintaining the essential emotional network of the most primary of groups is unappreciated and unresearched.

Response in case of illness involves the kin network with little differentiation according to social class or type of relative, with the major exchanges taking place among propinquitous kin (Sussman, 1959). In cases of critical or long-term illness, some additional assistance may come from distantly located relatives. With both near and distant relatives care of kin is largely the work of female members. This especially holds in generationally linked families (Litman, 1971). In a linked three-generational network, the mother of the middle generation will be the main provider of comfort both to her parents and her married children. Elderly family members in times of crisis were more likely to return to their daughters than any other family member.

The willingness to respond in the event of illness and the actual response should not be equated with feelings of competence to take care of an ill relative for any long period of time. Today's families do not have the structural, organizational, and economic resources to provide such care (Parsons and Fox, 1952). Litman reports that while four-fifths of families in his three-generation study feel convalescent care at home is most desirable, about one-third could not do this under any circumstances. About 75 percent of the younger generation families state that a family member has a "right" to such home care while the grandparent generation express some misgivings regarding the taking of such care (Litman, 1971). The ideology of "taking care of one's own"—familial responsibility—persists among the youngest generation, even though they allow the hospital and other health care systems to take on the major responsibility. The older generation's traditional response, "I do not want to be a burden to my children or grandchildren," is one that evokes a healthy skepticism. The need for emotional support is basic to survival, and one prominent feature of a family is its emotional network. Those elderly who cannot find emotional comfort among peers and in other primary groups probably crave family involvement.

A possible explanation for the attitude of the elderly and the willingness of the younger generation to use organized health care systems is that in highly differentiated societies where specialization of function is a fact of life and the economy is built around such complexities, one becomes conditioned to use such available systems. As the society shifts its policies and programs to encompass a national health insurance system with emphasis on entitlement rather than eligibility, one can anticipate greater use of nonfamilial systems not only in the health but in other societal sectors.

One overlooked dimension of family-aged member relationships is the consequence for the family system when middle-aged breadwinners or homemakers suffer a catastrophic illness or disability with consequent chronicity and requisite extensive rehabilitation. The 45-, 55-, or 60-year-old person in this instance is not elderly in chronological years but in physical capacity and has limited options for role performance. In a longitudinal study concerned with the maintenance of posthospital gains of patients whose age averaged 55 years and who

experienced a rehabilitative therapeutic regimen, the ability of the parent to resume tasks and responsibilities associated with the preillness role or to assume new or modified roles was a function not only of physical and psychological limiting factors but of his or her "centrality" in the family system (Stroud and Sussman, 1973). Centrality is defined as availability and capability of other family members to assume the disabled person's role responsibilities; degree of disruption and need for role reallocation whether real or perceived; economic and service burdens placed on other family members; and the impact of the system's role functioning as a consequence of the incapacitating illness.

The ability of the disabled member to maintain position, power, and high acceptance in a family depends upon the individual's ability to resume premorbid roles (Slater, Sussman and Stroud, 1970). The aura of familial piety, "to do the right thing" in the face of the limiting capacity of a member, pervades these family relationships. But this, by itself, is insufficient if the individual is dependent in ADL (Activities of Daily Living), unable to perform his premorbid activities. A reciprocal process of unequal exchanges is in operation. If the disabled member can contribute sufficiently to family activities or demand less of others so that psychological stress, physical strain, and economic distress are at a tolerable minimum, then there is less likelihood that outright rejection of the disabled person with concomitant relegation to a "deviant" status in the family will occur. The family is an emotional network, and the greater the involvement of members in various forms of interdependencies, routine and otherwise, the more likely it is that institutionalization of the older disabled member will be avoided.

Our discussion on kin networks may have been too idealistic in transmitting the advantages of connectedness and continuity. A case has been made for why membership in a network should be an option in a voluntary system in competition with other primary groups and networks. At the same time it is recognized that maintaining a viable kin network and successful intergenerational relationships involving the elderly person and other family members is problematical. It is no easy task, and all participants do not benefit equally. Each involved family member must weigh the costs, investments, and immediate and deferred rewards of their participation.

Intergenerational exchanges of help may have consequences for marital health if an aid-receiving or aid-giving couple cause a shift in the power relationship of a dyad and potentially exacerbate already existent strained marital relationships (Adams, 1970). The dynamics of exchanges catalyze shifts in behavior and relational styles within and between family units. The blue-collar husband's tie with his parent, a priority in his value system, may trigger both marital and in-law conflict (Sweetser, 1963).

Relocating one's household in reference to one's kin has implications for the mobility aspirations and patterns of members; the nature and quality of interpersonal service; and financial exchanges and internal dynamics of member units. While consequences of such a move cannot be accurately predicted, an announcement of intent may be a very effective trial balloon of expected results. The extent to which kin members are invited or just move close by will influence the quality and quantity of the exchanges.

Variant Family Forms

The discussion thus far has concentrated on the kin family network of the aged individual and indicated the viability of this structure as a voluntary network which under certain conditions can meet the emotional, physical, and social requisites of the members. A further understanding of the functionality of this network and knowledge of other types of "family" options are possible by a brief analysis of varied family forms and life styles.

In 1969 a task force of the 1970 White House Conference on Children began an examination of family structure, behavior, and linkages with nonfamily organizations (Sussman et al., 1971). It discovered that families varied along a number of dimensions—life styles, power relationships, competence, motivation, health, mobility, values, and modernity. In its report, "Changing Families in a Changing Society," Forum 14 made a strong case for the presence and continued existence of family pluralism in American society, and it strongly advocated that this pluralism be accepted and respected in legislation, policies, and service systems. Current policies and programs favor the traditional nuclear family, a unit consisting of husband, wife, and offspring living in neolocal residence, apart from other kin, the husband/father as the bread-winner, the wife/mother as homemaker. However, there are single-parent, dual-work, three-generation, and a variety of other type families that we shall describe subsequently. Yet most government and private sector programs still function to restore this so-called deviant family to the ideal. To counteract this effort and to reduce the professionalism and bureaucratization which accompanies these restoration efforts, organizations of working and welfare mothers, single parents, and retired persons have come on the scene and have transformed once isolated individuals and families into social groups offering support to each other and exerting pressure on the establishment for needed services (Haug and Sussman, 1969).

One critical point is that each of these forms has different problems to solve and issues to face in its dealings with the outside world and in its own internal family relationships. It also has needs for outside services and supports which differ from those of the traditional nuclear family and which, for the most part, remain unmet in the United States today. Highly standardized and often overbureaucratized service systems organized largely for the benefit and "efficiency" of their staffs, as a general rule, have either neglected to offer services to the wide array of family types or to vary programs and procedures so that relevant and needed services are geared to the special needs of each type.

The following taxonomy suggests the possible linkage of variant units that can make up one's family network (Table 2). The great variation of neolocal units opens new possibilities for reciprocal interactions and services, where physically and psychologically capable elderly persons can provide service, role modeling,

TABLE 2. FAMILY TYPE BY ESTIMATED PERCENT DISTRIBUTION IN THE U.S., 1976.[a]

Family type	Estimated percent distribution		
1. Nuclear family—husband, wife, and offspring living in a common household ("intact").	37		
a. Single career		18	
b. Dual career		19	
1. Wife's career continuous			no estimate
2. Wife's career interrupted			no estimate
2. Nuclear dyad—husband and wife alone: childless, or no children living at home.	11		
a. Single career		4	
b. Dual career		7	
1. Wife's career continuous			no estimate
2. Wife's career interrupted			no estimate
3. Nuclear family—husband, wife, and offspring living in a common household (*remarried*). No estimate of career patterns.	11		
4. Single-parent family—one head, as a consequence of divorce, abandonment, or separation (with financial aid rarely coming from the second parent), and usually including preschool and/or school-age children.	12		
a. Career		8	
b. Noncareer		4	
5. Kin network—three generation households or extended families where members live in close geographical proximity and operating within a reciprocal system of exchange of goods and services.	4		
6. Other single, widowed, separated, or divorced adults.	19		
Emerging experimental forms	6		
1. Commune family			
a. Household of more than one monogamous couple with children, sharing common facilities, resources and experiences; socialization of the child is a group activity.			
b. Household of adults and offspring—a "group marriage" known as one family—where all individuals are "married" to each other and all are "parents" to the children. Usually develops a status system with leaders believed to have charisma.			
2. Unmarried parent and child family—usually mother and child, where marriage is not desired or possible.			
3. Unmarried couple and child family—usually a common-law type of marriage with the child their biological issue or informally adopted.			
	100		

[a]Reformulated from M. B. Sussman, "Family Sociology," in *Current Research in Sociology*, Margaret S. Archer (ed.). The Hague: Mouton, 1974. Based on communication with James Ramey who suggested inclusion of item 6, Singles, based on 1970 census data on all adults.

socialization, and "parenting" equal or nearly equal in exchange to that which they receive.

The statistics in Table 2 are at best "guesstimates," interpretations of data collected from many sources, largely government health, marriage, and divorce statistics. Census data are not now collected to obtain family structural analysis of this kind, and it is unlikely that gathering of such data will occur in the near future. We recognize the limitations of the percent distribution; these prevalence data present at best a static picture that does not suggest any change in incidence over time. Even more discouraging is an absence of baseline data needed to determine the magnitude of change in family structures over any given period of time. Are these family forms a modern day phenomenon or have they always existed (during the past 75 years) but simply become more visible as a consequence of the social upheavals and people's movements of the 1960's? This may be the case for homosexual and lesbian family forms, but the phenomenon of divorce and remarriage and increased incidence of gainful employment of women, which in turn have increased the number of single-parent, and dual-work families, has a more recent history.

Reports from various family researchers (Ramey, 1972, 1975; Kanter, 1972; Conover, 1975; Somerville, 1972) and mass media indicate that more and more older persons, because of desire or necessity, are forming group marriages and communes that are becoming increasingly attractive to them. Reciprocal socialization between the older and younger generations is a possible explanation. Middle-aged elderly are "experiencing" the experimentation of their young in alternative forms of family. Some, in living independently of their children in new groupings that do not require remarriage and its concomitant obligations, are sustaining with these grown children the desired "intimacy at a distance" (Somerville, 1972). In one sense they are taking on the roles of their children and grandchildren and are enjoying doing it.

The following case history of communal living among the elderly not only illustrates what is possible in primary group relationships but also indicates changes in perceptions and legal definitions of family. In May 1971 the Orange County Board of Commissioners filed suit against the Share-A-Home Association contending that it was violating a zoning ordinance; being a boarding house it was not allowed in a single-family neighborhood (St. Petersburg Times, 1971). The Share-A-Home group was a nonprofit organization of eleven elderly persons, ages 61–94, who formed a communal family, moved into a 27-room

mansion that had been used formerly as a nursing home, and hired a staff to operate the household.

This case became a cause célèbre. The circumstances were ripe for recognizing that a commune was indeed a family in Winter Park, Orange County, Florida. There was public interest and support of a local publicist (Gray Associates, 1971); the concern of former President Nixon that nursing homes had become "dumping grounds for the dying" ["Nixon Hits 'Dumps' for Dying Aged" was one headline (Orlando Sentinel, 1971)]; the convincing Biblical evidence that communes were Christian families; the appealing arguments of the residents for their new family life and against the dire prospects of being sent to nursing and old age homes; and citizen support expressed by letters to editors of local newspapers, attendance at hearings, and visits with members of the "family." All these provided the setting for a favorable judicial ruling.

Dispositions were taken both in the courtroom and in the corridors; the judge visited the mansion and opinions were freely expressed. The major arguments for recognizing the commune as a family were: (1) the Bible approves living together; did not the disciples after Pentecost live together, having all things in common and each contributing in like manner according to one's ability? (Book of Acts); (2) the commune is really not new but is an old concept and is a family under the legal definition that a family is a group of people living under one roof with their servants (St. Petersburg Times, 1971). Specifically, the Orange County code defines a family as "one or more persons occupying a dwelling and living as a single housekeeping unit" (Orlando Sentinel, 1971). It followed that since these individuals were living in the same household, pooling their financial resources, helping one another when possible, and using the same kitchen they were indeed a family.

The major "against" argument was that the ". . . members were not related and, therefore, should not be living together in an area zoned solely for single family residences" (Orlando Sentinel, 1971). One editorial writer stated the official position in nonofficial terms, "a house is not a home, in the opinion of the Orange County Commission, when 12 senior citizens band together for comfort, companionship and ease of living, and name a manager to handle their finances and household chores" (*Orlando Sentinel*, 1971).

The presiding judge ruled that there was no violation of the zoning ordinance and that the Share-A-Home members were living as a family and entered a judgment for the defense. "'The whole atmosphere is very homelike and warm, everyone seems to genuinely care about each other, it is personalized and spotlessly clean and really, a delightful place where everyone seems to be extremely happy,' said the judge. He added, 'I think it's a great idea and it may be the forerunner of things to come, I hope so.'" (*Jacksonville Journal*, 1971).

INTERGENERATIONAL TRANSFERS AND FAMILY PATTERNS

In complex societies characterized by differentiation in work, service, and occupational systems, the financial and service supporters provided by such society-wide programs as social security and health care have eclipsed the importance of the single family's modus operandi for guaranteeing the well-being of older members because of the latter's control of wealth and the testamentary process (Kreps, 1962). A study of inheritance patterns in modern times reveals, however, that inheritance patterns reflect the web of the emotional fabric that links members of family networks together.

While society-wide economic transfers will be more fully discussed in Chapter 11 of this *Handbook*, a brief analysis will provide the base for discussing inheritance transfers and family relationships. In the modern period the development of society-wide welfare, social security, educational, and health care systems provides the very young and the aged with basic economic support and services which in the past were provided by the family or kinship group. A universal system of taxation provides for the old and young who are not gainfully employed and is the basis of society-wide economic transfers from one generation to the next. It is

apparent that such economic transfers and income redistribution have been largely a function of governmental and political superstructures of modern societies and have overshadowed the family's efforts to arrange for the economic maintenance of its own members. One consequence is reduced importance of the economic function of inheritance in providing the family with the necessary assets to sustain its members over generational time, educate its dependent young, and care for its ill or aged members.

The trend toward universal and society-wide support and care systems began in the United States at the turn of this century. The quality and extent of these systems are linked to the rate of modernization and level of modernity achieved in such diverse life sectors as economic, political, leisure, and religious. These systems of maintenance and care have diminished the obvious importance of inheritance as one process for sustaining the economic well-being of the family. Further, the corporate structure of modern economic systems reduces the necessity for an orderly intergenerational transfer of equity within family and kinship lines so as to enhance the continuity of the economic system, a prerequisite in the preindustrial period.

While the importance of inheritance to the economic maintenance of the family in modern times has diminished, and property holdings of families, kinship groups, or lineages have very little effect upon the workings of the economic market, the transfer of property, especially in modern industrial countries, is still a vital function. Inheritance may be viewed as an individually-based or society-wide transfer. Support of social security, welfare, and education by persons in their middle years may be interpreted as a legacy for the younger and older generations; they are society-wide transfers. Bequeathing one's property to another in a will is an individually-based transfer.

Inheritance patterns of 659 family systems, randomly selected from a court jurisdiction of approximately 2 million in the United States, were examined (Sussman, Cates and Smith, 1970). Findings relevant to the family and its aging members are:

1. Dual patterns of serial service and reciprocity are established as existing cotermi-

nously. Transfers from one generation to the next take place in the normal course of events as evidenced by the relatively small number of gifts given to charities, friends, and distantly related family members. With the bulk of transfers occurring within generational lines, it is obvious that serial service is a dominant pattern; parents help their young children, and when these children reach maturity they assume responsibility, doing what they can for their now aged parents. The cycle continues indefinitely over generational time.

Serial reciprocity complements this process of generational transfer. Specific allocations are made according to notions of distributive justice and actual exchanges of care, service, and material goods between members of the older and middle generations. Testators will their estates to designated children or other individuals according to the testators perception of their needs, emotional ties with them, and services exchanged among family members over the years. Serial service—the transfer of worldly goods from parents to lineal descendants—which occurs in due course, exists side by side with serial reciprocity which specifies the giver-taker relationship based on exchanges of goods and services and patterns of interaction.

2. Related to serial reciprocity and service is the occurrence of role reversals in which children begin to take care of their parents, a phenomenon previously described. These role reversals require new learning and place upon the middle generation potentially anxiety-provoking responsibilities. This generation, in addition to caring for the young, now has to care for the old parents.

3. Sibling members of the middle generation are sensitive to the problems they have in raising their own families. Therefore, they generally accept the notion that the sibling who has rendered the greatest amount of service to an aged parent should receive a major portion of the inheritance upon the death of that parent. If the sibling takes the parent into his home, other siblings usually expect that almost all of the parent's estate should go to that child. On the other hand, if the child went to live in the parent's home during the latter's declining years, then the payoff should be more equally distributed among the children since the one child has already profited from living in the parent's home. The data indicate general agreement that the child who performs the greatest amount of service should receive the greatest part of the estate. Where disagreements occur they focus on differences in perception among children concerning the amount of service actually rendered by the sibling who was left the largest share of the estate.

4. Children feel that they should maintain intimate contact with aged parents in order to provide them with emotional support and social and recreational opportunities, and that such contact maintenance is requisite for obtaining a share of inheritance. Exchanges may be of different orders. Children provide parents with physical care, emotional support, affection and the niceties of social interaction in their declining years; in return they receive financial compensation. What is suggested here is that the pattern of distribution to particular children is based upon services they have rendered, even among those who live in households apart from the aged parent. The child who provides the most physical and social services generally receives the largest reward.

The pattern of exchange of care for eventual financial reward does not function when the decedent does not require special attention. The normal testate pattern of distribution is for the decedent to leave his estate to the spouse if the spouse is still living. By leaving the estate to the spouse the testator provides the widow or widower with the means to continue an independent or nearly independent financial existence. This lateral transfer, which was identified as a "spouse-all" pattern, took place prior to a vertical estate distribution from parent to child. This occurred even under intestate conditions, where there is no will. Most beneficiaries, children for the most part, who stand to share under the law of descent and distribution, at least one-third of the estate in most jurisdictions, favored the spouse-all pattern. In the majority of cases, the testator's spouse was an aged parent and such a transfer enabled that individual to maintain independence for a longer period of time while still physically capable and sensorially alert.

Some implications of this orderly process are the reduction of potential turbulence which usually accompanies the loss of a network member. This is a conscious effort to effect a smooth continuity of relationships within the emotional network with minimal hassling among descendants over claims and priorities. A less desirable option is to take over the financial and moral responsibility for the aged person, if, by taking one's fair share, one increased the dependency of this person. Respondents proved to be very sanguine in harmonizing societal expectations of filial piety and the costing out of economic gains and losses. Knowledge that the equity, usually a nonmortgaged home, would eventually be passed on to them made the decision to keep things "as is" easy to come by.

In this analysis of generational transfers within family systems, the dynamics of the bonding relationship between adult children and their older parents have been mentioned only in passing. Significant research on intergenerational bonding and value transmission establishes that commonality of location of children and parents which increases opportunities for interaction approaches value congruity for members of both generations. Direct transmission of value orientations of parent to child via the traditional model of agent-novice socialization does not occur (Bengtson, 1975; Hill, Foote, Aldous, Carlson, and MacDonald, 1970).

Differences between the generations, commonly labeled as the "gap," are not as great as popularly portrayed. This is the case even though parents tend to minimize the differences between themselves and their children, while children indicate the reverse. Older members in linkages with adult children report high levels of affective relationships, while children perceive these ties more in terms of service and various exchanges of help (Black and Bengtson, 1973b). These perceptual differences should not inhibit the potential solidity of the intergenerational complement of the kin network. They infer complementary needs. Affection, real or otherwise, is desired and needed by the elderly and is sought in the exchanges with children. Children, in turn, who must invest in other affectual relationships such as their marriages, can best handle the "demands" for respect,

understanding, and trust of their parents by providing very specific services. The dynamics of specific parent-child relationships will influence specific testamentary transfers.

Two recent developments may modify the normal pattern of intergenerational transfers of equity along biological lines. The first is the increasing incidence of divorce and remarriage, and the second is the variety of life-styles now becoming available to the aged. In a 12-month period ending with August, 1974, there occurred an estimated 2,233,000 marriages and 948,000 divorces in the United States; 68,000 fewer marriages and 56,000 more divorces than in the prior 12-month period (U.S. National Center for Health Statistics, 1974). Remarriages since World War II have increased in incidence, with the expectation that four out of five of those who divorce will eventually remarry (U.S. Bureau of the Census, 1972a). Specific analyses of divorce patterns by socioeconomic levels indicate that men aged 35–44 in upper socioeconomic brackets, who have had consistently the lowest divorce rate among all men, have experienced both an increase in their numbers and a proportionate increase in the number of divorces (Glick, 1975).

Middle-aged women have experienced similar proportional increases in divorce. Glick reports that, "For all women 35 to 44, the proportion divorced went up, on average, by nearly one-half during the 1960's from 3.8 percent to 5.5 percent. . . . The percent divorced for professional women went up from 6.0 percent in 1960 to 7.8 percent in 1970; and the percent for women in the uppermost income group rose from 11.8 percent to 15.1 percent" (Glick, 1975, p. 19).

These trends suggest a potential redistribution of family acquired assets to pay for the costs of these new family formations and distributions to second marriage or a combination of first and second marriage heirs and legatees. Antenuptial agreements have been useful legal contracts for middle-aged and older persons entering a second marriage. Contractees agree not to claim their allowable share under state intestate laws, thus permitting inheritance transfers to biological issues of the first marriage. Even with such an arrangement, the testator can designate as beneficiaries spouses and offspring of second marriages, and this often occurs. The ante-nuptial agreement does not reduce the autonomy of the testator to freely will assets but nullifies a spouse's usual legal entitlement to a fair share of the estate.

The increased incidence of divorce and "a trend towards earlier first divorces, median age 31.6; and earlier separation after first marriage, median age 28.7" (U.S. Bureau of the Census, 1972b), along with a high rate of remarriage, suggests that traditional patterns of generational transfers may have to change to provide for multiple beneficiaries from more than one marriage. It is anticipated that ante-nuptial agreements will be employed less frequently among remarrying middle-aged individuals. Also, some elderly persons, especially those in the upper socioeconomic brackets, who have had more than one marriage may benefit by this shift away from the usual inheritance pattern which protects first marriage family members. Similar to the elderly progenitor of a large-sized family, the remarried older person has a larger number of relatives, especially children, with whom to develop linkages. The promise of an inheritance may provide motivation for family members to invest in a relationship with the elderly person, while the latter has a greater field of available relatives from which to choose.

Alternative life-styles and the prospects of elderly persons adopting these styles provide potentially divergent patterns of testamentary exchange. Glick (1975, p. 24) reports a "spectacular 8-fold increase occurred during the 1960's in the number of household heads who were reported as living apart from relatives while sharing their living quarters with an unrelated adult 'partner' (roommate or friend) of the opposite sex." The incidence of cohabitation is increasing in all age groups based on desire or necessity (Macklin, 1972). The Census reports that in 1970, among men over 65 who shared their living quarters with a nonrelative, one out of five shared it with a female (U.S. Bureau of the Census, 1973). This is but one example of a living arrangement involving non-relatives and the possibility that patterns divergent from traditional modes of testamentary exchange may emerge. Achievement rather than ascription may become the priority determinant in the transfer process. Elderly persons increasingly living more with nonrelatives in new family forms and becoming increasingly dependent and identified with such persons may move away from traditional familistic inheritance as the only possible outcome of the testamentary process (Parsons, 1954).

FAMILY-AGED MEMBER RELATIONSHIPS IN 1980'S

One major theme of this chapter is concern with the actual and potential role of family structures and networks in providing aging members a hedge against the controlling demands of organizational and institutional bureaucracies and, through network linkage activities and interaction, providing intimacy and human warmth, both requisites for the survival and quality living of aged members. Various forms of the family, as distinct from neighborhood peer groups and friends and acquaintances in institutionalized settings, may provide a more desirable option for older persons in obtaining physical, social, and psychological well-being.

These varied family structures, some created by societal conditions and others formed in the quest for more meaningful relationships than those found in the traditional nuclear family, have the potentiality for "humanizing" the aging process. The aged person can be in a family environment where his or her contributions are highly prized. The reasons are that the circumstances surrounding the beginnings of these varied family structures and the requisite activities for effecting survival indicate that these structures require reciprocal exchanges rather than one-sided dependencies, parity over superordinate-subordinate relationships, and effective utilization of individual and organizational resources.

Society-wide transfers in the form of financial support for health care, social service, medical service, nutrition, housing, and other living accoutrements are obviously lessening the importance of the individual family generational transfer of equities through inheritance. It is making the latter system more significant for its expression of family ties and intimacy but is still less than adequate as a total support system. Until entitlement, a universal right to available support systems, becomes the policy and law of the land, too many older citizens and member units of family networks will have insufficient resources to provide a quality home environment for themselves.

The provision of alternatives to the institutionalization of services and people in complex societies is difficult because of its potential effects upon all societal systems, institutions, and organizations. For example, to move to a client-centered human service system requires radical changes in the current professional-client model regarding the dispensation of services, and this can contaminate the operations of all other formally organized structures. To meet the needs and demands of aged individuals and families for health and social services, for example, may require bringing such activities into the home, or utilization of a decentralized organizational model with the provision of services at the client's call. Such proposed "business irregularities" from conventional practices immediately create linkage, relational, and communication problems; resistance from human service staffs; and if not reluctance at least controlled ambivalence from government and community elites. The threat of unknown consequences prevents a wholesale transformation of the current institutionalized patterns for doing business with aged members and their families.

Yet, the search for alternatives to institutionalization continues because there are neither enough institutions nor trained people to staff them to meet the expanding need for health and custodial care for the growing aged population. During the past decade federal health, welfare, and rehabilitation agencies have implicitly followed policies of reversing the trend of providing care and treatment for the chronically ill and aged in isolated, highly bureaucratized, and impersonal institutions. Providing services in the communities of those who require them is now being advocated, and comprehensive community health facilities are but one example of implementation of such a new policy. A

logical extension is to carry the services one step further, to the family.

As far back as 1962, Shanas (1962) foresaw the current situation in which the needs for health care for the elderly would exceed the supply of public funds and trained personnel. She raised the question at that time of how the family might be better utilized to meet these needs to the benefit of both the elderly and the general society. There are insufficient resources along with an unwillingness to reassess and revise current priorities of human services in other life sectors than health, such as nutrition, education, housing, and leisure. Breslau and Haug (1972) concluded as a result of a demonstration project on the delivery of paraprofessional services to the elderly: ". . . the needed social service would be more effective if it elicited the cooperation of the family and were perceived and formulated as a family enterprise. In other words, social service, instead of being an independent and alternative agent of intervention, ought to attempt to be a family ally that offers assistance when caring for the aged member is too great a burden." To effect this recommendation requires a basic modification of current models of service and their financial support.

One logical substitute for the continued proliferation of impersonal institutions and large bureaucratic agencies is the channeling of some of the funds used for service provision directly to the families of the elderly who can provide more personalized general care at perhaps less cost. In some societies with family-centered traditions, this "reversal" of the bureaucratic mode is not overly traumatic. For highly professionalized provider systems, however, the impact is potentially devastating. Experiments and demonstrations have yet to be tried. The cost benefits thus derived can mean improved resources for the short-term treatment in general hospitals of acute illness and injury among the aged and for the total care institutionalization which is essential for a very small proportion of the elderly.

The family network, while structured by blood and marriage ties, is essentially a "voluntary" system with few legal or cultural constraints to participate in it. The ties of

members are based largely on reciprocal exchanges of various kinds of aid, usually of
unequal value, and on some adherence to
filial responsibility. Although current statistics
indicate that most aged living with relatives
make their home with one of their children,
it is possible that other, more distant, members
of the family network would be willing to
undertake the care of elderly relatives if the
added responsibility were offset by certain
financial or service benefits. Consequently, a
particular service household within the family
network may be that of the child, grandchild,
nephew, niece, grand nephew, grand niece,
brother, sister, etc.

If circumstances facilitated the care of the
elderly within a unit of the family network,
the options available to the aged members of
the society could be increased. Many aged persons cling tenaciously to their independence and
participation in social activities as continuous
support for their self-images as productive self-
sufficient individuals. The institution represents
for such persons the abandonment of many of
these personal goals. Residence with a family
member, however, could ease the burden—
physical and economic—on the old person of
the total maintenance of a household, yet provide the opportunity to carry on accustomed
extrafamilial activities. As Peter Townsend
(1968) points out, the composition of one's
household determines to a significant degree
the individual's behavior both within and outside the family group.

A role for the family network in the care of
elderly, especially as a backup system for the
custody and treatment of those between independence and dependence in mental and physical
functioning, is inevitable. All research findings
and policy declarations maintain that in the remaining decades of this century:

1. There will be insufficient manpower for
the training of professional personnel to meet
the continuous demands and needs for quality
health care and rehabilitation.

2. The United States has reached its "absorptive capacity" in so far as professionalization is
concerned and cannot continue its current rate
of expenditure for professional and quasi-
professional training.

3. Skyrocketing hospital and rehabilitation
costs are draining family and third-party resources, and some other way for providing
quality care and treatment more economically
must be found.

4. Payoffs in improved functioning, if any,
of elderly persons as a consequence of extended
hospitalization for treatment of chronic disabilities are insufficient to warrant the high cost.

5. Further expansion or building of new
centralized care institutions will vitiate current
efforts to develop a client-centered program of
care therapy where the elderly relate to their
families and communities and have some say
regarding what is being done to and for them.

In many areas, however, a chipping away of
archaic structural forms is occurring, and this
may be the only tolerated process of institutional innovation. One fascinating alternative
is the creation of new forms of family, "fictive
kin," by having one group of self-sufficient
aged persons share an apartment with a second
group of less mentally and physically capable
elderly individuals, all residing together in a
boarding house. A team of counselor and activity
therapist play supportive roles to facilitate
reaching the objectives of self-responsibility and
independence of the competent and less competent participants. Another alternative is the
day hospital, a "grown up" ambulatory-care
clinic, where patients who do not require 24
hour in-hospital care come to the facility in
the morning and return to their households
in the evening after receiving medical care,
rehabilitation, and social services as required
(U.S. Department of Health, Education, and
Welfare, 1972). A modification of the day
hospital is the day care center whose major aim
is to maintain in the community with their
families aged persons who are not capable of
independent functioning because of physical
or psychosocial limitations (Cohen, 1973). The
leadership of such programs has been vested in
health professionals, although program components are geared to effect interaction, foster
intimacy, and overcome isolation associated
with long-term illness and impairment in the
aged (Robins, 1974).

All these experimental programs of alternatives to institutionalization have yet to be

evaluated in relation to their costs compared to other forms of care, participant and family satisfaction, relieving in-patient bed demand, staff interest and gratification, and maintenance of level of functioning of the elderly. Still, they are exciting in their potential as interstitial quasi-institutionalized care systems, between the family and bureaucratized human service systems, with the prospect of being people-oriented and -controlled.

These "halfway to institutionalization" programs, especially day care, with their short-term restorative, maintenance, and psychosocial activities for high risk elderly and post-hospitalized patients, cannot provide a long-term living environment for non-ambulatory or impaired elderly persons. The mandates of these programs at best can supply backstopping services to families which have elderly members in their households.

Considering that human beings require nurturance as well as health care, intimacy as well as privacy, interaction as well as isolation, emotional support as well as physical rehabilitation, and that these requisites are more critical to individuals as they become less sufficient and independent, the essential question is—where can these be found in a fee-for-service, contracting, contraceptive, and antiseptic society? Family networks still persist in the face of organization bureaucratization with its endemic structural properties and norms which result in treating people as commodities rather than as human beings. The simple and undeniable fact so obvious that it is overlooked—is that family networks are pervasive as functional systems for large numbers of individuals in the United States, and, for that matter, in societies worldwide. What is suggested here is to investigate the utility and viability of using the family network as an alternative or complementary living environment for its aged members. In this discussion, of course, family network refers to those persons who are "perceived" to be family and includes those who may be somewhat distantly related by blood or marriage such as second cousins and uncle- and aunt-in-law. Family network does not imply only members of the immediate family, e.g., children and parents of the nuclear (conjugal) family of procreation.

It is anticipated that the proffering of economic and service incentives to units of family networks for the care of the aged under a contractual arrangement will make a difference. These incentives, it is hypothesized, will increase the receptivity and willingness to provide an enhancing environment for the aged family member. The finding that the provision of incentives does not make a difference in the willingness of member units to provide creative environments for elderly members—they will provide in any case—should not diminish the potential significance of the incentive package. The availability of service and economic options should facilitate and buttress the family's efforts in such endeavors.

The contract provision supplies a family with a set of expectations for a given time period and in a real sense frees its members to develop the bonding relationship, the emotional components of family linkages. Expected benefits—such as (a) a direct monthly allotment of funds; (b) specific tax write-off for expenses incurred; (c) a low-cost loan to renovate or build an addition to the home in which the elderly person can maintain independence in a physical setting which would have few architectural barriers; (d) the provision of income tax relief for assuming this responsibility; (e) availability of specific services from established agencies which are necessary and convenient to the well-being of the family unit taking on the care-therapeutic role; and (f) property tax waiver with some formula proportional to dwelling usage—given singly or in combination to prospective providers of living environments for the elderly reduce the problematics of economic devastation and enhance family self-fulfillment.

The dumping of the impaired and frail elderly upon families by professionals has resulted in a mutually disastrous experience. The family sees its resources rapidly dwindling and is handicapped in its means to do things for its other members. It becomes guilt-ridden or neglectful; the thin rubber band of filial piety becomes stretched to the breaking point. By removing sacrifice and deficit living from the elderly member/family linkage, a modern version of filial responsibility can be effected. Removing the economic liabilities, and in their place offering a reward, and making available human service systems more responsive to the relief needs of families, such as the provision of day care and home bound services, provide motivation and time to develop mutual satisfactory interpersonal relationships. This is a prime function of family networks, the expressive component of filial responsibility.

This suggested late twentieth century living environment for the impaired elderly is an untested formulation. Research and demonstrations, one building on the other, can determine the viability of the approach. First, it would be important to determine the conditions and circumstances under which members of varied family networks and at different stages of the life cycle are willing to care for the elderly. This should be followed by demonstrations which will relate the most appropriate family network, stage of life cycle, and life-style with specific incentives, the physical and mental status of the elderly person, his attitudes and perceptions as well as those of his relatives, and the physical and social capabilities of relatives and household. These demonstrations will also determine social and economic cost/benefits for varied types of family network-home care arrangements.

Such demonstrations, after appropriate evaluation, should also consider the possible changes in service agencies which would result in the adjustment of services to the needs of home care. Returning the elderly to the care of the family would be compatible with recent efforts to reduce the inefficiency and the red tape which has come to characterize the operations of health, social, and welfare institutions and to return the responsibility for care to the community and ultimately to the family where it naturally resided in the past.

Serious attention should be given to the development of this auxiliary care system. This would require a reevaluation of current policies and programs of institutionalized care of the elderly, especially those of human service systems. Supportive activities to help the family in maintaining the elderly member in the home will undoubtedly increase. Currently, there is more interest and the beginnings of a social movement to develop more responsive client care systems around individuals (bringing services into the home), rather than requiring

clients to enter large-scale bureaucratized care and custodial systems. Discovering ways to combine family and professional labor power should auger well for existing human service systems. It provides a rationale for a new policy and changed functions, the basis for their continued existence in the future.

Not to be overlooked in the search for empirical data are the lobbying efforts of professionalized administrators for more institutionalized human service systems and larger budgets. The misperceptions of many practitioners and researchers about the bases for a family's involvement with elderly members are further indications of the need for empirical data on alternative care systems for the elderly. The lack of familism and nucleated family structure are major reasons given for the American family's inability to "care for its own." Incentives, e.g., payoffs, in the form of economic or social benefits are considered appropriate behaviors of nonfamily organizations and institutions, but these same rewards have been considered disconsonant with the ideology and ethos of the family and demeaning of its values. We do not accept this posture and find that rewards, incentives, reciprocity, exchange, and contracts are basic processes and products of everyday life. Families are not immune to these but, in fact, need them in order to survive. The proposed alternative to institutionalization of the aged in the remaining decades of this century integrates the normative, rational demands of a bureaucratic society for fiscal responsibility and cost-effectiveness with the more idiosyncratic norms of family networks where "blood is thicker than water" and where emotions are more powerful bonds than contracts.

SUMMARY

In this chapter I have presented a number of analyses which purport to explain historic and ongoing changes in family structure, the behavior of family members, and the factors which impinge on the survival and the quality of life of elderly persons. These have been organized around themes—each with its own set of assumptions, concepts, and hypotheses with clinical and empirical data to support them.

The family life of old people can be described variously, and a comprehensive presentation requires a book-length manuscript. The stance I assumed was to select specific themes and then to elaborate, thus providing the most robust explanation of family-elderly member life-styles and relationships.

The first of these themes was family-bureaucratic organization linkages, and how family members function as facilitators, protectors, and mediators for its elderly members in the latters' efforts to handle the normative demands of institutional and organizational bureaucracies. This is a critical modern day issue since the bureaucratization of provider systems is a worldwide phenomenon.

The task, therefore, is for the family to develop competence for handling and changing such bureaucratized social systems, largely human service ones which essentially control the life-styles of old people. To understand the potentialities of developing competencies in dealings with nonprimary groups through resocialization and other processes, exchange theory was indicated. Exchange theory components such as cost, reward, reciprocation, profit, reinforcement, power, and distributive justice provide logical explanations of family-elderly, family-organizational, and elderly-organizational linkage.

Understanding linkages, especially their conditions and processes, requires knowledge of what is a family, how to best describe it, and ways the family is perceived and used by functionaries of bureaucratized systems in their dealings with clients, patients, or customers. Suggested is a bipartite definition: the conjugal family form, spouses and their offspring, one established by contract, most visible and legitimized in relation to rights and responsibilities; and the "everyday family," a nonkinship based structure, composed of individuals in a cohabitating domestic relationship, one which provides love and emotional bonding and is sexually consequential. It, therefore, includes sanctioned and unsanctioned variant forms such as group marriage, communal, lesbian, and homosexual.

On the assumption that families are basic emotional networks and the search for such interactional support especially by elderly members is continuous, the emergence of forms of family which differ from the nuclear family of procreation and which may provide alternative emotional and economic supports is detailed. Special emphasis is on the kin family network and its potentialities for support of aged members living in their own households. For elderly individuals unwilling or unable to live independently, new forms of family such as communal are examined.

Intergenerational linkages and inheritance transfers along family lines have historically been basic processes of generational continuity and in the provision of emotional support for aged members. Patterns of serial reciprocity have characterized these transfers where equities controlled by the elderly testator are eventually conveyed to the young with the implicit understanding that the latter will care for their aged parents. The trend toward universal and society-wide support and care systems has diminished the importance of inheritance for sustaining the economic well-being of the family. This situation is examined and the functions of inheritance for emotional bonding are discussed. Also covered are the increasing incidence of divorce and remarriage and the plethora of life-styles which may modify the normal pattern of intergenerational transfers along blood lines.

While societies worldwide are increasingly assuming control over their members through the bureaucratization of their social systems and concomitantly are providing for those who are not producers, the ability of these societies to continue such support is problematic. Elites are asking whether their societies have reached the "absorptive capacity" to handle further development and organization of services for their citizens.

The profit from the production of goods and services is insufficient to pay for the high costs of services—services which, in societies such as the United States, are increasingly viewed as client entitlement rather than client qualification. While claimants of this economic view can be challenged, what is more salient from a humanistic perspective of aging with dignity is the prevention of too early an institutionalization of the elderly. Consequently, in the final section of this chapter, alternatives to institutionalization are discussed, and the feasibility of providing economic and human service supports (incentives) for member units of kin family networks is examined. Such recommendations fit the proposed exchange model: harmonizing the rationale demands and decreasing efficiency of bureaucratic organizations with the more idiosyncratic norms and emotional bondings of family and friendship networks. Such an accommodation is mandatory if the elderly are to be given increased options and autonomies in relation to roles, life-styles, and living arrangements.

REFERENCES

Adams, B. N. 1968. *Kinship in an Urban Setting.* Chicago: Markham.

Adams, B. N. 1970. Isolation, function, and beyond: American kinship in the 1960's. *J. Marriage & Fam.,* **32,** 575-597.

Adams, D. L. 1971. Correlates of satisfaction among the elderly. *Gerontologist,* Part II, **2,** 64-68.

Aldous, J., and Hill, R. 1965. Social cohesion, lineage type, and intergenerational transmission. *Soc. Forces,* **43,** 471-482.

Ball, D. W. 1972. The family as a sociological problem: Conceptualization of the taken-for-granted as prologue to social problem analysis. *Soc. Prob.,* **19,** 295-307.

Bengtson, V. L. 1975. Generation and family effects in value socialization. *Am. Soc. Rev.,* **40,** 358-371.

Bengtson, V. L., and Black, K. D. 1973. Intergenerational relations and continuities in socialization. *In,* P. Baltes and W. Schaie (eds.), *Personality and Socialization,* Chapter 9. New York: Academic Press.

Bengtson, V. L., Olander, E., and Haddad, A. 1975. The "Generation Gap" and aged family members. *In,* J. Gubruim (ed.), *Late Life: Recent Developments in the Sociology of Age.* Springfield, Illinois: Charles C Thomas.

Black, K. D., and Bengtson, V. L. 1973a. Solidarity across generations: Elderly parents and their middle aged children. Paper presented at annual meeting of the Gerontological Society.

Black, K. D., and Bengtson, V. L. 1973b. The measure of solidarity: An intergenerational analysis. Paper presented at the annual meeting of the American Psychological Association.

Blau, P. M. 1964. *Exchange and Power in Social Life.* New York: John Wiley.

Blau, Z. S. 1973. *Old Age in a Changing Society.* New York: New Viewpoints.

Blenkner, M. 1965. Social work and family relationships in later life with some thoughts on filial maturity. *In,* E. Shanas and G. Streib (eds.), *Social Structure and the Family: Generational Relations,*

pp. 46-59. Englewood Cliffs, New Jersey: Prentice-Hall.

Blenkner, M. 1969. The normal dependencies of aging. *In,* R. Kalish (ed.), *The Dependencies of Old People.* Ann Arbor: Institute of Gerontology.

Breslau, N., and Haug, M. R. 1972. The elderly aid the elderly: The senior friends project. *Social Security Bulletin,* **35,** 9-15.

Chevan, A., and Korson, J. H. 1975. Living arrangements of widows in the United States and Israel, 1960 and 1961. *Demography,* **12,** 505-518.

Cogswell, B. E., and Sussman, M. B. 1972. Changing family and marriage forms: Complications for human service systems. *Family Coordinator,* **21,** 505-516.

Cohen, M. G. 1973. Alternative to institutional care of the aged. *Social Casework,* **54,** 447-452.

Conover, P. W. 1975. An analysis of communes and intentional communities with particular attention to sexual and genderal relations. *Family Coordinator,* **24,** 453-464.

Cumming, E., and Henry, W. 1961. *Growing Old.* New York: Basic Books.

Dowd, J. J. 1974. Aging as exchange: A preface to theory. Mimeographed. Department of Sociology, Gerontological Center, University of Southern California.

Feldman, H. 1964. Development of the husband-wife relationship. Preliminary report Cornell studies of marital development: Study in the transition to parenthood. Department of Child Development and Family Relationships, New York State College of Home Economics, Cornell University.

Glick, P. 1975. A demographic look at American families. *J. Marriage & Fam.,* **37,** 15-26.

Gray Associates. 1971. Orange County starts lawsuit against Share-A-Home members—a new concept in care for aged. Publicity Release. June 28.

Gray Associates. 1971. Orange County to begin taking depositions. Publicity Release. July 3.

Hall, C. M. 1974. Variant family process. Draft paper.

Haug, M. R., and Sussman, M. B. 1969. Professional autonomy and the revolt of the client. *Soc. Prob.* **17,** 153-161.

Hill, R., Foote, N., Aldous, J., Carlson, R., and Mac Donald, R. 1970. *Family Development in Three Generations.* Cambridge: Schenkman.

Homans, G. C. 1960. *The Human Group.* New York: Harcourt, Brace & World.

Homans, G. C. 1961. *Social Behavior: Its Elementary Forms.* New York: Harcourt, Brace & World.

Jackson, J. J. 1971a. Sex and social class variations in black aged parent-adult child relationships. *Aging and Human Development,* **2,** 96-107.

Jackson, J. J. 1971b. The blacklands of gerontology. *Aging and Human Development,* **7,** 168-178.

Jackson, J. J. 1972a. Marital life among aging blacks. *Family Coordinator,* **21,** 21-27.

Jackson, J. J. 1972b. Comparative life styles and family and friend relationships among older black women. *Family Coordinator,* **21,** 477-485.

Jackson, J. J. 1973. Family organization and ideology. *In*, K. Miller and R. Dreger (eds.), *Comparative Studies of Blacks and Whites*. New York: Academic Press.

Jacksonville Journal, August 20, 1971.

Jourard, S. M. 1971. *The Transparent Self*. rev. ed. New York: John Wiley.

Kanter, R. M. 1972. *Commitment and Community: Communes and Utopias in Sociological Perspective*. Cambridge: Harvard University Press.

Kelley, H. H., and Thibault, J. W. 1954. Experimental studies of group problem solving and process. *In*, G. Lindzey (ed.), *Handbook of Social Psychology*, Vol. II. Cambridge: Addison-Wesley.

Kerckhoff, A. C. 1965. Nuclear and extended family relationships: Normative and behavioral analysis. *In*, E. Shanas and G. Streib (eds.), *Social Structure and Family: Generational Relations*, pp. 93–112. Englewood Cliffs, New Jersey: Prentice-Hall.

Kerckhoff, A. C. 1966. Family and retirement. *In*, I. H. Simpson and J. C. McKinney (eds.), *Social Aspects of Aging*. Durham, North Carolina: Duke University Press.

Kreps, J. M. 1962. Aggregate income and labor force participation of the aged. *Law and Contemporary Problems*, 27, 52–66.

Libby, R. W., and Whitehurst, R. N. (eds.) 1973. *Renovating Marriage: Toward New Sexual-Life Styles*. Danville, California: Consensus Publishers.

Linton, R. B. 1936. *The Study of Man*. New York: Appleton-Century-Crofts.

Litman, T. J. 1971. Health care and the family: A three-generational analysis. *Medical Care*, 9, 67–81.

Lowenthal, M. F., and Haven, C. 1968. Interaction and adaptation: Intimacy as a clinical variable. *Am. Soc. Rev.*, 33, 20–30.

Macklen, E. 1972. Heterosexual cohabitation among unmarried college students. *Family Coordinator*, 21, 463–472.

Moriwaki, S. Y. 1973. Self-disclosure, significant others and psychological well-being in old age. *J. of Health and Soc. Behavior*, 14, 226–232.

Munnichs, J. 1976. Linkages of older people with their families and bureaucracy in the Netherlands. *In*, E. Shanas and M. B. Sussman (eds.), *Older People, Family and Bureaucracy*. Durham, North Carolina: Duke University Press, forthcoming.

Nau, L. Y. 1973. Why not family rehabilitation? *Journal of Rehabilitation*, 39(3), 14–17+.

Noelker, L. S. 1975. Intimate relations in a residential home for the elderly. Ph.D. dissertation, Case Western Reserve University.

O'Neill, N., and O'Neill, G. 1972. Open marriage: A Synergic model. *Family Coordinator*, 21, 403–409.

Orlando Sentinel. 1971. July 21 and August 20.

Paillat, P. 1976. Bureaucratization of old age: Determinants of the process, possible safeguards and reorientations. *In*, E. Shanas and M. B. Sussman (eds.), *Older People, Family and Bureaucracy*. Durham, North Carolina: Duke University Press, forthcoming.

Parsons, T. 1954. The kinship system of the contemporary United States. *In*, *Essays in Sociological Theory*, 2nd ed., pp. 89–93. New York: The Free Press.

Parsons, T., and Fox, R. 1952. Illness and the modern American family. *J. Soc. Issues*, 8, 31–34.

Piotrowski, J. 1976. Old people in Poland: Family and bureaucracy. *In*, E. Shanas and M. B. Sussman (eds.), *Older People, Family and Bureaucracy*. Durham, North Carolina: Duke University Press, forthcoming.

Population Reference Bureau, Inc. 1975. The elderly in America. *Population Bulletin*, 30(3).

Ramey, J. W. 1972. Emerging patterns of innovative behavior in marriage. *Family Coordinator*, 21, 435–456.

Ramey, J. W. 1975. Intimate groups and networks: Frequent consequences of sexually open marriage. *Family Coordinator*, 24, 515–530.

Rapoport, R., and Rapoport, R. N. 1975. Men, women, and equity. *Family Coordinator*, 24, 421–432.

Robins, E. G. 1974. Therapeutic day care: Progress report on experiments to test the feasibility for third party reimbursement. Paper presented at 27th Annual Scientific Meeting of the Gerontological Society, Portland, Oregon.

Rosenmayr, L. 1976. The family—source of hope for the elderly of the future. *In*, E. Shanas and M. B. Sussman (eds.), *Older People, Family and Bureaucracy*. Durham, North Carolina: Duke University Press, forthcoming.

Rosenmayr, L., and Köckeis, E. 1965. Unwelt und familie alter menschen. Berlin: Luchterland-Verlag.

Rosow, I. 1967. *Social Integration of the Aged*. New York: The Free Press.

St. Petersburg Times. 1971. August 18.

Schneider, D. 1968. *American Kinship*. Englewood Cliffs, New Jersey: Prentice-Hall.

Schorr, A. 1960. *Filial Responsibility in the Modern American Family*. Washington, D.C.: Social Security Administration, Department of Health, Education and Welfare.

Shanas, E. 1962. *The Health of Older People: A Social Survey*. Cambridge: Harvard University Press.

Shanas, E. 1967. Family help patterns and social class in three countries. *J. Marriage & Fam.*, 29, 257–266.

Shanas, E. 1968. A note on restriction of life space: Attitudes of age cohorts. *J. of Health and Soc. Behavior*, 9, 86–90.

Shanas, E. 1971. Measuring the home health needs of the aged in five countries. *J. Geront.*, 26, 37–40.

Shanas, E., and Hauser, P. M. 1974. Zero population growth and the family life of older people. *J. Soc. Issues*, 30, 79–92.

Shaw, M. E., and Costanzo, P. R. 1970. *Theories of Social Psychology*. New York: McGraw-Hill.

Sherif, M. 1966. *In Common Predicament*. Boston: Houghton Mifflin.

Shimkin, D. B., Louie, G. J., and Frate, D. 1973. The black extended family: A basic rural institution and a mechanism of urban adaptation. Paper presented at IX international Congress of Anthropological and Ethnological Sciences, Chicago.

Shimkin, D. B., and Patterson, J. 1969. Recommendations for the improvement of health status among the disadvantaged. Study proposal.

Shimkin, D. B., and Shimkin, E. M. 1975. The extended family in United States black societies: Findings and problems. Unpublished paper. Urbana-Champaign, Illinois: Department of Anthropology, University of Illinois.

Shimkin, D. B., Shimkin, E. M., and Frate, D. A. (eds.). 1975. *The Extended Family in Black Societies*. The Hague: Mouton.

Slater, S., Sussman, M. B., and Stroud, M. W., III. 1970. Participation in household activities as a prognostic factor in rehabilitation. *Arch. Phys. Med. Rehabil.*, 51, 605–611.

Smith, J. R., and Smith, L. G. (eds.). 1974. *Beyond Monogamy: Recent Studies of Sexual Alternatives in Marriage*. Baltimore: Johns Hopkins University Press.

Somerville, R. M. 1972. The future of family relationships in the middle and older years. *Family Coordinator*, 21, 487–498.

Steinberg, F. 1971. Cited in Symposium: An institution looks at total community needs for the aging. Commentary by S. Zibit in *Gerontologist*, Part I, 2, 49.

Stroud, M. W., III, and Sussman, M. B. 1973. *The patient's Rehabilitation career: A ten-year longitudinal study*. Unpublished monograph.

Sussman, M. B. 1953. The help pattern in the middle class family. *Am. Soc. Rev.*, 18, 22–28.

Sussman, M. B. 1959. The isolated nuclear family: Fact or fiction. *Social Problems*, 6, 333–340.

Sussman, M. B. 1960. Intergenerational relationships and social role changes in middle age. *J. Geront.*, 15, 71–75.

Sussman, M. B. 1965. Relationships of adult children with their parents in the United States. *In*, E. Shanas and G. Streib (eds.), *Social Structure and Family: Generational Relations*, pp. 62–92. Englewood Cliffs, New Jersey: Prentice-Hall.

Sussman, M. B. 1971. Family systems in the 1970's: Analysis, policies and programs. *Annals*, 396, 40–56.

Sussman, M. B. (ed.) 1972. *Non-traditional Family Forms in the 1970's*. Minneapolis: National Council on Family Relations.

Sussman, M. B. 1973. Methodological problems in the study of the family. Unpublished paper read at the 81st Annual Convention of the American Psychological Association, Montreal.

Sussman, M. B. 1974. Issues and developments in family sociology in the 1970's. *In*, M. S. Archer (ed.), *Current Research In Sociology*, pp. 27–65. The Hague: Mouton.

Sussman, M. B. 1975. The four F's of variant family forms and marriage styles. *Family Coordinator*, 24, 563–576.

Sussman, M. B., Cates, J. N., and Smith, D. T. 1970. *The Family and Inheritance*. New York: Russell Sage Foundation.

Sussman, M. B., and Cogswell, B. E. 1972. The meaning of variant and experimental marriage styles and family forms in the 1970's. *Family Coordinator*, 21, 375–381.

Sussman, M. B., Cogswell, B. E., and Marciano, T. D. (eds.). 1975. *Family Coordinator*, 24.

Sussman, M. B. *et al.* 1971. Changing families in a changing society. *In*, *Report to the President: White House Conference on Children 1970*, pp. 227–238. Washington, D.C.: Government Printing Office.

Sweetser, D. A. 1963. Asymetry in intergenerational family relationships. *Soc. Forces*, 41, 346–352.

Thibault, J., and Kelley, H. 1959. *The Social Psychology of Groups*. New York: John Wiley.

Townsend, P. 1968. The structure of the family. *In*, E. Shanas, P. Townsend, D. Wedderburn, H. Friis, P. Milhoj, and J. Stehouwer (eds.), *Old People In Three Industrial Societies*, pp. 132–176. New York: Atherton Press.

Troll, L. E. 1971. The family of later life: A decade review. *J. Marriage & Fam.*, 33, 263–290.

U.S. Bureau of the Census. 1972a. Marriage, divorce, and remarriage by year of birth: June, 1971. *Current Population Reports*, Series P-20, No. 239. Washington, D.C.: Government Printing Office.

U.S. Bureau of the Census. 1972b. Marital status and living arrangements: March, 1972. *Current Population Reports*, Series P-20, No. 242. Washington, D.C.: Government Printing Office.

U.S. Bureau of the Census. 1973. Women by number of children ever born. *1970 Census of Population*, Vol. II, 3A. Washington, D.C.: Government Printing Office.

U.S. Department of Health, Education and Welfare. 1972. *Aging*, No. 215–216 (Sept.–Oct.).

U.S. National Center for Health Statistics. 1974. Provisional statistics (births, marriages, divorces and deaths for August, 1974). *Monthly Vital Statistics Report*, Vol. 23, No. 8. Washington, D.C.: Government Printing Office.

Vocational Rehabilitation Act. 1974. Amended. Title I, Section 102 (HR 14225).

Weber, M. 1947. *The Theory of Social and Economic Organization*. New York: Oxford University Press.

Youmans, E. G. 1963. *Aging Patterns in a Rural and Urban Area of Kentucky*. Lexington, Kentucky: University of Kentucky Agricultural Experiment Station.

10
HOUSING AND LIVING ENVIRONMENTS OF OLDER PEOPLE

Frances M. Carp

The Wright Institute

What does housing mean to the elderly? Aside from his spouse, housing is probably the single most important element in the life of an older person. (Proceedings of the 1971 White House Conference on Aging, 1973)

The domain of housing and living environments for the elderly has seen great activity in the United States since the early 1960's. A large number and some variety of housing facilities have been constructed, mostly supported by Federal funds. Concurrently there have been literally a flood of publications and a number of national and international meetings concerned with housing the elderly. These meetings and writings abound in both service and research content and, in addition, reflect efforts to bring together into a functional relationship planners, providers of service, and research investigators.

On the research side there is clear documentation that housing can have decisive impact upon the life-styles and well-being of older persons; and on the policy and service side, there is a growing commitment to provide adequate housing for the elderly. With regard to coordinate efforts on the part of planners, service providers, and researchers, progress seems less clear. Moreover, despite the activity, housing remains a major problem among the old, and the best solutions remain to be specified. Only a small fraction of the elderly have been rehoused, and most knowledge comes from studies of these persons in new housing for the elderly.

Housing is no longer considered by itself but as one element, albeit an important one, in the environment of the aging person. It is now clearly perceived that characteristics of housing interact with those of other aspects of the living situation to produce their effects, and therefore that predictions must be based upon multivariate models for independent (environmental) variables. It is increasingly recognized that the "human element" in the equation creates its usual complications: generalizations about "older people" are even less useful than those about other age groups. We still have not taken with sufficient seriousness what Kelly (1955) pointed out long ago: individual differences increase with chronological age so that the oldest population segment is the least homogeneous.

A further sign of growing sophistication is the appearance of more elegant research designs and statistical analyses which go beyond differences between group means and take into account the possibility that outcomes depend upon interactions between personal characteristics and environmental components and that, for example, a living situation which is "good" for most people may be detrimental to those with certain traits or background characteristics.

The growing acceptance of a transactional view of the person-environment interaction, in gerontology as elsewhere, suggests the futility of designing housing and living environments which will automatically produce the desired behavior on the part of elderly persons in a reflex manner. The need is rather to understand the complex interplay of physical and social environment with the characteristics of the resident. Conceptual models are moving toward the dynamics of field theory, and unidirectional predictions from housing stimulus to human response are less common.

DEFINING THE TERMS

It is necessary to define, for purposes of this chapter, the main elements of its title.

Housing and Living Environment

One sign of growing maturity in this field is recognition of the limited utility in considering housing out of context. A broader and more functional concept is now generally in use. The "real objectives" of housing for the elderly "go far beyond the provision of suitable independent housing and living arrangements" and are "to stimulate a fuller, more meaningful life for the residents and to encourage their continuing development as useful contributing members of society" (Gozonsky, 1966). Housing for the elderly is "the life setting in its physical and social entirety, the context for living" (Carp, 1966a). Elderly housing is "a very special concept—one that should relate to every aspect of living," and in this "total living environment," supportive services are as vital as convenience of location, and the atmosphere of activity and interchange may be more important than square footage or closet space (U.S. Senate Special Committee on Aging, 1973). The living environment does not stop at the walls of the dwelling or the property line: "successful housing must occur within a matrix of transportation, shopping, recreation, medical service, and social and other opportunities" and "the value of the matrix may well overshadow the value of the individual dwelling unit itself" (Grant, in press).

Housing for the elderly is no longer viewed in isolation from other aspects of the surround. The problem of understanding the role of housing and of improving the living environment are hardly solved by this strategem; indeed, they are compounded. With housing narrowly defined, the suggested procedure was to analyze the living unit into its relevant physical components, specify the relevant characteristics of older persons, and determine the relationships between housing and person variables.

Now the environment side of the equation has been immeasurably extended and complicated by the recognition that effects of "housing" depend to a marked degree upon contextual factors not in themselves necessarily related to or dependent upon attributes of the building in question. Simultaneously with expansion of the limited concept of "housing" into the broader and less well-defined concept of "living environment," the goals of housing programs have broadened from provision of physical shelter to improving the quality of life. The goal is "establishment of environments required to satisfy the total needs of the older adult" (Donahue, in press). Exactly what is to be included within "living environment" is as yet unclear; and "quality of life," while commendable as a national goal (Proceedings of the White House Conference on Aging, 1973), is similarly imprecise in definition and measurement.

Definitions of housing and living environment vary in scope and specificity. The residential environment has been defined "rather broadly to include characteristics of the neighborhood and community" (Schooler, 1969). Characteristics of the neighborhood rather than those of the dwelling unit may be decisive in determining satisfaction with housing (Carp, 1966b; Havighurst, 1969). Main elements of the living environment include (a) age and ownership of dwelling units, (b) physical condition (state of dilapidation) and availability of funds for maintenance and repair, (c) location with regard to services needed by this age group, (d) proximity to commercial and recreational activities, (e) proximity to relatives and age peers, (f) accessibility and usability of transportation, (g) congeniality or threat in the surrounding environment, whether related to physical hazards (unrepaired streets and sidewalks, outdoor lighting, park areas) or person hazards (robberies, attacks, high pressure salesmen, neglect) (Havighurst, 1969).

At levels of planning, service provision, and research, the primary implication of the new definition of terms is the need for awareness of and coordination with what is going on in all elements of the transactional field of person-in-living-environment. However, there is the additional need for determination of primary responsibility for various areas. Here the concept of focus seems relevant. For example, while the architect must design with full knowledge of the sensory-motor status of the clientele and of the location of community services and transportation to them, his task is to focus this nonarchitectural knowledge upon his design in order to improve it as one component of the living environment.

Without the consistent imposition of focus, "it will be very easy in our deliberations to drift into discussions of tangential subjects which seem to be important to housing, such as income, transportation, and the like" (Proceedings of the 1971 White House Conference on Aging, 1973), to the detriment of progress in regard to any topic. Without continual recognition that all the topics are simply names for aspects of a transactional field, progress on any one may be illusory in terms of the goal. Thus, the concept of living environment requires continual coordination and integration of efforts around various points of focus.

Older People

Like the first term in the title for this chapter, the second lacks definition as to scope; is sometimes taken to mean one thing, sometimes another; and it changes with time. Age, health, retirement, life events, and the viewpoints of planners, service providers, and investigators are frequently used to define "older persons."

Age. In regard to housing, "older person" is often defined as one who has reached the chronological age at which he becomes eligible for housing for the elderly or for services intended to enable him to remain elsewhere in the community. The age varies according to the housing and other services under consideration, and has tended to decrease, both for public-supported facilities such as public housing and for privately-sponsored retirement communities.

Health. It has been suggested that indexes of sensory-motor competence, physiological status, or functional health are more appropriate than age to considerations of housing, both in planning and providing facilities and in conducting research. Design of living environments must take into account that 85 percent of non-institutionalized elderly persons have one or more chronic health conditions (Havighurst, 1969). Moreover, increasing age means that the world is sensed less clearly and less fully, and response to the environment is less quick, less strong, and less assured. The implications of these age-related decrements to housing are many (Carp, in press a). A policy of designing and assigning living environments on the basis of physical status rather than chronological age may be evolving. For example, for purposes of determining eligibility for rent supplement, the Housing and Community Development Act of 1974 defines "elderly family" as one which includes an elderly person or a *nonelderly* person with a handicap.

Retirement. Because of the importance of finances in the problems of housing, retirement may be a more useful index than time since birth in defining the vulnerable group. Typically, at retirement income is reduced by half; and some third of the population aged 65 and older have incomes below the poverty line (Brotman, in press), a line which is lower for them than for younger adults (Orshansky, 1965). Even with good retirement benefits, the retired person must compete for housing with a fixed income which is approximately half that to which he is accustomed. The housing he can afford is likely to be of poor quality and not well located for access to community resources, and his limited financial capability restricts every other element of his living environment. As a larger percentage of income is preempted by shelter, there is less left, for example, for transportation which will provide access to needed services and facilities, family and friends, self-enrichment opportunities, and those for community service (Carp, 1971).

Definition of "older people" in terms of retirement status rather than age creates a larger and younger group, with somewhat different housing needs. Kreps (1968) has documented the declining age at retirement in this country. The trend is similar in other industrial nations: the proportion of older retired adults has increased (Townsend and Bond, 1971). It is reported that in the Republic of China, men now retire at 55 and women at 50 (Centre Internationale de Gerontologie Sociale, 1974).

In addition to the economic factor, retirement has a decisive effect on availability of time, which is a central problem for older people (Kleemeier, 1961). The sudden acquisition of "unlimited time," exactly when funds to make use of the resources of broader society are sharply diminished, makes the immediate living environment of preeminent importance. To a great extent it is retirement rather than age as such that keeps older people in their homes more hours a day than any other segment of the population over the age of five.

Life events. Yet another approach to defining "old persons" is through use of a Life Events Index. Occurrence of important events, favorable as well as negative, is postulated to involve stress and has been demonstrated to precede physical illness (Holmes and Masuda, 1970; Rahe, 1972). Following this logic, it has been suggested that the decisive chronological age for onset of the problems of aging is about 50 because of the tendency for many important life events to occur at about that time in life, creating a climate of stress which predisposes individuals to health and other adaptive problems.

Viewpoint. Another factor inevitably involved in definition of "older person" is the viewpoint of the planner, service provider, or investigator. Each tends to perceive, as representative of the elderly, those persons with whom he has contact (Carp, 1974a).

Implications

A matrix is needed which will enable these disparate viewpoints and pieces of information to be viewed in the context of their meaning for the older population at large. The various definitions of "older person" have one thing in common: all record the status as decremental, which implies provision of living environments to compensate for losses. Aside from that, the various definitions result in different populations at a given time, and any one definition provides different groups across time. The definition of "housing and living environments" is ambiguous and changing, and the meaning of "older person" is variable and undergoing change; the picture is further complicated by constant alterations in the living environment and in the population of older persons, however defined. Drawing valid generalizations is difficult under these circumstances.

Construction of Housing for the Elderly

Compared to other industrialized nations, the United States was slow to undertake the task of housing its older citizens. Since the inception of federally-assisted programs in 1956, however, there has been an impressive amount of construction. Under its various programs the Department of Housing and Urban Development (USDHUD) has rehoused approximately 750,000 older people, and about 600,000 live in special housing for the elderly. (For a summary of these programs see Carp, in press b; Lawton, in press a.) Most are low-cost high-rise apartment houses, but a sizeable minority are retirement communities which serve the relatively well-to-do.

Effects of these Living Environments

What have been the effects of living in these new settings? Favorable reactions following the move to a low-rent apartment house were reported by Donahue (1966) and positive reactions following the move to a relatively affluent retirement community by Hamovitch (1968). The absence of comparison groups of non-movers limits generalization from these studies.

Investigations which included comparison groups (Bultena and Wood, 1969; Lipman, 1968; Sherman, 1973) similarly reported associations between various indexes of well-being and moving to new and assumedly better housing and living situations. These studies are limited in assigning improvement in well-being to changed housing, as cause, because comparisons of movers with nonmovers were cross-sectional.

A study using before-and-after design and comparing movers with nonmovers confirmed the favorable effects of improved housing upon the social and psychological well-being of older people (Carp, 1966b, 1966c). Results of a cross-validation with data from five different housing environments were consistent with those of the original study, except in regard to functional health (Lawton and Cohen, 1974).

Both the original study and the cross-validation reported on the first year of tenancy, which might represent a "honeymoon" period. However, a "validation across time" using data over an eight-year interval supported the early conclusions. For example, satisfaction with housing and living environment continued to be higher (Carp, 1975) and death and institutionalization rates lower (Carp, in press c) among residents of the elderly-designated public housing than among members of the comparison group.

Investigations into the effects of housing and living environments quite understandably have been conducted primarily within the new settings which have been constructed. These are generally of two kinds, relatively affluent retirement communities (Hamovitch, 1968; Bultena and Wood, 1969) and low-cost publicly supported facilities for the elderly (Carp, 1966b, 1966c, 1975, in press c; Donahue, 1966; Lawton and Cohen, 1974; Lipman, 1968). All are age-segregated. It is hazardous for a number of reasons to generalize regarding "housing and living environments" from data collected in these special housing situations and often on recent inmovers.

Moreover, care must be taken in generalizing from reactions of their applicants and tenants to those of "older people." Residents of retirement communities differ from the general population not only in economic status but also in age, education, health, ethnic background, and other characteristics; not least among them is the availability of transportation which makes community services and facilities accessible, effectively expanding their "living environments" beyond the housing unit. In housing, as in all areas of living, these are the old who have the most options and are in the best position to exercise those options.

Respondents in the Carp (1966b, 1966c), and Lawton and Cohen (1974) studies have similar demographic characteristics to older people in general. However these studies, too, deal with special populations. All were screened by admission policies which stressed capacity for independent living, and all were self-selected for this type of living environment. Moreover, being aware of the new housing and completing application for it must produce resident groups of relatively well-informed, independent, persistent, and perhaps even aggressive people. It is likely that, among the elderly with limited opinions, they tend to be the most capable of exercising the options which are available.

Justifiable conclusions from these studies of housing impact are that (1) low-cost housing for the elderly can be beneficial for the competent, healthy, poor older people who choose and manage to live in it; and that (2) retirement communities can be satisfactory, at least over the short run, to the economically and otherwise privileged older persons who choose them. There is also evidence that (3) the factors which predict short-run adjustment in elderly-designed public housing tend to predict long-range adjustment (Carp, 1974b), implying that the new environment will benefit (and not benefit) the same people in the long run as in the short.

HOUSING AND LIVING ENVIRONMENTS FOR THE MAJORITY

The number of persons under Housing and Urban Development programs is impressive, but the total represents only about 3 percent of older persons. There is little doubt that those rehoused in low-rent units were taken from substandard housing and environments which imposed social isolation or serious conflict. To what extent have these programs met the need for better housing and living environments among the older population? No one knows the size or shape of the remaining need (U.S. Senate Committee on Aging, 1973). There are estimates and opinions. Niebanck (1966) viewed the effects as "limited" and estimated that in urban areas alone there are 40 elderly households in need of housing for every one in public housing. A special analysis of Census data prepared by the United States Department of Housing and Urban Development revealed that at least 400,000 elderly housing units could be absorbed through the conventional market and that another 400,000 are needed for older persons unable to meet purchase or rental costs (Donahue, in press). Another "conservative" estimate of those who want housing is 20 percent of the elderly population or about 4 million people (Lawton, in press a).

One obstacle to definitive assessment of the need for housing has been the lack of an accurate and reliable methodology to measure need. Sears (1974) devised an objective method for determining need among low and moderate income elderly persons which has been applied to every city and town in New York State. The results indicate that projected construction "can hope to meet considerably less than 29% of the state's need." The assessment will be valuable in deciding where to locate those units which can be constructed, and it supports more subjectively determined estimates in demonstrating the continuing need for housing.

Federally subsidized low-cost housing and retirement communities, together, affect the lives of a small fraction of the older population. About 90 percent or over 18 million persons live neither in institutions nor in special housing. Most older people reside in ordinary housing in their communities, and very little is known about their housing and how it accommodates them or about their needs in regard to the living environment. What is known about the quality of their housing is not encouraging. One in every five elderly persons lives in substandard housing, that is, a unit which lacks basic plumbing facilities (Brotman, in press).

More than half of all elderly households live in units built in 1939 or earlier, many of them much earlier. Old people tend to remain in or gravitate to older parts of cities and old houses in towns and on farms.

Location of Residence

More than 60 percent live in metropolitan areas, most of them (6.8 million) in central cities and fewer (4.3 million) in the suburbs. In this the elderly differ from the population as a whole, in which suburbanites outnumber central city residents.

Inner-city elderly. The old poor of the inner city are among the victims of urban decay as the inner city is abandoned by the more affluent and mobile who move into more desirable living accommodations in safer and more attractive areas. The inner city is apt to house predominantly ethnic minority groups and the frailest of the old from the ethnic majority. The old people who remain tend to be "block bound" (Keller, 1968). An inverse relationship has been demonstrated between age and distance traveled to secure needed services (Pastalan, in press). The old of the inner city must rely on the local area and its inhabitants to support their needs, while most of today's society reach far from home to meet the needs of everyday life (Keller, 1968). The local area of the inner-city resident is likely to be a poor provider of housing and furnishes a generally impoverished living situation. Because of reduced mobility, services and facilities become increasingly less accessible and may cease to exist for the older resident. "The old are no more citizens of the city than was the kitchen maid of former generations a citizen of her mistress' house" (Bott, 1957).

Inner-city residents are more likely than other people to rent their homes (U.S. Department of Housing and Urban Development, 1973a), and the renter's dwelling tends to be in worse condition than the owner's. Among older people in urban slums, one study (Clark, 1971) reports that looking for better housing is ceaseless, even if it is only within the same neighborhood; and another, that there is complete lack of predictability in moving behavior, which is interpreted as "evidence for a lack of control over one's behavior which is typical of the disenfranchised city dweller" (Lawton, Kleban, and Carlson, 1973).

Suburban. There is a growing migration of older persons to the suburbs where the quality of housing and the environment tends to be better. This trend has obvious implications for future housing needs. It involves the potential hazard that more of the future old will be trapped in their own homes when they can no longer drive automobiles as so often happens to the old of today who live in the suburbs, where public transit is scarce (Vecsey, 1973; Carp, in press d).

Rural and small town. Seventeen percent of the elderly population live in rural nonfarm areas and 5 percent on farms. The average older person in a rural area must house himself on an income that is $400 to $700 less than that of the person his age who lives in a metropolitan area, and his housing often lacks things most people take for granted. Though most have electricity, one in three lacks basic plumbing facilities, a similar number are without a telephone, and even more lack central heating.

Especially if black, the rural old have the worst housing and living arrangements. For example, consider plumbing. Overall, for blacks the proportion of households without basic plumbing is four times that for whites (Brotman, in press).

The rural poor not only are the most impoverished segment of the older population and in the poorest housing, they are also less healthy and have more disabilities which create problems in dealing with everyday tasks about the home. In addition, they are more isolated. Because of the distance to facilities and lack of transportation, the "living environment" of the rural old is often constricted to the dwelling unit. While some evidence supports the notion that small towns provide a favorable social setting for life in the later years (Montgomery, 1966; Britton, 1966), historical differences may change this picture for tomorrow's old.

The rural aged are at a special disadvantage because of the scarcity of younger family members to assist financially and physically in rehabilitation and maintenance of their housing and because of the more stringent credit terms for financing home improvements. It has been estimated that 90 percent of the substandard rural and small town dwellings need federal assistance for rehabilitation, while only 2 percent of the combined efforts of the U.S. Department of Housing and Urban Development and the Farmers Home Administration have been directed to the dire needs of rural families in substandard housing.

Households of the Elderly

Most (14 out of 20) elderly people live in family settings, but a quarter live alone or with nonrelatives, and the remaining 1 in 20 is in an institution. The tendency for the old to maintain independent households rather than to live with children or other relatives seems to be growing. For example, in 1970 a third of all older women lived alone (or in some cases with nonrelatives) and maintained independent households, while ten years earlier the proportion was a quarter. The same trend is less pronounced for men, among whom independent households rose from 13 percent to 16 percent in the same time period.

The demand for living units in which they can maintain their own households is not new among the elderly. Provision of independent housekeeping units for old people dates back to the Middle Ages when almshouses were built in England, *hofje* in Holland (small houses around a garden court), and *die fuggerei* in Germany, which are among the oldest social welfare establishments in Europe (Beyer and Nierstrasz, 1967).

It is assumed in many Western nations that the old prefer and deserve independent living as long as they are able. In Sweden there is "complete unity" on the principle that "to the largest possible extent . . . . old people with all means shall be able to live an independent life as long as possible in their own homes" (Berggren, 1960). In Norway "the fundamental idea is that the aged should stay in their homes as long as possible, because they feel happy there and because it is the most practical and economical arrangement" (Old People's Health Committee, 1960). In The Netherlands "not only should every possibility be explored which would enable the aged to continue to live independently, but special facilities should be provided for them in their homes" (Van Zonneveld, 1958). In Switzerland "our main idea is to enable the old persons to live in their own homes as long as they are in a position to look after themselves" (Roth, 1961).

The trend toward maintenance of independent households has important implications for the amount and type of housing which will be required. In 1970 persons over age 60 represented 14 percent of the U.S. population, and those over 65 constituted 10 percent of the total, a proportion that was only 4.2 percent in 1890. Four thousand people reach age 65, and 3000 die each day, for a net daily increase of 1000 new older people. The elderly are predicted to number 29 million by the year 2000 (Brotman, in press).

Moreover, independent living is more prevalent and increasing more rapidly, among women. There are three times as many women as men who live alone (U.S. Department of Housing and Urban Development, 1973a), and the trend of increase toward maintenance of independent households is much sharper among women. Meeting the future demand for independent living units is further complicated by the fact that in conjunction with this growing propensity to live independently is the wish to live near children (Schorr, 1960; Brody, 1970).

Types of Housing

Home Owners. Most older people live in ordinary houses, apartments, or rooms in their communities. Seven in every ten persons over 65 live in homes they own (Brotman, in press). There are many advantages to home owning, important among them rent-free housing and independence. Owning one's home, though, is also a burden which may be especially heavy to the old with reduced physical and financial resources. The renter can more easily move. The home owner must contend with deteriora-

tion, rising mortgage and insurance rates, the difficulties of selling and of buying a more appropriate (cheaper, smaller, more conveniently located) house, and the reluctance to leave a familiar neighborhood or to remain while it decays around him. "The special problems in housing the aged are in many cases due not to aging persons, but to urban decay, or to aging of the physical plant in which they live" (Gottesman, 1970).

The increasing problems of home ownership must be considered in conjunction with what seems to be a continuing and even increasing desire among older people to be home owners. In 1970, 72.4 percent of persons 60 or older were home owners, compared to 67.1 percent of the population at large (U.S. Department of Housing and Urban Development, 1973a). On the whole, a larger proportion of older than of younger people are home owners and, although this proportion falls off after age 65, even among the oldest group, the proportion in owner-occupied units is larger than for Americans generally. The need is obvious for programs to provide mortgage, insurance, and maintenance supports to enable older people to remain in homes they own, if that is their desire, without undue hardship.

Apartments. Most elderly renters live in apartments. These tend to be in older buildings in older parts of cities, where rents are relatively low but amenities are few, safety poor, and tenure often insecure. In older residential sections of cities, large homes are often partitioned into rental units. Facilitation of this process has been proposed as one natural solution to the problem of housing the elderly, especially considering the fact that it might assist older home owners who have too much space.

No data seem to exist on the extent of this conversion, the numbers of elderly persons occupying these residences, or of the physical and social conditions of the units in relation to the needs of their elderly tenants. The fact that one-room "apartments" subdivided out of large, old, formerly single-family dwellings are the situations from which many applicants for public housing for the elderly seek relief (Carp, 1966b) suggests that this living situation is a common and deleterious environment for the elderly poor.

Rooms and Boarding Houses. About 600,000 elderly persons live as roomers, either as non-relatives in households (456,000) or as occupants of rooming houses and other groups quarters (146,000). Old men in particular gravitate to old hotels and boarding houses. Hotels the old can afford tend to be in central cities and dilapidated, and tenure is often insecure due to programs of urban renewal and other more profitable use of the land. Boarding houses tend to be of varying but often poor quality because of the lack of local regulation.

Mobile Home Parks. A growing number of lower-middle class elderly are turning to the economic advantages of mobile home ownership and to the small homogeneous environment that the parks provide. Johnson (1971) maintains that residents feel a sense of community as well as one of security in this environment, and suggests that mobile home technology should be used to produce low-cost housing in other cultural and economic enclaves, possibly in urban as well as suburban areas.

College Campuses. With declining enrollment and the desire of many students to live off campus, it has been suggested that using vacated dormitories for elderly housing might benefit both aging people and colleges. Research is underway on a group of older persons who have taken up residence in a high-rise apartment house for the elderly on the Syracuse University campus.

Intermediate Housing. The concept of intermediate housing arose from observation of the need for housing among relatively independent elderly who do not need institutional care but who are unhoused, those on waiting lists for new housing, and those who cannot afford other housing. The Philadelphia Geriatric Center provided services designed to maximize tenant independence to the residents of a refurbished area of row houses adjacent to the Center which provide more protection and support than is usual in independent housing.

The first five years of this demonstration project led to expansion of the program (Lawton, in press a). This approach to housing fills a need for those who want to maintain their autonomy and for whom the move to a child's home or an extended care facility is not an appropriate choice, but it is available to very few persons.

In summary, there is a scarcity of data on how most elderly people live, and much must be left to conjecture. It is known that about three in each 100 have been rehoused under U.S. Department of Housing and Urban Development programs, most of them in low-rent apartments, but a significant minority in retirement communities. An additional, unknown but probably small, number are in facilities built entirely under private auspices. It is also known that out of every 20 old persons, 14 live in homes they own, and one is in an institution. The remaining five are distributed among apartments, boarding houses, and hotels. Within each of these categories, knowledge is lacking regarding the adequacy of living environments. The present review indicates that society faces a very large problem if there is genuine commitment to providing adequate living environments for older Americans.

Groups at Special Risk

The problems of housing and living environment are not distributed evenly across the elderly population but tend to accumulate for certain subgroups. Who are the people multiply handicapped in this regard? Ironically, they are likely to be not only the most isolated and most frail but also the least visible and least vocal of the older population. Those most in need of better housing and living environments are probably least capable of making their needs known. For them the various disadvantages common to the old are exaggerated: they tend to have even greater poverty, worse health, and less education. In addition, they must cope with racial and ethnic discrimination, language exclusions, and widowhood. The most disadvantaged elderly live in inner cities and on farms. They can also be identified as members of other population subgroups.

Mexican-American, Spanish-Speaking and Spanish-Surname. Elderly Mexican-Americans of San Antonio, Texas have less adequate housing than do Anglo-American old of the same city; they also are in poorer health and have lower levels of income and education (Carp, 1969a). Similarly, in the inner city of New York, the Spanish-speaking (mostly Puerto Rican) elderly live in the worst housing conditions and have the smallest incomes, the most health problems, and the least education (Cantor, in press).

Mexican-Americans seem far less likely than Anglo-Americans to seek low-cost housing for the elderly. In a city where Mexican-Americans comprised half the population, only 3 to 4 percent of the applicants for elderly public housing were Mexican-American (Carp, 1966b, 1969a). This may be due to location of the projects (Carp, 1969a, 1972), and it may reflect different life-styles and values (Carp, 1969b), the use of different information channels (Carp, 1970), and the economic advantage of home ownership (Carp, 1969b), as well as overt or subtle discrimination.

Asian-Americans. Elderly residents of America's Chinatowns probably are housed less adequately even than other urban aged, and they tend to have the lowest incomes, least education, and most health problems (Carp and Kataoka, in press). Asian-Americans, like Latin-Americans, have special barriers against access to the community as a result of language and culture differences not only between themselves and the majority society but also among themselves. Dialect differences bar communication even between Chinese-Americans. Like the Mexican-American, the elderly Asian-American's background is from another society, and because of recent immigration and rapid acculturation, a family may include not only several generations but also several levels of Westernization and wide educational differences.

There is need for research on how to house these and other cultural groups which is not localized nor biased by the views of Anglo-American investigators. On the other hand "Asian-Americans have less visibility and less power in obtaining services than members of

larger and more politically aggressive groups" and some housing programs should be promptly implemented rather than further studied. "We are not concerned about provisions that better housing improves health, adds to longevity, or betters social relationships. If older Asian-Americans wish the improved housing—and knowing how inadequate much present housing is—we will accept this as a given" (Kalish and Yuen, 1971).

Black. The housing problems of the black elderly are similar to those of older people in general, but "exaggerated and compounded by a more deeply embedded and concentrated poverty, as well as by other factors such as racial discrimination" (Jackson, 1971). About 70 percent of the black elderly live in poverty. "If you are black and live in a Southern state, your chances are 41 out of 100 of lacking one or more basic plumbing facilities" (Lawton, in press a).

In regard to housing the old, the black population has mostly relied on what resources they could mobilize themselves "because the larger society has refused to recognize them" (Jackson, 1971). Blacks are much less likely than their white counterparts to become "older persons" and therefore to qualify for special housing programs for the elderly. Twice the proportion of whites than of blacks reach age 75; blacks comprise 11.5 percent of the population under 65 and only 7.8 percent of the population 65 and older. The shorter life expectancy of blacks is consistent with the higher incidence of poor health and physical problems and the lower rate of medical care. These facts suggest the need for special attention to design features and inclusion of health services in the living environments of black elderly persons.

Jewish Slum-Dwellers. Aged Jewish residents of an urban slum, like elderly slum dwellers of other ethnic-racial backgrounds, were found to be in very poor housing; in addition, they were in less good health, less mobile, less socially interactive, participated in fewer activities, and had lower morale than aged Jewish persons in better parts of town (Lawton,

Kleban and Singer, 1971). They ascribed much of their difficulty to the living environment.

Widows. Widowhood for either sex typically brings with it a cluster of social, physical, economic, and psychological problems. Most older men are married and live with their spouses; most older women are widowed. Besides having longer life expectancies, women tend to marry men older than themselves. Almost 40 percent of husbands aged 65 and older have under-65 wives. This age discrepancy between spouses compounds women's chances of becoming widows.

Over half the elderly widows live alone or with nonrelatives (Brotman, in press); the older the widow, the more likely she is to live alone. Elderly widows comprise the most poverty-stricken population segment, with smallest budgets for housing and for other services. Their living environments tend to be dilapidated, isolating, and unsafe. In inner New York City poverty areas with the highest incidence of social disorganization (crime, welfare case load, deteriorated housing), the highest incidence of single person households is "among the frailest segment of the white population—older people in their 70's and 80's, particularly among widowed, single women" (Cantor, in press). The changing ethnic composition of the inner city accentuates the isolation of these elderly people.

Despite policy decisions and staff actions to create resident groups balanced with regard to sex, most public housing vacancies are filled by women alone. This supply of housing is far from adequate to accommodate their numbers, and the increasing preponderance of older women requires special attention to planning and design of living environments. The greater numbers of older women plus their attraction to public housing combine to saturate those living situations with females, while old men drift to old hotels and rooming houses. The result is a tendency toward sex as well as age segregation among the old, and particularly among the old who are alone. The consequences and determinants of this phenomenon are not well understood. When the concentration of women reaches some threshold, the social situation seems to become less attractive to men (Carp, 1966b). Physical design may contribute. For example, men may prefer the availability of meals and be more content with only a room to live in and take care of, while emphasis in public-supported housing has been on individual kitchens. Some variety of units might improve the sex-distribution of tenants.

Rosow's (1966, 1967) study in old apartment houses in Cleveland and Lopata's (1971) pilot study at a new retirement hotel in Chicago indicate that housing builders and managers can contribute to the welfare of older people who live alone by providing situations which facilitate social interaction.

Poorly Educated. Low levels of education characterize each multiple-handicap group. A study of the aged poor found that education figured prominently in regard to housing satisfaction: "As expected, those with less education, less income, and who lived alone tended to have more housing needs. But of these three variables, education was almost as important as the other two put together" (Palmore, 1971).

Housing and the Multiply-Deprived. There are many parallels among the problems of the various multiple-jeopardy groups. Low in social-economic status, with reduced mobility, little education, many health problems, and often alone, they are trapped by circumstances. "Deplorable housing conditions rank first in their complaints about their lot" (Clark, 1971).

Moreover, those most in need of housing may be least likely to obtain it. Jackson (1972) compared urban, low-income black aged applicants who were accepted into new public housing for the elderly with those who were not and observed "an apparent tendency for the selection process to favor those among the blacks who, in some sense, may be the *least deprived*." The most deprived elderly may be least likely even to *seek* better housing. When those of all racial/ethnic identities were considered, applicants for public housing for the elderly, while obviously deserving, were not the community residents in worst conditions of housing (Carp, 1969a). In the latter study there was no evidence of bias in the selection of tenants, but ethnic minorities, among whom housing tended to be least adequate, were grossly under-represented among the applicants.

Effects of Living Environments

Very little is known about the impact of the housing and living environments upon the well-being of the majority of the old, just as little is known about the housing and living environments themselves. Since practically all studies show improvement in well-being following the move to new housing, it is apparent that the former living environments of the rehoused had negative connotations. However, it is not known how much the current living environments of the majority resemble the environments from which the rehoused came. Also, as discussed earlier, those who have benefited from the new living situations are not representative of the older population at large. There have been significant selective biases. One source is institutional: "Both governmental and sponsoring groups tend to think of housing for the elderly as a resource for the very limited segment of the older population who a) have a housing problem and b) are healthy and independent" (Lawton, 1969). In addition, self-selection into the new facilities probably increases person-situation congruence, and this may be a major factor in adaptation and satisfaction there (Carp, 1968; Kahana, in press).

Information is sadly lacking on the housing and living environment of the typical old person and on its effects upon his life-style and well-being. Two indexes of its adequacy upon which there is some, though limited, evidence are (1) efforts to move and (2) stated satisfaction with the existing situation.

Residential Mobility. The elderly are less likely to move than are young adults. For example, during 1955-1960, 50 percent of the population but only 30 percent of persons 65 and older changed their place of residence (Lenzer, 1965). Rates of moving may be a poor basis for determining satisfaction on the part of the older population, in view of "the almost total lack of data on elderly people

who would like to move but cannot" (Havighurst, 1969). Clark (1971) found among urban poor elderly that the search for different housing was "ceaseless." Older people are much less successful than younger ones in realizing the wish to move. Among persons who planned and desired to move, 61 percent of young adults but only 37 percent of the elderly did so. "More than 6 out of every 10 of the older population did not fulfill their plans and desires to move, compared to less than 4 out of every 10 of the younger population" (Goldscheider, Van Arsdol and Sabagh, 1966). If the traditional age 65+ had been used to define the elderly, the difference might be even more extreme; these investigators used age 50 as the cutting point.

Within the older population, the degree of physical, mental, and economic competence of the individual tends to determine whether he moves or remains. In a residual, deprived population, the least competent did not want to move, and the most competent did, but "who actually leaves is likely to be determined by circumstances" (Lawton, Kleban, and Carlson, 1973). Available evidence suggests that residential mobility is an inadequate index of satisfaction with housing and living environment among older people.

Keller (1968) makes an important comment regarding the role of actual or perceived alternatives: "Where these are few, people may say that they are satisfied in their present surroundings, but they may be among the first to move once a realistic opportunity presents itself." Keller concludes that, for this reason, it is difficult to predict residential turnover solely on the basis of current attitudes.

Evaluation of Current Housing and Living Environment. Keller's finding also casts doubt upon the validity of older people's stated evaluations of their living situations. Verbal evaluation of present housing seems to be in part a function of the options available. From the fact that elderly people say they are "satisfied" with present housing, it is not safe to conclude they would not move or prefer some other mode. Many studies (for example, Britton, 1966; Carp, 1966b; Hamovitch, Peterson and

Larson, 1969; Montgomery, 1966; Lawton, Kleban and Carlson, 1973; Winiecke, 1973) report favorable assessment, by residents, of housing which investigators rated as poor. "The respondents' perception of self and of housing leads to speculation on how much of their evaluation was fact and how much was a defense mechanism to drive from their psychological field the threat of the inevitable" (Britton, 1966).

When the person has no option, evaluations of deleterious living environments may include some element of defense. This possibility is suggested by the comments of many investigators working with older people in poor housing to the effect that the evaluations of their situations by the old are consistently more favorable than those of data collectors and other observers. This possibility is supported by changes in evaluations when an option became available. In each of two situations of public housing for the elderly, when announcement was made regarding first admissions, and before anyone moved, evaluations of current housing became more negative among applicants who were offered apartments, but evaluations remained stable for those who were not (Carp, in press e).

THE NEED

The limited evidence suggests that housing continues to be a major problem among members of the older population and one which is underestimated by available data. The construction of facilities for the elderly, while apparently beneficial to those it serves, has touched the lives of a small fragment and an unrepresentative sample of the older population. It has tended also to be of two rather limited types: high-rise low-rent public housing for the elderly and relatively affluent retirement communities. In view of the diversity and changing characteristics of the older population, there is need to create a wider variety as well as a larger supply of beneficial living environments.

Innovation and Evaluation

As yet, planners and designers have no adequate basis for deciding what that variety of living

environments should encompass. "The most significant shortcoming in housing research is the failure to design and build purely experimental units" (Havighurst, 1969). In the absence of clear evidence, designers of policy and of physical facilities should be imaginative and try new concepts. "As a corollary, to provide more solid bases for subsequent action, evaluative studies of the effects of these innovations should be built into their implementation" (Carp, 1966a).

Involvement of Older Persons in Planning, Design, and Evaluation

An old person may be the first to discern design flaws (Carp, 1966b) but is "completely by-passed in the decisions regarding the kind of building he will have to use" (Lawton, in press a). Early involvement of persons similar to those for which a facility is being planned might elicit novel and practical suggestions while they could be implemented. Mock-ups and other simulation techniques to pretest these and other innovations might be highly cost-effective. Evaluation by users should be a normal follow-up on any environmental intervention and should be required for all which involve public funds.

Architectural solutions to problems of the elderly which are proposed by (usually younger) experts may even create special difficulties for older persons (Carp, 1966b). Such design features not only fail in their purpose but are financially wasteful. On a broader level of planning, while the expert and the elderly person agree in regard to the basic problems in the living environment, proposed solutions differ.

Riesenfeld, Newcomer, Berlant, and Dempsey (1972) found the needs identified by public administrators and by the elderly poor to be similar: good mobility, accessible health care, economic housing, consumer goods, and protective services. Proposed solutions were basically different. Agency personnel tended toward institution-based solutions such as low-rent elderly housing, mini-buses for the elderly, and health clinics. Elderly people suggested supportive services which would allow people maximum flexibility and choice while remaining where they were in the community: discount cards, special bus routes, reduced transit fares, consumer protection programs, and telephone assurance services. Solutions suggested by the old seemed to be directed toward improving present housing and providing access to facilities in the community rather than toward relocation and the creation of special facilities. For example, in regard to medical care they preferred adequate transportation to the clinic or hospital of their choice over moving to be near an elderly-care facility.

Improvement of Living Environments

Riesenfeld's data combined with other evidence of the preference of older people to remain in homes they own suggest the need to improve the quality of the present living environments of the elderly. Development and evaluation of programs for the better use of existing housing stock and neighborhoods are at least as important as construction and evaluation of new facilities, considering the proportions of older people who do and probably will reside in each. Information is badly needed concerning methods of improving the use of existing housing and of meeting the needs of elderly persons who prefer to remain in such housing.

In this regard the United States might learn much from the experience of other nations in housing their older citizens. Perhaps the task of caring for those among the elderly who are relatively intact and who desire their independence takes a certain sophistication which comes with experience in handling the problems of the old and their housing. In all countries it seems that the first step in providing for the old takes the form of institutional arrangements. A variety of nursing homes, nonhousekeeping homes for the elderly, and geriatric hospitals have been in operation for a number of years in many nations. However, "the special non-institutional housing programs for elderly and handicapped who under normal circumstances can shift for themselves if they live in suitable accommodations are of recent date" (Engberg, 1961). The movement to provide them began in several countries in the 1930's and accelerated after World War II.

Financial Assistance. Housing is less expensive for the old in some countries than it is in the United States. For example, in France old people pay a lower percentage of their income for housing and related costs than they do in this country (Centre Internationale de Gerontologie Sociale, 1974). Several countries provide financial assistance to elderly persons to enable them to remain in and to maintain their own homes. For example, in Norway elderly people whose residences are in need of repair may borrow money to modernize and recondition them from the State Housing Bank at favorable rates of interest (U.S. Department of Housing and Urban Development, 1973b). Assistance is graded according to the age of the building and the owner's income and is available for homes only ten years old. At age 65 every person in Sweden is entitled to an old-age pension, and about half the pensioners receive a supplemental housing allowance (U. S. Department of Housing and Urban Development, 1973b).

Home Services. In addition to assistance with the costs of housing and its maintenance, many nations have experience in providing additional services which help to define the quality of the living environment and which prolong independent living. In Norway there is not only home nursing but also an extensive home service which provides assistance with everyday tasks of housekeeping, such as housecleaning and window cleaning, bed making, shopping, food preparation, laundry, and clothes cleaning (U.S. Department of Housing and Urban Development, 1973b). Sweden also has an extensive home services program, with about a third of its staff on the government payroll and the larger number paid by other agencies. The purpose of these home services is to help old people remain in their own homes as long as possible, and toward this end it includes occupational therapy and home nursing as well as home care (U.S. Department of Housing and Urban Development, 1973b). Similarly, in Denmark an extensive domestic help service assists the old and the handicapped to maintain their own living arrangements as long as possible (Beyer and Nierstrasz, 1967).

Day Hospitals. Another type of program aimed at extending the period during which elderly people can live in their own homes is that of the day hospital. The day hospitals emphasize medical treatment and preventive care at the facility, including physical therapy, dental and podiatric care, and eye examinations in an atmosphere which they try to prevent from becoming "sick oriented." In order to prolong independent living they may also provide health services at home (McGuire, 1969).

Construction of New Living Environments

Attention to the housing needs of older people in the United States has largely focused on design and construction of special housing for the elderly, whether low-cost facilities or those for the relatively well-to-do. Obviously, it is in many ways easier to provide a homogeneous environment (Lawton, 1970) and to supply services to a concentrated and age-homogeneous population with similar life-styles (Sherman, Mangum, Dodds, Walkley, and Wilner, 1968).

Other nations have taken a somewhat different course in constructing housing, just as they have tended more to deliver services to people in their homes. In the countryside of England, clusters of two-story houses for young families include smaller numbers of one-story cottages for the old. In the suburbs of French cities, low-rise apartment buildings for the old share grounds with high-rise multi-age units. In Sweden, special housing for the old is built within housing for all ages.

Moreover, in Sweden "collective housing" has been designed to meet simultaneously the needs of young families in which both parents work, the unmarried, and the elderly who can afford it and are no longer able to remain in their former homes despite the program of home services (U.S. Department of Housing and Urban Development, 1973b). Collective houses provide the amenities of hotels, such as restaurants, cleaning, and laundry. Nursing care is available. These houses provide an old person the independence of a private apartment and the assurance of needed day-to-day and emergency services. While he is no longer in his earlier home, he remains within an environment which includes all age groups.

Clarification of the Role of Age Distribution

No doubt largely because housing constructed in this country for the elderly has been designed and specified for old-age tenants, interest in both planning and research tends to focus on the relative merits of age-segregated and age-integrated housing. To some extent this may be a semantic artifact: the appropriate and handy label "housing for the elderly" is used to refer to a complex concept which includes many components in addition to the age of occupants. Use of the label may oversimplify thinking: the fact that an event occurs *in* "housing for the elderly" may be but is not necessarily *because* it is housing limited to older people. Age segregation is one of many ways in which "housing for the elderly" in this country differs from alternative living environments. Low-cost housing for the elderly and retirement communities seem to have been largely successful, and there is a tendency to attribute this to the age homogeneity of their residents.

Rosow's Classic Study. The importance of having an adequate supply of age-peers in the immediate neighborhood was compellingly documented in a classic study by Rosow (1967). This landmark study had tremendous impact on the entire field of gerontology. Rosow found significant advantage in all aspects of socialization for apartment-dwellers whose buildings included a larger proportion of units with older tenants as compared to those in buildings with fewer units housing age-peers. Furthermore, he demonstrated that the advantage increased with the lower status or disadvantage of the old person.

Problems of Generalizing to Housing for the Elderly. Early evidence of the satisfactory experience with housing for the elderly coincided in time with Rosow's evidence pointing to the socialization benefits of a residential environment with a rich supply of age-peers. This coincidence may have influenced thinking toward the view that total age segregation in housing is ideal for older people.

Such a radical extrapolation from Rosow's

work seems questionable on several grounds: (1) Rosow's work was not conducted in new housing for the elderly but in old apartment houses; (2) Rosow defined "age dense" neighborhoods as apartment houses in which 40–50 percent of the living units had at least one elderly occupant, while public-supported housing for the elderly requires that 100 percent of the occupant households include at least one elderly (or handicapped) person. The difference in age homogeneity of neighbors between the two situations is obviously great. Retirement communities are more similar to Rosow's apartment buildings in regard to age composition of residents. According to Hamovitch (1968), who studied retirement villages in California where there has been a boom in this type of construction for the upper-middle class, these newer communities tend not to be as age-segregated as many believe.

(3) Rosow studied long-time residents of apartment houses while tenants in the newly constructed housing were the first inmovers. (4) Rosow studied people in old housing and old, established neighborhoods with which they were familiar. Most tenants of the low-cost facilities had moved from substandard and socially isolating housing to newly built projects which included special design features for the elderly as well as many accessible new neighbors, and residents of retirement communities had left their accustomed living environments for new and apparently preferred ones. All were in situations which were new, physically and socially; new to each inmover and new as physical facilities and communities. (5) Also important for purposes of making wide generalizations regarding effects of neighborhood age composition, both Rosow's respondents and the residents of age-segregated facilities are special population subgroups, and no one knows how they differ from one another or from the population of older people.

Studies in Age-Specified Housing. Early evidence from studies in age-segregated living situations found them to be satisfactory milieux for aging (Carp, 1966b, 1966c; Donahue, 1966; Hamovitch, 1968; Peterson and Larson, 1966; Sherman et al., 1968) as does limited long-term evidence (Carp, 1975, in press c). Generally, studies indicate higher rates of activity and social interaction in age-segregated housing. Findings on morale are less clear. Both Messer (1967) who studied elderly residents of age-segregated and age-integrated public housing, and Sherman (1974) who compared residents in special housing for elderly with people in dispersed housing, found social participation greater in the former. However, Sherman found "outlook on life only moderately related to activity" while Messer found "a high level of interaction to be associated with high morale among older people living in a mixed-age environment; the relationship disappears, however, in the age-homogeneous sample. (In fact, it is slightly reversed.)"

Confounding Variables. It is difficult to reconcile these findings or to generalize from them with respect to age segregation because special housing for the elderly is different from dispersed housing in many ways, just as public housing specified for the elderly is different in many ways, in addition to age of residents, from public housing for general use.

The fact that a facility is age-specified is only one of a number of its characteristics yet there seems to be a tendency to attribute favorable reactions to this feature. For example, Winiecke (1973) mentions "three salient advantages" of aged housing projects: improved living conditions, increased social contacts, and reduced rents. The respondents, who were poor (Old Age Assistance recipients), were informed of the low-cost public housing to be built for the elderly and then were asked about "special housing centers or apartment buildings for old people." The investigator seemed to conclude that the favorable-unfavorable tenor of their responses bore specifically upon the fact that facilities would be limited to the old—not to reduced rents or better living conditions. The conclusion regarding "interest in age-segregated housing" is particularly questionable in view of the fact that this tendency was *not* demonstrable in answers to a direct question about preference for living in a place with people the same age *vs.* other ages: "It remains unclear why respondents interested in aged housing wished to live around people like themselves but not specifically of the same age."

Use of the labels "age-segregated housing" and "aged housing" to describe living situations whose attractiveness to old people was *not* related to their attitude toward age homogeneity of residents may prove confusing. The author of this chapter contributed to the problem far earlier: the study of Victoria Plaza (Carp, 1966b) is cited as support for age segregation in housing the elderly. The favorable report is on "housing for the elderly" and, while an entire book describes the many facets of the living environment, it is the label that sticks in the mind of the reader.

The study of Victoria Plaza has no data on age segregation *vs.* age integration. The living situations from which applicants came were different from the new one in quality of housing, security of tenure, and imposition of social constraints or pressures, as well as age of neighbors. No one variable can be singled out as *the* operant or even predominant one in the favorable impact of the new situation. To the direct question, most residents were favorable to the age restriction (as they were to all characteristics about which they were queried) but open-end questions regarding good and bad features of the living situation evoked only a few negative comments about "living with nobody but old people" and not one favorable mention of the age composition of the tenant group.

With regard to gains in sociability, perceived health, longevity, delay of institutionalization, self-concept, and morale, it is scarcely tenable to conclude that favorable effects of new, inexpensive, good quality housing which provides access to activities and to other people is due to the age-segregation policy for admission. Such favorable effects may be the result of age segregation, but the data at hand do not warrant this attribution, and there are other legitimate contenders for the causal role.

The main problem in conducting decisive research on the age composition issue is the difficulty of locating sites for research which are otherwise equivalent and whose tenants are similar. The old who move into age-segregated housing generally move also into new, cleaner, more modern, and safer facilities. While it is true that tenants, as a consequence of the move, usually have easier access to old people, it is also true that this represents improved access to people of any sort. These improvements in the physical and social environment probably play some role in increasing the various indexes of well-being.

Such "halo" effects probably also influence evaluations of the policy of age segregation. Investigators must be more sophisticated and remember the imprecations of their mentors in measurement: stimulus materials to elicit reactions to age segregation must not incorporate other elements of the situation. Consider the "stimulus pull" of a typical question: "What do you think of a place like (this), designed for the elderly?" In the contexts in which they are often asked, even less explicitly "loaded" questions may evoke maximum halo.

Teaff, Lawton, and Carlson (1973) tried to control for the effects on self-report of life activities of certain physical environmental characteristics (number of apartment units, number of elderly-occupied apartments, number of apartments per acre, scatter of project and building height) as well as some background characteristics of the tenant group (social class, race, religion, and ethnicity). They found elderly tenants in age-segregated public housing to have higher rates of activity participation, better functional health, greater satisfaction with housing, higher mobility, higher morale, and more family interaction than those in age-integrated projects.

Even this degree of control may not be sufficient. The facilities did differ in age (as most age-segregated and age-integrated housing facilities do), and selective factors not revealed by the demographic items may have been in operation. For example, several studies demonstrate life-style and motivational differences between people who do and those who do not prefer age-segregated living situations. Hamovitch, Peterson, and Larson (1969) investigated the desired characteristics of housing with samples of persons in a wide variety of settings (congregate and isolated housing for upper-middle, middle, and low-income groups; church-related housing ventures; trailer parks; union persons in urban areas of both high and low age-density; those living in age-integrated communities, those who had moved to age-segregated communities, and those who had moved away from them). They found that preference for age-density was consistently related with characteristics of present housing (quality and single-family vs. apartment) and with personal and social characteristics (marital status, social class, and distance from children).

Other investigators report similar findings. Winiecke (1973) found that type of current living arrangement was related to interest in housing designated for the elderly. She points out that "the elderly are not being offered cheap age dense housing but cheap, age dense *apartment* housing." Understandably, then, various investigators find that older people who prefer or who move to housing for the elderly tend to be previous apartment-dwellers rather than among the large majority who are home owners. Winiecke also found that permanency of residence and security of tenure "figure strongly in an elderly person's decision to move to age segregated housing." Sherman *et al.* (1968) report that many retirement community residents had no children nearby and would like to see their children more often than they did.

With regard to views on age integration of neighborhoods to the extent of having families with children living nearby, Hamovitch, Peterson, and Larson (1969) found that the majority of those presently in high-density age-peer situations were negative, while those presently in low-density age-peer situations were about evenly split. (If these respondents were "weighted up" to approximate their representation in the population, the preference would of course be nearer the latter.) Winiecke's (1973) respondents who were "interested in age segregated housing" tended to be renters rather than home owners, dependent upon buses rather than automobile drivers, lonely and bored people who "would rather live in a place where everyone is pretty much like themselves rather than live among different types of people" though, as noted above, most of them did not prefer living only with people their own age.

The residents of age-specified housing tend to be different from others of their age-peers, and they comprise a small fraction of the older population. Generalizations regarding effects of age segregation in living situations on life-style and well-being are not warranted on the basis of existing data. Comparisons of the relative merits of age homogeneity and age heterogeneity in living environment are almost totally dependent upon stated preferences. Data regarding preferences include bias from respondent selection and halo effect.

The longer experience in other Western countries calls into question the wisdom of constructing disproportionate amounts of age-specific housing. In a study of three towns in France, a wish frequently voiced by the elderly, along with wishes for higher pensions and lower rents, was not to be isolated from other people, younger people as well as those their own age. "Avoiding segregation is one of the most important things; old people need to have youth around them, and the reverse is true" (Burch and Collot, 1972). In the Federal Republic of Germany, it is considered that collection of old people in housing for the aged can easily isolate them from society. To prevent this, housing provides for a mixture of generations (Blume, in press).

In regard to the characteristics old people in this country desire in housing, Hamovitch, Peterson, and Larson (1969) found that access to facilities and services ranked first, followed in order by climate, privacy, nearness to relatives, and, finally, neighbors similar in age, class, and race. Gottesman (1970) concluded that while many prefer to be among the old, "evidence is accumulating that a homogeneous concentration of disadvantaged individuals, whether old or not, yields negative effects on individuals' feelings about themselves and on their society's reactions to them."

A Gerontological Society Committee on Research and Development Goals in Social Gerontology commented: "That a preponderance of adults, in old age, will prefer or accept highly age homogeneous environments is an absurdity" (Havighurst, 1969). A study of TIAA-CREF beneficiaries concluded: "Clearly there are many people who wish to associate with persons other than those of the same age" and "in fact, there are few more recurrent themes, whether connected with 'where to live' or 'what to do,' than the wisdom of associating with persons of all ages, even with children— but perhaps not too much" (Ingraham, 1974).

Studies are needed with people who represent the entire range of the elderly population, in situations and formats which reduce response bias in questions relating to preferences, and which assess the impact of age composition of neighborhood within the context of other normally concurrent characteristics in such a way as to partial out their effects.

Theoretical Explanations of Age-Density Effects. The socially facilitating effect of *homogeneity* was Rosow's (1967) theory base and is perhaps the most common basis proposed to predict or explain advantages of age-segregated living environments. Age homogeneity is easily confounded and confused with other varieties of similarity. Most housing projects for the elderly seem to attract people who resemble each other in a number of ways. The most immediately apparent similarity is in income, due to the narrow range for admission to low-cost housing and the small percentage of elderly people who can afford retirement community living.

Sponsors try to select the healthy and competent. Normally, capacity for independent living is a formal requirement for admission. "Some housing administrators, very touchy about potential problems, bend over backward to exclude all but the most independent older people, or move quickly to seek other accomodations for them if their housekeeping or personal habits show a decline" (Lawton, 1970). In this, staff may be supported by other tenants (Carp, 1966b). The result of these formal and informal pressures is a resident community of continuing and even increasing homogeneity along a variety of dimensions.

Among members of a homogenous population, differences that exist seem to be highlighted and finer gradations of similarity to become important in social behavior, as homogeneity theory would predict. German-born Jews tend to choose each other rather than Jews born elsewhere as friends (Lawton and Simon, 1968). Black and white residents of the same housing tend to choose friends of their own "color" (Nash, Lawton and Simon, 1968).

Role theory has also been cited in explaining the advantages of age-specified housing. For example, Seguin (1973) reported on a participant observation study of a retirement community that the residents "generated social structures that established alternative family roles, work-type roles, and other roles, which were associated with the residents' sense of health, adequacy and well-being" and concluded that, since aging threatens feelings of adequacy because of the loss of work, family, and other roles, the retirement community may provide "a corrective experience in the development of alternative roles and functions."

Gubrium (1972) argues that, as the local environments of the aged become more concentrated with older people, it is increasingly likely for local *activity norms* to become age-linked, i.e., persons' expectations of each others' behavior become rooted in common experiences. A "subculture of aging" emerges if the norms provide congruence between what people expect of themselves and what is expected of them by significant others. Inconsistency between these expectancies should be related to dissatisfaction with self and situation; consistency, with satisfaction. Flexibility is no longer necessary because behavior in one situation is likely to be appropriate for others. Adaptation should be easier in age-homogeneous environments because of the consistency and lack of demand for flexibility.

On the other hand, there is the possibility that age-concentrated housing involves increased stress rather than less, due to the pressure for activity, sociability, and group conformity and to the lack of privacy (Carp, 1966b; Sherman et al., 1968).

There is the possibility also that the desirability of homogeneity or congruence has its limits. Uniformity and similarity can create a need for stimulation which is experienced as boredom and under which people seek variety, even to the extent of creating a problem or stress for themselves (Fiske and Maddi, 1961). The implications with regard to housing the elderly are that while the limits of tolerable stimulation must not be exceeded by physical design demands or those of the social milieu, it is also necessary to provide for the need for variety and the beneficial effects of exercising coping skills.

IMPLICATIONS OF STUDIES IN HOUSING FOR THE ELDERLY

It is understandable that much research has focused on the new types of housing and living environment which have been constructed in recent years. Moreover, it is essential that these facilities be carefully evaluated in terms of their attractiveness to older people and in terms of their impact upon the well-being of the elderly and of society at large. However, it is equally vital to be wary in drawing broad generalizations from currently available studies.

Selectivity of Environments and Residents

First, it must be recognized that recently constructed environments tend to be of a particular sort and do not by any means represent the range of possible designs and social milieux. Second, current tenants tend to be a very small and unrepresentative sample of the older population; what holds true for them may or may not hold true for the larger group. These reservations limit all generalizations regarding environmental impact upon well-being from studies in existing settings.

Moreover, conclusions regarding relationships between such variables as activity and morale must take into account the probably confounding effect of data source. Theory-relevant conclusions based on data collected in special housing and on its present occupants may or may not generalize in simple fashion to theory systems about the experience and behavior of older people in general. This is strongly suggested, for example, by Messer's (1967) finding that activity and morale were related among older people in age-integrated housing but not among those in age-segregated public housing for the elderly. For purposes of theory building as well as those of environmental design, there is need for studies on samples which represent the older population in general and which include the range as well as the extremes on variables of special interest such as age composition of neighborhood.

Need for Long-range Studies

Experience with the new environments remains of short duration. Sherman et al. (1968) warn that the residents of retirement communities they studied had not lived there long. Hamovitch (1968) qualifies the report of happiness on the part of upper-middle class people in an age-segregated living situation by reference to how they may feel ten years hence when they have become acclimated and are able to look more dispassionately at their surroundings, when deaths begin to mount, and when illness slows mobility and confines people within the community.

There is another reason for longitudinal investigations. Several studies point to the tendency for elderly inmovers to associate with others of their "own kind." This has been interpreted in terms of need for constancy and predictability. There is need also for variety and change. The optimal situation seems to be an appropriate balance of continuity or constancy with change or variety. It is conceivable that, in the early days after a move, the different environment creates all the variety and change that can be tolerated, and early formation of interpersonal relationships therefore reverts persistently to the basis of similarity, the known and familiar and undemanding. However, after a period of adjustment, when the setting is no longer new and adaptive demands become routine, people may begin to seek diversity and variety in interpersonal and other experiences, in order to maintain the appropriate balance.

Consistent with this hypothesis are the findings of Weinstock and Bennett (1969) that cognitive functioning was enhanced as a consequence of admission to a home for the aged, remained relatively stable among newcomers, but declined among long-time residents. The demands of this age-homogenous setting apparently provided stimulation to cognitive functioning for newly admitted residents while the same setting was ineffective in stimulating oldtimers. The stimulus quality of the environment is partly defined by the duration of the person-environment contact as well as by characteristics of the environment and of the person upon whom it impinges.

In addition, facilities age and resident populations age. The satisfaction of residents with their living environment and its attractiveness to prospective tenants may alter as a consequence. For example, when Victoria Plaza (Carp, 1966b) and Lurie Terrace (Donahue, 1966) were new and the first of their kind in the country as well as their cities, they probably presented quite different images to their tenants and to the communities than they do now, 15 years of age and the oldest of many similar projects. The reactions of the first applicants and inmovers to these facilities cannot be expected to represent those of today's.

Environmental Docility and the Loss Continuum

Conceptual models which summarize research on person-environment interaction suggest that the older person is more critically affected by his living environment than is the young person and that with increasing age living environments should be increasingly supportive. The "loss continuum" (Pastalan, 1970) indicates that with aging a person's world shrinks and his ability or willingness to deal with many people and with complex environments decreases. The "environmental docility hypothesis" (Lawton and Simon, 1968) proposes that the more competent the organism (in terms of health, intelligence, ego strength, social role performance, or cultural evolution), the less will be the proportion of variance in behavior attributable to physical conditions around him. Proponents of this hypothesis accept a generally negative relationship between competence and aging and perceive the solution to lie in

tailoring living situations to the current competency level of their occupants (Lawton, in press b).

A general problem for the designer of environments for the elderly is how much support and how much challenge should be built into such environments. The issue of how to build in support or challenge is a closely related but in some sense subordinate one. An overly supportive environment robs the individual of initiative and of the opportunity to exercise his adaptive ability, thereby maintaining it and enjoying the consequent sense of mastery and its favorable effect on self-esteem. An overly demanding environment frustrates, discourages, and further lowers competence and self-esteem. The problem of how much support and how much demand to build into living environments so that they will be optimal for older people is greatly complicated by the diversity of that group at present and the likelihood that it will become even more heterogeneous with time.

The Need for a Variety of Housing and Living Environments

The years of "aging" are long and now comprise a significant portion of the life span. The person is far different during his final year of life than in the first after he reached the chronological age, retirement, or other status which defines him as "old." The life-space must be made flexible and sensitive to the changing needs of its participants. It is likely that future elderly will be both older due to changes in life expectancies and younger as the various definitions of "old person" include more persons in younger age groups. At present the elderly are the most heterogeneous age group; in the future they will be even less homogeneous. "The younger aged, the older aged, and conceivably a middle group of aged, each will be confronted with a set of problems unique to that age level, but overlapping and impinging one on the other" (Brody, 1966).

Even when the stages or phases of later adult life are numbered and known, individual differences among people in any one of them will be great. As Pastalan pointed out in reference to the "loss continuum," it is unquestionably true that the average 80-year-old is not able to do some of the things easily done by the average 20-year-old. However, it is equally true that 20-year-olds are not identical and that 80-year-olds are even less so. Therefore, it is fruitless to contemplate design of "the" housing and living environment for the elderly or even for those in one "stage of aging." The primary orientation of innovation should be creation of a rich variety of milieux which express the aspirations and meet the characteristics of a rich variety of people.

Prosthetic and Therapeutic Environments

Lindsley (1964) contrasted therapeutic with prosthetic approaches to the environment-person interaction. Prosthetic environments cause favorable behavior change through elevating the support level; improvement in behavior lasts only as long as the prosthesis is applied. Therapeutic environments result in permanent changes, growth and development within persons, and environmental therapy can be withdrawn or reduced as competence is elevated.

The possibility of environmentally-induced growth and development among older people has been cited. Donahue (1966) observed some elderly inmovers to Lurie Terrace "move into a new and higher level of ego function" in the new milieu "which stimulates and furthers personality growth even at very late ages." Birren, Butler, Greenhouse, Sokoloff, and Yarrow (1963) noted that "when the environment is rich with social and cultural opportunities, security and permissiveness," at least some aging men show "qualities of growth and development."

Neither study tested the possibility that these changes were "therapeutic" in the sense of being internalized and enduring. This possibility should not be cast aside lightly, in view of the higher cost of more supportive living environments and because environments supportive beyond the need of their residents induce premature dependence and reduction in coping skill and self-esteem.

The possibility of a therapeutic environment has been tested in Israel where a ten-year study

was undertaken to see whether services provided to maintain community living could also be used to reinsert older immigrants into community living (Bergman, 1973). Housing was the service which most commonly (in 65 percent of the cases) allowed reentry into the community. Other effective services were ambulatory medical care insurance (55 percent) and household furnishings and equipment (52 percent); less frequent facilitators were household help (14 percent) and day care (10 percent).

To the extent that the Israeli situation provided a therapeutic environment, it was not limited to the inside of the institution but included support services in the community. Outmovers did not go from a totally supportive environment to one which provided no support, and they were reinserted into community living only when services in that community seemed adequate to meet their needs. The study does demonstrate the possibility of reversing the progression with aging from environments which allow maximum independence and provide minimal support to those which increasingly involve dependence and support.

Person-Environment Congruence

As Bergman (1973) pointed out, it is not known to what extent ability to leave the institution and resume community living was the result of faulty admission policy and procedure which institutionalized some older immigrants who could have coped with community living from the start. Neither is it known how much unhappiness and waste has resulted from faulty placements or unsuitable moves from which people are unable to extricate themselves. Even if a rich variety of environments is available, a person may choose or be assigned to one that is not optimally suited to his needs, competencies, life-style, goals, and values, or even to one that is detrimental to his well-being.

Lawton (1970) writes of the process of attempting to match person and environment as "placement" in distinction from "planning" those environments, and defines placement as "screening people in or out of a variety of environmental types" which should be based on "assessment of the individual's capacity to perform tasks which are most relevant to effective living in the various environments." There are other elements in person-environment congruence. For example, the move from a socially isolating or stressful living situation to one rich in opportunity for social involvement and planned activities was most beneficial to the happiness and adjustment of people who had been involved to some extent in the types of activity for which the new setting expanded opportunities and who preferred organized group activities. For people who were not involved in planned group activities prior to the move and who valued privacy, the move was less satisfactory, and a few of them were unhappy in the new setting and did not adapt well to it (Carp, 1968).

Because of the overwhelming importance of home to the older person, a mis-move can have pervasive and enduring negative consequences. Screening procedures to turn away those unable to perform tasks necessary to living in a facility clearly are necessary but must be supplemented with other considerations of congruence. Goals, values, and preferences are relevant as well.

The Living-Environment Counselor. It is unfortunate that admission must be handled by an agent of the housing provider rather than by an agent of the seeker of housing. The situation is parallel to that of the personnel office and the job seeker. The first is motivated to best fill the job vacancy so that the company will prosper; the second is motivated to take the next step upward in developing his career or other ends of his own. The elderly homeseeker does not usually have access to someone like the vocational or career counselor, whose job it is to look at the entire housing market in terms of what is best for his client at this point in his career and in view of the clients's own goals. This comment by no means impugns the motives or demeans the work of housing admission personnel. Their job, like that of the industrial personnel office, is to make best use of the facilities they represent, and most perform their task humanely and with compassion. There is, however, another legitimate view-

point which is not better but simply different: that of the older person wanting to meet his own needs and satisfy his own preferences and values in regard to the living environment in which he plans to age. His goal is to screen living environments to find the one most congruent to him.

Self-selection. The preeminence of the need for autonomy among older persons and the desirable effects of the exercise of options are constantly reiterated. The centrality of this motive and behavior opportunity suggests that the process of selecting a living environment should be, insofar as possible, one of self-selection. This requires the establishment of services to disseminate information regarding the entire range of available housing to old people and to provide them assistance in decision-making when desired. It is necessary not only to create a diversity of living environments but also to offer them as choices to older people. It is necessary not only to design living environments to support the capabilities and desired life-styles of the entire diverse range of older people, but also to provide a mechanism which assists each older individual to be aware of all alternatives available to him and to make the best decision regarding the environment which will best fit him.

Mechanisms of Transfer

Even if congruence is good at the time of matching living environment to person, changes occur in both. Each community needs a continuum of facilities (McGuire, 1969; Havighurst, 1969) each designed for a particular stage or phase of aging. Roughly, the first comprises independent housing and the second, congregate housing for the relatively independent and capable but with more services than those found in independent homes. The third step is the personal care home or perhaps intermediate housing for people who still value independence but need more attention and support. The fourth is a nursing home for those in need of skilled nursing care, and the last includes the hospital and extended care facilities where people go to die. Within each "stage of housing" there need to be appropriate types of variety, since this rough progression of housing represents only an environmental response to degrees of need for supportive services, and persons similar in need for supportive services vary on a wide variety of other dimensions.

The primitive state of knowledge about person-environment congruence, the lack of techniques for incorporating that knowledge into the selection of living environments by older persons, and the variety of changes which occur in person and situation over time indicate the need for what might be called mechanisms of transfer. These mechanisms would deal with person-situation congruence as an ongoing process.

When relocation is inevitable and alternatives limited or nonexistent, concomitant with provision of new quarters there should be a program to prepare, before they move, those aged who are to be rehoused. This has been done, with satisfactory results, in England by such techniques as telling the aged about the desirability of the new accomodations which are available and introducing them to new neighbors (Beyer and Nierstrasz, 1967). When relocation is desired and favorable alternatives are not readily discernible, information about possibilities should be provided.

The mechanisms of transfer should vitally involve in the decision-making process the older person who is considering or who is forced to move and should follow the model of the counselor for a student deciding upon a work career, providing information and an opportunity to discuss possibilities, rather than the "selection and assignment" model of industry. These transfer mechanisms would institutionalize society's concern with finding the best available living situation for Mr. X as well as the presently institutionalized societal need to utilize well the special living environments for the elderly.

The Exercise of Options. Elimination or reduction of the feeling of irrevocability about any move may be of tremendous value. In the Israeli experiment mentioned earlier, each self-dischargee, the family, and the local social service were given assurance that should any person be unable to function satisfactorily in the community, he would be speedily readmitted to the institution. This reassurance seemed to play a major role in allaying anxiety and strengthening resolution to try community reinsertion (Bergman, 1973). The plight of the poor old who exhaust their resources with a move to public housing has been mentioned, as has that of the more affluent investor in a retirement community which turns out to be not of his liking or in which fees expand to the detriment of other items in his budget. These problems reflect economic realities; transfer mechanisms must include fiscal as well as informational and counseling components.

Delaying the Move. Best use of a variety of facilities along stages of living environment corresponding to those of aging requires good timing of moves on the part of individuals. Some people wait too long to apply for more supportive living environments and are unable to qualify for them. This undue delay is often occasioned by the inadequate supply of facilities with supportive services and the consequent long waiting lists. It is probably due also to lack of information about the housing situation and lack of opportunity to come to terms with one's own aging and what it will mean in terms of environmental requirements. Mechanisms of transfer, along with more housing, should greatly relieve this problem of inappropriate delay.

Premature Moves. Other people move prematurely into housing situations which provide medical, nursing, and other services they may or may not someday need. This tendency is encouraged by the requirement of capacity for independent living at the time of admission to facilities which offer extended care. To insure care they may need in the future and to avoid becoming burdens on their children, people may move, while yet fully competent for independent living, to facilities which provide those potentially-needed services. A careful look should be taken at the economics of this situation as well as at its implications for maintenance of coping ability and morale. Assurance of the availability of extended care, if ever needed, might reduce the number of "premature movers" among the competent old. Again, this necessitates not only design and construction of facilities and provision of services but also programs of information dissemination and opportunity for counseling and the establishment of fiscal and interservice mechanisms to facilitate desirable relocations.

Research Utilization

The problem of communication between investigator and practitioner in the field of housing the elderly is a major obstacle to progress. The *relevance* of research-generated information is generally judged to be considerable and, despite limitations and inadequacies, findings are available which could be useful to the decisions of architects, builders, city planners, and other policy makers. These research findings, relevant to policy issues, are not being utilized adequately.

The utilization gap is partly the fault of investigators, who typically do not take sufficient initiative toward dissemination of their findings through multidisciplinary meetings, publications, and the public media, or by actively seeking communication with political decision-making groups, administrators, and other potential users of research findings.

A technology for communication between research investigators and potential users of research findings is required. Effort toward the development of a common language is highly desirable, despite the many difficulties involved.

In order to increase research utilization, the communication must be a two-way process. Despite the existence of research output which is relevant but not used, many of the relevant questions are not being addressed by research. Many of the problems confronting policy makers and practitioners can be translated into exciting research projects. These problems must be identified by practitioners and communicated to the investigators in ways the latter can comprehend sufficiently well to formulate cogent research designs to address them.

The initiative toward identifying researchable problems can be taken by any one of the actors in the system: planners, designers, adminis-trators, users, or researchers. Regardless of who takes the initiative, *mutual involvement of all actors* in problem definition is the ideal. Therefore, the initiator should seek the participation of others *early* in the process of problem formation. Similarly, involvement of all actors in the design process is a necessary ingredient of good design. Goals of a design-problem solution should be defined not by the sponsor or investigator alone, but by the potential user, administrator, design professional, and research evaluator, in interaction.

Postcompletion in-use *evaluative research with feedback* to the planner and designer should constitute a normal and mandatory part of every program, and provision for it should be included in the budget.

REFERENCES

Berggren, A. 1960. Quoted at National Health Council Meeting, Miami, March, 14, 1960. Comment based on 1956 report by the Royal Commission on Problems of Aging.

Bergman, S. 1973. Facilitating living conditions for aged in the community. *Gerontologist*, **13**, 184–189.

Beyer, G. H., and Nierstrasz, F. H. J. 1967. *Housing the Aged in Western Countries.* Amsterdam: Elsevier.

Birren, J. E., Butler, R. N., Greenhouse, S. W., Sokoloff, L., and Yarrow, M. R. (eds.) 1963. *Human Aging.* Washington, D.C.: Government Printing Office.

Blume, O. The problems of socio-gerontological housing research. *In*, W. Donahue (ed.), *Proceedings of the International Symposium for Housing and Environmental Design for Older Adults.* Washington, D.C.: International Center for Social Gerontology, in press.

Bott, E. 1957. *Family and Social Network.* London: Tavistock.

Britton, J. H. 1966. Living in a rural Pennsylvania community in old age. *In*, F. M. Carp (ed.), *Patterns of Living and Housing of Middle-Aged and Older People.* Washington, D.C.: Government Printing Office.

Brody, E. M. 1966. The aging family. *Gerontologist*, **6**, 201–206.

Brody, E. M. 1970. The etiquette of filial behavior. *Aging and Human Development*, **1**, 87–94.

Brotman, H. Every tenth American—the "problem" of aging. *In*, M. P. Lawton (ed.), *Community Planning for the Elderly*, in press.

Bultena, G. L., and Wood, V. 1969. The American retirement community: Bane or blessing? *J. Geront.*, **24**, 209–217.

Burch, G., and Collot, C. 1972. *Old People in Their Towns*. Translated by O. Neaman. Paris: Centre International de Gérontologie Sociale.

Cantor, M. *Study of the Inner-City Elderly*. New York: Office for the Aging, in press.

Carp, F. M. 1966a. Summary. *In*, F. M. Carp (ed.), *Patterns of Living and Housing of Middle-Aged and Older Adults*. Washington, D.C.: Government Printing Office.

Carp, F. M. 1966b. *A Future for the Aged*. Austin: University of Texas Press.

Carp, F. M. 1966c. Effects of improved housing on the lives of older people. *In*, F. M. Carp (ed.), *Patterns of Living and Housing of Middle-Aged and Older People*. Washington, D.C.: Government Printing Office.

Carp, F. M. 1968. Person-situation congruence in engagement. *Gerontologist*, **8**, 184–188.

Carp, F. M. 1969a. Housing and minority group elderly. *Gerontologist*, **9**, 20–24.

Carp, F. M. 1969b. Use of community resources and social adjustment of the elderly. *In*, *Proceedings of Seminars, 1965–1969*, Council on Aging and Human Development, pp. 169–176. Durham, North Carolina: Duke University.

Carp, F. M. 1970. Communicating with elderly Mexican-Americans. *Gerontologist*, **10**, 126–134.

Carp, F. M. 1971. The mobility of retired people. *In*, E. Cantilli and J. Smelzer (eds.), *Transportation and Aging*. Washington, D.C.: Government Printing Office.

Carp, F. M. 1972. The mobility of older slum-dwellers. *Gerontologist*, **12**, 57–65.

Carp, F. M. 1974a. The realities of interdisciplinary approaches: Can the disciplines work together to help the aged? *In*, A.N. Schwartz and I. N. Mensh (eds.), *Professional Obligations and Approaches to the Aged*. Springfield, Illinois: Charles C. Thomas.

Carp, F. M. 1974b. Short-term and long-term prediction of adjustment to a new environment. *J. Geront.*, **29**, 444–453.

Carp, F. M. 1975. Long-range satisfaction with housing. *Gerontologist*, **15**, 27–34.

Carp, F. M. Urban life-style and life-cycle factors. *In*, M. P. Lawton (ed.), *Community Planning for the Elderly*. New York: John Wiley, in press a.

Carp, F. M. Federal programs for housing the elderly, in press b.

Carp, F. M. Housing and living arrangements. *In*, *Improving the Quality of Life in the Later Years of Life*. Publishing Sciences Group, Inc, in press c.

Carp, F. M. Life-style and location within the city. *Gerontologist*, in press d.

Carp, F. M. Effect of viable alternatives upon evaluations of present living arrangements, in press e.

Carp. F. M., and Kataoka, E. Health-care problems of the elderly residents of Chinatown, in press.

Centre International de Gerontologie Sociale. 1974. *Newsletter* (August).

Clark, M. 1971. Patterns of aging among the elderly poor of the inner city. *Gerontologist*, **11**, 58–66.

Donahue, W. 1966. Impact of living arrangements on ego development in the elderly. *In*, F. M. Carp (ed.), *Patterns of Living and Housing of Middle-Aged and Older People*. Washington, D.C.: Government Printing Office.

Donahue, W. (ed.) *Proceedings of the International Symposium for Housing and Environmental Design for Older Adults*. Washington, D.C.: International Center for Social Gerontology, in press.

Engberg, E. 1961. Special housing requirements for the elderly and the handicapped. Working paper prepared for the Expert Committee on the Public Health Aspect of Housing, Geneva.

Fiske, D. W., and Maddi, S. (eds.) 1961. *The Functions of Varied Experience*. Homewood, Illinois: Dorsey Press.

Goldscheider, C., VanArdsol, M. D., Jr., and Sabagh, G. 1966. Residential mobility of older people. *In*, F. M. Carp (ed.), *Patterns of Living and Housing of Middle-Aged and Older People*, pp. 65–82. Washington, D. C.: Government Printing Office.

Gottesman, L. E. 1970. Long-range priorities for the aged. *Aging and Human Development*, **4**, 393–401.

Gozonsky, M. J. 1966. Preface. *In*, F. M. Carp (ed.), *Patterns of Living and Housing of Middle-Aged and Older People*. Washington, D.C.: Government Printing Office.

Grant, D. P. Creating living environments for older adults within existing contexts. *In*, W. Donahue (ed.), *Proceedings of the International Symposium for Housing and Environmental Design for Older Adults*. Washington, D.C.: International Center for Social Gerontology, in press.

Gubrium, J. F. 1972. Toward a socio-environmental theory of aging. *Gerontologist*, **12**, 281–284.

Hamovitch, M. B. 1968. Social and psychological factors in adjustment in a retirement process. *In*, F. M. Carp (ed.), *The Retirement Process*. Washington, D.C.: Government Printing Office.

Hamovitch, M. B., Peterson, J. A., and Larson, A. E. 1969. Perceptions and fulfillment of housing needs of an aging population. Paper presented at the 8th International Congress of Gerontology, Washington, D.C.

Havighurst, R. J. 1969. Research and development goals in social gerontology. A report of a special committee of the Gerontological Society. *Gerontologist*, **9**, 1–90.

Holmes, T., and Masuda, M. 1970. Schedule of recent events (SRE). *In*, *Proceedings of AAAS Symposium on Separation and Depression*, Seattle, December 1970.

Ingraham, M. H. 1974. *My Purpose Holds: Reactions and Experiences in Retirement of TIAA-CREFF Annuitants*. Philadelphia: Teachers Insurance and Annuity Association, College Retirement Equities Fund.

Jackson, H. C. 1971. National Caucus on the black aged: A progress report. *Aging and Human Development*, **3**, 226–231.

Jackson, J. J. 1972. Social impacts of housing relocation upon urban, low-income black aged. *Gerontologist*, **12**, 32–37.

Johnson, S. K. 1971. *Idle Haven: Community Building Among the Working-Class Retired*. Berkeley: University of California Press.

Kahana, E. A congruence model of person-environment interaction. *In*, M. P. Lawton and T. Byerts (eds.), *Theoretical Approaches to the Study of Environments and Aging*. New York: John Wiley, in press.

Kalish, R. A., and Yuen, S. 1971. Americans of East Asian ancestry: Aging and the aged. *Gerontologist*, **11**, 36–47.

Keller, S. 1968. *The Urban Neighborhood: A Sociological Perspective*. New York: Random House.

Kelly, L. 1955. Consistency of the adult personality. *American Psychologist*, **10**, 659.

Kleemeier, R. W. 1961. Time, activity and leisure. *In*, R. W. Kleemeier (ed.), *Aging and Leisure*. New York: Oxford University Press.

Kreps, J. 1968. The allocation of leisure to retirement. *In*, F. M. Carp (ed.), *The Retirement Process*. Washington, D.C.: Government Printing Office.

Lawton, M. P. 1969. Supportive services in the context of the housing environment. *Gerontologist*, **9**, 15–19.

Lawton, M. P. 1970. Assessment, integration, and environments for older people. *Gerontologist*, **10**, 38–46.

Lawton, M. P. *Planning and Managing Housing for the Elderly*. New York: John Wiley, in press a.

Lawton, M. P. Competence, environmental press and the adaptation of older people. *In*, M. P. Lawton and T. Byerts (eds.), *Theoretical Approaches to the Study of Environments and Aging*. New York: John Wiley, in press b.

Lawton, M. P., and Cohen, J. 1974. Housing impact on older people. *J. Geront.*, **29**, 194–204.

Lawton, M. P., Kleban, M. H., and Carlson, D. A. 1973. The inner-city resident: To move or not to move. *Gerontologist*, **13**, 443–448.

Lawton, M. P., Kleban, M. H., and Singer, M. 1971. The aged Jewish person and the slum environment. *J. Geront.*, **26**, 231–239.

Lawton, M. P., and Simon, B. 1968. The ecology of social relationships in housing for the elderly. *J. Geront.*, **8**, 108–115.

Lenzer, A. 1965. Mobility patterns among the aged, 1955–1960. *Gerontologist*, **5**, 12–15.

Lindsley, O. R. 1964. Geriatric behavioral prosthetics. *In*, R. Kastenbaum (ed.), *New Thoughts on Old Age*. New York: Springer.

Lipman, A. 1968. Public housing and attitudinal adjustment in old age: A comparative study. *Journal of Geriatric Psychiatry*, **2**, 88–101.

Lopata, H. Z. 1971. Widows as a minority group. *Gerontologist*, **11**, 67–77.

McGuire, M. 1969. The utilization of research data. *Gerontologist*, **9**, 37–38.

Messer, M. 1967. The possibility of an age-concentrated environment becoming a normative system. *Gerontologist*, **7**, 247–251.

Montgomery, J. E. 1966. Living arrangements and housing of the rural aged in a central Pennsylvania community. *In*, F. M. Carp (ed.), *Patterns of Living and Housing of Middle-Aged and Older People*. Washington, D.C.: Government Printing Office.

Nash, B. Lawton, M. P., and Simon, B. 1968. Blacks and whites in housing for the elderly. Paper presented at the 21st Annual Meeting of the Gerontological Society, Denver.

Niebanck, P. L. 1966. Knowledge gained in studies of relocation. *In*, F. M. Carp (ed.), *Patterns of Living and Housing of Middle-Aged and Older People*. Washington, D.C.: Government Printing Office.

Old People's Health Committee. 1960. Quote taken from Norwegian report "Our Aging Population."

Orshansky, M. 1965. Counting the poor: Another look at the poverty profile. *Social Security Bulletin* (January).

Palmore, E. 1971. Variables related to needs of the aged poor. *J. Geront.*, **26**, 524–531.

Pastalan, L. A. 1970. Privacy as an expression of human territoriality. *In*, L. A. Pastalan and D. H. Carson (eds.), *Spatial Behavior of Older People*. Ann Arbor, Michigan: University of Michigan.

Pastalan, L. Research and training in development and management of housing for older adults. *In*, W. Donahue (ed.), *Proceedings of the International Symposium on Housing and Environmental Design for Older Adults*. Washington, D.C.: International Center for Social Gerontology, in press.

Peterson, J. A., and Larson, A. E. 1966. Social-psychological factors in selecting retirement housing. *In*, F. M. Carp (ed.), *Patterns of Living and Housing of Middle-Aged and Older People*. Washington, D.C.: Government Printing Office.

Proceedings of the 1971 White House Conference on Aging: Toward a National Policy on Aging, November 28–December 2, 1971. 1973. Washington, D.C.: Government Printing Office.

Rahe, R. H. 1972. Subjects' recent life changes and their near-future illness reports. *Annals of Clinical Research*, **4**, 250–265.

Riesenfeld, M. J., Newcomer, R. J., Berlant, P. V., and Dempsey, W. A. 1972. Perceptions of public service needs: The urban elderly and the public agency. *Gerontologist*, **12**, 185–190.

Rosow, I. 1966. Housing and local ties of the aged. *In*, F. M. Carp (ed.), *Patterns of Living and Housing of Middle-Aged and Older People*, pp. 47–64. Washington, D.C.: Government Printing Office.

Rosow, I. 1967. *Social Integration of the Aged*. New York: The Free Press.

Roth, J. J. 1961. Old age insurance and welfare in Switzerland. *Geriatrics*, **16**, 203.

Schooler, K. K. 1969. The relationship between social interaction and morale of the elderly as a function of environmental characteristics. *Gerontologist*, **9**, 25–29.

Schorr, A. L. 1960. *Filial Responsibility in the*

Modern American Family. Washington, D.C.: Government Printing Office.

Sears, D. W. 1974. Elderly housing: A need determination technique. *Gerontologist*, **14**, 182–187.

Seguin, M. M. 1973. Opportunity for peer socialization in a retirement community. *Gerontologist*, **13**, 184–188.

Sherman, S. R. 1973. Housing and environments for the well-elderly: Scope and impact. Mimeographed. Albany: New York State Department of Mental Health.

Sherman, S. R. 1974. Leisure activities in retirement housing. *J. Geront.*, **29**, 325–335.

Sherman, S. R., Mangum, W. P., Jr., Dodds, S., Walkley, R. P., and Wilner, D. M. 1968. Psychological effects of retirement housing. *Gerontologist*, **8**, 170–175.

Teaff, J. D., Lawton, M. P., and Carlson, D. 1973. Impact of age integration of public housing projects. Paper presented at 26th Annual Meeting of the Gerontological Society, Miami Beach.

Townsend, P., and Bond, J. 1971. The older worker in the United Kingdom. *In*, Proceedings of a colloquium of the European Social Research Committee of the International Association of Gerontology: *Elderly People Living in Europe.* Paris.

United States Department of Housing and Urban Development. 1973a. *Older Americans: Facts About Incomes and Housing.* Washington, D.C.: Government Printing Office.

United States Department of Housing and Urban Development, Office of International Affairs. 1973b. *Special Supplement 10* (Dec.). Washington, D.C.: Government Printing Office.

United States Senate Committee on Aging. 1973. *Housing for the Elderly: A Status Report* (April). Washington, D.C.: Government Printing Office.

Van Zonneveld, R. M. 1958. Sociomedical investigations of housing for the aged. *Geriatrics*, **13**, 668–672.

Vecsey, G. 1973. Many of Nassau's aged find only isolation in suburbia. Special to the *New York Times* (December 4, 1973).

Weinstock, C., and Bennett, R. 1969. Relations between social isolation, social cognition, and related cognitive skills in residents of a home for the aged. Paper presented at the 8th International Congress of Gerontology, Washington, D.C.

Winiecke, L. 1973. The appeal of age-segregated housing to the elderly poor. *Aging and Human Development*, **4**, 293–306.

11
THE ECONOMY AND THE AGED

Juanita M. Kreps
Duke University

World-wide economic events of this decade are significantly different from those of the past in several respects: rates of inflation are accelerated in all industrialized countries; scarcities, particularly of food and fuel, now plague even the richest nations; serious pollution problems call into question past high rates of growth, and minority voices call into account traditional patterns of distribution. Shifts in the demand for food or energy or capital on one part of the globe are quickly transmitted to the international marketplace. No major economy can insulate itself from fluctuations generated by the problems in another country.

The shrinking of economic boundaries seems likely in time to reduce the income differentials between persons living in the various nations, just as the process has already narrowed the price range for goods sold in the international markets. For now, however, real incomes differ from one country to another because of cross-national differences in natural and human resource endowments and in the state of technology. In addition to variations in nations' resource and technological capacities, which together largely determine productivity, countries have also adopted different distributive arrangements. The rules by which a particular person or family shares in the consumption of goods and services reflect a wide range of societal views on such issues as economic and social equity, work incentives, and property rights.

In addressing questions of the economy's impact on the aging, or vice versa, it is necessary to disentangle the effect of resource constraints on total output from the effect of those rules that govern the distribution of that output among the persons and groups in the society. A highly developed economy, typified by the United States as well as by most western European countries, Japan, and Canada, enjoys large volumes of output along with growing amounts of free time for education in youth and retirement in old age (United Nations, 1962). Analysis of net years of working life in countries classified according to degree of industrialization indicates that the proportion of life spent in the labor force declines with industrialization. All developed nations have established systems of social insurance as well, with income claims provided to retired workers and their families.

There are differences in the proportions of earnings maintained in retirement in different countries (Gordon, 1963). A cross national survey of the aged by Shanas and her associates provides data on incomes maintained during old age in the United States, England, and Denmark and draws comparisons between living levels of the elderly and those of working age in the three nations (Shanas, Townsend, Friis, Milhøj, and Stehouwer, 1968). In some nations, such as the United States, earnings reflect high levels of output and recent rates of real economic growth that, although surpassed by certain other nations, have nevertheless brought steady improvements in levels of living for several decades. Widespread interest in the record of growth is now evident, not only because of the manner of its distribution among income, age, and racial groups, but also because of serious doubt as to whether the growth can or should continue. A corollary concern has to do with the rate of inflation and with the apparent trade-off between employment and price increase.

Since the economy's impact on any age group turns in large measure on the productivity and earnings of workers, it is important to direct attention first to the behavior of lifetime earnings and their implications for income in old age. Questions of whether these earnings will continue to grow as they have in the past, along with queries as to the effect of inflation on both the growth outlook and the prospect for full employment, are then raised. These macroeconomic influences set the stage within which the status of any age group is determined. Allocative patterns dictate the relative positions of youth, the middle- aged, and the elderly by specifying how each will share in total output. Finally, the question of impact is reversed to ask whether increasing numbers of older people are influencing the patterns of consumer demand, the use of free time, or the degree of conservatism in economic decision-making.

EARNINGS AND INCOME THROUGH THE LIFE COURSE

The significance of macroeconomic forces in determining the quality of life in old age is perhaps best illustrated by the role of economic growth. In order to examine the influence of growth on one's level of living both during and after worklife, we may study the behavior of earnings through the life course. Of particular importance are questions of the impact of overall growth versus improvements in the worker's ability and experience on the job; dif-

ferences in the relative influence of these two factors at different stages of the worklife; and the relationship of earnings levels to retirement income. Before turning to the analysis of lifetime earnings, focusing illustratively on the United States, it is important to note the centrality of income maintenance issues as they affect nonworkers in all industrialized countries in the second half of the twentieth century. (For a more detailed treatment of income maintenance see Chapter 22, Income Distribution and the Aging.)

Income for Nonworkers in Industrial Countries

The maintenance of income during the retirement years is an important social issue in all economically developed countries which, although productive enough to provide workers with substantial amounts of time free of work, find that in the absence of tax-benefit schemes, retirees lack adequate financial resources. Even those nations with established social security programs designed to supplant earnings with pensions are not without problems; public benefits frequently constitute only a small fraction of earnings, and private savings and annuities fail to bring total retirement income up to commonly accepted standards of adequacy.

Standards of adequacy vary from country to country and the extent to which various nations approximate the desired level of income also differs. Certain commonalities nevertheless exist among developed countries. For most persons in most developed economies, the major sources of lifetime income are wages and salaries earned for working. Lifetime earnings depend primarily on two factors: one's productivity as a worker, in combination with the capital equipment afforded him; and the length of time worked. These two dimensions are generally inversely related; the more productive the economic unit, the shorter the working time (Winston 1966), the reductions in working time occurring in the form of a reduced workyear or a decreased number of working years. Even when the worktime reductions begin to add to the time one spends in retirement, higher worker productivity should still provide adequate income claims to support retirees. Higher output also allows youth to remain in school longer, thereby increasing his education and skills and raising productivity even faster in the future.

It is nevertheless possible for lifetime output to increase without any resultant significant improvement in living standards during retirement years; the increase in output produced during the working years may also be consumed during those years. As the length of the retirement period grows, it becomes necessary to transfer more and more income claims in order to provide a given annual money income during the longer span. The value of money income, moreover, has been rapidly eroded under the impact of the inflation suffered by practically all nations in the past several decades. And even if retirement incomes rose at a rate necessary to offset the rise in living costs (or if the price level were stabilized), the standard of living of retirees would worsen relative to that of wage earners, whose incomes rise with economic growth (Rimlinger, 1971). This problem in the United States, analyzed in a subsequent section of the paper, does not appear when the social security benefit is tied to the change in real wages, as in the case of Western Germany. In the absence of such an attachment of benefits to real earnings, the faster the pace of the economy's growth and the longer the retirement period, the greater the deterioration in relative income position of retirees.

In most developed countries real annual income in retirement has been rising during the past several decades. The overall increase in productivity has enabled nations to afford higher levels of support not only for workers but for nonworkers as well. It is true that current rates of inflation are extremely high; fixed income recipients have suffered severe losses in levels of living within very short periods of time. Social insurance benefits are generally tied to the cost of living, and that portion of the retiree's income derived from these benefits now keeps pace with living costs after a short time lag. Other income claims that do not rise with prices are being rapidly eroded in value.

For the most part, however, the disadvantaged position of older people arises not from the fact that they have less real income than the previous generation of older people, but from two other possible circumstances: one, they are likely to have less income than they themselves enjoyed in their working years, and, two, they have less income than those still at work enjoy.

In summary, high productivity enables workers in industrialized nations to support themselves and their families at ever higher standards of living and in reduced working time (United Nations, 1973). Some of any annual increase in product is allocated to nonworkers, allowing youth to stay in school and older people to retire from work. But nonworkers and workers do not necessarily share equally in the increase in output; the consumption levels of workers tend to exceed that of retirees, and the degree of relative disadvantage deepens with greater growth and longer retirement periods. In developing countries, where poverty is common among all generations, the problem is particularly acute for the elderly, most often for older women.

Lifetime Earnings Patterns

The behavior of real earnings through the life course is dependent on productivity per man-hour (or man-year), which grows through time with technological progress and the worker's skill and experience on the job. The rise in output allows real income per worker to increase with age, albeit at different rates of increase at different stages of the worklife. Thus the earnings profile of a worker as he ages, reflecting the impact of economic growth as well as the improvement in his own capacities, is usually a rising curve that peaks near the end of worklife.

Cross-sectional income profiles showing the mean incomes for workers of different age groups are illustrated in Figure 1, which is based on average incomes (in 1967 dollars) for males with four years of high school. The pattern of income by age group at any point in time is the familiar inverted U, with average income rising until age 45-54, then falling gradually until retirement, when a sharp decline occurs. Finer measures, indicating the relationship of age and income by occupational group, show roughly the same pattern, although the age at which average income peaks varies with education and occupation. In general, the higher the level of education and/or skill level of the job, the later the age at which income is maximized (Kreps and Pursell, 1967).

The age-income relationship shown by the curves for 1939 and the three subsequent decades in Figure 1 does not indicate the behavior of income for one particular cohort of workers, however, as they move through worklife. From Table 1 (and Figure 1), we observe that the males born in 1905–1914 with four years of high school had average incomes that rose throughout worklife. Incomes rose fastest in the workers' mid-30's to mid-40's but continued to rise in their 40's to 50's and in their 50's to 60's. Thus, the average male born in 1905 and having a high school education would likely have enjoyed income increases from the beginning of his worklife at, say, age 18, until his retirement in 1969.

Reliance on cross-sectional data for lifetime

TABLE 1. MEAN INCOME CHANGES THROUGH WORKLIFE FOR MALES WITH 4 YEARS OF HIGH SCHOOL, IN 1967 DOLLARS.

| Cohort born in 1905–1914 | INCOME CHANGE | | |
	From cohort data	From cross-sectional data	Growth difference
1940–1949	$2365	$1549	$ 816
1950–1959	2094	955	1139
1960–1969	1493	56	1437
1940–1969	5952	2560	3392
Cohort born in 1895–1904			
1940–1949	1671	665	1006
1950–1959	1195	–196	1391
1940–1959	2866	469	2397

SOURCES: 1969 data from U.S. Bureau of Census, *Current Population Reports*, Series P-60, No. 75, p. 101; 1959 and 1949 data from Herman Miller, *Income Distribution in the United States*, U.S. Bureau of the Census, 1966, p. 130; 1939 data from Herman Miller, "Annual and Lifetime Income in Relation to Education: 1939–1959," *American Economic Review*, December 1960, p. 966. Consumer Price Index used to convert to 1967 dollars.

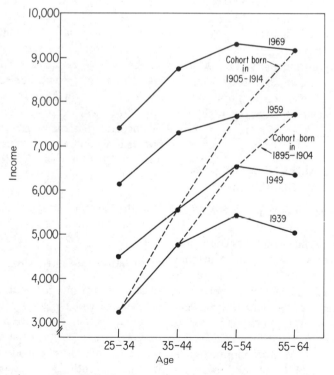

Figure 1. Age-income profiles of males with 4 years of high school (in 1967 dollars).

income estimates results in underestimation of income, since it fails to take account of the impact of economic growth. Table 1 separates the growth and the job experience components of income increase, inputing the cross-sectional difference to job experience and the remainder of the income increase to economic growth. It is important to note that the relative significance of the two components shifts during the course of worklife, with growth assuming a much greater portion of the increase in later years. Indeed, the change during the last decade of worklife would be minimal or negative (as in the case of the worker born in 1895, for example) if growth were not acting as an offset to the leveling-off or decline in the experience component of income.

The census data do not provide incomes for the 65-74 year age group, by education or previous occupational group, and it is therefore not possible to follow the cohort's income during the first decade (and then the subsequent years) of retirement. Herman Miller (1966) does give the figures for 1959, however. He shows a drop in median real income of 18 percent for the cohort born in 1885-1894, between 1949 and 1959 (from $6,333 to $5,184). This drop of nearly one-fifth came at the end of a lifetime of steady rise in income. The extent of the drop during the second decade of retirement is unknown, but there can be little doubt that real incomes continue to decline under the impact of inflation, if for no other reason.

CURRENT REAPPRAISALS OF THE MACROECONOMIC VARIABLES

The drift toward retirement before the usual age of 65, which has characterized the past decade or so in some industrialized economies, compounds the problem of retirement income by requiring larger aggregate transfers of income, and by increasing the number of years over which worklife savings and other assets must be spread. Moreover, gradual increases in life expectancy are clearly lengthening the retirement phase of life. Macroeconomic trends that reduce the availability of jobs to unemployed older workers, or increase the pressure

to move the retirement age downward, tend to offset the influence of rising productivity. Indeed, shortened worklife may slow real lifetime earnings significantly, perhaps to zero. The annual rate of economic growth, which is the major determinant of employment levels, is thus a critical force in setting the framework within which both earnings and retirement income are fashioned.

Current discussions of the future rate of growth are generally pessimistic because of two major problems: one, the growing concern over the environment, whose rate of deterioration appears to be related to the rate at which we increase productivity of goods and services, particularly goods; and two, the depletion of energy supplies under the continued pressure to increase the aggregate output. A third threat, that of higher rates of inflation that may accompany growth, is frequently cited also, although the fear that encouraging low growth in order to contain inflation will also generate higher levels of unemployment is just as often expressed.

In an attempt to relate the three major variables—economic growth, inflation, and unemployment—to the particular status of the elderly, each component will be examined, in turn, and then the state of the debate on growth will be reviewed briefly. The complex interaction of growth, prices, and income levels, and the manner in which these forces affect the aged's status, is further complicated by the fact that many aspects of social policy intervene to redirect the allocation of jobs and income. Distributional decisions made through tax policy, for example, may change the patterns of resource use in such a way as to protect the incomes of particular age or income groups, even when aggregate income is declining.

The Ambivalence of Growth

Even in a growing, affluent state, living levels are not particularly good for persons who are shut out of the productive process. In general, that age group currently at work receives the product, while those outside the labor force by reason of youth, old age, unemployment, or disability are supported by income claims transferred to them. These claims are increasingly public transfers which require tax collections, and incomes maintained via the tax mechanism are typically lower than earnings (Brittain, 1972). The aged's share in the national product is low because most aged do not work; conversely, the worker's share of the nation's output is high, although he enjoys much less free time than the elderly.

A systematic deterioration in the aged's relative income position occurs during periods of economic growth, even if price levels are constant or when pensions are tied to living costs. For while growth raises the living standards of workers and owners of capital each year, the real income of the aged person is fixed throughout retirement unless he or she is one of that small percentage of retirees who own equities. Indeed, the higher the rate of growth, the more rapidly the worker's earnings outstrip the fixed incomes of his predecessor on the job.

More specifically, we note from an earlier model that an annual rate of saving aimed at providing retirement consumption equal to 100 percent of current consumption during worklife would in fact provide 100 percent only when the rate of growth is zero (Kreps and Blackburn, 1967). Under assumed worklife and interest rate conditions, a growth rate of 1 percent throughout worklife allows the retiree 77 percent of the worker's consumption. When growth is 2 percent, the retiree's consumption is 60 percent; and when growth is 3 percent, only 48 percent of that of the workers. These levels of retirement income would be available, moreover, only at the beginning of the retirement period. A 60 percent consumption available at the time of retirement would decline to 45 percent of the workers' consumption in ten years of retirement, assuming the continuation of a 2 percent growth rate.

Economic growth is ambivalent in its consequences. By raising total output, growth makes it possible for a low-income group such as the aged to raise its absolute level of living above that achieved by the elderly in a preceding era. But since workers gain most if not all of the added growth, the nonworkers' relative position gradually worsens. What may have constituted an adequate level of living from the workers'

point of view thus falls below that acceptable standard in retirement, given the consumption standards of others in the society. As will be noted below, the prospect of no growth raises a different set of questions, with particular reference to the availability of jobs in the latter part of worklife.

Inflation

The impact of inflation on the economic status of the elderly has been widely discussed. After decades of debate, the United States Congress acted to tie the social security benefit to the cost of living, thereby mitigating inflation's effect on this group somewhat. Such an offset is not available to the worker; his real income has dropped in recent years, as the rise in prices has outstripped the rise in money wages. It is not surprising, therefore, that for the first time in the nation's history, inflation rather than unemployment has become the major public issue to labor and industry alike.

Public outrage at the current pace of inflation notwithstanding, predictions hold that prices will continue to go higher, in the United States, although the rate of increase is expected to slow somewhat. The most rapid rates of inflation are currently found in food and fuel, both of which loom large in the budget of the elderly. Moreover, the prevalence of poverty among the aged—about one couple in five had incomes of $3,000 or less in 1971, with half of all older couples on incomes of less than $5,000—would indicate that rising food prices, particularly, create extreme hardships.

One recent study of the impact of inflation on different racial, income, and age groups concluded that in the inflationary decade of the 1960's, the aged's share of the total income dropped by a larger percentage than was warranted by the decline in aged families as a fraction of all families. Specifically, the author compared the change in the income position of the elderly during the years 1961–65, when prices were rising at an annual rate of less than 1.5 percent, with the change occurring in 1964–68, when the annual rate was 3.3 percent. In the earlier period, the aged's share of total income fell by 0.9 percent while the proportion of all families headed by an elderly person declined by 0.4 percent. In the later, more inflationary phase of the decade, the aged again lost 0.9 percent of aggregate income, while their proportion of the total population remained constant. Although some redistribution from higher to lower incomes among the elderly occurred, thereby raising the median income of the group aged 65 and over, the elderly fell behind the income recipients in the economy as a whole (Brimmer, 1971).

The aged lost significantly, the author points out, in a period when most of the rise in the gross national product was due to price rise rather than growth in real output. In contrast to the late 1960's, however, when inflation rates reached 5 percent, current price rises are running at an annual rate of about 12 percent.

Inflation also has differential effects on the asset position or net wealth of individuals. Unanticipated inflation transfers real wealth from creditors to debtors, since the repayment of loans is made in the form of inflated dollars. A recent study calculated a "leverage ratio" that measures the exposure of an individual's asset position (monetary assets, variable-price assets, and debts). The lower the leverage ratio, the more vulnerable the group to inflation. The authors found that the elderly were the most heavily exposed age group since they have few debts and hold most of their limited wealth in the form of fixed assets. Conversely, young families are more heavily in debt; they tend to be in the process of buying houses, cars, etc. In summary, the leverage ratio of families whose head is over 65 is found to be .80, while that of families in the 25–34 age bracket is 1.75 (Bach and Stephenson, 1974).

The most recent analysis of the impact of inflation on different demographic groups concludes that the lower-income elderly, who depend primarily on OASDI and Supplemental Security Income, are cushioned against price rises to some extent. Since adjustments in these transfers lag the actual price increases, however (and do not always match the full rate of inflation), there may be some loss in the real income of this group. Higher-income elderly suffer a greater loss from inflation in proportion to their incomes because their sources include fixed dollar amounts such as those from private pensions. The elderly whose incomes include wage and salaries are subject to the inflation-induced rise in taxes falling on other age groups (Palmer and Barth, 1974).

Unemployment

Despite inflationary conditions, high levels of unemployment continue to hold sway. Even before fuel prices soared in 1974, forecasters expected a rise in unemployment to something over 5 percent. After the lack of fuel led to cutbacks in production, particularly in automobiles, the projected rate rose to 6 to 6$\frac{1}{2}$ percent—a significant increase in a labor force of 90 million persons. The early 1975 rate of more than 8 percent was far in excess of most projections, but even the current rate will probably rise in the course of the year.

Such an increase is unlikely to bring as much hardship to aged families as to those who are regularly full-time workers. Less than one-fourth of the males and less than 10 percent of the females aged 65 and over are in the labor force; hence their vulnerability to unemployment is lower than that of their younger counterparts. By far the highest rates of unemployment fall on teenagers, particularly nonwhites.

But the statistics on unemployment among the elderly do not tell the whole story. Most males aged 65 and over are classified as retired, whether or not they would prefer working part or full time. With the growing acceptance of retirement at or before age 65, men who would like to remain in the work force after that age are not likely to do so. Of the women who are now in their late 60's or older, only a small percentage held jobs outside the home, even when they were younger. The questions of relevance to the aged have to do with the adverse effect of rising unemployment on job prospects for the younger elderly (those aged 65 to 70) who make up the bulk of the aged who work, and with the possibility of a further decline in the usual retirement age generated by the pressure to balance the labor supply with the demand for workers.

Movements to lower the retirement age could

come from industry and the unions which, attempting to find jobs for young and middle-aged family heads, may reason that early pensioning for the 60 year old is an attractive alternative to displacing younger persons. As unemployment comes to be a major political issue, measures to lower the age of eligibility for social security benefits might also be initiated. Thus, age 62 or even 60 could come to be the normal retirement age. By defining more persons out of the labor force, the Congress, industry, and labor unions could reduce the recorded unemployment rate to a politically acceptable figure. In a similar fashion, social security legislation during the last major depression resulted from the need to draw older persons out of the labor force, thus helping to restore the balance between jobs and job seekers. Needless to say, a lowering of the age at which people are expected to retire merely shifts more and more of the burden of unemployment to the elderly, since pension incomes are seldom equal to foregone earnings. A major deterrent to such a shift at present is the fear of a shortfall in payroll tax revenues relative to social security benefits. A lowering of retirement age would of course worsen the revenue-benefit balance.

Income and Work Allocation under Conditions of Slower Growth

Should slower or even zero growth in output become a pattern, the relative status of the various age groups is difficult to predict. Economists are untutored in the implications of zero growth. And although there is no consensus on the inevitability of a steady state, recent and vivid description of the limits to growth force a consideration of the possibility of a much slower industrial pace. At a recent conference, economists posed the key questions:

What is the optimal rate of economic growth? . . . Should actions be taken to curb growth here and now? If so, what are the proper actions?. . . Can technological progress provide for the future? Is there an optimal population size? How would no-growth policy affect the incomes of disadvantaged groups?. . . How would individuals adjust

to a no-growth policy? (Weintraub 1973, p. xiii).

When these questions are focused on the particular position of the future elderly, the significance of growth in aggregate size and in patterns of income distribution are evident. The size of the retiree's income is fixed within the economy's capacity to support nonworkers along with workers, and this capacity is clearly set by the rate of growth. But the precise division of the total product depends on the manner in which society chooses to allocate that product. When the fruits of growth accrue to the current generation of workers, as is now the case in the American economy, worker's incomes exceed those of retirees. A reduction in the growth rate therefore tends to reduce this income differential. Under present distributive arrangements and zero growth, the incomes of workers and the incomes of retirees would move closer together, unless other changes acted to offset this movement.

Such an offset will likely occur in the form of reduced worklife. Slowed growth will almost inevitably reduce the number of jobs available, and higher unemployment could come to be translated into further downward pressure on retirement age. If this occurs the retiree will leave work with lower pension accumulations, which must then be stretched over a longer period of time. To the extent that the economy achieves its steady state by a reduced worklife, the problem of income in late life (which can no longer be referred to as old age, since many of the retirees will be in their late 50's and early 60's) is magnified.

As an alternative to reducing the length of worklife, a reduced growth rate could be accompanied by changes in work arrangements during worklife. Part-time work, particularly for teenagers and persons in their late 60's and early 70's as well as for women with family responsibilities, would effectively redistribute the available work. Free time, work, and earnings would then be spread over a longer portion of one's life, minimizing the income maintenance problems and increasing the value of leisure. These changed work patterns are now receiving a great deal of attention throughout western Europe, not because of a threat of zero growth but from a recognition of the need for a wider range of work-leisure options (Evans 1973).

Movement to zero economic growth for the United States is probably not acceptable. A number of compelling arguments for continued growth can be cited, not only on behalf of that large portion of the earth where present subsistence levels of living call for a continuation of improved technology and increased output, but also in order to improve the lot of the bottom income fifth of the American families.

In the United States of today, many families continue to struggle against the condition of poverty. The fact that the numbers of poor have been declining in the past decade and a half (as measured by the standard definition of poor, or low-income) is attributable primarily to economic growth, not to a redistribution of income. In particular, we have seen a decline in the numbers of poor persons from 39.5 million, or 22.4 percent of all people in 1959, to 25.5 million, or 13 percent in 1970 (Bureau of the Census, 1971). This improvement has occurred because fully employed heads of households have achieved the increases in real earnings that greater productivity made possible, with the result that their families were able to move beyond the poverty threshold. An ever-growing pie, not the way it was sliced, reduced poverty.

Were growth to cease, the poor's chances of further improving their lot would be greatly reduced; a redistribution of output would then be the only method remaining. It is doubtful that such a redistribution would be forthcoming, except perhaps very gradually. One may question also whether the poor, whose aspirations in recent years have grown dramatically, will accept this slow pace. Even in the past decade of high growth, the demands for increased opportunities, particularly on the part of minorities and women, have gone unmet. A period of slowed job prospects would augment the discontent already evident.

Despite these valid arguments in favor of continued high growth, there are unmistakable signs that resource constraints will force some change in the pattern of growth. It is easy to assume this problem away by proposing that we could grow without consuming resources too rapidly or destroying the environment by shifting from goods production, with all its waste and pollution to services—which presumably uses only "clean" human resources. But Lester Thurow reminds us that

> While it's quite true that services don't pollute directly, they generate a lot of indirect pollution. . . . Take education. Who is the largest consumer of electricity in the Boston area? . . . MIT. Who is the second largest? . . . the affiliated hospitals of Harvard. It's not at all obvious that we can have lots of health care and lots of education and still not have pollution or use of resources (Thurow, 1973, p. 145).

In short, there seems to be no easy way to take the purifying medicine of zero growth without suffering certain side effects. If these related imbalances are shared equally, as might be the case if all workers cut back their working time (and consequently their incomes), the impact of reduced growth on incomes would be absorbed with a minimum of hardship, and the time free of work would also be shared more evenly. But if the result is a growing number of unemployed and retired, current inequities in income will of course be magnified, and the additional free time would lack utility.

The economic status of the elderly would be improved by a trend toward longer, more flexible worklife in which work, earnings, and leisure time are apportioned more evenly through time. Such temporal allocation is not incompatible with slowed or even zero growth. But such a reallocation cannot occur unless working arrangements are changed. If present work arrangements are continued in a no-growth economy, the aged and other low-income groups are likely to suffer disproportionately. Such an outcome would mean that those least able to do so would absorb the major impact of reduced growth, and their particular hardship, although attributed to the cessation of growth, could have been mitigated by a change in work arrangements.

Earlier we noted the ambivalence of economic growth—an ambivalence due to its capacity to increase absolute levels of living for the elderly (along with others in the society), meanwhile lowering relative standards for the older group.

A no-growth condition is similarly ambivalent. Aggregate output is held constant by tightening the reins on income-producing effort, which has the immediate effect of dampening the incomes of workers vis-à-vis those of the nonworking elderly. The income differential between workers and nonworkers is reduced, and the aged's relative position improved. But there is a danger to the elderly: as growth slows, the reduced amount of work available is likely to be concentrated on those in their middle years, thus constricting even further the worklife and earning capacities of the oldest members of the labor force.

IMPACT OF THE AGED ON THE ECONOMY

Having directed attention to the ways in which social forces shape the lives of older people, the question may be reversed: how do the actions of the elderly affect the society? In particular, how are older people influencing consumer demand and patterns of leisure activity? To what extent do they determine the pattern of resource allocation? As the birthrate declines and the proportion of the population made up of older people rises, what changes will occur in market preferences and in economic decision-making? Does a rising median age bring a more conservative economy—one more security-conscious and less adventuresome in risk-taking?

Economic impact can come from the use of time, as well as money. "In an economic as in a philosophical or poetical sense," George Soule notes, "time must now be regarded as the scarcest of all categories of basic resources" (Soule, 1955, p. 99). The notion of scarcity of time has been emphasized by Wilbert E. Moore as well: "In the world of commonsense experience the only close rival of money as a pervasive and awkward scarcity is time" (Moore, 1963, p. 4).

Unfortunately, time and money are not always interchangeable. In many instances groups of people—the unemployed, the retired, for example—may not be able to transform time into goods. Time may therefore have little or no value in economic terms, its utility as leisure, when all time is free of work, being zero. The ability to exchange leisure for goods, or vice versa, is also limited for a large proportion of employed persons, whose annual hours of work are institutionally fixed throughout worklife.

A New Leisure Class?

In Thorstein Veblen's portrayal, those in the leisured group had money; not to have money meant that one worked for a living (Veblen, 1932). But in today's society free time has been generated in the process of growth in output, and much of that free time is being allocated to the retirement stage of life. As a result, persons in their 60's and over have an abundance of time free of work for pay, although most of them have quite modest incomes. Indeed, this "leisured class" has less money than the working class from which they graduated.

The total amount of nonworking time available to older people in the United States far exceeds that held by any other adult group. Even youth, whose leisure-time pursuits are highly publicized, particularly by advertisers, are far more constrained by education and work schedules than are retirees. The number of years accruing to people at the end of worklife will grow, moreover, as life expectancy improves and retirement age is lowered. In contrast to the earlier decades of this century, when the increase in free time was taken in shorter workyears, mid-century allocations of working time began to shorten worklife (Kreps, 1968). In other countries the free time accompanying increased productivity appears to be apportioned differently. During the two decades following the Second World War, the leisure pattern in Western European countries seems to have given more emphasis to workyear reductions and less to lowered retirement age than has been the case in the United States.

The forms in which nonworking time is apportioned have received little attention in the literature, although it is obvious that different degrees of utility would be associated with different allocative patterns. There is some question as to the value of leisure conferred in retirement, especially when it is accompanied by reduced incomes. The uneven distribution of leisure both among types of workers (Wilensky, 1961–62) and over a given life span has failed to elicit the interest aroused by income distribution; yet the portion of economic growth accruing in the form of leisure may be divided less evenly than income (Linder, 1970). In contrast to the leisure available to retirees, those in the work force are under some pressure to produce, to use time wisely, to work extra hours when possible. Steffan Linder points out that "we had always expected one of the beneficient results of economic affluence to be a tranquil and harmonious manner of life, a life in Arcadia. What has happened is the exact opposite. The pace is quickening, and our lives in fact are becoming steadily more hectic" (1970, p. 1).

Regardless of whether free time has utility to the retiree the amount of time so designated constitutes a major potential resource which can increasingly be turned to various uses: recreation, public service, education, work, if jobs are available. The extent to which older people will direct their time into these endeavors will depend in large measure on their income levels and the ease of entry to the different pursuits. In the field of education, some community colleges are now finding that retirees are eager to enroll in classes when the location, hours, and entry levels are appropriate to their needs. Since higher education is facing a period of depression because of a reduced number of college-age youth, an offset to the declining demand could come from the older age group. Although the median years of school completed by present retirees (about eight and one-half years) or even by those currently retiring (nine and one-half years) would seem to rule out most of the elderly's admission to college, nontraditional programs are being offered without reference to previous formal education.

Similarly, the potential contribution of older people to public service has not yet been realized, in part because there have been few attempts to organize the talents and time of this age group. Nor has it often been possible for retirees to contribute their time without also having to bear certain expenses (transportation, meals, etc.) which they can rarely afford. The impact of older people on the volunteer sector could be important and as in the case of educa-

tion, volunteer services are currently undersubscribed. As women enter the paid labor force, many community activities have gone unattended. The need for volunteers in such roles as teacher aides and health volunteers is particularly great. Neugarten has pointed out that a growth in numbers of the young-old—persons aged 55 to 70, who have higher levels of education and income, and who are more active politically—may produce important social changes in community participation (Neugarten, 1974).

Return of retirees to the paid work force in any large numbers does not seem a realistic goal in an era of rising unemployment. Any influence that older people exert on the economy will likely come from other roles, such as their role in public services or as a source of demand for education, for example. In neither case has the potential impact been analyzed in detail, perhaps because both education and volunteer services have so far been associated almost altogether with younger age groups.

The Older Consumer

Consumption patterns of the elderly were studied earlier by Goldstein who found that the total amount spent by an aged family was constrained by income in approximately the same manner as in the case of other age groups. Low levels of spending by older people appear to be due primarily to low incomes. Moreover, since the ability to borrow, particularly long-term funds, is quite limited for those whose remaining life expectancy is relatively short, older people find it necessary to live on current income to a far greater extent than do the young (Goldstein, 1960).

Growth in aggregate spending by the elderly results from an increase in their numbers as well as any rise in their money incomes. The numbers of people reaching age 65, less deaths among the elderly, now add about 300,000 per year to the total aged population. The increase in income per person is more difficult to predict, however, and projections of the aggregate income of the elderly therefore have only limited reliability. Earlier estimates of the total income going to the aged were aimed at identifying the components of the income and changes in the relative importance of these components in recent decades. In general, the shift has reflected two trends: one, a continued decline in the labor force activity of older men, causing the earnings portion of the aged's total income to drop; and, two, an expansion in public benefits and private pensions (Kreps, 1962).

Goldstein has also compared the composition of the aged's spending in 1950 with that of 1960, drawing on Survey of Consumer Expenditure data from the Bureau of Labor Statistics. The author shows that the proportions of expenditures made for certain groups of items—food, housing, and household operations and medical care—grow with increasing age of family head, whereas expenditures for household furnishings, transportation, personal care, clothing, and recreation are relatively lower for the old. These age-related comparisons held for both 1950 and 1960, but during the decade the relative importance of food and clothing expenditures declined, while medical care and housing grew as a proportion of the aged's budget. Two conclusions are drawn: one, different stages of the life cycle call for different patterns of consumption needs; but, two, a decline in income level requires shifts in expenditures in such a way as to ensure that the most basic needs can still be met (Goldstein, 1965). The clear implication that additional income in old age would increase the consumption of most goods has been borne out during the subsequent decade, as both the real incomes and expenditures of the elderly have grown (albeit less rapidly than those of the middle-aged). Conversely, an increase in particular prices (the cost of housing or medical care, for example) necessitates an increased expenditure for these essentials and a cut in spending for other goods, even food.

The aged can become a stronger force in directing the allocation of resources into the production of the particular goods they desire only if their incomes increase relative to those of the young; in fact, such an increase seems extremely unlikely. Nor has there been any strong representation of the elderly in the consumer field, except for Ralph Nader's recent investigation of nursing homes.

Very little advertising is aimed at the aged consumers, despite the growth in their aggregate expenditures. And although there have been predictions that producers would one day recognize the elderly's demand potential, no such recognition is apparent. Instead, the older consumer has access to the same goods and services markets as other age groups, with very little differentiation offered. For a wide range of products, no special markets are necessary. In the services areas, however, the aged obviously have needs that have long gone unmet, and many of these needs could have been paid for either by the older person himself or by public funds. Homemaker services, food preparation and delivery, and specialized transportation services would allow older people to live in their homes rather than go into congregate living arrangements which are frequently more expensive. Lack of market sensitivity to the range of goods and services the aged might well purchase if they were made available may be due in part to stereotyped notions of the aged as persons of very limited interests and capacities.

The aged's lack of consumer impact can be compared with their limited influence in political affairs. The threat of the aged's adverse vote has come to be reckoned with as the number of elderly has grown, however; improvements in social security benefits during election years are not uncommon. Achieving any consumer improvement by concerted action is much more difficult, even for the young and middle-aged who tend to be more active in promoting their interests. For the aged, the prospects of bringing direct pressure to bear on manufacturers or retailers are not good. An energetic public office that seeks to play an advocacy role for all consumers is probably a more realistic goal.

A Concluding Question: Do the Elderly Have Any Economic Impact?

Although neither the elderly nor any other age group wields a strong influence on the market for goods and services through concerted consumer pressure, any segment of demand plays its role in allocating resources. A competitive pricing system does respond to individual consumer choice; indeed, it is argued that the system remains competitive only to the extent that interferences aimed at favoring one person or group over another are avoided. The fact remains that one person is favored over another, when income allows different levels of consumer expenditures. The elderly's demand for goods and services, being constrained by lower incomes, has in the past had a minimum impact on resource allocation. The aggregate expenditure is now large and growing, nevertheless, and market response to this component of demand will follow.

The impact of older people in other economic areas seems more likely to diminish. Earlier withdrawal from work will reduce the influence of persons in their mid-60's and over. To the extent that early or compulsory retirements hasten the move of executives, managers, and other decision-makers from their jobs, there may be a significant erosion of older workers' power.

The relationship of age to the quality of business decisions—in particular, the correlation, if any, between age and willingness to assume risk—has had little study. It is therefore difficult to predict the outcome of a shift of decision-making authority from an older group to a younger one. The stereotype of the older executive as a conservative who avoids risk-taking while maximizing personal security cannot be confirmed or denied without careful research. But since the majority of corporate directors and practically all corporate officers are under age 65, the aged's representation on most top decision-making bodies is numerically too small to be of significance. Needless to say, the asset holdings of a relatively small number of very wealthy persons would seem to give them opportunities for exerting influence on business decisions.

Decisions made in the political arena increasingly affect the turn of economic events, as public sector activity increases relative to the private. The elderly's participation in public affairs, discussed in Chapter 15 of this volume, may offer an avenue through which older people can exert influence on the economy. Within the private sector the group's impact on resource allocation through their purchases of goods and services is significant and seems likely to grow, while their role in the labor force generally and in the important area of business decision-making appears more likely to decline.

The impact of macroeconomic trends on the welfare of the aged and conversely, the influence of a growing number of older people on the economy, are topics that have attracted little research interest. Yet sudden increases in the rate of inflation and the level of unemployment direct attention to the vulnerability of particular groups. If economic policy aimed at offsetting the effects of current hardships is to be effective, research is essential. Projections that indicate the future position of nonworkers under varying rates of change in growth and inflation would offer better policy guidelines than are now available.

REFERENCES

Bach, G. L., and Stephenson, James. 1974. Inflation and the redistribution of wealth. *Review of Economics and Statistics*, p. 5 (February).

Brimmer, Andrew F. 1971. Inflation and income distribution in the United States. *Review of Economics and Statistics*, pp. 37–48 (February).

Brittain, John A. 1972. *The Payroll Tax for Social Security*. Washington, D.C.: The Brookings Institute.

Bureau of the Census. 1971. *Income in 1970 of Families and Persons in the United States*. Current Population Reports, Series P-60, No. 80 (October).

Evans, Archibald A. 1973. *Flexibility in Working Life*. Paris: Organization for Economic Cooperation and Development.

Goldstein, Sidney. 1960. *Consumption Patterns of the Elderly*. Philadelphia: University of Pennsylvania Press.

Goldstein, Sidney. 1965. Changing income and consumption patterns of the aged, 1950-1960. *J. Geront.*, pp. 453–461 (October).

Gordon, Margaret. 1963. Income security programs and the propensity to retire. *In*, Richard H. Williams et al., *Processes of Aging*, pp. 436–458. New York: Atherton Press.

Kreps, Juanita M. 1962. Aggregate income and labor force participation of the aged. *Law and Contemporary Problems*, 27, 52–66 (Winter).

Kreps, Juanita M. 1968. *Lifetime Allocation of Work and Income*. U.S. Department of Health, Education and Welfare, Social Security Administration Research Report No. 22.

Kreps, Juanita M., and Blackburn, John O. 1967. *The Impact of Economic Growth on Retirement Income. Hearings before the Special Committee on Aging*, U.S. Senate, 90th Congress, pp. 58–64.

Kreps, Juanita M., and Pursell, Donald E. 1967. *Life-*

time *Earnings and Income in Old Age*. Joint Economic Committee, *Hearings on Old Age Income Assurance*, 90th Congress, 1st Session, Vol. II, pp. 260–279.

Linder, Steffan. 1970. *The Harried Leisure Class*. New York: Columbia University Press.

Miller, Herman. 1960. Annual and lifetime income in relation to education: 1939–1959. *American Economic Review*, p. 966 (December).

Miller, Herman. 1966. *Income Distribution in the United States*. U.S. Bureau of the Census.

Moore, Wilbert E. 1963. *Man, Time and Society*. New York: John Wiley.

Neugarten, Bernice. 1974. Age groups in American society and the rise of the young-old. *Ann. Amer. Acad.*, pp. 187–198.

Palmer, John L., and Barth, Michael C. 1974. *The Impacts of Inflation and Higher Unemployment: With Emphasis on the Lower Income Populations*. U.S. Department of Health, Education and Welfare, Office of Income Security Policy, Technical Analysis Paper No. 2.

Rimlinger, Gaston. 1971. *Welfare Policy and Industrialization in Europe, America, and Russia*. New York: John Wiley, Chapter 5.

Shanas, Ethel; Townsend, Peter; Wedderburn, Dorothy; Friis, Henning; Milhøj, Poul; and Stehouwer, Jan. 1968. *Old People in Three Industrial Societies*. London: Routledge & Kegan Paul.

Soule, George. 1955. *Time for Living*. New York: The Viking Press.

Thurow, Lester. 1973. Zero economic growth and income distribution. Andrew Weintraub *et al.*, *The Economic Growth Controversy*. New York: International Arts and Sciences Press.

United Nations, Department of Economic and Social Affairs. 1962. Sex and age patterns of participation in economic activities. *Demographic Aspects of Manpower*.

United Nations. 1973. *Question of Elderly and the Aged*. Report of the Secretary-General, pp. 33–37 (August).

Veblen, Thorstein. 1932. *The Theory of the Leisure Class*. New York: Vanguard Press.

Weintraub, Andrew. 1973. *The Economic Growth Controversy*. New York: International Arts and Sciences Press.

Wilensky, Harold, 1961–62. The uneven distribution of leisure. *Soc. Prob.*, 9, 32–56.

Winston, Gordon C. 1966. An International Comparison of Income and Hours of Work. *Review of Economics and Statistics*, **XLVIII**, 28–39 (February).

12
WORK AND RETIREMENT

Harold L. Sheppard
American Institutes for Research

BACKGROUND AND INTRODUCTION

The link between individual and work is especially important in studies of the elderly because of the relationship of the income of the aged to their previous and current work status. For nearly all persons, income during retirement is derived from some claim of attachment to the labor force in prior years. This is particularly so in countries in which age *per se* is not the almost exclusive ground for retirement income eligibility. As Atchley (1972) expressed it, "The idea that the right (to current income without current employment) must be earned is related to the fact that retirement is reserved for only older *workers*."

Thus, income during old age is primarily work-related, and work is defined as an activity for others for which the individual is rewarded monetarily. In the United States, retirement itself comes to be defined in monetary terms, as evidenced by the fact that in order to prove oneself eligible for Old Age and Survivors Insurance, the individual must pass a "Retirement Test," that is, must not be receiving more than a certain amount of *earned* income. Income from inheritances, investments, gifts, etc., is thereby *not* included in the test. Thus, the central importance of work in the life chances of the elderly lies in the fact that they (or their spouses) formerly worked. Also, their attitudes toward their retirement (before and during) and their actual retirement rates are accordingly affected by expected or actual incomes during retirement.

One of the several developments that continue to intrigue researchers and policy analysts in the field of industrial gerontology is the *increasing* percentage of persons out of every birth cohort who *survive* into "old age" (using 65 as an arbitrary cutoff age), accompanied by the *decreasing* percentage of those survivors who continue as active members of an employed, income-earning work force. For example, in 1905, the odds for white males born that year reaching the age of 65 were roughly 66 out of 100, in contrast to only 53 out of 100 for those born 40 years earlier, in 1865, the year that is frequently used as the launching of the Industrial Age in the United States. The figures are merely the factual basis for the generalized statement that "more people are living to be old," or more precisely, that a higher percentage of any birth cohort is living to be older than the previous cohort. Over the same period, however, the proportion of a given cohort of young workers continuing as members of the work force by the time they reach "old age" has been declining. The general explanation of these changes in work participation has focused on the shift from a predominantly rural-agricultural society—in which people were needed and in which a higher proportion had the option to continue working, if capable—to the contemporary urban-industrial-commercial society. As Dona-

286

hue, Orbach, and Pollak expressed it in the 1960 *Handbook of Social Gerontology*:

> Retirement is a phenomenon of modern industrial society. Previous socioeconomic systems in man's history have had varying numbers of older people, but none has ever had the number or proportion of aged that obtains in the industrialized societies of the present day. More important, *the older people of previous societies were not retired persons*; there was no retirement role. (Donahue, W., Orbach, H. L., and Pollak, O. Retirement: The emerging social pattern. *In*, C. Tibbitts (ed.), *Handbook of Social Gerontology*, p. 336. Chicago: University of Chicago Press. ©1960 by The University of Chicago.)

To be sure, the post-World War II period in Western industrialized countries has witnessed the most rapid rate of growth in the exit from the labor force. The bases for retirement as a somewhat unique sociohistorical phenomenon (over and above the influence of modernized health and medical practices) include the emergence of a *technology* capable of producing a gross national product and per capita income that allows for a decrease in the total man-hours necessary to provide a rising level of income and other forms of provisions for a living standard deemed acceptable and desirable; and an increase, due to mortality decreases, in average number of years in the labor force. Thus, even without any increase in the proportion of persons reaching 65 or older, it has been possible to "release" a higher percentage of such persons from having to produce goods and services, either for income or for other, nonmonetary motives. "Possible" is a critical word here, since it is conceivable that other patterns or forms of distributing the man-hours necessary for a desired living standard could have been developed during the past seven or more decades—patterns that would have resulted in, for example, a greater reduction in working hours among a working population of a given size, instead of a reduction of people at work.

At any rate, only industrial societies have undergone an *increase* in the proportion of people designated as "old" (about 65 and older); only industrial societies have simultaneously witnessed a *decrease* in the proportion of the old who are active members of those societies' labor forces. Labor force is defined as the population currently employed or seeking employment. This decline in the proportion of the old who participate in the labor force is not purely and simply a function of the fact that the category of "65-plus" is openended. That is, the decline is not due simply to the significant increase in the numbers and proportion of the "very old," i.e., those 75 and over, and presumably less "employable" than those 65-69.

The participation of men 65-69 in the work force has steadily declined. In 1950, approximately 60 percent of males in this age group in the United States were in the labor force, but by 1970, this proportion had declined to 41 percent. This low proportion, moreover, includes—much more than in the past—persons working part-time, and on less than a yearround basis. In 1972, out of all males in the population aged 65-69, only 21 percent had worked year-round (50-52 weeks) on a fulltime basis. Among all females in the same age group, the proportion was slightly under 7 percent.

EARLY RETIREMENT

The decline in labor force participation rates (and/or decline in the proportion of men working year-round and full-time) has not been taking place only among those 65-69. It can be seen in the population slightly younger than that group, those 60-64. The decline in the labor force participation rate in groups below the "normal" retirement age of 65 is partly attributable to the availability of retirement income programs, such as the right to reduced social security benefits at the age of 62, for men as well as women. Nevertheless, it remains unclear as to whether the mere availability of such programs is a sufficient explanation for the decline. Social security data on applicants for old age insurance benefits prior to the age of 64 show a disproportionate number with poor health, long-term unemployment experience, etc. Unfortunately, such information still provides us with insufficient insights into the reasons for early retirement among those under 65 who are *not* in ill health, and/or without poor labor market experience. The Social

Security Retirement History Study—initiated in 1969—will be a major contribution to a greater understanding of the forces affecting such retirement decisions because it will provide data on a longitudinal basis concerning the group that was 58-63 years old in 1969. Such a survey hopefully will take into account not only the characteristics of the individual (including occupation and industry), but also region, type of residence (urban size, etc.), and the state of the economy in each survey year. Thus, a multivariable type of analysis will be possible. However, it should be noted that few, if any, governmental national sample studies of this nature delve adequately into social-psychological variables which may also play a role in explaining variations in the labor force participation rates of (1) different age groups at any one time, (2) the same age cohort over a period of years, and (3) different *generations* of "older" workers. The latter approach would help us determine, for example, whether the older workers of 1950 were different in life-styles, work values, skill performance, and social character, than the older workers of 1980.

Data from this Retirement History Study suggest, as of its first cross-sectional survey in 1969, that marital status is a critical variable, with *married men* least likely to be early retirees. This suggests that persons with few or no family responsibilities are more likely to opt for retirement status (Irelan and Bond, 1974). But this interpretation is complicated by the additional facts that health, education, and occupation also play a role in such decisions, and that these three factors may be associated with marital status. According to the Retirement History Study, among the men and women no longer working in this age group (58-63) as of 1969, nearly two-thirds of the men and two-fifths of the nonmarried women reported that health was the primary reason for leaving their last jobs. Occupational status and race also figured heavily in their work incapacity. "Manual workers and Blacks with limitations were more likely to have stopped work on account of health." These facts about health and employment status can be misleading, however, if we ignore the further finding that most of the persons with physical limitations inter-

viewed were still working and had been disabled long before the survey year. Another critical factor in the retirement decision, of course, is the availability of a private pension and its adequacy. In the Retirement History Study's 1969 sample, fewer than one-half of the persons aged 58-63 were working for employers providing a private pension plan. Again, marital status was involved: the proportion with pension coverage in their present job was greatest among the married men, lower for nonmarried men, and least among nonmarried women. The status of the latter group is further aggravated by the fact that their median annual income is far below that of all other sex-marital status categories.

A critical age-sex group for industrial gerontologists is that of 55 to 64-year-old males, for it is in this group particularly that labor market experience, and actual or planned retirement, has undergone some marked developments. From 1947 to 1973, the labor force participation rate of this category declined from 90 percent to 78 percent.

The 1969 Retirement History Study by the Social Security Administration sheds further light on the reasons for withdrawal from the labor force on the part of the men aged 58-63 within that group. At the time these men were interviewed in 1969, 83 percent were still employed or actively seeking work. Ten years earlier—when they were ten years younger—the corresponding rate was about 96 percent. In 1969, nearly three-fourths were employed at full-time jobs, and 6 percent were working at part-time jobs. Contrary to a widely accepted belief, most of these nonactive men had withdrawn from the labor force before becoming eligible for social security benefits at the age of 62. Data from other government sources, nevertheless, show that a significant drop in labor force participation occurs after age 61, thus suggesting that for men—and women, too—62-64 years old, many do choose "early retirement" before the age of 65.

For males 58-63 years old in 1969, marital status was an important factor associated with labor force status: those married had the highest participation rate and were the least likely to retire early. For those 62-63, according to the

Social Security survey, the early retirement option was a major factor. It is not clear from the data, however, whether these men had actually stopped looking for work (and hence were not defined technically as "unemployed") due to the job-search discouragement process or were still looking in the months and years prior to their applying for benefits at age 62 or 63. (Workers exhausting their unemployment compensation benefits are disproportionately in the upper age groups.) But as Schwab (1974, p. 24) reports, "most nonparticipants are out because of other reasons."

Health was by far the reason most frequently mentioned by nonparticipants for leaving their last job. Compared to their male age-peers still in the labor force, a large majority of the nonparticipants (60 percent) viewed their health as poorer than that of people their same age. Only 12 percent of those still in the labor force answered similarly. The influence of poor health on labor force participation in pre-65 age groups has been noted in a number of other studies, for example, by United States Senate Subcommittee staff reports (1967b), Rosenfeld and Waldman (1967), and J. M. Davis (1972).

Occupation also played a major role among the factors influencing extent of participation in this group of men aged 58-63, as Table 1 indicates. When occupational category was taken into account, education *per se* surprisingly showed little relationship to degree of labor force participation. Education, of course, may affect the individual's chances for being in a given occupation, which in turn "predetermines" other life chances, including health status, job security, etc.

Black men are more typically to be found in the more disadvantaged occupational, health, and education categories associated with higher nonparticipation rates. Such factors provide much of the explanation for the greater decline in labor force participation rates of black men 45-64 by the time they are years older, in contrast to the white cohort.

The economic implication of labor force participation and differences in year-round, full-time employment can be seen in Table 2, which contrasts the median income of persons working year-round, full-time with the income of all employed persons by age and sex. The major feature of this table is the wide contrast in income, within each of the upper age groups, between those working year-round, full-time and the total employed population. A more meaningful comparison would present the median income of those *not* working year-round, full-time, but census data do not report this.

Educational level increases the probability, within each age group of both men and women, of working year-round, full-time as indicated in Table 3. Within each of the older age-sex groups shown, the greater the education, the higher the

TABLE 1. 1969 LABOR FORCE PARTICIPATION OF MEN 58-63, BY OCCUPATION.

Occupation of longest job	Percent in labor force
Professional	90
Farmer	88
Manager	87
Clerical	83
Sales	89
Craftsmen	84
Operative	79
Service	79
Farm Laborer	76
Nonfarm Laborer	73

Source: K. Schwab, *Social Security Bulletin*, August, 1974, p. 28.

TABLE 2. MEDIAN INCOME IN 1973 OF ALL PERSONS AND PERSONS WORKING YEAR ROUND, FULL TIME, BY AGE AND SEX.

Age	MALES		FEMALES	
	Total	YR–FT	Total	YR–FT
20–24	$ 5,157	$ 7,472	$3,027	$5,530
25–34	10,088	11,325	4,142	7,086
35–44	12,030	12,909	4,110	6,782
45–54	11,671	12,756	4,303	6,673
55–64	9,552	11,728	3,431	6,587
65 and older	4,106	8,923	2,119	5,560

Source: Census Bureau, *Current Population Reports*, P-60, No. 93, "Money Income in 1973 of Families and Persons in the Unites States," July, 1974, Table 2.

TABLE 3. PERCENTAGE OF MALE AND FEMALE INCOME
RECIPIENTS WORKING YEAR-ROUND, FULL-TIME,
BY AGE AND EDUCATION, 1972.

Education	MALES					
	All 25 and older	25–34	35–44	45–54	55–64	65 and older
Under 9 years	43	60	67	67	56	9
9–11	63	69	73	77	65	14
High School	76	80	86	84	74	17
13 or more years	78	76	90	89	75	23

Education	FEMALES					
	All 25 and older	25–34	35–44	45–54	55–64	65 and older
Under 9 years	16	21	32	38	26	2
9–11	29	27	36	44	33	4
High School	41	42	45	54	45	6
13 or more years	44	48	48	57	52	9

SOURCE: Census Bureau, *Current Population Reports*, P-60, No. 90, "Money Income in 1972 of Families and Persons in the United States," 1973, Table 51.

proportion working year-round on a full-time basis, excepting males 25-34.

The long-term decline in labor force participation rates for males applies especially to nonwhites, starting primarily at age 55. Census data (1974) reveal that from 1963 to 1973, the participation rates of nonwhite males (55-64) declined from 83 percent to only 71 percent—in contrast to a decline among white males of the same age group from 87 to 79 percent. Among nonwhite *females*, on the other hand, the decline was only from 47 to 45 percent over the same ten-year period. Among white women, the corresponding participation rates for 1963 and 1973 actually underwent a slight *rise*, from 39 to 41 percent. These data suggest, among other things, that race-sex categories (combined) are much more relevant than race or sex taken separately, in seeking to understand developments in the work behavior and lives of older workers, and of workers generally, as they go through the work-life cycle. The greatest decline in participation rates in this older group has taken place among *nonwhite males*; the second greatest, among white males; the third greatest, among nonwhite females; and an increase occurred in the case of the 55-64-year-old white women.

In the case of both older male and female nonwhites, ill health and disability as a reason for not being in the labor force is much more frequently cited than among older male and female whites.

WORK LIFE EXPECTANCY

From 1940 through 1960, working life expectancy of men (the average number of years worked during a person's life) at age 16 increased from 44.5 years to 45.2. Table 4, developed by Howard Fullerton (1972), shows the changes in expectation of worklife and retirement years (for 1940, 1950, and 1960). This type of table differs from others previously available, based on "period" life calculations. The latter have limited usefulness, according to Fullerton, because conventional tables calculate life expectancy at each age, "and ordinarily are based on mortality rates applicable to each age observed at one point in time." Fullerton's work is aimed at presenting a "generation" type of table which presents a more realistic approach to life expectancy and labor force participation rates. It is, in other words, of a much more "longitudinal" nature than the

TABLE 4. EXPECTATIONS OF YEARS OF LIFE, WORKLIFE, AND RETIREMENT FOR MEN ENTERING THE LABOR FORCE.

Age	Expectation of Life			Expectation of Worklife			Expectation of Retirement		
	1940	1950	1960	1940	1950	1960	1940	1950	1960
16	54.0	54.4	54.8	44.5	44.8	45.2	9.5	9.6	9.6
35	36.8	37.0	37.4	27.0	27.1	27.3	9.8	9.9	10.1
55	20.2	20.4	20.5	10.6	10.4	10.5	9.6	10.0	10.0
65	13.7	13.7	13.8	5.0	5.0	5.0	8.7	8.7	8.8

Retirement refers to final withdrawal from labor force at any age.
SOURCE: Howard Fullerton, *Monthly Labor Review*, July, 1972.

earlier period tables used by labor force analysts and social gerontologists.

Such a revised approach also suggests that retirement rates will be higher than previously projected. The contrast is greatest for men 65–70 as of 1960. The generation table approach reports a retirement rate of 195 per thousand, in comparison to only 119 when using the period table. The new calculations indicate that, on the average, for men 55, the proportion of remaining years spent in retirement increased slightly from 1940 to 1960. For men 65, the increase was even less, but nevertheless, as of 1960, nearly two-thirds of this group's average remaining life expectancy will be spent in retirement. Fullerton's calculations of retirement years for men 65 in 1960 arrive at an estimate of 8.8 years while the "period" table calculations resulted in an estimate of only 6.5. Such a discrepancy has serious implications for individual and public programs which base their service and financial plans on such estimates. Many of the projections for the future, more specifically, have reported a higher labor force participation rate in the upper age groups than have actually occurred or which can be expected in the future.

A NEW PHENOMENON: LABOR FORCE PARTICIPATION OF WOMEN

The growth of paid employment among women over the past quarter century is a phenomenon that cannot be overlooked when dealing with issues in industrial gerontology. From 1947 to 1973, their rate of participation in the work force of America increased at a rate of over 40 percent (from 32 to 45 percent). At the same time, male participation rates declined at a rate of over 8 percent. The full implications of this development have still to be spelled out by manpower and economic analysts and other social scientists.

One major explanation lies in the increasing "availability" of married women over this period, made possible by a decrease in home- and child-care responsibilities for such persons, a result of smaller family size. Neither can we exclude the influence of the increasing percentage of all persons residing in large urban areas, which typically offer greater job possibilities for women. The increased schooling of women is another factor. The "rising level of expectations" among American families, i.e., the desire for a "higher" standard of living, is yet another factor that must be considered.

By 1973, women constituted 38 percent of the employed labor force 16 and older; in 1947, only 23 percent. From 1959 to 1972, women as a proportion of *all* workers with year-round, full-time job experience rose from about one-fourth to nearly one-third. Indeed, the number of women working year-round, full-time increased, from 1959 to 1972, by over 60 percent, in contrast to only an 18 percent rise in the case of men.

How does all this relate to matters pertaining to work and aging? More specifically, over the more than a quarter of a century spanning from 1947 to 1973, the greatest increase in rate of labor force participation occurred among women 55–64 years old, followed by women

TABLE 5. LABOR FORCE PARTICIPATION RATES OF WOMEN, BY AGE, 1947 AND 1973 (16 AND OVER).

Year	Total	16–17	18–19	20–24	25–34	35–44	45–54	55–64	65+
1947	32	30	52	45	32	36	33	24	8
1973	45	39	57	61	50	53	54	41	9
Rate of Increase	*29*	*30*	*10*	*36*	*56*	*47*	*58*	*71*	*13*

SOURCE: *Manpower Report of the President, 1974*, Table A-2. Rates are rounded off.

in the next youngest age group, 45–54, as shown in Table 5.

The rates of increase in labor force participation substantially above the overall average increase of 29 percent since 1947 begin at the 25–34 age group and continue through the age group 55–64. Because the Labor Department data for those over 64 is "open-ended," it is not possible to ascertain with certainty whether the 65–69 age group also underwent substantial increases in labor force participation. But comparing Census data for 1940 with that for 1970, we do find a change from 9.5 to 17.0 percent of women 65–69 years old in the labor force, a change amounting to a 79 percent rate of increase. This is all the more remarkable, given the fact that in 1970, opportunities for women to retire as young as 62 were available under social security, which was not true in 1940. But statistics reporting "labor force participation rates" are not the same as those dealing with percentages of the population with "work experience." For example, in 1972, the Labor Department reported that among persons 16 and older, the *labor force participation* rate was about 61 percent. But in the same year, the percentage of such persons with any *work experience* was 67 percent. In 1972, the "labor force" was numbered at nearly 82.5 million men and women (civilians only). But those with "work experience" in the same year was reported at nearly 97 million! What is more important, for purposes of this chapter, is that the older the women's age (and for men, too, for that matter), the greater the discrepancy between the figure for labor force participation and that for those with any work experience, as Table 6 shows.

The increase of women as a percentage of the

TABLE 6. LABOR FORCE VS. WORK EXPERIENCE POPULATION FIGURES FOR WOMEN, 1970.
(in thousands)

	Labor Force	Work Experience	% Difference
All 16 and older	31,560	38,704	23
45–54	6,533	7,302	13
55–59	2,547	2,871	33
60–64	1,606	2,132	33
65–69	644	937	46
70 and older	412	678	65

SOURCES: Department of Labor data on 1970 labor force size and on persons with work experience in 1970.

total labor force will apparently continue, as Table 7 indicates.

In each of these upper age groups beginning with ages 55–59, women will constitute an increasing percentage of the labor force in that group—with the sharpest increase in the 70-plus group (in large part a reflection of the higher female-male sex ratio in this older group).

The most important single source for the in-

TABLE 7. OLDER WOMEN AS PERCENT OF TOTAL LABOR FORCE OF SELECTED AGES, 1960, 1970, AND 1990.

	1960	1970	1990 (projected)
All 16 & older	32	37	39
55–59	33	38	41
60–64	30	36	40
65–69	30	34	39
70 & older	26	32	41

SOURCE: *Manpower Report, 1974*, Table E-2.

crease in the proportion of women in the labor force over the past decades has been from the ranks of married women with husbands present (the rates for other women already being relatively high). Table 8 shows the changes, for selected years from 1953 to 1973, in labor force participation rates, by age of married women with husbands present.

In each age group, the presence of children under 18 influences the rate of participation and of extent of participation (part- or full-time). The percentage of older employed married women (with spouse present) working part-time (less than 35 hours per week) in 1970 was somewhat higher if they had children in the home than if they had no children at home. With the current trend toward smaller families among today's women of child-bearing age, we might expect an increased labor force participation rate—and increased full-time work—among such women as they themselves grow older. We have no way of knowing how this will affect

voluntary retirement rates in this group as they reach their mid-60's. But it is not unreasonable to speculate that these retirement rates may decline—despite the opportunities to retire. To repeat, we do know that among women aged 55–64, married and with husband present, labor force rates increased from 18 percent to 35 percent, from 1953 to 1973—a twofold increase during a period in which retirement before 65 became legally possible under Social Security Amendments. (Over the same time period, participation rates of 55–64-year-old *men* with spouse present *declined*—from 91 to 82 percent.)

Reference was made earlier to the relationship of urbanization to labor force participation rates of women. As an example, among white adult women of all ages, the 1970 rates in the central cities were higher than in places outside of central cities, but especially higher than the rates in rural areas (Census, 1973). Even when comparing Standard Metropolitan Areas by size

TABLE 8. FEMALE LABOR FORCE PARTICIPATION RATES OF MARRIED WOMEN, WITH SPOUSE PRESENT, BY AGE, 1953-73.

	Total[b]	Under 20	20–24	25–34	35–44	45–54	55–64	65+
1953	26	21	28	25	34	31	18	6
1957	30	24	30	27	36	37	25	6
1961	33	28	32	29	38	42	29	7
1965	35	27	36	32	41	44	31	8
1969	40	35	48	37	45	48	35	8
1973	42	42	53	44	49	48	35	7
"Stouffer" Index of Change[a]	22	27	35	25	23	25	21	1

[a] A measure that accounts for the fact that an increase from one level of percentage to some maximum percentage (such as 100 percent) will be affected by the size of the base percentage. It is a more sensitive and more relevant measure than the usual one that takes the percentage at one time and uses the absolute percentage points between that one and the succeeding one as a proportion of the original percentage. For example, an increase from 95 to 100 percent is greater, using the Stouffer approach (developed in his *American Soldier* volumes), than an increase from, say, 25 to 37 percent. The formula is:

$$\frac{\text{Difference in percentage points from time A to time B}}{\text{Difference between 100\% and time A percentage}}$$

In other words, when starting at 95 percent, an increase of only 5 is possible to reach 100. But when starting at 25, an increase of 75, to reach 100, is possible.
[b] Prior to 1967, participation rates were based on population 14 and older; starting in 1967, on 16 and older. The "total" and "under 20" columns reflect these changes.
SOURCE: *Manpower Report of the President, 1974*, Table B-2.

(including central city with suburb), the participation rates are highest in the largest areas (Sheppard, 1971). More pointedly, the rates for those in each of the subgroups of the population 60 and older living in central cities are generally twice the rates of those living in rural areas—especially in rural farm areas. Rural farm women are generally wives of farmers and typically are not defined in government reports as "members of the labor force" (despite the fact that they may be unpaid household workers in their own families). On the other hand, in the central cities female residents are more likely to be in lower income families (and not in husband-present families) and may be under greater pressure to seek employment.

Older single women and those widowed, divorced, or separated register the highest labor force participation rates when compared to married women with husbands present—despite the fact that the greatest rate of increase in such participation has been taking place among the latter group. In recent years the highest participation rate among all non-married women occurs in the age group 45-54.

The Social Security Administration's Retirement History Study sheds some new information especially on the labor force status of *nonmarried* women on the "threshold of retirement," those 58-63 as of 1969 (Sherman, 1974). Despite the eligibility for old age insurance, one-half of the nonmarried women in the Study aged 62-63 are in the labor force. In this same age group (62-63), widows have the lowest labor participation rate; those never married, the highest rate (46 *vs.* 62 percent). For the total groups aged 58-63, labor force participation rates were heavily affected by receipt or nonreceipt of social security benefits. Less than 30 percent of those receiving benefits were in the labor force as of 1969, in contrast to more than 70 percent of those not receiving benefits.

Among those in the labor force, their occupation distribution reveals a concentration in lower level jobs—clerical, operatives, private household, and other service occupations. "Only 15 percent were employed in the pro-

fessional and technical field." While the data reveal that education plays an important role in their level of occupation (for example, among those with a college degree, more than 80 percent are in professional and technical jobs), they do not shed any light on the "complicated issue of why women do not have more education or special training or experience so that more can qualify for jobs of higher status" (Sherman, 1974).

WORK PERFORMANCE, FUNCTIONAL AGE, AND TRAINING

Findings from research on the relationship between age and work performance and work capacities are difficult to interpret because of the difference in methods, populations studied, and theoretical approaches, etc. Often the use of simulated, laboratory settings will yield findings at variance with studies based on actual working conditions. On the other hand, older persons in actual work situations are themselves a selective group, since they omit those men and women out of the labor force whose performance on the job may differ from both younger and older persons who are in the labor force. Actual job performance evaluations, however, generally reveal findings more favorable than those based on "artificial" laboratory conditions, or on paper-and-pencil tests often used as a convenient proxy for actual job assessment evaluations (Laufer and Fowler, 1971).

Differences in productivity, of course, can vary depending on the nature of the work involved. Here the viewpoint of Charles Miller is pertinent. Dr. Miller has argued for ascertaining job-specific research data, as opposed to general laboratory data on memory, intelligence, dexterity, and other work-related performance phenomena. From his point of view, the literature on work performance and age is rather unsophisticated in terms of this failure to differentiate various aspects of a work-job situation (e.g., degree and type of physical efforts, as distinct from psychomotor facets which in turn should be distinguished from sensory perception, etc.)—and relative to specific types of job-tasks or occupations.*

Average rates of productivity will vary depending on the type of work involved. For example, among clerical workers, there are apparently no substantial age differences. Among mail sorters, marked productivity declines begin to appear, on the average, after age 60; among retail sales personnel, some decline is found somewhere in the 50's (Riley, Foner, Moore, Hess, and Roth, 1968, pp. 426–433; 460–463).

Laboratory tasks dealing with sensorimotor skills tend to indicate that older workers' experience may offset what otherwise might be expected as decrements due to aging. But equally important, the variation within age groups in job performance measures is such that large proportions of older workers frequently exceed the performance levels of many younger workers. Some studies also suggest that *consistency* of output may improve by age—with older workers performing at steadier levels. To be sure, although work injuries are not generally related to age (with some age differences appearing in certain types of work), once injured, the older the worker, the longer the recuperation period.

One of the unintended consequences of the use of cross-sectional research methodologies, and of the use of such statistical measures as the mean and the median, on the part of gerontologists studying such matters as age differences in intellectual and job capacities is the possible perpetuation of halftruths and misleading generalizations about such capacities. The typical report of this nature will accurately present the differences at any one time among the age groups studied, which generally reveal lower *average* score results as one goes up the age scale.

Averages obscure the phenomenon of heterogeneity within age groups and thus make difficult, if not impossible, the task of searching for those conditions, processes, and characteristics that might lead to possible practical solutions to the presumed problems of declining cognitive abilities, work performance, etc., that adversely affect the life chances of older persons as far as their work opportunities are concerned. The use of such averages also can reinforce negative stereotypes about adult and older workers as a group and thus result in discriminatory practices in hiring, promotion, and training.

Furthermore, as Baltes and Schaie (1974) have pointed out, even in cross-sectional analyses, there are separate dimensions of such measures of intelligence on which there are no differences according to age. In fact, on some of these dimensions, older persons tend to perform better than younger ones. But, a critical weakness of most studies on work performance is that they are not studies of changes in abilities as men and women grow older. They are only studies of differences between age groups at one point in time.

Longitudinal studies not only capture the changes, if any, occurring among a cohort of persons over time (i.e., as they grow older). They also can, when properly designed and implemented, reveal that an important phenomenon involved in performance is what might be called the "generation" factor—that is, the sociohistorical nature of the period of one's birth. Each generation of men and women in societies such as the United States undergoes certain unique kinds of experiences, for example, in the extent and nature of education, in living in periods of economic growth or decline, etc. Education in particular is highly critical in understanding the test performance of the elderly. The older the age group, the lower the average education. And the lower the level of education, the lower the group performance on certain dimensions of IQ tests. Future generations of "older" people— those who are now young—may turn out to be quite different from the old of the past and of today as far as job performance, occupational retraining, and job changing are concerned and may be much more capable of performing adequately in their work roles. This statement should be coupled with the further fact that in-

*From notes taken by the author from a presentation by Charles Miller, M.D., at a National Council on Aging Seminar on Industrial Gerontology, Washington, April, 1968.

creasingly the physically onerous nature of work (weight-lifting, the pace of the work cycle, etc.) is being reduced, and thus it constitutes less of a barrier to the employment of those persons, for example, who may be undergoing declines in physical ability.

The notion of "functional age" has received a great deal of attention in industrial gerontology. According to Ross McFarland (1973), one of the pioneers of research on this issue, interest in functional age emerged at the beginning of World War II, when industry found it necessary to hire previously retired workers to meet the demand for labor. In effect, it was found that it was inappropriate and even unfair to evaluate workers according to the year of their birth. In brief, the point is that functional age is not identical with chronological age.

Among the features of the literature focusing on the use of functional age in the world of work are the following:

1. The focus is on the abilities and not the disabilities (or the pathologies) of aging.

2. Special attention is paid to the determination of the conditions or characteristics that make for (or against) successful adaptation to work tasks, e.g., ignoring statistical averages and searching for variables that explain the heterogeneity within age groups vis-à-vis job performance.

3. Recognition is given to the "job-specific" dimension, and to the possibility that *experience* frequently can compensate for decrements that are either inevitable or results of not undergoing "refresher" training and retraining.

4. Recognition that decrements, function by function, do not occur within the individual at the same rate for each function, and that for some functions, the decrements may be only slight or irrelevant, insofar as job performance criteria are concerned. For McFarland, recent research on such phenomena as sense perception and age have far-reaching work-related implications. A larger number of workers could have their work years prolonged; expenditures of public funds might accordingly be reduced; with technological advances eliminating much of the physical stress in work, older workers' judgment, experience, and safety

of performance may come to be more valued in the future.

The work by McFarland (1973) and others with airline pilots has provoked controversy in that industry. Because of the rigid medical examinations required at periodic points in time, medical discharge data reveal that the average age for such forced retirement is about 40, with one-third involving cardiovascular disorders. Thus, it is possible to find pilots in their 50's who are in better physical condition than younger pilots. In other words, because of a careful screening process, a sort of "survival-of-the-fittest" phenomenon occurs. Yet the industry, with government sanction, requires automatic, compulsory retirement at the age of 60. On the other hand, researchers in this occupational sphere argue, as does McFarland, that "pilots should be evaluated on the basis of their ability to perform the complex task of operating high speed, high altitude aircraft, *not* in relation to chronological age alone."

Szafran, in his 1966 article on airline pilots concerning performance and health status, claims that until more systematic and careful research analysis is carried out, simple empirical knowledge is liable to reinforce existing stereotypes. ". . . All discussion about 'loss of capacity' in later adulthood is likely to arrive at the puzzling junction of biology and semantics where the terms become too elastic to be meaningful."

Research on functional aging in relation to problems of work and employment has led to certain solutions, including redesigning the job (the tasks as well as the physical technology or equipment), and in the development of special training principles and techniques for helping older workers adapt to changing technology and/or to new occupations. There is also the work of Leon Koyl (1974), developed and applied at deHavilland Aircraft in Canada. Koyl's approach and technique is designed to diagnose a specific, individual worker's physical capacities (and to some degree his mental qualifications) for performing specific work tasks, which thus requires detailed knowledge both about the specific individual and the specific tasks involved, leading, in other words, toward the matching of the worker and the job. Little is done, if anything, however, to modify the tasks to match the capabilities and potentials of the specific worker.

In recent years job redesign has become a more frequent subject for research, experimentation, and actual "installation" primarily because of such workplace problems as absenteeism, turnover, morale, and quality of output, along with productivity (Davis and Taylor, 1972). Stephen Griew (1964; also Marbach, 1968, and Barkin, 1970) has shown the importance of this approach to work environment improvements as applied to problems of aging. His contribution deals with age changes in working capacity, along with factors associated with stresses in the work environment, the importance of work movements and bodily postures while at work, etc.—and the possibilities of changing and modifying the physical environment, the workplace layout, equipment, and the actual organization of work itself.

Retraining has also been proposed as one approach in any multipronged set of solutions to problems of older workers. For some years, it has been taken more or less for granted that professional and skill obsolescence is a natural, normal but irremediable phenomenon in our type of rapidly changing society (Kaufman, 1974; Dubin, 1971). Retraining and "mid-career" development, however, are alternatives to skill obsolescence. Although older workers (around 45 and older) are not equitably distributed in the national manpower training programs, i.e., underrepresented in relation to their "share" of long-term employment, it has been found that their completion rates in such courses are higher than for younger enrollees; that the kinds of jobs for which they are trained differ from those for younger workers, with more being in agricultural and in non-manual nonagricultural occupations; that employment in training-related occupations is less likely for the older workers than for younger ones; and that continued employment status one year after completion of training is identical to that for younger trainees (U.S. Senate, 1967a, pp. 308–333).

Such training programs in the United States have not generally recognized the unique problems of adult retraining, nor the development of new principles and techniques for retraining of adults, such as those associated with the work of Eunice and Meredith Belbin (Belbin and Belbin, 1972; Belbin and Downs, 1972; Belbin, 1965, 1969) of the Industrial Training Research Unit, in Cambridge, England.

Their "discovery" or "activity learning" approach to adult retraining stresses the following: (1) experimental studies of learning among varying age groups tend to minimize the effect of prior knowledge in the learning situation, thus increasing the chances for older persons to show a decrement performance, resulting from a reaction to the nature of the laboratory material; (2) older persons lose their learning skills, due to lack of active practice, and the typical laboratory approach captures, therefore, initial and immediate ability, instead of potential learning ability; (3) most studies on human learning ability fail to adapt the training methods and instructions to the needs of older subjects. Given the use of especially developed training methods and appropriate learning conditions, the Belbins have shown that age differences in actual performance can be minimized. Part of the problem, therefore, seems to lie in the possibility that most training and teaching methods have been derived from experience with, and research on, younger subjects whose learning patterns differ in many ways from older subjects. The Belbins also take into account such psychological factors as anxiety and self-confidence which may interfere with the successful relearning among older workers.

Briefly, some of the methods applied are: defining the new task of learning less as an assignment and a duty, more as a "game," aimed at problem-solving; using visual and auditory signals, along with simulated learning situations, as opposed to expository teaching methods; breaking down a complex learning situation first into separate components easier to master (while still retaining the meaningfulness for the trainee); building in rapid, effective feedback, etc. These theories and methods have been extended beyond experimental stages and are already being put into use in industry, for example, in the postal service, air-freight handling, factory lathe work, aircraft production, steel factories, etc. The chief difficulty associated with the methods developed by the Belbins is that they require the retraining of trainers, and for each new type of occupational retraining, a "tailor-made," custom-built set of unique methods in order to achieve the successful progress of the older learners. On the other hand, continued reliance on the conventional methods of teaching and training older persons may only serve to perpetuate the stereotypes about "old dogs not being able to learn new tricks" and thus compound the problems of older workers.

UNEMPLOYMENT AND THE OLDER WORKER

A reading of the official statistics on unemployment rates suggests that the problem of unemployment among older workers is minimal, especially when compared to teen-age unemployment. But the data on unemployment rates fail to take into consideration some factors that can underestimate the saliency of older workers' unemployment experience. First, the proportion of teenagers seeking full-time, year-round employment is small compared to the proportion of older workers. Second, once unemployed, older workers remain unemployed longest. Third, persons 16–20 compared to old workers are rarely heads of families with dependents to support. Fourth, the official method for measuring and defining unemployment omits what has been called "hidden unemployment"—primarily made up of persons disproportionately older who have not actively sought employment in a given time period, although they had been looking prior to that period and would accept employment if offered.

Once unemployed, the older worker remains unemployed longer, is more likely to exhaust unemployment compensation benefits, becomes discouraged, and drops out of the labor force. The last stage in this process eliminates such persons from the "counts" on who is employed and who is unemployed, since the jobless individual must be seeking reemployment in order to qualify for being designated as "unemployed." A large portion of the applicants for retirement benefits—especially those before the age of 65—may consist of men and women who have undergone this process. While large-scale longitudinal studies are needed to verify the degree to which such speculation has an empirical foundation, it is worth noting that workers in their 60's constitute a disproportionate number of persons exhausting their unemployment benefits.

The special nature of the 55–64 age group's position in the labor market is reflected in the fact that despite the conventional presumption of the protection of seniority (first hired, last laid off), the unemployment rate of men in this age group, over the past 20 years, has consistently been higher than the rates of the younger adult male group (the 25–54 group). As for the "open-end" category of 65 and older, the male unemployment rates since 1962 have consistently been greater than the rates of those 55-64. This higher rate is significant not only because of their presumed higher seniority, hence job security, but also because of the other presumption, namely, their greater eligibility for retirement and hence exit from the rolls of the officially defined "unemployed." At the very least, the higher unemployment rates of the 65-plus group, relative to those 45-64, suggests that among such men who do not retire, their continued "membership" in the labor force is no guarantee of relatively safe job tenure.

The male 55–64 group is unique also because of the fact that their unemployment rates have been persistently higher than those of women of the same age. This greater disadvantaged position of the 55–64 males is all the more noteworthy when we consider the fact that, in the past, unemployment rates of women, in general, have always been higher than those for males as a whole.

The unemployment problem of the older job-seeker is frequently caused by plant shutdowns and mass layoffs, by such external factors as the overall economic growth rate in his or her local area or region, and by national economic conditions. But if the job seeker is handicapped in terms of schooling, physical capacity, and previous occupational experience, his unemployment is aggravated to the degree that "job-givers"—even in areas or times of economic opportunity—screen out applicants with less schooling or physical qualifications than the employer believes is necessary to perform the job being sought. We can add to this a "culture of age-ism"—a system of beliefs and behavior patterns about and toward older persons which operate against the welfare of older perons. In the job world, this means the use of the chronological age of a person as a negative indicator of his or her job abilities, motivation, and job absenteeism.

A critical point in this context is that age *per se* too frequently is a basis for not employing the older job applicant. Taking single ages among adult jobseekers, the percentage of workers of each age finding reemployment typically declines with increasing age. When the charge of "age-ism" is suggested, the lower educational levels of older workers is mentioned in defense of job-givers. However, in a multiple classification analysis of more than 2,000 hard-core unemployed in Detroit, in 1962, Wachtel (1966) found that age—even when such factors as education, along with sex, race, previous labor force experience, etc., were controlled—still remained a significant factor in their job-seeking experience.

In a study based on a group of men not usually in the "hard-core" population of the unemployed—engineers and scientists in the defense industries of the West Coast—R. P. Loomba (n.d.) found that even when measures of technical competence and education were held constant, (1) age was the most significant variable explaining their layoffs; and (2) among these unemployed engineers and scientists, duration of joblessness was a function of age—the older the professional, the longer he remained unemployed.

Analysis of declines in rates of male unemployment a decade after the two major recessions of 1958 and 1961 suggests that the "recovery rate" from unemployment differs according to age; the older the worker, the lower the recovery rate. For example, for males who were 25-34 in 1961, the unemployment rate in 1971 (when this cohort was 35-44 years of age) was 46 percent below the 1961 rate. The corresponding improvements (recovery rates) for the 35-44 group and the 45-54 group of 1961 were 35 percent and 33 percent, respectively. Because the recession period unemployment rates were substantially higher for nonwhite males, their recovery rate for each age group a decade later understandably was much greater. The limitations to such an approach to the study of reemployment are several, including nonaccountability for deaths, retirement, and new entries into the labor force. Nevertheless, the findings support the viewpoint that once unemployed, older workers (males in this case) face greater obstacles in seeking reemployment than younger ones. Such analyses tend to support the proposition that following a period of high unemployment, the older the worker, the greater the odds for his remaining unemployed or dropping out of the labor force altogether; and that such periods of unemployment accelerate the long-term downward trend in rates of participation in the labor force on the part of older workers.

It should also be noted that because most employees' health insurance benefits are tied to being employed, the loss of a job and its income, even for those without insurance coverage, increases the probability of worsened health care, thus aggravating the role of illness in labor force withdrawal. There is also some evidence (Cobb and Kasl, 1972; Kasl, Cobb, and Brooks, 1968; Slote, 1969) that the expectation of unemployment and the actual layoff itself can increase the probabilities of selected psychosomatic illnesses. Unemployment itself then becomes a basis for illness which, in turn, serves as an obstacle to reemployment. Furthermore, we do not know at the present time what the longer-term effects of unemployment are, as far as work-limiting illness is concerned. That is, the morbidity effects of unemployment among middle-aged and older workers may not be discernible at the time of job loss, but instead years later. In any event, we cannot ignore the possibility that "the move out of the labor force appears to be attributable to a combination of job loss and poor health which limits re-employability" (Parnes and Meyer, 1972, p. 83). Many persons with only mild types of illnesses or physical handicaps are employed, but if they then become unemployed, this combination can lead to withdrawal from the labor force after a period of unsuccessful job-seeking.

High national unemployment rates may substantially increase the number of persons applying for and receiving social security benefits. According to one analysis (Teeters, 1972):

> If the national unemployment rate remains at 6 percent . . . through the end of 1973, over 2.7 million people will receive OASI benefits who would not have done so if the . . . rate had remained at the 4.2 percent that prevailed in the first quarter of 1970 (p. 627).

While this study has been criticized by the Social Security Administration (Sander, 1974), it nevertheless is true that from 1969 to 1973—when the national unemployment rate rose—the number of 55-64 year old men and women not in the labor force increased by nearly 17 percent, while those in the labor force of the same age increased hardly at all, less than half a percent. In contrast, from 1965 to 1969, when the national unemployment rate declined, the number of 55-64-year-olds not in the labor force increased at a much lower rate, less than 7 percent—while those in the labor force increased at only a slightly higher rate, less than 8 percent.

In other words, during times of *rising* unemployment, the number of older persons (for example, 55-64) who are not in the labor force increases at a faster rate than the increase in total numbers of the 55-64 population; and during times of *declining* national unemployment, the rate of withdrawal from the labor force is hardly different from the general growth rate of the total population aged 55 to 64.

In 1967, Congress enacted the Age Discrimination in Employment Act, designed to protect most workers aged 40-65. There is as yet no systematic evaluation of its impact on the problems discussed in this chapter, but potentially the Act can have a positive effect on the success of older jobseekers and on the promotion chances of those employed.

A great deal of the literature on unemployment, among young and old workers alike, deals almost exclusively with the relationship of external factors or demographic characteristics (such as the general economy, sex, education, and previous occupation) to the job market experience of the unemployed. Few studies have attempted to supplement or enrich such analyses with behavioral and social-psychological dimensions of that experience. The survey by Sheppard and Belitsky (1966) of persons who had been, or were still, unemployed attempted to remedy this type of shortcoming. The authors found: (1) Length of time between loss of job and the start of the search for a new job was about the same for both old and young workers, except for those older workers who expected to be called back to their previous employers. This latter group of older workers had a longer callback waiting period than did the younger workers. (2) Older jobseekers used fewer job-seeking techniques and sources (such as using the public employment service, applying directly at company personnel offices, etc.) than younger jobseekers. (3) Even among all jobseekers using at least six of the eight techniques and sources covered in the survey, job-finding success was lower among the older workers. (4) Fewer companies, on the average, were directly contacted by older workers during the first month of unemployment. (5) This lower average number of direct company contacts on the part of older workers is partially explained by the further finding that older workers tended to restrict their job hunt to companies which they believed had job openings, and in which these older workers also believed age would not be held against them. (6) But the greater the number of companies visited, and the more likely the older jobseeker did not restrict himself to those companies believed to have openings, the greater the odds for job-finding success. (7) Social psychological factors played a significant role in this job-seeking process. When used in the analysis of factors contributing to degree of job-finding success, these factors tended to mitigate the importance of age *per se*. Among these social psychological factors were: (a) achievement motivation; (b) achievement values; (c) job interview anxiety; and (d) "subjective" age.

While general employer demand, previous skill level, education, and behavioral and social psychological factors are critical in explaining the fate of unemployed older workers, other forces are also operating. Especially important are the practices, policies, and beliefs regarding the use of, and capabilities of, older workers that prevail among employment service agencies and among employers and their representatives. Several studies have shown that older jobseekers must apply at more companies than younger ones before realizing success, thus suggesting age preference in company practices. Auto workers permanently laid off as a result of the Packard Motor Company shutdown were able to find reemployment in the other auto companies (in which, presumably, their Packard-acquired skills could be used), depending on their age: the younger the worker, the more likely he found a new position in the Detroit auto industry (Sheppard, Ferman, and Faber, 1960).

As indicated earlier, even the "gate-keepers" such as public employment agency personnel can affect the chances of job-finding success among older persons. Sheppard and Belitsky (1966) found that the older the jobseeker, the fewer number of services (e.g., being tested or counseled, referred to retraining programs or to employers for a job interview), on the average, were received from the Employment Service. The importance of this kind of prima facie evidence of age discrimination can be inferred from the further finding that degree of job-finding success was related to the number of such services received from the employment service agency.

Among workers temporarily laid off, but expecting eventually to be called back by their previous employers, older ones were more likely to wait for such a callback and not look actively for new jobs. If workers expecting a callback had high achievement values (defined and measured by Rosen), or high achievement motivation (defined and derived by McClelland), or had low job interview anxiety, age made little difference in extent of job-changing behavior (Sheppard, 1969). This finding is only one example of the point that the job-seeking problems of older workers are affected not only by "external" factors and their own education or skill levels, but also by factors of a self-selective nature, including the phenomenon of age self-concept.

RETIREMENT

The conventional use of the distinction between "voluntary" and "involuntary" retirement, according to some, loses its value to the degree that the decision to retire is less and less a function of the individual's own act of volition. Friedmann and Orbach (1974) point to the movement of production of goods and services out of the home into the factory and the office; the reduction in the proportion of the labor force who are self-employed; and skill obsolescence brought about by a constant change in technology and forms of work organization, as among the factors that make the decision to retire contingent on forces external to the worker. Generally speaking, the gradual acquisition of private pension coverage has also carried with it compulsory retirement provisions (Reno, 1972). General economic conditions and demographic composition of the total labor force play a part in the retirement decision.

The literature on attitudes toward retirement, especially among older persons not yet out of the labor force, is ambiguous and subject to a number of different interpretations. Furthermore, it would seem that both the general public and gerontologists lack any clear-cut consensus on how to judge and evaluate the increasing rates of retirement. Historically, it might be argued, retirement was originally looked upon as a rare and valued goal, since it would relieve workers from difficult and wearing tasks and allow them to spend a few remaining years in a well-earned relaxation. In the emerging market-industrialized society, especially after the social legislation of the 1930's, it meant, furthermore, some type of income maintenance for men and women unable to work or to find reemployment in the event of a job loss, after a given age level. But for some observers today, retirement is not the unmixed blessing that it may have been around the turn of the twentieth century.

The lack of widespread agreement may also be a reflection of differences in populations studied, methods used, and the kinds of measures applied in seeking answers to the issue of the degree of desirability of retirement.

Some of the lack of consistency may be, moreover, traceable to the fact that the existence of mass numbers of older persons no longer in the workforce—in a society in which work is still the primary source of social status and relatively adequate income—has not yet been accompanied by any clearly defined functions or behaviors for those in the "retirement role."

In the 1969 Social Security Retirement History Study of persons not yet fully in the "retirement years" (58–63), nearly one-half of the men and two-fifths of the nonmarried women indicated that they would not retire (or would not give any definite age at which they expected to retire). A large-sample study of persons 65 and older, conducted for the National Council on Aging by Louis Harris (1974), reached an estimate that there were 4.4 million retired persons in that age group who did not want to be retired and who would prefer gainful employment. In another large-sample (longitudinal) study of employed men 45–55 years old in 1966, it was found that 28 percent intended to retire before 65, but five years later interviews with the same cohort found an increase in such a proportion—39 percent—intending early retirement (Parnes, 1974). This type of finding contradicts other cross-sectional research reporting a negative relationship between age and early-retirement expectations.

According to the Social Security Study, the critical difference between those planning to retire ("prospective retirees") and those not planning any retirement lies in the economic sphere. The prospective retirees, first of all, were enjoying higher salaries, had a higher proportion covered by private pensions, and were more likely to judge their current income as adequate for their needs and desires. Educational level, on the other hand, did not play a uniform role in retirement intentions among men and women. Male prospective retirees had less education than those not planning to retire, while female prospective retirees had more education than women with no intention of retiring.

THE RETIREMENT DECISION AND PREFERRED RETIREMENT AGE

The typical study dealing with the conditions underlying or associated with the "retirement decision" rarely goes into fine enough detail beyond the generally studied factors such as expected retirement income, marital status, illness or incapacity levels, chronological age itself, and broad occupational categories. Recent studies tend merely to confirm the already recognized relationship of these and similar factors to the willingness to retire, or actual retirement status. For example, the older the nonretired person, the less favorable the attitude toward retirement (Harris, 1965; Katona, 1965).

But the field has much to benefit from adapting more refined and precise analyses that would, for example, explore the relationship of retirement choice to such features as (1) the detailed nature of the person's job, including degree of strain in performing these tasks and the degree of worker autonomy in task performance, etc. and (2) the individual's subjective perception and evaluation of his or her task attributes—e.g., degree of autonomy, variety, task challenge, etc. (perception and evaluation may overlap, but they are not identical). Such an approach makes it possible to ascertain variations and degree of heterogeneity within any of the otherwise broad occupational classifications.

One such study, using sophisticated measures and classifications, was carried out by Dan Jacobsohn (1972) among 55–64-year-old British male factory workers. Jacobsohn investigated the extent to which the job characteristics of blue collar workers—specifically degree of job strain and type of factory work—affected the willingness to retire. Using detailed items to measure these characteristics, Jacobsohn classified his sample into heavy, moderate, and light job-task categories. He found that these classifications helped to explain (1) workers' views as to what is an "ideal" retirement age; (2) self-appraisal of current health status; (3) expectations of effects of retirement on health status. The heavier the overall job-task level, the lower the ideal retirement age and the poorer the reported health status.

In addition to using this general measure of

job strain, Jacobsohn also classified the jobs into those involving (1) *conveyor* operations, i.e., mechanized line operations allowing the worker to operate at his own pace but having to pass the product to another worker; and (2) *individual* nonmechanized work, allowing maximum autonomy. His hypothesis that "the more rigidly fixed the work pattern, the higher would be the proportion of retirement-oriented respondents" was borne out. Fewer than one-half of the workers in individualized jobs were willing to accept the company's retirement age, while between 71 to 81 percent of the workers in less individualized types of factory work were willing.

Sheppard's research (1972) among white male blue collar workers included a measure of task-level quality (perceived autonomy, variety, responsibility, etc.) and found that the lower the task-level quality, the greater the percentage in each age group reporting that they would retire immediately if assured of an adequate income.

The 1969–70 national survey of all employed Americans conducted by the University of Michigan's Survey Research Center for the U. S. Department of Labor yielded data (supplied the author by the Department) showing that among white males 50 and older, responses to the question, "If you could get enough money to live as comfortably as you would like for the rest of your life, would you continue to work?" differed between blue and white collar workers. Nearly one-half (45 percent) of the blue collar workers, but less than one-fourth (24 percent) of the white collar workers, replied that they would not continue to work if provided with adequate income. This roughly two-to-one ratio also prevailed among workers 16–49 years old, but naturally at lower percentage levels.

Finally, data provided the author by the United Auto Workers indicates, on the behavioral level, that as of 1970–71, among Ford employees eligible for "early retirement," the proportion taking advantage of such provisions varied by skill level, with the lower skilled auto workers retiring before 65 at a rate much higher than among the highest skilled workers.

These attitudinal and behavioral data suggest the substantial role played by the nature of occupation—and within occupation, by specific job-task and skill level—in the retirement decision and perhaps in retirement adjustment. In this respect, retirement can be viewed frequently as an escape from an undesirable, unsatisfying work role, as a negative-type decision. The fact that most studies, if not all, of "retirement adjustment" reveal a high degree of satisfaction may partly be due to this "escape" function of retirement and also due to the tendency of people to accept to some degree whatever life status they may happen to be in. As Shanas (1972) found in her interviews of retired men, few, if any, referred—when asked what they missed about not working—to "work itself."

In this connection, what is lacking in the field of social and industrial gerontology is information concerning possible changes in "retirement propensity" resulting from improvements in quality of working life and specifically in the nature of task attributes and working environment.

Research by Charles Rose and John Mogey (1972) on the Normative Aging Sample survey of the Veterans Administration (males in the Boston area) concentrated on the "preferred age of retirement" as a dependent variable. Among the several independent variables used to test relationship to this retirement preference age (and the relative importance of each) were age at time of interview; social class; occupation; family context; and climate preference. The study should be noted for its reliance on more than gross measures of such independent variables. For example, in using an "occupational" variable, Rose and Mogey actually included 13 dimensions, including the extent to which the person's job was clearly related to the nature of his education, whether or not the subject originally had chosen to enter his current occupation, several job satisfaction measures, etc.

The older the respondent, the greater the tendency was to prefer a later age of retirement. Among some of the other major generalizations derived from the analysis by Rose and Mogey are the following: (1) As a person grows older, he tends to view himself in a higher rank (i.e., in a more favorable position in his place of employment) and will prefer to "stave off retirement to a later age." (2) As in other studies, education is positively correlated to preferred age of retirement, independent of age at time of interview. (3) When health status is held constant, older age and higher social class results in a higher age of preferred retirement. (4) Men with higher education and those expecting to retire later were more likely to prefer the local climate (climate preference was not related to age at time of interview). Furthermore, men choosing a climate different from Boston preferred younger retirement ages than those liking—or not rejecting—the Boston climate.

Concerning the overall measure of job satisfaction, the authors, contrary to other studies, found no overwhelming evidence of any relationship to preferred retirement age. Rose and Mogey go on to speculate that if and when the general population comes to approximate their special population (reduction of class and age differentials with regard to health status), "job satisfaction will be less important in the future for making predictions about retirement."

The authors conclude their analysis with a brief allusion to issues regarding retirement age policy, raised by the trend toward earlier compulsory retirement accompanied by the paradox of an increased capacity for longer worklife and a reduction of the alleged age decrements that in the past functioned as obstacles toward continued work roles—issues that will probably come increasingly to the fore in the next decade.

ADJUSTMENT

Studies concerning "retirement adjustment" show varying results, depending on definitions of the term *adjustment*, the types of populations studied, and the time when each study was made, including economic conditions at the time of the study.* Furthermore, the retirees' adjustment is related to whether or not the individual retires "voluntarily" (in good or

poor health) or is required to retire because of organizational rules. Level of retirement income has been found to be crucial, but few, if any, studies have used retirement income as a percent of preretirement income as a more refined variable involved in adjustment.

Friedmann and Orbach (1974) have classified the major criteria used in "retirement adjustment" studies: first, notations of personal happiness (measured by direct and indirect questions); and second, nature and degree of activity, such as social participation (again, ascertained typically through the subjects' reported responses pertaining to activity questions). These criteria have their obvious deficiencies, including those of the cultural nature of the meaning and substance of "happiness"; the wide variety of scales used to measure them; the lack of standardization, and the arbitrary choice of activity as an indisputable index of adjustment; the lack of congruity between other measures of adjustment and degree of activity, etc.

Rosow's research and conceptualization (1963) on the subject points to the strategic adjustment of attitudes of the individual before retirement, and Friedmann and Orbach refer to studies (for example, Streib, 1965; Streib and Schneider, 1971; Thompson, Streib, and Kosa, 1960) showing that such prior attitudes are the most important predictor of subsequent retirement adjustment (even for a variety of "adjustment" measures).

Research based on other measures of "adjustment" to retirement, such as physical and mental health, do not confirm the popular set of beliefs that suggest that retirement itself results in poor physical health (and/or morbidity and mortality) or aggravated mental health decline. To repeat, preretirement attitudes and expectations concerning retirement turn out to be generally related to type of current occupation (especially as type of occupation relates to how salient the job is as a source of intrinsic satisfaction), expected retirement income, health status, and education, to cite only a few of the range of related variables. Once retired, financial problems are high in the list of reasons for dissatisfaction among the sizeable minority of national samples expressing

---

*For an extended review of the subject, with reference to a number of retirement-adjustment studies, see Robert C. Atchley (1972), pp. 153–176.

nonfulfillment of retirement expectations. A Harris Poll of 1965 indicated that among all retirees, about 7 percent were dissatisfied with the very nature of retirement itself—that is, with the "retirement role." We have some knowledge concerning the issue of whether a given cohort of retirees over time would continue to report such a low percentage dissatisfied with the retirement role, or if it would rise or decline—or what factors might be related to those retirees reporting an increase, and those reporting a decrease, in such dissatisfaction. To some extent, Streib and Schneider's research (1971), discussed below, did attempt to trace such possible changes, but only over a short period of time. Barfield and Morgan (1969) found that among retired auto workers from 1967 to 1969 satisfaction with retirement declined in the group first reporting high satisfaction. At the same time, most of the retirees reported that their decision to retire when they did was a right decision and would advise others to retire at the same age they themselves did.

The cross-national survey by Shanas and colleagues in the United States, Britain, and Denmark (1968) stresses the importance of health status and of degree of physical capacity and mobility as basic conditions for whether or not the retired person enjoys his retirement. This study, conducted in 1962, was replicated in 1975 and 1976, and its findings—when reported—should shed light on differences, if any, between two "generations" of aged persons on a cross-national basis.

Streib and Schneider's study (1971), which was of a longitudinal nature (from 1952 to 1958), found that when comparisons were made between preretirement expectations and actual retirement experiences, persons tended to expect negative features in retirement much more than they actually experienced— for example, how much they would miss having a job and the social interaction rewards associated with work. Indeed, these two researchers report that after four to six years of retirement life, only 4 to 5 percent (depending on sex) felt that retirement was worse than they had expected at the time of their retirement; and one-third indicated that their retirement was actually better than originally expected.

We cannot claim any nomothetic value for such findings, given the fact that "times change" and so also may different generations of retirees. For example, given a sharp rise in the rate of inflation, without any corresponding change in retirement income, along with a possible difference in life expectation or "life-style" between different generations of retirees, it is possible that another longitudinal study, among workers retiring in the mid-1970's, might yield results varying from those reported by Streib and Schneider.

In 1969, Reno (1972) found that among newly retired workers aged 62–65 who retired compulsorily, more than one-half reported they did not want to retire. Friedmann and Orbach (1974) refer to older studies indicating that more than half of retired workers viewed their retirement as involuntary, either because of ill health or compulsory retirement requirements. They also refer to other studies in the 1950's which reported a great deal of widespread dissatisfaction with compulsory retirement and even a reluctance to accept 65 as an expected retirement age. But as already stated, "further analysis of workers' attitudes toward retirement during the period showed sharp variations according to income received or anticipated in retirement" (Friedmann and Orbach, 1974). The income factor was of greater concern than being cut off from their work.

Judging from more recent studies, there seems to be a growing percentage of men without any health impairments who are retiring "voluntarily," a trend that may be attributable to the growth in social security benefit levels, coupled with supplementary private pension plans. Nevertheless, the variation in the willingness to retire has also been found to be related to the nature of the work itself, as discussed earlier.

Any generalizations based on these and other specific studies, however, should be tempered by the observation that the relationship between job attitudes and retirement attitude may vary according to occupational level and also by a number of factors extrinsic to the job itself—such as expected retirement income, health status, personality characteristics, etc. (Fillenbaum, 1971). Other studies yielding contrary or different results from those cited here may have used different definitions, methods, and measures of such concepts as job satisfaction, social class, attributes of the job itself, occupational level, and attitude toward retirement. Finally, most of them are restricted to *intentions* to retire (or *preference* for given retirement ages), and not to the relationship of intentions to the actual, behavioral act of retiring, which would require a longitudinal approach.

One major study, based on a unique utilization of Census data, comes close to being what an ideal longitudinal study would be. This is the extensive analysis by A. J. Jaffe (1972), tracing data on males from the Census of 1950 to that of 1960. Because of its reliance on Census data, however, it excludes any social-psychological or attitudinal variables. Jaffe has listed and discussed a number of major generalizations about rates of retirement, especially among men. First, "retirement rates in recent decades seem to have been responsive to events in the economy, rather than to reflect basic changes in the individual's viewpoint about work or retirement." Second, most men who retire do so involuntarily ("involuntary" for Jaffe includes the decision to retire because of poor health). Third, retirement rates vary or differ widely, from industry to industry and from occupation to occupation. The self-employed in any industry are in a better position of autonomy concerning the option to retire or to continue working. Also, individuals with "high" education and in occupations requiring general—nonfragmented—skills are also more likely to be in less supply and greater demand than, say, individuals with less education and in occupations characterized by low, fragmented skills, labor oversupply, and frequent spells of unemployment (see also Kreps, 1967). Jaffe also found that the higher the ratio of men 45–54 to those 55 and older in any industry, the higher the retirement rate.

Another major industrial component affecting the retirement rate is the degree to which labor productivity increases along with extent of increases in employment in any given

TABLE 9. RETIREMENT RATES[b] FOR MEN BY SOCIOECONOMIC STATUS, 1950–1960.

Age in 1950	Highest SES I	II	III	Lowest SES IV	Farmers and farm laborers
45–49	a	2	2	5	15
50–54	5	9	7	14	24
55–59	30	42	42	44	39
60–64	36	49	48	49	42

[a]Less than 0.5.
[b]Retirements during 1950–60 per 100 men in 1950.
SOURCE: Derived from Census data by A. J. Jaffe, "The Retirement Dilemma," in *Industrial Gerontology*, Summer, 1972, p. 17.

industry. High rates of productivity progress, coupled with a low demand for more workers, can result in high rates of retirement. Socioeconomic status also had a primary influence on retirement rates as shown in Table 9.

Jaffe has summarized the three measures of occupation, education, and earnings, from the Census Bureau's 1963 Working Paper on socioeconomic scores, and has found that within each of four age groups in the 45–64 male population as of 1950, retirement rates by the year 1960 were closely related to this summarizing measure of socioeconomic status. Generally speaking, for each age group, the lower the socioeconomic score in 1950, the greater the retirement status by 1960. While such an analysis has not been carried out for the 1960–70 decade, there is no reason to believe that the relationship should have changed.

Finally, Jaffe makes the projection that relative to the supply of workers overall, the demand for workers in the current, and next decade perhaps, will not be great enough to provide employment for all willing and able older persons.

COMMENTARY

There are some countervailing influences and potential trends that should be noted when reflecting on these points made by Jaffe. One of these is the decline in the manual, blue collar occupations as a proportion of the total labor force. If it is true that nonmanual workers and the nonproduction industries have generally lower rates of retirement and that the projected nature of the labor force of the future will consist more of such workers, we might expect lower rates of retirement. This could be offset by the degree to which technological changes in nonproduction industries become more complicated relative to the competence and learning capacity of older workers.

Another factor relates to schooling, which seems to be negatively correlated to retirement rates. Given the fact that today's younger and middle-aged workers have a median schooling of more than a high school degree and a higher proportion with college education and that today's older workers with similar schooling have lower rates of retirement than less educated older workers, it is possible that in the decades to come, the uninterrupted trend characterizing the industrial society's pattern of lower and lower labor force participation rates among older workers (or retirement rates) may be stabilized.

A more tangible process may also be in the offing. Given the above factors (the shift in occupational structure and schooling) and others related to them, there is the debatable issue centering on how much the older workers of the future, say, those 60 to 69, perhaps even 70 to 74, will expect and demand a level of living commensurate with what they had been enjoying prior to reaching such upper ages. The issue may come down to whether or not they shall maintain that desired level of living through retirement income or through continued employment. A population of 28–30 million persons 60–74—better educated than their predecessors and not much less educated than the younger population—may have much more political influence than the same age group of today upon those institutions, private and public, that determine levels of retirement income, age of retirement, etc.

The trade-off between an adequate retirement income and adequate income through continued employment for older persons will create a major dilemma. There might ensue a resistance from private and public institutions responsible for financing and providing pensions and social security benefits, as well as from younger workers who may be called upon to deduct more from their current earnings in order to provide for greater retirement income to their older peers, coupled by difficulties for the economy as a whole to provide employment for an ever-increasing older person population. This pressure might be obviated to the degree that the demand for labor will have to be met by hiring and keeping older workers—to an extent greater than today—because of an expected decrease in the numbers of the young, a product of the current trend toward "zero population growth."

There is now a new possibility to reckon with: no one now knows how truly serious the "crisis" of energy and resource shortages will be by the end of the twentieth century. Our pattern of an ever-growing Gross National Product (nationally and on a per capita basis) in the past has relied in large part on a presumably bountiful and limitless supply of energy and resources, at least for North America and Western Europe, thus making it unnecessary to keep certain segments in the labor force, notably the young and the old. Preindustrial societies are marked by the high percentages of their young and old who are needed by the general population to produce, not only for others, but for themselves directly. A modern economy beset with shortages of energy and resource supplies may have to freeze or retard any otherwise increasing trend in increased age of entry into the workforce and decreased age of exit from that workforce. The sudden advent of a relatively high inflation rate in the early 70's and its possible continuity (at a minimum of 6–8 percent) can also be expected to influence downwardly the rate of "voluntary" retirement on the part of workers otherwise eligible for retirement. There already are signs of this change, among workers in industries providing "early retirement" options; these workers are not choosing that option to the extent expected originally.

Finally, we cannot ignore the role of government, through its laws, in affecting what may now seem to be inexorable trends—for example, the Age Discrimination in Employment Act of 1967, especially if that Act (already improved in 1974) is further amended to lift or eliminate the maximum age of 65 as the "ceiling" for which it provides protection.

REFERENCES

Atchley, Robert C. 1972. *Social Forces in Later Life: An Introduction to Social Gerontology*, Chapter 9, pp. 153–176. Belmont, California: Wadsworth.

Baltes, Paul B., and Schaie, K. Warner. 1974. The myth of the twilight years. *Psychology Today*, pp. 35–40 (March).

Barfield, Richard, and Morgan, James. 1969. *Early Retirement: The Decision and the Experience*. Ann Arbor: Institute for Social Research, University of Michigan.

Barkin, Solomon. 1970. Retraining and job redesign: Positive approaches to the continued employment of older persons. *In*, H. L. Sheppard (ed.), *Industrial Gerontology*, Chapter III, pp. 17–30. Cambridge: Schenkman.

Belbin, Eunice, and Belbin, Meredith. 1972. *Problems in Adult Training*. London: Heinemann.

Belbin, Eunice, and Downs, Sylvia. 1972. Activity learning and the older worker. *In*, Sheila M. Chown (ed.), *Ageing*, Chapter 16, pp. 190–202. Baltimore: Penguin Books.

Belbin, Meredith. 1965. *Training Methods for Older Workers.* Paris: Organization for Economic Cooperation and Development.

Belbin, Meredith, 1969. *The Discovery Method: An International Experiment in Retraining*. Paris: Organization for Economic Cooperation and Development.

Census Bureau. April, 1973. *Employment Status and Work Experience*, 1970. PC (2)-6A, Table 5.

Census Bureau. July, 1974. Current Population Reports. *Social and Economic Status of the Black Population in the United States*, 1973. P-23, No. 48, Table 25.

Cobb, S., and Kasl, S. 1972. Some medical aspects of unemployment. *In*, G. M. Shatto (ed.), *Employment of the Middle-Aged*, pp. 87–98. Springfield, Illinois: Charles C. Thomas.

Davis, J. M. 1972. Impact of health on earnings and labor market activity. *Monthly Labor Review*, 9 (October).

Davis, Louis, and Taylor, James (eds.). 1972. *Job Design*. Middlesex, England: Penguin Books.

Donahue, W., Orbach, H. L., and Pollak, O. 1960. Retirement: The emerging social pattern. *In*, C. Tibbitts (ed.), *Handbook of Social Gerontology*, pp. 330–406. Chicago: University of Chicago Press.

Dubin, S. S. (ed.). 1971. *Professional Obsolescence*. Lexington, Massachusetts: Lexington Books.

Fillenbaum, G. G. 1971. On the relation between attitude to work and attitude to retirement. *J. Geront.*, **26** (2), 244–248.

Friedmann, E., and Orbach, H. L. 1974. Adjustment to retirement. *In*, S. Arieti (ed.), *American Handbook of Psychiatry*, Vol. 1, 2nd ed., New York: Basic Books.

Fullerton, Howard. 1972. A new type of working life table for men. *Monthly Labor Review*, pp. 20–27 (July).

Griew, Stephen. 1964. *Job Redesign: The Application of Biographical Data on Aging to the Design of Equipment and the Organization of Work*. Paris: Organization for Economic Cooperation and Development.

Harris, Louis. 1974. Who the Senior citizens really are. Address delivered at Annual Meeting of National Council on Aging, Detroit.

Harris, (Louis) Associates. 1965. November poll of pre-retired adults. New York.

Irelan, Lola M., and Bond, Kathleen. 1974. Retirees of the 70's. Paper presented at Southern Conference on Gerontology (March).

Jacobsohn, Dan. 1972. Willingness to retire in relation to job strain and type of work. *Journal of Industrial Gerontology*, **13**, 65–74 (Spring).

Jaffe, A. J. 1972. The retirement dilemma. *Journal of Industrial Gerontology*, **14**, 1–89 (Summer).

Kasl, S., Cobb, S., and Brooks, G. W. 1968. Changes in uric acid and cholesterol levels in men undergoing job loss. *J. Am. Med. Assoc.*, **206**, pp. 1500–1507 (November 11).

Katona, G. 1965. *Private Pensions and Individual Savings*. Ann Arbor: Survey Research Center, University of Michigan.

Kaufman, H. G. 1974. *Obsolescence and Professional Career Development.* New York: American Management Association.

Koyl, Leon F., M. D. 1974. *Employing the Older Worker: Matching the Employee to the Job*. Washington D. C.: National Council on Aging.

Kreps, J. M. 1967. Job performance and job opportunity: A note. *Gerontologist*, **7**, 24–27 (March).

Laufer, Arthur C., and Fowler, William M., Jr. 1971. Work potential of the aging. *Personnel Administration*, pp. 20–25 (March-April).

Loomba, R. P., n. d. *A Study of the Re-employment and Unemployment Experiences of Scientists and Engineers Laid Off from 62 Aerospace and Electronics Firms in the San Francisco Bay Area during 1962-63*. Center for Inter-disciplinary Studies, San Jose State College. Mimeographed report to Manpower Administration, United States Department of Labor.

McFarland, Ross A. 1973. The need for functional age measurements in industrial gerontology, *Journal of Industrial Gerontology*, pp. 1–19 (Fall).

Marbach, G. 1968. *Job Redesign for Older Workers*. Paris: Organization for Economic Cooperation and Development.

Parnes, Herbert S., and Meyer, Jack A. 1972. Withdrawal from the labor force by middle-aged men, 1966-67. *In*, G. Shatto (ed.), *Employment of the*

Middle-Aged. Springfield, Illinois: Charles C. Thomas.

Parnes, Herbert S. *et al.* 1974. *The Pre-Retirement Years: Five Years in the Work Lives of Middle-Aged Men*. Columbus, Ohio: Center for Human Resources Research, Ohio State University.

Reno, Virginia P. 1972. Compulsory retirement among newly entitled workers. *Social Security Bulletin* (March).

Riley, Matilda White, Foner, Anne, Moore, Mary E., Hess, Beth, and Roth, Barbara K. 1968. *Aging and Society: Vol. 1, An Inventory of Research Findings*. New York: Russell Sage Foundation.

Rose, Charles L., and Mogey, John M. 1972. Aging and preference for later retirement. *Aging and Human Development*, 3, 45–62.

Rosenfeld, C., and Waldman, E. 1967. Work limitations and chronic health problems. *Special Labor Force Report*, Department of Labor, 90.

Rosow, Irving. 1963. Adjustment of the normal aged. *In*, R. H. Williams, C. Tibbitts, and W. Donahue (eds.), *Process of Aging*, Vol. 2, pp. 195–223. New York: Atherton Press.

Sander, Kenneth. July, 1974. The cyclical sensitivity of OASI beneficiary rolls. *Social Security Research and Statistics Note*, No. 22 (July).

Schwab, Karen. 1974. Early labor force withdrawal of men: Participants and nonparticipants aged 58–63. *Social Security Bulletin* (August).

Shanas, E. 1972. Adjustment to retirement: Substitution or accommodation? *In*, F. Carp (ed.), *Retirement*, pp. 219–243. New York: Behavioral Publications.

Shanas, E., Townsend, P., Wedderburn, D., Friis, H., Milhøj, P., and Stehouwer, J. 1968. *Old People in Three Industrial Societies*. New York: Atherton Press.

Sheppard, H. L. 1969. The relevance of age to worker behavior in labor market. *Journal of Industrial Gerontology*, pp. 1–11 (February).

Sheppard, H. L. 1970. The potential role of behavioral science in the solution of the 'older worker problem.' *In*, E. Shanas (ed.), *Aging in Contemporary Society*. Special Issue of *American Behavioral Scientist* (Sept./Oct.).

Sheppard, H. L. 1971. Age and migration factors in the socioeconomic conditions of urban black and white women. *In*, H. L. Sheppard, *New Perspectives on Older Workers*, pp. 43–51. Kalamazoo: Upjohn Institute for Employment Research.

Sheppard, H. L. 1972. *Where Have All The Robots Gone?–Worker Dissatisfaction in the 1970's*. New York: The Free Press–Macmillan.

Sheppard, Harold L., and Belitsky, A. Harvey. 1966. *The Job Hunt*. Baltimore: The Johns Hopkins Press.

Sheppard, H. L., Ferman, Louis, and Faber, Seymour. 1960. *Too Old to Work, Too Young to Retire*. Washington, D.C.: United States Special Committee on Unemployment Problems.

Sherman, Sally R. 1974. Labor force status of non-married women on the threshold of retirement. *Social Security Bulletin*, pp. 3–15 (September).

Simpson, I. H., Back, K., and McKinney, J. 1966. Orientation toward work and retirement, and self-evaluation in retirement. *In*, I. H. Simpson and J. McKinney (eds.), *Social Aspects of Aging*, pp. 75–89. Durham, North Carolina: Duke University Press.

Slote, Alfred. 1969. *Termination*. New York: Bobbs-Merrill.

Streib, G. 1965. *Longitudinal Study of Retirement*. Ithaca, New York: Cornell University Department of Sociology.

Streib, G., and Schneider, C. J. 1971. *Retirement in American Society*. Ithaca, New York: Cornell University Press.

Szafran, J. 1966. Age differences in the rate of gain of information, signal detection strategy, and cardiovascular status among pilots. *Gerontologia*, 12, 6–17.

Teeters, Nancy. 1972. Built-in flexibility of federal expenditures. *Brookings Papers on Economic Activity*, Vol. 3. Washington, D.C.: The Brookings Institute.

Thompson, W. E., Streib, G., and Kosa, J. 1960. The effect of retirement on personal adjustment: A panel analysis, *J. Geront.*, 15, 165–169.

United States Department of Labor. 1965. *The Older American Worker: Age Discrimination in Employment*.

United States Department of Labor. 1974. *Manpower Report of the President*, 1974.

United States Senate Subcommittee on Employment, Manpower, and Poverty. 1967a. Staff and Consultant Reports. *Examination of the War on Poverty*, Vol. 2, tables in pp. 308–333. Washington, D. C.: Government Printing Office.

United States Senate Subcommittee on Employment, Manpower, and Poverty. 1967b. Staff and Consultant Reports. *Examination of the War on Poverty*, Vol. 2. Washington, D.C.: Government Printing Office.

Wachtel, H. 1966. Hard-core unemployment in Detroit: Causes and remedies. *Proceedings of 18th Annual Meeting of Industrial Relations Research Association, 1965*, pp. 233–241. Madison, Wisconsin: Industrial Relations Research Association.

13
LEISURE AND LIVES:
Personal Expressivity across the Life Span

Chad Gordon
Rice University
and
Charles M. Gaitz
Texas Research Institute of Mental Sciences
with the assistance of
Judith Scott
Texas Research Institute of Mental Sciences

THEORETICAL ORIENTATIONS AND MAJOR OBJECTIVES

Most people everywhere have always longed for freedom from the struggle for subsistence; they have longed for time, for resources, and for opportunities to enjoy and fulfill themselves as well as support themselves. Freud expressed this basic dilemma of human existence most succinctly when he was asked what a person needs to learn in order to achieve maturity and health: "To love and to work."

Expressivity and Instrumentality as General Themes in Social-Psychological Theory

Freud's aphorism points to the distinction between *instrumental* and *expressive* activities. The essential contrast between instrumental and expressive meanings of human action has been emphasized in the "action theory" per-spective of Talcott Parsons (1951a, 1951b, 1955c, and 1959). Primarily, the distinction is based on the temporal position of gratification in the scheme of action. Instrumental activity (work and its routine preparations) has as its aim achievement of one or more goals or objectives and their attendant future gratifications. Expressive activity (symbolic and pleasurable material interchanges with the environment), on the other hand, involves primacy of rewards and gratifications intrinsic to itself, immediately in its doing. Thus, expressive action may involve the satisfaction of a deficiency or "need" such as drifting off to sleep when tired, but it also relates to symbolically defined "desires" or objectives of action such as expressing sexual feelings by means of strokes and caresses, expressing allegiance to some important group by appropriate ceremonials, or expressing rage and hostility through shouts and physical attacks.

This focus on immediacy of expressive action is not to say that it is limited to imperious bodily hedonisms or that it is free of normative regulation. Quite the contrary—just as instrumental activity is culturally patterned and normatively structured, so also is expressive activity. Here the standards are typically esthetic and stylistic rather than technical and are nested within major and minor cultural traditions (Parsons, 1951b, pp. 384–385). These standards regulate leisure and all other forms of expressive conduct.

Forms of Expressive Conduct Other Than Leisure Activity

It should be noted that the above formulation of conduct having expressive primacy is extremely general and includes many activities other than leisure. Specifically, we exclude from the conceptualization of leisure in this chapter expressive conduct that involves participation in large-scale public expressive activities, such as political demonstrations, religious ceremonials, military parades, and university inaugurations that primarily entail the individual's relation to institutions. Of course, any of these "nonpersonal" participations may serve some of the same objectives as do leisure activities, but their primary significance is their *intrinsically expressive* themes, not their *personally expressive* themes.

A Definition of Leisure from the Action Theory Perspective

Leisure may therefore be conceptualized from the action theory perspective as *discretionary personal activity in which expressive meanings have primacy over instrumental themes*, in the sense that gratification of present needs, wants, desires, or objectives is given precedence over practical preparation for later gratification (Gaitz and Gordon, 1972).

CONCEPTUALIZATIONS OF LEISURE IN THE LITERATURE

Classical approaches to the study of leisure focused on philosophical assertions concerning the very nature of leisure itself and on the relative value of leisure and work (DeGrazia, 1962, pp. 1–56). Aristotle meant by leisure both the *state* of being free from the necessity of being occupied (in work or any other form of obligation) and the wide range of intrinsically rewarding creative activities that fell under the Greek concept of *scholē*: composing and playing music, writing and reciting poetry, dancing, singing, fine conversation with worthy companions, and especially the form of mental cultivation that we would term "serene contemplation." He considered leisure to be the "first principle of all action" and the goal of all work (instrumental activity). Epicurus later added bodily pleasures, while Seneca and others stressed the unobligated character of contemplation as its prime virtue, symbolizing the nobility of freedom (and the freedom of nobles). Disraeli put this view more broadly in the context of nineteenth century Europe: "Increased means and increased leisure are the two great civilizers of man."

Christian doctrine (from St. Benedict through John Calvin and beyond) gradually elevated work and "good works" as moral and spiritual imperatives, while recasting leisure as, at best, necessary rest in preparation for greater efforts on the morrow, and, at worst, devilish temptation through which to indulge the carnal desires in sensuous sin and degradation (DeGrazia, 1962, pp. 23–25, 36–56; Berger, 1962, p. 35).

In the late 1800's, Thorstein Veblen (1899, especially Ch. 3–4) condemned the conspicuous consumption and honorific display of predatory prowess among the *nouveau riche* pecuniary elites he termed the Leisure Class. However, the spread of urbanism, industrialization, and material affluence, together with the rise of social science, brought an "objective" rather than normative approach to leisure study (Robinson, 1969b). Lundberg, Komarovsky, and McInerny (1934, and in Larrabee and Meyersohn, 1958, pp. 173–198) applied the seemingly precise method of time-budget analysis to nontheoretical lists of specific leisure activities, and DeGrazia (1961), Foote (1961), and other contributers to the Kleemeier collection (1961a) further developed the idea of leisure as essentially "time not spent in paid work" (Kleemeier, 1961b, p. 3).

At least six serious critical considerations reduce the meaningfulness of the time-budget approach: (1) the lists of categories are in reality neither exhaustive nor even mutually exclusive; (2) they are either too general or too specific for theoretical purposes; (3) the time-sampling procedures miss rare but important events in favor of repetitious and routine ones; (4) important forms of leisure activity such as sexuality are quite missing from the lists; (5) no explicit theoretical rationale controls the inclusion, exclusion, or specific formulation of the categories; and most importantly, (6) *time* spent in particular forms of leisure activity may not be of great theoretical importance and instead may be misleading because of lack of resources or opportunities necessary for more highly-desired forms.

Thus, it must be concluded that the Lundberg and later time-budget approaches were pioneering efforts in which numerical technique outran conceptualization and theoretical development.

The "negative definition" and clock-time approach to leisure remained rather sterile (both theoretically and empirically) until the social and psychological meanings of specific leisure activities were analyzed. Kaplan (1958, 1960a, 1960b, and 1961) returned to Aristotle's theme of "freedom" in leisure but focused on *minimized social role obligations* and further distinguished leisure from other nonwork activities that were nevertheless highly obligatory. Havighurst (1957, 1960, 1961, 1972, 1973; and with Feigenbaum, 1959) made especially important theoretical as well as empirical contributions by delineating a series of theoretical meanings of leisure (applied by coders, not by the respondents) that showed the great diversity of relevant social-psychological dimensions (autonomy, creativity, sociability, talent-development, services, relaxation, ego-integration). Havighurst's conceptual approach is the most comprehensive and yet subtle to appear in the literature to date (cf. Denny and Meyersohn, 1957).

David Riesman (1950, 1952, 1954, 1958, 1964; with Bloomberg, 1957; and with Roseborough, 1955) focused on leisure as personal consumption of the "standard consumer package" of material goods and cultural symbol systems and showed the intimate and complex interconnections between leisure styles and work situation across the individual's life span. He also added sexuality and mass communications involvement as key themes within leisure. Mass communications previously had been treated in relatively trivial categories (e.g. "listening to the radio") in time budgets, and sex had been repressed even more thoroughly from the social science literature than from the artistic literature (Foote, 1954). Throughout, Riesman perceptively characterized the intimate and two-way relationship between the instrumental activities and personal expressivity as these have changed over the centuries and over the course of a given individual's life span (especially in Riesman and Roseborough, 1955). Finally, Riesman was one of the first (1952) to specify a set of general objectives that persons frequently seek through the multitude of specific leisure activities—development (self-improvement), recreation (diversion), reverie, and creativity—and also illuminated the very pervasive feelings of ambivalence we may feel when our mundane attempts at seeking these values fail or go badly.

On a more literary, artistic, and psychological level, Berlyne (1969) has provided an excellent integration of a massive body of material on laughter, humor, and play in humans and other species. Detailed consideration of a wide range of theories of humor and play (variously emphasizing superiority, conflict, tension relief, fantasy aggression, etc.) led Berlyne to postulate a "collative" approach based on the idea of phased alternation among moderately novel and optimally complex physical, cognitive, and emotional processes. He also presents a wealth of information and insight regarding the symbolic content of games (such as engaged prowess, fantasy detachment from the real world, relief from boredom, strategy and skill versus luck, competiton versus mutuality, and alteration of the self in its reality context). He sees play and games as helping people to manage life pressures through chance, skill, and strategy as they experiment with and rehearse mental and physical activities that will be used later in life (see also Sutton-Smith and Roberts, 1964).

The anthropological literature on play in diverse cultures supports and extends these ideas (Norbeck, 1963, 1969, 1971, 1974a, 1974b; Turner, 1974). Play, games, sports, esthetic activities of all sorts, "public" sexuality, and, most particularly, transcendent psychological states serve important social as well as personal functions in relation to important cyclical events and have been shown to be highly institutionalized and regularized in most societies.

The "recreation" literature (see especially *The Journal of Leisure Research*) has concentrated on assessing current demands and future wants regarding public and private outdoor facilities for active sports and communing with nature (Witt and Bishop, 1970; Wennergren and Fullerton, 1972; Knopp, 1972). While short on theory, this literature does contain a great amount of specific information on consumer values, patterns of facility use, and monetary expenditures, and contains recurrent analyses of the National Recreation Survey (Cicchetti, 1972; Hendricks and Burdge, 1972).

More subtle and elaborate are the writings of Nels Anderson (1961) and Margaret Mead (1957, 1960) on the connections between leisure activities and other nonwork nonleisure activities such as family obligations, religious observances, political participation, etc. Both of these authors stress the fact that it is nonwork obligations (often more than work) that seems to absorb available time so that discretionary leisure activities may nearly vanish or not even be desired. On this basis, Anderson offered the interesting hypothesis that the greater the individual's integration into family and group life, the less leisure (presumedly unobligated personal expressivity) he will have (1961, pp. 105-106). Both Anderson and Mead stress the importance of the home context for leisure activity (as did Riesman), and Mead added explicit consideration of personal creativity, even in everyday matters, by people not labelled "artists."

Explicit theoretical and empirical work on the functions performed by leisure (either in terms of adaptive contributions to whole social systems or in terms of valued objectives sought by individuals) has appeared only recently, even though Berger articulated the need for this approach over a decade ago (1962). Havighurst (Donald and Havighurst, 1959; and in numerous other of his writings) formulated a list of 12 "derived benefits or satisfactions" from empirical studies, but there was little or no theoretical framework for this list.

Gross (1961) made the first attempt to outline systematically the functions that leisure (and especially play) might be performing for a national society. He used the Parsonian action theory perspective to suggest ways in which leisure might facilitate pattern-maintenance and tension-management, adaptation, goal-attainment, and integration. Though not validated with systematic empirical evidence, Gross's article illustrates a "theoretical" approach to leisure and also the value of social system analysis in addition to looking at the leisure of particular individuals.

Finally, Joffre Dumazedier's succinct conceptualization of leisure in his *Toward a Society of Leisure* (1967, pp. 16-17) has provided us with a clear view of five major functions or derived satisfactions that individuals frequently seek through one or more of the infinite number of diverse leisure activities. Not only is his a positive rather than negative conceptualization and one that stresses discretionary (nonobligated) activity rather than time, but his specification of relaxation, diversion, knowledge, social participation, and creativity takes us all the way back to Aristotle and integrates the insights of Riesman, Anderson, Mead, Havighurst, and others.

Now we can examine Dumazedier's objectives of leisure in the light of our general distinction between *expressive* and *instrumental* primacy in human conduct. We shall use the general concept of expressivity as a theoretical dimension along which to order the objectives. Also, we shall use the concept of expressivity to extend the set to include *sensual transcendence*, which has been touched upon by

Freud, Riesman, Anderson, Norbeck, and Turner but by few other analysts.

RECONCEPTUALIZATION OF LEISURE— A SYSTEMATIC ORDERING OF MEANINGFUL OBJECTIVES

In earlier papers we have suggested that *intensity of expressive involvement* is the theoretical dimension that underlies and provides for the meaningful ordering of the objectives of leisure formulated by Riesman, Dumazedier, and others (Gaitz and Gordon, 1972; Gordon, Gaitz, and Scott, 1973).

The Continuum of Expressive Involvement Intensity

Figure 1 shows our ordering of five major objectives of leisure derived from the literature

discussed above. Relaxation, diversion, self-development, creativity, and sensual transcendence are asserted to be forms of personal expressivity that are at increasing intensities of cognitive, emotional, and physical involvement. The more intense the activity, as we define it, the greater is the expenditure of energy, the need for focused attention, and the sensory stimulation.

Relaxation includes such low-intensity activities as sleeping and quiet resting, as well as solitude for daydreaming (Giambra, 1974), reverie, and thinking about future activities. While some may think that sleeping and resting are not really "activities" at all, research on dreaming and fantasizing (Freud, 1900; Faraday, 1973, 1974; Friday, 1973; Slatery, 1975) clearly shows that these may be very important forms of expressive behavior that

FORMS OF LEISURE ACTIVITY

INTENSITY OF EXPRESSIVE INVOLVEMENT (Cognitive, Emotional and Physical)		
Very High	SENSUAL TRANSCENDENCE	SEXUAL ACTIVITY PSYCHO-ACTIVE CHEMICAL USE ECSTATIC RELIGIOUS EXPERIENCE AGGRESSION, "ACTION" (physical fighting, defense or attack, verbal fighting) HIGHLY COMPETITIVE GAMES AND SPORTS INTENSE AND RHYTHMIC DANCING
Medium High	CREATIVITY	CREATIVE ACTIVITIES (artistic, literary, musical, etc.) NURTURANCE, ALTRUISM SERIOUS DISCUSSION, ANALYSIS EMBELLISHMENT OF INSTRUMENTAL (art or play in work)
Medium	DEVELOPMENTAL	PHYSICAL EXERCISE AND INDIVIDUAL SPORTS COGNITIVE ACQUISITION (serious reading, disciplined learning) BEAUTY APPRECIATION, ATTENDANCE AT CULTURAL EVENTS (galleries, museums, etc.) ORGANIZATIONAL PARTICIPATION (clubs, interest groups) SIGHT-SEEING, TRAVEL SPECIAL LEARNING GAMES AND TOYS
Medium Low	DIVERSION	SOCIALIZING, ENTERTAINING SPECTATOR SPORTS GAMES, TOYS OF MOST KINDS, PLAY LIGHT CONVERSATION HOBBIES READING PASSIVE ENTERTAINMENT (as in mass media usage)
Very Low	RELAXATION	SOLITUDE QUIET RESTING SLEEPING

Figure 1. Qualitatively varying forms of leisure activity (expressive primacy in personal activity), according to intensity of expressive involvement.

provide essential variety and re-creation for the mind as well as for the body.

Diversion provides change of pace and relief from mental tension or boredom with routine instrumental activities. Relatively passive absorption of mass media entertainment is in this category, as well as light reading, sedentary hobbies, and "passing the time of day" in conversation with friends and acquaintances (Kramer, 1974). Further discussion of play and games can be found in: Piaget, 1945; Berlyne, 1969; Norbeck, 1969, 1971; Erikson, 1972; of spectator sports in Huizinga, 1949; Stone, 1955, 1972; Roberts, Arth, and Bush, 1959; Sutton-Smith and Rosenberg, 1961; Sutton-Smith, Rosenberg, and Morgan, 1963; Sofranko and Nolan, 1972; Edwards, 1973; of sociability in Simmel, 1910; Riesman, 1964. Mass media research and theory constitute an immense field, but some key references are: Riesman, 1950; Wolfenstein, 1951; Rosenberg and White, 1957; Klapper, 1960; Robinson, 1969a; Turan and Zito, 1974.

Developmental activities (while often enjoyable in their own right) result in an appreciable increase in physical capacity, cognitive knowledge or more abstract ways of interpreting one's experience. These include learning about a subject of interest, not as preparation for later use, but simply because it is intrinsically interesting (Winthrop, 1966). Also included here is learning to do the cultural activities so highly regarded by Aristotle: learning to sing or dance, learning to paint or play a musical instrument or to act, as well as devoting serious attention to experiencing and comprehending works of art and beauty. Active involvement with others, such as attending a party, also falls under this rubric because one's attitudes and perceptions are inevitably altered through sustained and focused social interaction, and the level of emotional, cognitive, and physical involvement is often quite high.

Creative activities include the activities in which the person is performing actively in a contributory or independent fashion to create new cultural productions. These may be as ephemeral as amusing guests by playing the piano or as substantial as some of the amateurs' discoveries that have changed the technological face of the world. In these creative activities, the expressive and instrumental themes are inextricably bound and blended into a form of "useful play" (Fuller, 1973).

The *pursuit of sensual pleasure* is a key element missing from formulations of leisure by Dumazedier and other theorists working within the Western tradition. A partial explanation for this omission may be found in the residue of puritanical moralism. And yet, the pursuit of sensual pleasure has occupied much of the leisure time, as well as the fantasy life, jokes, stories, advertising, and mass media experiences, of ordinary persons everywhere and always. By sensual pleasure we mean not only primary and secondary sexual stimulation and activity (for example, see Masters and Johnson, 1966; Hunt, 1974; and Comfort, 1972, 1974), but also the activation of any of the senses by stimuli and actions that provide intense levels of pleasure, gratification, excitement, rapture, or joy (cf. Maslow, 1959; Schutz, 1967; Margolis and Clorfene, 1969; Weil, 1972; Inkeles and Todris, 1972; Playboy Editors, 1972; Lewis, 1973; Rhodes, 1974). Thus, we include sensual pleasure derived from the mystical awe that may be associated with intense religious experiences, use of psychoactive chemicals, emotion-laden conflict or competition (physical or verbal), erotic forms of dancing, dramatic expression, strong wit and humor, and many intense forms of play. Our concept of the transcendent states of mind, experience, or conduct concerns pleasures beyond the routine and ordinary instrumental activities necessary for life's basic requirements.

The truly transcendent sensual pleasures lie at the high end of the continuum of intensity of personal involvement, in which cognitive, emotional, and physical energies are aroused, focused and expended at very high levels. Furthermore, these high-intensity activities are characterized by combinations of the attributes delineated by Abraham Maslow (1959) as "being values" that constitute "peak-experiences": wholeness, perfection, completion, justice, aliveness, richness, simplicity, beauty, goodness, uniqueness, effortlessness, playfulness, truth, and self-sufficiency.

Costs, Risks, and Values of Leisure

Varying forms of leisure activities are sought by an individual for personal benefit or gratification—to make him "feel better" in some qualitative way. The activity may produce the desired result, but it also may fail to match expectations. Leisure activities frequently bring a sense of dissatisfaction and frustration. Beyond the obvious monetary costs, one may be bored by or addicted to mass media rather than being briefly diverted by them. Failure to learn to play a musical instrument or speak a foreign language can prove to be intimidating, while attempts at creative expression can reveal embarrassing lacks of talent, skill, style, or insight. In particular, the sensual pleasures carry the potential burdens of severe guilt feelings, a sense of undesirability after rejection, a sense of incompetence after failure, a sense of meaninglessness after success, and even the possibility of police action or disastrous economic and social effects if they involve prohibited sexual activity or psychoactive chemical use. Finally, some high-intensity leisure activities (e.g., sex or psychoactive chemicals) may be "psychologically addictive" so that the person cannot or will not give adequate attention to instrumental activities, while other high-intensity leisure activities (as in the case of skiing or skydiving) may be likely to produce physical injury.

Our arrangement of personally expressive activities is not meant to confer a higher or lower degree of value on these activities. Specifically, we are not arguing that the intense sensual leisures are necessarily "good" for people; such evaluations must be made by each person individually. While it is true that "all work and no play makes Jack a dull boy," Benjamin Franklin perhaps best articulated the goal of temporal alternation and ultimate balance between the instrumental and the expressive:

> The honest man takes his pains and then enjoys pleasure; the knave takes pleasure and then suffers pain.

On the basis of the foregoing considerations, we will use the following conceptualization of leisure as we review the empirical literature:

leisure is personally expressive discretionary activity, varying in intensity of involvement from relaxation and diversion at the low end of the continuum, through personal development and creativity at higher levels, up to sensual transcendence at the highest levels of cognitive, emotional, and physical involvement.

THE CONTEMPORARY LIFE SPAN, IN THEORY AND IN LEISURE RESEARCH

Consideration of typical leisure activities observed among different age groups or life-stage categories requires an explicit life span conceptual framework. Gordon (1971a, 1971b) has proposed an 11-stage developmental model incorporating major dilemmas of value-theme differentiation and integration in the culture of contemporary urban middle-class America.

Any new theory of life-stages inevitably draws upon previous formulations and then goes on to modify and add new features drawn from the particular theoretical perspective of the proposer. Since Shakespeare's delineation of the "seven ages of man," the most significant contributions to life-stage theory began with Sigmund Freud's *The Ego and the Id* (1923). Erik Erikson (1950a, 1956) emphasized the complex interrelations of sociocultural epoch and social roles and personality dynamics over the life cycle. Parsons (1955a, 1955b, 1955c) incorporated the Freudian stages of psycho-sexual development into a theory of action applicable to the family as a social system, to immediate parent/child interactions, and to the internal dynamics of the child's developing personality. Else Frenkel-Brunswik (1963) described five major shifts in social-psychological concerns that are loosely connected to the biological time clock of aging, and Charlotte Bühler (with Massarik, 1968) elaborated on the development of major life values, objectives, and plans over the life span. Three major collections of work dealing with diverse aspects of a life-stage approach were published in the 1960's (Kuhlen and Thompson, 1963; Sears and Feldman, 1964; Neugarten, 1968). These collections embodied a sociological and social-psychological perspective and went well beyond the Freudian psycho-sexual stage formulations

Life-cycle stage; approximate ages or timing	Most significant others	Major dilemma of value-theme differentiation and integration		
		SECURITY	vs.	CHALLENGE
I. Infancy 0–12 months	mothering one	affective gratification	vs.	sensorimotor experiencing
II. Early childhood 1–2 years	mother, father	compliance	vs.	self-control
III. Oedipal period 3–5 years	father, mother, siblings, playmates	expressivity	vs.	instrumentality
IV. Later childhood 6–11 years	parents, same-sex peers, teachers	peer relationships	vs.	evaluated abilities
V. Early adolescence 12–15 years	parents, same-sex peers, opposite-sex peers, teachers	acceptance	vs.	achievement
VI. Later adolescence 16–18/20 years	opposite-sex peers, same-sex peers, parents, teachers, lover(s), husband, wife, employers	intimacy	vs.	autonomy
VII. Young adulthood or youth 19/21–29 years	lover(s), wife or husband, children, employers, friends	connection	vs.	self-determination
VIII. Early maturity 30–44 years	wife or husband, lover(s), children, superiors, colleagues, friends, parents	stability	vs.	accomplishment
IX. Full maturity 45 to age of retirement	wife or husband, lover(s), grown children, colleagues, friends, younger associates	dignity	vs.	control
X. Retirement retirement age to onset of severe illness	remaining family, lover(s), long-term friends, neighbors	meaningful integration	vs.	autonomy
XI. Disability onset of severe illness to death	remaining family, friends, medical professionals, caregivers	survival	vs.	acceptance of death

Figure 2. Stage developmental model of the ideal-typical life cycle in contemporary, urban, middle-class America—giving approximate ages, the most significant other persons, and the major dilemmas of value-theme differentiation and integration. (From Gordon, 1971a, "Role and value development across the life cycle," a revision and expansion of Figure 2.)

in terms of roles and temporal span. Lidz (1968) integrated both social structural and psycho-dynamic levels of explanation and re-cast the insights of psycho-analytic perspective in terms of their connection with the social role demands and opportunities that are typically presented to the individual at each stage of the life span, even into the most advanced years.

Gordon's model of life-stages offers a consistent, comprehensive, and systematic formulation of the crucial dilemmas of *value-theme differentiation and integration* that are produced by the interaction of physical maturation, cognitive elaboration, social role acquisitions and relinquishments, and economic resource patterning throughout the life span. It is these interactions and dilemmas that structure the changing stages of the socio-cognitive development across a contemporary life span and which may in large part structure leisure desires and leisure behavior patterns.

"Value-theme" in this usage is intended to mean a cluster or complex of culturally defined, idealized aspects of human life and social interaction, such as achievement, acceptance, compliance, and self-control. These very general value-orientations are simultaneously *institutionalized* in the reward structures of the social system and *internalized* as evaluative standards and objectives in the personalities of individual social system members. This theory asserts that versions of these institutionalized value-themes become internalized in the personality and self-conceptions of most (if not all) of the social system's members and establish a set of significant dimensions of differentiation and integration in each successive stage of the life span.

Six unique assumptions underlie this socio-cognitive stage model of the contemporary life cycle:

1. The exact characteristics of the symbolic and behavioral interaction patterns at each stage are qualitatively distinct from those of the previous and subsequent stages. The differences center on the addition or relinquishment of particular significant others and on the qualitative character of the value-themes that these "others" make relevant to the person. Thus, it is implied that leisure activities will be differently valued and differently chosen at each stage.

2. Each of the proposed pairs constitutes a dilemma for the individual, in the sense that while he is being socialized to maximize his capabilities regarding both members of the pair, his actions in pursuit of one of the values may tend to block satisfaction in relation to the other. Many leisure activities call for particular skills and satisfy particular values that involve primarily one or the other value-theme at a particular stage. Beyond these, other leisure activities seem to "bridge" a value-theme dilemma or combine elements of both, and we may hypothesize that these bridging leisures will be chosen when possible.

3. It is not yet clear whether there are any essential or "critical" periods in which particular forms of socialization must take place, although there do seem to be "optimal" periods. Thus, we can expect that leisure activities matching the relevant values will also show this same temporal patterning, at least approximately.

4. The specification of these major stages and their combination of value themes and socializing agents have a wider application than merely to contemporary urban middle-class

Americans. Specific subcultures will stress somewhat different values and may have a different timing program, but the "official" socialization agencies of our country will make the specified value themes painfully relevant even to members of quite distinct subcommunities.

5. The left-hand member of each value-theme pair represents an empirical interpretation of the extremely general concept of *security*, while the right-hand members are differing versions of *challenge* from new and risky (although potentially rewarding) activity. Security and challenge occur as very important elements of most if not all cultures, especially those shaped by urbanism, industrialism, and rational secularism; therefore the proposed paradigm should apply, at least as a comparison or reference point, in relation to other cultures.

6. In most of these cultures, certainly in the past century, females have been socialized to focus on the left-hand (security) side of the value pairs, while males were taught to specialize on the right-hand (challenge) activities, only regressing to security concerns when failing in or anxious about new challenges. Thus, we can hypothesize that the leisure activities frequently chosen by females will emphasize home-centered, social, and relatively low-intensity forms, while those most frequently engaged in by men will include the more active, external-to-the-home, individual, and relatively high-intensity forms of leisure.

It should be pointed out that these value-theme dilemmas are hypothetical constructs, the validity of which can only be assessed in terms of their usefulness in helping us order and comprehend the empirical literature on leisure that constitutes the main material in this chapter.

Having set forth our theoretical approach to the general concept of leisure—as primacy of personally expressive meanings in discretionary activity—and our general stage-developmental model of the ideal-typical life span found in contemporary urban America, we now consider the major findings of leisure research and their relationship to life-stages.

Infancy and Childhood

Play (any "pretend" action) and games (play with a structure of rules) are the main leisure forms of the period from birth to adolescence. Berlyne (1969, pp. 840–843) has shown that playful activities typically follow a sequence of tension, uncertainty, or excitement followed by pleasurable reduction of this arousal and relief from conflict or tension. Bruner (1975) enumerated key functions of play as achievement without pressure, practice and experience with little anxiety, and interaction through language leading to effective learning. Thus, play serves as a forerunner of adult competence in both problem-solving and creativity (Caplan and Caplan, 1973). Spencer (1873, pp. 627–648) discussed the intrinsic value of play in overcoming boredom, discharging excess energy, and simulating predatory and conquest themes that come up later in "real life" activities of children. In addition, play produces intrinsically-rewarding states of consciousness (Weil, 1972). Erikson (1943) also indicated that children's play may be satisfying to them emotionally and may reflect largely unconscious problems (Escalona, 1943).

Theories of play stress the alternation of activities providing a sense of security with those presenting a form of challenge. Several studies (Piaget, 1945; Bateson, 1955; Sutton-Smith, 1966; Erikson, 1972; Murphy, 1972) support our position (Figure 2) that affective gratification and pleasurable body sensations represent the particular forms that security and challenge take during the first year of life. Socialization through playful activity strongly influences the child's general style of coping in interpersonal relationships.

A young child's play capacity expands rapidly as he develops control over major and minor muscle groups. At the same time that parents limit the forms of play a child may engage in, they also may provide warm and proud responses as the child shows independence, initiative, and self-control (Sutton-Smith, 1971). Psychoanalytic theory asserts that libidinal investment in the anal area is a primary focus of attention during the second year of life, and character traits of orderliness, perseverance, cleanliness, miserliness, and obsessive-compulsive neurosis may be traced back to this critical period. Sociological perspective suggests that parental response rewarding independence of action supports a child's senses of competance and self-determination, while the enforcement of limits raises the issue of *compliance*. Children's play with peers involves the same themes of leadership and control; general themes of expressivity and instrumentality emerge in group context, and the definition of the sex roles typically becomes much more rigid (see Figure 2). Writers such as Turner (1956, 1962), Mead (1934, pp. 149–164), and Parten and Newhall (1943) have demonstrated the importance of role-taking (the genesis of the self and of self-control) and the positive association of age with social participation and with direct personal leadership (MacDonald, McGuire, and Havighurst, 1949). With increasing age, there is an increase in the desire to engage in social and interactive forms of play and to be involved in both giving and carrying out "orders" regarding expressive and instrumental activities. Anderson (1959) has shown that overall energy expenditure rises dramatically from infancy through approximately age 20 and then declines steadily. The content of selected activities follows a very similar pattern of increasing variety and diversity over the years of childhood and, as one matures, is followed by sequential selective reductions in activities that are especially demanding of energy.

Sutton-Smith and Rosenberg (1961) and Sutton-Smith, Rosenberg, and Morgan (1963) consider the issues of historical change in the play activities of children. A move away from formality and power, the movement of both boys and girls in terms of rejecting previous "female" definitions of play, and the increasing tendency for girls to prefer games previously and currently played by boys may be seen as steps toward a more "democratic" and equalitarian approach to leisure among those in late childhood and early adolescence, and offer opportunities for relatively safe role experimentation in competence with peer relationships and development of evaluated abilities. A large

British study of children's street games (Opie and Opie, 1969) reaffirms the value of play for a child, stressing that both the uncertainty of outcome and the excitement of the game (within the context of a controlled situation) allow comprehension and joy far beyond "real life."

Adolescence

In the early stage of adolescence (about age 12–15) the primary developmental dilemma is the difficult interrelationship between acceptance and achievement. During late adolescence (about age 16–21) the concept of general social acceptance is concerned with and depends on intimacy with a small circle of loved ones, and the idea of achievement is directed toward responsible autonomy (Gordon, 1971a, pp. 88–94; 1971b). This frame of reference is in accord with findings in empirical literature on leisure interests and activities in this age period.

Major studies (MacDonald, McGuire, and Havighurst, 1949; Hollingshead, 1949, 1975; Whyte, 1943; Coleman, 1961; Sherif and Sherif, 1964) confirm that leisure activities of adolescents differ both quantitatively and qualitatively depending on social class structures. The literature (Friedenberg, 1959; Douvan and Adelson, 1966; Gordon, 1971b; Kagan and Coles, 1972; Dragastin and Elder, 1975) shows that late adolescents frequently use leisure activities to promote and maintain autonomy from their parents by first increasing degrees of solidarity with friends and then through intimacy with very close peers. The mass media contribute to the escape from the parental and occupational world (Kline and Clarke, 1971), and leisure and mass communications also serve to socialize adolescents into the roles and attitudes of adults. Studies on anticipatory socialization (Klapper, 1960; Larsen, 1964; Schramm, 1972; Noe, 1970) conclude that both male and female adolescents use leisure forms as a way in which to acquire "appropriate" male and female adult role attitudes and behaviors. Studies on the content of adolescent leisure activity are difficult to interpret, but generally the leisure activities seem to provide opportunities for explicit learning about "forbidden" topics such as sexuality, tolerance for others, and even seem to provide a special language through which one can look back on youth with nostalgic sentimentality. Adolescent leisure provides a margin of freedom within institutionalized constraints (Kraus, 1971, Ch. 13) and can increase self-esteem.

Studies by Bishop (1970) and Witt (1971) verify the assertion that leisure for adolescents tends to concern developing skills and competences to be rewarded within the youth culture and so provides an alternative to the school-based competences that are rewarded later in adult social structures. Sexual competence and other interpersonal skills foster social acceptance and later interpersonal intimacy (Hunt, 1974), all as a prelude to the development of specific connections to loved ones in the next life stage—young adulthood.

"Youth" and Young Adulthood (Age 19/21 to 29)

Gordon (1971a) defines the central problem of this stage as connection vs. self-determination. Problems arise as one attempts to maintain self-directed choices regarding future objectives while establishing and maintaining rewarding and stable connections to the larger social order through occupational and marital commitments.

The development of our post-industrial society is characterized by a prolongation of adolescence for a significant proportion of those aged 21–29, a "second adolescence" or "youth" stage involving an elaborate period of graduate training for the more complex professional roles, with the result that many young people remain outside the regular labor force for an extended period. A number of youth subculture features have impact on leisure activities—for example, the desires of youth for variety, autonomy, sensory experience through music, clothes, and a range of sensual pursuits including sexual indulgence and elaborated drug use (Erikson, 1950a, 1956; Berger, 1971; Keniston, 1970; Langman, 1971; Cottle, 1972; Playboy Editors, 1972; Rapaport and Rapaport, 1975; Gordon, 1976, Part IV).

The relationship of the young person and his family has an indirect impact on leisure. It should be noted that regarding attitudes, values, and behavioral patterns, there are still areas of basic agreement between the generations (Birren and Bengtson, 1970; Bengtson and Lovejoy, 1973). Gunther and Moore (1975), however, point out that the modern urban family has relinquished much of its leisure-providing function to the outside world and that the family must compete for the attention of its younger members against a wide range of external interests provided by peers, the mass media, and the university. The result is frequently an increased degree of age segregation in leisure activities.

The vast majority of young Americans marry before age 23, and the role of husband or wife makes substantial modification in leisure interests and activities. Kelly (1974, 1975) found in adult leisure studies that current activities had often been learned within parental families or at school. His studies, however, suggest that other crucial variables shaping leisure choices are: occupational situation, family roles, stage in the marital career, health status, available time, monetary resources, and personality factors. In complex analyses of leisure, Kelly indicates, as might be expected, that the arrival of the first child makes the most important changes in leisure behaviors of young marrieds.

The impact of leisure activities on the individual's marital and life satisfaction is complex. Orthner (1975a) holds that the importance of leisure has increased as the marriage form has shifted from hierarchical to companionate, and as the values placed on personal expressivity, creativity, and "fun" have become more important. In early stages of family formation, joint activities encourage interaction and development of shared commitments to the new life and are again an important factor when the household returns to its original dyad (Carise, 1975).

Further influences of leisure on marital satisfaction are dealt with by Orthner in a second article (1975b) tracing out several potential benefits for the nuclear family regarding leisure activity patterns: fulfillment of needs for some release from institutional conventionality, opportunity to consider alternatives to existing role relationships, increased personal communication with direct and honest feedback, experience of shared frustrations as well as happy experiences, compensation for inadequacies felt in other areas of life, increased cohesiveness of the family in planning future leisure activities, sharing of unique experiences and a sense of exclusiveness, and recollection of the shared happinesses or frustrations of the particular leisure activity forms chosen.

A few studies have analyzed the highly expressive forms of leisure, especially loving and sexuality, in terms of concepts that fit within our life cycle perspective of the dilemma produced in balancing security and challenge. The bulk of leisure research concerning the period after family formation deals primarily with the relationship between work and leisure, and so frequently focuses on later age groups that we will refer to it under the general concepts suggested by our life cycle theory for the next two periods: stability vs. accomplishment in early maturity, and dignity vs. control in full maturity.

Early Maturity (age 30–44 years)

For the age group 30–44 years, the primary value themes are stability vs. accomplishment. The husband is very likely to devote time, attention, and effort to his occupation and to attaining its rewards for accomplishment, while the wife has primary concerns with child care, household management, and maintaining family stability (Gordon, 1971a, p. 96). The degree of shared commitment to develop stability and growth in their marriage and family may ultimately determine both the success of the marriage and the emotional stability of the children. Leisure pursuits are among the significant means of achieving marriage and family growth as well as maintaining individual emotional health.

The most frequent leisure activities of this life-stage are home-and-family centered: TV viewing, visiting with family and friends, gardening, home workshop, individual hobbies, reading, walking, or some form of physical activity such as fishing, hunting, camping, swimming, golf, and so forth (Graham, 1959; Anderson, 1961, Ch. 7; Thompson and Streib, 1961; Sutton-Smith, Roberts, and Kozelka, 1963; Dumazedier, 1967, Ch. 5). Men are usually more active, more inclined to sports activity, and more likely to seek leisure pursuits away from the home (Havighurst, 1957, 1972).

The Interrelations of Work and Leisure. Richer nations have shorter workweeks, workyears, and worklives (Zuzanek, 1974, p. 248). The post-industrial society, however, is only just now getting back to the work time-commitments of fourteenth century craftsmen (Wilensky. 1961b; Carter, 1971). Within any country, the higher the socioeconomic status the longer the work-life allocation (Riesman, 1958; Kreps, 1968, 1972). Socioeconomic status also influences the form of leisure activities chosen. Lower status people generally seek relaxing, diverting, or sensually transcendent leisure activities: television viewing, family visiting, home workshop, hobbies, hunting, fishing, and drinking are particularly popular. Leisure activities in the context of same-sex groups are especially frequent (Komarovsky, 1964, Ch. 14; Whyte, 1943; Shostak, 1969; Aronowitz, 1973). Higher status people choose more developmental and creative leisure activities, as well as the less risky forms of sensual transcendence. They more frequently go to concerts and plays, join and take active or leadership roles in clubs and organizations, travel more extensively, and "party" more often (Riesman, 1954, 1964; Reissman, 1954; White, 1955; Clarke, 1956; Babchuck and Booth, 1969; Hyman and Wright, 1971). Financial resources obviously determine many of these differences, but most studies indicate that both gross and subtle class differences remain (Kaplan, 1960a; Weiss and Riesman, 1961; Bishop and Ikeda, 1970). Wilensky (1961a) has shown how "disorderly" career paths, more usual among working class people, tend to break down secondary attachments to community and organizations and even weaken many primary relationships to kin and friend.

Wilensky (1960, 1961c, 1962a, 1962b) has proposed two alternative hypotheses as possible causal mechanisms relating the actual nature of the occupation to particular leisure choices: compensation and "spillover" or generalization. The compensation hypothesis holds that leisure, especially the kinds of "expressive excesses" that involve drunkenness, nonmarital sexuality, and perhaps violence, will be chosen to provide just what the job lacks. The spillover hypothesis proposes that repetitive, dull, thing-oriented, and decisionless work will produce alienation, and thus low-level leisure activities characterized by apathy, isolation, and inertia. A number of investigators, trying to resolve the apparent contradiction in these two hypotheses, have reached only the concensus that additional factors must intervene between work and leisure: the tendency to blur work and leisure in professional careers, the amount of autonomy within the job situation, the different personal meanings attached to leisure, the influence of early family life, the interests of peers, the objectively-available leisure facilities, personality variables, the individual life-style, and the success with which the individual can derive self-esteem increments from leisure conduct (Jordan, 1956; Havighurst and Feigenbaum, 1959; Seligman, 1965; Burch, 1969; Noe, 1971; Haggedorn and Labovitz, 1968; Bishop, 1970; Spreitzer and Snyder, 1974; Shepard, 1974). Clearly, sophisticated research must ascertain the meanings of both work and leisure in relation to culture, subculture, and life-styles, in addition to attempting to measure the effects of education, income, and sex roles (see, for example, Havighurst and Feigenbaum, 1959; Neugarten, 1973; Shepard, 1974).

Full Maturity (Age 45 to Retirement)

At approximately age 45, the individual may experience physical changes (menopause for women, tension-symptoms and weight gain for men) that often lead to changes in self-conception. The value themes of dignity *vs.* control become central at this time, that is, the drive for accomplishment and acquisition become less important than maintaining one's dignity and receiving respect for one's past accomplishments. At the same time, there is concern for the loss of control over goals, decisions, resources, and other persons (Gordon, 1971a, pp. 98–99). Leisure serves three basic functions during this stage. First, it often brings acceptance and warm response from others, replacing the earlier focus on instrumental achievement. Second, expressive leisure can help to stave off the personal despair that Erik-son notes as the major potential demon of middle age (1950b, p. 98). Third, it structures time at a life-stage when there is more time free from responsibilities than has been true pre-viously. At this stage persons sometimes need to rediscover the significance of leisure and to explore latent or new interests and potentials.

Each "typical" household eventually returns to its original dyad, and the extent to which a couple enjoys interaction and sharing interests is again as important to their personal and life satisfaction as it was in young adulthood. Lei-sure activities may now be less home-centered and may begin to include more evenings out, more travel, and more personally-expressive leisure forms such as music, writing, or paint-ing. Fewer financial responsibilities may pro-vide more economic resources for leisure expenditures.

Research in this area emphasizes the impor-tance of evaluating past achievements, main-taining respect or dignity, and developing a sense of control over one's activities and life patterns as key features during the middle years (Cunningham and Johannis, 1960; Pfeiffer and Davis, 1971).

Retirement Age (Roughly Age 65 to the Onset of Severe Illness)

The important value themes apparent in the literature on old age and the transition to it from middle age are personal autonomy and meaningful integration (see Figure 2). It has been hypothesized that there may be parallel circumstances between later adolescence and old age, both periods in which autonomy be-comes a main concern. Retirement and other role relinquishments may follow the develop-mental pattern of adolescence in a reverse or-der (Linden and Courtney, 1953; Gordon, 1971a p. 100).

Meaningful integration refers to sharing and loving relationships with one or a few persons. It is likely that as energy declines and social roles are relinquished, bonds of highly valued integration to meaningful others may become the sole focus of cognitive and affective involve-ment. Yet most Americans value highly the continued capacity for autonomous decision-making and effective action. Close friends and family who are willing and able to provide both support and encouragement may establish the major context for selection of leisure activities within available resources.

The importance of a valued identity after retirement is a key issue in the leisure litera-ture (Havighurst, 1953, 1960, 1961, 1973; Havighurst and Albrecht, 1953; Michelson, 1954; Burgess, 1954; Kaplan, 1958, 1960b; Kutner, Fanshel, Togo, and Langner, 1956; Cavan, 1962; Miller, 1965; Rosow, 1966; Shanas, 1967; Maddox, 1970; Streib, 1971; Thompson, 1973; Boyack, 1974). Complex interaction of many factors determines such an identity: original commitment to the work role, economic and health resources, level of social involvement, role-flexibility, social competence, and the subcultural evaluation of older people and of leisure (Gordon, 1968a, 1968b, 1969; Gordon, Gaitz, and Scott, 1976).

In an interview study of several hundred retirees, Simpson, Back, and McKinney (1966) noted the close association between occupation and retirement leisure styles, even after control-ling for the social status of their respondents. They further reported that complex interac-tions of original commitment to the work role, economic level after retirement, levels of social involvement, and physical health were relevant to relationships among work style, retirement leisure, and morale or life satisfaction. Most time-budget studies relating age to allocations of leisure activities make no clear distinction between retirees and those persons 60 years old and over. Therefore, it is difficult to compare preretirement and retirement leisure patterns (Atchley, 1971). Major studies (DeGrazia, 1961, 1962; Hoar, 1961; Cowgill and Baulch, 1962; Havighurst and Albrecht, 1953; Campbell, 1969; Robinson, 1969b; Szalai, 1972) indicate that the older the respondent, the greater the amount of time devoted to leisure, but the nar-rower the range of leisure activities, and the more sedentary and homebound the forms.

Ethnic heritage is also an important variable of differentiation in leisure patterns of the elderly, perhaps even more so than with younger persons (Jackson, 1973; Clemente, Rexroad, and Hirsch, 1975). For example, Guttmann (1973) noted that elderly Jewish Community Center participants of European background preferred group activities and traditional Jewish cultural themes, while Jews reared in the American culture preferred leisure activities emphasizing individual and comparative themes, especially those based on self-enhancement.

Personality Styles. Much has been written about possible continuities or changes in personality style across the life span (see collections of articles in Neugarten, 1968, Parts I-IV; Havighurst, Neugarten, and Tobin, 1968; Riley and Foner, 1968, Part III; Kuypers, 1972). The interrelationship of personality characteristics and leisure choices, however, has not been carefully analyzed. Few studies consider the possibility that personality changes may be the consequences of altered leisure patterns (Neugarten, 1973). Havighurst (1953) emphasized flexibility through diverse leisure and other role experimentation during middle age in preparation for psychological health in old age. He also observed that personality variables were as important as social class, education, and chronological age in the selection of particular leisure activities (Donald and Havighurst, 1959; see also Maddox, 1968).

Social Participation in Old Age. Rose (1960) hypothesized that voluntary associations tend to develop in societies when the family no longer provides necessary nurturance and maintenance for the aged and that active participation in voluntary associations correlates positively with social adjustment. In partial support of this position, Videbeck and Knox (1965) found that persons in their 50's and 60's having relatively stable life circumstances tended to reduce participation in voluntary associations, whereas those respondents whose lives were disrupted by widowhood, changing jobs, or retirement tended to increase participation in voluntary associations. Two other studies (Cutler, 1973; Bull and Aucoin, 1975), however, found that the relationship between participation in voluntary organizations and life satisfaction becomes insignificant when socioeconomic status and health ratings are controlled. Wilensky

(1961c) recognized that voluntary associations help in the integration of the aged into the community, but that successful personal adjustment among the aged is more closely related to primary attachments with family and friends. The literature on this topic is extensive (Burgess, 1954; White, 1955; Taietz and Larson, 1956; Webber, 1954; Schmitz-Scherzer and Strudel, 1971; Guttmann, 1973; Thompson, 1973), but much research remains to be done on the complex interrelationship of voluntary association participation and psychological well-being.

Family Relationships and Leisure. Most older people have highly articulated networks of interaction and frequent encounters with immediate family members (Rosow, 1967; Riley and Foner, 1968, pp. 537-575). Expressivity is a very important element in such interactions (Thompson and Streib, 1961; Shanas, 1961, 1967; Shanas and Streib, 1965; Shanas, Townsend, Wedderburn, Friis, Milhøj, and Stehouwer, 1968; Shanas, 1970; Streib, 1970, 1971; Friedsam and Martin, 1973). Neighborhood friendships, as distinct from family relations, are closely connected to characteristics of the neighborhood itself and to the length of time the person has lived there (Riley and Foner, 1968, p. 565). Rosow's data (1967) show that longtime friendships among the elderly tend to be among those who are alike in age, experience, taste, preferences, and activity patterns.

Sexuality in Old Age. Research on sexual interest, behavior, and enjoyment has progressed from the physiological facts and their consequences through discussions of psychological and sociological processes that tend to inhibit or facilitate later-life sexual functioning (Kinsey, Pomeroy, and Martin, 1948; Rubin, 1965; Christenson and Gagnon, 1965; Masters and Johnson, 1966, 1970; Katchadourian and Lunde, 1972, pp. 75-79; McCary, 1973, Ch. 15; Pengelley, 1974, pp. 127-135; Helen Kaplan, 1974, Ch. 6; Jones, Shainberg, and Byer, 1975, pp. 37-47; Burnside, 1975). Sexuality is a form of leisure activity that can be continued into advanced years if the person has the physiological capacity, and if his value system and personality style are supportive of the search for pleasure, intimacy, and integration to loved ones.

A constant theme in the relevant literature is that sexual enjoyment is a capacity that is developed early in life and can be maintained throughout the entire life span, but only with continued reactivation in a meaningful and unthreatening environment (Pfeiffer, Verwoerdt, and Wang, 1969; Verwoerdt, Pfeiffer, and Wang, 1969; Pfeiffer, Verwoerdt, and Davis, 1972; Pfeiffer and Davis, 1972; Comfort, 1972). The best basis for an active and pleasurable sex life in the later years is an active and pleasurable sex life in the early and middle years (Comfort, 1972, 1974; Gordon, 1976, Part II, IV).

Physiological Decline and Debilitating Illness. The years after 70 or 75 are likely to bring a series of health problems that may prevent any but the most sedentary leisure activities, but even these can include many creative leisure forms.

The value-theme dilemmas in the very old age period become more centered around survival as opposed to any active form of integration with loved ones, and around acceptance of death as opposed to continuation of independent action. Expressive behavior—in the sense of religious concern, reverie, and fantasy as they play roles in getting one's thoughts, plans, and relationships to others straightened out—now take on special meanings (Neugarten, 1968, Part IX; Kastenbaum and Aisenberg, 1972, esp. Ch. 2 and 3).

THE HOUSTON STUDY OF LEISURE ACROSS THE LIFE SPAN

The Houston study of leisure and mental health contained operational procedures for measuring both forms and intensities of personal expressivity, and our analyses have focused on age and life-stage as key independent variables in shaping leisure choices and satisfactions.

Methodology

The data to be presented in this section were collected by a structured interview concerning

I. Relaxation
    1. Solitude: Having time to be alone to think, daydream, plan, or just do nothing.

II. Diversion
    2. Television viewing: Hours of TV watched on an average day.
    3. Cultural consumption: Looking at paintings or listening to music.
    4. Reading: Reading and finishing any book within the last year.
    5. Movies: Going to the movies.
    6. Spectator Sports: Watching sporting events either at the game or on television.
    7. Entertaining: Visiting with friends in one's home or going to someone else's house.

III. Developmental
    8. Outdoor activities: Going to the country, the beach, camping, fishing, walking in the woods, etc.
    9. Travel Taking trips to other cities for reasons other than business.
    10. Organizations: Belonging to social or civic clubs or organizations.

IV. Creativity
    11. Cooking Cooking, baking, barbecuing—fixing food for oneself, one's family or one's friends.
    12. Home embellishment: Sewing, mending, decorating, fixing, building, or working in the yard.
    13. Discussion: Talking about local or national problems and issues.
    14. Cultural production: Singing, drawing or painting, playing a musical instrument.

V. Sensual Transcendence
    15. Guns: Using firearms in sports like hunting or target practice.
    16. Participation in sports or exercise: Vigorous physical activity either inside the home or out.
    17. Dancing and drinking: Going out for an evening to a place where you can dance or drink.

Figure 3. Seventeen specific leisure activities arrayed according to increasing expressive involvement intensity.

leisure activities, value preferences, social attitudes, and various aspects of mental health from a sample of adults in Houston, Texas during the period of November, 1969 to February, 1970. The sample included 1441 persons and was stratified according to sex, ethnicity (anglo, black, and Mexican-American), two family occupational status levels, and six age groups that were later compressed to five groups for comparisons within the life-stage developmental model.

Age Group	Life-Cycle Stage	N
20–29	Young adult	248
30–44	Early maturity	308
45–64	Full maturity	425
65–74	Old age	242
75–94	Very old age	218
	Total sample	1,441

The interview included inquiries concerning 17 categories of leisure activities derived in part from Havighurst (1957). In addition, summary scores of key leisure dimensions were created from these 17 category frequency reports. Our leisure scores include a *participation* measure, six scores for participation in *active*, *passive*, *external*, *internal* (*homebound*), *social*, and *individual* leisure, five participation scores corresponding to the *levels* of the expressivity continuum (see Figure 3), and finally a *leisure pleasure* measure.

Results

Curvilinear associations between variables are common in social science research, but are frequently ignored in favor of the more convenient linear approximations. We present our data in the form of percentage graphs across the life span to highlight several nonlinear patterns. In these cases, the values of gamma (a measure of ordered association in cross-tabulations similar to the correlation coefficient; Somers, 1962) will be low, but inspection of the detailed pattern helps to clarify the form of the relationship.

Age and Total Leisure Participation

Our data show *the older the respondent, the lower the level of general leisure activity*. The

correlation of age and leisure participation is negative and quite substantial ($r = -.49$).

Figure 4 presents the percentage of persons showing high leisure participation within each of the five age groups, with "high participation" defined as scoring above the common median for the entire sample. The negative relationship between life cycle stage and leisure participation is dramatic: respondents in the youngest group (20-29) are almost four times as likely to report high levels of leisure participation (80+ percent) than are those in the oldest group (75 years and over, approximately 24 percent). Both males and females show similar strong negative associations between life-stage and leisure participation.

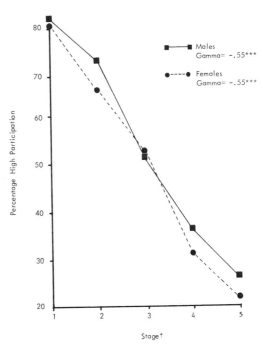

Figure 4. Percentage reporting high leisure participation, by stage and sex. Group size varies from 24 to 118.

Legend (in this and all following graphs):

$*p < .05$
$**p < .01$
$***p < .001$

†Stage 1: Age 20–29, young adult
 Stage 2: Age 30–44, early maturity
 Stage 3: Age 45–64, full maturity
 Stage 4: Age 65–74, old age
 Stage 5: Age 75–94, very old age

Age and Participation in Particular Leisure Categories

The relationship of life-stage, leisure category, and percentage of males and females reporting a high frequency of participation in each of the 17 leisure categories has been examined. Frequency of participation among the older compared to the younger age groups follows three patterns: lower, higher, or essentially the same.

Lower frequency of participation with increasing age was the pattern in eight categories: going out dancing and drinking, attending movies, participating in sports or physical exercise, using guns for hunting or target shooting (for men only), outdoor activities, traveling, reading, and cultural production (Figure 5). For the most part, these activities are done outside the home and involve a substantial degree of excitement, escape, physical exertion, and at least a moderately high intensity of involvement.

Equal frequency across the life span groups was the pattern for seven leisure categories: television viewing, discussion, spectator sports,

cultural consumption, entertaining, participating in clubs and organizations, and home embellishment (Figure 6). In contrast to the activities that are negatively correlated with age, these activities are likely to be engaged in by persons at home and within the context of family and friends; they are also more sedentary and have lower levels of involvement intensity. That older age groups have a lower frequency of external, high-intensity activities and that age does not appear to influence participation in homebound, moderate-intensity activities as suggested by these cross-sectional data lend support to the idea that the general notion of disengagement theory (Cumming and Henry, 1961) is in need of qualitative refinements. Our data suggest that what may be given up in the later years are the strenuous and outside-the-home activities, not the moderate-intensity and home-centered forms of sociability and media-based symbolic interaction. Thus, there may be disengagement from only some forms of interaction, not from interaction per se.

Higher frequency of participation among

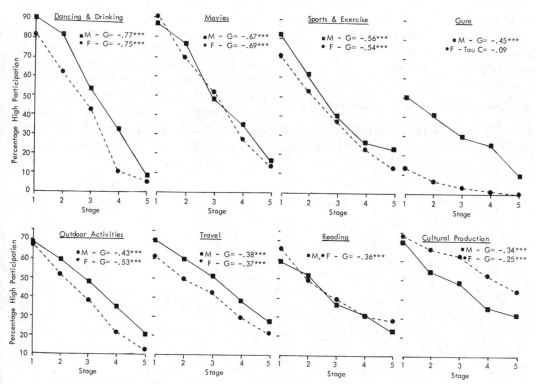

Figure 5. Patterns with lower frequency among older people, by stage and sex.

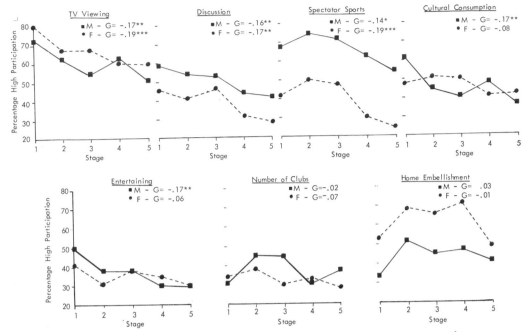

Figure 6. Patterns with similar frequency among older people, by stage and sex.

older persons was reported in two leisure categories: relaxation/solitude and, for men only, cooking (Figure 7). These differences probably relate to the reduced number of culturally provided roles, the fewer social opportunities available to older people, and decrements in monetary and physical resources.

Sex Role and Participation in Leisure Activity

The data reaffirm the importance of sex role patterning of leisure activity. While such sex role differences are expected, perhaps, for an activity such as cooking, differences are also noted for other categories. At almost every point in the life cycle, the curve of frequency participation is higher for men than women for dancing and drinking, sports or exercise, using guns, outdoor activities, travel, discussion of important issues, spectator sports, and membership in clubs and organizations. All of these are high-intensity, external forms that are well institutionalized American male roles. Three categories—attending movies, reading, and en-

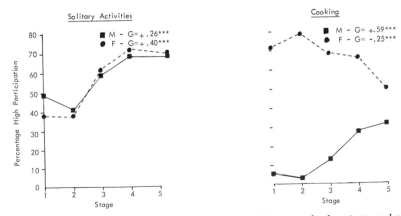

Figure 7. Patterns with higher frequency among older people, by stage and sex.

tertaining friends—show no differences between men and women in all age groups. In cultural consumption, however, males are higher in two stages (young adulthood and old age), and females are higher in early maturity, full maturity, and very old age. All of the other leisure forms show men, regardless of age, participating less frequently in activities than do women: cultural production, television viewing, relaxation and solitude, and especially cooking and home embellishment. The obvious internal/external and high/low intensity leisure-role differential between the sexes has been suggested (Komarovsky, 1964, especially Ch. 14) as part of total male-female life-style bifurcation, especially apparent among working class and lower-middle class populations such as those we studied.

Stylistic Dimensions of Leisure Activity: Activity, Externality, and Sociability

When the leisure categories are dichotomized into active/passive, external/internal, and social/individual forms, we are able to provide greater qualitative richness regarding the trends previously noted. In the active/passive and external/internal leisure forms, there are very strong negative associations between participation in activity and life cycle stage. The negative associations are stronger for active and external forms than for passive or internal forms. Although participation in all these leisure forms is negatively associated with age, this is not as marked for the passive and internal leisure forms. The negative relationship between participation and life-stage is even more strikingly illustrated in the social/individual dichotomy. The negative associations between social leisure participation and age are high for both men and women; however, there is a lack of association between age grade and the individual leisure forms.

Independent of the age dimension, men scored significantly higher than women on our measures of external and social leisure frequency, while women average higher on internal and individual forms. A particularly interesting finding was that men and women scored essentially the same on our measure of active leisure. Furthermore, and contrary to common expectation, the men scored slightly higher than the

women on our measure of passive leisure. These two findings lend further support to the basic sociological dictum regarding the necessity for studying the meaning of social actions in their context rather than simply asserting that men are more "active" than are women on either a biological or personal basis. Even in terms of very rigid sex-role separation during childhood and adult socialization, there are many active behavior patterns thought to be "appropriate" for females, just as there are many passive forms deemed suitable for men. Our active leisure measure reflects this availability and included frequency of participation in the following activity categories: entertaining friends, outdoor activities, travel, clubs and organizations, cooking, home embellishment, discussion of issues, cultural production, guns, sports or exercise, and going out dancing and drinking. In the same manner, our passive leisure measure includes relaxation and solitude, TV watching, cultural consumption, reading, going to the movies, and watching spectator sports. Although it can be argued that going out to the movies, being an avid sports fan, or being a rabid TV football watcher/shouter are quite active leisure forms (cf. Riesman, 1952, p. 422), we felt that (on the whole and for most respondents) movies and sports spectatorship carried much more quiescent and placid meanings than did the categories on the "active" list. In short, these data show that both men and women can and do engage in both active and passive forms of leisure and do so in about equal frequency (see Cunningham, Montoye, Metzner, and Keller, 1968, 1970).

Intensity Levels of Leisure Activity, Sex, and Life-stage

Figure 8 illustrates the associations between life-stage and leisure activity categorized in terms of the level of expressive involvement intensity of each activity, with separate pattern-designations for men and women. Level I, Relaxation and Solitude, shows the only upward trend by life-stages, while moderately negative patterns are displayed for Level III, Developmental Activity, and Level IV, Creativity. Women show a somewhat higher absolute level

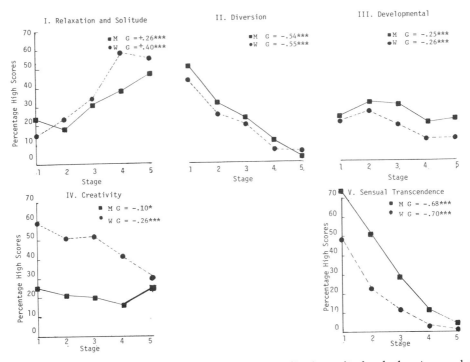

Figure 8. Percentages having high frequency scores on the five intensity levels, by stage and sex.

of Relaxation and Solitude than do the men even in the last two stages, probably reflecting their greater degree of social isolation within the home and within traditional roles (see especially Neugarten, 1970; Havighurst, 1973). Even greater sex differences are found regarding Level IV, Creativity. At every life-stage, women are appreciably more likely to report a high level of creative leisure activities (cooking for family and friends, home embellishment, discussion, and cultural production). In part, this difference is due to the inclusion of "cooking" which is a mixed instrumental-and-expressive item, but the other items classified as "creative," except for "discussion," show essentially the same pattern.

The two remaining categories, Level II, Diversion, and Level V, Sensual Transcendence, show very strong negative associations with life-stage. These most "pleasure-oriented" and "hedonistic" leisure categories in our sample are found to be almost the exclusive province of the relatively young. They also are primarily engaged in by men. Especially in the case of the outright "action" orientations of Level V

(use of guns, participation in sports or exercise, going out dancing and drinking), the workings of the "macho" masculine role definition are very clear.

The sex and life-stage patterns of differential engagement in the five functional categories of leisure (arrayed according to increasing intensity of expressive involvement) are understandable in terms of sociocultural value and role configurations (Gordon, 1971a). It is of course true that participation in the more intense forms may be attended by increased levels of anxiety or perhaps even guilt (Gaitz and Gordon, 1972), and thus the selection of any particular combination of leisure activities is an intensely personal matter of choice. It may be argued that a life focusing primarily on the various forms of security (the left-hand side of the value-theme dilemmas in Figure 2) to the near exclusion of the challenging or adventurous forms (the right-hand side of each value-theme dilemma) will be experienced by the person as flat and dull, without distinct "peak experiences" (Maslow, 1959) or the deep "downs" that may stimulate important personal growth. Theodore Roosevelt, known primarily for his advocacy of "ups," actually expressed quite well a philosophy of alternation and balance between the two valuable directions:

Far better it is to dare mighty things, to win glorious triumphs, even though checked by failure, than to take rank with those poor spirits who neither enjoy much nor suffer much, because they live in the gray twilight that knows neither victory nor defeat.

Leisure Pleasure, Life-stage, and Sex

Recent research indicates that chronological age and associated life-stage role circumstances will be associated with the amount of leisure pleasure obtained (Havighurst 1957, 1961; Neugarten, 1968, especially Part VI; Gordon, 1971a). Our data (Figure 9) reveal a substantial negative relationship between age and derived leisure pleasure. It should be noted that this measure includes self-rated importance and enjoyment as well as simple frequency of participation.

Examination of the evidence of variation across the life cycle reveals four distinct patterns of leisure pleasure scores. The first pattern—a successively reduced amount of pleasure de-

rived from a particular leisure activity in each succeeding age grade—was the pattern for dancing and drinking, movies, sports participation, outdoor activities, travel, and, to a slightly lesser degree, cultural consumption, cultural production, reading, and guns. For the most part, these activities have an active, outside-the-home orientation and are relatively high in intensity of involvement. The data provide empirical support for the assertion made by Robert Havighurst and others that role restriction is very likely to accelerate as the person passes through middle age towards old age and that this is especially evident in those patterns of interaction that relate the individual to persons outside his home and immediate family (Havighurst and Feigenbaum, 1959; Havighurst, Neugarten and Tobin, 1968).

The lower pleasure scores for reading and listening to music, both largely home-bound activities, may be the result of the lower educational level of older respondents. This interpretation for reading and listening to music implies a generational or cohort difference rather than a life-cycle change (see Chapters 6 and 8 in this *Handbook*). Only longitudinal

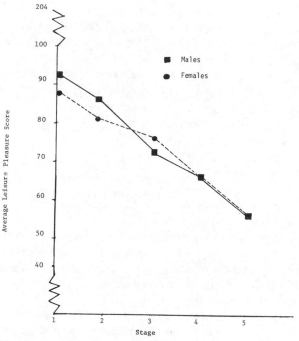

Figure 9. Average leisure pleasure score, by stage and sex.

information on the same individuals as they change over time could isolate the effects of life-cycle stage from those of generational cultural change (Schaie, 1967).

A second pattern of variation of leisure pleasure across the life span occurs when pleasure derived from a particular activity is greatest in the middle age grades. This was the pattern for spectator sports, discussion of important issues, organizations, and home embellishment. This pattern perhaps may be interpreted by drawing on Veblen's concept of conspicuous display through leisure activity (1899). Each of these leisure forms requires large blocks of time, active use of energy, and, frequently, substantial money, and thus serves to display "pecuniary prowess" to relevant audiences.

A third pattern is one in which there is little difference in the amount of leisure pleasure derived from a given activity across the life-stages. These activities—visiting with friends, cooking, and especially watching television— are typically carried out within the context of the home and immediate family and thus provide a leisure theme which is constant across the life span.

We found only one activity from which the amount of derived leisure pleasure showed a consistent positive relationship with increased age. This was "relaxation and solitude"— spending time alone thinking, day dreaming, planning, or in reverie. These data contrast sharply with the finding that active, external, social forms of leisure are less frequently engaged in and enjoyed by older persons. We do not assert that the increase in pleasure derived from solitude is the result of a *willing* disengagement from role-governed interaction (Cumming and Henry, 1961). The involuntary losses of various roles in the advanced years— widowhood, loss of friends through their death and mobility, and involuntary retirement— could produce the same results (Gordon, 1971a, pp. 100–105).

To summarize, active, physically demanding, and external-to-the-home forms of leisure were less frequently engaged in and enjoyed among each successive older age group. Conspicuous forms of leisure were found to reach their peak in the middle years and then decline again with age, while the strictly home-bound and family-centered forms such as cooking and watching television showed a pattern of essentially no variation across the life cycle. The leisure form called "relaxation and solitude" was found to be more frequent in each successive age group in accordance with the hypothesis of life-space restriction in the older years. Beyond any biological decrements in energy and any psychological tendencies toward self-absorption in the later years, the contraction of the social life-space commonly found in gerontological studies is due to normative prescription regulating and prohibiting the more intensely pleasureable leisure forms for older persons.

Sex role is also connected to the amount of leisure pleasure experienced, but the relationship is not a simple one. On the overall measure of leisure pleasure, there was no important difference between the sexes for any age group (Figure 8). Men scored higher on the amount of pleasure derived from outdoor activities, travel, dancing and drinking, discussion, sports and exercise, spectator sports, guns, and organizations. Women, on the other hand, scored higher on the pleasure derived from cultural consumption, cultural production, and cooking. Further, men derived pleasure from a slightly greater range of activities. Together, these findings show the moderate importance of sex role patterning of pleasure derived from various leisure categories but suggest that the qualitative form and breadth of leisure activities may be more related to sex roles than is the absolute amount of pleasure derived from the activity (cf. Havighurst, 1975; Neugarten, 1975).

CONCLUSIONS AND PROPOSED DIRECTIONS FOR FUTURE RESEARCH AND THEORY

Our basic theoretical assumption is that a human action is oriented toward the attainment of one or more socially-defined goals. Instrumental activity (work and its necessary preparations) aims toward goal attainment and its attendant gratifications at a later time, while expressive activity (symbolic and evaluated material interchanges with the environment) involves rewards and gratifications intrinsic to itself, immediately in its doing. Leisure may then be conceptualized, from this action-theory perspective, as discretionary, personal, expressive activity, in which expressive meanings are more important than instrumental themes in the sense that gratification of present needs, wants, desires, or objectives is given precedence over practical preparation for later gratification.

This concept of leisure draws on many philosophers and scientists. We specified the major objectives of leisure activities and placed them on an assumed continuum of expressive involvement intensity. The resulting arrangement of leisure objectives, as we pointed out earlier, is *relaxation, diversion, development, creativity*, and *sensual transcendence*. Positioning of the leisure forms on the expressive intensity continuum does not imply that higher intensity forms are "better," nor do we advocate particular forms. Every form of leisure activity has its costs, risks, and potential rewards.

We used a life-cycle paradigm (Gordon, 1971a, 1971b) as a device for relating the leisure activities typically engaged in by people at a given life-stage to the value themes generally emphasized at that particular life-stage in urban, middle class American settings. At each stage, we delineate two major value themes, and, in many ways, these are contradictory versions of *security* and *challenge*. Though there is no absolute "critical period" in which one particular socialization value must be internalized, there do seem to be certain "optimal" periods for such socialization. The value themes being taught in a particular life-cycle stage seem to be closely connected to both the instrumental (work) concerns of persons at that stage and to the expressive (leisure) activities that are typically selected at that time. In many instances, it is the leisure activities that are most able to perform a "bridging" function, bringing together and integrating major meanings from the security and the challenge themes at any particular stage.

We have also used this life-cycle stage perspective as a framework to order and gain better understanding of the extensive literature on leisure in the various life-cycle stages. In childhood, play and games are the major leisure forms; in adolescence, the themes of acceptance and achievement are woven tightly into the young person's use of mass media and into his or her early sexual experiences. We have then continued through the special "youth" stage in which young members of this society have yet to make clear connections to family and work establishments, and into young adulthood, when these connections become solidified and when self-determination plays such an important role in providing a margin of freedom within formal organizations and institutions.

In early and full maturity, the value themes of stability *vs.* accomplishment structure many of the leisure forms symbolizing "home and family" on the one hand, as contrasted with "living it up." We noted that differentiation into social classes and sex roles, relevant at all stages, is especially important at this age. The major interrelations of work and leisure were discussed, followed by an analysis of leisure after retirement, focusing on issues of social participation, personality styles, family relationships, and sexuality in the years following retirement and in that last period of life, when illnesses bring physical disability. During these later years the value themes become focused on the dilemma of the individual's survival as a continuing psycho-social entity versus the acceptance of death as the ultimate disintegration of the personal system.

Our own study of leisure and mental health served to illustrate the utility of the expressive involvement intensity continuum and its categorizations of leisure according to the major value objective they serve. We were also able to support the position that leisure activities must be viewed in the context of the social identity and the major life circumstances of the respondents. In brief, our findings were that the older the respondent, the lower the level of general leisure activity, the narrower its breadth, the less "intense" the forms, and the less likely a person to engage in the forms of leisure activity that can be characterized as highly active, external to the home, and physically demanding. Other leisure activities, the moderate intensity and home-centered forms of sociability and media-based symbolic interaction, continued into the oldest age group, and there was no evidence that individuals "disengage" from immediate relatives and friends.

We also found that active and external leisure forms are negatively associated with age, much more so than the passive and the internal leisure forms. Social leisure participations also are negatively associated with age, but what we have characterized as individual leisure is not. Reports of relaxation and solitude are positively correlated with age. Development and creativity do not vary with age, but diversion and sensual transcendence are negatively associated with age-position in the life span. The overwhelming majority of our respondents have either traded away the intense levels of potential happiness and even joy obtainable from some of these highly expressive leisure forms for a more sedate existence, or perhaps they had been socialized in a time when highly intense forms of leisure activity were not part of one's social-psychological repertoire.

While it is true that these intense forms of leisure activity may be attended by high levels of anxiety or even guilt (Gaitz and Gordon, 1972), and while it is also true that the challenge side of each value dilemma does tend to produce greater possible problems as well as greater possible gains, it remains for further research to discover whether active engagement in any particular leisure form can dramatically shape the mental health or psychological well-being of participants. Longitudinal research designs should be used to determine whether social-psychological orientations toward the world tend to shape the individual's selected patterns of leisure activity, or whether engagement in leisure activities tends to shape the consciousness and attitudes of the individual. We have no doubt that leisure activities will be found to play important roles in each of these ways; such activities may also prove to be those "bridges" that aid individuals in integrating the value theme dilemmas of each life-stage.

The scientific study of leisure still has many unanswered questions to investigate. In an affluent society, persons have an increasing amount of nonobligated time. As discretionary income increases, the so-called leisure industry expands. This industry was estimated to involve the expenditure of over 105 billion dollars in 1972 (U.S. News and World Report, 1972). This included expenditures for vacation, recreation, travel, sports, equipment, television and stereo systems, books and magazines, spectator sports, etc. Vast sums of money are spent on alcoholic beverages, tobacco, jewelry, and a large proportion of expenditures on clothing and automobiles are devoted to leisure uses. "Gather ye rosebuds while ye may" may well return as an important countervalue pattern, further weakening the work ethic.

Developing the kind of self-actualization that is creative, developmental, and innovative goes beyond the usual socialization of the person. We look upon the study of leisure as a potential contributor to such a development, filling out the content of what it means when we say, as did Freud, that the healthy, mature person must be able "to love and to work." Perhaps we can go beyond Marx's pronouncement that man's material circumstances determine his consciousness. In our leisure studies, we can take heart in a further step allowing us to say that man's leisure activities, in combination with his work and other material circumstances, determine his consciousness, and that his consciousness, in turn, can determine both his work and his leisure.

REFERENCES

Anderson, John E. 1959. The use of time and energy. *In*, J. E. Birren (ed.), *Handbook of Aging and the Individual*, pp. 769–796. Chicago: University of Chicago Press.

Anderson, Nels. 1961. *Work and Leisure.* London: Routledge & Kegan Paul.

Aronowitz, Stanley. 1973. *False Promises: The Shaping of American Working Class Consciousness.* New York: McGraw-Hill.

Atchley, Robert C. 1971. Retirement and leisure participation: Continuity or crisis? *Gerontologist*, 2, 13–17.

Babchuck, N., and Booth, A. 1969. Voluntary association membership: A longitudinal analyses. *Am. Soc. Rev.*, 34, 31–45.

Bateson, Gregory. 1955. A theory of play and fantasy. *Psychiat. Res. Rep.*, 2, 39–51.

Bengtson, V. L., and Lovejoy, M. C. 1973. Values, personality, and social structure: An intergenerational analysis. *American Behavioral Scientist*, 16, 880–912.

Berger, Bennett, M. 1962. The sociology of leisure: Some suggestions. *Industrial Relations*, 1, 31–45.

Berger, Bennett M. 1971. *Looking for America: Essays on Youth, Suburbia, and Other American Obsessions.* Englewood Cliffs, New Jersey: Prentice-Hall.

Berlyne, D. E. 1969. Laughter, humor, and play. *In*, G. Lindzey and E. Aronson (eds.), *Handbook of Social Psychology*, 2nd ed., pp. 795–852. Reading, Massachusetts: Addison-Wesley.

Birren, James E., and Bengtson, Vern L. 1970. The truth about the generation gap. *National Association of Retired Teachers Journal*, pp. 31–32 (May–June).

Bishop, Doyle W. 1970. Stability of the factor structure of leisure behavior: Analyses of four communities. *Journal of Leisure Research*, 2, 160–170.

Bishop, Doyle W., and Ikeda, Masaru. 1970. Status and role factors in the leisure behavior of different occupations. *Social. & Soc. Res.*, 54, 190–208.

Boyack, Virginia, L. (ed.) 1974. *Leisure and Aging Workbook.* Los Angeles: Andrus Gerontology Center, University of Southern California.

Bruner, Jerome S. 1975. Play is serious business. *Psychology Today*, 9, 81–84.

Bühler, Charlotte, and Massarik, Fred (eds.) 1968. *The Course of Human Life.* New York: Springer.

Bull, C. Neil, and Aucoin, Jackie B. 1975. Voluntary association participation and life satisfaction: A replication note. *J. Geront.*, 30, 73–76.

Burch, William R., Jr. 1969. The social circles of leisure: Competing explanations. *Journal of Leisure Research*, 1, 125–147.

Burgess, Ernest W. 1954. Social relations, activities, and personal adjustment. *Am. J. Sociol.*, 59, 352–360.

Burnside, Irene M. (ed.), 1975. *Sexuality and Aging.* Los Angeles: University of California Press.

Campbell, Donald E. 1969. Analysis of leisure time profiles of four age groups of adult males. *The Research Quarterly*, 40, 266–273.

Caplan, Frank, and Caplan, Theresa. 1973. *The Power of Play.* Garden City, New York: Doubleday, Anchor Books.

Carise, Collette B. 1975. Family and leisure: A set of contradictions. *Family Coordinator*, 24, 191–197.

Carter, Reginald. 1971. The myth of increasing non-work versus work activities. *Soc. Prob.*, 18, 52–67.

Cavan, Ruth S. 1962. Self and role in adjustment during old age. *In*, Arnold M. Rose (ed.), *Human Behavior and Social Processes*, pp. 526–536. Boston: Houghton Mifflin.

Christenson, C. V., and Gagnon, J. H. 1965. Sexual behavior in a group of older women. *J. Geront.*, 20, 351–356.

Cicchetti, Charles Joseph. 1972. A review of the empirical analyses that have been based upon the national recreation surveys. *Journal of Leisure Research*, 4, 90–107.

Clarke, A. C. 1956. Leisure and levels of occupational prestige. *Am. Soc. Rev.*, 21, 301–307.

Clemente, Frank, Rexroad, Patricia H., and Hirsch,

Carl. 1975. The participation of the black aged in voluntary association. *J. Geront.*, 30, 469–472.

Coleman, James S. 1961. *The Adolescent Society.* New York: The Free Press.

Comfort, Alex. 1972 *The Joy of Sex.* New York: Crown Publications.

Comfort, Alex. 1974. *More Joy.* New York: Crown Publications.

Cottle, Thomas J. (ed.) 1972. *The Prospect of Youth.* Boston: Little, Brown.

Cowgill, Donald C., and Baulch, Norma. 1962. The use of leisure time by older people. *Gerontologist*, 2, 47–50.

Cumming, Elaine, and Henry, William H. 1961. *Growing Old: The Process of Disengagement.* New York: Basic Books.

Cunningham, Kenneth R., and Johannis, Theodore R., Jr. 1960. Research on the family and leisure: A review and critique of selected studies. *Family Life Coordinator*, 9, 25–32.

Cunningham, David A., Montoye, Henry J., Metzner, Helen L., and Keller, Jacob B. 1968. Active leisure time activities as related to age among males in a total population. *J. Geront.*, 23, 551–556.

Cunningham, David A., Montoye, Henry J., Metzner, Helen L., and Keller, Jacob B. 1970. Active leisure activities as related to occupations. *Journal of Leisure Research*, 2, 104–111.

Cutler, Stephen J. 1973. Voluntary association participation and life satisfaction: A cautionary research note. *J. Geront.*, 28, 96–100.

De Grazia, Sebastian. 1961. The uses of time. *In*, Robert W. Kleemeier (ed.), *Aging and Leisure: A Research Perspective into the Meaningful Use of Time*, pp. 113–153. New York: Oxford University Press.

DeGrazia, Sebastian 1962. *Of Time, Work and Leisure.* New York: The Twentieth Century Fund.

Denny, Reuel, and Meyersohn, Mary Lea. 1957. A preliminary bibliography on leisure *Am. J. Sociol.*, 62, 602–615.

Donald, Marjorie N., and Havighurst, Robert J. 1959. The meanings of leisure. *Soc. Forces*, 37, 355–360.

Douvan, E., and Adelson, J. 1966. *The Adolescent Experience.* New York: John Wiley.

Dragastin, Sigmund E., and Elder, Glen H. (eds.) 1975. *Adolescence in the Life Cycle.* Washington, D.C.: Hemisphere.

Dumazedier, Joffre. 1967. *Toward a Society of Leisure.* Translated by Steward E. McClure. New York: The Free Press.

Edwards, Harry. 1973. *Sociology of Sport.* Homewood, Illinois: Dorsey Press.

Erikson, Erik. 1943. Clinical studies in childhood play. *In*, Roger G. Barker, Jacob S. Kounin, and Herbert F. Wright (eds.), *Child Behavior and Development*, p. 411–428. New York: McGraw-Hill.

Erikson, Erik. H. 1950a. Growth and crises of the healthy personality. *In*, E. H. Erikson (ed.), *Identity and the Life Cycle*, pp. 50–100. (Psychological Issues, Monograph 1: Vol. 1, No. 1.) New York: International Universities Press.

Erikson, Erik H. 1950b. Generativity and ego integrity, *In*, Bernice L. Neugarten (ed.), *Middle Age and Aging*, pp. 85–87. Chicago: University of Chicago Press.

Erikson, Erik H. 1956. The problem of ego identity. *Journal of the American Psychoanalytic Association*, 4, 56–121.

Erikson, Erik H. 1972. Play and actuality. *In*, Maria W. Piers (ed.), *Play and Development*, pp. 127–167. New York: W. W. Norton.

Escalona, Sybille. 1943. Play and substitute satisfaction. *In*, Roger G. Barker (ed.), *Child Behavior and Development*. New York: McGraw-Hill.

Faraday, Ann. 1973. *Dream Power*. New York: Berkley.

Faraday, Ann. 1973. *The Dream Game*. New York: Harper & Row.

Foote, Nelson. 1954. Sex as play. *Soc. Prob.*, 1, 159–163.

Foote, Nelson. 1961. Methods for study of meaning in use of time. *In*, Robert W. Kleemeier (ed.), *Aging and Leisure: A Research Perspective into the Meaningful Use of Time*, pp. 155–176. New York: Oxford University Press.

Fortune Editors. 1955. $30 billion for fun. *In*, Fortune Magazine's *The Changing American Market*, Chapter 10. New York: Time, Inc.

Frenkel-Brunswik, Else. 1963. Adjustments and reorientation in the course of the life span. *In*, Raymond G. Kuhlen and George G. Thompson (eds.), *Psychological Studies of Human Development*, rev. ed., pp. 161–171. New York: Appleton-Century-Crofts.

Freud, Sigmund. 1900. *The Interpretation of Dreams*. Translated by A. A. Brill. New York: Macmillan, 1913.

Freud, Sigmund. 1923. *The Ego and the ID*. Translated by Joan Riviere and V. Woolf. London: Hogarth Press and the Institute of Psychoanalysis, 1927.

Friday, Nancy. 1973. *My Secret Garden: Women's Sexual Fantasies*. New York: Trident Press.

Friedenberg, Edgar Z. 1959. *The Vanishing Adolescent*. New York: Dell.

Friedsam, Hiram J., and Martin, Cora A. 1973. Travel by older people as a use of leisure. *Gerontologist*, 13, 204–207.

Fuller, R. Buckminster. 1973. "Hyper": A concept for an integrated physical education facility. *World*, p. 38 (April 10).

Gaitz, Charles M., and Gordon, Chad. 1972. Leisure and mental health late in the life cycle. *Psychiatric Annals*, 2, 38ff.

Giambra, Leonard M. 1974. Daydreams: The backbone of the mind. *Psychology Today*, pp. 66–68 (December).

Gordon, Chad. 1968a. Self-conceptions: Configurations of content. *In*, Chad Gordon and Kenneth J. Gergen, (eds.), *The Self In Social Interaction*, Vol. I, pp. 115–136. New York: John Wiley.

Gordon, Chad. 1968b. Systemic senses of self. *Sociological Inquiry*, 38, 168–178.

Gordon, Chad. 1969. Self-conceptions methodologies. *J. Nervous Mental Disease*, 148, 328–364.

Gordon, Chad. 1971a. Role and value development across the life cycle. *In*, John W. Jackson (ed.), *Role: Sociological Studies IV* pp. 65–105. London: Cambridge University Press.

Gordon, Chad. 1971b. Social characteristics of early adolescence. *Daedalus*, 100, 931–960.

Gordon, Chad (ed.). 1976. *Human Sexuality: Contemporary Perspectives*. New York: Harper & Row.

Gordon, Chad, Gaitz, Charles M., and Scott, Judith. 1973. Value priorities and leisure activities among middleaged and older anglos. *Diseases of the Nervous System*, 34, 13–26.

Gordon, Chad, Gaitz, Charles M., and Scott, Judith. 1976. Self-evaluation of competence and worth in adulthood. *In*, *American Handbook of Psychiatry*. New York: Basic Books.

Graham, Saxon. 1959. Social correlates of adult leisure-time behavior. *In*, Marvin B. Sussman (ed.), *Community Structure and Analysis*, pp. 331–354. New York: Thomas Y. Crowell.

Gross, Edward. 1961. A functional approach to leisure analysis. *Soc. Prob.*, 9, 2–8.

Gunther, B. G., and Moore, Harve A. 1975. Youth, leisure and post-industrial society: Implications for the family. *Family Coordinator*, 24, 199–207.

Guttmann, D. 1973. Leisure-time activity interests of Jewish aged. *Gerontologist*, 13, 219–223.

Haggedorn, Robert, and Labovitz, Sanford. 1968. Participation in community associations by occupation: A test of three theories. *Am. Soc. Rev.*, 33, 272–283.

Havighurst, Robert. 1953. Flexibility and the social roles of the retired. *Am. J. Sociol.*, 59, 309–311.

Havighurst, R. J. 1957. The leisure activities of the middle-aged. *Am. J. Sociol.*, 63, 152–162.

Havighurst, R. J. 1960. Life beyond family, and work. *In*, Ernest W. Burgess (ed.), *Aging in Western Societies*, pp. 299–353. Chicago: University of Chicago Press.

Havighurst, R. J. 1961. The nature and values of meaningful free-time activity. *In*, Robert W. Kleemeier (ed.), *Aging and Leisure: A Research Perspective into the Meaningful Use of Time*, pp. 309–344. New York: Oxford University Press.

Havighurst, R. J. 1972. Life style and leisure patterns: Their evolution through the life cycle. *International Course in Social Gerontology*, 3, Proceedings, 35–48.

Havighurst, R. J. 1973. Social roles, work, leisure, and education. *In*, C. Eisdorfor and M. P. Lawton (eds.),

The Psychology of Adult Development and Aging, pp. 598–618. Washington, D.C.: American Psychological Association.

Havighurst, Robert J. 1975. The future aged: The use of time and money. *Gerontologist*, **15**, 10–15.

Havighurst, Robert J., and Albrecht, Ruth, 1953. *Older People*. New York: Longmans, Green.

Havighurst, R. J., and Feigenbaum, Kenneth. 1959. Leisure and life-style. *Am. J. Sociol.*, **64**, 396–404.

Havighurst, R. J., Neugarten, Bernice L, and Tobin, Sheldon S. 1968. Disengagement and patterns of aging. *In*, Bernice L. Neugarten (ed.), *Middle Age and Aging*, pp. 161–172. Chicago: University of Chicago Press.

Hendricks, Joe, and Burdge, Rabel James. 1972. The nature of leisure research: A reflection and comment. *Journal of Leisure Research*, **4**, 215–219.

Hoar, J. 1961. A study of free-time activities of aged persons. *Sociol. and Soc. Res.*, **45**, 157–163.

Hollingshead, August B. 1949, 1975. *Elm Town's Youth and Elm Town Revisited*. New York: John Wiley.

Huizinga, Johan. 1949. *Homo Ludens: The play element in culture*. London: Routledge & Kegan Paul.

Hunt, Morton. 1974. *Sex in the Seventies*. Chicago: Playboy Foundation Press.

Hyman, H., and Wright, C. 1971. Trends in voluntary association memberships of American adults: Replication based on secondary analysis of national sample surveys. *Am. Soc. Rev.*, **36**, 191–206.

Inkeles, Gordon, and Todris, Murray, with photographs by Robert Foothorap. 1972. *The Art of Sensual Massage*. San Francisco: Straight Arrow Books.

Jackson, Royal G. 1973. A preliminary bicultural study of value orientations and leisure attitudes. *Journal of Leisure Research*, **5**, 10–22.

Jones, Kenneth L., Shainberg, Louis W., and Byer, Curtis O. 1975. *Human Sexuality*. 2nd ed. San Francisco: Canfield Press.

Jordan, Millard L. 1956. Leisure time activities of sociologists, attorneys, physicians, and people at large from greater Cleveland. *Sociol. and Soc. Res.*, **40**, 290–297.

Kagan, Jerome, and Coles, Robert (eds.) 1972. *Twelve to Sixteen: Early Adolescence*. New York: W. W. Norton.

Kaplan, Helen S. 1974. *The New Sex Therapy: Active Treatment of Sexual Dysfunctions*. New York: Brunner-Mazel.

Kaplan, Max. 1958. Pressures of leisure on the older individual. *J. Geront.*, **13**, 36–41.

Kaplan, Max. 1960a. *Leisure in America: A Social Inquiry*. New York: John Wiley.

Kaplan, Max. 1960b. The uses of leisure. *In*, Clark Tibbitts, *Handbook of Social Gerontology*, pp. 407–443. Chicago: University of Chicago Press.

Kaplan, Max. 1961. Toward a theory of leisure for social gerontology. *In*, Robert W. Kleemeier (ed.), *Aging and Leisure*, pp. 389–412. New York: Oxford University Press.

Kastenbaum, Robert, and Aisenberg, Ruth. 1972. *The Psychology of Death*. New York: Springer.

Katchadourian, Herant A., and Lunde, Donald T. 1972. *Fundamentals of Human Sexuality*. New York: Holt, Rhinehart & Winston.

Kelly, John R. 1974. Socialization toward leisure: A developmental approach. *Journal of Leisure Research*, **6**, 181–193.

Kelly, John R. 1975. Life styles and leisure choices. *Family Coordinator*, **24**, 185–190.

Keniston, Kenneth, 1970. Youth: A "new" stage of life *American Scholar*, pp. 631–654 (Autumn).

Kinsey, A. C., Pomeroy, W. B., and Martin, C. R. 1948. *Sexual Behavior In the Human Male*. Philadelphia: W. B. Saunders.

Klapper, J. T. 1960. *The Effects of Mass Communication*. Glencoe, Illinois: The Free Press.

Kleemeier, Robert W. 1961a. *Aging and Leisure: A Research Perspective into the Meaningful Use of Time*. New York: Oxford University Press.

Kleemeier, Robert W. 1961b. Time, activity, and leisure. *In*, Robert W. Kleemeier (ed.), *Aging and Leisure*, pp. 3–14. New York: Oxford University Press.

Kline, Gerald F., and Clarke, Peter (eds.) 1971. *Mass Communications and Youth: Some Current Perspectives*. Beverly Hills, California: Sage Publications.

Knopp, Timothy B. 1972. Environmental determinants of recreation behavior. *Journal of Leisure Research*, **4**, 129–138.

Komarovsky, Mirra. 1964. *Blue Collar Marriage*. New York: Random House.

Kramer, Cheris. 1974. Folk-linguistics: Wishy-washy mommy talk. *Psychology Today*, **8**, 82–85.

Kraus, Richard G. 1971. *Recreation and Leisure in Modern Society*. New York: Appleton-Century-Crofts.

Kreps, Juanita M. 1968. The allocation of leisure to retirement. *In*, F. M. Carp (ed.), *The Retirement Process*, Chap. 13, pp. 137–144. Washington, D.C.: Public Health Service, U.S. Dept. Health, Education, and Welfare, No. 1778.

Kreps, Juanita M. 1972. Lifetime tradeoffs between work and play. *In*, G. M. Shatto (ed.), *Employment of the Middle-Aged*, Chap. 4, pp. 31–41. Springfield, Illinois: Charles C. Thomas.

Kuhlen, Raymond G., and Thompson, George G. (eds.). 1963. *Psychological Studies of Human Development*, rev. ed. New York: Appleton-Century-Crofts.

Kutner, B., Fanshel, D. Togo, A. M., and Langner, T. S. 1956. *Five Hundred Over Sixty*. New York: Russell Sage Foundation.

Kuypers, Joseph A. 1972. Changeability of life-style

and personality in old age. *Gerontologist*, **12**, 336–342.

Langman, Lauren. 1971. Dionysus–child of tomorrow: Notes on postindustrial youth. *Youth and Society*, **3**, 80–99.

Larrabee, Eric, and Meyersohn, Rolf (eds.) 1958. *Mass Leisure*. Glencoe, Illinois: The Free Press.

Larsen, Otto N. 1964. Social effects of mass communications. *In*, R. E. L. Faris (ed.), *Handbook of Modern Sociology*, pp. 348–381. Chicago: Rand McNally.

Lewis, Stephen. 1973. *Massage: The Loving Touch*. New York: Pinnacle Books.

Lidz, Theodore. 1968. *The Person: His Development through the Life Cycle*. New York: Basic Books.

Linden, M. E., and Courtney, D. 1953. The human life cycle and its interruptions. *Am. J. Psychiat.*, **109**, 906–915.

Lundberg, George A., Komarovsky, Mirra, and McInerny, Mary A. 1934. *Leisure, A Suburban Study*. New York: Columbia University Press.

McCary, James L. 1973. *Human Sexuality: Physiological, Psychological and Sociological Factors*. 2nd ed. New York: D. Van Nostrand.

MacDonald, Margherita, McGuire, Carson, and Havighurst, Robert J. 1949. Leisure activities and the socio-economic status of children. *Am. J. Sociol.*, **54**, 505–519.

Maddox, George, L. 1968. Persistence of life style among the elderly: A longitudinal study of patterns of social activity in relation to life satisfaction. *In*, Bernice Neugarten (ed.), *Middle Age and Aging*, pp. 181–183. Chicago: University of Chicago Press.

Maddox, George L. 1970. Adaptation to retirement. *Gerontologist*, **10**, 14–18.

Margolis, Jack S., and Clorfene, Richard. 1969. *A Child's Garden of Grass*. New York: Pocket Books.

Maslow, Abraham H. 1959. Cognition of being in the peak-experiences. *Journal of Genetic Psychology*, **94**, 43–66.

Masters, William H., and Johnson, Virginia E. 1966. *Human Sexual Response*. Boston: Little, Brown.

Masters, William H., and Johnson, Virginia E. 1970. *Human Sexual Inadequacy*. Boston: Little, Brown.

Mead, George H. 1934. *Mind, Self, and Society*. Chicago: University of Chicago Press.

Mead, Margaret. 1957. The pattern of leisure in contemporary American culture. *Annals*, **313**, 11–15.

Mead, Margaret. 1960. Work, leisure, and creativity. *Daedalus*, **89**, 13–23.

Michelson, I. C. 1954. The new leisure class. *Am. J. Sociol.*, **59**, 371–378.

Miller, Stephen J. 1965. The social dilemma of the aging leisure participant. *In*, Arnold M. Rose and Warren A. Peterson (eds.), *Older People and their Social World*, pp. 77–92. Philadelphia: F. A. Davis.

Murphy, Lois Barclay. 1972. Infant's play and cognitive development. *In*, Maria W. Piers (ed.), *Play and Development*, pp. 119–126. New York: W. W. Norton.

Neugarten, Bernice L. (ed.) 1968. *Middle Age and Aging*. Chicago: University of Chicago Press.

Neugarten, Bernice L. 1970. Dynamics of transition of middle age to old age. *Journal of Geriatric Psychiatry*, **1**, 71–87.

Neugarten, Bernice L. 1973. Personality change in late life: A developmental perspective. *In*, C. Eisdorfer and M. P. Lawton (eds.), *The Psychology of Adult Development and Aging*, pp. 311–335. Washington, D.C.: American Psychological Association.

Neugarten, Bernice L. 1975. The future and the young-old. *Gerontologist*, **15**, 4–9.

Noe, Francis P. 1970. A comparative typology of leisure in an industrialized society. *Journal of Leisure Research*, **2**, 30–42.

Noe, Francis P. 1971. Autonomous spheres of leisure activity for the industrial executive and blue collarite. *Journal of Leisure Research*, **3**, 220–249.

Norbeck, Edward. 1963. African rituals of conflict. *American Anthropologist*, **65**, 1254–1279.

Norbeck, Edward. 1969. Human play and its cultural expression. *Humanitas*, **5**, 43–55.

Norbeck, Edward. 1971. Man at play. *Natural History*, *Special Supplement on Play*, *Appendix B*, 48–53.

Norbeck, Edward. 1974a. The anthropological study of human play. *Rice University Studies*, **60**, 1–8.

Norbeck, Edward. 1974b. Anthrolpological views of play. *Amer. Zool.*, **14**, 267–273.

Opie, Peter, and Opie, Iona. 1969. *Children's Games in Street and Playground*. Oxford: Clarendon Press.

Orthner, Dennis K. 1975a. Leisure activity patterns and marital satisfaction over the marital career. *J. Marriage & Fam.*, **37**, 91–102.

Orthner, Dennis K. 1975b. Familia ludens: Reinforcing the leisure component in family life. *Family Coordinator*, **24**, 175–183.

Parsons, Talcott. 1951a. *Toward a General Theory of Action*. Cambridge, Massachusetts: Harvard University Press.

Parsons, Talcott. 1951b. *The Social System*. New York: The Free Press.

Parsons, Talcott. 1955a. The American family: Its relations to personality and to the social structure. *In*, T. Parsons and R. F. Bales, *Family: Socialization and Interaction Process*, pp. 13–33. Glencoe, Illinois: The Free Press.

Parsons, Talcott. 1955b. Family structure and the socialization of the child. *In*, T. Parsons and R. F. Bales, *Family: Socialization and Interaction Process*, pp. 35–131, Glencoe, Illinois: The Free Press.

Parsons, Talcott. 1955c. The organization of personality as a system of action. *In*, T. Parsons and R. F. Bales, *Family: Socialization and Interaction Process*, pp. 133–186. Glencoe, Illinois: The Free Press.

Parsons, Talcott. 1959. An approach to psychological theory in terms of the theory of action. *In*, S. Koch (ed.), *Psychology: The Study of a Science*, Vol. 3, pp. 612–711. New York: McGraw-Hill.

Parten, Mildred, and Newhall, S. M. 1943. *In*, Roger G. Barker (ed.), *Child Behavior and Development*, pp. 509–525. New York: McGraw-Hill.

Pengelley, Eric T. 1974. *Sex and Human Life*. Reading, Massachusetts: Addison-Wesley.

Pfeiffer, Eric, and Davis, Glenn C. 1971. The use of

leisure time in middle life. *Gerontologist*, **11**, 187–195.

Pfeiffer, Eric, and Davis, Glenn C. 1972. Determinants of sexual behavior in middle and old age. *J. Am. Geriat. Soc.*, **20**, 151–158.

Pfeiffer, Eric, Verwoerdt, Adriaan, and Davis, Glen C. 1972. Sexual behavior in middle life. *Am. J. Psychiat.*, **128**, 1262–1267.

Pfeiffer, Eric, Verwoerdt, Adriaan, and Wang, Hsioh-Shan. 1969. Sexual behavior in aged men and women. *Arch. Gen. Psychiat.*, **19**, 756–758.

Piaget, Jean. 1945. *Play, Dreams and Imitation in Childhood.* English translation. New York: W. W. Norton, 1951.

Playboy Editors. 1972. *The Pursuit of Pleasure.* Chicago: Playboy Press.

Rapaport, Rhona, and Rapaport, Robert. 1975. *Leisure and The Family Life Cycle.* London: Routledge & Kegan Paul.

Reissman, Leonard. 1954. Class, leisure and social participation. *Am. Soc. Rev.*, **19**, 76–84.

Rhodes, Richard. 1974. A very expensive high. *Playboy Magazine*, pp. 131ff. (December).

Riesman, David. 1950. *The Lonely Crowd.* Garden City, New York: Doubleday, Anchor Books.

Riesman, David. 1952. Some observations on changes in leisure activities. *The Antioch Review*, **12**, 417–436.

Riesman, David. 1954. *Individualism Reconsidered.* Glencoe, Illinois: The Free Press.

Riesman, David. 1958. Leisure and work in post-industrial society. *In*, Eric Larrabee and Rolf Meyersohn (eds.), *Mass Leisure*, pp. 363–385. Glencoe, Illinois: The Free Press.

Riesman, David (ed.) 1964. *Abundance for What?* Garden City, New York: Doubleday.

Riesman, David, and Bloomberg, Warner, Jr. 1957. Work and leisure: Fusion or polarity? *In*, David Riesman (ed.), 1964, *Abundance for What?*, pp. 147–161. Garden City, New York: Doubleday.

Riesman, David, and Roseborough, Howard. 1955. Careers and consumer behavior. *In*, David Riesman (ed.), 1964, *Abundance for what?* pp. 113–137. Garden City, New York: Doubleday.

Riley, Matilda White, and Foner, Anne. 1968. *Aging and Society*, Vol. I. New York: Russell Sage Foundation.

Roberts, John M., Arth, Malcolm, and Bush, Robert R. 1959. Games in culture. *American Anthropologist*, **61**, 597–605.

Robinson, J. P. 1969a. Television and leisure time: Yesterday, today and (maybe) tomorrow. *Public Opinion Quarterly*, **33**, 210–222.

Robinson, John P. 1969b. Social change as measured by time budgets, *Journal of Leisure Research*, **1**, 75–77.

Rose, Arnold. 1960. The impact of aging in voluntary association. *In*, Clark Tibbitts (ed.), *Handbook of Social Gerontology*, pp. 666–697, Chicago: University of Chicago Press.

Rosenberg, Bernard, and White, David Manning (eds.) 1957. *Mass Culture.* New York: The Free Press.

Rosow, I. 1966. Retirement leisure and social status. *In*, F. C. Jeffers (ed.), *Duke University Council on Aging and Human Development, Proceedings of Developers 1965–1969*, pp. 249–257.

Rosow, Irving. 1967. *Social Integration of the Aged.* New York: The Free Press.

Rubin, Isaac. 1965. *Sexual Life After Sixty.* New York: Basic Books.

Schaie, K. Warner. 1967. Age changes and age differences. *Gerontologist*, 7, 128–132.

Schmitz-Scherzer, R., and Strudel, I. 1971. Age-dependency of leisure-time activities. *Hum. Develop.*, **14**, 47–50.

Schramm, Wilbur (ed.) 1972. *Mass Communications.* 2nd ed. Urbana, Illinois: University of Illinois.

Schutz, William C. 1967. *Joy.* New York: Grove Press.

Sears, Robert R., and Feldman, S. Shirley (eds.) 1964. *The Seven Ages of Man.* Los Altos, California: William Kaufmann, 1973. Originally published as a series of articles in the British magazine, *New Society.*

Seligman, Ben S. 1965. On work, alienation and leisure. *The American Journal of Economics and Sociology*, **24**, 337–360.

Shanas, Ethel. 1961. *Family Relationships of Older People.* New York: Health Information Foundation.

Shanas, Ethel. 1967. Family help patterns and social class in three countries. *In*, Bernice L. Neugarten (ed.), 1968, *Middle Age and Aging*, pp. 296–305. Chicago: University of Chicago Press.

Shanas, Ethel (ed.) 1970. *Aging in Contemporary Society.* Beverly Hills, California: Sage Publications, *Sage Contemporary Social Science Issue*, 6.

Shanas, Ethel, and Streib, Gordon F. (eds.) 1965. *Social Structure and the Family: Generational Relations.* Englewood Cliffs, New Jersey: Prentice-Hall.

Shanas, Ethel, Townsend, Peter, Wedderburn, Dorothy, Friis, Henning, Milhøj, Poul, and Stehouwer, Jan. 1968. *Old People in Three Industrial Societies.* New York: Atherton Press.

Shepard, Jon M. 1974. A status recognition model of work-leisure relationships. *Journal of Leisure Research*, 6, 58–63.

Sherif, Muzafer, and Sherif, Carolyn. 1964. *Reference Groups: Exploration into Conformity and Deviation of Adolescents.* New York: Harper & Row.

Shostak, Arthur B. 1969. *Blue Collar Life.* New York: Random House.

Simmel, Georg. 1910. Sociability. *In*, Kurt H. Wolff (translator and ed.), 1950, *The Sociology of Georg Simmel*, pp. 40–57. Glencoe, Illinois: The Free Press.

Simpson, I. H., Back, K. W., and McKinney, J. C. 1966. Continuity of work and retirement activities, and self-evaluation. *In*, I. H. Simpson and J. C. McKinney (eds.), *Social Aspects of Aging*, pp. 106–119. Durham, North Carolina: Duke University Press.

Slatery, William J. 1975. *The Erotic Imagination: Sexual Fantasies of the Adult Male.* Chicago: Henry Regnery.

Sofranko, Andrew J., and Nolan, Michael F. 1972.

Early life experiences and adult sports participation. *Journal of Leisure Research*, **4**, 6–18.

Somers, Robert H. 1962. A new asymmetric measure of association for ordinal variables. *Am. Soc. Rev.*, **27**, 799–811.

Spencer, Herbert. 1873. *The Principles of Psychology*, Vol. **II**. New York: Appleton and Co.

Spreitzer, Elmer A., and Snyder, Eldon E. 1974. Work orientation, meaning of leisure and mental health. *Journal of Leisure Research*, **6**, 207–219.

Stone, Gregory P. 1955. American sports: Play and dis-play. *In*, Eric Larrabee and Rolf Meyersohn (eds.), 1958, *Mass Leisure*, pp. 253–264. Glencoe, Illinois: The Free Press.

Stone, Gregory P. (ed.) 1972. *Games, Sport and Power*. New Brunswick, New Jersey: E. P. Dutton.

Streib, Gordon F. 1970. Old age and the family. *In*, Ethel Shanas (ed.), *Aging in Contemporary Society*, pp. 25–39. Beverly Hills, California: Sage Publications.

Streib, Gordon F. 1971. New roles and activities for retirement. *In*, George Maddox (ed.), *The Future of Aging and the Aged*, pp. 18–53. Atlanta, Georgia: Southern Newspaper Publishers Association Foundation.

Sutton-Smith, Brian. 1966 Piaget on play: A critique. *Psych. Rev.*, **73**, 104–110.

Sutton-Smith, Brian. 1971. Children at play. *Natural History*, Special Supplement on Play, Appendix B, 54–59.

Sutton-Smith, Brian, and Roberts, J. M. 1964. Rubrics of competitive behavior. *Journal of Genetic Psychology*, **105**, 13–37.

Sutton-Smith, Brian, Roberts, J. M., and Kozelka, Robert M. 1963. Game involvement in adults. *Journal of Social Psychology*, **60**, 15–30.

Sutton-Smith, Brian, and Rosenberg, B. G. 1961. Sixty years of historical change in the game preference of American children. *Journal of American Folklore*, **74**, 17–46.

Sutton-Smith, Brian, Rosenberg, B. G., and Morgan, E. F., Jr. 1963. Development of sex differences in play choices during preadolescence. *Child Development*, **34**, 119–126.

Szalai, Alexander (ed.) 1972. Daily activities of urban and suburban populations in twelve countries. *In*, *The Use of Time*. The Hague: Mouton.

Taietz, Philip, and Larson, Olaf F. 1956. Social participation and old age. *Rural Sociology*, **21**, 229–238.

Thompson, Gayle B. 1973. Work versus leisure roles: An investigation of morale among employed and retired men. *J. Geront.*, **38**, 339–344.

Thompson, Wayne E., and Streib, Gordon F. 1961. Meaningful activitiy in a family context. *In*, Robert J. Kleemeier (ed.), *Aging and Leisure: A Research Perspective into the Meaningful Use of Time*, pp. 177–211. New York: Oxford University Press.

Turan, Kenneth, and Zito, Stephen F. 1974. *Sinema*. New York: Praeger.

Turner, Ralph H. 1956. Role-taking, role-standpoint, and reference group behavior. *Am. J. Sociol.*, **61**, 316–328.

Turner, Ralph H. 1962. Role-taking: Process versus conformity. *In*, Arnold M. Rose (ed.), *Human Behavior and Social Process: An Interactionist Approach*, pp. 20–40. Boston: Appleton-Century-Crofts.

Turner, Victor. 1974. Liminal to liminoid, in play, flow, and ritual: An essay in comparative symbology. *In*, Edward Norbeck (ed.), *The Anthropological Study of Play*. Rice University Studies, **60** (3), 53–92.

U.S. News and World Reports. April 17, 1972. Leisure boom: Biggest ever and still growing. pp. 42–45.

Veblen, Thorstein. 1899. *The Theory of the Leisure Class*. New York: Mentor Books, 1953.

Verwoerdt, Adriaan, Pfeiffer, Eric, and Wang, Hsioh-Shan. 1969. Sexual behavior in senescence. *Geriatrics*, **24**, 137–154.

Videbeck, Richard, and Knox, Alan B. 1965. Alternative participatory response to aging. *In*, Arnold M. Rose and Warren A. Peterson (eds.), *Older People and Their Social World*, pp. 37–48. Philadelphia: F. A. Davis.

Webber, Irving L. 1954. The organized social life of the retired in two Florida communities. *Am. J. Sociol.*, **59**, 340–346.

Weil, Andrew. 1972. *The Natural Mind*. New York: Houghton Mifflin.

Weiss, Robert S., and Riesman, David. 1961. Some issues in the future of leisure. *Soc. Prob.*, **9**, 78–86.

Wennergren, E. Boyd, and Fullerton, Herbert H. 1972. Estimating quality and location values of recreational resources. *Journal of Leisure Research*, **4**, 170–183.

White, R. C. 1955. Social class differences in the use of leisure. *Am. J. Sociol.*, **61**, 145–150.

Whyte, William F. 1943. *Street Corner Society*. Chicago: University of Chicago Press.

Wilensky, Harold L. 1960. Work, careers, and social integration. *International Social Science Journal*, **12**, 543–559.

Wilensky, Harold L. 1961a. Orderly careers and social participation: The impact of work history on social integration in the middle mass. *Am. Soc. Rev.*, **26**, 521–539.

Wilensky, Harold L. 1961b. The uneven distribution of leisure: The impact of economic growth on "free time." *Soc. Prob.*, **9**, 32 56.

Wilensky, Harold L. 1961c. Life cycle, work situation, and participation in formal associations. *In*, Robert W. Kleemeier (ed.), *Aging and Leisure: Research Perspectives on the Meaningful Use of Time*, pp. 214–242. New York: Oxford University Press.

Wilensky, Harold L. 1962a. Labor and leisure: Intellectual traditions. *Industrial Relations*, **1**, 1–12.

Wilensky, Harold. 1962b. *Work and Leisure*. New York: The Free Press.

Winthrop, Henry. 1966. Developmental leisure time activity in the United States in relation to cultural ideals. *Journal of Human Relations*, **14**, 267–286.

Witt, Peter A. 1971. Factor structure of leisure behavior for high school age youth in three communities. *Journal of Leisure Research*, **3**, 213–219.

Witt, Peter A., and Bishop, Doyle W. 1970. Situational antecedents to leisure behavior. *Journal of Leisure Research*, **2**, 64–77.

Wolfenstein, Martha. 1951. The emergence of fun morality. *J. Soc. Issues*, **7**, 3–16.

Zuzanek, Jiri. 1974. Society of leisure or the harried leisure class? Leisure trends in industrial societies. *Journal of Leisure Research*, **6**, 293–304.

14
AGING AND THE LAW

Leonard D Cain
Portland State University

LEGAL AFFIRMATION OF AGE STATUSES

Evolution of Law

The specification of a chronological age or age span for the purpose of status demarcation and differentiation is replete in the statutes, codes, and other legal expressions of a wide variety of government entities and governmentally validated agencies. Eligibility to vote, to receive a pension, to seek public office, to maintain the right to employment, to receive various protections or services or exemptions is typically determined in part by the chronological age of members of a society. References to age-related attributes (minor, elderly, grandparent), without specificity of chronological age, also abound.

Surprisingly, scholars in jurisprudence and in sociology of law have given limited attention to the utilization of age to distinguish among statuses, although ancient laws identified distinctions based on age, especially between the minor and the adult, and recent laws reflect a continually expanding use of age differentials, especially to separate old age from adulthood.

Law is frequently identified as a means of preserving social order through coercion, or threat of coercion. Max Weber (1947) distinguished between *convention* and *law*:

A system of order will be called *convention* so far as its validity is externally guaranteed by the probability that deviation from it

within a given social group will result in a relatively general and practically significant reaction of disapproval. Such an order will be called *law* when conformity with it is upheld by the probability that deviant action will be met by physical or psychic sanctions aimed to compel conformity or to punish disobedience, and applied by a group of men especially empowered to carry out this function (p. 127).

Many components of age-status systems historically have been enforced and maintained apparently more by convention than by law, and this continues today. However, as societies have become more complex and more secular, the effectiveness of convention has not been sufficient to maintain order. Thus, resort to law to clarify age statuses and to protect rights related thereto has emerged. In addition, as rapid changes in society at large have dramatically altered the needs of the elderly, law has been employed to promulgate a new network of statuses for the elderly.

Theories of the origin and purposes of law are complex, a source of continuing controversy. Roscoe Pound (1922) suggested that legal history is

the record of a continually wider recognizing and satisfying of human wants or claims or desires through social control; a more embracing and more effective securing of social interests; a continually more complete and effective elimination of waste and precluding of friction in human enjoyment of the goods of existence—in short, a continually more efficacious social engineering (p. 99).

Montesquieu, in *L'Esprit des Lois*, in the eighteenth century challenged the then generally held notion that the ideal rules of law were constant, both through time and among different societies. Rather than accepting the premise that ideal law is discovered through the contemplation of man's ideal nature, Montesquieu directed scholars in jurisprudence to the local manners and customs of a people in order to determine the roots and the rationale of a particular legal system. This shift of focus from "natural law" to "social context" gave impetus to a new discipline, sociological jurisprudence (Stone, 1966).

Although the impact of Montesquieu was felt through much of Europe in the nineteenth century—note Bismarck's pioneer effort to respond to new needs of older workers by providing economic support (Cain, 1974a)— sociological jurisprudence was not felt in the American legal system until shortly before World War I (Stone, 1966). Resistance to the contextual response to needs continued to come from social and economic ideologies, from common-law resistance to innovative statutes, and from continuing efforts to guard local government prerogatives in the face of centralized welfare plans. The inadequacy of the legal system to meet the social needs of the United States in the early twentieth century gave to early sociological jurisprudence an activist orientation which prompted *ad hoc* remedies to various identified inadequacies in the legal order (Stone, 1966, p. 26).

The burgeoning, both in the United States and in Europe and elsewhere, of such social movements as those concerned with child labor and juvenile courts in the early part of the century, and with gerontology more recently, may be closely tied to the shift in jurisprudence since the time of Montesquieu. Stone (1966) noted that the greatest development in law based openly and fully upon response to social need has been made since World War II. The last three decades have seen "the steady continuance of humanitarian concern with the backward, the handicapped, the underprivileged, and the oppressed."

Stone's admonition about emerging demands upon jurisprudence has relevance for modifications of age statuses:

> ... the sociological jurist of the future will also have to approach his characteristic problems through a vast effort at understanding the wider social context, seeking by the light of available social knowledge the key points of the systems of action from which adjustments can be effectively made (p. 28).

Definitions of Age

Before considering the surfacing of age in law, it is important to recount several applications of the concept age. Undoubtedly *chronological age* is currently most widely accepted and most easily understood. In the industrialized societies vital statistics are relied upon heavily; the birthday has become among the most convenient of classifiers. However, statuses based on other than chronological definitions of age are evident in these societies.

Bell (1972), in reporting on the Normative Aging Study, sponsored by the Veterans Administration in Boston, identified six separate nonchronological *age indicators*: biochemical; auditory; anthropometric; ability; personality; and social. Increased understanding of these several possibly disparate indicators of aging has, according to Bell,

> practical significance in providing guidelines for ... planning in behalf of aged population in such matters as ... health care and economic assistance, to indicate therapeutic intervention, and to design optimal conditions for working and retirement (p. 147).

Clark and Anderson (1967) have distinguished between *functional age* and *formal age*. It is the onset of biological deterioration sufficient to interfere with the performance of adult work tasks, for example, which signals the onset of old age in those societies which accept *functional age* as a status determinant. Old age is associated with "observed changes in physical condition—and its onset corresponds with the individual's need to restrict his activities substantially."

Formal age, in contrast, is pegged "to some external event which is arbitrarily invested with symbolic significance." A foremost external event is "time," which lead Clark and Anderson to classify *chronological age* as a type of *formal age*.

> In most American commercial and industrial enterprises a worker is defined as "old" at the age of sixty-five . . . The Federal Government, through its Social Security Act, has given official sanction to this definition . . . This . . . definition of old age, based on chronology, becomes even more removed from the realities of [functional old age] (p. 8).

Clark and Anderson also illustrated, but did not designate, a third type of age. Let us call it *social age*. They observed, for example, that among the Western Apache "single persons are regarded as 'youths' or 'maidens' regardless of their physiological [that is, functional] or chronological [that is, formal] age—only marriage can confer adult status" (p. 6). A generally age-related status is conferred, not on the basis of personal attributes such as those related to chronological or functional age, but on the basis of a particular association with another person—such as spouse, parent, widow, or worker with seniority over another worker.

Cain (1959) identified status complications for the elderly in those societies which have turned increasingly toward chronological age to determine the status of the elderly:

> [There] is the task of establishing legal bases for determining old age which are consonant with the attributes of the aging [functional age] as well as the resources and values of the society [including social age]. There are complications and unanticipated consequences . . . , however . . . [P]aradoxically, as the legal terminus for adulthood has been established [by chronological age] . . . , studies which confirm vast variations in rate of maturation and in retention of skills . . . in old age have been reported. Thus, as chronological age has increasingly become a determinant for assignment to the old age status, researchers confirm the inadequacy of chronological age as an appropriate method for determining old age (p. 58).

Challenges to the efficacy of chronological age are very much in evidence in American courts and legislatures, as shall be indicated shortly in a review of challenges to mandatory retirement regulations.

Obstacles to the Analysis of Age-Law Relationships

It is impossible to determine when law was first used to delineate among age statuses. In folk and peasant societies, there are difficulties in distinguishing among theological rules, moral guidelines, traditional age status patterns, and what may be called emergent law. Therefore, historical and comparative analyses are vulnerable to the charge that age status differentials may not have involved law at all. Although there are clear indications that age differentials have been validated by law for many centuries, it is only in recent decades that law has been used to provide a distinctive status to the elderly.

Reference in law to a chronological age or age span is typically unambiguous. However, reference to functional age or social age is often more difficult to isolate, to label. Some of our interpretations may be open to challenge.

Law itself is cloaked in a variety of forms. Law may be expressed through a formal constitution or in resolution of constitutional and other legal issues in courts. Law is also manifested in legislative decisions. It furthermore is exhibited in administrative orders and policies. In addition, there is the question of the legal standing of contracts, for example, those which may be made between management and labor to determine rules regarding seniority, compulsory retirement, age quotas, and the like.

Any effort to analyze the impact of legal age on status is faced with the fact that in many societies laws are made at different levels of government. The United States, for example, has three levels, federal, state, and local, which are likely to enact laws regarding age.

Law may be age specific, or it may specify an age span. Law may be prescriptive, proscriptive, or permissive. There will be little opportunity to apply this or related classificatory schemes, since historical and anthropological, and even current, data on law and age seldom have reflected concern over such factors.

An additional significant status determinant needs early consideration, the variable of sex. In a number of societies the use of chronological age, or application of functional age and social age, varies with sex. As evidence will show, a female may be eligible to marry at a younger age than her male counterpart or to become eligible for retirement benefits at a different age from a male. The direct bearing of the sex variable on age status and how this relates to such values as equal protection of the laws remain poorly explored.

Because of the paucity of interest on the part of both those in legal professions and in the social sciences regarding the age-law relationship and its consequences for individuals and societies, this chapter is perforce exploratory. But laws which incorporate age to distinguish among statuses continue to be adopted; courts are increasingly called upon, at least in the United States, to reconsider the soundness and fairness of use of age criteria in restricting or extending rights and duties; administrative agencies continue to turn to age as a means of authorizing access to services of many kinds. Therefore, to make an effort to identify the uses of age in law and to begin an assessment of the ramifications of such usage are vital to gerontology.

THE EMERGENCE OF AGING IN LAW

Although our time frame is primarily contemporary, an examination of historic legal systems can provide examples of humankind's persisting task of confronting age differences of members of society. The survey is not exhaustive. But through a brief review of the Code of Khammurabi, of some ideas of Plato and the Greeks, of uses of age in Rome, of the British Common Law through Blackstone, and of the Code Napoleon, many of the boundaries of current issues already can be identified.

Quickly in evidence is that age, law, and status have been intertwined for a long period. Indications of the use of age to make sharp status distinctions, of the interplay of chronological, functional, and social age, and of age status ambiguity and asynchronization provide opportunity to sharpen contemporary tools of analysis. The review also highlights the recency of efforts to use law to separate old age from adulthood.

The Code of Khammurabi

The oldest surviving legal code, the Code of Khammurabi, was compiled in approximately 2300 B.C. by the king who united several states in the Euphrates Valley to consolidate the Babylonian Empire (Williams, 1907). Although there are no direct references to chronological age in the Code, rudiments of social age distinctions are to be found. Application of age is associated with intergenerational obligations, with responsibilities toward dependents (orphans, widows, the ill), and with relationships between older and younger siblings.

In the Code's Epilogue, King Khammurabi declared:

I am the peace-bringing shepherd whose staff is straight, the good shadow which is spread over my city; to my heart the people of Sumer and Accad I have taken, under my protection have I caused them to live in peace, sheltered them in my wisdom, so that the strong may not oppress the weak, to counsel the orphan and the widow, their head have I raised in Babylon.

The Code dealt at length with kinship matters. Clause 14 proclaimed: "If anyone steals the minor son of a man, he shall be put to death." If a husband wanted to divorce his wife, he was compelled to pay alimony sufficient to bring up the children. Clause 148 is especially humanistic: "If anyone has taken a wife and a sickness has seized her, and if his face is set toward taking another wife, he may take her, but the wife whom the sickness has seized he may not repudiate her; she shall live in the house he has built, and as long as she lives he shall support her."

Protection for the young is provided. Clause 166 declared: "If a man has taken wives for his sons, for his little son a wife has not taken, if afterwards the father has gone to his fate, when the brothers divide the goods of their father's house, to their little brother, who has not taken a wife, besides his portion, money for a dowry they shall give him, and a wife they shall cause him to take."

A series of clauses on the adoption of children reveals a strong desire to provide maximum protection to the adopted child. Clause

88 stated: "If an artisan has taken a child to bring up, and has taught him his handicraft, no one can make a complaint." However, Clause 189 countered: "If he [the artisan] has not taught him [the child] his handicraft, that foster child shall return to the house of his father."

The Code emphasized the protected status to be afforded children. Yet, references to widows, to lifelong protection to an ill wife, and similar issues suggest that King Khammurabi was concerned with more than distinctions between a minor and an adult, that he was concerned with additional life course issues which occupy our attention today.

The Ancient Greeks

Important contributions of the Greeks of Plato's era include the introduction of chronological age criteria in establishing a status system and the designing of that system to promote efficiency in government affairs. However, some of the references to chronological age may have been more Plato's advocacy than Athens' adoption. At least Richardson (1933), in prefatory remarks to her study of the elderly in Greece, highlighted the difficulty in reconstructing an age-status system based often on references to functional age criteria:

> Several difficulties have been encountered, one of the most obvious being the lack of chronological boundaries for the periods of man's existence, and secondly, the difficulty of dealing with an indefinite and abstract term [age] which does not yield to investigation so readily as one of more concrete designation (pp. xiii–xiv).

Richardson provided infrequent glimpses of the legal status, from both chronological and functional perspectives, of the elderly in ancient Greece. Certain criminal acts, including robbing the gods or performing acts of treason, were to be excused if the perpetrator was in a state of madness, or was affected by disease, or was "under the influence of extreme old age." An individual "could bequeath his property to whomever he wished, provided his judgment was not influenced by physical pain, violence, drugs, old age, or the persuasion of a woman." She also reported that a key element in the Athenian system of justice was a body of men, all 60 years of age, who were chosen annually by lot to sit as a review board on issues which came before magistrates.

Richardson also reviewed age status recommendations advanced by Plato for his ideal republic. Responsibility for "the care of orphans was to be entrusted to the fifteen oldest guardians of the law." If children brought charges of maltreatment by their parents, decisions were to be rendered by a group of parents who were more than 60 years of age. Charges by the elderly that their children were providing them insufficient care should be "brought before a court composed of the eldest citizens," who were authorized to inflict serious punishment if errant children "were over thirty (in the case of a man) or forty (in the case of a woman)." If the children were younger than these specified ages, "the penalty should be scourging or imprisonment."

Also, according to Richardson, when a son was faced with the prospect of charging his aging father with insanity, the son was called upon to present his case "before the eldest guardians of the law." Plato also advised that the minister of education should be an old man. But retirement from important governmental positions should take place at age 70. Plato, however, proposed "no pension system, and no philanthropic institutions to care for the aged."

Richardson saw in the Greeks' attitude toward the elderly a "most redeeming feature" in Greek character. She was impressed with legislation which called upon adult children to maintain support for their elderly parents. She noted the absence of any pension plan, or institutions for the care of the aged, "but it is likely that contributions were made by friends for these purposes as the need arose" (p. 58).

To what extent Plato's ideas should be interpreted as reflections of the actual state of affairs in Greek city states, and to what extent they were unrealized recommendations to establish an ideal social order, cannot be dealt with here. But from Plato (1960), especially the *Laws*, written when Plato was in his 70's, we do obtain evidence that legal age is an ancient concept, and that policy needed to implement a status system based on chronological age was fully understood.

To implement his age-status system, Plato found it necessary to maintain an accurate record of births and deaths:

> A man's first year is the opening of his whole life; it should be registered with that title— "beginning of life"—in the shrines of the kindred. There must be also, for each boy and girl in the phratry, a further record on a whitened wall bearing the number of the magistrates after whom dates are reckoned; in the vicinity there must be a record of such members of the phratry as are alive at each date, the names of those who decease being expunged (p. 169).

Since there was no such system of keeping records of vital statistics established in Athens at the time of Plato, it is suggested that Plato may have been the originator of the major precondition for the maintenance of a system of statuses based on chronological age in a complex society, that is, accurate recording of and provision of public access to the day of birth of all citizens.

Maintenance of birth records was recognized as important if there were to be proper observance of such laws as those which prescribed the age for marriage, military service, and qualifications for various official roles. The age span which Plato specified for marriage was between 30 and 35 years for males, 16 and 20 years for females. If there should be a man "who comes to five-and-thirty unwedded, he shall pay a yearly fine." Liability for military service stretched from age 20 to age 60, as was the actual case in Plato's Athens. When women were given military tasks, they should be beyond the child bearing period but under the age of 50. Plato proposed that no man under 30, and no woman under 40, be appointed to any office. Among the most important of the magistracies in Plato's state is the Curators of Law, which was to be composed of 37 members, all of whom must be over age 50 and under age 70 (Book VI; also see pp. xxxvii–xl).

Thus, the early Greeks used chronological age supported by law to differentiate among statuses throughout the life course.

The Roman Application

Roman law contributed at least three innovations in the use of chronological age. Adulthood was partitioned into two distinctive statuses, with age 46 the beginning of senior, but preelderly status. Preadult status was partitioned into a series of developmental stages, each associated with increased responsibleness. The concept of career, including a minimum age requirement for transfer to each successive stage, was well developed.

Hunter (1885) has provided substantial evidence on Roman contributions to legal age status. The Assembly of the Centuries, ascribed to the innovation of King Servius Tullius (sixth century, B.C.), diminished power based on kinship and descent and strengthened power based on a combination of property ownership and age. Five classes, in each of which membership was based on ownership of property, were established. Each class was subdivided into political units called centuries. In each class there were equal numbers of centuries composed exclusively of either *seniores* (male citizens aged 46 to 60) or *juniores* (male citizens aged 17 to 45). Functionally, it was the duty of the younger to serve in the field during military operations, whereas the older served as defenders of the city itself (pp. 8–9).

The most systematic consideration of age in law in Rome is evident in the institution of *tutela*. *Tutela* was "a right and power over a free person, given and allowed by the *jus civile* in order to protect him while by reason of his [young] age he is unable to defend himself." Children under the age of puberty, defined to be 14 for boys, 12 for girls, were in *tutela* (that is, had tutors assigned to them). Essentially the tutor's role was to supervise, and give consent to, such legal acts of the *pupillus* (the prepubertal client) which the law would otherwise not accept as mutually binding.

The age of seven was crucial in determining tutor-pupil relationships. After age seven the child was presumed to have *intellectus* and thus became capable of participating in the procedures of law; however, the law asserted that there was not yet *judicium*, the ability to decide whether there was advantage in assuming a particular obligation. From age seven to puberty the pupil was to receive judicious counsel from the tutor.

The tutor was obligated to terminate his jurisdiction over his pupil when the pupil became 14 and to encourage him to seek the services of a *curator* to manage his property during the remaining 11 years of minority status (until age 25). The postpubertal minor could avoid the services of a curator, except in lawsuits, although Justinian declared that "males above the age of puberty . . . receive curators till they complete their twenty-fifth year [since] they are still of such an age as to be unable to manage safely their own affairs" (Hunter, 1885, pp. 696-708).

As early as 180 B.C. a code, *Lex Villia Annalis*, had spelled out the chronological age at which a citizen could become eligible for each stage of a governmental career. Prerequisite to entering the first stage was to have served in ten annual military campaigns, which began no earlier than age 17. Thus, a young man may be admitted to the lowest ranking magistracy, the Quaestorship, at age 28, followed by eligibility to enter the Praetorship at age 40, and the Consulship at age 43.

Eventually, two types of career sequences were open to citizens; there were the "higher" career routes, either Senatorial or Equestrian, and the "lower" routes, either civil or military. During the later stages of the Empire, the career of officials had become strictly defined, and a system of seniority was strongly upheld (Homo, 1962, pp. 344, 359).

Blackstone's Commentaries on Age

The remarkable feat of Sir William Blackstone (1967) in his compilation and commentary upon British law, produced between 1755 and 1765, preserves for us today some important insights into the development of legal age distinctions. Although his observations essentially are limited to the distinctions between the infant and the adult, they are nonetheless vital to our understanding of current complications in use of chronological age in law.

Several innovations in law-age relationships in British common law were identified by Blackstone. The Roman theme of a developmental process for reaching the age of responsibility has been further developed. Eligibility to own property has become related to age. The expression of age in law has become established as an instrument of social control. The sex variable has achieved a new specificity. Most important of all, there has been granted to jurors the opportunity to evaluate, on a case by case basis, the functional capacity of individuals to exercise responsibility, although chronological age continued to provide parameters.

The greatest age specificity is found in Blackstone's report on "persons capable of crimes" (Blackstone, Book 4). The very young have no discernment. "Where there is no discernment, there is no choice; and where there is no choice, there is no act of will." The first age status, infancy, is labeled by Blackstone "nonage," and it follows that there was no criminal punishment at all for this age category, regardless of behavior.

A problem immediately arises: What is the age in which discretion, and therefore responsibility for one's own acts, arrives?

What the age of discretion is, in various nations, is a matter of some variety. The civil law [in England] distinguished the age of minors, or those under twenty-five years old, into three stages: *infantia*, from the birth till seven years of age; *pueritia*, from seven to fourteen; and *pubertas*, from fourteen upwards. The period of *pueritia*, or childhood, was again subdivided into two equal parts: from seven to ten and a half was *oetas infantoe proxima*; from ten and a half to fourteen was *oetas pubertati proxima* (Book 4, p. 22).

During the first stage of *pueritia*, the child ordinarily was presumed to be incapable of discretion, for purposes of imposing punishment for a criminal act. During the second stage, up to age 14, the child may be punishable for a crime, if the court adjudged him to be "capable of mischief." Beyond age 14, minors were liable to be punished for commission of a crime on the same basis as adults.

But Blackstone noted exceptions to this rule:

The law of England does in some cases privilege an infant, under the age of twenty-one, as to common misdemeanors, so as to escape fine, imprisonment, and the like; and particularly in cases of omission, as not repairing a bridge or a highway, and other similar offences; for, not having the command of his fortune till twenty-one, he wants the capacity to do those things which the law requires (Book 4, p. 22).

Already in Blackstone's day there was evidence of age status ambiguity, or asynchronization, built into law.

A male at twelve years old may take the oath of allegiance; at fourteen is at years of discretion, and therefore may consent or disagree to marriage ... ; at seventeen may be an executor; and at twenty-one is at his own disposal ... A female at seven years of age may be betrothed ... ; at nine is entitled to dower; at twelve is at years of maturity ... at fourteen is at years of legal discretion ... at seventeen may be executrix; and at twenty-one may dispose of herself and her lands (Book I, 463).

Although Blackstone used chronological ages as though they firmly depicted status differentials, he also indicated that functional age was, in practice, often more important in predicting a court's ruling:

By the ancient Saxon law, the age of twelve years was established for the age of possible discretion ... and from thence till the offender was fourteen ... he might or might not be guilty of a crime, according to his natural capacity or incapacity. This [the period from twelve to fourteen] was the dubious stage of discretion. . . . But by the law, as it ... has stood at least ever since the time of Edward the Third, the capacity of doing ill, or contracting guilt, is not so much measured by years and days, as by the strength of the delinquent's understanding and judgment. For one lad of eleven years old may have as much cunning as another of fourteen ... If it appears to the court and jury that an infant under fourteen could discern between good and evil, he may be convicted and suffer death (Book 4, p. 23).

Blackstone indicated that in all cases of those under age fourteen it was vital that the evidence of discretion "be strong and clear beyond all doubt and contradiction."

On another subject, Blackstone identified "want of age" as a legal disability in validation of a marriage contract. Under the civil law, if a boy under 14, or a girl under 12, married, either, upon coming of age, may declare the marriage to be void, without divorce proceedings. There was also a statute which declared that a male who married a female under age 16 without her parents' consent was subject to fine or imprisonment. Another later statute declared that "all marriages celebrated by license where either of the parties is under twenty-one, without the consent of the father (or guardian), shall be absolutely void."

Of importance for our purpose is the fact that Blackstone followed his report of the extension of the age in which the young could marry without parental consent with an analysis of the consequences of such modification in legal age:

Much may be said both for and against this innovation ... On the one hand, it prevents the clandestine marriage of minors, which are often a terrible inconvenience to ... families ... On the other hand, restraints upon marriages, especially among the lower class, are evidently detrimental to the public, by hindering the increase of people; and to religion and morality, by encouraging licentiousness and debauchery among the single of both sexes (Book 1, p. 438).

A search of the four volumes of the *Commentaries* revealed no direct references to an old age status separable by law from an adult status. Two references to old age were discovered, however:

[Our parents], who protected the weakness of our infancy, are entitled to our protection in the infirmity of their age: they, who by sustenance and education have enabled their offspring to prosper, ought in return to be supported by that offspring ... (Book 1, p. 453).

If witnesses to a disputable fact are old and infirm, it is very usual to file a bill to perpetuate the testimony of those witnesses, although no suit is depending ... (Book 3, p. 450).

The tracing of the origin of a distinctive old age status defined and upheld by law has yet to be accomplished by legal historians. Blackstone is of little assistance. However, the legacy preserved by Blackstone reveals that during the eighteenth century a systematic use of age, primarily chronological, had developed in Great Britain.

The French Civil Code

The *Code Napoleon* (1841), decreed and promulgated in 1803 and 1804, in the wake of the French Revolution, is replete with references to chronological age and occasionally to social age. Both Book I, "Of Persons," and Book III, "Of the Different Modes of Acquiring Property," make repeated reference to distinctions between minority and majority status and occasional reference to other age criteria as well.

The Code provided for thorough implementation of Plato's proposal to record births and deaths of all citizens, and for repeated use of such recording as well. Limits on the rights of minors were spelled out in meticulous detail. Differential ages based on sex were adopted, especially in matters related to marriage; a peculiar "seniority" principle restricted divorce after 20 years of marriage. Jural discretion, as in the British common law, was promoted. Age status asynchronization was produced when "majority" for eligibility to marry was made an older age than for achieving majority status otherwise. Very importantly, the Code used middle and older chronological ages to provide for several status differentials, although no clear, systematic distinction between the adult and the elderly is yet in evidence. Also of importance was the utilization of social age in identifying, for example, special statuses for grandparents, great-grandparents, and widows.

A minor is defined as "an individual of either sex who has not yet accomplished the age of twenty-one years" (Article 388). As a reciprocal, "majority is fixed at twenty-one years completed; at this age a person is capable of all acts regarding civil life, save the restriction contained under the title, 'Of Marriage' " (Article 488).

Under the "Of Marriage" title are the following variations from the above definitions:

A man before the age of 18, and a woman before 15 complete, are incapable of contracting marriage (Article 144).

However:

The government shall be at liberty, nevertheless, upon weighty reasons, to grant dispensations of age (Article 145).

There follow other qualifications, including occasions in which variations by sex appear in the Code:

The son who has not attained the full age of 25 years, the daughter who has not attained the full age of 21 years, cannot contract marriage without the consent of their father and mother; in case of disagreement, the consent of the father is sufficient (Article 148). If the father and mother are dead, or . . . under an incapacity . . ., the grandfathers and grandmothers shall supply their place; . . . (Article 150). Where the children of a family have attained the majority fixed by Article 148 [25 years for sons, 21 years for daughters], they are required, previously to contracting marriage, to demand, by a respectful and formal act, the advice of their father and mother . . . (Article 151). From the majority [25 years and 21 years] to the age of 30 years completed for sons, and until the age of 25 years completed for daughters, the respectful act required by the preceding article [to demand, by formal act, parental advice] and on which consent to marriage shall not have been obtained, shall be renewed [monthly]; and one month after the third act it shall be lawful to pass on to the celebration of the marriage (Article 152).

After the age of thirty years, it shall be lawful, in default of consent, upon a respectful act, to pass on, after the expiration of a month, to the celebration of the marriage (Article 153).

The significance of chronological age is accentuated by the pronouncement that civil officials who officiate at marriage ceremonies for those who are under the prescribed ages and who have not previously received consent of the designated relatives are subject to fines and six months imprisonment (Article 156). Provision was made for the civil officer to have "transmitted to him the act of birth of each party about to be married" (Article 70).

A complicated set of age, and tenure, factors was included in provisions for "Divorce by Mutual Consent" (Book I, Chapter III). If the husband is under 25 and the wife under 21 years of age, mutual consent in divorce proceedings is not admissible (Article 275). Mutual consent is not acceptable until the marriage has lasted at least 2 years (Article 276), nor is it acceptable after 20 years of marriage or after the wife has become 45 years old (Article 277).

Thus, it was imperative that the chronological age of each citizen was recorded and fully available. Indeed, the Code provided for such recording:

> Declarations of birth shall be made, within three days after delivery, to the civil officer of the place: the child shall be shown to him (Article 55). The act of birth shall be immediately reduced to writing, in the presence of two witnesses (Article 56).

There were also special provisions for the registration of abandoned new-born infants, and for infants born at sea (Articles 57, 58).

The chronological age at death was also considered necessary to record:

> The act of death shall contain the Christian names, surname, age, profession, and domicil of the deceased person; . . . [and] the Christian names, surnames, age, profession, and residence of the deponents; . . . (Article 79).

Rules related to adoption incorporated age in distinctive ways.

> Adoption is not permitted to persons of either sex, except to those above the age of fifty years, and who . . . shall have neither children nor legitimate descendants, and who shall be at least fifteen years older than the individuals they propose to adopt (Article 343).

In addition, to become eligible to adopt, one must have provided assistance and uninterrupted care to the proposed adopted person during at least six years before the adopted one became 21 (Article 345). However, if a person's life has been saved during a fight, or from fire or water, he may seek to adopt the rescuer, even if rules must be waived.

> It shall suffice . . . that the adopter have attained majority, be older than the adopted, without children, or lawful descendants, and if married, that his conjunct consent to the adoption (Article 345).

Closely linked to the adoption process was the role of "friendly guardianship" (Book I, Chapter II). To become a guardian one must be at least 50 years of age, without legitimate descendants, and willing to assume legal responsibility for a minor assigned to him (Article 361). The ward of the guardian must be at least 15 years of age when assignment is made (Article 364).

If both parents of a minor child die without prior agreement of guardianship for the child, rights of guardianship accrue to kinship generations in ascending order.

> [If parents of a minor child die] the guardianship belongs of right to his paternal grandfather; and in default of such to his maternal grandfather . . . (Article 402).
>
> Where, in default of the paternal grandfather, and likewise of the maternal grandfather . . ., an equal claim shall appear to be established between two [great-grandparents], who shall both belong to the paternal line of the minor, the guardianship shall pass [to the] paternal grandfather of the father of the minor (Article 403).

If by default the great-grandfathers in competition are in the maternal line, the family council chooses between the two (Article 404).

It is important to note that the factor of gender takes precedence over the factor of age of grandparents in the above elaborate procedure to determine guardianship. However, the family council, an agency of last resort, apparently operated on the opposite principle:

> The family council shall be composed . . . of six relations, . . . half on the father's side, and half on the mother's side, and according to the order of [kinship] proximity in each line. . . . amongst relations of the same degree, the elder to the younger [shall be preferred] (Article 407).

One of the three references to old age, apart from the social ages of grandparents and great-grandparents, refers to the right to refuse a guardianship role:

> Every individual who has completed his sixty-fifth year may refuse to become a guardian. He who previously to this age shall have been nominated such, may, at seventy years, cause himself to be discharged from the guardianship (Article 433).

A second reference to old age deals, strangely, with group death in which it is impossible to ascertain the order of death:

> If several persons, respectively called to the succession of each other, perish by one and

the same accident, so that it is impossible to ascertain which of them died first, the presumption of survivorship is determined . . . by force of age and sex (Article 720).

If those who perished together were under fifteen years, the eldest shall be presumed to have survived.

If they were all above sixty, the youngest shall be presumed to have survived.

If some were under fifteen years, and others more than sixty, the former shall be presumed to have survived (Article 721).

If those who perished together were of the age of fifteen years complete, but less than sixty, the male is always presumed to have survived, where there is equality of age, or if the difference which exists does not exceed one year.

If they were of the same sex, the presumption of survivorship which gives rise to succession according to the order of nature must be admitted: thus the younger is presumed to have survived the elder (Article 722).

The third reference to old age provided immunity from arrest for *stellionate*, which is where an individual sells or mortgages an immovable property which is knowingly not owned by the individual, or where the individual understates the mortgage on property he is selling (Article 2059). The immunity is granted both to minors (Article 2064) and to "persons of seventy years of age . . . It is sufficient that the seventieth year have begun in order to enjoy the indulgence granted to persons of seventy years" (Article 2066).

The Code awarded considerable power to parents, especially the father. "A child, at every age, owes honor and respect to his father and mother" (Article 371). The child remains subject to parental control until age 21, or until emancipation (Article 372). A child cannot leave home without the permission of his father before age 21, except for voluntary military enlistment after age 18 (Article 374). A father who is grievously dissatisfied with the behavior of his child under 16 years of age may have the child confined for a period not to exceed one month (Article 376). After the child is 16 but not yet 21, the father may seek the child's confinement not to exceed six months, although the court may overrule the father entirely or reduce the period of confinement (Article 377).

Finally, the complexity of the age-law relationship is illustrated in the Code's procedures for the "emancipation" of minors. First, the minor is emancipated (that is, more or less becomes an adult) by marriage (Article 476). Likewise, by simple declaration of the father, routed to the justice of the peace, a minor at the age of 15 may be emancipated (Article 477). If the minor is an orphan, he may be emancipated by his family council after he has reached the age of 18 (Article 478).

An emancipated minor may make leases of short duration (Article 481); he may not borrow without a resolution from his family council (Article 483); but "the minor emancipated, who enters into trade, is reputed an adult for the acts relative to such trading" (Article 487).

With the *Code Napoleon*, age—chronological, social, and, to a degree, functional—has become a vital component of law. Unfortunately, there is not opportunity here to explore either the rationale for the particular designations of age or the consequences upon actual application of the designated ages in French life.

LAW AND AGE STATUS: AN OVERVIEW OF THE LIFE COURSE

The brief review of selected historical codes reveals rather convincingly that a major concern of societies is to distinguish between the pre-adult and the adult. Efforts to distinguish between the adult and the elderly appear to be a phenomenon of the nineteenth and, mainly, of the twentieth centuries. To a considerable extent, legal age issues have become bimodal, that is, age based laws focus upon either the withholding of adult status from the minor or the withdrawal of adult status from the elderly. The rise of gerontology has, of course, accompanied the emergence of the latter task. It needs to be stressed, however, that legal age issues are evident throughout the life course, and that decisions regarding modification of status due to aging are likely to have relevance for understanding the emerging status of the elderly.

The Importance of Determination of Chronological Age

In the presentation thus far there has been the presumption of the close link among age, law, and status. By altering rights and obligations of individuals as changes in chronological age occur, laws provide means of maintaining an age-status system through time. Crucial to the operation of such a system is accurate representation of the ages of individuals. And this can sometimes become complicated.

Shaki (1969) has reported that the Israel Supreme Court (among other courts) has accepted age as a factor in status determination since age conveys a source of rights and duties under the law. He also indicated that the determination of an individual's chronological age may have consequences for the rights and duties of others, including public officials (as, for example, the *Code Napoleon* gave evidence). Likewise, the broader public interest is related to the determination of an individual's age because of the large number of public enactments which depend on knowledge of persons' ages for their implementation.

Many individuals in Israel have needed confirmation of their own chronological age by the courts, since, for one reason or another, documentary evidence of date of birth has been lost or is probably in error. It is with this particular issue that Shaki supplies strong evidence of the importance of legal age in complex, industrialized societies and obliquely points to complications ahead for those nations now undergoing rapid industrialization and whose records of age of its citizens may not be accurate.

In a nation such as Israel, populated by people many of whom have endured the ravages of war and dislocation, and who are to a great extent immigrants, and who furthermore may have had persuasive reasons for manufacturing one or more birth dates for themselves, determination of age from sources other than birth certificates or local registration of birth is important. Israel in 1963 passed the Determination of Age Law, which assigned to the Magistrates' Courts the task of determining the age of individuals when difficulties arose. Previously, when District Courts were assigned this task, the Israel Supreme Court underscored the importance of age in law:

For many years now it has been the practice of the District Courts in [Israel] to give declaratory judgments as to a person's age. We see no justification to annul this practice . . . whereby the rights of hundreds of persons have been determined (Dorfman v. A. G., 1950, quoted by Shaki).

Curiously, in an article so informative about the use of age in law, Shaki advanced the position that age is not a factor in status. He argues that a person's age cannot be arbitrarily determined; rather, a court's duty is to declare a person to be a certain age and to rest the case. He insists that age is not a legal institution, because age has a "temporary and transient nature."

Each . . . age group has its own set of rights and duties, appropriate in the view of the legislator for that particular age group, and these will undergo a continual process of change . . . There is thus lacking a continuous and clear identity of the content of age in point of law, since age itself lacks and always will lack continuous identity (p. 385).

It is not necessary to rebut Shaki's arguments that age is not a matter of status. Rather, let it simply be pointed out that the evidence presented by Shaki himself indicates that courts and legislatures have been involved in using age (not of an individual at a random period of time, but as a classificatory device) as a means of determining eligibility, of imposing demands and restrictions and extending privileges on individuals. Shaki himself, after observing that the concepts "minority" and "majority" have attributes similar to that of age, concludes that these two categories should "be regarded as matters of status." Insofar as statutes, executive orders, constitutions, court decisions, contracts, and similar legal documents identify age criteria—chronological, functional, or social—as a determinant in distinguishing rights or obligations of one age category from another, it may be concluded that an age-status system defined by law is in evidence.

Law and the Termini of Life

Plato proposed, and the *Code Napoleon* fully utilized, the recording of births as a prelude to status assignment. In recent years, however, legal age, both chronological and functional, has become operative before birth (Anonymous, 1970). "When does life begin?" remains one of the unresolved issues both in law and morals. Those who oppose birth control measures typically associate life with the human right to be conceived. Those who support abortion do not attribute life to the fertilized ovum, or to the embryo, but rather, in one way or another, to a fetus. Another logic has life beginning at birth. Many societies have not attributed human life to the infant until some form of initiation has taken place.

Recent court decisions have leaned toward the principle that human life begins when the fetus has reached the stage of viability, that is, when a premature separation of the fetus from the mother's womb would not in itself terminate life. There is a prospective conflict in law between the right of life to be given to the fetus and the right of a prospective mother to undergo an abortion without being charged with murder.

California courts have ruled that the decision which decides that the slaying of a viable fetus is a homicide is not in conflict with the state's abortion laws, "since abortions are not sanctioned after the twentieth week of pregnancy and a fetus reaches the stage of viability only after a minimum of 26-27 weeks." Thus, in seeking to reconcile the right of the pregnant woman not to give birth and the right of the fetus to continue its development toward eventual birth, society has turned to a combination of functional and chronological age, geared to the time of conception rather than the time of birth, to formulate law.

That current solutions are tentative and stand in need of reappraisal has been recognized in that "the determination [of the viability of the fetus] may become more difficult as the use of incubators and artificial wombs increases." Soon the problem of reintegrating medical knowledge and judicial decision will recur (Anonymous, 1970, pp. 857, 858).

Similarly, law has been used to distinguish between a fetus and a stillborn, premature infant, for example, to provide instructions for the disposal of remains. An embryo or fetus, removed from the womb through abortion, spontaneous or otherwise, in many jurisdictions may be disposed of without certificate of death or record of burial. In contrast, disposal of the remains of a stillborn infant typically requires a death certificate and record of burial.

The perfecting of skills in organ transplantation, and the intensifying debate over legalizing euthanasia, turn us toward legal issues at the ending of life, from the right to begin life to the right to terminate it. Scher (1972) reminds us that euthanasia is in law still defined as homicide, although increasing numbers of physicians admit privately that they practice euthanasia on occasion. Many who promote dignity in dying advocate its legalization. Louisell (1973) portrays the trap we have produced for ourselves as he quotes Hillaire Belloc:

> Of old when men lay sick and sorely tried,
> The doctors gave them physic and they died.
> But here's a happier age, for now we know
> Both how to make men sick and keep them so! (p. 737).

Louisell, in a lengthy review of euthanasia, refuses to lend support to its legalization. His final note is in part about overindulgence in application of legal age:

> Our era is one that seeks, and often for good reason, a constant expansion of juridical order in human affairs. But not every human relationship stands to profit from complete juridicalization. The refusal so far of legislatures to intrude into the mercy-death area has been prudent . . . (p. 745).

Apart from the issue of euthanasia is that of what has been called "death with dignity." Legislation calling for regulation of nursing homes and of medical practices regarding the elderly, and consideration of the wishes of the elderly or near relatives in application of new technology and pharmaceuticals to prolong life of the human organism, attest to development of new legal age definitions in the years immediately ahead.

Some Current Issues in Moving into Adulthood

Recent decades have seen the emergence of age status asynchronization in the application of law to define advent of adulthood (Cain, 1964). The declaration that "majority is fixed at twenty-one years completed" no longer is adequate. In many nations the age of suffrage has been lowered to age 18. Those under 21 are frequently eligible for military draft. Age of adult responsibility for illegal acts has been variously defined. Eligibility to marry, to enter the labor force, to sign contracts, to obtain an automobile driver's license, vary from jurisdiction to jurisdiction.

To illustrate the difficulty in differentiating the minor from the adult, it must suffice at this time to quote from a recent United States Supreme Court decision (Application of Gault, 1967):

> From the inception of the juvenile court system [in the late nineteenth century] wide differences have been tolerated—indeed insisted upon—between the procedural rights accorded to adults and those of juveniles. ... the proceedings were not [interpreted as] adversary; [rather] the state was proceeding as *parens patriae*. ... but there is no trace of [this] doctrine in the history of criminal jurisprudence. ... Beyond [the age of seven in British common law] the state was not deemed to have authority to accord [children] fewer procedural rights than adults. ...
> The essential difference between [Gerald Gault's] case and a normal criminal case is that safeguards available to adults were discarded in Gerald's case. ...
> We [court justices] conclude that the constitutional privilege against self-incrimination is applicable in the case of juveniles as it is with respect to adults. We appreciate that special problems may arise with respect to waiver of the privilege by or on behalf of children, and that there may well be some differences in technique—but not in principle—depending upon the age of the child and the presence and competence of parents (pp. 14, 16, 17, 29, 55).

On Being an Adult

To be an adult has been typically to be a "person" or a "citizen." Once the age of majority is reached (although this is sometimes asynchronous), societal expectations of persons become fully operative, barring mental or physical defect. Therefore, seemingly no special effort to define adulthood in law is necessary. However, as the *Code Napoleon* so vividly illustrates, the span of years ordinarily associated with adulthood may be divided into two or more age statuses: rights of marriage (before and after age 30), of adoption (before and after age 50), restrictions on divorce (before and after age 45, for women), as examples. There are also statutes in various countries which limit eligibility to public office to those of mature years, which protect middle-aged workers in employment rights, and which provide for vocational rehabilitation for older workers.

Generally, speaking, however, legal age issues have been based either on how early in life an individual should be granted full rights and obligations of adults, or on how late in life adult rights and obligations should be maintained.

Aristotle has been credited with the aphorism:

> Injustice arises when equals are treated unequally, and also when unequals are treated equally (Ginsburg, 1965).

Laws have been utilized to determine when a young person is to be considered equal to an adult, with the rights and obligations of status related thereto, and when a young person is to be considered unequal to an adult, with denials of rights and obligations, and with protections related thereto. The case, Application of Gault, referred to above, attempts to resolve part of this issue but leaves other parts unresolved.

Similarly, law is increasingly being relied upon to determine how long an adult is to continue in that status and when an aging person is to be redesignated an old person with status modifications related thereto.

In a sense, the gerontological movement is currently caught in the trap of trying simultaneously to promote the case of equality by maintaining adult status into old age—e.g., the proposal to abolish mandatory retirement—and to promote the case of inequality by insisting that the elderly have special needs.

A vital component of the advocacy for legislation which gives distinctive service-oriented status to the elderly is the amassing of evidence, usually generated by social and biological scientists, which indicates either the inferior competitive prowess of the elderly in obtaining goods and services or their greater need for medical or other services. The gerontological movement has concentrated on developing and utilizing such data [to persuade lawmakers that the elderly are unequal to adults].

. . . the politics of aging—whether it is exhibited in gerontological efforts to provide special benefits to the elderly [as unequal to adults] or in attempts to extend adult benefits or rights until the onset of functional [in contrast to chronological] old age—has yet to encounter thoroughgoing assessment by the Court. That time is likely to come soon. (Cain, 1974b, pp. 74, 75).

Although most legal age cases have been framed to consider extension of adult status, there are occasions in which the legal question has been modified to ask whether special status granted to the young (or old) is a denial of justice to the adult.

A prime example is an issue which is likely to continue to be before the American courts, the constitutionality of age-variable fees and services in public transportation. In a case involving reduced bus fares for youth, Transcontinental Bus System, Inc. v. C.A.B. (1967), the court declared that "unjust discrimination occurs when there is different treatment of like traffic for like and contemporaneous service under substantially similar circumstances and conditions." This includes the offering of a service to a particular class of passengers which is not offered to others.

During the 1960's a number of air lines began to offer discounted fares for youths between ages 12 and 21. The Civil Aeronautics Board (1972) conducted extensive hearings on this and related subjects, guided by the Federal Aviation Act, Section 404(b), which requires that "no air carrier . . . shall . . . subject any particular person . . . to any unjust discrimination . . . in any respect whatsoever." The CAB found that "The youth . . . fares, . . . available only to limited classes of persons, . . . defined by age, . . . are therefore *prima facie* discriminatory." Subsequent to the investigation the CAB ordered a phasing out and eventual cancellation of discount fares for youth and certain others (Civil Aeronautics Board, 1973). A separate investigation of reduced fares for the elderly is currently in process.

Yet, reduced fares for children to ride buses to school or elsewhere, reduced or canceled fares for the elderly to ride buses or rapid transit, and reduced fares for infants on many types of public conveyances, are in force today in many jurisdictions.

A workshop on transportation and aging in Washington, D.C., in 1970 (Cantilli and Shmelzer, 1971) reviewed both the distinctive transportation needs of the elderly and a number of demonstration projects which offer special services to the elderly through reduced fares or special conveyances, routes or time schedules. A difficulty in determining the age status ramifications of this report relates to the offering of services variously to "retirees," "senior citizens," "the elderly," as well as the "poor" and the "handicapped." The workshop provided no consideration of the constitutional justification for special services to the elderly, at the expense of the adult population. But if an adult, ineligible for service solely because of age, challenges the special treatment of the elderly, will the court rule that the special services are *prima facie discriminatory*"?

How to provide economic protection to the fare paying consumer (that is, the adult), profit to the carrier through filling otherwise unoccupied seats, and equity to the young and the old who may not have resources to pay full fare or may have destinations different from adults remains a formidable challenge to legislatures and to courts.

A SEPARATE LEGAL STATUS FOR THE ELDERLY

A distinctive legal status for the elderly, based essentially on the presumption that those who reach a specified old age are, as a class, unable to provide basic needs for themselves as adults are called upon to do, has been in evidence in Europe for well over a century. The important study by Hatzfeld (1971), which reports that France had begun to consider the special needs of the elderly, along with those who may be ill, invalid, or unemployed, by mid-nineteenth century, is a case in point.

However, it has been the success of a post-World War II gerontological movement which has led to the adoption of a plethora of laws which have contributed to the creation of a distinctive status for the elderly. Other sources of laws, including those related to issues of surrogate management of properties of older people (Alexander and Lewin, 1973) and to support of mandatory retirement policies, have also contributed to a new, complex legal status for the elderly.

Most of these recent laws utilize chronological age, although the specific age denoting a change in status may vary from issue to issue and from jurisdiction to jurisdiction. It would appear that age status asynchronization, which has long beset the young as they seek to enter adulthood, has become a characteristic of growing old (Cain, 1964, p. 298; Cain, 1974a, p. 171).

Efforts by lawmaking agencies to relate chronological age in law to the actual functional attributes of those involved appear to be minimal. Age criteria may hold rather firm through time, although life expectancy and developments in health have improved dramatically in recent decades in many countries. And age for retirement, for example, varies greatly from country to country. Jural attention to matters of social age among the elderly has to date been slight, although, for example, a worker forced to retire because of age may be required by law to provide financial support for a young child or an elderly parent.

Examples to follow are indicators of the near ubiquity of legally defined old age in industrialized societies. The task of reviewing the diverse and complex developments in law related to the elderly is too formidable to undertake at this time. Rather, a brief review of age of eligibility for pensions, of efforts to provide legal protection for older workers, and a rather comprehensive examination of the issue of age-based mandatory retirement are provided.

Age of Eligibility for Retirement Pensions

A study of the age of eligibility to participate in the public pension systems of 21 member nations of the Organization for Economic Co-Operation and Development reveals a wide diversity among nations with similar demographic patterns, economies, and political systems (Hyden, 1971). Table 1 shows that 9 of the 21 nations have established a lower age for

normal retirement for women than for men. Whether this age discrimination is to be interpreted as against male or against female is not clear. The range of ages for retirement is from 60 to 70 for men, 55 to 70 for women.

Four of the nations provide for early retirement with reduced pension payments; three nations permit early retirement with full benefits for workers who have contributed to the pension fund for a specified extended period; involuntary unemployment for at least 12 consecutive months provides older workers in two nations with eligibility for early pension payments; physically debilitating work assignments provide for early eligibility in three nations; illness may provide for early eligibility in three nations.

Twelve of the nations do not require substantial retirement from all work to maintain eligibility, whereas five do so specify. Only seven nations increase benefits to those who continue to work at their long term job beyond normal retirement age.

These descriptive data presented by Hyden direct both policy makers and theorists to some fundamental questions about aging and the law. It is unlikely, for example, that the 55-year-old woman in Italy or Japan or Turkey is functionally equivalent, for work purposes, to the 70-year-old woman in Ireland or Norway. Then why the great disparity in age of retirement and in other aspects of pension systems as well?

Undoubtedly there are differential labor force needs, at least when the system was adopted for each country. Types and strengths of pressure groups vary among nations. There may be poorly understood ideological differences among peoples regarding the right of the elderly to earn a living or to be unburdened from toil and strain. We need to know much more about origin of legislation and of the persistence of laws through changes in social structure before there can be understanding of the differences among, and adequacies of, pension systems.

Employment Protection for Older Workers

In response to evidence of discrimination against older workers, governments in many nations have adopted fair employment practices

TABLE 1.[a] PENSION SYSTEMS IN OECD COUNTRIES, BY NORMAL AGE OF RETIREMENT, QUALIFICATIONS FOR EARLY RETIREMENT, REDUCED PAYMENTS FOR EARLY RETIREMENT, BY REQUIREMENT FOR RETIREMENT, AND BY INCREMENTS PAID FOR DEFERMENT OF NORMAL RETIREMENT.

	NORMAL AGE FOR RETIREMENT		EARLY RETIREMENT QUALIFICATIONS						
Country	Male	Female	Work 35–40 years	Unemp. 1 year	Tiring work	Long illness	Early retirement, less pay	Substantial requirement to retire	Increments if retirement deferred
Austria	65	60	x	x		x		x	
Belgium	65	60					5 yrs	x	
[b]Canada	65	65						b	
Denmark	67	62				x			
France	60	60							x
West Germany	65	65		x					
Greece	62	57			x		2 yrs	x	
Iceland	67	67							x
Ireland	70	70							
Italy	60	55	x		x				x
Japan	60	55						x	
Luxembourg	65	65	x						
Netherlands	65	65							
Norway	70	70							
Portugal	65	65						x	
Spain	65	65		x				x	
Sweden	67	67					4 yrs		x
Switzerland	65	63							
Turkey	60	55				x		x	x
United Kingdom	65	60						x	x
United States	65	65					3 yrs	x	x

[a]Adapted from Hyden (1971), Tables I, II, and III, pp. 35, 36, and 37.
[b]In Canada the universal pension program does not require retirement, but the social insurance program does require substantial retirement.

and related legislation. Boglietti (1974), in a review of international conditions related to this form of discrimination, noted that frequently age discrimination in the private sector of the economy is given impetus by discriminatory civil service policies. A typical pattern is for a government to establish a minimum age for employment by statute but to permit maximum age for employment to be established by administrative regulation (United Nations: Department of Economic and Social Affairs, 1966).

Boglietti, in seeking an explanation for age discrimination, cites the frequent argument of employers, "diminished working capacity" of older workers. However, not every worker displays diminished capacity in synchronization with the calendar:

At the age of 50, or indeed at any other age, tremendous variations can be observed in the "apparent age" of different individuals ... Occupational health services and personnel departments have often deplored their inability, for lack of technical facilities, to establish objective differences between persons of the same age who, subjectively, can be seen to vary greatly (p. 356).

The Commission on Human Rights, United Nations, issued a declaration in 1949 which argued that the interplay of age prejudice and discriminatory practices produces

detrimental distinctions which do not take account of the particular characteristics of an individual as such, but take into account only collective qualifications deriving from the membership in a certain social or other group (quoted in Boglietti, 1974, p. 363).

Boglietti reported that since this declaration by the Commission on Human Rights, many of the member nations have sought to reduce the vulnerability of older workers through both legislative and contractual measures, although the precise means varies greatly among nations. Ironically, none of the cases cited by Boglietti incorporates "particular characteristics of an individual" into legislation, except possibly those which relate to years of work, but all do resort to the application of the criticized "collective qualifications."

The Netherlands pioneered in antidiscriminatory measures as early as 1945: West Germany adopted similar measures in 1956. In 1965 Czechoslovakia adopted a law which provided for a three weeks' notice for dismissal of workers over 40. In 1967 Hungary adopted a provision which calls upon employers to refrain from age discrimination; the United States adopted a comprehensive law which made discrimination against workers 40 to 65 years of age illegal in most cases. Since 1968 in the Netherlands, workers are entitled to two weeks' notice for each year of service after age 45 and to three weeks' notice for each year after age 50. A Belgian law passed in 1969 requires the period of notice to be calculated on the basis of the length of employment. In enforcing this, Belgian courts have taken into account both seniority and age, and have on occasion required advance notice of three years or more, or payment of equivalent compensation to a dismissed older worker. In Japan and Colombia it is necessary for employers to hire on an age quota basis. And Canada, Finland, France, and Costa Rica, among other nations, have recently adopted fair employment practice laws.

Proposals before the European Economic Community in 1972 include a recommendation of a quota system and another which would extend the period of notice of dismissal, e.g., a three months' notice for those aged 40, but six months' notice for those aged 50.

Several relevant points are to be found in Boglietti's report. Foremost is that chronological ages have been incorporated into law in a variety of ways in efforts to reduce discrimination against older workers. A second point is that, although there is recognition of the inadequacy of chronological age to provide equity in protecting the rights of older workers, legislatures as yet have found few attractive substitutes for chronological age in specifying eligibility for legal age protections.

However, the legal issues related to overcoming a "minority group status" for older workers are more complex than Boglietti suggests. Age is not a good predictor of performance capability. Some jobs require more strength or concentration or endurance than some older workers can maintain. But there are also some indicators that many older workers in bureaucratized societies actually are favored over younger workers. The seniority principle is a major case in point. If competency rather than age *per se* is to become a guidepost in hiring and promoting, does it follow that seniority protections and privileges will perforce be abolished?

There is an emergent issue even more complicated. In time of recession, cutbacks in labor force are often required. Seniority rules and fair employment legislation would seem to shelter the older worker. However, in recent years, through affirmative action incentives in the United States, new minority employees have been added to labor ranks. Ought the rights of older workers prevail over the rights of newly employed minorities? Should those who have the prospect of immediate, albeit reduced, financial support through a pension be permitted to continue work when younger workers with family obligations are forced into the ranks of the unemployed? An economic recession will test the strength of laws and court decisions won after long and arduous struggle by gerontologists.

The Issue of Mandatory Retirement

Among the most controversial legal age issues, at least in the United States, is that of mandatory retirement. To date courts have generally rejected appeals to have age *per se* accepted as a basis for removing a person from employment declared unconstitutional. With this issue there is opportunity to interrelate the jural perspective as test cases move through the courts, the evidence of researchers regarding the attributes and needs of older workers, and social theories which pertain to social system maintenance. In addition, the relative merits of chronological age criteria and functional age criteria can be reappraised.

A prosecutor in Commonwealth v. Moore, in 1827, declared:

> ... [The employers] had an undisputed right to discharge any workman ... when they conceived that his continuance was no longer conducive to their interest ... They were at perfect liberty to dismiss every journeyman [tailor] ... (quoted in Fisher, 1973, p. 4).

Employers in the United States could, for the most part, dismiss employees capriciously until the Depression of the 1930's prompted preventive legislation (Fisher, 1973, p. 5). Title VII of the Civil Rights Act of 1964 and the Age Discrimination in Employment Act of 1967 have made it illegal for employers to discriminate, including dismissal, on the grounds of race, color, religion, sex, national origin, and age (between the years of 40 and 65).

An issue increasingly before the courts is whether old age, generally past age 65, will be added to the list of personal attributes which cannot be used legally for discriminatory purposes.

In 1953 a special project, Criteria for the Continued Employment of Older Workers, was undertaken by The National Committee on the Aging in the United States. Its goal was "to encourage the creation of adequate yardsticks for determining whether a worker should continue in employment or not," based on the critera of continuing productive capacity, the worker's desire, and the employer's preference (Mathiasen, 1957, p. 10).

Difficulties in achieving that goal were clearly recognized. On the one hand, mandatory retirement curtails earning and spending power of workers; industry is deprived of the productive skills of individuals; and for the worker forced to retire there may be serious consequences for personal and familial well-being. "Fixed retirement negates the principle that work is a value in itself, a principle which has been basic to the great industrial development of our nation" (Mathiasen, 1957, p. 5.). Mandatory retirement at a specified chronological age "makes no allowance for individual differences and goes counter to the basic tenet of democracy which upholds the right of every man to the full

development and the exercise of his inherent abilities" (p. 6).

On the other hand, "a fixed retirement program facilitates some aspects of personnel planning, simplifies the funding of retirement benefits, and operates impersonally" (p. 15). That is, "the objectivity of chronological age as a criterion for retirement makes it an attractive instrument *in lieu of a better arrangement*" (p. 6, italics added).

The National Committee on the Aging held out hope for a resolution of the issue:

> Perhaps at some future date the results of [a combination of medical and psychological measurements of performance capabilities] will be found to be so closely related to productive capacity that the proponents of [flexible retirement policies] can confidently assert their objectivity and utility (p. 16).

In the two decades and more since the Committee's project was launched, a "better arrangement" has yet to be confirmed. In this continuing state of ambiguity and inadequacy, the courts increasingly are being called upon to provide resolution on behalf of individuals to be permitted to continue to work beyond a specified retirement age. The courts continue to uphold the constitutionality, but not necessarily the fairness, of mandatory age retirement policies.

Finally, the Committee complicated the task of courts and legislatures by pointing out the variable historical context for employment opportunities:

> In a time of full employment, the capable older person finds it comparatively easy to continue at work, or ... to get a new job. When, however, there is a shortage of jobs, other considerations come into play. The relative equities of various age groups become a matter for discussion. It is often felt that the individual newly out of school and anxious to take his place as a worker should be given priority. Older workers are regarded as having had their chance, and it is thought that these should be content to retire to a subsistence level of income rather than being active participants at work (p. 16).

Although the origins of mandatory retirement policies are not clearly known, they appear to be associated with early government social legislation, private insurance programs, and with various pension plans. One interpretation is that retirement had its origins within the framework of public relations, before there were studies on the link between age and ability, and before there were economic concepts to relate retirement and pensions to benefits to a company or the national economy (Mathiasen, 1957, pp. 43, 133).

Notably absent from recent court deliberations, both by appellants and the courts, has been consideration of the actual function of mandatory age provisions and of the function of alternative means of providing for retirement if chronological age is declared unconstitutional. One seldom mentioned function of mandatory retirement is to protect the worker who has reduced productive capacity before the age of normal retirement. Roth (1963), in very perceptive comments on the structuring of the passage of time through what he labels "timetables," observed:

In [for example] many universities and in large, well-established businesses there is often an obligation to provide a job for the professor or executive even when he is no longer considered useful to the organization . . . the unwanted incumbents cannot be moved off to a dead-end sidetrack (p. 106).

Roth noted that "systems of compulsory retirement with loopholes for excepting individuals who are still wanted sometimes operate as such a sidetrack at the upper age range" (p. 106).

When the span of time to complete a specified stage in the life course is highly uncertain—for example, the span of time to cure a tubercular patient, or to rehabilitate a criminal, or to train for a job—it may seem appropriate to provide "considerable leeway in timing the sequence of events" in each of these stages of a career, thereby "promoting a wider area of bargaining between superior and subordinate, professional and client" (p. 109). However, the tested social response typically is exactly the opposite: "a standardized timetable is imposed or maintained as a way of avoiding the disruptive consequences of uncertainty and widespread bargaining" (p. 109).

Roth concluded, "Perhaps standardization results from a combination of a high degree of uncertainty and a powerful authority to impose a timetable without compromise" (p. 109). Mandatory retirement represents at present "a timetable without compromise." Courts are currently being pressed to remove the "powerful authority" of the employer and possibly the union. A recent public opinion poll discovered an overwhelming 86 percent of older citizens want abolition of mandatory retirement policies (Harris, 1975, p. 216). The "disruptive consequences," if any, of providing for considerable leeway in "timing the sequence of events" leading to retirement await thorough consideration by the courts, by workers, and by gerontologists.

However, several recent articles in law journals have consistently supported abolition of mandatory retirement, with little reflection on the consequences of shifting to functional age criteria. Work (1972), for example, concluded:

The cut-off age of sixty-five should be eliminated from [fair employment] legislation, and the opportunities for employment should be provided for all, regardless of age, based solely on their ability to do the work involved. Such legislation should eliminate arbitrary age discrimination among workers by requiring employers to assess the functional age of an individual rather than rely on his chronological age (p. 345).

August (1974) summarized:

A balancing of the very serious problems now caused by discrimination against the older worker against the virtually insignificant costs of prohibiting such discrimination would . . . require the elimination of the [1967 Age Discrimination in Employment] Act's upper age limit [of sixty-five] (p. 1352).

Another recent article (Anonymous, 1974) suggested that "it is time now for the legislative and judicial branches to extend meaningful protection to the worker over age sixty-five" (p. 513).

But it is currently the courts which are sharpening the issues. We turn finally to court arguments which continue to uphold mandatory retirement policies.

THE CONSTITUTIONALITY OF MANDATORY RETIREMENT PRACTICES

In Norman v. United States (1968), the court held that mandatory retirement of military officers was not a deprivation of a vested right.

The Weiss v. Walsh (1971) case was based on

the charge of a distinguished professor of philosophy that his constitutional rights, under the
First and Fourteenth Amendments, had been
denied by administrators at Fordham University
when they refused to hire him for a faculty
position after having shortly before offered the
position to him, solely because of his age. The
judge's ruling, which was against the plaintiff,
has great significance for students of aging and
the law:

> [I]t is, according to plaintiff, that notwith-
> standing that Fordham found him preemi-
> nently qualified . . . , the actual or intended
> offer was withdrawn because of the eleventh-
> hour interjection of an arbitrary age limita-
> tion by some state board or official.
>
> Plaintiff, now in his seventieth year . . .
> states that his physical health and mental
> capacity are excellent . . . In this litigation,
> however, the court is called upon to judge
> neither the brilliance nor worthiness of a
> man, but the merit of his legal claims.
>
> . . . Even assuming that equivalent impor-
> tance is accorded to employment opportunity
> in our constitutional scheme, and given the
> protection afforded such opportunity by the
> Due Process and Equal Protection Clauses, I
> am constrained to hold that Professor Weiss is
> not the victim of an invidious and impermis-
> sible discrimination. Notwithstanding great
> advances in gerontology, the era when ad-
> vanced age ceases to bear some reasonable
> statistical relationship to diminished capacity
> or longevity is still future. It cannot be said,
> therefore, that age ceilings upon eligibility for
> employment are inherently suspect, although
> their application will inevitably fall unjustly in
> the individual case. If the precision of the law
> is impugnable by the stricture of general
> applicability, vindication of the exceptional
> individual may have to attend the wise discre-
> tion of the administrator. On its face, there-
> fore, the denial of a teaching position to a
> man approaching seventy years of age is not
> constitutionally infirm (pp. 76, 77).

In McIlvaine v. Pennsylvania State Police
(1972) the court held that a state law establishing a mandatory retirement age, in this case 60,
for police officers, when uniformly applied, was
reasonable and did not violate constitutional
rights.

Both the Weiss and the McIlvaine rulings were
cited by the court in Retail Clerks Union, Local
770 v. Retail Clerks International Association
(1973) in the dismissal of charges that the Asso-

ciation had violated the rights of union employees who, as a result of provisions in newly
adopted by-laws for mandatory retirement at
age 65, were to be deprived of their livelihood.
The court ruled:

> Not all discrimination between classes of
> persons is violative of the law. The test is
> whether distinctions which are drawn are
> rationally related to the purpose for drawing
> of the distinctions. Here, this Court cannot
> say that the mandatory retirement provisions
> do not achieve a permissible end, or that the
> means chosen are impermissible or irrational
> (p. 1287).

The case of Armstrong v. Howell (1974) continues to deny the relevance of Fourteenth
Amendment arguments. The plaintiff, Armstrong, had been hired at age 66 by a county
hospital. Subsequent to her hiring the state
passed a new Civil Service Act which called
upon counties to establish personnel policies.
County officials did develop a policy which included mandatory retirement for employees at
age 65, although with a provision for gradual
rather than abrupt termination of employees
who were already past 65. The court admitted
that

> there is no controversy over the fact that at
> the time of her mandatory retirement and
> termination . . . , plaintiff was an employee
> in good standing, was highly respected by her
> supervisors, was fully capable of performing
> the duties connected with her job and was, in
> fact, capably performing those duties and
> physically and mentally able to perform her
> duties as of the date of her termination (p. 50).

The court reviewed the charge:

> [T]he plaintiff has challenged the Act [which
> forced her retirement] . . . on the grounds
> that her rights under the Fourteenth Amend-
> ment of the Constitution are violated and
> abridged, this for the reasons that plaintiff's
> classification which requires mandatory
> retirement at age sixty-nine (for her) has no
> reasonable basis to the purposes of promotion
> of economy and efficiency . . . And . . . plain-
> tiff claims to be the victim of an irrebuttable
> presumption of unfitness to work . . . (p. 51).

In rejecting the relevancy of these claims, the
court ruled:

> [T]here appears to be no question but what
> age is a classification which bears a reasonable

relation to the law in question and that age has an inevitable and definite relationship with the ability to perform work (p. 51).

The premise that age has a definite relationship to work performance has been challenged by Kaplan (1971):

As a matter of scientific fact there is no objective evidence to support any generalized relationship between age and ability as measured by productivity. . . .

This arbitrary standard [mandatory retirement because of age] coupled with the adverse consequences of retirement and the inability of the elderly worker to find substitute employment make retirement based solely on age violative of . . . the Constitution (p. 169).

If the proposition that there is no "generalized relationship between age and ability as measured by productivity" is to be incorporated into law, and if functional age, as measured, for example, by productivity, is to substitute for chronological age as the criterion for retirement, it surely follows that employers can justify before the court the forced early retirement of a worker whose productivity has begun to decline. The confusion and strain noted by Roth when timetables were absent may well result from the abolition of chronological age criteria for retirement.

A prospective basis for challenge to the arguments in support of mandatory retirement laws and policies is to be found in the dissent of Justice Rehnquist to the majority opinion of the United States Supreme Court in Cleveland Board of Education v. LaFleur (1974). The Court invalidated a policy of the School Board which required pregnant school teachers to take a leave without pay after a pregnancy of a specified number of months, to which Justice Rehnquist responded:

Since this right to pursue an occupation is presumably on the same lofty footing as the right of choice in matters of family life, the Court will have to strain valiantly in order to avoid having today's opinion lead to the invalidation of mandatory retirement statutes for governmental employees. In that event federal, state, and local governmental bodies will be remitted to the task, thankless both for them and for the employees involved, of individual determinations of physical impairment and senility.

Thus, a fundamental legal issue is joined. Repeatedly an older chronological age used to remove an individual from a position of employment has been upheld in the courts as defensible. Rehnquist sees the invalidation of such use of age as producing a thankless task. Yet, a report drafted by the National Institute of Industrial Gerontology and released by the United States Senate, Special Committee on Aging (1969), declared:

Until we achieve the ideal goal of making one's year of birth irrelevant in the minds of employers and employees, the greatest protection for older workers is the joint effect of economics and legislation . . .

In granting *certiorari* on May 20, 1975, in Murgia v. Massachusetts Board of Retirement (1974), the United States Supreme Court agreed to undertake for the first time this so called "thankless task" of examining the issue of the relevance of the year of birth in determining retirement requirements.

A fundamental legal problem, that of consistency, emerges at this point. Political pressure to abolish mandatory retirement rules continues. If chronological age is declared to be unjust as a determinant in restricting employment, does it follow that the courts will rule, or legislatures will decide, that chronological age is unfair as a determinant for eligibility for the vast array of services and protections and exemptions built into law which now benefit mainly those over 65? How practical, efficient, and fair are functional criteria as a substitute for currently used chronological criteria? (Botelho, Cain, and Friedman, 1975)

LEGAL AGE: OPPORTUNITIES FOR GERONTOLOGY

This chapter has introduced a number of issues which have seldom been confronted by gerontologists. Specialists in legal history, in jurisprudence, in political processes, and social status must devote additional attention to the entire question of legal age before a more definitive statement can be advanced.

Two remaining themes call for comment. The first relates to the relative strengths of chronological, functional, and social age as prospective determinants of status; the second relates to the prospects of dramatic innovations in legal approaches to the status of the elderly.

Age: Chronological, Functional, Social

Chronological age is thoroughly imbedded in law. Recent developments in computer technology make it increasingly attractive as a means of regulating the flow of individuals through the status systems of a complex society. There is little question but that birthdays will continue to count heavily in status determination for years to come.

However, many of those factors which make chronological age attractive also make functional age possible. Efficiency in production made possible through computer technology could also provide the luxury to a society of permitting individual differences in rate of maturation and aging to be fully respected. Philosophers of education have long emphasized the need to consider the readiness of the individual pupil to learn. If court decisions overturn mandatory retirement policies, societies will shortly have the task of establishing institutions which incorporate "readiness" to retire into their operations.

The most unexplored, and probably the most intriguing, type of age is social age. Illustration of our understanding of the term is better accomplished by possibilities rather than by existing practices. For example, both a 65-year-old man and a 25-year-old man may be fathers of young children. Their social age in this instance is the same. Both are expected to join the school Parent Teachers Association; both are expected to provide nurture and guidance to their children. Regarding legal age, there is the question of whether the two will equally have opportunity to obtain resources to fulfill the obligations to their children. Mandatory retirement suggests a negative answer.

But there are some rather concrete examples. Among the more intriguing examples of social age is that of widowhood, as defined in many pension systems. According to Laroque (1972), current social security systems in most industrial societies have tacitly accepted the premise that a wife is financially dependent on her husband. Generally, also, widowhood is associated with old age, or near old age. The issue of survivors' rights, expressed in so called reversionary pensions, arises when the husband at the time of death was receiving, or had worked long enough to have become eligible to receive, an old age pension. According to Laroque:

> The rules applying to survivors [of eligible pensioners] are then seen as an integral part of the old-age scheme, and the same legislation and institutions provide for old-age pensions and widows' pensions (p. 2).

Whereas it is relatively easy to incorporate data about the worker himself into actuarial dimensions of pension plans—length of service, age of retirement, projected years of survival after retirement—there is complication and financial risk involved in providing reversionary pensions for widows. Major premises in pension schemes appear to be that, one, widows are likely to begin this status when chronologically relatively old, and therefore will draw pensions for a relatively few years, and, two, a widow is likely to be functionally incapable of earning a decent income herself, primarily because of old age.

But these premises, built upon the assumption that the social age of widowhood is correlated with older chronological age, do not always hold true. Young widows of old military veterans have drawn pensions more than a century after a war. At least one union which planned to accumulate pension funds sufficient to provide decent pensions for widows has found that the growing and unanticipated practice of older union members to divorce their wives and remarry younger women, who in turn become widows at an early age, has put heavy strain on the pension fund.

Laroque, in fact, proposed that social security schemes be redesigned so that reversionary principles be abolished, to be replaced by policies which would provide women with their own personal rights to a pension. Scandinavian countries already provide a pension to both men and women upon reaching a legally specified age.

The policy of assigning pension credits to the worker (male) only, and not equally to worker and spouse, except in reversionary ways reviewed above, has led to additional legal age complications. Divorce has triggered much of the controversy. Until recently in the United States, a divorced woman, who may have been married for many years to a worker who was accumulating years of eligibility for benefits, was deprived of all rights to a share of those benefits when the worker became eligible to receive them. Recent changes in social security laws provide that a woman who was married to the same worker for at least 20 years becomes eligible to receive the social security benefit she would have been eligible to receive if no divorce had taken place.

A variation of the divorce question has been reviewed by Gudebski and Jovovich (1973). Laws and contracts which associate the accrual of rights to a pension upon retirement with the worker only, and not with the spouse of the worker also, have come under challenge in the courts. In most pension agreements payments made to a widow of the worker eligible for pension payments are greatly reduced upon the death of the worker, although expenses for the widow may be reduced by only a small amount. Often more complicated still is the issue of rights to a pension fund for a spouse who becomes divorced from the contributing worker, especially if the divorce takes place before retirement. The right to economic well-being in old age for divorced older women hinges upon future court decisions regarding whether or not pension funds are interpreted as community property.

Gudebski and Jovovich have argued that recent decisions by courts in California lend support to the proposition that the principle of community property now can be extended to the ex-spouse who was a nonemployee to include right to an equal share of unmatured retirement benefits which heretofore have been credited to the worker only. They base their interpretation partly on a recent decision in California:

[We] do not believe the Legislature has declared the employee's right to a pension so sacrosanct that it is incompatible with his spouse's ownership of her community share in it. Both employee and non-employee own community property rights in the pension

fund that are of equal stature . . . Because the employee participates in the pension program he does not thereby strip his spouse of vested community property rights in that fund [through divorce] (Phillipson v. Board of Administration, 1970).

As far as can be ascertained at this time, social age as discussed above is not in the mainstream of legal theory or decision making. Possibly future decisions regarding widows, divorcees, and employees with seniority will correct this deficiency.

Prospects for Innovations in Legal Age

Stone (1966), who was referred to earlier, suggested that jurisprudence had been led to support *ad hoc* remedies to social ills at the turn of the century. The gerontological movement, for the most part, has continued in this tradition. But the success of the movement in promoting particular solutions to particular problems has produced such a myriad of laws that the elderly, instead of becoming independent, may have become increasingly dependent on intermediaries to interpret and administer the programs sustained in law.

A labor-management contract recently negotiated in France (Anonymous, 1973), which sets new rules for increasing financial assistance to older unemployed workers, is a case in point:

[Workers to qualify for added benefits] must have been at least 60 at the time of their dismissal (but persons dismissed during the 20 months preceding their sixtieth birthday . . . may apply); . . . They must have been receiving . . . special unemployment allowances . . . for a period depending on their age on dismissal (i.e. nine months for dismissal between 60 and 61, six months for dismissal between 61 and 62, and three months for dismissal between 62 and 64).

. . . The payment of this supplement ceases on the day when the beneficiary either reaches the age of 65 years and three months, or begins to receive an old-age pension, . . . or re-enters employment before reaching that age (pp. 439–440).

A United States Senator recently testified:

Upon reaching 65 the aged taxpayer is oftentimes confronted with an entirely new set of rules, usually far more complex than the tax provisions during his preretirement years. . . .

For the untrained . . . elderly taxpayer, these complex tax relief measures can prove to be mind boggling (United State Senate, Special Committee on Aging, 1974, p. 13).

In a report on legal problems of older Americans (United States Senate, Special Committee on Aging, 1970) a similar observation was made:

Federal benefit programs—though designed to aid elderly individuals—frequently produce a myriad of complex legal problems which completely overwhelm the untrained [elderly] layman (p. 7).

Clearly, a major challenge facing gerontologists is to move beyond advocacy for particular measures to a perspective which calls for consistency and coherence of status, for programs which can be comprehended and managed more fully by the elderly themselves.

All the materials reviewed for this chapter have counted age from birth (or, in the case of abortion, from conception). But the farther an individual moves from the year of his birth, the less significant is that fact for the purposes of gauging functional capacity. A major breakthrough is likely to come as indicators of the length of time until death become perfected (Bryson and Siddiqui, 1969; Palmore and Jeffers, 1971). We know a bit about the significance of longevity of parents; we know that cigarette smoking shortens life; we predict how long a cancer patient is likely to live. The practice of retiring everyone at an age counted from birth results in some workers' receiving only a few months' return from many years of contribution to pension funds; others will receive payments for decades. If age could be counted backward from death, rather than forward from birth, more equitable opportunity to receive return on pension investments could be accomplished, housing and health service planning could be improved, and a larger percentage of the elderly could have the option of a few years of leisure at the end of their lives.

There are already practical ramifications to this recommendation. In the United States, the Equal Employment Opportunity Commission, in an amendment of the rules released in February, 1968, indicated that sex based differences for retirement, either compulsory or optional, violates federal law. However, a spokesman for the Wage-Hour Administration at about the same time opined that the Equal Pay Act, on which the commission ruling was based, did not prevent provisions for different ages for retirement.

What the law really is on this subject is a matter of conjecture. Part of the reason for the difficulty is that on a statistical basis . . . women live longer than men and consequently a pension for them costs more (Tolan, 1969, p. 64).

More practically, gerontologists have before them the task of determining measurements for functional age and training specialists to administer those measurements.

It is apparent that the amount of activity and interest in law and politics of old age, as reflected in the gerontological movement, far surpasses the scholarly efforts to understand the processes by which those political endeavors create status alterations and to assess their consequence upon the rights and the self-identity of the elderly.

Cohen (1967) identified a "legal Gordian knot" in efforts simultaneously to maintain adult status for the elderly and to provide special services:

There is a deep and growing concern . . . that older people may, from time to time, require special services and special protections. There is a growing recognition that older people are not always dealt with in the same way as younger people in the same condition . . . The dilemma then is this: The elderly are first and foremost adults with all the rights and privileges that accrue to free adults in our society. They enjoy, as a general rule, no special status analogous to that of children in the eyes of the law . . . In our zeal to provide them with the protections and rights that are stated in the Older Americans Act, we must not pierce the shield which guarantees independence except under conditions which make it clear and certain that we have done so only to avoid disaster (pp. 96–97).

Cohen (1974) proposed an analytical framework to facilitate the monumental task of ordering the data and the issues on aging and the law. He proposes three major components:

(1) Exploration of statutory law and common law in pursuit of further recognition of

the impact of legal age in determining the status of the elderly . . .
(2) The issue of access to legal services by the elderly . . .
(3) Substantive issue analysis [including] analysis of legal problems which are old age specific . . .; issues where impact on the elderly is extremely high . . .; and old-age-affecting issues (pp. 265-266).

Cain (1974b) sought to raise the status question by posing the issue of equity versus equality for the elderly. He concluded:

Perhaps the most important aspect of the problem [of a gerontology of legal age] is the recognition of the fact that no concerted efforts have been made to ascertain the links among social and biological research of the attributes of the elderly, the political activism which builds upon research discoveries to promote new laws regarding the elderly, and the actual consequences of these new laws upon the status of the elderly (p. 79).

Both Cohen and Cain are calling for examination of interrelationships among theoretical interests, research ventures, advocacy thrusts, and political activities regarding the elderly, for the purposes both of understanding what is happening to the status of the elderly, as well as other age categories, and of protecting the freedom and the dignity of those who are called upon to accommodate to the ever changing status demands imposed by law.

REFERENCES

Alexander, G. C., and Lewin, T. H. D. 1973. *The Aged and the Need for Surrogate Management.* Syracuse, New York: Syracuse University Press.

Anonymous. 1970. Criminal law—Homicide—Fetus is a human being within meaning of the homicide statutes when it reaches age of viability. *Vanderbilt Law Review*, 23, 854-859.

Anonymous. 1973. France: Guaranteed income for the older unemployed. *International Labour Review*, 108, 439-442.

Anonymous. 1974. Age discrimination in employment: The problem of the worker over sixty-five. *Rutgers-Camden Law Journal*, 5, 484-513.

Application of Gault. 1967. 87 S.Ct. 1428.

Armstrong v. Howell. 1974. 371 F. Supp. 48.

August, R. L. 1974. Age discrimination in employment: Correcting a constitutionally infirm legislative judgment. *Southern California Law Review*, 47, 1311-1352.

Bell, B. 1972. Significance of functional age for inter-disciplinary and longitudinal research in aging. *Aging and Human Development*, 3, 145-147.

Blackstone, William. 1967. *Commentaries on the Law of England.* 4 Vols. New York: Oceana Publications. (Lithograph of the American Edition of 1772.)

Boglietti, G. 1974. Discrimination against older workers and the promotion of equality of opportunity. *International Labour Review*, 110, 351-365.

Botelho, B. M., Cain, L. D., and Friedman, S. M. 1975. Mandatory retirement: the law, the courts, and the broader social context. *Willamette Law Journal*, 11, 398-416.

Bryson, M. C., and Siddiqui, M. M. 1969. Some criteria for aging. *Journal of the American Statistical Association*, 64, 1472-1483.

Cain, L. D. 1959. The sociology of ageing: A trend report and annotated bibliography. *Current Sociol.*, 8, 57-133.

Cain, L. D. 1964. Life course and social structure. In, R. E. L. Faris (ed.), *Handbook of Modern Sociology*, pp. 272-309. Chicago: Rand McNally.

Cain, L. D. 1974a. The growing importance of legal age in determining the status of the elderly. *Gerontologist*, 14, 167-174.

Cain, L. D. 1974b. Political factors in the emerging legal status of the elderly. *Ann. Amer. Acad.*, 415, 70-79.

Cantilli, E. J., and Shmelzer, J. L. (eds.) 1971. *Transportation and Aging: Selected Issues.* Washington, D.C.: Government Printing Office.

Civil Aeronautics Board. 1972. *Domestic Passenger-Fare Investigation: Phase 5—Discount Fares. Docket 21866-5.* Washington, D.C.: The Board.

Civil Aeronautics Board. 1973. *Domestic Passenger-Fare Investigation: Phase 5—Discount Fares. Docket 21866-5. Supplemental Opinion and Order on Reconsideration.* Washington, D.C.: The Board.

Clark, M., and Anderson, B. G. 1967. *Culture and Aging: An Anthropological Study of Older Americans.* Springfield, Illinois: Charles C. Thomas.

Cleveland Board of Education v. LaFleur. 1974. 414 U.S. 632.

Code Napoleon (The French Civil Code)—Decreed and Promulgated in Sections, March 1803-March, 1804. 1841. New York: Halsted and Voorhies.

Cohen, E. S. 1967. Old age and the law. *Women Lawyers Journal*, 53, 96-97, 100-103.

Cohen, E. S. 1974. Legal research issues on aging. *Gerontologist*, 14, 263-267.

Dorfman v. A. G. 1950. Israel Supreme Court, 9 P.E. 203.

Fisher, R. W. 1973. When workers are retired—An overview. *Monthly Labor Review*, 96, 4-17.

Ginsburg, M. 1965. *On Justice in Society.* Ithaca, New York: Cornell University Press.

Gudebski, J. J., and Jovovich, S. 1973. Retirement pay: A divorce in time saved mine. *Hastings Law Journal*, 24, 347-358.

Harris, L., and Associates. 1975. *The Myth and Reality of Aging in America.* Washington, D.C.: The National Council on the Aging.

Hatzfeld, H. 1971. *Du Paupérisme a la Sécurité Sociale*. Paris: Librairie Armand Colin.

Homo, L. 1962. *Roman Political Institutions: From City to State*. New York: Barnes & Noble.

Hunter, W. A. 1885. *A Systematic and Historical Exposition of Roman Law*. 2nd ed. London: William Maxwell and Son.

Hyden, S. 1971. Flexible retirement provisions in public pension systems. *In*, Organisation for Economic Co-Operation and Development, *Flexibility in Retirement Age*, pp. 21–37. Paris: The Organisation.

Kaplan, T. S. 1971. Too old to work: The constitutionality of mandatory retirement plans. *Southern California Law Review*, **44**, 150–180.

Laroque, P. 1972. Women's rights and widows' pensions. *International Labour Review*, **106**, 1–10.

Louisell, D. W. 1973. Euthanasia and biathanasia: On dying and killing. *Catholic University Law Review*, **22**, 723–745.

McIlvaine v. Pennsylvania State Police. 1972. 6 Pa. Cmwlth. 505, 296 A.2d 630.

Mathiasen, G. (ed.) 1957. *Flexible Retirement: Evolving Policies and Programs for Industry and Labor*. New York: G. P. Putnam's Sons.

Murgia v. Massachusetts Board of Retirement. 1974. 376 F. Supp. 753, D. Mass. (Certiorari granted, 43 U.S.L.W. 3609, U.S. May 20, 1975.)

Norman v. United States. 1968. 183 Ct. Cl. 41, 392 F 2d 255.

Palmore, E., and Jeffers, F. C. (eds.) 1971. *Prediction of Life Span: Recent Findings*. Lexington, Massachusetts: D. C. Heath.

Phillipson v. Board of Administration. 1970. 3 Cal. 3d 32, 50, 473 P. 2nd 765, 777, 89 Cal. Rptr. 61, 73.

Plato. 1960. *Laws. Translated*, *with an Introduction by A. E. Taylor*. New York: E. P. Dutton, Everyman's Library No. 275.

Pound, R. 1922. *An Introduction to the Philosophy of Law*. New Haven: Yale University Press.

Retail Clerks Union, Local 770 v. Retail Clerks International Association. 1973. 359 F. Supp. 1285.

Richardson, B. E. 1933. *Old Age Among the Ancient Greeks*. Baltimore: Johns Hopkins Press.

Roth, J. 1963. *Timetables: Structuring the Passage of Time in Hospital Treatment and Other Careers*. Indianapolis: Bobbs-Merrill.

Scher, E. M. 1972. Legal aspects of euthanasia. *Albany Law Review*, **36**, 674–697.

Shaki, A. H. 1969. Is age a matter of status? *Israel Law Review*, **4**, 371–391.

Stone, J. 1966. *Law and the Social Sciences in the Second Half Century*. Minneapolis: University of Minnesota Press.

Tolan, T. L. 1969. Discrimination: Sex and age questions. *Proceedings of New York University Twenty-First Annual Conference on Labor*, 59–76.

Transcontinental Bus System, Inc. v. C.A.B. 1967. 383 F, 2d 466.

United Nations Organization: Department of Economic and Social Affairs, Public Affairs Branch. 1966. *Handbook of Civil Service Laws and Practices*, pp. 427–428. New York: The Organization.

United States Senate, Special Committee on Aging. 1969. *Employment Aspects of the Economics of Aging. A Working Paper in Conjunction with the Overall Study of "Economics of Aging: Toward A Full Share in Abundance."* Washington, D.C.: Government Printing Office.

United States Senate, Special Committee on Aging. 1970. *Legal Problems Affecting Older Americans: A Working Paper*. Washington, D.C.: Government Printing Office.

United States Senate, Special Committee on Aging. 1974. *Protecting Older Americans Against Overpayment of Income Taxes*. Washington, D.C.: Government Printing Office.

Weber, M. 1947. *The Theory of Social and Economic Organization*. Translated by A. M. Henderson and Talcott Parsons. New York: Oxford University Press.

Weiss v. Walsh. 1971. 324 F. Supp. 75.

Williams, H. S. 1907. *The Historians' History of the World*, *Vol. I: Prolegomena; Egypt, Mesopotamia*, pp. 498–514. New York: The History Association.

Work, M. 1972. Age discrimination and the over-sixty-five worker. *Cumberland-Samford Law Review*, **3**, 333–345.

15
POLITICAL SYSTEMS AND AGING

Robert B. Hudson
and
Robert H. Binstock*
Brandeis University

The basic issues considered in this chapter are threefold: How does aging become manifest politically, either through older individuals or through groups? Is aging expressed in distinctive political patterns and does it have any unusual consequences for political systems? To what extent and in what fashions have political systems responded to aging as a social concern?

The first section of this chapter deals with the political attitudes and behavior of aging persons. The second section examines the politics of aging-based organizations. The final section considers the ways in which aging has become a concern of political systems and how older people fare in them.

POLITICAL ATTITUDES AND BEHAVIOR OF AGING PERSONS

Only a small portion of the research literature that provides data on the political attitudes and behavior of the aging has the politics of aging as its primary focus. Much of the evidence available on older persons' politics can be found in literature on social change, political system stability, political socialization, mass political

*The authors wish to acknowledge the research assistance of Martha Burns and Myrna Weiner, associates of the Brandeis University Program in the Economics and Politics of Aging.

attitudes, voting, party identification, elite political behavior, and systemic policy responses. In most of these studies, age has been treated rather cursorily as one of many variables and rarely has it been interpreted with appropriate care. Consequently, before considering the variety of evidence available on the politics of aging individuals, it will be useful to consider briefly the interpretive perspectives that one should have in mind.

Issues of Interpretation

Interpreting the political attitudes and behavior of aging persons involves an intriguing interplay among three analytically distinct perspectives—processes of aging through the life cycle; characteristics of different age cohorts; and the effects of historical periods upon all individuals and cohorts. Since these perspectives are discussed in greater detail elsewhere in this volume, it is only necessary here to identify them briefly in a political context.

First, one must consider whether the political attitudes and behavior of older persons, observed longitudinally, can be explained by developmental patterns—physiological, psychological, social, and economic—intrinsic to the processes of aging in the human life cycle. To the extent that some persons may be found to reduce their active participation in political life as they grow older, the changes may be interpreted in terms of physical declines and patterns of social isolation associated with older ages. Were aging found to be associated with increasingly liberal views on economic issues, one might hypothesize that this attitudinal change could be explained by the severe reductions in income that many persons experience when they retire. Conversely, maintained levels of participation and stability of political views might be interpreted in terms of the persistence of certain behavioral and attitudinal characteristics through the life cycle.

Second, the age cohort to which older persons belong must be taken into account when interpreting their political activities and behavior. Data on persons who are old at the time of measurement may reveal more about the shared experiences and perceptions of that particular older generation—exposure at approximately the same age and time to common patterns of schooling, family life, economic cycles, wars, and political events—than about anything intrinsic to the processes of aging. Some older persons have lived their entire lives within stable political systems; others have seen their political regimes undergo total transformation during their politically formative years. In many countries considerable proportions of the electorate, particularly women, were not enfranchised until they were well into middle or later life. Cohort interpretations look to these exposures to outside events, and emphasize the possibility that a particular age cohort may perceive and internalize these experiences differently from those cohorts that precede and follow them. It is in this sense that many scholars as well as journalists term those persons who entered the polity in the 1930's as "The Depression Generation."

A third perspective emphasizes the homogenizing effect of "environmental changes which simultaneously alter attitudes [or behavior] of all or most individuals . . . ." (Searing, Wright, and Rabinowitz, 1975). By looking at historical or period effects on an entire population over several decades one can provide a larger context for examining life-cycle and cohort interpretations of older persons' political attitudes and

behavior. If persons seem to become more conservative as they grow old, this may be explained by data that show that the total population (all age groups) has become more conservative in parallel fashion over the decades examined. Or, if a particular older age cohort is found to be liberal in its outlook, one may find that all cohorts are displaying parallel trends toward liberalism.

Analysis of older persons' political attitudes and behavior has reached a stage of sophistication in which the importance of these different interpretive perspectives has been recognized. But appropriate use of these perspectives has been too recent to have yielded unequivocal generalizations about the effects of aging as a variable. Nonetheless, some promising generalizations can be drawn. The next two subsections will review the data available on age as a variable in political attitudes and behavior. Then the generalizations that can be drawn from these data will be considered in the light of the complexities outlined above.

Political Orientations and Issue Beliefs of Older Persons

Analyses of political orientations and attitudes can legitimately focus on a number of variables, including among others: ideologies; attachments and loyalties to political parties and other institutions; perceptions, affect, and evaluations directed toward political objects (Easton and Dennis, 1969); and personality type (McClosky, 1967). Political scientists have not yet developed a single recognized model for clearly delineating and functionally integrating such variables. Consequently, it seems advisable here to adopt the approach of Searing, Schwartz, and Lind (1973) by positing for discussion purposes a continuum by level of generality. Considered at the more general end of the continuum will be *orientations*, including ideological dispositions and attachments to political institutions. At the more specific end will be attitudes or views on *specific issues* expressed in response to operational political propositions.

A substantial majority of studies examining political orientations and issue beliefs as they relate to aging address the issue of whether older persons tend to be conservative in outlook. Yet the term conservative is extremely ambiguous. Substantively, it may connote a pessimistic view of the nature of man, or a natural ordering of society, or a preference for a particular social and economic hierarchy, or a fear of activist government. Temporally, it may connote an attachment to things past or simply an aversion to change.

While this overview of the literature cannot report on concepts of conservatism that were not clearly delineated in studies that have already been executed, it is possible to consider separately the substantive and temporal aspects of conservatism. Accordingly, the first part of this subsection will deal with the content of political orientations and the second part with the stability of orientations over time. A third part will consider specific issue beliefs of older persons and the extent to which they do or do not flow from more general orientations.

The Content of Orientations. The comparatively few studies that examine directly the basic political orientations of the aging indicate—if one puts aside questions of causality, variations in attitude on specific issues, and degrees of differentiation between older persons and the remainder of the population—greater conservatism among older people than among younger groups. Glenn (1974, p. 181), perhaps the foremost student of the question, states that "the preponderance of evidence from some contemporary Western societies shows that in any point in time older people as a whole are more conservative than young adults." Free and Cantril (1968) find a grouping age 50 and above somewhat more conservative than younger groups in responding to both "ideological" and "operational" versions of the same propositions. Both Lipset (1959) and Campbell (1962) note the tendency of older persons to disproportionately defend traditional social values.

Considerable additional evidence can be marshalled pointing to the relative conservatism of older persons, if one is willing to assume that preference for a "conservative" party is a true indication of conservatism and that voting behavior is an accurate manifestation of a set of underlying attitudes. Campbell, Converse, Miller, and Stokes (1960) record older age groups as having greater identification with the Republican party than younger groups; Crittenden (1962) finds the same relationship; and Riley and Foner's (1968) survey of the literature concurs.

Linkage between conservative party identification and advanced age is not confined to the United States. Lipset (1959) reports similar findings for Germany, Sweden, Italy, and France. In Great Britain, Rose (1964), McKenzie and Silver (1968), and Butler and Stokes (1971) cite older persons' disproportionate support of the Conservative party. Edinger (1970) finds a positive relationship between older age and votes for the Christian Democratic party in West Germany continuing through the 1969 election. Ehrmann (1968) reports that data from *Sondages* polls yield a positive linear relationship between age and intentions to vote for DeGaulle rather than the Socialist Mitterand in the 1965 French presidential election. *Sondages* polls also indicate that DeGaulle's party received disproportionate support from the more conservative elements of French society—meaning women, the well-to-do, and those who are old and religious (Lipset, 1959). Watanuki (1967) reports clear support by older persons for the Japanese Liberal Democratic (conservative) party.

More recent studies provide some interpretive dimension to these cross-sectional findings. Abramson (1974) finds that the historical relationship between partisan choice and social class in the United States has weakened during the post–World War II years. He attributes this change to cohort rather than to life-cycle effects, finding a continuing decline in class-based partisanship among successive cohorts entering the electorate after World War II. A parallel study (Abramson, 1971), using Western European data, also supports the cohort interpretation, although the findings reported reveal a less consistent decline in relationships between social class and partisanship.

Inglehart (1971) also employs a cohort interpretation in discussing data that show greater attachment among older cohorts than among younger ones to moderately conservative ideological orientations. Using only cross-sectional data, he finds that younger cohorts in six European countries are consistently less "acquisitive" (posited as a conservative value) than older ones, a relationship that holds even when education and socioeconomic status are controlled. He argues that the affluence of the modern era, by affecting the younger cohorts during a formative period, is largely responsible for the differences.

One further study adding an interpretive perspective to the relations between old age and conservative orientations is McKenzie and Silver's (1968) analysis of "working-class Tories" in Britain, suggesting the ways in which cohort effects can influence findings of old-age preference for conservatism. When they examined a sample of working-class voters whom they identified as "deferentials," they found a strong relationship between older age and Conservative party voting. Noting that deference is an orientation that does not develop at older ages, but rather is internalized at some early point in life, the authors underline the "traditional preindustrial" values to which some contemporary older persons have been socialized.

The Stability of Orientations. Considerable evidence exists that older persons tend to retain political orientations they have developed earlier in life. These orientations may have been regarded by society as liberal in the era when a person first developed them; but if subsequent generations have "new" orientations—in whatever direction—the retained orientations of earlier generations inevitably reflect "old" ideas. To the extent that this is the case, older persons will be a conservatizing or a temporally conservative element in the political system.

Much evidence on this temporal aspect of conservatism can be found in studies of party identification and voting patterns (insofar as they can be interpreted to reflect orientation). Campbell et al. (1960) report a number of American findings. Stability and strength of party identification increases with age; older persons are the least likely to consider themselves "independents" and are the least likely to engage in split ticket voting. However, when the relationships between age, party identification, and duration of attachment are sorted out, age is shown to be only an indirect cause. Attachments of longer duration, which are in turn highly correlated with age, seem the principal indicators of continuing stability.

Parallel findings have been observed in Great Britain by Butler and Stokes (1971) who show that strength of partisan self-image increases monotonically from age groupings in the 20's through to the 80's. They also find a marked consistency in party voting over time, concluding that "with the aging of the voter the relatively plastic attitudes of youth tend to harden and the acquired habits of the early voting years begin to become more deeply fixed" (Butler and Stokes, 1971, p. 40).

The importance of the duration of an attachment can be understood by noting the independent role of the political party in orienting its followers to the political world. "Once a person has acquired some embryonic party attachment, it is easy for him to discover that most events in the ambiguous world of politics redound to the credit of his chosen party" (Campbell et al., 1960, p. 165). Butler and Stokes (1971) argue that the voter's experience over a series of campaigns can be regarded as a kind of "learning" in which the rewards of increased clarity and

TABLE 1. STRENGTH OF PARTISAN SELF-IMAGE BY AGE.

Age range	20	21–24	25–30	31–40	41–50	51–60	61–70	71–80	80+
Percent describing selves as 'very' or 'fairly strongly' attached to party	47	58	62	65	73	74	73	76	88

SOURCE: Butler, D., and Stokes, D. 1971. *Political Change in Britain*, p. 40. New York: St. Martin's Press, and by permission of Macmillan London and Basinstoke.

simplicity reinforce the party ties that supply them. Converse (1964) notes that the stability of party identification over time is extraordinarily higher than stability for any given issue position.

Despite this evidence on the relative stability of older persons' attachments, one cannot conclude that older persons do not change their orientations. Studies showing the relative stability of older persons' attachments also indicate that they can and will change. Glenn and Hefner (1972) found that there is no apparent tendency for cohorts to become more resistant to influences for change as they grow older, although changes may be somewhat delayed in comparison with younger cohorts. Searing, Wright, and Rabinowitz (1975) find that the "primacy principle"—that basic political orientations are learned in childhood and are relatively enduring throughout the adult years—is fundamentally sound, but argue that it has been overstated in the literature on childhood political socialization.

Specific Issue Beliefs. There is considerable support for the proposition that persons of all ages have more loosely structured attitudes on specific issues—or at least attitudes subject to greater change—than on basic political attachments and orientations. There is little evidence to suggest that older persons vary from the larger population in relation to either (a) the overall structuring of their issue beliefs or (b) greater variability regarding specific issues.

In a study comparing attitudes of two metropolitan mass populations, for example, Prothro and Grigg (1960) found broad consensus on major principles of democratic life (democracy itself, majority rule, minority rights), but on a series of questions tapping these same beliefs in specific operational form, the consensus broke down sharply. Older people were no more likely than younger people to express specific operational beliefs contradicting their general principles.

Similarly, Free and Cantril (1968) discovered wide variation between the "ideological" and the "operational" dispositions of the American populace, finding that respondents in their sample simultaneously supported conservative ideological statements and liberal operational ones.

While older persons (50 years and over) in their sample were marginally more conservative on all responses, they showed the same tendency as the total sample in expressing contradictory ideological and operational views.

Foner (1972), while taking the position that each age cohort becomes more conservative ideologically as it grows older, suggests that older persons can become more liberal on specific issues in line with general political trends in a society. Her argument can be supported by studies in which older persons displayed favorable attitudes toward labor unions (Evan, 1965) and toward the admission of the Peoples Republic of China to the United Nations (Glenn, 1974).

Douglass, Cleveland, and Maddox (1974) provide a slightly different explanation for seeming inconsistencies in the ways that persons respond to ideological principles and specific issues that operationalize such principles. They suggest that age may account for views on specific issues in accordance with the degree to which the issue is perceived to have direct and immediate relevance to a respondent. While their study implies one explanation for why specific issue responses may often contradict expressions of basic political attachments, they do not indicate that older persons are either more or less likely than younger persons to have specific issue beliefs that contradict their views on more general principles.

While older persons are similar to persons of all ages in their tendency to contradict their basic orientations when responding to specific issues, there are data to indicate that aging persons respond somewhat differently than younger people to certain specific issues. The data available analyzing older persons' responses to issues do not, however, comprise a structured, systematic overview. The current literature only provides findings from isolated studies.

A few studies conducted since the mid-1950's suggest that contemporary older persons may not be as tolerant and permissive as younger ones on selected issues involving civil rights and civil liberties. On government civil rights intervention in general (Campbell, 1971), and on school integration (Killian and Haer, 1958) and housing integration (Hunt, 1960), older persons have been reported as comparatively resistant.

On issues of "law and order" intervention, however, older persons tend to be somewhat more in favor of an activist governmental posture (Campbell, 1971, and Glamser, 1974). In an earlier study, Stouffer (1955) found less toleration among older people on issues of communism and civil liberties.

On other issues, older persons seem generally less in favor of governmental intervention than do younger groups. In matters of foreign policy, the predominant attitudes of older persons have been rather consistently opposed to overseas involvement, even though what was once called "isolationist" has since become "dovish" and what was once "conservative" has now become "liberal" (Campbell, 1971). On specific issues regarding government's domestic role, some studies have shown older persons to be relatively less favorable toward government ownership and collectivism (Riley and Foner, 1968) and central planning of the national economy (Allardt and Pesonen, 1967).

On some specific issues that can be interpreted as directly affecting the aging, older persons show distinct signs of supporting old age interests, but the significance of this is limited since younger people can sometimes be found to support the same matters in equal or greater proportions. Campbell reported that persons age 65 and above are considerably more in favor of "help[ing] people get doctors and hospital care at low cost" than younger groups (1971, p. 114) but reported few differences by age in views on greater governmental responsibility for full employment and for a minimum standard of living. Allardt and Pesonen (1967) found 70 percent of Finnish Conservative respondents 50 years and older favoring state aid to help the sick; but they also found younger conservatives to favor it even more. Similarly, while Butler and Stokes (1971) found older persons most heavily in favor of increased pension benefits, they found very considerable support for the entire range of British social service programs in their sample generally. On education issues, some studies show older persons to be less in favor of public expenditures (Campbell, 1971, and Clemente, 1975) from which they would seem to have the least to gain. Although there are frequent observations

that older persons have disproportionately opposed school expenditures in local referenda, the accuracy of these reports remains in question because of methodological and inferential difficulties.

Political Interest and Participation of the Aging

In both their degree of expressed interest in political questions and in formal expression of that interest, older persons are relatively active. Many forms of political participation do not decline in old age. And, even though some cross-sectional data indicate that older persons are less active politically than younger ones, a number of studies shows lower levels of political activity to be more a function of female sex and low education than of age. The aged are less involved in the more active forms of participation, but it seems quite certain this results more from physical infirmity and lack of mobility rather than from any significant falling off in interest about political matters.

Older persons are, however, highly represented in the most active of all political roles—incumbency of political office. While such incumbency is most frequently a continuation of roles assumed earlier in life, major offices in most societies are, nonetheless, held by older persons. Literature suggesting the larger consequences of incumbency of office by older persons is reviewed toward the end of this section.

Political Interest. Considerable evidence exists pointing to relatively high interest in political matters on the part of old people. There is a roughly linear relationship between age and political interest, although the greatest increases come more during the transition from youth to middle age than from middle age into old age. Milbrath (1965, p. 46), in citing findings from the early studies by Lazarsfeld, Berelson, and Gaudet (1944), and Berelson, Lazarsfeld, and McPhee (1954), states that "persons of middle age, presumably with greater understanding of politics, expose themselves to more stimuli about politics than persons of young ages do." Riley and Foner's (1968) inventory concludes that the political interest reached at maturity holds into old age, and Berelson, Lazarsfeld,

TABLE 2. PERCENTAGE OF WHITE PERSONS REPORTING A GREAT DEAL OF INTEREST IN POLITICS, BY AGE, SEX, AND EDUCATION.

Years of school completed	AGES		
	21–39	40–59	60 and up
Males			
8	18.2 (33)	15.2 (112)	26.8 (97)
9–11	20.8 (72)	21.2 (99)	31.1 (45)
12	23.1 (173)	26.6 (139)	28.6 (42)
All education levels	27.4 (456)	24.9 (502)	29.5 (298)
Females			
8	5.3 (38)	14.4 (111)	21.2 (104)
9–11	18.5 (130)	21.1 (90)	26.2 (42)
12	16.1 (192)	25.5 (165)	48.2 (56)
All education levels	19.0 (496)	22.7 (520)	34.5 (330)

The sample is inflated by about 100 percent by a weighting procedure used to increase representativeness. Therefore, the reported N's (in parentheses) are about twice the number of respondents represented. The data are from Gallup survey 637 (1960). SOURCE: Glenn, N., and Grimes, M. 1968. Aging, Voting and Political Interest. *American Sociological Review*, v. 33, p. 570.

and McPhee (1954) report higher interest among older persons. Early media studies by Schramm and White (1954) found that, with age, there was a notable increase in reading public affairs news and editorials and a decline in reading sports news and the comic pages.

The most detailed evidence focusing on the relationship between political interest and age are found in Glenn and Grimes (1968) and Glenn (1969). Controlling for sex and education, Glenn and Grimes find a positive monotonic relationship between age and reported political interest. "The highest reported interest is consistently at age 60 and higher, and the difference between the middle-aged and the elderly is pronounced at most educational levels for both sexes" (Glenn and Grimes, 1968, p. 570). While the authors take considerable pains to note the limitations on generalizing their findings to other age cohorts or to other countries, they conclude that their evidence is very convincing that average political interest has increased from young adulthood to old age among their United States samples. In his article on opinionation, Glenn (1969) concludes that

there is no evidence that older persons become either less interested in national or international affairs or that old people become less likely to express their opinions to interviewers. And, when controlling for education, there is no appreciable variation by age in interest or opinionation. His analysis of 35 different longitudinal and cross-sectional surveys also suggests that the aging take greater interest in current public figures than do younger counterparts with similar education. If, as some have suggested, older persons "disengage" from society, a variety of data indicates that such disengagement is not manifested in reduced amounts of political interest or opinion.

Voting. Evidence regarding age and voting also shows a positive linear relationship, at least up until the beginnings of old age. Moreover, where selected controls are introduced, the fall-off attributed to old age largely disappears.

Numerous cross-sectional studies have shown that voting participation increases with age, peaks shortly after age 60, and then falls off, but never back to the lower levels of the 20's and early 30's. Tingsten's (1937) early work reported this finding in Europe; the inventory of Milbrath (1965) and data reported by Crittenden (1963), Glenn and Grimes (1968), and Verba and Nie (1972) all document this pattern for the United States. Nie, Verba, and Kim's (1974) recent cross-national study finds the same bell-shaped relationship in the United States, Austria, India, Japan, and Nigeria.

Where appropriate controls have been introduced, however, there is equally general agreement that the fall-off in voting participation by older persons is probably not attributable to their age, but rather to other characteristics. Cross-sectional studies consistently show women voting less than men at virtually all educational, income, and age levels (United States Bureau of the Census, 1965; Campbell et al., 1960; Foner, 1972), and that this occurs cross-nationally (Nie, Verba, and Kim, 1974). Due to the higher mortality rate among men, older populations are disproportionately female; consequently, the fall-off in voting participation by older persons can be traced in part to the general tendency of women to vote less (Glenn and Grimes, 1968). Similarly, because contemporary older populations have consistently possessed less formal education than younger groups, some of the lower voting rate attributed to older persons may well result from less education than from greater age. Data reported by Glenn and Grimes (1968), U.S. Bureau of the Census (1965), Verba and Nie (1972), and Nie, Verba, and Kim (1974) all show controls for education reducing the drop-off in voting among older persons. Verba and Nie (1972), Nie, Verba, and Kim (1974), and Maddox (1974) also report that length or stability of residency lessens the effect of age on voter turnout.

When these controlling variables are applied simultaneously, the fall-off in voting frequency attributed to older age is reduced still further. Glenn and Grimes (1968) report that the moderate decrease reported after the 50's is either reversed or eliminated for persons from their 50's up to age 80 when controls are introduced for both sex and education. Verba and Nic (1972) find that when controlling for socioeconomic status and length of residency, there is no decline for even the oldest group.

Participation beyond Voting. Voting is an infrequent and essentially passive form of political participation. A person who decides to vote simply chooses among a very limited number of predetermined alternatives, an act of limited impact with largely unknown consequences. Beyond voting, there is a variety of more active forms of participation. Milbrath (1965) lists 14 formal alternatives, divided into "spectator," "transitional," and "gladiatorial" activities. Verba and Nie (1972) create an overall participation index based on four factor scales of participation—voting, communal activity, campaign activity, and making personal contacts.

The relative frequency with which older persons, compared to younger ones, engage in these more active forms of participation is largely parallel to that found for voting. And, as is the case with voting, when controls for education, sex, residency, and overall socioeconomic status are introduced, the role assigned to age as a variable in explaining the lower participation among older persons declines markedly. Among the different types of participation, data show the aging to engage actively in the more moderate forms of participation while being underrepresented in the more intensive ones.

While there are cross-sectional data reported in Campbell (1971) and Lane (1965) suggesting that the aging tend to be somewhat underrepresented on various forms of participation, by far the most thorough investigations are to be found in the works of Verba and Nie (1972) and Nie, Verba, and Kim (1974). Using a combined measure of participation, Verba and Nie find (a) that older persons' participation is higher than the population average; (b) that correction for socioeconomic status results in yet higher participation scores for older persons; and (c) that this same correction moves

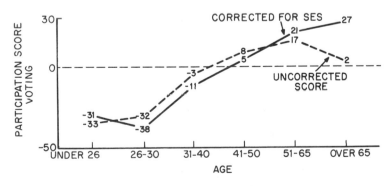

Figure 1. Life cycle and voting: corrected for socioeconomic status. (From Fig. 9-3 "Life Cycle and Participation: Corrected for Socioeconomic Status" (p. 141) in *Participation in America: Political Democracy and Social Equality* by Sidney Verba and Norman H. Nie (Harper & Row, 1972).)

the peak period of activity from the 40's into the 50's. The authors conclude that, while there remains some fall-off in overall participation after 66, "[w]hat was originally a pattern of steady increase throughout the life cycle followed by a sharp decline in later years [before correction for both socioeconomic status, including education, and length of residency] becomes a somewhat more gradual increase in participation . . . ." (Verba and Nie, 1972, p. 148).

In addition to devising this overall participation score for different age groupings, Verba and Nie also create "clusters" of participant types and then determine the distribution of different social categories among each of the types. The six types are: inactives (those engaging in no political activities); voting specialists (those voting quite regularly, but engaging in no other forms of participation); parochial participants (those contacting at least one public official and voting with average frequency); communalists (those working actively with others in community problem-solving organizations and voting with considerable frequency); campaigners (those working actively around elections—persuading others how to vote, working for a party or candidate, attending meetings, and contributing money); and complete activists (those highly involved in each of the preceding activities except for contacting public officials). When the clusterings of individuals among these six participation types are broken down by age, those 65+ are shown to be: slightly overrepresented on the inactive index, highly overrepresented on the voting index, slightly overrepresented as parochial participants, moderately underrepresented as communalists, moderately underrepresented as campaigners, and highly underrepresented as complete activists. Older persons thus distribute heavily on the moderate forms of participation, becoming increasingly underrepresented on the more intensive forms.

The intriguing cross-national data reported by Nie, Verba, and Kim (1974) can only be given cursory treatment here. Most notable is their finding of largely parallel patterns of participation through the life cycle, cross-nationally. With only minor variations, they find (a) participation rising through the early years, peaking in middle age, and falling in later life; (b) this holding for both men and women; and (c) men consistently participating more than women. With education controlled, the activity scores for the oldest age groups are higher in each of the countries except Japan, and the downturn in participation is either substantially reduced (United States and Nigeria) or eliminated altogether (India). They also control for retirement and find that in each of three countries—India, Japan, and the United States—those persons who are still active in the work force participate more in politics than those who are not. Finally, Nie, Verba, and Kim compare voting to overall participation and find that, while the age trends for the two are largely parallel, the following differences emerge: (a) younger adults increase their participation in voting more rapidly than in other activities; (b) the decline in voting in the later years is less steep than for other activities; and (c) the higher male rate of participation is more pronounced in other political actions than it is in voting.

These studies indicating high levels of participation by middle-aged and older persons in a variety of political activities beyond voting have led Neugarten (1974) to speculate regarding the political implications of trends toward retirement at earlier ages than 65 years old. In discussing "the rise of the young-old"—that is, the age group 55 to 75, who constitute 15 percent of the population—she points up that they are relatively healthy, less tied to traditional work and family responsibilities, and increasingly well educated. These characteristics of the group, together with its high level of political activity, bring Neugarten to argue that the young-old have enormous potential as agents of social change. Whether that potential is indeed likely to be realized can be evaluated best in the light of the generalizations one can draw about the impact of older persons' political attitudes and behavior, considered below.

Aging and Political Leadership. Persons in late middle age and early old age, as widely believed, disproportionately occupy positions of leadership in most industrialized societies, although in the wake of revolutionary change, leadership tends to be younger. Moreover, a positive relationship between older ages and the importance of leadership positions continues well into old age. It is not entirely clear from the existing data that older leaders are more conservative than younger ones, although some evidence indicates that members of political elites may become more conservative over time.

Incumbency of Leadership Positions. The proposition that political leadership positions are held by relatively old persons is confirmed by a great deal of evidence. Lehman's (1953) data show this general pattern for a variety of political contexts—American presidential candidates, members of the British cabinet, "chief ministers" in early England, American ambassadors and Supreme Court justices, and cabinet members. Schlesinger's study, *Ambition and Politics* (1966), correlates importance of the office (House, Governor, Senate, President) with the age at which it was first attained.

In addition, it seems that the older an incumbent may be, the higher the office that he or she is likely to hold. In American state governments, Schlesinger (1966, p. 192), finds "the age timetable parallels the office hierarchy showing a progressive rise in the typical age at

which office is achieved," and "the age focus is sharper the higher the office." Reporting on legislative data from five countries, Schlesinger (1967) presents a roughly similar cross-national pattern of age and political leadership in which upwards of 50 percent of legislators have attained middle age by the time of their first election to national assemblies. Not surprisingly, the average age of first attaining cabinet status is higher than the age of first election, supporting the notion of a positive relationship between age and achievement.

In a study of Congressional candidates in the 1958 elections to the House of Representatives, Walker (1960) tentatively concludes that older candidates are nominated (1) when a "dominant" party is reasonably sure of success, and when the candidate is an incumbent; and (2) when a local, nonincumbent party is weak and feels a nearly sure sense of impending defeat. Younger candidates are selected (1) by the nonincumbent party "in almost any variety of two-party situations where there is at least an outside chance of success and a determination to wage an aggressive campaign" (Walker, 1960, p. 25), and (2) where a district has been disturbed by serious economic dislocations and has a recent record of marginal or shifting vote patterns. Fishel (1969) provides additional

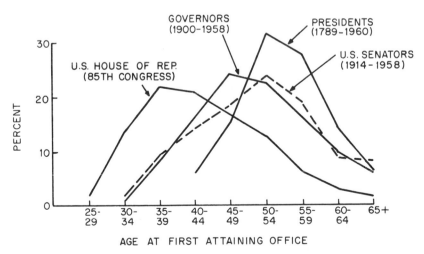

Figure 2. Age and achievement of major office in the United States. (From Joseph A. Schlesinger, *Ambition and Politics: Political Careers in the United States*, © 1966 by Rand McNally & Company, Chicago, Figure IX-1, p. 175. Reprinted by permission of Rand McNally College Publishing Company.)

evidence that candidacy opposition to incumbents comes predominantly from younger challengers.

Ideological Orientations of Older Incumbents. Evidence on whether older members of political elites tend to be conservative and whether individuals become more conservative as they age while in office is inconclusive. Lehman (1953, p. 283) suggests a conservative bias in older elites by contending that "elderly leaders are more likely to be chosen by groups long established, firmly entrenched, and relatively complacent or satisfied with the status quo." And Schlesinger (1966) suggests that younger candidates are more flexible than older ones because of career ambition considerations. Fishel (1969), however, does not find that younger challenging candidates are necessarily more liberal than older ones. In responses to questions on the domestic economy, civil rights, and foreign policy, candidates under 40 of both major parties who were nominated for the first time proved to be more conservative than older candidates. This finding held when controlled for the urbanization of candidate's districts. Eisele (1972), in a study of trends in voting (conservative-liberal) among "careerist Senators" (reelected two or more times), found a net increase in liberal voting in his sample over the period 1947-1970. The net result was accounted for by liberal votes of new entry cohorts; in fact, many careerists increased the frequency of their conservative votes in their later terms.

Putnam's (1971) study of legislators in Great Britain and Italy addresses itself explicitly to two different meanings of ideology. He finds that, while older legislators do not differ markedly from their younger counterparts in viewing politics through a coherent set of beliefs ("ideological style"), they do exhibit greater "interparty hostility" than do younger legislators. The causal elements regarding the age relationships in Putnam's findings are not definite (he emphasizes cohort over life-cycle effects), but his evidence does indicate that in the face of considerable lessening of inter-party ideological divisions in the last half century, older legislators have tended to retain the hostility those earlier divisions produced whereas the younger legislators have not assumed the same posture. Thus, in Great Britain: "For the older Tories, the Labour party remains, as it has always been for them a slightly sinister intruder. Their younger colleagues, by contrast, entered a political world in which Labour was simply 'the other side'" (Putnam, 1971, p. 676).

Macropolitical Change and Older Incumbents. Students of social change and revolution have given a good deal of attention to relations between the stability of political systems and elite age patterns and the duration of incumbencies. The sense of much of this literature is stated by North and Pool (1966, p. 383): "It is only in times of revolutionary change . . . that one finds an elite whose average age is in the thirties or early forties."

North and Pool document the relatively young ages of both Kuomintang and Chinese Communist elites starting with the 1920's and observe that even by 1945 none of the Kuomintang Central Executive Committees had an average age membership above 45. Even as Chinese elites have aged while holding power, the Soviet Politburo has been marked by a great "aging" process since the time of the 1917 Revolution to more modern times; the average age has been continually increasing since 1917, with only three exceptions (Schueller, 1966). Rigby (1972), Lewytzkyi (1967), and Blackwell (1974) note the aging of Politburo members and the resistance of these early members to recruitment of younger generations into Soviet leadership, one obvious explanation being their concern with self-preservation.

Modern Germany may represent the clearest case of aging and generations linked to questions of regime stability and change. In the study of the Nazi elite, Lerner, Pool, and Schueller (1966) find that relative youth is associated with centrality of revolutionary role. Party propagandists—the captains of persuasion who "spearheaded" the movement—were the youngest of all leaders; Nazi administrators were somewhat older, and the average age of all Nazi members older yet. In contrast, the postwar leadership in West Germany has been relatively old. Whereas the average age of the Nazi elite was under 50, 61 percent of the post-war West German political elite was over 50, and 27 percent over 60 years of age (Edinger, 1968).

Generalizations and Interpretations

Given the evidence available, can one draw generalizations about patterns of political attitudes and behavior among aging persons? In the aggregate, contemporary older persons are somewhat more conservative than younger persons in the content of their basic political orientations. However, to the extent that the mean orientation of today's older persons is comparatively conservative, it reflects a general tendency of all people to retain their orientations as they age throughout the life cycle, or at least to change them more slowly as they grow older. In effect, the aggregate conservatism of contemporary older persons is properly understood in the relative sense that their liberalization has not kept pace with changes in the total population (Glenn, 1974). Consequently, the relative conservatism of today's aging may be a transitory phenomenon. Indeed, if societies enter long periods of political stability, the tendency of age cohorts to retain their basic orientations as they grow older could bring about a future situation, as Lipset speculates (1959), in which older age groups will have political orientations to the left of younger groups. Some indication that this might be occurring already is provided by data from the 1972 U. S. Presidential election showing that the proportion of votes for McGovern was slightly less among 32 to 49 year olds than among persons 50 and older (Cantor, 1975).

While political orientations remain fairly stable throughout life, people of all ages will sometimes contradict their basic attachments and ideological outlooks when expressing their beliefs on specific operational issues. Accordingly, older persons tend to support specific propositions that can have immediate and direct impacts on their presumed aggregate interests, even if these specific views may contradict the more basic political orientations they have maintained.

A rather consistent pattern emerges from examinations of older persons' political interest and participation. When age is isolated as a variable, by controlling for sex and education, interest in politics increases with age and never diminishes. Voting participation increases until about age 60 and then falls off somewhat; but even this fall-off is largely attributable to other characteristics than aging. In more active forms of political participation, aged persons are involved nearly as much as all adults, except in such activities as working to form groups to deal with general local problems and taking active roles in such organizations.

Persons of older ages are overrepresented in positions of political leadership, except in the wake of revolutionary change. While longer-term incumbents of leadership positions tend to be more conservatively disposed than new leaders, it is not clear from the evidence that this contrast can be attributed to aging.

To the extent that one can isolate aging as a variable associated with distinctive patterns of political attitudes and behavior, how are such patterns properly explained? As indicated at the outset, three types of interpretive perspectives can and should be employed in explanatory attempts: the processes of aging through the life cycle; the characteristics of different age cohorts; and the effects of historical periods upon all individuals and cohorts. However, the efforts of scholars to analyze age as a variable in political attitudes and behavior have not revealed a clear, single formula for the use of these perspectives in establishing the presence or absence of causal relations.

The life-cycle interpretation was emphasized by Crittenden (1962) in a study of the relations between aging and identification with the Republican party. Cutler (1969), however, employed a cohort perspective in reanalyzing Crittenden's data and found that cohort phenomena were at least as and, perhaps, more important than life-cycle changes in explaining the tendency of older persons to favor Republicanism. Glenn and Hefner (1972) confirmed Cutler's findings by introducing more refined techniques while analyzing new data and brought out the importance of period effects by revealing the distortions that could take place due to limitations on the time frames used for observation. Searing, Wright, and Rabinowitz (1975) cast further doubt on the independent salience of cohort explanations. They find considerable instability within particular age cohorts and show that patterns displayed by "political generations" may lose their distinctiveness. For instance, they find that by 1968 even the so-called Depression Generation was no more Democratic in identification than the rest of the electorate. While finding that life-cycle processes of aging have some salience, they emphasize the contextual influence of historical periods in reducing the importance of age as a distinctive variable in explaining political attitudes. As a consequence of the work of these various scholars, it currently appears that all three perspectives—life cycle, cohort, and period—must be utilized for proper analyses (Cutler and Bengtson, 1974). But the ways in which they interact are yet to be precisely delineated.

Regardless of the explanations for patterns of political attitudes and behavior that can be identified among the aging, what consequences, if any, do these patterns have for political systems? The aggregate tendency of older persons to be somewhat more conservative in basic orientations than the total population undoubtedly has some marginal "conservatizing" effect on political systems. To the extent that basic orientations may be said to influence political decisions, the aging may provide somewhat more support for stability and continuity than do their fellow citizens.

Although there is some evidence to indicate that older persons' views on specific issues will be influenced if their presumed interests seem immediately and directly affected, it is not clear that a voting bloc can be organized around old-age interests. As Campbell (1971) has noted, the political differences within age groups are far more impressive than the differences between age groups. No evidence has been assembled to show an instance in which an "old-age interest" or an "old-age candidate" can be presumed to have shifted older persons' votes in a concerted bloc. And, in fact, it would be very difficult to document such a phenomenon because of problems in disaggregating

election returns and inferential difficulties in interpreting the motivations that underlie votes. Some of the inferential difficulties can be reduced in research on referendum propositions that seem to have immediate and direct consequences for aging voters (although the problem of disaggregating returns by age still remains).

To the extent that valid studies have shed light on this issue, they have not shown the existence of an "aging vote." However, given current demographic trends indicating substantial increases in the numbers and proportion of older persons in many nations (see Chapter 3), the possibility of concerted voting behavior in response to "old-age interests" will undoubtedly remain of interest to researchers.

THE POLITICS OF AGING-BASED ORGANIZATIONS

Although the political activities of most organizations have some implications for older persons and processes of human aging, this section is focused on the politics of a particular set of organizations that can be termed *aging-based*. (The political activities of other, differently-based organizations and institutions as they are relevant to aging will be treated in the final section of this chapter; discussions of relations between aging and organizations, not involving societal politics, can be found in other chapters of this volume.)

An aging-based organization is one that depends in large measure for its activities upon the existence of older persons: as membership for the organization (e.g., in Great Britain, the National Federation of Old Age Pensioners Association); as consumers of the organization's goods and services or those offered by its members (e.g., American Nursing Home Association); as clients for the practitioners who belong to the organization (e.g., Associazione Medici Geriatri Italiani); or as subjects for study by researchers and educators who comprise the organization's membership (e.g., Société Française de Gerontologie). Such organizations have often been termed "interest groups" or "pressure groups" in the literature but are not so termed here because to do so would imply from the outset the choice of a particular theoretical perspective for interpreting the political significance of these organizations, a choice which is not necessarily warranted.

In analyzing the politics of aging-based organizations there are two central issues. First, are the political activities of aging-based organizations and their political significance different from other organizations active in politics? Second, does or can the political behavior of these organizations make a difference in the situation of aging persons—that is, do or can the organizations exercise power to benefit older persons? To shed light on these issues one must consider: reasons why such organizations develop; the internal features of organizational life that characterize leadership-membership relations and which may shape external political behavior; the types and effectiveness of external political activities; and whether the existence of such organizations is likely to have major consequences for the nature of a political system.

The literature that addresses these issues can be grouped into two general categories. One category consists of detailed analyses focused directly on the origins and developments of such organizations, their internal features, and their external political activities. The other category is peripheral literature, in that it consists of little more than assertions about the power of these organizations, assertions which are made in the context of: more general works on the politics of organizations; case-history analyses of the evolution and implementation of public policies; and speculative essays on aging-based organizations.

While both categories of literature have something to say about the power of aging-based organizations, the observations based on the direct studies are more equivocal than those in the peripheral literature. The reasons for equivocation in the direct studies can best be understood once the problems with the unequivocal statements in the peripheral literature are examined. Consequently, the first part of this section will review the direct, detailed studies of aging-based organizations, and identify priority areas for further research.

A second part will critically examine assertions about power in the peripheral literature, outline the problems involved in measuring power, and consider what properly can and has been done to identify the limits of power through direct studies of aging-based organizations.

Origins, Internal Characteristics, and Political Activities

Although there has been a considerable amount of writing in which the politics of aging-based organizations have been alluded to, scholarly research devoted directly to the topic has been sparse and appears to have been confined to the American scene.

Riley and Foner (1968) concluded from their inventory of the literature that "little evidence has been brought to bear . . . apart from descriptions . . . of the scattered political movements centering upon old age" (p. 478). The direct sources then available dealt largely with organizations which had already passed from the scene or had ceased vigorous political activity: the Railroad Employees Pension Association of the early 1930's (Polner, 1962); the Townsend Movement of the 1930's and 40's (Messinger, 1955; and Holtzman, 1963); and the McLain organization in California politics of the 1940's and 50's (Pinner, Jacobs, and Selznick, 1959).

Since then, Putnam's (1970) general history of old age politics in California has provided updated information on the remnants of the McLain organization, and additional works have focused directly on the politics of newer, contemporary aging-based organizations. Pratt (1974, 1976), and Binstock (1972, 1974) have dealt with several membership organizations active in American national politics and with a variety of customer, client, and research organizations, as well. And Henretta (1973) has analyzed the Massachusetts Legislative Council for Older Americans, an organization active in state politics.

Common to the studies of contemporary and earlier aging-based organizations is the finding that such organizations can play a role in shaping the issues of public policy debate. Moreover, they can gain access to legislators, to administrative officials, and to parties and other political institutions and thereby have some opportunity to influence policy and program decisions. None of the organizations studied has displayed a capacity to organize and deliver a bloc of old age votes. All of these organizations seem to be characterized by a centralized decision-making process; whether leadership is embodied in a single personality or is more diffused may be related to the stage of organizational development. The researchers employ various interpretive frameworks to explain the origins and significance of these organizations: social movements; interest groups; and protest. But a generalization about why and when aging-based political organizations develop would be difficult to draw from these studies.

Earlier Organizations. The pre-1968 studies deal with pension reform organizations that reached peaks of membership and political activity years ago and only survive in the form of nominal vestiges. The Townsend Movement had members in every state at its peak in 1936, including as many as 1½ million members (Holtzman, 1963); by 1953 it had dwindled to 23,000 members, had become inactive politically, and was largely engaged in recreational activities (Messinger, 1955). The McLain organization in California, known for most of its history as the California Institute for Social Welfare, reached a peak of about 70,000 members in the 1950's (Pinner, Jacobs, and Selznick, 1959). Since McLain's death in 1965, the organization has been carried on by his son and a long-time associate, but the political vitality of the organization has dwindled (Putnam, 1970). The Railroad Employees National Pension Association was vigorous from its founding in 1930 to 1934 when the Railroad Retirement Act, its sole objective, was enacted; it has since been a hollow organization (Polner, 1962).

Since these aging-based membership organizations had their origins in the Great Depression and were developed through the efforts of individual leaders, scholars have been hesitant to draw generalizations from the studies by Messinger, Holtzman, Polner, and Pinner, Jacobs, and Selznick for application to more contemporary organizations. Clearly those studies indicate that aging-based membership organizations can in some circumstances frame issues for public policy debate; gain access to public officials, political parties, and other political institutions; conduct letter-writing campaigns directed at legislators and voters; and exert some amount of political influence in governmental decision-making. But since these organizations had their origins in the Great Depression and were organized through the efforts of unusual individual leaders, one might well conclude that the political significance of these organizations was bound up with societal phenomena peculiar to their era, and with the special characteristics and skills of their founders who exercised highly personal styles of leadership.

This problem of generalization has been addressed by Carlie (1969), who argues that the aging-based organizations active in pension politics during the Depression are properly interpreted as expressions of a broader social movement and not as old-age interest groups. He does not view the history of these organizations' political activities, and whatever power they had, as providing general evidence that older persons have deep-seated and enduring interests that they are inclined to concert through aging-based organizations to further an isolable old-age interest. Rather, he sees these pension organizations as time-bound, dependent for survival upon broader Depression-era social forces that gave rise to general societal anxiety over status dislocation and economic dependency. Pinner, Jacobs, and Selznick's (1959) study of the McLain organization and Messinger's (1955) analysis of the Townsend Movement can be read to support Carlie's social movement interpretation. While Holtzman employs the term "interest group" in discussing the Townsend Movement, its use does not reflect the conceptual distinction posed by Carlie. Holtzman's book (1963) and his cross-national discussion of old age politics (1954) can also be read to support the social movement interpretation. Polner's (1962) case of the Railroad Employees can be construed as an interest group phenomenon, but can just as easily be interpreted in the context of a Depression-generated social movement.

Contemporary Organizations. A recent study by Henretta (1973) introduces a different interpretive dimension to the origins and meaning of aging-based membership groups. His subject is the Massachusetts Legislative Council for Older Americans, an organization of about 10,000 members, established in 1967. Within a few years this organization became prominent in Massachusetts legislative politics, largely because of the personal leadership efforts of its founder, Frank Manning. In contrast to Townsend and McLain, Manning developed and mobilized his membership through a preexisting set of senior citizen recreational and social clubs. Much like the earlier organizations, however, the Council's internal politics have consisted of centralized decision-making by Manning. Externally, he has articulated policy issues to the legislature and the public-at-large, endorsed political candidates and referendum propositions, brought out older persons to a (calculatedly) limited number of political rallies and legislative hearings, had access for personal consultation with state administrators and legislators, and discreetly exercised an electoral bluff—implying that older persons will follow his position, but never testing his ability to swing their votes. Despite these similarities to the earlier organizations, Henretta does not see the Council as part of a broader social movement; nor does he find a cohesive, sharply-focused interest group. Rather he interprets the Council as a protest organization through which Manning has provided political definition to a range of problems that have been inadequately perceived by older persons.

The contemporary membership organizations active in national politics show a pattern similar to the Townsend, McLain, and Manning organizations in that the impetus for articulation of issues comes from the leadership rather than the membership. However, the leadership styles of these contemporary national organizations, to the extent they have been studied (Pratt, 1974), seem far more bureaucratized than personalized. They are well financed, have developed secondary leadership, and are manned by relatively large staffs. Their maintenance and survival are not dependent upon the manipulative skills of a single personality or upon the persistence of a single, aggravated problem that evokes a response from older persons. The identification of this comparatively bureaucratized leadership in these contemporary national organizations may reflect the fact that by the time they were studied they had reached a stage of organizational development and permanency that the organizations analyzed by Holtzman, Henretta, and Pinner, Jacobs, and Selznick have never attained.

The richest source of information on the politics of contemporary aging-based organizations is Pratt's book (1976). The vast majority of his data on the origins and internal characteristics of organizations is focused on three membership organizations active in American national politics: the National Council of Senior Citizens (NCSC) founded in the early 1960's to work for the passage of Medicare, and claiming a current membership of over 3 million persons; the National Retired Teachers Association-American Association of Retired Persons (NRTA—AARP), started by a California educator in 1947, with a membership purported to be over 6 million persons in 1974; and the National Association of Retired Federal Employees (NARFE), organized in 1921, with a present membership of just under 200,000. Pratt's data on external political activities not only encompass these membership organizations, but extend as well to national organizations that depend on older persons as clients and as subjects for study. Most prominent among these in Pratt's analysis are: the National Council on the Aging (NCOA), a loose confederation of some 1,400 public and private social welfare agencies; the National Association of State Units on Aging (NASUA), consisting of the administrators and committee members of the government agencies in each state which are supported by federal grant-in-aid funds under the Older Americans Act of 1965; and the Gerontological Society, a multidisciplinary professional society with a membership of about 3,500 researchers, educators, and practitioners.

Pratt views these contemporary organizations as expressions of a social movement rather than as responses to specific problems and interests of older persons requiring urgent, focused solutions. In contrast to the Depression-generated movement that Carlie (1969) identifies as a context for interpreting the significance of the earlier Townsend and McLain organizations, the movement perceived by Pratt is a long-term twentieth-century politicization of the aging. It has been brought about gradually by the breakdown of agrarian society and the disintegration of the extended family, with concomitant developments of social, economic, physical, and psychological problems of old age. Pratt regards non-aged sectors of society as part of this movement to the extent that they have developed increasingly benign views toward old age.

In identifying the political activities undertaken by these organizations, Pratt concurs with earlier treatments by Binstock (1972, 1974) and documents them in much greater detail. Both Pratt and Binstock portray these organizations as very active and skilled in gaining access to elected and appointed public officials, to career bureaucrats and legislative staff, and to political parties and other politically active organizations in Washington. This access enables them to frame many issues of policy and implementation relevant to the aging, as well as to play a role of some influence in the debates and implementive processes that ensue.

One reason for the organizations' success in gaining access to governmental leaders and political organizations is that the millions of members belonging to NCSC and NRTA-AARP represent an implicit electoral force that politicians are not eager to alienate. Nonetheless, despite the statements of journalists and the propaganda claims of organizational leaders, these organizations have not and do not dare attempt to make the apparent potential of an old-age electoral force more explicit. The reason, both Pratt and Binstock observe, is that the electoral potential is a bluff; if it were called by politicians, the inability of these organizations to swing a significant bloc of older voters would probably be revealed.

Other explanations for the success of the aging-based organizations in gaining access and shaping policy agendas, as well as explanations of the policy goals the organizations seek and the relations among the organizations, vary according to the interpretive framework employed. Pratt's observations are shaped by his social movement interpretation; Binstock's are shaped by an interest-group interpretation.

Because Pratt's social movement framework postulates a benign societal view towards the problems of aging, he argues that the leaders of aging-based organizations are sought by the political system for their specialized information on the needs of older persons. Politicians and political organizations recognize the legitimacy of aging needs, want to do something to help out, and, moreover, require the help of the aging organizations for both finding out what to do and for legitimizing what is done. At the same time, the social movement interpretation leads Pratt to see the organizations as comfortable collaborators who are able to interpret their interests in a way that identifies them with "the general good" without encountering an institutionalized adversary in the sense that labor is a frequent opponent of management. Whether the interests advocated and the advice tendered by the organizations' leaders are responsive to their memberships is not clear. While Pratt does suggest that decision-making is centralized in these organizations, he does not undertake analyses of their internal politics. Consequently, neither relations between members' views and the substance of leaders' advice and advocacy, nor the ways in which internal politics may affect external political activities emerge from his analyses.

Binstock's (1972) analysis of the organizations' political activities is interpreted in terms of Lowi's (1969) characterization of American politics as "interest-group liberalism." According to Lowi, it is a normative (if unfortunate) assumption of American politics that the interests of citizens are properly and best represented through organized interest groups. Consequently, government has parceled out to private groups the power to make public policy, acquiescing in the notion that "the public interest" is brought about through conflicts and accommodations among organized groups, each seeking fulfillment of its own interests.

Within this framework, Binstock argues that government provides access to aging-based organizations, as well as other groups, because it feels a responsibility to do so. While Pratt emphasizes the value of aging-based organizations to government as sources of technical advice, Binstock points up the desire of government officials to legitimate their policies by giving the old age interests a seat in conference rooms and at bargaining tables.

Within this interpretive framework of interest-group liberalism, the objectives that the aging-based organizations try to achieve through their political activities emerge primarily as efforts to maintain their financial stability and symbolic authority. Far from seeing the organizations as collaborators, Binstock suggests that they compete and conflict with each other in order to carve out their own shares of material rewards, legitimacy, and other incentives distributed through the political system. He observes that the organizations only collaborate for brief periods when government officials, alienated by heightened interorganizational competition among the aging-based groups, threaten to cut off access for all of them.

Distinctions among the political activities of the different types of aging-based organizations are found by Binstock, consonant with an interest-group interpretation. While the membership organizations are active in relation to income transfer policies, the client and research-based organizations—NCOA, NASUA, and the Gerontological Society—are not. Customer-based organizations—such as the American Association of Homes for the Aged, the American Nursing Home Association, and the National Council of Health Care Services—are active in seeking favorable adjustments in legislation and regulations governing their roles as vendors in the income transfer process. In relation to what Binstock terms "middleman" programs, he finds that the different types of organizations behave similarly to each other, each seeking a handsome portion of the middleman's share of funds and legitimacy distributed through a variety of governmental agencies. Although the organizations are vigorously competitive in this middleman domain, they have apparently managed to arrive at a fairly stable pattern of reward distribution and mutual accommodation.

Both Pratt (1976) and Binstock (1974), each within his slightly different interpretive framework, see the political activities of these organizations as roughly comparable to those of other organized groups in American politics. In their judgment, aging-based organizations are unlikely to have any major implications for the nature of the American political system. Neither the goals that these organizations seek, nor the power that they have for attempting to implement them, seem likely to engender a marked reordering of political processes or public priorities. Indeed, Pratt's and Binstock's investigations suggest that the political activities of aging-based organizations tend to reinforce typical patterns of behavior in American politics, and therefore provide data for better general understanding of contemporary American politics.

Areas for Further Research. Although recent research has helped to update knowledge about aging-based organizations and to clarify some issues, far more needs to be known. Most of the organizations already looked at by Pratt and Binstock, for example, deserve further attention. Especially worth some detailed study may be consumer-based organizations such as the American Nursing Home Association and its state and regional counterparts, reputed to be extremely powerful in gaining immunity from public accountability and from enforcement of regulations (Mendelson and Hapgood, 1974).

In American politics, alone, there are a great many aging-based organizations about which little is known other than through statements written by the organizations' leaders. Jackson (1974), for instance, a founder and Vice-President of the National Caucus on the Black Aged, provides a brief and intriguing account of her organization's activities. Established in 1970 "to help improve qualities and quantities of life for blacks . . . through effective and concentrated political action . . . " (p. 139), it has articulated policy issues affecting black older persons, lobbied federal agencies for research and training grants to black organizations, and engaged in protest activities such as convening a Black House Conference on Aging several weeks prior to the White House Conference on Aging of 1971. An organization such as this presents many interesting issues for investigation in addition to comparison along the dimensions for investigation examined in previous studies of old-age organizations. To pose just a few: Is the fact that the Caucus is based on a concern for a distinctive subgroup of the aging population reflected in its external politics? Has it formed alliances with other aging-based or black organizations? How do its political activities compare with those of other black organizations? How does its behavior compare with that of other minority-group aging-based organizations such as Asociacion Nacional Pro Personas Mayores? Can the political activities of the Caucus be better understood as those of a black-based or aging-based organization?

Beyond a number of state and local membership organizations that are potential subjects for comparative analysis, there are several organizations which seem distinctive enough for special attention. The Urban Elderly Coalition, founded in 1972, represents the efforts of about 75 directors of big city commissions on aging to represent the positions of their mayors on legislation and regulations developed in Washington. The Gray Panthers, founded in 1970, are a self-styled militant organization of young and old persons who, in an attempt to publicize and redress relatively specific grievances, have occasionally employed protest tactics similar to those developed by Saul Alinsky (1946).

Cross-national comparisons present another opportunity for important research. As will be indicated below, much has been asserted about the politics of old age organizations in countries other than the United States, but none of those organizations has been directly studied. Are the origins, internal features, and political activities of the organizations that have been studied peculiar to American society?

Finally, the issue of how internal organizational politics may shape an organization's external political activities has barely been touched upon in examinations of old age politics. As Lowi (1974) has pointed out, it is common for a group to represent its constituency in a distorted fashion. And as Wilson (1962) and others have shown, the distinctive style that an organization has in its internal politics may have direct consequences for its external political behavior. For these reasons it may well be worth examining just who and what the aging-based organizations represent, and the ways in which the strategies and substance of representation are shaped by internal politics.

Assessments of Power

Although the direct studies of aging-based organizations, discussed above, do treat questions bearing on the power of these organizations, they do not do so in the clear, unequivocal terms that partisans of the aging would like. The reasons for this are very complex, and can be better understood if one first looks at more peripheral literature in which generalizations are made about the power of aging-based organizations. By examining samples of that literature, and seeing the difficulties and dilemmas reflected in generalized statements about power, one can then better appreciate the more equivocal statements found in the detailed studies of these organizations.

Assertions about Power. The vast majority of treatments of the political activities of aging-based organizations are little more than assertions and speculations regarding the power or potential power of membership organizations. Friis (1969, p. 144) declares that the Association of Old Age and Invalidity Pensioners in Denmark "has been an influential pressure group." Cottrell, discussing aging-based organizations in the United States, characterizes the National Council of Senior Citizens and the American Association of Retired Persons as having "a great deal of political clout" (1971, p. 35). Finer observes that in Great Britain the National Federation of Old Age Pensioners Association is "of some importance politically" (1958, p. 123). Havighurst suggests that in Sweden "the Old Age Pensioners Association is a potential political force which has the leaders of all parties interested" and that in the Netherlands, "the old people's associations have a potential, if not an actual, political significance" (1960, p. 308, p. 325). Countless other statements of this nature can be found in the literature— in monographs and articles on the interest group politics, in general, of a particular nation; in case histories and political analyses of the evolution of public pension and health programs and other policies affecting older persons; and in essays dealing with the political and social aspects of aging.

Because such assertions are frequently cited as authoritative sources, it is important to stress that they are severely limited as foundations for knowledge about the political significance of aging-based organizations. There are essentially three reasons why these general statements about the power or potential power of membership organizations cannot be used as bases for generalizations.

First, most of these observations are unsupported by the presentation of evidence and analysis, or even by reference to an authoritative source. As Havighurst properly observes in his introduction to a chapter in which he makes many such general assertions about the power of aging-based organizations in eight western nations: ". . . because there are not many scientific studies available on these topics . . . . [the] chapter . . . must be regarded as tentative in its conclusions and open to considerable correction by more careful studies which may be made in the future" (1960, p. 301).

Second, when sweeping statements about the power of particular organizations can be compared with analyses based on extensive research, the general statements seem to be contradicted by evidence. One can compare, for example, Finer's and Havighurst's observations about the importance of the pensioners' associations in Britain and Sweden with Heclo's book-length monograph (1974) on the political processes through which pension policies evolved in those two nations from the nineteenth century through the early 1970's. Heclo's conclusion, based on a detailed analysis of extensive evidence, is that "at no time did

organizations of the aged or pensioners themselves play any prominent part" (1974, p. 156). Similarly, Sundquist's (1968) and Marmor's (1970) analyses of the enactment of Medicare in the United States do not provide evidence to substantiate many assertions that the National Council of Senior Citizens played a powerful role in the passage of that legislation.

Third, in the relatively few instances in which arguments are presented to support general assertions about the power of aging-based organizations, the arguments tend to rest upon problematic assumptions. The typical arguments point to facts showing that older persons constitute a substantial proportion of the electorate in a given political system, sometimes as much as 20 percent (Friis, 1969), and imply or explicitly state that "a considerable block of votes could be influenced by the older people [the Swedish Old Age Pensioners Association] in their own behalf" (Havighurst, 1960, p. 308). Such arguments not only rest on the assumption that a capacity to affect the outcome of elections is an important source of power—a proposition that is debatable with respect to many so-called democratic political systems—but they also contradict the evidence available on the voting behavior of older persons. As the review of the literature in Section I of this chapter indicates, the voting behavior of the aging appears relatively stable and not susceptible to being changed substantially by age-based appeals. Moreover, when the assumption that the vote of older persons can be organized to affect the fate of a particular candidate, party, or proposition has been put to the test, it has proven to be invalid. Hence, while Havighurst argues that the older persons of Sweden are a potentially powerful voting bloc for furthering their own interests, Heclo's (1974, p. 289) analysis of old age pension politics in that nation states that when a distinctive electoral appeal has been made on the issue of old age provision, "the advocate as often as not has lost in the election." In fact, Heclo concludes that "elections were of little direct significance" to the evolution of old-age programs in Sweden and Great Britain (1974, p. 288).

Defining and Measuring Power. Even though the many sweeping assertions about the power of specific organizations cannot be relied upon as bases for generalization, it would be foolish to assume that aging-based organizations do not have political power. To be sure, one can safely generalize from common observation that aging-based organizations do not have sufficient power to control political systems. On the other hand, it is clear from relatively detailed contemporary accounts (Binstock, 1972; Henretta, 1973; Pratt, 1976) that these organizations have at least some power, enough power to ensure that elected officials, legislative staffs, and bureaucrats will not totally ignore the existence and aspirations of aging-based organizations. The issues, however, lie between these extremes of the power continuum—the extreme of controlling power, and the extreme of powerlessness.

Cottrell, Finer, Friis, Havighurst, and others are undoubtedly correct when they characterize specific organizations as having power or potential power. But how much power? Enough to force radical or incremental changes in governmental policies toward the aging? Sufficient power to change the votes of legislators? To have an administrative ruling reversed? To get more police protection in certain neighborhoods? Enough power to elicit the proclamation of a "senior citizens' month"?

Answers to questions of this nature are difficult to develop because the phenomenon of power is not easily susceptible to rigorous, systematic analysis. The very meaning of the term is elusive, despite—or perhaps because of—more than two milleniums of consideration by political philosophers.

The only assumption that seems common to the many definitions and theories of power that have been developed is that power is the ability to fulfill one's wishes and protect one's autonomy (Cranston and Lakoff, 1969, p. 126).*

Power is even more difficult to measure reliably than it is to define. As Bachrach and

Baratz (1962) have pointed out, the evidence of power that is sought and the data found are largely shaped by the political theory, explicit or implicit, underlying the investigation. Research based on elitist theoretical assumptions can be expected to find relatively little evidence of power exercised by aging-based organizations. An investigation using a pluralistic political model is likely to characterize aging-based organizations as interest groups or pressure groups. In so doing, it may tend to overemphasize the power of the group (Macridis, 1961), impose an unrealistic rational framework for interpreting organizational objectives (Wilson, 1973), and generate a distorted view of the relationship between the organization's political activities and the aspirations of its constituent members (Lowi, 1974).

The most severe challenge to be faced in measuring an organization's political power, regardless of the definitions and theoretical perspectives that may be employed, is generated by the inherent difficulties in identifying causal relations (Banfield, 1961). This problem of measurement is especially severe if one poses issues of causation in terms of one-to-one relations for specific policy outcomes: Did the power of the Townsend Movement hasten the enactment of Social Security legislation in the United States in 1935? Were Sweden's superannuation pension reforms of the 1950's brought about by the political activities of the two major Swedish pensioners' organizations, *Sveriges folkpensionärers Riksförbund* and *Sveriges folkpensionärers Riksorganization*? The answers to such questions cannot be obtained through methods of experiment and control. While Holtzman (1963) answers "yes" to the first question and Heclo (1974) answers "no" to the second question, the authoritativeness of their answers rests solely with the persuasiveness of their arguments; their conclusions are perennially subject to reversal by more persuasive counterarguments that may be marshalled. Perhaps because of this limited state of the art, many researchers understandably shy away from making categorical statements about the power of an organization, and from presenting conclusions as to whether one or several organizations'

---

*Although many important distinctions can be made between "power" and "influence," the two terms are treated here as if they were synonymous in order to avoid a tedious presentation; see Dahl (1960) and Banfield (1961).

political activities brought about the enactment of a specific public policy. Nowhere in their lengthy analysis of the McLain organization, for instance, do Pinner, Jacobs, and Selznick (1959) present categorical statements about the power of the organization or resolve the issue of whether or not the organization's political activities were responsible for particular policies.

Identifying the Limits of Power. Because of these obstacles to systematic analysis of power, Lakoff observes, "it is small wonder that some political scientists prefer to leave the term power to propagandists or to specify what they mean by it whenever they use it. The trouble is, of course, that it is virtually impossible to dispense with the term completely—as impossible as it would be for an economist to dispense with the similarly elusive concept of value" (Cranston and Lakoff, 1969, p. 127).* Given that social scientists and partisans of the aging will not ignore power as it bears on relations between older persons and political systems, how can the power of aging-based organizations be analyzed more systematically and rigorously? Should scholars contrive narrow definitions of power that are so artificial and pedantic that analyses based upon them will throw little light on issues of general interest? Alternatively, must scholars simply rest their cases on persuasive arguments, leaving juries of readers to draw their own conclusions?

At the very least it is possible, as indicated by the direct literature reviewed above, to identify the existence of sufficient power to participate actively in the processes of political systems. The existential facts that aging-based organizations do frame policy issues and gain access to bureaucrats, legislators and their staffs, and to other political institutions have been clearly documented. It is the consequences of that participation, of any power exercised through these opportunities, that is more difficult to pin down and express reliably.

Certainly one method for establishing systematic information about the consequences of

*From *A Glossary of Political Ideas*, edited by Maurice Cranston and Sanford A. Lakoff, © 1968 by Maurice Cranston and © 1969 by Basic Books, Inc., Publishers, New York.

power exercised by aging-based organizations is to focus on its limits. While cause-effect relations are inherently impossible to identify for reasons outlined earlier, it is possible to develop a reasonably reliable picture of what such organizations cannot do. Many of the direct studies reviewed earlier (Polner, 1962; Holtzman, 1963; Pinner, Jacobs, and Selznick, 1959; Binstock, 1972; Henretta, 1973; and Pratt, 1976) provide clear evidence of aging-based organizations failing to gain certain objectives that they have sought through extensive and vigorous efforts to exercise power. To be sure, these failures may or may not be attributed to poor strategic management of potential power resources; but strategic skill is part of existential power.

A seeming corollary of this method is to define the limits of power by selecting for a frame of reference some consequence or policy that has not been achieved. Binstock (1972), for instance, sets forth as a desirable policy goal a radical redistribution of income to the aged; since that goal has not been realized, he can conclude that whatever the power of aging-based organizations, it has not redressed the economic problems of the severely disadvantaged aged. Yet, this observation does not establish limits to the organizations' potential for power because, as Binstock makes clear, the organizations have not tested their potential by attempting to achieve a radical redistribution.

In considering the potential power of aging-based organizations, an issue of particular concern to partisans of the aging, one cannot overly stress the importance of directing attention to the goals the organizations are trying to achieve. A common though not necessarily warranted assumption of most journalists and many scholars is that organizations and persons active in politics only have sufficient power to achieve incremental changes in policy and in the nature of political systems. But if the goals sought by aging-based organizations are incremental, examination of their activities in the political system does not provide evidence of what it might be possible for them to achieve. If they do not pursue radical changes, it is not possible to identify reliably the limits to their potential for power.

Whether, and in what circumstances, contemporary aging-based organizations will seek to achieve radical goals can only be understood by investigating the relations between their intraorganizational incentives and processes and their external political activities. This is why a priority need for further research is systematic investigation of the ways in which external goals and strategies are shaped by the internal politics of aging-based organizations.

AGING AS A CONCERN OF POLITICAL SYSTEMS

The two preceding sections of this chapter have examined the political attitudes and behavior of the aging and the politics of aging-based organizations. This final section considers the ways in which aging has become and remains an active concern of political systems.

Given the patterns through which modern nation states have developed since the early sixteenth century, there was no *a priori* reason to assume that aging would necessarily become a focus for collective activity by governments and other political institutions. The late nineteenth century was a major turning point; for the first time the industrialized nations—with the notable exception of the United States— undertook major governmental actions toward ameliorating the lives of their older citizens. In the ensuing years, those initial steps have been modified and expanded substantially as the modern welfare state has grown along with the economies of the industrial nations. Today, public policies affecting the aging make up very considerable portions of the expenditures of national governments.

The enormous range of governmental policies affecting older persons precludes any detailed catalogue here of the relevant contemporary programs; in-depth treatment of specific policies can be found in other chapters (living arrangements, Ch. 10; employment, Ch. 12; income maintenance, Ch. 22; health, Ch. 23; social services, Ch. 24). The discussion here will have three general aims. The first is to present an overview of when and why political systems initially responded to aging as a collective concern. The second is to examine three different types of responses which governments have made to the needs of older persons. The

final aim is to consider how the aging fare in contemporary political systems and to speculate on how they will be treated in the future.

Development of Social Policy Toward the Aging

Literature dealing with the evolution of governmental responses to the aging varies in approach, method, and conclusions. Some studies are detailed histories of developments in one country; others explicitly examine economic and political trends cross-nationally. Some have tended to emphasize the differences in particular programs or combinations of programs for the aged in different countries; others have emphasized overall similarities, finding individual differences small in the face of alternative responses which could have been adopted.

Regardless of their approaches, scholars generally agree that aging persons first became a major concern of political systems in the late nineteenth century. The birth of the modern welfare state, with economic relief for older persons as a major feature, can be pinpointed at the enactment of German health, accident, and old age/invalidity programs of the 1880's. During the ensuing 25-year period, modest yet revolutionary pension schemes were enacted in most of the industrial world: Denmark (1891), Belgium (1894), New Zealand (1898), the Australian states (1901), France (1903), the Australian federation (1908), Britain (1908), and Sweden (1913). The time lag between these governmental commitments and the relatively late enactment of the United States social security program in 1935 has been attributed to a variety of factors; principal among them has been the peculiarly monolithic American attachment to classical liberal economic and political ideology (King, 1971).

Since these initial commitments, the income maintenance policies of industrial nations have undergone innumerable modifications and expansions (see Kaim-Caudle, 1973; and Schulz, Carrin, Krupp, Peschke, Sclar, and Van Steenberge, 1974). Moreover, political systems have expanded their efforts for helping older persons to include not only divisible personal needs such as shelter, medical care, and employment training, but also to encompass a concern for the design and operation of transportation systems and other features of the broader environment that have differential consequences for older segments of the population.

The evolution of governmental policies toward the aging can be traced to a number of factors ranging from the zealous efforts of individual reformers to a variety of fundamental societal changes brought about by long-term technological, economic, and social trends. Additionally, in selected contexts, political parties, trade unions, economic elites, professional and commercial organizations, and other politically active institutions have found reason to advocate or oppose governmental action toward the aging. While selected activities of such political institutions with respect to aging have been discussed in various contexts (e.g. Cottrell, 1960; and Duncker, 1970), their efforts have not been studied systematically.

In the absence of literature specifically designed to explain the origins of collective concern for the aging, it is necessary to turn to works that consider the overall development of social welfare policies. In this more general literature, one can isolate three categories of factors that played some role in the development of aging as a concern of political systems: historical, cultural, and ideological forces; proximate political forces; and patterns of allocative competition.

Historical, Cultural, and Ideological Forces. It is widely held that industrialization and its concomitant social and economic dislocations made public social intervention for the aging virtually inevitable, regardless of specific variations in national responses. While improvement in life expectancy increased the numbers of older persons, many of them were unable to stand the rigors of industrial employment and found that industrialization was eroding traditional patterns of support through the extended family. But industrialization alone does not account for political systems responding to the plight of the aged through collective intervention.

Also at work were ideological forces, patterns of belief that tended to limit as well as suggest policy measures. Many observers agree that in

Britain and France (Rimlinger, 1971) and in the United States (Lipset, 1967), strong attachments to the tenets of nineteenth century liberalism precluded the intervention by the state for many decades. In Britain, these attachments had lessened among the upper and middle classes by the end of the century; in France they were displaced in part as new forces emerged on the Left; in the United States, the break was longer in coming. That neither economic nor political liberalism were central elements in nineteenth century German political ideology, however, allowed easier justification for the early social insurance policies of Bismarck (Dahrendorf, 1969). A force of comparable magnitude in a number of countries well into the twentieth century was an unswerving belief in pre-Keynesian orthodox economics; severe economic dislocation was met by cuts in governmental spending rather than by any new stimulus (Heclo, 1974).

On the other hand, the importance of ideological forces in constraining or facilitating the emergence of major policy innovations can be overemphasized. As indicated in the first section of this chapter, mass publics do not possess highly structured belief systems, particularly at the operational level, and their role in policy development appears marginal in any event. Political elites may have more structured belief systems than mass publics, but formal beliefs are only one of many considerations that these more proximate political actors bring to questions of policy.

Proximate Political Forces. Many conventional models of the political system hold that interest groups, political parties, and elections provide the major avenues through which societal demands come to be met through governmental action. Cross-national studies do not, however, reveal these political institutions and channels to have been consistently important forces in the processes through which governments' concerns for aging came about. In his study of pension developments in Britain and Sweden, Heclo (1974), for example, concludes that (a) the British National Pension Committee was of considerably greater consequence than the Swedish Committee for Public Pensions;

(b) the Friendly Society movement and private insurance sector in Britain served to forestall the development of contributory pensions, while their Swedish counterparts never showed comparable interest and vigor; and (c) the sponsorship and analysis of superannuation by the Swedish *Landsorganisationen* was never matched by Britain's central labor organization, the Trades Union Congress.

In general, trade unions, insurance associations, and other interest groups have limited their involvement in policies affecting aging to those specific issues in which their group self-interest has been seen as directly at stake. Such perceptions, however, have changed over time. The Friendly Societies in Britain (Briggs, 1961) and the AFL in the United States (Greenstone, 1970) long opposed a number of social intervention policies, including those for the aging, until they were convinced that their own organizations were not endangered or until they became part of the public administrative apparatus itself. Similarly, the British Life Offices Association, representing private insurance companies, came to support Conservative party superannuation proposals when it "had been persuaded to the view that its member companies' interests would be served by a partnership that accepted a state role in providing earnings-related pensions" (Heclo, 1974, p. 276).

The more general political situation of interest groups may have also affected the timing and scope of policies related to aging. Heidenheimer (1973) argues that when class consciousness has been high and one labor federation has been dominant, organized labor has overcome parochial tendencies and supported governmental proposals for social insurance. In contrast, some governmental policies have been enacted before cohesive organizational opposition could develop. Titmuss (1959) notes this phenomenon regarding the medical profession's response to British health policy, and Heidenheimer (1973) sees it in relation to the real estate interests' weak opposition to public housing programs in the United States.

In some instances, political leaders have employed social policies for the aging as a means of forestalling development of social movements opposed to their regimes. Such a preemptive strategy was used by Bismarck toward the German Social Democrats and by Lloyd-George toward the emerging Labour party.

The roles of political parties and elections in the development of policies toward the aging show no consistent pattern. Policies toward the aged, whether breakthroughs or incremental changes, have been developed during periods of rule by conservatives (Germany under Bismarck and during the 1957 pension reforms, Britain's Beveridge proposals), by liberals (Britain and Sweden's initial pension legislation, American social security), and by the Left (post-World War II social security reorganization in France). In election campaigns, "pensioneering" tends to be practiced by all parties, and has been noted particularly in Britain (Beer, 1965). But as Heclo finds, while elections may sensitize policy makers to the need for action, "[p]arties have not served as the unfettered transmission lines between public demand and government social policy, partly because those responsible for the latter were not interested in, and could not understand the messages, but mostly because the public was sending no clear signals on concrete social policies" (1974, p. 293).

Patterns of Welfare Allocation. Development of social policies for the aged must also be viewed in the context of the full range of demands for social intervention. Although the emergence of aging as a concern was common to industrialized political systems in the late nineteenth and early twentieth centuries, subsequent policy expansions and elaborations have varied among nations. Some countries that first responded to the aging at a time when few competing social demands had achieved recognition could more easily expand and elaborate these responses because the needs of the aging had been established prior to alternate claims. On the other hand, where the initial response to the aging came after other concerns had been firmly established, later policy actions toward the aging have been less extensive. Attention to the aging in France, for instance, has been inhibited by a long-standing concern with the nation's birthrate, which has led to heavy emphasis on family allowance policies designed to encourage population growth (Laroque, 1969).

In discussing how certain programs drive out others, Wilensky (1975) notes the relative neglect of social security in a number of nations in favor of generous spending in higher education. Nonetheless, benefits for the aging in the United States have been *relatively* generous, even though the initial American response to older persons came several decades later than that of most nations. The 1935 Social Security Act gave firm recognition to older persons as a social concern prior to many competing claims. Since then, outlays for the aging have continued to dwarf other governmental social expenditures in the United States. In absolute terms, American public pensions are not as generous as comparable programs in many other nations. Yet, as a proportion of the total national welfare budget, expenditures for public pensions in the United States rank highest among the 22 most industrial nations (Wilensky, 1975). This top ranking can be partially explained by the comparatively slow American response to competing welfare demands—universal health insurance, social services, public health programs, and public housing.

The political consequences of early recognition of the aging as a deserving constituency are, indeed, most clearly visible for the United States. The Old Age Assistance provisions of the original Social Security Act were not only the most popular, but without them it is doubtful that the remaining titles would have been enacted (Witte, 1962; and Steiner, 1966). Provisions for loss of income due to disability, for example, never had the same popularity and were not enacted until 1950. All accounts of the passage of the American Medicare legislation in 1965 agree that opposition to direct governmental involvement in health care financing—particularly that coming from and organized by the American Medical Association—could not have been overcome had the legislation's coverage extended beyond the aged (Marmor, 1970; Sundquist, 1968; Rose, 1967). Coverage of additional constituencies was not, in fact, even an issue at the time.

Support for the legislation emerged from pressures to help the aged in meeting one of their most urgent needs rather than from any constellation of forces wishing to involve the American government in the medical field more generally. Similarly, it was not surprising that the Supplemental Security Income program enacted by the United States in 1973—a program confined to the aged, blind, and disabled—was able to emerge from the legislative shambles of the Nixon administration's Family Assistance Plan which attempted to move away from categorical stipulations toward a universal guaranteed income.

Because aging has been so well established as a proper concern of government, policies helping older persons have often been strategically valuable to partisans of other causes. Sometimes those who espouse concerns other than aging have supported legislation for the elderly as a tactic for opening the way for their own constituencies. Or they have pointed to existing programs for the aging as precedents and justifications for responses to other causes. In the United States, especially, this has occurred in relation to health insurance, in property tax relief, and particularly in housing where tenant groups have sought expansion of rent ceilings and rent supplementation programs originally confined to housing for the elderly.

Kinds of Governmental Responses to the Aging

Although initial recognition of aging as a concern of political systems took the form of remedying a specific problem of older persons —lack of a source of adequate income— governments' continuing responses have taken a variety of forms. Contemporary governmental efforts directed toward the aging are numerous and extensive in range, but can be seen as comprising three general kinds of public response.

Specific Problem Legislation. The first category of public policies affecting aging—as exemplified by income maintenance legislation—consists of programs specifically designed through legislation to alleviate distinct problems experienced by older persons. In addition to public pensions, many nations have developed programs earmarked to solve specific and immediate problems through such efforts as: building residential and institutional facilities for the elderly; job retraining and job placement for older workers; and regulating such specific matters as the management of private pension plans, the operation of nursing homes and other long-term care facilities largely serving the aged, and discrimination against older workers in employment. These and other legislatively designed programs are discussed in detail elsewhere in this volume, particularly in Chapters 10, 22, 23, and 24.

General Concern Mechanisms. A second, more generalized kind of governmental response has been to establish mechanisms that have at least nominal concern for all matters relating to aging, without focusing on a specific or single set of problems. In addition to interventional effects these mechanisms may have, they legitimize the broad category of "the aging" as a policy constituency in political systems.

One approach in this category has been for legislatures to establish special committees on aging. Such a committee may stimulate proposals for governmental action affecting the elderly and serve as a focal point and arena for policy debates. The U. S. Senate Special Committee on Aging, for example, although having no legislative authority, served as a major communications link in the political processes leading to the enactment of Medicare (Sundquist, 1968). According to Vinyard (1972), the Special Committee functions as a legislative catalyst, a career advancement vehicle for incumbent Senators, a monitor of executive agency operations relating to aging, and a symbol of government's concern for older persons.

Similarly, executive branches of government establish commissions, councils, and task forces on aging—both ongoing and *ad hoc*—to take broad looks at their governments' efforts toward the aging. They are expected to propose legislation, to facilitate administration and coordination of activities affecting older persons, and to stand as symbols of public concern for the elderly. In general, they have little power to effect changes and to establish themselves as influential forces within governmental affairs (Binstock, 1971).

Another type of mechanism created by political systems as a generalized response to older persons is the governmental institute for research and education in aging. For some years the Soviet Union has maintained a national institute of Gerontology in Kiev. The United States, through legislative enactment of a National Institute on Aging in 1974, has been the most recent government to develop such a mechanism. These public gerontological institutes, through both intramural and extramural programs, undertake biomedical and behavioral studies for adding to basic knowledge about processes of aging, without necessarily focusing on the solution of immediate problems.

Still another type of generalized approach that political systems undertake in response to aging is exemplified by the Administration on Aging (AoA) in the United States. Created by the Older Americans Act of 1965, the agency was charged with a series of general responsibilities toward older Americans that could be interpreted to include virtually any dimension of life related to processes of aging. With an initial appropriation of $10 million for combined functions of services, research, and training, it began as little more than symbolic affirmation of the aged as a policy constituency (Hudson, 1973).

In the years since 1965, AoA has enlarged substantially to a point where it is currently administering programs with a combined budget of approximately $400 million. In this process of growth some legislatively-earmarked programs focused on specific problems (such as nutrition) have been added to its portfolio, and it has devised a broad strategy for implementing its more open-ended responsibilities for providing social services (Gold, 1974). But throughout most of its development AoA has largely been an administrative vehicle for passing on national funds to states which, in turn, have been left with the specific decisions as to which of the needs and problems of older citizens these resources might be applied.

The rationale for this open-ended arrangement has been to facilitate the expression of local political priorities in responding to the needs of the aging. However, in an analysis of how states responded to this opportunity Binstock, Cherington, and Woll (1974) found that patterns of choice among the states depended far more on administrative and personnel factors than upon demographic, social, economic, and political variations among the states. A relatively new set of local mechanisms to receive AoA funds, area agencies on aging, has not yet been examined systematically. Hudson (1974), however, suggests that ambiguous mandates to these area agencies will make it difficult for them to make effective responses to the needs of aging constituents.

Coordination of Broader Programs and Services. A third category of governmental responses to aging has been an effort to make more sensitive to aging-related concerns all of the public programs, services, and regulations that have relevance to the adult population. Most prominently identified among such general areas of relevance have been: health, mental health, transportation, housing, employment, legal reform, and social services.

As special concerns affecting the aging have been identified in these and other areas, one kind of response of governments has been to designate staff specialists on aging to serve within the more general bureaucratic or legislative structures of responsibility. Although these specialists inevitably play some role in promoting day-to-day sensitivity to aging, the imperatives of organizational life and career survival limit severely the impact they can have.

An additional pattern of governmental response has been to attempt redirection of general adult programs, services, and regulations by impacting them from a position outside the structures that administer them. Thus, AoA and its state counterparts have been charged with planning and coordinating the activities of public agencies that affect aging. They have not been notably successful in carrying out this charge, however, because they have lacked the power to be effective (Binstock, 1971) in overcoming the inherent and inevitable resistance to coordination manifested by the other organizations (Estes, 1973, 1974).

Aging and the Future of Governmental Concerns

Given the responses that political systems have already made to the aging as a constituency, what can be said about how older persons fare in their political systems? To be sure, a conclusive answer to this question would require extended discussion. Nonetheless, in a chapter on relations between political systems and the aging, some brief observations ought to be made.

If one sets a *minimum* standard of adequacy —perhaps comprised of sufficient food for survival, ready delivery of requisite medical care, and shelter that is free of dangerous hazards and disease—it is clear that substantial proportions of the aging do not fare well in their political systems. On the other hand, if one sets a *relative* standard of equity, comparing the situation of the aged with other mass categories of citizens in a given political system —racial minorities, younger persons, the sick and disabled, the socially or politically deviant —it is possible to come up with a different answer. Binstock (1972, p. 278), for instance, argues that in the American political system, "the symbolic responses [the aging] elicit and material rewards they receive at least equal and may exceed those gained by comparable categories of citizens and organized interests, if not matching those of the very wealthy, party leaders, 'big' business, and 'big' labor." At the same time, he points out that the relatively good political position of the aging as a whole does little to help the situation of those millions of older persons among them who have not attained a standard of minimum justice. The differential impacts that a public policy may have on a total class of citizens, and on subcategories of that class, make it possible for "the aging" to fare reasonably well while many older persons continue to suffer severe deprivation.

In some areas of collective concern there are already signs that discrepancies between the situations of the aggregate category labeled "the aging" and certain subcategories of older persons will continue to grow. While public policies are improving the income situation of the aging in general, substantial numbers of older persons remain in severe poverty (see Ch. 22). Similarly, as many public programs and services for the elderly are generated, the help extended to aging persons who are members of ethnic minority groups does not seem to increase proportionally (Jackson, 1974).

If public policies continue to improve conditions for the aging in general without substantially alleviating the problems of severely disadvantaged older persons, it is possible that governments may eventually stop focusing on the needs of the total aging constituency. Current tendencies to direct policies toward the elderly may be submerged within policies that are directed toward other characteristics than age—toward poverty, ethnic and cultural deprivations, physical and mental disabilities, living arrangements, educational and training needs. On the other hand, given the strongly-rooted development of aging as a governmental concern, public policy may well remain focused on older persons in general. In that case, alleviation of the severe problems of certain subcategories of older persons will require far more complexities of differentiation and fine-tuning than embodied in current policies.

As much as the concern of governments for aging has developed since the early income maintenance programs of the nineteenth century, there is no inherent reason why the response of political systems cannot become more elaborate and extend further to meet any number of needs of older persons. Some students of aging have suggested, for instance, that the dissolution of traditional patterns of the extended family has left many older persons in social isolation and lacking psychological support (see Ch. 9). It is not unreasonable to speculate that governments might attempt to restore extended families or to create artificial ones. The American government has already taken a small step in this direction through its Foster Grandparents program in which older persons were recruited to provide and to receive social and psychological support from retarded and chronically disabled children in institutions.

Ironically, the future of governments' concerns for the aging may be limited by expansion of the aggregate needs of older persons. Continuing low birth rates and trends toward earlier retirement from the labor force could very well bring about substantial increases in the numbers and proportions of persons who are chronologically aged and who otherwise could be regarded and might regard themselves as aging. If so, governments will be hard-pressed to fulfill the responsibilities toward the aging which they have already undertaken. The politics of resource allocation may lead to retrenchments in or abrogations of existing governmental commitments to meet the needs of the aging.

While some observers have speculated that larger numbers and proportions of aging citizens could lead to gerontocracies, evidence from throughout this chapter indicates that a marked increase in the political power of older persons is unlikely. If governments respond positively to the challenge of meeting or expanding their commitments, it will probably be because of broad ideological changes in political systems, and not because of major growth in the political strength of the aging.

REFERENCES

Abramson, P. R. 1971. Social class and political change in Western Europe: A cross-national longitudinal analysis. *Comparative Political Studies*, 4, 131–155.

Abramson, P. R. 1974. Generational change in American electoral behavior. *Amer. Pol. Sci. Rev.*, 68, 93–105.

Alinsky, S. D. 1946. *Reveille for Radicals.* New York: Random House.

Allardt, E., and Pesonen, P. 1967. Cleavages in Finnish politics. *In,* S. M. Lipset and S. Rokkan (eds.), *Party Systems and Voter Alignments: Cross-National Perspectives*, pp. 325–351. New York: The Free Press.

Bachrach, P., and Baratz, M. S. 1962. Two faces of power. *Amer. Pol. Sci. Rev.*, LVI, 947–952.

Banfield, E. C. 1961. *Political Influence.* New York: The Free Press of Glencoe.

Beer, S. 1965. *British Politics in the Collectivist Age.* New York: Alfred A. Knopf.

Berelson, B., Lazarsfeld, P. F., and McPhee, W. 1954. *Voting*. Chicago: University of Chicago Press.

Binstock, R. H. 1971. *Planning*. Washington, D. C.: 1971 White House Conference on Aging.

Binstock, R. H. 1972. Interest-Group liberalism and the politics of aging. *Gerontologist*, **12**, 265–280.

Binstock, R. H. 1974. Aging and the future of American politics. *Annals of the Am. Acad. of Pol. and Soc. Sc.*, **415**, 201–212.

Binstock, R. H., Cherington, C. M., and Woll, P. 1974. Federalism and leadership-planning: Predictors of variance in state behavior. *Gerontologist*, **14**, 114–121.

Blackwell, R. 1974. Political generation and attitude change among Soviet Obkom elites. Paper delivered at the 1974 annual meeting of the American Political Science Association, Chicago.

Briggs, A. 1961. The welfare state in historical perspective. *Archives Européennes de Sociologie*, **11** (2), 221–258.

Butler, D., and Stokes, D. 1971. *Political Change in Britain*. New York: St. Martin's Press.

Campbell, A. 1962. Social and psychological determinants of voting behavior. *In*, W. Donahue and C. Tibbitts (eds.), *Politics of Age*, pp. 87–100. Ann Arbor: University of Michigan.

Campbell, A. 1971. Politics through the life cycle. *Gerontologist*, **11**, 112–117.

Campbell, A., Converse, P., Miller, W., and Stokes, D. 1960. *The American Voter*. New York: John Wiley.

Cantor, R. 1975. *Voting Behavior and Presidential Elections*. Itasca, Illinois: F. E. Peacock.

Carlie, M. K. 1969. The politics of age: Interest group or social movement. *Gerontologist*, **9**, 259–263.

Clemente, F. 1975. Age and the perception of national priorities. *Gerontologist*, **15**, 61–63.

Converse, P. 1964. The nature of belief systems in mass publics. *In*, David Apter (ed.), *Ideology and Discontent*, pp. 206–261. London: The Free Press of Glencoe.

Cottrell, W. F. 1960. Governmental functions and the politics of age. *In*, C. Tibbitts (ed.), *Handbook of Social Gerontology*, pp. 624–665. Chicago: University of Chicago Press.

Cottrell, W. F. 1971. *Government and Non-Government Organizations*. Washington, D. C.: 1971 White House Conference on Aging.

Cranston, M., and Lakoff, S. A. 1969. *A Glossary of Political Ideas*. New York: Basic Books.

Crittenden, J. 1962. Aging and party affiliation. *Public Opinion Quarterly*, **26**, 648–657.

Crittenden, J. 1963. Aging and political participation. *Western Political Quarterly*, **16**, 323–331.

Cutler, N. 1969. Generation, maturation, and party affiliation: A cohort analysis. *Public Opinion Quarterly*, **33**, 583–588.

Cutler, N., and Bengtson, V. 1974. Age and political alienation: Maturation, generation and period

effects. *Annals of the Am. Acad. of Pol. and Soc. Sc.*, **415**, 160–175.

Dahl, R. A. 1960. The analysis of influence in local communities, *In*, C. R. Adrian (ed.), *Social Science and Community Action*, pp. 25–42. Lansing, Michigan: Michigan State University.

Dahrendorf, R. 1969. *Society and Democracy in Germany*. Garden City, New York: Doubleday, Anchor Books.

Douglass, E., Cleveland, W., and Maddox, G. 1974. Political attitudes, age, and aging: A cohort analysis of archival data. *J. Geront.*, **29**, 666–675.

Duncker, A. E. 1970. Policies for the aged in New York State. Unpublished doctoral dissertation, New York: Columbia University.

Easton, D., and Dennis, J. 1969. *Children in the Political System*. New York: McGraw-Hill.

Edinger, L. 1968. *Politics in Germany*. Boston: Little, Brown.

Edinger, L. 1970. Political change in Germany: The Federal Republic after the 1969 election. *Comparative Politics*, **2**, 549–578.

Ehrmann, H. 1968. *Politics in France*. Boston: Little, Brown.

Eisele, F. 1972. Age and political change: A cohort analysis of voting among careerists in the U. S. Senate, 1947–1970. Unpublished doctoral dissertation, New York University.

Estes, C. L. 1973. Barriers to effective community planning for the elderly. *Gerontologist*, **13**, 178–183.

Estes, C. L. 1974. Community planning for the elderly: A study of goal displacement. *J. Geront.*, **29**, 684–691.

Evan, W. 1965. Cohort analysis of attitude data. *In*, J. Beshers (ed.), *Computer Methods in the Analysis of Large-Scale Social Systems*, pp. 117–142. Cambridge, Massachusetts: Joint Center for Urban Studies of M. I. T. and Harvard University.

Finer, S. E. 1958. Interest groups and the political process in Great Britain. *In*, H. W. Ehrmann (ed.), *Interest Groups on Four Continents*, pp. 117–144. Pittsburgh, Pennsylvania: University of Pittsburgh Press.

Fishel, J. 1969. Party ideology and the congressional challenger. *Amer. Pol. Sci. Rev.*, **63**, 1213–1232.

Foner, A. 1972. The polity. *In*, M. W. Riley, M. Johnson, and A. Foner, *Aging and Society*, Vol. 3, pp. 115–159. New York: Russell Sage Foundation.

Free, L., and Cantril, H. 1968. *The Political Beliefs of Americans: A Study of Public Opinion*. New York: Simon and Schuster.

Friis, H. 1969. Issues in social security policies in Denmark. *In*, S. Jenkins (ed.), *Social Security in International Perspective*, pp. 129–150. New York: Columbia University Press.

Glamser, F. 1974. The importance of age to conservative opinions: A multivariate analysis. *J. Geront.*, **29**, 549–554.

Glenn, N. 1969. Aging, disengagement, and opiniona-tion. *Public Opinion Quarterly*, 33, 17-33.

Glenn, N. 1974. Aging and conservatism. *Annals of the Am. Acad. of Pol. and Soc. Sc.*, 415, 176-186.

Glenn, N., and Grimes, M. 1968. Aging, voting and political interest. *Am. Soc. Rev.*, 33, 563-575.

Glenn, N., and Hefner, T. 1972. Further evidence on aging and party identification. *Public Opinion Quarterly*, 36, 31-47.

Gold, B. 1974. The role of the federal government in the provision of social services to older persons. *Annals of the Am. Acad. of Pol. and Soc. Sc.*, 415, 55-69.

Greenstone, J. D. 1970. *Labor in American Politics*. New York: Random House, Vintage Books.

Havighurst, R. J. 1960. Life beyond family and work. *In*, E. W. Burgess (ed.), *Aging in Western Societies*, pp. 299-353. Chicago: University of Chicago Press.

Heclo, H. 1974. *Modern Social Politics in Britain and Sweden: From Relief to Income Maintenance.* New Haven, Connecticut: Yale University Press.

Heidenheimer, A. J. 1973. The politics of public education, health and welfare in the U. S. A. and western Europe: How growth and reform potentials have differed. *British Jour. of Pol. Sci.*, 3, 315-340.

Henretta, J. C. 1973. Political protest by the elderly: An organizational study. Unpublished doctoral dissertation, Cambridge, Massachusetts: Harvard University.

Holtzman, A. 1954. Analysis of old age behavior in the United States. *Gerontologist*, 9, 56-66.

Holtzman, A. 1963. *The Townsend Movement: A Political Study.* New York: Bookman Associates.

Hudson, R. B. 1973. Client politics and federalism: The case of the Older Americans Act. Paper delivered at the 1973 annual meeting of the American Political Science Association, New Orleans.

Hudson, R. B. 1974. Rational planning and organizational imperatives: Prospects for area planning in aging. *Annals of the Am. Acad. of Pol. and Soc. Sc.*, 415, 41-54.

Hunt, C. 1960. Private integrated housing in a medium size Northern city. *Soc. Prob.*, 7, 196-209.

Inglehart, R. 1971. The silent revolution in Europe: Inter-generational change in post-industrial societies. *Amer. Pol. Sci. Rev.*, 65, 991-1017.

Jackson, J. J. 1974. NCBA, black aged and politics. *Annals of the Am. Acad. of Pol. and Soc. Sc.*, 415, 138-159.

Kaim-Caudle, P. R. 1973. *Comparative Social Policy and Social Security.* London: Martin Robertson.

Killian, L., and Haer, J. 1958. Variables related to attitudes regarding school desegregation among white Southerners. *Sociometry*, 21, 159-164.

King, A. 1971. Ideologies as predictors of public policy patterns: A comparative analysis. Paper delivered at the 1971 annual meeting of the American Political Science Association, New York.

Lane, R. 1965. *Political Life: Why and How People Get Involved in Politics.* New York: The Free Press.

Laroque, R. 1969. Social security in France. *In*, S. Jenkins (ed.), *Social Security in International Perspective*, pp. 171-189. New York: Columbia University Press.

Lazarsfeld, P. F., Berelson, B., and Gaudet, H. 1944. *The People's Choice.* New York: Duell, Sloan, & Pearce.

Lehman, H. 1953. *Age and Achievement.* Princeton, New Jersey: Princeton University Press.

Lerner, D., Pool, I. de S., and Schueller, G. 1966. The Nazi elite. *In*, H. Lasswell and D. Lerner (eds.), *World Revolutionary Elites: Studies in Coercive Ideological Movements*, pp. 194-318. Cambridge, Massachusetts: The M. I. T. Press.

Lewytzkyi, B. 1967. Generations in conflict. *Problems of Communism*, 16, 36-40.

Lipset, S. M. 1959. *Political Man: The Social Bases of Politics.* Garden City, New York: Doubleday.

Lipset, S. M. 1967. *The First New Nation: The United States in Historical and Comparative Perspective.* Garden City, New York: Doubleday, Anchor Books.

Lowi, T. J. 1969. *The End of Liberalism.* New York: W. W. Norton.

Lowi, T. J. 1974. Interest groups and the consent to govern: Getting the people out for what? *Annals of the Am. Acad. of Pol. and Soc. Sc.*, 413, 86-100.

McClosky, H. 1967. Personality and attitude correlates of foreign policy orientation. *In*, H. Rosenau (ed.), *Domestic Sources of Foreign Policy*, pp. 51-109. New York: The Free Press.

McKenzie, R., and Silver, A. 1968. *Angels in Marble: Working Class Conservatives in Urban England.* Chicago: University of Chicago Press.

Macridis, R. C. 1961. Interest groups in comparative analysis. *Jour. of Politics*, 23, 25-45.

Maddox, G. 1974. Is senior power the wave of the future? Paper delivered at the 1974 annual meeting of the American Association for the Advancement of Science, San Francisco.

Marmor, T. R. 1970. *The Politics of Medicare.* London: Routledge & Kegan Paul.

Mendelson, M. A., and Hapgood, D. 1974. The political economy of nursing homes. *Annals of the Am. Acad. of Pol. and Soc. Sc.*, 415, 95-105.

Messinger, S. L. 1955. Organizational transformation: A case study of a declining social movement. *Am. Soc. Rev.*, 20, 3-10.

Milbrath, L. 1965. *Political Participation.* Chicago: Rand McNally.

Neugarten, B. 1974. Age groups in American society and the rise of the young-old. *Annals of the Am. Acad. of Pol. and Soc. Sc.*, 415, 187-198.

Nie, N., Verba, S., and Kim, J. 1974. Political participation and the life-cycle. *Comparative Politics*, 6, 319-340.

North, R., and Pool, I. de S. 1966. Kuomintang and Chinese communist elites. *In*, H. Lasswell and D. Lerner (eds.), *World Revolutionary Elites: Studies in Coercive Ideological Movements*, pp. 319-455. Cambridge, Massachusetts: The M.I.T. Press.

Pinner, F. A., Jacobs, P., and Selznick, P. 1959. *Old Age and Political Behavior*. Berkeley: University of California Press.

Polner, W. 1962. The aged in politics. A successful example, the NPA and the passage of the Railroad Retirement Act of 1934. *Gerontologist*, **2**, 207–215.

Pratt, H. J. 1974. Old age associations in national politics. *Annals of the Am. Acad. of Pol. and Soc. Sc.*, **415**, 106–119.

Pratt, H. J. 1976. *The Gray Lobby*. Chicago: University of Chicago Press.

Prothro, J., and Grigg, C. 1960. Fundamental principles of democracy: Bases of agreement and disagreement. *Jour. of Politics*, **22**, 276–294.

Putnam, J. K. 1970. *Old-Age Politics in California: From Richardson to Reagan*. Stanford: Stanford University Press.

Putnam, R. 1971. Studying elite political culture: The case of 'ideology.' *Amer. Pol. Sci. Rev.*, **65**, 651–681.

Rigby, T. H. 1972. The Soviet Politburo: A comparative profile, 1951–1971. *Soviet Studies*, **24**, 3–23.

Riley, M. W., and Foner, A. 1968. *Aging and Society*. New York: Russell Sage Foundation.

Rimlinger, G. 1971. *Welfare Policy and Industrialization in Europe, America, and Russia*. New York: John Wiley.

Rose, A. 1967. *The Power Structure: Political Process in American Society*. New York: Oxford University Press.

Rose, R. 1964. *Politics in England*. Boston: Little, Brown.

Schlesinger, J. A. 1966. *Ambition and Politics: Political Careers in the United States*. Chicago: Rand McNally.

Schlesinger, J. A. 1967. Political careers and party leadership. *In*, L. Edinger (ed.), *Political Leadership in Industrialized Societies*, pp. 266–293. New York: John Wiley.

Schramm, W., and White, D. 1954. Age, education, and economic status as factors in newspaper reading: Conclusions. *In*, W. Schramm (ed.), *The Process and Effects of Mass Communications*, pp. 71–73. Urbana, Illinois: University of Illinois Press.

Schueller, G. 1966. The Politburo. *In*, H. Lasswell and D. Lerner (eds.), *World Revolutionary Elites: Studies in Coercive Ideological Movements*, pp. 97–178. Cambridge, Massachusetts: The M.I.T. Press.

Schulz, J., Carrin, G., Krupp, H., Peschke, M., Sclar, E., and Van Steenberge, J. 1974. *Providing Adequate Retirement Income: Pension Reform in the United States and Abroad*. Hanover, New Hampshire: Brandeis University Press.

Searing, D., Schwartz, J., and Lind, A. 1973. The structuring principle: Political socialization and belief systems. *Amer. Pol. Sci. Rev.*, **LXVII**, 415–432.

Searing, D., Wright, G., and Rabinowitz, G. 1975. The primacy principle: Attitude change and political socialization. *British Jour. of Pol. Sci.*, forthcoming.

Steiner, G. 1966. *Social Insecurity: The Politics of Welfare*. Chicago: Rand McNally.

Stouffer, S. 1955. *Communism, Conformity, and Civil Liberties*, Garden City, New York: Doubleday.

Sundquist, J. L. 1968. *Politics and Policy: The Eisenhower, Kennedy, and Johnson Years*. Washington, D. C.: The Brookings Institution.

Tingsten, H. 1937. *Political Behavior: Studies in Election Statistics*. London: P. S. King and Son.

Titmuss, R. 1959. Trends in social policy: Health. *In*, M. Ginsberg (ed.), *Law and Opinion in the 20th Century*, pp. 299–318. Berkeley: University of California Press.

United States Bureau of the Census. 1965. Current Population Reports, p. 20, No. 143.

Verba, S., and Nie, N. 1972. *Participation in America: Political Democracy and Social Equality*. New York: Harper & Row.

Vinyard, D. 1972. The Senate Special Committee on the Aging. *Gerontologist*, **12**, 298–303.

Walker, D. 1960. The age factor in the 1958 congressional elections. *Midwest Jour. of Pol. Sci.*, **4**, 1–26.

Watanuki, J. 1967. Patterns of politics in present-day Japan. *In*, S. M. Lipset and S. Rokkan (eds.), *Party Systems and Voter Alignments: Cross-National Perspectives*, pp. 447–466. New York: The Free Press.

Wilensky, H. 1975. *The Welfare State and Equality: Structural and Ideological Roots of Public Expenditures*. Berkeley: University of California Press.

Wilson, J. Q. 1962. *The Amateur Democrat: Club Politics in Three Cities*. Chicago: University of Chicago Press.

Wilson, J. Q. 1973. *Political Organizations*. New York: Basic Books.

Witte, E. 1962. *The Development of the Social Security Act*. Madison, Wisconsin: University of Wisconsin Press.

4 AGING AND INTERPERSONAL BEHAVIOR

16
PERSONAL CHARACTERISTICS AND SOCIAL BEHAVIOR:
Theory and Method

Kurt W. Back
Duke University

INTRODUCTION

Perspectives on Personality

Philosophers, writers, and poets have wondered at the puzzle of the sequence of human life, so different in various settings, but exposing a unity for the individual from birth to death. Modern science has dealt with this question, as with other problems of philosophy, mainly by ignoring it. There is hardly a term for the developing, changing, yet persisting nature of the person, much less a theory connecting this term to other concepts.

The metaphors of the poet can be a helpful introduction to the metaphor of scientific theory. Peer Gynt puzzles over the layers of an onion and sees in them the different aspects of his life, but misses a center representing the essence of him. He is sure that there is a kernel to himself, but he cannot put his finger on it. He has to admit that he lived in many different ways, but he asserts that it was *he* doing the living, and that his life was not a sequence of disconnected acts.

In the language of the social psychologist studying human development, the two corresponding problems are the character of the individual self and its vicissitudes in the course of human development. The empirical question is how to find it and how to recognize it in different stages of the life cycle.

Sartre (1956) has stated the paradox: take away all social roles—the "self-deception" which people present to the world—and nothing remains, but this "nothing" is also the unifying force of the person. Thus this "nothing" exists, and we can experience it immediately in the same way we can "see" one person whom we are looking for but who is not at a party. The plethora of quotation marks in the preceding sentence indicate the verbal sleight-of-hand in Sartre's approach. But it can be treated as a metaphor illustrating the difficulties of stating what is meant by the term, the "self."

If the concept of the crucial part of the human being is so hard to define, the difficulty becomes staggering if development over time is taken into account. There is the inevitable course of the life cycle as well as social relations and unique experiences. In this cycle we want to distinguish a permanent core and temporary adaptations. This distinction has given rise to scientific as well as to poetic and philosophic metaphors. Controversies over the relative importance of heredity and environment is only one expression, though currently the most popular one, of this scientific dilemma. The ancient metaphor of the left hand (what one is given) and of the right hand (what one achieves) is a convenient organizing principle for biography, and this division also can be useful as a scheme for human development. For the child, the family, the ancestral background is all important; youth and adulthood look to personal achievement and the peer group; and in later years the left hand, personal idiosyncracies, take over again (Sitwell, 1944). To understand the aged we are led back to the whole life history, the history as it organizes itself around the individual.

Theoretical Biology and Developmental Social Psychology

In effect, the differences are not so unrelated to the onion: in any organism it is difficult to specify what makes it or its type unique and to recognize this identity, whether from the seed to the full grown plant, or from infancy to senescence.

Thus biologists, especially those interested in development, have a similar problem to that of the social scientist: What is the unity of the organism which develops from the zygote to the full organism? How is the species represented in the egg? This question had seemed to be so unanswerable that preformation—the existence of the whole organism in the original cell—seemed to be the only tenable hypothesis (Jacob, 1974). This would be a physical representation of the essence of the organism. But after preformation was abandoned, biologists tried to avoid the general issue and contented themselves with descriptions of the several aspects of development from zygote to full-grown individual. Renewed interest in a theoretical approach has led biologists, like social scientists, to the search for a principle which shows the permanence of aim in a changing world and a language which can represent the developmental point of view (Waddington, 1968-1972). This language has its source in the previous work of biologists, but as will be seen, it is as appropriate to social psychological development as it is to physiological development.

An organism keeps an equilibrium of its internal and external environment; this has been called homeostasis. If the equilibrium is disturbed, the organism will create conditions which will restore a viable situation. This describes the short range efforts of the organism to maintain itself. However, each organism has its own cycle of growth, development, and decay. This development too maintains a quasi-equilibrium; however, it is an equilibrium of changing conditions, along a path as it were. A fetus disturbed during its development will still tend toward becoming an organism of the correct species; a child deflected from its normal development can still return in some way to regular adult status; unusual experiences at early life stages can be corrected in old age. Something in the individual follows a predetermined path and, after some disturbances, will regain this path; this is true for the biological development of the organism as well as for the socio-psychological development of the individual.

C. H. Waddington (1957) has coined the term chreod (necessary path) for the identifiable units of an individual. Chreods are conformations (topological units) which are defined throughout a period of time. An organism will return to its path after disturbance, compensating for past disturbances in some way, in a "channeled trajectory." In the same way a traveler may catch up with a tour group after losing it—the group maintains its unity to him, although the composition may have changed.

A chreod has a definite goal, a capacity to maintain itself, but can be defined without any mystical or teleological conception. One need only to define the region, i.e., the range of characteristics which one will accept as homogeneity, and the limiting change which can occur while keeping identity in order to define a chreod over a certain time period. Such a chreod would be the development of an egg into groups of cells. One can then define the end of the chreod as the time when the cell differentiates into the different dermal layers, and each layer then becomes a new chreod developing into its specific organ system. Such a change from a chreod to another or a group of others is called catastrophe; a formal study of development can be undertaken by determining the chreods and catastrophic conditions (Thom, 1972).

This scheme has been devised to analyze physical development in which the content or changing characteristics are visible or can be easily visualized. It is, however, applicable to the development of living organisms in general, within the psychological and social contexts. One can look at many theories and methods as partial attempts to explain development, to define chreods, catastrophe, and resulting changes.

In common, everyday life we seem to have an intuitive grasp of the essential unity of the person and of extreme changes which may occur. In general, we treat a person as being one identity over most of his lifetime; only extreme changes are recognized by speaking of a different person and reacting to the difference—a child to an adult, a status change, such as entering a religious order, or some of the changes accompanying old age, such as retirement, bereavement, or institutionalization. The intuitive knowledge has been incorporated slowly into the systematic corpus of social science; impatience with the partial results from long scientific studies into a state of affairs which seems immediately obvious has led to dispute over research methods and their use. We can give a direction to the needs of research by assessing the answers to the questions which we have asked about development and the measurement of continuity and change.

The concepts of developmental biology which we have outlined are directly applicable to developmental social psychology, and important trends in current theory can be seen this way. A scheme which provides a direct sociological analogue to the biological model has been proposed by Peter Marris (1974).

Reviewing the experience gained from several studies of transition to new conditions, among them a study of widowhood, he found in a common pattern a trait which he called conservation. People act conservatively, attempting to keep a self-image undisturbed, even when subjected to many jolts; in changed conditions, as after bereavement, the maintenance of the self-image may lead to novel looking kinds of behavior, and in this sense conservation is the basis of innovative behavior. The maintenance of the self through this conservative function can be defined as a chreod maintaining itself through the vicissitudes of life crises. Catastrophic changes occur when it is not possible to maintain the chreod and a new constellation has to be found.

Thus, Marris describes the catastrophic reaction, the destruction of a chreod and the construction of a new one. His description of the grieving process, for instance, starts with the ambivalence toward a situation which has lost immediate support (Marris, 1958). The intensive involvement with the other person which has been quite stable is profoundly disturbed. The bereaved person has to determine the essential meaning of the previous relationship and incorporate it into a pattern for a new life. We find in any transition several common features: (1) a self-concept which was realized in certain social relations; (2) a shattering of these relations which leads to a reevaluation of their meaning—the grieving reaction; (3) a new understanding of the nature of this relationship and the conditions of preservation of the self (conservation); (4) the incorporation of this new knowledge into the current situation which may result in a new combination (innovation).

Marris' scheme is a concrete illustration of abstract developmental geometry. There is a certain set of attitudes and values connected to social situations which stay constant over a long period. Stability is maintained and can be measured. This "field" extending over time will resist changes and return to its essential form after a disturbance; if it cannot adjust, it will form new fields, preserving some of the characteristics of the old ones. The definition of these processes in the interpersonal sphere is the task of developmental social psychology as the definition in the biologic sphere is the task of developmental biology.

The Individual, Nature, and Society

The study of personal traits and the self in aging is intimately connected with development in the whole life cycle, and this process can be seen as analogous to the biological development of the organism. We began our discussion, therefore, by exploring general concepts and analytic procedures which could apply to the whole field. We must now inquire about distinctions within the field and the usefulness of restrictions to particular systems or periods of development.

There is, to be sure, one fundamental distinction between biological and psycho-social development: development of the human personality is determined to a great extent by interaction with others, by the types of associations, and by the norms of the society. In particular, these social interactions, elaborated by the whole symbolic process of human language and culture, can change the meaning of the purely biological development. Thus any differences which are biologically irrelevant may be exaggerated through social norms, while differences which are biologically important may be ignored. Discussion of sociopsychological development thus cannot concentrate solely on the characteristics of the individuals concerned, but has to take into account the social conditions of the time; individual traits acquire their meaning only through social interaction.

Social classification of the individual becomes, therefore, a precondition to the development of individual traits and the complex of self and personality. Continuity of a person will also depend on social definition. Different societies use different criteria in making classifications. The work of sociologists and anthropologists, especially the structural school, has shown the variety of classifications and logical systems which govern these classifications.

We must stress the difference between the natural units of development, as they can be observed by the biologists, and their transformation into social categories. Appropriate behavior by a person as well as toward a person, the social role, can depend on many criteria, some immediately obvious to perception, such as physical characteristics, some less so, such as ancestry, abilities, or achievements. Societies may function, stressing one kind or another, facilitating and frustrating the life of individuals.

The importance of age as a social criterion depends on the classification system of the society. Contemporary society has shown an interesting tendency to disregard those traits which are most obvious to immediate perception. Thus, such characteristics as sex or race are not supposed to be taken into account for most social role performance, while less visible traits, such as ability or training, are. In fact, the existence of roles linked to these traits, such as sex roles, is taken to be an unfortunate anachronism, almost the result of a conspiracy. There are even attempts to purge the language of these classifications, using "person" instead of "man" or "woman," or similarly omitting race descriptions.

Age seems to be in a similar position as those other visible traits. Efforts are made to prove that chronological age has little to do with role performance and legal limits based on age alone are diminished. Again, efforts at purging the language are indicative of the social trend: "old people" become "senior citizens," "old' itself becomes "elderly" or even "middle-aged," and "old age asylums" become "nursing homes" or even "sun cities." Thus, one can deny that the immediate perception of a person has something to do with his social role.

The effort at elimination of biological and perceptual categories has created new problems. A clear description of appropriate behavior at each age can ease the path of the aged (Rosow, 1974), although it violates rules of equal rights. The same society which tries to obliterate the differences of age, sex, and race has also witnessed the rise of gerontology, feminism, and ethnic consciousness. This may look like a paradox, but it also may be a reaction to this ambiguous situation.

The development of personality and its relation to social behavior is affected by social standards. Personality development will conform, within biological limits, to social requirements, and therefore one cannot in our society discuss a clear picture of the aged personality—defined by a rigid age limit—as compared to the middle-aged or young one. In fact, one would have difficulties in setting an age which would separate the old from the rest. Thus, we will give attention to theories of group membership, human development, and methods for studying them, which would apply to human beings in general. But we must make assumptions or "wagers" (Duvignaud, 1972) about the characteristics of individuals in contemporary society. Because we do look at one person as the same individual during his lifetime, we shall generally assume a continuity of the self. In other societies, discontinuities may be marked: in some cultures in India, a man can leave his home, after having fulfilled his duties to his family and community, become a hermit, and really become another person in his own eyes as well as everyone else's. These abrupt changes are not normative in our society, however, although they may occur. As a general working hypothesis, we shall accept a continuity of personality—the perseverance of one chreod—and look at changes as exceptions, as catastrophies, in the terminology of theoretical biology.

This point of view has two immediate consequences for our discussion. We cannot concentrate on aging only (partly because old age is becoming an arbitrary definition), but must discuss the life cycle with emphasis on the later stages. Secondly, we must assume continuity or at least continued identity of a person and seek for continuity—conservatism—even in seemingly complete breaks.

SOCIAL GROUPS

Human individuality tends to be preserved and reestablished throughout the vicissitudes of life. This is the state of affairs which is represented by the concept of chreod. Individuality is preserved in the context of groups most relevant to the person. We can classify groups into those which give extension in time and those which give extension in space. The most important of the first is the family, but other groups, such as community and ethnic groups, have the same function. These are long, enduring groups which give a person a sense of identity. The other type of group, such as friendship and work groups, provides immediate contact with the contemporary world; these provide spatial continuity. An individual's life is affected by the kind of groups he uses for each purpose, as well as by the interplay between the two groups.

Family

The importance of the family as the link for the individual between the past and the future does not have to be documented in detail. The sociologist who is measuring generational mobility acknowledges this fact as does the biographer who searches for a person's ancestors even if he does not acknowledge any influence of heredity. Thus, family relations stay with a person throughout his life, even if he rejects them. In this case the family does not simply come down to a nonexisting level, but the act of rejection is one more significant aspect of the family relationship. Another aspect of the family relationship is its primacy. It is present at the beginning of life when the individual is most dependent on others. It then leads to an intense emotional relationship. Intensity and continuity are the main characteristics of the family relationship and characterize this group from all others (Back, 1965).

In addition to these general characteristics, however, there are variations in what family means to different people. For instance, the extent of family ties for different individuals may differ, not only cross-culturally but within the same culture (White, 1962). Throughout the life cycle the family has different aspects for the same individual: in youth the family of origin is important; in later stages of life the family of procreation is more important. The connection between these aspects of family has been little investigated but is most important. However, studies of links in three generation families show symmetry between the older (grandparent-parent) and younger (parent-child) links (Hill, 1970). We can see that different patterns of family formation and of fertility will lead to different family conditions when older ages are attained. Thus a declining birth rate leaves the current young generation with the likelihood of having very little close family once they have themselves grown older (Shanas and Hauser, 1974). Then because the nuclear group is missing, collateral groups of the family may become more important again. Thus the larger kinship group may assume a stronger hold.

The family endures through an individual's lifetime, but the importance of different relationships varies in intensity. Intensity of emotional involvement could be related to patterns of physical or social contact but not necessarily so. We may think, therefore, that changes in household composition and residential propinquity of relatives will lead to major changes in the importance of family relations. Increased urban living has had this effect. Much theory has assumed a decline in intensity as well as in extent of family relations. Research has shown, however, that the actual changes in household composition were not as definite as had been assumed, and that the importance of family ties persists even under conditions of residential separation (Anderson, in press). Thus, at least in Western societies, conjugal family units have always been the preferred arrangement; the lack of common residence has not led to low emotional ties between aged parents and adult children.

Community

A similar argument can be made about the importance of the community, namely, that increased flexibility does not lessen its importance for identity. The impact of greater residential mobility, in addition to the improvement of transportation and of communication connecting people to different parts of the world, might be considered as decreasing the importance of one's immediate local community. However, this is not necessarily true; neither residential mobility nor heightened communications inevitably results in decreased emotional ties with the local community. Greater mobility may make it possible to adopt a new community easily. New patterns of emotional ties may be brought into play so that the individual can adjust to changes. A whole new culture of quick adaptation and individual interaction has arisen, which may make people strongly attached to a community, even if only for a short time (Rogers, 1968; Henry, 1965). Communities have sprung up mainly to cater to this; retirement communities are one example of this general trend.

Work Groups

In contrast to such groups, we have immediate groups, face-to-face contact groups, such as peer groups, with which an individual can identify momentarily. During adulthood and in later life the most important such groups

are those connected with work, the associations made through the working life. Work identity is probably an individual's most important identity, second only to identity based on family and community relations. Work identity, however, has a more voluntary character to it than the other two. A person may accept a certain position or job, but he can also give it up or change to another. However, work identity can be lost completely through unemployment or retirement. In aging, the loss of the work role becomes a social loss as important as the monetary loss, and it is a real giving up of certain important associations. Thus retirement can represent a more complete break with previous conditions, more radical than temporary dissolution of family ties such as are meant by the so-called "empty nest stage," i.e., the stage in which one's children leave home (Back, 1971; Simpson and McKinney, 1966; Streib and Schneider, 1971; Streib and Thompson, 1958).

Voluntary Groups

The work role, as said, is in part voluntary, and a variety of other roles important to the individual can be substituted for it. These may range from the role taken within friendship groups to the identity established through hobbies or recreational activities, or finally, to identification with other people. Professionals working with the aged have assumed that these groups are substituted for the supposed loss of family, work, or community affiliations and have promoted their formation for the aged. These are voluntary associations: hobbies, golden age clubs, and interest clubs. Because of commonality of attitudes and beliefs, a person can enter into various associations, be influenced by them, feel identity with them—but only for an immediate time (Kleemeier, 1961). All such groups are dependent on immediate patterns of interaction and can be usefully studied from this point of view.

Generations

There is an additional kind of group which is not yet well-defined, but which provides a transition between long range groups and immediate groups. This could be called a generation or the subjective cohort. People identify with a certain group of individuals of their own age, especially people whom they have known in youth. Strict age-grading, as practiced in the extreme by the East African tribes (Eisenstadt, 1956), where an age cohort moves officially through its places in society, is not common in Western society. However, certain events such as school or initiation rituals pull some common age groups together. Several scholars, among them Ortega y Gassett (1923) and Mannheim (1952), have proposed the concept of a generation as meaningful even in Western society. Generational boundaries are made by major historical events, but in most writers' hands the concept is mainly useful for an intellectual elite. However, it may become an important tool for understanding morale and behavior of the aged if we consider that the generation serves as a reference group; for instance, relative deprivation, which would be severe if considered in relation to the young in society, is not felt if considered in reference to one's own generation. The subjective experience of generation has not been studied to a great extent, and although this kind of group may not be formally developed, it is latently important in order to understand individual identities (Bengtson, Furlong, and Laufer, 1974).

The relationship of aging to this array of possible associations raises the question of whether there is a regular transition from one to the other. The importance of the different and predictable relationships can be related to different ages, and conversely, the aging process is reflected in a different pattern of social relations. Effective group membership is a social equivalent of individual aging (Rosow, 1974). We can look at the different group conditions in their relation to the life cycle. The most important group memberships in temporal as well as spatial affiliation (family and work) are tied to the life cycle; the lesser affiliations (community and voluntary organizations) are rather independent of it. The social conditions of individual development can be described as the differential involvement in different types of groups. Regularities as well as individual variations of the aging process are functions of their shifting importance.

THEORY

Dimensions of Theory

The task of developmental social psychology is to determine a configuration which defines an individual over a considerable period of time, to describe its characteristics and its conditions of origin, maintenance and dissolution, and to analyze the boundary regions and the changes which can be expected after sudden disruption. The theoretical approaches to the development of social interaction are usually not motivated by a central interest in the field itself, but treat more general questions or those which overlap social psychological development. They are likely to be appropriate to some aspects of development, perhaps defining persistence or conditions of change. They define parts of the chreod, its nature or its boundary, and are attuned to different time slices. They may thus treat transition to aging or the persisting aging personality.

Whatever the emphasis of the theory, it is faced with the fact that human development proceeds at two levels; the biological organism is determined by the rise and decay within the natural life span and by the social experience which can organize life according to voluntary standards. A related contrast is that between subjective self-determination and the press of external circumstances. Theorists can be said to be optimistic or tragic to the degree to which they accept the discrepancy between human aspiration and biological necessity; they are also active and passive according to their emphasis on the feeling of self-determination.

The importance of the tragic-optimistic contrast or the active-passive orientation becomes apparent when considering the later part of life. The path of the biological individual turns downward and points toward individual death but survival of the species. In considering man as a social being, it is always possible for society to arrange institutions such that either youth or age can be peaks or depressions in life. Thus different kinds of time perspective in the whole life cycle can determine the expectation as well as the experience of self-development in aging.

We shall thus discuss the theories and methods which are relevant to the development of personality. They are mostly concerned with fragments of the person, simple variables or observations. After discussing these several aspects we shall attempt to discuss aspects of the self in general: time perspective, the interplay of different kinds of group affiliation, such as family and work groups, social and demographic influences, and the relation of the development of the self to the meaning of life.

Theories differentiated according to the time range considered will also be divided according to their concern with continuity and change. Contemplation of the long range impresses one with regularity and perseverance, while attention to the moment impresses the observer with the importance of change. Consideration of theories according to their time range is also important for questions of personality and the social environment. We shall, therefore, discuss applicable theories according to such a scheme.

Continuity Theories

Taking an extremely long range view with genetic and evolutionary emphasis, one looks only at slow and gradual adaptations. Each person is simply a step in a long sequence of generations. Socially we find the analogue of this approach in family histories where each character is taken as a whole representing his own generation. Sociological family studies show a prevailing influence over the whole life span, leading to extreme creative or pathological results (Goddard, 1912; Simpson, 1956). Not much attention is given to change. For the new generation, the aged person represents only the memories of his own youth.

More central to questions of individual development are the physiologically oriented theories which derive human behavior from some constitutional pattern that persists throughout life. This approach has a long tradition, from the "humors" of the ancients to phrenology. Recent theories have taken a variety of physiological conditions into account. Among the more popular ones, Sheldon's (1942) typology uses a number of measurements to determine the somato-types which are related to corresponding character types. Other theories do not try to explain the whole personality constellation, but only specific tendencies or traits. In addition, research on particular physiological effects, such as glandular deficiencies and nervous development, has been used to explain some constitutional patterns. To a smaller degree the same sources may explain long lasting personality differences. These theories take the biological developmental work as a model and are, therefore, led to the same question: What is it which controls the consistent creation of particular forms over the life span?

Some theories try to ascribe single causes for human behavior; they are usually designed to treat extreme or pathological cases. Conditions such as body build, glandular secretions, and development of nerve nets (Rimland, 1964) can determine behavior if they are beyond the normal range. However, small variations within this range are not sufficient to guide the whole life course.

A modern variant of these somatic theories puts the predetermining causes into early experiences of the individual. These theories propose that some event or constellation in early childhood will determine the course of life. Orthodox psychoanalysis can be taken as the model for this perspective. The work of the psychoanalysts and psychodynamically oriented theorists has established clearly the importance of early childhood experiences, especially of unusual or painful ones. Again, we must stress the point that this work was principally designed to expose sources of pathological behavior, not to deal with variations in the normal range.

The strict psychoanalytical theories look for lifelong determination of character during the pregenital stages, that is, before adolescence. The way in which a person reaches genital maturity and the completeness of maturation will determine character, personality tendencies, and behavior in future years. One implication of this view is that basic tendencies of the personality do not change appreciably after this time. Thus we have here an equation, setting equal on the one side the deep-seated, interacting tendencies of the personality and on the other, earlier events in the lifetime. Biographies of two of Freud's classical cases (Freeman, 1971; Gardiner, 1971) have shown how circumstances in the later parts of life can modify the personality of individuals who seemed to be caught in a neurotic pattern established in childhood.

Although this classical, Freudian approach is not generally applied in its pure form today, its general ideas have great influence in theoretical consideration of adult behavior. In general, most textbooks or theoretical discussion will devote more time to childhood or adolescent development than to changes during the adult and later years. The middle years are considered to be the standard from which all other ages are to be explained as either leading to this period or leading away from it; thus most discussion is devoted to the stages which build up the personality patterns which are then supposedly stable during the middle years.

Developmental Theories

The importance of early childhood experiences is undoubted, and correspondingly, a psychodynamic investigation made into the present condition of a person will show that many personality traits are quite stable. However, it has been recognized even by many scientists working within the psychoanalytic tradition that adult development can be important and that it leads to definite personality changes. To put it another way, it has been recognized that people face new problems after adolescence which they have to solve in their own way. Thus several varieties of neo-Freudians have extended development into later paths and periods of life and in this way discovered personality traits which are more appropriate to adult and elderly ages. Probably the most complete attempt of this kind was made by Eric Erikson (1959) who began as a child psychoanalyst and later extended his work to cover the whole life span. He discovered a major problem during the postadolescent

years—the search for an identity or the identity crisis, which is different from the Freudian sexual developmental stages. Starting with this crisis, he isolated a series of problems which must be solved at the appropriate age. Eventually he described a sequence of seven stages, each characterized by a certain kind of problem which must be solved so that the individual can pass easily into the next stage. Personality traits will develop at each stage depending on the resolution of each previous conflict. In fact, however, in the description of his theory even Erikson devotes much more space to the earlier stages which take an individual through adolescence than to the later stages which describe the rest of the individual's life cycle.

The great importance of early childhood and the attention given to it by psychologists are not confined to those who work within the psychoanalytic framework. We find the same imbalance in cognitive and structural theories. In establishing a theory related primarily to intellectual and cognitive development, Piaget (Inhelder and Piaget, 1958) defines a development of steps toward a logical understanding of the world, but once this is achieved, he seems to assume a future leveling out of development. The achievement of cognitive maturity is cumulative and is not unlearned in the later stages of life. Thus the achievement of logical understanding, accomplished by the end of adolescence, is considered the main developmental task.

Some special theories have tried to take into account some of the facts of development in the later ages. The first one was the so-called disengagement theory of Cumming and Henry (1961), which fastens on the restriction of individual life and interests in the older ages. This theory tries to account for such disengagement by assuming that, as a natural development, withdrawal from the physical and social environment occurs during old age. An obvious corollary or perhaps a causative agent is the lack of purely physical means of interaction with the environment: the decline both of sensory abilities and muscular activities. Application of this development to a more personal and social withdrawal from society may be an obvious step, but, since its proclamation, disengagement theory has been controversial. It explains some puzzling findings: the relatively high morale of the aged, even under conditions that might seem distressing to a younger observer, and the seeming acceptance of a more contemplative life, which some cultures feel to be appropriate to the aged. On the other hand, it does not correspond to observations of some aged who are either extremely active and creative in old age or extremely distressed at being forced to withdraw from social contacts. We can see how this theory has clashed with the opposite one (Maddox, 1963): the so-called activity theory, which says that the more active an aged person is, the better his morale will be. Clearly, a combination of the two theories will account for almost any event or development we can think of. We are reminded again of the fact that one-sided theories may be very appropriate for some part of the range. Disengagement theory may fit the development of some people quite well, especially within the middle range of possible adaptations. People who are extremely creative may be able to adapt even during older years by staying very active, but people who are maladapted during most of their adult life will find the maladaptation and the lack of social support insufferable in later age. This whole controversy, therefore, might be better framed in Erikson's terms as a problem to be solved in old age, perhaps in a balance to be achieved between withdrawal and activity.

One might go to the opposite extreme from the Freudian theorists and state that the personality asserts itself gradually over the life span. Although few would claim that the aged exhibit the basic personality in its purest form, the emphasis on self-realization and similar terms by some personality theorists points in this direction. They see human development as a struggle to realize one's essence, to reach the possibilities of one's being in the purest form; one could say that they see a continuous progression of a chreod to a pure form (Maslow, 1962).

We may stop at this point to see to what extent personality theories have solved the problems we have posed as questions of theoretical understanding. As theories, they have been chiefly concerned with extending continuities through time (Campbell, 1958). The very concept of personality assumes a continuity in time over the course of life. For practical purposes, any personality theory assumes that one can learn more about the actions of a person by knowing something of his past and previous adaptations rather than by knowing about his immediate situation. In general, therefore, personality theories are better able to explain continuity than to explain change. In the same way, they concentrate on the individual and not on the situation in which he moves. Therefore, the changes are conditioned through events within the individual and not through events that might impinge on him. This is, of course, not entirely true. To be handled effectively, individual problems and changes must be worked out within the environment and in relation to it. However, even in discussing environmental effect, personality theories discuss intrinsic change—a change which would occur within the individual, based on previous experience or because of inevitable workings within him. This may explain, in part, the greater concentration of personality theories on early development rather than on later stages. The young organism, still physically growing and changing, can easily lead the observer to assume that there are similar and necessary changes within his personality and intellectual development. These intrinsic changes are less obvious in the relatively stable and physically unchanging adult. Even physical changes in senescence are not comparable to the physical development of the first 10 or 15 years of life; hence, a necessary assumption of an intrinsic change is less defensible in the later stages of life. This may explain why the intrinsic theory of personality development in aging, namely the disengagement theory, has been more subject to attack than corresponding theories about childhood and even about later stages such as adolescence. In general, we may find a weakness of all personality theories in consideration of the individual by himself and therefore a corresponding disregard of the fit of the individual to the environment. In fact, most theories have concentrated chiefly on misfits or pathological relationships between individual and environment. The main interest in personality development occurs among researchers attempting to explain deviations and maladaptations of the individual within the environment. Research also concentrates on independent development of the individual. Unusual or pathological courses of life have always been evident in personality theories and discussion. The first subjects who draw attention to themselves are those who seek help, and it becomes difficult to find a large sample of normal subjects. Thus we find that most personality theories can better explain pathological than adjustive behavior, and one must turn to situational theories to understand this.

Situational Theories

Is it possible to understand a person's actions solely within contemporaneous relationships? Some theories try to approximate this by concentrating on a minute analysis of interactions. A conversation between strangers or between familiars can be analyzed for its own sake without reference to previous structures or memories. The main concepts which are used to make this possible focus on "role." A role, in contrast to personality, is something assumed by an individual to create an interaction or to help him function in a certain scene. The term has been taken from theater, and theorists have accepted a similar metaphor to dramatize their use of this concept.

There is a whole range of interactionist theories which have grown up around the concept of role and the corresponding general perspective of the theater (Biddle and Thomas, 1966; Foote, 1958). Their central concern is not, as in personality theories, with the continuity and identity of the person, but with individual transactions. Their common core or background is the heritage of "symbolic interaction," that is, an emphasis on the propensity of the human being to use symbols. The role taken by a person will depend on the needs of the situation and the expectation of the other participants. In the development of symbols and the roles people take, theories differ in their insistence on the importance of

a common understanding of the situation. The classic symbolic interaction theories emphasize shared expectations and shared understanding of the situation (Mead, 1934). Thus observation and research concentrate on the kinds of roles people tend to take, different requirements for the role, and the way in which role performance is acted out (Denzin, 1970). Recent writers, such as Goffman (1959), emphasize the voluntary character of role-playing and theatrical performance and the distinction between the actual performance and the other life of the participant—as it were, a backstage situation.

By contrast, other theorists, especially those connected with ethno-methodology, point to the problematic nature of the common understanding and the underlying suppositions of any situation. They concentrate, in even more detail than classic theorists, on the way in which the understanding of a situation is established or arrived at by negotiation (Garfinkel, 1968). Thus they show how supposedly stable situations are based on a tenuous agreement and the fact that this agreement is arrived at through painful effort. Of more immediate concern to our problem here is the way in which biographies are constructed in each situation, and how the meaning of biographical background, that is, of the personality, may change depending on the situation and the ways in which the definition of the situation has been formed. This theory goes, in a sense, to a different extreme from orthodox psychoanalytic personality theories. Ethno-methodologists are rarely concerned with the reality of long ranging personality tendencies; on the contrary, they try to show how these tendencies are re-created in each individual situation. For them, personality tendencies are really convenient fictions to explain certain kinds of behavior to other participants and to one another. In another way the two theories contrast with each other. As we have seen, personality theories are particularly useful in explaining extreme and pathological behavior which will override every constrained situation. Ethno-methodological theories and other theories which have come out of the symbolic-interactionist tradition say that they deal with everyday life, with everyday interactions, and try to explain the interactions which do occur; they concentrate on those people who are not constrained by an internal reason from acting in a way appropriate to the situation. Even more, they like to explain pathologies as social definitions, that is, as products of environmental conditions. Thus they would not say that the personality of the aged differs from that of a younger person in a particular way, but that the powerful majority, the middle-aged, use age as a criterion, a stigma, to ascribe undesirable traits (Goffman, 1963). In practice, just as personality theorists are more comfortable dealing with an extreme type of person, interactionist theorists prefer to deal with unusual situations, such as confidence games, emergency wards, or total institutions.

The extremes of the personality theories show that it is possible to consider only the reality of a long ranging trait within a person, taking the whole life of a person as a unit while disregarding the situation in which he has to live. On the other hand, it is also possible to take each situation as a new event, as a new problem to be solved, and to study the way in which each situation can be solved as an event in itself. These theories then regard continuity almost as a construction which people make to justify their own acts. Such theories consider only extrinsic events: how people react to situational requirements, how situations develop, and how social life can work smoothly, contrary to individual desires. However, according to the criteria we have shown for theories of human life, these two approaches are at opposite ends. For a look at specific problems then—especially pathology on the one hand and unusual situations on the other—it becomes more efficient to use a one sided approach. The main problem with which one has to deal, however, is the question of the connection between the two. How do personality and society interact? How do people learn how to negotiate or establish an identity? How do they learn to perform in specific situations?

Transitional Theories

We find two basic approaches to a connection between personality and situations, depending on which side one wants to start. One way is more individual, an approach to show how different persons can be proficient in adapting to new situations. In this case, the process of learning becomes the prime focus of interest. Learning, when all is said and done, is a concept which explains how previous experiences of an organism effect later orientation and activities. One feature of learning as a mechanism is that it is not restricted to any concrete situation: strictly speaking, no situation is completely repeatable. Thus the essence of any kind of learning is generalization. The theories show how individuals abstract from one situation and apply the learned responses to another situation. We can explain continuity of behavior over a long time because of learning; yet at the same time, we can understand change because of the imperfection of learning and the impossibility of exact replication of a situation. Learning theories and behavior theories typically show how one set of stimuli changes an organism sufficiently to enable it to behave similarly but differently in a future situation. In this way we can transcend the distinctions between continuity and change. Learning theories, in the same way, try for a middle ground in the other criteria set up, and in some ways they do show the connections between external evidence and internal reactions, and the way in which the organism gradually adapts to its environment.

The diversity in the development of learning theories almost encompasses the history of modern psychology. Theories differ partly in their relative emphasis on internal and external factors. For instance, one group emphasizes the preexistence of experiences which may cause differences among people and the way these different experiences are reacted to later. These theories are summarized under the title of social learning (Bandura and Walters, 1963) and are particularly important in the study of the development of motives. The other approach is more externally directed and in some circumstances may ignore what happens within the individual; it connects a certain stimulus pattern to a certain response pattern on a statistical basis. This is behavior theory (Skinner, 1953), which is especially important in purposeful modification of behavior. This is done by discovering the kind of pattern of stimuli which may lead to the desired outcome (Franks, 1969). Its particular strength is its parsimony: it is possible to select just a few stimulus items and disregard many features of the situation, including the personality of the individuals concerned. Its defects, however, lie in the same direction: it may lead to dangerous over-simplification and the disregard of possibly complex interactions of the organism. It may, therefore, be better adapted to purposeful control than to the explanation of actual ongoing events.

Learning theories may be seen as a building of bridges from the individual to the situation. They build a society from the actions of individuals. Another way of performing this operation is building the bridge from a different direction. This is the purpose of the so-called field theory, which tries to encompass the individual as well as surrounding the situation in one concept, sometimes called the life-space (Deutsch, 1968). This represents a slice of time. The field at a given time includes the individual and all his surroundings which are present, remembered, or anticipated. Field theory begins by placing each person at a point in the total field of forces of attraction and rejection and defines paths and barriers which enable him to reach a point of attraction or to retreat from rejection. By taking the person as a point, of course, one neglects individual differences, that is, personality. However, one also can construct a field within a person and present in a special way different personality aspects or different aspects of a person's development. One can distinguish, for example, people who are relatively simple, that is, in whom we can recognize few regions, and one can distinguish complex persons, in whom we can recognize many regions distinct from each other. We can also distinguish people who are very rigid, who cannot jump from one idea to another, and more fluid persons, for whom internal boundaries are less definite (Kounin, 1941). As a matter of fact, it may be possible to make a completely developmental theory based principally on changes of this kind. Field theory tries to relate the life-space, that is, the external field of a person to the internal field of a person. As a spatial representation of the process we are discussing, field theory is a convenient representation and is almost seductively convincing. It may, however, sometimes be difficult to transform the attractive pictures into concrete facts by which we can describe and measure.

In reviewing the different theories, we have considered the complications of looking at human life with one fixed trajectory, determined by initial conditions or as acted in different roles according to the script which happens to be played at the moment. The variability of human personality according to the possible situation in which an individual finds himself, however, is so large that one or the other of these models might be applicable depending on conditions. While we have lists of personality traits, we have very few classifications of situations. Certain combinations are necessary when dealing with an actual problem. We have seen how such concepts as learning or the abstract looking at a field at a given time may help to consider a combination of personality and situational factors. We can conclude this theoretical section by discussing several approaches which may help in understanding life cycles and stages in particular social conditions.

Biographical Theories

In concentrating on the personal problems of the aged and the psychological aging process, one may neglect the nonrecurring, historical situation in which aging occurs. The particular experiences of any group born at about the same time, the generation, or cohort in scientific terms, are important for the aging process (Ryder, 1965). In this way the influence of specific historical events on patterns which continually change over the years can be investigated. Cohort analysis has been specifically a demographic tool, used to show the effects of demographic conditons, such as natality, maturation, and mortality. Cohorts are used less in social psychological studies to identify those social conditions in a person's childhood which become important in social interactions during the adult and later years. A cohort analysis of changing family and social situations is very important in this context. If the social situation at a crucial time impinges on a child's socialization, this will affect his later life. As children grow up they have different patterns in aging. It can be reasonably assumed that the children can see in the aged what they can expect in their own lives when they reach that stage. Thus the acceptance and rejection of this status becomes important not in early life but at the end, at the life-stage of aging. For instance, a study of the housing and living arrangements over the human life cycle and different life cycles over history will help to understand the life of the aged during a particular time period. A rural cohort will age differently in the city than an originally urban group.

Unfortunately very little data of this kind has been systematically collected: generational effects are pulled out for explanations of isolated facts. Data on family and social life, systematically collected in different time periods, lends itself to cohort analysis. It is only now that systematic work by historians and demographers has given some idea of possible variability and change in family relationships. At present, probably the best we can do is to become aware of the consequences of this effect. Looking at any theory which is too generalized, we would do well to test it against specific, historical periods. On the other hand, we may be able to test a relationship on different historic data which would give us, therefore, a wider range of application and measure than we could have obtained in a simple, contemporary study.

Studying historical cohorts may be chiefly a framework by which one can look for specific problems. One of these problems is identification of crises which a person has survived in his life. One set of these crises (abrupt changes of status and life conditions), occuring during the earlier stage of a normal life, will have a great effect on adjustment during the second half of the life cycle. Entering school, jobs, leaving home, or marriage are such events. There may be idiosyncratic factors, such as early bereavement, migration, or sudden change in economic or family condition. All these events affect the cohort as well as the individual himself. Similar crises during the life cycle occur in the latter stages of life. Retire-

ment, children leaving (the empty nest stage), and bereavement are the most common events in a person's life cycle at that time. We can test the different ways in which a person handles a crisis. Is there a common way of handling crises which would show a common personality trait; is there an interaction of the personality with different kinds of crises (Janis, 1974)? We also have those crises which specifically affect each cohort. Such events as war, economic crises, and political and natural events may affect a whole cohort at some time and have an impact on its aging pattern. The old veteran or the survivor of a disaster has a certain behavior pattern impressed upon him which lasts into old age. In this way we can study those crises common to mankind and the different effects of personality on cohorts and cohort membership.

On a very small scale we can use a similar system of crisis conditions to look at any particular decision to be made. A series of factors which can be analyzed in a systematic way impinges upon the decider. We find here again different sets of conditions which may lead a person to make a decision. Some are completely dependent on the situation, optimizing a gain at that time by looking at future outcomes and planning where the risk is least and the payoff best. It is in this kind of decision that businessmen and politicians can be guided by analyzing the same statistical theories (Snyder, Bruck, and Sapin, 1962; Wilensky, 1967). This is, however, also a pattern which may guide a person throughout life in making decisions. Again, if we start with some personality definition, we can find those people who are repeating crucial decisions of early life over and over—usually said to be a neurotic symptom. However, to a certain lesser degree, a tendency to react in a certain way, whether it fits the situation or not, is a common personality tendency. Reaction in different decisions, especially in crises throughout our lifetime, can become an indicator of a person's personality and also of a group or cohort which might be affected in a certain similar way. Decision theory can, therefore, be considered as a technique that tries to combine personality and situational factors (Back, 1961, 1968).

Summary

Let us look back at the theories we discussed. We find surprising agreement in the main outlines obscured by a variety of different emphases on details. Taking our original point of view, that we have to look at a stable configuration, a person whom we can recognize through the vicissitudes of development, we realize that the person reacts differently in different situations and that these configurations change with individual development and social conditions. The nature of human development ensures that the person changes in a regular way and that we easily accept a person in old age as being the same as he was in his youth. In fact, we feel that complete stability is suspect, as the eternal youth of Dorian Gray. Theoretical biologists have used the concept of chreod for an equivalent situation and we have employed it for use in this context. Different theories look at different aspects of the chreod. Continuity theories look at some of the characteristics of the chreod; their main effort has been to identify this main characteristic early in the life cycle and trace its persistence and impact on other traits. Situational theories, on the other hand, try to identify adjustments in the chreod according to immediate conditions, sometimes neglecting the conformation itself. The theories which combine continuity and situation try, from this point of view, to define several characteristics of the chreod. Learning theories accept the person who learns, as well as what is learned; field theory tries, with varying success, to talk about the person-in-the-field as a unit (in fact, Lewin (1938), its main representative, used a similar term, "hodology," in defining a "science of the path"), and decision theory tries to determine conditions of significant change in the chreod.

METHOD

The Framework in Current Methodology

We have identified the basic problem of developmental social psychology as the persistence of certain configurations—chreods—through time and the conditions of their destruction and replacement (catastrophe). We have also noted that the nature of the chreod does not preserve all its traits in a static fashion, but exhibits a lawful change which is consistent within a wide range of disturbance; this is what is meant by identity of a person. This model supports various theories which concentrate on different aspects of the development process. It also gives guidance in assessing research strategies.

The methodological problems of developmental social psychology follow from the description of the process. One must define: (1) the essential dimensions of the chreod— the characteristics of the personality which determine the identity, (2) the regular changes of the chreod in the developmental process, (3) the variations of the chreod in the course of events—the possible distortions of the chreod which still lead back to the original trajectory, and (4) the catastrophic changes—the complete changes of the personality and the self. These necessary tasks comprise the methodological questions in the development of the self and its conditions.

We shall discuss now how these tasks fit into the traditional techniques of social psychology. Most of the data in which social scientists place any trust, at least officially, are derived from one standard method: the social survey. The standards by which facts are judged to be acceptable in the compendium on aging by Riley and Foner (1971) are the standards of the social survey.

The definition of "hard data" as those collected by one method, the social survey, has some consequences: some advantageous, some doubtful. Among the latter has been an increasing cleavage between those who follow the rules of survey research and develop more and more refined analytic models, and those who reject this approach completely and look for other, intuitive methods. We can compare the offerings of each one-sided approach with the needs of a social psychology development.

The use of quantitative techniques imposes upon the observer a very restrictive system, abstracting from the totality of experience. What we study must be countable, must be seen in a relationship of more or less. To achieve this, we must take out the qualitative aspects of a situation. The social survey is a model of quantification in social science. Its logic of design and analysis intends to establish the frequency of a certain trait or condition among a well-defined population and to measure the relation of the conditions by assessing relative frequencies. At each step of the procedure, therefore, one looks for the best possible means of determining frequencies and of relating these frequencies to each other. Standards of excellence in surveys relate mainly to these factors. A population can be defined, a sample taken, data collection techniques instituted which will conform to random selection of the sample and, therefore, make it possible to make precise statistical limits about the data collected. Standardized interviewing, editing, and coding techniques make it possible to treat one unit like another, a necessary condition for quantitative research. Analysis techniques, such as scaling, index construction, use of diverse measures of association and significance then translate into statements the importance of the different conditions on behavior and action (Lazarsfeld, 1972).

The ideal of the survey analyst is to arrange data collection and processing in a way that foresees the need for human judgment at each point and substitutes for that need an automatic method which will insure understandable and reasonable numbers. The system makes possible the quantitative assessment of the importance of different factors. We can measure traits which represent general personality conditions by asking people about things they do generally, habitually, or have done in the past. We can take aged people, who belong to certain clubs, who live with their families, who live in some institution, or who live alone, and assess the importance of personality and background factors in their reaction to their present situation. We do this in such a way that the sample selected represents a population of people in this specific condition. Then we can assess the contribution of different factors to the respondents' living patterns. Every subject generalizes to a general condition, at least as long as circumstances do not change too much. In order to judge the appropriateness of the method of hard data and to evaluate the

alternative and supplementary procedures which have been suggested, we will now compare this ideal of the survey with the needs of the developmental model sketched before.

1. The essential dimensions of the chreod. The diversity in analyses of questionnaires leads to precisely defined variables. However, when one wants to look at the configuration which represents the individual, the aim is less to discern the particular variables and their possible associations than it is to perceive a geometrical patterning.

The unity of the individual is an elusive concept to put into the definite language and operations of the social scientist. Few people can state what they are in comprehensive terms or prepare an explicit philosophy of life. Even persons who might be able on consideration to make such a definite statement about their principles will think of them rarely; people are not usually consciously guided by them. The unity of the person is sometimes more easily inferred by outsiders than expressed by the person concerned.

The intuitive concepts of the unity of the person have been watered down because of the vagueness of concepts and a variety of only partially meaningful techniques. The all-encompassing term used has been the *self* or *self-concept*. This term, so masterfully introduced by William James (1890), has found acceptance in readers and been seminal for future analysis. Much of more meaningful analyses of the self has come usually from philosophical approaches, not from social science. Probably the most strenuous effort to define the self has come from existentialists.

In the aged subject it is possible to find a thread of continuity in summarizing past life. A person may organize the story of his life around themes which were salient throughout the life course. The life review has been shown to be a useful instrument in studying the aged (Butler, 1968). In a sense, life review is a short autobiography, leaving it to the respondent to organize the objective data of his history around a concept of the self. It may, however, be difficult to use in a large scale, systematic way but may be useful as a way of developing patterns of the self-image.

Transformation of these patterns into types and the presenting of them to subjects so that the dimensions of the self are recognizable challenge the ingenuity of the researcher. One approach we may notice has come from a philosopher, Charles Morris (1956), who distinguished a number (7–14 depending on the test) of ways of life which have validity in historical and religious examples, but can also be reduced to a small number of dimensions. The last includes a lengthy description of each way and is, therefore, designed principally for highly literate subjects. Endorsement of the different ways gives a meaningful pattern of the person.

Detailed description of the self-concept becomes either an intolerable burden on the respondent or provides a morass of data for the analyst. It is no wonder, therefore, that the ambition of social scientists has been scaled down, and some practical simplifications have been used to represent the self-image. One simplification is the analysis of values. Values expressed by a person are still an indication of a general predisposition for acting and can indicate a stable position of the self within a universe. Values are determined by content analysis of material produced by the respondent or by aspect, e.g., age or occupational role in the self-image (Back, 1971).

Again, it would be more efficient for large scale research to determine the categories ahead of time. This has been done in an adaptation of the semantic differential, a set of bi-polar scales on which a term is rated (Osgood, Suci, and Tannenbaum, 1957). One can use as the stimulus term "myself" or an equivalent and by choosing the appropriate scales determine the aspects of the self which one wants to measure. Further, it has been found that the best use of this device is not concentration on the scales themselves but comparison of the terms, which can be done through simple, geometric technique. Thus one can assess the relation of one's current self with the past self, ideal self, or self-presentation. The simplicity of data collection and analysis makes this technique for some researchers a synonym for measurement of the self-image.

2. Changes of the chreod in the developmental process. We used the unfamiliar term of chreod instead of a more current one to draw attention to the fact that we are talking about a tendency preserved in development which manifests itself in many different ways. The measurement of this constant is elusive; one would need to determine the normal way of development within which one could still accept the continued existence of a chreod. We must remember that the concept was originally employed for the biological development of the organism, and was only useful after different types (species) were defined and a general theory of the development process was accepted. In the study of personality we are still in the process of sorting out different types, and it is unlikely that such definite personality categories as the different animal species will emerge, but we may succeed in producing a measure of individuality, the unique essence of a person. It has been frequently objected that the design of surveys and the extraction of numerical variables make it impossible to determine unique patterns of action (Blumer, 1956). Some techniques have been devised to assess development. Two contrasting approaches are the longitudinal survey and biography. One is an extension of the survey method, the other of the artistic apperception of human life.

To study the development of personality and social interaction, we can take surveys of different times in the life of one person; that is, we may make a longitudinal study instead of a cross-sectional study. The usual way of doing this, of course, is to combine both: to take a cross-sectional sample which represents a certain kind of population and follow the sample through a few years to see the development of the persons involved. This technique has many advantages. It may combine the exactness of the cross-sectional survey with the time dimension and also give enough data on one person at different times to get an overall picture of that person. For many conditions and problems this technique has been valuable and has given us a way of checking many data which have been obtained in cross-sectional studies. Longitudinal studies thus could provide standards for the regular development of a personality, namely, a progression of the organization of attitudes and behavior around a certain kernel representing the personality constellation. Some large scale studies have successfully identified certain patterns and employed types which may be meaningful summaries of certain kinds of development (Block, 1971). However, these groupings are intuitions going beyond the strict application of statistical techniques to the data at hand.

The difficulties in longitudinal designs are so immense that frequently the methodological problems are either insufficiently dealt with or the methodology overwhelms the analysis. Such designs should be justified by a great increment in knowledge. Presumably, if a sensible analysis system could be devised, almost any question of human development could be settled by taking a national sample of respondents and following them through a considerable number of years. This could provide all possible facts of interest. The difficulties which we have enumerated before as well as some others are so large, however, that many a longitudinal design is in reality quite useless. It may be more useful under certain conditions as specific questions are being asked, or for a population with special problems. Wiggins (1973) has shown the subtleties and difficulties in just treating one question in panel analysis. For instance, we may want to study special personality conditions or special environmental conditions: to know how some people react to crises such as bereavement or retirement, or to check up on some groups as they make specific decisions such as giving up a home and moving into a retirement community, and then follow the subjects closely to see how their decisions are reached. In cases of this kind the complicated and costly longitudinal design is justified.

Studying the course of life and organizing it around an integrating concept is the topic of another branch of investigation, that is, biography. The use of biography and biographical techniques can give large scale longitudinal studies focus and even a reason for existence.

Like the biographer, we can distinguish between primary and secondary material; that is, we can take already worked out biographies as secondary material, or use the material which biographers have used: the diaries, letters, memoirs, and relevant documents of other people (Allport, 1942; Dollard, 1935). The primary materials, of course, are similar to the kind of data that are collected by case studies. They are sometimes similar to data solicited by interviews or other techniques in contemporary case studies. The use of personal documents as material for psychological-sociological study forms a type of bridge between the clinical case study and historical material. The more consciously collected memoir, written perhaps with an eye for publication, might be a little more suspect of trying to present a flattering picture of the subject to an audience. Of course, that is only a question of degree: any communication by a person is given with an audience in mind, even if it is only the investigator. In the case of an interview there is more spontaneity, and the subject may reveal himself to the investigator in a stylistic manner of talking or writing not introduced in any material prepared for publication. Discussion with friends, family, and other associates might be even more telling than a preparation designed to reach a larger audience.

Perhaps a step further away from a spontaneous communication is a complete description of a person by himself—an autobiography. An autobiography, as a matter of fact, may be a case study, as in many case study techniques a person is asked to write a complete autobiography up to the present time. However, in a literary sense, autobiography can usually be judged as a work of art as well as a work of self-presentation. The possible purpose behind writing it is the individual's wish for self-expression: to make a point, to express certain opinions, to help other people find a way to happiness, or to warn them of their own mistakes. The most famous autobiographies of all time, such as St. Augustine's or Rousseau's, had all these purposes in mind. They are certainly composed in a spirit of unity within a not too unified life. They can be considered as a work of art and appreciated for their form, but they are also genuine personal documents.

If we look at documents as having possible distortions, we can study biography as another problem: as it were, a double refraction

(Cockshut, 1974). First, biography is a presentation a person wants to give of himself, and second, it is the point of view which the biographer is trying to impose on the subject. The biography has the advantage of using a variety of points of view on the same subject. Although the same facts will be presented, we can compare the subject from very different perspectives as described by different biographers. Of course, different biographers may have access to different material, but this is not necessarily the reason for the discrepancy. The good biographer keeps in mind the essential unity of the person and shows how the person has developed and changed through the different vicissitudes of the life course. The biographer may strain the available evidence to impose an exaggerated unity on his subject, but the basic hypothesis of unity of the person throughout the life course makes it possible to see all events, all associations in proper perspective. True, different biographers and different episodes have interpreted individual lives in different ways; this reinterpretation is equivalent to the new discovery of important variables with new analysis techniques.

3. Variation of the chreod in the course of events. Judicious selection of indices, definitions of combinations, or the insight of the biographer can give us some definitions of the essence of the personality preserved through time. However, this applies only to a regular life course within a small range. In theory, the self may be distorted but still basically the same in a variety of vicissitudes. The question is: How can we determine the basic unity in these many shifts and trace the return to the basic configuration? It is here that one starts to distrust computational methods and turns more to sensitive intuition, that is, to qualitative methods.

This question concerns the depth and subtlety in contrast to the superficiality of survey questions. One might think that the more data we have about an individual, the more we would know about his most deeply held opinions. But in cold fact, the real question is: What does one want to do with these painfully collected data? One can quantify them again and put them into a form in which they can be manipulated by standard statistical techniques: treat them as if they were the regular survey data. In this case one could have orginally designed the questionnaire in a way manageable for such use. One can also continue describing particular cases and summing them up, but too many interviews become unmanageable, and the results can become very confusing. In fact, the usual procedure has been to combine the two approaches: to use depth data as a base for later construction of a quantifiable interview, or maintain them as case studies to be used later as illustrative cases for a large scale quantitative study. In either case it is recognized that the main value of a survey interview will come largely from the quantitative relationships. Depth data will only supplement the survey.

Thus it seems that social surveys in more or less standard form are still the most effective technique for studying the interactions between the aged personality and social behaviors. For special problems, however, additional techniques may be needed. Let us now turn to the biggest contrast, the individual case study.

It has been said that a complete understanding of a small event could lead to complete understanding of all the forces actuating it. In such a way a study of individual cases can lead us to the interrelationships between personality and social interaction. We can begin by realizing that we can also trace the development of a relationship in an individual case and from it see how the person operates; at least we can immerse ourselves in the point of view of the person concerned. Thus in a case study we can use great detail to see how conditions can be related and obtain insight into the actual process of the events studied.

A researcher immersing himself into the intricacies of a single life can gain new and unexpected insights. The intricate constellations which are lost in a statistical analysis of a limited set of variables can be demonstrated. Themes can be developed which are meaningful for one person and cannot be determined by comparisons with others. The single case is, in a sense, the beginning and the end of all social research. If we could trace back the development of insights, we would find that they derive usually from a personal experience or experience with another person, which is then put to the test in a large scale study. This is most explicit in those theories which derive from clinical work, but it is likely to be so in many other cases. At the other end, one would want to put together all the findings of large scale research into the pattern of actual human beings. There is great intellectual satisfaction in doing a well-reasoned case study. Understanding one person wholly is to a certain degree the entire aim of the scientist.

Just as the case study technique complements the social survey in its achievements, so it has also complementary deficiencies. The deficiencies lie in the question of representativeness and in the way of reasoning within a single case. Although we may hope that any one case could give us all the information, we really do not get total understanding. Thus we still have to make some inferences from similar or contrasting cases. We do not know whether a particular case is enough similar to or representative of most other cases, and so do not know how much importance we can give to data of this one person. Usually the cases are not even selected in a random manner, because other considerations enter into the selection. One of the best sources of case studies, of course, is clinical material, and we have seen in the discussion of personality theories how clinical material can distort the perception of the researcher. People who come voluntarily to be studied because they have troubles usually have one trait in great excess, and that trait tends to dominate much of their behavior. Thus in clinical material we will probably find pure cases of extreme personality conditions or extreme situational stresses. Even in cases selected purposefully by the investigator to be representative, there are difficulties because of limited accessability. People who are willing to act as case studies are rarely in the mainstream of society; otherwise, they would not have the time and leisure to devote to the research. Frequently in cultural anthropology, it turns out that case studies supposed to be illustrative of the whole culture are actually deviant or different from the modal traits demonstrated. Further, the researcher naturally tends to find people who communicate easily or who are self-directed and can provide the richness of data necessary for a good case study.

Another difficulty with the case study is that the reasoning derived from it is to some degree subjective. This may be an advantage or disadvantage depending on the skill of the investigator, but in any case it gives findings the nature of art rather than science; it is difficult for another person to repeat what the original investigator did with the same data. A combination of inferences made on a few cases becomes a collection of intuitive flashes of insight. This, frequently happening in the case study analysis, may lead the research astray and result in a self-perpetuating approach to pursuit of the theory. The technique thus lends itself well to discovery, but not to the openness of disproof, which is the mark of scientific inquiry. In effect, what is bias in a survey is clinical insight in a case study.

4. The catastrophic changes. Beginning with the main hypothesis of the unity of human experience, we have identified techniques by which the essence of the self, the abstract concept of the chreod, can be established. These methods are designed to recover the unity of the individual through all its aberrations. Sometimes, however, one is drawn to the conclusion that there is a real break in the course of life, that there is a real difference in the person, and that one is justified in treating this change as a complete reorganization of the self—a catastrophe in the language of theoretical biology.

Such changes do not occur without some precipitating event. There is some push, internally or externally, which stretches the elasticity of the self so far that one is led beyond the boundaries of the identity of self, leading in extreme cases to a complete reorganization of the self, sometimes a complete upheaval of the person.

Again, we can look at the process in different ways: from the intensive study of individual, sometimes prominent cases, to the large scale analysis of likely situations. One might also propose that the definition of the change is in the eyes of the receiver, that it is arbitrary whether we call something a change in a chreod or a new chreod. In principle, this is not so: the catastrophe is irreversible, and the reorganization will be around a different set of equilibria. The most striking examples are conversion experiences, like the proverbial "Road to Damascus." Surprising major changes in aging can be looked upon as catastrophies as well, whether they are occasioned by changes within the individual like arteriosclerosis, or situational changes like institutionalization.

We face here the fact that the conditions with which we deal are less definite in their classification than the visible organization of biological development. There is a plethora of possible variables which could be considered as important, and even conversion, from one extreme point of view to another, might be an indication of continuous extremism. It is likely that one can always find some sense in which the continuity of the person can be claimed to exist under even the most obvious changes. This corresponds to the fact that we do recognize the unity of the individual over the whole life time, in many social, legal, and interpersonal ways. Thus the question of a break, of destruction of a chreod, depends on the original definition of the chreod, which is in some sense arbitrary. This definition will depend exactly on the theory which one espouses; the efficiency of the theory is shown by its fit to common observation and understanding.

Even if we could take stages of life as units and transition from one stage to another as breaks or "catastrophes" we do not even find any agreement on how many stages in aging there are. The definition of different age groups becomes an individual variable, and even the number of age states is a question of perception (Jeffers, Eisdorfer, and Busse, 1970).

Acknowledgement of the destruction of a chreod can be viewed as a residual category. It is an event where the methods we have been discussing do not indicate a continuity of the person. When the measures of a person or the observations of behavior do not admit the hypothesis of continuity, it becomes economical for the observer to construct a completely new picture of the person. In this case the whole understanding of the person or the set of interrelation of variables will be changed.

The general supposition is that of continuity of the person—this is the general assumption, the "wager" which we make when we study the person at all. Both common usage and scientific analysis start with this assumption, and one experiences surprise, even shock, when there is a complete break. At the extreme, this happens in psychotic or hysteric conditions; in the more usual cases, the burden is on the researcher to show that there is a break and to define what it means.

There are basically no special methods for determining abrupt changes. All the methods which we have discussed, as well as their problems, determine the conditions of continuity and transformation; failing to find continuity, we can define a complete break and the characteristics of a new constellation. This can be done in a case study, as well as with a quantitative method, when it becomes clear that a new stage of life or a new self has to be introduced. However, biographical studies frequently ignore the last development in later ages under some explanation that this does not represent the real person. In quantitative studies abrupt changes of relationships may occur after a certain event; thus the designs which concentrate on certain crises may use a completely different scheme for before and after the crises. In all cases the assumption of the destruction of the chreod is the only viable alternative.

SOCIAL GROUPS, SELF, AND TIME

Time Perspective

Aging consists of both accumulated experience and the realization that there is little time left. Attitude toward time, past and future, can be taken as an organizing principle. We can extricate the leading issues in the relation of personality and social groups in old age from a consideration of changing time perspective. Perception of time connects the biological, social, and historical realms. Consciousness of death is a profoundly human characteristic, and changes in the life span have had a corresponding effect on human personality throughout the life cycle. We shall, therefore, discuss first time perspective in general and then give special consideration to demographic conditions. Time perspective can also organize the influence of different social groups.

The shifting importance of these groups, such as family, work, and community, is one of the most important factors in adult personality change. At this time we can conclude the discussion by looking at the personal meaning of the later stages of life, of how they fit into the picture on one's whole life experience. Self, development, and social interaction lead back to a general interpretation of the human condition.

The course of life can be seen as an alternation of expanding to contrasting time perspective, from a stage of expression of one's capacities to the realization of one's limitations. It would be reasonable to suppose that the transition to aging occurs at the point when the realization of time limitations becomes salient. Several theorists of the human life course, especially those who look more to psychodynamic features have put the late 30's as the time of significant change. Jung (1933) talks about the crisis at this age; Elliot Jacques (1970) as well has shown the difference in creativity before and after this age, using as evidence the higher death rate of very creative people just in their mid-30's and the corresponding occurrences of depression around that age. Other observers have put this crisis a little later, and general studies of the life cycle have shown a dip in morale around age 50 which is then followed by a surprising degree of happiness (Back and Gergen, 1966). It can be looked at as a period when capacity deteriorates but interests and ambition are still strong, while at the later stage there may be a reconciliation between desire and capacity. This discrepancy among various ages may also result from the effect of the lengthened life expectancy. Shakespeare, who considered forty as old age—"when forty winters shall beseech thy brow"—would hardly have understood a crisis of middle age occurring at this age. The prolongation of life span also would push this crisis toward a later time.

In different ways then researchers speak of a time for the beginning of an aging personality. It follows a time when the course of life is mainly a question of expanding, of looking for the future, of training, and of preparation. Then comes the point which we have been discussing: where one feels the preparation finishing and the point for which one prepares is arriving. At this time the main problem of the person becomes acknowledging one's own achievement, maintaining this achievement, and gradually letting go. A view of this kind of the whole life cycle is pervasive from the change of the tasks which Erikson discusses to the experiences of public opinion researchers which show the climax or high point of life to be around 40-50. The questions remain, however, which were discussed in the theoretical section of this section: whether this is an intrinsic development coming from the human organism; whether it is a question of events which occur at this time; and finally, what the nature of this development is.

In effect, the difference between biological and social aging might not be as large as one may suppose. Based on a biological foundation, aging may simply be seen as an accumulation of averse events, small in themselves but with which the organism is finally unable to cope (Strehler, 1962). Thus intrinsic changes of the organism might depend on exposure to external events, just as the social condition of aging does. We can look at these events which lead to aging without committing ourselves to a specific intrinsic or situational theory.

Demographic Conditions, Generations, and the Path of Life

The clearest analog to the personal, biological condition is the social situation of the family and the change of generations. As a result of increased longevity, it is within the family that the changing role and the changing effect of roles is becoming most pronounced. Anthropologists have pointed out that the unfounded, malleable character of the human infant as well as the need of transmitting culture has made the family a necessary feature of human development. From the long range point of view we can see biological functions of the family. It is to enable the older generation which rears the child and brings him to maturity to surrender this function to the next generation which in turn begins the process again. The question of the role for the older generation after this point has never seemed particularly important because of the usually short, normal life span. Three generations living together has been the exception rather than the rule in society (Laslett, 1972). The problems heretofore connected with such a situation have been more on the order of individual conflict or noticed tragedy than a general social problem. Balandier (1974) has pointed out the situation of conflict of generations, that is, two adult generations trying to assert their place in society. It is the unique problem of a long-lived society, and thus, unique for ours. It is difficult to reconstruct the prevalence of different family situations in different societies; hence, an example of the most prominent ones may suffice. In the English royal family, there had not been a number of adult sons of a reigning king from about 1300, the sons of Edward III, to 1800, the sons of George III, and in the first case this condition resulted in a century of civil war—the War of the Roses. The living conditions of the royal family are, of course, superior to the rest of the population and, therefore, we can expect similar conditions to be even rarer in the bulk of the population. A similar conflict might, however, still occur although it would not have such great consequences for the whole country.

This consideration shows that the role of the older person in the family is a novel and unique one, and we must, therefore, be careful in discussing the effects of family relationships on the personality of the aged. During most of history, this is not a situation people expected. The uniqueness of the persons who reach old age gives them honor in the society. It is also likely that only quite superior individuals survive to old age. We might project into the future and look at the conditions of the aged in a society which has a stable population with relatively long life expectancy and low fertility. We cannot, of course, describe any psychological relationships, but we can predict what the situation would be. While a great proportion will be older in such a population, in effect, there will be about the same proportion or slightly less of those over 65 as those below age 14. With the lower fertility there will be a greater lengthening of generational span, and we shall find a great number of three generational configurations and even four generational groups in the population. On the other hand,

because of the low fertility, we shall also find many individuals without any living relatives, either descendants or collateral (Shanas and Hauser, 1974; Back, 1974). Thus the role within the family might become less important, as compared to the generational role within the whole society. There will be much more importance placed upon an age group rather than on a specific position within the family system.

The demographic situation will, therefore, be the determinant of personality development in the later stages of life. In fact, this is so because the definition of later stages of life depends on the mortality experience and the kinds of associations a person can be exposed to as well as his demographic situation. We can see these changes as affecting the social psychological development of the aging as part of a longer term trend related to the establishment of a stable population with low mortality and low fertility. Over the long run the situation will lead to the establishment of small families, not only in the nuclear family itself, but also in extended family relationships. This might lead to more intensive involvement with the relations one has, but failing this, it would also lead to a greater dependence on other groups with which one may have contact. Perhaps it will also lead to a heightened ability to move quickly in and out of intensive relationships without great harm (Rogers, 1968). The lower time perspective which is supposedly characteristic of the aged, in this way, may diffuse through the whole society. We may say that modern demographic trends, in the consequence of the life cycle, takes the future from the young, and the past from the old.

In assessing personality development, therefore, we have to look at the interplay of three conditions: the general tendency of preserving a self-concept, changes by passage through different stages of the life cycle, and the changes imposed on this pattern through the different effects of demographic and social changes. We can evaluate this interplay by discussing the different changes in primary groups with occur in aging in our society.

Family

Alterations in family life and household composition are frequently the first changes the aging person notices. Children are suddenly adults. The conventional place to date the change into later life is the empty nest stage, the stage when children leave home and the household loses its function to raise and socialize children. The household ceases to be a place where the future for some of its members outside the household is being prepared. This is a time for a reorganization of roles in the household, and it has been supposed by many family theorists to be a traumatic experience for the older couples, especially for the wife and mother. However, research has shown that this transition is less detrimental than has been presumed. Studies of this separation process itself cannot find much upset of the parents concerned. and in many cases even reveal feelings of relief (Back, 1971; Harkins, 1974; Glenn, 1975). There may be several reasons for this condition: one is that this transition corresponds to the normal development of the organism and may come at the appropriate time. The belief that it is a break corresponds to the belief that personality pattern is an unchanging kind of unity which depends on the person while extending the life of the person. However, the term which we have used, the chreod, implies that the self has a normal development and will be different in a child-adolescent than an adult or old person, and that the development is part of the identity of the self, just as seeds grow into a tree. The separation from children occurs when the older generation is getting weaker, becoming less adapted to changing conditions, and is possibly in conflict with the younger generation. On the other hand, separation is to be expected and is functional. The younger generation can bring up its own children; this fits the picture of life to which most people look forward.

Not only is separation from children the result of an expected development, but is not as abrupt as one would think. In cases of large families, some children might have left the home and established their own families while others still remain at home; thus the establishment of a third generation comes at the time when there is still a nuclear family unit itself in the home. Marriage or leaving home to look for an occupation in a strange city is a fairly abrupt formal separation, but often children leave for school, a temporary job, or other tentative experiences, which keep the possibility of returning open. The family unit then still exists. It thus makes it possible to adapt materially to the situation as it is and still keep psychologically the position of the self, the psychological self-image, constant until it dies on its own, as it were. Both the gradual change in many cases and the common feeling of relief toward separation allows the preservation of the self-image in the transition to old age. One can find that most often there is an expectation from youth to marriage to having children to seeing children grow up and leave home to leading an independent life in old age without children. Each of these steps can be viewed as a continuous path of achievement, and although there may be loss of contact, dissolution of the household would not necessarily be seen as a loss and a threat to the self.

Work Life

We may say that in this case the development of the personality conforms, as it were, to the biological destiny of man, the sequence of generations, the ebb and flow of life, which is represented socially in family relations. However, work in another sequence comes in social affiliations whose requirements are not adapted to the rhythm of life. A continuous work career during life looks like a straight line function, and separation from the work environment, especially symbolized by retirement, may be more of a loss and a crisis situation than corresponding events in family life.

The lengthening of the life span which has made changes in the meaning of family life and relations has also affected the work span. The proportion of life which individuals spend in the labor force has decreased at both ends; however, this has not lessened the degree of identification of many people with their work role. In fact, with some increase in the labor force by women, especially in the white collar occupations, the identifications of people with the work role has increased and may be the primary way of identification in family as well as other groups. This also corresponds to trends in society of increasing emphasis on achievement and ability, and to disregarding those roles which depend on immediate interpersonal perception. Emphasis by psychologists on measuring the real decrease in work capacity through the age range has shown that the belief in the decrease is a social stereotype. However, this fact only emphasizes the social importance of retirement and is best shown by the fact that most permissive rules on retirement very quickly become social standards for the process (Back, 1976). In some occupations, such as the military and civil service, retirement can come so early that it really has become a cue for a second career; this almost corresponds to the middle life crisis around age 40 which we discussed above. However, retirement in later life does become an important break in one's life career, but is not based on criteria of ability. It does force on the retiree a complete readjustment of attitudes and self-concept.

If one forgets for the moment the purely material benefits of working, the main values of the work roles consist in association, achievement, and organization of time. The latter is clearly the one which leads most to the organization of total life, immediately changes with retirement, and influences the organization of one's personality concepts. Most studies have shown that the experience of retirement itself is more of a problem than long range adjustment to living in retirement (Stokes and Maddox, 1967). The disruption of the time schedule in effect usually means that one has to structure his own time. Scheduling is usually dictated by circumstances and rules and can be accomplished in different ways: work similar to that done in preretirement can be done on a part-time or nonpaid basis; some new interest can be put in the foreground of life, perhaps something which might have been a hobby before; or one's social situation can be altered, for instance, by moving to a community which is organized around retirement (Kleemeier, 1961). We can see in each case a different way of trying to protect the essence of what one has considered oneself. This will also depend on different ways in which the self was originally involved in the work life. In failing to maintain the self-image, the feeling of loss might predominate for the rest of one's life; these are the cases of unsuccessful retirement.

Community and Interest Groups

Family and work settings provide the two overarching social settings in which an individual finds himself. These are the group formations which might and usually do organize the life cycle over a long time. The human task in a biological sense is to provide continuity in the chain of generations, and in a social sense is to provide for an impact on society through one's work and achievement; that is the function of family and work. Two others, however, have a different time perspective which is not so much tied to the human life cycle. The community, the larger scale social-ethnic or racial identity, remains throughout one's life as a group with which one can always identify. Purely associational groups are voluntary and based on conflict. It is these kinds of groups and associations which may provide the backing for people of older ages when the family and work associations become less important. Involvement in a community may allow a new role for old people by providing those civic duties which people with other responsibilities are not able to perform. However, purely political movements based on age have not been very successful (Pinner, Jacobs, and Selznick, 1959). This shows that there is a lack of identification with an aged group, and older people are still more dependent on earlier associations, on the interests of their family, their work, and other ideological interests learned in their youth. Some local communities have been noted to be more interested in bonds for parks than for schools, but this is about as far as the political concern for the aged goes. On the other hand, the interest in associations has been exploited as a great future for the aged. The availability of different interest clubs and other activities at the time when a person can pursue his own interests may make possible new development of the aged and new identification based on a different principle. When the function of the family diminishes, the work role is complete, and even the community doesn't feel the need of their involvement, the aged might turn to temporary, associational groups which are concerned only with a certain aspect of personality or certain aspects of interest or work. At this point in life, this may be the only way in which a person can find spontaneous expression (Lowenthal and Haven, 1968).

The "Real Self" and Aging

At this point, one might consider what the interplay of person and association of life cycle can teach us about the nature of a person's basic personality. We have started with the general principle which we may identify as a self which stays the same in one respect but keeps changing in the course of normal development throughout life. We have identified this by the term *chreod*: the necessary path which the individual follows, different at different stages of the path but still an organizing and attracting force along the path and throughout life. The theoretical as well as the practical problem in analyzing the life cycle and aging is finding a way of understanding and measuring the essential dimensions of the chreod. The chreod might be a more abstract mathematical concept for the self which has been so fruitful a concept yet so hard to define. We can see here the same theoretical and corresponding methodological difficulties produced by the slow evolutionary changes of the organism and the rapid historical changes of human society. In order to understand the regular changes within the self or the chreod, the dimensions and measures we expect to be different in different stages of life, we have to take into account: (a) the development of the individual chreod; (b) regular changes which we can expect along the path; and (c) the particular historical conditions which might make the development different.

These differences correspond to the development of three kinds of models for studying change: life cycle analysis, cross-sectional analysis, and cohort analysis [which may be unimportant in slow-changing biological development but may become important with the fast occurring demographic and social changes (Riley, Johnson, and Foner, 1972)].

We began with the question of where we can find the self. We can only observe different reactions, different roles of a person, and never be able to understand the total essence of the self. Peer Gynt peels the layers from the onion, but we never find the center. We can and have analyzed the different types of social conditions which may necessitate playing different roles: child, parent, grandparent, worker or retiree, community insider or outsider, or a member of an interest group. Changes, for instance, from worker to retiree, may affect the personality or they may show the personality emerging in different ways. It was in this context we discussed the theory of conservation and innovation. However, in considering such developments we can look at three ways in which aging can direct us to a consideration of the self.

The first way of looking at the self in the aging process is not by examining the individual, but by viewing a whole succession of individuals through a series of generations. From a life cycle point of view—the point of view from which we might look at other societies and other species—we may only understand the development of the self in the context of continuous sequence. By losing sight of the individual in his long range development, we are able to take a neutral and detached stance toward the development of the self and the meaning of human life. This meaning cannot be found in the individual life cycle, neither in the earlier stages nor in its final stages, but can only be assessed by its transmission to the next generation—either directly to individuals or indirectly through one's contribution to the general culture. We look, therefore, at the self as being realized not within the life of one individual but through the sequence of several generations until we can see in historical development the real meaning of how the self relates to its internal symbols and the development of society.

The second way presents a more optimistic outlook. It views the self as something within the person which is restricted by cultural as well as group affiliation but which gradually tries to develop and be realized. In this theory of self-realization, we do not look at the long range, but only at the immediate, the here-and-now, at the point where self-realization occurs. This corresponds to certain modern theories of philosophy, including existentialism, which call acting according to social and role prescriptions self-deception which can only be transcended at certain points. Thus in looking at aging one may find that the self will tend to this realization; at the later stages of life, attachment to society becomes weaker, and the real self can develop, emerge, and show itself in its full beauty. In this case aging will be a real golden age—not in the past but at the point where the self is able to realize itself.

The third way views the self in the perspective of the life span. It accepts the general curve of life, rising at first and then declining until death. Thus the self may develop to a certain point only, expressing itself in different ways, but ending finally in total destruction. Again, as in other theories, we may find that it changes at many points, and that it may be even more reasonable to speak of a different self at different times. But whatever this transition and transformation is, it will deteriorate at the end, and judging from the whole time span, the self cannot be distinguished from the life in which it occurs, biologically as well as socially and historically. It cannot be separated from its temporary triumphs and its ultimate defeats. This might be called a tragic view of life, but its acceptance may cause realization of the meaning of the essence of the human self.

REFERENCES

Allport, G. 1942. *The Use of Personal Documents in Psychological Science*. New York: Social Science Research Council.

Anderson, M. The impact on the family relationships of the elderly of changes since Victorian times in governmental income-maintenance provisions. *In*, E. Shanas and M. Sussman, *Older People, Family and Bureaucracy*. Durham, North Carolina: Duke University Press, in press.

Back, K. W. 1961. Decisions under uncertainty: Rational, irrational and non-rational. *American Behavioral Scientist*, 4, 14–19.

Back K. W. 1965. A social psychologist looks at kinship structure. *In*, E. Shanas and G. Streib, *Social Structure and the Family: Generational Relations*, pp. 326–340. Englewood Cliffs, New Jersey: Prentice-Hall.

Back, K. W. 1968. New frontiers in demography and social psychology. *Demography*, 6, 90–97.

Back, K. W. 1971. Transition to aging and the self-image. *Aging and Human Development*, 2, 296–309.

Back, K. W. 1974. Human nature, psychological technology, and the control of population growth. *J. Soc. Issues*, 30, (4), 279–296.

Back, K. W. 1976. The ambiguity of retirement. *In*, E. W. Busse and E. A. Pfeiffer, *Behavior and Adaptation in Later Life*. 2nd ed. Boston: Little, Brown.

Back, K. W., and Bourque, L. B. 1970. The life graph: Aging and cohort effects. *J. Geront.*, 25, 249–255.

Back, K. W., and Gergen, K. J. 1966. Personal orientation and morale of the aged. *In*, I. Simpson and J. McKinney, *Social Aspects of Aging*, pp. 306–321. Durham, North Carolina: Duke University Press.

Balandier, G., 1974. *Anthropo-Logiques*. Paris: Presses Universitaires de France.

Bandura, A., and Walters, R. H. 1963. *Social Learning and Personality Development*. New York: Holt, Rinehart & Winston.

Bengtson, V. L., Furlong, M. J., and Laufer, R. S. 1974. Time, aging, and the continuity of social structure: Themes and issues in generational analysis. *J. Soc. Issues*, 30 (2), 1–30.

Biddle, B. J., and Thomas, C. J. (eds.) 1966. *Role Theory, Concepts and Research*. New York: John Wiley.

Block, J. 1971. *Lives Through Time*. Berkeley: Bancroft Books.

Blumer, H. 1956. Sociological analysis and the "variable." *Am. Soc. Rev.*, 21, 683–689.

Butler, R. N. 1968. The life review. *In*, B. Neugarten (ed.), *Middle Age and Aging*, pp. 486–496. Chicago: Chicago University Press.

Campbell, D. 1958. Common fate, similarity and other indices of the status of aggregates of persons as social entities. *Behavioral Science*, 3, 14–25.

Cockshut, A. O. J. 1974. *Truth to Life*. London: Collins.

Cumming, E., and Henry, W. E. 1961. *Growing Old: the Process of Disengagement*. New York: Basic Books.

Denzin, N. 1970. *The Research Act*. Chicago: Aldine.

Deutsch, M. 1968. Field Theory. *In*, G. Lindsey and E. Aronson (eds.), *Handbook of Social Psychology, Vol. I*, pp. 412–487. Cambridge: Addison-Wesley.

Dollard, J. 1935. *Criteria for a Life History*. New York: Yale University Press.

Duvignaud, J. 1972. *The Sociology of Art*. New York: Harper & Row.

Eisenstadt, S. N. 1956. *From Generation to Generation*. Glencoe, Illinois: The Free Press.

Erikson, E. H. 1959. Identity and the life cycle. *Psychological Issues*, 1.

Foote, N. N. 1958. Anachronism and synchronism in sociology. *Sociometry*, 21, 17–19.

Franks, C. (ed.) 1969. *Behavior Therapy*. New York: McGraw-Hill.

Freeman, L. 1971. *The Story of Anna O*. New York: Walker.

Gardiner, M. (ed.) 1971. *The Wolf Man*. New York: Basic Books.

Garfinkel, H. 1968. *Studies in Ethnomethodology*. Englewood Cliffs, New Jersey: Prentice-Hall.

Glenn, N. D. 1975. Psychological well-being in the postparental stage: Some evidence from national surveys. *J. Marriage & Fam.* pp. 105–110 (February).

Goddard, H. H. 1912. *The Kallikak Family*. New York: Macmillan.

Goffman, E. 1959. *The Presentation of Self in Everyday Life*. New York: Doubleday, Anchor Books.

Goffman, E. 1963. *Stigma*. Englewood Cliffs, New Jersey: Prentice-Hall.

Harkins, Elizabeth, 1974. Stress and the empty nest transition: A study of the influence of social and psychological factors on emotional and physical health. Unpublished dissertation, Duke University.

Henry, W. E. 1965. Social mobility as social learning: Some elements of change in motive and social context. *In*, M. B. Kantor (ed.), *Mobility and Mental Health*, pp. 30–47. Springfield, Illinois: Charles C. Thomas.

Hill, R. 1970. *Family Development in Three Generations*. Cambridge: Schenkman.

Inhelder, B., and Piaget, J. 1958. *The Growth of Logical Thinking*. New York: Basic Books.

Jacob, Francois 1974. *The Logic of Living Systems*. London: Allen Lane.

Jacques, Elliott 1970. *Work, Creativity, and Social Justice*. New York: International Universities Press.

James, W. 1890. *Principles of Psychology*. New York: Holt.

Janis, I. L. 1974. Vigilance and decision making in personal crises. *In*, C. V. Coelho, D. A. Hamburg, and J. E. Adams (eds.), *Coping and Adaptation*, pp. 139–175. New York: Basic Books.

Jeffers, F. C., Eisdorfer, C., and Busse, E. W. 1970. Measurement of age identification. *In*, E. Palmore (ed.), *Normal Aging*, pp. 389–394. Durham, North Carolina: Duke University Press.

Jung, Carl Gustav 1933. *Modern Man In Search of A Soul*. New York: Harcourt, Brace & World.

Kleemeier, Robert W. (ed.) 1961. *Aging and Leisure*. New York: Oxford University Press.

Kounin, J. S. 1941. Experimental studies of rigidity. *Character and Personality*, 9, 251–282.

Laslett, P. 1972. *Household and Family in Past Times*. Cambridge: Cambridge University Press.

Lazarsfeld, P. F. 1972. *Qualitative Analysis*. Boston: Allyn and Bacon.

Lewin, K. 1938. The conceptual representation and measurement of psychological forces. *Contributions to Psychological Theory*, 1, no. 4.

Lowenthal, M. F., and Haven, C. 1968. Interaction and adaptation: Intimacy as a critical variable. *Am. Soc. Rev.*, 33, 20–30.

Maddox, G. 1963. Activity and morale: A longitudinal study of selected elderly subjects. *Soc. Forces*, 42, 195–204.

Mannheim, K. 1952. The problem of generations. *Essays on the Sociology of Knowledge*. London: Routledge & Kegan Paul.

Marris, Peter 1958. *Widows and their Families*. London: Routledge & Kegan Paul.

Marris, Peter 1974. *Loss and Change*. London: Routledge & Kegan Paul.

Maslow, A. H. 1962. *Toward a Psychology of Being*. New York: D. Van Nostrand.

Mead, G. H. 1934. *Mind, Self and Society*. Chicago: University of Chicago Press.

Morris, C. W. 1956. *Varieties of Human Value*. Chicago: Chicago University Press.

Ortega y Gasset, J. 1923. *The Modern Theme*. New York: W. W. Norton.

Osgood, C. E., Suci, C. I., and Tannenbaum, P. H. 1957. *The Measurement of Meaning*. Urbana, Illinois: University of Illinois Press.

Pinner, F. A., Jacobs, P., and Selznick, P. 1959. *Old Age and Political Behavior*. Berkeley: University of California Press.

Riley, M. W., and Foner, A. 1971. *Aging and Society, Vol. I: An Inventory of Research Findings*. New York: Russell Sage Foundation.

Riley, M. W., Johnson, M., and Foner, A. 1972. *Aging and Society, Vol. III: A Sociology of Aging*. New York: Russell Sage Foundation.

Rimland, B. 1964. *Infantile Autism*. New York: Appleton-Century-Crofts.

Rogers, C. 1968. Interpersonal relationships U.S.A. 2000. *J. Applied Behavioral Science*, 4, 208–269.

Rosow, Irving. 1974. *Socialization to Old Age*. Berkeley: University of California Press.

Ryder, N. 1965. The cohort as a concept in the study of social change *Am. Soc. Rev.*, 30, 843–861.

Sartre, J. P. 1956. *Being and Nothingness*. New York: Philosophical Library.

Shanas, E., and Hauser, P. 1974. Zero population growth and the family life of old people. *J. Soc. Issues*, 30 (4), 79–92.

Sheldon, W. H. 1942. *The Varieties of Temperament*. New York: Harper.

Simpson, G. L. 1956. *The Cokers of Carolina*. Chapel Hill, North Carolina: University of North Carolina Press.

Simpson, I. H., and McKinney, J. C. 1966. *Social Factors in Aging*. Durham, North Carolina: Duke University Press.

Sitwell, O. 1944. *Left Hand, Right Hand*. Boston: Little, Brown.

Skinner, B. F. 1953. *Science and Human Behavior*. New York: Macmillan.

Snyder, R. C., Bruck, H. W., and Sapin, B. 1962. *Foreign Policy Decision Making*. New York: The Free Press.

Stokes, R. G., and Maddox, G. L. 1967. Some social factors on retirement adaptation. *J. Geront.*, 22, 329–333.

Strehler, B. L. 1962. *Time, Cells and Aging*. New York: Academic Press.

Streib, G. F., and Schneider, C. J. 1971. *Retirement in American Society*. Ithaca, New York: Cornell University Press.

Streib, G., and Thompson, W. E. 1958. Adjustment in retirement. *J. Soc. Issues*, **14.**

Thom, Rene. 1972. *Stabilité Structurelle et Morphogénèse*. Reading, Massachusetts: W. A. Benjamin.

Waddington, C. H. 1957. *The Strategy of the Genes*. London: Allen and Unwin.

Waddington, C. H. 1968–1972. *Towards a Theoretical Biology*. 4 vols. Chicago: Aldine-Atherton.

White, H. 1962. *Anatomy of Kinship*. Englewood Cliffs, New Jersey: Prentice-Hall.

Wiggins, Lee M. 1973. *Panel Analysis*. New York: Elsevier Scientific Publishing.

Wilensky, H. 1967. *Organizational Intelligence*. New York: Basic Books.

17
SOCIAL NETWORKS AND ISOLATION

Marjorie Fiske Lowenthal
and
Betsy Robinson
University of California, San Francisco

INTRODUCTION

In this chapter, the authors' intent was to focus primarily on the socio-psychological characteristics of older persons comparatively isolated from social networks of various types; the extent to which this isolation represented a change from earlier life-stages; and the consequences for well-being of age-linked as compared with lifelong patterns. Inasmuch as the literature tends to stress the beneficial aspects of high network involvement, much of the evidence we are able to proffer about the isolated elderly must be largely inferential.

In the best of all possible research worlds, we could also have reported on both the rhythm and the relativity of isolation and interaction, but here too there is as yet little to report. By rhythm, we mean personal patterns of oscillation between social involvement and withdrawal that may well be established quite early in life, with some people having alternating needs that are essentially daily, others weekly, monthly, or even annual; the latter are reflected by such decisions or ruminations as "this is going to be my social year," or "my year for catching up on reading." While the preferred phasing of withdrawal and in-

volvement may change somewhat across the life course, we suspect that there is considerable continuity in the favored rhythm. One of the serious and little studied problems of aging is the extent to which the individual, especially but not only if handicapped or institutionalized, loses control of his chosen pattern and is forced to be with others when he prefers solitude, and to be alone when he would like company.

By the relativity of isolation we refer in part to the traditional concept of relative deprivation, that is, cognitive and comparative assessment of the "usual" behavior of whomever one considers to be one's peers. In later life such reference groups tend to consist of a kind of semiabstract notion of other people one's age, reflected in the increasing use of such phrases as "considering my age." But perhaps of even more importance, at least in advanced old age, is the concept of the former self as the referent other. Autobiographies and diaries that include life-stages through the 80's and 90's are replete with this sort of reference (Berenson, 1963; Russell, 1969; Tolstoy, 1960), as were our own life history interviews with aged subjects (Lowenthal, Berkman, and Associates, 1967). At this stage of our knowledge, however, we have no way of assessing whether this form of retrospective yardstick is relevant for persons other than articulate and introspective artists and intellectuals.

A host of other intrapersonal qualities are relevant to the inquiry into the causes and consequences of isolation, at any age or life-stage. Despite the traditional disciplinary fences between psychology and sociology, subjective and social factors must be examined simultaneously if we are to understand the consequences for adaptation of the balance between interaction on the one hand and isolation or solitude on the other, especially in old age. The ideal overall framework for such inquiry would include not only the usual dimension of amount of interaction in dyadic (paired, interpersonal relationships) and multiple networks, and the identification of the significant others, but a subjective or involvement dimension as well. This "involvement" dimension should include cognitive, motivational, and affective factors and how they are associated with the behavioral measures of amount of interaction.

A review of the literature in adult development and aging yields considerable material on the interactional dimension, primarily in networks other than dyadic, and little on the subjective sense of involvement. Efforts to integrate the two are rare. From a life-course perspective, the total framework is important because it will enable us to assess (a) the extent to which the two types of networks (dyadic and multiple) may complement or substitute for each other at various life-stages; (b) the extent to which cognitive awareness and perceptions of the various networks change; (c) whether increases in degree of commitment in one or more networks may compensate for age-linked losses in others; and (d) whether past commitments have continuing symbolic significance, thus at least in part compensating for lack of current behavioral involvement. By making use of an involvement dimension, we could further test the hypothesis that it is unwanted relationships that tend to be sloughed off in later life, not in the mode of disengagement but in one of "good riddance" (Lowenthal, Thurnher, Chiriboga, and Associates, 1975).

Such a two-dimensional framework would also enable us to assess, more adequately than we have as yet done, the usefulness of various typologies proposed for describing dominant patterns of involvement with social networks and related value systems (Bengtson and Martin, 1970; Blau, 1973; Merton, 1968; Rosow, 1965; Seeman, 1959, 1972; Williams and Wirths, 1965). When empirically rounded out with data on adaptive level, the schema should also help us to draw conceptual distinctions between isolation and loneliness (Blau, 1973; Dubos, 1965; Rose, 1965; Rosenberg, 1970), and perhaps more importantly, between loneliness and aloneness (Fromm-Reichmann, 1959; Shanas, 1970; Townsend, 1968b). All of which, of course, brings us very close to symbolic interaction theory (Blumer, 1969; Mead, 1934; Strauss, 1956) and the phenomenology of Husserl (Farber, 1940) and Schutz (1971) which we believe are highly promising theoretical orientations to the issues with which we are concerned in this chapter.

Because much is missing in the subjective dimension of this proposed model, we shall organize the material to be reported here largely in terms of the behavioral, or interactional, dimension, incorporating references applicable to the subjective or involvement dimension wherever available. To the extent that the data permit, we shall discuss the relevance of an individual's "location" in terms of this model for his or her adaptive level. In conclusion, we shall venture some suggestions as to where more attention to the subjective sphere might lead us, and its implications for theory and research.

DYADIC RELATIONSHIPS

The formation of dyadic relationships and the development of a capacity for mutuality and intimacy have been of major concern in studies of child development and adolescence, and the intimacy stage is of course a critical one in Erikson's (1963) developmental schema. Over the past ten years, other research, not clinically based, has indicated that, whether subjectively defined or objectively assessed, intimacy and the capacity for mutuality continue to be vital personal resources through very old age (Lowenthal and Haven, 1968; Lowenthal *et al.*, 1975, Ch. 8). Although she was not primarily concerned with the qualitative aspects of dyadic relationships, Blau's classic study (1961) strongly implies, for women, a certain flexibility in the object of close relationships, in this instance a shift after widowhood from the intimacy of marriage to that of same-sex friendships. The prevailing lack of mutuality and intimacy in friendships between men at several life-stages (Lowenthal *et al.*, 1975, Ch. 3) may be a major explanation for the fact that men adapt to loss of spouse less flexibly than women (Lowenthal, Berkman, and Associates, 1967) and in general seem to be able to satisfy the need for intimacy only through remarriage. Indeed, the recent study of adult life-stages referred to above suggested that men, especially in late middle age, were very aware of, and regretted, the lack of depth in their friendships. In real life, in the middle and lower socioeconomic group studied, dyadic relationships between men often resembed parallel play or met work-oriented goals rather than truly interpersonal needs.

Current or recollected relationships described as intimate underscore the relativity of the concept. For some people at all stages of life, regular contact with a hairdresser, a barber, a bartender, a delivery boy, or a public health nurse may be construed as having a confidant. Nor is intimacy, for example, as conceptualized by Erikson (1963) necessarily a prerequisite to the full attainment of his later stages of generativity (the concern with establishing and guiding the next generation) or integrity (the acceptance of one's life as one has lived it). Indeed, some of the great contributors to the arts, the sciences, and statesmanship seem to have become so only by avoiding, or freeing themselves from, close dyadic bonds. On a less exalted level, it may well be that strong involvement in extended family networks, in voluntary associations, and in sociopolitical affairs tends to be formed among persons whose need for intimacy is not great, or who, for psychological reasons, avoid it. Further, the need for intimacy appears to vary across the life course, and the trajectories of men and women differ (Lowenthal, 1975).

Except for the marital relationship, very little research has been done on the quality of dyadic relationships. For example, the extent to which siblings may become increasingly important with advancing age, with or without loss of spouse, is as yet not clear. Although some studies reported that bonds between same-sex siblings strengthened in later life (Adams, 1968; Irish, 1964), our study found that it is opposite sex siblings with whom bonds were tightened (Lowenthal *et al.*, 1975, Ch. 2). There is also anecdotal if not empirical evidence that friends, as well as cousins or others from the extended family of childhood, adolescence, and young adulthood may be searched out and the relationships renewed in later life, through correspondence if not in person. With or without widowhood or widowerhood, old loves also have a way of cropping up in the thoughts if not the lives of older people, though this phenomenon is not necessarily age-linked.

A life-course perspective on dyads emerges primarily from marital studies. Among persons over 65 most men, but few women, are married and living with a spouse (U.S. Bureau of the Census, 1972). This, of course, is a reflection of higher mortality rates among older men. There has been, however, a long-term decline in mortality rates, and together with a trend toward earlier marriage, this has meant that increasing proportions of married couples survive jointly in two-person households into the later years (Shanas and Streib, 1965). Blood and Wolfe (1960) report that during the child-rearing years the marriage relationship is subordinate to the demands of children, and husbands and wives tend to grow apart. Inasmuch as the frequency of marital interaction is reported to once again increase in postparental years, and particularly after retirement, we must ask what is known about the stresses and strengths of older marriages.

Most older people tend to have positive perceptions of their marriages, and many report improvement and an increase in satisfaction in the later stages (Gurin, Veroff and Feld, 1960; Stinnett, Carter, and Montgomery, 1972; Stinnett, Collins, and Montgomery, 1970). Rollins and Feldman (1970) found a steady decline in general marital satisfaction from the beginning of marriage, a leveling off in satisfaction throughout the middle years, but improvement after the children leave home. However, this study also reported marital crises among men anticipating retirement, and our own recent work reported marital crises among women facing the empty nest, suggesting that anticipated loss in one network threatens others (Lowenthal *et al.*, 1975, Ch. 2). Several studies reported that after age 60 love, companionship, and being able to express true feelings are the most rewarding aspects of marital life (Stinnett, Carter, and Montgomery, 1972; Stinnett, Collins, and Montgomery, 1970). Blood and Wolfe (1960) also found that companionship was highly valued between older couples, particularly by older women. They went on to indicate, however, that for some older women satisfaction with companionship tapered off in old age as the husbands began to lose interest in (or perhaps energy for) keeping as active as their wives might like. Stinnett, Carter, and Montgomery (1972) found the most troublesome aspects of older marriages were in different values and philosophies of life and in lack of mutual interests. Husbands were dissatisfied by the alleged lack of respect they received from their wives, while wives were dissatisfied with poor communication. Thompson and Chen (1966) noted that while young couples may get along fairly well without much verbal communication, lack of such communication may cause serious problems among older couples. McKain (1969), in a study of older couples who had married in later maturity, found that although a few remarried to allay anxiety about health, and some to avoid dependency on their children, the most frequently given reason was the desire for companionship.

Changes in the husband-wife relationship have primarily centered on role changes at retirement. Such change was characterized by a shift away from instrumental, largely work-oriented, behavior on the part of the husband to mutually expressive behavior, usually brought about by a loosening of former sex roles in the division of labor in the household (Clark and Anderson, 1967; Troll, 1971). Lipman (1960, 1961, 1962) has pointed out that the increasing equalitarian nature of the relationship can contribute to the happiness of the older couple. He further emphasized that older couples who rigidly defined their respective roles prior to retirement adjusted to it less successfully. The retired male who prided himself mainly on accomplishment was more likely to have low morale than his counterpart who placed a high value on interpersonal relationships. Similarly, the wife whose sense of self-esteem depended on having full control of the household did not adjust well if her husband began to encroach on her domain after retirement.

Veroff and Feld (1970) have found that older men who remarried after a divorce or after the death of their wives had higher "affiliation motivation scores" (or "the disposition to strive to establish, maintain, and restore positive affective relationships with other people" [p. 20]) than either still-married men or married and remarried women. Since a strong affiliation motivation is associated with seeking out and attaining the married state to avoid the discomfort of loneliness, they suggest that men may be less capable of being alone than women and add to the accumulating evidence of men's difficulty in establishing close relationships with anyone but a wife.

MULTIPLE PERSON NETWORKS

A number of studies have noted that with advancing age there is a decline in number of roles (another way of saying that there are fewer networks to which the individual relates), in amount of interaction, and in the variety of social contacts (Riley and Foner, 1968, pp. 410–414). The less active, however, are likely to be older, in poorer health, poorer economic circumstances, and of lower intelligence (Maddox, 1966). As a consequence, considerable controversy has arisen regarding the sociopsychological impact of declining involvement in various social networks (Cumming and Henry, 1961; Havighurst and Albrecht, 1953; Maddox, 1964, 1965; Neugarten and Havighurst, 1969; Tobin and Neugarten, 1961). To complicate the picture, there is also evidence that a low level of interaction may not necessarily be age-linked (Lowenthal, 1964; Maddox, 1963).

Some findings from the studies testing disengagement theory (Cumming and Henry,

1961) are that (a) personality characteristics have a strong bearing on the relationship between activity and morale (Havighurst, Neugarten and Tobin, 1968); (b) the extent to which social networks encourage or discourage continued participation is an important factor (Carp, 1968a; Roman and Taietz, 1967); and (c) therefore a distinction must be made between voluntary and involuntary withdrawal (Lowenthal and Boler, 1965; Tallmer and Kutner, 1970). On the other hand, Lemon, Bengtson, and Peterson (1972) conducted a formal test of hypotheses drawn from activity theory and found most were not supported. They did find that belonging to an informal friendship network was related to life satisfaction, but frequency of interaction was not. They concluded that it is the quality or type of interaction, rather than quantity, that is important for the saliency of social networks.

We still have much to learn about the origins and consequences of the wish to be alone, and the extent to which it remains constant across the life course. We agree with the observations of Blau (1973) and Rosenberg (1970) that composite indices which assess only the extent of social interaction and social isolation have tended to give a holistic emphasis to the concepts (one of the dangers when methodology precedes conceptualization). The individual stands at the center of concentric circles of social networks which have varying significance for him and which differentially integrate him with the broader society. It is to these multiple person networks that we now turn.

Family Networks

Social norms stressing independence between parents and adult children lead to the inevitable question as to the extent to which older persons in this country are isolated from kinship networks. Stemming from a sociological tradition which assumed that the nuclear family system was required to meet the demands of a developing industrial society, much of the focus on family life in American society has centered on the nuclear family (Sussman, 1965). There is growing evidence, however, that nuclear units are linked together both within and across generations (Hill, 1965; Kerckhoff, 1965; Shanas, 1968; Sussman, 1965; Sussman and Burchinal, 1968; Townsend, 1968a). Much of this research approaches the problem in terms of frequency of contact which, not surprisingly, indicates that interaction is largely a function of proximity. Most older persons are reported to have close relatives within easy visiting distance, and contacts are relatively frequent (Rosenberg, 1970; Rosencranz, Pihlblad, and McNevin, 1968; Rosow, 1967; Shanas, 1962, 1968; Stehouwer, 1968). Further, proximity is apparently more salient for interaction in the kinship network than is consanguinity. Rosenberg's (1970) working class sample, for example, saw close relatives less frequently than more distant ones, when the former lived geographically further away (in terms of city blocks).

Contacts with relatives are also more common among persons in higher socioeconomic levels (Riley and Foner, 1968, pp. 545-546). The pattern is reversed for contact with children, however. Shanas (1968) notes that although there are no differences by class in having children nearby, older persons with middle class rather than working class backgrounds are less likely to have recently seen a child. Working class parents are also more likely to have more children and to live with them than are middle class parents.

Rosenberg (1970) found no differences in kin contact among older (70-79) compared to younger working class aged, nor between the widowed and married. There were also no differences among retired, partially retired, and working men. The working class people who were separated, divorced, or who had never married did have more restricted kin contact, however, than did the married or widowed. He suggests that, in the culture of the American working class, those who are separated, divorced, or remarried may be ostracized. A cross-national study of three countries—Denmark, Britain, and the United States—found that married older couples tended to live near their children, and more widowed people than married lived with a child (Stehouwer, 1968). In the United States, the latter tended to be older working class women (Shanas, 1968). In a study of the help patterns among older people and their adult children in these countries, Shanas also found that older people turned to their children, particularly daughters, for help in meeting many daily responsibilities. When daughters were not available, then help flowed from sons to parents; when no children were available, siblings were a source of support. Although there were class differences in all three countries in terms of whether old people lived with children or other relatives, in none of the countries was living with kin considered a form of mutual aid.

Rosencranz, Pihlblad, and McNevin (1968) in a rural older sample, substantiate the relationship between health status of the older person and kinship relations. Thus, visits to older people by children or other relatives tend to be more frequent than visits to children by older people. Ill health, then, may function to strengthen the kinship network in terms of frequency of interaction, but we know little about the quality of the relationship between ill older persons and their children. Blau (1973) infers that sickness eventually demoralizes older persons and alienates those close to them, who are burdened with their needs and demands. Kerckhoff (1965) notes that evidence indicates intrafamilial mutual support, but that at the same time it conflicts with a general acceptance of a norm of nuclear family independence. As Shanas (1968) notes, family size is important, because several children can share physical and psychological demands which would be onerous to one. In short, the increase in contact required by an ill parent reverses the dependency flow in the previous parent-child relationship, and the conscious or unconscious resentment of the caretaking child may serve to psychologically isolate the older person from the family network.

Although most research has been directed to interaction between parents and children, it has also been suggested that with increasing age the involvement with relatives of one's own generation becomes strengthened (Cumming and Schneider, 1961, cited in Rosenberg, 1970). While there is a decrease with age in the number of persons who have living siblings, Clark and Anderson (1967) found among their samples of

older people that siblings outnumbered other relatives. In other studies, the nature of the sibling relationship showed great variability, ranging from estrangement to mutual support or dependency. Sibling interaction occurred less often than that between older people and their children and was primarily dependent upon proximity (Rosencranz, Pihlblad, and McNevin, 1968; Youmans, 1962). Older persons who had never been married had more contact with siblings, but they were not as likely to live with siblings as with other relatives, at least in the United States (Shanas, 1968; Stehouwer, 1968). As noted in the discussion of dyadic relationships, the interaction and affective or other types of commitment among older siblings has been a relatively neglected aspect of the study of family networks.

Similarly, although studied in somewhat greater depth, there has also been relatively little research on the relationships between older people and their grandchildren. Not only do most older people have grandchildren, but due to changing mortality, birth, and marriage rates, a good many older people have great-grandchildren as well (Stehouwer, 1968; Townsend, 1968c). By the same token, an "old-old" generation of relatively frail people is also increasing, and Townsend suggests that in the future it will be women in their 60's who will be faced with caring for infirm mothers in their 80's or 90's, and that the demands of the parents, on the one hand, versus the demands of the grandchildren, on the other, may weaken relationships with both.

Taking note of the paucity of knowledge about the quality of involvement with grandchildren, Neugarten and Weinstein (1968) examined three dimensions: degree of comfort in the relationship, its significance, and the style with which the role was enacted. While grandparenthood was often a welcome and pleasurable event, it was also frequently accompanied by some dismay, arising from a sense of being prematurely old, from strained relations with the adult child, and from indifference to caretaking responsibilities for the grandchild. While most people perceived grandparenthood as a kind of biological renewal or continuity, or in terms of emotional self-fulfillment, about a

third nevertheless felt remote from their grandchildren and did not consider the relationship
meaningful. Neugarten and Weinstein's data
also found more traditional forms of grand-
parenting to be more frequent among persons
over 65, while the "fun-seeker" and the "distant" grandparents were younger. In other
words to the extent that estrangement exists, it
is difficult to determine whether it is imposed
on the grandparent or determined by them.
These authors also noted that the anticipation
of, and the initial adjustment to, grandparenthood need study. Reversing this perspective,
Goldfarb (1965) subsequently remarked on the
notable paucity of information about how interaction with grandparents affects the personality and psychological development of grandchildren. Another important question for
research is the changing relationship between
grandparents and grandchildren as each grows
older.

A recent study by Maas and Kuypers (1974)
illustrates the complexity of determining the
degree and depth of interpersonal relations
within the immediate and extended kinship network, as personality characteristics, established
life-styles, and environmental contexts must all
be taken into account. Some older men and
women in this study, for example, had developed a sociable life-style, but whether their
interpersonal relationships were centered primarily on their marital partner, their immediate
family, or extended well beyond the family
often depended on whether the husband was
retired or still working, and the scope and
proximity of the family network. Others had
developed a more detached style in which frequency of interaction was high, but psychological involvement low. Women with this life-
style were well educated and of high economic
status, and focused on clubs and other formal
group activities. While they did not exclude the
family, familial relationships did not appear to
be intimate. Men with this life-style had typically climbed into supervisory and executive
positions, meeting many people, but not enjoying a significant relationship with any. In
contrast, men of lower socioeconomic status
tended to be "loners," leading home-based
lives focused on leisure-time activities. Their relationships with their wives were not close or

expressive, and in general, they were not sociable, even when members of the kinship network lived close by. Women no longer married,
but relatively young, healthy, and employed,
made children and grandchildren an integral
part of their lives. Older women in poor health,
also no longer married, tended to be comparatively uninvolved, with infrequent and passive
interaction with others, accompanied by a
sense of dissatisfaction. In general, the unwell,
disengaged older men and women alike were
dissatisfied with their marriages and their relationships with their children, and they were
remote from their grandchildren. Entrenched in
the sick role, they presented a picture of
negativism and dissatisfaction.

One senses, in reviewing most of the literature
on the familial networks of older people, a
mixture of sterility, formality, and ritualism in
the responses. A pervasive stereotypy runs
through the reports coming from adult children, as though, anticipating their own possible
future needs, they are trying to set an example
for their own children. Their aging parents pick
up the stereotype and say "my children have to
live their own lives." It is not quite clear
whether involvement with middle-aged or aging
parents is construed by adult children as precluding the possiblity of living one's own life,
or whether the kind of attitudinal and behavioral research which our methods by and large
ordain prevents adequate understanding of the
complexity of the relationship between adult
children and their parents and vice versa. Our
current norms do not sanction older people
making demands on the young except in matters of illness or other dire necessity. Possibly
reacting to this norm, most older persons report
that they see their children and grandchildren
as often as they would like (Riley and Foner,
1968, p. 547). In fact, it is those older people
who had expected to have close interpersonal
relationships with their children who feel most
isolated and neglected (Brown, 1970). Perhaps
the anomalies between norms and needs in these
familial networks explain why friendships in
old age boost morale but relationships with
children have an equivocal effect, as suggested
by both Blau (1973) and Rosenberg (1970).

Many of the "young-old" people reporting in
the studies we have reviewed here were exposed

to the child-rearing literature of the late '30's and early '40's, with its emphasis on permissive child-rearing, and a policy of noninterference with, and no demands on, adult offspring and their own children. It would be challenging to try to distinguish between superficially assimilated norms and personal needs or wishes in this young-old group. And it will be interesting to see how they and their children respond to the pressing needs of physical and psychological dependency when they become "old-old" (Goldfarb, 1965). There is some suggestion that those who were "old-old" at the time when most of the studies reported here were conducted, many born before the turn of the century, may have less trouble accepting the dependency needs which are inevitable consequences of the increasing frailties of very old age, than those persons who come after them. Some tentative support for this thesis (for women only) is suggested by the differences between younger and older women among elderly first admissions to a psychiatric facility (Simon, Lowenthal, and Epstein, 1970) and by the sharp drop in the suicide rate for women after age 74 (Dublin, 1963).

Oddly enough, although the Japanese (and Japanese American) cultures are considered to be even more instrumental than the American, Japanese in their 70's, despite the rapid post–World War II "modernization" of their norms, seem to have less trouble accepting dependency than their American age-peers. This may, however, be due in part to a survival factor, since the suicide rate among Japanese males increases steadily and sharply from age 40 to 80 and over (Gibbs, 1966). Despite the traditional ritualism of the Japanese culture, the relationships of the elderly with their adult children seem richer than is true for the Euro-American culture (Kiefer, 1974). On the other hand, it may be that the cultural differences are more apparent than real, resulting from the methodologies customarily used by cultural anthropologists.

Friendship Networks

As noted earlier, most studies of friendship among older persons focus on scope of networks and interaction, rather than on the quality of dyadic friendships. Indeed, it is dismaying to note how little attention has been paid to individual preferences for, and participation in, dyadic as compared with group friendships across the adult life course, and to sex differences therein. Among older persons, themselves, distinctions are often blurred between the availability of (or interaction with) friends and the maintenance of close relationships, with some people professing that their friendships embrace the entire community (Rosencranz, Pihlblad, and McNevin, 1968). Although it can be concluded in such instances that the reported number of close friends is unrealistic, differing concepts of friendship perhaps may account for the inconsistent findings on frequency of interaction with friends.

Among the friendship studies cited in Riley and Foner (1968, pp. 562–563), some report that friendships tend to be maintained into old age; others, that there is a decrease primarily because friends had died or moved away and because older persons themselves had difficulty in getting about and making new friends. Not surprisingly, older persons in good health (and thereby more mobile) were more likely than the less healthy to visit with friends. At the other extreme are studies reporting that the loss of old friends was offset by the acquisition of new ones, and there are even some studies which report that old people have more friends than they did when younger.

There is little difference in friendship associations by sex (Shanas, 1962), although as noted in the discussion of dyadic relationships, the quality of friendships differs markedly between men and women. As to scope and amount of interaction with friends, Rosencranz, Pihlblad, and McNevin (1968) report that widowhood narrowed the circle of friends for men, but Blau's (1961) study of widows reported quite the opposite effect for women. In view of the traditional prerogatives of women in our society as the initiators and decision-makers in regard to the family's social networks, this is scarcely surprising. There is also some evidence that women who have had sustained career commitments may resemble men and have a more restricted social network after retirement or widowhood, because they have not had time to fulfill the role of social life facilitator (Lowenthal, Berkman, and Associates, 1967).

Studies cited in Riley and Foner (1968, p. 563) also indicate that friendship contacts are more frequent among persons of higher socioeconomic status. The more recent Maas and Kuypers (1974) study, however, indicates, as in the case of family networks, that personality characteristics and life-style are also important attributes for involvement with friends. Older persons highly involved with spouses and family also had more enduring relationships with old friends, while others, most of whom were middle class, appeared to have evolved a socially busy life-style wherein they knew many people, none or few of whom were close. This study highlights the fact, then, that frequency of interaction with friends irrespective of socioeconomic status tells us very little about the subjective saliency of the social network.

As noted previously, it has been suggested that although the rate of interaction among relatives may be higher than the rate of association with friends, it is the latter which is more meaningful. Adams (1967) reports that for people of all ages, interaction with friends is valued more highly than interactions with relatives because of the voluntary nature of friendship. Two studies of the elderly, one focusing primarily on older couples in an age-heterogeneous but congregate setting (Johnson, 1971) and the other focusing primarily on older widows in an age-segregated setting (Hochschild, 1973), report that relations with kin and with friends are usually managed separately. When commitments conflict, kinship usually wins out over friendship ties. It appears that it is affection, not obligation, that accounts for this priority, which is somewhat of a contradiction to the report of Adams mentioned above, as well as to those of Blau and Rosenberg mentioned earlier. Relations with kin and those with friends are, then, not really competitive—those with children being based on emotional ties, those with friends on reciprocity. In both contexts, considerable mutual aid was evident. Although relatives were first turned to in case of a health crisis, friends and neighbors were helpful in relieving relatives of care (Johnson, 1971; Hochschild, 1973). In a similar vein, Carp (1966) found that the longer residents lived in retirement housing the less contact they had with family members. However, satisfaction with family relations improved. Friendship networks may serve a complementary function to kinship networks, and indeed may help to strengthen the latter by relieving some of the burden from caretaking kin.

Homogeneity in the social milieu has a strong bearing on friendship patterns. Thus, people in age-segregated housing are more likely than those in age-integrated housing to associate with neighbors (Rosow, 1967). In either type of context, the more characteristics neighbors have in common, such as socioeconomic status, marital status, and value orientations, the more integrated the friendship networks (Bultena and Wood, 1969; Rosenberg, 1970). Blau (1961) reported that where unlike statuses were prevalent, social life became restricted. Widowhood among younger women, for example, may decrease social contact earlier in life than is true for most women in their milieux, where activities are mainly planned for couples. In a community consisting primarily of older couples, however, those who became widowed after entering the community continued their friendships as before, but those who were widowed before entering found it difficult to make friends (Johnson, 1971). Similarly, in a planned retirement community, persons who became dependent upon extensive health care were sanctioned by the rest of the group to withdraw from community life, whether or not they were physically or psychologically ready to do so (Seguin, 1973). On the other hand, people who by preference are "loners," may be placed in an uncomfortable position in such age-homogeneous residence areas because they are pressured to join the activities of the group (Hochschild, 1973). Rosow (1967) has noted that when isolated older persons who had previously expressed a wish for more friends moved to a neighborhood where age-peer density was greater their morale actually decreased. This group, wishing for contact but unable to make it, appears to be similar to the marginal isolates (people who throughout their lives kept trying and failing to achieve close relationships) reported in another study of community-resident aged. Such marginal isolates in general have much lower morale than lifelong isolates (Lowenthal, 1968).

It is also clear, however, that the effect of

structural constraints, presence or absence of normative expectations, and availability of age-peers are highly relevant factors in the sustaining of old friendships and the creation of new ones. But, according to Hess (1972), friendship patterns are less dependent upon age-homogeneity than on the total cluster of networks in which the individual is active. Family, work, and community networks often compete with relationships between friends. On the other hand, friendships offer complementary gratifications and, on occasion, may also serve as a substitute for other relationships. The salience of friendship, too, may change as the salience of other networks change across the successive stages of the adult life course. It is by now a truism that an individual's self-image, role identity, and attitudes toward self and others are to a considerable extent developed and sustained through interaction with others. Consequently, stability in a friendship network lends a sense of continuity of self to the individual. One might also speculate that age-homogeneous friendships may vary in significance by life-stage. One hypothesis is that age, as a basis for friendship, is most pronounced at those stages where the individual's ties to other networks are loosened. Those undergoing similar life-course experiences may find a new solidarity through sharing them. This has been recognized as an almost universal phenomenon in adolescence when the role of child-in-family is being relinquished. It no doubt also accounts for the notable degree of cohesiveness found in many retirement communities—indeed it may in large part account for their popularity. Opportunity permitting, we suspect there would be a similar cohesiveness at other life-stages involving role loss, say among empty-nest women who are looking for something to fill the gap in their lives.

On the other hand, when friendship is fused with work and family roles, disruption in the friendship network develops as the saliency of the other networks diminishes or disappears. Blau (1973), for example, suggests that retired and widowed people whose friends had previously been co-workers and couples may thus become very quickly isolated should both events occur close together. Rosow (1973) rather reluctantly suggests that a practical solution to such problems would be to increase the association of such persons with age-peers, which, except for loners and marginal isolates, is most likely to take place in an age-homogeneous residential setting.

There is some evidence that perception of friendship networks and definitions of friends vary by sex, socioeconomic status, and geographic location. With some exceptions, we found little on the nature of the commitment to friends or on the possible continued relevance of old friendships in which interaction has been weakened by geographic distance or illness, or disrupted by death. But perhaps the most serious shortcoming of the friendship literature—by no means limited to studies of the aging—is in its ambiguity. The emphasis is on "networks" of friends, and the very use of the word implies that one's friends also have a relationship with each other, constituting a kind of cohesive reference group. We have little information about the extent to which friends are perceived in terms of an interacting network or in terms of the kinds of dyadic relationships exalted by Emerson and Tennyson. By their standards a friendship network constituted of a group of people all interacting with each other might well preclude a dyadic friendship, and, conversely, an individual may have several truly intimate friends none of whom are intimate with each other.

Work and Leisure Networks

Work and leisure networks are reviewed together in this section because each is usually defined in juxtaposition to the other. Work involves certain prescribed activities and usual schedules around which people program their lives. Leaving the work force, therefore, creates a void presumably to be filled by leisure pursuits. These assumptions essentially outline an activity theory, and much resulting research has been devoted to leisure activities after retirement. The extent to which either the work or the leisure networks are socially integrative, the circumstances under which retirement leads to social withdrawal, and the degree to which participation in leisure activities includes interpersonal relationships has received only limited attention. Neugarten (1975) has noted that in another 25 years the retirement age will lower to around 55, and that most people will have twice as many retirement years, many of them shared for a longer time by husband and wife in the same household. As retirement becomes both more widespread and of longer duration, it is not enough to report that people do one thing or another when they retire. More attention must be given to retirement as a process, taking into account varying degrees of prior involvement with the work as well as other networks.

Most of the studies which focus on informal social interaction on the job have arisen from industrial sociology and relate the significance of interaction to productivity and other work-related behavior. The extent to which work friendships, initiated through work, exist; whether they are retained after retirement; among what kinds of people in which kinds of work networks these relationships develop; and the meaning they have—all of these issues have received but scant attention. The little evidence available indicates that work-related friendships, both on the job and in retirement, vary by occupation and socioeconomic status.

One study (Sofer, 1970) found that the social aspects of the job were valued among all categories of employed persons, many respondents reporting that if they did not work they would miss the friends and associates at work. This study also indicated that the kind of associations one enjoyed with co-workers—whether primarily social or work-related—was associated with the context of the work situation. Dubin (1956), however, reports that although some social interaction on the job may be required, it is not necessarily very important to the individual. In his study of industrial workers, only a minority of persons reported significant social relationships with people at work. Similarly, Kornhauser (1965) found that white collar employees and the highly skilled factory workers were more sociable than those who had routine jobs. The latter tended to be withdrawn, with fewer friends and less satisfactory family relationships than the other groups.

Evidence for the continuance of friendship relations with former colleagues after retirement is also somewhat conflicting. Several personal accounts indicate that former associates are lost at retirement and to sustain interpersonal contacts the retiree has to make a special effort (Mitchell, 1972; Pressey and Pressey, 1966). A study of retired blacks, while showing that visiting with friends and relatives was a main source of pleasure, found only one group—service workers for the city—where contact with former co-workers was sustained perhaps because they were working out-of-doors, making them more readily accessible (Lambing, 1972). It has been suggested that professional workers are the least likely to experience an abrupt transition between work and retirement (Moore, 1963). Indeed, one study of retired scientists found that retirement did not necessarily imply a cessation of professional activities, including attendance at meetings. Continued engagement with still-working colleagues, however, appeared to depend to a certain extent on one's eminence in the profession and whether one had been university or business based (Rowe, 1973). Neither of these studies considered the degree of involvement or quality of relationships thus sustained. In contrast, a study by Sparks (1973) reports that among male workers in Japan, close friends are developed primarily on the job, which, therefore, has implications for a continuing relationship after retirement. Since many Japanese men turn to other jobs, often in different geographical locations, after their mandatory retirement from long-term positions, old relationships may be drastically disrupted, and new ones are difficult to develop. In our own society, retirement usually reduces opportunity for social contacts, but whether it also entails the degree of personal isolation experienced by many older men in Japan merits further investigation.

The problems of retirement, particularly for men it seems, arise from (1) the belief that work is essential to their personal and social identity and (2) the influence of work in structuring other aspects of the life course, including that of one's family as well. Despite their increasing role in the labor force, less attention has been paid to the general problems of retirement of women, and still less to the possible isolating consequences thereof. There is evidence that they retire earlier than men and that most of them do so voluntarily (Spence and Robinson, 1966). There is also evidence that it is the still married and the lifelong singles who retire early, while the widowed and divorced continue working longer, possibly for economic reasons (Streib and Schneider, 1971). Among middle and lower-middle class, middle-aged working women, the husband's future retirement is viewed as a far more important event than their own retirement. For their male counterparts, the stresses, suffered once-removed by their wives, are twofold: boredom with the present jobs and little or no hope of change; and anxiety about retirement income (Lowenthal et al., 1975). This recent research makes it clear that we need to know much more about the anticipation of retirement, and in the study of retirement, we must cover a far longer time period than we have thus far. We know that some middle-aged men are busily building up or strengthening new social relationships or networks in anticipation of retirement and that others are planning new careers entailing new work networks. But neither of these strategies is employed by many of the men in the above mentioned study (who average about 50 years of age) and thus they do not account for the relaxed mellowness of men much closer to retirement, reported on in this same study, most of whom have no such plans at all. For these men, simple release from boring and frustrating routine in the near future has such appeal that strategies for substitution may not occur to them. There seems to be little anticipated nostalgia for work-related social networks.

As more than one recent retiree has been surprised to learn, just slowing down the daily routine greatly reduces the amount of free time left—and one can spend a long time with the newspaper. Such a path of least resistance notwithstanding, social gerontologists have traditionally viewed engagement in leisure activities, including organizational and political pursuits, as one way in which older persons may replace or reinforce weakened or lost networks. Actually, very little research has been devoted to the interpersonal relationships, dyadic and otherwise, that may develop or be strengthened in the context of leisure pursuits at any stage of life. While there is indication that styles in the uses of leisure developed in early life have a strong bearing on adaptation throughout the life course (Brooks and Elliott, 1971; Maas and Kuypers, 1974; Zborowski, 1962), most studies of those now old were conducted among people who had little leisure in their youth and therefore no lifelong patterns of leisure use to fall back on. In Kornhauser's (1965) study of industrial workers, nearly half of the men in the sample had no special interests or hobbies of any kind. Moore (1963) has noted that the demand for leisure occurs primarily among those who have found interesting ways of using it and who are deeply enmeshed in networks of social life. That so few workers in Kornhauser's sample had either solitary or social leisure interests during their worklife raises the serious question of what these men will do in retirement to replace the social satisfactions many received from work.

Despite the optimism of social philosophers and social scientists about new and better life-styles, if not worlds, being created by an increase in leisure at all life-stages, the availability of more free time is not always viewed as a blessing. Kleemeier (1961) noted long ago that a major problem of the aged is having too much free time. Proportions of older people who say they do not know what to do with their time increase with age, and few complain about not having enough time, nor do they want more of it (Riley and Foner, 1968, p. 533). The relevance of networks in these leisure studies emerges most clearly in a fondness for visiting, most often with relatives. Reading between the lines, one might interpret "too much leisure" to mean "I have more free time than most of the people I want to be with."

Meyersohn (1972) proposes four functions of leisure, at least three directly tied to the concept of work and none discussed in terms of social networks or relationships. One function is "rest, respite, and restoration," to recover from work. A second, which he calls "self-realization," is really a different form of work, with the emphasis (in Meyersohn's terms) on craftsmanship and an accompanying active consumption. "Spiritual renewal" or contemplation, is a third form of leisure, and presumably solitary, though, he reports, seldom pursued. The fourth function of leisure, "entertainment," is not so directly tied to the concept of work by this author. He views it as a relatively new phenomenon, which he relates to the growth of the mass media (exposure to which can at best constitute a kind of symbolic network). Actually, escapism is by no means a new phenomenon—the outlets offered by the Roman Circuses, for example, have been an object of philosophical and historical interest for centuries. And, with the advent of the printing press, a whole flurry of discussion was sparked among such authors as Pope, Goldsmith, Addison, Fielding, and Johnson about the function of popular escapist literature (Lowenthal and Fiske, 1957). Their criticisms, of course, were not that it was passive or solitary, but that it was neither morally uplifting nor intellectually stimulating.

In many respects, these views of leisure, none of which are specifically "set" in a network of social relationships, suggest that our education and culture are largely responsible for the dissatisfaction of that great majority of older people, who as they age increasingly value interpersonal relationships. In direct conflict with this deeply human need, most people age 60 and over spend their leisure time at home, half of it in solitude, watching television, engaging in hobbies, and reading (Cowgill and Baulch, 1962).

Theoretically, since for some time this country has been the world's greatest consumer of leisure time and leisure goods, we would expect not only scholars but people in general, and especially those who have the most leisure time, to be skilled in its functions and uses, balancing solitude and interpersonal involvement to meet their needs. Perhaps the triviality of what is most accessible is not only an unsatisfying substitute for networks of real people, but deadening to any impulse to seek them out. Until the late 1930's, at least in the recollections of the senior author of this paper, the working class old, to say nothing of the middle class, used to talk, with each other and with the young, on buses, in cafeterias, and on the streets. Now, at least in large cities, they seem strangely silent. Are they benumbed and dazed by the media?

Has the one-way communication of the TV world become their principal social reality? No doubt the media are better than no contacts at all for the house- or nursing-home bound, but do they also tranquilize those who need not be confined, so that they come not to venture forth except for dire necessities?

Although this section, as the chapter as a whole, is supposed to be devoted to social networks, the literature thus far has seldom elaborated on the social contexts of either work or leisure. It has, however, conveyed a strong impression that, even among those who have not yet reached very old age and who are in comparatively good health, there are few who are ensconced in anything that could be called a network of people sharing common leisure activities and that those who are belong to the privileged sectors of society whose activities include concerts, theater, and golf. That for the majority there is no such interpersonal cluster may account for the fact that with extra free time most prefer to work. Work settings, at the very least, usually involve some interaction with real people.

The next two sections of this chapter offer further cases to the same point. Involvements in voluntary associations, including religious, and in sociopolitical affairs, are usually included in the checklists of "leisure activities," but rarely are we able to detect the extent to which they involve social networks in the sense of groups of people interacting in face-to-face situations.

Voluntary Associations

In social gerontology, voluntary associations have often been viewed as a means of continuing the involvement of older people in extra-familial social networks. A review of the studies cited in Riley and Foner (1968, pp. 483–510), however, indicates that in fact, the majority of persons do not belong to such groups, and, of those who do, most belong to only one. Church membership is an exception and tends to be maintained well into the 70's. But membership *per se* tells us little, and participation in church-related groups declines at an earlier age. By and large, participation in voluntary associations is more related to sex, social class, and the continuance of activity in other social networks than it is to age. Older people are more likely to be actively involved in such networks if they are still working, married, and entertaining friends occasionally. This suggests the importance of dyadic relationships and participation in one or two other networks as conditions for involvement in voluntary associations. Retired persons show a substantial decline in involvement in those voluntary organizations associated with an occupational role, though this decline is more noticeable among men than among women and, again, is less true of the more privileged classes (Rosencranz, Pihlblad, and McNevin, 1968).

Women are also more likely than men to continue to attend church regularly and to participate in other forms of religious activities. Atchley (1972) reports that while church groups are willing passively to accept the participation of older people, few actively solicit it. Decrease in church attendance among the elderly as in other organizational activities is also associated with poor health and transportation problems; thus we find older people increasingly substituting televised church programs for actual attendance. Since religious memberships appear to be the principal form of organizational participation sustained in later life, such reliance on the media has ominous implications for even greater isolation of the elderly.

The evidence on whether major life changes influence participation in voluntary associations is ambiguous. As we have noted, studies indicate that older people reduce such involvement when they make a geographic move (Riley and Foner, 1968, p. 506) or when they retire. Streib (1956), on the other hand, reports that retirement has no such effect; and a study of a multipurpose senior center revealed that half of the members joined within two years after a major life change (Storey, 1962). This study, it should be added, also found that members of such groups were continuing a lifelong pattern of voluntary network involvement. To summarize the majority of studies, it appears, as with other leisure patterns, that direct participation in voluntary associations in old age depends to a considerable extent on styles established earlier in life. And as Wilensky (1961) suggests, the

small proportion of older persons who do thus participate in such associations have generally established their leisure routines by midlife, and for most this was focused on family and neighborhood networks, which, short of illnesses, deaths, and geographic moves, continue into old age. Wilensky also notes that, low though it is reported to be, the active involvement of older people in the social networks provided by voluntary associations is probably overestimated because of an undersampling of social isolates in most studies. Large rooming houses are often bypassed as sources for respondents, and contacting widows, widowers, and other older adults living alone is difficult. In addition, since the norm in American society is that older people are expected to maintain voluntary association networks and involvements (Britton and Britton, 1972), self-reports on participation may well be inflated.

Another form of voluntary association is the political network; since this is the subject of another chapter in this volume (Ch. 15), we shall here briefly review the evidence for social involvement in such networks as a potential deterrent to isolation in later life. In the political arena, just as with other voluntary associations, it is often difficult to distinguish between membership and active participation. The research findings tend to be limited primarily to voting behavior, which tells us little about networks offering the possibility for social interaction. Unlike "activities" listed as memberships, however, voting at the polls at least potentially offers a modest opportunity for mingling, though the "network" is geographically, rather than politically, contained.

As is true of other voluntary associations, much of the literature on political participation in the United States describes how various demographic characteristics relate to such involvement. Although there are some exceptions, higher socioeconomic status and educational level, being male, and living in an urban environment are positively associated with such activity, and this is generally true at all age levels (Milbrath, 1965). Glenn and Grimes (1968), analyzing material from 28 nationwide surveys and from a cohort analysis of voter turnout, found that when both sex and education were held constant, voting among older respondents remained fairly constant up to age 80. They reported a sharp decline after age 80 and attributed it to physical impairment. Although membership in voluntary political associations is quite low at all age levels, in general, persons 55 and over are somewhat more likely than younger people to belong to such groups (Riley and Foner, 1968, p. 468).

Gubrium (1972) found that disruptions in the lifelong pattern of activities of the elderly occur when they experience major interpersonal crises in primary relationships. Thus, discontinuities in dyadic relationships such as those brought about by widowhood and divorce may lead to a feeling of apathy or desolation, with a subsequent decrease in activities, including political. Although Gubrium was not concerned with sex differences, such crises could help to explain the earlier and more pronounced decrease in participation at the polls among older women than among older men.

In the light of the number of studies which compare political involvement among the young and the old, evidence on the amount of interest in gaining political information, from whom, and how, is sparse, although there is some indication that older people are more likely than younger to follow public affairs through the mass media (Riley and Foner, 1968, p. 468). This suggests the possibility of decline in whatever informal "political networks" (located in an earlier time at the village store or pump) may have existed. Several studies, however, infer that the greater use of the media by older persons represents an increased interest in public affairs, because the older the respondent, the more likely he is to select serious content rather than entertainment (Riley and Foner, 1968, pp. 524–526). Schramm (1969) also reports that public affairs news and educational programs, in particular, engage the attention of older persons.

As to the possibility of the impact of sociohistorical change on the active group involvement of older people in political affairs, it should be born in mind that most studies available for review when this volume was prepared were conducted in a period of relative safety on the streets and of increasing social and economic benefits for older citizens. For some groups, especially the lower-middle and lower class "young-old," the recent and rather drastic changes in both of these conditions seems to be having a strong impact. This increase in sociopolitical and economic grievances, combined with a relative lack of established channels for active political participation, and with a strong predilection for television viewing, suggests a latent susceptibility of the "young-old" to charismatic leaders able to present convincing "solutions" to the issues which concern them most (Lowenthal, 1975).

One consequence of the assumption that voluntary associations are important mechanisms for reducing social isolation among the aged has been the establishment of senior centers and programs drawing on the services of older volunteers. The stated purpose of such organizations is to fill personal voids created by constricted life-space (Katz, 1970), but as we have noted earlier, the majority of the members of such centers are lifelong joiners. From a somewhat different perspective, however, in an analysis of survey data concerning the need for substitutes for work-related networks, Preston and Helgerson (1972) found only 9 percent of an older sample who would be willing to serve as volunteers. They conclude that since almost a fifth of their sample considered themselves to be unemployed rather than retired, they were perhaps unwilling to identify themselves as interested in unpaid work. Carp (1968b) also examined whether voluntary activity fulfilled needs similar to those filled by paid work and concluded that the latter is far more highly valued because it denotes that one is still doing something really worthwhile. These findings, then, challenge the assumption that the elderly will volunteer their services in new networks as replacements for lost roles, especially in the work network, particularly if they perceive themselves as still able to function in the work role. As to reduction of social isolation, Bley, Dye, Goodman, and Jensen (1973), exploring self-reports of clients of a community center, found that the elderly participated in it primarily because of the content of the program and *not* because they were seeking social contacts. The staff, on the other hand, perceived social relationships as significant incentive for participation. Brown (1974) found that elderly persons who become even slightly dissatisfied with group relations tended to voluntarily withdraw from them. He also reported that the pattern of changing relationships among the elderly is not toward more participation in formal organizations, but toward more intimate relationships, especially within the immediate family. This corresponds to the anticipations of many younger men facing retirement, who look forward to the possibility of strengthening interpersonal relationships, particularly familial (Lowenthal *et al.*, 1975). On the other hand, another study, this one of a Jewish center, found that while those of American backgrounds preferred activities enabling them to express their individuality, those of Eastern European background were indeed primarily interested in activities in which their sense of belonging to a network was paramount (Guttmann, 1973). We also know from studies of age-segregated housing environments that not only may organizational structure require formal responsibilities, but that the residents themselves form groups on the basis of common interests, which in turn provide for leadership roles (Hochschild, 1973; Johnson, 1971; Seguin, 1973). In such environments responsibility and involvement are usually broadly distributed, and offer evidence for Rosow's (1974) conclusion that the needs of older citizens for social involvement can probably best emerge in the context of age-homogeneous social structures.

The kind of participation indices traditionally used in studies of voluntary associations tell us little about the critical issue of locus of control. While the individual may, perhaps as an ego-strengthening maneuver, report himself as voluntarily decreasing his participation for good and sufficient reasons such as a decline in energy, we also know that the resources of most individuals of all ages are grossly underused and that the demands of a crisis or of being seriously needed in some social context often activate latent energy and talents which surprise the individual himself as well as others in his milieu. We suspect that if a need to have older people actively involved were articulated and formalized

by voluntary organizations, as they may be in age-segregated housing, their energies would be replenished to meet the occasion.

Helping Networks

Maddox (1970) has noted that attention to the problematic aspects of the aged in modern urban societies was initially focused on institutional living arrangements. The old were, in these circumstances, usually characterized as socially isolated, impoverished, disabled, and mentally impaired. Since the institutionalized represent only about 5 percent of those over 65, it is not surprising that research reviewed here, based primarily on community-resident elderly, provides a more optimistic view of their social networks. In the community, too, however, the evidence indicates that the isolated tend to be of low socioeconomic status, in poor rather than good health, and unmarried (Lowenthal, 1964; Maddox and Eisdorfer, 1962; Scotch and Richardson, 1966). These are also characteristics of elderly persons permanently or temporarily residing in institutions (Lowenthal, Berkman, and Associates, 1967; also studies reported in Riley and Foner, 1968, p. 580). The studies by Shanas, Townsend, Wedderburn, Friis, Milhøj, and Stehouwer (1968) have shown that utilization of institutional and community services is closely related to family structure and relationships. When older people have no close relationships or when the family can no longer cope with serious and long-term nursing needs, community services are required not only to complement the services of the family, but to replace them. Consequently, the extent to which institutions help residents in maintaining meaningful ties with the outside world, and the likelihood that significant social networks with other residents and staff may develop may be queried.

Some 20 years ago when national concern developed about the institutionalized elderly, the reference was usually to those confined to mental hospitals. Since that time, there has been a movement to return the elderly to their own homes or communities, with a subsequent influx to community-based institutions. The results of this process remain relatively unassessed.

Kahn (1975) notes that the "mental health revolution" has resulted in older persons dropping out of the psychiatric system. This does not mean, however, that they are no longer institutionalized. Citing an analysis by Redick (1974), Kahn suggests that the aged are now being displaced to nursing homes, and it is these kinds of long-term facilities which are becoming the custodial institutions of the aged.

Among studies of the social consequences of such settings, Curry and Ratliff (1973) found that almost a quarter of the residents of intermediate and larger sized homes were totally isolated from friends and relatives. Residents in the smaller homes were less isolated than those in larger homes in terms of frequencies of social contacts, apparently because they made friends and interacted with them within the home itself. Handschu (1973) has also noted that nurses' aides are more likely to develop companion relationships with residents in smaller, rather than larger nursing homes. Social interaction among residents of nursing homes is also influenced by social class. Those placed in institutions by welfare agencies are usually located further from relatives than are self or private referrals, and, perhaps as a consequence, it has been found that the elderly poor are not visited as often by friends or relatives as are their more affluent counterparts (Kosberg, 1973). It has also been noted that patients who are visited by relatives get more care and attention by staff (Glaser and Strauss, 1968; Gottesman and Bourestom, 1974; Kosberg, 1973), a circumstance which again benefits the affluent more then the nonaffluent resident.

Traditionally, long-term care facilities have seen their primary responsibility as that of meeting basic physical needs ("custodial care") and disregarding psychological and social ones. As a consequence, the elderly may well have perceived legitimacy in the "sick role," living up to the institutional expectations for illness, and at the same time, isolating them from others (Kahana, 1973; Kahn, 1975; Petroni, 1969). That residents spend most of their time alone is a common phenomenon. In one study of 40 nursing homes in a mid-Western city, for example, it was observed that over half of the residents' waking time was spent alone and do-

ing nothing (Gottesman and Bourestom, 1974). They were in contact with another person, primarily with staff, less than a fifth of their time awake. Another study also found extreme isolation; the patients themselves, however, perceived more of it than did the staff (Jones, 1972). Most contacts also appear to have been of a rather superficial nature, since the residents made a distinction between just talking to someone and "really getting to know them." Many nursing homes have undergone significant change, and in some there is certainly a trend toward more attention being paid to psychosocial needs (Hammerman, 1974). We tend to agree with Kahana (1973, p. 283), however, that "there are few studies of the quality of life in nursing homes along humanistic lines."

Several experimental projects have been conducted and evaluated as a basis for introducing more interaction in such settings. The aforementioned study by Jones (1972), for example, introduced recreational therapy as a means to this end. Although communication increased within the group, it resulted in only a slight increase outside of the sessions, and even that was not sustained for any length of time. Jones also found a considerable amount of overt conflict, hostility, and mistrust between patients which seemed to be exacerbated by the sessions as patients vied for positions in the group. He suggests, therefore, that perhaps the need for self-protection keeps such patients at a distance from each other. Another experiment, which introduced 10 undergraduate students to serve as volunteer companions to 30 residents of a nursing home met with somewhat more success (Arthur, Donnan, and Lair, 1973). The morale scores of the residents who received such companionship, compared to those who did not receive it, improved significantly. The variety of such contacts is also important, as indicated by the fact that a group visited by a different student each week for the duration of the program improved more than one visited by the same volunteer during the same period. The adjustment of the former group also continued to improve after the volunteer program was terminated.

These latter experiments in meeting the social needs of residents were introduced into the institution from the outside. Yet it is the staff of such organizations which comprise the day-to-day life of the residents. Putnam (1973) notes that many such staff members realize they are a center of human warmth. While the more competent elderly manage social interactions with other residents quite satisfactorily, the less competent cling to the nurse or nurses' aide and are often comforted by sitting near the desk and listening to staff conversations. It should be noted, however, that when attention was more clearly focused on patients by asking nurses to attend to the psychosocial needs of the patients, there were no significant changes in patients' functioning. At the same time, Putnam points out, patients did not deteriorate, suggesting that increased attention may help older patients to at least stabilize for a time.

Indeed, the lack of meaningful social contacts is one of the paradoxes of institutional living. Continued contact with friends and relatives outside helps to keep the person from becoming too isolated, but it is clear that supportive relationships with staff are important if not decisive. Given adequate staff, interpersonal relations can be enhanced somewhat if both staff and residents share a common cultural heritage. Kahana and Harel (1972) have noted that such a shared orientation leads to improved communication and greater empathy. In general, however, the parameters within which residents in institutions might respond to a positive, supportive, "friendship" relationship with staff or other residents have not yet been well defined.

In other types of age-homogeneous settings, it appears that the informal and loose structures of older persons who are residentially linked, by their own choice, are often more satisfying than family networks where the health-related or other needs of the older person may adversely influence both affect and spontaneity. The voluntarily chosen age-homogeneous community (such as trailer camps or age-segregated public and private housing) may also have a strong advantage over the more institutionalized forms of living arrangements. A hypothetical comparison between a comparatively healthy group of older people in the former type of setting and a similarly healthy group in an "old

age home," or in one of the many complexes that provide a range from independent living to total care immediately, suggests the essential structural differences. On the one hand, we have a freely associating group of "equals" while on the other we have a group of "equals" situated within two vertical institutional hierarchies of authority (one administrative, one health-care related, themselves often conflicting) and a third hierarchy of residents who are graded by the authority hierarchies in terms of degree of socioeconomic, social, physical, and mental resources. These more or less visible hierarchies foster elitist groups among residents at one extreme, and at the same time they may well encourage or perpetuate the sick role among the less privileged, which the latter may use as a means of competing with the elitist groups for attention from the institutional hierarchies.

Those older people who choose to enter any one of the voluntary "adult communities," while they may evolve their own hierarchies, are not forced to do so by built-in structural ones. These persons appear spontaneously to assume more responsibility for each other and to develop more meaningful relationships in the process. This kind of spontaneity, say in a helping role, is implicitly if not explicitly discouraged in the institutional arrangements, partly because of the existence of a network of professional helpers within the institution who have control over their residents. This analysis is largely an impressionistic conclusion from the research we have reviewed, but one which has also been reached by other observers (Hochschild, 1973; Kleemeier, 1961).

The situation in nursing homes is even more difficult to evaluate, partly due to the remarkable paucity of professional research attention to those proliferating institutions and partly to the fact that the few studies extant do not systematically take into account such salient factors as the range of debilitation of the patients and the staff/patient ratio. The impression one gains is of overworked, undertrained, and highly harassed staff who are unable to cope with the physical needs of their patients, to say nothing of their psychosocial needs. A major, interdisciplinary, and sophisticated study of a representative sample of such institutions is long overdue, and may well be underway before this volume is published.

INVOLVEMENT AND ISOLATION: IMPLICATIONS FOR RESEARCH AND THEORY

The social networks we have reviewed in this chapter range from the primarily interpersonal (family and friendship) to those which are or may be a combination of the interpersonal, the anonymous, and the remote or symbolic. The extent to which leisure, voluntary association, and sociopolitical networks include or exclude close, dyadic relationships, closely knit subgroups, anonymous "theys," and symbolic reference groups is the result of the interrelationship among three sets of factors. First there are the structural and normative characteristics of the networks themselves; second, the perceptions and predilections of the individuals related to them; and, third, the objective position of particular individuals within them (voluntary/involuntary, passive/active, low or high in any power structures that may exist).

To fully understand the causes and consequences of age-linked changes in involvement in or isolation from the various networks to which an individual relates, therefore, we need to learn much more about (a) the structural, the normative, and the latent characteristics of such networks, particularly in regard to age-grading; and (b) the location of the individual in his networks, including both his objective role in terms of behavioral and hierarchical measures, and his subjective perceptions, degree of commitment, and amount and nature of his affect toward the network. Whether studied longitudinally or retrospectively, the location of the individual first must be assessed at a point in his career in the network prior to the time when age-linked changes, voluntary or imposed, might be presumed to take place. Such studies should be undertaken in two ways: using a given network as the object of research as well as a sample of all of the people related to it; and using the individual as the point of departure and assessing the nature of his relatedness, both objective and subjective, to all of his relevant networks. The first type of study is the only way in which we can realistically begin to assess the extent to which withdrawal or isolation from a network is voluntary, or implicitly or explicitly coerced. The second type of study, starting with the individual and all of his significant networks, is the only means for filling in the gaps in our knowledge about such issues as preferred rhythms of involvement and isolation, how or whether they change in the adult life course, the extent to which some networks may be interchangeable in terms of meeting the needs of the individual, and the extent to which the wish or need for dyadic versus multiple person networks may change across the life course or differ between the sexes.

As the individual reaches more advanced old age, and especially if he or she becomes physically and/or mentally impaired, many of the networks mentioned above may actually become, or be perceived as "helping." But if the need for help is both considerable and longterm, the multiple person networks are unlikely to meet it. Even in the most devoted family constellations, unless full-time nursing help can be afforded, the psychic and physical resources of the care-taking others will eventually become overtaxed, although it is surprising how long some families are able to assume care for a completely helpless old person (Lowenthal, 1964). When such situations develop, the research questions bearing on social networks and social isolation change not only in degree, but in kind. They have been studied in detail in the period when state mental hospitals were the major recourse for the mentally and physically chronically impaired elderly (Blau, 1966; Gaitz, 1969; Goldfarb, 1961; Lowenthal, Berkman, and Associates, 1967; Simon, Lowenthal, and Epstein, 1970). They have been seriously neglected since the dismantling of many state hospitals has returned thousands of such seriously impaired old persons back to whatever their families or communities may be able to offer.

From a conceptual and theoretical view, the material we have reviewed, and the very title of the chapter, strongly imply a continuum from high network involvement to extreme isolation, the one presumably associated with "good" adaptation, the other with poor. We have tried to suggest the need for a less dichotomous conceptual framework. Ranking low on network involvement at any life-stage does not necessarily result in low morale or poor mental health or whatever measure we wish to use. As the research literature has indicated, it tends to be those predisposed to gregariousness in earlier life-stages who suffer from withdrawal (or being excluded) from such networks in old age.

Locus of control is of critical importance to the individual in the social network context. For many older people the new freedom of choice of the post–child-rearing stage (and beyond) is cherished, and symptoms of maladaptation show up when other demands (grown children who remain dependent, aged parents who become so) interfere with this freedom. For many men this freedom or potential freedom often evokes both wishes and actions directed toward closer interpersonal, often dyadic relationships. Such men relinquish the more formal networks with relief. The obstacles they face are that close friendships are often, as yet, uncultivated, and their grown children who rarely were close to their fathers at any time, whose interests and needs are centered in the world outside their family of origin, are often indifferent to them, if not resentful. At the same time, the broader networks show little interest in welcoming older women, who express the need for more involvement in fields beyond the family and close friends. The subsequent frustrations of these women aggravate those of their husbands who may be seeking intimacy but are at a loss as to how to achieve it.

As a chapter in a companion volume to this one (Lowenthal, 1976) suggests, what is needed in the conceptual framework for studying isolation/social involvement on the one hand, and adaptation on the other, is an elaboration of an adult life-course perspective on concepts of commitment—interpersonal, moral, and self-expressive (or, in slightly different terms, competence/effectance, White, 1963)—which have varying degrees of centrality for women and men at successive life-stages. Nor must a fourth type of commitment, not necessarily but often age-linked, be overlooked, namely, preoccupation with self-protection and

survival. At any given stage of life, a strong commitment in any one of these areas may offset weaknesses in others. The extent to which a social network context is essential to the fulfillment of any one of them, and whether this importance changes across the life course, is a challenging question. As we have suggested, with increasing age former networks, or networks envisaged by the individual but not necessarily participated in, may be as meaningful, or more so, as those where social interaction currently takes place. A strong involvement in friendship and familial relationships may come to meet the generative (Erikson, 1963) or the consultative (Berezin, 1963) needs of older men more effectively than various types of more formal network affiliations within which the elderly are rarely called upon for advice or leadership. A strong moral or religious commitment may, as the data have suggested, be more gratifyingly reinforced by self-selected television programs which one may absorb in relative peace and solitude than by actual involvement in religious networks, which requires the economic resources and the physical energy to dress properly to get to a house of worship.

For those who have had a strong commitment to competence, men in the work context, for example, and women in their familial roles, the former networks, co-workers and superiors at work, one's peers in PTA, Den Mothers, and other groups primarily centered on child-rearing, may have long since dissolved, but nevertheless these continue to serve as meaningful frames of reference long after active involvement in them has ceased. While such former networks become, in a sense, symbolic, they continue to be evoked, and such evocation often strengthens the sense of a job well done.

Among older people with a strong commitment to self-preservation and survival, there are some for whom this has been a lifelong preoccupation, the origins of which may best be traced to psychic problems stemming from infancy and childhood. Others acquire such commitment along with the infirmities of age. Unlike some of the other forms of commitment, networks, for such people, become more salient. For the lifelong self-protective person, helping networks may not be needed by any objective standards relating to infirmity, but in our culture only in old age does it become acceptable to seek help for rather vague or minor symptoms of psychological or physical fragility. Those old persons whose self-protectiveness is forced upon them by economic, social, or physical deprivations (most frequently all three) are likely to be conflicted by their dependency needs. Unlike the lifelong self-protective, who may professionally be classified as "good" clients and patients, they may prove difficult if not recalcitrant. These persons will increasingly constitute a prime challenge to the helping family and professional networks unless the "helpers" find some way to reinforce the salience of former networks, dyadic and otherwise, and real or symbolic opportunities for the sustainment of commitment in the other areas that have been important to them.

REFERENCES

Adams, B. N. 1967. Interaction theory and the social network. *Sociometry*, 30(1), 64–78.

Adams, B. N. 1968. *Kinship in an Urban Setting*. Chicago: Markham.

Arthur, G. L., Donnan, H. H., and Lair, C. V. 1973. Companionship therapy with nursing home aged. *Gerontologist*, 13(2), 167–170.

Atchley, R. C. 1972. *The Social Forces in Later Life*. Belmont, California: Wadsworth.

Bengtson, V. L., and Martin, W. C. 1970. Alienation and age: An inter-generational study. Presented at 23rd Annual Meeting of the Gerontological Society, Toronto.

Berenson, B. 1963. *Sunset and Twilight: From the Diaries of 1947–1958* (edited by Nicky Mariano). New York: Harcourt, Brace & World.

Berezin, M. A. 1963. Some intrapsychic aspects of aging. *In*, N. E. Zinberg and I. Kaufman (eds.), *Normal Psychology of the Aging Process*, pp. 93–117. New York: International Universities Press.

Blau, D. 1966. Psychiatric hospitalization of the aged. *Geriatrics*, 21, 204–210.

Blau, Zena Smith. 1961. Structural constraints on friendships in old age. *Am. Soc. Rev.*, 26(3), 429–439.

Blau, Zena Smith. 1973. *Old Age in a Changing Society*. New York: Franklin Watts.

Bley, Nina, Dye, D., Goodman, M., and Jensen, Kathryn. 1973. Clients' perceptions—A key variable in evaluating leisure activities for the elderly. *Gerontologist*, 13(3), Part I, 365–371.

Blood, R. O., Jr., and Wolfe, D. M. 1960. *Husbands and Wives: The Dynamics of Married Living*. New York: The Free Press.

Blumer, H. 1969. *Symbolic Interactionism: Perspective and Method*. Englewood Cliffs, New Jersey: Prentice-Hall.

Britton, J. H., and Britton, Jean O. 1972. *Personality Changes in Aging*. New York: Springer.

Brooks, J. B., and Elliott, D. M. 1971. Prediction of psychological adjustment at age thirty from leisure time activities and satisfactions in childhood. *Hum. Develop.*, 14(1), 51–61.

Brown, A. S. 1974. Satisfying relationships for the elderly and their patterns of disengagement. *Gerontologist*, 14(3), 258–262.

Brown, R. G. 1970. Family structure and social isolation of older persons. *In*, E. Palmore (ed.), *Normal Aging*, pp. 270–277. Durham, North Carolina: Duke University Press.

Bultena, G. L., and Wood, Vivian. 1969. The American retirement community: Bane or blessing? *J. Geront.*, 24(2), 209–217.

Carp, Frances M. 1966. *A Future for the Aged*. Austin, Texas: University of Texas Press.

Carp, Frances M. 1968a. Some components of disengagement. *J. Geront.*, 23(3), 382–386.

Carp, Frances M. 1968b. Differences among older workers, volunteers, and persons who are neither. *J. Geront.*, 23(4), 497–501.

Clark, Margaret, and Anderson, Barbara G. 1967. *Culture and Aging*. Springfield, Illinois: Charles C Thomas.

Cowgill, D. O., and Baulch, Norma. 1962. The use of leisure time by older people. *Gerontologist*, 2(1), 47–50.

Cumming, Elaine, and Henry, W. E. 1961. *Growing Old: The Process of Disengagement*. New York: Basic Books.

Cumming, Elaine, and Schneider, D. M. 1961. Sibling solidarity: A property of American kinship. *Am. Anthropologist*, 63, 498–507.

Curry, T. J., and Ratliff, B. W. 1973. The effects of nursing home size on resident isolation and life satisfaction. *Gerontologist*, 13(3), Part I, 295–298.

Dubin, R. 1956. Industrial workers' worlds: A study of the central life interests of industrial workers. *Soc. Probl.*, 3(3), 131–142.

Dublin, L. I. 1963. *Suicide: A Sociological and Statistical Study*. New York: Ronald Press.

Dubos, R. 1965. *Man Adapting*. New Haven: Yale University Press.

Erikson, E. H. 1963. *Childhood and Society*. 2nd ed. New York: W. W. Norton.

Farber, M. 1940. *Philosophical Essays in Memory of Edmund Husserl*. Cambridge, Massachusetts: Harvard University Press.

Fromm-Reichmann, Frieda. 1959. Loneliness. *Psychiatry*, 22(1), 1–15.

Gaitz, C. M. 1969. Functional assessment of the suspected mentally ill aged. *J. Amer. Geriat. Soc.*, 17(6), 541-548.

Gibbs, J. P. 1966. Suicide. *In*, R. K. Merton and R. A. Nisbet (eds.), *Contemporary Social Problems*, 2nd ed., pp. 281-321. New York: Harcourt, Brace & World.

Glaser, B. G., and Strauss, A. L. 1968. *Time for Dying*. Chicago: Aldine.

Glenn, N. D., and Grimes, M. 1968. Aging, voting, and political interest. *Am. Soc. Rev.*, 33(4), 563-575.

Goldfarb, A. I. 1961. Mental health in the institution. *Gerontologist*, 1(4), 178-184.

Goldfarb, A. I. 1965. Psychodynamics and the three-generation family. *In*, Ethel Shanas and G. F. Streib (eds.), *Social Structure and the Family*, pp. 10-45. Englewood Cliffs, New Jersey: Prentice-Hall.

Gottesman, L. E., and Bourestom, N. C. 1974. Why nursing homes do what they do. *Gerontologist*, 14(6), 501-506.

Gubrium, J. F. 1972. Toward a socio-environmental theory of aging. *Gerontologist*, 12(3), Part I, 281-284.

Gurin, G., Veroff, J., and Feld, Sheila. 1960. *Americans View Their Mental Health: A Nationwide Interview Study*. New York: Basic Books.

Guttmann, D. 1973. Leisure-time activity interests of Jewish aged. *Gerontologist*, 13(2), 219-223.

Hammerman, J. 1974. The role of the institution and the concept of parallel services. *Gerontologist*, 14(1), 11-14.

Handschu, Susan Stellar. 1973. Profile of the nurse's aide—Expanding her role as psycho-social companion to the nursing home resident. *Gerontologist*, 13(3), Part I, 315-317.

Havighurst, R. J., and Albrecht, Ruth. 1953. *Older People*. New York: Longmans, Green.

Havighurst, R. J., Neugarten, Bernice L., and Tobin, S. S. 1968. Disengagement and patterns of aging. *In*, Bernice L. Neugarten (ed.), *Middle Age and Aging*, pp. 161-177. Chicago: University of Chicago Press.

Hess, Beth. 1972. Friendship. *In*, Matilda White Riley, Marilyn Johnson, and Anne Foner (eds.), *Aging and Society*, Vol. Three: *A Sociology of Age Stratification*, pp. 357-396. New York: Russell Sage Foundation.

Hill, R. 1965. Decision making and the family life cycle. *In*, Ethel Shanas and G. F. Streib (eds.), *Social Structure and the Family*, pp. 113-139. Englewood Cliffs, New Jersey: Prentice-Hall.

Hochschild, Arlie Russell. 1973. *The Unexpected Community*. Englewood Cliffs, New Jersey: Prentice-Hall.

Irish, D. P. 1964. Sibling interaction: A neglected aspect in family life research. *Soc. Forces*, 42(3), 279-288.

Johnson, Sheila K. 1971. *Idle Haven: Community Building Among the Working-class Retired*. Berkeley: University of California Press.

Jones, D. C. 1972. Social isolation, interaction, and conflict in two nursing homes. *Gerontologist*, 12(3), Part I, 230-234.

Kahana, Eva. 1973. The humane treatment of old people in institutions. *Gerontologist*, 13(3), Part I, 282-289.

Kahana, Eva, and Harel, Z. 1972. Social and behavioral principles in residential care settings for the aged: The residents' perspective. Presented at the Annual Meeting of American Orthopsychiatric Association, Detroit.

Kahn, R. L. 1975. The mental health system and the future aged. *Gerontologist*, 15(1), Part 2, 24-31.

Katz, A. H. 1970. Self-help organizations and volunteer participation in social welfare. *Social Work*, 15(1), 51-60.

Kerckhoff, A. C. 1965. Nuclear and extended family relationships: A normative and behavioral analysis. *In*, Ethel Shanas and G. F. Streib (eds.), *Social Structure and the Family*, pp. 93-112. Englewood Cliffs, New Jersey: Prentice-Hall.

Kiefer, C. 1974. *Changing Cultures, Changing Lives: An Ethnographic Study of Three Generations of Japanese Americans*. San Francisco: Jossey-Bass.

Kleemeier, R. W. (ed.) 1961. *Aging and Leisure*. New York: Oxford University Press.

Kornhauser, A. 1965. *Mental Health of the Industrial Worker*. New York: John Wiley.

Kosberg, J. I. 1973. Differences in proprietary institutions caring for affluent and nonaffluent elderly. *Gerontologist*, 13(3), Part 1, 299-304.

Lambing, Mary L. Brooks. 1972. Social class living patterns of retired negroes. *Gerontologist*, 12(3), Part 1, 285-288.

Lemon, B. W., Bengtson, V. L., and Peterson, J. A. 1972. An exploration of the activity theory of aging: Activity types and life satisfaction among in-movers to a retirement community. *J. Geront.*, 27(4), 511-523.

Lipman, A. 1960. Marital roles of the retired aged. *Merrill Palmer Quarterly*, 6(3), 192-195.

Lipman, A. 1961. Role conceptions and morale in couples in retirement. *J. Geront.*, 16(3), 267-271.

Lipman, A. 1962. Role conceptions of couples in retirement. *In*, C. Tibbitts and Wilma Donahue (eds.), *Social and Psychological Aspects of Aging*, pp. 473-485. New York: Columbia University Press.

Lowenthal, L., and Fiske [Lowenthal], Marjorie. 1957. The debate over art and popular culture in eighteenth century England. *In*, Mirra Komarovsky (ed.), *Common Frontiers of the Social Sciences*, pp. 33-112. Glencoe, Illinois: The Free Press.

Lowenthal, Marjorie Fiske. 1964. Social isolation and mental illness in old age. *Am. Soc. Rev.*, 29(1), 54-70.

Lowenthal, Marjorie Fiske. 1968. The relationship between social factors and mental health in the aged. *In*, A. Simon and L. J. Epstein (eds.), *Aging in Modern Society*, Psychiatric Research Report #23, pp. 187-197. Washington, D.C.: American Psychiatric Association.

Lowenthal, Marjorie Fiske. 1975. Psychosocial variations across the adult life course: Frontiers for research and policy. *Gerontologist*, 15(1), Part 1, 6-12.

Lowenthal, Marjorie Fiske. 1976. Toward a sociopsychological theory of change in adulthood and old age. *In*, J. E. Birren and K. W. Schaie (eds.), *Handbook of the Psychology of Aging*. New York: Van Nostrand Reinhold.

Lowenthal, Marjorie Fiske, Berkman, P. L., and Associates. 1967. *Aging and Mental Disorder in San Francisco*. San Francisco: Jossey-Bass.

Lowenthal, Marjorie Fiske, and Boler, Deetje. 1965. Voluntary vs. involuntary social withdrawal. *J. Geront.*, 20(3), 363-371.

Lowenthal, Marjorie Fiske, and Haven, C. 1968. Interaction and adaptation: Intimacy as a critical variable. *Am. Soc. Rev.*, 33(1), 20-30.

Lowenthal, Marjorie Fiske, Thurnher, Majda, Chiriboga, D., and Associates. 1975. *Four Stages of Life: A Comparative Study of Women and Men Facing Transitions*. San Francisco: Jossey-Bass.

Maas, H. S., and Kuypers, J. A. 1974. *From Thirty to Seventy*. San Francisco: Jossey-Bass.

McKain, W. C. 1969. *Retirement Marriage*. Storrs, Connecticut: University of Connecticut Press.

Maddox, G. L. 1963. Activity and morale: A longitudinal study of selected elderly subjects. *Soc. Forces*, 42(2), 195-204.

Maddox, G. L. 1964. Disengagement theory: A critical evaluation. *Gerontologist*, 4(2), Part 1, 80-82, 103.

Maddox, G. L. 1965. Fact and artifact: Evidence bearing on disengagement theory from the Duke geriatrics project. *Hum. Develop.* 8(2-3), 117-130.

Maddox, G. L. 1966. Persistence of life style among the elderly: A longitudinal study of patterns of social activity in relation to life satisfaction. *Proceedings, 7th International Congress of Gerontology*, *Vienna*, 6, 309-311.

Maddox, G. L. 1970. Themes and issues in sociological theories of human aging. *Hum. Develop.*, 13(1), 17-27.

Maddox, G. L., and Eisdorfer, C. 1962. Some correlates of activity and morale among the elderly. *Soc. Forces*, 40, 254-260.

Mead, G. H. 1934. *Mind, Self, and Society* (edited by C. W. Morris). Chicago: University of Chicago Press.

Merton, R. K. 1968. *Social Theory and Social Structure*. New York: The Free Press.

Meyersohn, R. 1972. Leisure. *In*, A. Campbell and P. E. Converse (eds.), *The Human Meaning of Social Change*, pp. 205-228. New York: Russell Sage Foundation.

Milbrath, L. W. 1965. *Political Participation: How and Why Do People Get Involved in Politics?* Chicago: Rand McNally.

Mitchell, W. L. 1972. Lay observations on retirement. *In*, Frances M. Carp (ed.), *Retirement*, pp. 199-217. New York: Behavioral Publications.

Moore, W. E. 1963. *Man, Time, and Society*. New York: John Wiley.

Neugarten, Bernice L. 1975. The future and the young-old. *Gerontologist*, 15(1), 4-9.

Neugarten, Bernice L., and Havighurst, R. J. 1969. Disengagement reconsidered in a crossnational context. *In*, R. J. Havighurst, J. M. A. Munnichs, B. L. Neugarten, and H. Thomae (eds.), *Adjustment to Retirement*, 2nd ed., pp. 138-146. Assen, The Netherlands: Van Gorkum.

Neugarten, Bernice L., and Weinstein, Karol K. 1968. The changing American grandparent. *In*, Bernice L. Neugarten (ed.), *Middle Age and Aging*, pp. 280-285. Chicago: University of Chicago Press.

Petroni, F. A. 1969. The influence of age, sex, and chronicity in perceived legitimacy to the sick role. *Sociol. & Soc. Res.*, 53(2), 180-193.

Pressey, S. L., and Pressey, A. 1966. Two insiders' searching for best life in old age. *Gerontologist*, 6(1), 14-16.

Preston, Caroline E., and Helgerson, S. 1972. An analysis of survey data obtained by a service agency for older people. *Gerontologist*, 12(4), 384-388.

Putnam, Phyllis A. 1973. Nurse awareness and psychosocial function in the aged. *Gerontologist*, 13(2), 163-166.

Redick, R. W. 1974. Patterns in use of nursing homes by the aged mentally ill. *Statistical Note 107*. Biometry Branch, Rockville, Maryland.

Riley, Matilda White, and Foner, Anne. 1968. *Aging and Society. Volume One: An Inventory of Research Findings*. New York: Russell Sage Foundation.

Rollins, B. C. and Feldman, H. 1970. Marital satisfaction over the life cycle. *J. Marriage & Fam.* 32(1), 20-28.

Roman, P., and Taietz, P. 1967. Organizational structure and disengagement: The emeritus professor. *Gerontologist*, 7(3), 147-152.

Rose, A. M. 1965. The subculture of the aging: A framework for research in social gerontology. *In*, A. M. Rose and W. A. Peterson (eds.), *Older People and Their Social World*, pp. 3-16. Philadelphia: F. A. Davis.

Rosenberg, G. S. 1970. *The Worker Grows Old*. San Francisco: Jossey-Bass.

Rosencranz, H. A., Pihlblad, C. T., and McNevin, T. E. 1968. *Social Participation of Older People in the Small Town*, Vol. 2, No. 1, Department of Sociology, University of Missouri-Columbia, September.

Rosow, I. 1965. Forms and functions of adult socialization. *Soc. Forces*, 44(1), 35-45.

Rosow, I. 1967. *Social Integration of the Aged*. New York: The Free Press.

Rosow, I. 1973. The social context of the aging self. *Gerontologist*, 13(1), 82-87.

Rosow, I. 1974. *Socialization to Old Age*. Berkeley: University of California Press.

Rowe, A. R. 1973. Scientists in retirement. *J. Geront.*, 28(3), 345-350.

Russell, B. 1969. *The Autobiography of Bertrand Russell*. New York: Simon & Schuster.

Schramm, W. 1969. Aging and mass communication. *In*, Matilda White Riley, J. W. Riley, Jr., and Marilyn E. Johnson (eds.), *Aging and Society, Volume Two: Aging and the Professions*, pp. 352-375. New York: Russell Sage Foundation.

Schutz, A. 1971. *Collected Papers*, Volumes I and II. The Hague, The Netherlands: Martinus Nijhoff.

Scotch, N. A., and Richardson, A. H. 1966. Characteristics of the self-sufficient among the very aged. *Proceedings, 7th International Congress of Gerontology*, Vienna, 8, 489-493.

Seeman, M. 1959. On the meaning of alienation. *Am. Soc. Rev.*, 24, 783-791.

Seeman, M. 1972. Alienation and engagement. *In*, A. Campbell and P. E. Converse (eds.), *The Human Meaning of Social Change*, pp. 467-527. New York: Russell Sage Foundation.

Seguin, Mary M. 1973. Opportunity for peer socialization in a retirement community. *Gerontologist*, 13(2), 208-214.

Shanas, Ethel. 1962. *The Health of Older People: A Social Survey*. Cambridge, Massachusetts: Harvard University Press.

Shanas, Ethel. 1968. The family and social class. *In*, Ethel Shanas, P. Townsend, Dorothy Wedderburn, H. Friis, P. Milhøj, and J. Stehouwer, *Old People in Three Industrial Societies*, pp. 227-257. New York: Atherton Press.

Shanas, Ethel. 1970. Aging and life space in Poland and the United States. *J. of Health and Soc. Behavior*, 11(3), 183-190.

Shanas, Ethel, and Streib, G. F. 1965. *Social Structure and the Family*. Englewood Cliffs, New Jersey: Prentice-Hall.

Shanas, Ethel, Townsend, P., Wedderburn, Dorothy, Friis, H., Milhøj, P., and Stehouwer, J. 1968. *Old People in Three Industrial Societies*. New York: Atherton Press.

Simon, A., Lowenthal, Marjorie Fiske, and Epstein, L. 1970. *Crisis and Intervention: The Fate of the Elderly Mental Patient*. San Francisco: Jossey-Bass.

Sofer, C. 1970. *Men in Mid-career: A Study of British Managers and Technical Specialists*. London: Cambridge University Press.

Sparks, D. E. 1973. Retirement and the relocation of older workers. *Area Development in Japan*, 7, 24-33.

Spence, D. L., and Robinson, Betsy. 1966. Patterns of retirement in San Francisco. *In*, Frances M. Carp (ed.), *The Retirement Process*, pp. 63-75, Public Health Service Publication #1778. Washington, D.C.: Government Printing Office.

Stehouwer, J. 1968. The household and family relations of old people. *In*, Ethel Shanas, P. Townsend, Dorothy Wedderburn, H. Friis, P. Milhøj, and J. Stehouwer, *Old People in Three Industrial Societies*, pp. 175-226. New York: Atherton Press.

Stinnett, N., Carter, Linda Mittelstet, and Montgomery, J. E. 1972. Older persons' perceptions of their marriages. *J. Marriage & Fam.*, 34(4), 665-670 (November).

Stinnett, N., Collins, Janet, and Montgomery, J. E. 1970. Marital need satisfaction of older husbands and wives. *J. Marriage & Fam.*, 32(3), 428-434.

Storey, Ruth T. 1962. Who attends a senior activity center? *Gerontologist*, 2(4), 216-222.

Strauss, A. L. 1956. *Mirrors and Masks*. Glencoe, Illinois: The Free Press.

Streib, G. 1956. Morale of the retired. *Soc. Prob.*, 3, 270-276.

Streib, G. F., and Schneider, C. J. 1971. *Retirement in American Society*. Ithaca, New York: Cornell University Press.

Sussman, M. B. 1965. Relationships of adult children with their parents in the United States. *In*, Ethel Shanas and G. F. Streib (eds.), *Social Structure and the Family*, pp. 62-92. Englewood Cliffs, New Jersey: Prentice-Hall.

Sussman, M. B., and Burchinal, L. 1968. Kin family network: Unheralded structure in current conceptualizations of family functioning. *In*, Bernice L. Neugarten (ed.), *Middle Age and Aging*, pp. 247-254. Chicago: University of Chicago Press.

Tallmer, M., and Kutner, B. 1970. Disengagement and morale. *Gerontologist*, 10(4), Part 1, 317-320.

Thompson, P., and Chen, R. 1966. Experiences with older psychiatric patients and spouses together in a residential treatment setting. *Bulletin of the Menninger Clinic*, 30(1), 23-31.

Tobin, S. S., and Neugarten, Bernice L. 1961. Life satisfaction and social interaction in the aging. *J. Geront.*, 16(4), 344-346.

Tolstoy, L. 1960. *Leo Tolstoy Last Diaries* (edited by L. Stilman). New York: G. P. Putnam's Sons, Capricorn Books.

Townsend, P. 1968a. The structure of the family. *In*, Ethel Shanas, P. Townsend, Dorothy Wedderburn, H. Friis, P. Milhøj, and J. Stehouwer, *Old People in Three Industrial Societies*, pp. 132-176. New York: Atherton Press.

Townsend, P. 1968b. Isolation, desolation and loneliness. *In*, Ethel Shanas, P. Townsend, Dorothy Wedderburn, H. Friis, P. Milhøj, and J. Stehouwer, *Old People in Three Industrial Societies*, pp. 258-287. New York: Atherton Press.

Townsend, P. 1968c. The emergence of the four-generation family in industrial society. *In*, Bernice L. Neugarten (ed.), *Middle Age and Aging*, pp. 255-257. Chicago: University of Chicago Press.

Troll, Lillian E. 1971. The family of later life: A decade review. *J. Marriage & Fam.*, 33(2), 263-290.

U.S. Bureau of the Census. 1972. *Census of Population: 1970. Subject Reports. Marital Status*. Final Report PC (2)-4C. Washington, D.C.: Government Printing Office.

Veroff, J., and Feld, Sheila. 1970. *Marriage and Work in America*. New York: Van Nostrand Reinhold.

White, R. W. 1963. *Ego and Reality in Psychoanalytic Theory. Psychological Issues*, Vol. 3, No. 3, Monograph 11. New York: International Universities Press.

Wilensky, H. L. 1961. Life cycle, work situation, and participation in formal associations. *In*, R. W. Kleemeier (ed.), *Aging and Leisure*, pp. 213–242. New York: Oxford University Press.

Williams, R. H., and Wirths, Claudine G. 1965. *Lives Through the Years*. New York: Atherton Press.

Youmans, E. G. 1962. Leisure-time activities of older persons in selected rural and urban areas of Kentucky. Progress Report 115, Kentucky Agricultural Experiment Station, Lexington, Kentucky.

Zborowski, M. 1962. Aging and recreation. *J. Geront.*, 17(3), 302–309.

18
STATUS AND ROLE CHANGE THROUGH THE LIFE SPAN

Irving Rosow*
University of California, San Francisco

You should live so long.
—Ancient Chinese valediction

After a meticulous review of the relevant literature, John Clausen recently concluded that we have no comprehensive theory of the life cycle. He wrote (1972, pp. 498, 412):

> If we have been able to discern certain links and certain patternings . . . in life course lines, they are by no means a basis for a general theory of the life course . . . . They remain largely unintegrated insofar as a general theory of the life course is concerned. Perhaps it is unrealistic to think of a theory of the life course. Perhaps we can only look forward to more limited theories relevant to aspects of the life course.

Clausen's implicit call for modest middle-range theories is sound. Its basis warrants a skeptical view of the prospects for any comprehensive theory of the life cycle in the near future. Clearly, any possible overall theory is complicated by at least two factors: (1) The empirical and normatively appropriate patterns at each life-stage are quite diverse. When these variations *within* life-stages are compounded into sets of permutations *across all*

*I am indebted to my colleague, Dr. Corinne Nydegger, for her thoughtful, searching review of the draft of this article.

life-stages, their variety and complexity are quickly exponentialized. These permutations are neither random nor completely independent but have some correlation between stages. However, there is enough slippage and independence across stages for the number of patterns to become unmanageable, exceeding the capacity of any comprehensive theory to deal with them economically, if at all. (2) Also, social change itself compounds this problem insofar as it imposes on life-stage differences additional generational differences with selective effects. This cohort problem simply underscores the importance of cross-sequential analysis in distinguishing developmental from social change effects.

For similar reasons, it is hardly surprising that, despite some preliminary groundwork (Riley, Johnson, and Foner, 1972), we also have no viable theory or conceptual schema for status and role change through the life span.

But before a coherent theory of this process will even be possible, especially one that includes aging, the notions of status and role themselves must be clarified. For these concepts are fraught with ambiguities that are problematic enough to vitiate any comprehensive theory of role change through the life span. Insofar as age is a major status and age-grading involves roles, any discussion of their change in the course of life is subject to the same ambiguities that affect the basic concepts and require clarification. This is especially true whenever old age is involved (Rosow, 1974).

Therefore, in this paper, I want to address one underlying confusion that has plagued social scientists for 40 years: *the assumption that status and role are invariably complementary*. For as I shall propose, the relationship between the twin concepts is *not* constant, it probably varies along lines that I shall indicate, and this variation is consequential. Accordingly, in this chapter, I want to: (1) trace the source of confusion about status and role; (2) clarify the ambiguity by *separating* the two concepts; (3) construct a set of role types based on their independence of one another; and (4) examine some changes in the life cycle in terms of this typology.

STATUS-ROLE CONFUSION

The concepts of *status* and *role* have recently been judged to accommodate much of sociology's substantive concern (Komarovsky, 1973). They are fundamental to social structure and to many of its processes. As primary social units, status and role become organizing concepts in the analysis of most norms, relationships, conformity and deviance, stability and change. Accordingly, as basic elements of social intercourse, they are essential to the analysis of group and institutional functioning and to the formulation of diverse problems.

The two concepts are presently quite adequate for most workaday sociological discourse. Informally, they are treated as synonymous and interchangeable; typically in professional writing, the two terms are even alternated to avoid the stylistic awkwardness of repetition. Occasionally they are even fused, as in "status-role." Colloquially, the terminology suffices.

The basis for this lies in Linton's (1936) classic formulation that made them not simply complementary concepts, but opposite sides of a single coin that were irrevocably and indissolubly bound together. Status and role were treated as conceptual Siamese twins, one structural and the other functional. Their

complementarity presumably made them inseparable. This is abundantly clear from Linton's definition and explication of the concepts (1936, pp. 113-14; italics of *complete sentences* inserted):

> The polar positions in such patterns of reciprocal behavior are technically known as *statuses*. The term *status*, like the term *culture*, has come to be used with a double significance. A *status*, in the abstract, is a position in a particular [interaction] pattern. It is thus quite correct to speak of each individual as having many statuses, since each individual participates in the expression of a number of patterns. However, unless the term is qualified in some way, *the status of any individual means the sum total of all the statuses which he occupies. It represents his position with relation to the total society* . . . .
>
> A status, as distinct from the individual who may occupy it, is simply a collection of rights and duties . . . .
>
> A *role* represents the dynamic aspect of a status. The individual is socially assigned to a status and occupies it with relation to other statuses. When he puts the rights and duties which constitute the status into effect, he is performing a role. *Role and status are quite inseparable, and the distinction between them is of only academic interest. There are no roles without statuses or statuses without roles*. Just as in the case of *status*, the term *role* is used with a double significance. Every individual has a series of roles deriving from the various patterns in which he participates and at the same time *a role*, general, which represents the sum total of these roles and determines what he does for his society and what he can expect from it.

Here, status is treated as a position in a social structure and role as the pattern of activity intrinsic to that position. The distinction is perfectly familiar, and this usage has certainly been standard since Linton's time.

Sociologists will readily see that Merton's later concept of *status set* assimilates Linton's notion of a person's many statuses; but Merton also appreciated that each specific status involves multiple relationships, and he formulated this in his concept of *role set* (Merton, 1957, pp. 368-370). His deceptively simple refinement opened up an array of complex new issues about differentiation within roles. In itself, this qualification of only the one rather than both concepts belies Linton's view that the distinction between status and role is always unimportant.

Linton's analysis was clear enough and a major advance when it appeared. But this is not to say that all difficulties suddenly vanished, for some other problems remained that subsequent efforts have still not resolved (Biddle and Thomas, 1966). Linton's formulation ultimately proved to be incomplete, leaving in its wake various undefined issues (viz., Merton's role set) and a residue of haziness. It predictably gave rise to the familiar problem of single terms with multiple referents and multiple terms for single referents, as well as a host of other difficulties (Biddle and Thomas, 1966, pp. 3–19). It blurred some vital distinctions that are necessary in certain analyses, notably non-institutionalized roles and other significant phenomena. Accordingly, there has been an intermittent, but abiding confusion when the heart of a problem has been focused specifically on status and role or has involved atypical role activity. Where precision is needed, the terminology is wanting.

FOUR PROBLEMS

The most important ambiguities involve four major role issues, those of: (1) presence, (2) boundary criteria, (3) interaction, and (4) levels. We will consider them briefly.

(1) The *presence* problem: *is there a role?* Roles are not always delineated sharply enough to establish "when" there is a role, to identify its type, and to indicate clearly when behavior is actual role activity. Consequently, certain roles that are integral to group structure and process have not been related to role theory, but to personality or other factors. Non-institutional and deviant roles have particularly suffered from such exclusion.

(2) The *boundary criteria* problem: *what is the role?* Given the fact that there is a role, we cannot always set its boundaries sharply enough to distinguish role from non-role behavior, particularly around the edges. We have not been able to judge clearly what is intrinsic and what is extrinsic to the role, what is specifically role activity, and what is residual or

idiosyncratic. The central elements have been less problematic. But beyond these, vagueness quickly sets in, and precision bleeds off at the boundaries. Merton's (1957, p. 133) treatment of the constraints on and options open to the actor provides some entree to the distinction between central and peripheral requirements. But subsequent work has not appreciably developed such leads. Neither the most ambitious role taxonomy yet devised (Biddle and Thomas, 1966, pp. 23–63) nor one of the leading role theorists (Sarbin and Allen, 1968; Sarbin, 1968) has made significant inroads on the criteria of setting boundaries.

(3) The *interaction* problem: *roles affect each other.* This might also be called the "permutations" issue. The total status set provides the context of its specific parts, and the norms of a given position are affected by those of a person's other statuses. While some positions are rather segregated from others, few are hermetically sealed. So various roles spill over to modify the norms of other roles. In other words, there is an interaction effect within the status set that qualifies the norms for any particular position (cf. Rosow, 1974, pp. 42–50).

This may be one of two kinds. (a) Sometimes it is a *simple* qualification of other roles. In that case, for example, the sexual norms for an adolescent girl might differ if she were the daughter of a minister or a psychologist, an engineer or an artist, not to mention a devout Catholic or an atheist. (b) In other cases, the statuses in a set may be ordered in a *hierarchy* of importance so that some roles have more pervasive effects than others. Then the interaction effects are asymmetrical, with more central roles taking clear precedence and coloring others more strongly than they are affected in return. These may reflect sheer subcultural influences, as in the case of the proverbial middle class Jewish mother in the United States. With *all* other things being equal, the norms for maternal nurturance, solicitude, and control over children are significantly greater for such a stereotypical Jewish mother than a Protestant of comparable social class and position.

However, the basic point is that the configuration of a particular status set and the relation among its components may significantly modify the norms for any specific role. To illustrate again, the normative expectations for *widowhood* may differ drastically as variations occur in other factors, such as the actor's sex, race, social class, religion, family situation, and residence. Thereby, the role of widowhood is quite different for a black Baptist washerwoman living with her adult children in Tuscaloosa than it is for a retired white Jewish businessman without any family who lives alone in Miami Beach. Thus, the interaction effects within status sets may diversify and obscure the norms for any particular role across a sample of respondents. While these may appear as a set of variations on a common theme, this is not always clear. The unequal weights of the different statuses in a series of role permutations may blur the specific norms in question. And if we consider the full range of contexts, the common elements of a role may even account for less behavior than the differences arising from varying status sets. In other words, it remains unclear how the basic norms of a particular role are infused and qualified by the diversity of other roles across a series of cases.

This problem certainly confounds the study of age and sex positions. The reciprocal effects make it difficult to separate the pure age factor from a person's other statuses or to see clearly how age operates differently in various status sets. In the analysis of data, there is now no practical alternative to holding these other status patterns constant while trying to abstract the distinctive age factor cleanly (Rosow, 1974). The tremendous variation among status sets makes this extremely difficult. And at best, this is only an interim expedient that may blur precisely those interaction effects that might be the most crucial for age roles (cf. Clausen, 1972).

(4) The *levels* problem: *overall status and role.* This is the most general form of the interaction problem, requiring the integration of Linton's specific and general levels. It goes beyond simple reciprocal influences between roles and poses the problem of how to translate an actor's entire status set or all his role sets into a single, general social status or role. How does one systematically combine his many separate statuses into *one* abstract social status? How does one convert a person's many role complexes at a concrete level into *the* role at a comprehensive level? The criterion issue is formidable. This problem may press somewhat harder on anthropologists and analysts of small communities where status consistency and convergence may be fairly common, with the same people continually interacting in different status capacities. But the role segregation of larger, more complex societies, with separate groups of actors in interaction, does not clarify the conceptual difficulty. The specific and general levels reflect the pervasive problem of diverse status patterns and role combinations in a person's life.

Obviously this paper cannot even begin to address all four of these problems. Therefore, we will concentrate only on the first as the logical starting point. This analysis will mainly concern the *presence problem: "when" there is a role and its type.* But it will not consider the last three: the boundary criteria problem (what is included in the role); the interaction problem (the reciprocal effects of various roles within status sets); and the levels problem (synthesizing a discrete status set into a general social status or an array of role sets into an overall social role).

We must readily concede that as basic as they are, status and role may ultimately prove to be the kind of sensitizing concepts (such as "culture") that help to orient theory, but which in themselves are resistant to precise, rigorous application, free of any ambiguity. However, the limits on such precision cannot be established without efforts at clarification, even by chipping away at one problem at a time. Certainly the four problems mentioned here are not exhaustive, but they do indicate some basic dilemmas in determining what does or does not qualify as role behavior, whether in terms of age or other factors.

NON-INSTITUTIONALIZED ROLES: THE EXCLUDED CASES

The deviant cases of non-institutionalized roles are extremely awkward, if not embarrassing. As residual cases, they reflect Linton's lack of closure. What does one do with them? Where do they fit? In the course of actual analysis, they are usually handled in one of two ways. They are often arbitrarily excluded from consideration and effectively ignored. Or else they are consigned to some residual category, such as symbolic interaction or ethno-methodology, that typically lies outside the perspective of conventional structural analysis.

Both of these alternatives are succinctly mooted in the Presidential Address at the 1973 meetings of the American Sociological Association. On that occasion, Mirra Komarovsky included in her introductory remarks several apposite caveats (1973; italics inserted):

> The substantive content of roles would appear to span much of the subject matter of sociology . . . [and] any theoretical propositions concerning the normative content of these roles would hardly be distinguishable from the general fields of political, economic, or family sociology . . . . [Accordingly,] I shall deal only with *institutionalized roles, linked to recognized social statuses.* Excluded, then, are many 'regularities in interpersonal relationships' (Newcomb, 1966) or forms of interaction like the 'family scapegoat,' 'the big wheel,' or 'the rebel,' lacking the normative content of institutionalized roles (Popitz, 1972). Moreover, the emphasis will be primarily on social structural analysis rather than on symbolic interactionism of the descendants of Cooley and Mead.

It is quite legitimate, of course, to address only a selected set of problems. But in terms of *role theory*, where do such patterned social relationships of the family scapegoat, the big wheel, the rebel, or others actually fit in? It may be comforting to prejudge them all as lacking in social norms, but surely this is an empirical issue. It is arbitrary, if not cavalier, to dismiss by definition what must at least be regarded as a legitimate, open question. In view of competing reference groups, conflicting expectations, and various role options, it is rather foolhardy to foreclose the possibility of normative content in these atypical cases. For even much deviance, especially of marginal groups, is heavily normative.

The regrettable fact is that we still lack a frame of reference that can accommodate the atypical forms of status and role that arise in non-institutionalized contexts. Many of these are relevant to role theory, though in terms that remain to be clarified. But aside from their more general significance, they are also germane to various age roles and norms (cf. Neugarten, Moore and Lowe, 1965), particularly for the elderly who systematically lose major institutionalized roles simply with the passage of time.

THE CENTRAL PROBLEM

Clearly, Linton cannot be held responsible for all the ambiguities of role theory, for many difficulties were not appreciated before they gradually crystallized in later work. But the heart of the immediate problem is his treatment of status and role as inseparable twins. His most basic premise was that status and role must occur together and cannot vary independently: if there is a status, there must be some significant role; if there is a role, there must be some specifically related status position. If status, then role; if role, then status. This is the essence of their complementarity.

But this formulation is not exhaustive. That is, the coexistence of status and role is not the only form in which they occur. While their inseparability is integral to most institutionalized roles, this is not invariant, and as we have seen, it does not apply to the difficult classes of deviant cases. For some statuses and roles do *not* neatly correspond; each does not have its "natural" complement in a binary pair but *may appear by itself.* Significant discrepancies and anomalies recur with disquieting persistence, usually but not exclusively with non-major statuses. In these cases, status and role simply unravel and come unbound.* The assumption of their necessary and invariant linkage, as in Siamese twins or binary stars, cannot accommodate such separation.

Yet the severing of this tie is necessary, and this paper undertakes to examine its implica-

---

*In a similar vein, Alice Rossi (1968, especially pp. 36–39) criticized the careless assumption that the actual relationship of paired concepts, such as instrumental-expressive or authority-support, is necessarily as given. She showed that their occurrence and effects were empirical issues that could only be verified if the concepts were treated as independent factors rather than constrained by definition.

tions. The separation of status and role will cast role change through the life span into a fresh perspective.

Therefore, we want to treat status and role as independent, to formulate an inclusive typology of their variations, and then to relate these to the life cycle. If one is willing to abandon Linton's restrictive premise, a simple, exhaustive schema is readily available. Accordingly, we will waive Linton's proviso and assume instead that status and role may occur *separately*, regardless of the relative frequency of their different combinations. If we regard the concepts as independent, all patterns can be distinguished and classified in an inclusive typology. This provides for not only the major institutionalized roles, but also the deviant and non-institutionalized.

ASSUMPTIONS

But before presenting the typology, we should make several assumptions clear, not as a token genuflection, but as a set of premises on which the analysis is based. Hopefully this will defer some premature secondary questions that would distract from and vitiate the main point. In other words, we want to examine the forest, not the trees.

Now to our premises. First, in the matter of definitions, our use of the concepts is fairly conventional in Linton's terms. *Status* represents a formal office or social position that can be designated by name or a clear term of reference. This classifies and locates a person in a social structure and *may* denote "a collection of rights and duties" for that position—although this implication is moot and at the very crux of our problem. *Role* consists of the expected behavior considered appropriate to *any* set of rights and duties. This involves the activity and interaction connected with a position *or* a set of relationships for which the person is held responsible or which he is accorded.

Secondly, we will speak of the "presence" or "absence" of status and role *in relative, not absolute terms*. Some normative expectations, as in many institutionalized roles, are reasonably explicit and commonly understood by the actor

and his associates. But in other roles, including some of the non-institutionalized, expectations are often limited, superficial, and vague. We shall regard a role as *developed* (+) if the following conditions are met: if the expectations refer to a definite status or person and if they are normative, shared, and reasonably consensual within some significant reference group. But we shall regard a role as diffuse or *minimal* (−) when expectations are vague, limited, variable, or unpatterned, with negligible consensus or normative elements. That is, it is minimal if the norms are few, weak, amorphous, or subject to little accord. Therefore, as a convention of terminology, the following typology will classify status and role simply as "developed" (+) or "minimal" (−), with the proviso that this dichotomy is only a gross distinction between those that are significant and clear or relatively limited and amorphous.

Finally, the designation of role types in the following framework is purely arbitrary. The names are simply convenient labels for purposes of discussion, no more and no less. They are not evaluative, nor are they literal concepts, but only convenient terms of reference.

THE TYPOLOGY

With these caveats firmly in mind, the typology of status-role permutations in which the two concepts are treated as independent appears in Figure 1. What do these respective types portray and include? The Institutional represent statuses with roles; the Tenuous, statuses without roles; the Informal, roles without statuses; and the Non-Role, neither. We will consider them seriatim.

Role Types	Status	Role
1. Institutional	+	+
2. Tenuous	+	−
3. Informal	−	+
4. Non-Role	−	−

Figure 1. Status-role combinations of various role types.

Institutional: + +

These represent the major institutionalized statuses *with* roles to which Komarovsky (1973) referred. They are the least problematic prototypes of the most commanding sociological importance and interest. They involve the central positions of occupation, family, social class, race, ethnicity, religious affiliation, sex, for the most part age, and so on. These factors are neither exhaustive nor homogeneous, for the Institutional include diverse offices, positions, and statuses—formal and informal, ascribed and achieved. But the Institutional roles are all those in which normative expectations are clearly linked with definite positions or attributes: men, women, professionals, manual workers, parents, children, Catholics, Baptists, public officials, organizational members, racial and ethnic identity, and so on.

Aside from the interaction effects among statuses, the basic problem in Institutional age roles is the delineation of age norms. These have only recently come under focal study (Neugarten, Moore and Lowe, 1965; Rosow, 1974), and their social meanings and functions are yet to be intensively examined. Most important is the extent to which age norms are a *matter of consensus, for this may eventually compel a careful reexamination of the concept, "institutionalized."* Age norms may vary in clarity and consensus, and these remain to be explicated. For many norms that are now *assumed* to be commonly held may prove to be nothing of the kind; they may actually conceal widespread ignorance about a great diversity of underlying views. Therefore, any significant variation in the *degree of agreement* about norms would oblige us to specify a threshold of consensus, a minimal level, that would be necessary before we would regard a pattern as "institutionalized." But this is a generic problem of social structure that transcends the sheer issue of Institutional roles.

Empirically, Institutional roles may well be the modal type of all roles. Following Linton, this is the dominant frame of reference for role analysis and the least problematic category in our types. It provides one basis for examining a diversity of roles. However, the key point *for our problem* is that in Institutional roles, expectations are directly linked to definite social statuses. The main difficulties arise in the remaining types that do not meet this condition.

Tenuous: + −

This is the case that consists of definite social positions *without* roles or only vague, insubstantial ones. Ernest Burgess (1950) pointed out long ago that the position of the aged is essentially roleless, an observation occasionally resurrected for ritual acknowledgement by gerontologists, but whose implications have been largely ignored by old age specialists and role theorists alike. The effects of role attrition for the aged have been amply demonstrated in many contexts: the results are to divert them from the mainstream of social participation, to undermine their group integration, and commonly to demoralize them (Riley and Foner, 1968; Rosow, 1967). But the elderly are only prototypical of the Tenuous, and others belong here as well.

In general, the Tenuous consist of several basic subtypes: (A) *titular* positions or offices, whether honorific or nominal; (B) the genuinely *amorphous* of several kinds. (A third possible subtype, pariahs and outcasts, are not properly roleless, for they are hedged in with powerful sanctions that are quite clear and to which compliance can readily be judged.)

(A) Among the titular, (A1) the *honorific* involve statuses in which high prestige is publicly bestowed for valued characteristics or achievements. The prototypes here include Nobel Laureates or members of the British peerage who are *not* invited to participate actively in the House of Lords. The honors are symbolic, and no specific role activities beyond the most token are associated with the position. This does not minimize the collective social values that such honors represent, but simply recognizes that they involve an extremely limited role. (A2) The *nominal* positions or offices are also basically token, whether in organizational or personal terms. Many public and even private bureaucracies harbor divisions, departments, or posts that are literally obsolete and have no essential functions, but nonetheless continue to survive. In these instances, vacuous roles take on a group quality. In other cases, people are effectively disposed of by token promotion or by being "kicked upstairs" in a face-saving gesture that gracefully removes them from positions of power or consequence to ones where their influence is reduced. (The process of face-saving in such situations has long been a concern of Erving Goffman [1958b].) Such procedures are not limited to formal organizations; they also occur in families or informal groups where others sharply curtail a person's actual functions, but maintain a facade of deference to him. The basic condition is that such roles are shorn of effective resources and significant activities.

Whereas honorific positions symbolically reward valued attributes or performance and thereby constitute social "promotions," nominal positions represent "demotions" that signify loss, obsolescence, superannuation, or exclusion from influence or authority. Role functions are drastically stripped away or limited.

(B) The genuinely amorphous are the most problematic of the Tenuous types. They include many that are devalued, both deviants and others who exemplify social loss, failure, stigma, or marginality. Though commonly deprecated as deviant, people who are "failures" typically are *not* assimilated in those coherent subcultures that afford them significant group support and clear behavioral expectations. Rather, these roles tend to occur under conditions that provide the actor with few normative guidelines and often, though not invariably, oblige him to face his role dilemmas privately.

Aside from the aged to whom we shall presently return, there are at least four forms of amorphousness. (B1) Goode (1956) described a classic *ambiguous* situation in his 1948 study of younger divorced mothers. For these women, there were virtually no significant norms by which they could restructure their lives as divorcees in most institutional contexts: in relation to their children, ex-husbands, other men, work, leisure, social life, friendships, and the potential remarriage arena. Divorce has been increasing steadily over recent decades, including the period of Goode's research. By 1950, the divorce rate for married women 15 years and older had reached 10.3, and during the 50's, the ranks of divorcees were swelled by almost 400,000 per year (Bureau of the Census, 1973, p. 90). But for our problem, the crucial factor is that so many women were entering this marital status—in a central institution—without clear norms about their appropriate role and their proper relations with others. Indeed, the very composition of a suitable role set remained equivocal. We may also note that, except in countries where illegitimacy has been reasonably institutionalized, similar ambiguities mark the position of the unwed mother.

(B2) A second form of amorphousness is *de facto*, exemplified by the chronically unemployed, the jobless high school dropout, and similar cases. In this type, the person retains obligations (to work and support his family), but objective circumstances deny him the opportunity to perform. The effects of long-term unemployment during the depression have been well documented (Bakke, 1934, 1940a, 1940b; Ginzberg, 1943; Jahoda, Lazarsfeld, and Zeisel, 1971; Komarovsky, 1940; Sletto and Rundquist, 1936). Millions of men lost jobs. As household heads, they were still financially responsible for their families, but their economic effectiveness was destroyed. They were technically role failures, but in circumstances for which they were not personally responsible. Without work, their financial functions were nil, and their occupational role was empty. They had no economic activities, and their authority within the family was often undermined. Their main obligation became to seek jobs unremittingly in a stagnant labor market that had effectively disappeared. Even this unemployment status became virtually roleless, for those who daily pounded the pavements and conscientiously pursued the few ads that appeared usually finished off their rounds early and quickly exhausted any prospects. In this process, many men underwent the corrosive conversion from the unemployed to the unemployable. Yet, whether or not they suffered this particular fate, all the chronically unemployed exemplified men with financial responsibilities, but without corresponding economic activities. In our usage, they had status obligations, but their economic roles were de facto Tenuous. While the literature has described their situation, it has not analyzed the data systematically in relation to role theory nor abstracted the appropriate propositions in those terms.

(B3) Amorphousness is also expressed in two forms of *role attrition*. (B3a) The first may be called *role emptying* in which the responsibilities and normative expectations within a position simply dwindle away. This is seen to a large extent in old age when there is significant shrinkage *within* roles. It is also particularly reflected in some incarcerated populations. Some inmates of total institutions have contrived to develop adaptive survival mechanisms (Goffman, 1958a, 1961), but this has by no means applied to all. Particularly relevant in this sense are long-term state mental hospital patients, primarily the burnt out chronic schizophrenics and the senile dementias, who have wasted away for decades in the back wards of custodial institutions. Commonly admitted in an emergency to the "front wards," they often received some treatment and were given time to recover, with some guidelines and expectations of them as patients. But if they were not well enough to leave the hospital within a year, they seldom left at all but were transferred to the chronic wards. Once consigned to these back wards, they were perceived and labeled as lifelong institutional patients. Processes of degradation and depersonalization effectively wrote them off as human beings and rendered them socially invisible. Nothing further was expected of them, including even the rudiments of personal hygiene, and any rights that they might have formerly claimed were virtually forfeit. The process of institutionalization to the chronic back wards rapidly shriveled their status to one of an empty role, with no residue of rights and duties.

(B3b) The second type of role attrition and the final case of the amorphous Tenuous is that of *status loss*. This is the contraction of the status set that results in the loss of roles. It is exemplified by the most problematic aged, those who have lost central institutional positions in the family, the labor force, and so on, whose social participation has become marginal, and whose life-styles have been vitiated by the various decrements of aging. Their major status losses start with retirement, widowhood, failing health, and drastically reduced income, and then they spread to other areas as their social contacts and activities dwindle.

As their statuses diminish, roles of the elderly tend to become increasingly Tenuous, for these sociological decrements are largely irreversible and not compensated by substitutes. Few of the widowed remarry, few of the retired return to full-time work, few of the ill recover their health, and reduced income is almost never restored. Unlike previous life transitions, losses in old age are seldom replaced. Thus, there is an interruption of two normal earlier processes: status *accretion* in which new positions are added to those already held, and status *succession* in which new roles replace those that are outgrown or left behind. For the aged, such losses are usually irreversible, and the attrition leaves their roles Tenuous.

Why is this? In a rapidly changing technology, the older worker may become obsolete, but economic utility is not invariably an exhaustive value. Vacuous roles are not simply a function of *personal* imcompetence, obsolescence, or worthlessness. Rather, the problem lies in judgments of people's *social* utility. Sociologically, the loss of roles reflects a steady decline in major *responsibilities* and thereby the possibility that old people's actions and performance can affect others significantly. So long as they are not unusually dependent, whether through incapacity or deprivation, their behavior has relatively little effect on other persons and is thereby *socially inconsequential*. If they create no trouble and perform few functions on which the social system depends, then they have little impact on that system. By the same token, if the system has replacements to take over their previous functions, then there is little social stake in their decisions and behavior so long as these are not particularly problematic. Thus, even though the elderly do have an age status, the loss of responsibility and functions is the basis of their role limitation. The loss of statuses leaves them with few normative expectations, with lives that are unstructured by *social* guidelines (Rosow, 1974). Society simply has little stake in establishing special requirements and standards for those in positions with little social effect and few consequences.

I have examined various aspects of this problem in several different contexts (Rosow, 1962, 1967, 1974). But because the aged are the subject of this *Handbook* and the major exemplars of the amorphous Tenuous, the concomitants of their status (and here, also role) loss warrant more detailed attention than has been devoted to the other role types. I have previously analyzed their case in the following terms (Rosow, 1973):

First, *the loss of roles excludes the aged from significant social participation and devalues them*. It deprives them of vital functions that underlie their sense of worth, their self-conceptions and self-esteem. In a word, they are depreciated and become marginal, alienated from the larger society. Whatever their ability, they are judged invidiously, as if they have little of value to contribute to the world's work and affairs. In a society that rewards men mainly according to their economic utility, the aged are arbitrarily stigmatized as having little marginal utility of any kind, either economic or social. On the contrary, they tend to be tolerated, patronized, ignored, rejected, or viewed as a liability. They are first excluded from the mainstream of social existence, and because of this nonparticipation, they are then penalized and denied the rewards that earlier came to them routinely.

Second, *old age is the first stage of life with systematic status loss for an entire cohort*. All previous periods—childhood, adolescence, and various phases of adulthood; from education through marriage, parenthood, raising and educating a family; from modest occupational beginnings through successively higher positions—all are normally marked by steady social growth. This involves gains in competence, responsibility, authority, privilege, reward, and prestige. But the status loss of old age represents the first systematic break in this pattern of acquisition. Not only are the gains and perquisites disrupted, but the sheer loss of [prestige] actually reverses the trend. People pass through a vague period of transition in which they are redefined as old and obsolete. The norms applied to them change quickly from achievement to ascrip-

tion, from criteria of performance to those of sheer age regardless of personal accomplishment. People who were formerly judged as individuals are then bewilderingly treated as members of an invidious category. They are dismissed as superannuated, peculiarly wanting in substance and consequence, almost in character, and thereby lacking any moral claim on the normal social values available for distribution.

To be sure, there are other patterned [social] losses in our society, but none uniquely connected with age. People do have illegitimate children, go to prison, get divorced, wind up in mental hospitals, or otherwise fall from grace. But they are deviants who are in the minority; age has nothing to do with their status. They are construed as personal failures in some fundamental sense. Yet the losses of old age ultimately overtake everybody, not because they have significantly failed, but only because they have survived. This raises perplexing problems of social justice for the aged: to comprehend a loss of [esteem] when there has been no personal failure.

Third, *persons in our society are not socialized to the fate of aging*. This, too, is a major discontinuity from previous experience. Usually people are rather systematically, if not always formally, trained for their next stage of life. They are indoctrinated about future roles and expectations, about the values and norms that will govern them. While the role losses of old age are institutionalized, the socialization to them is not [Rosow, 1974]. People must adapt to the strains and develop a way of life without clear definitions, expectations, and standards [Lipman, 1961]. Our society generally does not prepare people for defeats and losses of status and certainly not for those of old age.

Fourth, *because society does not specify an aged role, the lives of the elderly are socially unstructured*. Even though people are classified as old, they have almost no duties. Shorn of roles, their responsibilities and obligations are minimal. Their position is part of no division of social labor and does not mesh with any definite group of others that sociologists call a "role set" (Merton, 1957). Consequently, they tend to live in an imperfect role vacuum with few standards by which to judge themselves and their behavior. Others have few expectations of them and provide no guides to appropriate activity. They have no significant norms for restructuring their lives. There are no meaningful prescriptions for new goals and experience, no directions to salvation as occasionally accompany sin, loss, or failure at younger ages [Rosow, 1974]. There are only platitudes: take care of yourself, stay out of drafts, keep active, hold onto the banister, find a hobby, don't overdo, take your medicine, eat. The very triviality of these bromides simply documents the empty *social* role of the aged, the general irreversibility of their losses, and their ultimate solitude in meeting their existential declines.

In this sense, it is virtually impossible for them to be literal role failures. This is not necessarily reassuring, however, for psychologists know that unstructured situations generate anxiety. Certainly with a broad horizon of leisure and few obligations, many old people feel oppressively useless and futile. They are simply bored—but not quite to death.

Although freedom from responsibility may sound heavenly to the young, it actually demands strong personal interests and motivation. In earlier periods, life is mainly structured by social duties. People's social positions and role obligations largely govern their general activities and time budgets. This is not true in old age for, *within objective constraints*, life is essentially shaped by individual choice and personal initiative. Because many people lack the interest and initiative to fashion a satisfying existence independently (Hunter and Maurice, 1953), life patterns range from the highly active and imaginative to passive vegetation. To be sure, almost the entire spectrum of possible styles is socially acceptable (Rosow, 1967). But this broad range of permissible alternatives simply documents the role vacuum: there are few prescriptions, norms, and expectations; weak definitions of what an old person should be like and how he should spend his time; and only a clouded picture of the good life in old age.

Finally, *role loss deprives people of their social identity*. This is almost axiomatic, for sociologists define the social self as the totality of a person's social roles. These roles identify and describe him as a social being and are central to his very self-conceptions. The process of role loss steadily eats away at these crucial elements of social personality and converts what is to what was—or transforms the present into the past. In psychological terms, this is a direct, sustained attack on the ego. If the social self consists of roles, then role loss erodes self-conceptions and sacrifices *social* identity.

These then are the social inputs of the crisis of aging. For the first time in life, the elderly are excluded from the central functions and social participation on which self-conceptions and self-esteem are based. They systematically lose perquisites and [value] solely on the basis of age. Social pressures that they are powerless to dispel result in invidious judgments of them, and their personal efforts cannot significantly affect their various losses. Because they lack major responsibilities, society does not specify a role for the aged, and their lives become socially unstructured. This is a gross discontinuity for which they are not socialized, and role loss deprives them of their very social identity.

Clearly, the aged are not the only amorphous Tenuous in our society, but they do represent the largest prototypical case. Analytically, they expose one of the key factors that govern the social position of most others of this type: the loss of major responsibility and authority. Hence, the retention of statuses without functions (including old age) earmarks many of those who have little substance or consequence in the normal operation of the system, who are generally depreciated.

Informal: – +

This type represents role behavior that is *not* connected with any particular status or position, but which *serves significant group functions*, whether positive or negative. Such informal roles may or may not be present in a setting. When they do occur, they involve patterned activities that have perceptible consequences for a group and the relations among its members. While these are neither required nor indispensable to its operation—and their absence certainly signifies no vacant positions—informal roles do affect group processes, if not structure. To this extent, they have social functions that are associated with a particular person or subgroup. As a definite pattern of conduct or relations, such regularities of behavior in a relatively stable group may even become semi-institutionalized, with incipient expectations and norms crystallizing about the actor(s). The basic conceptual distinction of this type is that its functions are not intrinsic to a status, to the "collection of rights and duties" that are integral to a social position.

Who may be included in this category? Certainly all of Komarovsky's (1973) casual examples: The family scapegoat, the big wheel, the rebel. There are also numerous others: heroes, villains, and fools (Klapp, 1962), rabblerousers, charismatic figures, and other symbolic leaders (Klapp, 1965), roues, playboys and boulevardiers, tough guys, manipulators and operators, mediators, patsies, blackmailers, prima donnas, confidants, gossips, informal leaders and influentials, shills, ratebusters, scabs, locals and cosmopolitans, earth mothers and nymphomaniacs, stoolpigeons, certainly homosexuals, flirts, and "gold diggers." Such examples can be extended considerably, but these suffice to make the point.

This category provides a place for many of the "residual" cases that have embarrassed role theorists. Because they could not be linked with institutionalized statuses, they have been treated almost as a form of sociological detritus or as a conceptual dandruff to be hastily brushed away before anyone took notice. Yet how can sociologists conscientiously ignore what Newcomb (1966) properly termed "regularities in interpersonal relationships"? To which we might add, regularities of social function.

The general point can be emphasized with several examples of informal influence, though they will be balanced by other cases as a reminder that it is not limited to influence. Kitchen cabinets and executive confidants are inner circles of advisors often without (or independent of) any position. Among community influentials, power groups may coalesce around specific issues and then dissolve when these are resolved; or, relatively stable power elites commonly function purely informally, without the sanction of public office. Locals and cosmopolitans may have quite different orientations and reference groups, though these are not necessarily built into their formal statuses, including their social class positions. Crisis situations may cry out for charismatic leadership which may not always be forthcoming, for those waiting in the wings do not always have the symbolic and personal qualities that can effectively capture the popular imagination and retrieve the situation. One may advertise in the want ads with fair assurance of success for a competent accountant, but it is quite another matter to advertise successfully for one with

charisma (or "hustle") no matter how desirable this might seem. For charismatic qualities cannot be required and built into an institutional (much less an official) status, no matter what the imperatives, any more than happiness can be required of a spouse or the incumbent of any other status. Similarly an old widow might well have an old next-door neighbor, but not necessarily one whom she could trust as a confidante who would be so important for her stability and integration (Lowenthal and Haven, 1968).

Clearly, all informal roles without statuses are not equally significant, for some are obviously more consequential than others. They exist at different institutional levels and have quite different scope. Those at the primary or small group level certainly have more limited effects than those in large groups, organizations, or broader institutions. The pool hall hustler and the village gossip affect far fewer people than a Bernard Baruch quietly conferring with a President, but their informal roles within their spheres are equally amenable to analysis, probably in similar analytic terms.

Informal roles assimilate what appear in Sarbin and Allen's taxonomy as "character roles" (1968). Other psychologists who enter this arena commonly refer to them as *psychological types*. They assume that social behavior and relationships result from individual personality characteristics or predispositions that are reflected in personal styles or adaptations to given situations. This may be quite true, but questions about the *psychological causes* of action are quite different from those about behavior's *social effects*. Self-selection may cast the actors in informal roles, but the social consequences of their activity are a separate issue.

On the other hand, various sociologists, such as Goffman, Klapp, Becker, and Strauss, discuss such figures in the rhetoric of *social types*. Aside from his interest in the informal mechanisms within bureaucracies, Goffman has been mainly concerned with the face-work and social psychology of interpersonal relations. Klapp's (1962, 1965) interest in social types has focused on their symbolic reflection of prevailing and changing social values. Becker (1963) and Strauss (1959) have dealt with the emergence and maintenance of social identities. While these various issues are not the same, they share a common core of interest and afford a reasonably similar basis of discourse.

Both the psychological and the social perspectives have been legitimately concerned with various problems of personality or social psychology. Clearly, personality factors do operate in individual adaptations and in various other sociological contexts. This appears not only in problems of social structure and personality, but also in such processes as leadership, decision-making, self-selection procedures, social perception, stereotyping, and others. But neither the psychological nor the social tradition has tried to integrate its social psychological concerns systematically with role theory as such.

Our immediate problem is not the personality aspects or social psychology of unusual roles. Our interest in Informal roles concerns their consequences for various groups or systems. That is, in their effects on the social units in which they occur. The typology proposed here constitutes a framework for the classification of various status-role patterns and offers one possible entree to their integration with role theory. (It may even provide one base of a bridge between role theory and work in other traditions, such as symbolic interactionism.)

Non-Role: – –

This is a logical, but irrelevant "type" that is extraneous to role problems. It includes those miscellany, such as idiosyncratic behavior, personality elements, personal style, and so on that have *no* significant patterned social consequences. Accordingly, though we note the category here for the sake of logical closure, it has no importance for our problem. Because Non-Role behavior is peripheral to our interests, it should not distract us, and we will simply exclude it from the rest of the analysis.

DISCUSSION

The preceding considerations make it clear that Linton's premise of the necessary complementarity of status and role is too restrictive.

Major Institutional roles are complementary, but they do not cover all important social relationships nor exhaust the problems of role theory. Our analysis shows that status and role do not invariably occur together but may arise separately. This was previously handled by disregarding the Tenuous and Informal types as conceptually deviant. Tenuous roles empty statuses of functions, while Informal roles involve processes that are independent of social positions. These pose significant problems for role theory in any structural analysis.

The Tenuous include many of the "unsuccessful" and the social "misfits." Ours is a competitive society whose ideology of progress is paralleled by values of personal striving, acquisition, and success. Accordingly, theory has been absorbed with aspiration, growth, mobility, and success. But there has been no equal attention to the analysis of the unsuccessful, to the fringe and vacuous roles. When such analytic categories are provided, as in the present typology, it is not surprising that so many of the social "failures" appear among the Tenuous. Except for the honorific, the Tenuous contain several varieties of role loss, ineptitude, and deprivation, before and during old age.

The later years approximate social "failure" in many respects. Particularly with the decrements of retirement, widowhood, and declining health and income, the aged commonly move on to fewer and emptier roles. They drop out of organizations, see less of their friends and neighbors, and their social world outside the family shrinks significantly, often drastically. While disengagement theorists have arbitrarily interpreted the shrinkage as a function of a normal social psychological process, they have not articulated this view with a coherent theory of adult development. Yet there are more economic explanations of reduced social participation: role loss and devaluation. In both role emptying and status loss, people often withdraw and fail to exercise options that would provide alternatives, such as joining voluntary associations. In other words, social decline and failure are invidious, and as a consequence, people frequently restrict their public participation.

The common element here is the social definition of failure, whether by omission or commission, by obsolescence or inadequacy, by performance or ascription. On a *societal* level, *we do not socialize people to deviance or failure.* Nor do we accord them any but the most limited claims on available social values when their responsibilities and consequential actions are minimal. Therefore, when major problems of disruption or social control are not involved (as exemplified perhaps by criminals or contagious sanatoria patients), those that do not conform acceptably to performance norms or are devalued in ascriptive terms are often stigmatized and cut off from conventional opportunities. In either case, the roles presumably connected with their statuses (or expected sequences) are usually limited and may even become vacuous (cf. Veevers, 1972, 1973). Among the aged, these pressures systematically push them toward the Tenuous category.

As far as Informal roles are concerned, whether positive or negative, their implications for future work in role theory become almost axiomatic, and we can present them briefly without elaborate discussion. (a) Informal roles without statuses operate within and outside the formal system. (b) They are heterogeneous and exist at virtually all levels of the social structure. (c) They are not inconsequential, but have significant functions, whether positive or negative, within their respective groups or institutional spheres. (d) While some may be correlates of or supplements to various statuses, *Informal roles are neither intrinsic to nor reducible to these positions.* One cannot readily infer role from status or vice versa. (e) Their social functions in various contexts usually have either been related to a given substantive field or analyzed in conventional institutional or systems terms. But they have seldom been addressed specifically as role problems or systematically related to role theory. Their significance in this respect has been largely overlooked but warrants attention.

Finally, (f) Informal roles represent a large, diverse range of second-order activities and patterned relationships. They provide essential functions that the major Institutional roles do not cover, filling gaps in the processes by which a social structure operates—especially as it becomes more differentiated and complex.

Thus, they flesh out the functions of the skeletal structure. Clearly, they may supplement, overlap with, or deviate from the Institutional roles in any group or level of the system. Thereby, their possible functions are understandably diverse: to innovate or improvise, to compensate for inadequate provisions of Institutional roles, to help moderate role conflicts, to meet crises and accommodate strains, to integrate or disrupt groups, to lubricate or create frictions in various systems, to generate or mediate personal conflicts, and so on.

Indeed, the analogy between Informal roles and informal systems becomes almost inescapable. In this sense, one can express the conceptual correspondence with systems analysis in the following terms:

$$\frac{\text{Informal Roles}}{\text{Institutional Roles}} = \frac{\text{Informal Systems}}{\text{Formal Systems}}$$

That is to say, Informal roles bear the same relationship to Institutional roles that informal systems do to formal systems. The development and elaboration of Informal roles are integral to the status structure but are not provided by it. Institutional status positions generate the most essential roles of a system, but ultimately, even in the central institutions, these tend to be incomplete. They certainly represent the necessary, but not sufficient (much less optimal) conditions of operation. The bare bones need fleshing out. Just as a structure requires the development of an informal system for flexibility, so are its processes virtually dependent on the elaboration of Informal roles that are not inherent in Institutional statuses. A central problem for future theory remains the explication of these relationships in role terms and the modification of existing theory in light of such analysis.

EN PASSANT: AN ILLUSTRATIVE APPLICATION

To illustrate the generality of our schema, we can apply it to selected elements of a particular model. In this case, a most suitable example is that of Riley, Johnson, and Foner (1972, p.9) which describes the channeling of cohort members into age roles. From their complete flow

Role Types	Social Allocation (P3)	Normative Expectations (4)	Socialization (P4)
1. Institutional	+	High	+
2. Tenuous			
Titular	+	Low	–
Amorphous[a]	+/–	Low	–
3. Informal			
Group selected[b]	+	Moderate	±
Self-selected	–	Variable	–

[a]Viz.: + (aged) and – (divorcee)
[b]Viz.: scapegoat

Figure 2.   Allocation, norms and socialization of role types.

chart, we can select three key components on which our respective role types are differentially processed—not only for age roles, but more generally as well. This appears in Figure 2 where the notations of the column headings refer to Riley, Johnson, and Foner's original diagram, and examples of subtypes are footnoted.

The contents of Figure 2 are straightforward and can be read accordingly. For our immediate purposes, certain qualifications that would be necessary in a refined analysis (viz., the actual variation in socialization to different Institutional roles) need not divert us here. What is more to the point is that the various role types may be allocated differently, but this is not invariably consequential for their subsequent processing. For example, even though the Amorphous aged (+) are allocated by ascription and the divorced (–) are recruited by choice, their normative expectations and socialization patterns are similarly vague and diffuse. On the other hand, among the Informal roles, the normative expectations and socialization processes differ for those that are filled by group designation or by self-selection.

These details warrant a more refined, systematic analysis than we can undertake here. But the central point is that the role typology offers some new perspective on the Riley-Johnson-Foner model and affords leads for deeper examination of its elements. To this extent, it provides an entree to the more systematic analysis of particular role problems that have been neglected but warrant careful study.

Our immediate interest is simply to establish this rather than to pursue its complex implications here. But we will presently apply the typology to variations in role activity through the life span.

THE MEANINGS OF ROLE CHANGE

The concept of role change has several different usages that should be distinguished prior to any discussion. All are legitimate, but their referents and implications differ. So, before applying our typology to the life span, we should indicate which of the meanings concern us here. I hope that this clarification will avoid some troublesome misunderstanding.

Role change involves at least five different temporal connotations. (a) The first is that of the *simple movement* between two positions that a person holds simultaneously. This is clearly illustrated by his moving between family and work roles. Or, within each sphere, by movement between being a father (to a child) and being a son (to an older parent); or between being a supervisor and a subordinate to different people at work. These involve routine shifts between different role relationships in a short time. But the remaining changes represent significantly longer time perspectives.

The next pair entail important *internal* role alterations. (b) Roles may be modified and redefined as a function of *social change*. Thereby, they are transformed in their content, normative expectations, and so on in response to historical events. The changing position of

American women in the family, the labor force, and other institutions illustrates such a fundamental restructuring of their roles in scope, quality, and focus.

(c) Third, there are also comparable changes within single roles through time as correlates of age that are essentially functions of different *life-stages*. For example, being a son or a daughter involves progressive role changes as people traverse the life cycle, growing from childhood through adolescence to adulthood and on through the successive stages of maturity. Clearly, different normative standards govern the expectations and reciprocities of a daughter and her parents when she is a child, an adolescent, a young woman, a wife, a mother, a matron, and a grandmother. She remains a daughter during all these periods, but her role and its content are steadily modified. These changes within a role may be construed in human developmental or sociological frames of reference. The essential factor is that specific role expectations and relationships vary by life-stages and implicitly by age-appropriate norms (Neugarten, Moore, and Lowe, 1965).

The final two connotations involve alteration of the *status set* by the acquisition of new roles or the loss of existing ones. (d) A status set may simply be enlarged by *accretion* or reduced by *attrition*. The person adds or loses a role by joining or leaving a group or association, whether formal or informal. While the activity or membership he acquires or drops is usually quite voluntary, this certainly is not a requisite. But the particular character of such changes is often age-related. Thus, people's roles may fluctuate in number by joining or leaving a church, the Girl Scouts, a union, the PTA, a bowling team, the local Democratic party, a Little League team, a bridge club, a professional society, or a social circle. The age relationship is commonly linked to life stages, and it may vary from attendance at nursery school to senior citizens clubs. Such roles may be added or dropped singly. But the processes of accretion and attrition are often integral to evolving life-styles at different periods, with several new roles being acquired or lost during a rather limited period. These changes commonly involve role complexes (correlated, if not integrated, multiple roles) that are related to expanding or contracting life-stages.

(e) Fifth, a change of role may also refer specifically to *status passages*, the transition between positions that are sequentially ordered. This invariably involves the relinquishment of one status and the acquisition of the succeeding one, for the two positions are mutually exclusive within a status succession, and their order is usually irreversible. In the prototypical case, such as the professional career ladder, the statuses are often hierarchically arranged, with the preceding stage a prerequisite of the succeeding one. The classic formulation of status passage was set forth by van Gennep (1960) who traced the three-step process of separation-transition-induction. Clear illustrations of such role change include getting married, graduation from school and entrance to a profession, having a child, and so on. To be sure, not all statuses are arranged in sequential chains. Even when they are, deviations from the typical pattern of role succession occasionally do occur (as in an annulment effacing a marriage, with the parties reverting to the "single" status). However, in the life cycle, despite the wonders of cosmetology and surgery, age is progressive and not reversible. The crucial element here is that in these status passages, the transition occurs between mutually exclusive, successive roles.

Now for the caveat. In this paper on the life span, we are mainly interested in statuses and roles that change as functions of new *life-stages*. Therefore, we are concerned only with the relevant variations, those pertaining to the last three connotations of role change: (c) *modifications of single roles* between age grades or periods, (d) *accretion and attrition*, and (e) *sequential status passages*. So we will *not* deal with the two extraneous referents of role change: routine movement between current roles and the alteration of roles by social change.

CHANGES THROUGH THE LIFE SPAN

We will trace the different status-role types as they fluctuate over the life cycle, tentatively proposing their gross profiles as these wax and wane in relative importance through time. We should also like to distinguish the role changes according to their kind: modification across periods, accretion-attrition, or status passage. Then, ideally, we could assess the relative salience of the three kinds of change in different life-stages.

But this poses some difficulty, for the *relative importance* of the role types is not simply reducible to *quantitative* terms, to their respective shares of the person's total role activity. The Tenuous type emphasizes role attrition and contraction, in a word, loss or inactivity. The conception of role as activity does not accommodate the notion of role as *in*activity. In quantitative terms, as Tenuous roles increase, their activity values come to approximate zero. Yet, their *relative importance* among the role types may be increasing. So there is a contradiction between declining amounts of activity and its greater importance. There is no meaningful way to express this growing *qualitative* importance in a declining *numerical* index. Hence, this precludes the possible equation of importance with nominal amounts of role activity.

Accordingly, the gross profiles of change throughout the life cycle must reflect the prominence of the three types in some other fashion. For the moment, we will simply leave this as an arbitrary judgment. I will express their relative importance schematically as *hypothetical curves in a model of comparative change*. This will indicate their shifting significance at different life-stages without regard to the particular sources of change. While these sources (role modification, accretion-attrition, and status passage) may vary considerably across periods, their relative salience and relation to role types remain problems for future research. Therefore, this model will simply trace the tentative curves of our three role types as I conceive their shifting importance throughout life. In this presentation, the profile of the major Institutional roles will be the basic frame of reference to which the others will be compared.

To simplify the model, we will assume that the life span is divided into the most basic, fundamental stages—with the full understanding that all of them can be embellished, subdivided,

and refined much further. Clearly, "young adulthood" can be broken down into completion of school, starting work, getting married, having children, and so on, even with courtship inserted somewhere along the way. Or "middle age" can simultaneously involve sex differences in a waxing career line for men and the waning of an emptying nest for women as children grow up and successively leave home. By the same token, "old age" may similarly be subdivided. An excellent summary of the substantive trends is readily available in Clausen's (1972) fine treatment of this difficult, nebulous subject. But in this paper, we will assume such substages and take them for granted without further consideration, for at the moment it is the principle rather than the details that concerns us.

Furthermore, there is an important difference in the clarity of movement within and between major life-stages: transitions between larger life-stages are often more indefinite and blurred than changes within them. The ostensibly "lesser" movements tend to be the most specific, sharpest, and clearest. This is most apparent in those based on sheer age criteria, as when another birthday qualifies one to enter school, secure a driver's license, vote, buy liquor, or forces one to retire. These are scheduled and legalistic. Other specific status changes, role acquisitions and losses are also often punctuated by public or private rites of passage that sharply denote the transition. For example, ceremonies of baptism, bar mitzvah, engagement, marriage, graduation, funerals, and the like not only signify an actor's status change, but also his new reciprocal relationships with significant others. Status changes such as these are typically sequential, very specific and clear cut. But they do not invariably and automatically delineate major life-stages in social terms. Widowhood or retirement may change one's status, but *not* necessarily one's life-stage.

Other role changes tend to be vaguer and more blurred. They are not so clearly tied to any specific sequence of statuses, yet they are linked, if only loosely, to major life periods. They tend to be one of two kinds: (a) The first marks the *gradual* changes within a role through time, such as the evolving roles of parents as their children grow from infancy to adulthood, or conversely those of adult children as their parents pass from middle age to old age and into senility. These modifications tend to develop somewhat slowly and gradually. Though they are sometimes precipitated by immediate events, the changes are not scheduled (Glaser and Strauss, 1971), they are usually independent of any particular status passages, and they may cover several stages of the life cycle.

The second set concerns the *timing* of role changes in relation to age-appropriate norms. Certain status transitions and other behavior tend to be judged by what is appropriate at given ages. In other words, there are informal, but definite expectations that reflect age-appropriate norms (Neugarten, Moore, and Lowe, 1965). These do not incorporate a precise deadline or cut-off point, but rather a loose period of time whose flexibility varies with the particular change in question. While the marriage ceremony itself signifies a sharp status change, the period during which a person is normatively expected to get married is relatively flexible before informal social pressures are brought to bear. Other examples of such flexible periods that tend to stiffen at their boundaries include: the timing of parenthood (Nydegger, 1973a, 1973b; Veevers, 1972) and other family changes (Olson, 1969), progress along career lines (Huyck, 1970), and the timing of different status changes in related institutional contexts (Huyck, 1973). Both types of change, modification within roles and normative timing, may emerge within life-stages, but in a framework of relatively loose, blurred transition zones. Yet the normative shifts are extremely significant.

Finally, the demarcations that distinguish one major life-stage from another may be the vaguest of all. Here the transitional periods are the broadest and their boundaries the most ambiguous. Legal criteria, individual attributes, and social definitions are often so disparate that few meaningful cutting points can be established. Indeed, the definition of life-stages may vary more by people's life-style (viz., social class) than by the stages themselves. Therefore, it is wisest at this point simply to acknowledge the ordering of the life cycle, with the full understanding that its phases are not always sharply separated from one another so much as buffered by broad zones of transition. For purposes of this paper, this implies that at present too precise or refined a division of major life-stages is premature and unwarranted, an invitation to misplaced concreteness.

Accordingly, we will construe the basic life-stages in quite simple terms, such as infancy/childhood, adolescence, youth/adulthood, middle age, and old age. We will not pin them to specific chronological ages. Also, these stages obviously cover significantly different lengths of time, but no matter. This is not crucial for our

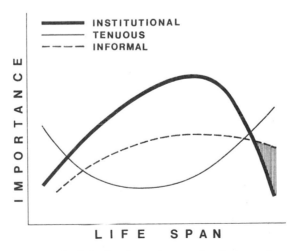

Figure 3. Relative importance of role types in the life span.

immediate problem. Now we can turn to consider how our role types shift in relative importance during the course of life. This is schematized in Figure 3.

Institutional: + +

Changes in the relative importance of the major Institutional roles show a clear profile across the life span. Elsewhere, I have indicated that significant status transitions *before* old age are marked by basic role continuity, net social gains, and various rites of passage; but the movement *into* old age reverses these patterns, with major role discontinuity, systematic social losses, and few rites of passage. Such discontinuities and losses often precede rather than follow the change in status (Rosow, 1974 Ch. 2).

For our purposes, the key factor is the asymmetry of the Institutional curve. (This is the heavy reference line in Figure 3.) There is a fairly steady increase in importance and in social gains that reach their peak and level off in late middle age and then decline with the losses of old age. These social gains and decrements are basically a function of the changing dependence and responsibilities of a person as he traverses the life course. The sequence of roles and their increase in number generally involve growing responsibilities, both within and among roles. These new obligations also involve correlates of greater social resources: power and authority, privileges and rewards, a diversity of options, and so on. While these prerogatives are usually valued by the actor, this is not always the case. They are not necessarily an unmixed blessing, and they are not always psychologically welcome. On balance though, they usually are construed as gains and advantages. But in terms of status and role structure, the curve of responsibility and its social gains generally grows steadily and relatively smoothly into late middle age. This obtains in virtually all major institutional spheres, notably the family, education, and work; in civic, religious, political, and community affairs; in formal and informal groups; in voluntary organizations; and even in leisure activities. The pattern of growth marks both single roles and role complexes as well.

In this growth curve, then, the person moves from stages and positions of lower responsibility and privilege to higher ones. In childhood, this starts with the reduction of dependency and the acquisition of skills that reduce the necessity for his care and supervision. With greater independence, the person is expected to be more responsible for himself and to attain greater autonomy. Eventually he moves on to roles where he assumes increasing responsibility for others who are socially less competent, typically younger persons. This profile of change occurs within and between life-stages, that within them being a dampened version of the larger curve of gain across stages.

This correspondence with social maturation is reflected in the succession of statuses. An actor's movement through most of life shows a growing share of available values. He has larger spheres of decision, greater recognition, rewards, and prerogatives; his span of authority increases as the number of people exercising authority over him declines. These gains are age-related and integral to life-stages. Because successive phases impose greater responsibility, they are accorded greater authority. And, because such obligations are socially consequential, systematic incentives and prerogatives are provided. Accordingly, during the life-stages of social gain, the major Institutional roles increase in relative importance until late middle age.

After the leveling off of social gains in late middle age, the declines of old age begin to set in. There is a steady attrition of statuses and some emptying of roles, with the major Institutional ones clearly declining in importance. But this process will be discussed in the next section.

We must remember, of course, that the slope of this curve varies somewhat, not only for individuals, but also for different institutional spheres and subgroups in the population: sex, occupation, social class, and so on. But here we are concerned only with the generic profile through life-stages.

Tenuous: + –

The relationship between the Tenuous and major Institutional roles can be succinctly summarized. They are moderately, but inversely correlated throughout the life span. Thereby, the relative importance of the Tenuous type presents a contrary profile to the Institutional curve, but not its precise opposite because of the modifying influence of the Informal roles. Clearly, the interaction effects among the three curves remains a problem for future research that the gross schematization of Figure 3 can only reflect.

Obviously, minimal roles are most conspicuous and important at the extremes of the life span, early and late in life. In infancy and childhood, the person is being socialized into the most basic elements of his culture and is being weaned from a position of extreme dependence. In the preschool period, his roles are few and limited, almost confined to the family and play group and perhaps nursery school. With the start of school, he begins to take on a few more roles with gradually increasing responsibility as he moves into a slowly expanding social world. This increase in roles, in life space, in membership groups, and in responsibilities continues steadily throughout adolescence and as he approaches maturity. Each social gain reflects his diminishing dependence and greater competence in the adolescent transition from childhood to adulthood. As he moves into new institutional spheres, especially in education, sex, and work, two things occur: his existing activities *expand* and he also *acquires* new roles. So there is both a growth within roles and an increase in their number. Correlatively, his role restriction has declined steadily since childhood, it reaches a rather low point during adolescence, and it remains relatively unimportant for several decades of adulthood until late middle age and the onset of old age. In effect, role limitation lies dormant during most of adulthood.

The first stirrings of a revival of the Tenuous appear well into middle age. The obverse form of the adolescent pattern is gradually set into motion, involving both the decline of activity within roles (despite the retention of statuses) and the reduction in their number. This is reflected in both the titular (honorific and nominal) and the amorphous subtypes. Later middle age is the main period when adult honors start

to arrive and also when some persons are deflected into relatively empty positions. The amorphous varies somewhat by category. The ambiguous (viz., divorcee) and the de facto (viz., chronically unemployed) are less sensitively geared to life-stages than the two forms of role attrition (role emptying and status loss). Though they are subject to objective market factors and other institutional forces, yet they do display a perceptible relationship to life-stage. In our immediate examples, for instance, the probability of divorce is greater in early adulthood, and extended unemployment is more likely in middle and old age. But the two forms of role attrition definitely make their incipient appearance in most cases in the heart of middle age, by the mid-40's. For women, role contraction begins domestically when the first child leaves home and continues into the so-called empty-nest stage when the youngest child departs. The decline of mothering and managing a menage reflects the reduction of role activity, although the status is retained. During this period, some men who are well established begin to relax a bit at work and shift into a lower gear. At the same time, a few secondary activities may even be given up. These, however, are simply the first harbingers of future trends. The relative importance of the Tenuous in middle age is not yet great, for many Institutional roles remain viable and are actively maintained.

But the Tenuous begins to grow steadily with the onset of old age and the increase of role attrition, both in the emptying and loss of roles. With retirement, widowhood, illness, failing income, and their correlates in the lapse of organizational memberships and so on, the person loses roles and enters a stage of reduced activity, a contracting social world, more marginal social participation, and possibly greater dependency. This involves the normal decrements of aging that have been so amply documented in the gerontological literature and are brought up to date in other chapters of the *Handbook*.

What is crucial is that during old age, people lose Institutional roles in most spheres, and this loss increases precipitously after age 75. That the age status of the elderly is evaluated in ascriptive rather than performance terms (Rosow, 1973) testifies to both forms of role attrition, particularly the loss of Institutional and other statuses. But, we shall suggest that Informal roles may well be retained longer than the Institutional.

In summary, the relative importance of the Tenuous type in the course of life describes a "U"-shaped curve, biased toward the late stages. It is high at the extremes of childhood and old age, and it is relatively low and flat during most of adulthood and maturity. During childhood and adolescence, it declines steadily in importance with the acquisition of statuses and the expansion of roles. Conversely, it begins to revive again by later middle age, and its tempo mounts increasingly with the progressive attrition of old age. In general, gradual role contraction may be somewhat more typical of late middle age and both contraction and status loss of old age.

Informal − +

The Informal roles present a novel perspective and are more interesting in some respects than the others, regardless of whether they exemplify integrative or disruptive functions. As Figure 3 illustrates, Informal roles describe an irregular, fluctuating, flatter curve than either of the other types. And, for most life-stages, those between childhood and old age, their relative importance tends to fall between the other two. Then, in the later years, when the Tenuous increases as Institutional roles are lost, the Informal type changes significantly less than either.

Figure 3 shows that the profile of the Informal roles starts low and slightly later than the Institutional curve. By adolescence, it rises to intermediate levels. Then it fluctuates irregularly through adulthood and middle age as a constrained, flattened, muted echo of the Institutional profile. In other words, there is a loose, moderate correlation between the two types prior to old age.

But at that point, there is a sharp divergence between them. When the Institutional curve declines quickly with the attrition of major roles, the relative importance of Informal roles drops off much less. It does drop to some extent because of older people's generally lower social participation. But of the three types, the relative importance of the Informal roles changes least from the earlier life-stages and remains the most stable throughout life. This is probably true whether the persons involved are self-selected or group selected, although this is subject to future research.

The flatter profile of the Informal curve probably involves four main factors. (a) Informal roles encompass a broader range of contexts than the Institutional type. They occur in both the major and lesser institutional spheres, in formal and informal settings, in organized and more amorphous groups. But regardless of setting, they belong to the *informal* system. To this extent, they may operate within formal structures to supplement and modify Institutional roles and adapt these to the particular local context. This is the basis for their moderate correlation with the Institutional curve. However, insofar as they also operate within informal groups that are not so institutionalized, this tends to reduce their correlation with the Institutional profile. Therefore, their straddling of purely informal social groups and the informal subsystems of major institutions tends to have contrary effects that operate in somewhat different directions. Because there are two loci of activity, one with major Institutional roles and the other without them, Institutional roles can account for only part of the variance. This reduces the possible correlation between them.

However, insofar as Informal roles appear in purely informal settings that remain viable spheres of participation in the later years, they are not subject to the sharp attrition that characterizes the loss of major Institutional roles. Therefore, even in retirement and widowhood, people may continue to operate in their informal groups of friends and neighbors, preserving some significant basis of their Informal roles. Thereby, these may remain more stable and decline less than the Institutional.

(b) These considerations also make it clear that Informal roles are *less* correlated than the Institutional type with social responsibility. Therefore, the Informal curve should not vary so sensitively through the life-stages with the ebb and flow of social duties and obligations. This factor alone would prevent these roles from reaching the relative importance of the Institutional type. To the extent that the Informal occur in major institutionalized contexts, they may echo the other profile, but only partially and with considerable modulation. Accordingly, the Informal curve is relatively flatter.

(c) The sheer number of persons with Informal roles is fewer than those with Institutional roles. For any particular individual, the ratio of his Informal/Institutional roles is almost certainly lower prior to old age than when he is elderly. During most of adulthood, people's lives are basically structured by their Institutional role obligations, and these almost invariably take precedence over other considerations. This is to say that, regardless of the deviant minority (viz., the never married, the imprisoned, and so on), virtually all adults have major status and role commitments. But within any given group or setting, only some members, but not all, have significant Informal roles. Not all are leavening jokesters or scapegoats serving to unify other group members. Not all have special functions for the group that distinguish them from other members, whether in formal or informal settings. Therefore, in contrast to the Institutional type, fewer persons perform Informal roles, and there are fewer of these in any actor's total role repertoire. This also limits the correlation between the two curves and keeps the relative importance of the Informal type below that of the Institutional prior to old age. By the same token, because fewer people are involved, the overall Informal profile may vary irregularly, but within a narrower, flatter range, over the life course.

(d) Finally, Informal roles are also the major repository of people's more stable personal styles. These may evolve from and reflect personality characteristics which are refined in adolescence and adulthood into fairly regular attributes that confer individual tone and flavor on people's social identities. As nominal personal qualities, they may set a common manner in which the person fills different roles. The actor develops a style that may be perceived in personality terms and evokes similar reactions across situations and groups. His relatively basic, stable style may underlie his similar relation to these groups and the nature of his Informal roles. The sheer fact that such particular patterns may develop from personality characteristics may reflect a selection process in th. casting of characters. But otherwise, they may have little effect on the social functions that these styles may serve. From the group perspective, it may make little difference *who* performs certain functions. On the other hand, the personal styles may also affect what functions are served. Needless to say, such styles are not always expressions of personality, for many are purely socially or culturally determined, as the women's liberation movement has insisted and other professional literature has borne out (Clausen, 1968; Inkeles and Levinson, 1968; Lieberman, 1950; Goslin, 1969). But at the moment, regardless of source and their reinforcing interaction, personal styles may play themselves out in similar ways across groups and situations. So an individual may develop a style—as a kittenish coquette, as an irascible grouch, as a pollyanna *Luftmensch,* as a braggart, as a cynic, or whatever—that colors his relations to others and his participation in diverse groups. In the process, his personal style may well predispose him or others to cast him in various Informal roles. To the extent that these inhere in relatively settled, well developed forms, they should help to stabilize the curve of Informal roles throughout a person's life.

These four factors, then—the straddling of Institutional and Informal contexts, lower social responsibility, fewer persons, and personal styles—seem to be the key variables that account for the profile of the Informal type: its relatively greater stability than the other two in the course of life, its lower overall importance than the Institutional type before old age, and its greater importance during old age when the loss of major roles becomes significant.

POLICY IMPLICATIONS

As an added note, the theory underlying these curves contains one implication for the aged that policy makers and practitioners might consider. This is illustrated by the shaded section at the right of Figure 3, between the Institutional and Informal profiles after they intersect in old age. If we assume that one major social policy objective is the maintenance of roles for the elderly, then the curves in later life in Figure 3 shed some light on the possible resources for this. The shaded area shows the relatively greater stability of Informal over Institutional roles. The blank area between the Informal and Tenuous profiles represents an effective role "deficit." The policy objective of role maintenance would be to minimize this role deficit. Under different conditions—certainly in another social system, or perhaps in a less imperfect or a more idealistic and sentimental world—one might try to preserve the rights, duties, and participation of the aged by maintaining their Institutional roles and thereby reduce their Tenuous posture. But there is little prospect for this in modern, advanced societies, for our social organization systematically undermines the position of the elderly and deprives them of major institutional functions (Rosow, 1962). So it is quite fatuous to hope that policy makers can preserve their central roles simply through good will and ingenuity. Other drastic social changes in our institutional structure and its dominant values would be necessary. And such fortuitous developments cannot simply be taken for granted. Under these conditions, the maintenance of Institutional roles presents no viable alternative to the reduction of the Tenuous-Informal gap.

If an alternative and a possible resource for such a policy exist, they must be sought in enlarging the shaded area of Informal roles. In other words, any prospective flexibility must lie there. This has two major implications: (a) Attention would have to be focused primarily on the *informal* social system, mainly on the networks of friendship, neighboring, and similar links that develop from spontaneous associations and voluntary activities which generate cohesive social groups. The applied problem is not simply to contrive artificial programs to be imposed from above in an effort to induce old people to participate. Rather, it indicates the need to recognize and

work with those conditions that stimulate spontaneous social ties and provide natural opportunities for Informal roles within our present institutional structure. Then social policy could undertake to support and strengthen those favorable conditions. In other words, from a strategic standpoint, there is less likelihood of a significant *role* payoff in direct service programs for the aged than there might be in those efforts that address the social context of their lives, their environment, and the world in which they live and move. This means very simply to optimize those normal social forces that are congenial to spontaneous relationships, voluntary groups, and Informal roles. Once these favorable conditions have been strengthened and contextual obstacles to association minimized, the factors that are conducive to interaction could then come into play and operate more freely. Thereby, the chances of increasing Informal roles at the expense of the Tenuous would be enhanced.

(b) Furthermore, the prospective success of such intervention would increase to the extent that it mobilized and capitalized on old people's *status similarity*. This would ideally rest not simply on age alone, but generally on as many of their shared statuses as possible: sex, marital position, race, ethnicity, social class, religion, and other aspects of common social background. This reflects the fact that insofar as people share a similar cultural heritage, history, social position, life style, experience, and fate, then the greater will be their potential for spontaneous interaction and group stability. In other words, the closer one approximates social homogeneity, the greater the likelihood of informal group life, continued participation, and the development of Informal roles.

Such integration has viable prospects when based on old people's other voluntary associations or formal organizations, even if membership or participation has lapsed. The success of many enterprises for the aged is greatly enhanced when there is self-selectivity (or even eligibility) based on other shared statuses or identities. It is for this reason that senior citizens programs attached to an established church or ethnic center are more successful than those organized by agencies with which old people have not been previously affiliated. The same principle applies to various retirement housing or communities that limit recruitment to selected groups, such as Florida's Salhaven (upholsterers' union) and Moosehaven (the Moose Lodge), the retired teachers' apartment in Omaha, and others. Arlie Hochschild's (1973) study provides an excellent example of the solidary effects of common background, shared statuses, and social homogeneity in providing continuity and generating Informal roles. Formal organizations and voluntary associations afford an entree to persons of similar identity and status, both past and present. To the extent that such former memberships were salient and meaningful, they retain a significant status potential that could be mobilized with imaginative contextual management. Thus, shared statuses, both current and previous, including formal organizational affiliations, could well be capitalized upon in the maintenance and even increase of Informal roles in old age. But clearly, regardless of how common statuses may be used, the essential leverage remains within the system of Informal roles.

CONCLUSION

We have offered here an inclusive taxonomy of status and role types to incorporate the deviant cases that Linton's formulation failed to take into account. This enabled us to clarify several abiding ambiguities associated with these concepts, notably the Tenuous and Informal types in which status and role occur separately rather than together. This made these atypical cases more amenable to analysis within a role framework, and eventually we proposed separate profiles of role change through the life cycle.

The aged represent the prototype of Tenuous roles in which statuses are emptied of functions. While the Tenuous describe a "U" shaped curve in the course of life, their relative importance is biased toward the later stages. Role contraction typifies late middle age, and both contraction and status loss mark old age.

The declining social responsibility and role attrition of the elderly are reflected in their shrinking social world. Sociologically, they display the decrements of retirement, widowhood, declining health and income, reduced group memberships, and social interaction. This involves the loss and emptying of roles, both in number and content. For women, the contraction of domestic roles begins well into middle age when the first child leaves home and continues into old age, especially after widowhood. For men, role attrition starts about the same time with an easing of work activity and continues after retirement. In the vestibule to old age during the preretirement period, people enter a phase of declining social activity, including formal organizational memberships, and a gradually contracting social world. This reflects their increasingly marginal social participation. Institutional roles wither away, and other decrements rise precipitately after 75.

This general pattern appears in the inverse relationship between the curves of Institutional and Tenuous roles. In later life, the Institutional decline in relative importance and the Tenuous correspondingly increase. Indeed, this process makes such residual ascribed statuses as age more prominent and, in the social evaluation of the elderly, supports the shift from standards of role performance to ascriptive criteria.

Although Informal roles have significant group and individual functions, they are neither integral nor reducible to particular status positions. In contrast to Institutional and Tenuous roles, the Informal curve through the life span varies less and is relatively flatter. In old age, its comparative importance falls off much less than the Institutional and does not rise as the Tenuous does. This relatively greater stability inheres in the facts that Informal roles are not closely linked with social responsibility, they straddle formal and informal contexts, and they absorb personal styles across situations. Accordingly, as we have seen, Informal roles afford the most viable prospect for role maintenance in the face of the Institutional deficits of later life, particularly if this capitalizes on status homogeneity among the aged and on continuities from their earlier life-stages.

The present formulation is an interim refinement of current perspectives on status and role, hopefully one that will stimulate further research and theoretical development, not only on the elderly *per se*, but on a sociology of the life course where aging properly belongs.

REFERENCES

Bakke, E. W. 1934. *The Unemployed Man.* New York: E. P. Dutton.

Bakke, E. W. 1940a. *Citizens Without Work.* New Haven: Yale University Press.

Bakke, E. W. 1940b. *The Unemployed Worker.* New Haven: Yale University Press.

Becker, Howard. 1963. *Outsiders: Studies in the Sociology of Deviance.* New York: The Free Press.

Biddle, Bruce, and Thomas, Edwin (eds.) 1966. *Role Theory.* New York: John Wiley.

Bureau of the Census. 1973. *Statistical Abstract of the United States, 1973.* Washington, D.C.: Department of Commerce.

Burgess, Ernest. 1950. Personal and social adjustment in old age. *In,* Milton Derber (ed.), *The Aged and Society,* pp. 138–156. Champaign, Illinois: Industrial Relations Research Association.

Clausen, John (ed.) 1968. *Socialization and Society.* Boston: Little, Brown.

Clausen, John. 1972. The life course of individuals. *In,* Matilda Riley, Marilyn Johnson, and Anne Foner, *Aging and Society, Vol. 3: A Sociology of Age Stratification,* pp. 457–514. New York: Russell Sage Foundation.

Ginzberg, E. 1943. *The Unemployed.* New York: Harper and Brothers.

Glaser, Barney, and Strauss, Anselm. 1971. *Status Passage.* Chicago: Aldine-Atherton.

Goffman, Erving. 1958a. The characteristics of total institutions. *In, Symposium on Preventive and Social Psychiatry,* pp. 43–84. Washington, D.C.: Walter Reed Army Institute of Research.

Goffman, Erving. 1958b. *Presentation of Self in Everyday Life.* Edinburgh: University of Edinburgh.

Goffman, Erving. 1961. *Asylums.* Garden City, New York: Doubleday.

Goode, William. 1956. *After Divorce.* New York: The Free Press.

Goode, William. 1960. Norm commitment and conformity to role-status obligations. *Am. J. Sociol.* 66, 246–258.

Goode, William. 1970. *World Revolution and Family Patterns.* New York: The Free Press.

Goslin, David (ed.) 1969. *Handbook of Socialization Theory and Research.* Chicago: Rand McNally.

Hochschild, Arlie. 1973. *The Unexpected Community.* Englewood Cliffs, New Jersey: Prentice-Hall.

Hunter, Woodrow, and Maurice, Helen. 1953. *Older People Tell Their Story.* Ann Arbor: University of Michigan, Division of Gerontology.

Huyck, Margaret. 1970. Age norms and career lines in the careers of military officers. Unpublished Ph.D. Thesis, University of Chicago.

Huyck, Margaret. 1973. Social class and age cohort patterns in timing of education, family and career. Paper delivered at the 26th Annual Meetings of the Gerontological Society, Miami Beach.

Inkeles, Alex, and Levinson, Daniel. 1968. National character: The study of modal personality and sociocultural systems. *In,* Gardner Lindzey and Elliot Aronson (eds.), *Handbook of Social Psychology,* 2nd ed., Vol. 4, pp. 418–506. Reading, Massachusetts: Addison-Wesley.

Jahoda, Marie, Lazarsfeld, Paul, and Zeisel, Hans. 1971. *Marienthal: The Sociography of an Unemployed Community.* Chicago: Aldine-Atherton.

Klapp, Orrin. 1962. *Heroes, Villains and Fools.* Englewood Cliffs, New Jersey: Prentice-Hall.

Klapp, Orrin. 1965. *Symbolic Leaders: Public Dramas and Public Men.* Chicago: Aldine.

Komarovsky, Mirra. 1940. *The Unemployed Man and His Family.* New York: Dryden.

Komarovsky, Mirra. 1973. Some problems in role analysis. *Am. Soc. Rev.* 38, 649–662.

Lieberman, Seymour. 1950. The effects of changes in roles on the attitudes of role occupants. *Hum. Rel.* 9, 385–403.

Linton, Ralph. 1936. *Study of Man.* New York: Appleton-Century.

Lipman, Aaron. 1961. Role conceptions and morale of couples in retirement. *J. Geront.,* 16, 267–271.

Lowenthal, Marjorie, and Haven, Clayton. 1968. Interaction and adaptation: Intimacy as a critical variable. *Am. Soc. Rev.* 33, 23–30.

Merton, Robert. 1957. *Social Theory and Social Structure.* rev. ed. New York: The Free Press.

Neugarten, Bernice, and Datan, Nancy. 1973. Sociological perspectives on the life cycle. *In,* Paul Baltes and K. Warner Schaie (eds.), *Life Span Developmental Psychology: Personality and Socialization,* pp. 53–69. New York: Academic Press.

Neugarten, Bernice, Moore, Joan, and Lowe, John. 1965. Age norms, age constraints and adult socialization. *Am. J. Sociol.* 70, 710–717.

Newcomb, Theodore. 1966. Foreword. *In,* Bruce Biddle and Edwin Thomas (eds.), *Role Theory,* pp. v–vi. New York: John Wiley.

Nydegger, Corinne. 1973a. Timing of fatherhood: Role perception and socialization. Unpublished Ph.D. thesis, Penn State University.

Nydegger, Corinne. 1973b. Late and early fathers. Paper delivered at the 26th Annual Meetings of the Gerontological Society, Miami Beach.

Olson, Kenneth. 1969. Social class and age-group differences in the timing of family status changes. Unpublished Ph.D. thesis, University of Chicago.

Parsons, Talcott. 1951. *The Social System.* New York: The Free Press.

Popitz, Heinrich. 1972. The concept of social role as an element in sociological theory. *In,* John Jackson (ed.), *Role,* pp. 11–39. New York: Cambridge University Press.

Riley, Matilda, and Foner, Anne. 1968. *Aging and Society, Vol. 1: An Inventory of Research Findings.* New York: Russell Sage Foundation.

Riley, Matilda, Johnson, Marilyn, and Foner, Anne. 1972. *Aging and Society, Vol. 3: A Sociology of Age Stratification.* New York: Russell Sage Foundation.

Rosow, Irving. 1962. Old age: One moral dilemma of an affluent society. *Gerontologist,* **2,** 182–191.

Rosow, Irving. 1967. *Social Integration of the Aged.* New York: The Free Press.

Rosow, Irving. 1973. The social context of the aging self. *Gerontologist,* **13,** 82–87.

Rosow, Irving. 1974. *Socialization to Old Age.* Berkeley: University of California Press.

Rossi, Alice. 1968. Transition to parenthood. *J. Marr. & Fam.* **30,** 26–39.

Sarbin, Theodore. 1968. Notes on the transformation of social identity. *In,* Leigh Roberts, Norman Greenfield, and Milton Miller (eds.), *Comprehensive Mental Health,* pp. 97–115. Madison: University of Wisconsin Press.

Sarbin, Theodore, and Allen, Vernon. 1968. Role theory. *In,* Gardner Lindzey and Elliot Aronson (eds.), *Handbook of Social Psychology,* 2nd ed., Vol. 1, pp. 488–567. Reading, Massachusetts: Addison-Wesley.

Sletto, Raymond, and Rundquist, E. 1936. *Personality in the Depression.* Minneapolis: University of Minnesota Press.

Strauss, Anselm. 1959. *Mirrors and Masks: The Search for Identity.* New York: The Free Press.

van Gennep, Arnold. 1960 (1908). *Rites of Passage.* Chicago: University of Chicago Press.

Veevers, J. E. 1972. The violation of fertility mores: Voluntary childlessness as deviant behavior. *In,* Craig Boydell, Carl Grindstaff, and Paul Whitehead (eds.), *Deviant Behavior and Societal Reaction,* pp. 571–592. Toronto: Holt, Rinehart & Winston.

Veevers, J. E. 1973. Voluntarily childless wives. *Sociol. & Soc. Res.,* **5,** 356–366.

19
DEATH AND DYING
IN A SOCIAL CONTEXT*

Richard A. Kalish
Graduate Theological Union

What is death? The answers are numerous, varying according to culture, age, health, cognitive capacities, one's life situation, perhaps sex, the nature of dependents, projects finished and unfinished. Death means different things to the same person at different times; and it means different things to the same person at the same time.

Death is a biological event, a rite of passage, an inevitability, a natural occurrence, a punishment, extinction, the enforcement of God's will, absurd, separation, reunion, and time for judgment. It is a reasonable cause for anger, depression, denial, repression, guilt, frustration, relief, absolution of self, increased religiousness, and diminished religiousness. It is a disruption of the social fabric by removing a significant person from the scene; it strengthens the social fabric by removing those less capable of doing their tasks and by permitting others, who otherwise chafe at being restricted, to move into more demanding roles. It has one set of meanings for the dying person, another for those who love him, yet another for those responsible for his health care, and still another set of meanings for those involved with funerals, legal documents, insurance, estates and trusts, public health statistics, wars, and executions.

*With gratitude to Vern Bengtson, Robert Binstock, and Charles Garfield for their valuable comments on previous drafts of this chapter.

The human being, as far as we know, is the only living creature that can anticipate his own future and, therefore, anticipate his own death. This awareness arises from his interactions with others, and it is through these interactions that meaning—most particularly the meaning of death—develops. Although the death of an individual is a deeply personal and highly idiosyncratic event, every death takes place in a social context and gains meaning from this context. The symbols—both verbal and nonverbal—through which death is perceived and understood are a significant component of every culture and are part of the cognitive awareness of every individual. The clarification of some of these symbols, particularly of the concepts of *aging*, *dying*, *death*, and *being dead*, is a first step to understanding the meanings of the phenomenon.

Dying is a process that we all know exists, that we can observe, and that can be influenced by the social environment as well as by the individual who is dying. *Death* "is the transition from the state of being alive to the state of being dead" (Kass, 1971, p. 699); it is an abstraction when used in this fashion, although it is often used—and correctly so—as synonymous with being dead. *Being dead* is a state that we all know exists, and that we cannot influence by any empirically verifiable intervention. We can speculate as to its nature, but we cannot know it with certainty, given our present state of knowledge.

The process of dying needs to be differentiated from the process of aging. In one sense, we are all dying, i.e., we are all being processed toward our death. Living is dying, and dying begins at conception. Unfortunately, such an approach to the definition of dying may provide food for thought but can only obscure the phenomenological significance of dying in the real world. Medawar (Kass, 1971) defines senescence as those changes in bodily capacities that accompany aging and that make the individual increasingly likely to die from random accidental causes; since no one dies merely of old age but must also be affected by some other condition, e.g., illness, physical trauma, dying can be defined as "the process leading from the incidence of the 'accidental' cause of death to and beyond some border, however ill-defined, after which the organism (or its body) may be said to be dead" (Kass, 1971, p. 699).

The most important unique characteristic of the process of dying is that it eventuates in the state of death. The physical and emotional pain, the loss of others, the inability to function in familiar ways, the ascribed role of "dying person" are all occurrences that can be comprehended through other experiences. Only death itself, the end result, remains unique.

What is unique about the state of being dead is the inability to experience, i.e., to think, to perceive, to behave, to have feelings. We have no prior history that enables us to understand what this state means, although theologians, philosophers, and others have presented their ideas and many people have accepted these ideas, in whole or in part. Nonetheless, death is still an unknown.

Freud (1959) recognized that, while death was obviously natural, undeniable, and unavoidable, people behaved as though death would only occur to others. "Our own death is indeed unimaginable, and whenever we can make the attempt to imagine it we can perceive that we really survive as spectators" (Freud, 1959, pp. 304-305). Because of the impossibility of truly conceptualizing oneself as dead, Freud insisted that fear of death was in actuality the displaced fear of castration or some other experience

(Rank, 1936). Jung (1959), however, stipulated that the major focus of the later years was one's death, and Becker (1973) contends that the major concern of *all* ages is death and what it represents. Contemporary writers would probably follow Becker, although without necessarily positing that death is *the* major focus for all ages. Nonetheless, the evidence supports his claim that strong feelings about death exist throughout the life span.

DEATH AND AGING

The relationship between age and death has altered greatly over the centuries. During prehistoric times, the life expectancy was probably around 18; this increased to about 20 in the Greco-Roman period, then to 35 by the Middle Ages (Dublin, 1965). Turn-of-the-century Americans could anticipate living for nearly 50 years. Even allowing for the substantial contribution to these low life expectancies of high rates of infant mortality, only a small proportion of the population survived into their 60's or 70's.

Death is now highly predictable as a function of age; moreover in much of the Western world and Japan, it is the old who die. Although the old have always died, the dying have not always been old. It is only in very recent decades that death has become primarily the province of the elderly, rather than an event scattered erratically across the life span.

If death is highly distressing, a supposition not contradicted by the observation that life for some is so painful that death is actively sought, and if the elderly are—with obvious exceptions—those who are going to die, then being old is in itself frightening, not only to those who are old but to those who work with or live with the elderly. Indeed, it may well be more frightening to the nonelderly, for whom experience with death is limited and who perceive themselves as having more to lose by dying. Therefore, because of the close association between old age and death in modern industrial societies, the individual and social issues relating to death are in many ways individual and social issues of aging. We may certainly hypothesize that one of the significant reasons that the old are avoided and isolated is their proximity to death.

ISSUES IN AGING

The basic theme of this chapter is the many meanings of death and dying. These meanings are found in the way death is defined, in how death affects the individual both when he is confronted by imminent death and when he is not, in what happens in the dying process both for the dying person and for his caretakers, and in the encounter with the deaths of others.

Thus the issues take shape. What is the meaning of death? How does its eventuality affect behavior? How can we cope with the knowledge of death so as to make living most satisfying? What happens in the dying process? Are there predictable stages? When is death? How are the dying cared for and how can this care be improved? How do individuals cope with the loss of others? How does the social structure handle this loss?

Of particular concern throughout the chapter is the dying process and the death of the elderly. In some ways the death of the elderly differs from the death of the young or the middle-aged. Research and observations have shown that attitudes toward death, preferred styles of dying, and dying trajectories all differ considerably among age groups. Not only is age a factor in the ways individuals confront their own deaths, but it is a factor in the perceptions of and responses to the dying person found in family members, friends, and caretakers. These various meanings of death—to the individual and to the society—are still relatively unexplored facets of death and dying of the elderly, in spite of the recent awareness that the terminally ill need improved health and personal care.

The focus throughout the chapter is on the individual, particularly the elderly individual, and those in his social milieu. This has required that some important issues be omitted. Thus, the chapter contains no discussion of suicide, abortion, capital punishment, or deaths in war. Space limitations have led to the unfortunate exclusion of the historical context of death and bereavement and to ignoring the significance of death in other cultures. There has been no op-

portunity to describe legal ramifications of wills, bequests, and the transmission of property, or of customs such as the levirate or sororate in which the brother or sister of the deceased marries the widow or widower. Funerals and mourning are insufficiently explored. The circumstances of widows and widowers have not received adequate attention. Little is said about the difficulties facing death-related professionals, e.g., police, coroners, morticians, military, health caretakers, clergy, or about death-related industries, e.g., the life insurance industry, the florist industry, the relevant segment of the chemical industry. Epidemiological data on cause of death and on death rates of different populations have been omitted. The terminal decline, in which altered cognitive capacities seem to prognosticate deaths, does not receive its due attention. Death education, death in literature and the arts, economic costs of death, all have been ignored.

These important issues have been excluded not because they lacked significance to the meaning of death and dying, but because they failed in competition with other issues to be relevant to the theme. Other authors would have devised other criteria and made other decisions. However, these criteria and these decisions will need to stand for this chapter.

The organization of this chapter has been presented indirectly in the previous paragraphs: The Meanings of Death, Common Reactions to Death, The Process of Dying, Caring for the Dying, Encountering the Death of Others, and a concluding section that attempts to bring together the threads and to look to the future. Where a data base is available, it has been presented; where empirical research is lacking, the lack has been made obvious.

THE MEANING OF FACING DEATH

Whether an individual faces a death that is imminent or whether he is facing a demise presumably much later in time, this death has many different meanings. These meanings obviously vary as a function of age, for several reasons. First, with increasing age, the anticipated life span is normally foreshortened, requiring constant readjustment in the allocation of time, effort, and other resources. Second, older persons tend to be perceived—and often perceive themselves—as not having sufficient futurity to deserve a major investment of the resources of others: the state, the family, the community, the work organization, and so forth. Third, older persons receive more reminders of impending death through signals from within their bodies and through the responses of other individuals and social institutions, as well as through the deaths of their age-peers.

All these factors tend to encourage the process of disengagement, both psychological and social (Havighurst, Neugarten, and Tobin, 1968). Much of the present controversy regarding the adequacy of the disengagement model dissolves when applied to persons facing their own death. Ross (1969) considers the final stage of dying, *acceptance*, as highly adaptive. She describes this stage as pertaining to a dying person who is well advanced in reducing his attachments to people, groups, material possessions, and ideas, a course of action that permits him to focus his remaining energies on only those attachments that are most vital to him. The dying individual's sense of loss diminishes as his attachments diminish in importance. That this stage closely resembles the concept of disengagement is not generally recognized (Kalish, 1972).

Apparently the pressures for disengagement that so often confront the elderly individual also confront the dying person at any age. These pressures encourage a turning inward, contemplation of meaning of the past through reminiscence, concern for the meaning of the present and the future, and pulling back from the emotional pain that occurs when attachments are lost or broken. When an elderly person enters the terminal phase, he has presumably already begun to disengage as a function of being old, and the additional detachment that is apparently induced by an imminent death encounter may be easier for him to cope with than for a younger person facing the same circumstance. Therefore we might hypothesize that the death of an older person would be less stressful than the death of an individual whose disengagement only began in response to the dying itself. Such a hypothesis is in need of empirical testing.

Two meanings of death with particular significance for the elderly are suggested by the previous discussion. First, death as an organizer of time: old people are known to have limited time. Second, death as loss: old people are known to have suffered many death-imposed losses, as well as other losses that are often associated with the dying process. A third meaning is also important: death as punishment. Since death and dying are normally perceived as intensely negative occurrences, and since negative occurrences are readily seen as punishments for transgressions, then logically death might be considered a punishment. Further, since it is old people who die, then the elderly may be thought of as victims—perhaps deserving victims—of punishment. These three meanings of death will be explored in the following discussion.

Death as an Organizer of Time

The meaning of anything, whether it is a physical object or a feeling or a human relationship, is defined in part by its boundaries. Our life is similarly defined and understood, in part, by conception, birth, and death, and we organize our lives in terms of these boundaries, even though we rarely know with more than moderate certainty where the boundary of death is. Nonetheless, we do know with complete certainty *that* it will be, and this knowledge influences our planning.

The end of life serves to organize life in two ways. First, the awareness that life will end makes all possessions, all experiences, all of everything transient. If all is recognized as transient and if detachment occurs appropriately, then more can be experienced without emotional disruption. If life were infinite, we might not need to withdraw our affect from people and things, since we might not need to experience their loss.

Second, the finitude of life alters the meaning of the way in which we use time. If time were infinite, we could have time to do many things and we would not need to establish priorities or to give up desirable options. To the elderly, death is a clearly perceived parameter that directly limits their personal futurity. Older persons were found to project themselves into a much more limited time futurity than younger persons, when asked to report coming important events in their lives and the timing of these events (Kastenbaum, 1966b). There was, however, no difference in their ability to use the concept of time to organize and interpret experience in general.

Many people have noted that retrospective time seems to pass with increasing rapidity as they age, while on-going experienced time varies not so much with age as with the nature of the experience, mood, fatigue, and anticipation. A graphic illustration of this was an 80-year-old man in a geriatric institution who made the following two comments within the same interview: "When you're as old as me, you'll learn that time devours you." ". . . nothing I could do with the time" (Kastenbaum, 1966a).

Thus, on the one hand, the coming of death speeds up the feeling of being "devoured" by time when contemplated retrospectively in weeks and months; on the other hand, death makes the moments and minutes creep by because there is nothing to do, i.e., nothing *meaningful* to do, because whatever is attempted will be transient or unfinished, a situation that renders a person helpless to achieve what he feels is important.

Back (1965) reports on a study with elderly residents of rural communities in the West. When they were asked what they would do if

	AGE		
	20–39	40–59	60+
Marked change in life style, self-related (travel, sex, experiences, etc.)	24%	15%	9%
Inner-life centered (read, contemplate, pray)	14%	14%	37%
Focus concern on other, be with loved ones	29%	25%	12%
Attempt to complete projects, tie up loose ends	11%	10%	3%
No change in life style	17%	29%	31%
Other	5%	6%	8%

Figure 1. Responses of 434 residents of Los Angeles County to the question: If you were told that you had a terminal disease and six months to live, how would you want to spend your time until you died? (From Kalish and Reynolds, 1976.)

they knew they were to die in 30 days, they were less likely than younger respondents to indicate that their activities would change at all. A more recent study of 434 respondents in the Greater Los Angeles area, divided approximately equally into three age groups (20–39, 40–59, 60+) supported and expanded Back's figures. Given a similar situation, except that the duration was 6 months instead of 30 days, more of the older group would not change their life style at all, and nearly three times as many older persons as younger would spend their remaining time in prayer, reading, contemplation, or other activities that reflect inner life, spiritual needs, or withdrawal (Kalish and Reynolds, 1976). How much these results reflect physical and health-related changes, how much is due to the pressures of disengagement, and how much results from a preference for inward-directed rather than interpersonal involvements is not known.

Death as Loss

An elderly person, in contemplating his own death, is likely to be aware that he will suffer a variety of losses. He will lose self, which includes his body, all forms of sensory awareness, his roles, and his opportunities to have experiences; he will also lose others, and he may be able to empathize with the grief others will feel in losing him.

Diggory and Rothman (1961) developed a list of seven values that they stated were lost through death: (1) loss of ability to have experiences, (2) loss of ability to predict subsequent events (e.g., life after death), (3) loss of body (and fear of what will happen to the body), (4) loss of ability to care for dependents, (5) loss suffered by friends and family (e.g., causing grief to others), (6) loss of opportunity to continue plans and projects, and (7) loss of being in a relatively painless state. A questionnaire was administered to several available populations, with usable responses coming from 563 people. They then compared the relative salience of each consequence for age, sex, religion, social class, and marital status categories. They found, for example, that the greatest concern for men was their inability to care for dependents, while the greatest concern for women was causing grief to friends and family. Persons between 15 and 39 selected causing grief to friends as their major anticipated loss through death, while those over 40 (there were relatively few respondents over age 55) chose the inability to care for dependents.

Kalish and Reynolds (1976) modified the statements slightly for their study of 434 people in four ethnoracial communities in Los Angeles and asked that they be responded to in terms of importance. Caring for dependents and causing grief to friends and relatives were found to be less important to the older respondents than to the younger, a finding that might well arise from their having fewer dependents and their awareness of their reduced impact on others. That older persons also felt less reluctant to give up experiencing is readily explained, since the potential for satisfying future experiences for the elderly is often less, both quantitatively and qualitatively, than for other age groups.

Other kinds of losses are associated with the dying process and death. One of these is loss of control, which takes place in a variety of ways. People are well aware today that dying often occurs in a milieu where the dying individual himself has little control over what is put into or taken out of his body. Decisions are made by family members, hospital personnel, and physicians with little or no input by the dying person, although these decisions are presumably made for his welfare. The ascribed role of the dying patient is certainly one that would rearouse any prior anxieties connected with loss of mastery. Caution is required in applying the global concept of loss to the great diversity of specific kinds of losses discussed above. While the notion of loss as a generic construct has heuristic value, it is necessary to remember that the meaning to an older person—or, indeed, to anyone—of loss of his physical body is vastly different than the meaning to him of the loss of loved ones (resulting from his own death) or the loss of ability to retain control of the self.

Death as a Punishment

Death is often seen as a punishment for "sins," although this tends to be the case more with the death of a younger person than with the death of an elderly person. A large proportion of people in our society maintain the implicit assumption that the actions of an individual will be rewarded or punished by what happens to him during his lifetime. Therefore, in order to make sense of what is seen as a premature death, one alternative is to seek some wrongful mode of behaving in the functioning of that individual that—in this magical thinking—"caused" him to die. For older people, the comment is made, "Well, their time has come," implying that their death was not out of sequence, was not a punishment. This belief lies deep in our history, since Western theology ascribes the advent of death itself as having arisen from human transgressions.

Kalish and Reynolds (1976) included two relevant questions in their survey, asking for agreement or disagreement with the following statements: "Accidental deaths show the hand of God working among men." "Most people who live to be 90 years old or older must have been morally good people." Nearly two-thirds of those who responded agreed with the former statement, while only slightly more than one-third agreed with the latter. However, significantly more older people than younger people agreed that the morally good live longer, while no age differences were found concerning the punishment by God through accidents. The results suggest that nearly twice as many people believe in death as a divine retribution as believe in long life as a divine reward. In some instances, when the process of living has become too painful—whether the suffering of a terminal patient or the despair of a presumably healthy person—death is seen as a welcome relief rather than a punishment. This mood often affects the survivors of an elderly individual, especially if they have observed him suffer physical pain, emotional stress, or cognitive confusion. His death is perceived as his release from a terrible existence—and, more covertly, as *their* release from the agonies of involvement in his dying process.

Death, Physicalness, and Transcendence

A totally different view of the meaning of death is presented by Ernest Becker (1973), who explores the tension established by being aware that man's physical nature leaves him vulnerable to death and prevents him from transcending these physical qualities at least during his lifetime. He suggests that people are caught in a dilemma. Of all living organisms, only humans know that they shall die. The same creatures who write poetry, make laws, develop and maintain (and destroy) cultures, and achieve the heroic also die and decay. People seek meaning for themselves, but the same self that seeks meaning is finite, while the meaning sought often transcends the finite.

In past eras, Becker contends, people coped with their physicalness, their "creatureliness," as he terms it, through religious ideologies that enabled them to transcend the body that eventually will die and rot. Today, with the dominant ideology strongly influenced by scientific rationalism, such transcendent views are difficult or impossible to maintain. People are forced to look closely at their creatureliness, and this means that they must recognize their lack of control over the forces that are causing their aging and eventual death. People once talked of having a soul, and that soul could transcend the body; now people talk of having self, and transcendence must occur through progeny, memories, or some other influence on the future, albeit almost always a very finite future.

When belief systems do not provide for the possibility of transcendence, death marks the ultimate loss of control and power, the ultimate separation from people and all else, the ultimate cessation of self and any meaning or purpose that resides in self. Thus, the traditional rituals and beliefs that mitigated the terror of death lose their value, and death becomes immensely frightening. Initially, the response of our society to the present mood of rationalism was to ignore or deny death, but when that became impossible, an all-out attempt was generated to cope with death. And that is where we are now.

COMMON REACTIONS TO DEATH: FEAR AND DENIAL

People react to death in general and their own death in particular in many ways. It is not unusual for one person to undergo several different, often contradictory, feelings about his death within a fairly short period of time—or even simultaneously. Two familiar responses to death are fear and denial. Undoubtedly the denial of death is one way of coping with the fear of death, so the two feelings are closely intertwined, although they are handled separately in research and discussion since they are not truly identical concepts.

Fear of Death

That fear of death exists is undebatable. The basis for such fear is much less certain. Becker (1973) posits two alternative stances. The first, which he terms the "healthy-minded" argument, contends that reactions to death are learned and that, therefore, fear of death is not natural. With proper early learning, with appropriate human relationships, the meaning of death, whether perceived as annihilation or as a rite of passage to another existence, can be assimilated as a natural process that need not be feared. Those who try to introduce death education into school curricula and elsewhere most likely accept this view implicitly.

The alternative, the "morbidly-minded" argument, insists that "the fear of death is natural and is present in everyone, that it is the basic fear that influences all others, a fear from which no one is immune, no matter how disguised it may be" (p. 15). This view does not exclude the role of early learning and lifetime experiences as influencing fear and anxiety, but essentially stipulates that fear of death is part of the human condition.

Becker himself opts for the morbidly-minded position. Because the fear of death is so powerful, people have developed belief systems and rituals to cope with their terror. The success of these beliefs and rituals varies from society to society and also from individual to individual within societies. The apparent calmness with which certain people meet death is a tribute to the effectiveness of their beliefs but does not rule out the universality of the terror.

Attitude surveys do not support Becker's position. When people were asked directly, they placed fear of their own death fairly far down on their list of fears, indicating the fear of the loss of others through death as their primary concern (Geer, 1965). Similar results are found in other studies. Depending on the wording of the items, the population studied, and the setting, the actual percentages vary, but the general conclusions remain the same: in response to direct questions, relatively few people indicate a fear of death. About one-fourth of a multiethnic sample indicated such fear (Kalish and Reynolds, 1976); 16 percent of a reasonably alert, institutionalized geriatric group stated their fear (Kimsey, Roberts, and Logan, 1972); only 10 percent of a group of 260 older community volunteers directly admitted fear of death, although another 31 percent indicated mixed feelings or ambivalence (Jeffers, Nichols, and Eisdorfer, 1961). These are typical of the many relevant studies.

Several studies have compared death attitudes of the elderly with those of other age groups. These show, with fair consistency, that the elderly think and talk more about death, whether they were asked to respond in terms of the frequency with which they contemplated death (Kalish and Reynolds, 1976; Riley, 1970) or in terms of having had such a thought during the previous five minutes (Cameron, Stewart, and Biber, 1973). Nonetheless, death appears less frightening for those who are older; this has been found in a variety of groups and using a variety of instruments and procedures (e.g., Feifel and Branscomb, 1973; Kalish and Johnson, 1972; Kalish and Reynolds, 1976; Kogan and Wallach, 1961; Martin and Wrightsman, 1965). A study in India found not only highly significant differences in death fear between young and retired persons, but a still significant difference between 55–60-year-old respondents and those who were 61 years old or older (Sharma and Jain, 1969). Not all studies, however, are in agreement; Templer, Ruff, and Franks (1971) obtained no age trends at all.

Initially it might seem contradictory that the old, for whom death is more imminent and who admit to finding it more salient, are still less fearful, yet the data make sense. Three reasons may be proposed:

(1) In old age, there is a diminished social value of life, i.e., the elderly person places less value on his own life while others in his environment tend to share his evaluation (Glaser, 1966). The older person recognizes his limited futurity; he is likely beset by health problems and economic restrictions; earlier roles, once very satisfying, are often closed to him. At the same time, our future-oriented social value system emphasizes the need to expend its energies on the producers of tomorrow rather than those of yesterday. As is sometimes said of the elderly, their future is behind them.

(2) People in industrialized nations can anticipate a life span of 65 to 75 years, women a few years longer, men a few years less. Perhaps this life expectancy becomes incorporated as a given in the thinking of many people. When they face their own deaths in advance of that time, they feel deprived; when they outlive their own expectations, they feel they have received their entitlement or even more.

(3) As people become older, they are socialized to their own death. The rehearsal for widowhood is well-known and begins at a fairly early age (Kalish, 1971). As older family members and, eventually, age-peers begin to die in larger numbers, each death must be worked through in some fashion. By the time the elderly person faces his own death, he has dealt with death sufficiently often, perhaps even rehearsing his own death, that he has been socialized to death. However, this does not in any way mean he is inured to death.

The latter point may also help explain why older people think and talk more about death. Not only is their death more imminent and, therefore, more on their minds, but they have experienced the deaths of others more frequently and have more death-related experiences to recall (Kastenbaum, 1969). Supporting data come from a British study of the bereaved: the proportion of bereaved who visited physicians, required medicine for shock or anxiety, or reported sleeplessness decreased with age (Cartright, Hockey, and Anderson, 1973). These are presumably indications of less fear of death among the elderly, which the authors interpret much as has been done here.

What about fear of death in those who are dying? The work of Feifel is relevant here. He studied four populations (seriously and terminally ill, chronically ill and disabled, mentally ill, and healthy), applying a variety of psychological measures. On many measures, those who faced imminent death did not differ from the other groups; the seriously and terminally ill did display significantly more anxiety and depression than the healthy, and they were more likely to use denial as a coping defense, while the healthy used intellectualization as a modal response. The terminally ill also blocked more frequently in their attempts to explain verbally their concepts of death. These same persons considered time to be both "valuable" and "meaningless" and indicated the future as the time of greatest concern, as opposed to the healthy who focused on the present (Feifel and Jones, 1968).

Correlates of Death Fear

If the life of a person has been full and satisfying, we might hypothesize that he is (a) more ready to die because he has been fulfilled or (b) less ready to die because he desires more of the fulfillment and his sense of loss of self by death is greater or (c) both of the above. The truth is that we have no good basis for knowing which column on the answer sheet should be filled in. Although (c) is probably the most accurate, this author's observations and experiences suggest (a) as more valid than (b). As Weisman states, ". . . to say that people die as they have lived is from a psychological viewpoint meaningless" (1972, p. 122). So many other factors are involved that the richness and satisfaction of the life that has been lived may account for only a very small portion of the variance.

Undoubtedly age is a major factor in the way an individual accepts his own death, but we know little of how age interacts with other variables. We might speculate, as an example, that a young or middle-aged person living a full, rich life would find death more distressing than an age-peer whose life was uneventful for him, while the exact opposite might be found in contrasting two groups of older persons. It is the interaction between age and other factors that must be probed. Feelings about the process of one's own dying can undoubtedly be related to physical suffering, the nature of the illness and the dying trajectory (Glaser and Strauss, 1968), the level of medical care, and the warmth of human relationships. Whether these would be factors in the fear of personal death when not imminent is problematic. Restricting his sample to retired persons, Templer (1971) found no relationship between his Death Anxiety Scale and the Cornell Medical Index somatic score.

Several studies have attempted to relate fear of death and personality variables. High scores on depression measures seem to correlate with overt fear of death as do measures of hypochondriasis, impulsivity, and hysteria (Magni, 1972; Rhudick and Dibner, 1961; Templer, 1971). A Death Concern Scale was constructed by Dickstein (1972) and correlated with the Edwards Personal Preference Schedule scales and the Taylor Manifest Anxiety Scale using university students. Correlations were significant for the Manifest Anxiety Scale and for needs for Change, for Succorance, and for Heterosexuality: those with high death concern (which consists primarily of items that involve fear and anxiety) displayed greater manifest anxiety, greater need for heterosexual activity, greater need to be succorant (to receive nurture from others), and less need for change.

The relationship between religious beliefs and fear of death is also a very complex one. A major source of confusion is the frequently simplistic measures that are used in the research for operationalizing both religiousness and fear of death. It has been suggested that some acceptance of personal transcendence or transcendent meaning to one's life makes dying an easier process (Augustine and Kalish, 1975). With reasonable consistency, people who are more religious are found to have lower death anxiety than those less religious. This has been found the case among religiously involved churchgoers (Martin and Wrightsman, 1965; Templer, 1972), among the active elderly (Swenson, 1961), among psychology students at a southern university (Williams and Cole, 1968), among a combined sample of physically ill, emotionally disturbed, and normal persons (Feifel and Branscomb, 1973), and among a multiethnic sample (Kalish and Reynolds, 1976). Other studies have found a curvilinear relationship, with the very religious (defined as adhering to the traditional Judaic-Christian views) having the least fear of death and the most nonreligious (defined as affirmed agnostics or atheists) having moderate fear of death: those with the highest death anxiety are irregular churchgoers or intermediate in their religiousness (Kalish, 1963a; Nelson and Nelson, 1973). Perhaps in these latter studies, the major independent variable is a belief system that is confused and uncertain, rather than specific religious views.

A most fascinating recent study (Garfield, 1974) explored differences in reactions to death-related stimuli of graduate students in psychology and in religion, Zen meditators, and psychedelic drug-users. Most dramatic was the contrast between the two student groups and the two altered-state groups. Thus, the latter displayed significantly less physiological responsivity to death-related stimuli on galvanic skin response and heart rate response measures than did the student groups but did not differ in these measures in response to a non–death-related aversive stimulus. Differences on a standardized death anxiety scale also showed less anxiety among members of the altered-state groups. Perhaps because the altered-state groups have had transcendent experiences and have also encountered the blurring of ego lines, so that the difference between self and nonself is diminished, the prospect of death does not pose a condition that is different from what they have already experienced. The blurring of ego lines may also occur in very old age, an issue that Peck (1968) explores in his discussion of developmental tasks of Body Transcendence *vs.* Body Preoccupation and Ego Transcendence *vs.* Ego Preoccupation. Peck uses transcendence to mean "overcome" the pains of the body or the limitations on futurity, but his work provides an intriguing parallel to Garfield's nonetheless.

Denial of Death

To deny that one is dying is to repress in some fashion the awareness that the process is going forward. The dynamics can be understood in the same fashion that other forms of denial through repression occur. To deny that death has taken place—or will take place—requires that we deny the cessation of experiencing. Traditionally Western culture denied death through such assumptions as having a transcendent soul that would abide in a self-aware hereafter or having an identity that would permit bodily

resurrection. In recent years, as these traditional forms of denial have become less acceptable, people have searched for alternatives, such as dwelling in the memory of others or living on through progeny or through works and accomplishments. When the temporary nature of these became obvious, people have had to develop either an acceptance of their own eventual and total extinction or else a belief system akin to the Asian philosophies of rebirth in other earthly forms.

In working with persons who are denying their dying, we are working with a psychological process based on personal dynamics, and we may very well need to enable the dying person to face what is taking place. In working with the denial of death (or of being dead), we are working with a belief system, closely related to psychodynamic processes, that is embedded in the sociocultural and theological values the person has internalized throughout a lifetime.

The obvious question that arises from the previous discussion is whether the elderly and others really lack a fear of death or whether they are denying the immense fear that they have. Further, how likely is it that the lower death fear stated by the elderly merely masks a greater actual fear through a more powerful form of denial? Although we cannot give definite answers to these questions, the vacuum is not total.

Feifel and Branscomb (1973) attempted to measure reactions to death at the conscious, fantasy, and below-the-level-of-awareness levels. One might debate the adequacy of reaction time to a word association test or the other two similar instruments they operationalized as measuring fear of death below the level of awareness. Nonetheless, their conclusions merit attention: "The dominant conscious response to fear of death is one of repudiation [of the *fear*] ; that of the fantasy or imagery level, one of ambivalence; and at the nonconscious level, one of outright negativity" (p. 286). This can certainly be interpreted as the mechanism of denial serving to deal with fear.

A Stockholm investigator offers some probable support. Magni (1972) selected three death attitude scales for his conscious death fear measures (Boyar, 1964; Kalish, 1963b; Lester,

1966) and then developed a psychophysical approach to the measurement of nonconscious death fear. The latter consisted of flashing on a screen a death-related picture and a neutral picture, each being displayed for gradually increasing periods of time beginning with an exposure duration too brief for the picture to be recognized and extending in exposure duration until the individual can properly identify the subject matter. Correlations between scores on the various attitude scales and the duration of exposure time required to identify the neutral subject matter all hovered around 0.00. Correlations between the same scales and the exposure duration for recognition of the death-related picture were all negative!! Thus, two measures of the same phenomenon (i.e. death fear) correlated negatively with each other. Even though, technically speaking, only the correlation between the Boyar scale and the response time latency was statistically significant (at the 1 percent level of confidence), the Kalish and Lester scales came within a hair's breadth of showing a significant correlation (i.e., at the 6 percent level of confidence) (Magni, 1972).

Perhaps Magni's findings that consciously expressed fear of death is inversely related to one measure of nonconscious death fear arises from cultural differences or from some idiosyncrasy of his sample (nurses) or his experimental setting or measures. It is too easy, however, to discard inconsistent information on the basis of inadequacy in design or procedures, while accepting the results of comparable studies when these results are consonant with one's theories. The most parsimonious explanation for Magni's data is that denial intensified as fear of death increased, so that the survey responses were actually negatively related to feelings that were less amenable to direct questioning.

Other studies have also found different kinds of relationships between predictor variables and fear of death, depending on the level of consciousness tapped by each measurement. Alexander and Adlerstein (1959, 1960) found higher galvanic skin response and longer response time latencies to death words than to neutral words when each were flashed tachistoscopically on a screen, although verbal responses to direct questions indicated no fears of death in the same population. Subsequent studies by other investigators have confirmed the essential results (e.g., Golding, Atwood, and Goodman, 1966; Williams and Cole, 1968). Unfortunately, none of this work has been done with older persons nor was age even noted as a variable. Research opportunities in this area seem promising.

Denial is certainly a powerful mechanism. Physicians often discuss patients whom they told, directly and clearly, that their condition was terminal, yet learned at a subsequent meeting that their words had not been "heard." Ross (1969) cites denial as the initial reaction of persons just informed that they have a probably terminal prognosis. However, Hinton (1966) described his own interviews with 102 terminally ill patients whom he visited weekly during their hospitalization, then stated that only 8 of these persons were denying their deaths. Hinton and Ross are, of course, describing people at different points in the death trajectory. That denial operates is obvious; the extent to which it operates and how it operates are still unknowns.

THE PROCESS OF DYING

The process of dying obtains its unique qualities because it eventuates in the irreversible state of being dead. The dying process, nonetheless, is a stage in the life of a person, and one of the major tasks of many professionals who study the meaning of death is finding ways to add some enrichment to the remaining life of those who have been defined as terminal.

The *dying trajectory,* as defined by Glaser and Strauss (1968), consists of two properties, that of duration (it takes place over time) and that of shape (it can be charted). The pacing of a dying trajectory may be sudden or slow; it may be fairly regular or erratic. Its shape may signify only a downhill direction or it may go down, then up, then plateau, then down again. Moreover, the dying trajectory as perceived by the dying person himself may not accord with the trajectory as perceived by his caretakers in or out of the health facility (Kalish, 1970).

Probably the major determinant of the dying

trajectory is the nature of the condition from which death is occurring. Dying from lung cancer marks a much different trajectory than dying from a myocardial infarction; the completed suicide off the Golden Gate Bridge may be represented by a chart resembling a rectangle, while the slowly deteriorating elderly woman will show a gradually descending line that reaches the baseline only after covering considerable distance.

The sudden and unexpected death is most often the preferred form of dying, although the elderly consider sudden death and slow death as equally tragic (Kalish and Reynolds, 1976). Those desiring sudden, unexpected death probably wish to avoid physical pain and suffering, as well as the emotional stresses for themselves and their survivors. However, this kind of death can be more brutal for the survivors, since there has been no opportunity for them to prepare, nor does it permit the dead person to get his affairs in order, to try to finish those projects that were important to him, or to participate in the grieving process with those he has loved. In many ways, a sudden and unexpected death has less impact on the survivors of an elderly person, where the rehearsal for death has probably been in process for some time and where preparations for death are more probably made (Lipman and Marden, 1966; Kalish and Reynolds, 1976).

Stages of Dying

The best known set of stages is undoubtedly that proposed by Ross (1969): (1) denial and isolation; (2) anger and resentment; (3) bargaining and an attempt to postpone; (4) depression and sense of loss; (5) acceptance.

The applicability and universality of these five stages are still undetermined. As guidelines for what can occur or as a hypothesis to be verified against a rigorous collection of empirical data, these stages are extremely valuable. Whether they chart a necessary path to "good" dying is debatable; to a large extent, it is a personal rather than a medical or behavioral issue.

There is little question that many dying persons do exhibit denial, anger, bargaining, depression, and (less often) acceptance. Denial

is probably most evident during the early periods of awareness; acceptance is probably most evident during the later periods. However, any of these kinds of behavior may occur at any time during the dying process: the terminally ill do not move through any regular progression, but they move back and forth, sometimes rapidly and sometimes displaying denial and repression or bargaining and acceptance in consecutive moments or even simultaneously, perhaps at different levels of awareness. Also, even the stage of acceptance, which Ross emphasized is not attained by everyone, may subsequently give way to denial or anger. In a later publication, Ross (1974) points out that her stages are not rigidly adhered to: "Most of my patients have exhibited two or three stages simultaneously and these do not always occur in the same order" (pp. 25-26).

Ross's writing and her talks have led to some unexpected outcomes, resulting from the popularity of her ideas among hospital nurses and other health professionals, as well as from her following among the dying themselves and their family members. In effect, her stages are in danger of becoming self-fulfilling prophecies. Some health caretakers have been observed trying to encourage, or even manipulate, their dying patients through Ross's stages; patients occasionally become concerned if they are not progressing adequately, with adequacy also defined in terms of the stages. Ross herself has expressed great concern over these abuses.

Another issue altogether is the moral question as to whether acceptance of death is a proper way to die. Weisman (1972) states that "Acceptance ... is not synonymous with capitulation" (p. 20), in other words, the dying person can accept his imminent death without giving up the life that remains for him. On the other hand, "not going gently into that good night, but raging ... " may well be an equally acceptable way to die for the person doing the dying, if not necessarily for his survivors or the health care professionals. Perhaps "raging" and acceptance are not completely mutually exclusive. And we should never confuse acceptance of death with wishing to die—they are not at all the same phenomenon.

Weisman continues by encouraging the concept of *appropriate death* as the goal for those working with the dying. Such a death means that the person has died in a fashion that resembles as much as possible the way that he wished to die. Although the fact of death is an inevitability, the process of dying (or of living until the moment of death) can be influenced by those in the dying person's social milieu.

The Where of Dying

Most people die in health care institutions, both in the United States (Lerner, 1970) and in England (Cartwright, Hockey, and Anderson, 1973), and by far the greater proportion of these die in general hospitals. Although only about 4 percent of the elderly are in a convalescent care home at any given time, upwards of 20 percent of death certificates stipulate that such a facility had been the residence at the time of death (Kastenbaum and Candy, 1973).

But where do people want to die, i.e., where does an appropriate death take place? And how do their survivors feel? Most people of all ages would prefer to die at home although this was significantly less true for those between 40 and 59 than either younger or older adults (Kalish and Reynolds, 1976). And the majority of the family members of those who did die at home were glad that the death took place where it did; however, the burden on the caretakers was often heavy, and retrospectively one-third of them were either uncertain as to the wisdom of the decision or else felt a hospital would have been preferable (Cartwright, Hockey, and Anderson, 1973).

New options for the dying are now being explored. Already successful in London and recently operative in the United States and Canada in varied forms is the hospice, a facility for patients whose physicians believe they are no longer amenable to restorative medical treatment. St. Christopher's Hospice near London, originally established by Dr. Cicely Saunders, provides excellent human care, necessary medical treatment, unlimited visiting hours, and optimum amelioration of pain for persons whose life expectancy is measured in days or weeks.

The When of Dying

People want to live to an older age than they expect to live (Reynolds and Kalish, 1974) and black Americans are especially eager for a long life; over 65 percent of blacks interviewed wished to live past 90, compared to 25–28 percent of Japanese, Mexican, and Anglo Americans (Reynolds and Kalish, 1974). The desire for a long life, however, does not preclude an awareness that conditions do not always make such longevity desirable. Slightly over half the blacks and Anglos, about half the Japanese, and about one-third of the Mexican Americans favored allowing people to die if they want to. The proportion favoring this position diminished with age. Conditions under which people should be permitted to die were categorized as "dying anyway" (48 percent) and "in pain" (23 percent); the reasons given opposing such an option were based on the right of God alone to take life (48 percent) and the assumption that there is always hope (32 percent).

The parameters of a human life are now being reevaluated, both by the health professionals and by the community as a whole. Although investigators have studied beliefs as to when life begins (e.g., Knutson, 1967) and when life ends (e.g., Kalish, 1966), the problem is less amenable to medical answers than to the religious, social, and political pressures existing in society.

For centuries, physicians and others have agreed with Galen that the cessation of heart activity marked the moment of death, although there have always been some who contended that, biologically speaking, no such "moment" existed (Ackerknecht, 1968). Nonetheless, the vast majority assumed that being dead was a readily observable phenomenon. With modern medical methods, the vast majority of deaths can be easily diagnosed with complete certainty.

But a new element has been introduced. Heart activity and respiration can be continued mechanically in comatose persons who come to exist only at the discretion of the individual who controls the machine's switch. Mechanical devices may soon be available that will be capable of maintaining heart activity indefinitely. Although extremely few individuals are affected, those few present a matter of great concern in and of themselves; the future potential of these contrivances suggests that many others may soon be similarly affected.

The key issue becomes the conflict between the death of the brain and nervous system and the death of the heart or respiratory system. An Ad Hoc Committee of the Harvard Medical School has proposed new criteria for death that they specify as (1) unreceptivity and unresponsivity, (2) no movements or breathing, and (3) no reflexes, all of which can be confirmed by (4) a flat electroencephalogram (Cassell, Kass, and Associates, 1972). These criteria have been incorporated into law in some states. They do not, however, define the status of the patient who retains the vital functions but lacks higher brain function, i.e., where there has been death of the forebrain (Morrison, 1973).

Physical death itself is not an all-or-none event. Neither the body nor the self dies all at once. Certain organs may continue to function even after clinical death is declared. "Psychological death" has been applied to the cessation of cognitive functioning, presumably irreversible; "social death" takes place when the individual is perceived as dead or "as good as dead" by those in his environment. Conversely, a person may be biologically or clinically dead, yet still be talked to or related to by the survivors as though life continued, so that he remains socially alive while being clinically or psychologically dead (Glaser and Strauss, 1965; Kalish, 1968).

In addition to the question of maintaining existence after the irreversible cessation of brain function, the issue of how long to continue life when the future is filled with pain and suffering based on an irreversible condition also needs to be considered. The alternatives are three-fold: (1) to use all possible means to keep the patient alive; (2) to eliminate extraordinary or heroic measures, but to continue normal medical procedures; and (3) to permit steps that will accelerate the downhill trajectory and eventual death (Morrison, 1971). Such decisions have often been made by the physician, sometimes in concert with family members and, less often, with input from the dying person himself. Elderly residents of a Veterans' Home were asked their preference among situations comparable to these three alternatives, given the conditions that they would be fatally ill, in great distress, and under heavy medical expense. Nearly half wished that the physicians try to keep them alive; about one-fourth accepted elimination of heroic methods, but rejected any attempt to speed the downhill trajectory; and the rest were open to both elimination of extraordinary methods and the possibility of speeding up the dying process (Preston and Williams, 1971).

Some dying patients, because they are very old or extremely deteriorated, do not receive heroic methods. They are seen as having "earned their deaths . . . " (Glaser and Strauss, 1968, p. 60). These individuals are often beyond the point at which they could have meaningful input into the decision-making process. Recently the use of a "living will" has been suggested so that the patient's wishes can be better represented. A living will is a document completed by an individual in control of his cognitive capacities that stipulates the conditions under which he would oppose the use of extraordinary measures or would prefer to be permitted to die. The document has no legal force, although some state legislatures have initiated proposals to make these legally binding. One drawback, of course, is that a person facing imminent death may feel quite differently about his desires for heroic methods than he had anticipated when his death appeared much farther removed in time, yet his condition may well preclude any opportunity to alter his living will.

Many elderly have asked their family members or their physicians to permit them to die rather than to suffer the pain and ignominies that can accompany terminality. Nonetheless, any decision that curtails the life potential of a given individual is filled with significant social hazards. Even the living will may be filled out in order to ease the burden on the eventual survivors, rather than in response to the more basic feelings of the person. Many elderly are so sensitive to their potential drain of family resources, both financial and personal, that they might request to die rather than ask for the help they need to live a while longer.

SOCIAL AND PSYCHOLOGICAL ASPECTS OF CARING FOR THE DYING

Before any consideration is given to letting someone die more quickly than is medically necessary, a careful evaluation should be made of the person's inner resources and of the care he is receiving. The wish to die is frequently the wish to avoid the emotional and physical pain of continuing to live through what is to come. It might be valuable to develop a concept parallel to that of heroic methods in medicine, i.e., heroic methods in providing social and emotional support. Weisman (1972) contends that fears of abandonment, humiliation, and loneliness are among the most powerful forces motivating the dying; this certainly coincides with Becker's (1973) assumptions about death anxiety arising from fear of helplessness and vulnerability.

Three factors have been suggested as paramount in enabling people to die an appropriate death: (1) a warm and intimate personal relationship, preferably with a family member or friend, but if necessary with a health caretaker; (2) an open awareness context, in which the dying person and the important people of his social environment are aware of the prognosis and can relate to each other in terms of the terminal condition; (3) a belief system that provides for meaning. These three circumstances can be integrated with each other to provide a sense of transcendence that permits the dying person to retain self-esteem and the belief that his past, his future, however brief, and his life in toto had significant meaning and that this meaning extends beyond his short existence on earth (Augustine and Kalish, 1975).

Following these comments to their logical conclusion suggests that good care of the dying includes seeing that close intimate relationships be maintained or, if lacking, established. It is difficult, sometimes impossible, to have such relationships with a dying person unless the topic of death can be openly discussed (ignoring death in these circumstances is like ignoring the horse eating the daisies in the dining room). Patients who talk about death and dying do not necessarily wish or need to dwell on what it is going to be like. What they often need is to share their feelings about what their final months, days, or hours will be like.

The pros and cons of open awareness have been carefully outlined by Glaser and Strauss (1965) and subsequently by Share (1972), who labels the alternatives as the Open Approach and the Protective Approach. The elderly appear more favorable to the Protective Approach, while nonelderly favor the Open Approach; among all age groups, however, people are more likely to feel that they themselves could be told than they are that others should be told (Christ, 1961; Kalish and Reynolds, 1976). Weisman (1972) again says it cogently: " ... to be informed about a diagnosis, especially a serious diagnosis, is to be fortified, not undermined" (p. 17).

Psychotherapy with the Dying

Providing the dying with psychotherapy is an idea whose time has come. Up until very recently, psychotherapists preferred working with people who might be able to return to a more productive life, an attitude that they shared with physicians and other health caretakers. A change seems to have occurred recently, and some mental health professionals, as well as a small but increasing number of students and others, are seeking roles as counselors to the dying.

Well over a decade ago, LeShan (LeShan and Gassman, 1958; LeShan, 1969) reported on his psychotherapeutic relationships with terminal cancer patients. He attempted to mobilize the will to live, since he found the fear of death an inadequate motive for successful therapy. Rather than trying to prepare his patients for death (they all died within a year or so after completion of the project), he focused on the availability of their own resources so that they could live out their remaining months as richly as their disease permitted.

Becker (1973), while emphasizing the immense rewards that psychotherapy can provide, cautions against expecting too much when used with the dying. New insights may be felt as arriving too late, and the dangers of intellectualization can be even greater with the dying, for whom the time to overcome their self-protectiveness is not sufficient. Becker, consistent with his other views, encourages the fusion of psychotherapy with a religious belief system. LeShan contends that the patient must overcome his despair, which reflects negative views of himself, views that are not newly obtained but that are made worse through the ravages and isolation caused by illness. Both emphasize the importance of the therapist in enabling the individual to work through his denial and despair.

The relationship of altered states of consciousness to psychotherapeutic processes with the dying has been discussed recently, aiming to shed light on both processes and to improve the effectiveness of the therapy. Fisher (1970) expresses this well: "When an individual is not allowed to work out interpersonal conflicts before his death, he experiences his days of dying as burdensome, is often guilt-ridden and resentful, and suffers terrible loneliness. As a result of his altered states of consciousness, he very often experiences new insights into his relationships and he wishes to share them with his significant others. Often these insights are laden with conflict resolution, and when he is unable to share this knowledge with his loved ones, he experiences sadness" (p. 4). And later: "One of the very significant results of his having experienced a transcendental state of consciousness is his willingness to engage in the life process. No longer is death an excuse for not living" (p. 5).

Pahnke and his associates (e.g., Pahnke, 1969; Pahnke and Richards, 1966; Richards, Grof, Goodman, and Kurland, 1972) have moved farther into the realm of mystical experience by exploring the use of LSD in providing psychotherapy for the dying, permitting the patient to experience transcendence himself. They observed that the effects of their techniques seemed to produce dramatic change, with the altered state experience permitting the patient to perceive death as a transition, rather than as an ultimate cessation, opening up the possibility of continued consciousness. No data are available regarding the age distribution of dying persons who have their states of consciousness altered, but some of the cases described by clinicians are older persons.

Other Interventions with the Dying

Medical and psychological interventions in the dying process are only two general ways of altering the trajectory. There are many others:

(1) Voodoo death. Initially applied to the Haitian use of magical rites to cause death, this concept has been expanded to include such phenomena as death caused by induced helplessness. Richter (1957) observed this process in rats and drew parallels with human behavior.

Hinton (1972) discusses well-authenticated instances in which sudden death resulted from an abrupt shock. "These tragedies are probably due to the heart stopping from a catastrophic over-action of the autonomic nervous system. Whether the emotional aspect of shock plays a causal role in such events, or the vital sequence is mediated through nervous reflexes with or without some parallel emotion, is hard to say" (p. 91).

(2) Relocation. Several studies have indicated that relocating the elderly, especially the very old and confused, may accelerate the dying trajectory, although certain personality types seem to be predictive of better adjustment than others (Aldrich, 1964; Turner, Tobin, and Lieberman, 1972). Whether this results from increased stress or from other factors is not fully known.

(3) Will-to-live. The extent to which people can intervene in their own dying trajectory is far from understood. In an attempt to document the will-to-live, Phillips & Feldman (1973) systematically looked at dates of death in relationship to birthdates and important holidays. They found that significantly more people died shortly after these occasions than died in the equivalent period prior to the date. Certainly, one interpretation of these results is that a will-to-live was operative. Conversely, the will-to-die is often described by workers in longterm care facilities and elsewhere, following the death of an elderly resident subsequent to some particularly depressing event. The words are often said: "After that happened, he just turned his face to the wall and died."

ENCOUNTERING THE DEATH OF OTHERS

Whether or not we can conceive of our own deaths, we can certainly conceive of the deaths of others. Except for very young children, such deaths are very real events in the lives of everyone. These deaths are encountered at the personal level, through family members, friends, and neighbors, or through the deaths of those whose loss is significant, e.g., a political figure, a famous entertainer or athlete, a professional confrere. Death is encountered at the impersonal level, through statistics on wartime casualties, the rampages of a mass murderer, a flood or earthquake or other disaster. For obvious reasons, deaths are much more likely to occur to friends, relatives, and acquaintances of the elderly than of young or middle-aged persons.

Before the Death

Physicians sometimes discuss a terminal diagnosis with family members prior to any explanation to the dying person himself. They may also use this occasion to enlist the support of the family in following an appropriate medical regimen that may be very demanding of their energies, emotions, and finances. From this discussion may come decisions regarding how much information the patient will receive concerning his terminal diagnosis. If the decision is reached during this time to let the patient know his prognosis, further discussion may ensue as to who will tell him and how he will be informed; conversely, if the decision is made that the dying person should not be informed, the role of the family in this deception may also be discussed. In other instances, the terminal prognosis is presented to the patient first, who in turn discusses it with his family.

As the survivors-to-be of the dying person come to understand the implications of the prognosis, they often begin the process of anticipatory grieving (Lindemann, 1944). If the dying trajectory is lengthy, with a slow downhill trend, the survivors may have worked through many of their feelings regarding the loss prior to the actual death. Social death (see earlier) can occur, and they may even show irritation that clinical death is taking so long. When the clinical death finally does occur, it may be met with more relief than grief. Health caretakers and other friends and relatives may perceive this as unfeeling or callous behavior, not realizing how painful the anticipatory grief process actually was (Fulton and Fulton, 1971).

When a sudden, unexpected death occurs, there is no opportunity for anticipatory grieving, and the survivors must cope with the real-ity of the death immediately. Denial can only be shortlived, if it occurs at all. Pine (1972) points out that survivors tend to create their own history of the death, enabling them to make the death more comprehensible and, perhaps, to provide some of the facilitation of anticipatory grief. Thus people discuss the events that led up to the death, the feelings that they had about the dying person, their involvements with him prior to his death.

The intensity of anticipatory grieving is a function of the relationship between the dying person and each of the survivors-to-be. To some extent, it reflects the history of the relationship, but it also reflects what the forthcoming loss will mean to the survivors. A middle-aged woman is about to suffer the loss of an elderly father, to whom she had been extremely close. The father's death will remove an important person from her life, but it will not disrupt her day-to-day existence in the same way her husband's death would, even though tensions in the marriage have caused her to wonder about a separation.

Blauner (1966) states, "The disruptive impact of a death is greater to the extent that its consequences spill over onto the larger social territory and affect large numbers of people" (p. 534). The same is true of the period prior to the actual death. More to the present point, Blauner's sociological construct can be applied in the psychological field. To paraphrase: The disruptive impact of a death on a given surviving individual is greater to the extent that its consequences spill over into more roles of his life and affect larger numbers of behaviors and activities.

There are no rituals or ceremonies for the dying person in Western society, unless the "last" rites of the Catholic Church are considered as such, but even this brief ritual is primarily a sacrament for the sick rather than a rite for the dying. The death vigil occasionally occurs, but with most deaths occurring in institutions, these are not common, although some ethnic groups, e.g., Mexican Americans, still attempt to see that some family member remains with the dying person. It is easy to see why the death vigil is not popular among health caretakers: just visualize a room of four or more very sick persons, one of whom will probably die in a matter of a few days, and seven or eight not-always-silent mourners surrounding the bed of that dying person. Clearly the needs of institutional management clash with the needs of the dying person and his family members; it is not difficult to determine who has the greatest amount of power.

At the Time of Death

Even the diagnosis of death occurs in a social setting and is affected by age-related social values. Older people in the hospital ward or emergency room, according to Sudnow (1967), are less likely to receive as thorough a medical examination, should they seem for all intents and purposes dead, than younger people. Others whom the medical staff will more quickly judge as dead or beyond hope are "the suicide victim, the dope addict, the known prostitute, the assailant in a crime of violence, the vagrant, the known wife-beater, and generally, those persons whose moral characters are considered reproachable" (p. 105). Welu's (1972) observations in hospital emergency rooms provide independent support.

Nothing has been written as to how death is communicated to the family when it takes

Length of time following a death before it is "all right" to:

| | AGE | | |
	20–39	40–59	60+
Remarry:			
Unimportant to wait	23%	28%	20%
One week to six months	11%	9%	10%
One year to five years	54%	53%	37%
Five years or more	12%	11%	34%
Return to work:			
Unimportant to wait	29%	38%	33%
One day to one week	37%	37%	29%
One month to one year	24%	19%	24%
More than one year	11%	7%	14%
To start going out with other men/women:			
Unimportant to wait	19%	25%	23%
One week to one month	10%	8%	7%
Six months to five years	56%	53%	42%
More than five years	15%	14%	29%

Figure 2. Preferred mourning practices expressed by 434 residents of Los Angeles County for others of their own age, ethnicity, and sex. (From Kalish and Reynolds, 1976.)

place at home, except that one or two people tend to accept responsibility for informing others, and someone will usually emerge to begin to make arrangements for funeral and burial. In the hospital setting, the best description is provided by Sudnow (1967) who states that a typical interaction would include the following:

(1) The relative is informed in a quiet, subdued voice by the physician who is standing close to him; the information will be given without much preface.

(2) "While the informed relative is actively engaged in crying . . . . the doctor maintains as passive a stance as the fact of his presence will allow. He looks away, or downwardly, and says nothing" (Sudnow, 1967, p. 141). He does not shuffle papers or smoke or behave in any way that might seem unduly casual.

(3) Although the physician seldom offers further sympathy in any overt fashion, he remains in the room, silently, as a sign of support. He does not respond to bursts of anger, disbelief, or self-pity, since such comments are usually not addressed to anyone in particular.

(4) When the relative ceases crying, often due to his own embarrassment with the display of emotion, he will initiate additional conversation with the physician. The topics often include the cause of death, whether pain was involved, whether it might have been prevented, and—depending on hospital procedures and the determination of the physician—autopsy permission.

(5) The relative usually initiates leaving, although the physician sometimes provides the cue that the interview should end. They part.

After the Death: The Individual Survivor

Many kinds of physiological changes accompany grief, although there is no single pattern that is universally observed. Averill (1968) evaluates claims that (1) physiological activity diminishes during grief and (2) grief is a catabolic state; he concludes that the evidence is too meager and inconsistent on both issues to take a firm position. Lindemann (1944) describes the characteristics of a person suffering acute grief (Averill did not limit himself to that stage) as including "sensations of somatic distress occurring in waves lasting from twenty minutes to an hour at a time, a feeling of tightness in the throat, choking with shortness of breath, need for sighing, an empty feeling in the abdomen, lack of muscular power, and an intense subjective distress described as tension or mental pain" (p. 187). In addition, he found changes in respiration, especially when the person was discussing his grief, and in physical strength and digestion. These, it must be emphasized, are normal grief reactions.

The behavioral responses to loss are also numerous:

—anger, often accompanied by expressions of blame directed against others who might or might not have had any objective role in the death, e.g., physicians and other health caretakers, God, another member of the family;

—guilt, based on real or fantasized responsibility for the death or on real or fantasized inadequacies in the course of the relationship, increased by the realization that it is too late to make amends;

—depression, described by Parkes (1972) as being episodic and acute rather then chronic and prolonged;

—anxiety and restlessness, inability to sit still, but all accomplished without zest; (Parkes, 1972, mentions that 18 out of 22 nonelderly widows reported restlessness and increased muscular tension during the first month following their loss);

—preoccupation with the image of the deceased, often so vivid and so real and immediate that those suffering recent losses frequently feel they have encountered the dead person in reality, while simultaneously knowing it is "impossible" (Kalish and Reynolds, 1976; Lindemann, 1944; Parkes, 1972).

Lindemann (1944) also refers to the tendency on the part of some recently bereaved persons to take on the characteristics of the deceased, by emulating his walk or mannerisms, adopting the views of the deceased, making career choices to coincide with the vocation of the dead person. This might be interpreted as an attempt to deny the loss by identifying the dead person as oneself.

Averill (1968) postulates that grief has survival value in an evolutionary sense, by bringing the protection of the group to serve the needs of the bereaved, without which the vulnerability of the grieving person would be far greater. The grieving person often initiates behavior that can be seen as a search for a lost person (Parkes, 1970), but whether this is adaptive as Averill seems to imply, or not, seems very ambiguous.

Parkes (1970) has identified four phases of grief: (1) numbness, during which the loss is partially disregarded; (2) yearning, during which the desire to recover the lost object is paramount and leads to searching behavior; (3) disorganization and despair, when the permanence of the loss is accepted and searching ceases; (4) reorganization of behavior. These are, of course, descriptive trends and not rigidly defined and exclusive stages.

A modest body of literature has developed, discussing what happens as surviving spouses are socialized to their roles as widows and widowers. These have been reviewed by Berardo (1968, 1970): a recent and extremely comprehensive study by Lopata (1973) has added considerably to the available sources of information.

After the Death: The Social Structure

The death of an individual tears the fabric of society and leaves some holes in it. If the dead person is elderly, the impact of his death on the social structure is likely to be considerably less than that of a younger person. When the death removes from society a person with family or work or significant community responsibilities, his roles need to be filled in some fashion. Another worker must be recruited and trained; the tasks of the parent must be given to another person or distributed among several people.

Also, there is some evidence that death in one generation can also affect the next generation. Those who suffered the loss of a parent through death in their childhood seem more disposed to emotional difficulties in their own adult years (e.g. Hilgard and Newman, 1959; Hill, 1972). Although the loss of a parent through divorce seems much more frequent today than the loss through death, both situations leave the children (and often the surviving spouse) with feelings of having been abandoned. Child care can become a problem. At the other end of the age spectrum, the removal of a spouse through death may leave an elderly survivor feeling extremely vulnerable to what seems to become a more hostile society.

When a death does occur, "...the newly bereaved person is often treated by society in much the same way as a sick person. Employers expect him to miss work, he stays at home, and relatives visit and talk in hushed tones. For a time, others take over responsibility for making decisions and acting on his behalf" (Parkes, 1972, p. 5). The suggestion that the bereaved person is like a sick person can be carried beyond the perception of his role by others. People who have suffered a recent loss of a loved one show a higher level of both morbidity and mortality than actuarially predicted (e.g., Maddison and Viola, 1968; Parkes, 1972). These figures may result from a combination of the psychological stress produced by the period preceding the death and the impact of the loss itself, and the physical stress induced by the caretaking process that often leads to inadequate sleep, lack of exercise, and poor eating habits. Interestingly enough, only non-elderly people are found to have rising illness and death rates following a loss; the elderly appear unaffected (Rees and Lutkins, 1967). It needs to be added, however, that Clayton (1973) is sharply critical of the interpretations of these studies. While recognizing that physician visits and the prescribing of tranquilizers and sedatives sharply increase after bereavement, she feels that little if anything definitive can be stated beyond that.

Clayton and her associates are conducting studies with a randomly selected panel of widows and widowers, whom they are following longitudinally. They have found that those who could effectively be diagnosed as depressed 1 month after the loss were very likely to be depressed 12 months later. Also, those who were depressed described themselves as more irritable, had more difficulty in accepting the fact of death, were more angry about the death, and displayed many more symptoms of poor physical health, when these were mea-sured about one year later (Bornstein, Clayton, Halikas, Maurice, and Robins, 1973).

Women who have lost husbands, especially during their later years, are likely to find a sufficiently large community of other widows that they are not left without options for friends and companions. Nonetheless, there are numerous factors that prevent adequate establishment of good relationships, at least for many, and certainly the potential companionship of men is limited. Widows suffer from loss, stigma, and deprivation. The loss leads to grief; the stigma leads to altered self-concept and isolation; the deprivation leads to loneliness (Parkes, 1972).

A number of programs have been established specifically for widows, many based on the widow-to-widow program, first begun in Boston. This program trains women who have been widowed to serve as out-reach workers for those more recently widowed (Silverman, 1969, 1970). It attempts to ameliorate the loneliness and isolation of widows, while simultaneously hoping to enable them to do their necessary grieving in an emotionally healthy fashion.

Rituals and Ceremonies to Aid the Bereaved

Wakes, black attire and armbands, funerals, cemetery processings, "sitting shiva," these are just a few of the many rituals and ceremonies that serve the dual role of providing a rite of passage for the dead and serving the psychological needs of the living. Arguments over the efficacy of funerals, over open casket versus closed casket, over burial versus cremation are well-known (see, for example, Harmer, 1971; Raether, 1971). Some form of ceremony,

	AGE		
	20–39	40–59	60+
Relative, family member	58%	58%	37%
Priest, minister, God	19%	24%	48%
Friend	11%	11%	7%
Other, including physician	2%	1%	1%

Figure 3. Individual named by 434 residents of Los Angeles County as person they would be most likely to turn to for comfort following a significant death. (From Kalish and Reynolds, 1976.)

preferably a ceremony individualized for the family, will presumably offer a meaningful way of coping with the initial grief; it seems to help make the death more real, to reduce the "search for the lost object." Research evidence, unfortunately, is lacking. It has also been argued that funeral directors, like physicians and nurses, receive part of their abuse because of the guilt of the survivors for behavior committed and uncommitted. Displacing the guilt one feels for having neglected the dead person onto the physician or nurse for real or imagined neglect or onto the funeral director for his business practices may be a temporarily effective way to assuage these feelings of guilt. At the same time, some of the complaints concerning business practices in the health professions and the funeral industry are undoubtedly warranted.

One major function of the funeral and related rituals is to provide the support of the extended family and the community for those who have suffered the loss. In the early stages of dealing with such loss, the bereaved are not as capable of effective functioning, and they require the resources given by others so that they can deal with the shock, distress, depression, and other feelings engendered by the severance of ties. "The wake and the funeral reaffirm the group identity of the survivors, often with the help of the religious collective representations extending all members into afterlife" (Lopata, 1973, p. 53). Lopata voices much the same sentiment as Becker (see earlier) in describing the need of the survivors to develop some sense of transcendence or transcendent meaning both for their loved one and for themselves. The sharing of ritual and of food and drink is an affirmation of family and community ties at a time of stress.

The graveyard is also part of this ritual, serving simultaneously the sacred function of providing appropriate symbols of continuity for the deceased, in the context of religious belief, and the secular function of disposing of the corpse which becomes a public health problem (Warner, 1959). Whether the method of disposal is land burial, water burial, or cremation, both sacred and secular functions are found. When the body no longer exists,

as occurs in some wartime deaths or in airplane or boat accidents or drownings, some symbolic alternative is often utilized.

There seems little doubt that traditional death-related rituals are in a state of transition today. Many people now request that charitable donations be made in lieu of sending flowers; others desire cremation, with the ashes sprinkled over a mountain or in the ocean, instead of land burial. Neither money donations (which have long been used in many cultures and American subcultures to help the survivors get through what is often a period of acute financial crisis) nor sprinkling of ashes suggest a secularization of death. Rather, they point to the development of new kinds of sacred rituals.

SOME FUTURE PRIORITIES

Each section of this presentation opens up extensive possibilities for both research and programs, with the potential for the research to aid in the development and improvement of programs and the programs to provide new insights and new hypotheses for additional research. Specific research priorities are extremely difficult to establish, but some general areas of major concern can be outlined.

First, research methodologies require greater consideration. By now we should have progressed beyond asking someone if he is afraid of dying as a measure of fear of death; we should no longer be assuming that simple agreement to a direct question asking whether one believes in God is a sufficient measure of religiousness. Innovative measures and methods have been developed, e.g., the psychological autopsy (Weisman and Kastenbaum, 1969), physiological reactions to death-related stimuli (e.g., Garfield, 1974; Golding, Atwood, and Goodman, 1966), the relationship of death dates to birth dates (Phillips and Feldman, 1973). Additional efforts in this direction are necessary.

Second, at the same time, a more effective use of traditional methodologies can be encouraged. Depth interviews, projective techniques, and naturalistic observations can be used more fruitfully and more rigorously.

Third, some of the clichés of the field require testing. They may indeed be valid, but workers with the dying and the bereaved are already developing their own mystique that is in need of critical evaluation. Therefore, we need research to consider Ross's stages in a more empirical and controlled fashion; to investigate the kinds of impact various physician approaches to informing a person of terminality have on the dying person; to study much more closely and critically the meaning of the various awareness contexts (Glaser and Strauss, 1965); to evaluate the significance for a dying person of perceiving transcendent meaning in his own existence; to know much more about those factors that permit appropriate recuperation of the bereaved after serious loss.

Fourth, more attention should be paid to individual differences. That is, although most people appear to wish to know if their diagnosis is terminal, some people do not; although open awareness contexts may indeed be found, as is now normally assumed, more adaptive than mutual pretense, the latter may be more effective for some persons; although most dying persons very likely do wish a close personal relationship, some may very well prefer to remain alone. Present research has approached these principles too globally. It would be a worthwhile effort to look at correlates of individual differences and to try to understand these differences.

Fifth, these individual differences may be a partial function of subcultural and role identification. Therefore, we should attend to the potential influence of ethnoracial, sex, family status, religious, regional, nationality, social class, linguistic, and other bases for explaining individual differences.

Sixth, the effects of the many newly-established programs should be carefully scrutinized, both in order to make them more significant in the lives of persons being helped and in order to add new knowledge for all concerned. At the same time, there is a great need to monitor traditional ways of caring for the dying, to see how they functioned, where they succeeded and failed. For example, the familiar criticism of the medical profession for inadequately caring for the dying and for the survivors needs to be tested by sound research and to be supplemented by the description of new options.

All six of these global priorities require special attention to age as a variable and the elderly as a group (or, preferably, to intragroup variability within the group categorized as elderly). The older person who is dying, who has suffered a loss, or who is concerned with finitude may not always respond in the same fashion as a comparable younger person. Methodologies in both basic and applied research need to consider age differences. Further, age and personality differences interact, so that a social value or a personality quality that might cause a young person to perceive death in one fashion would cause an elderly person to see death quite differently. In the same context, age and subcultural variation also interact in ways that need investigation.

The accomplishments of the past two decades have been considerable, most noteworthy probably being breaking through the taboo surrounding death. Fairly sophisticated attitude scales have been developed, and some additional measures have been tried out. More people are now cognizant of death and dying as worthy of attention, a fact that in itself adds valued informants and increases professional and lay sympathies for relevant research. A modest body of information and a substantial body of opinion and exhortation are now in print.

Research on death has moved out of its infancy, but has barely attained "toddler" stage. Many articles depend more on opinion and unorganized observations than on rigorous quantitative *or* qualitative research. Nonetheless, enough of the issues have been defined and enough preliminary theorizing, description, and research have been accomplished that the topic is ready for more sophisticated investigation. This would seem to offer special opportunities to gerontologists who operate in a realm where death and dying are constantly visible on the near horizon.

REFERENCES

Ackerknecht, E. 1968. Death in the history of medicine. *Bull. Hist. Med.*, **42**, 19–23.

Aldrich, C. K. 1964. Personality factors and mortality in the relocation of the aged. *Gerontologist*, 4, 92-93.

Alexander, I. E. 1959. Death and religion. *In*, H. Feifel (ed.), *The Meaning of Death*, pp. 271-283. New York: McGraw-Hill.

Alexander, I.E., and Adlerstein, A. M. 1960. Studies in the psychology of death. *In*, H. P. David and J. C. Brengelmann (eds.), *Perspectives in Personality Research*, pp. 65-92. New York: Springer.

Augustine, M. J., and Kalish, R. A. 1975. Religion, transcendence, and appropriate death. *Journal of Transpersonal Psychology*, 7, 1-13.

Averill, J. R. 1968. Grief: Its nature and significance. *Psychological Bulletin*, 6, 721-748.

Back, K. 1965. Cited in R. Kastenbaum. 1966. Meaning of time in later life. *Journal of Genetic Psychology*, 109, 9-25.

Becker, E. 1973. *The Denial of Death*. New York: The Free Press.

Berardo, F. M. 1968. Widowhood status in the United States: Perspectives on a neglected aspect of the family life cycle. *Family Coordinator*, 17, 191-203.

Berardo, F. M. 1970. Survivorship and social isolation: The case of the aged widower. *Family Coordinator*, 19, 11-25.

Blauner, R. 1966. Death and social structure. *Psychiatry*, 29, 378-394. Reprint. 1968. *In*, B. Neugarten (ed.), *Middle Age and Aging*, pp. 531-540. Chicago: University of Chicago Press.

Bornstein, P. E., Clayton, P. J., Halikas, J. A., Maurice, W. L., and Robins, E. 1973. The depression of widowhood after thirteen months. *British Journal of Psychiatry*, 122, 561-566.

Boyar, J. I. 1964. The construction and partial validation of a scale for the measurement of the fear of death. *Dissertation Abstr.*, 25, 2041.

Cameron, P., Stewart, L., and Biber, H. 1973. Consciousness of death across the life-span. *J. Geront.*, 28, 92-95.

Cartwright, A., Hockey, L., and Anderson, J. L. 1973. *Life Before Death*. London: Routledge & Kegan Paul.

Cassell, E., Kass, L. R., and Associates. 1972. Refinements in criteria for the determination of death: An appraisal. *J. Am. Med. Assoc.*, 221, 48-54.

Christ, A. E. 1961. Attitudes toward death among a group of acute geriatric psychiatric patients. *J. Geront.*, 16, 56-59.

Clayton, P. J. 1973. The clinical morbidity of the first year of bereavement: A review. *Comprehensive Psychiatry*, 14, 151-157.

Dickstein, L. S. 1972. Death concern: Measurement and correlates. *Psychological Reports*, 30, 563-571.

Diggory, J. C., and Rothman, D. Z. 1961. Values destroyed by death. *Journal of Abnormal and Social Psychology*, 30, 11-17.

Dublin, L. L. 1965. *Factbook on Man*. New York: Macmillan.

Feifel, H., and Branscomb, A. B. 1973. Who's afraid of death? *Journal of Abnormal Psychology*, 81, 282-288.

Feifel, H., and Jones, R. 1968. Perception of death as related to nearness to death. *Proceedings of the 76th Annual Convention of the American Psychological Association*, 3, 545-546.

Fisher, G. 1970. Psychotherapy for the dying: Principles and illustrative cases with special references to the use of LSD. *Omega*, 1, 3-15.

Freud, S. 1948. (Originally published, 1915). Thoughts for the times on war and death. *In*, S. Freud, *Collected Papers*, Volume 4, pp. 288-317. London: The Hogarth Press.

Fulton, R., and Fulton, J. 1971. A psychosocial aspect of terminal care: Anticipatory grief. *Omega*, 2, 91-100.

Garfield, C. A. 1974. Psychothanatological concomitants of altered state experience: An investigation of the relationship between consciousness alteration and fear of death. Doctoral dissertation. University of California, Berkeley. Department of Psychology.

Geer, J. H. 1965. The development of a scale to measure fear. *Behavior Research and Therapy*, 3, 45-53.

Glaser, B. G. 1966. The social loss of aged dying patients. *Gerontologist*, 6, 77-80.

Glaser, B. G., and Strauss, A. L. 1965. *Awareness of Dying*. Chicago: Aldine.

Glaser, B. G., and Strauss, A. L. 1968. *Time for Dying*. Chicago: Aldine.

Golding, S. L., Atwood, G. E., and Goodman, R. A. 1966. Anxiety and the two cognitive forms of resistance to the idea of death. *Psychological Reports*, 18, 359-364.

Gorer, G. 1967. *Death, Grief, and Mourning*. New York: Doubleday, Anchor Books.

Harmer, R. M. 1971. Funerals, fantasy, and flight. *Omega*, 2, 127-135, 150-154.

Havighurst, R. J., Neugarten, B. L., and Tobin, S. S. 1968. Disengagement and patterns of aging. *In*, B. Neugarten (ed.), *Middle Age and Aging*, pp. 161-172. Chicago: University of Chicago Press.

Hilgard, J. R., and Newman, M. F. 1959. Anniversaries in mental illness. *Psychiatry*, 22, 113-121.

Hill, O. W. 1972. Childhood bereavement and adult psychiatric disturbances. *J. Psychosomatic Res.*, 16, 357-360.

Hinton, J. M. 1966. Facing death. *J. Psychosomatic Res.*, 10, 22-28.

Hinton, J. M. 1972. *Death.* 2nd ed. Baltimore: Penguin Books.

Jeffers, F. C., Nichols, C. R., and Eisdorfer, C. 1961. Attitudes of older persons toward death: A preliminary study. *J. Geront.*, 16, 53-56.

Jung, C. G. 1959. (Originally published, 1934). The soul and death. *In*, H. Feifel (ed.), *The Meaning of Death*, pp. 3-15. New York: McGraw-Hill.

Kalish, R. A. 1963a. An approach to the study of death attitudes. *American Behavioral Scientist*, 6, 68-80.

Kalish, R. A. 1963b. Some variables in death attitudes. *Journal of Social Psychology*, 59, 137–145.

Kalish, R. A. 1966. A continuum of subjectively perceived death. *Gerontologist*, 6, 73–76.

Kalish, R. A. 1968. Life and death: Dividing the indivisible. *Social Science and Medicine*, 2, 249–259.

Kalish, R. A. 1970. The onset of the dying process. *Omega*, 1, 57–69.

Kalish, R. A. 1971. Sex and marital role differences in anticipation of age-produced dependency. *Journal of Genetic Psychology*, 119, 53–62.

Kalish, R. A. 1972. Of social values and the dying: A defense of disengagement. *Family Coordinator*, 21, 81–94.

Kalish, R. A., and Johnson, A. I. 1972. Value similarities and differences in three generations of women. *J. Marriage & Fam.*, 34, 49–54.

Kalish, R. A., and Reynolds, D. K. 1976. *Death and Ethnicity: A Psychocultural Study*. Los Angeles: University of Southern California Press.

Kass, L. R. 1971. Death as an event: A commentary on Robert Morison. *Science*, 173, 698–702.

Kastenbaum, R. 1966a. As the clock runs out. *Mental Hygiene*, 50, 332–336.

Kastenbaum, R. 1966b. On the meaning of time in later life. *Journal of Genetic Psychology*, 109, 9–25.

Kastenbaum, R. 1969. Death and bereavement in later life. *In*, A. H. Kutscher (ed.), *Death and Bereavement*, pp. 28–54. Springfield, Illinois: Charles C. Thomas.

Kastenbaum, R., and Candy, S. E. 1973. The 4% fallacy: A methodological and empirical critique of extended care facility population statistics. *Aging and Human Development*, 4, 15–22.

Kimsey, L. R., Roberts, J. L., and Logan, D. L. 1972. Death, dying and denial in the aged. *Am. J. Psychiat.*, 129, 161–166.

Knutson, A. L. 1967. The definition and value of a new human life. *Social Science and Medicine*, 1, 7–29.

Kogan, N., and Wallach, M. 1961. Age changes in values and attitudes. *J. Geront.*, 16, 272–280.

Lerner, M. 1970. When, why, and where people die. *In*, O. G. Brim, Jr., H. E. Freeman, S. Levine, and N. A. Scotch (eds.), *The Dying Patient*, pp. 5–29. New York: Russell Sage Foundation.

LeShan, L. 1969. Mobilizing the life force. *Ann. N.Y. Acad. Sci.*, 164, 847–861.

LeShan, L. and Gassman, M. 1958. Some observations on psychotherapy with patients suffering from neoplastic disease. *American Journal of Psychotherapy*, 12, 723–734.

Lester, D. 1966. A scale measuring attitudes toward death: Its consistency, validity, and use. Unpublished manuscript.

Lindemann, E. 1944. Symptomatology and management of acute grief. *Am. J. Psychiat.*, 101, 141–148. Reprint. 1965. *In*, R. Fulton (ed.), *Death and Identity*, pp. 186–201. New York: John Wiley.

Lipman, A., and Marden, P. 1966. Preparation for death in old age. *J. Geront.*, 21, 426–431.

Lopata, H. Z. 1973. *Widowhood in an American City*. Cambridge, Massachusetts: Schenkman.

Maddison, D., and Viola, A. 1968. The health of widows in the year following bereavement. *J. Psychosomatic Res.*, 12, 297–306.

Magni, K. G. 1972. The fear of death. *In*, A. Godin (ed.), *Death and Presence*, pp. 125–138. Brussels: Lumen Vitae Press.

Martin, D. S., and Wrightsman, L. 1965. The relationship between religious behavior and concern about death. *Journal of Social Psychology*, 65, 317–323.

Morison, R. S. 1971. Death: Process or event? *Science*, 173, 694–702.

Morison, R. S. 1973. Dying. *Sci. Am.*, 229 (3), 54–62.

Nelson, L. P., and Nelson, V. 1973. Religion and death anxiety. Presentation to the annual joint meeting, Society for the Scientific Study of Religion and Religious Research Association. San Francisco.

Pahnke, W. N. 1969. The psychedelic mystical experience in the human encounter with death. *Harvard Theological Review*, 62, 1–32.

Pahnke, W. N., and Richards, W. A. 1966. Implications of LSD and experimental mysticism. *Journal of Religion and Health*, 5, 175–208.

Parkes, C. M. 1970. "Seeking" and "Finding" a lost object. *Social Science and Medicine*, 4, 187–201.

Parkes, C. M. 1972. *Bereavement*. New York: International Universities Press.

Peck, R. C. 1968. Psychological developments in the second half of life. *In*, B. Neugarten (ed.), *Middle Age and Aging*, pp. 88–92. Chicago: University of Chicago Press.

Phillips, D. P., and Feldman, K. A. 1973. A dip in deaths before ceremonial occasions: Some new relationships between social integration and mortality. *Am. Soc. Rev.*, 38, 678–696.

Pine, V. R. 1972. Death, dying, and social behavior. *In*, B. Schoenberg, A. C. Carr, A. H. Kutscher, D. Peretz, and I. K. Goldberg (eds.), *Anticipatory Grief*, pp. 31–47. New York: Columbia University Press.

Preston, C. E., and Williams, R. H. 1971. Views of the aged on the timing of death. *Gerontologist*, 11, 300–304.

Raether, H. C. 1971. The place of the funeral director in contemporary America. *Omega*, 2, 136–149, 154–158.

Rank, O. 1936. *Will Therapy and Truth and Reality*. New York: Alfred A. Knopf.

Rees, W. D., and Lutkins, S. G. 1967. Mortality of bereavement. *Brit. Med. J.*, 4, 13–16.

Reynolds, D. K., and Kalish, R. A. 1974. Anticipation of futurity as a function of ethnicity and age. *J. Geront.*, 29, 224–231.

Rhudick, P. J., and Dibner, A. S. 1961. Age, personality and health correlates of death concerns in normal aged individuals. *J. Geront.*, 16, 44–49.

Richards, W., Grof, S., Goodman, L., and Kurland, A. 1972. LSD-assisted psychotherapy and the human encounter with death. *Journal of Transpersonal Psychology*, 4, 121-150.

Richter, C. P. 1957. On the phenomenon of sudden death in animals and man. *Psychosomat. Med.*, 19, 191-198.

Riley, J. W., Jr. 1970. What people think about death. *In*, O. G. Brim, Jr., H. E. Freeman, S. Levine, and N. A. Scotch (eds.), *The Dying Patient*, pp. 30-41. New York: Russell Sage Foundation.

Ross, E. K. 1969. *On Death and Dying*. New York: Macmillan.

Ross, E. K. 1974. *Questions and Answers on Death and Dying*. New York: Macmillan.

Share, L. 1972. Family communication in the crisis of a child's fatal illness: A literature review and analysis. *Omega*, 3, 187-201.

Sharma, K. L., and Jain, U. C. 1969. Religiosity and fear of death in young and retired persons. *Indian Journal of Gerontology*, 1, 110-114.

Silverman, P. R. 1969. The widow-to-widow program: An experiment in preventive intervention. *Mental Hygiene*, 53, 333-337.

Silverman, P. R. 1970. The widow as a caregiver in a program of preventive intervention with other widows. *Mental Hygiene*, 54, 540-547.

Sudnow, D. 1967. *Passing On*. Englewood Cliffs, New Jersey: Prentice-Hall.

Swenson, W. M. 1961. Attitudes toward death in an aged population. *J. Geront.*, 16, 49-52.

Templer, D. I. 1971. Death anxiety as related to depression and health of retired persons. *J. Geront.*, 26, 521-523.

Templer, D. I. 1972. Death anxiety in religiously very involved persons. *Psychological Reports*, 31, 361-362.

Templer, D. I., Ruff, C., and Frank, C. 1971. Death anxiety: Age, sex, and parental resemblance in diverse populations. *Developmental Psychology*, 4, 108.

Turner, B. F., Tobin, S. S., and Lieberman, M. A. 1972. Personality traits as predictors of institutional adaptation among the aged. *J. Geront.*, 27, 61-68.

Warner, W. L. 1959. The city of the dead. *In*, W. L. Warner, *The Living and the Dead*. New Haven: Yale University Press. Reprint. 1965. *In*, R. Fulton (ed.), *Death and Identity*, pp. 360-381. New York: John Wiley.

Weisman. A. D. 1972. *On Dying and Denying*. New York: Behavioral Publications.

Weisman, A. D., and Kastenbaum, R. 1968. The psychological autopsy: A study of the terminal phase of life. *Community Mental Health Journal Monograph No. 4*. New York: Behavioral Publications.

Welu, T. C. 1972. Psychological reactions of emergency room staff to suicide attempters. *Omega*, 3, 103-109.

Williams, R. L., and Cole, S. 1968. Religiosity, generalized anxiety, and apprehension concerning death. *Journal of Social Psychology*, 75, 111-117.

PART 5 AGING AND SOCIAL INTERVENTION

20
THE POLITICAL DILEMMAS
OF INTERVENTION POLICIES

Robert H. Binstock

and

Martin A. Levin

Brandeis University

The fundamental notion that governments should intervene in the social condition of aging persons has been firmly established in industrialized societies. As social scientists and other professionals have increased their knowledge of aging and its social contexts, they have identified a number of social issues that, from one ideological perspective or another, seem to call for public intervention.

Yet, accompanying the growing commitment of modern societies to public intervention for the solution of social problems is a deepening sense of despair over our seeming incapacity to intervene effectively. Expectations regarding the amelioration of social conditions have been heightened by the grandiloquent promises of political leaders. At the same time, improvements in the material situations of most nations have enabled governments to allocate greater resources to policies for curing social ills. But as governments have committed themselves to policy initiatives directed at an ever-increasing range of social issues and problems, reformers have begun to lose some of their optimism as they observe the results of intervention efforts.

Certainly in the United States the record of ineffective performance has begun to accumulate at a staggering and frustrating rate. Few if any contemporary Americans would argue with the assertions that: the Model Cities Program did not develop model cities; although Social Security provides retirement income to approximately 20 million persons each year, at least several million older Americans experience severe economic deprivations; Medicare does not make adequate medical care available to the aged; and the War on Poverty has not been won, it has been abandoned. Indeed, most persons who have observed and participated in the adoption and implementation of contemporary social policies did not even have to read a policy study by Pressman and Wildavsky in order to understand why they entitled it *Implementation: How Great Expectations in Washington Are Dashed in Oakland; Or, Why It's Amazing that Federal Programs Work at All, This Being a Saga of the Economic Development Administration as Told by Two Sympathetic Observers Who Seek to Build Morals on a Foundation of Ruined Hopes* (1973).

Most of us recognize that the onus for our despair rests in part with theoretical and empirical inadequacies in our capacity to develop and design effective modes of social intervention. But we also tend to place some of the onus on politics. Those of us who would prefer to see more radical and redistributive policies adopted are frustrated by an apparent bias of our political system toward the adoption of incremental and distributive policies. And those of us who are more or less satisfied with the kinds of policies we adopt, because we regard incrementalism and distributiveness as reasonable prices to pay for the values of maintaining a democratic political process, are frustrated by the political difficulties of implementing those policies as effective solutions to social problems.

The purpose of this chapter is to provide a perspective on the politics of public policy through which social scientists and their professional colleagues—interested in aging and other social issues—can be somewhat more optimistic in their outlooks toward policy interventions and more effective as participants in policy processes. We will assume for purposes of this discussion that social science is capable of developing intervention models (see Chapter 21) that would be effective if political processes did not "interfere" with the adoption and implementation of those models. We will also assume for purposes of discussion that fundamental changes in political systems might bring about more effective policies without sacrificing democratic values. Although both of these assumptions warrant extended examination, they cannot be considered within the scope of this chapter.

The central issue of this chapter is: if social scientists explicitly confront what we do know about the contemporary political contexts in which policies are adopted and implemented, what can they do within those contexts to optimize social intervention efforts?

In order to treat this issue within a single chapter it will be necessary to emphasize certain political structures and processes to the exclusion of others. Although we will make a few general observations about the politics of public policy in modern democratic systems, we have chosen to deal with the American political system as a context for most of the discussion. As American political scientists, the authors are naturally more equipped to interpret the relevant scholarly literature within the context of politics in the United States. An important benefit of this choice is that a predominant characteristic of the American system is its frag-

mentation of power, a characteristic that is central to the difficulties of adopting and implementing effective policies for social intervention. If one conceives of modern democratic systems arrayed on a continuum ranging from centralized to fragmented or dispersed power, the American system is located among those near the extreme characterized by dispersion. Consequently, while most of our discussion will be about the politics of public policy in the American political system, a great deal of what we will say is germane, in some degree, to other political systems.

The scope of this chapter also makes it necessary to eschew a number of intriguing theoretical and definitional issues. The very word *policy* presents a problem. Neither scholarly definitions (e.g., Lasswell and Kaplan, 1970; Friedrich, 1963) nor popular conceptions of the term provide an adequate definition because they assume that policies are relatively clear, authoritative expressions of public goals that provide a fundamental context within which other governmental decisions and activities can be viewed and interpreted. The assumption is unrealistic because this reification of "policy" disintegrates when political behavior is examined. The language of a legislative act (and "the intent" behind it) is no more or less a policy than the decisions made by bureaucrats who implement the act by interpreting it and undertaking action (and their intentions in doing so). As Pressman and Wildavsky (1973) have observed, one can neither work with a definition of policy that excludes any implementation nor one that includes all implementation. The full range of governmental actions that one can observe—executive decisions, legislative processes, program planning and administration, regulatory and judicial decisions, referenda, and many other kinds of public decisions—are important for understanding the politics of social intervention. Equally important, moreover, are the failures of a government to act, which can obviously have as much or even greater consequences than action (Bachrach and Baratz, 1963). In short, the definition and organization of a discussion of policy must largely be a function of the phenomena and issues one chooses to examine.

The two kinds of political phenomena that will receive attention in this discussion are those involved in processes of legislative decisions and those which legislative decisions set in motion. Accordingly the discussion will be facilitated by a simple distinction between *policy adoption*—the enactment of a piece of legislation (other than appropriation bills)—and *policy implementation*—the variety of activities set in motion by the adoption of legislation. In choosing to label the enactment of legislation as policy adoption we are excluding from consideration many other forms of public action to which this term can be properly applied, such as executive orders and court decisions. One reason for this choice is that in all democratic political systems, legislative decisions are among the most important initiatives for domestic social intervention. Another reason is that the central importance of power fragmentation in shaping social policy is most readily perceived and illustrated in the context of legislative behavior.

The balance of this chapter is organized into four major sections. In the first section we will briefly examine some of the sources and manifestations of political limitations on effective policy intervention. The second section will consider how political limitations which are endemic to the American system tend to shape policies that are adopted through legislation. The third section will discuss some of the ways in which these political characteristics limit the efficiency and effectiveness of policy implementation. And a final section will suggest means through which social scientists and other professionals can optimize policy adoption and implementation by confronting the political dilemmas that limit the effectiveness of policy intervention.

SOURCES AND MANIFESTATIONS OF POLITICAL LIMITATIONS ON EFFECTIVE POLICY INTERVENTION

The adoption of a social policy not only requires politicians to choose among policy proposals, but it also characteristically requires them to sacrifice some of the substance of the proposal that they choose. In the United States,

as in all nations that have some form of representative government, an ongoing concern of politicians is their prospects for reelection. Because of this concern they are eager to be identified with policies that are regarded favorably by the electorate. Accordingly, they seek to espouse and support policies that evoke favorable reactions even if they do so at the expense of alternative policies that may be more effective for solving problems, but less popular.

The desire of politicians to be identified with popular policies is reflected in a number of more specific tendencies. First, politicians prefer to espouse and support policies that are immodest—dramatic and ambitious—in promise. Rather than announcing policies for getting more and better qualified personnel in nursing homes, they will declare policies that promise to older Americans "The best possible physical and mental health which science can make available. . ." and "Immediate benefit from proven research knowledge which can sustain and improve health and happiness." (Older Americans Act of 1969, Public Law 89-73, Title I, Sec. 101, subsecs. 2 and 9.)

Second, regardless of the immodest terms in which policies may be couched, politicians want those policies to lend themselves to tangible, particularly quantifiable results, for which they can take credit in reelection campaigns. For example, a policy proposed to improve nutrition among older persons would not lend itself to the kinds of tangible outcomes preferred by politicians if its design were such that reports of results could only be expressed in terms of an assessment of the nutritional status of aging persons. In contrast, the Nutrition Program for the Elderly designed in Title VII of the Older Americans Act is very suitable. Since it lends itself to reports from each Congressional district on the number and location of nutrition programs in operation, and on the number of meals served to older persons, assessments of either the nutritional value of the meals or the nutritional status of those who have eaten them are not politically necessary.

Third, because the time span between elections is relatively short, policies that embody goals which can be achieved quickly are preferred to policies that may require a generation, a decade, or perhaps just five years to be effective. This preference is especially unfortunate in its implications for some of the possible policies that could be undertaken in relation to aging. Many of the characteristics of persons who will join the ranks of the aged each year between now and the first decade of the twenty-first century will be different from those of the contemporary aged (Neugarten, 1974). Since these future aged are already well along in their life courses, it is possible to make use of our knowledge about them to undertake policy initiatives to deal with some of the social issues that their continuing maturation may involve (Binstock, 1975). But the tendency of politicians to favor policies that quickly show results of some kind makes the adoption of such initiatives difficult.

There are exceptions, of course, to each of these three patterns. One could argue, for instance, that: the Age Discrimination in Employment Act of 1967 is undramatic and modest in its prohibitions and enforcement objectives; the research objectives of the National Institute on Aging do not lend themselves to reports of tangible results; and the pension reform law, the Employee Retirement Income Security Act of 1974, is designed for effectiveness in the mid to distant future. While these are possible exceptions, the preference of Congressmen for policies that are immodest, and that lend themselves to tangible and quick results, are generally at work along with many other forces in shaping the outcomes of policy adoption processes.

A desire to appeal to the electorate, however, is but one of the elements at work in shaping the behavior of politicians as they engage in policy processes. Far more important are their struggles to cope with the peculiar fragmentation of power that is a predominant characteristic of the American political system. Power is dispersed among innumerable private entities— economic, social, professional, and religious elites; commercial, industrial, and trade organizations; political parties, political action groups, and organized citizen constituencies—that not only have influence in nongovernmental spheres of activity, but which also have influence on governmental structures and decisions. In addi-

tion, public power (authoritative or official power) is dispersed among tens of thousands of units of government, semiautonomous structures within these units, and a number of quasi-public entities.

In any given effort to adopt or to implement a policy, numerous fragments of private and public power are able to come into play. A political leader desiring to have a legislative proposal adopted must concert power by securing the support and neutralizing the opposition of those who control power fragments. The same need to concert power is confronted by those who implement policy. But the price of concerting these fragments is often paid by sacrificing the substance of what might be regarded as an "ideal proposal" for policy adoption, or an "ideal policy" for implementation.

Before we examine the patterns through which power fragmentation leads to modifications in proposed and adopted policies, it is worth considering briefly the sources and manifestations of public power fragmentation in the United States. It is important to note that the dispersion of public power which is a central factor in the difficulties of effective policy intervention is also an expression of central values in American political culture.

The fragmentation of public power that characterizes the American political system can be accounted for by a number of factors in the nation's early history and in its 200 years of subsequent development. Given the prenational development of distinct colonies, a virtual precondition of union was the choice of a federal structure of government in which each state retained sovereignty. Moreover, most of the framers of the national and state governments were wary of consolidated power because of their colonial political experiences. Their fears of centralized authority, reinforced by the political philosophies of Locke and Montesquieu, were expressed in structures which separated powers within the national and state governments. In part this was done to make it more difficult for informal factions—"a number of citizens, whether amounting to a majority or minority of the whole, who are united and activated by some common impulse of passion or of interest"—to assemble sufficient influence to tyrannize through controlling the powers of government (Madison, 1937). The prospect of political leadership sufficiently powerful to be able to adopt and implement its version of an ideal policy was and remains for most Americans a fear, not an aspiration.

In the two centuries of the United States' existence, the proliferation of public fragments of power has been exponential. In the contemporary United States there are 80,000 distinct units of government—counties, townships, municipalities, special district governments, metropolitan governments, and school districts, as well as the states and the national government. Most overlap in jurisdiction. Each has a specific set of formal powers, and within a substantial proportion of these units, that power is divided among executives, legislatures, and judiciaries. In addition, during the last two decades the national government has sponsored and financed thousands of local and regional entities—regional and area planning units, community action agencies, coordinating councils, citizen committees, technical commissions—and delegated to many of them independent authority affecting local policies that draw on federal resources. The federal government's role in proliferating such entities can be grasped by simply noting the impact of one piece of national legislation, the 1973 Comprehensive Services Amendments to the Older Americans Act of 1965. In accordance with this legislation, in less than two years, over 400 Area Agencies on Aging (AAAs) had been created through the dispersal of federal funds, many of them functioning independently of state and local governmental auspices.

In addition to this proliferation of governments and governmental entities, public power has been further fragmented due to the persistent influence of a major tenet of American political culture: the belief that public decisions, whenever feasible, should be based on the widest possible participation of the governed and not left to a governing elite. Under the influence of the Progressives of the late nineteenth and early twentieth centuries, this tenet became expressed in constitutional provisions requiring that many important state and local policy decisions be made through direct popular referenda. It has also become manifest since the early 1960's through federal legislation mandating establishment of mechanisms for citizen participation in poverty programs and urban renewal decisions and in local demands for "community control" of neighborhood schools and other facilities and services.

This highly fragmented and overlapping distribution of public power—among governments, governmental entities, and the public at large, as well as within governments and between governments—in the larger societal context of a dispersion of private power among elites, interest groups, political parties, political action groups, and organized citizen constituencies, makes the challenges involved in exercising policy leadership seem overwhelming. Not only does policy leadership require a general capacity to concert and/or neutralize fragments of public and private power, but the sets of fragments involved may vary substantially from one policy to another, each set comprising an *ad hoc* system defined by the policy proposal to be adopted or by the policy to be implemented.

When the difficulties of overcoming power fragmentation are added to some of the difficulties engendered by politicians' desires to espouse popular policies (discussed earlier), the possibilities of adopting and implementing effective social intervention policies are considerably limited. In the next two sections, we will examine some of the ways in which these political difficulties influence policy adoption and implementation.

THE POLITICS OF POLICY ADOPTION

The need to overcome power fragmentation in order to undertake public initiatives for social intervention poses one of the central dilemmas of policy leadership in American politics. To overstate somewhat for purposes of clarification, policy leadership is typically carried out in either a "power-costly" or "power-costless" pattern. Through one pattern the policy leader expends his store of political resources in order to obtain the support of some persons and entities who control fragments of power (or "requisite actions") and to neutralize the opposition of some others; in this pattern the leader realizes the adoption of his power-costly proposal at the expense of the political power he has managed to acquire as well as at the cost of opportunities to maintain and enhance his power. The other prototypical approach is for the political leader to bargain away the substance of a policy proposal, or let it be altered, until it is a power-costless proposal, providing a distribution of rewards to "requisite actors"—persons and entities controlling requisite actions—that is sufficient to obtain necessary support and neutralize opposition; in this pattern the leader tends to maintain and often enhance his store of political power, but at the cost of substantive goals (see Banfield, 1961).

While these two characterizations may represent the extremes of the situation, they capture a central dilemma of policy leadership within the American political system and, to greater or lesser degrees, within many other political systems. Only rarely will politicians expend sufficient power to have a proposal for intervention adopted as policy without alterations in its substance. More commonly, the adoption of a proposal for intervention is achieved because elements of the proposal itself are modified in return for the supporting actions requisite to the enactment of a policy.

Adoption of policy through legislation is especially susceptible to this dilemma. The President and the Congress share the authority to make legislation become law but derive, maintain, and seek their power from different electoral bases. Within the Congress individual legislators cannot and do not rely wholly on a party organization to keep them in office. They tend to develop voting patterns that are based on their own conceptions of what is necessary to maintain the support of their constituencies. Similarly, the major legislative committees within the Congress develop behavioral patterns that are keyed to groupings of organized interest constituencies both within the bureaucracy and outside the government. In addition, it has become an article of faith in American politics that interest groups should participate in the legislative process, certainly on proposals affecting the aging (Vinyard, 1972), by helping to

shape and criticize legislation in formal hearings and through informal sessions with Congressmen and Congressional staff. This faith is so central to contemporary American political culture that if interest groups do not seek to participate in the legislative process, the President and Congress recruit their active participation in order to legitimate the process and product of policy-making (see Chapter 15).

To have a policy proposal adopted in such a legislative context, its proponent must act as a broker among Congressmen and Congressional Committees, among bureaucracies and interest groups, and between Congress, the President, and bureaucracies and interest groups. He or she may be willing and able to expend a sufficient store of power to obtain enough support for the policy to be adopted in a form that closely resembles the initial or ideal proposal. But more often than not, the costs of building adequate support for the adoption of a policy are a number of changes in the policy proposal itself and, as will be considered in a later section of this chapter, a concomitant reduction in the probability that the policy adopted will be effectively implemented.

Policy proposals calling for allocations of public resources to be highly concentrated in relatively few specific geographic areas or electoral constituencies often become enacted as legislation distributing those resources widely among legislative districts. The development of the Model Cities program was a striking case of this. It started with the original proposal by a leader of organized labor to rebuild two cities, Detroit and any other, through a massive infusion of federal funds. The proposal was modified by a Presidential Task Force to obtain broader political support by expanding it to 66 neighborhoods distributed among a number of cities. By the time the Presidential proposal had been subjected to brokering in Congress to obtain adequate legislative support, the policy adopted provided $212 million for 150 cities (Banfield, 1973). The tendency toward wide distribution of resources made available through national social policies is often expressed in an explicit formula stated in legislation which allocates funds among implementing agencies. Title III of the Older

Americans Act is one of the typical legislated provisions spelling out such a formula for distribution; as enacted in 1965 it provided an equal sum of money to all state implementing agencies, plus an additional sum to each in accordance with a formula based upon the number of older persons in the state. For certain types of social legislation the use of such formulas has become routine (Wright, 1968), eliminating the need for *ad hoc* processes of brokering.

Also typically modified to obtain support are proposals that call for focusing expenditures of resources upon a social problem or social grouping that is defined in relatively narrow terms. This takes place through several characteristic patterns.

One pattern is to *add* to the initial target problem or group several other narrowly-defined targets that have an apparent relationship. The apparent relationship may not bear up to careful scrutiny, but close examination may be fended off through the use of a legislative title that is broad enough to cloud the picture. In the late 1960's, for example, the National Association for Retarded Children sought federal legislation to provide funds to the states to develop services and facilities for the mentally retarded. Sufficient political support to enact legislation, however, was only obtained by the development of a coalition adding on organized advocates of public initiatives for the epileptic and the cerebral palsied. The policy adopted, dealing with three relatively narrow problems—mental retardation, epilepsy, and cerebral palsy—was symbolically rationalized by the use of broad language; it was labeled the Developmental Disabilities Act of 1970 (Cherington, 1972).

In another classic pattern broader support is obtained not by including in several additional narrowly-defined targets, but by broadening the definition of the initial target. In some senses the use of the terms "older American," "senior," and "aging" in many policies that have been adopted, and particularly the official applicability of these policies to the largest possible categories of citizens implied by these names, may be seen as examples of this phenomenon. As indicated throughout this *Handbook*, the

aging are a heterogeneous category of citizens, and many of the social issues associated with aging populations apply to relatively small proportions of the category. Yet the need to obtain legislative support for policies that deal with problems affecting relatively small proportions of older persons exerts a pressure for broadening policies toward aging so that they apply to the largest possible aggregate constituency of citizens (see Chapter 15).

Through still another pattern, the target or problem is not added to or broadly redefined, but the nature of what is to be done about the problem is changed to directly provide benefits to interest groups and constituencies so that they will support legislation. A classic illustration of this is provided by the evolution of various proposals for "senior service corps," that have ultimately become embodied in Title VI of the Older Americans Act. When a bill for such a program was sponsored in Congress in 1967, conflicts among interest groups over which of them would share in the benefits of administering the policy as middlemen killed the legislative proposal and also delayed by a year the reauthorization and amendment of the Older Americans Act. Only when an accommodating pattern of resource distribution among aging-based interest groups was finally arrived at, were they able to join in supporting senior service corps legislation (Binstock, 1972).

Which of these several patterns may come into play, singly or in combination, can often be traced to the specific nature of the proposal under consideration. Even within the same area of social concern, the distribution and intensities of support, opposition, and indifference among and between sets of requisite actors—individual legislators, committee chairmen, bureaucrats, organized interests, elites, and citizen constituencies—can vary from one proposal to another. In relation to policies affecting the aging, Binstock (1972) has illustrated that the kinds of reactions among aging-based interest groups shift in relation to the substance of the legislation proposed. The patterns of legislative modification that are used to secure sufficient support for the adoption of a policy seem to shift accordingly.

Various schemes for classifying proposed

and adopted policies have been developed which are of some value for identifying recurring patterns of brokering that occur in the legislative process. In considering policies affecting the aging, Binstock (1972) has distinguished among regulatory, direct income transfer, and middleman policies, applying the latter two categories in his analysis. In a more general scheme of classification, Lowi (1964) has distinguished among distributive, regulatory, redistributive, and constituent policies. Similarly, Wilson (1973) has developed a four-fold classification of policies that are characterized by: distributed benefits and distributed costs; concentrated benefits and distributed costs; distributed benefits and concentrated costs; and concentrated benefits and concentrated costs. Each of these, as well as other typologies, are useful for examining a number of issues relating to political behavior and public policy. But it is neither necessary nor of any special value to choose a particular scheme for making certain generalizations about the central issue under consideration here—namely, what can be said about the cumulative impacts of the various patterns of legislative modifications that take place as domestic social policies, particularly those of relevance to the aging, are adopted?

One generalization that clearly emerges from the literature is that very few, if any, policy proposals are adopted without undergoing modifications that are made to secure legislative support and to neutralize opposition. To be sure, it is plausible to argue that the greater the sense of crisis that pervades the nation, the less a proposal to deal with that crisis is likely to be modified through legislative brokering and the more it is likely to be effective as an instrument for social intervention. Proponents of this thesis argue that while social, economic, and political conflicts in the United States are numerous, they are shallow rather than deep, cross-cutting rather than reinforcing. Consequently, in the context of a dramatic crisis, an underlying American liberal consensus (Hartz, 1955) makes it possible for differences to be transcended through effective mobilization of powerful, if temporary, coalitions, while opponents are placed at a severe disadvantage. Frequently cited to support this thesis is the New Deal

legislation enacted during the Great Depression, especially the Social Security Act of 1935—as Lowi (1969) terms it, "Old Welfare." However, if one compares the Social Security Program and its contributory "insurance" rubric with more radical schemes of the era such as the Townsend Plan, both the efforts to secure widespread support for the legislation and the moderate character of the intervention it authorized become evident (Holtzman, 1963). Opponents of this thesis cite crises such as "the urban crisis" of the 1960's in which the legislative response was the adoption of highly-compromised policies including the Model Cities Program, described earlier in this chapter. On the other hand, as Banfield (1970) has pointed out, one can debate the breadth and intensity with which the so-called urban crisis and other presumed crises have been felt.

Another generalization that emerges is that many policy proposals which are relatively uncompromised when enacted, perhaps in the context of a widespread mood of crisis, tend to become modified in substance over time much as if the process of securing political support and neutralizing opposition were being carried out longitudinally rather than cross-sectionally. Regulatory policies adopted in the wake of popular outrage at abuses against the public interest are commonly vitiated because the parties to be regulated are later able to exercise their fragments of power so as to effectively neutralize or capture the machinery of regulatory implementation. One need only consider, for instance, the ongoing cycle through which media exposure of nursing home conditions engenders a sense of public outrage, a commission is appointed to investigate conditions and to recommend legislation to deal with them, and reasonably strong regulatory standards are legislated. Nonetheless, the nursing home industry is able to remain remarkably immune to regulation (Mendelson and Hapgood, 1974). Similarly, organized interests and constituencies whose powers may have been neutralized by a public sense of crisis or some other contextual factor at the time when a policy was initially adopted are often afforded a new opportunity for legislative brokering through the process of amendment. Several years later in the different context of a deadline for reauthorization of legislation, new patterns of support, opposition, and indifference often emerge, and organized interests may be able to extract substantive policy changes in return for their support. "Community action" policies adopted in the crisis atmosphere of urban rioting in 1967, for instance, were modified later in legislation responsive to the interests of big city mayors and middle income constituencies (Sundquist and Davis, 1969).

A third observation to be made, perhaps the most important one for understanding why many scholars of public policy have directed their attention to issues of policy implementation, is that Congress has developed a "circuit-breaker" that enables it to cope with an overload of popular demands for adopting policies of social intervention. The American electorate since the New Deal has continually broadened the scope of activities that it considers legitimate for intervention by the federal government. As the range of government activities deemed inappropriate has become smaller, and as the proportion of Americans with middle incomes, white-collar occupations, and college educations has become greater, there have been fewer debates over the wisdom and propriety of public initiatives to solve social problems. There are some indications that such debates may be renewing on economic if not philosophical grounds, as resources become scarcer (see Chapter 25 of this *Handbook*), but the tendency of the 1960's and 70's has been toward a presumption that if a social problem can be identified it requires a governmental response. And as television has become a major source of political information, the number of issues that can be politicized as "crises," if only temporarily, is limited by little more than the reformer's imagination.

The circuit-breaker that Congress has developed for coping with the overload of demands for public initiatives is a legislative pattern through which specific substantive issues of policy implementation are avoided in legislative adoption of policies. The pattern became especially manifest in the 1960's and early 1970's in the enactment of policies for the development of services and facilities. Several

phrases, such as "The Great Society Programs," have been used to describe these policies which mandate a number of complex implementing actions to be undertaken by federal, state, and local agencies. Since the term coined by Lowi (1969) to describe these policies, "New Welfare," has already been applied in analyses of policies toward the aging (Binstock, 1972), and because this term is less time-bound than others, we will employ it for convenience in this discussion. However, the term should *not* be understood to stand for public assistance programs or even for a broader category of welfare policies in the usual sense. It is intended to represent a full range of social policies— Employment Development, Model Cities, Community Action, the Older Americans Act, and so on—that mandate implementing agencies to develop services and facilities within a legislative context that is outlined below.

The central ingredient in the New Welfare legislative pattern is a distribution of funds to state and local entities, with only the most general rules about what should be done with the distributed resources. Sometimes the funds are to be distributed to existing entities, but often, the legislation calls for the designation and creation of new entities that can be directly identified with the issue to which the legislation is responding. In either case, the composite nationwide administrative apparatus is a hybrid comprised of whatever entities may exist, or be designated and created, in the various state and local jurisdictions (Binstock, Cherington, and Woll, 1974). The substantive responsibilities of these implementing entities are usually described in the most general of terms: develop services and comprehensive plans; coordinate; undertake advocacy. And a flexible, competitive process is usually established for distributing funds to organizations that are directly engaged in operating programs.

The Older Americans Act, especially in its Title III provisions as enacted in 1965 and amended in 1969 and 1973, is a clear example of New Welfare legislation. It initially authorized funds to encourage each state to designate a State Unit on Aging. Each state received one annual sum to help meet the costs of "statewide planning, coordination, and administration," and another sum to be distributed by the State Unit in response to grant proposals from public and nonprofit organizations that would establish, demonstrate, and expand programs and services for older Americans. The content of these programs only needed to be in keeping with the very vague objectives declared in Section 101 of the Act, for example: "Efficient community services which provide social assistance in a coordinated manner and which are readily available when needed." (Public Law 91-69, Sec. 101, subsec. 8.) Operating under these conditions, the State Units were little more than "pipelines" for the distribution of federal funds to local organizations in almost random fashion, unrelated to developmental strategies (Binstock, 1971).

The 1973 Amendments to the Act added a provision for the creation and funding of additional implementing substate regional entities known as Area Agencies on Aging, which can be structured in a dozen or more ways to be specified in state plans. These Agencies are to develop a plan for each of approximately 600 areas in the nation, that will:

> . . . provide for the establishment of a comprehensive and coordinated system for the delivery of social services within the planning and service area covered by the plan, including determining the need for social services in such area (taking into consideration, among other things, the numbers of older persons with low incomes residing in such area), evaluating the effectiveness of the use of resources in meeting such need, and entering into agreements with providers of social services in such area, for the provision of such services to meet such need; . . . .
>
> (Public Law 93-29, Sec. 304
> subsec. c, paragraph 1)

Having developed these plans, the Area Agencies are expected to obtain most of their funding to implement them by securing through their own efforts "state resources, resources of county and local governments, . . . user fees; resources of voluntary social agencies; and other federal resources, such as those available under Title VI of the Social Security Act or Title VII of the Older Americans Act." (Gold, 1974)

When the ingredients of New Welfare legislation, so well illustrated by Title III of the Older

Americans Act are blended with some of the patterns of legislative modification discussed earlier, the result is a recipe for political triumph, though not one for effective social intervention. Through the adoption of legislation based on this recipe, national politicians can maintain and reinforce their legitimacy as public leaders. The cadres of state and local entities that receive federal funds, as well as their associated participating constituencies and interest groups, are grateful supporters of the policy although they inevitably regard as inadequate the amount of funds made available to them. Constituencies and interests that are unable to gain access to the resources distributed by such policies decry them, but they tend to be accommodated through inclusion in subsequent amendments. While legislation is vague about the social outcomes to be achieved through policy, it is relatively specific about the allocation of funds to newly-designated or newly-created implementation entities and their need, in turn, to expend effort and to distribute money for developing programs. Consequently, "successful results" can ensue relatively quickly and in tangible form. Virtually all that is required is to report on the number of entities and programs that have been established, and the number of dollars that have been widely distributed among constituencies throughout the nation.

Although the New Welfare recipe provides Congress with an excellent means of responding symbolically to a variety of politicized issues, it also leaves policy effectiveness highly dependent upon the agencies that implement it—the federal bureaucracy which must interpret the vague responsibilities described in legislation to make them somewhat operational, and the existent and newly-created state and local entities that receive the funds and the broad mandates to develop programs and services, to plan comprehensively, to coordinate, and to advocate. The effectiveness of these implementing agencies is partly limited by the amount of funds that policies provide to them. But they are more severely limited because their efforts at implementation encounter problems of power fragmentation and other political dilemmas endemic to the American political system. As we shall see in the next section, the ability of Congress to evade these dilemmas through its New Welfare pattern of legislation hardly eliminates the need for those dilemmas to be confronted by the agencies expected to implement policy.

THE POLITICS OF POLICY IMPLEMENTATION

All policies require implementation, and most implementation efforts encounter political difficulties. As indicated earlier, for instance, even very clear and specific regulatory policies are often vitiated by the capacity of powerful private interests to neutralize or capture regulatory implementing machinery. New Welfare policies, however, mandating the development of services and facilities, inevitably seem to encounter more of the political difficulties of implementation than other kinds of policies. Consequently, our examination of the politics of policy implementation in this section will emphasize New Welfare policies. In the final section of the chapter we will draw on this examination in a comparative discussion of the political difficulties in implementing different types of policies.

Although the New Welfare policies adopted in the early 1960's were obviously not designed upon the basis of social science knowledge, many of these policies gave hope to social reformers who had come to recognize how the political dilemmas of the legislative process make it difficult for Congress to adopt highly redistributive or regulatory policies that will be effective for a sustained period. The new policies represented a somewhat innovative approach to intervention and frequently, because they remained vague and general in substantive content, could deal with relatively controversial issues. Most importantly, by often passing to state and local communities the responsibility for determining the specific substantive choices of intervention, these policies seemed to reduce the scope of conflicts to be resolved.

During the 1960's many social scientists, planners, social workers, and other professionals became active participants in the policy processes of the New Welfare. They were sought by federal agencies that needed advice in developing guidelines to operationalize legislation and by local agencies needing advice on what to do within the guidelines. They were funded to undertake research for evaluating the impact of programs and for designing improved models of local intervention. And they were lured by a general liberal optimism about the new approach to social reform. However, the New Welfare policies that promised so much were disappointments when implemented.

The implementation of these policies has unquestionably provided benefits to citizen constituencies, as well as to interest groups and to state and local governments. Some of these have been benefits manifest in the policies adopted. Implementation of the Older Americans Act, for instance, has provided many older persons with free meals, recreational and leisure activities, educational opportunities, homemaker and home health services, and a great variety of other services and facilities (see Chapter 24).

Implementation of New Welfare policies has also provided to citizen constituencies some latent benefits which have not usually been anticipated in officially adopted policy. Chief among these benefits has been the way in which many citizens' groups, organized as part of efforts to develop services and facilities, have become vehicles for political action which enable citizen constituencies to exercise some power in public decisions. Implementation of federal policy in juvenile delinquency in the early 1960's, for example, led to the development of citizen constituencies which were able to challenge with some effectiveness the discretionary powers of public welfare bureaucracies (Marris and Rein, 1969). Similarly, councils on aging funded in Massachusetts through implementation of Title III of the Older Americans Act provided an organizational base for some of the power exercised by the Massachusetts Legislative Council for Older Americans (Henretta, 1973).

Despite manifest and latent benefits from the implementation of New Welfare programs, they have been disappointing for several reasons. One reason is they tend to be inefficient, with incredibly high cost-benefit ratios. Manifest or intended benefits are achieved after long delays and adaptations, with much larger expenditures than initially planned, and reaching a relatively small proportion of the intended constituencies (Pressman and Wildavsky, 1973). A second reason is that latent benefits do not prove politically viable for a sustained period. A classic example is the case of the Economic Opportunity Act of 1964. Implementation of the program generated political action groups among poor and ethnic minority constituencies in urban communities throughout the nation. Yet, as these groups became stronger, legislative support for the policy that nourished them became weaker and ultimately disappeared. If strong political action groups develop among the aged poor as a latent benefit of implementation of the Older Americans Act's "advocacy" policy, Congressional support for that policy may erode in similar fashion.

The most important reason for disappointment with New Welfare policies is that they do not seem effective in solving social problems. Regardless of the benefits distributed through their implementation, they do not make a substantial dent in *aggregate* social problems. Employment training programs can provide training, but they do not make much of an overall impact on problems of unemployment (Goldstein, 1972). Older worker training programs, the Foster Grandparents Program, senior volunteer programs, home care programs, and a variety of programs implemented under the Older Americans Act have unquestionably provided economic, social, and health benefits to many older persons. But as many chapters in this *Handbook* indicate—especially Chapters 22, 23, and 24—millions of older Americans whom policy declares should benefit from these programs undergo severe economic and social deprivations and experience substantial health care problems.

Since the implementation of such programs can be successful in distributing benefits, could they be reasonably effective instruments of amelioration if cost-inefficiencies were reduced? It is plausible to argue that research can identify social impact variables that lend themselves to more efficient models of program implementation. As indicated in Chapter 21 of this *Hand-*

book, there is room for considerable improvement in the validity and applicability of theories and empirical research available from the behavioral and social sciences. Moreover, interpretations of legislation by the federal bureaucracy could establish administrative procedures that might facilitate less cumbersome and costly patterns of program implementation. Pressman and Wildavsky (1973) have recommended, for instance, that administrative designs interpreting Congressional legislation should be geared more directly to the difficulties likely to be encountered by those who must implement programs, and that the number and complexity of difficulties that need to be overcome for successful implementation could be drastically reduced through program designs that are simple and direct, with fewer required steps. But even if one stipulates that more efficient intervention designs and administrative machinery could be used, the inefficiencies of program implementation would not be reduced enough to make these policies efficient enough to be relied upon as measures for solving social problems. The reason is that most of the difficulties that incur inefficiencies—delays, exorbitant cost-benefit ratios, and goal adaptations and attenuations— can be traced to the political dilemmas that are endemic to American politics.

A central dilemma in implementation of New Welfare policies is that implementing agencies do not have sufficient power resources of their own to deal effectively with the dispersion of public and private power that they must confront if they wish to accomplish anything at all. They are rarely armed with more than their dedication, some amount of technical expertise, an official mandate to implement, and a relatively small amount of funds that can be expended at their discretion. Yet, as a study of public and private agency efforts in "community organization for the aging" has shown, virtually any attempt to develop or change service programs and facilities requires, at some point, obtaining the support and neutralizing or overcoming the opposition of public organizations— county, municipal, and state agencies; special district and metropolitan governments; regional planning authorities; advisory commissions, committees, and councils—as well as private organizations, interest groups, organized citizen constituencies, and local elites that control relevant fragments of power. To the extent that the implementing agencies are unable to exercise some form of power to secure support and to neutralize or overcome opposition, the results are: initial objectives are substantially altered and attenuated; success in implementation is greatly delayed; and many efforts at implementation are unsuccessful, even with altered and attenuated objectives (Morris and Binstock, 1966).

Examination of efforts to implement programs in other fields reinforces these findings, regardless of whether there is initial consensus (Pressman and Wildavsky, 1973) or substantial conflict (Derthick, 1972) among the relevant parties. A generalization that emerges from these and a number of additional implementation studies (Bardach, forthcoming; Bailey and Mosher, 1968; Murphy, 1971) is that the greater the number of parties that are involved and need to be dealt with in an implementation effort, the greater the probabilities of failure, delay, and goal alteration and attenuation. But even if comparatively few parties are involved, perhaps two or three target organizations or constituencies, inefficient implementation is virtually inevitable.

The tendency of public and private organizations to resist innovations, whether generated externally or internally, has received extensive treatment in scholarly literature. In the context of considering organizations as targets of implementation efforts, it is sufficient to note a major reason for this tendency. An "organization does not search for or consider alternatives to the present course of action unless that present course is in some sense 'unsatisfactory'" (March and Simon, 1958). Or, to state it another way, an organization's "existing pattern of behavior has qualities of persistence; it is valuable in some way or it would not be maintained" (Simon, Smithburg, and Thompson, 1961). Since implementation efforts almost always pose some change in a target organization's existing pattern of behavior, an implementing agency needs to be able to exercise some form of power in an attempt to overcome or at least neutralize the target's resistance. In turn, organ-

izational targets are able to employ a variety of effective defensive strategies—delay, domain exclusiveness, and many others (Bardach, forthcoming).

Organized citizen constituencies and other avowedly political organizations may often be relatively unsusceptible to the exercise of power by an implementing agency because such organizations are primarily maintained through purposive incentives (the attainment of political objectives), rather than through material or solidary incentives (Wilson, 1973). For this reason, and because of the stress that American political culture exerts in favor of participatory processes, attempts to secure the support of constituencies customarily take the form of having them participate in the decision-making processes of policy implementation. Such participation frequently engenders delays and goal adaptations and attenuations that make for inefficient and ineffective implementation, and sometimes leads to outright failure. The costs that constituent participation can have for policy effectiveness have been noted in efforts to implement poverty programs (Greenstone and Peterson, 1973), water fluoridation programs (Crain, Katz, and Rosenthal, 1969), and in a variety of other policy areas. A study of advisory commissions, councils, and committees of State Units on Aging identified patterns of association between the participation of various constituencies on these bodies and selections of goals that were comparatively noninnovative (Binstock, Cherington, and Woll, 1974).

If the objectives of implementation are not vitiated and frustrated through the trade-offs of constituency participation, an implementing agency has opportunities, in theory, to be reasonably efficient by exercising power to secure support and to neutralize or overcome opposition. But as indicated earlier, few implementing agencies have an impressive stock of resources for exercising power, and New Welfare legislation adds little to that stock: relatively small amounts of funds, and vague official mandates from Washington to carry out implementation missions. Although the amounts of funds and the importance of the missions may be greater under some policies than others, in no cases are these sufficient resources for efficiently and effectively coping with state and local fragments of public and private power—certainly not, for instance, in the case of the Older Americans Act (Binstock, 1971). From our earlier discussion of power fragmentation as it comes into play in the legislative process, it should be clear, in any event, that sufficient resources for power to deal with the many state and local actions requisite for efficient implementation are not likely to be conferred upon implementing agencies through legislation.

An occasional public implementing agency may have substantial power at its disposal if it is part of a very strong local political organization like the Daley "machine" in Chicago. But the power of the machine is unlikely to be expended in its public agency's efforts to implement national policy. One of the primary reasons a machine is able to build and maintain power is that it only chooses to spend its power resources rarely and on favorable terms (Banfield, 1961). Public agencies administering New Welfare policies in Daley's Chicago, for example, have tended to distribute as patronage the federal resources made available (Greenstone and Peterson, 1973). This enhances the machine's store of power, but does little to achieve effective implementation of national policies.

The recognition that some implementing agencies with substantial power at their disposal do not tend to expend it for effective implementation has led to a number of policies that call for bypassing established bureaucracies and creating new agencies for implementation. A theory behind this has been that newly-created bureaucracies will be unfettered by organizational stasis, committed to the innovations of the policy that created them, and willing to expend what power they have directly for the goals of implementation (Marris and Rein, 1969). But this strategy has not been an improvement, let alone solved any of the underlying dilemmas of implementation. The advantages of being a new implementing structure vanish quickly over time. Moreover, as Hudson has observed in analyzing the creation of Area Agencies on Aging, the incentives leading these new structures to work for their political survival are in conflict with implementation efficiency (1974).

Another device that has been frequently put forward as a panacea for dealing with the fragmentation of power that impedes implementation is a mandate for coordination. However, legislation and administrative regulations that charge implementation agencies with a mission to coordinate are simply restating the underlying dilemma of policy implementation in a somewhat misdirecting and confusing fashion. For coordination is a "buzz-word" or euphemism for exercising power to secure support and to neutralize or overcome the opposition of organizations, constituencies, and other parties that control relevant fragments of power (Binstock, 1971). Efforts to coordinate are frustrated by the customary difficulties of implementing policies in a political system characterized by a dispersion of power. In analyzing 184 coordination objectives sought by 48 State Units on Aging, Hudson and Veley (1974) found a remarkable degree of goal displacement and attenuation.

If one could ignore the underlying political dilemmas that render implementation inefficient and ineffective, the extraordinary number of highly talented personnel that New Welfare policies require for implementation, in itself, would severely limit their feasibility. A central implementing responsibility of staff for Area Agencies on Aging, for example, is to develop local programs in conjunction with municipalities, counties, special district governments, local and state planning agencies, state governments, private health and welfare agencies, and consumer constituencies. To be properly equipped, personnel need to possess considerable political skills and to have sound training in at least: state and local government; administrative and planning techniques; state, local, and intergovernmental finance; and issues of special pertinence to the social conditions of aging persons. Given a projected total of 600 Area Agencies, 600 professionals of this caliber would be needed to provide just one such staff person for each Agency. Similarly talented personnel are required to implement policies of social reform in education (Dennison, 1969), police behavior (Wilson, 1968), prison rehabilitation (Martinson, 1974), and dozens of other fields. Even if the employment incentives offered by implementing agencies were sufficiently attractive for obtaining the services of such highly-qualified persons, an administrative dilemma is that they are simply not available in the quantities needed.

In view of the basic dilemmas that render implementation inefficient and ineffective, why have so many New Welfare policies been adopted and maintained? To be sure, some of them have been abandoned as federal programs; but the overwhelming majority of New Welfare policies have survived, despite their lack of effectiveness as ameliorative measures.

One reason is that cadres of implementing agency personnel, consumer constituencies, and organizations that directly receive the benefits distributed through implementation quickly develop a vested interest in the maintenance of these policies. When the issue of continuing the policy through legislative reauthorizatiori is at stake, they are well-equipped and prepared to pursue their interests effectively in the legislative arena. Shortly after State Units on Aging were authorized by the Older Americans Act of 1965, for instance, the staff of these agencies had established a National Association of State Units on Aging. Together with a number of other organizations having a stake in aging policies, the Association has provided political support for the continuation of the Act through stages of reauthorizing legislative amendments (Pratt, 1976; Binstock, 1972). When the 1973 Amendments mandated the creation of Area Agencies on Aging, the personnel of these agencies formed their own association shortly thereafter, as an instrument for advocating their continuing interest in the policy.

Another reason New Welfare policies have tended to survive is that they meet the requirements of political symbolism for instant and quantifiable "success." Since legislation expresses objectives in vague and general terms, the principal tangible measures of results are the number of dollars expended and the number of program units established through implementation. These measures can almost always be reported back to Congress with favorable results.

The successful expenditure of allotted funds is virtually ensured because of the pressures exerted upon implementing agencies by the federal agency that distributes the dollars to them and by state and local politicians. A prime concern of a federal agency is to expend its allotted funds, without scandal, before the fiscal year is up. A failure to do so may raise questions about the need for its continuing existence, and at least reduces its chances of obtaining increased appropriations in the years ahead. As Pressman and Wildavsky express it:

> [The federal granting agency] . . . is a mover of money. Its task is to remove a certain amount of money from its coffers in the time period allotted. Spending, to be sure, is not the prime goal of the granting organization. It may wish to further economic growth, to see that the money is used efficiently, to reduce population. But it is difficult to determine whether these goals have been achieved, and in any event the results would not be in for a number of years. The one major criterion of success that is immediately available, accordingly, is ability to spend the allotted amount (1973, p. 137).*

This imperative to move money ensures that implementing agencies are quickly designated or created. Once the implementing agencies receive their allotments, state and local political leaders naturally take a dim view of any sign that "free" federal dollars will be "wasted" by returning them to Washington. Given the pressures to spend funds, implementing agencies inevitably use them to create programs, regardless of how efficiently those programs distribute social benefits and ameliorate social conditions.

The American political system tends to reward its legislators for the causes they espouse and the policies they adopt. Neither the American public nor the media demand that Congressmen give continuous oversight to policy implementation. Responsibility for implementation failure tends to be placed upon federal, state, and local bureaucrats and attributed to their administrative inadequacies. For New Welfare policies to be legislatively sustained, it is sufficient that members of Congress receive reports on the amount of money expended and the number of implementation and program units established in their separate constituencies, as well as throughout the nation. The underlying political dilemmas endemic to the system remain, limiting efficient and effective implementation.

*Copyright © 1973 by The Regents of the University of California; reprinted by permission of the University of California Press.

SOCIAL SCIENTISTS AND THE POLITICS OF INTERVENTION

In the late eighteenth and early nineteenth centuries, economics was thought of as the "dismal science." The problems of scarcity, especially in relation to population growth and cyclical economic instability, seemed to be intractable. However, the seemingly successful mid-twentieth century application of Keynesian economic theory in Western nations turned economics into a more optimistic science. Now, near the end of the twentieth century, politics seems to have become the dismal science for democratic societies, especially if they seek to cope with social problems through policy intervention. Certainly the political dilemmas of policy adoption and implementation that have been examined here would seem to suggest a pessimistic assessment.

Many social scientists whose studies have pointed to the political dilemmas of policy intervention have attempted to avoid drawing dismal conclusions from their research by setting forth proposals for improving policy processes. In their attempts to be optimistic they, unfortunately, ignore the implications of their own analyses of political behavior. One of the more perceptive analysts of American policy processes, for instance, is Lowi (1969). He characterizes the functioning of American politics as "interest group liberalism" and suggests that Americans have come to accept the notion that "the public interest" or social justice is brought about through conflicts and accommodations among organized groups, each seeking fulfillment of its own interests. Yet his proposal for reforming American politics to achieve social justice requires the adoption of legislation that clearly states objectives and the specific means through which they are to be achieved; he would have the Supreme Court declare "invalid and unconstitutional any delegation of power to an administrative agency that is not accompanied by clear standards of implementation." (Lowi, 1969, p. 298). What he fails to explain in his proposal is how such legislation for social justice can be adopted in a system in which—as he has pointed out—the public interest is determined by the outcome of conflicts and accommodations among organized groups.

Attempts to maintain or develop optimistic perspectives regarding the prospects for social amelioration have also taken other forms. One traditional approach has been to look to nongovernmental mechanisms as instruments of social change. As recently as 1960 most economists viewed the economic market as the best available mechanism for the allocation of resources and for determining what should be produced and for whose consumption. During the ensuing ten years, however, this position has crumbled as the inadequacies of the market as a means for decisions on resource allocation, production, consumption, and distribution have been pointed up (Liebman, 1974).

Another familiar approach is to focus upon forces through which the basic features of a political system may change, perhaps through the inexorable impact of social and economic trends, or through the revolutionary efforts of political movements. What such changes could be and whether they would be desirable are philosophical issues that cannot be addressed in the scope of the present discussion. In any event, if basic changes occur in the nature of the American political system, there is no likely reason to expect that they will come about in the immediate decades ahead. At the same time, there are many reasons to expect that severe social problems and political pressures for public initiatives to solve them will persist in the context of a system that has many endemic political limitations upon the adoption and implementation of effective solutions.

It is possible, however, to develop a reasonably optimistic perspective regarding the prospects for improved intervention policies without ignoring underlying political difficulties. Indeed, a foundation for constructive results is more likely to be built by fully recognizing these political difficulties rather than by minimizing them. The political structures and processes that limit policy effectiveness also present opportunities to reformers through which the effectiveness of policy initiatives may be somewhat improved. The final portion of this chapter considers some of the ways available to social scientists and other professionals for influencing choices in processes of policy adoption and implementation so that public interventions may be optimized.

Optimizing Policy Adoption

An exponential growth in the amount of social information used in public policy processes took place between the Great Depression and the 1960's, leading to a "professionalization of reform" in which many social scientists and other professionals have become heavily involved in the development of policy proposals (Moynihan, 1965). In addition to generating data that are used to develop and justify policy proposals, social scientists are able to offer their policy advice and ideas, and are listened to, in a variety of public and private settings: through Congressional testimony, service on commissions and task forces, and articles and speeches; and by working directly with politicians and their staffs, bureaucrats, political parties, and organized interests.

Despite the political dilemmas that make it very difficult for effective social policies to be legislatively adopted, the substance of policy advice and proposals put forward can make a difference for several reasons. First, as indicated earlier, proposals adopted when there is a sense of crisis pervading the nation tend to undergo less modification through legislative brokering than at other times. When a crisis comes, politicians under heavy pressure to respond will turn to whatever social scientists and other professionals have made available to them, and they will tend to use it. To be sure, even if "the ideal policy" is adopted in relatively unmodified form, it may be vitiated through subsequent processes of amendment and implementation. But as will be indicated below, some of the basic decisions that can be made in choosing among several general policy approaches can reduce the probability of subsequent goal adaptation and attenuation in the implementation process.

If proposals for comparatively effective policies are less likely to be modified in a crisis, it may seem tempting to the designer or advocate of a policy to cry "wolf"—to engender a sense of crisis in order to facilitate the adoption of his proposal. But to do so is self-defeating, for the high costs of indulging oneself in this temptation had become clear by the mid-1970's. Through some 15 years of an overload of demands on Congress to deal with readily-politicized issues, legislators and much of the public were numbed by declarations of "crisis." As suggested earlier, Congress developed a prebrokered pattern of legislative response that led to a proliferation of inefficient and ineffective policies. Among the unfortunate though perhaps temporary outcomes in the Congress and in the American public have been: a blurring of priority distinctions among social problems even though some—such as racial discrimination or the extreme poverty experienced by several million older Americans—may be far more severe than others; and a growing conviction that social policies comprise "a great social pork barrel" and are not effective measures for ameliorating social conditions (Stockman, 1975).

It is not necessary for a crisis to be at hand for the social scientist to play some part in influencing policies that are adopted. There are some considerable differences in content and strategy among approaches that can be chosen as proposals for coping with a particular social problem or set of problems. The choice proposed, though altered and diluted, is usually reflected to some extent in the policy ultimately adopted. Aggressive advocacy of proposals by social scientists and other professionals can optimize legislative outcomes by emphasizing basic approaches to intervention that seem to work better than others given the nature of American politics.

One choice that is clearly indicated by our earlier analysis of the endemic political limitations on effective policy implementation is to de-emphasize approaches to intervention that require complex strategies of implementation and to emphasize approaches that come closest to approximating "self-implementing" or "self-executing" policies. No policy, of course, is self-implementing. And, given the nature of the legislative process, only in rare circumstances does legislated policy state clear objectives and specify the means for achieving them; even in those rare circumstances, implementing machinery and administrative discretion are necessary for policy to be carried out. Yet, there can be substantial contrasts in the degree and complexity of implementation required to carry out different types of policies. The administrative machinery and discretionary operations required to distribute predictable and tangible Social Security income benefits to older persons, for example, seem quite complex when viewed in isolation. When contrasted, however, with the machinery and operations required to distribute relatively unpredictable and intangible service benefits under the Older Americans Act, the implementation of Social Security seems comparatively simple and direct.

An emphasis on policies that are relatively self-implementing would seem to imply that direct income transfer policies should be chosen for advocacy when issues like the severe economic, social, and health care problems of older persons are considered for legislative attention. Direct income transfer policies—like Social Security, Supplemental Security Income, Railroad Retirement Benefits, and the much-discussed "negative income tax"—are the best approximations of self-implementing policies. They avoid most of the problems of administrative discretion because they specify benefit levels and relatively clear-cut eligibility requirements, which are uniform throughout the nation. While implementation of such policies necessitates some decentralization and involves a certain number of administrative problems, the *political difficulties* of state and local implementation are minimized if not totally eliminated.

Some income transfer policies, however, in which the purchasing power transferred is restricted to a particular category of goods, services, and facilities, entail relatively complex administrative machinery and do involve substantial political difficulties of implementation. Policies like Medicare and Medicaid require the participation of a variety of middlemen between program administrators and beneficiaries, providing goods, services, and facilities, and then receiving reimbursement from the government which has issued credit to the beneficiaries. These indirect income transfer policies necessitate somewhat greater administrative

discretion than Social Security and the other income policies listed above and certainly encounter far more political difficulties in the implementation process because of the varieties and numbers of middlemen involved (Binstock, 1972). The inefficiencies generated by the political difficulties of implementing such policies are primarily ones of financial cost rather than of goal alteration and attenuation.

Policies for developing services and facilities to be made available to citizens without charges or reimbursement provisions are even more—substantially more—discretionary, complex, politically difficult to implement, and uncertain in outcome. As indicated earlier, New Welfare policies like the Older Americans Act, Foster Grandparents, and a variety of senior service corps programs, have comparatively vague objectives and do not specify the precise nature of benefits and the patterns through which they are to be distributed. They pass on to a complicated, costly, and hybrid administrative apparatus of state and local implementing agencies the responsibility of clarifying policy through the processes of spending money and assembling and coordinating programs. Because these processes are limited by political difficulties, especially the need to deal with the fragments of power controlled by the many public and private parties that must be involved in program development, implementation does not produce reliable patterns for clarifying objectives or for providing benefits and distributing them. Implementation of these policies not only tends to be very inefficient in financial terms; it also tends to alter and attenuate the objectives of policy, vague as they may be.

Although an emphasis on income policies is indicated by the far greater political difficulties of implementing policies for the development of services and facilities, it is not at all clear that we can do without service and facility policies. In debating the prudence of income *vs.* service and facility policies on the basis of considerations other than the endemic political limitations on effective implementation, proponents of both views have acknowledged that something needs to be done to improve the quantitative and qualitative inadequacies of social and health services and facilities available to the low-income aged and other poverty groups. Proponents of income policies argue that needed services and facilities should and can be developed by the private sector, as an alternative mechanism to government policies (Solomon, 1974); however, this argument rests on problematic assumptions about market elasticity, speed, and information.

Regardless of the relative merits of the two sides of this debate, what we do know about the politics of policy adoption indicates that service and facility policies will most likely continue to be adopted. As indicated earlier in this chapter, they are especially well-suited for meeting the political needs of Congressmen and are strongly supported by aging-based organizations and other groups that have a vested interest in generating and maintaining them (also see Chapter 15). The social scientist who advocates an emphasis on income policies because they involve less political difficulties of implementation need not be concerned that service and facility policies will be ignored by Congress, although contemporary disenchantment with New Welfare policies may lead to transformations in their current characteristic patterns.

Given that Congress will probably continue to adopt policies for the development of services and facilities, what can social scientists advocate for optimizing these kinds of policies? First, as Pressman and Wildavsky (1973) recommend, patterns of implementation that are simple and direct should be emphasized rather than complicated procedures that require an extensive sequence of numerous interdependent steps. Each step in a sequence of implementation procedures encounters political difficulties, particularly the dilemma of fragmented power. The greater number of steps in the sequence, the greater the probabilities of delay, financial inefficiencies, and goal adaptations and attenuations. The policy creating Area Agencies on Aging and mandating them to implement, described in detail earlier, is an excellent illustration of the kind of policy that social scientists should not advocate. It not only requires the Agencies to execute an incredibly complex set of interdependent steps with a constituency participating in decisions throughout the process, but also expects them to do so through

securing the bulk of program development funds by exercising their own competitive initiatives in extracting money from other public agencies. In contrast, the Nutrition Program for the Elderly authorized under another Title of the same legislation, provides an approach to implementation that is much closer to what should be advocated. This policy provides funds to the State Units on Aging which, in turn, simply pass them on to organizations in the state that are willing and able to operate a program. Although this policy is hardly an ideal model for implementation, the political difficulties encountered in implementing it are comparatively few and so, too, are occurrences of delays, cost inefficiencies, and goal adaptations and attenuations.

Another approach that should be emphasized, for which the Nutrition Program is also a reasonably good example, is advocacy of policies that are intended to achieve rather intangible and long-term results, but which are designed to involve a short-term phase that meets politicians' needs for relatively tangible and quick results. Among the stated goals of the Nutrition Program are promotion of "better health among the older segment of our population through improved nutrition," and reduction of the social "isolation of old age, offering older Americans an opportunity to live their remaining years in dignity." (Public Law 92-258, Sec. 701, subsec. b.) As indicated earlier, reports on the Program are not in terms of assessments of its consumers' states of health, social integration, and dignity. But it does lend itself well to reports from each Congressional district on the number and location of programs in operation and the number of meals served to older persons in congregate settings. These kinds of reports help to maintain political support for the Program. To be sure, alternative implementation designs— e.g., nutritional counseling programs for retirees and preretirees, or a series of educational television programs—might or might not be better for promoting improved nutritional health, social integration, and dignity. They would not, in any event, lend themselves nearly as well to the kinds of tangible, quick results that politicians like. Whether the Nutrition Program will achieve its long-term, intangible objectives remains to be seen. It will, however, probably survive for some time, distributing very specific benefits to some older persons.

Still another approach that social scientists can undertake is to advocate policies which emphasize intervention variables that are subject to a greater degree of control through public initiatives than variables which, though better predictors of the desired social outcome, are less subject to policy control. The reasons for this emphasis are similar to those that imply a stress on direct income transfer policies as the best approximations of self-implementing policies. Some social issues, however, such as age discrimination in employment or health care and safety conditions in nursing homes, are not particularly susceptible to the effects of income policies and lend themselves better to regulatory policies.

As indicated earlier, implementation of regulatory policies is frequently ineffective because interests expected to be the targets of regulation are often able to neutralize or capture implementing machinery. Moreover, the political and administrative difficulties of enforcing regulatory policies and the need to report tangible success may lead the implementing agency to redefine and attenuate its policy goals. Kraft (1966) has pointed out, for example, how the FBI was able to narrow its task to manageable areas—apprehending bank robbers and calling them "public enemies," solving kidnappings, infiltrating the American Communist Party— and to minimize public expectations that it should deal with more politically and administratively difficult problems like civil rights violations or organized crime of the post-Prohibition era.

Regulatory policies, therefore, while designed to operationalize those variables that are the best predictors of reducing the social problem under consideration, may not in fact operationalize those variables through implementation. For example, there is evidence indicating that the degree of likelihood of apprehension by the police is a comparatively good predictor of reduction in crime (Levin, 1976); but studies of police behavior show that police administrators have very limited ability to influence the behavior of patrolmen in efforts to have policies

carried out (Skolnick, 1966; Westley, 1970; Wilson, 1968). Similarly, the best predictor of improved health care and safety conditions in nursing homes may be vigorous and rigid enforcement of regulatory standards which have been adopted as policy. Yet as Mendelson and Hapgood (1974) observe, not even moderately vigorous enforcement takes place.

One alternative to regulatory policies that social scientists can advocate, through which relevant variables can be controlled somewhat better, is an approach in which the federal government directly develops and operates a demonstration of a service or facility. The classic example of this kind of policy, which has been termed "yardstick regulation," is the Tennessee Valley Authority, a program operated directly by the federal government, which was supported by reformers as a means of demonstrating to the American citizenry that electric power could be produced with better service and lower costs than private firms had claimed was possible (Derthick, 1974). Following this approach it would not be unreasonable to suggest as an alternative to nursing home regulatory policy, for instance, that the federal government begin to undertake direct development and operation of a small number of demonstration nursing homes.

To be sure, the implementation of a policy for direct federal development and operation of one or several demonstration nursing homes or some other kinds of model programs would encounter, as did implementation of the Tennessee Valley Authority (Selznick, 1966), some of the political dilemmas of citizen participation and power fragmentation that are confronted in state and local implementation of service and facility policies. But development and operation of such model or demonstration programs by the federal government would bypass some of the political difficulties encountered in implementation of contemporary service policies which require securing cooperation and operational compliance from assembled networks of existing public and private organizations over which the implementing agency has no control. If an avoidance of some of the political difficulties of implementation were to yield demonstration results that were even moderately efficient and effective, public recognition of what could be done might produce the "yardstick regulation" effect. That is, the political pressures generated by public approval of the demonstrated program might act as a countervailing force to the power of nursing home interests. This might reduce the political difficulties of implementing existing policies of nursing home regulation.

Although federally-developed and operated demonstration programs are likely to evade many political difficulties of implementation, it is a matter for conjecture whether a yardstick regulatory effect can take hold. Much depends on the larger societal context within which such a policy is implemented. Public attitudes toward a demonstration policy of federally-operated nursing homes might be clouded by ideological and practical concerns about government eventually taking over direct operation of all nursing homes. On the other hand, such concerns have often tended to erode when it has become widely apparent that the mechanisms of the market, even when combined with public regulation, are inadequate for coping with severe problems of service.

In any event, even if a demonstration policy for direct federal operation of several nursing homes did not result in a moderately efficient and/or effective program model, and/or did not turn out to have some kind of yardstick regulation effect, the financial costs of this approach are not great, and the policy would provide some citizens with nursing home care. As is the case with the Nutrition Program discussed earlier, neither consumers nor society would be harmed.

Some social scientists and related professionals may find the notion of federally-operated demonstrations, and certain earlier policy emphases that we have suggested in this discussion, to be unsatisfactory on ideological or other grounds. Perhaps we would agree with them on some such considerations. However, our attention has been primarily directed to one consideration, namely, that the particular type of policy adopted substantially determines conditions of implementation. Accordingly, our suggestions regarding the types of policies to be advocated for legislative adoption have been based upon criteria for reducing the inefficiency and ineffectiveness of subsequent implementation. However, some of the conditions of implementation can, in fact, be determined after a policy is adopted.

Optimizing Policy Implementation

There are two principal roles in which social scientists and their professional colleagues can have some influence on the processes of implementing policies that have already been adopted. One is as advisers to federal bureaucrats who implement policy by developing regulations and making administrative decisions which interpret legislation in operational terms. The other is as advisers to implementation agencies that function within those administrative regulations and decisions. Opportunities to undertake either of these two advising roles are usually available in relation to what we have termed New Welfare policies—policies for the development of services and facilities.

Just as policy proposals are modified because of the political dilemmas at work in the legislative process, advice to federal, state, and local implementing agencies tends to be adapted by them to meet the political conditions of their survival. Nonetheless, the advice offered to them can be reflected in their decisions and need not, in any event, always be at odds with the political pressures that they confront.

Our earlier analysis of the endemic political difficulties that limit efficient implementation has several implications for giving advice to federal bureaucrats who interpret the implementing conditions set forth in legislation. First, to the extent that legislation does not spell out complicated, interdependent steps and procedures for implementation, such complications should not be created or elaborated through interpretive decisions. Legislation is typically rather specific regarding procedures for allocating funds to state and local implementing agencies, especially when a formula distribution pattern is used. But provisions regarding the development of state and local implementing plans, and dealing with the parties that should participate in implementing processes, are often rather vague. Officials interpreting legislation should be advised to set forth requirements for the development of plans in a fashion that enables plans to be relatively simple and flexible. More importantly, they should be advised to keep to a minimum the number of public and private organizations and citizen constituencies required to participate in the processes of implementation. The fewer number of such parties participating, the fewer fragments of power that will have to be dealt with, and the less likely that implementation will be characterized by delay, financial inefficiency, and goal adaptations and attenuations.

A second strategy in advising federal administrators, is to emphasize the need to provide to implementation agencies every possible chance to build power that will facilitate their capacities to implement. For instance, under Title III of the Older Americans Act as amended in 1973, each State Unit on Aging was required to designate Planning and Service Areas within the state for which, in turn, Area Agencies on Aging would be designated. Some State Units, in submitting their designations to the federal Commissioner on Aging for review and approval, chose to tailor their proposals in a fashion that would make it possible for them to use as power bases the existing Councils on Aging, home care corporations, and other organizations they had nurtured and developed in preceding years. The Commissioner had a choice, within the language of the legislation, to review and approve these submissions in terms of relatively rigid demographic considerations or in terms of strategic considerations reflected in some of the State Unit submissions. A social scientist, concerned with optimizing implementation would have advised the Commissioner to choose the latter course. Given the inadequate resources that are available to most implementing agencies for exercising power, and given the difficulties of power dispersion with which they must cope, federal officials should generally be advised to enhance the power stock of implementing agencies whenever they can.

Advice to implementing agencies, of course, should generally follow the same lines. That is, they should be urged to use every chance they can to build their stocks of power, and to keep their processes as simple and as direct as they can.

An additional issue for implementing agencies, however, is how to minimize goal adaptation and attenuation, given that they have limited resources for exercising power. Morris and Binstock (1966) have argued that it is often possible for an implementing agent with limited power resources at his command to avoid failure and to minimize goal adaptation and attenuation by reformulating the immediate strategic objectives of his efforts. In this way, they suggest, he can make an effective match between the kinds of power he has for overcoming the resistance of target organizations and the particular array of targets that must be overcome, without sacrificing the substance of policy objectives. It should be noted, however, that this construct did not emerge from an empirical test, but was developed from an analysis of what went wrong in a number of very inefficient implementation efforts.

One further important issue confronting many implementing agencies, especially those that are new entities engendered by federal policy, is whether to use what power they have for political survival and maintenance in their state and local environments or for the implementation of federal policy. As Hudson has pointed out, the implementation requirements of federal policy can tend to make these two objectives mutually exclusive (1974). Advising an implementing agency on this issue is probably pointless. Even if one were disposed to urge an agency to risk its survival in a vigorous attempt to implement the goals of national policy, it could hardly be expected to heed such advice. This is especially so in view of a frequently-demonstrated pattern in which minimal efforts to implement national policy—observance of federal regulations and expenditure of funds—seems sufficient to maintain continuing federal support.

As illustrated by the small number of suggestions that can be made regarding the advice that social scientists and other professionals can give for optimizing implementation of service and facility policies, the difficulties of effective implementation are endemic to the American political system. Recognizing that these difficulties are endemic, however, does not in itself imply that attempts to ameliorate social conditions through policy intervention should be abandoned. We have already indicated a number of approaches that can be emphasized in the processes of policy adoption for avoiding some of the problems of implementation. And we have also suggested a few approaches for optimizing implementation efforts. Still to be addressed is the issue of whether efforts to optimize policy interventions are worth the struggle to do so in view of the inherent political limitations on policy effectiveness.

Policy Ineffectiveness and the Decision to Intervene

To this point we have been considering approaches that can be taken for improving the effectiveness of policy interventions to deal with social problems. In doing so we have intended to make clear that the major limitations on policy solutions to social problems are political difficulties endemic to the American system, particularly the dispersion of power in innumerable private and public fragments. Moreover, we have indicated that the dispersion of public power reflects central values in American political culture.

Americans tend to view politics as a process for resolving value differences through compromise and accommodation, rather than through the triumph of some values over others. But the difficulty with this view is that political resolutions characteristically tend to accommodate some interests more than others, especially those interests that control some of the larger fragments of private power. The weighting of values that reflect concern for the severity of social ills experienced by some members of society is not heavy, and even if it were it would not be sufficient to make policy intervention in social conditions more effective than it is.

Nonetheless, the difficulties posed by such a political process hardly justify an abandonment of public initiatives to cope with social problems. In view of the conditions of deprivation and suffering that pervade the lives of millions of older persons and many other Americans, the fact that policy effectiveness is inherently limited by political dilemmas is no reason for social scientists and other professionals to cease aggressive efforts at social reform. Ineffective and inefficient policies may provide some benefits to those in dire need. Also, reductions in ineffectiveness and inefficiencies can be made and provide still greater benefits. Moreover, in many policy interventions, the costs of ineffectiveness and inefficiency are largely in terms of time, effort, and money, and not in terms of social harm.

For these reasons, the social scientist can enter into processes of policy adoption and implementation with greater aggressiveness and optimism in using the decision rules that he customarily employs in evaluating evidence. In scientific research, decision-making is appropriately biased against making errors through "false acceptance" of evidence and biased in favor of the "false rejection" of evidence. In the context of policy advocacy and advisory roles, however, one might consider the value of reversing these biases (Levin and Dornbusch, 1973). Emphases on false rejections of measures for social interventions lead to an overwhelming preponderance of decisions to maintain the *status quo*, decisions which are important policies in themselves, and especially unfortunate ones for those persons who are experiencing severe deprivation. Emphases in favor of false acceptances of measures for intervention engender the risk of costs in time, effort, and money, but provide potential avenues for social amelioration that can be explored.

It is important to exercise caution, however, in using a decision rule that emphasizes false acceptances over false rejections of policy intervention measures. As Levin and Dornbusch (1973) have observed, not all of the costs of policy ineffectiveness are measured in terms of losses in time, effort, and money. Other kinds of costs which can substantially outweigh the benefits provided through policy intervention must be considered.

One moderating concern that should receive attention in policy advocacy is the opportunity costs that may be incurred by the adoption of a relatively ineffective policy. For instance, the Congress appears ready to enact some form of universal health insurance policy in the mid-to-late 1970's. Adoption of a highly-compromised policy, however, *might* be worse than no policy at all. The current politicization of health care inadequacies as a public issue seems to have concerted sufficient power to bring about a legislative response from Congress. Once the pressure of contemporary public concern is relieved by a legislative response, it may be some time before such pressure again builds up sufficiently to overcome a new pattern of power fragmentation that might be generated and sustained by a highly-compromised policy.

Aggressive optimism in policy advocacy should also be tempered by wariness toward the unanticipated consequences of intervention. For example, the adoption of legislation eliminating age-specific mandatory retirement policies *might* swiftly lead to the development of personnel practices through which older workers would be dismissed in selectively discriminatory and less predictable patterns than at present, perhaps engendering severe problems for many persons in coping with unanticipated unemployment status and/or imposed early retirement.

Exercising caution to identify opportunity costs and unanticipated consequences, however, can be overdone. Attempts to elaborate alternative strategies and the possible social contexts in which they might be employed can be endless. And no matter how extensive the process of elaborating alternatives and contexts may be, it cannot provide a basis for deciding among alternatives (Rapoport, 1962). The decision to advocate intervention must turn upon the value preferences and priorities of the social scientist, the professional, the reformer who wishes to engage in the politics of policy intervention.

REFERENCES

Bachrach, P., and Baratz, M. 1963. Decisions and non-decisions. *Amer. Pol. Sci. Rev.*, 57, 632–642.

Bailey, S. K., and Mosher, E. K. 1968. *ESEA: The Office of Education Administers a Law*. Syracuse, New York: Syracuse University Press.

Banfield, E. C. 1961. *Political Influence*. New York: The Free Press of Glencoe.

Banfield, E. C. 1970. *The Unheavenly City*. Boston: Little, Brown.

Banfield, E. C. 1973. Making a new federal program: Model Cities, 1964–68. *In*, A. Sindler (ed.), *Policy and Politics in America*, pp. 125–158. Boston: Little, Brown.

Bardach, E. *The Implementation Game: What Happens After A Bill Becomes a Law*. Forthcoming.

Binstock, R. H. 1971. *Planning*. Washington, D.C.: 1971 White House Conference on Aging.

Binstock, R. H. 1972. Interest-group liberalism and the politics of aging. *Gerontologist*, 12, 265–280.

Binstock, R. H. 1975. Planning for tomorrow's urban aged. *Gerontologist*, 12, 42–43.

Binstock, R. H., Cherington, C. M., and Woll, P. 1974. Federalism and leadership planning: Predictors of variance in state behavior. *Gerontologist*, 14, 114–121.

Cherington, C. M. 1972. Interest groups in the evolution of the Developmental Disabilities Act of 1970. Unpublished paper, Brandeis University.

Crain, R., Katz, E., and Rosenthal, R. 1969. *The Politics of Community Conflict*. Indianapolis, Indiana: Bobbs-Merrill.

Dennison, G. 1969. *The Lives of Children*. New York: Random House.

Derthick, M. 1972. *New Towns In-Town*. Washington, D.C.: Urban Institute.

Derthick, M. 1974. *Between State and Nation*. Washington, D.C.: The Brookings Institution.

Friedrich, C. J. 1963. *Man and His Government*. New York: McGraw-Hill.

Gold, B. 1974. The role of the federal government in the provision of social services to older persons. *Annals of the Am. Acad. of Pol. and Soc. Sc.*, 415, 55–69.

Goldstein, J. H. 1972. The effectiveness of manpower training programs. *In*, Subcommittee on Fiscal Policy of the Joint Economic Committee, Congress of the United States, *Studies in Public Welfare*, paper no. 3. Washington, D.C.: Government Printing Office.

Greenstone, D., and Peterson, P. E. 1973. *Race and Authority in Urban Politics*. New York: Russell Sage Foundation.

Hartz, L. 1955. *The Liberal Tradition in America*. New York: Harcourt, Brace.

Henretta, J. C. 1973. Political protest by the elderly: An organizational study. Unpublished doctoral dissertation, Cambridge, Massachusetts: Harvard University.

Holtzman, A. 1963. *The Townsend Movement*. New York: Bookman Associates.

Hudson, R. B. 1974. Rational planning and organizational imperatives: Prospects for area planning in aging. *Annals of the Am. Acad. of Pol. and Soc. Sc.*, 415, 41–54.

Hudson, R. B., and Veley, M. B. 1974. Federal funding and state planning: The case of the state units on aging. *Gerontologist*, 14, 122–128.

Kraft, J. 1966. *Profiles in Power.* New York: New American Library.

Lasswell, H. D., and Kaplan, A. 1970. *Power and Society.* New Haven, Connecticut: Yale University Press.

Levin, M. A. 1976. *Urban Politics and Criminal Courts.* Chicago: University of Chicago Press.

Levin, M. A., and Dornbusch, H. D. 1973. Pure and policy social science. *Public Policy,* pp. 383–423 (Summer).

Liebman, L. 1974. Social intervention in a democracy. *The Public Interest,* **34,** 14–29.

Lowi, T. J. 1964. American business, public policy, case studies, and political theory. *World Politics,* **16,** 677–715.

Lowi, T. J. 1969. *The End of Liberalism.* New York: W. W. Norton.

Madison, J. 1937. The federalist no. 10. *In, The Federalist,* pp. 53–62. New York: Random House.

March, J. G., and Simon, H. A. 1958. *Organizations.* New York: John Wiley.

Marris, P., and Rein, M. 1969. *Dilemmas of Social Reform: Poverty and Community Action in the United States.* New York: Atherton Press.

Martinson, R. 1974. What works?–questions and answers about prison reform. *The Public Interest,* **35,** 22–54.

Mendelson, M. A., and Hapgood, D. 1974. The political economy of nursing homes. *Annals of the Am. Acad. of Pol. and Soc. Sc.,* **415,** 95–105.

Morris, R., and Binstock, R. H. 1966. *Feasible Planning for Social Change.* New York: Columbia University Press.

Moynihan, D. P. 1965. The professionalization of reform. *The Public Interest,* **1,** 6–16.

Murphy, J. 1971. Title 1 of ESEA: The politics of implementing federal education reform. *Harv. Edu. Rev.,* **41,** 35–63.

Neugarten, B. 1974. Age groups in American society and the rise of the young-old. *Annals of the Am. Acad. of Pol. and Soc. Sc.,* **415,** 187–198.

Older Americans Act of 1965, As Amended, (Public Laws 89-73, 90-42, 91-69, 92-258, 93-29).

Pratt, H. J. 1976. *The Gray Lobby.* Chicago: University of Chicago Press.

Pressman, J. L., and Wildavsky, A. B. 1973. *Implementation: How Great Expectations in Washington Are Dashed in Oakland.* Berkeley: University of California Press.

Rapoport, A. 1962. The use and misuse of game theory. *Sci. Am.,* **207,** 108–118.

Selznick, P. 1966. *TVA and the Grass Roots.* New York: Harper & Row, Torchbook.

Simon, H. A., Smithburg, D. W., and Thompson, V. A. 1961. *Public Administration.* New York: Alfred A. Knopf.

Skolnick, J. H. 1966. *Justice Without Trial.* New York: John Wiley.

Solomon, A. P. 1974. *Housing the Urban Poor.* Cambridge, Massachusetts: The M.I.T. Press.

Stockman, D. A. 1975. The social pork barrel. *The Public Interest,* **39,** 3–30.

Sundquist, J. L., and Davis, D. W. 1969. *Making Federalism Work.* Washington, D.C.: The Brookings Institution.

Vinyard, D. 1972. The Senate Special Committee on Aging. *Gerontologist,* **12,** 298–303.

Westley, W. A. 1970. *Violence and the Police.* Cambridge, Massachusetts: The M.I.T. Press.

Wilson, J. Q. 1968. *Varieties of Police Behavior.* Cambridge, Massachusetts: Harvard University Press.

Wilson, J. Q. 1973. *Political Organizations.* New York: Basic Books.

Wright, D. 1968. *Federal Grants-in-Aid: Perspectives and Alternatives.* Washington, D.C.: American Enterprise Institute.

21
STRATEGIES OF DESIGN AND RESEARCH FOR INTERVENTION*

C. L. Estes
University of California, San Francisco

and

Howard E. Freeman
University of California, Los Angeles

In every civilization, community, and family, and in the minds of most individuals, there are ideas on the proper course of growing old, on the ways persons of advanced age are to behave and be responded to, and on the precautions and means which persons, individually and collectively, should take in order to obtain the desired state of affairs for the aged. All persons and groups are confronted with the process of aging and the phenomenon of the old person.

Romantics and others have contended that earlier in human history, and in some so-called "primitive" and agrarian societies, relative consensus among community members existed on what was right and proper for old people and on what was "normative aging" (Rosow, 1962). Yet, Pearl Buck's novels contradict ideas on the respect and treatment of the aged in preindustrial China; the old-age farms found in rural Europe and the United States hardly suggest a responsible welfare policy for the aged; and the ill-fed and ill-clothed elderly beggars found today in Latin America, Asia, and Africa dispute the existence anywhere of

either a consensual or humane social posture toward old persons.

Certainly, it is clear that there is much more heterogeneity than homogeneity on views and values about the aged, and on their care, treatment, and place in the contemporary community. Disagreement exists on a spectrum of issues, from so-called basic moral matters such as euthanasia, to practical concerns, such as what constitutes a moderate level of economic living (Clark and Anderson, 1967). This point, of course, is an inevitable theme of many chapters in this compendium. It requires reemphasis here, and considerable discussion subsequently in this chapter, since any effort to consider the strageties of design and research for intervention cannot ignore the diversity that exists in these times concerning the aged, either as a population aggregate or as individuals occupying roles in a plethora of groups and social settings.

Another point raised repeatedly in this book, which has critical relevance here—and indeed is the *raison d'être* for this chapter—is the emphasis in modern society for the fate of the aged, to be determined collectively and not on an individual basis. No doubt, we will continue to

*We gratefully acknowledge the assistance of Phyllis Keats Gross.

socialize children to the idea that respect for the aged is virtuous, to the notion that we must save for our old age, and to the view that each generation is personally responsible for its elders. But, the key determinants of the standards of living enjoyed, more often endured, by our aged are the country's social policies, political actions at all levels of government, decisions of bureaucratic administrators, and the power and influence of various organized groups.

The purpose of this chapter is to direct attention to some of the current issues and requirements for the design, implementaiton, and evaluation of social intervention programs for older persons. For purposes of this discussion, our definition of intervention is deliberately broadly defined—as pragmatic attempts at alteration which aim at social change (Baltes, 1973, p. 4).

Our premise is that the application of social science knowledge and perspectives, both conceptual and methodological, can codify, reduce, and refine the range of conceivable ideas about the prevention, treatment, and management of the problems community members face as they advance in age, thereby providing a degree of order and consistency, as well as validity, to programmatic efforts for this age segment of the population. Our approach toward social intervention—which we regard as a rational approach—calls for the application of a set of procedures and a posture not uniquely endemic to the field of gerontology, but which are applicable to the development of strategies of intervention of dealing with the matrix of social problems which confront members of our society. We are proposing a general outlook that is urgently needed in the field of gerontology.

The major obstacle to the rational approach to intervention may be found in the organizational, professional, and political constraints on the types of research, policy, and practice which have emerged in the entire human resource field (see Rossi and Williams, 1972). Gerontology suffers in particular, however, as an arena of social action, and efforts to "modernize" programs in it have been limited in innovative scope and continuity of political and financial support.

Research in gerontology has received relatively minor federal support. Also, support has been negligible in the intervention-relevant areas of evaluation and demonstration research. The consequent lack of empirically-verified strategies for accomplishing specified objectives augments the influence of ideological and political considerations in gerontological policy-making and intervention design. Conventional wisdom and well-meaning service programs have not, however, managed to dent the social-reality that has been constructed—namely that the aged are a problem group whose behavior and lot in life have undesirable ramifications for themselves and for the general community.

The dimensions of research strategy outlined in this chapter provide an alternative. But the approach set forth assumes there is a trajectory toward rationality in collective efforts in the planning and development of interventions in the aging field.

To the extent that there is progress toward rationality in the field, there are both opportunities for remedying the existing conditions and the lives of the aged, and additional responsibilities for the social strategist, the planner, practitioner, and researcher. Indeed, as we see it, under the scheme of things advocated, he or she becomes a new kind of influential and change agent. This necessarily requires constant refinement of methods and procedures, and explication of the processes of research and utilization of research results. Without this refinement and explication, what we are advocating is the substitution of one mystique for another.

KNOWLEDGE AS A BASIS FOR INTERVENTION

It is important to remember that what is done for and about the elderly, as well as past and contemporary research in the field, is a product of our conceptions of aging. In an abstract philosophical sense, the aged have only the problems we "create" for them. Therefore, a consideration of the determinants of such conceptions and the knowledge and opinions on which they are based is necessary.

The Social Construction of Problems of the Aging

There are few analyses in the gerontological literature on the social genesis of the knowledge which has been accumulated; little attention is paid to the impact that social researchers, politicians, policy-makers, and practitioners have in shaping the very problems of the aged with which they are concerned. Yet, professional gerontologists necessarily contribute to what sociologists of knowledge have called the "social construction of reality" about aging and the aged. As their perceptions and definitions of reality are widely disseminated and shared with the general community, these views and ideas become institutionalized—part of the "collective stock of knowledge" (Berger and Luckmann, 1966, p. 60). Although *socially generated*, such "knowledge" and expert opinion take on the character of *objective reality*, regardless of whether or not they are valid (Mannheim, 1936).

The essential point is that theories and perspectives in the field of gerontology are versions of reality which are socially constructed. Current conceptions of the aged and aging, as well as appropriate intervention strategies in the aging field are not determined solely by objective facts but by (1) the *interpretation* and *ordering* of perceptions of those facts into paradigms or ways of perceiving and explaining the world (Kuhn, 1970), and (2) the *power* and *influence* of the perceivers and interpreters (Gouldner, 1970). Thus, in an important sense, the aged do not have social problems other than the ones we have "given" them.

The position that reality is social is not to assert that the elderly face no problems independent of those that are socially constructed (Cottrell, 1972). There are phenomena associated with growing old and population characteristics which may be said to be fundamentally "real" regardless of how they are perceived. For example, biological age is a fact, independent of how it may be perceived and consequently treated. Friedson (1970, p. 223) notes a similar distinction in regard to disease and illness:

> . . . a social state is added to a biophysical state by assigning the meaning of illness to

disease. It is in this sense that the physician creates illness . . . and that illness is a kind of social deviance analytically and empirically distinct from mere disease.

Relevance of perceptions of aging to the identification of social problems and development of intervention programs is illuminated by the work of Howard Becker and others (Becker, 1963; Matza, 1969). Neither social problems nor deviance are inherent in the personality, socialization, or behavior of particular groups and individuals. Rather, they reside in the *reactions of others* to such groups and individuals. This perspective, called "labelling theory," holds that:

> Deviance . . . is created by society. . . . Social groups create deviance by making the rules whose infraction constitutes deviance. . . . The deviant is one to whom that label has successfully been applied (Becker, 1963, p. 8).

The designation of a social problem "depends on how other people react to it" (Becker, 1963, p. 11). Viewed in this light, the aged and the consequences of aging are "social problems" only when they are labelled as such:

> The social problem, then, is *not inherent* in the aging process or the aging individual; instead, growing old is a social problem as a consequence of the labelling applied by others. . . . Further, the more influential the group doing the labelling, the more widespread the acceptance of the labels. . . . A form of power accrues . . . to those . . . who are in a position to construct reality regarding the problems of aging, for their definitions may become institutionalized (Estes, 1972, p. 4).

The development of intervention strategies is intertwined, then, with the "societal reaction," to the phenomenon of aging, including that of professionals in the field (Lemert, 1951, 1973; Coser, 1965). Study of the societal reaction involves looking at both the *subjective and objective* aspects of the phenomenon of aging. This issue has been touched upon by gerontologists in calling for the study of (1) perceptions of aging, both by the aged themselves and others (Peterson and Peters, 1971; Freeman, 1973; Birren, Woodruff, and Bergman, 1972), (2) aging research as a social process (Birren, Woodruff, and Bergman, 1972), and (3) the organization and practice of planning efforts and intervention programs and their relation to the vested interests of the professionals, groups, and institutions involved (Estes, 1972, 1975; Freeman, 1973).

The impact of the professionals' labelling on the older person may be compounded because as persons become older they experience new problems and role changes as a consequence of biological aging. These modifications are likely to make the older person more vulnerable to the cues and perceptions of others in their interactions, thereby augmenting the potential influence of others in revising the self-images which older persons hold of themselves. Thus, in the long run, the professionals who research, legislate, plan, or implement interventions for the elderly influence how different individuals *experience* the aging process (Estes, 1975). Social researchers, planners, and practitioners involved in intervention programs are not neutrals. Rather, they are actively engaged in modifying and structuring social reality for the aged.

An Overview of Intervention Strategies

Any discussion of intervention strategies must be both philosophical and political at the same time. The philosophical aspects emanate from the ultimately value-based identification and social construction of conditions deemed undesirable and the assumption that a social science perspective is a viable point of departure for the development and implementation of social policies about the aged. The political aspects lie in the fact that research for social change inserts social scientists into the essentially political process of policy determination (Benveniste, 1970; Schultze, 1968).

Although the fields of policy analysis, planning, and social research are far from mature and lack specificity of procedures, there is general agreement on the major elements in developing an intervention strategy. Following the identification of a set of conditions or behaviors deemed undesirable, it is critical to (1) explicate the objectives of the intervention; (2) designate the target population; (3) posit a theory on how such changes can be effected; (4) develop an operational program or treatment; (5) select organizations and practitioners to implement the program; and (6) develop a research design that permits the study of both program implementation and impact (Freeman and Sherwood, 1970).

Before proceeding with a discussion of these individual elements, we should note that in the field of aging, as in other areas of human concern, methodologies must be developed and research must be conducted not only for the design of intervention in the present but also for anticipating the direction of program activities for the future. This problem is particularly important given the expected differences between generations of the elderly. For example, the elderly of the next decade will arrive at retirement age with more education, more urban experience, and, it is hoped, more experience with service institutions (Havighurst, 1969) than previous generations of the elderly. Of relevance to this point are empirical findings indicating that "cohort differences may be greater than age changes" (Birren, Woodruff, and Bergman, 1972, p. 67) in attitudes and personality, suggesting the policy implication that programs suitable to one age cohort may not be suitable to another. This finding on age cohorts calls for a built-in flexibility in intervention strategies if they are to endure over the long run.

We do not advocate, however, any single theoretical perspective or practice model over another. Further, all existing service programs cannot be restructured immediately. What is proposed is a special and particular *commitment to innovation and experimentation as a basis for gradually restructuring the field of intervention in gerontology.* This commitment is required among those with responsibility for the allocation of resources for the implementation of a systematic set of intervention strategies, as well as among planners and practitioners in the field.

Gerontological Knowledge as a Basis for Intervention

Development and design of effective intervention strategies must be linked with some view or perspective of the aged and the aging process. Such perspectives are likely to emanate from some interaction between one or more of the following—naturalistic observation, experimental reports, systematic research, social values, and political commitment.

Social gerontological perspectives include viewing aging as a life-cycle, life-span developmental process (Neugarten and Berkowitz, 1964; Riegel, 1972; Lowenthal, 1974), as a process of social disengagement (Cumming and Henry, 1961), as a phenomenon of changing social activity (Havighurst, 1963), as an arena of symbolic interaction (Rose, 1965), and as a set of deviant behaviors (Rosow, 1963, 1974; Birren, Woodruff, and Bergman, 1972, p. 54). The aged, as an aggregate are seen as a minority group (Barron, 1953; Streib, 1965); as a subculture (Rose, 1962); and as a political influence group (Trela, 1971; Pratt, 1974). Others in the field view the aged as a consumer group, as either a peripheral or residual work force, and as a socially and economically dependent aggregate. The aged can also be viewed as an integral part of a family support system (Shanas, Townsend, Wedderburn, Friis, Milhøj, and Stehouwer, 1968).

Other chapters in this volume elaborate these different perspectives on the aged and the aging process. Here, it is sufficient to indicate the diversity of these perspectives and their consequences for the design, implementation, and evaluation of intervention strategies. By way of illustration, take what many would call the major social science perspective or paradigm in gerontology—the life-cycle, life-span developmental perspective.

From this perspective, a number of different intervention approaches may be called for, depending upon which aspects of this general perspective are emphasized. Blending into a biopsychological perspective, this view of aging stresses developmental change which is observable at all stages of life span and linked to biophysical maturation. But adherents of the perspective accord different degrees of influence to the contribution of environment, culture, and normative codes to development and aging. At issue is the impact of developmental versus generational and cultural determinants on the rate, directionality, and sequentiality of an individual's life changes as he or she moves along a trajectory from birth to death. The theoretical and empirical rationale for a life-span developmental view remains vague and perhaps even misunderstood (Baltes and Schaie, 1970).

Rather than detail the multitude and complex versions or themes within this general life-span framework or paradigm, it is sufficient to say that different theorists, researchers, and practitioners draw from different perspectives within this one major paradigm. These varying perspectives have relevance to the gerontological issues of continuity, disengagement, and activity theories.

Of major significance is the fact that the prescriptions for intervention based on this singular paradigm are startlingly ambiguous and potentially contradictory. For example, they might involve modification of the environment or of the opportunities for activity, or some version of behavior modification, dependent on the assumed or empirically verified influence of environment (Hoyer, 1973; Lawton, 1970). Further, they might involve either interventions directed primarily on the individual at one developmental stage rather than another, or they might involve a conception of intervention throughout the life span (Beattie, 1970; Birren and Woodruff, 1973; Looft, 1973; Lowenthal, 1974), as in the case of recent proposals for life-span supportive services and education. Developmentally-relevant intervention strategies might involve either modification of the environment in addition to or in place of the above (Estes and Schooler, 1966; Rosow, 1967) or of the larger social institutions to the extent they are perceived as interacting with or affecting personality development in aging.

The life-span, developmental perspective is probably the most debated and researched theory which the social sciences have offered in gerontology. Yet, as our brief discussion of it demonstrates, even within this general perspective, there are embodied a multitude of contradictory and conflicting ideas about aging and the aged which result in inconsistent, disparate, and elusive objectives for intervention in the field. This is a major problem in the design of intervention strategies.

Thus, a general problem in ascertaining the direction for intervention efforts relates to the lack of ". . . well supported and articulated theories which permit . . . exposition of intervention principles" (Baltes, 1973, p. 5). As stated by Labouvie (1973, p. 13):

> The challenge . . . on a theoretical level . . . is to develop . . . models that specify how the environment interacts with aging and that explicitly spell out the possible experiential bases of aging. At the present, however, it is not possible to formulate specific prescriptions as to what strategies of intervention are suitable or even necessary. This uncertainty reflects the current state of theorizing. . . .
> As long as our understanding of the causes of aging is in such a fragmentary state, we need to be 'cautious in our advice and energetic in our research' (Watson, 1971).

Theory in gerontology not only is still in its infancy, but the existing knowledge in the field is not easily codifiable into coherent frameworks. Also, problems emanate from the different definitions and conceptualizations of aging employed and the inadequacy of much of the existing data due to methodological design problems.

Major gaps in knowledge are created by the lack of adequate research strategies to test some of the key questions in the field. An example of this issue involves the difficulty in distinguishing between generational change and developmental change (or cohort *versus* life-cycle change). Findings from cross-sectional studies, typically focused on the contrasting views and characteristics of different age-cohorts of persons at a given point in time, cannot validly address questions of age change, that is, the process of aging. The problem of differentiating life-cycle from generational or cultural differences has been addressed in detail elsewhere, and alternative design models, or sequential strategies, have been developed to meet some of the objections to both cross-sectional and longitudinal designs (Schaie, 1965; Ryder, 1965; Baltes, 1968; Riley and Foner, 1968; Baltes and Schaie, 1970; Birren, Woodruff, and Bergman, 1972). Unfortunately, however, sequential strategies are costly and require reasonably large samples studied at least at two points in time. But, significantly, early

findings from studies employing this strategy indicate that cohort differences may be greater than age changes in many instances (Birren, Woodruff, and Bergman, 1972; Schaie and Strother, 1968; Woodruff and Birren, 1972).

Another difficulty emanates from the potentially different results from studies utilizing chronological age versus ones employing sociologically or psychologically-derived definitions of aging. In most cases, chronological age has been employed in research due to the lack of adequate indicators of nonchronological definitions. But the use of chronological age may well obscure the very characteristics or consequences of the aging process which the researcher seeks to study. Several gerontologists have discussed this problem in relation to the necessity for defining aging in terms of the personal perceptions and experiences of, and the meaning of aging to members of the society (Sparks, 1973; Birren, Woodruff, and Bergman, 1972). Data based on these latter conceptions are seen to differ importantly from data based on the use of objective standards which are socially defined, such as age 65.

Because of the conceptual confusion in gerontology, two tactics are likely to be part of program planning and development. One is to avoid stating, with specificity, the guiding perspective on aging and the aged which is linked to a particular effort. An example of such an approach would be one which emphasizes process rather than outcome—whether it be an innovative program in the area of recreation, the creation of a new health-care delivery system or the founding of an unusual political organization for the aged. The effort is to show that a certain process can be undertaken (taking for granted its inherent value), but with little commitment to the question of results or impact—for to do so would require a commitment to a perspective on aging as well as to the research evaluation process.

The second tactic is to create broad-scale and so-called comprehensive innovations, in which there are a large number of program inputs with many vague objectives. The sub-state (area) planning strategy of the 1973 Comprehensive Services Amendments to the Older Americans Act may be classified as an example of this tactic. The approach is akin to the physician who treats a patient with multiple diseases by means of a number of broad-spectrum antibiotics. Even if the patient improves in some respects, the doctor cannot either duplicate his results in other patients suffering from only some of the diseases or know what parts of the regime to discontinue in the case of the particular patient.

Arguing against comprehensiveness in the human services field is heresy—but *for the purposes of understanding the impact of innovation, it is necessary to know about the consequences of each specific innovative input before there is an attempt to "package" different programs.*

For many professionals and policy-makers in the field of aging, this position may be seen as destructive to program efforts. While acknowledging the number of different and often competing perspectives and practice orientations, and the difficulty in explicating and linking program objectives to particular perspectives, they are likely to insist that there is little choice but to continue the so-called comprehensive efforts—even if uncertain as to objectives of the programs or without knowledge of their outcome. From a practical, i.e., political standpoint, they may be correct with respect to existing programs which involve large populations and extensive commitments. We recognize that all current programs cannot be rendered immediately consistent with the views on explicating objectives expressed here. The issue must be met head on, however. Explicating the perspectives underlying programs and identifying their objectives is essential to the design of social interventions if rigorous evaluations of program impact are to be undertaken. It may be necessary to give up ideas of comprehensiveness and the emphasis on process in order to undertake programs that can be carefully evaluated in terms of results. Unless this is the approach, future large-scale service programs, with their vast costs, are no more likely to be responsibly promulgated than current ones.

Prime illustrations of the lack of explicit frameworks and objectives are the programs and policies embodied in the 1973 Amend-ments to the Older Americans Act, amendments that only partially were developed with the benefits of severely limited research. Indeed, most of the relevant research did not provide data on what programs "worked" and should be implemented nationally on a broad scale. Instead, available studies provided mostly "negative findings," documenting the inability of state units on aging (SUAS) to carry out their "leadership planning" functions and to implement coherent statewide program strategies with their Title III community grants (Binstock, 1972; Hudson, 1973). The 1973 Amendments were designed to correct some of these problems through a strategy of sub-state planning, which is yet to be demonstrated as an effective approach (Warren, 1971; Estes, 1974).

The same can be said about the Title VII nutrition program. Research on nutrition demonstration projects illustrated many negative findings.

> *participating ... did not bring about change in dietary habits ... it did not effect change in living patterns of participants ... [although] findings indicate some increase of acceptance of their present status* (Bechill and Wolgamot, 1972 pp. 22, 25).

These and the few other findings regarding the nutrition program impact, however, had to be qualified with statements like, "it is not known whether this change was due to participation in the nutrition program."

Thus, both the Title III and Title VII programs under the 1973 Amendments appear to be based on little or no knowledge of whether these strategies will work. These illustrations dramatize the urgency and critical necessity for intervention design and evaluation which permit the critical examination of component program elements.

Requirements for Policy Research

Even social scientists studying social problems with an "applied" orientation have frequently failed to provide findings useful for policy purposes. As described by Scott and Shore (1974), policy-relevance is determined by the policy salience and "tractability" of conditioning or independent variables that are hypothetically associated with the outcome or dependent variables. Tractability is related to the potential for manipulability and control of the conditioning or independent variables in an operating program. These authors convincingly argue that "the assumption that policy implications are inherent in and forthcoming from . . . [sociological] research findings requires a giant leap of faith" (Scott and Shore, 1974, p. 52). Instead, the intentional selection of variables from the virtually inexhaustable array of potentially associated variables found in the sociological literature should be based on "its practical importance in the operation of a program and its potential interest to legislatures and other public groups that would be asked to appropriate money to support a . . . program" (Scott and Shore, 1974, p. 55).

Many persons in the aging field believe that all research is inherently useful in the development of programs. On the contrary, it is important to distinguish research on social phenomena, on social problems, and on social policy in the field. But "basic" research often addresses issues which are neither appropriate nor relevant to the problem areas of interest to policymakers. The traditional schism between research and application is at least as evident in gerontology as in other fields. It is found at all levels of research—from the formulation and design of research to the translation of research findings for practical application, the problem of research utilization.

Basic research on social phenomena may be either descriptive or analytical, in the sense of hypothesis-testing. But, in and of itself, this type of research is neither likely to address policy considerations, nor is it likely to result in the selection of input variables which are programmatically relevant (i.e., manipulable or "tractable"). As noted by Baltes (1973), Kastenbaum (1968), and others, social gerontologists seem preoccupied with simply describing aging and with lamenting the negatives of being old and, even worse, they appear to have left efforts at explanation and modification (i.e., intervention) primarily to the biologically-oriented disciplines (Baltes, 1973).

Similarly, research on social problems of aging may be descriptive or analytical. But unless designed to answer policy questions, both the delineation of research problems and variable selection may be irrelevant to prescriptions for intervention strategies. For example, research which concludes that older people would be healthier if they had exercised more in their middle years and happier if they had had better relations with their parents in infancy has little policy relevance for the current cohort over the age of 65, because there is no program intervention which can modify these "given" past experiences of older persons.

Policy research on the other hand, while addressing many of the same issues and employing identical theories, concepts, and variables, is generated by specific concerns, concentrates on studying tractable input variables, and is more immediate in terms of its time-frame for completion (Coleman, 1973). Policy research, then, is pragmatic, political, and value laden. There is a strain between adhering to the canons of science and the rules of social research while also attempting to satisfy the demands and expectations of policy-makers. Unless social research is accurate and usable by policy-makers, they are just as likely to use inadequate research as none at all. This suggests a special kind of responsibility for the researcher, if he is going to meet the dual commitments to the policy-maker and to his academic peers.

Developing Intervention Strategies

In the development of intervention strategies, there must be a constant interplay between the activities, experiences, and ideas of persons on the firing line—practitioners and service personnel—and the views, orientations, and thinking of those engaged in both research and political roles. This interplay needs to be framed and undertaken in the light of available data and theories, products of research studies, and information provided by indicators and population information.

Social Indicators. In all areas of social concern including gerontology, there is a recently developing interest in the construction of time series (Taber and Flynn, 1971) which not only reflect the economic aspects of community life, but also the social qualities of life as well (Freeman and Sherwood, 1971; Duncan, 1973). Social and economic indicators, as well as carefully analyzed census data, are essential for the development of social policies and for selection of priorities of particular interest for intervention programs (Birren, Woodruff, and Bergman, 1972).

Given the extensive body of recent literature on social indicators, both directly related to the aging field and on general social considerations, there is little point in extended review here. It should be pointed out, however, that gerontology resembles other fields in that there are serious matters, including a lack of consensus among investigators, that limit progress in the field of social indicators and related work. This is the case even though a serious effort has been made to develop such indicators specifically in this field (Administration On Aging, 1971). Both selection of the social indicators and variables for disaggregation require full knowledge and understanding of the policy-utilization potential of the indicators.

Disagreements exist, first, regarding the criteria for the selection of valid and reliable variables on which to measure the social and interpersonal conditions of the aged and their environment. Second, there is lack of agreement about the variables on which to disaggregate time series (Freeman and Sherwood, 1970), e.g., is race important, or urban-rural residence, or what? Time-series are useful only when meaningfully disaggregated, and this need in the aging field is obvious. For example, the current debate on the different ages at which men and women are eligible for social security clearly requires data on labor force participation, broken down by sex. Systematic attention must be directed at the selection and operationalization of key variables for purposes of disaggregation.

There is a third related matter. In using variables of key interest for time-series analyses, as well as for cross-sectional studies, too little attention is given in social gerontology to the categorization and classification of basic characteristics such as permanently disabled and mentally impaired.

The widely used key parameter in this field—chronological age—is a clear example. As discussed previously in this chapter, and elsewhere in the volume, studies vary widely in their categorization and analysis of study data by age. Consequently, close comparisons between parallel investigations simply are not possible with respect, for example, to measures of medical utilization, social participation, and so on. For indicator research, as well as for cross-sectional and panel studies of a shorter time-frame, the field of aging can benefit from more consensual agreement regarding the measures and categorization of age and aging that are used, enhancing the possibility of comparing the results of different investigations.

Service Statistics. Virtually all agencies, large and small, public and private, make some effort to collect and summarize data on the characteristics of their client-populations, on services and treatments provided, and often on something about the impact of their programs. In general however, such service statistics are notoriously useless for systematic purposes for both the development of social interventions and policy analysis.

There are numerous criticisms on the limitations and lack of utility of most such data. Despite reviews going back well over a half-century, the situation remains pitiful. In the aging field, in most specialized and private agencies as well as in large public programs (with the possible exception of information from the Social Security Administration), gross biases in the collection and processing of the data result in its minimal value for the stimulation and development of intervention programs or for assessing their implementation and impact. For example, hospitals and social agencies often rate patients that they do not see again as recovered simply because they do not return for treatment.

The reasons for the extant situation are many, ranging from a lack of technical expertise and manpower, to a lack of interest and minimal motivation by service personnel to engage in data collection and processing efforts. The potential usefulness of such data is great, however. Thus, a future goal should be to improve the quality and comparability of service statistics so they can contribute to the various phases of social intervention efforts.

PERSPECTIVES ON CAUSATION

Despite the plea for orderly development of intervention models, there is no inevitable sequence to their development. As in the case of the genesis of most research problems in the social sciences, a number of inputs—including extant theoretical notions, visibility of social concerns, political considerations, and availability of funding—play a role in the development of particular interventions. Sometimes specification of the target population and the choice of a level of intervention are early steps; other times they occur subsequent to the formulation of other elements in an intervention design.

Nevertheless, at some point it is essential to take a position with regard to causation. In general, it is reasonable to think of three causal models as guiding the development of intervention models in the aging field.

Proximal Cause

Continued scientific investigation into the human condition has provided considerable evidence against the simplistic idea that single causes can be isolated to explain any of the individual, interpersonal, or social ills that confront us. The model that "A causes B," the single cause view, in most cases neither provides a sufficiently satisfying explanation nor allows full development of interventions to prevent, restore, or manage the problems which confront the aged or any other aggregate.

At the same time, specific interventions both for purposes of the design of programs and their evaluations often must be satisfied with the economical approach of concentrating upon a single determinant which is hypothesized to directly affect some condition and whose modification will result in a change in the condition. This is the idea of proximal cause.

At all levels of intervention in which biologi-cal phenomena are involved, the concept of proximal cause is clear. For example, while a complex causal model is necessary to explain diabetes, control of sugar intake by either diet or drug provides the means of managing this illness. So too, at a preventive level, vaccinations protect against a number of serious diseases including polio, smallpox, and so on.

At first glance, it seems reasonable to argue that proximal causes should be given priority in developing interventions. But there are reasons as well to argue against taking this view of causation.

From a practical standpoint, as we have noted, in addition to assessing the proximal relevance of a cause or determinant, it is essential to consider the opportunities for modification and tractability. For example, the proximal cause of unhappiness among older persons may be feelings of estrangement from their children. But to remedy this matter may require changing the general community's concept of aged persons, not merely counseling of the parties directly involved. The proximal cause, in some cases at least, must remain unattended until more distant conditions are attended to.

From a realistic standpoint, furthermore, some proximal causes cannot be the direct foci of interventions. Sexual frustrations among widowed aged persons cannot be approached by a social agency pandering for them; instead, either indirect means (e.g., social clubs) or substitute activities (e.g., athletic and social games) may be the only expedient alternatives.

Finally, attention to proximal causes may direct activities unduly to interventions at the level of management of social and medical problems, to the neglect of preventive types of interventions. This is not always the case. But often interventions addressed to proximal causes do not touch the underlying etiological problems. Social as well as medical concerns among the aged are more likely to be "chronic" than acute, and long-term rather than short-term. Dealing with proximal causes often can be likened to holding one's finger against a spigot rather than replacing the faucet's washer.

Multi-Causal Models

There are two different conceptions of multi-causal models that are often used as a basis of intervention programs. One view holds that a number of different determinants exist for a particular behavior or condition, e.g., inadequate housing for the aged. The deficiency is believed to be a function of lack of interest on the part of architects and physical planners, the shortage of public funds, the residential mobility of urban and suburban families, and the confusion in political boundaries. Correction or modification in any one of these areas may have an impact on the housing needs of the elderly. Or to take another example: poor nutritional status among the aged may be related to a lack of funds, inadequate knowledge of good nutritional practice, inability to shop in stores having appropriate foods because of handicaps, and so on. Each of these determinants could be the focal point of the current Title VII Nutrition Program intervention effort.

The illustrations above are examples of causal models in which the various determinants may be *independent* of each other. The second multi-causal model is one in which a series of determinants are thought to be *interrelated*, e.g., depression among the aged may be related to the geographic distance from relatives and friends, the social commitments of these people, and the lack of adequate transportation. In these circumstances, modification of any one of these determinants is unlikely to have much of an impact on the mental health of older persons. Rather, what would be required is a program that seeks the remedy of all of the explanatory phenomena.

In fact, rarely are the various determinants of particular social concerns in any area, and particularly in the field of aging, either entirely independent or completely interdependent. Rather, there usually is a partial connection between various determinants of particular problems. The dilemma is that one must begin many intervention programs without definitive knowledge of causation; at the same time, however, one needs a hypothetical model in order to design a program and provide proper evaluation of it.

The complexities for evaluation research that ensue as a consequence of multiple causation are well recognized. First, it is the recognition of multi-causality that leads to complex intervention programs. Second, it is these complex programs which make rigorous evaluation research so difficult. There is no ready solution to this situation. On the one hand, highly simplistic intervention programs, particularly when the determinants are interdependent, are clearly doomed to failure. On the other hand, overly complex programs become almost impossible to administer consistently and also are exceedingly difficult to evaluate.

In the field of aging, the tendency has been to overextend the design of programs and to argue that only extremely broad programs will have an impact at all, as illustrated by the Title III area planning and comprehensive services legislation. Programs under Title III require everything—coordination, planning, advocacy, direct service, pooling of untapped resources, and other elements. Programs and strategies so designed may thwart intervention efforts, wasting not only human resources but also prohibiting adequate research on outcome. The solution must be economical programs in which each program element is tied to a particular anticipated outcome, with specification of the hypothetical interactive relationships between program elements. This requires that a multi-causal model be explicated—including clear statements of the direction and, if possible, the magnitude of relations between the various inputs and determinants of the particular condition.

A popular approach to the complex problems of multi-causality is a specific procedure referred to as "path-analysis." Path analysis is nothing more than a flow-chart indicating the various pathways and directions of relationships among the relevant variables (Land, 1969). As discussed subsequently, existing data may be available from descriptive surveys and predictive studies which can be utilized in the specification of relations between variables.

The Epidemiological View

A third way of thinking about cause is derived from work in the field of public health. In efforts to control epidemics, public health physicians observed that there were often three sets of related conditions which might be modified, and that it made little difference in outcome except in expediency, regarding which set was modified. These sets of conditions are often labelled "host," "agent," and "environment." The classic illustration is the eradication of malaria, a disease carried by a germ in mosquitoes living in swamps. One approach is to provide a vaccination against the germ; a second is to develop a means of killing the mosquitoes that carry the germ; and the third is to contaminate the swamps in which mosquitoes live by placing oil on them, so that the environment is no longer compatible for the insects. The host-agent-environment idea can be thought of as three links of chain; it makes little difference which of the links is broken to render the chain useless.

The epidemiological view has relevance to the field of aging, particularly for programs of prevention. For example, in dealing with problems of accidents, emotional and physical illness, and selected social aspects of the lives of older persons, this type of conceptualization has important relevance.

In some intervention efforts, the epidemiological model may be a means of simplifying the program, thereby facilitating the tasks of planning and evaluation. If one uses this model, and concentrates on modifying only a single link among the three, the interventions are likely to require several and markedly different component parts. For example, it is possible to think about reducing accidents among the aged by modifying the environment, but this may require considerable reconstruction including the building of ramps, guard rails, and improved interior lighting. Compare such a program with the easier one of dumping oil on swamps.

In developing a strategy of intervention, there is no formula for what model will make the most sense. What is essential is that whatever the model developed, it should be as explicit as possible. Models arise from special and unique combinations of conceptual ideas or theories, empirical data, and personal experiences. In some instances models stem mainly from theoretical ideas. This is particularly so in dealing with physical health problems, for through centuries of study medical scientists have developed conceptual and theoretical

bodies of knowledge. In the development of interventions of a social character, where the concern is with interpersonal and community life phenomena, there is much less theory available. More often these are based on fragmented pieces of existing data which are organized into a hypothetically constructed causal scheme. The needs in this instance are twofold: for more adequate theorizing and for developing bodies of reliable and valid empirical information.

CONCEPTUAL AND OPERATIONAL FRAMEWORKS FOR INTERVENTION

There are three general orientations which guide most of the intervention efforts in the field of aging. These involve efforts aimed at change at the psychological, social psychological, and social structural levels.

Individual Change

Many gerontological programs emphasize the individual, as in the efforts to manage and ameliorate physical and mental illnesses and to deal with the numerous problems of physical deterioration which occur with aging. Programs of individual counseling for both emotional and environmental problems often include ideas concerning the individual psychology, as well as the biology of aging.

There are a number of attractions to using a framework which focuses on the individual, including the relative ease of identifying inputs and outputs and constructing adequate evaluation designs. Currently, however, there is reluctance to emphasize frameworks that concentrate on individuals. The reasons are twofold: first, it is clear that many of the problems which confront the elderly cannot be prevented and ameliorated by a focus on the individual alone. For example, to the extent that there is no transportation enabling older persons to obtain medical or other services, intervention aimed at the social structural level of transportation experimentation may be deemed more efficacious than that aimed at the individual level. Also, there is an increased emphasis on the interpersonal and social aspects of the quality of life. Such a shift is likely to decrease the relative emphasis on individual and psychological frameworks.

The second reason for looking beyond the individual in the development of frameworks for intervention programs is the cost of such efforts, which are regarded by many as insufferable given the numerous demands for resources. Also, as one moves beyond biomedical problems and into areas of emotional and interpersonal concern, there is considerable skepticism about the value of individual interventions. The possibilities of modifying the styles of an older person's life and feelings of social and economic deprivation through case work and individual counseling, for example, are slim. Psychotherapy seems to benefit a select group of persons treated whether they are young or old.

In discussing individual interventions, we should make clear that there still remain many current efforts that are unstudied from the standpoint of program design, testing, and evaluation. Even many of the therapeutic drugs and certainly much of the advice regarding health care for the aged are based primarily on clinical impressions and, in some cases, on folklore. Further, most individual interventions consist of private relationships between practitioner and patient or client and like much medical treatment, there is little or no information about the actual processes that are involved. This lack of knowledge and the attendant latitude and variations permitted in the application of such interventions inhibit the standardization of the treatment variables and their applicability to rational intervention strategies.

Social Psychological Change

Many programs are based on the viewpoint that, in one way or another, it is essential to change the thinking, values, and attitudes of one group or another. Some of these programs focus directly on the aged; they include efforts to provide information on nutrition and opportunities for participation in social activities and to modify the value stances of different groups. Such programs may be directed toward the elderly, toward others in the community,

and sometimes toward an entire community population (Cohen, 1970). Some may be essentially political in character, to provide popular support for various actions believed appropriate by politicians and politically appointed administrators. It is absolutely necessary, of course, that such activities take place if there is to be public support for programs of extended health insurance, public housing, and the like for the aged.

In addition, although less prevalent, there are social psychological programs directed toward changing the attitudes, beliefs, and values of the professionals who interact with the aged. Regardless of what profession is involved, it is fairly well documented that the aged are often regarded as "uninteresting," "disreputable," and "difficult" (Butler, 1969; Coe, 1967; Mutschler, 1971). Medical practitioners and others in the health field have been accused of neglecting the aged. Long-term terminal cases in particular are frequently regarded as burdensome by health practitioners (Spence, Feigenbaum, Fitzgerald, and Roth, 1968). The same observation holds for those engaged in a variety of social programs, including recreation activities and educational efforts (Troll and Schlossberg, 1970). Efforts to change the perspectives and interests of professionals have filtered into formal education programs of all sorts (Birren, Woodruff, and Bergman, 1972), the most serious of which have been the National Institute of Child Health and Human Development (NICHD) and Administration on Aging (AoA) funded training programs for professionals in gerontology.

Social psychological interventions attempted in fields such as race relations and mental health provide important lessons for gerontology. The first generalization supported by considerable research is that "knowledge" is relatively easy to modify through a variety of different communication methods. Most studies of efforts to modify values and deep-seated attitudes, however, have not proved particularly successful. Many argue that these more fundamental changes occur only when the social environment of persons is modified and are subsequent rather than antecedent to major modifications in the values held by individuals (Rose, 1965;

Scott and Freeman, 1966). The current view, for example, is that racial prejudice is reduced following the curtailment of discrimination.

Second, in most areas of concern about the human condition, there are pluralistic ideas on what are right and proper standards. It is argued that these ambiguities are intense with regard to social norms for the elderly (Clark and Anderson, 1967; Rosow, 1974). Also, it has been claimed that there is no coherent national policy toward the aged because of the range of different perspectives on their problems (Cohen, 1970; Taber and Flynn, 1971). Consequently, different social psychological intervention efforts may support program objectives which compete with one another. For example, clergymen may stress the importance of family responsibility for the aged while, at the same time, voluntary groups are seeking to inculcate views of community responsibility for old persons. Some would argue that the competition between programs is an inevitable aspect of the general pluralism of American society; others maintain that the variation which exists diminishes the impact of all such efforts.

In-between frameworks that focus on individual change and on social psychological intervention are the now popular interpersonal efforts. Some are fads, such as encounter groups, and others are more systematically developed group-dynamic efforts to mediate psychological or environmental problems of the aged. The impact of most of these efforts remains to be tested, although undoubtedly the enthusiasm for these approaches will spill over to programs for old persons.

Social Structural Change

The idea that important modifications in the lives of persons and in their environments require intervention at a social structural level clearly is not a new viewpoint; it can be traced to the religious movements that occurred throughout history and to numerous social, political, and economic philosophers who have stressed the need to modify the outlines of society. Current emphasis on social structural change has been particularly strong

in the U.S. since the late 1950's when, in order to combat poverty and racial discrimination, there was governmental recognition and acceptance of the concept of social structural change.

Social structural change implies that some major social institution in a community can and will be modified. Some social structural change is based upon legal action including promulgation and enforcement of laws about age-discrimination. Other social structural change is related to shifting opportunity structures for groups of individuals by modifying the physical and social environment. It may involve developing special types of transportation for groups, reorganizing housing arrangements, or developing new employment or social opportunities.

Social structural change need not occur at the general level of the community. Although some analysts consider modifications in groups and organizations in the service delivery system as too narrow to be regarded as social structural change, they can represent important changes. For example, the implementation of legislation requiring all agencies and organizations to have 10 percent of their patient and client loads consist of persons 60 years of age or older, or to require all hospitals and outpatient clinics to have special geriatric units, would undoubtedly result in major social changes. Particularly with respect to the problems of the elderly, change in the delivery systems for health care and personal services are required as well as in the methods and means by which economic support is given to old people (e.g., a guaranteed minimum income without restrictions on ways to spend it, rather than a welfare dole that may include food stamps and specific requirements for categorical expenditures).

The social structural framework continues to be popular in the thinking of many planners and program professionals in the field. In part this is because of pessimism regarding individual and social psychological approaches, and in part it is related to a general dissatisfaction with the way communities have developed programs rooted in these psychological conceptions.

At the same time, it is necessary to be skeptical of program efforts of a social structural nature. In the first place, while much lip-service is given to the importance of making social structural changes, the political reluctance of most community members to modify their own positions limits the applicability of this framework. This is as true of social agency practitioners as it is of members of the general community (Estes, 1973), because practitioner interests in the maintenance and enhancement of their organizations may displace their social concerns for the problems of the group to which they provide services. Further, even when there is readiness for change, or at least a climate which allows it to be accomplished, implementation is difficult. For example, it is frequently impossible to demonstrate that there has been planned and active discrimination against aged persons with respect to employment, obtaining credit, and the like. Thus, although the legal statutes are now quite clear, the social structural realities remain the same.

Levels of Intervention

Public health practitioners and researchers often conceptualize interventions in terms of the time-frame for action. At one end are efforts designed to *prevent* the onset of a condition; intermediate are programs to *restore* the situation or *cure* a problem; at the other end are attempts to *manage* or *contain* conditions. This model can perhaps most clearly be illustrated in terms of individual health problems, although it has relevance for all interventions in the aging field. A long and active life clearly is associated with the absence of circulatory disease; and therefore, it is generally believed wise to control cholesterol intake among older persons. At a preventive level, intervention calls for good nutritional practices from childhood; at an intermediate, restorative level, it calls for changed eating habits and programs of exercise to reduce fat levels for prospective cardiac cases; at a management level it requires medication and changes in regimen for those with circulatory afflictions.

The concept of levels of intervention becomes more obtuse when applied to nondisease specific concerns. For example, those who hold a perspective of the aged as a minority group might suggest that prevention of such a status requires classroom programs of education and value inculcation during early school years; the intermediate level would consist of implementing attitude and value-change among employers and community leaders; and at the restorative or management level it would include vigorous enforcement of laws against discrimination of the aged. If one had the option of unlimited resources for programs and for the necessary research and development, one can argue that prevention, restoration, and management should all be attended to with equal commitment. But this is not a realistic possibility and, in the competition for resources, priorities must be established. Political expediency and humanitarianism tend to put emphasis on "management" level interventions. At the same time, recognition of the increasingly high cost of restorative and management efforts on a never ending basis calls for attention to programs of prevention.

There is also the matter of the time-frame of studies, for action oriented persons and policymakers are almost by nature impatient. Most interventions of a preventive character require much longer periods before outcome can be judged. As a consequence, it is difficult to gain support for research projects which may extend over decades. From the standpoint of the politician and the administrator, the expediency of short-term studies often limits testing intervention of a preventive type.

There can be no formula for the distribution of interventions by level. It is clear that a complex mosaic of political views, values, professional and researcher interests, funding agencies, priorities, and so forth, determine the scope of activities in this respect. But it is critical that the formulation of interventions be explicit regarding the level of intervention desired, for it provides the framework for defining the target population.

EVALUATION RESEARCH AND PROGRAM FEEDBACK

Evaluation research is an important component of any intervention strategy. It represents the feedback mechanism which enables those responsible to assess the effects of intervention programs. In gerontology, evaluation is essential to decision-making regarding the design and refinement of program operations. For example, it is necessary to assess the relative merits of nursing home *versus* independent home care, retirement communities *versus* age-integrated living arrangements, and categorical *versus* noncategorical medical and rehabilitation programs.

Evaluative research differs from "basic research" primarily in terms of purpose rather than method; that is, general canons of good methodology apply to both types of research and the research question can be said to determine the most appropriate design. However, the purpose of evaluative research is determined by policy questions residing in legislative mandates, the requirements of the persons awarding grants, and planners and practitioners administering and implementing them. The researcher designing and implementing an evaluation study must, to a greater degree than is necessary with basic research, work directly with those persons overseeing the project or program being evaluated in order to institute appropriate measurement criteria and to assure utilization of the results by the staffs concerned.

Evaluation research is often contracted for by a specific group or agency to provide information to be used for internal purposes; consequently, evaluation data all too often never reach the public domain. Contracting agencies are reluctant to lay bare the faults which evaluation may reveal; therefore, the dissemination of results is likely to be characterized by a limited and self-serving release of evaluation data. The researcher, as a member of the scientific community, has the responsibility to see that the information gained in his research reaches the public domain in the form of conference papers, journal articles, and so forth. Evaluation research adds to the empirical data-base of the social sciences primarily in this manner. However, even when evaluation research results are published and available, the problems of their utilization are still great. For example, the researchers' objectives and those of policy-makers and practitioners may differ widely regarding the use and presentation of the research data (e.g., the scientific community is likely to be more interested in

testing theories than the effectiveness of specific program inputs).

Also, because of the multi-disciplinary character of social gerontology, location and integration of completed investigations is very difficult since research results may appear in specialized gerontological journals, in disciplinary publications, or in monographs that have narrow audiences and distribution. At the same time, the problems of access to studies and data are widely recognized in the aging field, indeed perhaps more in this area than in many others. The effort to set up a National Information and Research Clearinghouse on Aging is a hopeful example of a means for remedying the problem of access to research results. The recent volumes on social research in aging by Riley and her associates (1968, 1972) are exemplars of an effort to review, categorize, and organize research, as well as to conceptualize various problem domains. Such compilations are an important starting point for the development of intervention efforts, for selecting methods of intervention, and for designing evaluations to assess both process and impact.

Evaluation Research Perspectives

As with methods utilized for basic research, controversies exist regarding appropriate methodologies for evaluating specific types of major programs and individual projects within them. These have centered on (1) the advantages and disadvantages of experimental, quasi-, and nonexperimental designs, and on the more qualitative process-oriented methods (Suchman, 1967; Caro, 1971; Weiss, 1972; Rossi and Williams, 1972); (2) whether such research should document only program inputs, or program outputs—or whether it is essential to compare inputs and outputs in some formal way, as in cost-benefit analysis (Greenberg, 1968); and (3) the extent to which the research should assess impact on individuals (attitudinal or behavioral), organizations, institutions, or on processes of decision-making (Weiss and Rein, 1969; Freeman, 1972). These issues are further complicated by the extent to which the research is focused on immediate, intermediate, or long-run objectives and effects (Freeman, 1964).

There is general agreement regarding the basic elements requiring investigation in evaluation research, although the emphasis given to one element or another will vary depending on the needs of the agency commissioning the evaluation. As stated by Suchman (1967), there are five components relevant to evaluation: (1) the effort expended (amount of activity or input), (2) the effect (results of the effort), (3) the adequacy of impact, (4) efficiency (the effect in relation to cost), and (5) the process (how the effect was achieved).

Steps in Research Evaluation

The evaluation of social intervention has been the topic of a large number of recent papers and monographs (see Bernstein and Freeman, 1975, for a recent bibliography). Although space prohibits detailed discussion of evaluation procedures, it is important to note that sound evaluation requires not only the empirical testing of the three research hypotheses that make up the impact model, but also involves a number of "steps" including the specific identification of the target population, the measuring process, and impact assessment.

Development of an Impact Model. In all fields, including gerontology, the controversy continues regarding which particular evaluation research strategy is most practical and efficient to study specific interventions (Riecken and Boruch, 1974). In general, most evaluation researchers argue for the experimental design (Houston, 1972). Such designs impose a useful type of specification on the investigator, for he or she must develop an impact model. Impact models are not only essential for experimentally-designed evaluations but also for rational and systematic program development as well.

Ideally, the development of an impact model is inherent in the design of an intervention program. The impact model is a statement about the expected relationship between the intervention program and the movement toward the goal it hopes to achieve. The impact model delineates the hypotheses to be tested by the

evaluation research. It is impossible to either duplicate or evaluate an intervention program unless an impact model is provided (Borgatta, 1959).

Unfortunately, in many social service programs, the intervention is implemented without there ever being consensus as to the outcome goals, i.e., without an impact model being developed (Lind and O'Brien, 1971). When this is the case, the researcher must attempt to construct an *ex post facto* impact model in order to evaluate the intervention program.

An impact model is the translation of ideas formulated about the regulation, modification, and control of social behavior or community conditions into a hypotheses upon which intervention programs and action effort can be based. The absence of an extensive and explicit model prevents the extension of programs on a general basis and limits opportunities through evaluation research for confirming the implementation and the effectiveness of intervention programs. Impact models are predicated not only on conceptual and experiential knowledge but on some view of cause and effect.

Concerning the expected relationship between program activities and the movement required to obtain the goal, the impact model is a statement of strategy for closing the gap between the standard or goal specified during the design of the intervention and the behavior or condition currently existing. An impact model must contain, at a minimum, three hypotheses: (1) a causal hypothesis, (2) an intervention hypothesis, and (3) an action hypothesis.

The Causal Hypothesis. Central to any impact model is a hypothesis about the influence of one or more characteristics or processes (as independent variables) on the condition or behavior, the modification of which is the object of the program. For example, many social scientists believe that, among the aged, there is a relationship between extent of social isolation and suicide. That is, lack of integration between the individual and the social structure is hypothesized as a primary determinant of suicidal actions among population groups, including the aged.

In the development of the causal hypothesis, it is necessary that it be stated in a way that permits its testing. A restatement in operational terms of the suicide illustration above might be: suicide is most likely among persons who have minimal participation in the community's political activities and voluntary associations and whose contacts with their families are intermittent and limited both in number and intensity. Of course both the independent or causal variable (social integration) and the dependent or outcome measure (suicide reduction) have been derived from the intervention program and thus, as part of the evaluation process, it is critical that the variables be stated in measurable form.

The Intervention Hypothesis. The intervention hypothesis is the statement which specifies the relationship between the program and the behavior or condition to be modified, changed, or eliminated. One intervention hypothesis, in our example of suicide reduction, might be that knowledge of community resources and organizations by the aged is related to their participation in political and voluntary groups. A program could then be specified to increase knowledge of resources and organizations. Thus, the impact model for the reduction and prevention of suicide would specify that a program increasing the knowledge of available resources and organizations would increase social and political participation leading toward a reduction in suicide.

The Action Hypothesis. A third hypothesis also is required. The action hypothesis is necessary to assure examination of whether or not the intervention, even if the results are in the desired direction in "real life," necessarily occurs when the intervention effort tries to replicate what takes place ordinarily.

This third hypothesis is necessary because events that occur *in vivo* may not be duplicated when they are brought about by an intervention. To continue the example considered before, increasing older persons' participation in community activities by an educational program that makes them aware of voluntary associations may not make them any less prone to suicide than before. Despite an existing general relationship between lack of social integration and suicide in the population as a whole, it might be, for example, that there are particular characteristics among individuals who have failed on their own to participate in community activities and that these variables diminish or contradict any utility to the action effort. Indeed, older persons may learn about associations, and join them, but may actually be more stressed and depressed by their additional interpersonal experiences. Thus, the action hypothesis and its testing is as important as the other two hypotheses in evaluations of interventions.

Identifying the Target Population. It is critical that the characteristics of the population to be subjected to an intervention be specified prior to the development and execution of the intervention program. Intervention evaluation attempts to estimate the extent to which the program actually was directed at those identified as the target population. This may be done by means of surveys, analysis of agency records, or observation of persons served.

It is important to develop refined procedures for estimating the congruence between the persons or units actually included in a social intervention and those for which the intervention was intended. The reasons are twofold. First, most social interventions are small-scale experiments, and the major basis for their implementation and study is applicability to much larger populations. Extension of programs is possible only if the characteristics of the study group in the experiment are well documented. The second reason for carefully identifying the population is to have measures available on which to distinguish those who are willing to participate in programs and those who are not from the pool originally defined as the target population. Similar analyses also are necessary if one is to understand the differential impact of programs on sub-aggregates within the study population.

While the rationale for precise and explicit identification of the target population may appear fairly obvious, in practice the matter is subject to numerous constraints. From the standpoint of the design of innovations, on the one hand, study groups should comprise a representative sample of a known population, one for which there is evident concern. On the other hand, from the standpoint of the evaluation of the impact of social innovations, the study group should be as homogeneous as possible. Even in cases where classic experimental designs are used, minimal subject heterogeneity reduces the risk that internal differences within the study group will be a source of contamination that obscures the results.

There are political problems in restricting study groups when either potential participants or community leaders are convinced of the benefits and desirability of participating. It may be seen as immoral to exclude anyone in need of either a treatment or service although it might be beneficial to do so from the researcher's perspective. Thus, for example, although it may be sensible for program implementation and evaluation purposes to limit the target population by age, race, sex, role, socioeconomic status, mobility, and geographic location, the actual choice is a compromise between program needs, research aspirations, and political considerations. When the evaluation of the intervention requires assignment of some subjects to "control groups" or competing programs, the political problems and the strains of taking into account the characteristics of the study group are often greatly intensified.

Further, the inclusion of cases on the basis of identifiable characteristics is often resisted by practitioners who wish, or insist, that clinical judgment about "amenability for treatment," "responsiveness to therapy," "cooperativeness," and the like are valid requirements for inclusion in programs. Since it is difficult to reliably reproduce such judgments, taking them into account and restricting participants in such ways limits generalizability of the findings regarding the effects of the interventions.

The design constraints also may involve excessive costs and problems of case-finding. Programs limited by some condition of the study group (e.g., mental health problems requiring protective services intervention) and by a set of personal characteristics (e.g., ethnic or economic) often require considerable surveying and outreach in order to secure the required study group, particularly in providing a systematic sample of the population to insure representativeness.

Moreover, there is increasing concern with the rights of human subjects and that persons involved in any intervention program be fully informed about the requirements, procedures, and anticipated outcomes of participation. Since most intervention programs involve sustained and frequent participation, interest and motivation can lag with consequent attrition of the target population. Identification of knowledge of the properties of the study group is necessary in estimating bias resulting from such losses.

There is, of course, a limit to the quality of data that can be collected about a study group. Selection must be based upon a framework which provides guidelines for "what counts." Also, it is sometimes difficult to develop valid and reliable measures of characteristics. Economical selection of measures rather than excessively broad batteries of tests and instruments is important for methodological development.

A final complexity to be noted is the increased difficulty of providing identifying data when the targets are not persons but geographical, ecological, or organizational units. For example, a program may be concerned with modifying the procedures and activities in nursing homes by shifting the character of the organization. The target population in this case is organizations with selected characteristics such as number of beds, staff to patient ratio, and source of funding. Despite attention to characteristics of organizations, communities, and ecological units in recent years by organizational analysis, the measurement of these types of variables is still rudimentary. Notwithstanding the difficulties of measurement and avoiding political controversy in delimiting the target population, if interventions are to be extended and are to provide efficacious alternatives to current programs, explanations of both level of intervention and the characteristics of target population are critical requirements.

Measuring Process. Equally critical is the knowledge of whether the program was executed in a format similar to that described in the impact model. As previously discussed, it is important that programs are specifically described in terms of the procedures, practices, and personnel arrangements. Unless one knows that programs were actually undertaken in ways consistent with the program design, there is no point in being concerned about the efficacy of the intervention. The examination of operating programs usually requires a combination of research approaches. Direct observation of what takes place often is a critical means for determining congruence between program design and implementation (Weiss and Rein, 1969). In addition to direct observation, interviews with clients as well as agency reports may be used.

In part, studying the process of social intervention is a quality control function. It serves to alert planners and program developers about what is actually taking place. But this is only one purpose of what is commonly called "process research." If programs are going to be expanded to different locations or situations, and if larger numbers of individuals are going to be used as agents of social change, it is necessary to be able to tell practitioners with clarity and specificity what they are supposed to do. Only if there is a process evaluation of the actual implementation content of a program can this occur.

Assessing Impact

The essense of an experimental design involves a "before and after" comparison of control (no treatment) and experimental (treatment) groups to which subjects have been randomly assigned. This enables the researcher to infer equivalence of the two groups in all respects but the treatment (i.e., the program) and thereby to distinguish the effects of the program from those attributable to other factors. The randomization requirement is often difficult to fulfill completely in action programs because program agencies are very reluctant to deny service to persons who are in the control group.

In response to these and other problems, a variety of alternative quasi-experimental designs have been suggested. In one way or another, quasi-experimental designs involve attempts to adjust statistically for differences between experimental and control or compari-

son groups. There are numerous warnings about the extent to which such an approach leads to faulty conclusions regarding the effect or effectiveness of programs (Riecken and Boruch, 1974).

There is some question of whether experimental designs are appropriate to study broadgauged programs focused on altering participation in decision-making or planning rather than on altering individual behavior or attitudes. It has been argued, for example, that if the target of change is the service delivery system rather than the client, an experimental design is inappropriate for evaluation (Weiss and Rein, 1969). Weiss and Rein discuss the research problems which occur when the primary aim of a program is to make an impact on a situation and, only secondarily, an impact on individuals. In such cases, researchers often study individuals because they cannot decide how to assess the broader types of impact which the program attempts to make.

It is argued by some that experimental designs do not permit consideration of the more dynamic aspects of programs, in which many variables are essentially uncontrolled. Weiss and Rein suggest that such programs must be studied with more descriptive and inductive methodologies focusing on the details of the interrelationship between the programs and its surroundings, on the reactions of individuals and institutions to the programs, and the consequences for them and the larger community. Studies using field methods combined with interviewing have been conducted to evaluate the impact of action programs in a number of communities (Vanecko, 1969; Department of Housing and Urban Development, 1970) which illustrate the use of a process-oriented qualitative method for comparative community studies.

There are numerous difficulties with implementing true experiments because of ethics and political concerns regarding the denial of treatment (see, for example, Fox, 1959). Further, there are administrative difficulties in undertaking experiments. There is little doubt that, with adequate cooperation of action groups and sufficient resources from funding agencies, many more social interventions can be appropriately studied by means of true experiments. There is a legitimate concern with the amount of time that evaluation experiments take, as well as the barriers to their completion provided by politicians and practitioners who fundamentally do not wish to be confronted with the results of experiments which assess the utility of their pet ideas and programs.

It is critical, however, that impact be measured. Periodically, as noted, arguments are raised for simply studying the process of program implementation, implying that we need know only whether practitioners do what they claim they are doing. The assumption is that, if they are, the program is a success. Were there no measures of impact, for example, housing and institutional relocation efforts for the elderly would undoubtedly have become national policy because we would not know the potentially deadly effects of such moves for older persons (Lieberman, 1961). Even though evaluation of impact may more often than not result in negative findings regarding effective social interventions, it is critical that ineffective programs be discarded and the search continue more intensively for efficacious means of dealing with the problems of all groups, including the aged.

The importance of research utilization is reemphasized by this very statement—that is, given that research is applicable to the development, evaluation, and change of intervention strategies, how does one assure the utilization of such findings?

Research Utilization

Numerous factors contribute to the lack of research utilization. Weiss organizes them into five major areas:

(1) the evaluators' perception of his role in the utilization process, (2) the organization's resistances to change, (3) inadequate dissemination of results, (4) the gap between evaluation findings and clear courses for future action, and (5) the tendency of much evaluation to show little or no positive effect (Weiss, 1972, p. 110).

In this and earlier portions of this chapter, we have discussed obstacles to research utilization. Here our attention is directed to possible solutions to the obviously complex problem.

One solution which has been proposed to improve utilization of research and evaluation findings is the creation of a new profession of translators sufficiently trained in the techniques of research (Clark, 1969; Lowenthal, 1974) to interpret and translate data into recommendations for those who plan and conduct action programs. Coleman's (1973) concern regarding the lack of involvement of researchers in politics where policy is made suggests the need for advocacy skills for such translators in the political arena as well.

Other solutions have been suggested, some of which assign the researcher primary responsibility for resolving this problem. The Administration on Aging (AoA) has attempted a number of efforts of this type for improving research utilization in the field, initially through conferences of researchers and practitioners and more recently via the required inclusion of research utilization plans in all research proposals submitted to AoA. Since none of these efforts proved sufficiently beneficial to be institutionalized on a regular basis, AoA currently is attempting to assure at least its own utilization of the results of research it funds by (1) employing a narrowly defined "research strategy" which delimits the type of research which the agency will fund (requiring such research to provide specific types of data relevant to program requirements as legislatively mandated) and (2) offering a series of competitive bid contracts, most of which are designed to meet AoA's own monitoring and evaluation requirements and which are essentially designed and directed by an AoA "project officer."

It is obvious that the solution to the general problem of disparity in the applicability of much research and in negligible research utilization will be a long time in coming—in no small part due both to the lack of widely shared concern and of financial commitment to its resolution. Related and obviously important considerations are how policies regarding intervention strategy design are actually made and how practitioners implement these strategies so that the issues of research utilization can be addressed at both levels. Additionally, consideration must be given to altering the incentive systems operating in the academic and professional communities to augment the probability that policy research is conducted and disseminated by their members.

Another problem related to research utilization is the lack of confidence by policy-makers in the reliability of research findings (Maddox, 1971). One proposed solution to this problem is the support of replication studies "by different investigators in different places so that . . . evidence of the accuracy of findings . . . [is] accumulated . . . [however] to date lack of funds prevents this" (Maddox, 1971, p. 10). Other obstacles are described as the tendency by legislators and administrators of programs to resist change.

Increased funding, improved communication, and the systematic review and dissemination of policy-relevant research findings in the field have been proposed as partial solutions. The National Institute on Aging and National Clearinghouse for Research and Information in Aging reflect these concerns; however, their capacity to resolve these problems is unknown. Nevertheless, to our knowledge, no efforts are being directed at the problems of the resistance to change.

THE CHALLENGES AHEAD IN INTERVENTION RESEARCH

Well-conceived and executed interventions are rare across the entire spectrum of human and social problem areas. The reasons for the limited success of social experiments (and biomedical ones are not much more successful) are almost infinite: diffuseness in the planning and implementation of intervention designs, political opposition, lack of adequate economic resources and human talent, and faulty research procedures are perhaps the most frequently cited reasons for the failure of action efforts.

Nevertheless, it is clear that the systematic development, execution, and study of ways to remedy the human condition has become a major endeavor (Bernstein and Freeman, 1975) involving a massive investment of economic and human resources (Abert, unpublished). We are, in brief, moving toward what Campbell (1969) has termed an "experimenting society," albeit more slowly and hesitatingly than many would wish.

Although the field of gerontology has been part of the trend to innovate, experiment, and test ways of improving quality of life, it has been argued that intervention in this area has been aimed primarily toward "alleviation of seemingly deficient behaviors rather than on enrichment and prevention" (Baltes, 1973, p. 5). In biomedical research, experimentation and field trials historically have been viewed as a means for developing programs of prevention as well as of treatment. This dual emphasis has not emerged in gerontology.

As indicated in Maddox's Background Paper prepared for the 1971 White House Conference on Aging, annual expenditures for all health and welfare programs were estimated at $2 billion. Of this, the research investment was estimated to be *two-tenths of one percent.* Maddox and others argued then that if the standards in most fields of industrial research and development are applied, "research related to aging should be at least *ten times as high as it is*" (Maddox, 1971, p. 6). Unfortunately, since 1971, no significant dollar increases have been made for aging-related research. Thus, the limited amount available for model projects, research and demonstration, evaluation, and basic research discourages the systematic development of new intervention strategies.

Our comments on research support are not a digression. There is a paradox. On the one hand, the social reality shared by the general community population, by the aged themselves, and by experts is that the aged are a major social problem aggregate. A 1974 Harris Poll found that both the aged and their younger community counterparts regard old persons as unalert, physically inert, narrow minded, sexually inactive, and rotting away without proper medical care and enough money to live on (National Council on the Aging, 1975). On the other hand, resource programs for the aged are conceded to be of unknown efficacy, inadequate in scope, and fluctuating in support. They are not responsive to the social reality.

What is needed is a major shift in emphasis, a qualitative change in outlook that joins the emerging field to the social movement for an experimenting society (see Bernstein and Freeman, 1975, for a discussion of the development of the area). The current scarcity of research funds, the questionable priority-setting resulting from decentralization of responsibilities under "New Federalism," and the ambiguities of current program objectives of federal agencies need to be overcome for activities in the field to move in the direction we propose—toward a set of social change efforts of proven benefit in improving the lives of older persons and the conditions under which they live.

REFERENCES

Abert, James. *Case Studies in Evaluation Research*. Unpublished.

Administration on Aging. 1971. A social indicator system for the aged: A summary report. Washington, D.C.: USDHEW, SRS.

Baltes, P. B. 1968. Longitudinal and cross-sectional sequences in the study of age and generation effects. *Hum. Develop.*, 11, 145–171.

Baltes, P. B. 1973. Strategies for psychological intervention in old age. *Gerontologist*, 13, 4–5.

Baltes, P. B., and Schaie, K. W. 1970. On life-span developmental research paradigms: Retrospects and prospects. *In*, L. R. Goulet and P. B. Baltes, *Life-Span Developmental Psychology: Research Strategy*, pp. 365–395. New York: Academic Press.

Barron, M. 1953. Minority group characteristics of the aged in American society. *J. Geront.*, 8, 477–482.

Beattie, W. M. 1970. The design of supportive environments for the life-span. *Gerontologist*, 10, 190–193.

Bechill, W. D., and Wolgamot, I. 1972. *Nutrition For The Elderly*. Washington, D.C.: DHEW, SRS, AoA.

Becker, H. 1963. *The Outsiders*. New York: The Free Press.

Benveniste, G. 1970. *The Politics of Expertise*. Berkeley: Glendessary Press.

Berger, P. L., and Luckmann, T. 1966. *The Social Construction of Reality*. Garden City, New York: Doubleday.

Bernstein, I. A., and Freeman, H. E. 1975. *Academic and Entrepreneurial Research*. New York: Russell Sage Foundation.

Binstock, R. H. 1972. The roles and functions of state planning systems: Preliminary report of a nationwide survey of state units on aging. Brandeis University, Waltham, Massachusetts.

Birren, J. E., and Woodruff, D. S. 1973. Human development over the life-span through education. *In*, P. B. Bates and K. W. Schaie (eds.), *Developmental Psychology*, pp. 305–337. New York: Academic Press.

Birren, J. E., Woodruff, D., and Bergman, S. 1972. Research, demonstration and training: Issues and methodology in social gerontology. *Gerontologist*, 12, 49–83.

Borgatta, E. F. 1959. The new principle of psychotherapy. *J. Clin. Psych.*, 15, 182–186 (July).

Butler, R. 1969. Age-ism: Another form of bigotry. *Gerontologist*, 9, 243.

Campbell, Donald T. 1969. Reforms as experiments. *American Psychologist*, 24, 409–429 (April).

Caro, F. (ed.). 1971. *Readings in Evaluation Research*, pp. 1–34. New York: Russell Sage Foundation.

Clark, M. F. 1969. Creating a new role: The research utilization specialist. *Rehabilitation Record*, X, 32–36.

Clark, M., and Anderson, B. 1967. *Culture and Aging*. Springfield, Illinois: Charles C. Thomas.

Coe, R. 1967. Professional perspectives on the aged. *Gerontologist*, 7, 114–119.

Cohen, E. 1970. Toward a social policy on aging. *Gerontologist*, 10, 13–21.

Coleman, J. M. 1973. Ten principles governing policy research. *American Psychological Association Monitor*, 6 (February).

Coser, L. 1965. The sociology of poverty. *Soc. Probl.*, 13, 140–148.

Cottrell, W. F. 1972. *Technology, Man and Progress*. Columbus, Ohio: Charles E. Merrill.

Cumming, E., and Henry, W. 1961. *Growing Old*. New York: Basic Books.

Department of Housing And Urban Development, 1970. The Model Cities Program: A report prepared for Model Cities by Kaplan, Gans, and Kahn of San Francisco. Washington, D.C.

Duncan, Otis D. 1973. Social Indicators. *Social Science Frontier Papers*. New York: Russell Sage Foundation.

Estes, C. L. 1972. Community planning for the elderly from an organizational, political, and interactionist perspective. Unpublished Ph.D. dissertation, University of California, San Diego.

Estes, C. L. 1973. Barriers to effective community planning for the elderly. *Gerontologist*, 13, 178–183.

Estes, C. L. 1974. Community planning for the elderly: A study in goal displacement. *J. Geront.*, 29, 684–691 (November).

Estes, C. L. 1975. Constructions of reality: Perceptions of aging. University of California, San Francisco, unpublished paper.

Estes, C. L., and Schooler, K. K. 1966. Effects of residential mobility and changed physical environment on the individual's adjustment to the aging process. *Proceedings of the 7th International Congress of Gerontology*, Vienna, June 27.

Fox, Renée C. 1959. *Experiment Perilous*. New York: The Free Press.

Freeman, Howard E. 1964. Conceptual approaches to assessing impacts of large scale intervention programs. *Social Statistics, Proceedings of the American Statistical Association*, 192–198.

Freeman, Howard E. 1972. Outcome measures and social action experiments: An immodest proposal for redirecting research efforts. *American Sociologist*, 7, 17–19 (November).

Freeman, H. E., and Sherwood, C. C. 1970. *Social Research and Social Policy*. Englewood Cliffs, New Jersey: Prentice-Hall.

Freeman, Howard E., and Sherwood, Clarence C. 1971. Research in large-scale intervention programs.

In, Frances G. Caro (ed.), *Readings in Evaluation Research*, pp. 233–261. New York: Russell Sage Foundation.

Freeman, M. 1973. Some sociological perspectives on aging. Human Development Program, University of California, San Francisco, unpublished paper.

Friedson, E. 1970. *Profession of Medicine*. New York: Dodd, Mead.

Gouldner, A. W. 1970. *The Coming Crisis of Western Sociology*. New York: Basic Books.

Greenberg, B. G. 1968. Evaluation of social programs. *Review of International Statistical Institute*, 36 (3), 260–277.

Havighurst, R. J. 1963. Successful aging. *In*, R. Williams, C. Tibbitts, and W. Donahue (eds.), *Processes of Aging*, pp. 299–320. New York: Atherton Press.

Havighurst, R. J. 1969. Committee on research and development goals of the Gerontological Society, status of research in applied social gerontology. *Gerontologist*, 9, entire issue.

Houston, T. R., Jr. 1972. The behavioral sciences impact-effectiveness model. *In*, P. Rossi and W. Williams (eds.), *Evaluating Social Problems*, pp. 59–67. New York: Seminar Press.

Hoyer, W. J. 1973. Application of operant techniques to the modification of elderly behavior. *Gerontologist*, 13, 10–14.

Hudson, R. 1973. State politics, federalism and public policies for older Americans. New Orleans: paper presented to American Political Science Association, September 4 to 8.

Kastenbaum, R. 1968. Perspectives on the development and modification of behavior in the aged: A developmental-field perspective. *Gerontologist*, 8, 280–283.

Kuhn, T. 1970. *The Structure of Scientific Revolutions*. Chicago: University of Chicago Press.

Labouvie, G. V. 1973. Implications of geropsychological theories for intervention: The challenge for the seventies. *Gerontologist*, 13, 10–14.

Land, K. 1969. Principles of path analysis. *In*, E. F. Borgatta (ed.), *Sociological Methodology: 1969*, pp. 3–37. San Francisco: Jossey-Bass.

Lawton, M. P. 1970. Assessment, integration and environments for older people. *Gerontologist*, 10, 38–46.

Lemert, E. 1951. *Social Pathology*. New York: McGraw-Hill.

Lemert, E. M. 1973. Beyond Mead: The societal reaction to deviance. Presidential address, Society for the Study of Social Problems, New York.

Lieberman, M. A. 1961. Relationship of mortality rates to entrance to a home for the aged. *Geriatrics*, 16, 515–519.

Lind, S. D., and O'Brien, J. E. 1971. The general problem of program evaluation: The researchers' perspective. *Gerontologist*, 11 (4), Part II, pp. 43–50.

Looft, W. R. 1973. Reflections on intervention in old age: Motives, goals and assumptions. *Gerontologist*, 13, 6–10.

Lowenthal, M. F. 1974. Psychosocial variations across the adult life course: Frontiers for research and policy. Portland, Oregon: Robert W. Kleemeier Memorial Lecture, Gerontological Society, October.

Maddox, G. 1971. Behavioral and social research on aging, *Work Book on Research and Demonstration*, pp. 6–11. Washington: Administration on Aging, SRS, DHEW.

Mannheim, K. 1936. *Ideology and Utopia*. New York: Harcourt, Brace & World.

Matza, D. 1969. *Becoming Deviant*. Englewood Cliffs, New Jersey: Prentice-Hall.

Mutschler, P. 1971. Factors affecting choice of and perseveration in social work with the aged. *Gerontologist*, 11, 231–241.

National Council On The Aging. 1975. The Myth and Reality of Aging In America. Washington, D.C.

Neugarten, B. L., and Associates. 1964. *Personality in Middle and Late Life*. New York: Atherton Press.

Peterson, W. A., and Peters, G. R. (eds.) 1971. Perceptions of aging. *Gerontologist*, 13, 59–108.

Pratt, H. J. 1974. Old age association in national politics. *Annals*, 415, 106–119.

Riecken, H. W., and Boruch, R. F. (eds.) 1974. *Social Experimentation*. New York: Academic Press.

Riegel, K. 1972. The influence of economic and political ideology upon the development of developmental psychology. *Psychological Bulletin*, 78, 129–141.

Riley, M. W., and Foner, A. (eds.) 1968. *Aging and Society, Vol. 1: An Inventory of Research Findings*. New York: Russell Sage Foundation.

Riley, M. W., Johnson, M., and Foner, A. 1972. *Aging and Society, Vol. 3: A Sociology of Age Stratification*. New York: Russell Sage Foundation.

Rose, A. M. 1962. The sub-culture of the aging: A topic for sociological research. *Gerontologist*, 2, 123–127.

Rose, A. M. 1965. A current theoretical issue in social gerontology. *Gerontologist*, 4, 46–50.

Rosow, I. 1962. Old age: One moral dilemma of an affluent society. *Gerontologist*, 2 (4), 182–191.

Rosow, I. 1963. Adjustment of the normal aged. *In*, R. Williams, C. Tibbits, and W. Donahue (eds.), *Processes of Aging*, 2 (38), 195–220. New York: Atherton Press.

Rosow, I. 1967. *Social Integration of the Aged*. New York: The Free Press.

Rosow, I. 1974. *Socialization to Old Age*. Berkeley: University of California Press.

Rossi, P., and Williams, W. 1972. *Evaluating Social Programs: Theory, Practice and Politics*. New York: Seminar Press.

Ryder, N. B. 1965. The cohort as a concept in the study of social change. *Am. Soc. Rev.*, 30, 843–861.

Schaie, K. W. 1965. A general model for the study of development problems. *Psychological Bulletin*, 64, 92–107.

Schaie, K. W., and Strother, C. W. 1968. Cross-sequential study of age changes in cognitive behavior. *Psychological Bulletin*, **70**, 671-680.

Schultze, C. L. 1968. *The Politics and Economics of Public Spending*. Washington, D.C.: The Brookings Institution.

Scott, John F., and Freeman, Howard E. 1966. A critical review of alcohol education for adolescents. *Community Mental Health Journal*, **2**, 222-230.

Scott, R. A., and Shore, A. 1974. Sociology and policy analysis. *American Sociologist*, **9**, 51-59 (May).

Shanas, E., Townsend, P., Wedderburn, D., Friis, H., Milhøj, P., and Stehouwer, J. 1968. *Old People in Three Industrial Societies*. New York: Atherton Press.

Sparks, P. M. 1973. Behavioral versus experiential aging: Implications for intervention. *Gerontologist*, **13**, 15-18.

Spence, D. L., Feigenbaum, E. M., Fitzgerald, F., and Roth, J. M. 1968. Medical student attitudes toward the geriatric patient. *J. Am. Geriat. Soc.*, **16**, 976-983.

Streib, G. 1965. Are the aged a minority group? *In*, A. Gouldner and S. M. Miller (eds.), *Applied Sociology*, Ch. 24. New York: The Free Press.

Suchman, E. 1967. *Evaluative Research*. New York: Russell Sage Foundation.

Taber, M., and Flynn, M. 1971. Social policy and social provision for the elderly in the 1970's. *Gerontologist*, **11**(4), Part II, pp. 51-54.

Trela, J. 1971. Some political consequences of senior center and other old age group membership. *Gerontologist*, **11**(2), Part II, pp. 118-123.

Troll, L. E., and Schlossberg, N. A. 1970. A preliminary investigation of "age bias" in helping professions. *Gerontologist*, **10**(3), Part II, p. 46.

Vanecko, J. J. 1969. Community mobilization and institutional change. *Social Science Quarterly*, **50**(3), 609-630.

Warren, R. 1971. *Truth, Love and Social Change*. Chicago: Rand McNally.

Watson, J. S. 1971. Cognitive-perceptual development in infancy: Setting for the seventies. *Merrill Palmer Quarterly*, **17**, 139-152.

Weiss, C. H. 1972. *Evaluation Research*. Englewood Cliffs, New Jersey: Prentice-Hall.

Weiss, R. S., and Rein, M. 1969. The evaluation of broad aim programs: A cautionary case and a moral. *Annals of the Am. Acad. of Pol. and Soc. Sci.*, **385**, 133-142 (September).

Woodruff, D., and Birren, J. E. 1972. Age changes and cohort differences in personality. *Developmental Psychology*, **6**, 252-259.

22
INCOME DISTRIBUTION
AND THE AGING

James H. Schulz*

Brandeis University

The economic situation of the elderly population has been undergoing significant change during the past few decades. In the not too distant past, the aged were almost all poor or near-poor; they faced a variety of economic hardships which were exceedingly difficult to justify, given the generally high standard of living prevailing among the rest of the population.

It is now much more difficult to generalize about the aged's economic situation. First, the wide disparities in economic status among different groups of the aged have become more visible and, in some cases, have probably increased. Second, it is difficult to be definitive about the economic status of the aged, given that changes in public and private pension programs are only slowly reflected in the statistics upon which such conclusions are based. The problem of determining the economic status of the aged is a highly dynamic issue at this time. Unprecedented economic changes have and are taking place in countries throughout the world which will have a profound impact on the current and future aged populations.

The focus of this chapter is almost exclusively on developments in the United States. While statistics and events would be different in other countries, many of the analytical and programmatic issues discussed, however, are also quite relevant to the situation in other countries. The interested reader may wish to consult a number of excellent cross-national aging studies which have recently been completed. These studies provide a variety of viewpoints on international economic developments in aging, especially the evolution of social security systems. (See Shanas, Townsend, Wedderburn, Friis, Milhøj, and Stehouwer, 1968; Rimlinger, 1971; Kaim-Caudle, 1973; Wilson, 1974; and Schulz, Carrin, Krupp, Peschke, Sclar, and Van Steenberge, 1974.)

The first part of this chapter presents a brief review of the statistics existing at the time the chapter was written. The reader is warned, therefore, that the data presented are, in an important sense, illustrative. They demonstrate the sources and kinds of information available to investigate the economic status of the elderly; in order to keep up to date, the reader must seek out the most recent data.

The latter part of the chapter presents a brief overview of the various income maintenance programs in the United States which make a major contribution toward the economic welfare of the elderly. The chapter ends with a discussion of some major issues confronting

*Appreciation is expressed to the following persons who read all or part of initial drafts of this chapter: Lenore E. Bixby, Alan Fox, Mollie Orshansky, Alfred Skolnik, Gayle Thompson, Dorothy Wedderburn, Robert Binstock.

policy-makers as they seek to improve these programs and respond to changing conditions and new problems.

THE AGGREGATE ECONOMIC STATUS OF THE ELDERLY

The Aged's Share of National Income

Data on the total amount of money and non-money income received by the aged are not published very often by government statistical agencies. The Social Security Administration has provided one estimate of the aggregate money income received by the aged population for the year 1967. Bixby (1970) reports that persons age 65 or older (and their spouses) received about $60 billion in money income that year. Thus, the aged's share of the nation's total personal income before taxes in 1967 was about 10 percent. In that year those aged 65 or older constituted slightly less than 10 percent of the total population.

The major portion of that 1967 income came from retirement benefits, the income being distributed as follows:

Source	Percent
Retirement benefits	37
OASDHI	26
Other	11
Earnings	30
Income from assets	25
Veterans' benefits and public assistance	6
Other income	2

The second most important source of income was earnings, reminding us of an important economic distinction between those elderly who are partially or fully retired and those who are not.

A more recent estimate of the aged's share of total personal income is provided by the U.S. Bureau of Census (1974a). In 1973 persons age 65 and over received $95.2 billion, which represented 11.2 percent of aggregate household money income.

Both the Social Security Administration and Census Bureau estimates are for money income before taxes. Using the Brookings Institution tax file of U.S. family units with incomes projected to calendar year 1972 levels, Fried, Rivlin, Schultze, and Teeters (1973) estimate the elderly population's *after-tax* share of total personal income. Figure 1 shows the proportion of 1972 total income received by persons age 65 and over before and after taxes and transfers. The percent of total income held by the elderly rises slightly after income and payroll taxes are deducted but rises to nearly 14 percent after transfers are taken into account.

These income share statistics must be used cautiously in evaluating the economic status of the aged relative to the nonaged. The aggregate totals, for example, combine persons still in the labor force (often at the peak of their earnings) with those retired on very low pension income.

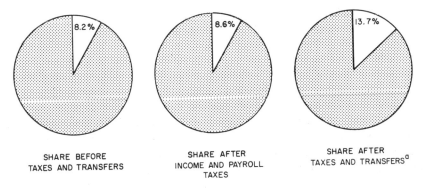

SHARE BEFORE
TAXES AND TRANSFERS

SHARE AFTER
INCOME AND PAYROLL
TAXES

SHARE AFTER
TAXES AND TRANSFERS[a]

Figure 1. The U.S. aged's share of personal income, 1972. (From Fried *et al.* (1973), based on Table 3-5.)

[a]Includes old-age, survivors, and disability insurance, unemployment and workmen's compensation, public and general assistance (welfare), veterans' benefits, and military retired pay.

Median Income

An alternative way of contrasting the aged and nonaged populations is to examine median income for various age groups in the population. Figure 2 shows how the median incomes of males and females (white and black) change with age. Figure 3 then shows the change in median income by age for male- and female-headed families and unrelated individuals. Median income drops for the three male age groups and one black female age group after age 45; for white females and female-headed families there is also a decline, but one which starts with the age group after age 54.

These statistics should not be interpreted as showing that the income of particular individuals typically drops after age 45. Many, if not most, individuals continue to have rising incomes up until retirement. However, as a group, a particular cohort of older workers finds its income position lower relative to younger cohorts. The younger cohort comes into the work force with higher beginning

wages and receives, on average, higher salary increases—reflecting, among other things, prior technological change, higher educational levels, and placement in high-productivity industries.

While various economists (e.g., T. Paul Schultz, 1964) have warned against interpreting cross-sectional earnings data as reflective of lifetime earnings patterns for individual workers —economic data to support this warning have only recently become available. Nancy and Richard Ruggles (1974), using a 1 percent longitudinal sample of the United States social security files, examine cross-sectional age-earnings profiles and longitudinal cohort profiles by single years of age:

The. . .cohort patterns for the period 1957 to 1969 make it apparent that *each cohort enjoys a continual rise in average earnings over its lifetime.* The shape of the age-earnings profile results from younger generations growing at faster rates than older generations, passing them, and in turn being passed by still younger generations. In this way, the rise and fall observed in the age-earnings

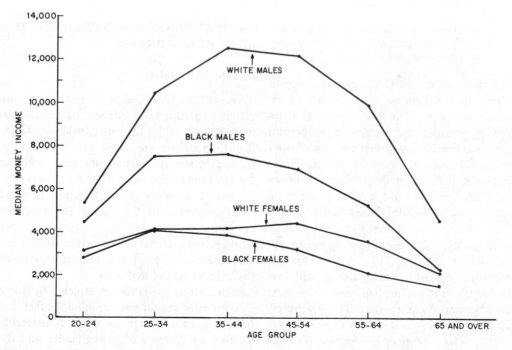

Figure 2. Median income of persons[a] by age, sex and race, 1973. (From Table 53, U.S. Bureau of the Census (1975a).)

[a]Excludes persons without any income.

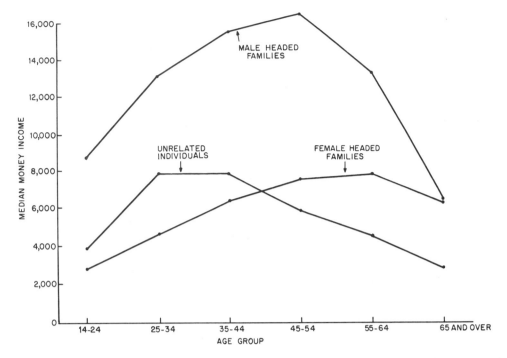

Figure 3. Median income by age and family type, 1972. (From Table 25, U.S. Bureau of the Census (1975a).)

[cross-sectional] profile can be fully reconciled with ever-rising. . . .cohort earnings patterns. [emphasis added]

The data do indicate the aggregate drop in incomes in the later ages as a result of increasing numbers of persons retiring. Compared to younger age groups, older persons clearly have much lower incomes. And among the elderly themselves, there are significant differences. Figure 4 presents information from the "1968 Survey of the Aged" on median income of social security beneficiaries. Beneficiaries with work experience had significantly higher median incomes. More aggregate but more recent data for 1973 show that the median income of all men age 65 and over was $4,106. But the median income for those men who were "year-round full-time workers" was $8,923. (U.S. Bureau of the Census, 1974b). The comparable median incomes of older women were $2,119 and $5,560, respectively.

THE DISTRIBUTION AND ADEQUACY OF AGED MONEY INCOME

Income Distribution

Annually, the U.S. Census Bureau surveys the incomes of American families and individuals. Each March, in the Current Population Survey (CPS), questions are asked to determine the income of survey units for the year ending in the December prior to the March interview.

Table 1 presents the distribution of total money income for the elderly in 1973. The table shows that in 1973, 77 percent of aged families had incomes of more than $4,000 but that only 27 percent of unrelated individuals had incomes above that level.

In evaluating the situation depicted by Table 1, the reader should keep in mind the fact that family income figures are often considerably inflated by earnings of young adults, and the figures for "unrelated individuals" by definition leave out the aged who live with relatives.

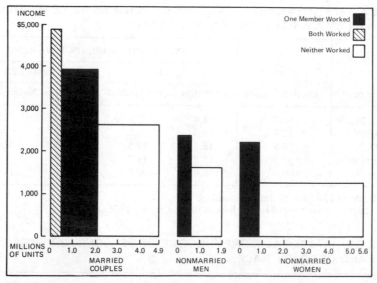

Figure 4. Median income by work status, social security beneficiaries, 1967. (From Bixby (1970), Chart 4.)

Tables 2 and 3 show additional summary distributions of income for the aged (age 62 or older), differentiated on the basis of sex and

TABLE 1. TOTAL MONEY INCOME FOR AGED[a] FAMILIES AND UNRELATED INDIVIDUALS, 1973.

Income	Families	Unrelated individuals
Under $1,000	0.8	5.3
1,000–1,499	1.1	9.7
1,500–1,999	2.0	13.0
2,000–2,499	3.1	16.0
2,500–2,999	4.9	13.2
3,000–3,499	5.5	9.0
3,500–3,999	5.8	6.5
4,000–4,999	12.4	8.9
5,000–5,999	10.6	5.3
6,000–6,999	8.8	3.2
7,000–7,999	6.5	1.8
8,000–8,999	5.7	1.8
9,000–9,000	4.2	1.4
10,000–11,999	6.7	1.8
12,000–14,999	7.6	1.2
15,000–24,999	9.9	1.3
25,000–49,999	3.4	0.4
50,000 and over	1.0	0.1
Total percent	100.0	100.0

[a]Head age 65 or over.
Source: U.S. Bureau of the Census (1974b).

race. The data in these tables illustrate the wide differentials existing among various subgroups of the aged population and emphasize the importance of disaggregating data used to examine the economic status of the aged.

More often than not, statistical tabulations group the retired and working elderly together. This, of course, is true for the data thus far presented. But for many policy issues this aggregation makes evaluation difficult, if not meaningless. One of the most helpful steps which can be taken in disaggregation is to at least separate the aged into two broad categories: the retired and the nonretired aged. For evaluating the economic "needs" of the aged, this separation is most important.

In recent years the U.S. Bureau of the Census has begun to publish some income statistics which include work status. Table 4 presents 1973 income distributions for the aged which distinguish by work status. Again, the distribution data show the much better economic situation of many of those working. For example, nearly half of the households with aged heads working had incomes greater than $8,000. Only 21 percent of households without working heads had as much income.

The data presented in Tables 1 through 4

TABLE 2. 1973 TOTAL MONEY INCOME OF PERSONS 62 YEARS OLD AND OVER BY MARITAL AND FAMILY STATUS.

| Income class | Married couples | SINGLE, WIDOWED, OR DIVORCED | | | |
| | | MALES | | FEMALES | |
		In families	Not in families	In families	Not in families
Less than $3,000	11.3	51.4	45.6	73.4	57.3
3,000–4,999	22.4	19.3	25.6	14.3	24.3
5,000–9,000	35.6	18.1	17.5	9.6	14.1
10,00 or more	30.5	11.2	11.3	2.7	4.3
Total percent	100.0[a]	100.0	100.0	100.0	100.0

[a]May not add to 100 percent due to rounding.
SOURCE: Derived from Table 54, U.S. Bureau of the Census (1975a).

TABLE 3. 1973 TOTAL MONEY INCOME OF PERSONS 62 YEARS OLD AND OVER, BY RACE.

| Income class | MARRIED COUPLES | | SINGLE, WIDOWED, OR DIVORCED | |
	White	Black	White	Black
Less than $3,000	10.1	29.8	56.8	81.9
3,000–4,999	21.8	30.8	22.6	11.7
5,000–9,999	36.4	26.3	14.8	6.4
10,000 or more	31.8	13.0	6.0	.9
Total percent	100.0[a]	100.0[a]	100.0[a]	100.0[a]

[a]May not add to 100 due to rounding.
SOURCE: Derived from Table 54, U.S. Bureau of the Census (1975a).

TABLE 4. AGED[a] MONEY INCOME BY EMPLOYMENT STATUS OF HEAD, 1973.

Income	Head not in labor force	Head in labor force
Less than $2,000	15.9	4.3
2,000–3,999	32.5	17.0
4,000–6,999	19.8	17.8
7,000–7,999	10.5	13.7
8,000–11,999	10.4	18.1
12,000–24,000	9.0	22.3
25,000 or more	1.8	6.8
Total percent	100.0[b]	100.0

[a]Age 65 or more.
[b]May not add to 100 due to rounding.
SOURCE: Derived from data in U.S. Bureau of the Census (1974a).

(and Tables 5 and 6 to follow) do not include: capital gains "income"; nonmoney transfers such as food stamps, health benefits, and subsidized housing; and nonmoney employee fringe benefits (which sometimes are available to retirees). It is important to remember these limitations and also the fact that there is a tendency for survey respondents to *under*report their income. The U.S. Census Bureau (1974c) reports, for example, that "recent CPS [Current Population Survey] income data on Social Security and public assistance payments to beneficiaries have averaged approximately 84 and 73 percent, respectively, of their benchmark estimates."

Who are the Poor Aged?

The picture of poverty among the elderly might change significantly as a result of the new Supplemental Security Income Program (SSI) which went into effect nationally in January, 1974. Unfortunately, at the time this chapter was written data were not available reflecting the increased income levels made available to elderly persons through SSI. Instead, the discussion below focuses on the pre-SSI situation.

The most commonly used measure of poverty in the United States is an index originally developed by the Social Security Administration in the early 1960's. In 1969 this index was adopted by a Federal Interagency Committee for purposes of reporting statistics for the "low income" population. The index is based on the Department of Agriculture's 1961 Economy Food Plan and reflects the different consumption requirements of families based on their size and composition, sex, age of the family head, and farm-nonfarm residence. A later section of this chapter discusses other concepts of retirement income adequacy and various poverty indexes.

Using the Social Security/Interagency index, we can look at poverty among the aged relative to poverty among all age groups in the United States. Table 5 presents a breakdown of poverty level incomes among various age groups. In 1973 the poor aged represented 14.6 percent of the total poor population, with 16.3 percent of persons age 65 or older receiving money incomes below the poverty standard for that year.

Table 6 presents data on the changes in aged

TABLE 5. PERSONS WITH INCOME LEVELS BELOW THE POVERTY STANDARD, 1973.

	Number	Percent
All persons with income below the poverty standard	23.0 million	100.0
Aged	3.4	14.6
Nonaged	19.6	85.4
Proportion of each age group with incomes below the poverty standard		
Under 3 years	1.5	15.9
3 to 5 years	1.6	15.5
6 to 13 years	4.5	14.5
14 and 15 years	1.1	13.3
16 to 21 years	2.8	11.8
22 to 44 years	4.7	7.6
45 to 54 years	1.6	6.9
55 to 59 years	.8	7.7
60 to 64 years	1.1	11.7
65 years and over	3.4	16.3

SOURCE: U.S. Bureau of the Census (1974c).

TABLE 6. PERCENT OF PERSONS AGE 65 AND OVER WITH POVERTY LEVEL INCOMES—1966, 1970, 1973.

	1966	1970	1973
All persons age 65 or more	28.5	24.6	16.3
White aged	26.4	22.6	14.4
Negro aged and other races	53.4	45.9	35.5
Aged persons in families with male head and unrelated males	21.7	16.8	10.5
Aged persons in families with female head and unrelated females	41.0	38.2	34.9

SOURCE: U.S. Bureau of the Census (1974c).

poverty over the 1966–73 period. The data also show the significant differences in poverty incidence among whites, nonwhites, males, and females.

As discussed above, it is also important to distinguish between the retired and working elderly. Data for 1973 give a very different picture of aged poverty for the two groups. In Table 7 poverty rates are given for men and women according to their work status. As would be expected, this table (and Table 4) shows a much higher incidence of poverty

TABLE 7. POVERTY RATES[a] AMONG AGED[b] FAMILIES AND UNRELATED INDIVIDUALS, BY WORK STATUS AND SEX, 1973.

	PERCENT POOR			
	NOT RETIRED[c]		RETIRED[d]	
Family status	Men	Women	Men	Women
All 65 and over	4.9	10.9	15.5	33.6
Family head	4.2	*[e]	11.5	17.9
Unrelated individual	9.8	11.4	31.9	37.3

[a] Percent poor.
[b] Age 65 or older.
[c] Worked year-round, full time; data for part-year or part-time workers not shown.
[d] Head or unrelated individual did not work during the whole year.
[e] Percentage not computed for case less than 50,000.
SOURCE: Unpublished data provided by the Social Security Administration, derived from special Office of Economic Opportunity tabulations.

among the *retired* elderly—especially among unrelated individuals.

How will the Supplemental Security Income (SSI) program which began in 1974 affect the economic status of the aged poor? Mollie Orshansky, the developer of the government's poverty index, has observed:

> The Federal guarantee under SSI remains below the poverty line, though State supplementation may raise income above it for some persons not on assistance before SSI. The poverty tally then may decrease little because of SSI, but the resultant poverty gap [the gap between the income of the poor and the poverty level] might be reduced considerably. . . .
>
> Moreover, the SSI payment schedule with its added differential for living alone may be large enough to coax out some new independent aged one- or two-person households, particularly those just approaching age 65 who are still pondering over living arrangements for their retirement years. We may, thus, by providing better support for our older citizens, achieve the paradox of moving some of our now hidden aged poor—about 1.3 million persons, almost all women at latest counts—and raising the count of the needy (Orshansky, 1974).

Another source of aged poverty relates to the inability of some workers to continue working until age 65. A Social Security Administration survey designed, among other things, to gather information on why workers retire before receiving full social security benefits at age 65 identified a large group of disadvantaged workers who end up receiving low, actuarially reduced benefits:

> Nonworking men claiming benefits at the earliest possible age include some of the most advantaged and most disadvantaged new retirees. A fourth of the nonworking men entitled at age 62—representing 15 percent of all men entitled at this age—retired willingly with second pensions; they had a median income of $4,000 from their retirement benefits. Yet 45 percent of the group aged 62 had no [second] pensions and did not want to retire when they had to leave their jobs. These men had a median income of only $930 from their actuarially reduced social security benefits (Reno, 1971).

Similar findings were reported by Abbott (1974) based on an analysis of data from the Social Security Administration's Continuous Work-History sample.

Perhaps most significant in the historic trend of poverty among the aged is the economic situation of aged women, especially widows. "In our society, at every age and every stage, women are more vulnerable to poverty than men, especially if they must do double duty as both family head [i.e., no husband present] and homemaker" (Orshansky, 1974). Table 8 shows the separate poverty rates for men and women in 1973. In almost every category the rates for women are higher, often higher by a wide margin. Focusing on aged women in poverty, Table 9 shows that the largest number of such women are widowed (about 1½ million) and that the group with the highest in-

TABLE 8. PERCENT OF MEN AND WOMEN IN POVERTY, 1973.

Age	Men	Women
Total age 16 or older	7.4	11.6
16–21 years	10.4	13.2
Family head	13.2	75.6
Other family member	8.3	9.3
Unrelated individual	38.1	49.6
22–64 years	5.8	9.7
Family head	4.6	33.4
Other family member	5.7	5.2
Unrelated individual	15.2	22.8
65 or older	12.4	19.0
Family head	9.5	16.8
Other family member	8.0	8.0
Unrelated individual	27.1	33.5

SOURCE: U.S. Bureau of the Census (1975b).

TABLE 9. AGED WOMEN WITH POVERTY LEVEL INCOMES, 1973.

	BELOW POVERTY LEVEL	
Marital status	Number[a]	Percent
Married, husband present	375	8.3
Married, husband absent	29	*[b]
Widowed	1,578	24.9
Divorced	97	31.4
Separated	55	54.5
Never married	165	21.6

[a] Thousands.
[b] Base less than 75,000.
SOURCE: U.S. Bureau of the Census (1975b).

cidence of poverty is "separated women" (55 percent).

Finally, there is a group of aged persons who usually do not appear in published poverty statistics but by one definition of poverty are indeed poor. If an individual's income drops sharply, his ability to maintain his accustomed standard of living also drops—unless savings are utilized or borrowing takes place. A great many elderly persons have found that this is exactly what happens when they retire: the pensions they receive are much less than their prior earnings and cause a dramatic change in the standard of living which can be maintained without supplementation. Such persons—confronted with a substantial drop in their living standard—can be characterized as experiencing relative poverty.

Data from the Social Security Administration's Survey of New Beneficiaries provide us with the only available comprehensive information on the amount of earnings replaced (in the recent past) by public and private pensions. Fox (1974) reports on the replacement rates of pensions for social security recipients retiring in 1970. It is unfortunate that data are not available for a year later than 1970. However, regardless of year, the data and analysis by Fox (and by Kolodrubetz, 1973) represent a major breakthrough in efforts to evaluate the role of pensions in providing adequate income for the nonworking aged.

Table 10 shows pension replacement rates using as a measure of preretirement earnings the average of "estimated total earnings" in the three years of highest earnings (during the last ten years prior to award of social security benefits to recipients). "This measure uses a crude estimation of total earnings for those whose reported earnings were equal to or greater than

TABLE 10. PENSIONS AS A PERCENT OF ESTIMATED PRERETIREMENT EARNINGS FOR MALE WORKERS ACHIEVING ENTITLEMENT IN EARLY 1970[a]

Replacement	Men Receiving:		
	Social security pension only, earnings *below* maximum	Social security pension only, earnings at or *above* maximum	Social security and a private pension
Number[b]	61,800	31,500	64,800
Total percent	100	100	100
0–20	1	21	1
21–30	21	68	6
31–40	45	11	19
41–50	15	0	28
51–60	5	0	23
61–70	4	0	13
71 or more	10	0	11
Median	36	24	49

[a] Social security benefits and private pensions as a percent of total earnings in the 3 years of highest earnings in the 10 before award: Percentage distribution of wage and salary workers entitled to benefits payable at award or at time of survey, January–June 1970.
[b] Excludes not only persons with less than 3 years earnings in last 10 but also those who were self-employed in their longest job, who were receiving public employee pensions, or who failed to report the amount of private pensions. Also excluded are those whose earnings attained the taxable maximum in the first or second quarter of any of the 3 highest years.
SOURCE: Fox (1974) and unpublished data provided by the Social Security Administration.

the [social security] taxable maximum in any of the three highest years" (Fox, 1974).*

About half of male wage and salary workers in the survey (and 78 percent of the women) did not have any pension other than social security. Table 10 shows that social security provided many of these men with very low earnings replacement. The highest replacement rates tended to be achieved by men (and women) with irregular employment (Fox, 1974) or low earnings. (See Table 11.)

Looking again at Table 10, we see that men with private pensions had much higher earn-

*The earnings estimating procedure is described in the appendix of Fox (1974).

ings replacement. About half of them received income equal to 50 percent or more of their preretirement income. Those with less than 50 percent tended to be concentrated in the 30–50 percent range.

If we look at the total group of retiring males, we see there is a large group of "middle-income workers" without private pensions who have very low earnings replacement and many high and low income workers with relatively high replacement.

While the Fox study provides important and very useful replacement data, it suffers from some limitations. Estimates of replacement rates using after-tax earnings are not calculated. Also, no earnings replacement ratios

TABLE 11. SOCIAL SECURITY BENEFITS AS A PERCENT OF AVERAGE TAXABLE EARNINGS, 1970[a].

Percent replacement	Total	AVERAGE MONTHLY TAXABLE EARNINGS IN THREE HIGHEST YEARS						
		Under $100	$100–199	$200–299	$300–399	$400–499	$500–599	$600 and over
				Men				
0–20	1	0	0	1	3	2	1	1
21–30	45	0	1	14	38	42	67	72
31–40	36	0	23	50	50	53	31	27
41–50	9	0	35	33	10	3	0	0
51–60	3	5	22	2	0	0	0	0
61–70	2	15	14	0	0	0	0	0
71–80	1	12	3	*[b]	0	0	0	0
81–90	1	11	1	0	0	0	0	0
91 and over	3	57	*[b]	0	0	0	0	0
Total percent	100	100	100	100	100	100	100	100
				Women				
0–20	1	0	0	*[b]	1	3	3	2
21–30	22	0	2	19	26	37	65	59
21–40	35	0	15	49	58	58	31	39
41–50	18	0	42	27	15	2	0	0
51–60	8	6	27	5	0	0	0	0
61–70	4	15	8	*[b]	0	0	0	0
71–80	2	10	3	0	0	0	0	0
81–90	2	11	1	0	0	0	0	0
91 and over	9	58	1	0	0	0	0	0
Total percent	100	100	100	100	100	100	100	100

[a] Social security benefits as percent of average taxable earnings in the 3 years of highest earnings in the 10 before awards, by size of such earnings: Percentage distribution of persons newly entitled to benefits payable at award or at time of survey, by sex, January–June 1970 awards.
[b] Less than 0.5 percent.
SOURCE: Fox (1974).

are available for families. The pension amounts reported in Table 10, for example, do not include any spouse benefits. But for many purposes, it would be useful to know the ratio of total family pension income to total average family earnings. Unfortunately, many difficulties arise in estimating such family ratios. For example, husbands and wives are often of different ages and, hence, reach pension eligibility at different times.

OTHER FACTORS AFFECTING THE ECONOMIC STATUS OF THE AGED

The distribution of economic welfare is imperfectly measured by statistics presenting only the distribution of money income. However, almost all of our discussion thus far has relied on this measure.

The discussion of this section focuses on three major limitations of money income statistics:*

1. Assets and debts (i.e., net worth) are also important determinants of consumption potential over time.
2. Benefits derived from government services

*See Morgan, Smith, and Jones (1962) and, more recently, Taussig (1973) for a more exhaustive list of problems and a discussion of some of the conceptual issues.

add to economic well-being but are excluded from income measures.
3. Tax laws affect persons differently and, hence, after-tax income distributions are usually a better measure of economic well-being than before-tax distributions.

Assets and Debts

Surveys to determine asset holdings of individuals have been undertaken very infrequently in the United States. As with surveys attempting to assess the distribution of income, asset surveys have been plagued by the underreporting of survey units. Moreover, this problem has been even worse for the asset surveys.

The most recent comprehensive information on the assets of the elderly is almost a decade old.** The 1968 Social Security Survey of the Aged presents detailed information on the assets of the elderly in 1967. Table 12 shows the proportion of elderly units holding various amounts of financial assets and equity in an owned home. What is most striking about the information in Table 12 is the large number of older families with relatively insignificant amounts of *finan-

**The Social Security Administration's "Income and Wealth Survey Pilot Project" (currently underway) is the initial phase of what may become a major new data collection effort.

TABLE 12. AGED[a] FINANCIAL ASSETS AND HOMEOWNER EQUITY, 1967[b].

| Asset amount | FINANCIAL ASSETS ONLY | | EQUITY IN HOME | |
	Couples	Unrelated individuals	Couples[c]	Unrelated individuals[c]
None	26	42	*[d]	*[d]
$1–999	17	19		
1,000–2,999	15	11	13	18
3,000–4,999	8	6		
5,000–9,999	12	9	24	26
10,000–19,999	11	7	40	39
20,000 or more	13	5	23	17
Total percent	100[e]	100	100	100

[a] Age 65 or older.
[b] Asset information does not include value of business and farm assets and equity in rental.
[c] Homeowners only.
[d] Not applicable.
[e] Totals may not add to 100 due to rounding.
SOURCE: Based on data in Murray (1972).

cial assets. About two-thirds of elderly couples and almost 80 percent of unrelated individuals had less than $5,000 in financial assets in 1967. In fact, 43 percent and 61 percent respectively had less than $1,000.

Some people have argued that the poor asset situation of past and current aged cohorts reflects in part the economic vicissitudes of past decades—especially the Great Depression and the post-War II inflation—and might improve. Since the aged population is increasingly composed of elderly who worked and saved in the relatively prosperous years of the 50's and 60's, will not the future elderly asset picture change?

Unfortunately, information to answer this question is almost nonexistent. Data from the Social Security Administration's Retirement History Study (Irelan, 1972), however, provide 1969 asset statistics for a cohort of individuals approaching retirement. Table 13 contrasts the financial asset situation of the 1967 aged population with the asset picture for "preaged" persons age 58 to 63 in 1969. The data show that there has been little improvement in the financial asset status of this preretirement group as compared to the current elderly. In fact, the two distributions are almost identical.

Also included in Table 13, to provide some historical perspective, is the financial asset situation for the elderly five years earlier (1962). Again, the data show that the distribution in that year is virtually identical with the 1967 situation.

Finally, it should be noted that the assets of most elderly persons are not held as financial assets but as equity in an owned home (see Table 12). About 80 percent of elderly couples lived in an owned home, compared with about 40 percent of nonmarried elderly persons. The amount of mortgage debt on these homes is very low; in fact, about four-fifths of elderly homeowners own their homes free of any mortgage.

Government Nonmoney Benefits

In addition to the cash transfer programs which increase the income of the elderly, there are a number of nonmoney benefits and services by the federal government which seek to improve the economic and social welfare of the elderly.*

*Each year a summary of federal activities in aging is published by the U.S. Senate Special Committee on Aging. This summary includes reports from federal departments and agencies with regard to their programs or activities which affect the current and future aged persons. Many states and local governments also provide special services to the elderly.

TABLE 13. FINANCIAL ASSETS[a] OF THE AGED AND A "PRERETIREMENT" COHORT.

Asset amount	Survey units with head age 58–63 in 1969[b]	Survey units with head age 65 or more in 1967[b]	Survey units with head age 65 or more in 1962
None	25	36	35
$1–999	22	19	19
1,000–2,999	14	12	12
3,000–4,999	7	7	7
5,000–9,999	10	10	9
10,000–19,999	9	8 }	18
20,000 or more	12	8 }	
Total percent	100[c]	100	100

[a] U.S. savings bonds, checking accounts, savings accounts, stocks, corporate bonds, mutual funds, and money owed by others.
[b] Tabulation of married couples and nonmarried individuals.
[c] Does not add to one hundred due to rounding.
SOURCE: Based on data in Murray (1972), Sherman (1973), and Epstein and Murray (1967).

The major ones are:
1. Medicare and Medicaid
2. Housing subsidies
3. Food stamps
4. State planning, services, and information provided under the Older Americans Act, including meals served by the Nutrition Program
5. The national nutrition program for the elderly
6. Operation Mainstream—older worker manpower program
7. Research programs
8. Veterans Administration services

From time to time various studies have measured the magnitude and distribution of some of these nonmoney benefits, but no really comprehensive study of them has been undertaken.

Tax Benefits

A U.S. Bureau of the Census (1973b) analysis of data from the 1970 Census of Housing reported that the aged paid about twice as high a percentage of their income (8 percent) for real estate taxes as any other age group. However, property tax relief laws for the elderly have been legislated by about 80 percent of the state governments in the United States (NRTA/AARP, 1975). Such legislation has been stimulated by the relatively low economic status of many elderly persons, the high proportion of home ownership (as discussed above) among the elderly, and a perceived inequitable tax burden caused by the property tax as a result of the first two factors and the assumption that the incidence of the property tax falls primarily on the homeowner.

Based on the research that has been done, economists remain uncertain regarding the incidence of the property tax; a recent summary and evaluation of the literature is provided in Break (1974). Aaron (1973), for example, argues that "the theory of tax incidence embodied in numerous studies now influencing public policy...[is] an atavistic attachment to naive and obsolete theory in defiance of published theoretical advances that demolish the previous orthodoxy."

One form of property tax relief which has gained growing acceptance in state legislatures is "circuit-breakers" which provide partial or complete relief for property tax payments that exceed a stipulated fraction of income. Aaron (1973) argues that such tax relief is unrelated to the real burdens of the property tax:

> If the conclusion of general equilibrium analysis is accepted that the property tax is borne substantially by owners of capital, then circuit-breakers are not compensation for tax burdens, but rather a form of negative income tax based on current income and property tax payments... The question most advocates of circuit-breakers have failed to answer is why one relatively minor element of household expenditures should be singled out as an index for financial support....

In addition to property tax relief, one or more state governments grant to the elderly the following other types of tax relief:
1. Exemption of prescription drugs from sales tax
2. In paying income tax:
   a. Special income levels for filing returns
   b. Higher "personal exemptions"
   c. Special medical deductions
   d. Special treatment of retirement income
   e. Tax credits

Federal tax benefits to the elderly through the income tax laws are very large. These benefits include:
1. A double personal exemption: Persons age 65 or older can deduct from their taxable income an additional personal exemption, which in 1974 was equal to $750. Thus, an older person can deduct a total of $1,500, and an older couple filing jointly can deduct $3,000.
2. Exemption from taxation of benefits received under the Social Security and Railroad Retirement Systems: Social security benefits are excluded from gross income by administrative ruling, and railroad retirement benefits are excluded by law (Surrey, 1967).
3. Retirement income credit: "The retirement income credit is a very complex provision intended to extend tax benefits, somewhat comparable to the tax benefits resulting from the exclusion of social security and railroad retirement from gross income, to retired individuals

who are not covered (or only partially covered) by the social security and railroad retirement programs" (Surrey, 1967).

4. Sale of personal residence capital gains exclusion: Persons who sell their home for $20,000 or less on or after their 65th birthday and who owned and used it as their principal residence for at least five of the last eight years need not include in their income any gain on the sale. If the property is sold for more than $20,000, they may have to report part of the gain as income.

In addition to the above tax benefits which exclusively or primarily benefit the elderly, there are a number of tax provisions for people of various ages which are of particular importance to the elderly:

1. Deductibility of mortgage interest and property taxes on owner-occupied homes: Some elderly who have not yet paid off their mortgage are able to take advantage of the first deduction if they itemize their deductions (i.e., do not take the standard deduction).

2. Deductibility of certain medical expenses and medical insurance premiums: Persons itemizing deductions can deduct one-half (up to $150) of the amount paid for medical care insurance even if they have no other out-of-pocket medical expenses. Also, they may deduct certain medical and dental expenses which exceed 3 percent and certain medicine and drugs which exceed 1 percent of "adjusted gross income."

3. Deductibility of state taxes: Especially important to the elderly, given the large proportion who own homes, is the deductibility of property taxes.

4. Exclusion of private pension contributions for employees and the self-employed: Employers can deduct contributions which they make to private pension plans for their employees, and income earned by these plans is also exempt from income tax. In addition, under the Employee Retirement Income Security Act of 1974, individuals who are not covered by any qualified pension plan can take a tax

deduction for contributions to an individual retirement plan—up to 15 percent of earned income or $1,500 (whichever is less). And self-employed persons can contribute tax-free to such a plan 15 percent of earned income up to $7,500 a year.

Surrey (1973) has calculated the revenue lost to the government by various federal income tax provisions. He estimates that the retirement income credit and additional exemptions for the aged and the blind cost about $2.5 billion and that the exclusion of social security and railroad retirement income costs an additional $1.0 billion. More importantly, Surrey argues that "while the general impression is that the tax expenditures for the aged are to assist those elderly who are hard pressed, their effect is such that nearly half of the assistance in dollar terms goes to individuals with incomes above $10,000...[and that] no assistance is given by these tax expenditures to individuals too poor to pay an income tax." (See Table 14)

Measuring Economic Welfare

Marilyn Moon (1974) has studied the changes in the ranking of elderly families when a more general measure of economic welfare than in-

TABLE 14. ESTIMATED DISTRIBUTION OF AGED TAX PREFERENCES[a] FOR INDIVIDUALS, 1972[b].

Adjusted gross income class	Amount of benefit[a] (millions of dollars)
0–$3,000	880
3–5,000	820
5–7,000	460
7–10,000	640
10–15,000	265
15–20,000	135
20–50,000	235
50–100,000	75
100,000 and over	40
Total	3,550

[a] Additional exemption, retirement income credit, and exclusion of OASDHI for aged.
[b] Calendar year.
[c] Includes some benefits to nonaged disabled.
SOURCE: Surrey (1973).

come alone is used. Using data for 1967 from "The Survey of Economic Opportunity," Moon constructs a "well-offness" measure which includes income, net worth, certain in-kind transfers (Medicare, Medicaid, and public housing), taxes, and intrafamily transfers. The measure is standardized to compare across families of varying size.

Moon estimates intrafamily transfers to be about $6 billion per year—half flowing to the younger extended family from the aged nuclear family but the other half flowing in the opposite direction. Of much greater importance is the value of the aged net worth annuity (i.e., yearly value of total assets), estimated by Moon to be $35 billion for 1967.

Table 15 shows Moon's estimated shifts of families from one income class to another as a result of taking into account more than gross money income. "Families at the bottom of the income distribution tend to move up. How-ever, for higher income classes a substantial minority of families fall by two or more dollar classes when ranked by the measure of eco-nomic welfare. Thus, families do change in ordinal ranking when a measure of economic welfare is used" (Moon, 1974).

MAJOR PENSION AND WELFARE PROGRAMS

Social Security

There are many excellent discussions which re-view the historical development of social security in the United States and abroad.* The focus of this section, therefore, is on resulting benefit levels, rates-of-return, and develop-ments in other countries.

Figure 5 shows the growth of the American social security system (OASDHI: old age, survivors, disability and health programs) and, for comparative purposes, changes in welfare expenditures and private cash benefits. Whereas OASDI was an almost unmeasurable percentage of gross national product (GNP) in 1950 (.3 percent), the expenditures for OASDHI in 1974 were about 5 percent of GNP. Restricting attention to just OASDHI, Table 16 compares expenditures in the United States with selected industrialized countries. Comparability is mea-

*See, for example, Jenkins (1969), Schottland (1970), Rimlinger (1971), Brown (1972), Schulz et al. (1974). For a good summary of social security pro-visions in the United States, see U.S. Social Security Administration (1974).

TABLE 15. CHANGE IN INCOME CLASS USING AN "ECONOMIC WELFARE" MEASURE FOR AGED FAMILIES, 1967.

	PERCENT OF FAMILIES IN EACH INCOME CLASS WHO:				
Current Money Income Class	Fall by two or more classes	Fall by one class	Stay in same class	Move up one class	Move up two or more classes
$ -5,000--1	–	–	29.10	.00	70.90
0	–	.00	.00	1.28	98.72
1–499	.00	.00	2.65	13.37	83.98
500–999	.04	.32	7.16	20.72	71.76
1,000–1,499	.03	1.68	6.42	23.21	68.66
1,500–1,999	.64	2.03	5.01	21.16	71.16
2,000–2,499	3.06	2.24	6.23	16.44	72.03
2,500–2,999	2.63	.34	4.90	39.03	53.10
3,000–3,999	5.84	1.11	18.17	28.59	46.29
4,000–4,999	3.71	2.95	20.94	22.41	49.98
5,000–5,999	4.14	4.86	19.04	32.88	39.07
6,000–7,999	5.33	3.87	36.02	32.75	22.02
8,000–9,000	5.04	14.38	25.70	48.35	6.52
10,000–14,999	14.07	8.41	40.73	36.80	–
15,000 or more	1.73	11.05	87.22	–	–

SOURCE: Moon (1974).

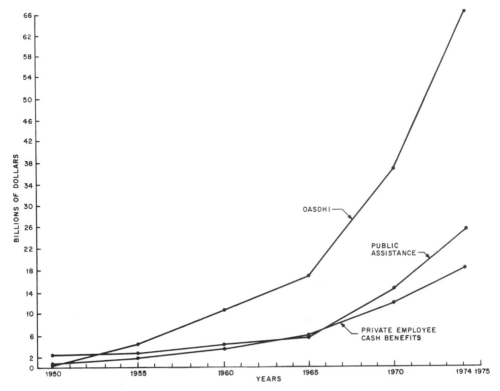

Figure 5. OASDI[a], public assistance, and private cash benefits[b] 1950–1974. (From Skolnik and Dales (1975).)

[a]Old-age, survivors, disability and health insurance.
[b]Cash benefits under private pension plans, group life (including government civilian employee programs), accidental death and dismemberment, and cash sickness insurance, paid sick leave; and supplemental unemployment benefit plans.

TABLE 16. EXPENDITURES FOR OLD-AGE, SURVIVORS, AND DISABILITY INSURANCE, 1968 AND 1971.

Country	PERCENT OF GNP	
	1968	1971
Belgium[a]	4.7	5.0
Canada[c]	2.2	2.4
France	4.2	4.2
Germany, Fed. Rep.	8.0	7.6
Japan	.3	.3
Netherlands[b]	6.9	6.3
Sweden	5.1	6.0
United Kingdom	3.8	3.6
United States	2.8	3.4

[a]Excludes disability, which is administratively incorporated into Belgium's health insurance.
[b]Excludes disability benefits because the three income replacement elements of disability, cash sickness, and workmen's compensation are combined.
[c]Covers disability by an assistance program.
SOURCE: Horlick (1974).

sured by determining what percentage such expenditures represent of GNP.

Social security coverage has now been extended (along with higher benefits) to all but a very small minority of the regular workforce. All gainfully employed workers are now covered except (a) federal government employees and some state and local government employees, (b) farm and domestic workers who are not regularly employed, and (c) self-employed persons with very low incomes. As a result, in 1955 only 42 percent of the population aged 65 and over was receiving social security benefits, but by 1973 there were over 19 million aged social security beneficiaries—representing 89 percent of the over-65 population (*Social Security Bulletin*, 1974).

Benefit Levels and Earnings Replacement. In August, 1974, the average social security benefit

TABLE 17. HISTORY OF PERCENTAGE INCREASES IN SOCIAL SECURITY BENEFIT AND CONSUMER PRICES (1939-1972).

Effective date	Across-the-board increases	Average increases for all beneficiaries	Increases in CPI between the effective dates[a]
9/50	77%	81.3%	75.5%
9/52	12.5[b]	14.1[c]	9.3
9/54	13	13.3	0.5
1/59	7[d]	7.7	7.9
1/65	7[e]	7.7	7.9
2/68	13	14.2	9.3
1/70	15	15.6	10.8
1/71	10	10.4	5.2
9/72	20	20.7	5.9
3/74	7	–	–
6/74	4	–	–

[a] 1957–1959 = 100%.
[b] Greater of 12.5% or $5.
[c] 15.2% for old-age beneficiaries.
[d] Guarantee of 7% or $3.
[e] Guarantee of 7% or $4.
SOURCE: First nine entries: Social Security Administration as prepared by Congressional Research Service and distributed by Special Senate Committee on Aging. Last two entries: Lingg (1974).

paid to a retired worker was about $2,200 per year, and the average spouse benefit was about $1,100 (*Social Security Bulletin*, 1974). These benefits are more than double the average amount paid to beneficiaries a decade ago. As shown in Table 17, this increase in benefit levels results in large part from the extraordinarily large benefit increases that have been legislated in recent years.

Looking to the future, Rettig and Nichols (1974) have calculated replacement of earnings ratios for hypothetical male workers retiring between 1974 and the year 2050. Three lifetime earnings patterns are used; workers are assumed to have earnings each year equal to either

a. social security "*maximum* taxable earnings"* applicable for that particular year,

*Maximum taxable earnings is the legislated amount of earnings upon which employer and employee contributions must be paid. Contributions are calculated as a percentage of all earnings below *the maximum and on no* earnings above it.

or

b. *median* taxable earnings in each year, or
c. "low" taxable earnings—defined by Rettig and Nichols as representative low earnings for a steady worker.

Rettig and Nichols assume increasing price and earnings levels and take into account the social security law's automatic adjustment provisions. It is important to recognize, however, that the Rettig and Nichols calculations do not deal with workers whose earnings exceed "maximum taxable earnings" for part or all of their lifetime. Table 18 shows, however, that a substantial portion of covered worker earnings were above the maximum—typically between 20 and 25 percent in the later years. However, the 1972 social security legislation raised the taxable earnings ceiling significantly and introduced an escalator provision which raises the ceiling as the Consumer Price Index rises. Consequently, the percent of workers with earnings above the maximum has declined significantly. In 1972, 25 percent of workers had earnings above the maximum. Preliminary estimates for 1973 indicate 21 percent, and projections for 1974 and 1975 are about 14 percent (Bixby, 1975).

TABLE 18. EARNINGS ABOVE THE MAXIMUM TAXABLE EARNINGS CEILING.

Year	Amount Not Taxable (millions)	Percent Not Taxable
1940	$ 2,694	7.6
1945	8,615	12.0
1950	22,306	20.3
1955	38,559	19.7
1960	58,219	22.0
1961	61,290	22.6
1962	69,906	24.2
1963	76,752	25.4
1964	88,104	27.2
1965	100,973	28.7
1966	78,139	20.0
1967	92,297	21.9
1968	84,135	18.3
1969	100,740	20.1
1970	116,500	21.9
1971	134,400	24.1
1972	129,500	21.1

SOURCE: Based on data presented in the *Social Security Bulletin*, July 1974, Table M-14 (Current Operating Statistics).

TABLE 19. PROJECTED SOCIAL SECURITY PENSION AND REPLACEMENT RATIO FOR A MALE RETIRING AT AGE 65.

Year	ASSUMED EARNINGS PATTERNS[a]					
	Maximum taxable earnings[b]		Median taxable earnings[b]		Low taxable earnings[b]	
	Pension	Ratio	Pension	Ratio	Pension	Ratio
1975	$ 3,882	.29	$ 3,275	.43	$1,954	.61
1980	5,582	.33	4,342	.44	2,530	.62
1985	7,102	.33	5,655	.45	3,169	.61
1990	8,976	.33	7,279	.46	4,033	.61
1995	11,442	.33	9,130	.45	5,222	.62
2000	15,082	.34	11,868	.46	7,122	.66

[a]Earnings assumed to increase 5 percent annually. See text.[b]
[b]PIA at award times 12. Consumer Price Index assumed to increase 3 percent annually.
[c]Ratio of PIA at award (base pension only, excluding any spouse benefit) to monthly *taxable* earnings in the year just prior to retirement.
SOURCE: Based on data in Rettig and Nichols (1974).

Limiting earnings to those below the maximum gives deceptively higher earnings replacement ratios for the working population in the United States than if total earnings were used. With this qualification in mind, the reader can use Table 19 to contrast current benefits with future benefits which would result from the 1973 benefit formula. For the "maximum earnings" worker replacement is very low (29 to 34 percent) and is highest for the low earner (61 to 66 percent).

TABLE 20. PROJECTED REPLACEMENT RATES OF SOCIAL SECURITY PENSIONS, RETIRING U.S. COUPLES,[a] 1960–1980.

Replacement Ratio[b]	Percentage Distribution[c]
Less than 0.20	15
0.20 to 0.29	21
0.30 to 0.39	26
0.40 to 0.49	17
0.50 to 0.59	8
0.60 to 0.69	5
0.70 to 0.79	2
0.80 to 0.89	2
0.90 to 0.99	1
1.0 or more	4

[a]Retired married couples where the husbands were between the ages of 45 and 60 (inclusive) in 1960.
[b]The replacement rate is calculated for the initial year of retirement by dividing total social security pension income of a couple by average family preretirement earnings for the five years prior to retirement.
[c]Does not add to 100 due to rounding.
SOURCE: Schulz *et al.* (1974).

Using 1960 census data, alternative projections have been made by Schulz *et al.* (1974) for persons retiring between 1960 and 1980. These projections are based on the 1972 old-age pension benefit formula but do not limit earnings to those below the maximum taxable earnings ceiling. Table 20 presents estimates of the earnings replacement rates for couples. In contrast to the Rettig and Nichols projections for hypothetical workers, the Schulz *et al.* projections estimate replacement ratios for all social security old-age pension recipients. Hence, the latter projections show a wide range of replacement rates, with most couples projected to receive less than 50 percent replacement.

Is Social Security a "Good Buy"? With frequent changes in benefit levels and contribution rates, one question which continues to receive a great deal of attention is determining who, if anyone, "loses" in the United States because of compulsory social security. Pechman, Aaron, and Taussig (1968) discuss, for example, the calculations which have been made "to show that payments to social security by new entrants into the labor force will be much greater than the retirement benefits that they can expect to receive subsequently. These calculations have influenced the views of some members of Congress and others who have begun seriously to question the fairness of the social security system as it is developing in the United States." As Pechman, Aaron, and Taussig correctly point out, these calculations unrealistically *assume* that currently legislated contribution rates and benefit levels will remain unchanged in the future.*

Other critics argue that even if workers get more back than they contribute, they could get a better return by investing their funds privately. In an important study by John Brittain (1972), "lifetime rates of return" for social security are estimated using 1966 tax and benefit levels. Projected yields for average earners ranged from 2.78 to 6.28 percent, depending on assumptions with regard to the economic growth rate, birth/mortality rates, the interest rate, and the age when entering the work force. Brittain concludes that "if the model and the official demographic projections are fairly realistic, new contributors will in the aggregate get neither a very good 'buy' nor a very bad one, but they will fare moderately well."

A more recent study by Chen and Chu (1974) of 1974 retirees and entrants calculates similar lifetime rates of return for 1974. The rates for 1974 *retirees* range from 6.1 percent to 16.9 percent. *Entrants* into the labor force in 1974 are estimated to have rates of return between 1.1 percent and 7.7 percent.

The study by Brittain and the more recent one by Chen and Chu demonstrate the difficulty of giving an unequivocal answer to the question of whether social security is a "good buy." Both studies fail to include in the analysis federal and state income tax treatments of contributions and benefits. McClung (1974) has speculated that "although it is a fact that the OASI PIA [primary insurance amount] computation is weighted in favor of persons with low AME [average monthly earnings], a rate of return calculation on an after-tax basis might well

reveal that, just with respect to OASI, system redistribution is from poor to rich."

The two studies do effectively spotlight possible differences between groups. Brittain, for example, notes that the wide spread in the rates of return indicates substantial income redistribution among categories of participants. For example, "the college graduate who starts work at twenty-two fares much better than the high school graduate who starts work at eighteen if both earn the average wage. . ." It remains for an after-tax study to determine whether any of the differentials change when tax laws are taken into account.

Social Security Programs Throughout the World. Periodically the U.S. Social Security Administration publishes comprehensive summaries of social security programs for all countries of the world where the necessary information is available. The latest summary of programs in 127 countries (U.S. Social Security Administration, 1973b) reports that 105 countries have old-age/invalidity/survivors programs. While there is wide variation from country to country, some generalizations can be made:

1. Slightly more than half of pension programs under social insurance (as distinct from provident funds or universal systems) have tripartite financing (employee, employer, and government contributions).
2. In most countries old-age benefits become payable between age 60 and 65, although in some countries the age is as low as age 50, and in a few it is as high as age 70.
3. Over half of the programs have the same pensionable age for women as for men; the others permit women to retire earlier.
4. A majority of programs impose a retirement test in determining benefit eligibility (i.e., limit earnings).
5. Pensions in most countries are wage-related but computation methods vary greatly.
6. The majority of programs add supplements to pensions if a recipient has a wife or young children.
7. Of the countries providing the automatic or semiautomatic revaluation of benefits during retirement, 14 base the adjustment

*See, for example, Buchanan and Campbell (1966).

on wage changes, 10 take the price index into account, and 2 use both.

8. Most countries provide survivor's benefits; typically this benefit is a fixed percentage of the prior pension (although a few pay only a lump-sum amount).

Private Pensions

Analysis of private pensions continues to be an area of research virtually ignored by the academic community.* What we know about the impact of private pensions on the economy and their role in providing economic support to the aged comes mostly from a few government studies. What we know most about is the growth in private pension assets and the extent of worker coverage.

Figure 6 shows the growth of reserves for private pension and deferred profit-sharing plans from 1950 to 1972. By 1972 these reserves had reached a total of $167.8 billion, with that

---

*Despite its age, Bernstein (1964) remains a good starting point for anyone wishing to become acquainted with the nature, terminology, issues, and growth of private pensions. See also Schulz (1970), Nader and Blackwell (1973), and Taggart (1973).

year's contributions to finance current and future benefit commitments reaching $18.5 billion.

Based on a survey of households conducted by the Bureau of the Census in April 1972, the Social Security Administration has revised an earlier estimate of private pension coverage (Kolodrubetz and Landay, 1973). The Census survey indicated that prior estimates of pension coverage had been too high. The Social Security Administration now estimates that 44 percent of wage and salary workers in private industry were covered by private pensions in 1972 (Kolodrubetz, 1974).

Table 21 shows how pension coverage in the United States varies by work status, sex, race, industry, and earnings. Among full-time workers, women, nonwhites, and low earners have the lowest coverage. The industries with the lowest coverage are wholesale and retail trade, construction, and the service industry.

Private Pension Benefits. With regard to those workers covered by private pensions, two of the most important questions are: how many of these workers lose their right to a benefit due to voluntary or involuntary employment

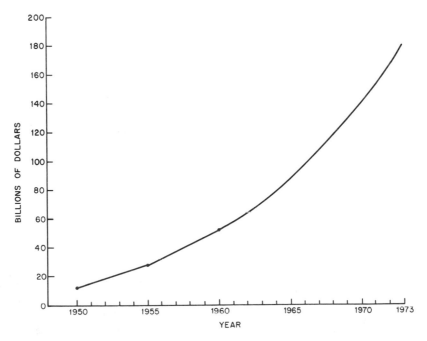

Figure 6. Reserves in private pension and deferred profit-sharing plans—1950, 1955, 1960–73. (From Kolodrubetz (1975).)

TABLE 21. PRIVATE PENSION COVERAGE, APRIL 1972.

	Percent
Wage and salary workers in private industry	
All full-time and part-time employees	43.7
Full-time employees only	47.0
Men	52.0
Women	36.0
Whites	48.0
Nonwhites	39.0
Full-time employees, by industry	
Communications and public utilities	82
Mining	72
Manufacturing	
Durable goods	63
Nondurable goods	57
Finance, insurance, and real estate	52
Transportation	45
Trade	
Wholesale	48
Retail	31
Construction	34
Services	29
Full-time employees, by earnings	
Men earning less than $5,000	26
Women earning less than $5,000	31
Men earning $5,000–9,999	58
Women earning $5,000–9,999	58

SOURCE: Kolodrubetz (1974) and Kolodrubetz and Landay (1973).

shifts, and how large a benefit will eligible workers ultimately receive?

The first question revolves primarily around the issue of vesting (i.e., a nonforfeitable right to a pension). The April 1972 Census survey discussed above also obtained data on vesting. Survey respondents were asked: "If you should change to a job not covered by this plan, would you still be eligible to receive the plan's benefits at retirement age?" A relatively high proportion (15 percent) of workers with private pension coverage answered the vesting question with "don't know." As to who had vested pensions, Kolodrubetz and Landay (1973) report:

Given the conditions for vesting found in retirement plans, it is not surprising that the proportion of workers who had vesting rose as job tenure lengthened. About 60 percent of the workers with less than 10 years of employment did not yet have vesting rights. The rate of vesting rose as job tenure increased— from 20 percent of those having worked less than 5 years to 47 percent for those who had

worked 15–19 years. . . . The low rate of vesting (or qualification for early retirement) for workers aged 50 and older is somewhat surprising, especially among those workers with long tenure. Only half of the men aged 50 or older who were employed 10 or more years had vested status. . . .

With regard to private pension benefit levels, there have been numerous reports over the years on the formulas used by various plans to calculate retirement benefits (U.S. Bureau of Labor Statistics, 1966; Bankers Trust Company, 1970; and Davis and Strasser, 1970). Most plans calculate benefits in one of the following ways:

1. A uniform benefit to all retirees meeting minimum age and/or years of service requirements.
2. Relating benefit levels to prior years of service.
3. Relating benefit levels to both prior earnings and years of service.

Kolodrubetz and Skolnik (1971)—using a limited sample of 30 "well-known" private plan formulas in effect during or before 1968— explore different methods of measuring the benefit promises of plans and show the degree of sensitivity and variability in benefit levels and wage-replacement ratios to various assumptions and variables. Strasser (1971) calculates hypothetical pension benefits based on 1969 pension plan provisions. Using a sample of plans from all industries, Strasser calculates the benefit for a "typical" worker retiring in 1969 with 30 years of service and career average earnings of $4,800. The private pension benefits ranged from about $1,400 a year (the average benefit in mining) to about $2,400 (the average benefit in communications and public utilities). For all industries the average was about $1,700.

We can contrast the hypothetical benefits calculated by Strasser with the actual pensions received by retiring workers. The Social Security Administration surveyed the 1.2 million persons who became entitled to retired worker benefits under social security between July 1969 and June 1970. Kolodrubetz (1973) reports on the level of benefits received by those workers who had achieved private pension eligibility and were receiving benefits at the time of the survey. This study found the median annual private pension to be $2,080 for men but only $970 for women.

Pension Reform Legislation. In September, 1974, the "Employee Retirement Income Security Act" became federal law. This major legislation extended previous legislation regulating and supervising private pensions and, for the first time, established certain minimum pension standards. The major provisions of the legislation are:*

1. Plans must minimally vest benefits using one of three alternatives:
    a. Vesting of 25 percent after 5 years of service, going up by 5 percent each year of the next 5 years and by 10 percent thereafter until 100 percent vesting after 15 years.
    b. Vesting of 100 percent after 10 years of service.
    c. Vesting of 50 percent when age and service add up to 45 years, with 100 percent vesting 5 years thereafter— subject to the constraint that employees must be 50 percent vested after 10 years service and 100 percent vested after 15 years.
2. Plan termination insurance is established, up to $750 monthly for employees whose plans terminate with insufficient funds.
3. Funding and fiduciary standards are strengthened.
4. Individual retirement accounts (exempt from federal income taxation) may be established by workers without private or public employee pension coverage, investing up to $1,500 annually or 15 percent of annual compensation (whichever is less).
5. New disclosure regulations permit participants to request once each year a statement from the plan administrator of total benefits, both vested and nonvested, which have accrued and the earliest date on which unvested benefits will become nonforfeitable.

*See Skolnik (1974) for a more comprehensive summary of the law.

6. The Social Security Administration receives reports (through the Treasury Department) from employers of vested benefits held by separated workers; Social Security notifies employees of all vested pension rights at the time of social security entitlement.
7. With the consent and cooperation of their employers, employees may transfer upon separation vested pension rights on a tax-free basis from one employer to another; or the employee may transfer the funds to an "individual retirement account."

Welfare Programs

In 1974 the major welfare program for the aged, blind, and disabled, "Old Age Assistance" (OAA), was replaced by a new "Supplemental Security Income" (SSI) program. As set out in a staff report by the U.S. Joint Economic Committee (Storey and Cox, 1973), it was hoped that the new program would result in:

1. Poor people having more cash to spend.
2. A *national* minimum income for the aged, blind, and disabled.
3. Uniform eligibility conditions instead of conditions which differed widely from state to state under OAA.
4. A start in unraveling the administrative snarl enveloping welfare programs (SSI is federally administered by the Social Security Administration).

There are two types of benefits under SSI: the basic federal payment and *optional* state supplementary payments. However, legislation passed in 1973 obligated states to supplement the federal payment in order *to at least maintain 1973 state OAA levels* (in cases where these 1973 levels were higher than the 1974 federal minimum income). The maximum federal SSI benefits for an individual and a couple without other income and living in their own household were $1,752 and $2,628 in 1974. At the time this chapter was written the latest published data were for August 1974. At that time about 3.7 million aged, blind, and disabled persons were receiving SSI; of that number, 2.2 million were aged (*Social Security Bulletin*, 1974).

To allow for variations in need in various states, the SSI legislation allows states to supplement the basic benefit. Rigby (1974) reports that 33 states and the District of Columbia had optional supplementation programs in 1974. In four states, however, the payment standards were below the federal payment and limited to individuals with special/emergency needs and to individuals with supervised living arrangements.

In May, 1974, 70 percent of aged SSI recipients (in federally administered programs) were receiving only federal SSI payments (Bell, 1974). There were an additional 209,200 aged receiving state supplementation only. In May, 1974, the average monthly payment to individuals was $82 (federal only) and $136 (federal plus state supplementation). For couples, the average monthly payment was $102 and $163, respectively.

SOME POLICY ISSUES

Adequate Retirement Income

The most popular method of evaluating the economic status of the aged (and other groups) is to look at the aged population at a given moment in time and compare their actual incomes to some standard level. The two most widely used measures for aged families are the U.S. Social Security Administration's "poverty" and "low income" indexes and the U.S. Bureau of Labor Statistics' "Budget for a Retired Couple." These indexes have been useful for setting levels of income above which minimum income adequacy is indicated. But the levels established by these indexes are somewhat arbitrary—being based in the case of the Social Security index on an emergency food budget and the assumption that these food costs constitute one-third of total required living expenditures. In the case of the Bureau of Labor Statistics' budgets, the designated levels are above a minimal level and seek to provide something called a "modest but adequate" living standard.

Derek Bok (1967) has succinctly summarized the major limitations of such *absolute* budget standards as follows:

. . .Experience in other countries has revealed how difficult it is to determine the expenditures that are appropriate for any group of people. Moreover, it is not enough simply to establish a single retirement budget. Separate determinations would have to be made for each of many income classes reaching retirement age, since a budget suitable for a day laborer would hardly seem adequate to a highly paid technician. Furthermore, the standard budget is probably too static a conception for the task at hand. While it may be possible to define the minimum living expenses which should be guaranteed here and now to the poorest of the aged, it is much more difficult to determine what standard of living will be considered adequate many years hence when present generations of workers begin to retire. Yet under our contributory system this question is important. We must concern ourselves with future benefit levels if employees are to have an adequate notion of the pensions they can count on in retirement and if they are to make contributions bearing some reasonable relation to the benefits they will eventually receive. In view of these problems, any effort to establish an adequate social security policy should aim at defining the proportion of prior wages which each worker can count on receiving when he retires. (*Harvard Law Review*, **80**, 717–764. Copyright 1967 by the Harvard Law Review Association.)

Viewing the adequacy of retirement income in terms of preretirement earnings replacement is becoming more common in developing pension policy. Schulz *et al.* (1974), in their book *Providing Adequate Retirement Income— Pension Reform in the United States and Abroad*, discuss the earnings replacement concept at great length. They then review and analyze Swedish, West German, Belgian, and Canadian social security pension reforms which were based upon the earnings replacement concept. Using simulation analysis, comparative pension replacement rates are estimated for the four countries.

One of the replacement rates estimated by Schulz *et al.* is for the "average worker." The hypothetical earnings pattern used for this average worker assumes that earnings grow in the early work years at a rate greater than the growth of average earnings of *all* workers but that eventually the wage growth declines and falls below the average prior to retirement. This

TABLE 22. SOCIAL SECURITY EARNINGS REPLACEMENT RATES FOR AN "AVERAGE WORKER" IN FOUR COUNTRIES.

Country	PERCENT OF FINAL EARNINGS	
	3% Growth economy	5% Growth economy
Sweden	69	55
West Germany	72	81
Belgium	73	84
Canada	39	39

SOURCE: Schulz et al. (1974).

hypothetical earnings pattern, however, is subject to the constraint in the model which specifies that the average lifetime earnings of this "average worker" must equal the average of "average earnings" for all workers over the same period. Table 22 presents the estimated earnings replacement for a hypothetical average worker provided by social security in the four countries.

In contrast to the recommendation of the 1971 White House Conference on Aging (undated) which defined adequate income in terms of the Bureau of Labor Statistics' "modest but adequate" budget for a retired couple, Schulz et al. (1974) "believe this country [the United States] should formulate new policies to improve both private and public pensions...starting not with a *poverty* standard of adequacy but rather using a standard which recognizes the desirability and reasonableness of maintaining living standards in retirement."

The Public/Private Pension Mix

The first compulsory social insurance system was adopted by Austria in 1854. The German social security system (the first *comprehensive* plan) was instituted by Bismarck in 1883–1889. In the United States, the American Express Company established a pension plan in 1875. For an excellent summary of the historical evolution of private pensions see Charlet (1968).

Despite the fact that the first pension plans were established about a century ago, there is still little agreement about the relative virtues of public versus private pensions and what the ideal mix of the two types should be. There is

great diversity in the mix of pensions existing in the various countries—but with fewer countries where private programs assume a major role than there are countries relying primarily on public pensions.

This lack of agreement on the mix of pensions is quite different from the general consensus which has developed over time as to the need for some type of compulsory public pension or insurance arrangement to provide at least minimum economic security in retirement (and for other situations such as liability, illness, etc.). While individual self-reliance and voluntary preparation for retirement—together with family intradependence—dominated the early discussions of old-age security provision, it is now generally accepted that this is not the appropriate cornerstone of an income maintenance policy for the aged. Instead, there is widespread support for relying on compulsory pensions.*

Given widespread disagreement over the appropriate pension mix and the large number of political debates which have occurred in various countries on the question, one would expect to find a large professional literature devoted to this topic in various countries. Surprisingly, this is not the case. While there has been quite a lot of popular writing on the subject, and some writing on the question of compulsion (as cited above), very little has been written which attempts to objectively approach the question of the most desirable pension mix and accumulate data for evaluation purposes. In this regard, Kincaid (1973) has provided a good discussion of the public/private mix issue in the British context.

In hearings before the U.S. Senate Special Committee on Aging, Edwin S. Hewitt, partner in a firm of pension consultants and actuaries, argued the case for a dual pension system:

> By establishing different methods of allocation, private plans accomplish different goals.

*See Roy Lubove (1968) for an extensive discussion of the debate over voluntarism versus compulsion which occurred prior to the passage of the initial social security legislation in the United States. See also Brown (1972) for a discussion of the Clark Amendment proposed for the original Social Security Act and why it was defeated. This amendment would have permitted approved company group annuity plans as substitutes for compulsory coverage under old-age insurance.

In fact, it is extraordinary how flexible an instrument for providing adequate security the private plan has proved to be.

There are two kinds of flexibility and perhaps this fact is underrated when we appraise what private plans are doing.

First, is their flexibility in terms of adapting to different needs. Very real differences in security problems exist among different companies, different industries, different age groups.

Retirement at an earlier age than 65 may be necessary in some cases. Sometimes the risk of disability is higher than at others. An older work force may mean past service credits; a younger group may provide some kind of account accumulation. The variations are important and should not be understated.

The second dimension is the flexibility between periods of time. Private plans have exhibited amazing flexibility to make their provisions meet the different needs that a group may have at different times.

The initial job of most pension plans when first established is to concentrate on retirement income for the older worker, hence the importance of past service benefits.

As plans become better funded, they tend to branch into other areas. Variety increases as plans are able to spend more money and give attention to tailormade benefits to meet specific needs.

Currently, for example, many plans are wrestling with such problems as protecting the value of benefits against inflation, providing adequate survivors' income, getting supplemental arrangements for longterm savings.

So, these two elements of flexibility between plans and over time periods demonstrate the role that private plans should be expected to play in the provision of old-age income. They are compensation payments which allocate money to where it should do the most good.

It is not possible, in our judgment, for either the public system or the private plans to do the whole job in an efficient, economical manner. Private plans can't be universal and they cannot be a basic layer of protection. A public system cannot be as flexible and it cannot be as changeable over time as individual private plans (Hewitt, 1970).

But experience has shown that there are many problems connected with private pensions. Some of the major ones are:

1. It is difficult to cover all workers; in the United States a major segment of the work force still remains uncovered (Kolodrubetz, 1974).

2. It is difficult to make private pensions inflation-proof; in the United States very few private pensions adjust for general price increases during retirement (Norwood, 1972).

3. The economic costs of private pension (a) administration, (b) funds investment, (c) mobility, (d) disclosure to recipients, (e) supervision and regulation, and (f) reinsurance are much higher than for social insurance (Schulz et al., 1974).

4. It is difficult to make private pensions "portable"—that is, to allow workers to have job mobility without a reduction in the value of their pension rights relative to what the value would be if they did not change jobs (Bernstein, 1964).

5. Private pensions may discourage the hiring of older workers because it is usually more costly to provide such workers with a specified pension benefit (Latimer, 1965; Taggart, 1973).

6. Private pensions contribute to the concentration of corporate ownership and control (Murray, 1967).

In the United States, Myers (1970) has presented the arguments for no further increases in real social security benefit levels and reliance on private pensions and individual saving for additional improvements.

Schulz et al. (1974) present the alternative view. They recommend "the adoption of an adequacy of income standard for social security old-age benefits which would provide inflation protected benefits equal to at least 55 percent of the individual's or family's (if married) preretirement average earnings during the best ten of the last fifteen years prior to retirement. . ." The balance of retirement income would come from private pensions and savings. (See Paul, 1974, for a pension consultant's view.)

If we look at the pension systems currently existing in various countries, what we find is that there is a tendency to rely heavily on public pensions or a private/public combination *with extensive regulation* of the private sector (Schulz et al., 1974).

Financing Social Security Old-Age Pensions

A wide variety of mechanisms are used in various countries to finance social security. In the United States three major financing problems have arisen:

1. The payroll contribution is regressive, with the proportion the contribution represents of total earnings falling, for earning levels above the maximum taxable earnings ceiling. As benefit levels are increased by Congress, these contributions become an increasingly burdensome and inequitable tax on the poor worker.
2. Congress has used the social security system as a welfare system for the aged (minimum benefits, weighted benefit formulas, and early eligibility) but has not financed these welfare benefits with general revenue financing, therefore exacerbating the previous problem as a result of the higher required tax rates.
3. As the population "ages" with a rising percentage of the population age 65 or

older, rising pension costs are projected to exceed payroll tax contributions.

Quite a lot of attention has been focused on the first two problems.* The third problem is relatively new but promises to be one of the most important questions influencing the future of social security. A good summary of information on this topic is provided by Crowley (1974).

Figure 7 shows past and projected long-run costs of OASDI as a percent of taxable payroll. About 2005, the costs begin to increase sharply:

> Although most of the increase in cost is expected to occur after the turn of the century (when the effects of the changes in the population projections are fully felt), part of it will already occur within the next few years, thereby producing a marked decline in the near future in the ratio of assets to expenditures in the absence of an immediate increase in income to both the OASI [Old Age and Survivors Insurance] and DI [Disability Insurance] Trust Funds. . .

*See Brittain (1972), Pechman, Aaron, and Taussig (1968), Eckstein (1968), McClung (1969), Cruikshank (1970), and Atkinson (1972).

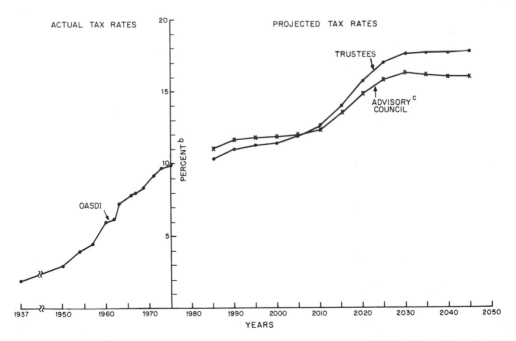

Figure 7. Past OASDI tax rates and projected current costs, 1940–2045[a]. (From Data in Board of Trustees, OASDI (1974) and Advisory Council on Social Security (1975).)

[a]Both employer and employee contributions.
[b]Percent of covered earnings.
[c]Assumes that recommendations in Advisory Council on Social Security (1975) are enacted.

The increasing costs. . .are due principally, but not totally, to the demographic effect of the projected large aged population as compared to the working population. Some of the cost, however, is due to what could be considered anomalies in the automatic benefit adjustment provisions in present law. . . The present automatic provisions are projected to result in awarded benefits that would increase faster than average earnings in the future. The differential in trends between average awarded benefits and average covered earnings would be relatively minor during this century. . . .but it is projected to increase substantially thereafter (Board of Trustees, OASDI, 1974).

The Advisory Council on Social Security (1975) gave considerable attention to future costs of the social security system. With regard to long-term costs, the Advisory Council—accepting the projections of the Office of the Actuary—warned of serious financial problems in the future. While stipulating that they did not have time to present comprehensive recommendations on this issue, the Council recommended some interim action:

1. Financing aged health care insurance (Medicare) out of general revenue and using the released funds for old-age pension financing.
2. Removing the 7 percent limitation on the tax rate for the self-employed and raising the tax to 150 percent of the employee contribution rate.
3. Studying the merits of raising the age of eligibility for social security retirement benefits.

In trying to predict how soon and how great will be the economic burden of aging populations in the United States and various other nations, we are faced with the difficulty that the key variables—fertility, pension levels, and the age of retirement—are in a state of flux and essentially unpredictable (Schulz, 1973). This means that long-range planning becomes very difficult. However, at the same time, all these variables are subject to influence by national policy, and, therefore, the magnitude of future problems is subject to control—should a nation desire to do so.

The trend of a lengthening retirement period resulting from medical advances and, more importantly, from retiring at an earlier age needs to be watched closely. Serious thought will have to be given to reevaluating or, in many cases, establishing a national policy in this area.

Adjusting Social Security Benefit Levels

In looking at the question of whether and how old-age pensions are adjusted, it is useful to distinguish among four cases:

1. Adjustment of *new* pensions at the time of initial payment for past *inflation* effects on the pension calculation;
2. Adjustment of *new* pensions at the time of initial payment for past *economic growth*;
3. Adjustment of *old* pensions for *inflation*;
4. Adjustment of *old* pensions for *economic growth*.

The United States now has a provision in the social security law which automatically adjusts pensions during retirement for general increases in the price level. The adjustment mechanism finally became law in 1972 after many years of debate over whether such a provision would discourage significant (and "needed") improvement in the general level of social security pensions adjusted for price changes.

In 1963, Kreps and Spengler proposed that retirees be provided some share in economic growth through the establishment of a social credit scheme (Kreps and Spengler, 1963). Since then there has been relatively little discussion of this issue and few advocates of an automatic adjustment mechanism using, for example, an earnings index.

Support for such a reform depends on the relative desirability of competing public expenditures and most especially on the adequacy of retirement pension benefits *at* retirement. Certainly the lack of discussion of this issue in the United States has been in large part a result of public debate and action being focused on aged poverty and the very low levels of pensions both at and during retirement.

The attempt to index for inflation the social security system in the United States created a major and complicated problem. Analyzing the 1972 adjustment provisions, Thompson (1974) concludes that ". . .inflation will cause [social security] replacement ratios to increase over time—with higher rates of inflation causing faster increase in replacement ratios. . ." and "that changes in replacement ratios and, consequently, in the payroll tax necessary to finance Social Security benefits will be the capricious result of future rates of inflation and the future rates of growth of wages." Thompson believes that Congress legislated an adjustment procedure which "introduces an unintended over-adjustment into the benefit levels due" workers who will retire in the future.

The Advisory Council on Social Security also criticizes the indexing mechanisms:

> The provisions of present law for computing average monthly earnings, on which benefits are based, and for adjusting the benefit table in the law to changes in prices may result over the long range in unintended, unpredictable, and undesirable variations in the level of benefits.

The problem results from the fact that the 1972 indexing legislation specified that the social security benefit formula (not benefits) was to be adjusted for changes in the Consumer Price Index. The legislation was written so that the adjusted benefit formula was to be used to increase benefits not only for those *currently* retired but also for those *retiring in the future*. Since benefits for future retirees would be based on earnings levels which already reflected wage adjustments for past inflation, the mechanism results in a double adjustment.

The Advisory Council recommended that the adjustment process be changed so that the pension formula provided pensions which were a constant proportion of preretirement earnings, these pensions to be adjusted upward for inflation during the retirement period.

Thompson's analysis and the recommendations of the Advisory Council lend additional evidence to the case for encouraging policy-makers to evaluate pension programs in terms of their current and future earnings replacement potential (see Schulz *et al.*, 1974). Moreover, as the aging of the United States population develops, there will be a need for a greater awareness of the intra- and intergenerational equity considerations arising out of developing pension systems. As the national cost of aged income maintenance rises, simultaneous attention must be given to both adequacy and equity issues in order both to maintain public confidence in and support for the programs and to use with maximum effectiveness the retirement funds available.

REFERENCES

Aaron, Henry J. 1973. What do circuit-breaker laws accomplish? *In*, George E. Peterson (ed.), *Property Tax Reform*. Washington, D.C.: The Urban Institute.

Abbot, Julian. 1974. Covered employment and the age men claim retirement benefits. *Social Security Bulletin*, **37**, 3-16 (April).

Advisory Council on Social Security. 1975. *Reports*. Washington, D.C.: Government Printing Office.

Atkinson, A. B. 1972. Income maintenance and income taxation. *Journal of Social Policy*, **1**, 135-148.

Bankers Trust Company. 1970. *1970 Study of Industrial Retirement Plans*. New York: Bankers Trust Company.

Bell, Richard. 1974. *Payments, Social Security Benefits, and Living Arrangements Under the Supplemental Security Income Program, May 1974*. Research and Statistics Note No. 36-1974. Washington, D.C.: Office of Research and Statistics, U.S. Social Security Administration.

Bernstein, Merton C. 1964. *The Future of Private Pensions*. New York: The Free Press.

Bixby, Lenore E. 1970. Income of people aged 65 and older: Overview from 1968 survey of the aged. *Social Security Bulletin*, **33**, 3-34 (April).

Bixby, Lenore E. 1975. Communication with the author.

Board of Trustees, OASDI. 1974. *1974 Annual Report of the Board of Trustees of the Federal Old-Age and Survivors Insurance and Disability Insurance Trust Funds*. Washington, D.C.: Government Printing Office.

Bok, Derek C. 1967. Emerging issues in social legislation: Social security. *Harvard Law Review*, **80**, 717-764.

Break, George F. 1974. The incidence and economic effects of taxation. *In*, Allan S. Blinder, George F. Break, Dick Netzer, Robert M. Solow, and Peter O. Steiner, *The Economics of Public Finance*. Washington, D.C.: The Brookings Institution.

Brittain, John A. 1972. *The Payroll Tax for Social Security*. Washington, D.C.: The Brookings Institution.

Brown, J. Douglas. 1972. *An American Philosophy of Social Security*. Princeton, New Jersey: Princeton University Press.

Buchanan, James, and Campbell, Colin. 1966. Voluntary social security. *Wall Street Journal*, Dec. 20.

Charlet, Pearl E. 1968. Public policy and private retirement programs—a suggestion for change. *In*, U.S. Joint Economic Committee, *Old Age Income Assurance*. Part I. Washington, D.C.: Government Printing Office.

Chen, Yung-Ping, and Chu, Kwang-Wen. 1974. Tax-benefit ratios and rates of return under OASI: 1974 retirees and entrants. *The Journal of Risk and Insurance*, **41**, 189–206.

Crowley, F. J. 1974. Financing the social security program—then and now. *In*, Subcommittee on Fiscal Policy, U.S. Joint Economic Committee, *Studies in Public Welfare*. Paper No. 18. Washington, D.C.: Government Printing Office.

Cruikshank, Nelson H. 1970. *The Stake of Today's Workers in Retirement Security*. Committee Print, U.S. Senate Special Committee on Aging. Washington, D.C.: Government Printing Office.

Davis, Harry E., and Strasser, Arnold. 1970. Private pension plans, 1960–1969—an overview. *Monthly Labor Review*, **93**, 45–56 (July).

Eckstein, Otto. 1968. Financing the system of social insurance. *In*, William G. Bowen (ed.), *The Princeton Symposium on the American System of Social Insurance*. New York: McGraw-Hill.

Epstein, Lenore A., and Murray, Janet H. 1967. *The Aged Population of the United States*. Social Security Administration Research Report No. 19. Washington, D.C.: Government Printing Office.

Fox, Alan. 1974. *Earnings Replacement from Social Security and Private Pensions: Newly Entitled Beneficiaries, 1970*. Preliminary Findings from the Survey of New Beneficiaries, Report No. 13. Washington, D.C.: Office of Research and Statistics, U.S. Social Security Administration.

Fried, Edward, R., Rivlin, Alice, Schultze, Charles L., and Teeters, Nancy H. 1973. *Setting National Priorities—The 1974 Budget*. Washington, D.C.: The Brookings Institution.

Hewitt, Edwin S. 1970. Testimony. *In*, U.S. Senate Special Committee on Aging, *Economics of Aging: Toward a Full Share in Abundance*, Part 10B—Pension Aspects. Washington, D.C.: Government Printing Office.

Horlick, Max. 1974. *National Expenditures on Social Security in Selected Countries, 1968 and 1971*. Research and Statistics Note No. 29-1974. Washington, D.C.: Office of Research and Statistics, U.S. Social Security Administration.

Irelan, Lola M. 1972. Retirement history study: Introduction. *Social Security Bulletin*, **36**, 3–8 (November).

Jenkins, Shirley (ed.) 1969. *Social Security in International Perspective*. New York: Columbia University.

Kaim-Caudle, P. R. 1973. *Comparative Social Policy and Social Security*. London: Martin Robertson.

Kincaid, J. C. 1973. *Poverty and Equality in Britain*. Baltimore: Penguin Books.

Kolodrubetz, Walter W. 1973. Private retirement benefits and relationship to earnings: Survey of new beneficiaries. *Social Security Bulletin*, **36**, 16–36 (May).

Kolodrubetz, Walter W. 1974. Employee-benefit plans, 1972. *Social Security Bulletin*, **37**, 15–21.

Kolodrubetz, Walter W. 1975. Employee-benefit plans, 1973. *Social Security Bulletin*, **38** (May).

Kolodrubetz, Walter W., and Landay, Donald M. 1973. Coverage and vesting of full-time employees under private retirement plans. *Social Security Bulletin*, **35**, 20–36 (November).

Kolodrubetz, Walter W., and Skolnik, Alfred M. 1971. *Pension Benefit Levels: A Methodological Analysis*. Office of Research and Statistics, Social Security Administration. Staff Paper No. 11. Washington, D.C.: Department of Health, Education, and Welfare.

Kreps, Juanita, and Spengler, J. J. 1963. Equity and social credit for the retired. *In*, Juanita Kreps (ed.), *Employment, Income and Retirement Problems of The Aged*, pp. 198–229. Durham, North Carolina: Duke University Press.

Latimer, Murray W. 1965. *The Relationship of Employee Hiring Ages to the Cost of Pension Plans*. Washington, D.C.: U.S. Department of Labor.

Lingg, Barbara A. 1974. Effects of the OASDI benefit increase in June 1974. *Research and Statistics Note*, No. 24. Washington, D.C.: Social Security Administration.

Lubove, Roy. 1968. *The Struggle for Social Security, 1900-1935*. Cambridge, Massachusetts: Harvard University Press.

McClung, Nelson. 1969. The economics of pension finance. *The Journal of Risk and Insurance*, **36**, 425–431.

McClung, Nelson. 1974. Old age, survivors and disability insurance in a general scheme of wage replacement. A paper prepared for the Social Security Advisory Council, Washington, D.C. Mimeo.

Moon, Marilyn. 1974. A measure of the economic welfare of the aged. Unpublished Ph.D. dissertation. University of Wisconsin.

Morgan, James N., Smith, Robert, and Jones, John. 1962. *Income and Welfare in the United States*. New York: McGraw-Hill.

Murray, Janet. 1972. Homeownership and financial assets: Findings from the 1968 survey of the aged. *Social Security Bulletin*, **35**, 3–23 (August).

Murray, Roger F. 1967. Economic aspects of pensions: A summary report. *In*, U.S. Joint Economic Committee, *Old Age Income Assurance*, Part V. Washington, D.C.: Government Printing Office.

Myers, Robert J. 1970. Government and pensions. *In*, *Private Pensions and the Public Interest*. Washington, D.C.: American Enterprise Institute for the Public Policy Research.

Nader, Ralph, and Blackwell, Kate. 1973. *You and Your Pension*. New York: Grossman.

NRTA/AARP (National Retired Teachers Association and American Association of Retired Persons). 1975. *1975 Tax Facts—A Comparative Guide to State Tax Regulations*. Washington, D.C.: The Associations.

Norwood, Janet L. 1972. Cost-of-living escalation of pensions. *Monthly Labor Review*, **95**, 21–23 (June).

Orshansky, Mollie. 1974. *Federal Welfare Reform and the Economic Status of the Aged Poor*. Staff Paper No. 17. Washington, D.C.: Office of Research and Statistics, U.S. Social Security Administration.

Paul, Robert D. 1974. Can private pension plans deliver? *Harvard Business Review*, beg. on p. 22 (September–October).

Pechman, Joseph A., Aaron, Henry J., and Taussig, Michael K. 1968. *Social Security–Perspectives for Reform*. Washington, D.C.: The Brookings Institution.

Reno, Virginia. 1971. Why men stop working at or before age 65: Findings from the survey of new beneficiaries. *Social Security Bulletin*, **34**, 3–14.

Rettig, Albert, and Nichols, Orlo R. 1974. *Some Aspects of the Dynamic Projection of Benefits Under the 1973 Social Security Amendments* (P.L. 93–233). Actuarial note. no. 87. Washington, D.C.: Social Security Administration.

Rigby, Donald E. 1974. State supplementation under federal SSI program. *Social Security Bulletin*, **37**, 21–28 (November).

Rimlinger, Gaston. 1971. *Welfare Policy and Industrialization in Europe, America, and Russia*. New York: John Wiley.

Ruggles, Nancy, and Ruggles, Richard. 1974. The anatomy of earnings behavior. *In*, National Bureau of Economic Research, *The Economics of Well-Being*. Conference on Research on Income and Wealth, Vol. 41, forthcoming.

Schottland, Charles I. 1970. *The Social Security Program in the United States*. 2nd ed. New York: Appleton-Century-Crofts.

Schultz, T. Paul. 1964. *The Distribution of Personal Income*. U.S. Joint Economic Committee. Washington, D.C.: Government Printing Office.

Schulz, James H. 1970. *Pension Aspects of the Economics of Aging: Present and Future Roles of Private Pensions*. Committee Print, U.S. Senate Special Committee on Aging. Washington, D.C.: Government Printing Office.

Schulz, James H. 1973. The economic impact of an aging population. *Gerontologist*, **13**, 111–117.

Schulz, James H., Carrin, Guy, Krupp, Hans, Peschke, Manfred, Sclar, Eliot, and Van Steenberge, J. 1974. *Providing Adequate Retirement Income–Pension Reform in the United States and Abroad*. Hanover, New Hampshire: Brandeis University Press/New England Press.

Shanas, Ethel, Townsend, Peter, Wedderburn, Dorothy, Friis, Henning, Milhøj, Poul, and Stehouwer, Jan. 1968. *Old People in Three Industrial Societies*. New York: Atherton Press.

Sherman, Salloy R. 1973. Assets on the threshold of retirement. *Social Security Bulletin*, **35**, 3–17 (August).

Skolnik, Alfred M. 1974. Pension reform legislation of 1974. *Social Security Bulletin*, **37**, 35–42 (December).

Skolnik, Alfred M., and Dales, Sophie. 1975. Social welfare expenditures, fiscal year 1974. *Social Security Bulletin*, **38**, 3–19 (January).

Social Security Bulletin. 1974. Current operating statistics (December).

Storey, James R., and Cox, Irene. 1973. *The New Supplemental Security Income Program–Impact on Current Benefits and Unresolved Issues*. Paper No. 10. *In*, Subcommittee on Fiscal Policy, U.S. Joint Economic Committee, *Studies in Public Welfare*. Washington, D.C.: Government Printing Office.

Strasser, Arnold. 1971. Pension formula summarization: An emerging technique. *Monthly Labor Review*, **94**, 49–56 (April).

Surrey, Stanley S. 1967. Congressional testimony. *In*, Ways and Means Committee, U.S. House of Representatives, *Hearings: President's Proposal for Revision in the Social Security System*, Part 1. Washington, D.C.: Government Printing Office.

Surrey, Stanley S. 1973. *Pathways to Tax Reform– The Concept of Tax Expenditures*. Cambridge, Massachusetts: Harvard University Press.

Taggart, Robert. 1973. *The Labor Market Impacts of the Private Retirement System*. Paper No. 11. *In*, Subcommittee on Fiscal Policy, U.S. Joint Economic Committee, *Studies in Public Welfare*. Washington, D.C.: Government Printing Office.

Taussig, Michael K. 1973. *Alternative Measures of the Distribution of Economic Welfare*. Princeton, New Jersey: Industrial Relations Section, Princeton University.

Thompson, Lawrence. 1974. An analysis of the factors currently determining benefit level adjustments in the social security retirement program. Technical Analysis Paper No. 1. Office of Income Security Policy. Washington, D.C.: Office of the Assistant Secretary for Planning and Evaluation, Department of Health, Education and Welfare.

U.S. Bureau of Labor Statistics. 1966. *Private Pension Plan Benefits*. Bulletin No. 1485. Washington, D.C.: Government Printing Office.

U.S. Bureau of the Census. 1973a. *Consumer Income*. Current Population Reports, Series P-60, No. 90. Washington, D.C.: Government Printing Office.

U.S. Bureau of the Census. 1973b. *Real Estate Tax Data for Homeowner Properties for the United States and Regions: 1971*. 1970 Census of Housing, HC(S1)-17. Washington, D.C.: Government Printing Office.

U.S. Bureau of the Census. 1974a. *Consumer Income*. Current Population Reports, Series P-60, No. 96. Washington, D.C.: Government Printing Office.

U.S. Bureau of the Census. 1974b. *Money Income in 1973 of Families and Persons in the United States*. Current Population Reports, Series P-60, No. 93. Washington, D.C.: Government Printing Office.

U.S. Bureau of the Census. 1974c. *Characteristics of the Low-Income Population: 1973* (Advanced Report). Current Population Reports, Series P-60, No. 94. Washington, D.C.: Government Printing Office.

U.S. Bureau of the Census. 1975a. *Consumer Income*. Current Population Reports, Series P-60, No. 97. Washington, D.C.: Government Printing Office.

U.S. Bureau of the Census. 1975b. *Characteristics of*

the Low-Income Population: 1973. Current Population Reports, Series P-60, No. 98. Washington, D.C.: Government Printing Office.

U.S. Social Security Administration. 1972. *Social Security Bulletin: Annual Statistical Supplement.* Washington, D.C.: Government Printing Office.

U.S. Social Security Administration. 1973a. *Social Security Programs in the United States.* Washington, D.C.: Government Printing Office.

U.S. Social Security Administration. 1973b. *Social Security Programs Throughout the World, 1973.* Office of Research and Statistics, Research Report No. 44. Washington, D.C.: Government Printing Office.

U.S. Social Security Administration. 1974. *OASDI Digest.* DHEW Publication No. (SSA) 74-11917. Washington, D.C.: Department of Health, Education and Welfare.

1971 White House Conference on Aging. Undated. *Toward a National Policy on Aging.* Final Report, Vol. II. Washington, D.C.: Department of Health, Education and Welfare.

Wilson, Thomas (ed.) 1974. *Pensions, Inflation and Growth.* London: Heinemann Educational Books.

23
AGING, HEALTH, AND THE ORGANIZATION OF HEALTH RESOURCES

Ethel Shanas
University of Illinois, Chicago Circle
and
George L. Maddox
Duke University

HEALTH AND ILLNESS AS SOCIAL CONCERNS

Physical and psychological well-being are matters of great social as well as personal concern. The reasons for this can be easily understood. Health and illness affect an individual's performance of basic personal tasks of daily living and of expected social roles. Impairment and disability increase the probability of failure in carrying out personal tasks and social roles; and such failures in turn increase dependency which, particularly for adults, challenges widely shared personal and social expectations and preferences for independence. Moreover, loss of autonomy tends to have a negative effect on self-evaluation and life satisfaction. Illness also exacts economic costs in terms of both lost opportunities for productive work and charges for the health services required to restore functioning. Health is thus both a key personal resource for any individual and a social concern, because performance of social roles in economic, kinship, and community organizations requires individuals who can function competently.

All societies develop definitions of illness which exempt an individual under specified circumstances from the obligations to perform expected social roles. Such exemptions are typically based on the assumed legitimacy of the disabling illness and on indications that the sick person wants the exemption to be temporary. Social groups recognize that an individual may feign sickness in order to be relieved from social obligations and to elicit helping behavior from others. Hence social groups look for and frequently require official confirmation of sickness claims and, in any case, search for evidence that the sick individual does not want to remain in this special exempt status any longer than necessary.

Society, like an individual, is concerned about the economic cost of illness. Modern industrial societies in recent decades have committed an increasingly large proportion of their economic resources to the development and maintenance of organizations designed to control illness and to restore sick individuals to maximum functioning. In Western European societies, for example, the capital investments, manpower development, and operating expenses committed to health constituted about 7 percent of their Gross National Product in the early 1970's; in the United States the annual investment in health services in 1972 was 7.7 percent of the Gross National Product and exceeded 99 billion dollars (Somers, 1971; Cooper, Worthington, and Piro, 1974).

Average life expectancy has increased markedly in economically developed countries during this century and similar trends are now evident in developing countries (United Nations, 1973). Improved social conditions, coupled with advances in medical technology and sanitation, have not only insured the survival of increasing numbers of persons into the later decades of life but have also encouraged people's expectations that the benefits of the best health care available are a social right. What constitutes "best care" in any society is not easy to define; but universally the provision of that care has proved to be expensive. Consequently, all societies currently share a set of common basic problems in the provision of health care. According to Somers (1971) these are: control of expenditures; development of adequately comprehensive care systems; manpower development; and achievement of consensus about the equitable distribution of basic services. Any discussion of these common problems in the provision of health care inevitably involves consideration of the relationship between aging and illness. The risk of illness and impairment increases with age and, correspondingly, the personal and social costs of illness in late life are very high. A brief review of the relationship between aging and illness and of the implications of this relationship for the allocation of societal resources will illustrate the basis of some important social concerns.

Aging and Illness

The relationship between chronological age and illness is well-known and well-documented in life tables and epidemiological reports on the distribution of disease and impairment. Chronological age is a basic and the best single general predictor of mortality as indicated by death rates; age is also associated with morbidity as indicated by an age-related incidence and prevalence of disease and disability. These observations will be documented in some detail later in this chapter. Whether as a result of intrinsic biological mechanisms which are inherited at birth, exposure to hostile environmental factors, or both, the older the biological organism, the greater its risk of disease, impairment, and death (Lasagna, 1969). As we shall see, factors other than chronological age must be considered in understanding observed patterns of mortality and morbidity. Nevertheless, the middle and later years of life are characterized by a series of biological changes, usually gradual ones, which result in a decreased capacity for functioning and survival. We are not surprised therefore to see reports on health and illness which summarize findings by age categories such as 45 to 64, 65 to 74, 75 and older, and which demonstrate repetitively the expected association between age and illness.

A variety of disciplines are interested in understanding illness and responses to illness among older persons. Scientists are interested in charting human performance over the life span and the factors which affect functioning and survival. One aspect of this interest is the possibility and probability of interventions that might lengthen the currently observed life span and enable more individuals to achieve the longer than average life now enjoyed by a relatively few persons in their 80's and 90's. Scientists also wish to understand how human performance is affected by the complex relationship between the physical and psychological aspects of health and illness and between the objective and subjective aspects of these states. Furthermore, there is interest in the complex and imperfect way in which illness and the need for health care are translated by individuals into demand for and utilization of health services.

While social administrators are interested in scientific issues related to health and illness, they have particular concerns of their own. They are likely to take note, for example, that older persons have high rates of illness and disability and generate high demand for health services, and that this older age category is increasing at a higher rate than other age categories in developing as well as in developed countries. Health practitioners, in turn, take special note of older persons not only because they are at high risk for disease and disability and generate demand for services at a high level but also because particular kinds of health problems are observed in late life. The problems most frequently observed among older persons tend to be chronic, often degenerative, rather than acute; the older individual's health problems are frequently multiple, including physical, psychological, and social components in a complex mixture.

Further, it appears that the particular manifestation of illness and disability in late life does not mesh well with modern systems of health care. The organization of health resources tends to be mismatched with the patterns of illness and disability displayed by older persons. Health care tends to be organized primarily to concentrate on the specialized management of acute disease in hospital settings which, in turn, are not well-articulated with community-based primary, preventive, or rehabilitative care (McKeown and Cross, 1969; U.S. Department of Health, Education and Welfare, 1971b). This mismatch between the health care needs of older persons and the organization of resources to meet those needs has become increasingly obvious. The increasing proportion of older persons in the populations of all societies and the escalating cost of their health care underlie a general widespread sense of urgency in the devising of more efficient and effective health care systems.

Economic Aspects of Health Care

The documented high risk of illness and impairment in late life predicts that utilization of health services increases with age. Correspondingly, the private and public economic costs of health care in late life are high. In 1973 in the United States, for example, persons 65 years of age and older (approximately 10 percent of the population) accounted for 28 percent of the $80 billion bill for personal health care in that year. The personal health care costs of older persons are between two and three times higher than the amount that might be expected on the basis of chance alone (Andersen, Kravits, Anderson, and Daley, 1973; Cooper and Piro, 1974). Recent experience in the United States

provides an illustration: older persons had an average annual medical bill of $1052 as compared to a bill of $384 for persons aged 19 to 64 and $167 for persons under the age of 19. Moreover, the average hospital bill for an older person and his average physician's bill was three times greater than the average bill for other adults. Comparable estimates of the high cost of health care in late life have been made in Great Britain where older persons comprise 13 percent of the population but consume about 40 percent of the resources of the National Health Service (Logan, 1966). In Great Britain health bills are primarily a public rather than a personal responsibility. Even in the United States, however, where health care bills are considered to be primarily a private responsibility, public expenditures covered about two-thirds of the total expenditures for health services to older persons. Despite the high level of public expenditures, the individual older person in the United States insured under Medicare in 1973 could expect to have only 40 percent of his health bill paid from this source and could expect to pay a total of $311 on the average "out of pocket."

The recognized cost of health care significantly understates the real cost of illness borne by sick individuals and the kinsmen on whom they depend for informal care and support. An estimated 5 percent to 10 percent of older individuals living outside institutions require home care which, to a substantial degree, is provided by relatives. The psychological burden of such care has received very little attention (Grad and Sainsbury, 1968), and the real economic cost of such care has not been systematically studied. We do not know, for example, the economic cost implicit in having an adult family member forego employment in the interest of remaining at home to care for a disabled individual. Generally, home care provided by family members has been treated as though it had no economic cost although the cost of publicly financed home health care programs is demonstrably high (Stiefel, 1967).

The cost of health care is rising in all industrial societies. The percentage of the Gross National Product in the more economically developed countries allocated to health services has essentially doubled in the last several decades alone. In the United States and Western European countries, 6 percent to 8 percent GNP is currently allocated to health services. Older persons contribute significantly to the rise in health costs. The proportion of older persons in the populations of the developed countries has essentially doubled in the first three-quarters of this century.

Inflation of health care cost plus uncertainty about levels of demand for services among high utilizers of services, such as older persons, have made projections of the total cost of health services quite difficult. In 1965, at the inception of Medicare in the United States, for example, the projected 1970 cost of Part A (hospital care) of that program was $3.1 billion. The actual cost for services in this program in 1970 proved to be $5.8 billion. Similarly, in 1965 the projected 1990 cost for hospital services under Medicare was $8.8 billion, while in 1969 the revised estimate for 1990 was $16.8 billion. Comparable underestimations of cost were initially made for Part B (supplemental medical insurance); a fivefold increase in the cost of this program was observed between 1965 and 1970 (U.S. Senate Committee on Finance, 1970).

The economics of health care systems is quite complex and not fully understood. We understand only partially, for instance, how various options for organizing and financing health care affect both demand and the total cost of care. We know only partially how the providers of service respond to the stress of increased demand for care. We have very limited understanding about the specific effects which an alternative organization of health care may have on the morbidity and mortality experienced by a population generally or by older members of a population in particular.

In a recent analysis of the probable effects of various policy options for organizing and financing health care in the United States, Newhouse, Phelps, and Schwartz (1974) provide an extensive review of current evidence related to three interrelated issues of considerable relevance in considering alternative approaches to health insurance: (1) How do various options affect demand for services and the total health bill? (2) How does a health care system adapt under pressure? (3) What is the expected return on various health care investments? For purposes of discussion they estimate the effects of two prototypical national health insurance schemes, one offering total care and the other 25 percent coinsurance option (i.e., the patient is responsible for one-fourth of the cost of care). Using evidence from a number of small experiments in health care organizing and financing, they conclude that a publicly financed total health care program would increase inpatient demand between 5 percent and 15 percent and that a program that required 25 percent coinsurance might increase inpatient demand not at all or no more than 8 percent. On the other hand, they anticipate that ambulatory care would be dramatically and differently affected by the two options. The total care option was projected to increase demand for ambulatory care by as much as 75 percent and 25 percent coinsurance was projected to increase demand by as much as 30 percent. Were such increases in demand to occur, the total cost of health care annually would be increased substantially by as much as $16 billion in the case of total care option and $7 billion in the case of the 25 percent coinsurance option.

While increased demand for health services potentially could generate additional resources and personnel to meet the demand, according to Newhouse, Phelps, and Schwartz, other responses tend to be more probable. These more likely responses include, at least in market economies, increased prices for services; and in all types of economies, a probable increase in the time required to receive services. Waiting for service is costly in terms of time and when it occurs, individuals who are time rich but dollar poor (e.g., unemployed or retired persons) are most likely to benefit from health care programs in which all or most of the cost of care is provided by insurance. Health care providers under the stress of increased demand, however, tend to change the character of services offered (e.g., they offer less preventive and more acute care). Newhouse, Phelps, and Schwartz conclude somewhat pessimistically that "even a substantial investment in delivery of more health services is not likely to produce any clearly measurable changes in any dimension of health, whether length of life or physical well-being." There is no other convincing evidence to the contrary from economically developed countries. Such a conclusion sheds some light on why the organization and financing of health care for older persons is increasingly a matter of public discussion in all societies. If the best available health care for all individuals is a right insured by removing price as a barrier and equilibrating supply and demand, the total health bill of a society will be predictably high. In the U.S., as a case in point, a health system designed to cover total cost of illness might require an investment of 11 percent of the Gross National Product. Current discussion of National Health Insurance options in the United States reflects concern about the high cost of health care to older persons. Most options now under discussion include various provisions for coinsurance and a wide range of exclusions from coverage.

MEASURING HEALTH AND THE DEMAND FOR HEALTH CARE

Problems Inherent in Defining Health

Any discussion of health, whether focused on the aged or any other population group, must begin with a definition of what is meant by health. Such a definition is essential for describing the status of a population or individual, for allocating resources for health care, and for organizing services to meet health needs (Sullivan, 1966; Andersen, 1968; Fanshel and Bush, 1970; Maddox, 1972; Aday and Eichorn, 1972; Patrick, Bush, and Chen, 1973). Definitions of health may focus on the individual, his disease state and/or his ability to function, or they may be global definitions of the extent of a given disease state or disability in the population.

If one focuses on the individual and his disease state, attention is typically directed to the medical diagnosis, the treatment plan, and its impact on the person who is ill. If one concentrates on the ability of the individual to function, one observes the behavior of an individual. Illness must be distinguished from illness behavior. With a given complaint a person may

or may not go about his usual activities. He may or may not spend time in bed because of illness. The global statistic, in contrast to the description of the individual case, presents a summary of the experience of the population; e.g., all persons with a given disease or all persons who spend time in bed because of illness (Simmons, 1963).

In practice, health in the aged is usually defined in one of two ways: either in terms of the presence or absence of disease, or, alternatively, in terms of how well the older person is functioning. A definition of health in terms of pathology or disease states is commonly used by health personnel, particularly physicians. We can call this a medical model or perspective on health. A judgment of health based on the presence or absence of pathology is the result of observation, examination, and the findings of laboratory tests. While such a judgment strives for objectivity, it reflects the health professional's overall attitudinal set, his medical sophistication and training, the skill of technicians administering given tests, and the conditions the physician expects to find in a patient of a given age and sex. Further, even though the physician may use pathology as a basis for his judgment, his overall assessment and response characteristically reflect the social climate of the time (Simmons, 1963). The introduction of health insurance for the aged (Medicare) in the United States, for example, was followed by an increase in the proportion of old persons admitted to hospitals; presumably the health status of older persons did not change in response to the enactment of Medicare, but medical judgments about hospitalization of older persons did.

An alternative way of defining health among the elderly is based not on pathology but on level of functioning (Haber, 1967, 1969, 1970; Katz, Downs, Cash, and Grotz, 1970; Harris, Cox, and Smith, 1971; Lawton, 1971; Shanas, 1971, 1974). This perspective has been summarized by a World Health Organization Advisory group (1959). This group states "... health in the elderly is best measured in terms of function; ... degree of fitness rather than extent of pathology may be used as a measure of the amount of services the aged will require from the community." Thus the things that an old person can do, or thinks he can do, are useful indicators of both how healthy he is and of the services he will require. The implications of this perspective for the development of health resources will be discussed in greater detail below; but, in effect, a functional approach assumes that both the individual and the physician may have relevant and possibly conflicting information about health status. Functional definitions of health, however, tend to de-emphasize global statistics or the knowledge of disease states prevalent among the elderly as predictors of their demand for services and tend to stress individual assessments.

The points of view of those who prefer the medical model of health needs and of those who prefer the functional model are not irreconcilable, and efforts have been made to assess the two models by comparing the self-reports of old people with the findings of physical examinations (Sachuk, 1963; Maddox, 1964; Sullivan, 1966, 1971; Van den Heuvel, 1974). Piotrowski and his colleagues in Poland (1970) have demonstrated the value of the functional model in assessing health needs by comparing old people's responses to a standardized set of questions widely used in cross-national studies to assess the functioning of the elderly, with the result of physician examinations of these old people. The greatest disparities between self-reports of health and medical examinations in the Polish sample occur between the overall global judgments of health made by an elderly individual and by his physician. It is the general judgment of the old person that his health is "good," or "poor" that is most likely to differ from the physician's comparable overall assessment. When actual behavior of an old person in each of the areas investigated is compared with the medical evaluation of the possibility of such behavior, the degree of convergence in judgment of the physician examiner and the elderly subject is quite high.

Maddox and Douglass (1973), in their discussion of the findings of the Duke University longitudinal study of the elderly, compare the medical and functional evaluation of an initial sample of 270 elderly persons in a study which covered 15 years and 6 observations. Over time, the old person's and the physician's rating of health tended to be congruent. Perhaps the most significant finding of Maddox and Douglass was that from one observation to the next the self-health rating of the individual was "a better predictor of future physicians' ratings than the reverse." Thus, while self-reported health is not a substitute for clinical diagnosis, it is useful as well as reliable information.

Specialists in geriatrics, that branch of medicine dealing with older people, largely have accepted a position that represents a compromise between the view of health in the elderly as the presence or absence of pathology and the view which defines health in terms of functional abilities. In a report on the planning and organization of geriatric services, a World Health Organization Expert Committee (1974) states: "It is now accepted by the medical profession that morbidity should be measured not only in terms of the extent of the pathological process but also in terms of the impairment of the function in the person affected by a pathological condition . . . Functional diagnosis is one of the most important elements that has been introduced in geriatrics. In this approach a distinction is made between an impairment and a disability caused by a pathological condition."

The Expert Committee then goes on to define impairment and disability, the first as a physiological or psychological abnormality that does not interfere with the normal life activities of the individual, and the second as a condition which results in partial or total limitation of the normal activities of the individual. A similar distinction was made by Amelia Harris and her associates (1971) in their study of the impaired in Britain. They defined impairment as "lacking part or all of a limb, organ, or mechanism of the body," which in turn limits getting about, working, or self-care, and disability as "the loss or reduction of functional capacity." Harris points out that a person may be impaired but not necessarily disabled, even though in general usage "disablement and handicapped are often used interchangeably."

The formal statement of the W.H.O. Expert Committee (1974) reflects the growing consensus regarding the desirability of functional assessment of the health of the elderly. The measurement of health, once considered solely a prerogative of the physician and of his interpretation of objective laboratory tests, has now been broadened to include some measure of how well the individual copes with his impairments and the extent to which such impairments interfere with life routines. In this chapter we argue that the functional model provides a more useful conceptual tool than the medical model because it will better predict how pathology is translated into illness behavior and ultimately into the sick role.

Measuring Health Status and Forecasting Utilization

Measures of the health status of the aged become increasingly important as one attempts to forecast the demand for health services and facilities. Irrespective of developments in medical diagnosis, treatment, and care systems, the elderly in the future will make greater demands on the health establishment than they do now. They will require more physicians' care, more places in hospitals and nursing homes, and more home health services. This can be predicted from the changing age distribution of populations. Both developed and developing countries will have substantial increases in their numbers of older persons (United Nations, 1973). In the United States, for example, persons aged 65 and over, about 20 million in 1970, are expected to increase almost 40 percent to a projected 27.8 million persons by 1990. Even more important in terms of the demand for health services is the expected change in the "population mix" among the elderly. The proportion of younger aged (65 to 69) in the total older population is steadily becoming less, while the proportion of those 75 years of age and over is increasing. By 1990, 39 percent of all older persons, 11 million people, will be 75 years of age and older (Current Population Reports, P-23, No. 43, February, 1973) compared to about 37 percent, 7.5 million persons, in 1970. The aging of the population alone will mean an increase in the use of health services. As people become older, they are more likely to need such services.

The changing ratio of men to women within the older population also forecasts an increase in the demands for services. In the present population 65 and older, there are 80 men for every 100 women; by 1990, there will be only 68 men for every 100 women. Women are more likely to utilize health services than men. Further, the usual pattern in illness in old age is for women to look after their husbands and to provide nursing care and after-hospital care. As the ratio of older men to women decreases, however, the older population becomes increasingly a population of widowed, divorced, and single women. These persons are likely to have no one who can serve as surrogate trained nurse or household helper. Adult daughters and daughters-in-law are often employed outside the home. Thus, the increase in the proportion of women in the older population, like the aging of the population itself, predicts a rise in the demand for health services, whether such services are delivered in or out of institutions.

Studies of the utlization of medical care among the elderly show that the heavy users of such care, compared to other old people, are more likely to be over 75; they are more likely to be widowed, and they are more likely to be women (Shanas, 1962; Maddox, 1975). The demographic structure of the aged in the United States in 1990 will show an increase in both the absolute numbers and the proportions of the elderly who have these characteristics. An increase in the utilization of services therefore seems inevitable.

The Predictors of Health Status and the Utilization of Medical Care

The development of prediction models for the utilization of medical care is a long-time and continuing interest among both physicians and social scientists. The available models range from those which predict the utilization of medical care in the population from the estimated prevalence of a disease, to mathematical models, to psycho-social analyses of why people use health services (Chiang, 1965; Rosenstock, 1966; Andersen, 1968; Moriyamo, 1968). Currently, studies of the characteristics of people using health services have yielded very little definitive information on the basis of which sound predictions about health care utilization can be made. Findings of certain of the psycho-social studies of health and illness, however, seem relevant to understanding patterns of utilization among the elderly.

Despite general agreement that more health services will be required by the elderly in the future, some investigators argue that clinically diagnosed disease and impairments alone are inadequate predictors of the use of medical care by this age group. Two themes emerge in these arguments, one primarily psychological, the other related to social policy. Kasl and Cobb (1966) distinguish *health behavior*, activity undertaken for the purpose of preventing disease by a person who believes himself well; *illness behavior*, activity undertaken by a person who feels ill for the purpose of diagnosis; and *sick-role behavior*, activity engaged in for the purpose of cure by a person who considers himself ill. According to Kasl and Cobb, whether an individual engages in one of these behaviors or not is a function of whether he feels threatened by disease or illness and what the value of taking action is to him. In their review of the literature, these authors found no studies which specifically indicated that age and sex were related to the perception of symptoms. On the other hand, studies which correlate reports of an individual's health with physician's reports typically conclude that the underreporting of symptoms is more prevalent than overreporting among the elderly. Further, the attitudes of elderly subjects toward personal happiness as well as their evaluation of their own age group as middle-aged or old correlate better with their own health self-assessment than with a physician's evaluation (Suchman, Phillips, and Streib, 1958; Friedsam and Martin, 1963; Maddox, 1964).

Andersen (1968) has evaluated families' use of health services in terms of three categories: *predisposing* factors, in which he includes family attitudes, social structure, and health beliefs; *enabling* factors including family and community resources; and *need*, which would include illness and the individual's response to it. Need was to be measured objectively by the number of symptoms reported by respondents. In a Swedish study using this framework, Andersen and his associates found that the social class and income of an individual were more important in predicting use of health services than either age or sex (1968), both demographic factors which have been widely used to predict need. Shuval and Antonovsky in an Israeli study (1970) also have demonstrated that, while diagnosed medical need is an important predictor of services, a position also taken by both Kasl and Cobb and Andersen, medical care has other functions for the individual. The user of medical care may be seeking general reassurance, or, on a more mundane level, in Israel he may be seeking a physician's excuse so that he may absent himself from work.

Shanas (1962; and with collaborators, 1968) has analyzed both the predictors of health status among the elderly and the use of medical care by this age group. She points out that old people in the United States, irrespective of advanced age and infirmity, prefer and attempt to be active and self-sufficient. They seem to feel that an admission of illness or incapacity is somehow a sign of weakness. Shanas states that the reasons many old people in the United States do not use medical care are primarily psychological, not financial. Many older people, despite their health complaints, believe that a doctor cannot help them, or that they are not really sick enough to require medical attention. A common statement among the respondents in a national study was "I don't want to bother the doctor." Contemporary old people tend to accept aches, pains, and other symptoms of physical distress as being the usual accompaniments of advanced years. By the time an old person sees a physician he, or those responsible for him, have decided that he is ill and needs treatment.

The introduction of a national health insurance scheme for the elderly in the United States (Medicare) and the behavior of older persons subsequent to its introduction reinforce the impression outlined above. The availability of Medicare did not result in a substantial rise in the number of doctor visits reported by older people. In 1973, persons aged 65–74 averaged 6.5 physician visits per year, persons 75 and over 6.6 (U.S. Department of Health, Education and Welfare, Vital and Health Statistics, 1974b). Sixteen years earlier, in 1957, the National Health Survey (U.S. Department of Health, Education and Welfare, 1958) reported that persons aged 65 and over averaged 6.8 annual out-of-hospital contacts with physicians.

Kalimo and associates in Finland (1968) have attempted to estimate the need for medical care for the elderly as well as other population groups from survey data. They have used self-reports from individuals combined with physicians' assessments of how much care would be required for those persons reporting given diseases, certain restrictions on mobility, given amounts of time spent in bed because of illness, and physicians' visits within a given time period. Their data indicate that patients with chronic ailments, patients confined in bed for more than three days, and patients who had recently visited a physician—all characteristics positively associated with age—had the greatest need for medical care. The Kalimo study thus translates qualitative reports of disease states into quantitative scores which are considered as predictive of probable need for services; the result confirms the expectation that need increases with age. On the other hand, Svane in a Danish study (1972) and Harris and Clausen in Britain (1968) both show that the use of medical care by the elderly rises in response to how need is defined by those offering services. Use is a function of the availability of service. As services increase, the definition of need for the service is often broadened. With limitations in services for whatever reason—reduction in funds or lack of personnel—need is defined more rigidly and service utilization declines. This is a critical observation. Subjective and objective assessment of need for service actually translates differently into utilization of services depending on the availability of services.

STUDIES OF THE PHYSICAL AND MENTAL HEALTH STATUS OF ELDERLY PERSONS

A Health Profile of the Young Old, the Old, and the Very Old

In preparation for the 1971 White House Conference on Aging in the United States, the National Center for Health Statistics (1971) produced a particularly useful profile on physical health in the later years of life. The profile was constructed from four continually updated data collection and analysis resources of the National Center for Health Statistics: vital statistics, health interview statistics, health examination statistics, and health resources statistics. In addition to the collection of vital statistics from which annual life tables are constructed, the Center uses continuing surveys of national probability samples to obtain data which can only, or best, be obtained through household interviews (e.g., social factors related to illness, injury, disability, and cost and uses of medical services); data from direct examination regarding the prevalence of illness in the population by disease category, including previously undiagnosed illness; and data on health facilities and their utilization, including nursing homes. The origin, program, and operation of the national health surveys are described in a continuing series of reports of the National Center for Health Statistics (1965), and numerous substantive reports on particular topics are identified in cumulative annual listings and topical indices (for example, National Center for Health Statistics, 1973). The continual updating of data from the National Center is a reminder of the time-boundness of health statistics and, hence, a reminder that while the patterns of information about health tend to be relatively stable, specific details change rapidly and must be checked regularly.

We have chosen in this section, therefore, to give only limited attention to detailed reports of the distribution of illness and disability among older persons and to indices of the utilization of health resources by older persons.

While it is important to provide the reader with some sense of the relevant current evidence, it is equally important to emphasize that such evidence goes out of date quickly. We will provide illustrations of types of data available and direct the reader to the best source of relevant data.

Several characteristics of U.S. National Health survey reports are worth noting. The age categories used in data presentation distinguish those who might be called the *young old* (45–64) from the *old* (65–74) and the *old old* (75 and over). Moreover, these reports give specific attention to functional definitions of health status.

We will begin by reviewing the most recent profile of physical health status of older persons in the U.S. now available and then introduce some cross-national comparisons. We suggest that, while the profile of physical health of older persons in the U.S. may differ in detail from the profile of similar persons in other industrial societies, the profile will probably be generally applicable to such societies.

Life Expectancy. Average length of life is a traditional measure of health status. Age-specific estimates of average remaining years of life illustrate both the use of chronological age as a predictor of mortality and cohort differences in life expectancy. In 1969, for example, the average future lifetime for an individual born in the United States was 70.5 years; the expectation of life was 67.9 years for a white male, 75.1 for a white female, 60.7 for a nonwhite male, and 68.4 for a nonwhite female. The average life expectancy for males in the U.S. ranked 18th among nations in the world, considerably behind Sweden's 71.6 years which headed the list. Females in the U.S. ranked 11th behind the Netherlands whose 75.9 years ranked first (National Center for Health Statistics, 1971, pp. 2–3).

In the United States individuals 45 years of age in 1968 (cohort born in 1923) had already lived almost as long as the average person born in 1900 could have expected to live, and the 45 year old still had on the average about 30 years of life remaining, specifically 26.8 years for men and 32.5 years for women. Similarly,

men and women who had survived to age 65 could expect 12.8 and 16.3 years of life remaining, and those who had survived to age 75 could expect 8.2 and 9.9 years. In interpreting such data, one should keep in mind the distinction between life expectancy at birth and age-specific life expectancy. Average life expectancy at birth is, to a substantial degree, a function of infant mortality. Hence increasing average life expectancy at birth reflects substantial decreases in infant mortality in developed countries. Decreasing death rates in the adult and later years of life affect average remaining years of life at particular ages; age-specific life expectancy has been increasing in recent years, even for very old persons. However, these increases have been small. The sex differences in life expectancy illustrated in Table 1 are characteristic of all developed countries. For females, from 1940 through 1968, the trend in average remaining years of life at ages 45, 65, and 75 was upward. This increase in life expectancy was true for males only at age 75.

Average life expectancy, as we have noted, reflects the death rate at various ages. Generally, the lower the death rate, the higher the average life expectancy. A steady decline in death rates began in the late nineteenth century, leveling off in 1955 but in the 1960's increasing slightly for men. Recent trends in age-specific mortality have accentuated the differences in life expectancy among men and women. For example, among cohorts, the death rate between the ages of 45–64, which was 50 percent higher for white

TABLE 1. AVERAGE REMAINING YEARS OF LIFE AT AGES 45, 65, AND 75, BY SEX AND COLOR: UNITED STATES, 1968.

Sex and color	AVERAGE REMAINING YEARS OF LIFE		
	At age 45	At age 65	At age 75
Sex			
Men	26.8	12.8	8.2
Women	32.5	16.3	9.9
Color			
White	30.0	14.7	9.0
All other	26.2	13.7	10.8

SOURCE: National Center for Health Statistics, *Health in the Later Years of Life*, 1971, p. 4.

men than for women in 1940, became 80 percent higher by 1950, and in 1968, 100 percent higher. A similar but smaller divergence is observed between the death rate of nonwhite men and women.

Patterns of Morbidity. Although we wish to stress in this chapter the social and social psychological implications of disease and disability, a brief review of observed patterns of morbidity in relation to age is warranted. Currently, major causes of death in late life in the United States are diseases of the heart, malignant neoplasms (cancer), and cerebrovascular disease (mainly strokes). These three conditions account for 70 percent of deaths of persons 45 years of age and older; 40 percent of these deaths are accounted for by disease of the heart alone. Similar patterns, with minor variations, are observed in other industrial societies.

In general, the lower the socioeconomic position of an individual, the higher the prevalence of disease and the higher the age-specific death rate. These commonly observed associations between socioeconomic position, illness, and life expectancy have a complex explanation. Indices of socioeconomic position usually include measurements of income, occupation, and education. Such factors, singly or in combination, are reflected in different styles of life and differential access to and use of health resources. For instance, low income, a manual occupation, and minimal education generally predict a high incidence of disease and elevated death rates in all industrialized countries.

The prevalence of chronic disease increases markedly with age. Of individuals 65 years of age and older living outside institutions, 85 percent report at least one chronic disease and about 50 percent report some limitation of normal activity related to chronic health conditions.

Dental problems also increase with age. Over one-fourth of persons aged 45–64 have lost all their teeth, and almost nine out of ten have diseases of the tissues supporting or surrounding remaining teeth.

Poor vision is increasingly common after age 45, particularly among women. Good vision (20/20+) without correction is demonstrated for 39.2 percent of men and 30.9 percent of women aged 45–64 in contrast to 7.6 percent of men and 2.7 percent of women aged 65–79. Correspondingly, the proportion of moderate to severe visual defects among those aged 65–79 is twice as high as that observed among those aged 45–64. Even with corrected vision, 5 percent of the younger age category still exhibit severe visual impairments, and this triples in the older age category.

Hearing impairments also increase with age. For individuals aged 65–79, about one-third have significant impairment of hearing in the frequencies essential in the range associated with normal speech. The rate of impairment in this age category is 40 times greater than that found among individuals aged 18–24 and 4 times greater than among those 45–64.

Although chronic conditions are the most frequent health problems in late life, acute episodes of illness and injury which occasion restriction of activity or medical attention are also common. In recent years older persons have reported on the average at least one acute episode of illness each year, most commonly respiratory disease.

Following this brief review of morbidity statistics, we wish to stress again that the pattern of disease and impairment observed in old persons currently is not necessarily an accurate indication of the health profile of subsequent cohorts of older persons.

Some Social and Social Psychological Implications of Illness

Observed patterns and trends in the distribution of disease and disability are substantially a function of age and hence are relevant for understanding factors which affect the total as well as average length of the human life span. Disease and disability also affect economic costs for individuals and society both in terms of income foregone and the expense of health care as noted above. We wish to stress here the social and social psychological implications of disease and disability particularly as they result in handicaps or restricted social functionings.

Illness affects the energy available to an individual and his capacity to direct the energy at his disposal toward the achievement of personal goals and the meeting of social obligations. Illness and related disability handicap an individual in the role performances required in everyday life and reduce the social space effectively available to him. An individual who is ill, for example, loses days at work and may be forced into early retirement. About half of the individuals who retire prior to age 65 report that poor health was involved in some way with their decision to give up work. Illness and disability also affects the capacity to play marital roles. And, since we know that body image is an important aspect of an individual's conception of self and that social involvement and integration contribute positively to life satisfaction, illness and disability predictably and demonstrably have a negative effect on self-esteem and on a sense of well-being. From these arguments we would expect physical illness and impairment to be correlated negatively with intellectual functioning, with the correct perception of and adaptive responses to environmental stimuli, and hence with mental health. We will see subsequently that this is, in fact, the case. The reports of the surveys of the U.S. National Health Survey, there-

fore, appropriately concentrate not only on illness and impairment but also on the associated limitations of activity and inability to carry out important social roles.

Since illness and impairment increase with age, so predictably does limitation of activity and disability. Table 2 indicates the extent and seriousness of limited activity associated with age. In the United States in 1968-1969, about one in five males aged 45-64 reported some limitation of activity. One in ten reported a restriction in amount or kind of major activity, and one in sixteen indicated an inability to carry out a major activity. For males aged 65 and over, over two in five reported restricted activity, and one in four indicated an inability to carry on major activities. The extent and kind of disability experienced by nonwhite men and women were somewhat higher than that observed among whites.

The observed patterns of activity restriction due to illness in part reflect sex-linked role expectation. Females, although they tend to report a higher prevalence of disease, have been more likely to play roles that are less demanding physically and which are less visible socially. The higher observed limitation of activity among

TABLE 2. DEGREE OF LIMITATION OF ACTIVITY DUE TO CHRONIC CONDITIONS AT AGES 45–64 AND 65 AND OVER, BY SEX AND COLOR: UNITED STATES, 1968-69.

Sex, color, and age	No limitation of activity	PERSONS LIMITED BECAUSE OF CHRONIC CONDITIONS			
		Total	But not in major activity[a]	In amount or kind of major activity[a]	Unable to carry on major activity[a]
Sex			Percent in specified group		
Men					
45–64 years of age	79.7	20.2	2.8	10.4	7.0
65 years and over	54.1	46.0	3.1	17.7	25.2
Women					
45–64 years of age	82.7	17.3	3.1	12.3	1.9
65 years and over	60.3	39.7	4.9	25.9	8.9
Color					
White					
45–64 years of age	81.9	18.1	3.0	11.1	4.0
65 years and over	58.4	41.6	4.2	22.3	15.1
All other					
45–64 years of age	76.0	24.0	2.4	13.9	7.7
65 years and over	48.6	51.5	3.4	23.1	25.0

[a]Major activity refers to ability to work, keep house.
SOURCE: National Center for Health Statistics, *Health in the Later Years of Life*, 1971, p. 32.

nonwhites is probably best explained by their relatively depressed socioeconomic status and by the related higher incidence of illness and disability among them.

Illness as a Handicap. As we noted earlier, from the standpoint of a health professional, an individual is considered to be diseased, impaired, or ill if the signs and symptoms presented by the individual deviate significantly from prevailing professional judgments of physiological, psychological, or social normalcy. From a layman's point of view, an individual is ill if he feels he is ill or experiences signs and symptoms usually associated with illness. In fact, there is typically substantial congruence between professional and lay views of illness (Maddox and Douglass, 1973); among older persons realistic assessments of health and illness predominate. And, among the approximately one out of three older persons whose subjective view of health status is incongruent with a professional assessment, an optimistic denial of illness is as commonly observed as a pessimistic accentuation of illness. While it is known that illness is not automatically translated into disability, the rates at which adults discount or accentuate illness is not known. Both denial of illness and hypochondriacal accentuation of illness are observed among older persons, but there is no evidence that such discounting or accentuation are a function of age.

These observations are important for understanding the use of reported disability in the U.S. National Health Survey home interview study. An individual's report that he is disabled is not, in an epidemiological sense, to be simply equated with underlying illness or impairment. But there is reason to believe that the correlation among disability and illness and impairment is high and, in any case, so far as social consequences are concerned, an individual is ill if he says he is ill and behaves as though he is ill.

The data in Table 3 reflect succinctly the typical and expected patterns of reported disability days in relation to age. The data also illustrate variations of this basic pattern by sex and socioeconomic position. Restricted-activity days and bed-disability days increase with age,

tend to be higher for women than for men, and are highest among those with the lowest socioeconomic position. Older men and women who are currently employed report on the average fewer days lost from work than younger workers. It should be noted, however, that after age 65 only a small proportion of individuals remain in the work force and that among them work-loss days are unrelated to income level. As will be noted later in the chapter when utilization of health services is discussed, days in hospital reflect essentially the same age, sex, and status patterns as that observed for disability days. And the same is true for the utilization of long-term care facilities.

Physical illness and impairment clearly increase in the later years of life and, by any standard, are quite common. After age 65, a minority of individuals are free from diagnosed chronic disease or impairment; a majority experience some limitation of normal daily activity. It is equally important to point out, however, that a very substantial majority of older individuals continue to function in a community setting. And most function reasonably well in carrying out the activities of daily living. Again, there is evidence that this generalization is applicable to all industrialized countries.

Cross-National Evidence of Functional Capacity

We have noted earlier that life expectancy in economically developed countries is quite similar. Although life expectancy in the United States is slightly lower for women and considerably lower for men that in the most nearly comparable countries, the pattern of disease and impairment and related limitation of activity and disability in developed countries can reasonably be presumed to be similar to that we have described in the United States. We also have direct evidence from a cross-national study of health status among older persons in the United States, Great Britain, and Denmark (Shanas, Townsend, Wedderburn, Friis, Milhøj, and Stehouwer, 1968).

In the early 1960's, observed rates of institutionalization of older persons were quite simi-

TABLE 3. DISABILITY DAYS, NUMBER AND AVERAGE PER PERSON PER YEAR
AT AGES 45-64 AND 65 AND OVER, BY SELECTED CHARACTERISTICS: UNITED
STATES, 1968-1969.

Selected characteristics	Restricted-activity days	Bed-disability days	Work-loss days among currently employed
Sex	Average number of days per person per year		
45–64 years of age			
Men	19.8	7.3	6.4
Women	20.9	7.9	6.2
65 years and over			
Men	31.7	12.7	6.1
Women	36.2	14.4	5.2
Color			
45–64 years of age			
White	19.5	7.2	6.0
All other	29.1	11.6	9.0
65 years and over			
White	33.1	13.1	5.4
All other	47.6	20.5	10.1
Family Income			
45–64 years of age			
Under $3,000	42.8	15.6	8.6
$3,000–3,999	29.3	11.2	8.7
$4,000–6,999	20.8	7.4	7.1
$7,000–9,999	16.9	6.8	6.3
$10,000–over	14.1	5.3	5.2
65 years and over			
Under $3,000	43.0	15.4	6.1
$3,000–3,999	32.0	13.6	6.2
$4,000–6,999	28.0	11.5	6.4
$7,000–9,999	28.7	14.7	6.1
$10,000–over	24.5	11.6	6.1

Source: National Center for Health Statistics, *Health in the Later Years of Life*, 1971, p. 36.

lar in these three industrialized societies. About 3.7 percent of all older people were institutionalized in the United States; 4.5 percent in Britain; and 5.3 percent in Denmark. These differences probably reflect public policy regarding institutionalization as much or more than differences in underlying illness and impairment. In these societies, among persons 75 years of age and older, the percentage institutionalized was essentially the same, about 8 percent. Also, the proportion of those found to be bedfast at home was essentially the same, in the range of 2 percent to 3 percent. The index of incapacity which was used in this survey to assess the ability of older individuals to be ambulatory, to negotiate stairs, and to carry out personal acts such as washing, dressing, and trimming toe-

nails indicate comparable patterns of capacity and incapacity in the three societies.

When individuals in the three societies were asked to assess their health status in terms of "good," "fair," or "poor," again comparable patterns of response were found. In the United States, 18 percent considered their health to be poor; 16 percent responded in this way in Denmark; 14 percent in Great Britain.

In a study of the handicapped and impaired in Great Britain, Amelia Harris (1971, Part I) documents the expected association between age and disability. The probability of being appreciably or severely handicapped was found to increase with age. Those 65 years of age and older comprised more than half the handicapped persons 16 years of age and over in this study.

Moreover, among the very severely handicapped adults, almost six in ten were 65 or older.

Aging and Psychological Impairment

Disease and disordered behavior vary in the degree to which their etiology, natural course, and a definitive therapy are known. Some disorders, particularly those that are traceable to a particular noxious agent, have clearly recognizable symptoms, a well-known natural course, and are amenable in predictable ways to prevention, amelioration, or cure. Common childhood diseases are cases in point. Other disorders, particularly those that involve complex malfunction of organ systems, such as disorders of the heart or lungs, tend to have multiple etiologies, variable natural courses, and less than definitive therapies. Still other human disorders appear to be quite unspecific; etiology is debatable, natural course is highly variable, and nothing approximating a definitive therapy exists. For these phenomena, such as obesity or alcoholism, there is likely to be a debate over whether *behavior disorder* is a more appropriate designation than *disease*.

On a continuum of specificity/nonspecificity, mental illness (or disorder) is relatively nonspecific. Predictably, what we call nonspecific diseases or disorders present difficulties for diagnosticians as well as laymen. And difficulty in classification makes it difficult for the epidemiologist to identify reliably the incidence and prevalence of various types of psychological impairments.

Riley, Foner, Moore, Hess, and Roth (1968, Part 3, Ch. 16) provide a useful introduction to the conventional terminology of research on mental health and illustrate typical findings. The classification *psychosis* refers to impairment of mental processes and a related inability to evaluate reality in a socially tolerable way. Psychosis is usually distinguished from neurosis or psychoneurosis, which refers to an impairment of psychological functioning but without a sharp break with conventionally defined reality. Another distinction of special relevance for understanding psychological impairment in late life relates to the presumed organic or non-organic (or functional) etiology of the impairment.

A number of excellent summaries of comparative epidemiological research on the prevalence of psychological impairment in late life exist (e.g., Lowenthal, Berkman *et al.*, 1967; Busse and Pfeiffer, 1969; Kay, 1972). In spite of differences in detail, which reflect differences in classification and in sampling, the picture which emerges from this research is quite consistent. Among persons 65 years of age and older living in a community setting, about 20 percent appear to be at least moderately impaired in psychological functioning, 5 percent of them severely so.

The rate of hospitalization for mental disorders increases with age. Older persons account for about one-fourth of the new admissions to state mental hospitals and constitute a high proportion of the long-term residents in such institutions (Kramer, Taube, and Redick, 1973). Attempts to reduce long-term hospitalization in the United States have resulted in a decrease in the number of older residents in mental hospitals. But as the populations of mental institutions have decreased, there has been an increase in the number of older persons treated for psychiatric disorders in general hospitals. Between 1966 and 1967, for example, the number of older persons treated in general hospitals for psychiatric disorders increased by 29 percent, days of care for such cases increased by 49 percent, and the average length of stay increased by 15 percent. Moreover, it has been estimated that by 1967 the mentally ill elderly in nursing homes alone surpassed the residents of all other types of psychiatric facilities (Kramer, Taube, and Redick, 1973).

The association between physical illness and mental disorder is especially marked among older persons. Of a sample of older persons in the San Francisco Geriatric Screening Clinic, 87 percent were reported to be in need of full-time psychiatric care at the time they were seen; and 42 percent were found to be seriously impaired physically. The seriousness of the physical impairments exhibited is indicated by a very high death rate following institutionalization. Twenty-five percent of the institutionalized older persons in the San Francisco study died within one year, 44 percent within two (Simon, Lowenthal, and Epstein, 1970).

In the absence of appropriate longitudinal data, the association between age and functional mental disorders remains somewhat ambiguous. It is possible that the relationship is curvilinear, with the highest rates appearing in the middle adult years and lower rates in late life. However, the association between aging and organic brain diseases is quite clear.

Kay (1972) has reviewed the evidence on aging and organic brain disease and concludes that, of all mental and physical handicaps of the old, chronic organic brain disease is the most disabling and the most costly. Acute or subacute forms of this problem, which is characterized by a clouding of consciousness and confusion or delirium, have multiple causes and are potentially reversible. Chronic forms of the problem, however, usually reflect widespread organic damage and are both degenerative and progressive. A high proportion of first admissions to state and county mental hospitals in the United States are diagnosed as chronic brain syndrome according to Kay. For first admissions aged 65–74, about 75 percent present this problem; for those 75 and older, 90 percent. Kay indicates a similar trend in Great Britain. In many parts of the world an estimated 4–6 percent of all persons 65 years of age and older have chronic brain disease, and a larger proportion experience acute confusional states at one time or the other. Studies in Japan, England, and Denmark indicate that at age 65 about 2 percent of all individuals manifest chronic brain disease; at age 70, 4 percent, and at age 80, 20 percent.

THE ORGANIZATION OF HEALTH CARE AND ITS UTILIZATION BY OLDER PERSONS

Review of Sites of Health Care Facilities

Health care for older persons may be delivered to the old person as an out-patient (that is, in his own home or in the doctor's office or clinic) or as an in-patient (that is, in a hospital or nursing home). Different countries place differing emphases on the site of health care for the elderly, taking into account their allocation and organization of available resources for the delivery of health services.

Home/Out-patient Care. The day-to-day care of the patient in his own home may be given by family members alone or it may be given by home health services, an array of services which may include skilled nursing care, occupational and physical therapy, and even podiatry and home dental care in addition to physician visits. Brahna Trager in a report prepared for the United States Senate Special Committee on Aging (1972) distinguishes between three types of home health services: *concentrated* or intensive service, *intermediate* service, and *basic* service. *Concentrated* services are needed for patients who otherwise would require admission to institutions. Such service could include frequent physician visits, daily nursing visits, physical and occupational therapy, social services, the provision of special equipment such as a hospital bed, and the services of a homemaker-home aide. The designation *intermediate* implies a lesser number of home health services. This range of service is most often applicable to those persons who are temporarily disabled. *Basic* home health service is the least elaborate and refers to medical supervision, home nursing visits, and perhaps the services of a homemaker or home health aide. Although this basic package of services is described as simple, the organization and delivery of such services is still very complex and involves the integration and cooperation of a variety of health professionals.

A 1966–68 survey by the National Center for Health Statistics (U.S. Department of Health, Education and Welfare, Monthly Vital Statistics Report, 1971a) estimated that about 499,000 persons aged 65–74 and 886,000 persons aged 75 and over received some type of health care at home. About 30 percent of the younger group and 24 percent of the older group received medical care, such as changing bandages, receiving injections, and other related treatments. Four of every five persons, however, had personal care ranging from having meals served in bed to help with bathing. Most of this home care was given by family household members. Only about 7 percent received care from a registered nurse, and about 34 percent had care provided by other sources.

Ambulatory or out-patient care in combination with home health care, it is argued, can keep some older people in their own homes and out of institutions. But ambulatory care assumes that the services of a physician will be available, whether that physician be an individual practitioner, a member of the staff of a neighborhood health center or family care center, or a representative of a hospital out-patient department. Ambulatory care as an alternative to institutional care also assumes that transportation be available to bring the patient from his home to the health center or hospital and back again when required. Most important of all, ambulatory care means either that the old person can manage by himself with such care or that someone is available to look after him. The emphasis on avoiding institutionalization and on keeping frail and sick people in the community assumes, and inappropriately in many instances as Maddox (1975) has noted, the availability of a family unit which can be mobilized in the care of the old person. Carefully evaluated ambulatory care systems for older persons in the United States do not exist, and hence their effectiveness and cost vis-à-vis other alternatives are not known.

Great Britain has an organized home health service which includes, in addition to physician visits, health visitors, nursing care, chiropody, homemakers, home-delivered meals, and social services. There are wide variations from area to area in the provision of these services, however, because of differences in the allocation of funds, difficulties in recruiting staff, and the differing criteria adopted by local bodies in assessing an elderly person's need for help (Wroe, 1973). The cost-effectiveness of this approach vis-à-vis alternatives has not been documented.

Under the legislation establishing Medicare in the United States, payments for some home health services are possible. The problems attendant in the implementation of such services, however, have limited their development. Under the present Medicare regulations, previous institutionalization in a hospital or nursing home is a condition for receiving Medicare payments for home health services. Thus, a program with the potential for keeping some older people out of institutions encourages admission to institutions.

In-patient Care. In-patient care is available to older persons as it is to other persons, in short-stay and long-stay hospitals and in nursing homes. In the United States, the proportion of older persons admitted to hospitals has risen steadily since the introduction of Medicare. The rise in rates for admissions to short-stay hospitals is particularly impressive, from 259.6 per 1,000 Medicare enrollees in 1967 to 315.8 per 1,000 in 1973. Admission rates for long-stay hospitals, such as chronic diseases or tuberculosis hospitals, have actually declined slightly, from 4.7 per 1,000 enrollees in 1967 to 4.2 per 1,000 in 1973 (U.S. Department of Health, Education and Welfare, Health Insurance Statistics, 1974c). Admission to skilled nursing homes certified for payments under Medicare, which rose immediately after the introduction of Medicare, have also declined in recent years, from 24 per 1,000 enrollees in 1970 to 19.3 per 1,000 in 1973. This decline in nursing home admissions on the one hand reflects stricter standards for certification of the patient as eligible for payments under Medicare and, on the other hand, the withdrawal of certain nursing homes from the program in protest against what they consider its inadequate level of payments.

Nursing homes have become increasingly important as an in-patient facility serving the elderly in the United States. It is estimated that there were 16,100 nursing homes in that country in 1973-74 including both skilled and intermediate care facilities certified to receive payments under Medicare or Medicaid (Title XVIII and Title XIX of the Social Security Act) and those not certified by either program but giving some level of nursing care (U.S. Department of Health, Education, and Welfare, Monthly Vital Statistics Report, 1974a).

Between 4 and 5 percent of the elderly population, about 1 million persons, predominately women (70 percent) of whom the great majority were over 75, were residents in nursing homes in 1973. The turnover of patients in nursing homes is substantial. In 1972, about 1.1 million persons were admitted to nursing homes, and almost a million were discharged (U.S. Department of Health, Education and Welfare, Monthly Vital Statistics Report, 1974a). Of these, almost seven out of every ten were live discharges, that is, persons discharged either to go into institutional settings, such as hospitals or homes for the aged, or to return to their own homes. Since sick people may move back and forth between the hospital and the nursing home, admission figures for both hospitals and nursing homes tend to overstate the actual number of individuals who used such facilities. The National Health Survey, using survey data, estimated that about one-fifth of all older persons in short-stay hospitals in 1973 had more than one hospital episode that year (U.S. Department of Health, Education and Welfare, Vital and Health Statistics, 1974b).

Goldfarb's (1969) studies of the elderly in New York have demonstrated that many sick old people are living in homes for the so-called well aged. The population using nursing homes and long-stay hospitals and those using other kinds of institutions may be quite similar. Goldfarb believes that while some of these persons may be placed in an inappropriate institution, very few among them could function outside the institutional setting. In general, then, the decision to place an older person in a nursing home, a long-stay hospital, or in another kind of congregate setting reflects medical custom and the availability of facilities rather than any careful decision on the part of the older individual or his family. The decision tends to be not whether to institutionalize but where to institutionalize.

The Role and Function of the Institution in Health Care

Institutional living is not common among the elderly either in the United States or in European countries. At any one time, only about 5 percent of the elderly in the United States live in institutions, whether these be homes for the well aged, nursing homes, or long-term care facilities. The proportion of old people who are likely to spend some time in an institution

in later life has been variously estimated. Kastenbaum and Candy (1973) working backwards from newspaper death notices estimated that one of every five persons would be in an institution before the end of his life. Shanas (1962) in a 1957 survey of a cross-section of American adults found that four of every ten adults knew personally or had known someone who had gone to a home for the aged or nursing home. One of every ten adults said that a parent, grandparent, or other close relative had lived in a home for the aged. The move to a sheltered environment was always reported to be a result of the old person's being in frail health. The 1972 study of nursing homes referred to earlier indicated that nursing homes beds were likely to have two different occupants in the course of a year, suggesting an institutional population during 1972 of about 10 percent of the elderly (U.S. Department of Health, Education and Welfare, Monthly Vital Statistics Report, 1974a).

Old persons in institutions differ markedly in demographic characteristics from other old people. They are older than the rest of the elderly population; they are more likely to have never married or to be widowed; and they are more likely to have only one child or no children. For persons in any marital status, the proportion of those institutionalized is likely to rise with age. Peter Townsend, the British sociologist, has hypothesized that "the likelihood of admission to an institution in old age is partly contingent on family composition, structure and organization, and not only on incapacity, homelessness and lack of socio-economic resources" (1965). The institution meets the need of the frail and the sick who lack family supports and whose families are no longer able to care for them (Maddox, 1975). The widely-held belief that families reject old people and forget them in institutions for the aged or nursing homes is not supported by the facts. Families turn to these living arrangements for their aged members when all other resources for care are exhausted. Where home care programs are limited, as in the United States, institutionalization of an elderly person is often the only option available to those with responsibility for his care. Despite the efforts now underway to develop options for institutionalization in that country, it is not at all clear that many people now institutionalized can appropriately be returned to the community.

At the present time, the Netherlands, among the developed countries, has the highest proportion of its population age 65 and over in institutions, 10 percent (Munnichs, 1973). This does not mean that the older Dutch are more sickly than old people in the other countries. Indeed, average expectancy of life in the Netherlands is among the highest in the world, 77.4 years. The Netherlands since World War II has stressed a program of group care for the aged which has resulted in the proliferation of institutions. This policy has now been modified, and a new policy designed to encourage family members to keep old people at home is now underway. The present policy encourages the use of state-supported home helpers and other supportive home services for the elderly. Its expressed goal is the reduction of institutionalization.

The Role of the Family in Health Care

The actual and potential role of the family in providing care for its aged sick members only recently has been seriously considered in the formation of policy in the United States and in other countries. The resurgent interest in the family and in family responsibility for the aged is in part an emotional reaction to the long-term care institution with all its negative connotations. Further, the consideration of the family as caretaker for its aged sick also represents a search for a possibly cheaper alternative to the cost of institutional care (Maddox, 1975). Morton Kramer (1969), the demographer and epidemiologist, has suggested that in determining the need for health care in the future, the proportion of men and women who are single, widowed, and divorced may be a more important factor regulating the demand for care than changes in the age structure of the population itself. A somewhat similar position has been taken by an expert group dealing with mental illness in the elderly. They state that in considering such illness ". . . sociological studies of various types of family structure and kinship and their association with the emotional well-being of the elderly, might prove more useful

than the traditional studies of social class, economic status, and isolation as assessed by the usual criteria" (World Health Organization, 1972).

The family is the actual, as well as potentially the major, caretaker for the sick old person. In the United States and in other countries studied (Britain, Denmark, Israel), from two to three times as many persons are bedfast and housebound at home as are in institutions of all kinds (Shanas et al., 1968; Nathan, 1970). In Poland and Yugoslavia, with limited institutional facilities, this proportion is reported to be even higher (Piotrowski, 1968; Nedeljkovic, 1970). Adult children are the major social support of the elderly sick. Where there are no children, other relatives arrange for medical care, and indeed, like children, serve as nurses, housekeepers, chauffeurs, and health worker surrogates. Simon, Lowenthal, and Epstein (1970) found that among elderly mental patients seen at a metropolitan hospital the majority were brought in by family members. Shanas, in a national survey, asked older people who, other than their spouse, they would turn to in a health crisis. In nine cases of every ten, an older person with a child would turn to the child. Seven of every ten persons who had no children said they would depend on a relative. "The average individual to whom an older person would turn for help in a health crisis is a middle-aged woman, either a daughter or other relative, married and herself the mother of children, at least one of whom is under eighteen" (Shanas, 1962). On the other hand, in a study of three generation families in Minnesota, Litman (1971) found that regardless of generation, almost half of the families studied said that they would find it difficult to care for a sick member at home for any length of time. One-third said that they would be unable to care for a sick member at home under any circumstances, with the elderly most likely to express this feeling, largely due to their own physical limitations.

In any decision concerning care for their aged parents, most sons and daughters of aged parents would have to consider the welfare of their own children. They would have to evaluate the sacrifices and stress that their own children might experience with a sick old person in the home. The childless relatives of many older people would also be faced with difficulties if they were called upon for help. Many of them are age contemporaries of the old person. Their incomes are equally limited; their health may be equally precarious. Despite the findings from national studies that, when an older person with children is in poor health, he will live with or close to the children so that they can take care of him (Shanas, 1962; Shanas *et al.*, 1968), the increasing proportion of women in the labor force, the decline in family size, and increased urbanization all indicate sources of continuing strain in efforts to maintain the family as a caretaker for the sick aged. Maddox (1975) has pointed out that the capabilities of families to cope with impaired and disabled members is very limited and that the real costs to family caretakers in terms of physical and psychic stress have yet to be determined.

Patterns and Profiles of Health Care Utilization

We have discussed earlier the overall utilization of hospitals and nursing homes by the elderly. In this section we will consider the differences in the utilization of such facilities by men and women and by geographic regions of the United States. We will then discuss some of the trends in hospital usage as well as the utilization of physicians and other health personnel by older people. Finally, we will evaluate the reliability of the sources of data used in this chapter and in other reports of health care utilization.

Hospitalization rates in the United States are higher for older men than for older women. They are also higher for white persons of both sexes than for all other persons. Overall, the elderly are hospitalized least in the Middle Atlantic States—New York, New Jersey, and Pennsylvania—and most in the West South Central States of Arkansas, Louisiana, Oklahoma, and Texas. This regional difference in hospitalization is related to the use of alternative forms of care, particularly skilled nursing home facilities. While 19 persons in every thousand were admitted to skilled nursing home facilities in the Middle Atlantic States in 1973, only 5 persons in every thousand were admitted to such facilities in the West South Central States (U.S. Department of Health, Education and Welfare, Health Insurance Statistics, 1974c). For the

United States as a whole, admissions to skilled nursing facilities totalled about 6 percent of hospital admissions, while for the Middle Atlantic States, those with lower hospital rates, they were 7.2 percent, and for the West South Central states, those with higher hospital rates, they were only 1.3 percent.

Total hospital utilization by aged persons increased substantially from 1966, following the introduction of Medicare, to 1969. Between 1969 to 1971 the increase in utilization slowed to about 1 percent a year; but there was again a substantial rise in such utilization beginning in 1972 (Pettengill, 1972). The recent rise in hospital utilization by the aged is partly a result of the hospital replacing and augmenting the physician's office as the center of the health care delivery system. At the same time, as has been said earlier, Medicare legislation which links residence in a nursing home to stays in hospitals has been an important factor in increasing hospital admissions.

In contrast to the rise in hospital rates, old people's use of physicians outside of the hospital has risen very little since the introduction of national health insurance for the aged. Nine percent of all older men and 6 percent of all older women interviewed in 1973 said that they had not seen a doctor for five years or more. Women were more likely to see a doctor than men. About seven of every ten older women compared to about six of every ten older men reported that they had seen a doctor outside of a hospital in 1973. Men aged 65 to 73 averaged about six visits to physicians during the year compared to seven visits for women; but among persons 75 and over the number of physicians' visits by both men and women was slightly less than 7 a year.

Dental care is not now covered by health insurance for the elderly. In contrast to physician visits, almost half of all older men and women had not seen a dentist for five years or more. The proportion of old people seeing a dentist in 1973 was estimated at 27 percent, with women again more likely than men to see the dentist.

Data on the utilization of medical and dental care and medical facilities by the elderly in the United States are collected by the federal government through the National Center for

Health Statistics and the Social Security Administration, and by private groups such as the American Hospital Association. Data on the use of physicians and dentists largely comes from household interview studies of a sample of the American population. In such studies each person in the household 19 years and over present at the time of the contact is interviewed individually. For adults not present at the time of the interview, a related household member is usually asked to supply information. This method of collecting these data on the use of physician and dentist care tends to obscure their actual usage by the elderly. Information for many elderly persons is not secured from them directly but from other household members and is therefore often incomplete and fragmentary. Further, no information is collected about persons who may have died during the survey year.

Data on hospital utilization is also collected in the Health Interview Survey of the National Center for Health Statistics, but these data represent a substantial understatement of the actual level of hospital use. They exclude the hospital experience of persons who died in the hospital or who died after being discharged but before the survey. The National Center for Health Statistics also collects discharge data from hospitals but excludes in its collection the hospital departments of long-term and custodial institutions. The Social Security Administration has produced data on hospital utilization for the elderly through two sources, the Current Medicare Survey which is derived from a sample of admission notices received by the Administration each month, and the Medicare Control Records data which represent the hospital utilization of the part of the enrolled population for which benefits are paid. These latter data, the basis for the utilization reports in this section, also slightly understate hospital use by aged persons since some persons who have exhausted their benefits during the year are nevertheless hospitalized, and some few persons, not eligible for hospital insurance, also are among those hospitalized. The material for persons in nursing homes reported earlier, like other utilization data, is also derived from a sample survey, in this instance one which employed a combination of mail and personal interview survey techniques.

In general, because of the methods of data collection outlined above, all medical utilization data for the aged in the United States tend to underestimate the actual utilization of both hospitals and physicians and dentists by this age group. In the instance of hospitals, the amount of underestimation may indeed be quite large.

Cross-National Experience in Attitudes Toward and Utilization of Medical Care

The aged are a vulnerable group, at high risk for physical and mental health deterioration. This is true in all countries. Yet it is obvious that the actual health behavior of the elderly differs from country to country; these observed differences reflect variation in cultural styles, social and physical environments, organization of health facilities, and in family relationships and living arrangements. Further, within any one country, the health needs of the younger aged in contrast to the needs of the very old may be quite dissimilar both in kind and degree; and this in turn will be reflected in their health behavior.

Comparable studies made in six countries (Denmark, Great Britain, the United States, Israel, Poland, and Yugoslavia) demonstrate both the similarities and the differences among the elderly in their health behavior. With health behavior measured in the same way, more than three-fourths of the entire elderly population in each country were found to be ambulatory. An index of the capacity for self-care among the ambulatory aged showed that the United States has the lowest proportion of people who lack the capacity for self-care living at home and that Poland and Israel have the highest (Shanas, 1974). There are greater differences in incapacity scores among the very old from country to country than among their total aged population, 65 years and over. Those who were 80 and over in Poland and Israel had the greatest limitation in their capacity for self-care. Since Israel has a much higher proportion of its elderly in institutions than does Poland (about 5 percent compared to 1 percent), one may assume from the findings on the functional capacity of the very old living in the community that Israel has the highest proportion of elderly in need of health care. Thea Nathan (1970) has offered an explanation for the marked incapacity reported by the elderly in Israel. She says: "It may be that the upheavals in the lives of so many aged persons in Europe during the last generation (war, bombing raids, concentration camps, living in hiding during long periods of time) had a special effect on their physical health and on the process of aging."

When old people in Western Europe and the United States are compared with those in Eastern Europe and the Near East, the former appear to be health optimists, the latter, health pessimists (Maddox, 1964; Shanas *et al.*, 1968; Shanas, 1974). In Denmark, Britain, and the United States, more than half of all people over 65 describe their health as "good," while about one in six describe their health as "poor." In Poland and Yugoslavia, only about a quarter of all older people describe their health as "good," while about one in every two think their health is "poor," and in Israel only one-fifth of all old people think their health is "good," while about one in three think their health is "poor." The elderly in Britain put the most optimistic interpretation on their impairments and incapacities. Americans, too, are likely to be optimistic but for different reasons. The British optimism appears to be a result of people not wanting to complain, or of not wanting to make trouble or to create difficulties. The American optimism instead is the result of an American self-image of activity and wellness in which any admission of illness is a sign of weakness. To be ill in the United States is a form of alienation contrary to American achievement values (Parsons, 1958). The old person, a sharer of these common cultural beliefs, feels that he must deny any signs of physical weakness.

It may be that old people in the two Eastern European countries and in Israel are really in poorer health than their Western counterparts, as has been suggested. After all, these are the people whose lives were most disrupted by the second World War, who experienced personal deprivations much greater than that of their counterparts in the Western countries. Interviews with those responsible for health care in the different countries suggest another interpretation of the health pessimism of the elderly Eastern European. Apparently, older persons in Eastern Europe and Israel live within cultures in which the old are expected to have health complaints, and such health complaints are both accepted and tolerated.

The expression of health complaints by the elderly, as has been mentioned earlier in this chapter, does not necessarily mean that the complaining elderly will adopt the sick role or use medical care. The Poles and the Yugoslavs were far less likely to use doctors than the Israelis. About 45 percent of the former compared to 53 percent of the latter said they had spent some time in bed because of illness during the year before they were interviewed. In Israel, however, 80 percent of these persons were visited by a doctor, in Poland 66 percent, and in Yugoslavia 37 percent.

The studies of social and cultural factors affecting the health behavior of old people in the United States and Europe highlight the necessity for studies of the physical, social, and cultural environment of the elderly in the developing countries. The situation in those countries is changing rapidly as a result of urbanization and industrialization, and it would seem essential that they be alert to the effect of changes in their traditional cultural and social patterns on the health behavior of old people.

The WHO Expert Committee on the planning and organization of geriatric services (1974) outlines three objectives of health services for the elderly. Such services, they conclude, should aim (1) to maintain old people in their homes as long as possible, (2) to offer alternative residential accommodation to those who are in need of special care and accommodation, and (3) to provide hospital accommodation for those who need a full medical assessment or special medical or nursing care. The expert committee further suggests a model program for health care of the elderly. The model program they suggest is organized around the concept of a health center where general practitioners or family physicians work in teams of 8 to 12 and serve a population of 20,000 to

30,000 of whom 2,000 to 3,000 are elderly. At the health center the entire health team concerned with the older person can meet, and representatives of home health services for the elderly, of community services, and of various medical care specialties (the hospital services in many countries) can be linked for the benefit of the older person. In such a scheme it is expected that a physician specializing in geriatric medicine will visit the health service regularly and will engage in assisting the general practitioners in detecting early illness, see older patients referred by the general practitioner, provide consultant advice for local physicians, and be available to give advice to social workers and representatives of community agencies. The expert committee also recommended a geriatric unit for assessment and treatment of old people as an integral part of major general hospitals, as well as the use of day hospitals for frail persons who can be kept in their own homes. In addition, they pointed out the necessity for long-term care facilities. A major caveat of the WHO experts is that "any elderly individual admitted to a home for the physically or mentally frail should not be regarded as having arrived at a final destination." The experts state that many old people improve markedly in such situations and can often return to their homes or to some other form of supervised housing. The discharge of older people from in-patient care, however, requires adequate home care and community services, and the experts state that discharge is not "efficient" if such services are not available.

At the present time the model program suggested by the expert group, while a desirable goal, is nowhere implemented throughout a country, although some places, for example, Denmark, have made concerted efforts to implement such a program of health services. The United States has neither the hierarchical organization of health services suggested by the plan, nor a medical specialty in geriatrics. Should the United States adopt health maintenance organizations (H.M.O.'s) on a broad scale, the model plan could be modified for use in that country. Further, although geriatric medicine is not a medical specialty at this time, many clinicians in the United States are specializing in the care of older people whether by force of circumstances or design. Various aspects of the model program suggested by the expert group, however, such as geriatric day hospitals, health assessment schemes, etc., are now underway in parts of the United States, usually as demonstration programs.

SUMMARY

Health is of major importance both to the aging individual and to society. For the individual, health is a determinant of his ability to perform those personal tasks which enable him to participate in social life. Society, on its part, depends on the good health of its members to enable them to function adequately in their economic, community, and family roles. Health then may be thought of as a social resource. In most societies health is also viewed as a social right; thus the organization of health care and its delivery to individuals reflects not only necessary social concern but also social policy. In this chapter, health, as it relates to both older individuals and society and in the aggregate as a social resource, is considered under four major headings: health and illness as social concerns; measuring health status and the demand for health care; the physical and mental health of older persons; and the organization and utilization of health care.

There is a demonstrated high risk of illness and impairment in late life. For many persons growing old is associated with chronic illness and with limitations on physical and mental abilities. A variety of scientific disciplines are interested in understanding not only how such illness develops but also the responses to illness by older persons. For reasons not yet clearly understood, persons with what appear to be the same degree of impairment show different degrees of disability. Policy makers and social administrators, on their part, are concerned with the organization of health care and health services for the aged and their economic costs. At this time there appears to be a mismatch between the health needs of older persons and the organization of resources to meet these needs. Present health care systems are primarily organized to deal with acute illness; the illnesses of old age, however, tend to be degenerative and chronic.

Illness, measures of health in the elderly, and health needs are defined in various ways. Definitions of health may focus on the individual or they may be global statistics of the extent of a disease state in a population. Definitions of health may be based on medically determined disease states or on some measure of physical or mental functioning. In practice, health in the elderly is commonly defined in terms of disease states. Illness or impairment, so defined, however, does not necessarily translate either into disability or into demand for health services. In this chapter we argue that the functional model of health in the elderly provides a more useful conceptual tool than the model based on pathology, because the former is a better predictor of illness behavior. Efforts to analyze the health needs of the elderly and how these needs predict the demand for medical care are confounded by the fact that not only are clinically diagnosed disease and impairment inadequate predictors of the demand for services, but both subjective and objective assessments of needs for service translate differently into the utilization of service depending on service availability. Both older people and the health establishment assess health needs differently depending on the circumstances under which care can be delivered.

Our discussion of the physical and mental health of older persons considers the differences in life expectancy between men and women, the major causes of death in late life, and the effect of illness and disability on the performance of the usual social roles of older people. Life expectancy of both men and women has risen markedly in the last half century, although while the life expectancy of women is still increasing, that of men seems to have stabilized. Because women outlive men, the very old, who make the greatest demands for health care, are largely a population of women. The limitation of activity and disability among individuals increases with age. Old people have the longest hospital stays and the highest admission rates to mental hospitals. However, although only a minority of older individuals are free from diagnosed chronic disease states, the great majority of older persons continue to function in the community.

Health care for the elderly can be given in the patient's own home or as in-patient care in the hospital or long-term care institutions. In our discussion of the organization of health care, we point out that the economic, physical, and psychological costs to the family of providing care for the elderly at home are not known. The facts seem to be that families are now the major caretakers of old people who are ill; the elderly in institutions include a disproportionate number of the very old, the never married or widowed, and those who have had no children. Actual health behavior of old people differs from country to country, reflecting differences in length of life, cultural styles, environments or living arrangements, and the organization of health facilities. Nevertheless, in all countries there is now an effort to maintain old people in their own homes as long as possible, to offer alternative residential accommodations to those who need them, and, finally, to provide proper hospital care and specialized medical attention for the acutely ill.

REFERENCES

Aday, L. A., and Eichorn, R. 1972. *The Utilization of Health Services: Indices and Correlates, A Research Bibliography*. Washington, D.C.: The National Center for Health Services, Research and Development.

Andersen, R. 1968. *A Behavioral Model of Families' Use of Health Services*. Chicago Center for Health Administration Studies. Research Studies No. 25. Chicago: University of Chicago Press.

Andersen, R., Anderson, O. W., and Smedby, B. 1968. Perceptions of and response to symptoms of illness in Sweden and the United States. *Medical Care*, 6, 18–30 (January–February).

Andersen, R., Kravits, J., Anderson, O. W., and Daley, J. 1973. *Expenditures for Personal Health Services: National Trends and Variations, 1953-1970*. Rockville, Maryland: Public Health Service.

Busse, E. W., and Pfeiffer, E. 1969. Functional psychiatric disorders in old age. *In*, E. W. Busse and E. Pfeiffer (eds.), *Behavior and Adaptation in Late Life*. Boston: Little, Brown.

Chiang, C. L. 1965. An index of health: Mathematical models. *Vital and Health Statistics*, Series 2, No. 5 (May). Washington, D.C.: Government Printing Office.

Cooper, B. S., and Piro, P. A. 1974. Age differences in medical care spending, fiscal year 1973. *Social Security Bulletin*, 37(5), 3–14(May).

Cooper, B. S., Worthington, N., and Piro, P. A. 1974. National health expenditures, 1929–1973. *Social Security Bulletin*, 37(4), 3–40(April).

Fanshel, S., and Bush, J. W. A. 1970. A health status

index and its application to health services outcome. *Operations Res.*, **181**, 1021–1066.

Friedsam, H. J., and Martin, H. W. 1963. A comparison of self and physicians' health ratings in an older population. *Journal of Health and Human Behavior*, **4**, 179–183.

Goldfarb, A. I. 1969. Institutional care of the aged. *In*, E. W. Busse and E. Pfeiffer (eds.), *Behavior and Adaptation in Late Life*. Boston: Little, Brown.

Grad, J. C., and Sainsbury, P. 1968. The effects that patients have on their families in a community care and a control psychiatric sample, a two year follow-up. *British Journal of Psychiatry*, **114**, 265–278.

Haber, L. D. 1967. Identifying the disabled: Concepts and methods in the measurement of disability. *Social Security Bulletin*, **30**(12), 17–35(December).

Haber, L. D. 1969. *Epidemiological Factors in Disability: I. Major Disabling Conditions*. Social Security Survey of the Disabled, Report No. 6 (February). Social Security Administration.

Haber, L. D. 1970. *The Epidemiology of Disability: II. The Measurement of Functional Capacity Limitations*. Social Security Survey of the Disabled, Report No. 10 (July). Social Security Administration.

Harris, A. I., assisted by Clausen, R. 1968. *Social Welfare for the Elderly, 1 and 2*. Government Social Survey. London: Her Majesty's Stationery Office.

Harris, A. I., with Cox, E. and Smith, C. R. W. 1971. *Handicapped and Impaired in Great Britain, Part I*. Social Survey Division, Office of Population Censuses and Surveys. London: Her Majesty's Stationery Office.

Kalimo, E., and Sievers, K. 1968. The need for medical care: Estimation on the basis of interview data. *Medical Care*, **6**, 1–17(January–February).

Kasl, S. V., and Cobb, S. J. 1966. Health behavior and sick-role behavior. *Arch. Environ. Health*, **12**, 246–266(February).

Kastenbaum, R., and Candy, S. E. 1973. The 4% fallacy, a methodological and empirical critique of extended care facility population statistics. *Int. J. Aging and Hum. Devel.*, **4**, 15–21.

Katz, S., Downs, T. D., Cash, H. R., and Grotz, R. C. 1970. Progress in development of the index of ADL. *Gerontologist*, **10**, Part 1, 20–30(Spring).

Kay, D. W. K. 1972. Epidemiological aspects of organic brain disease in the aged. *In*, C. M. Gaitz (ed.), *Aging and the Brain*. New York: Plenum.

Kramer, M. 1969. Statistics of mental disorders in the United States: Current status, some urgent needs and suggested solutions. *The Journal of the Royal Statistical Society*, **132**(3), 353–407.

Kramer, M., Taube, C., and Redick, R. 1973. Patterns of use of psychiatric facilities by the aged: Past, present, and future. *In*, C. Eisdorfer and P. Lawton (eds.), *The Psychology of Adult Development and Aging*. Washington: American Psychological Association.

Lasagna, L. 1969. Aging and the field of medicine. *In*, M. W. Riley, J. W. Riley, Jr., and M. E. Johnson (eds.), *Aging and Society, II: Aging and the Professions*. New York: Russell Sage Foundation.

Lawton, M. P. 1971. The functional assessment of elderly people. *J. Am. Geriat. Soc.*, **19**, 465–481.

Litman, Theodor J. 1971. Health care and the family: A three generational analysis. *Medical Care*, **9**(1), 67–81(January–February).

Logan, R. F. L. 1966. The burden of the aged in society and on medical care. *In*, J. N. Agate (ed.), *Medicine in Old Age*. London: Pittman Medical.

Lowenthal, M. F., Berkman, P. L. *et al.* 1967. *Aging and Mental Disorder in San Francisco: A Social Psychiatric Study*. San Francisco: Jossey-Bass.

McKeown, T., and Cross, K. 1969. Responsibilities of hospital and local authorities for elderly patients. *Brit. J. Prevent. & Social Med.*, **23**, 34–39.

Maddox, G. L. 1964. Self assessment of health status: A longitudinal study of selected elderly subjects. *J. Chronic Diseases*, **17**, 449–460.

Maddox, G. L. 1972. Social determinants of behavior. *In*, F. Hine, E. Pfeiffer, G. L. Maddox, and P. Hein (eds.), *Behavioral Science: A Selective View*. Boston: Little, Brown.

Maddox, G. L. 1975. The patient and his family. *In*, Sylvia Sherwood (ed.), *The Hidden Patient: Knowledge and Action in Long-Term Care*. New York: Spectrum Publications.

Maddox, G. L., and Douglass, E. B. 1973. Self-assessment of health: A longitudinal study of elderly subjects. *J. of Health and Soc. Behavior*, **14**, 87–93.

Moriyamo, I. M. 1968. Problems in the measurement of health status. *In*, E. B. Sheldon and W. E. Moore (eds.), *Indicators of Social Change*. New York: Russell Sage Foundation.

Munnichs, J. M. A. 1973. Linkages of older people with their families and bureaucracy in a welfare state, the Netherlands. Paper prepared for a Conference on Family, Elderly and Bureaucracy, Quail Roost, North Carolina (May).

Nathan, T. 1970. Health needs and health services. *In*, United Nations, *Symposium on Research and Welfare Policies for the Elderly*. New York: United Nations.

National Center for Health Statistics. 1965. *Vital and Health Statistics Programs and Collection Procedures*, Vol. 1, No. 1. Washington, D.C.: Government Printing Office.

National Center for Health Statistics. 1971. *Health in the Late Years of Life: Data From the National Center for Health Statistics*. Washington, D.C.: Government Printing Office.

National Center for Health Statistics. 1973. *Current Listing and Topical Index to the Vital and Health Statistics Series, 1962–1972*. Washington, D.C.: Government Printing Office.

Nedeljkovic, Y. 1970. *Old people in Yugoslavia*. Analytical tables. Belgrade: Institute of Social Policy.

Newhouse, J. P., Phelps, C., and Schwartz, W. 1974. Policy options and the impact of national health insurance. *New Engl. J. Med.*, **290**(24), 1345–1359.

Parsons, T. 1958. Definitions of health and illness in the light of American values and social structure. *In*, E. Gartley Jaco (ed.), *Patients, Physicians and Illness*. New York: The Free Press of Glencoe.

Patrick, D. L., Bush, J. W., and Chen, M. M. 1973. Toward an operational definition of health. *J. of Health and Soc. Behavior*, 14(1), 6–23.

Pettengill, J. H. 1972. Trends in hospital use by the aged. *Social Security Bulletin*, 35, No. 7 (July).

Piotrowski, J. 1968. *Report to the Social and Rehabilitation Service, U.S. Department of Health, Education and Welfare*. Warsaw.

Piotrowski, J. 1970. *Old People in Poland and their Vital Capacity*. Warsaw.

Riley, Matilda White, Foner, Anne, Moore, Mary E., Hess, Beth, and Roth, Barbara K. 1968. *Aging and Society: An Inventory of Research Findings, I*. New York: Russell Sage Foundation.

Rosenstock, I. M. 1966. Why people use health services. *Milbank Memorial Fund Quarterly*, XLIV(3), Part 2, 94–124.

Sachuk, N. N. 1963. Some general studies of the health of the aged. *In*, World Health Organization, *Seminar on the Health Protection of the Elderly and the Aged and on the Prevention of Premature Aging*. Copenhagen: World Health Organization.

Shanas, E. 1962. *The Health of Older People: A Social Survey*. Cambridge, Massachusetts: Harvard University Press.

Shanas, E. 1971. Measuring the home health needs of the elderly in five countries. *J. Geront.*, 26, 37–40.

Shanas, E. 1974. Health status of older people, cross-national implications. *Am. J. Public Health*, 64, 261–264.

Shanas, E., Townsend, P., Wedderburn, D., Friis, H., Milhøj, P., and Stehouwer, J. 1968. *Old People in Three Industrial Societies*. New York: Atherton Press; London: Routledge & Kegan Paul.

Shuval, J. T., in collaboration with Antonovsky, A., and Davis, A. M. 1970. *Social Functions of Medical Practice*. San Francisco: Jossey-Bass.

Simmons, W. R. 1963. The matrix of health, manpower and age. *In*, R. H. Williams, C. Tibbitts, and W. Donahue (eds.), *Processes of Aging: Social and Psychological Perspectives*, Vol. 2. New York: Atherton Press.

Simon, A., Lowenthal, M. F., and Epstein, L. 1970. *Crisis and Intervention: The Elderly Mental Patient*. San Francisco: Jossey-Bass.

Somers, A. R. 1971. The nationalization of health services: A universal priority. *Inquiry*, VIII(1), 48–60.

Stiefel, J. B. 1967. Use and cost of AHS coordinated home care programs. *Inquiry*, 4(1), 61–68(October).

Suchman, E. A., Phillips, B. S., and Streib, G. F. 1958. An analysis of the validity of health questionnaires. *Soc. Forces*, 36, 223–232.

Sullivan, D. F. 1966. Conceptual problems in developing an index of health. *Vital and Health Statistics*, Series 2, No. 17. Washington, D.C.: Government Printing Office.

Sullivan, D. F. 1971. Disability components for an index of health. *Vital and Health Statistics*, Series 2, No. 42. Washington, D.C.: Government Printing Office.

Svane, O. 1972. *Vurdinger af aeldres behov for pleje og omsorg*. Copenhagen: The Danish National Institute for Social Research.

Townsend, P. 1965. On the likelihood of admission to an institution. *In*, E. Shanas and G. F. Streib (eds.), *Social Structure and the Family: Generational Relations*. Englewood Cliffs, New Jersey: Prentice-Hall.

United Nations. 1973. *Question of the Elderly and the Aged: Report of the Secretary General on Conditions, Needs and Services, and Suggested Guidelines for National Policies and International Action*. New York: General Assembly, A/9126.

U.S. Bureau of the Census. 1973. Some demographic aspects of aging in the United States. *Current Population Reports*, Series P-23, No. 43 (February). Washington, D.C.: Government Printing Office.

U. S. Department of Health, Education, and Welfare. 1958. *Selected Survey Topics, United States, July 1957–June 1958*. National Health Survey. Public Health Service. Washington, D.C.: Government Printing Office.

U.S. Department of Health, Education and Welfare. 1971a. Persons 55 years and over receiving care at home, July, 1966–June, 1968. *Monthly Vital Statistics Report*, 19, No. 10 (January), Supplement.

U.S. Department of Health, Education and Welfare. 1971b. *Toward a Comprehensive Health Policy for the 1970's*. Washington, D.C.: Government Printing Office.

U.S. Department of Health, Education and Welfare. 1974a. Nursing homes: An overview of national characteristics for 1973–1974. *Monthly Vital Statistics Report*, 23, No. 6 (September), Supplement.

U.S. Department of Health, Education and Welfare. 1974b. Current estimates from the health interview survey: United States–1973. *Vital and Health Statistics*, Series 10, No. 95 (October). Washington, D.C.: Government Printing Office.

U.S. Department of Health, Education and Welfare. 1974c. *Health Insurance for the Aged: Hospital and Skilled Nursing Facility Admissions, Fiscal Year 1973*. Health Insurance Statistics (December). Washington, D.C.: Social Security Administration.

U.S. House of Representatives, Committee on Ways and Means. 1974. *National Health Insurance Resources Book*. Washington, D.C.: Government Printing Office.

U.S. Senate Committee on Finance. 1970. *Medicare and Medicaid: Problems, Issues, and Alternatives*. Washington, D.C.: Government Printing Office.

U.S. Senate Special Committee on Aging. 1972. *Home Health Care Services in the United States*. 92nd Congress, 2nd session. Washington, D.C.: Government Printing Office.

Van den Heuvel, W. J. A. 1974. *Older people and their*

health. Some notes on health measurement in gerontology. Nijmegen: Gerontologisch Centrum.

World Health Organization, Regional Office for Europe. 1959. *The Public Health Aspects of the Aging of the Population*. Report of an advisory group, Oslo, 28 July-2 August 1958. Copenhagen: World Health Organization.

World Health Organization. 1972. *Psychogeriatrics*.

Technical Report Series 507. Geneva: World Health Organization.

World Health Organization. 1974. *Planning and Organization of Geriatric Services*. Technical Report, Series 548. Geneva: World Health Organization.

Wroe, D. C. L. 1973. The elderly. *In*, Muriel Nissel (ed.), *Social Trends*, No. 4. London: Her Majesty's Stationery Office.

24
AGING AND THE SOCIAL SERVICES

Walter M. Beattie, Jr.
Syracuse University

INTRODUCTION

Throughout the world the majority of older persons are unreached and unserved by social service programs. The emergence of such services is a twentieth century phenomenon. All have their roots in the historical and cultural identities of the societies in which they are to be found.

There is little agreement in the literature or among the social systems of different countries as to the definition of social services and what is to be included under this rubric. Although they have many commonalities, there is much variation in the goals, organization, and content of social services to the aging throughout the world. The approach in this chapter is a broad one.

Social services are here defined as organized societal approaches to the amelioration or eradication of those conditions which are viewed at any historical point of time as unacceptable and for which knowledge and skills can be applied to make them more acceptable. Such services, therefore, are based upon scientific knowledge and humanistic values out of which are defined the roles, responsibilities, and acceptable conditions for the individual, family, community, and society. In recent years, with increased scientific research on the

biological, psychological, and social processes of aging as well as a greater awareness of environmental factors which restrict or enhance the capacities of older persons to participate in social life, specialized social services for the aging have emerged. Such services are based upon knowledge and skills which can be applied to improve the social functioning and self-actualization of the older individual, his family, or community. Social services for the aging thus broadly defined are affected and, in turn, affect a variety and range of settings in which older persons function—the home and family, community, congregate and group dwellings, and institutions.

Any approach to an understanding of the role and place of social services for the aging must be considered within a life-span and inter-generational framework. It also must be based upon a recognition of the vast range of differences to be found among individuals of the same chronological age in later life and among individuals who have been commonly classified as "old," "the aged," or "the elderly." This age range may embrace 30 to 45 or more years. Social services must be based upon a recognition that the biological, psychological, and sociological processes of aging continue to differentiate individuals at any one chronological point in the life span. A guiding philosophy of services to the aging is to assure that their provision supports the individualized and unique needs and capacities of the older person.

What follows is an overview of social services to the aging as they have begun to emerge in recent years. Beyond a discussion of specific services, their development, and characteristics, some underlying issues—historical and ideological—as well as social forces and policies which have a marked influence on the content, availability, and delivery of social services to the aging, are examined.

Planning for the provision of social services to the aging and the development of delivery systems is then discussed, followed by a brief look at the emerging family-oriented English approach and the recent area agency approach to services in the United States.

Manpower resources, training programs, and research needs for the provision of social services to older persons are identified. This discussion is followed by a prospective look at the continuing development of social services to the aging during the last quarter of the twentieth century.

OVERVIEW OF SOCIAL SERVICES TO THE AGING

Specialized social services to the aging have their roots in antiquity as well as in the medieval and emerging modern eras. Because the place of the aging in past societies, as well as the roles of governments, are discussed elsewhere in this book, this chapter will not attempt to trace the development of such services.

It is also not possible to include within the scope of this chapter a full discussion on each of the social services relevant to the needs of older persons. What follows, therefore, is a brief overview of specific characteristics of such services and, where possible, some emphasis on their development.

Public Social Services

The advent of social security systems throughout the world, beginning in the late nineteenth century, while emphasizing contributory social insurance programs and noncontributory assistance or supplemental income programs, also gave impetus to public responsibility for the provision of a limited range of social services. In some countries such services as shelter, individual counseling, and group activities are recognized as rights of all older persons, while in others limited services, such as social casework, are restricted to recipients of assistance-supplemental income programs.

With the development of national health systems, particularly in Western Europe, medical-health programs for the aging were included as part of a comprehensive social security program. In others, health insurance, such as Medicaid in the United States, also provided for medical assistance to the medically indigent, which provided a new clientele for public social services beyond those who were financially indigent. Gold (1974) has identified for the United States that in the late 1960's the federal government, through Title I (Old Age Assistance) of the Social Security Act, provided for an expansion of social services to the aging, including the beginning purchase of services from nonpublic sources. Such services were provided not only for those receiving cash assistance but also for past and potential recipients. At the same time, such public social services for the aging have had the lowest of priorities, except in major metropolitan centers where homemakers and group social services, such as senior centers, were considered appropriate public responsibilities. In more recent years public social welfare agencies have been responsible for a number of "in-kind" assistance programs including: vendor payments, primarily through Medicaid, to doctors, hospitals, nursing homes, and other providers of medical-health services; food stamps; and rent supplement programs.

Services into the Home

Although the historical trend has been that of institutional based services for the elderly, the past 30 years has seen a progressive momentum developing toward community and institutional based services (see section on the emergence of geriatric centers) reaching into the home of the older individual and his family. In some countries this movement has been more accelerated than in others. These differences are accounted for by differences in public policy, financial mechanisms, and value systems which emphasize, to a greater or lesser extent, kinship and family ties and community responsibilities toward older persons. Such services include home-helps (also called homemakers, home-health aides), portable meals (or meals on wheels), friendly visitors, day-care (also called geriatric day hospitals), respite services, and substitute family care (foster homes).

Home-help Services. Although the development of home-help services for the aging has accelerated only in the past three decades, the first Home-Help Association was founded in Frankfurt on the Main, Germany, in 1892. Its early development by Western European countries has since spread throughout the world. As Winston (1975) has identified, this service may be used alone or as a foundation to other services. She identifies it as "basic and generic" to health and social welfare programs. It includes a broad range of supportive help to the older individual and his family, including personal care. The National Corporation for the Care of Old People (1972) in England reported that in 1970, 84 percent of the recipients of home-help services were 65 years and over, with nearly 70 percent of the aged served being 75 years and over. This report also notes that more than one-fourth (27.4 percent) were housebound and about 90 percent had difficulty with personal mobility. In England men were more likely than women to receive such services and were more often living alone. As the report states, "elderly recipients were worse off in respect of accommodation, amenities and equipment than other categories of recipient." (p. 5). Official policy in England and Wales is to discontinue minimum charges for home-help service, which previously had been the case, and by January, 1971, only 13 local authorities in England and Wales retained such charges.

A 1965–66 survey, as reported by the National Corporation (1972), showed wide variation in the proportion of elderly who have the services of home-helps, with the conclusion that such differences may be related to the criteria adopted by authorities for supplying such services and the amounts allocated for such services. It went on to state that "in order to satisfy the unmet needs of present recipients and to provide home-help for those who are eligible by present standards but are not currently receiving it, the home-help service would need to be increased to between two and three times the present size. This estimate takes no account of the possibility of modifying present standards of assessment so as to render more people eligible for the service" (p. 9). It is also important to note that there is a major lack of knowledge about home-help services and their availability among the oldest age group, that is, the group most in need of the services. It was mandated as the duty of all local health authorities to provide home-help services on a scale adequate to the needs of their areas.

In the United States, this service has traditionally been called homemaker service and more recently, as a function of national health insurance (Medicare), home-health aides. The goal of such a service has been to enhance the quality of daily living and is usually provided under the supervision of a nurse or social worker. It was first developed around the needs of children by the Community Service Society of New York in 1904, and in the depression years of the 1930's was expanded under the Works Progress Administration where women in financial need were assigned to help in the homes of families with children and homes of the aged and chronically ill. In 1962, the National Council for Homemaker Services was established, and during that year public assistance funding was first made available for this service. By mid-1970 over 1,800 agencies were identified, employing over 20,000 homemakers. Prior to the 1960's, the majority of agencies offering this service were voluntary; however, since that time they have increasingly become a part of public agency responsibilities (Hunt, 1971).

In 1959, the International Council of Home-Help Services was established. Winston (1975) reports that today 19 countries have significant programs to help older persons to remain in their homes. Such programs tend to be administered under local auspices, with an increasing use of the team approach, that is, nurses, social workers, physicians, therapists, etc.

In her study of in-home services throughout

the world, Little (1975) has ranked countries according to the number of home-helps per 100,000 population. They are:

Group A (100-plus)—Sweden, Norway, Netherlands, Great Britain.
Group B (19–99)—Finland, Belgium, Switzerland, Canada, Germany.
Group C (2–18)—United States, France, Israel, Japan, Austria.
Group D (less than 1)—Australia, Italy.

She raises the question as to what the "ideal" ratio of home-helps should be for a developed country and reports that a British study by L. G. Moseley suggests between 300–400 home-helps per 100,000 households for Britain as an appropriate goal for national planning. This represents a ratio double or more that which local authorities were asked to plan by 1983, that is, 150/100,000. It is greater than the present ratio attained by all but the leading countries of Sweden, Norway, and the Netherlands (Little, undated, p. 20).

For the developing areas of the world, Little (1975) has reported that there are a large number of countries with home-health services not affiliated with the International Council of Home-Help Services. She points out that although many services are not reflected in statistical reports, they do exist. The main Asian service is to be found in Japan, with heavy emphasis upon the approaches of Great Britain and Sweden. In other areas of the Far East, such as Hongkong, the services are provided under private auspices. Some countries use this service as a means of strengthening family life through teaching, while others, through government personnel, train local persons with relatives and neighbors performing necessary care tasks. As Little points out, no one pattern fits the historical and changing social and economic conditions found throughout the world. The alternative to institutionalization may be housing with no services and forced isolation. Developing countries have the opportunity to avoid some of the mistakes which lead to such isolation and abandonment found in some developed sectors of the world.

Meal Services. Meal and nutritional services for older persons were developed in response to the high incidence of malnutrition and dehydration found among older persons, particularly those living alone. The importance of food as a stimulus to socialization was also recognized. Originating in England as meals-on-wheels, largely out of the work of the Women's Royal Voluntary Service, the service, while still largely voluntary, has expanded over the last decade. At the same time, a 1965–66 survey (Harris, 1968) estimated that this service reached, in England and Wales, only 1.2 percent of people age 65 and over, with a further 2.9 percent who could not get even one cooked meal a day without difficulty. This study of nine areas in England and Wales found that the portable meals service would need to be at least doubled in all but one area and increased considerably more than this in most areas if all those in need were to accept the service. The National Corporation for the Care of Older People (1972) points out that although voluntary organizations in England and Wales provide over 60 percent of meals at home and 50 percent of meals elsewhere for older persons, with increased service control and provision of portable meals by local authorities, the role of voluntary organizations is diminishing.

In the United States such programs for the elderly began under voluntary auspices in the early 1950's and enjoyed limited expansion. It was recognized as one important component of a full range of services to reach into the homes of older persons and was often accompanied by socialization and friendly visiting on the part of the person delivering the hot meal.

Senior centers and clubs often provided hot meals at a common site. Such programs, however, were but one component of other services. It was not until the 1973 Comprehensive Services Amendments to the Older Americans Act that federal policy provided funding for nutrition services for the aging. The emphasis was on the establishment of local sites for congregate dining services to provide nutritionally sound meals for older persons. Emphasis was placed upon the impoverished, isolated, and minority aging. Although portable meals may be a component of such community services for the elderly, the highest priority is given to congregate dining as a means of reducing isolation and increasing socialization among the elderly. One essential component of such services is the provision of transportation and, where needed, escort services between their homes and the congregate dining site. In 1974, the Congress authorized extensions of the program to 1977 with an increased fiscal authorization of 250 million dollars. Due to recent inflationary trends and the increased cost of meals, some programs have been reduced in scope, such as reductions in supportive services for home delivered meals, as well as therapeutic diets. As of early winter 1974, 178,000 elderly were being served, with 116,583 on the waiting lists (Special Committee on Aging, 1975, pp. 92–93).

Friendly Visitors. Possibly the oldest of social welfare services were provided by volunteers. In situations involving the breakdown of the family or in the absence of the family, which is particularly the case for older persons, neighbors and community representatives provided assistance and aid. In more recent years, particularly during the past 30 years, there has emerged a more formalized structure of into-the-home visits of volunteers called friendly visitors. This program, at first organized by voluntary organizations, especially church-related groups, expanded in the 1950's as components of public welfare programs. It is recognized for its therapeutic and socialization contributions to the well-being of the housebound elderly. Often such visitors provide additional help services beyond that of establishing bonds of friendship.

Friendly visitor programs are characterized by the training of volunteers not only for their "listening" role but also to develop a capacity to recognize problems or situations to which their supervisor can be alerted. Such volunteers, therefore, are not only trained but also supervised by a professional person, usually a social worker. They have been increasingly viewed as part of the helping team of professionals and paraprofessionals.

Transportation-Escort Services. Possibly one of the most critical problems facing older persons, particularly those 75 years and over, is that of transportation. Despite the fact that numerous community studies in the 1950's and 1960's noted community environmental barriers restricting the mobility of older persons, the issue of transportation as an essential ingredient of service access and provision was not given major policy attention in the United States until the 1971 White House Conference on Aging. Today, it is considered of critical importance, not only in giving older persons access to services beyond their home but equally so for those providers of service who cannot reach into the home of the older person because of the absence of appropriate public transportation systems. Increasing attention is being given to vehicles especially designed to transport the elderly, such as hydraulically operated "kneeling" buses, wheelchair buses, and dial-a-buses (by telephone), where vehicles will come to the door and assistants can help escort the older person from his home into the vehicle and from the vehicle into his place of destination.

Today, in the United States the federal Department of Transportation has mandated a proportion of its funding to be directed toward the special needs of the elderly and the handicapped. Federal regulations in the United States also mandate that transportation services be avilable to older persons as components of federally supported service programs. This service, therefore, is a basic component of services into the home and provides a bridge between the home and other health and social services located in the community.

Home Repair Services. For older persons living alone or for couples of advanced years, one of the critical issues, both in the core of urban centers where decay and deterioration are to be found more frequently and in more rural areas, is the lack of ability or capacity to maintain the repair of their property. They may be living under hazardous conditions. Increasing attention is being given to the development of home repair services whereby older persons, often retirees, are employed on a part-time basis to provide minor repair and household maintenance services for other older individuals who cannot purchase such services on the open market. This service includes a broad range of maintenance activities, such as plumbing, electrical, heating, painting, and roofing.

Day Care-Geriatric Day Hospitals. There is a major debate as to the appropriate place of institutional care in the range of services and facilities available to older persons. The majority of older persons who are institutionalized, particularly in psychiatric facilities, are there for social and economic reasons, as well as for medical-psychiatric reasons. The literature has noted that many of the persons who end up in such facilities do so because of the absence of a family or because working children cannot care for them in the day. This has given rise to a new form of service called geriatric day hospitals and in other areas, day-care centers.

This service, available to older persons who have mental and/or physical impairments but who can remain in the open community if professional and supportive services are provided, is primarily an outreach service of institutions (see section on the emergence of geriatric centers). It is usually provided on an eight-hour-a-day, five-day-a-week basis and includes a full range of medical, psychiatric, social, and rehabilitative services and recreational activities. Transportation service from the older person's own residence to and from the center is provided, as well as meals while attending the center. Such services often relieve family members throughout the day and/or prevent premature institutionalization of older persons who can function in the community through such support.

Respite Services. An emerging service focused on relieving primary caretakers of their continuing responsibilities for older persons, such as adult children over weekends or vacation periods, is called respite service. An increasing number of geriatric care centers are offering this service. (See section on the emergence of geriatric centers).

Registrant Service. Another new service offered to older persons who continue to reside in their own home by geriatric care centers is that of registrant service. Through such an approach older persons, residing in the community, may register and be identified and have available to them the multiservice components of such centers on a continuing basis, where needed, in order to prevent breakdown and crisis from occurring. Such an approach permits the center to reach into the home and provide a range of professional and supportive services, such as those already discussed.

Social Group Activity Programs. One of the critical needs of older people is that of the meaningful use of time. With losses of child-rearing and occupational roles and the changing structure of the society, with more and more older persons concentrated in cities rather than living in rural areas, options and alternatives for activities which are satisfying to the social and psychological needs of the older person are of vital importance. Social group activity programs for the aging emerged over the past 20 to 30 years, some with therapeutic goals and others with recreation and options for the use of leisure as the goal (see Kaplan, 1953).

Social group activity programs are to be found in a variety of settings, ranging from public social services to neighborhood and settlement houses to hospitals and institutions caring for older persons. Recreational and leisure time programs for the aging are increasingly to be found under public auspices of parks and recreation departments, with some states and local communities in the United States providing funding for the training of leadership and for special leisure-time programs for older people.

Senior Centers. Emerging in the 1940's out of the same traditions as social group activity programs, the senior center movement has grown not only in the United States but also abroad. Under the pioneering leadership of the Gertrude Landau and William Hodson Day Center in New York City, recognition was given to the socialization and activity needs of older persons who, often residing alone and in isolation, had little group activity and personal-social identity.

Beyond providing opportunities for creative growth and socialization, as well as communal dining, such centers have increased not only in numbers but in range and scope of activities and functions. In less than a decade, the number of centers and clubs has increased tenfold. In 1966 a national directory of centers in the United States identified fewer than 400 such programs, while in 1974 they had increased to nearly 5,000 (National Institute of Senior Centers, 1974). Such centers, usually neighborhood based, today provide a broad spectrum of services—health, social, educational, and recreational. Many serve as a bridge between the older person and the community and afford opportunities for employment and voluntary services for older persons.

Rehabilitative Services. Traditional rehabilitation services have been concerned primarily with the physical rehabilitation of the individual. In more recent years, rehabilitation has been associated with mental health and psychiatric programs. The majority of such programs have been biased toward the young and the adult worker. Emphasis has been placed on a vocational orientation to rehabilitation, including educational programs, to prepare handicapped persons for employment. This bias has effectively prevented the majority of older persons from having access to rehabilitation programs and has condemned many to lives of physical, emotional, and social impairment. For example, in 1970, of the 7,632 referrals made to the Ohio Rehabilitation Services Commission, only 35 were persons 65 and older, and only 1,309 (17 percent) were between the ages of 45 to 64 (Scripps Foundation for Research in Population Problems, 1972, p. 51). With an aging population, increased emphasis must be given to social and emotional rehabilitation, as well as to physical rehabilitation. If older persons, following strokes or cardiovascular accidents, could learn to once again use their hands in order to feed themselves or to comb their hair, this would do much for self-dignity and would improve, if only slightly, the quality of their existence.

Public policies and service programs must focus on the potentials and capacities of each older individual. This is particularly important in regard to social and rehabilitative services for the aging.

Services to the Blind and Hard of Hearing. It should be noted that at least one-half of all legally blind persons in the United States are 65 years and over, with a higher rate of visual impairment among older nonwhites. Some changes and losses associated with vision are normal changes associated with aging. Others are related to disease processes more frequently to be found among the aging, such as diabetes, glaucoma, macula degeneration, and senile cataracts. It should also be noted that an even larger proportion of the deaf population is to be found among the elderly.

Despite these facts, services to the blind and to the deaf populations focus upon education and retraining for employability, with little emphasis on the specialized needs of older persons with visual and hearing impairments. The majority of social and environmental services for the aging are not organized around these special need groups within the aging population, representing a major gap in service provision. Beginnings are now being made at federal, state, and local levels to relate the specialized needs of such populations to the developing aging service system.

Legal Services. One of the emerging services for older persons is related to their legal needs. Some are in the areas of consumer rights and protection, while others are in the more specialized areas of guardianship, conservatorship, and protective services. The civil rights of older persons and the need for legal advocacy is only now beginning to develop and be recognized as a related component of social services.

Protective Services. Possibly one of the most complex service areas related to social, medical, and legal services is that of protective services for the aging. Work in this area was pioneered in the United States in the early 1960's by the National Council on the Aging and the American Public Welfare Association. The Benjamin

Rose Institute of Cleveland has pioneered in developing a carefully designed study of this service under the leadership of the late Margaret Blenkner. Essentially, the service focuses on the mentally impaired older person without anyone available to provide help and support (Blenkner, Bloom, Nielsen, and Weber, 1974). Despite the recognition of the need for this service over the past 15 years, it is for the most part unavailable to the majority of elderly. Where it is developing, it is increasingly related to public social services and legal service centers.

Information and Referral. It is well documented that a large proportion of older persons with the greatest service needs are less likely to have information concerning available services. This is particularly true for those of advanced age, who are more likely to be living alone, socially isolated, and with reduced income. Information and referral services, although not new in regard to broad community health and social services, are recent in their approach to the special information needs of older persons and their families. Such services are increasingly attempting to locate the isolated, sometimes called the "invisible," aging and make them aware not only of the services that exist but how they can use them. Such outreach services also attempt to identify unmet needs of such isolated older persons and relate them to the appropriate service.

Information and referral services are, however, not restricted only to the isolated aging. It is a basic service for any community social service system in order to assure that information is available and is useful to the wide range of conditions and needs of the aging. Such services, therefore, identify and evaluate services which exist; refer older persons to requested and/or needed services; evaluate whether or not the older person got to the needed service and whether the service was useful; identify, through keeping a record of requests made, gaps in available services; and provide information on use as well as gaps to social planning agencies in order that such information is used as part of an ongoing planning process.

The Emergence of Geriatric Centers. One of the recent trends is the development of the geriatric center, historically rooted in the home

for the aged tradition. In a number of locations throughout the United States, such facilities are reaching into the community and providing a wide range of housing and service alternatives, as well as providing a means whereby older persons may come to their facilities on a limited basis, that is, for the day (see day care), or for periods of one or two weeks (see respite services), etc. Such centers, under a single administrative structure, can assure continuity of care as well as the full range of services which are preventive, treatment, and rehabilitation oriented. They also can provide structured approaches to the relocation of older persons from one level of service and setting to another and, through appropriate planning and intervention, can prevent some of the relocation shock which has led to increased morbidity and mortality among those older persons relocated.

Such centers usually combine service functions, research functions, and training functions which enable them not merely to respond to the needs of the present day aging but also to build knowledge out of practice in order to modify old services and anticipate the need for new services. In addition, they provide a valuable resource for in-service training and often enjoy relationships with institutions of higher learning.

IDEOLOGICAL CONSTRAINTS AND PERSPECTIVES ON THE DEVELOPMENT OF SERVICES TO THE AGING

It was not until the 1940's that social policies, programs, and services to meet the specialized needs of the aging began to emerge. Since that time, such policies, programs, and services have been constrained and limited. They have had low priority.

Much of the lag between the needs of older persons and the provision of services to meet such needs is related to historical and cultural ideologies which have influenced the goals and content of the health and social services as well as the values and attitudes of those providing such services. Such ideologies have also influenced the political decision-making process of resource allocation and utilization.

The professions of public health, medical

care, and social work were largely developed in the first two decades of this century. This was a period when emphasis was on the control of infectious and communicable diseases, environmental sanitation, as well as maternal and child health. High infant and maternal mortality rates and the plight of children who were exploited economically gave rise to protective legislation and social reform. The major emphasis was on the earlier stages of the life span. Medicine emphasized curative approaches to treatment, and physicians were largely trained to provide periodic and episodic intervention and care at times of crises. Medical and public health education focused on acute, infectious, and communicable diseases. Hospitals were emerging as facilities for acute care and emergency treatment. Those individuals with long-term, chronic illness were, for the most part, relegated to custodial care facilities, with little professional service or treatment provided. During this period hospitals were moving from private control and auspices to public nonprofit corporations.

Much of the foundation for present mental health services and treatment was being evolved along Freudian psychotherapy theories and practices with their emphasis on early developmental psychosocial behavior. Mental hospitals were for the most part custodial in orientation, and often the traditions and practices of the nineteenth century almshouses and poor farms were confused and combined administratively and servicewise with those of the mental hospitals (asylums). Such institutions were overrepresented in the proportions and numbers of elderly who were warehoused there.

Social work as a profession grew out of the traditions of the charity organization, social reform, and settlement house movements of the later nineteenth and early twentieth centuries. Its concerns were on the individual, the family, and the community. However, as it moved from volunteerism to professionalization, it built much of its theories on the current behavioral and social science developments of the early part of the twentieth century, especially Freud. Again, the emphasis was on the psychosocial dynamics of the developmental stages of life and focused on the child and parent relationship. It was not until the 1940's that social group methods and even later, the 1950's, that community organization and planning were accepted as legitimate components of social work education and practice.

Stemming from the earliest social welfare ideologies of the poor laws, rehabilitation—physical and later mental—emphasized as its goal the restoration of the individual to employability in the labor force. Where educational programs were involved, such as in special programs for the blind or the deaf, the emphasis was on preparing such handicapped persons for occupations and to prevent their becoming welfare recipients.

Each of the helping professions, therefore, due to historical and cultural influences in its development, was biased toward the young and the potentially employable as the legitimate recipients of service. As older persons continue to increase in numbers and as policies and practices, such as compulsory retirement, remove them from significant social roles, they are turning to community resources for help. Yet, the majority of community services are not available to them or they received the lowest of priorities. There is widespread documentation as to the failure of the professions and the services to respond to the health, environmental, and psychosocial needs of the aging.

Added to the above are central values, particularly of Western and urbanized industrialized nations, which devalue the older person and his place in the social structure. These contribute to what Robert Butler (1969) has termed ageism, that is, social practices including prejudices and stereotypes which are negative in their appraisal of older persons and their role in the society. Ageism is pervasive in most industrialized urbanized societies. It discounts the value of older persons and subtly raises barriers to the availability of resources and services required by them. It excludes the aging from continuing participation and contributions to social life.

For the professions, ageism means giving little or no priority to the unacceptable situations and conditions in which the elderly are to be found. It also means not recognizing service responsibilities and priorities in addressing these situations and conditions. For the majority of professions and services, the aging are either the least served or are not served at all. Only today are beginnings being made in the development of educational and training programs to prepare people for services to older persons. The majority of faculties of professional schools either do not recognize or give lip service to the legitimacy of including content on aging in the curricula and fail to prepare students for specialized careers for working with older people. Students often reflect in their personal attitudes the fears and prejudices of faculty and service providers. These fears are associated with their own personal aging, and their prejudices reflect the broader ageism of the society.

Despite the development of gerontological knowledge over the past three decades, these negative perspectives on aging still prevail and are reflected in policies and processes affecting services to the aging. In fact, in the United States, in the 1960's the so-called war on poverty gave little recognition to the fact that the elderly constituted one of the major segments of poverty. Levitan (1969), in *The Great Society's Poor Law: A New Approach to Poverty*, reviews in detail each of the programs developed for this "war." No reference or identity to aging is included.

The Model Cities program of the 60's with its emphasis on new approaches to physical and social planning in the core cities of America, also failed to recognize that the highest concentrations of older persons in the United States were to be found in the inner-cities of its metropolitan areas. It was only after such programs were established and attention was called to the special needs of the elderly that a response to such needs developed.

The lack of priority given to aging is reflected in the limited interest of research, education, and training to develop and apply appropriate knowledge required for service intervention. Not only have services been inadequately funded through public and voluntary sources, equally so, research and experimentation have been limited. It should also be noted that there has been a wide gap between the development of knowledge and its translation into services for older persons. The effect has been to deprive the elderly of needed environments and services and to fail to recognize aging as a normal stage to the life cycle. As Riley, Riley, and Johnson (1969) have noted, the intrusion of aging into

the clientele of the professions has been a gradual and subtle process, often unremarked and unrecognized by practitioners and those preparing others for practice.

Beyond the ideological professional and societal constraints to serving the aging are fundamental changes in family structure and organization which have emerged as a consequence of aging. Such changes have a profound influence on the need for and the content of social services to older persons.

It has only been during the twentieth century that the family has extended itself from a two and three generation system to one which increasingly includes four and, at times, five generations. Two of these generations may be within the older age period of the life cycle. For example, in the United States today, one out of three persons reaching the age of 60 has an older parent living. Those family members in their middle years, the 40's to mid-50's, may be the only economically productive generation within a four to five generation family system. Social policies and practices which stress family and relative responsibility for aging family members are being challenged by the realities of the extension of the family over time, as well as by increased mobility of family members, separating the generations over space. Research specifically focused on the aging and the family identifies networks of mutual assistance and aid, as well as emotional strengths and ties which are not confined to the generations living within a household or within a limited geographic area (Shanas and associates, 1968).

The perception by service providers of the family has been that of the nuclear household. Yet, the realities of aging demand a social service delivery system which addresses itself to each of the life-stages and their interdependence to one another. How social services to the aging can and should be focused on the family and the older individual within an intergenerational context is of critical importance.

Much as the family is responding to and being affected by impersonal forces of an increasingly complex society, so are the service organizations and agencies which, particularly in the public sector, are organized around mass needs and conditions. Large-scale organizations, with rules, regulations, and impersonal standards, all too often approach the service needs of older individuals and their families in a stereotypical and bureaucratic manner. Yet, the limited gerontological research available identifies that the aging processes increasingly differentiate persons of the same chronological age from one another as they grow older. No other life-stage categorizes as similar so many persons with differing needs and identities. A major question, therefore, is how to humanize and individualize large scale organizations and the services they provide in order that they may be responsive to the individualized and, at times, unique needs and conditions of older persons and their families.

Within the aging population there is a wide range of ethnic, cultural, racial, and national identities. Only in recent years has gerontological research recognized such differences and the need for knowledge on the specific characteristics and needs of older members of such subpopulations. One of the increasing challenges, especially in the United States, is to provide services which are in keeping with the ethnic traditions and identities of older persons and, indeed, support their life-styles. Such differences also occur in other societies and cultures which again place great emphasis on the need for pluralistic approaches to services.

Special issues in regard to the acceptability and the availability of services are dependent upon cultural identities. In some cultures it has been noted that language is related to facial and bodily gestures through which meaning is derived from words. The telephone is seldom used. In others, television may be inappropriate as a means of communication in regard to services, while in others the newspaper may have little value or relevance (Carp, 1970).

The issue of service access, beyond the older consumer knowing that a service exists, is dependent upon his ability to get to the provider or upon the service reaching out to the consumer's place of residence. Many social agencies report that they have few requests for service by older individuals. Often the request must be made at the office of the agency providing the service. One of the problems confronting the elderly is increasingly limited mobility. Public transportation has been, until most recently, unresponsive to the specialized needs of the aging. Social agencies have not adapted their services to the specialized requirements of older people.

There is also great unevenness between services available to the rural aged as compared to the urban aged. This is true not only in large nations, such as the United States, which has major problems and issues in regard to the accessibility and availability of services to the aging in rural areas, but it is equally so in smaller Western European countries, such as the Netherlands, where a broad array of services exist in urban centers, but to a much lesser extent in rural areas. This is also an issue in developing countries where resources and services to the aging are scarce in both urban and rural areas and where the structure of family roles and responsibilities is undergoing fundamental change.

Where few services exist, it is not possible to provide alternatives and choice. Yet, a stated goal among applied social gerontologists is that of providing options and alternatives to respond to the unique and changing needs of the older person. The capacity to fit the service to the individual rather than following the more traditional approach of fitting the individual to the service is a major challenge in providing services to the aging.

Related to individualization are the concepts of independence and dependence. As a reflection of our social ideologies, the aging are often referred to as a dependent population along with infants and children. Much of this definition arises out of the fact that they are removed from economically productive endeavors. At the same time, in the social and psychological sense, at each stage of the life span, all human beings are dependent on a number of other individuals. This is the basis for social organization. Many of the dependencies associated with aging are normal and are not pathological (Blenkner, 1969). A challenge of the social services is to respond to the older person's needs, while at the same time not increasing his state of dependency. The goal of such services should be to foster interdependence. A particular value again cited in cross-national research on aging is the desire of older persons not be dependent on their children. In this sense the concept of independence gives way to mastery over one's self, one's environment, and one's destiny. This sets the goal for continuing self-actualization and self-realization well into the later years. The challenge to the social services is to support such a goal, rather than to destroy the capacity for self-mastery.

Much as gerontology is a field related to many disciplines, so the needs and conditions of older persons are multifaceted. Housing needs are linked to health status and condition, and both, in turn, may be directly related to income level. Service interventions, therefore, require linkages between medical, health, social, environmental, and, at times, legal services. One of the primary barriers to the effective provision of services to the older person is all too often a lack of organizational approaches to bring together medical, health, and social service systems on a coordinated and, at times, integrated approach to the needs of the older individual and his family. The need to develop such linkages is of high priority. This need appears to be international in scope. Kahn and Kamerman (1975), in a preliminary report on cross-national studies of social service programs and systems for the aging in France, Israel, Canada, the United Kingdom, Poland, the Free Republic of Germany, and Yugoslavia, stress the essential need for interdisciplinary approaches between medical and social service components of care and the need for case management and case accountability functions which may be carried out by the social services.

This need for coordination by means of an interdisciplinary structure is important not only from the viewpoint of the individual recipient but equally so to avoid costly duplication and waste of resources. Riley, Riley, and Johnson (1969), in their monumental review of research and professional perspectives on aging, point to service duplication and competition in both present services and in anticipated roles of the service professions. They also suggest new organizational approaches to service provision to foster the emergence of "new and imaginative" solutions to many problems.

Perhaps one of the larger issues confronting the development of social services for the aging

is related to the place of institutional and congregate care facilities in the continuum of services, care, and settings for older persons. In the more urbanized and industrialized sectors of the world, there have occurred in recent years a negative stereotyping of the institution as the place of last resort for the elderly and movements toward de-institutionalization of the present aging population. This has led to a stress on the need to develop community based social and health services to prevent institutionalization. The question of the appropriate place as well as the content of service for older persons is not, however, an *either* institutional based *or* community based service question. There is an appropriate place for congregate care and protective shelter and services in the continuum of social services and settings for the aging. The requirement is that an appropriate range of settings and service alternatives be available, accessible, and acceptable to the needs of older persons at a particular point of time and place. As the needs and conditions of the older person change, so will the components of service and settings change.

Among the many public policy issues affecting the availability, adequacy, and utilization of social services are those related to cash income versus services and the development of service standards and licensure. It has been suggested that if older persons were to receive sufficient income, the marketplace would respond to their needs through the provision of such services. It would not, it is argued, be necessary for governments to provide such services.

The cash approach presumes that there will be a response in the marketplace to the specialized needs of older persons. Where this has occurred, as in the United States in the area of nursing home care, there is still a major subsidization from the public sector. There is also the value laden question of whether profit should be made out of the service needs of older people. It can further be argued by advocates of public responsibility in providing services to the aging that there is a great shortage in the availability of services, and that even with cash in hand the majority of older persons would not be able to purchase such needs.

Another responsibility of the public sector is the development of standards and licensure to assure that the older public is protected. Few standards currently exist except in regard to institutional care. In this area such standards have tended to emphasize fire, sanitation, and safety codes rather than services provided the older person. Other standards are beginning to emerge in such areas as day care; however, they are still in their beginning stages of development.

SOCIAL SERVICE PLANNING

Planning is based upon the premise that goals can be formulated and achieved which will enable present conditions and situations, which are considered unacceptable, to be ameliorated or eliminated in the near (short-range) or distant (long-range) future. It is also based on the premise of achieving a better or more ideal state of being for all or part of society.

Social planning for the aging narrows the scope of such planning. It is based on a view that the consequences of an aging population have been to a large extent dysfunctional both to older people and society at large. It also is based on the premise that the rational approach of goal formulation and resource allocation can improve the quality of life for older persons. Social planning for the aging, therefore, requires an identification of those unacceptable conditions and situations which affect the *social* functioning of the older person. Such situations and conditions may be due to normal biological, physiological, and psychological processes and changes associated with growing old, such as loss of perceptual capacities—vision, hearing, etc. They may also be related to disease processes more prevalent among those in their middle and later years, such as chronic diseases— diabetes, neoplasms, heart disease, etc. Other unacceptable conditions may be related to the environments in which older persons are to be found, such as physically deteriorated neighborhoods, rural isolation, substandard and poorly designed housing, etc. Still others may be related to a social environment which provides inadequate, irrelevant, or inaccessible information and

communications for older persons, or transportation and mobility systems which are not designed for or responsive to the decreasing locomotion capacities of the elderly.

Unacceptable conditions or situations most commonly found among the aging of the western world, and which are usually associated with urbanization and industrialization, are those associated with changes and losses related to social arrangements and practices. Such conditions are increasingly found in developing areas of the world, but to a lesser extent (United Nations, 1975). These include: loss of work role (compulsory retirement); reduction in income and/or purchasing power (associated with retirement, widowhood, and advanced longevity); age-segregation and at times isolation (associated with specialized and congregate housing and institutional care); personal and social isolation (associated with living alone without appropriate community services reaching into the home); personal and social vulnerability (associated with a combination of physical, mental, and social losses—usually associated with advanced stages of the life span).

Social service planning for the aging, which is but one component of social planning, must have as its basic concern the mobilization, allocation, and utilization of resources—fiscal, facility, and manpower—to provide ways to enable the aging individual and his family to function at optimal levels. Further, it has as its central goal the development of services that will permit the older person to continue to experience the opportunity for maximum personal growth, self-actualization, mastery, social participation, and contribution, regardless of age, physical and mental limitation, or social-environmental setting.

Because of the wide range of age, social, cultural, and racial differences to be found within the aging population of communities and nations, it is important that planning and service delivery systems be comprehensive in scope and in their range of alternatives. Unacceptable conditions and situations differ not only among and between persons at various stages within the aging life span, but equally so among and between subpopulations and groups within each of the advanced stages of life. The goal of supporting and meeting the individualized needs of older persons and their families is dependent upon a comprehensive network of service alternatives.

Because the composition of the aging population changes continuously, with the young-old constantly bringing new identities, life-styles, and experiences into old age, values, orientations, and expectations will continue to change within the older age group. Planning and service delivery systems need to be designed to assure flexibility in response to this ever changing nature of the aging population.

Because the conditions and situations of individual older persons also change—for better or worse—planning and delivery systems for the aging must be based on evaluative designs and organizational patterns which will assure the movement of the older person among and between settings and services in a coordinated manner. Continuity of service delivery must be assured. In addition, the service and setting must be responsive to the unique and changing individualized needs and conditions of the older person rather than fitting the older person to the service.

It is essential that the fundamental questions as to the goals of services for the aging and the design of delivery systems be predicated upon scientific knowledge and a conceptual and philosophical understanding of aging. To date, only limited attention has been given to the design of social service delivery systems for the aging. Rather, the services have emerged piecemeal and often unrelated to one another. The situation as reported for England is similar to that of the United States where many local services for the elderly are piecemeal and inadequate. This is tragic because it means they may be almost irrelevant, making almost no impact on the needs of those they seek to serve, neither giving support to family and friends who urgently need it nor preventing unnecessary demands being made on institutional care (The National Corporation for the Care of Old People, 1972).

One of the main requirements of social service planning is the identification of the range and characteristics of unacceptable conditions confronting older individuals. This implies situation finding, as well as assessing and

evaluating such situations and conditions. There are a number of methods employed by social researchers and surveyors to establish this information. Based upon measures of the gravity or severity of the condition, for example, starvation or substandard nutrition, the service goal is formulated—that all older persons will be assured the right to one nutritious meal a day. Beyond the statement of the service goal is the need to establish quantitative measures of the numbers of older individuals affected by the condition or situation. As an hypothetical example, 1 out of 100 older persons is starving; 50 out of 100 are suffering from malnutrition; 20 out of 100 require special diets—salt free or low-carbohydrate, etc. Through such an approach, projections of needed fiscal, facility, and manpower resources to ameliorate or eradicate the unacceptable condition can be made.

Knowledge gained from biological, behavioral, and social research on the processes and conditions of aging, while at times tentative and in beginning stages of development, is essential as a basis for formulating service goals. For example, there is a high rate of functional illiteracy among today's elderly. Psychological research indicates that the capacity to learn continues into the most advanced stages of life, although differently as to speed and motivation than among those of younger ages. Within the broad goal of adult education to promote lifetime learning, the most specialized goal of adult education programs for the elderly can be formulated upon such knowledge about the unacceptable condition (illiteracy) and the capacity to continue to learn in old age.

There are a number of similarities to be found among all age groups within a population. Some are similarities of advantage and others are similarities of disadvantage. Because of its emphasis upon time related changes over the life span, gerontology tends to emphasize differences related to age. However, there are some common similarities among all ages and some common conditions which are shared and which require a broad array of basic community services. Often, as Riley, Riley, and Johnson have noted (1969, p. 4), "the old do not differ from the young in every respect nor are the differences always to their disadvantage."

If basic services, such as public health services, for all in a population do not exist, a planning goal would be to see that they are provided for all in the population, including for older persons. Because public health services developed historically prior to the large increases in numbers and proportions of older persons (indeed, such increases are to a large extent due to public health services themselves), they often fail to provide basic preventive services related to the aging. For example, well-baby clinics are often considered as a significant component of community public health services. Geriatric well-clinics, however, which could provide for health and social screening of older persons to identify potential risk factors and prevent their developing into crisis situations, are seldom offered.

A planning goal in such instances would be to develop such services within existing public responsibilities. Other basic services offered by both public and voluntary agencies include family and individual counseling, financial assistance, group services, public recreation, etc. It would be unfortunate as a planning goal to emphasize the establishment of specialized services for the aging in the absence of such services for the total population. In the developing areas of the world, where resources are scarce, it would be an essential planning goal to include older persons and their specialized needs as part of the developing basic service patterns of a community. This is particularly important in view of the recent report of the United Nations (1975, pp. 17-18) which indicates that by the year 2000, 60 percent of the world's 60-years-and-over population will be found in the developing areas of the world.

Beyond the development of basic community services and the inclusion of the aging as legitimate consumers of such services, it is important to conceptualize predictable life changes associated with aging and those unacceptable conditions and situations which will be confronted by increasing numbers of older persons. It is possible, based upon present knowledge of aging and events which occur for the majority of older persons in the last one-third of the life span, to identify changing and often dysfunctional situations which can and should be addressed by appropriate service interventions to change the unacceptable to a more acceptable way of life for the older individual. Because such life events also occur to significant numbers within the aging population, it is possible to predict numbers of persons affected by a given situation and to develop ratios of service need, that is, the number of persons requiring such service within a given size, such as 1000, 10,000 or 100,000 (see discussion on home-helps).

For the young-old, identified by Neugarten (1974) as somewhere in the 50's and extended until the mid-70's, there are a number of service needs which may be called adjustment and integrative services. Included in the specific conditions associated with aging to which these services are related are loss of work role due to age discrimination, or inability to find new employment because of age, generally occurring among the 45-65 age group; retirement in many countries occurring at increasingly younger ages, somewhere between 55 and 65; income reduction; bereavement, especially loss of spouses by women, etc.

Specific goals toward which services would be directed include the participation of older persons in the life of the community; the retention and use of capacities and potentials in a way that is personally satisfying and socially approved and recognized; and adjustment by older persons to new social roles in the family and in the broader community.

Specific services to achieve such goals include new careers through adult and continuing education; specialized employment and volunteer placement programs for older workers and retirees; preretirement and postretirement counseling; specialized casework and group work services to the older person and/or his family, including bereavement counseling; income security and maintenance programs—public and voluntary—such as supplemental assistance, social security, and private pensions; specialized recreational programs for the aging; and senior center programs.

As aging progresses in the life span, there is an increasing requirement for supportive services which have as their goal to aid the older person to remain in his familiar habitat or to retain his usual living arrangement (with adult children, friends, etc.) when this is no longer possible through his own efforts. This broad goal is related to a number of specific conditions to be found among the aging, particularly those 75 years of age and older. These include those elderly persons living alone who may be bedfast or housebound; those unable to manage their homes and environments due to mental impairment and/or increased energy loss; isolation from others due to age, physical disability, illness, and increasing deprivation of friends and relatives. Services directed toward achieving this goal would include outreach services; organized day care; geriatric day hospitals; escort services; homemaker/home-health aides; friendly visiting; portable meal services; organized home care including medical, psychiatric, nursing, social work, rehabilitation, and homemaker components; substitute family care–foster care; home repair services; transportation services; and telephone lifelines.

It is difficult for some older individuals, particularly those in advanced old age, the mid to late 80's and above, to maintain an independent living arrangement. Often they are unable to meet or satisfy their basic needs for self-maintenance, care, or protection. A full range of congregate and shelter care services—day care and geriatric day hospitals; substitute family care; specialized housing, including health, social, and recreational services; in-patient long-term care and treatment facilities; temporary in-patient emergency service; and, respite-family vacation care—are required to meet the requirements of this age group. The goals of such services are to protect older persons from the hazards of living in the open community or from their inability to cope with independent or family living situations due to physical and/or mental infirmity.

Another service area, particularly related to those of extremely advanced age and with limited mental functioning due to mental deterioration, emotional disturbances, or extreme infirmity, is that of protective services. The condition confronted by such persons in need of such services is their inability to manage their own affairs in such areas as providing for personal and physical needs, planning and decision making, and in the handling of finances. Such services require a coordinated and focused

organization of legal, medical, psychiatric, and social services. The goal of such services is to protect the civil rights and personal welfare of the older person from the neglect and/or exploitation by relatives, friends, the community at large and, at times, himself.

A service area now in its developmental stage is that associated with the situations and conditions of death and dying. This area of need, which has been traditionally avoided and denied by the professions and society at large, requires social, psychological, and medical components. Specialized terminal care facilities and services are beginning to emerge, particularly in Great Britain. There is increased recognition of the importance of providing services which relate to the dying process and enable the dying person to maintain his personal integrity. It also attempts to support him and his family to deal with feelings and experiences related to separation and loss.

Although the above social service planning model identifies services within broad age categories within the aging population, such services may be required by others in their early and middle years, as well as by those in their later years, such as protective services for those in their 60's or 70's. However, most of the events associated with aging can be identified within chronological age ranges for a specified population, if not for an individual. For instance, if 62 is the modal age of retirement, it is possible to determine the number of persons who will reach age 62 for a given year in a given community, to project within that population what proportion will be facing retirement, and to plan appropriate services for their needs. This is also true for widowhood, specific chronic diseases, etc. At the same time, particular services and facilities may be inappropriately utilized due to the absence of other alternatives. For example, if services are available and accessible into the home of the older individual, there is some evidence enabling us to predict that premature institutionalization will not occur.

A community plan of services must develop priorities organized around such measures as the number of persons negatively affected by a condition associated with aging, or the gravity of a situation. In the latter instance, although only a few older persons within the population may be affected, it may still be considered as completely unacceptable and require immediate attention. This might include such situations as abandonment, gross neglect, or starvation. The need is to develop measures of those conditions affecting older persons and the number of persons so affected if planning is to begin to address itself to such questions as effectiveness and efficiency.

Through the efforts of the Ford Foundation and under the leadership of Miss Ollie A. Randall, a number of demonstrations in community planning for the aging were carried out throughout the United States in the early 1960's. These were assessed by Morris and Binstock (1966) in *Feasible Planning for Social Change*. One of their significant findings was the lack of involvement of or access to community power structures and decision makers. Indeed, the politics of planning is a critical element at all levels of government, as well as in the voluntary sector. It is important, therefore, to distinguish between a model for planning in regard to the life span as discussed above and the processes of planning itself, which require political strategies as well as substantive content about aging *per se*.

Finally, increasing awareness is being given to the importance of older persons participating in the planning process, as well as in the decisions affecting how services shall be organized and delivered to meet their needs. Organizations of older persons have begun to emerge over the past several years at national and local levels and increasingly are involved in what has come to be known as advocacy planning for social change to improve the quality of life and the range of options and alternatives available to older persons.

MODELS OF SOCIAL SERVICE SYSTEMS

Although there has been limited attention to the development and design of social service systems to the aging, in recent years some have been suggested. One suggested by Stanley J. Brody (1973) argues that medical care is but one important part of the continuum of health care and that health-social services are equally important and "not ancillary" to any other service. He suggests the parallel functions to be met by the health-social service system in both the community and the in-patient acute hospital. These include personal services; supportive or extended medical services; maintenance services; counseling—including listening skills and the mobilization and utilization of resources; and, linkage services (information, referral, and education).

Bell (1973, p. 395), on the other hand, emphasizes the concept of community care and identifies five basic components of a home delivered service system. These, he suggests, may be enlarged through other program components. All should be coordinated and made available within a given geographic region by a single public agency. The components of such community care include: health maintenance; home-help; mobile meals; transportation services; and counseling, crisis intervention, and advocacy.

The developmental concept is emphasized by Elaine Brody as one most useful for social gerontology and social work practice. This concept stresses that there are tasks to be mastered in the later stages of life as in the earlier phases. This concept, she suggests, helps to counter the negative and pessimistic attitudes in work with the elderly and provides more positive goals. Its approach recognizes the range of differences within the aging stage of life and the "unique potentials" of psychological well-being for older persons. She further suggests that the developmental concept brings into focus the need to critically examine the usefulness and appropriateness of knowledge and techniques borrowed from work with the young (Elaine Brody, 1971, p. 55).

Gold has recently provided a listing of social services to the elderly which he describes as "suggestive," some of which are mutually exclusive (Gold, 1974, pp. 59-60). His listing is arranged according to the levels of capacity and incapacity of older persons, as well as those with special needs. In addition, it includes a category of services which assure access to other social services.

Robert Morris and his associates at the Levinson Gerontological Policy Institute, Brandeis University, have proposed a service delivery model to respond to the needs of the long-term sick, handicapped, and disabled, with the elderly representing the largest majority of this population. As pointed out by Morris, "major medical and social agencies seldom consider the slow-moving long-term case as their primary responsibility; they are to be 'referred' to some 'other agency' for social-economic and psychological conditions" (Special Committee on Aging, U.S. Senate, 1971b, p. 1). Because no other agency can or is willing to take such sustained responsibility, such individuals end up in inappropriate institutions, such as nursing homes, which cannot meet their needs.

Their proposal is for a Personal Care Service System to maximize residential choice for the elderly and disabled. Hopefully, such a service system would decrease inappropriate institutionalization and optimize the functional capacities of such individuals in the housing and neighborhoods of their preference. One or more Personal Care Organizations would be established and developed at the local community level and funded through nonprofit corporations, which would purchase care for beneficiaries within a given geographical area. P.C.O.'s would assume responsibility for maintaining the elderly and disabled in the community by taking on maintenance roles and through offering a range of services, such as home-finding, foster care, and group living, as well as home-helps, shopping, housecleaning, meal preparation, personal grooming, exercise, laundry, and necessary local travel. They would also arrange and finance other care services provided by other agencies. Further, P.C.O.'s "would not provide professional medical care, rehabilitation or counseling services nor would they replace present income maintenance programs" (see Caro, 1972, pp. 5–6). One of the chief features of such an approach would be that levels of payment for services would be negotiated in advance based upon the degree of the individual's functional impairment. Such an approach, it is suggested, would focus on the development and implementation of a service plan appropriate to the individual's specific needs, emphasize efficiency in delivering services, and assure a coordinated approach to continuity of care among a number of service providers.

Tobin suggests that there are likely to emerge in the foreseeable future community based social-health service systems that will provide for continuing supportive care as the individual's needs change. He suggests that neighborhood based centers, placing a priority on services to the aging, will emerge out of the higher expectations and demands of older persons and the increased sensitivity to their needs by service providers. This will be part of what he calls the local primary care system backed up by small local institutions developed by those responsible for the local-neighborhood care systems. This would allow for a more decentralized approach, keeping the majority of older persons in their familiar habitat and environment. It would be "a flexible resource for the community provision system. In the long run, if effectively linked to the secondary and tertiary components of the health system, it could be less costly than other forms of care, possibly less costly than our present reliance on the proprietary nursing home industry which articulates with neither other community providers nor hospitals" (Tobin, 1975, p. 36). He further postulates the emergence of the terminal care facility or hospice which could reach into the home of the older person and his family, as well as provide supportive services within an institutional setting.

THE EMERGING BRITISH SYSTEM

It was not until the early 1970's that services for the elderly in England, which heretofore were located in a number of national and local agencies, were transferred and centralized as the responsibility of local authorities through implementation of the Health Services and Public Health Act of 1968. Such authorities were given the responsibility to provide a broad range of services and arrangements "to meet the needs of the elderly," including meals, recreation, information and outreach, transportation facilities, boarding homes, visiting and social work services, and home facilities. Such services were to be provided in addition to present services offered by local authorities and within the limits of their available funding and staff. In addition, local authorities were given the obligation to provide old people a variety of supplemental services directly related to medical care, such as home-helps, home-delivered meals, sheltered care, supervision of the mentally ill, special housing for the handicapped, and modifications of home facilities to meet their needs.

The official government position was to bring about the closest integration between health and social services at the local level. It also emphasized a rethinking of welfare services, the use and relationship of voluntary efforts to public services and to develop priorities to meet local conditions. High on the priorities were to be services to support and promote independent living arrangements for older people.

As Shanas points out, the British policy is for the integration of health and social services to the elderly wherever possible with an emphasis on a "family-oriented" approach to meeting the needs of older people (Special Committee on Aging, U.S. Senate, 1971a, pp. 3-4.)

EMERGING DELIVERY SYSTEMS IN THE UNITED STATES—THE 1973 COMPREHENSIVE SERVICES AMENDMENTS TO THE OLDER AMERICANS ACT

As official public policy, the federal government of the United States, through the 1973 Comprehensive Services Amendments to the Older Americans Act of 1965, established a beginning structure for the development of comprehensive and coordinated delivery systems for Americans 60 years and older at the local community level. By July 1, 1975, such area agencies on aging numbered nearly 475 and were established in geographical areas where 70 percent of the aging in the United States reside.

The Act defined social services as including:

1. health, continuing education, welfare, informational, recreational, homemaker, counseling, or referral services;
2. transportation services where necessary to facilitate access to social services;
3. services designed to encourage and assist older persons to use the facilities and services available to them;
4. services designed to assist older persons to obtain adequate housing;
5. services designed to assist older persons in avoiding institutionalization, including pre-institutionalization evaluation and screening, and home health services; or
6. any other services, if such services are necessary for the general welfare of older persons.

Funding from the federal government was provided for the establishment of local sites for congregate dining services to provide nutritionally sound meals for older persons. Such nutritional programs by definition are required to provide transportation to assure accessibility to meal sites and outreach to the nonserved and the underserved, as well as opportunities for socialization and other social and psychological needs. In addition to local organizations, each state and territory, in order to receive federal funding for services, their administration, and provision, must have an established unit on aging. Public policy, therefore, in the United States has given explicit recognition to the need for state level organization, as well as community based, organized, and coordinated service delivery systems to the aging.

MANPOWER, TRAINING AND RESEARCH

As community and institutional-based services for the aging expand and governmental, voluntary, and private financing is made more available, one of the major barriers to the provision of quality services will be the lack of trained personnel to provide such services. The vast majority of persons now providing services to the aging at the skilled-professional, allied-paraprofessional, and voluntary levels are untrained. They have little or limited knowledge as to the aging processes, the specialized needs of the elderly, and the optimal ways of providing services to older people.

Career ladders in the field of aging are for the most part unformulated. Dead-end jobs and tasks with few incentives are by and large the nature of beginning and less-skilled positions in the present emerging system of services to older people. At the professional level, as previously noted, aging as a field of concentration or specialization has been given limited or no priority. Persons who are presently providing leadership in service settings and educational institutions have only recently acquired knowledge, skills, and commitment to the needs of older persons through personal motivation and self-education. Until most recently aging has had low priority in the majority of academic institutions, much as services to the aging have had low priority among the professions and the community.

Despite the above, throughout the United States innovative and new approaches are beginning to emerge through the provision of specialized class and field learning and educational programs in aging both at the undergraduate and graduate levels. In addition, a number of two-year community colleges are moving toward specialized curricula for paraprofessional responsibilities in service provisions for the aging. They are also providing a wide range of training and community service programs for older persons (Korim, 1974).

Increasingly, the place and role of older persons as teachers, students, and service providers is being raised with new careers for older persons developing in the area of service provision to other older persons. In addition to the specialized efforts of the Social Research, Planning and Practices Section of the Gerontological Society (U.S.A.), which has sponsored several workshops for faculty of schools of social work in the area of faculty and curriculum development, additional efforts are being made by universities working with state units on aging to develop faculty competencies and teaching materials in two- and four-year colleges and university programs within their states. A newly established national Association for Gerontology in Higher Education, which has developed over the past three years, is providing leadership to institutions of higher learning throughout the United States in the area of aging.

Despite these efforts, however, there is a paucity of career programs preparing persons for work with the aging. Training needs may be divided into the following categories:

- Those already working in the provision of social services and who have yet no formal training in the field of aging. For such persons in-service short-term and continuing education courses are being increasingly offered to provide opportunities to bridge the gap between new knowledge and its utilization, as well as to deal with the philosophical and conceptual dimensions of aging. At times such training is task-oriented relating to specific staffing functions of serving the needs of the aging.
- Those persons seeking careers in working with the aging. Training and educational programs at two-year, four-year, and graduate professional educational levels are required for the young student as well as those in their mature years seeking new careers.
- The need to "gerontologize" faculty and professional leaders through programs of continuing education into commitments to educational and service delivery programs in the field of aging.

The Expert Group Meeting on Aging of the United Nations, in May, 1974, stressed the need for national programs to consider manpower needs for the aging in the following areas: training of trainers; training of supervisory, administrative, and paraprofessional personnel of various sectors, including the voluntary; developing curricula and training materials (United Nations, 1975). The Group also expressed the need for an international expert group of educators in gerontology to consider the core knowledge and skills required in services to the aging and for the development of training materials.

The role of the United Nations Regional Centers for research and training in social welfare and development was also recognized, with the recommendation that they should address themselves to the training needs for the aging, as well as include aging within curricula and manpower development, giving priority attention to manpower research and studies for the aging. Education and training needs for the provision of services for the aging is an essential worldwide priority.

Gerontology is comprised of many disciplines, and the requirements of older persons are multidimensional. Traditionally, those responsible for service provision and those responsible for education, training, and research have had limited communications and relationships. In addition, each of the disciplines and professions, as well as the separate systems of services, have not related to one another in carrying out educational, research, or service delivery responsibilities. There is a need to build linkages among and between the professions and disciplines, as well as those responsible for service provision, education, and training and research.

In the United States, at the community level, as already stated, geriatric centers are combining service provision functions with those of knowledge building (research) and knowledge and skill transmission (training). There is also the development of gerontology centers and institutes in major universities combining the same broad functions. Such centers and institutes may serve national, regional, state, or local needs. They provide opportunities for interdisciplinary linkages and disciplinary depth in research and education in theoretical and applied approaches to aging.

It has been well documented that often behavioral and social research is so designed and carried out that it is of limited use for those who must act on and apply knowledge derived from such research. The problems in regard to the translation of research for use were discussed by an international group of experts following the 1971 White House Conference on Aging in Washington, D.C. As stated by this group, "one of the more consistent findings in the various areas of human functioning is that individual differences increase in range during the later years. Its translation of findings into practical significance is enormously complicated by this spread. Making provision for majority needs may be harmful to minority needs. Coping with this problem is not really in the province of the research worker but is considered to require a political or administrative decision" (Birren and Woodruff, 1972, p. 72). The issue

was seen essentially as that of translation from the language of the researcher to that of the practitioner. This continues to be a major barrier to the use of research by those providing services.

DEMOGRAPHIC DATA

It has only been in recent years that demographic data and analysis throughout the world has occurred beyond age 60 or 65. Where such analysis has occurred, it has shown that the 75 and older population is the most rapidly increasing proportion of the population in the majority of urbanized industrialized countries. Where data has been collected and analyzed for the 85 years and over population, a proportionate increase has occurred. It is among those in the advanced stages of life that the greatest proportionate increase is occurring and where the demand on health and social services is the greatest.

As recommended by the Expert Group Meeting of the United Nations (May, 1974), "demographic data collection and analysis be developed with five year intervals for those beyond the age of 45 years; and projections of life expectancies for males and females be made at various points of the life span" (United Nations, 1975, p. 79). The specialized needs of the very old, while increasingly recognized, require specific demographic projections to assure appropriate planning and delivery of services.

The support of applied social research has been exceedingly limited. For too long, demonstrations, that is, the application of an innovative or new approach to services for older persons, have been equated with social research. However, the majority of such demonstrations have not been based upon carefully developed designs and controls. They have, for the most part, resulted in an *a-posteriori* description of how a service was provided.

There is a need for experimental designs in the areas of population served; the effects of alternative settings and the characteristics and roles of service providers still need to be developed and carried out. Such approaches are costly and are fraught with value-laden issues. Nonetheless, it is possible and necessary for the development of appropriate and effective services for older persons that experimental research be carried out (United Nations, 1975, p. 79).

PROSPECTS FOR THE LAST QUARTER OF THE TWENTIETH CENTURY

Projections into the future are always hazardous. Yet, most of those institutes and organizations dealing with the future have, for the most part, as has the society as a whole, given little attention to the impact of aging on institutional and social arrangements. Demographically, older persons will continue to increase in numbers and proportions throughout the world and especially in the developing areas. The attributes of each successive age cohort will be different from those preceding and following them. At the same time the very old will continue to increase significantly and will place increased strain and pressure on all forms of community and institutional social service delivery systems. One of the critical issues will be that of resource allocation among the various need groups within the society and the political framework within which such decisions will be made.

Binstock, noting this growth of the aging and their broad range of service needs which are greater than the available personnel and facilities, suggests, particularly in American society, that the gap between the federal government's already established policy of providing services to older persons and its capacity to implement it will be enormous. He further suggests that if government responds positively to the challenge of expanded services and facilities, it will not be due to increased pressures on government by older persons themselves, but rather on "pervasive" ideological considerations (Binstock, 1974).

At the same time, advocacy by older persons on their own behalf, as well as on behalf of others, which is only in its beginning stages, will continue to expand, and it is highly possible that it will feed into the political process, particularly at the local level. Professionals responsible for administrative planning and service delivery needs of the aging will increasingly recognize older persons as a constituency group with which they will have to work in partnership at all levels—community, state, and federal. The participative role of older persons in both the planning and the service delivery processes will continue to grow along the line as argued for by Estes, that is, in defining the problem, planning the strategies, and implementing the process for the development and delivery of services and facilities for the aging (Estes, 1973).

The world, at this writing, is involved in a period of major change and, at times, crisis in regard to the "haves" and "have-nots." A redistribution of power relationships in regard to natural resources, their control, and allocation is occurring and already is having an impact on all in the population, including the elderly. Issues of energy, its cost, allocation, and distribution and of the availability of food and shelter are and will continue to be critical issues and concerns in the decades ahead. The economic inflationary trend, which is worldwide, as well as the counter-trend of deflation, is having a profound effect on the lives of today's elderly and will have a continuing effect on the social and economic status of older persons in the future. The conditions in which older persons are to be found will have to take into account these complex and impersonal forces, and recognition will have to be made by policymakers, as well as by service providers, of the impact of such forces on the lives of the present and future populations of the aging. Although much has been stated in gerontological literature concerning the preparation of those in their young and middle years for their own later years, such preparation may be insufficient if it does not take into account the specialized meaning of world and social change and their implications for tomorrow's aging. Such preparation must be based upon uncertainty and complexity rather than on formula approaches to adjustment and satisfaction in old age.

At the same time, as Neugarten suggests, older persons, particularly in the more industrialized and urbanized countries, are bringing into the world of the later years attitudes and values which are beginning to reformulate their self-perceptions and identities (Neugarten, 1974). The "young-old" may not only formulate new political and social roles but will increasingly be viewed as resources in themselves. The vast untapped reservoirs of such resources, as providers of health and social services, will begin to break down the stereotypical image of the aged as impaired and in need.

Despite the uncertainties of the present and the future, responses to the facts of an aging population and the specialized needs of the young-middle and old-old will continue to occur and expand. As the special needs for locomotion and mobility of the aging are reflected in environmental design, transportation systems, and communication networks, and as alternatives to support the individual identities of older persons continue to be recognized and developed, particularly at the neighborhood and community levels, changes will occur in the fundamental organization and delivery of services. Community health systems, combining environmental, social, health, education, and recreational needs, will increasingly come together in new organizational forms which will respond to the multidimensional needs of the older persons through interdisciplinary linkages. Special issues in regard to the centralization of planning and administration and the decentralization of services will occur. Through such approaches, hopefully, life as well as death for older persons will increase in dignity and meaning.

REFERENCES

Bell, William G. 1973. Community care for the elderly: An alternative to institutionalization. *Gerontologist*, 13(3), 349–354.

Binstock, Robert H. 1974. Aging and the future of American politics. *In*, Political consequences of aging. *Annals*, 415, 199–212.

Birren, James E., and Woodruff, Diana S. 1972. Research demonstration, and training: Issues and methodology in social gerontology. *In*, International research and education in social gerontology: Goals and strategies. *Gerontologist*, 12(2), 49–83.

Blenkner, Margaret. 1969. The normal dependencies of aging. *In*, Richard A. Kalish (ed.), *The Dependencies of Old People*, pp. 27–37. Ann Arbor, Michigan: University of Michigan/Wayne State University, Institute of Gerontology.

Blenkner, Margaret, Bloom, Martin, Nielsen, Margaret, and Weber, Ruth. 1974. *Final Report—Protective Services for Older People: Findings from the Benjamin Rose Institute Study*. Cleveland, Ohio: The Benjamin Rose Institute.

Brody, Elaine M. 1971. Aging. *In*, *Encyclopedia of Social Work*, pp. 51–74. New York: National Association of Social Workers.

Brody, Stanley J. 1973. Comprehensive health care for the elderly: An analysis. *Gerontologist*, 13(4), 412–418.

Butler, Robert N., M.D. 1969. The effect of medical and health progress on the social and economic aspects of the life cycle. *Industrial Gerontology*, 2, 1–9.

Caro, Francis G. 1972. Organizing and financing personal care services: An alternative to institutionalization for the disabled. Mimeographed. Waltham, Massachusetts: Levinson Gerontological Policy Institute, Brandeis University.

Carp, Frances M. 1970. Communicating with elderly Mexican-Americans. *Gerontologist*, 10(2), 126–134.

Estes, C. L. 1973. Barriers to effective community planning for the elderly. *Gerontologist*, 13(2), 178–183.

Gold, Byron D. 1974. The role of the federal government in the provision of social services to older persons. *In*, Political consequences of aging. *Annals*, 415, 55–69.

Harris, Amelia. 1968. *Social Welfare for the Elderly*. London: Her Majesty's Stationery Office.

Hunt, Roberta. 1971. Homemaker service. *In*, *Encyclopedia of Social Work* (16th Issue), Vol. 1, pp. 583–586. New York: National Association of Social Workers.

Kahn, Alfred J., and Kamerman, Sheila B. 1975. Preliminary findings of cross-national studies of social services systems. Unpublished, used with permission of authors. New York: Columbia University, School of Social Work.

Kaplan, Jerome. 1953. *A Social Program for Older People*. Minneapolis: The University of Minnesota Press.

Korim, Andrew S. 1974. *Older Americans and Community Colleges: A Guide for Program Implementation*. Washington, D.C.: American Association of Community and Junior Colleges.

Levitan, Sar A. 1969. *The Great Society's Poor Law: A New Approach to Poverty*. Baltimore: The Johns Hopkins Press.

Little, Virginia C. 1975. Factors influencing the provision of in-home services in developing countries. Unpublished mimeo.

Little, Virginia C. Undated. Present status of homemaker-home-help services in developed countries. *In*, *Home-Help Services Around the World*, pp. 16–21. Washington, D.C.: International Federation on Aging.

Morris, Robert, and Binstock, Robert H. 1966. *Feasible Planning for Social Change*. New York: Columbia University Press.

National Corporation for the Care of Old People, The. 1972. *Services for the Elderly at Home*. London: Bedford Square Press, paperback.

National Institute of Senior Centers. 1974. *Directory of Senior Centers and Clubs*. Washington, D.C.: The National Council on the Aging.

Neugarten, Bernice L. 1974. Age groups in American society and the rise of the young-old. *In*, Political consequences of aging. *Annals*, **415**, 187–198.

Riley, Matilda White, Riley, John W. Jr., and Johnson, Marilyn E. (eds.) 1969. *Aging and Society, Vol. 2: Aging and the Professions*. New York: Russell Sage Foundation.

Scripps Foundation for Research in Population Problems. 1972. *Ohio's Older People*. Oxford, Ohio: Miami University.

Shanas, Ethel, and Associates. 1968. *Old People in Three Industrial Societies*. New York: Atherton Press.

Special Committee on Aging, U.S. Senate. 1971a. *Making Services for the Elderly Work: Some Lessons from the British Experience*. Washington, D.C.: Government Printing Office.

Special Committee on Aging, U.S. Senate. 1971b. *Alternatives to Nursing Home Care: A Proposal*. Washington, D.C.: Government Printing Office.

Special Committee on Aging, U.S. Senate, 1973. *Older Americans Comprehensive Services Amendments of 1973*. Washington, D.C.: Government Printing Office.

Special Committee on Aging, U.S. Senate. 1975. *Developments in Aging: 1974 and January–April 1975*. Washington, D.C.: Government Printing Office.

Tobin, Sheldon S. 1975. Social and health services for the future aged. *In*, Aging and the year 2000: A look at the future. *Gerontologist*, **15**(1), 32–37.

United Nations. 1975. *The Aging: Trends and Policies*. New York: United Nations, Dept. of Economic and Social Affairs.

Winston, Ellen. 1975. Homemaker-home-help services to the elderly: Efforts to maintain independent living. *In*, *Home-Help Services for the Aging Around the World*, pp. 1–2. Washington, D.C.: International Federation on Aging.

25
THE FUTURE OF SOCIAL INTERVENTION

Sanford A. Lakoff
University of California, San Diego

THE FUTURE OF AGING AS A SOCIAL CONCERN

Although in times past the care of the elderly was mainly a problem for families or philanthropic institutions, in recent decades it has also come to be regarded as another of the responsibilities of government. The reasons for this shift of responsibility are readily apparent. Thanks to the extraordinary progress of biomedical research, as well as to improved nutrition and public health, more people than ever survive into old age. Since old age is still debilitating, however, more people than ever require assistance. This assistance is no longer fully provided by the traditional sources, in part because of the increased scale of the problem, but also because of complex changes in social structure and social attitudes, as a result of which the agencies of government have come to replace private institutions and the family as the providers and overseers of social welfare.

Given the general change in expectations which affects all welfare policy, it is not surprising that in modern times "old age has become the object of a policy" (De Beauvoir, 1972, p. 222) or that governments everywhere should be expected to formulate policies for the care of the elderly. It is a fact that social intervention on behalf of the elderly is now a well-established practice in every advanced country. The practice, however, is not always well grounded, either in a consciously adopted social ethic or in an analytical understanding of the changing historical context in which aging as a social phenomenon—and not simply as a physiological one—requires attention. Instead, social policy with respect to the elderly is apt to be an unstable compound formed of the traditional belief in the virtues of charity for the "old and infirm" (with the taxpayer, however, replacing the private donor), an exaggerated conception of the incapacities of the elderly, and a pragmatic political recognition that older people are too significant a fraction of the population to be altogether ignored. (Not only do they vote, but to subject them to gross neglect is to invite embarrassment and public scandal, which can be more costly politically than the danger of electoral reprisals by the elderly themselves.) The result, especially in the United States, is a patchwork of policies rather than a coherent and farsighted effort of social planning and foresight.

The Future of Aging

For the immediate future, the failure to undertake an adequate effort of social planning for the needs of the elderly will pose the most acute difficulties for the advanced countries. It is in these countries that the proportion of

643

older people to the total population has become large enough to require the formulation of careful policies, and it is only in these countries that government action has become imperative because the elderly tend to live apart from their children and to be excluded from the labor force.

The experience of the United States shows clearly that the emergence of aging as a social problem is one of the corollaries of modernization. In 1850, when the average life span in the United States was 40 years of age, the population over the age of 64 comprised only 3 percent of the total. Today, it stands at close to 10 percent (Riley, Foner, Moore, Hess, and Roth, 1968, p. 3). In 1900, two-thirds of the American male population over 64 was still in the labor force; today, fewer than one-third remain employed beyond this conventionally established age of retirement (Riley *et al.*, 1968, p. 5). In previous times, older Americans were likely to reside with their children; today, nearly 80 percent, married or widowed, maintain separate households (Riley *et al.*, 1968, p. 5).

The American pattern is typical of the experience of other industrially advanced countries. In these countries, persons over 64 comprise 9.6 percent of the population, on the average, as compared with an average of only 3.3 percent in the developing countries (see Chapter 3 in this *Handbook*). Although the advanced countries contain only 30 percent of the world's population, they have 45 percent of its older people. If current trends in fertility and mortality rates are maintained, the proportion of the population over 64 in the advanced countries will rise to 11.4 percent by 2000 and to 4.6 percent in the developing countries (see Chapter 3 in this *Handbook*). Barring an unlikely devolution of recently acquired public functions to the private sector, public provision for the needs of the elderly will continue to be an issue of relatively high priority on the public agendas of all the advanced countries and will be an increasingly critical issue in the developing countries. It is easier, however, to predict the absolute numbers of older people who will be alive during the next several decades (since they are all now alive) than their proportion to the total population, which will depend upon future fertility rates. In political terms, the absolute number may be less significant than the proportion. If there are fewer young people, the elderly will have fewer competitors making rival claims for social services, but if the proportion of the elderly rises relative to that of the total employed population, the demand for income transfers from the employed to the retired could pose a burden that would result in political friction between the age groups.

There are other uncertainties as well which make it hazardous to try to discern the shape of future policies by extrapolating from present tendencies. Since the social definition of old age is virtually synonymous with retirement from the labor force, the lowering of the age of retirement, which is a trend strongly in evidence in recent years, could make the division between those under 64 and those above this age much less meaningful than it is now. The rise of the "young-old," the age group comprising retired people aged 50 to 75, could seriously complicate the job of the policy-maker fixated upon the old distinction (Neugarten, 1974, 1975). Another difficulty is that those who will become part of the elderly population, however defined, are likely to exhibit different characteristics from those whose experience of aging has been the basis of existing studies and existing policy conclusions. They will very likely have different values, a higher standard of education, perhaps a better preparation for retirement, and they may well expect more from government than have previous generations of elderly people, for whom the welfare state was still a novel experiment.

The Rationale for Intervention

Such uncertainties, however, do not alter the fundamental consideration which forms the premise of social intervention on behalf of the elderly. Simply put, this premise is that the process of aging tends to make people dependent upon others for assistance at a time when the state has come to be the overseer and dispenser of social welfare.

It is not simply because the elderly have

become more numerically significant that they pose a problem for governments, but rather that this numerically significant group has certain characteristics that make it a claimant for attention. As has been abundantly demonstrated by many studies, older people are prone to suffer declines in mental and physical capacities and therefore to become physically and mentally incapable of accomplishing the routine tasks of living. They are more prone to chronic illnesses than other groups in the population. In the United States, four of five persons over 64 have at least one chronic condition (Riley *et al.*, 1968, p. 3). Because of their diminished participation in the labor force, they are considered unproductive and a burden on society, and they may also receive significantly lower incomes than other adult age groups. Even those who survive into old age without physical handicaps are stereotyped as incapable, with the result that they find it difficult to keep or obtain employment. In addition to their economic problems, the elderly are likely to suffer a sense of psychic dispossession that reflects loss of roles and status, as they are deprived of identities defined by parental or employment functions.

The political response to the problems of the elderly is in part a reflection of a general commitment to social welfare that has become a standard element in modern government. Older people are classed, for this purpose, with children and the handicapped, on the assumption that people in these categories must be regarded as dependents and that society as a whole has a responsibility to assure that all who are dependent are not deprived of some measure of assistance. In addition, however, the elderly form a significant part of the polity, and as such are in a position to compete against other interested groups for a share in the distribution of the social product. In the United States, where the proportion of the population over 64 is almost 10 percent, the proportion of the same age group in the general electoral population is 15 percent (Binstock, 1974, p. 200). Although older people tend not to play a unified role in politics, their political power, real and potential, gives them considerably more leverage in the competition for scarce welfare resources than is available to other dependent populations.

It would therefore be misleading to construe the policy-making process in which the problems of the elderly must be addressed as an exercise in apolitical rationality based solely on the responsibilities of the state to provide welfare to the dependent. The reality is that policy for the elderly will inevitably reflect political considerations, especially those that relate to the balance of influence among competing groups. There is reason to believe, however, as will be shown later in this discussion, that the influence of interest-group conflict in political decision making may be waning, as the complex interdependence of interests compels planning and coordination by agencies responsible to large and diverse constituencies. There will still be a need for the debate of alternate policies, and considerations of group interest will undoubtedly color such debates. Increasingly, however, the policy debate will require a clarification of the issues at stake and a recognition of the values to be served by a policy, rather than the play of political forces alone.

In order to provide a foundation for such future efforts at policy making, it is necessary to pose two sets of questions, ethical and historical. What is the ethical basis of the social obligation toward the elderly? How will the problem of the elderly be affected by the transformation of industrial into "post-industrial" society? With the general answers to these questions in mind, we can proceed to consider initiatives that can plausibly be taken by governments concerned to develop a policy for the elderly which is grounded both on a principle of social justice and on an appreciation of the impending transformation of industrial society.

EQUITY AND THE ELDERLY: THE IDEAL OF SOCIAL JUSTICE

In certain primitive societies, the elderly are venerated, sometimes to the point of worship. Modernization appears to reverse this attitude dramatically and in some ways cruelly. No longer is age held to be synonymous with wisdom, or a useful fund of experience, or ripeness of judgment. Instead, the knowledge acquired by the elderly in their youth becomes obsolete because of the rapid progress of learning, even in the less esoteric vocations, and the wisdom claimed for experience stands in contrast to the innovative temperament prized as the mark of vitality. As the "tradition of the new" becomes the aesthetic standard, those who cling to previous styles and accustomed ways are dismissed as out of touch with reality or quaintly old-fashioned.

This change of attitude is reflected in the broader evolution of the ideal of social justice. When this ideal was first stated, it took the form of a belief in an enduring order in which age confers a special place. In modern societies, this belief tends to be replaced, or at least supplemented, by the belief in personal freedom and self-development. Since this freedom is to apply to all without exception, "place" is either the same for all or achieved rather than ascribed. When this modern ideal expresses itself in a radically competitive form, age is frequently a serious handicap, and the very belief in the impartiality of social justice based upon the principle of equal rights may inhibit the state from recognizing a responsibility to aid those who cannot fend for themselves.

It would be a mistake, however, to conclude from the contrast between primitive and modern values that the ideal of social justice has undergone so drastic a change as to remove the ethical basis for any concern with the condition of older people. Paradoxically, the full development of the modern belief in universal autonomy provides the basis for a surer, more defensible response to the problems of the elderly than the older ideal even though it denies the special claim of the elderly. Precisely because the social responsibility to protect human rights is defined so as to apply to *all* members of society and not simply to one class of the population, assistance (or social provision) becomes a matter of right, not on ground of any special claim, but rather on the ground of the universal claim made for all human rights on behalf of all members of society.

The Nature of the Classical Ideal

The ideal of justice is perhaps the most ancient of all human aspirations. In classical times, it was regarded by the best minds as the central issue of government. Plato's great dialogue, *The Republic*, is also entitled *On Justice*, and it is an open question whether Plato was not more concerned with the definition of justice in this dialogue than with ascertaining an ideal form of government.

It is worth noting that the discussion of justice in the dialogue begins when Socrates inquires of an elderly Athenian, Cephalus, whether he regards old age as a blessing or a curse (Plato, *The Republic*, pp. 327–331). Cephalus replies that old age confers a great sense of calm and security. Socrates wonders whether, in Cephalus' case, this sense results from his having acquired considerable wealth. Cephalus replies that money is a comfort, not because of the pleasures it can buy but rather because it enables him to pay the debts he owes to men before departing to the world below. Socrates is reminded of the folk saying which holds that to be just is to speak the truth and to pay one's debts.

Although Socrates quickly dismisses this folk definition and Cephalus himself immediately departs from the scene of the dialogue, having served to spark the discussion, the conclusion which Socrates and his pupils reach is actually a refined, philosophical version of the folk wisdom artfully introduced at the outset. Justice is defined as the pursuit and application of philosophical truth by those capable of understanding it; "paying one's debts" is restated in philosophic terms as "giving everyone his due." The result is the well-known social structure outlined in the *Republic*, in which the Guardians rule as philosopher-kings, with the aid of military auxiliaries, over a mass of ordinary people who are thought to be incapable of self-government and whose lives are necessarily devoted to thoughts and activities less exalted than those of the Guardians.

This Platonic ideal of social justice was claimed to be an expression of equality, not of equality as the term was understood by democrats, but of "equality for equals." Both Plato and Aristotle defined justice as an expression of equality, but both introduced a distinction which made the association highly ambiguous, to say the least. Justice (and with it, the ideal of equality) was said to have a double aspect, one retributive, the other distributive. The first corresponds to what we mean when we say that it is just to repay like with like. Retributive justice is an application of the principle of proportional equality and provides benefits according to some standard of merit. Plato and Aristotle both rejected the view that justice could be understood in terms of only one of these two principles, but in doing so they left considerable room for interpretation, especially in the case of the concept of distributive justice. Each society was presumably free to set standards of merit of its own choosing. These standards might include birth or wealth as well as learning and service to the community, with the result that patterns of privilege of all sorts could be said to be just and in accordance with the principle of equality—a result which has been bitterly criticized as an underhanded effort to make aristocracy and oligarchy seem justified (Havelock, 1957, pp. 339–375).

The Greek philosophers generally took a highly favorable attitude toward maturity, or old age as it was then. They regarded youth with suspicion, as a period in which the mind had not yet been fully formed and in which spirit and passion could well succeed in casting off the reins of reason. They favored restrictions on political participation according to age, which in effect would have created a gerontocracy.

Justice as Liberty: Origins of the Modern Perspective

The early philosophic effort to define social justice presupposed an organic model of society in which individual claims were clearly subordinate to the good of the whole and in which individuals were identified in accordance with their functional role in society, whether as head of family, housewife, or slave. Subordina-

tion, even in the form of slavery, was held to be just because the premise of equality was generally not understood to mean that all people, regardless of their actual social condition or function, were to be considered as of equal worth. Equality was thought to be an ideal which applied either to a remote golden age or to a perfect state to come in the indefinite future (Lakoff, 1964). This conception continued to be in accord with the prevailing notions of social justice throughout the Middle Ages, even though Christian teachings had introduced the idea of the brotherhood of mankind, reinforcing the earlier Stoic break with the classical belief in the naturalness of inequality. The Christian conception was held to apply only in an ultimate or spiritual sense, but not to require social reform. Thus medieval society, with its feudal hierarchy and its distinctions of estates and orders, was said to fulfill the requisites of the Christian idea of social justice.

The Protestant revolt was in part the expression of an unwillingness to accept this interpretation of Christian social teachings. The Protestant reformers did away not only with many of the distinctions introduced within the ecclesiastical estate, but with the principle that distinctions of rank could be drawn among Christians in any capacity. The only recognized distinctions were those of function. The body of Christians was said to be a priesthood of believers, all alike capable of knowing the moral law by reading the Bible for themselves. Even Calvin, who believed that no individual effort could overcome predestination, claimed that membership in the elect could not be known with any certainty. It followed, therefore, that the claim of superiority could neither be ascribed nor advanced (lest it lead to an accusation of sinful haughtiness and pride).

In the short run, Protestantism did not bring about any wholesale change in social structure or social attitudes. Its largest immediate impact was in ending the ecclesiastical monopoly of the Roman church and establishing a new, heterogeneous religiosity. Nevertheless, the social implications of the reform of the Christian religion and its ecclesiastical organization were to be profound and long-lasting. The demand for "Christian liberty"—from the yoke of Rome and from the control exercised by its priesthood—was to give rise to the demand for secular liberty. In the process, a new understanding of social justice came into being, which stood in pointed contrast with the older, organic view.

According to this new conception, which emerges with greatest clarity in the writings of the natural rights–social contract theorists, social justice consists primarily in the recognition of natural rights enjoyed by all as equal partners in the social compact. These rights are generally understood as claims based either upon the moral injunctions contained in the law of nature or upon universally accepted conventions. Since the law of nature ordains that man is to preserve his life, it follows that everyone has the right to life. Beyond this fundamental issue, the contract theorists differ. John Locke, the most influential theorist in the Anglo-American tradition, argued that the right to life could not be secure unless it were joined and supported by the right to liberty and to property. Society is created by mutual compact, in order to make the enjoyment of these rights more secure than they would be in a "state of nature" or in a condition in which the interpretation and execution of the law of nature is left to every individual. Locke did not suppose that men were equal in all respects. "Age or virtue may give man a just *Precedency*: Excellency of Parts and *Merit* may place others above the common level...." (Locke, 1689, pp. 6, 54).

Locke believed that the best way to preserve the terms of the contract would be to create a government in which a representative legislature is the seat of power. He was not a democrat in the strict sense of the word, because although he maintained that the contract required unanimity (and dissenters would therefore have to found their own societies "*in vacuis locis*"), he did not believe that all citizens ought to be represented in the legislature. Instead, he acknowledged that representation should be kept in proportion to "public assistance", or in other words to taxes paid in accordance with wealth and income. Nevertheless, he also acknowledged that the legislative

power was fiduciary in nature and that if the legislature were to use its authority to invade or abrogate the rights of the people—by which he seems to have meant a majority—the power would be forfeit.

The concept of social justice established by Locke and by the later liberal political economists, notably Adam Smith, put a premium on individual initiative. The main function of government was to assure that individuals were free to organize their own lives, to enter into contracts, to benefit from the exercise of reason and industry, and to suffer the consequences of following blind passion or succumbing to indolence. The liberals were not opposed to charity for those who were unable, because of infirmity, to provide for themselves, but they were anxious above all to avoid the paternalism of the system of absolute monarchy because they knew it could easily turn into an oppressive tyranny and because they were determined to overcome the unfairness of feudal privilege. Although in retrospect they have been accused of promoting a callous competitiveness, in their own historical times they stood as champions of universal emancipation. It was they who first insisted upon what Napoleon was to call "the career open to talent." It was they, more than any other group or movement, who established the principle of religious toleration and who laid the groundwork for the achievement of universal suffrage —even though in many cases they resisted this expansion at first out of fear for the consequences to property.

Their reforms, then, were aimed at redistributing the power that had either been monopolized by the monarchy or shared only with a limited group of aristocrats. Power was now to be exercised by a broader body of citizens, and those who were most diligent and most successful in their economic affairs could acquire the largest share.

The liberal or "laissez-faire" definition of social justice therefore departed radically from the more organic and more hierarchical classical and medieval views. Instead, it sought to create a system of competition in which the distribution of both rewards and power would be accomplished by the "invisible hand" of the market rather than by the state and government. A "free enterprise" economy was thought to be the necessary basis of free society.

Out of the attempt to limit the functions of the state to the provision of minimal security of life and property, the development of private charitable activities was a logical outgrowth. The traditional association of the churches with charitable activities was maintained and accentuated as the state removed itself from them. In addition, voluntary associations sprang up around particular charitable concerns, to support orphanages and hospitals and otherwise take up the slack left by the withdrawal of the state or the insufficiency of church efforts. Private charities therefore became one of the hallmarks of liberal society.

The replacement of public by private charity was in part a reflection of the rise of individualism as well. Public charitable efforts were widely viewed as unnecessary and likely to have harmful consequences. The Elizabethan Poor Law was taken as the classical case of failure. This law, which, in effect, guaranteed a minimal annual wage, only produced a class of people permanently on the dole. The result has lately been cited to discredit the concept of the guaranteed annual wage as well to point up the more general danger of public charity. Instead, it is held to be better to stress full employment coupled with relief for those unable to support themselves. This view has been criticized as a rationalization of exploitation. Critics of the welfare state have charged that in reality the system has served as a device for guaranteeing the availability of low-wage labor and for lulling the poor into a contented attitude toward the social system (Piven and Cloward, 1971).

Righting the Balance: The Rise of the Collectivist Ideologies

As the industrial revolution produced grave social discontents and disorders, social thought moved in a more collectivistic direction. Agitation over the "social question" led to the demand for "socialism" as the antidote to individualism (Lakoff, 1974a). Much of the intellectual energy of the nineteenth century went into a debate over the rights of the individual—especially over his supposed absolute right to private property. The socialists argued that there were no rights anterior to the creation of the community, and that the right of property in particular ought not to be considered sacred or immune from abridgment in the name of the common good.

Although the socialist movement led to revolutionary outbreaks throughout Europe, in the Western European countries and in North America socialism has in effect been incorporated with liberalism, in the manner of the "social liberalism" advocated by L. T. Hobhouse. Certain industries have been nationalized; others have been closely regulated. The socialist critique of the anarchy of capitalism has led to government efforts to control the economy and to redistribute income to alleviate social distress. Governments have also greatly expanded their responsibility for public welfare. The result is that the attention to welfare needs in the Western mixed economy systems proceeds from both individualistic and collectivistic premises. In many of the advanced industrial nations, state social insurance schemes provide a floor, upon which individually arranged private pension and insurance arrangements are supposed to provide adequate supplements.

In the United States, especially, there is no settled consensus on the functions to be performed collectively and those to be assigned to individuals on their own behalf. In other words, there is no simple formula defining the balance to be struck between individual self-reliance and social responsibility. As a result, every welfare measure proposed becomes a new occasion for debate on the question of whether private or public instrumentalities are most appropriate. If there is any general consensus, it would seem to be in favor of "pluralism"—the mixture of public and private efforts under the watchful but often remote eye of government.

"POST-INDUSTRIAL SOCIETY" AS A MATRIX FOR ANALYSIS

The term "post-industrial society" has been coined by a contemporary sociologist (Bell, 1974). The presupposition of all such theorizing is that it is possible and useful to construct abstract models, "ideal types" in Max Weber's term, or paradigms, which embody the salient features of a particular historical period. This procedure had its modern origin in the work of such nineteenth century periodizers as Karl Marx, Auguste Comte, and Herbert Spencer.

The Paradigm of Industrial Society

According to this theory, post-industrial society is preceded by an earlier transformation in which agrarian society is gradually replaced by industrialization. From roughly the middle of the eighteenth century, the point at which the historians usually date the start of the "industrial revolution," the first transformation has been under way, spreading from Europe to North America and then elsewhere, and involving certain fundamental changes including especially:

1. The replacement of human and animal power by mechanical systems relying on fossil fuels and hydroelectric power as sources of energy.
2. A vast increase in agricultural productivity, providing capital for industrial expansion and freeing labor for industrial pursuits.
3. A transfer of human labor from agriculture to primary (extractive) and secondary (manufacturing) industry.
4. A shift of population from rural to urban areas.
5. A differentiation of industrial states from nonindustrial, or advanced from developing industrial societies.
6. A change in social values from traditional and other-worldly to materialistic and secular systems of belief.

In the first societies to undergo this process, the change also brought about a highly individualistic social system. Industrialization was thought best achieved by personal initiative, and state paternalism was decried as an interference with the "simple system of natural liberty" (Adam Smith) which was the best guarantor of progress. The latecomers to industrialization have generally adopted more collectivistic ideologies, such as nationalism and socialism, on the ground that progress requires

positive direction by the state and that considerations of justice make individualism, with its inevitable inequalities of result, intolerable.

Another consequence of the change was to put a new emphasis on the development of industrial capacity for purposes of war and upon the acquisition of colonies, both as military bases and as sources of raw materials and markets.

In the more advanced countries, the individualistic emphasis of the first stages gradually yielded not to a general collectivism but to a pluralistic organization emphasizing competition among organized and unorganized social groups, including social classes. A quasi-market system developed, in which bargains were struck by these competing groups, alongside and through the more formal institutions of parliamentary government, and under the aegis of federalism. Complementing the institution was a "work ethic" which made it socially onerous to be unproductive, although great wealth, even when it exempted its possessors from the need to take gainful employment, was, however unaccountably, often taken as a sign of achievement. Rising living standards created expectations of improvement among all sectors of the population, and economic growth made it possible to improve the general standard of living without significantly redistributing shares of income.

Industrialization is of course a continuing process. Nevertheless, it is analytically rewarding to consider it as a terminal process to be contrasted with a later phase of development labeled post-industrial.

The Paradigm of Post-Industrial Society

Among the most salient points of contrast are these:

1. Fossil fuels are exhausted and tend to be replaced by forms of energy developed by scientific discovery, such as atomic energy.
2. As manufacturing becomes increasingly automated and industrial productivity and affluence increase, the demand for labor decreases in the primary and secondary sectors of the economy and rises in the tertiary or service sector. This sector

includes government services, demand for which tends to increase as government assumes burdens previously left to the private sector and acquires others resulting from the complexity of industrial society.

3. As a result of the growing demand for highly trained workers, especially those with technical and scientific skills, the pattern of education changes. Whereas in industrial society, education is primarily directed at the training of large numbers of low-skilled workers, now secondary and post-secondary education must be redirected to emphasize a higher level of preparation for employment.

4. The urbanization of society appears to lead to a later differentiation in which the suburbs are separated from the central city, a development, however, which may simply lead to a fuller amalgamation in the form of the integrated metropolitan area.

5. International differentiation comes to be defined not only by the single measure of industrial production, but also by the degree of commitment to scientific and technological excellence. Thus, such figures as the proportion of gross national product devoted to research and development, or the number of qualified scientists and engineers in the population, are considered part of the index of advancement, in the belief that physical and human resources committed to science and technology produce a multiplier effect reflected in future economic growth as well as in military capacity.

6. The social values of industrial society, especially those emphasizing work and its rewards, come into question, along with the emphasis on economic growth as an index of progress. Instead, an ethic based upon a vague but widely held stress on "the quality of life" emerges as a challenge, and possibly as a harbinger of a "scientific" rather than an industrial value system.

These changes are accompanied by many others which serve as functions or corollaries. Satisfaction of minimal economic needs leads to a growing interest in luxury and leisure among groups of the population previously forced to remain preoccupied with security and subsistence. The social standard of expectation comes to include a higher level of consumer satisfaction, even though comparatively few find this level within reach. While an absorption in consumption and leisure activities is particularly pronounced in the affluent societies, it is not far from the surface in those countries (however socialistic their ideological professions) which stand at an intermediate level in the race to affluence.

In post-industrial society, issues in which scientific and technological considerations are paramount tend to become pressing matters of public policy. These issues arise in every area of public concern, from national security to health and welfare. They include problems of whether to allocate large amounts of resources to the development of ever more sophisticated weapons systems, whether to subsidize high technology projects of potentially great economic consequences, and how to balance the benefits and costs of innovations. Because such issues come to loom so large in social controversy and in the agendas of government, scientists and technologists in virtually every area of disciplined knowledge come to play a more significant role than previously in the formulation of public policy, both as advisers to government agencies and as participants in the adversary process by which the debate over public issues tends to be conducted.

Government in "Post-Industrial" Society

During the development of industrial society, politics is predominantly a play of interested groups, including social classes. Government is often depicted as an umpire or arbiter among these groups, sometimes as an instrument by which one group succeeds in coercing another. In general, however, the functions of government are limited and the most important concerns of individuals are treated by private arrangements.

A marked change takes place, however, as industrialization proceeds, especially because regulation of industrial activities becomes necessary, both for reasons of protecting safety and health, and because of the harmful effects of unrestrained economic competition. How far governments should go in imposing regulation and planning becomes a subject of intense debate. Although the debate cannot easily be resolved in principle, in practice what happens is that governments become much more than "nightwatchman states," as socialists in the nineteenth century derisively characterized the liberal state. Governments regulate competition, negotiate the terms of international trade, and in general influence economic life at every turn. Growing bureaucracies not only preside over such efforts of regulation, but also respond to demands for services, including welfare services.

As industrialization advances to such a point that the focus of attention turns increasingly to the provision of such services, intense government intervention in all aspects of social and economic life becomes commonplace. Thus, in the period of post-industrial history, which is marked by the increasing emphasis on services, the expectation develops that government will play a central role in the organization of social as well as economic life.

Advocates of social planning would have this role performed in a highly centralized, highly rationalized way. According to them, governments ought to develop a capacity to gather information on the most comprehensive basis and ought to use this information to make comprehensive analyses and assessments. On the basis of the data, it is argued, governments can set policies which would stand in sharp contrast to the unplanned, often chaotic and pathological developments which result from inequities in the distribution of income and opportunity, and from different rates of achievement among individuals and groups. Some advocates of increased governmental planning argue that a political consensus must be reached on the goals to be achieved by social policy, which would then be implemented by a neutral civil service. Others would have the civil service design alternative strategies so as to allow differing political perspectives to be brought to bear on commonly recognized problems.

Critics of planning, especially when it is conducted by a remote and oversized central government, prefer techniques which devolve responsibility upon different levels of government and upon the private sector. Radical critics of planning contend that governments should not intervene unless absolutely required for public safety, on the ground that individuals, operating in the economic market and in its political equivalent, will make choices that best reflect their own priorities and serve their own needs. Government action, it is said, is both wasteful, because it entails the creation of large bureaucratic and professional establishments, and likely to be counterproductive, because the programs must be designed for aggregates rather than individuals and because the programs must be devised and implemented by agencies hamstrung by bureaucratic red tape, lack of imagination, and insensitivity.

A middle position, which is the one that currently prevails in most Western governments, sees government as the developer of general policies and in some cases as the implementer of these policies. In other cases, government provides incentives to other public agencies and to those in the private sector, in an effort to influence the actual operation of the social system in accordance with public priorities. The post-industrial state is apt to put a heavy emphasis on the analysis of social problems and the development of government policy with respect to these problems, but it is also apt to resist further expansion of its own efforts to cope with these problems. This resistance arises partly from the frustrations of experience. When too many programs are administered directly by the central government, the quality of service suffers, and government becomes unwieldy. Ideological beliefs also come into play, and these account for considerable variations. Countries in which a socialist ideology is strong, such as the Scandinavian countries, are apt to stress a greater role for public institutions. Countries in which a liberal suspicion of big government is strong are apt to take the opposite course. In these cases, however, the alternative to planning at the centralized level may not be a total absence of planning but rather the diffusion of planning among various levels. Such programs as revenue sharing aim to revitalize the federal character of the American political system as an alternative both to big centralized government and to reversion to the old reliance on the private sector.

The new emphasis on the role of governments in setting policy means that policy will no longer be so heavily influenced by the play of interested groups as it has been in the past. While these groups continue to play an important role, it is the new skilled elites, or professional purveyors of information and analysis in every field, who come to be relied upon by governments for the design of policies and programs. This tendency is reflected in the increasing role for professionals assigned in the upper reaches of the civil service, and to a lesser extent, in the political realm as well. The need for policy analysts in government creates a demand for trained specialists and generalists who will come to play a vital role in the setting of policy.

Thus, the tendency of government in the post-industrial stage of society will be toward a strong, positive role for government, not necessarily in the performance or implementation of policy, but certainly in the setting of policy. The contours of policy will be shaped less by interested groups, as was the case previously, and more by the relatively disinterested efforts of professional analysts. Since these professionals are not completely disinterested or unbiased, there will be conflicts among them as to the character of the policies to be followed. As the experience of the natural scientists indicates, these conflicts are all but inevitable when what is at stake is not an issue of fact or of accepted interpretation, but where the evidence is incomplete and there is a mixture of scientific and "transscientific" policy at issue (Lakoff, 1974b). What has been true for such issues as arms control will also be true for such issues as welfare policy.

Policy making, however, cannot take place in a political vacuum. No matter how important the role of professionals or of interested groups, the public and its representatives will play an equally crucial role, especially in demanding action or responding to experiments. The parliamentary system imposes constraints on governmental action which come into play sporadically but are nonetheless effective.

It is conceivable that the social priorities of

post-industrial society will shift away from the preoccupation with security and economic growth toward those loosely grouped under the rubric of the "quality of life." This assumes that governments are capable of managing the economy and of creating the conditions of stable world order—assumptions yet to be borne out. Should they prove justified, there can be no doubt that the attention of governments will be drawn increasingly to the improvement of the conditions of life.

THE SERVICE STATE: SOCIAL INTERVENTION IN THE POST-INDUSTRIAL ERA

In a post-industrial era, some degree of state intervention in virtually every sector of social life is all but inevitable. Governments will be expected not only to regulate and stimulate economic activity but also to provide a comprehensive range of social services. Ideological and cultural differences will probably preclude the emergence of a single pattern either in social structure or in the character of public intervention. All post-industrial societies will resemble each other in certain respects, including the attention they must all give to the education and utilization of technically qualified specialists and to the development of the service sector of the economy. In other aspects they will probably continue to differ, at least marginally, and perhaps more than marginally. Certainly, the mix of public and private emphasis will vary from country to country. In political terms, the need for expertise will have a similar effect in all the post-industrial countries, whether individualist or collectivist in ideology. This effect can perhaps best be characterized as a modification in the group basis of political conflict and accommodation resulting in a greater emphasis on the articulation and debate of alternatives by experts, politicians, and relatively fragile, issue-based constituencies.

Beyond Interest-Group Politics

Because of the growing technical complexity of the issues that must be dealt with and the diffuse character of electoral "interest" in policy outcomes, all governments will need to rely more heavily on the advice and assistance of professionals and scientists than in the past. In more and more cases, they will find the inter-action of interest groups an even more dubious guide to effective policy making than it may have been when the function of government was to act simply as a broker among power blocs.

The case of the elderly is a particularly good example of the reasons governmental reliance on the play of political influence is not always appropriate. The elderly do not vote as a bloc, despite common interests, because previously formed identifications based upon other characteristics tend to override identification in terms of age. The various "middleman" interest groups claiming to represent the needs of the elderly tend to be exclusively concerned with incremental improvements in existing programs of benefit to their constituents and almost never address themselves to the long-term needs of older people in society (Binstock, 1974). Reliance on special-interest groups in this area is especially inappropriate because it proceeds on the patently erroneous assumption that policy for the aged concerns only a limited seg-ment of society, an assumption which is true only at any particular point in time and there-fore distinguishes policy toward the elderly from many other types of welfare policy.

In post-industrial society, governments and their advisers will need to consider the effects of particular policies on the rest of society and on future generations. Governments which permit special interests to dictate or veto policy will simply become ineffective. At the same time, no government can ride roughshod over the will of powerful groups. Especially in representative systems, governments pursue such a course only at great peril. It will there-fore become more essential than ever that alternate courses of action be proposed for public discussion before commitments are made, and that the virtues of preferred policies be amply explained so that political leadership can mobilize support in issue-based constituen-cies sufficient to override a narrowly conceived special-interest position.

Sponsoring Social Experiments

It will also be important that new programs be tested before being legislated as universal panaceas. In the past, the fact that so much real authority was located in the private sector or in regional governments meant that a wide range of experiments would be undertaken as a matter of course. As government becomes more centralized and bureaucratized, such diversity cannot be assumed. On the contrary, the danger is that the central government will feel com-pelled to establish a single program to be im-plemented with only marginal variations. Such a policy risks compounding any error incorpo-rated in the program, and since errors are all but unavoidable, it is a much better idea to introduce programs on an experimental basis, with ample opportunities for evaluation, and to encourage experiments with a variety of dif-ferent approaches, before embarking on nation-wide reforms.

Improving Policy Planning in Government

In this connection it must be pointed out that most governments are as yet ill-equipped to perform the function of long-term analysis of social needs. Most are overwhelmed by the immediate burdens placed upon them and by the need to meet these burdens with limited resources. They could all profit from the crea-tion of long-term policy planning staffs, both at the highest centralized levels (such as the office of the President in the United States) and at the level of departments and agencies. These staffs could in turn enlist the assistance of policy analysts in other agencies of government, in the universities, foundations, and private industry, in identifying trends and opportuni-ties and in framing imaginative proposals.

The Congressional Office of Technology Assessment in the United States is an example of the kind of structural arrangement that needs to be added. Existing agencies are apt to be preoccupied with immediate issues and con-flicts and to be reluctant to become embroiled in proposals which represent more than incre-mental changes in existing practice.

Once analyses and proposals are formulated,

they need to be made politically feasible. Here the best analysis will not be sufficient unless it benefits from public recognition of the need for action coupled with the desire of politicians to respond to inchoate public demands. Post-industrial society will be as much a "political" system as any, in the sense that policies will need to be debated and choices registered. The main difference between the politics of industrial and post-industrial societies will probably be the openness of the electorate to persuasion. Since the issues will not as often be those that readily fit the neat lines of interest groups, it will be necessary to create constituencies in support of major proposals, as has recently been the case with much environmental legislation.

Broadening the Concept of Welfare

In recent years, practice has run ahead of theory in broadening the traditional view of human needs and rights and the corresponding social responsibility to care for human needs. It is now tacitly accepted not only that people need the security that only society can provide in case of dire emergency, but that it is the business of the state to make it possible for all citizens to fulfill their potentialities as individuals and as contributors to the common good.

This tacit agreement has been rationalized in economic terms on the grounds of the economic costs of unproductiveness. The high costs of social deviance and unproductiveness make it economically sensible for society to attempt to avoid incurring these costs by fostering individual self-reliance and if necessary by providing training and employment for those unable to make their way in the system.

The agreement need not be rationalized on economic grounds alone, however. It is also a function of political ideology. In all democracies, the guiding principle is the belief in universal autonomy. Such autonomy is possible only if all citizens are enabled to fulfill their potentialities. This means that they must be provided with opportunities for education and for the pursuit of careers for which they are qualified. It also means that they must be protected against the debilitating effects of handicaps and accidents.

The traditional liberal version of this democratic idea has been criticized, especially in recent years, by those who argue that individual talent and industry, as measured by the market system, should not be permitted to foster gross inequalities of result. Instead, the productive system should be regarded as a common instrument and the rewards apportioned in accordance with some standard of need rather than merit. Ethnic pluralism has been invoked to support the idea that minorities, who have in the past been deprived of equal opportunities, must now be compensated by a proportional assignment of employment, so as to attain a proportional distribution of the more desirable jobs. Some advocate minimum quotas for previously disadvantaged minorities. It is said in support of such measures that they are the best practical means of redressing a social injustice, and against them, that they would do so by inflicting injustice upon others and would result in a lowering of standards of competence and a dampening of the aspiration to excellence.

Apart from the issue of equity, there has also developed a belief that society must also take a more active role in affecting the character of the work experience, and the character of leisure activities, which will come to absorb the time of a larger and larger segment of the society. It is now well understood that to invoke the concern for the protection of privacy and individual rights in every context is to condemn people to lives devoid of opportunities for self-expression and maturation, with the result that some individuals may come to regard themselves almost as outcasts within their own society. They will certainly be unfit for the responsibilities of citizenship and in many cases will be open to appeals to resentment and frustration. Work which makes the individual a mindless appendage of some machine not only robs him of dignity but does not encourage him to develop a sense of initiative and responsibility. It diminishes his capacity and interest for the cultivation of a sense of craft and at the same time of a sense of citizenship, for he thinks of the social process as another automatic system operating independently of his role in it. Similarly, a culture in which the manipulation of consumer attitudes is a predominant influence may create a mass of like-minded people easily made into a pliant political support system, incapable of exercising independent judgment.

If leisure is defined as the total sum of activities outside work, it is clear that as work becomes a smaller, less consuming part of life activity—especially with the encouragement of earlier retirement and the prolongation of the life span—the organization of leisure will determine the character of society as much as the organization of work has traditionally affected it. Demands are therefore being made upon government not only to concern itself with the work experience but even with leisure activities.

At each stage of the life cycle, whether in work or in leisure, the "sense of self" must also have a bearing on the degree of contentment or frustration experienced as people find themselves induced or compelled to adapt to various life roles. This sense of self is influenced by changing patterns of social approbation and disapprobation. The aging are especially sensitive to such changes, particularly when the society begins to value youth rather than age. In traditional society, individuals move through the stages of the life cycle in such a way as to receive honor as they grow older, perhaps as a compensatory device for the loss of youthful vigor. It may be that the emphasis on novelty and change which is so pronounced in modern society is responsible for the decline in the veneration of the old.

The social approach to welfare and to the evaluation of life roles is itself strongly influenced by changes in the social and economic structure. The structure of power and status may never exactly mirror the distribution of social responsibility, which often falls heaviest on those who receive the smallest rewards. Nevertheless, the rationale for social assistance reflects both a sense of the need to provide for those who cannot provide for themselves and a sense of obligation toward those who contribute to the welfare of society. The welfare legislation of the present century has been justified on both grounds.

The elderly, however, especially the elderly poor, are in a more vulnerable position than those sectors of the population whose contributions are present rather than past. They cannot press their case by means of strikes or some other similar means of negotiation or bargaining. Their electoral leverage is more apparent then real. Their major case has therefore been put in terms of an appeal on humanitarian grounds. There has not been a clear social consensus, however, as to the need for such support from society, in view of the emphasis on individual self-reliance and the stigma attached to a reliance on public charity.

In the era of the welfare state, the general approach of Western societies has been to redistribute income, to a limited extent, so as to remove some of the burden of private philanthropy, but otherwise to design schemes of social insurance and subscriber-supported retirement programs, to which employers contribute, as a method of insuring the minimal security of the elderly by prior provision during the working years. The crucial change in recent years has been the decision made by some countries to tie retirement benefits to changes in the price or wage level (Schulz, 1972).

This mixture of approaches is likely to be maintained for the foreseeable future, although the demand for further changes to take account of inflation is virtually certain to arise. Very likely, there will be further efforts to tie assistance more directly to social productivity rather than to individual contributions. The proposal for a negative income tax would offer minimal compensation to all, including the elderly, from a general social fund. This approach has the support of radicals as well as conservatives because it is said to encourage self-respect and to obviate the need for a welfare bureaucracy. If it should be adopted, it will also signal a social recognition that productive labor has ceased to be the moral norm it has been for industrial society.

The Ethical Foundation of Social Policy

The responsibility to care for the elderly is both an ethical and a pragmatic matter. From an ethical point of view, it is hardly surprising that "honor thy father and mother" should have been one of the first of the great ethical injunctions to be laid upon civilized humanity.

This injunction serves to remind us of the obligation we bear to those who have given us existence and have nurtured us—an obligation which reflects the classical view of justice as a return of like for like.

At the same time, this injunction has a practical aspect. In the animal realm, where ethical injunctions cannot arise, offspring desert their parents at an early age. In the human case, parental devotion and sacrifice is essential, and instinct alone could not be relied upon to sustain the long period of parental care. The injunction therefore serves a practical social purpose by helping to assure parents that their services to the young will be reciprocated.

In agricultural societies, reciprocal services are likely to be performed even while children are young and parents are not yet unable to provide for themselves. The family, moreover, remains a cohesive social unit. It is not as though the children can readily leave the family and pursue a separate existence. "Social security" is to some extent tribal or community security.

In modern industrialized societies, little remains to shore up the ethical injunction. Not surprisingly, perhaps, people discover that they have interests which compete with the instinct of paternity, and some therefore decide not to have children at all. It is not as though children are necessarily a comfort and support in old age. Since comparatively few families are occupied with agriculture and those which are so occupied usually go beyond the family for assistance, there is no need to raise children to serve as "hands." The ethical responsibility to care for those who cannot care for themselves has passed to society at large. And society has acted on the assumption that the best course is to encourage individuals to plan for their own retirement, so that their provision can be their own responsibility. Increasingly, the inability of many people to make such preparations, or to meet the heavy burden of expenses which may befall them, especially for medical services, has led to demands for social intervention and assistance. Any society which takes a measure of pride in itself and aims to minimize distress and resentment will take steps to meet these demands. Some degree of social intervention can therefore be safely assumed. The extent to which more than minimal goals are set and pursued, however, will test the imagination and the resourcefulness of every modern state.

Beyond the Industrial Work Ethic

In policy terms, the issue facing post-industrial societies as concerns the elderly is how to assist a large and growing sector of the population which, though comparatively unproductive, is likely to have acute needs that will not be met without public assistance. In one important respect, a post-industrial society may be in a better position to meet such needs than an industrial society. In an industrial society, contribution to productivity is considered a defining characteristic of social worth and desert. In post-industrial society, it may come to be understood that productivity is a function less of actual labor than of the application of scientific intelligence in the form of technology. The character of each specific contribution of labor will therefore come to seem less important as a basis of compensation than it did when productivity was so much a function of sheer work. The danger in this development is that the end of the "work ethic" could promote a casual assumption that social rewards should be a function of demand rather than contribution. Those who contribute their skills and energy would nurse resentments against those who did not, and those who found that society was ready to compensate them, regardless of their contribution, would become a potentially disruptive and demoralizing force.

To avert this danger, governments will certainly find it advisable to stimulate activities in the service sector, where labor productivity may be more difficult to measure, but where vital functions need to be performed. At the very least, such employment will make it possible to avoid the need to compensate people regardless of their willingness to contribute to society.

While the principle of encouraging public and private employment in the service sector for those whose labor is not required elsewhere in the economy is especially relevant to the needs of the industrially unemployable, it also has some bearing on the condition of the elderly. If resources are to be made available significantly to increase provision for the needs of the elderly, it may well be advisable to expand the role of the industrial "retired" in the service areas of the economy. This could entail a host of specific measures, such as those already undertaken to form "senior service" corps, to encourage the employment of the elderly, usually on a part-time basis, in day care centers for working parents, as teacher-assistants in schools, etc. By providing socially useful employment for older people, governments would be able to justify increasing their compensation (even if much of this compensation might be devoted to medical insurance and other such programs). Such employment could also make retirement less the total transition from work to nonwork that it has been in industrial society (U.S. Senate, 1969).

The End of Aging As a Special Problem

By such particular changes, post-industrial societies could inaugurate a far-reaching set of social transformations, as a result of which work and leisure and education and employment could be better integrated and made lifelong activities. One reason the elderly face problems of adjustment now is that the life cycle has been associated with a social program in which roles and statuses are assigned on an age-related and work-related basis. To the extent that this relationship can be minimized, the problems of adjustment will be minimized. It is at least conceivable that in a post-industrial society, where grinding labor for the great majority ceases to be necessary for economic growth, much more effort could be devoted to the development of a better balance in human activity throughout the stages of the life cycle, to allow for more variation in types of employment, continuation of education, and a mix of leisure and work now enjoyed only by the affluent. In this process some of the social problems of aging would become far less acute.

If government policy could modify the sharp alteration between work and retirement, it could also significantly influence the equally sharp transition from integration into family and community to the separation of the elderly from both. In the United States, the rapid expansion of the "nursing home" as a depository for increasing numbers of old people is a direct consequence of government policy, as incorporated in the medicare legislation. If other incentives were provided, more older people might remain in the care of their families or in their own separate residences. Others could enjoy the amenities of retirement communities now foreclosed to them on account of cost. Short of such measures as these, which are admittedly costly, there are also ways of improving the standard of care in the nursing homes, by requiring affiliation with high quality public institutions, such as hospitals and universities, or by requiring the appointment of public directors to the boards governing profit-making nursing homes.

Aging and the "Quality of Life"

In a sense, the treatment of the elderly could prove to be a test case of the character of post-industrial society and of the meaning of the ambiguous phrase, "the quality of life." The deplorable treatment of the needy elderly is an indictment of modern society, and an indication that the progress made in mastering nature and overcoming material necessity has so far not been matched by developments in social organization and social responsibility. It is here that the challenge and opportunity for government is most apparent.

If post-industrial society is to represent an advance over an industrial society, it is reasonable to expect that advance to be registered above all in the provision not only of charity and care for those who cannot fend for themselves, but even more in the development of systems of provision which will make extraordinary assistance unnecessary. The overhaul of private and public pension schemes is one element in such an effort at provision. Another would be an increase in the availability of preventive medical care. A third might be the regular provision of education, to enable people to develop new talents and interests as they pass from one stage of life to the next. A considerable number of such proposals is already on the public agenda. It remains to be seen whether and when governments will consider them seriously in the context of an effort at fairly long-run planning.

Ideology and the Elderly

In general, it will probably not be necessary to revise attitudes completely in order to achieve a reasonable degree of consensus with respect to the condition of the elderly. To the extent that provision for the elderly is built into wage-benefit arrangements, it should be possible to avoid any difficulty over the work ethic. Since aging is universal, social policy toward aging can and should be presented as a general policy, affecting all members of society, rather than as an attempt to provide for a particular narrow group. The objection to excessive social planning can be met by providing alternatives and by leaving implementation in the hands of intermediate organizations and individuals. Insofar as the treatment of the elderly suffers from false stereotypes, deliberate efforts could be made to erase such stereotypes by media campaigns and by rigid enforcement of non-discrimination laws.

It may be that the most serious barrier to the improvement of the treatment of the elderly lies in a modern predilection for youth and vitality and the corresponding disdain and dread of aging. This attitude may be too deeply established to be uprooted by governmental decree or even by some set of programs aimed at improving the image of the elderly. The best remedy for the social effects of this set of attitudes is to achieve a social condition in which aging is no longer a period of decline in respects other than physical. Only if aging does not bring with it a loss of social function or status and only if retirement comes to be seen as an opportunity for a rich experience deferred until late in life will attitudes change. The task for government policy-makers is to create an environment in which such a change may come about. The problem they will face is that in order to mobilize support for such an effort, they will have to overcome the prevailing set of often negative attitudes.

Alternate Futures: The Choices Ahead

It was suggested at the outset that it would be foolhardy to attempt to predict the course of governmental action with respect to the elderly as though this course could safely be extrapolated from present tendencies or as though it must necessarily follow a single certain path. The possibilities, however, are not infinite. Social policy must be shaped within the context of emerging realities, and it is likely to be shaped in accordance with the evolving pattern of social values. As modern society comes to depend more and more on the advances of science and technology, and less on sheer physical labor, the possibility that aging need not be a prospect to be dreaded becomes increasingly realistic. Indeed, as Neugarten suggests, the tendency for people to retire well before the age of 65 could effectively eradicate some of the customary distinction between middle and old age (Neugarten, 1974, 1975). The passing of industrial society could signal the passing of the great emphasis upon employment as the definition of a meaningful life. The way could be opened to a broader and more subtle view of the entire life process, in which work and leisure, industry and creativity, could be more readily mingled than they were in the heat of the blast furnaces that powered the industrial revolution.

The ideological barriers to a new integration of aging and the life process—whether in the form of an individualism that denies collective responsibility or a collectivism that stultifies individual choice—need not be thought insuperable obstacles. These polar alternatives have now often been blended, and much of the passion has left the halls in which these themes were debated during the past century.

To say, however, that the way is clear for a new social understanding in which the special problems of the elderly will be reduced to a comparative few, because the aging will find a new place in society, assumes that governments will be capable of recognizing a change in social conditions and of adapting to them. Nothing in life is certain, however, and even less is certain in politics. Since the aging are not likely themselves to become the catalyst of this political change, it will come about only if there is a growing recognition of the need to move beyond the provision of special assistance to the elderly to the integration of aging into a new and comprehensive role for government in promoting human development.

POSTSCRIPT: A CAVEAT ON SOCIAL FORECASTING

The Nature and Limits of Social Forecasting

Since the effort to transcend existing approaches to social welfare must take account of trends and future possibilities, there is bound to be a strong temptation on the part of governments to embrace the technique of social forecasting. For that reason, it may be appropriate to add a note of caution with respect to the use of this technique, especially by governments.

In the past, speculation about the shape of the future was generally thought an activity for supernatural clairvoyance, best left to seers claiming occult powers. Lately, such speculation has become a widely practiced if not completely accepted professional activity. "Futurology" or social forecasting is an intellectual undertaking with a place in some academic curricula and in considerable vogue in government and industry. One practical application which has been made of this activity is what is known as "technology assessment." An "Office of Technology Assessment" was created by the Congress of the United States in 1974 in order to assess the likely social consequences of new technologies before they are so widely adopted that it becomes too difficult to withdraw or modify them without causing major dislocations.

The attempt to anticipate the impact of new technologies arises from bad experience with a variety of recent technological advances. Wonder drugs, pesticides, supersonic aircraft, and many other technical innovations have always seemed to their promoters to be agents only of benefit. As the unforeseen consequences of certain of these advances, and their indirect costs, have also had to be taken into account, governments have beome warier of technological "hard sell" techniques. Technology assessment is one of

the remedies adopted to attempt to identify the negative consequences and to compare them with likely benefits.

That policy-makers should feel the need for such assistance on a regular, institutionalized basis, and that specialists in the various academic and practical disciplines should be willing to try to provide the service, reflects some of the profound impact science and technology have had in recent times. Because scientists have been able to establish the predictive validity of their research, it has been assumed that it should be possible to predict social consequences, at least where a new technology is in question. The trouble with such an assumption, of course, is that the more the framing of the problem for analysis shifts from terms appropriate to the laboratory and from physical, chemical, or biological considerations into a social context, the more uncertain analysis becomes. Uncertainty is especially acute when qualitative questions must be answered in quantitative terms and when changeable human values must be assumed constant for purposes of analysis. In recognition of such uncertainties, forecasters tend to resist the temptation to identify a single certain outcome. Instead, they usually construct a variety of "scenarios" or "alternate futures."

Even so, social forecasting is a hazardous business at best, as is well indicated by the example that has attracted the most attention, the warning of impending limits to growth advanced by the Club of Rome.

The Doomsday Prophets and Their Critics

The Meadows study (Meadows, Meadows, Randers, and Behrens, 1972) can be regarded as a prime example of social forecasting. It was conceived and executed in accordance with the analytical principles developed by Jay Forrester, a leading exponent of computer simulation, and it is designed to allow for wide variations in the crucial parameters. As is well known, the results of the exercise indicate that even under the most optimistic assumptions, the world system is headed for disaster in the none-too-distant future. The course of disaster is plotted along five curves, all rising exponentially and all intersecting at some point with the finite character of the human environment. The curves plotted are those for population increase, the depletion of resources, the exhaustion of arable land (along with diminishing returns in agricultural productivity), technological advances, and global pollution.

The least controverted of the Meadows projections is that concerning population. Some critics argue that since rates of population increase tend to decline with prosperity (and also with increasing awareness of the cost of population to economic growth), it is a mistake to expect present trends to continue until the planet becomes so crowded that survival will become impossible. Even these critics tend to agree, however, that population pressures, especially in the developing areas of the world, represent a grave and continuing threat. Population becomes somewhat less threatening if the other projections can be shown to be faulty. And these are in fact widely challenged.

Resource depletion is subject to one set of challenges. As resources become scarcer, economists point out, the price they bring tends to rise. Users are therefore induced to find cheaper substitutes or to lower their consumption of the resource. Economic incentives are also created for the discovery of new sources and the exploitation of known sources that were previously uneconomical. As the price of fossil fuels rises, for example, risk taking in exploring for new sources is encouraged, as is the development of substitute energy sources such as atomic fission, thermonuclear fusion, and solar energy. Synthetic materials are substituted for natural fibers, animal skins, and even for animal proteins—though these substitutions require other materials such as petroleum which are also being depleted. In general, critics maintain, doomsday can be considerably deferred, if not altogether abrogated, by a judicious use of market incentives, human ingenuity, and conservation measures (Maddox, 1972).

In the case of food production, it is pointed out in criticism of the Meadows study that there is no good reason to assume that further advances in agricultural technology are unlikely.

The recent example of the so-called green revolution brought about by the introduction of improved varieties of rice and wheat, which have dramatically increased yields in South Asia, is an example of what can reasonably be expected from continuing research and from the diffusion of agricultural knowledge to areas of the world where land remains undercultivated. By combining the support of continuing research with the diffusion of known technologies, along with incentives for cultivators in the advanced countries and some export of capital to the developing areas, the advanced countries could alleviate the food supply problem significantly.

Curbing pollution imposes costs, it is admitted, but these are not necessarily unacceptable. Economic growth can be sustained not only by activities that cause pollution but also by those that check it. There is no inherent reason why water and air resources must continue to become more and more polluted. In some cases, all that is necessary to prevent the extrapolation of present trends is to change existing laws framed when the problem of pollution was neglected. In other cases, the need can be served best by calculating the indirect costs of pollution and assigning them to the producers or users responsible for them. In other cases, government policies can encourage the use of relatively nonpolluting technologies. Pollution control is not always simple, but it is by no means impossible (Cole, Freeman, Jahoda, and Pavitt, 1973).

Underlying all of these criticisms is one common assumption, which is that the intelligent social use of science and technology can confound predictions based solely on extrapolations from existing tendencies. Critics of the "doomsday syndrome" point out that Thomas Malthus' gloomy prediction that population was destined to outrun food resources has so far proven erroneous precisely because he took no account of the role of scientific progress in increasing agricultural yields. For the same reason, it is argued, neo-Malthusian forecasts, even though they now assume a certain steady rate of technological progress (except for diminishing returns in some areas), are likely to prove ill-founded in such critical areas as energy supply. Without minimizing the acute problems due to maldistribution of resources, industrial capacity, and scientific talents and equipment, it can nevertheless be argued plausibly that there is no necessary reason to believe that Malthus' theory is shortly to be vindicated.

The critique of the limits to growth argument is especially salutary in pointing out the dangers of forecasting by extrapolation. If this had been done in earlier times on the Malthusian model in areas other than food production, similar errors would have resulted. If an effort had been made to extrapolate patterns of fossil fuel consumption from a point in the nineteenth century, it would have missed entirely the significance of oil as a heating fuel, a fuel for the internal combustion engine, and as the chemical basis for plastics. To have extrapolated transportation patterns from the days of the horse-drawn carriage would have missed entirely the introduction of road, rail, and air transport.

This is not to suggest that advances in science and technology can be relied upon to alleviate all shortages or all problems. Sometimes, an advance in one respect raises new problems in others. The deaths due to traffic accidents are a sobering reminder of the high costs of technological progress, as are the estimates of the mutations likely to result from atmospheric nuclear testing. Advances in science and technology can no longer be assumed automatically to produce benign effects; all that can plausibly be contended is that certain such advances, if intelligently used, can yield benefits and that there is no good reason to think that all technology is inherently malevolent and de-humanizing.

In the belief that technology should not determine social patterns, Denis Gabor, the developer of holography, has argued that it is up to society to "invent the future," or in other words to control the use of technology and encourage development thought likely to be beneficial. While there is much merit in this suggestion, there is also some real danger that an overreliance on the capacity to manipulate not only the complexities imposed by nature but also those imposed by man himself can induce an illusion that there is a "technological

fix" for every social problem, provided only that governments are willing to commit resources and talents to it.

There is now ample if dismaying evidence that efforts to frame new Manhattan or Apollo projects in order to deal with urban decay or with crime and deviance are apt to be much less successful than the efforts upon which they are modeled. The reasons are fairly obvious. In the first case, the object can be precisely defined and achieved by the production of some set of equipment. The project is almost entirely based on the use of laws of nature or the development of testable innovations. Margins of error can be left and opportunities for correction can be provided because the process can proceed by stages and the components and assemblies can be tested and refined. The actual operation of the end-product can be monitored in reasonably controlled conditions. Urban problems, as well as the problems of crime and deviance, require an attempt to understand and influence human behavior, and not simply to develop some new technological system. They cannot easily be dealt with in laboratory conditions. It is not possible to bring to bear upon them a well-constituted body of scientific knowledge, because in most cases such knowledge simply does not exist. The applications that are made of the results of research, furthermore, are not subject to controlled monitoring.

What is true for projects of urban renewal and crime control is also true for other projects of social reform. In Europe, where the tendency is to doubt that long-standing social problems can be eradicated, programs have been less ambitious and therefore less controversial. In the United States, where idealistic impulses are regularly harnessed to pragmatic efforts of social reform, the field is strewn with partial successes and outright failures—among them urban renewal, public housing, preschool education, the "war on poverty," the "model cities program," medicare, and the racial integration of the schools. The difficulties experienced in such efforts need not be taken as a justification for neglect but they should exert a serious caution against the casual assumption that because mankind is capable of extraordinary achievements in technology, it must also be possible to plan a preferred future, no matter how intractable the obstacles.

For these reasons, any effort to anticipate or to urge social action with respect to the problems of the elderly should be hedged with caution. The biological and psychological infirmities of age are given by nature. They may prove to be less intractable than they are presently thought to be, as medical research extends the magnificent progress recorded in this century. There can be no certainty, however, that even if adequate resources are allotted to medical research, the results will dramatically alter or reverse conditions which have always been associated with the life cycle. This means that the biological and psychological characteristics of aging must be taken as given in efforts to frame government policy, granted that the tendency to reduce these characteristics to stereotypes rather than take account of the diversity of real experience is deplorable.

The difficulty of making projections concerning the approach to social problems is only compounded by the fact that social policy is inevitably framed and implemented in a political context. Relatively nonpolitical specialists may identify the problems; social planners may propose solutions; but it is in the political process—which is to say in the context of a play of forces mixing interests, values, budgetary constraints, institutional inertia, and the imperfections of social bargaining and experimentation—that policy is decided upon and put into effect. Since the elements of politics will vary from society to society, no universal projection of the prospects for social intervention on behalf of the elderly, unless it is very general, is apt to be realistic.

REFERENCES

Bell, D. 1974. *The Coming of Post-Industrial Society*. New York: Basic Books.

Binstock, R. H. 1974. Aging and the future of American politics. *Annals of the Am. Acad. of Pol. and Soc. Sc.*, 415, 201-212.

Cole, H. S. D., Freeman, C., Jahoda, M., and Pavitt, K. L. R. (eds.) 1973. *Thinking About The Future; A Critique of The Limits to Growth*. London: Chatto & Windus.

De Beauvoir, S. 1972. *The Coming of Age*. New York: G. P. Putnam's Sons.

Havelock, E. A. 1957. *The Liberal Temper of Greek Politics*. New Haven: Yale University Press.

Lakoff, S. A. 1964. *Equality in Political Philosophy*. Cambridge, Massachusetts: Harvard University Press.

Lakoff, S. A. 1971. Knowledge, power and democratic theory. *Annals of The Am. Acad. of Pol. and Soc. Sc.*, 394, 4-12.

Lakoff, S. A. 1974a. Socialism from antiquity to Marx. *Dictionary of the History of Ideas*, Vol. IV, pp. 284-294. New York: Charles Scribner's Sons.

Lakoff, S. A. 1974b. Scientists and the adversary process. Paper presented to the annual meeting of the American Political Science Association, Chicago, Illinois, September, 1974.

Locke, J. 1689 (1964). *Two Treatises of Government*. P. Laslett (ed.). Cambridge: Cambridge University Press.

Maddox, J. 1972. *The Doomsday Syndrome*. New York: McGraw-Hill.

Meadows, D. H., Meadows, D. L., Randers, J., and Behrens, III, W. 1972. *The Limits to Growth*. New York: Universe Books.

Neugarten, B. 1974. Age groups in American society and the rise of the young-old. *Annals of the Am. Acad. of Pol. and Soc. Sc.*, 415, 187-198.

Neugarten, B. 1975. The future and the young-old. *Gerontologist*, 15 (1), Part II, 4-10.

Piven, F. F., and Cloward, R. 1971. *Regulating the Poor*. New York: Pantheon Books.

Plato. *The Republic*. Translated by A. Bloom, 1968. New York: Basic Books.

Riley, M. W., Foner, A., Moore, M. E., Hess, B., and Roth, B. K. 1968. *Aging and Society: An Inventory of Research Findings*, I. New York: Russell Sage Foundation.

Schulz, J. H. 1972. Aging societies: International trends in social security reform. Paper presented at the 25th annual conference on Aging, Michigan-Wayne State Institute of Gerontology, September, 1972.

U.S. Senate. 1969. Proposal for the American community service forces. *Usefulness of the Model Cities Program to the Elderly*. Hearings before the Special Committee on Aging, 91st Congress, 1st session, part 6, pp. 573-602. Washington D.C.: Government Printing Office.

AUTHOR INDEX

SUBJECT INDEX